DATE DUE

			PRINTED IN U.S.A.

CLASSICAL
AND MEDIEVAL
LITERATURE
CRITICISM

Guide to Gale Literary Criticism Series

For criticism on	Consult these Gale series
Authors now living or who died after December 31, 1959	*CONTEMPORARY LITERARY CRITICISM (CLC)*
Authors who died between 1900 and 1959	*TWENTIETH-CENTURY LITERARY CRITICISM (TCLC)*
Authors who died between 1800 and 1899	*NINETEENTH-CENTURY LITERATURE CRITICISM (NCLC)*
Authors who died between 1400 and 1799	*LITERATURE CRITICISM FROM 1400 TO 1800 (LC)* *SHAKESPEAREAN CRITICISM (SC)*
Authors who died before 1400	*CLASSICAL AND MEDIEVAL LITERATURE CRITICISM (CMLC)*
Black writers of the past two hundred years	*BLACK LITERATURE CRITICISM (BLC)*
Authors of books for children and young adults	*CHILDREN'S LITERATURE REVIEW (CLR)*
Dramatists	*DRAMA CRITICISM (DC)*
Hispanic writers of the late nineteenth and twentieth centuries	*HISPANIC LITERATURE CRITICISM (HLC)*
Poets	*POETRY CRITICISM (PC)*
Short story writers	*SHORT STORY CRITICISM (SSC)*
Major authors from the Renaissance to the present	*WORLD LITERATURE CRITICISM, 1500 TO THE PRESENT (WLC)*

ISSN 0896-0011

Volume 13

CLASSICAL AND MEDIEVAL LITERATURE CRITICISM

Excerpts from Criticism of the Works of World Authors from Classical Antiquity through the Fourteenth Century, from the First Appraisals to Current Evaluations

Jelena O. Krstović
Editor

Michael Magoulias
James E. Person, Jr.
Anna J. Sheets
Brian J. St. Germain
Joseph C. Tardiff
Associate Editors

Gale Research Inc.

An International Thomson Publishing Company

I(T)P

NEW YORK • LONDON • BONN • BOSTON • DETROIT • MADRID
MELBOURNE • MEXICO CITY • PARIS • SINGAPORE • TOKYO
TORONTO • WASHINGTON • ALBANY NY • BELMONT CA • CINCINNATI OH

Library of Congress Catalog Card Number 88-658021
ISBN 0-8103-2434-2
ISSN 0896-0011

Printed in the United States of America
Published simultaneously in the United Kingdom
by Gale Research International Limited
(An affiliated company of Gale Research Inc.)
10 9 8 7 6 5 4 3 2 1

The trademark **ITP** is used under license.

Contents

Preface

Since its inception in 1988, *Classical and Medieval Literature Criticism* has been a valuable resource for students and librarians seeking critical commentary on the writers and works of these periods in world history. Major reviewing sources have assessed *CMLC* as "useful" and "extremely convenient," noting that it "adds to our understanding of the rich legacy left by the ancient period and the Middle Ages," and praising its "general excellence in the presentation of an inherently interesting subject." No other single reference source has surveyed the critical reaction to classical and medieval literature as thoroughly as *CMLC*.

Scope of the Series

CMLC is designed to serve as an introduction for students and advanced readers of the works and authors of antiquity through the fourteenth century. The great poets, prose writers, dramatists, and philosophers of this period form the basis of most humanities curricula, so that virtually every student will encounter many of these works during the course of a high school and college education. By organizing and reprinting an enormous amount of commentary written on classical and medieval authors and works, *CMLC* helps students develop valuable insight into literary history, promotes a better understanding of the texts, and sparks ideas for papers and assignments. Each entry in *CMLC* presents a comprehensive survey of an author's career, an individual work of literature, or a literary topic, and provides the user with a multiplicity of interpretations and assessments. Such variety allows students to pursue their own interests; furthermore, it fosters an awareness that literature is dynamic and responsive to many different opinions.

CMLC continues the survey of criticism of world literature begun by Gale's *Contemporary Literary Criticism (CLC)*, *Twentieth-Century Literary Criticism (TCLC)*, *Nineteenth-Century Literature Criticism (NCLC)*, *Literature Criticism from 1400 to 1800 (LC)*, and *Shakespearean Criticism (SC)*. For additional information about these and Gale's other criticism series, users should consult the Guide to Gale Literary Criticism Series preceding the title page in this volume.

Coverage

Each volume of *CMLC* is carefully compiled to present:

- criticism of authors and works which represent a variety of genres, time periods, and nationalities

- both major and lesser-known writers and works of the period (such as non-Western authors and literature, increasingly read by today's students)

- 4-6 authors or works per volume

- individual entries that survey the critical response to each author, work, or topic, including early criticism, later criticism (to represent any rise or decline in the author's reputation), and current retrospective analyses. The length of each author or work entry also indicates relative importance, reflecting the amount of critical attention the author, work, or topic has received from critics writing in English, and from foreign criticism in translation.

An author may appear more than once in the series if his or her writings have been the subject of a substantial amount of criticism; in these instances, specific works or groups of works by the author will be covered in separate entries. For example, Homer will be represented by three entries, one devoted to the *Iliad,* one to the *Odyssey,* and one to the Homeric Hymns.

Starting with Volume 10, *CMLC* will also occasionally include entries devoted to literary topics. For example, *CMLC*-10 focuses on Arthurian Legend and includes general criticism on that subject as well as individual entries on writers or works central to that topic—Chrétien de Troyes, Gottfried von Strassburg, Layamon, and the Alliterative *Morte Arthure.*

Organization of the Book

An author entry consists of the following elements: author heading, biographical and critical introduction, principal English translations or editions, excerpts of criticism (each preceded by a bibliographic citation and an annotation), and a bibliography of further reading.

- The **Author Heading** consists of the author's most commonly used name, followed by birth and death dates. If the entry is devoted to a work, the heading will consist of the most common form of the title in English translation (if applicable), and the original date of composition. Located at the beginning of the introduction are any name or title variations.

- A **Portrait** of the author is included when available. Many entries also feature illustrations of materials pertinent to the author or work, including manuscript pages, book illustrations, and representations of people, places, and events important to a study of the author or work.

- The **Biographical and Critical Introduction** contains background information that concisely introduces the reader to the author, work, or topic.

- The list of **Principal Works** and **English Translations** or **Editions** is chronological by date of first publication and is included as an aid to the student seeking translated versions or editions of these works for study. The list will focus primarily on twentieth-century translations, selecting those works most commonly considered the best by critics.

- **Criticism** is arranged chronologically in each entry to provide a useful perspective on changes in critical evaluation over the years. All titles by the author featured in the critical entry are printed in boldface type to enable the user to ascertain without difficulty the works being discussed. Also for purposes of easier identification, the critic's name and the publication date of the essay are given at the beginning of each piece of criticism. Anonymous criticism is preceded by the title of the journal in which it appeared. Publication information (such as publisher names and book prices) and parenthetical numerical references (such as footnotes or page and line references to specific editions of works) have been deleted at the editors' discretion to provide smoother reading of the text. Many critical entries in *CMLC* also contain translations to aid the users.

- A complete **Bibliographic Citation** designed to facilitate the location of the original essay or book precedes each piece of criticism.

- Critical excerpts are also prefaced by **Annotations** providing the reader with information about both the critic and the criticism, the scope of the excerpt, the growth of critical controversy, or changes in critical trends regarding an author or work. In some cases, these notes include cross-references to excerpts by critics who discuss each other's commentary. Dates in parentheses within the annotation refer to a book publication date when they follow a book title, and to an essay date when they follow a critic's name.

- An annotated bibliography of **Further Reading** appears at the end of each entry and lists additional secondary sources on the author or work. In some cases it includes essays for which the editors could not obtain reprint rights. When applicable, the Further Reading is followed by references to additional entries on the author in other literary reference series published by Gale.

Topic Entries are subdivided into several thematic rubrics in which criticism appears in order of descending scope.

Cumulative Indexes

Each volume of *CMLC* includes a cumulative **author index** listing all authors who have appeared in Gale's Literary Criticism Series, along with cross references to such biographical series as *Contemporary Authors* and *Dictionary of Literary Biography*. For readers' convenience, a complete list of Gale titles included appears on the page prior to the author index. Useful for locating an author within the various series, this index is particularly valuable for those authors who are identified with a certain period but who, because of their death date, are placed in another, or for those authors whose careers span two periods. For example, Geoffrey Chaucer, who is usually considered a medieval author, is found in *Literature Criticism from 1400 to 1800* because he died after 1399.

Beginning with the tenth volume, *CMLC* includes a cumulative index listing all topic entries that have appeared in the Gale Literary Criticism Series *Classical and Medieval Literature Criticism, Contemporary Literary Criticism, Literature Criticism from 1400 to 1800, Nineteenth-Century Literature Criticism,* and *Twentieth-Century Literary Criticism*.

Beginning with the second volume, *CMLC* also includes a cumulative nationality index. Authors and/or works are grouped by nationality, and the volume in which criticism on them may be found is indicated.

Title Index

Each volume of *CMLC* also includes an index listing the titles of all literary works discussed in the series. Foreign language titles that have been translated are followed by the titles of the translations—for example, *Slovo o polku Igorove (The Song of Igor's Campaign)*. Page numbers following these translated titles refer to all pages on which any form of the title, either foreign language or translated, appears. Titles of novels, dramas, nonfiction books, and poetry, short story, or essay collections are printed in italics, while those of all individual poems, short stories, and essays are printed in roman type within quotation marks. In cases where the same title is used by different authors, the author's name or surname is given in parentheses after the title, e.g. *Collected Poems* (Horace) and *Collected Poems* (Sappho).

Critic Index

An index to critics, which cumulates with the second volume, is another useful feature of *CMLC*. Under each critic's name are listed the authors and/or works on whom the critic has written and the volume and page number where criticism may be found.

A Note to the Reader

When writing papers, students who quote directly from any volume in the Literary Criticism Series may use the following general forms to footnote reprinted criticism. The first example pertains to material drawn from a periodical, the second to material reprinted from books.

Rollo May, "The Therapist and the Journey into Hell," *Michigan Quarterly Review,* XXV, No. 4 (Fall 1986), 629-41; excerpted and reprinted in *Classical and Medieval Literature Criticism,* Vol. 3, ed. Jelena O. Krstović (Detroit: Gale Research, 1989), pp. 154-58.

Dana Ferrin Sutton, *Self and Society in Aristophanes* (University of Press of America, 1980); excerpted and reprinted in *Classical and Medieval Literature Criticism,* Vol. 4, ed. Jelena O. Krstović (Detroit: Gale Research, 1990), pp. 162-69.

Suggestions Are Welcome

Readers who wish to make suggestions for future volumes, or who have other comments regarding the series, are cordially invited to write or call the editors.

Acknowledgments

The editors wish to thank the copyright holders of the excerpted criticism included in this volume, the permissions managers of many book and magazine publishing companies for assisting us in securing reprint rights, and Anthony Bogucki for assistance with copyright research. We are also grateful to the staffs of the Detroit Public Library, the Library of Congress, the University of Detroit Mercy Library, Wayne State University Purdy/Kresge Library Complex, and the University of Michigan Libraries for making their resources available to us. Following is a list of the copyright holders who have granted us permission to reprint material in this volume of *CMLC*. Every effort has been made to trace copyright, but if omissions have been made, please let us know.

COPYRIGHTED EXCERPTS IN *CMLC*, VOLUME 13, WERE REPRINTED FROM THE FOLLOWING PERIODICALS:

Greek, Roman and Byzantine Studies, v. 16, Winter, 1975. Reprinted by permission of the publisher.—*Journal of Jewish Studies*, v. XXXI, Autumn, 1980; v. XXXIII, Spring-Autumn, 1982. © Oxford Centre for Postgraduate Hebrew Studies. Both reprinted by permission of the publisher.

COPYRIGHTED EXCERPTS IN *CMLC*, VOLUME 13, WERE REPRINTED FROM THE FOLLOWING BOOKS:

Allen, Richard F. From *Fire and Iron: Critical Approaches to "Njál's Saga."* University of Pittsburgh Press, 1971. Copyright © 1971, University of Pittsburgh Press. All rights reserved. Reprinted by permission of the publisher.—Bergin, Thomas G. From *Boccaccio*. The Viking Press, 1981. Copyright © 1981 by Thomas G. Bergin. All rights reserved. Used by permission of Viking Penguin, a division of Penguin Books USA Inc.—Bilde, Per. From *Flavius Josephus between Jerusalem and Rome: His Life, His Works, and Their Importance*. Journal for the Study of the Pseudepigrapha, 1988. Copyright © 1988 Sheffield Academic Press. Reprinted by permission of the publisher.—Branca, Vittore. From *Boccaccio: The Man and His Works*. Edited by Dennis J. McAuliffe, translated by Richard Monges. New York University Press, 1976. Copyright © 1976 by New York University. Reprinted by permission of the publisher.—Cassell, Anthony K. and Victoria Kirkham. From an introduction to *"Diana's Hunt—Caccia di Diana": Boccaccio's First Fiction*. Edited and translated by Anthony K. Cassell and Victoria Kirkham. University of Pennsylvania Press, 1991. Copyright © 1991 by the University of Pennsylvania Press. All rights reserved. Reprinted by permission of the publisher.—Cohen, Shaye J. D. From *Josephus in Galilee and Rome: His Vita and Development as a Historian*. E. J. Brill, 1979. © 1979 The Trustees of Columbia University in the City of New York. All rights reserved. Reprinted by permission of The Trustees of Columbia University in the City of New York.—Dover, K. J. From "Classical Oratory," in *Ancient Greek Literature*. Edited by K. J. Dover & others. Oxford University Press, Oxford, 1980. © K. J. Dover, E. L. Bowie, Jasper Griffin, M. L. West 1980. All rights reserved. Reprinted by permission of Oxford University Press.—Feldman, Louis H. From "Josephus as an Apologist of the Greco-Roman World: His Portrait of a Solomon," in *Aspects of Religious Propaganda in Judaism and Early Christianity*. Edited by Elisabeth Schüssler Fiorenza. University of Notre Dame Press, 1976. Copyright © 1976 by University of Notre Dame Press, Notre Dame, IN 46556. Reprinted by permission of the publisher.—Grant, Michael. From *The Ancient Historians*. Charles Scribner's Sons, 1970. Copyright © 1970 Michael Grant Publications Ltd. All rights reserved. Reprinted by permission of the author.—Grossvogel, Steven. From *Ambiguity and Allusion in Boccaccio's "Filocolo."* Leo S. Olschki Editore, 1992. Reprinted by permission of the publisher.—Guarino, Guido A. From an introduction to *Concerning Famous Women*. By Giovanni Boccaccio, translated by Guido A. Guarino. Rutgers University Press, 1963. Copyright © 1963 by Rutgers, The State University. Renewed 1991 by Guido A. Guarino. All rights reserved. Reprinted by permission of the author.—Hastings, R. From *Nature and Reason in the "Decameron."* Manchester University Press, 1975. © 1975 R. Hastings. Reprinted by permission of the publisher.—Hollander, Robert. From *Boccaccio's Two Venuses*. Columbia University Press, 1977. © 1973 Columbia University Press, New York. All rights reserved.

PHOTOGRAPHS AND ILLUSTRATIONS APPEARING IN *CMLC*, VOLUME 13, WERE RECEIVED FROM THE FOLLOWING SOURCES:

From *Freud in the Iceland Saga*, by Jesse L. Byock. University of California Press, 1982. Reproduced by permission of the author: **p. 325.**

Giovanni Boccaccio

1313-1375

Italian short story and novella writer, poet, essayist, novelist, nonfiction writer, and critic.

INTRODUCTION

Heralded as one of Europe's foremost storytellers, Boccaccio is renowned for the *Decameron*, a collection of one hundred novellas widely recognized as a masterpiece of world literature. Praised for its narrative unity and tenable character delineation, the *Decameron* has been deemed paramount to the development of short fiction. Although most literary works of the Middle Ages were composed in Latin, the *Decameron*—like Boccaccio's earlier prose and poetry—was written in the Italian vernacular, implicitly elevating the language of the middle class, and their values and concerns, to the status of literary subject matter. Boccaccio, lauded for his dialectical investigations into morality and human behavior, is also credited with establishing *ottava rima*—the verse meter of popular minstrels which eventually became the characteristic vehicle for Italian poetry—as a respectable verse form. While he is best known for his vernacular writings, Boccaccio also devoted himself late in his career to humanist scholarship, producing several allegorical eclogues, biographies, and encyclopedias in Latin. His manifold works are considered transitional because they incorporate both the spiritualism of the Middle Ages and the intellectualism of the Renaissance.

Biographical Information

Although Boccaccio customarily alluded to his aristocratic background, most modern biographers have contended that he purposefully misrepresented his family in order to conceal his illegitimacy and bourgeois origins. It is generally believed that Boccaccio was born in Tuscany, the son of an unknown French woman and a prosperous Italian merchant. He spent his childhood in Florence and is said to have composed poetry before the age of seven. In 1327 Boccaccio was sent to the "great, sinful city" of Naples, as he described it, to learn the family business and study law. While there, he made the acquaintance of several prominent intellectuals, and, inspired by their love for scholarship, resolved to devote himself to a literary career. Boccaccio produced several noteworthy works during his Neapolitan period, including the short poem *La caccia di Diana* (*Diana's Hunt*), the five-volume prose composition *Il Filocolo*, and the twelve-canto epic poem *Teseida* (*Book*

of Theseus). He returned to Florence around 1340 and shortly thereafter published the *Elegia di Madonna Fiammetta (Fiammetta)*, which is widely regarded as the first modern psychological novel, as well as the *Decameron*. Having distinguished himself as a poet and scholar, Boccaccio became active in politics and was appointed the city state's emissary. In this capacity he went to Padua in 1351 to induce the poet Francesco Petrarch to reside in Florence; although Petrarch refused, Boccaccio became one of his most enthusiastic admirers. Over the course of the next two decades, Boccaccio studied classical languages and the Homeric poems, and wrote several works in Latin, notably the encyclopedic mythology *De Genealogia deorum gentilium* (*Genealogy of the Gentile Gods*); a collection of biographies on famous men and women—*De casibus virorum illustrium* (*On the Fates of Illustrious Men*) and *De claris mulieribus* (*Concerning Famous Women*); and a compilation of geographic names entitled *De montibus, silvis, fontibus, lacubus, fluminibus, stagnis seu paludibus, et de nominibus maris*. He still occasionally composed in Italian, namely lyrics, essays in honor of Dante Alighieri, and satires like *Il Corbaccio*. Boccaccio died in 1375 in Certaldo, a town not far from Florence.

Major Works

Scholars have generally divided Boccaccio's ouevre into three periods. The Neapolitan period (1327-40) is dominated by narratives and epic poems dedicated to Boccaccio's early love, a woman to whom he gives the name Fiammetta. Most important among these are two works with themes derived from medieval romances: *Il filocolo*, a prose composition adapted to the fashionable world of Naples which relates the attachment between the lovers Florio and Biancofiore; and *Il filostrato*, a short poem in the *ottava rima* meter which recounts the love of Troilus for his unfaithful Criseida. Another noteworthy work of this period, the *Teseida*, is an epic based on Vergil's *Aeneid*; here, the wars of Theseus serve as a backdrop for the love of two friends, Arcita and Palemone, for the same woman, Emilia. Boccaccio's Florentine years (1340-52) are widely considered the period of his full maturity. His most notable compositions include the novel *Fiammetta*, the story of a woman who longingly awaits the return of an exiled lover, and the *Decameron*. Based on humorous French tales popular throughout the Middle Ages, the *Decameron* centers on seven women and three men who, hoping to escape the Black Plague of 1348, retreat to the hills of Fiesole above Florence, where for ten days they candidly tell each other stories dealing with such topics as love, intelligence, and human will before returning to the city. Although the one hundred novellas comprise numerous themes and characters, critics have observed that Boccaccio's use of framing structures and narrative devices—like his proem, or preface, his introductions to the first and fourth days, and his epilogue—lend a sense of thematic and stylistic unity to a work which otherwise might have appeared disordered or fragmented. Several voluminous works in Latin constitute the final period of Boccaccio's literary career (1342-75). The *Genealogy of the Gentile Gods*, the most famous of these treatises, served as the standard handbook of mythology until the nineteenth century and was translated into all the major European languages.

Critical Reception

Although commentators throughout the centuries have admired both Boccaccio's sophisticated prose and his highly elegant verse attuned to the manners and morals of fourteenth-century Italy, most critical attention has focused on the *Decameron*. When it first appeared in manuscript form in 1370, the *Decameron* attained enormous popularity among the literary middle class; however, writers and scholars were indifferent to the work, and it was rarely included in aristocratic and scholarly libraries. The *Decameron* did not receive serious critical recognition until 1870, when Francesco De Sanctis, in his *Storia della letteratura italiana* (*History of Italian Literature*), described it as the "Human Comedy," thus suggesting that it is worthy of comparison to Dante's *Divine Comedy*. Since De Sanctis's study, criticism on the *Decameron* has been voluminous, with much of it centering on Boccaccio's use of allegory and irony, his attitude toward women, and the significance of various metaphors, symbols, and allusions in the individual novellas. In contrast to the intellectual elite who once shunned the book, modern scholars have now recognized the *Decameron* as a multifarious composition that addresses the most complex, fundamental, and eternal questions facing humankind. In English literature alone, many great writers—Geoffrey Chaucer, John Dryden, William Shakespeare, John Keats, Alfred, Lord Tennyson, Henry Wadsworth Longfellow, and others—have found subjects for poems, stories, and dramas in the *Decameron* as well as in Boccaccio's other prose and poetry. Thus, critics have universally concurred that Boccaccio's influence on modern letters is incalculable, acknowledging him as one of the world's most popular and enduring literary figures.

PRINCIPAL WORKS

La caccia di Diana [*Diana's Hunt*] (poetry) 1334
Il filostrato (poetry) 1335
Il filocolo (prose) 1336-38
Teseida [*Book of Theseus*] (poetry) 1339-41
L'amorosa visione [*Amorous Vision*] (poetry) 1342
Elegia di Madonna Fiammetta [*Fiammetta*] (poetry) 1343-44
Decameron (novella) 1348-53
De Genealogia deorum gentilium [*Genealogy of the Gentile Gods*] (treatise) 1350-74
Il Corbaccio (satire) 1354-55
Vita di Dante Alighieri [*Life of Dante*] (essays) 1354-55
De casibus virorum illustrium [*On the Fates of Illustrious Men*] (mediations and history) 1355-74
De montibus, silvis, fontibus, lacubus, fluminibus, stagnis seu paludibus, et de nominibus maris (nonfiction) 1355-74
De claris mulieribus [*Concerning Famous Women*] (biography) 1360-74

PRINCIPAL ENGLISH TRANSLATIONS

Amorous Fiammetta (translated by Bartholomew Young, 1587; revised by Edward Hutton, 1926)

The Filostrato (translated by N. E. Griffin and A. B. Myrick, 1929)

Boccaccio on Poetry, Being the Preface and Fourteenth and Fifteenth Books of Boccaccio's Genealogia Deorum Gentilium (translated by Charles G. Osgood, 1930)

Concerning Famous Women (translated by Guido Guarino, 1963)

The Life of Dante (translated by James Robinson Smith, 1963)

The Fates of Illustrious Men (translated by Louis Brewer Hall, 1965)

Nymphs of Fiesole (translated by Joseph Tusiani, 1971)

Decameron (translated by G. H. McWilliam, 1972)

The Book of Theseus (translated by Bernadette Marie McCoy, 1974)

Corbaccio (translated by Anthony K. Cassell, 1975)

Decameron (translated by Mark Musa and Peter E. Bondanella, 1982)

Diana's Hunt—Caccia di Diana (translated by Anthony K. Cassell and Victoria Kirkham, 1991)

CRITICISM

Giovanni Boccaccio (essay date c. 1370)

SOURCE: "Author's Epilogue," in *The Decameron*, translated by G. H. McWilliam, Penguin Books, 1972, pp. 829-33.

[*In the following excerpt from the epilogue to the* Decameron *(first manuscript version, c. 1370), Boccaccio, anticipating negative critical reaction to the work, justifies his use of Italian vernacular, his focus on women characters, and his interjection of eroticism and irony.*]

Noble young ladies, for whose solace I undertook this protracted labour, I believe that with the assistance of divine grace (the bestowal of which I impute to your compassionate prayers rather than to any merit of my own) those objectives which I set forth at the beginning of the present work have now been fully achieved. And so, after giving thanks, firstly to God and then to yourselves, the time has come for me to rest my pen and weary hand. Before conceding this repose, however, since I am fully aware that these tales of mine are no less immune from criticism than any of the other things of this world, and indeed I recall having shown this to be so at the beginning of the Fourth Day, I propose briefly to reply to certain trifling objections which, though remaining unspoken, may possibly have arisen in the minds of my readers, including one or two of yourselves.

There will perhaps be those among you who will say that in writing these stories I have taken too many liberties, in that I have sometimes caused ladies to say, and very often to hear, things which are not very suitable to be heard or said by virtuous women. This I deny, for no story is so unseemly as to prevent anyone from telling it, provided it is told in seemly language; and this I believe I may reasonably claim to have done.

But supposing you are right (for I have no wish to start a dispute with you, knowing I shall finish on the losing side), I still maintain, when you ask me why I did it, that many reasons spring readily to mind. In the first place, if any of the stories is lacking in restraint, this is because of the nature of the story itself, which, as any well-informed and dispassionate observer will readily acknowledge, I could not have related in any other way without distorting it out of all recognition. And even if the stories do, perhaps, contain one or two trifling expressions that are too unbridled for the liking of those prudish ladies who attach more weight to words than to deeds, and are more anxious to seem virtuous than to be virtuous, I assert that it was no more improper for me to have written them than for men and women at large, in their everyday speech, to use such words as *hole,* and *rod,* and *mortar,* and *pestle,* and *crumpet,* and *stuffing,* and any number of others. Besides, no less latitude should be granted to my pen than to the brush of the painter, who without incurring censure, of a justified kind at least, depicts St Michael striking the serpent with his sword or his lance, and St George transfixing the dragon wherever he pleases; but that is not all, for he makes Christ male and Eve female, and fixes to the cross, sometimes with a single nail, sometimes with two, the feet of Him who resolved to die thereon for the salvation of mankind.

Furthermore it is made perfectly clear that these stories were told neither in a church, of whose affairs one must speak with a chaste mind and a pure tongue (albeit you will find that many of her chronicles are far more scandalous than any writings of mine), nor in the schools of philosophers, in which, no less than anywhere else, a sense of decorum is required, nor in any place where either churchmen or philosophers were present. They were told in gardens, in a place designed for pleasure, among people who, though young in years, were nonetheless fully mature and not to be led astray by stories, at a time when even the most respectable people saw nothing unseemly in wearing their breeches over their heads if they thought their lives might thereby be preserved.

Like all other things in this world, stories, whatever their nature, may be harmful or useful, depending upon the listener. Who will deny that wine, as Tosspot and Bibber and a great many others affirm, is an excellent thing for those who are hale and hearty, but harmful to people suffering from a fever? Are we to conclude, because it does harm to the feverish, that therefore it is pernicious? Who will deny that fire is exceedingly useful, not to say vital, to man? Are we to conclude, because it burns down houses and villages and whole cities, that therefore it is pernicious? And in the same way, weapons defend the liberty of those who desire to live peaceably, and very often they kill people, not because they are evil in themselves, but because of the evil intentions of those who make use of them.

No word, however pure, was ever wholesomely construed by a mind that was corrupt. And just as seemly language leaves no mark upon a mind that is corrupt, language that is less than seemly cannot sully a mind that is well ordered, any more than mud will contaminate the rays of the sun, or earthly filth the beauties of the heavens.

What other books, what other words, what other letters, are more sacred, more reputable, more worthy of reverence, than those of the Holy Scriptures? And yet there have been many who, by perversely construing them, have led themselves and others to perdition. All things have their own special purpose, but when they are wrongly used a great deal of harm may result, and the same applies to my stories. If anyone should want to extract evil counsel from these tales, or fashion an evil design, there is nothing to prevent him, provided he twists and distorts them sufficiently to find the thing he is seeking. And if anyone should study them for the usefulness and profit they may bring him, he will not be disappointed. Nor will they ever be thought of or described as anything but useful and seemly, if they are read at the proper time by the people for whom they were written. The lady who is forever saying her prayers, or baking pies and cakes for her father confessor, may leave my stories alone: they will not run after anyone demanding to be read, albeit they are no more improper than some of the trifles that self-righteous ladies recite, or even engage in, if the occasion arises.

There will likewise be those among you who will say that some of the stories included here would far better have been omitted. That is as may be: but I could only transcribe the stories as they were actually told, which means that if the ladies who told them had told them better, I should have written them better. But even if one could assume that I was the inventor as well as the scribe of these stories (which was not the case), I still insist that I would not feel ashamed if some fell short of perfection, for there is no craftsman other than God whose work is whole and faultless in every respect. Even Charlemagne, who first created the Paladins, was unable to produce them in numbers sufficient to form a whole army.

Whenever you have a multitude of things you are bound to find differences of quality. No field was ever so carefully tended that neither nettles nor brambles nor thistles were found in it, along with all the better grass. Besides, in addressing an audience of unaffected young ladies, such as most of you are, it would have been foolish of me to go to the trouble of searching high and low for exquisite tales to relate, and take excessive plains in weighing my words. And the fact remains that anyone perusing these tales is free to ignore the ones that give offence, and read only those that are pleasing. For in order that none of you may be misled, each of the stories bears on its brow the gist of that which it hides in its bosom.

I suppose it will also be said that some of the tales are too long. To which I can only reply that if you have better things to do, it would be foolish to read these tales, even if they were short. Although much time has elapsed from the day I started to write until this moment, in which I am nearing the end of my labours, it has not escaped my memory that I offered these exertions of mine to ladies with time on their hands, not to any others; and for those who read in order to pass the time, nothing can be too long if it serves the purpose for which it is used.

Brevity is all very well for students, who endeavour to use their time profitably rather than while it away, but not for you, ladies, who have as much time to spare as you fail to consume in the pleasures of love. And besides, since none of you goes to study in Athens, or Bologna, or Paris, you have need of a lengthier form of address than those who have sharpened their wits with the aid of their studies.

Doubtless there are also those among you who will say that the matters I have related are overfilled with jests and quips, of a sort that no man of weight and gravity should have committed to paper. Inasmuch as these ladies, prompted by well-intentioned zeal, show a touching concern for my good name, it behoves me to thank them, and I do so.

But I would answer their objection as follows: I confess that I do have weight, and in my time I have been weighed on numerous occasions; but I assure those ladies who have never weighed me that I have little gravity. On the contrary, I am so light that I float on the surface of water. And considering that the sermons preached by friars to chastise the faults of men are nowadays filled, for the most part, with jests and quips and raillery, I concluded that the same sort of thing would be not out of place in my stories, written to dispel the woes of ladies. But if it should cause them to laugh too much, they can easily cure themselves by turning to the Lament of Jeremiah, the Passion of Our Lord, and the Plaint of the Magdalen.

There may also be those among you who will say that I have an evil and venomous tongue, because in certain places I write the truth about the friars. But who cares? I can readily forgive you for saying such things, for doubtless you are prompted by the purest of motives, friars being decent fellows, who forsake a life of discomfort for the love of God, who do their grinding when the millpond's full, and say no more about it. Except for the fact that they all smell a little of the billy-goat, their company would offer the greatest of pleasure.

I will grant you, however, that the things of this world have no stability, but are subject to constant change, and this may well have happened to my tongue. But not long ago, distrusting my own opinion (which in matters concerning myself I trust as little as possible), I was told by a lady, a neighbour of mine, that I had the finest and sweetest tongue in the world; and this, to tell the truth, was at a time when few of these tales remained to be written. So because the aforementioned ladies are saying these things in order to spite me, I intend that what I have said shall suffice for my answer.

And now I shall leave each lady to say and believe whatever she pleases, for the time has come for me to bring all words to an end, and offer my humble thanks to Him who assisted me in my protracted labour and conveyed me to the goal I desired. May His grace and peace, sweet ladies, remain with you always, and if perchance these stories should bring you any profit, remember me.

Petrarch (letter date 1373)

SOURCE: Letter to Boccaccio in 1373, in *Petrarch: The*

First Modern Scholar and Man of Letters, by James Harvey Robinson with Henry Winchester Rolfe, 1898. Reprint by Haskell House Publishers Ltd., 1970, pp. 191-96.

[An Italian poet and scholar, Petrarch is regarded as one of the greatest literary figures of the Renaissance. An ardent humanist and Latinist, he is primarily known for the passion, lyric expressiveness, and psychological power of his verse, collected in Canzoniere *(1374), which exerted a tremendous influence on European literature. In the following excerpt from a letter to Boccaccio dated 1373, Petrarch defends the unscholarly subject matter and relaxed narrative style of the* Decameron, *stating: "It is important to know for whom we are writing, and a difference in the character of one's listeners justifies a difference in style." This letter also originally contained Petrarch's Latin translation of the story of Griselda, the last narrative in the* Decameron.]

Your [**Decameron**], written in our mother tongue and published, I presume, during your early years, has fallen into my hands, I know not whence or how. If I told you that I had read it, I should deceive you. It is a very big volume, written in prose and for the multitude. I have been, moreover, occupied with more serious business, and much pressed for time. You can easily imagine the unrest caused by the warlike stir about me, for, far as I have been from actual participation in the disturbances, I could not but be affected by the critical condition of the state. What I did was to run through your book, like a traveller who, while hastening forward, looks about him here and there, without pausing. I have heard somewhere that your volume was attacked by the teeth of certain hounds, but that you defended it valiantly with staff and voice. This did not surprise me, for not only do I well know your ability, but I have learned from experience of the existence of an insolent and cowardly class who attack in the work of others everything which they do not happen to fancy or be familiar with, or which they cannot themselves accomplish. Their insight and capabilities extend no farther; on all other themes they are silent.

My hasty perusal afforded me much pleasure. If the humour is a little too free at times, this may be excused in view of the age at which you wrote, the style and language which you employ, and the frivolity of the subjects, and of the persons who are likely to read such tales. It is important to know for whom we are writing, and a difference in the character of one's listeners justifies a difference in style. Along with much that was light and amusing. I discovered some serious and edifying things as well, but I can pass no definite judgment upon them, since I have not examined the work thoroughly.

As usual, when one looks hastily through a book, I read somewhat more carefully at the beginning and at the end. At the beginning you have, it seems to me, accurately described and eloquently lamented the condition of our country during that siege of pestilence which forms so dark and melancholy a period in our century. At the close you have placed a story which differs entirely from most that precede it, and which so delighted and fascinated me that, in spite of cares which made me almost oblivious of myself, I was seized with a desire to learn it by heart, so that I might have the pleasure of recalling it for my own

benefit, and of relating it to my friends in conversation. When an opportunity for telling it offered itself shortly after, I found that my auditors were delighted. Later it suddenly occurred to me that others, perhaps, who were unacquainted with our tongue, might be pleased with so charming a story, as it had delighted me ever since I first heard it some years ago, and as you had not considered it unworthy of presentation in the mother tongue, and had placed it, moreover, at the end of your book, where, according to the principles of rhetoric, the most effective part of the composition belongs. So one fine day when, as usual, my mind was distracted by a variety of occupations, discontented with myself and my surroundings. I suddenly sent everything flying, and, snatching my pen, I attacked this story of yours. I sincerely trust that it will gratify you that I have of my own free-will undertaken to translate your work, something I should certainly never think of doing for anyone else, but which I was induced to do in this instance by my partiality for you and for the story. Not neglecting the precept of Horace in his *Art of Poetry,* that the careful translator should not attempt to render word for word, I have told your tale in my own language, in some places changing or even adding a few words, for I felt that you would not only permit, but would approve, such alterations.

Although many have admired and wished for my version, it seemed to me fitting that your work should be dedicated to you rather than to anyone else; and it is for you to judge whether I have, by this change of dress, injured or embellished the original. The story returns whence it came; it knows its judge, its home, and the way thither. As you and everyone who reads this knows, it is you and not I who must render account for what is essentially yours. If anyone asks me whether this is all true, whether it is a history or a story, I reply in the words of Sallust, "I refer you to the author"—to wit, my friend Giovanni.

My object in thus re-writing your tale was not to induce the women of our time to imitate the patience of this wife, which seems to me almost beyond imitation, but to lead my readers to emulate the example of feminine constancy, and to submit themselves to God with the same courage as did this woman to her husband. Although, as the Apostle James tells us, "God cannot be tempted with evil, and he himself tempteth no man," he still may prove us, and often permits us to be beset with many and grievous trials, not that he may know our character, which he knew before we were created, but in order that our weakness should be made plain to ourselves by obvious and familiar proofs. Anyone, it seems to me, amply deserves to be reckoned among the heroes of mankind who suffers without a murmur for God, what this poor peasant woman bore for her mortal husband.

My affection for you has induced me to write at an advanced age what I should hardly have undertaken even as a young man. Whether what I have narrated be true or false I do not know, but the fact that you wrote it would seem sufficient to justify the inference that it is but a tale. Foreseeing this question, I have prefaced my translation with the statement that the responsibility for the story rests with the author; that is, with you. And now let me tell you my experiences with this narrative, or tale, as I prefer to call it.

In the first place, I gave it to one of our mutual friends in Padua to read, a man of excellent parts and wide attainments. When scarcely half-way through the composition, he was suddenly arrested by a burst of tears. When again, after a short pause, he made a manful attempt to continue, he was again interrupted by a sob. He then realised that he could go no farther himself, and handed the story to one of his companions, a man of education, to finish. How others may view this occurrence I cannot, of course, say; for myself, I put a most favourable construction upon it, believing that I recognise the indications of a most compassionate disposition; a more kindly nature, indeed, I never remember to have met. As I saw him weep as he read, the words of the Satirist [Juvenal] came back to me:

> Nature, who gave us tears, by that alone
> Proclaims she made the feeling heart our
> own;
> And 't is our noblest sense.

Some time after, another friend of ours, from Verona (for all is common between us, even our friends), having heard of the effect produced by the story in the first instance, wished to read it for himself. I readily complied, as he was not only a good friend, but a man of ability. He read the narrative from beginning to end without stopping once. Neither his face nor his voice betrayed the least emotion, not a tear or a sob escaped him. "I too," he said at the end, "would have wept, for the subject certainly excites pity, and the style is well adapted to call forth tears, and I am not hard-hearted; but I believed, and still believe, that this is all an invention. If it were true, what woman, whether of Rome or any other nation, could be compared with this Griselda? Where do we find the equal of this conjugal devotion, where such faith, such extraordinary patience and constancy?" I made no reply to this reasoning, for I did not wish to run the risk of a bitter debate in the midst of our good-humoured and friendly discussion. But I had a reply ready. There are some who think that whatever is difficult for them must be impossible for others; they must measure others by themselves, in order to maintain their superiority. Yet there have been many, and there may still be many, to whom acts are easy which are commonly held to be impossible. Who is there who would not, for example, regard a Curtius, a Mucius, or the Decii, among our own people, as pure fictions; or, among foreign nations, Codrus and the Philaeni; or, since we are speaking of woman, Portia, or Hypsicratia, or Alcestis, and others like them? But these are actual historical persons. And indeed I do not see why one who can face death for another, should not be capable of encountering any trial or form of suffering. . . .

North American Review (essay date 1824)

SOURCE: "Boccaccio's Decameron," in *The North American Review*, Vol. XIX, No. XLIV, July, 1824, pp. 68-86.

[*Here, the anonymous critic surveys Boccaccio's life and career, relates the* Decameron's *literary history and artistic merits, and briefly comments on the* Decameron's *impact on subsequent European literature. The critic also laments the* Decameron's *immorality, stating that "many of the tales in the* Decameron *are disgraced by the most unpardonable impurities.*"]

Italy, it has been observed by one of the most ingenious and elegant historians of modern times, has peculiar cause to exult in the state of her literature during the fourteenth century. At that period the north of Europe still continued buried in the night of darkness, which attended and followed the dismemberment of the Western Empire; or, if a ray of light shone out here and there in the British Isles, in Germany, or among the remoter tribes beyond them, it seems to have been but a faint and fitful glimmering, only just enough to illuminate and render visible the capricious barbarism of the conquerors of the Caesars. The literature of the south of Europe, however, was just springing into being, with the flush and freshness of youth upon it. The songs of the troubadours, and the romances of chivalry, exhibiting all the charm of simplicity, raciness, and vigor, began ere now to be produced, in the fertility of a virgin soil, all over the contiguous countries of Italy, Spain, Portugal, and France. The people of these favored lands spoke kindred dialects of one great language, formed by incorporating the Teutonic idioms with such scattered fragments of the Roman tongue, as had survived the destruction of the Roman power; and their poetry displays an age not of imitation, nor of improvement on the past, but an age of first creation, like that in the times before among the primitive Greeks.

But there was this remarkable particular in which the Italians were distinguished in literature, from their sister nations in the south of Europe. The literature of the latter, as observed by Sismondi, belongs to the respective nations themselves, and not to individuals; but Italy, while in the general progress of intellectual culture she was not behind either France or Spain, gave birth to three men of extraordinary genius, who stood then, as they stand now, preeminent among all their contemporaries, and who, each in his peculiar kind, bequeathed the noblest models of excellence to an admiring posterity. They were all Florentines, children of that proud republic, whose destiny it was to renovate, in commercial splendor and in taste for letters, the glories of ancient Athens. Dante, the oldest of the three, and he among them, whose mind was of the most sublime and original cast, gave to the world the first great poem after the revival of letters in Western Europe; Petrarca created lyric poetry anew; and Boccaccio that rich, easy, mellifluous, flexible prose, which is so finely adapted to the national character of the Italians.

Boccaccio is the least celebrated of these illustrious names, because the department of literature, which he most successfully cultivated, wants the elevation of lyric or heroic poetry, and because the licentiousness of a part of his writings has fixed a lasting stigma upon his fame; owing to which, the incidents of his life and the merits of his writings are, perhaps, less familiarly known at the present day than those of Dante or Petrarca. But as Boccaccio was in fact the creator of the classic prose style of his nation, and as the ***Decameron,*** the most popular of his works, and that on which his reputation as a writer chiefly rests, is possessed of sterling excellencies, which, in our own day, as well as in preceding times, have endeared it to all the lovers of Italian literature, an account of his life, with a particular examination of the **Decameron,** may not be devoid of interest.

Neither the birthplace, nor the parentage of Boccaccio is known with certainty. His family, which maintained a respectable rank in the republic of Florence, belonged to Certaldo, a small village in the Val d'Elsa, about twenty miles from the city, from which our author himself was called Giovanni di Boccaccio da Certaldo. His father, Boccaccio di Chellino di Buonaiuto, was a merchant extensively engaged in commercial speculations, who, nevertheless, in the spirit which created the grandeur of his country, had been appointed to important offices in Florence. Giovanni, his son, was born in the year 1313, and, as some authors contend, in Florence; but Tiraboschi concludes, from the testimony of his oldest biographer, Villani, and of Domenico d'Arezzo, that he was born at Paris, where his father was then casually residing, and was the fruit of an intrigue with an obscure French woman. Manni, and other admirers of Boccaccio, strive hard to free his escutcheon from the sinister bar; but the fact, as we have stated it, is nearly certain.

Boccaccio was placed at Florence in his childhood under the care of Giovanni, father of the famous poet Zanobii da Strada, for instruction in liberal knowledge; but was soon removed from school by his father to be devoted to mercantile affairs, in the transaction of which he travelled constantly through the various provinces of Italy, and the neighboring countries. But in the short space of time, which he spent in study, he had acquired or developed a decided predilection for literature, which no exertions of his father could extinguish, nor any of the pleasures or cares of the world dissipate. On the contrary, he returned from his travels, not with that taste for business, which his father was anxious to inspire, but with increased intellectual accomplishments, and a more ardent thirst after knowledge. In this manner he wasted his youth and the prime of his manhood, reluctantly fastened down to the detail of commerce, doing constant violence to his feelings, and struggling in vain to accomplish his filial duties, while a more powerful and irresistible impulse was forcing him forward into the career of fame, on which he was destined to enter.

His example strikingly illustrates the uselessness of attempting to constrain the dispositions of the youthful mind, when they are once decidedly formed. The same intellect, that, in the situations to which nature and acquired taste adapt it, flourishes luxuriantly, and puts forth its hardy and healthful blossoms, will, if torn from the genial skies and earth, which it demands, droop away into a stinted and languishing growth. So it was with Boccaccio until his twenty eighth year, when a little incident, which occurred at Naples, emancipated his genius from the fetters, wherein it had hitherto lain imprisoned. While residing at Naples as a merchant, he happened to visit the tomb of Virgil, the sight of which so inflamed his poetic enthusiasm, and so heightened the disgust he felt towards com-

merce, that his father finally suffered him to follow the bent of his inclinations. The only condition imposed on Boccaccio was, that he should learn the canon law, which, in his eagerness to devote himself to study, he was willing to do, although he himself complains that the years thus occupied were thrown away, so invincible and exclusive was his attachment to letters. His father's death, soon afterwards, left him unconstrained master of his actions, when he gave himself up unreservedly to his favorite studies, and pursued them with all the energy of his ripened faculties. He collected and copied the manuscripts of ancient classics, and studied their works with enthusiasm; he eagerly sought for the society and instructions of all contemporary scholars in Italy, France, and Germany; in fine, he left unexplored no source of knowledge, which his age or country supplied, until he had mastered the severer sciences, as well as politer arts, and became not only one of the most cultivated writers, but also one of the most learned and accomplished men of his times.

The voluminous works of Boccaccio in mythology, geography, and history, to which we shall advert hereafter, fully attest his various and profound erudition. The acquisition of learning is the more honorable to him, as he commenced the study of letters late in life, and pursued it under an accumulation of disadvantages, of which it is not easy for us to form an adequate conception in our day. The invention of the art of printing has so immensely multiplied the copies of books, that learning is now as common as the very air we breathe. But then the scholar was obliged to plunge into the darkness of conventual cells in quest of the treasures of ancient lore, which lay buried there beneath the cobwebs and dust of centuries. He was compelled to proceed in his solitary path, without the illumination of criticism to guide his footsteps, painfully gathering up the strains of poetic inspiration from rolls of torn, defaced, and worm eaten parchment, or transcribing the oracles of philosophy from the lines of a *palimpsesta,* which the barbarism of monkish bigotry had sacrilegiously obscured for the reception of its superstitious legends. Nor, in the fourteenth century, did they possess any of those ample and abundant helps to learning, which have since rendered it as accessible to the peasant as the prince. The land was not then thronged with able professors in every department of human knowledge; nor was a multitude of schools established to diffuse the elements of science throughout the whole body of the people; nor were colleges and universities sprinkled all over the civilized world. We, therefore, in times when science has spread open her portals, and beckons all mankind to enter freely and bend before her shrine, cannot easily realise the situation of one, who aspired after her favor, and who, at the revival of letters, slowly won his way up the steep and laborious ascent, which then led to her temple. This consideration ought to increase our respect for men, who surmounted all these difficulties, and attained to so much well earned celebrity as did Boccaccio.

Among the remarkable circumstances in the studies of Boccaccio, we may mention his close intimacy with Petrarca. Their acquaintance began in 1350, Boccaccio being thirty seven years of age and Petrarca forty six, in the memorable year of the great jubilee, at which time they met in Florence, as Petrarca passed through it on his way to Rome, to unite there with the general assemblage of all the learning, wealth, rank, and beauty of christendom. The friendship, which arose between these two great scholars at this period, continued with them through life, each of them, in the constant interchange of letters and other friendly services, contributing to the improvement of the other, mutually communicating all their most secret thoughts, and zealously combining their common faculties for the advancement of learning. They cherished and admired each other's talents; and the tribute of public respect, which Boccaccio was the means, on one occasion, of communicating to Petrarca, served greatly to cement their union.

The family of the poet, as the admirers of him well know, was banished from Florence by the faction of the *Neri* in 1302, in the same year with Dante Alighieri, for his father's adhesion to the fallen party of the *Bianchi*. But in 1351, after the fame of Petrarca had spread far and wide throughout all Italy, after he had been solemnly crowned in the capitol as the prince of poets, before the applauding multitudes of Rome, when Naples, Venice, Padua, Milan, were contending for the possession of him, who was the glory of the Italian name, then it was that the Florentine republic, deeming the political sins of the parent atoned for by the celebrity of the son, strove to reclaim the poet to the land of his fathers, by restoring to him his confiscated patrimony, and soliciting him to fix his residence in the city of Florence. To enhance the value of the compliment, Boccaccio was charged with the grateful duty of presenting the request of the republic to his friend Petrarca, who, however, declined their solicitations, preferring to retire among the delightful solitudes of Vaucluse. But from this day the intimacy of the two friends continued close and unshaken till Petrarca's death, which was only a year before that of Boccaccio.

To Petrarca, and his friend Boccaccio, belong the merit of having introduced into modern Italy the study of Greek, and that, too, long before the dispersion of the Constantinopolitan exiles by the conquests of the Turks. Petrarca preceded his friend a few years in the study of a language and literature, which had so long been neglected by their countrymen; but Boccaccio applied to it with greater zeal than Petrarca, acquired more extensive knowledge of it, and did more towards rendering it familiar to the Italians. While Petrarca was learning the Greek language of the celebrated Calabrian monk Barlaamo, Boccaccio was acquiring it of Leonzio Pilato. These teachers were both natives of Calabria, where the Greek was still a spoken tongue. Leonzio had become deeply imbued with Greek erudition at Constantinople, and, being invited to Florence in 1360 by Boccaccio, founded there the first chair of public instruction in Greek, which, in modern times, was established in Western Europe. Leonzio is described by his patron and pupil as a man of rough aspect, deformed features, with a long beard, and a profusion of black hair, always immersed in thought, and of manners as rude as his person, but whose mind was, nevertheless, an inexhaustible storehouse of the history and literature of Greece. His immense erudition induced Boccaccio to overlook his defects of temper, manners, and person, to re-

ceive him into his own house, and to procure him a stipend from the city for a course of public lectures on Homer.

Boccaccio, after the death of his father, resided sometime at Naples, but chiefly at Florence; and in the mean time wrote and published various works, mostly of poetry and romance. His uncommon merits were soon discerned by his countrymen, and his fame passed rapidly from Florence over the rest of Italy. He was repeatedly employed by the state in the most important and most delicate negotiations, for which, by his enlarged mind and extensive travels, he was peculiarly fitted. His first embassy was to Romagna, whither he was sent to treat with Ostasio, or with Bernardino da Polenta, lord of Ravenna. The precise date of this mission is not well ascertained, being placed in 1347 by Tiraboschi, but three years subsequent by Baldelli, the latest biographer of Boccaccio. In 1351 he was sent to Padua, as we have already noticed, to invite Petrarca to Florence. The same year he was the ambassador of the republic to Lewis, Marquis of Brandenburg, son of Lewis the Bavarian, whom the Florentines solicited to cross the Alps, and reduce the power of the Visconti of Milan, then all powerful in Italy. In 1353, when it was rumored that Charles Fourth was about to enter Italy, the Florentines charged Boccaccio with an embassy to Pope Innocent Sixth at Avignon, to concert with him in what manner to receive the Emperor. He was invited to Naples in 1363 by Niccolo Acciajoli, grand seneschal of the kingdom; but, dissatisfied with his reception, which he considered less honorable than his merits demanded, he soon returned to Florence. Two years afterwards he was despatched a second time to the court of Avignon, to explain to Urban Fifth some circumstances in the conduct of the Florentines, at which the pontiff had been dissatisfied; and, again, in 1367 he was sent on another mission to the same pope, who was then at Rome, whither the papal see was just returned from Avignon. This was the last public embassy in which Boccaccio was employed by his countrymen; although not the last proof of their esteem for his character; for in 1373 he was appointed by the city to deliver a course of public readings on Dante. His lectures were received with great applause; and lectures on the Commedia, in imitation of them, were afterward pronounced by the historian Filippo Villani at Florence, and by Benvenuto da Imola at Bologna.

Boccaccio was accustomed to retire from the tumult, dissensions, and popular conflicts of the city to his little patrimony of Certaldo, to pursue his studies in tranquillity.; and there he died, on the 21st of December, 1375, shortly after the death of Petrarca. He was honorably buried, and the following inscription, written by himself, was placed over his grave.

> Hac sub mole jacent cineres ac ossa Johannis.
> Mens sedet ante Deum, meritis ornata laborum
> Mortalis vitæ; Genitor Boccaccius illi,
> Patria Certaldum, studium fuit alma poesis.

The morals of Boccaccio, we regret to say, partook of the prevailing looseness and licentiousness of the times. His private life was by no means praiseworthy, and many of his writings, parts of the *Decameron* especially, bespeak a man of libertine principles, and a scoffer at things the most sacred and venerable.

A very singular incident in the private life of Boccaccio was his sudden conversion. His friendship for Petrarca, who, amid all his foibles, preserved a sincere respect for religious institutions, in some degree conduced to elevate the morals of Boccaccio. Petrarca frequently admonished him of the evil example and pernicious consequences of his conduct; but without a very marked permanent effect, until the enthusiasm, or the artifice, of a Carthusian friar produced an instantaneous change in his course of life, and rendered it as austere and ascetic as it before had been licentious. The circumstances are related by many authors; but the most particular account of them, which we have read, is that given by the Abbé de Sade. A Carthusian of Sienna, named father Petroni, who, after having wrought a multitude of miracles to the great satisfaction of the populace, while he lay on his deathbed, charged father Ciani, a monk of his order, to repair to Boccaccio and Petrarca, inform them that they had but a few years to live, and warn them instantly to reform their manners and writings, and to renounce poetry, and all profane studies, that they might dedicate the residue of their lives to the sole service of God. To convince Boccaccio of the supernatural source of this communication, the wily Carthusian acquainted him with a secret, which he thought was known to himself alone, on the discovery of which, seized with superstitious dread, and terrified by the idea of the near approach of death, he immediately reformed his manners, assumed the monastic habit, applied to the study of the saints and fathers, and determined to abandon love and poetry, and even part with his library, which consisted almost exclusively of profane authors. Petrarca, who viewed the subject a little more dispassionately, and pretty clearly intimated, that he looked upon the pretended prophecy as a pious fraud, dissuaded his friend from carrying his devotion to such extravagant excess; but thenceforth Boccaccio was an altered man. This happened in 1362, thirteen years before his death, and so far not altogether in accordance with one part of the good father's prophetic denunciation.

In proceeding to give some account of the voluminous writings of Boccaccio, we shall begin with his Latin treatises, although the composition of them was chiefly the work of his later years. Of these the most celebrated is a book on the genealogy of the gods, in which he assembles all the apparatus of learning, which was then accessible, for the illustration of the fantastic mythology of the Greeks and Romans. Another book of his, on the Names of Mountains, Forests, Lakes, Rivers, and Seas, was among the first of modern geographies, in the compilation of which he derived no little aid from his own extensive personal knowledge of many parts of Europe. These works are neglected now, because the discovery of a great number of manuscripts then unknown, and the facilities afforded to study by the art of printing, have enabled us to push farther our researches into antiquity; and the use of them is now superseded by more learned and critical works on the same subjects. But, in the times when they were written, they attained the highest repute, and were

considered little less than prodigies of erudition; and on these forgotten compilations, singular as we may now deem it, our author relied for his literary immortality. Two other works, the first on the Calamities of Illustrious Persons, and the second on Famous Women, were very popular reading in their day, so much so as to have been translated into many languages. These books are not composed in the pure and elegant Latinity of our classical models; but they gave Boccaccio the character of an unequalled scholar.

Of poetry, Boccaccio published sixteen Latin Eclogues, which, however, do not display the greatest felicity of composition, and are not to be compared in merit with the Latin poems of Petrarca. He also composed a considerable number of poems in Italian; but, according to the consenting voice of the best critics, he possessed neither the elegance of style, nor quickness of fancy, nor force of sentiment, which should place him in the first rank of poets.

Still his poems are remarkable in more than one point of view. Among them are two heroic poems, *La Teseide* and *Il Filostrato,* which were the earliest attempts, in any modern tongue, to revive the ancient epopoeia. Boccaccio perceived that the essence of epic poetry consisted in the invention, interest, and development of the action; and although he overdid the thing, and composed romances instead of poems, yet, as a later writer observes, 'abandoning the dull repetition of dreams and visions, he imagined a regular action or fable, and conducted it through different stages of adventure to its close,' and thus pointed out the proper course for his more gifted successors to follow. The *Teseide* has some additional claims on our attention, as having been translated, or rather imitated by Chaucer and Dryden. The *Knight's Tale* of Chaucer is not properly a translation of the *Teseide*; for the sire of English verse has abridged the prolix, and enlarged the poetical parts of his original, and compressed the whole into a concise and beautiful heroic tale; and when the language of Chaucer was grown obsolete, and his rich pages a sealed book to the common reader, Dryden transfused the ideas and the imagery of Chaucer into his spirited poem of Palamon and Arcite.

But the great merit of Boccaccio lay in his Italian prose. His life of Dante, and Commentary on the *Divina Commedia,* and the several larger romances, written by him, entitled *Il Filocopo, La Fiammetta, L'Ameto,* and *Il Corbaccio,* we may pass lightly over to arrive at the great monument of his genius and foundation of his fame, the *Decameron.* Of all the rest of his works, except this, we are not ashamed to say we know little ourselves. Few of them are ranked at this day among the Italian classics. We will merely pause, therefore, to remark, that they are the oldest specimens of romances of love; for they lead the way in that department of literature in modern times; and the ancients were utterly destitute of anything that deserves the name of a romance. These did not, like the romances of chivalry, flatter the imagination by recounting marvellous and impossible adventures; but went directly to domestic life, and the human heart, as it is found in society, for the sources of their interest. But all that we have

The oldest portrait of Boccaccio, from a manuscript of the Filostrato.

to observe, on this point, will arise more appropriately out of the examination of the **Decameron.**

The scene of this celebrated performance is placed at Florence in the year 1348, when that proud and populous city was laid low in sorrow by the scourge of one of the most destructive plagues, which history records; a plague, which, in the complication of its horrors, and the extent of its ravages, is entitled to a mournful eminence beside those of Athens, Marseilles, and London. The description of this malady, which forms the introduction of the work, is justly esteemed one of the choicest morsels of the kind in the whole range of literature. The perfect truth of the description, the masterly skill with which the most striking circumstances are selected, to give us a distinct idea of the dreadful moral and physical effects of the pestilence, and yet to awake no disgust in our minds, and the unaffected emotion of the writer in unfolding the desolation of his beautiful city, invest this piece with all those attributes of genuine historic eloquence, which belong to the celebrated description by Thucydides of the plague of Athens.

This plague first broke out in the Levant, and moving on from place to place, finally, notwithstanding every precau-

tion that human foresight could devise, made its appearance in the spring of the year at Florence. The malady was soon found to be contagious, and spread with frightful rapidity through the crowded population of the city. No sooner had the contagion become general, than all social order was at an end; the constituted authorities of the city ceased to possess any control over the people; every one became undisputed master of his own actions; and in this universal anarchy and misrule, abandoned miscreants rose up, who made the desolation of their fellow citizens the means of unhallowed gain, going from house to house, and despoiling the deserted palaces of their sumptuous plate and furniture, and even plundering the dead, or the dying in their last helpless agonies, of the very jewels they wore on their persons. Indeed the morbid selfishness and hardness of heart, engendered by constant familiarity with these scenes of horror, which sometimes led the best to abandon their friends to fate, and tempted the bad to such acts of profligate pillage, manifested itself in the whole conduct of the inhabitants. It was the usage in the city for the friends of a deceased person to assemble at his house, and sympathise with the afflicted family; but all the accompaniments of grief were now no more; the surviving relations, given up to a kind of intoxication of despair, converted the funeral solemnity into a revolting scene of laughter and noisy merriment.

But the manner in which those persons, who were yet in health, spent their time, was the most remarkable. One class, thinking to avoid the contagion by moderation in diet and by shunning all excesses, formed little parties, who shut themselves up from the world, paid no regard to whatever was passing without their doors, and, living temperately on the best of wines and viands, occupied their minds entirely with music and other agreeable but moderate recreations. Others, on the contrary, maintained free living to be the surest preservative, and accordingly they passed day and night in drinking, feasting, and every excess of vice, moving continually from tavern to tavern, taking possession of the untenanted mansions of the rich, and using all they contained as common property. Another class held a middle course between these two extremes, neither binding themselves to a strict diet like the one, nor indulging in intemperance like the other, but eating and drinking as their feelings dictated, going about as usual, only smelling constantly of spicery and aromatic herbs, by way of protection against the influences of contagion. A more numerous class, however, of those in easy circumstances, hurried away from the city, their friends, and their possessions, into the country, postponing every consideration to the love of life, and seeming to hold it a tempting of their fate to abide in a place thus doomed to destruction. But, not to dwell any longer on these painful objects, it is confidently affirmed that, within the space of five months, what by the neglect to which the sick were exposed, what by the inherent virulence of the pestilence, more than a hundred thousand souls perished within the walls of the city; so that many a magnificent dwelling was depopulated to the last servant; thousands in the prime of youthful vigor, who rose in the morning seemingly in perfect health, were carried out to their last long home before night; large families became entirely extinct, as if they had never been; and a multitude of vast possessions remained, without any living person to claim the inheritance.

It is amid these scenes of distress, that our author, with the truest insight into human nature, has laid the action of one of the most delightful and enchanting works of imagination. There is no inconsistency here; nothing could be more finely conceived. It is not merely, that the tragic nature of everything around places the smiling hilarity of the fable in higher relief, although this too has its weight; but it is the exquisite accordance of the design with the emotions of the heart in such a situation, that we most admire in the conception of the *Decameron.* We might have imagined, that melancholy objects would harmonise best with feelings of profound sorrow; but in that case we should judge superficially; for in fact the constant menace of death presented to us at every instant, in all we see, produces a moral inebriation; and then our passionate desire to escape from the contemplation of our dangers will cause a torrent of gaiety to flow over the heart, at the very moment when each exterior circumstance would seem calculated to dry up the fountains of joy.

At the height of the plague, then, our author imagines seven young ladies to have attended divine service in the city on a Tuesday morning, they being the whole congregation. After their devotions were over, being all intelligent, nobly descended, beautiful, highly accomplished in manners and mind, and united by close ties of blood or friendship, they withdrew into a vestibule of the church, and began to speak of their melancholy situation. At last, Pampinea, the eldest of the group, first observing that the desire to preserve life was among the strongest instincts of our nature, asked, why they should not follow the example of so many before them, who had forsaken the devoted city. If we walk out, said she, we are saluted only by the litters of the sick, or the palls of the dead borne along in the streets, or by the scum of the city insulting our grief with songs and indecent ballads; and if we remain at home, we must wander in solitude through our gloomy apartments, with the phantoms of our departed friends continually before our eyes. She proposed, therefore, that they should retire together into the country, and occupy their different villas in succession, where the fresh air, the warbling of birds, the green hills and vallies waving with the future harvest, and the clear, bright canopy of heaven above them, might, in some degree, relieve their spirits from the pressure of calamity.

This plan was applauded by all her companions; only Philomena, one of them, objected, that their situation would be open to calumny, and even to danger from the lawless wretches, who were roaming about the country, unless they had some gentlemen in their company to afford them countenance and protection. This difficulty embarrassed the ladies exceedingly; but while they were consulting on the point, three gentlemen of their acquaintance entered the church, who were delighted with their project, and declared themselves ready to depart at a moment's warning. Orders were despatched into the country to prepare for their reception; and the next morning the whole party set off for a villa about two miles from the city. After they were arrived, one of the gentlemen, Dioneus, under

which name Boccaccio is said to have described himself, told the ladies that, in accepting their invitation, he had left all his cares behind him, and unless they were of the same mood, he should speedily bid them farewell. Pampinea replied, that they were fully disposed to merriment

Within the limit of becoming mirth;

and, in order to regulate their diversions, she proposed that each of the company in rotation should act as head one day, the first to be elected by the whole, and each successor to be appointed by the king, or queen, of the preceding day. Accordingly Pampinea was chosen queen; and crowned with a laurel's wreath, as the ensign of sovereignty. The next day, when the sun became high, they retired into a meadow of deep grass sheltered from his rays; and in order to pass the time away agreeably, it was proposed, that each person should relate a story, or *novel,* of some kind, for the entertainment of the company. The ten stories being concluded, they spent the rest of the day as they had the afternoon and evening before, in dancing, and singing, and conversation; and the next, and the following days, after the same manner; and thus are related the hundred novels, ten novels each day for ten days, which compose the *Decameron.*

The novels of the first day are on miscellaneous subjects. Those of the second are concerning persons, who, after being conducted by fortune through a variety of adverse vicissitudes, finally, beyond all hope, arrive at a happy issue. The two following days being Friday and Saturday, it was agreed to suspend their amusements, to be resumed again on Sunday; and on that day they removed to another more beautiful villa, which is depicted here with great fidelity, minuteness, and uncommon elegance of description, and is still pointed out to strangers as *Boccaccio's Villa.* The estate is called, *Il Podere della Fonte,* or the Farm of the Fountain, from a jet of water, which spouts up from a natural spring through a statue placed over a marble basin, and which supplies a constant stream of sufficient size to irrigate the whole of the grounds. This villa was formerly a domain of the Neroni di Nigi, but now belongs to the Pandolfini. Here the 'gay hermits' continued their amusements, and the subject of the third day was still the mutability of fortune; on the fourth, they discoursed of those whose love had terminated unfortunately; on the fifth, of what had terminated happily for lovers after the most cruel mischances; on the sixth, of persons who had successfully retorted some stroke of wit by a keen repartee, or by some prompt reply, or happy foresight, had averted peril or derision; on the seventh, concerning stratagems, with which wives had deceived their husbands; on the eighth, of tricks, such as are daily practised between different persons; on the ninth, concerning any subject which struck each one's fancy; and on the tenth and last, of persons, who, in whatever situation, had displayed uncommon liberality or magnificence. At the close of the tenth day, the party agreed to separate, and on the day following they returned to their respective homes in Florence.

Hoping we shall not have trespassed on the indulgence of our readers by going thus fully into a detail of the plan, we will now proceed to advert briefly to the literary history and merits of the *Decameron.* It was published in two parts, the first in 1353, and the second in 1358; and immediately upon the invention of printing, it was printed and circulated freely in Italy, until it was condemned, in the middle of the sixteenth century, by the Council of Trent; but the printing of corrected and *expurgated* editions was afterwards licensed by the popes, at the earnest solicitation of the grand duke of Tuscany. Since then innumerable editions of it, with every species of critical and historical illustration, have been printed in the original; and it has been translated and circulated in all the languages of Europe.

Some authors have accused Boccaccio of plagiarism; the French particularly, whose *sçavans,* like her warriors, are a little too prone to claim what is not theirs of right, undertake to say many of his tales are borrowed from the *fabliaux* and old romances. There can be little doubt, however, as to the fact. Boccaccio does not pretend to invent the fable of his novels. He simply gathers up the popular tales of the day, such as his reading, travels, or friends could furnish him with, adorns them with new incidents, and embodies the whole into his own spirited and beautiful narrative, the admitted model of Italian prose. The great passion then was for narrative poetry and narrative prose; and the novellists, like the trouveurs, drew from the same common source; and, therefore, neither are chargeable with plagiarism, because neither aspire to the merit of originality. The origin of that whole school of literature itself is another and wider field of inquiry, which we may not enter here; although the result of such inquiry, we imagine, would be to trace the whole up to an oriental fountain. The praise, however, which will not, and cannot be denied him, is that of having first rescued these entertaining compositions from the mouths of court buffoons and street jesters, and elevated them into a new class of literature, while succeeding ages, and other nations, have been proud to imitate their great master, without surpassing him in excellence.

What then is the extraordinary merit, which has conferred this rank on Boccaccio? It is the elegance of his style, his felicity and choice of expression, the rich variety of his subjects, the spirit and faithfulness of his delineations, the unaffected naïveté of his narrative, the dramatic eloquence of his dialogue, the poignancy of his satirical touches; it is from qualities like these, that he derives the celebrity of his name. He raises before us a moving panorama of life in all its complicated varieties. We cannot give an idea of the nature of the animated scene more clearly, than by translating the words of Ginguené. 'Priests, crafty and libertine as they were then,' says he,

> 'monks abandoned to luxury, gluttony, and debauch; duped and credulous husbands; artful and coquettish wives; the young devoted to pleasure, the old to gain; oppressive and cruel lords, frank and courteous knights; ladies either frail and addicted to gallantry, or else generous and proud, often the victims of their weakness, and tyrannised over by jealous husbands; pirates, banditti, hermits, workers of false miracles, and of tricks of jugglery; persons, in short, of every condition, country, age, all with their appropriate costume of passions, habits, and language; these a. · the objects, which fill up this immense

picture, and which men of the severest taste are never weary of admiring.'

Nothing could be more exact than the view Ginguené thus gives of the **Decameron.** And yet Boccaccio looked upon the work as a slight thing thrown out, if we may so speak, in a frolic of the imagination, and prized himself on his heavy compilation of heathen criticisms; but posterity, more just than himself to his fame, has allowed the latter to sink, as they were floating down the tide of time, while the lighter graces of the former have kept them buoyant above the stream, to remain an imperishable monument of his genius.

We will not stop to recount the numerous imitators of Boccaccio, who immediately sprang up in Italy. Nor will we examine how much the poets and dramatists of later times are indebted to him; just observing, as we pass, that many of La Fontaine's fables, two of Molière's best comedies, *George Dandin* and *L'Ecole des Maris,* Lope de Vega's *Discreta Enamorada,* and several others of the best pieces in foreign literature, are extracted from the treasures of the **Decameron.** We will pause only on English literature a moment, where we find, not to speak of meaner authors, that Chaucer, Shakespeare, and Dryden, are under great obligations to Boccaccio. Witness several of the finest among the *Canterbury Tales,* which Chaucer took from our author, and which Dryden wrought up into some of the most gorgeous and majestic of his Fables. Witness the whole plot, many of the particular incidents, and the very names of the principal persons in *All's Well that Ends Well,* which may be traced to Boccaccio's Giletta di Nerbona. Witness, finally, some of the finest parts of *Cymbeline,* borrowed, the commentator Stevens to the contrary notwithstanding, from the Bemabo da Genova of the **Decameron.** All these instances will attest the early and wide popularity, and the genuine merits of Boccaccio.

We wish we could close our [essay] here, and were not obliged, in justice to historic truth, to subjoin that many of the tales in the **Decameron** are disgraced by the most unpardonable impurities; a circumstance, which, as we have already intimated, fastens a deep stain, indelibly deep, on the memory of Boccaccio. But, in his latter years, he most bitterly lamented the immoral tendency of portions of his writings, and desired in vain to recall the winged messenger of corruption, which had flown forth among men, and could no longer be stayed in its course. The taste and moral sense of our own days would effectually interdict the composition of such tales; but Boccaccio did only what the feelings and manners of his age sanctioned. And yet this was an age of incipient illumination; and slight as must have been the elevation, or the influence of women, it was an age, when Italy was the commercial medium of the world, and the asylum of letters, arts, and refinement, adorned with the superb paintings of the modern masters, and all those magnificent structures, which signalised the pomp of the great cities and families, the taste of the Medici of Florence, the splendor of the Visconti of Milan, of the Gonzaghi of Mantua, and of the yet more princely Ferrarese House of Este.

But, notwithstanding all these outward indications of highly cultivated manners, the fact that a work, like the one we have examined, was avowedly published for the recreation of the female sex, is enough to show what was, in truth, the moral standard of the times. The **Decameron** abounds in the delineations of domestic incidents, manners, and scenery; and we cannot suppose the character of women, as it then existed, would be mistaken or misrepresented by so acute an observer, and so faithful a painter as Boccaccio. The brilliancy on the surface of things, of which we have spoken, arose more from the political revolutions of wealthy states, than from genuine refinement. Many of the first cities of Italy were just becoming subject to absolute princes, either elected by the people, who flew to despotism as a refuge from anarchy, or exalted into dominion by intrigue and arms. These new masters of governments, which before were popular, displayed an unbounded profusion of luxury, that they might intimidate their enemies, and retain the respect of their friends by the show of power, and still more, that they might divest the minds of their freeborn subjects from the galling sense of subjection. The magnificence of the Estensi, the Gonzaghi, the Carraresi, the Scaligeri, and the Visconti, was nothing but the *panis et circenses,* with which Augustus amused the turbulent populace of Rome.

Ugo Foscolo   (essay date 1826)

SOURCE: "Boccaccio," in *Critical Perspectives on the "Decameron,"* edited by Robert S. Dombroski, Hodder and Stoughton, 1976, pp. 15-25.

[*A prominent Italian poet, essayist, and critic, Foscolo is renowned for his autobiographical novel* Le ultime lettere di Jacopo Ortis *(1802) and the poem* I sepolcri *(1807; On Sepulchres). In the following excerpt from an article originally published in the* London Magazine *in 1826, Foscolo considers the* Decameron *from philological and historical perspectives, explaining that the work, while rhetorically and stylistically accomplished, is most notable as a record of Italy's cultural and civic history.*]

[Boccaccio] died not only without the hope, but without the desire, that his **Decameron** should outlive him. His autograph copy has never been found, and from what we shall presently have occasion to observe about his handwriting, we derive very strong presumptive evidence that he destroyed it himself. A young friend of his [Francesco Mannelli], eight or ten years after his death, transcribed it with the most scrupulous exactness, frankly confessing that the copy he used was full of errors. After the introduction of printing, copies and editions were multiplied with mistakes, which, it was clear, were partly accumulated by the negligence of printers, while their art was yet in its infancy. But from the age of Boccaccio to that of Lorenzo de Medici and the pontificate of Leo X, the Italian language was so barbarised that it seemed lost to the learned men of Italy; for more than a century they wrote in Latin, which had fixed rules and was common to all Europe. The critics of that illustrious epoch strove by every means to form the language spoken by Italians into a literary language, well adapted for written composition and for being understood by the whole nation, and in the penury of authors who could furnish observations, and examples, and principles, from which a right method might be

derived, they had recourse, with common consent, to the tales of Boccaccio; they found words at once vernacular and perfectly elegant, distinct and expressive; skilful construction, musical periods, and diversity of style; nor perhaps could any expedient at that time have been found better adapted for obviating numerous difficulties which presented themselves. But the maxims and the practice of the literary men of that age consisted not so much in constructing rules from observations as in imitating punctually, servilely, and childishly the most admired writers. In poetry they were implicit copiers of Petrarch, and sang of pure and sacred love. In Latin they imitated Virgil and Cicero, and treated sacred things in profane words. Thus the system of restricting a whole dead language to the works of a few writers was still more absurdly applied to the living tongue of Italy, and the critics were almost unanimous in decreeing that no example was to be adduced from any poem except the Canzoniere Amoroso of Petrarch.

From this circumstance, the Protestants took occasion to impute to the literary men of that time very small regard to manners, and no sense of religion. The first accusation is exaggerated, and was common to them with all orders of society in Europe; the other is most absurd, but has prevailed in Protestant universities from that day, and has been handed down by long tradition, on the testimony of the first religious reformers, who, in order to open every possible way for the reception of their doctrines, imputed infidelity to all the learned men of the court of Leo X. But most, if not all of these men believed the faith they possessed, and which was then attacked by hostile superstition. Some made a vow never to read a profane book, but being unable long to observe it, got absolution from the Pope; others, that they might not contaminate Christian things with the impure latinity of monks and friars, tried to translate the Bible into the language of the age of Augustus. This system of servilely imitating excellent authors did not prevent some men of genius, particularly historians, from attempting to relate in a style at once original, dignified, and energetic, the events of their country. But they were living writers, nor had long celebrity and prescriptive authority yet stamped them as models. To this reason, which holds good of every age and country, was added, that the liberty of the numerous republics of Italy which had sprung up in the barbarism of the Middle Ages, declined in the most fertile and splendid period of her literature, and the historians who were witnesses of the misfortunes and degradation of their country, wrote in a manner which was not agreeable to her tyrants. Hence Machiavelli, Guicciardini, Segni, and others who are now studied as masters of style, were not then read, except by a few; their works were hardly known in manuscript, and if published they were mutilated; nor were any complete editions of their histories printed until two centuries after they were written. Thus the *Novelle* of Boccaccio held the field, and their popularity was greatly increased by the abhorrence and contempt which they inspired against the wickedness of the monks.

Certain young men of Florence conspired against Duke Alexander, bastard of Clement VII, with the design of driving him from their country, and re-establishing the republic. They held meetings under the colour of amending the text of Boccaccio by the collation of manuscripts, and by critical examination. Such was the source, and such the authors, of the celebrated edition of Giunti, in 1527, now regarded as one of the rarest curiosities of bibliography, and preserved from that time as a record of the Florentine republic, almost all these young men having fought against the house of Medici, and died at the siege of Florence or in exile. The work subsequently became more scarce, because it was constantly exposed to the danger of being mutilated or prohibited through the interest of the monks. Leo X made a jest of those things, and crowned the abbot of Gaeta, seated on an elephant, with laurel and cabbage-leaves. Adrian VI, who succeeded him, had been immured in a cloister, and the cardinals of his school shortly after proposed that the Colloquies of Erasmus, and every popular book injurious to the clergy, should be prohibited. Paul III was of the opinion that the threat was sufficient, nor was it at that time put in execution; but when the *Decameron,* which had already been translated into several languages, was quoted by the Anti-Papists, the Church ceased to confine herself to threats, and began actually to prohibit the reprinting and the reading of Boccaccio's tales; nor could any one have a copy in his possession without a licence from his confessor. The Protestant Reformation provoked a reform in the Catholic Church, which though less apparent was perhaps greater and more solid. The Protestants took as the basis of theirs the liberty of interpreting the oracles of the Holy Spirit by the aid of human reason; while the Catholics admitted no interpretations but those inspired by God as represented by the Popes. Which of these two was the most beneficial to the interest of religion is a difficult question. Perhaps every religion which is subjected to the scrutiny of reason ceases to be faith; while every creed inculcated without the concurrence of the reason degenerates into blind superstition. But, as far as literature was concerned, liberty of conscience, in many countries, prepared the way for civil liberty, and for the free expression of thoughts and opinions; while in Italy, passive obedience to the religious power strengthened political tyranny, and increased the debasement and long servitude of the public mind. The Protestant Reformation was principally confined to dogmas—the Catholic wholly to discipline; and, therefore, all speculations on the lives and manners of ecclesiastics were then repressed as leading to new heresies. The Council of Trent saw that the people of Germany did not stop short at complaining that the monks were traders in Indulgences, but went on to deny the sacrament of confession, the celibacy of the clergy, and the infallibility and spiritual power of the Pope. It therefore decreed that any attack upon, or insinuations against, the clergy, should be followed by immediate registration of the book containing them in the index of prohibited works; and that the reading or the possession of any such book, without licence from a bishop, should be regarded both as a sin and as an offence punishable in virtue of the anathema. These laws, of ecclesiastical origin, were thenceforth interpreted and administered by civil tribunals subjected to the presidency of inquisitors of the order of St Dominic; who, moreover, by the consent of the Italian governments, were invested with authority to examine, alter, mutilate and suppress every book,

whether ancient or modern, previously to its being printed.

The Spanish domination in Italy, the long reign of Philip II (the most tyrannical of the tyrants), and the Council of Trent, had imposed silence upon genius. Cosmo I, Grand Duke of Tuscany, kept in his pay one or two historians of the house of Medici; he caused all books of a less servile character to be collected together from every part and burnt. The *Decameron* was, therefore, by an absolute political necessity, resorted to by literary men as the sole rule and standard of the written prose language. To cancel every memorial of freedom, Cosmo I suppressed all the academies instituted in Tuscany during the republican government of its cities; the only indulgence he showed was to an assembly of grammarians, who afterwards became famous rather than illustrious under the name of the Accademia della Crusca; and then, when the indolence of slavery deadened and chilled the passions; when education, committed to the Jesuits, had enfeebled all intellect; when men of letters became the furniture of courts, often of foreign courts; when universities were in the pay of kings, and under the direction of inquisitors—then did the Accademia della Crusca begin to claim supremacy over Italian literature, and to establish the tales of Boccaccio as the sole text and rule for every dictionary of grammar, and the basis of every philosophical theory regarding the language.

Nevertheless the academicians found that the *Decameron* had never been printed in a genuine and correct form, fitted to serve as the ground-work of language. After many years spent in consulting, correcting, and collating manuscripts, they prepared an edition which they hoped to consecrate as the oracle in all grammatical questions: but the Holy Office interposed in the most furious manner, and did not allow it to be printed. They therefore consented, as they could do no better, to publish a mutilated edition. The grand dukes of Tuscany, in order to put an end to these difficulties, deputed certain learned men to negotiate with the Master of the Sacred Palace in the Vatican, of whom one was a bishop, and nearly all dignified ecclesiastics. The Master of the Sacred Palace, a Dominican friar and a Spaniard, attended their meetings in his own right. Writing his opinions in a bastard language, he gave his advice as an official grammarian: they did not, however, come to any conclusion.

At length an Italian Dominican, of a more facile character, was added to the council, and having been confessor to Pius V he prevailed on Gregory XIII to allow the *Decameron* to be printed without any other alteration than what was necessary for the good fame of the ecclesiastics. Thus, abbesses and nuns in love with their gardeners were transformed into matrons and young ladies; friars who got up impostures and miracles into necromancers; and priests who intrigued with their parishioners' wives into soldiers; and by dint of a hundred other inevitable transformations and mutilations, the academy, after four years' labour, succeeded in publishing the *Decameron* in Florence, illustrated by their researches. But Sextus V ordered that even this edition, though approved by his predecessor, should be infamized in the Index. It was therefore necessary to have recourse to fresh mangling and interpolation, and of texts so fabricated, therefore, the academicians of La Crusca weighed every word and every syllable of the *Novelle,* exaggerated every minute detail, and described every thing under the high-sounding names of the richness, propriety, grace, elegance, the figures, laws, and principles of language . . . .

This singular destiny of a work composed as a mere pastime, threw into comparative oblivion its other literary merits, which were more useful to the civilisation of Europe, and stamped upon the name of its author an infamous celebrity, which has always hidden from the world the true character of his mind. . . . It is unquestionable, that if Petrarch had expended on writing Italian prose the tenth part of the labour which he bestowed on his poetry, he would not have been able to write so much as he did. This reason, among many others, contributed to induce him to write in Latin: the chief motive, however, was the glory which then attached to the Latin poets, and which, in the universities and the courts of the princes, was scarcely granted to those who write in Italian. Few however, if any, had any real conception of the spirit and merits of the Latin tongue. Coluccio Salutato was a man of great learning and enjoyed a high reputation among the scholars of that age; yet he pronounced that the pastoral poems of Boccaccio, written in Latin, were only inferior to Petrarch, and that Petrarch was superior to Virgil! Erasmus, a critic of another age, and of a different turn of mind, when commenting on the literature of the fourteenth century, detracts a little from the praises bestowed upon Petrarch, and enhances those of Boccaccio, whose Latinity he esteems the less barbarous of the two.

The injury which Petrarch did to his native tongue, by his ambition of writing in Latin, was compensated by his indefatigable and generous perseverance in restoring to Europe the most noble remains of human intellect. No monument of antiquity, no series of medals, or manuscript of Roman literature was neglected by him wherever he had the least hope of rescuing the one from oblivion, or of multiplying copies of the other. He acquired a claim to the gratitude of all Europe, and is still deservedly called the first restorer of classical literature. Boccaccio, however, is entitled not only to a share, but to an equal share, to say the least, of this honour. We are perfectly aware that our opinion on this subject will be at first regarded as a paradox put forth from a mere ambition of novelty; the proofs, however, which we shall briefly adduce, will convert the surprise of our readers at our temerity into wonder at the scanty recompense which Boccaccio has hitherto received, in spite of his gigantic and successful endeavours to dispel the ignorance of the Middle Ages.

The allegorical mythology, together with the theology and metaphysics of the ancients, the events of the history of ages less remote, and even geography, were illustrated by Boccaccio in his voluminous Latin Treatises, now little read, but at that time studied by all as the chiefest and best works of solid learning. Petrarch knew nothing of Greek; and whatever acquaintance, in Tuscany or Italy, they had with the writers of that language, they owed entirely to Boccaccio. He went to Sicily, where there were still some remains of a Greek dialect, and masters who taught the language, and put himself under two preceptors of the greatest merit, Barlaamus and Leontius. Under them he studied several years; he afterwards prevailed on the republic of Florence to establish a chair of Greek literature for Leontius. Had it not been for Boccaccio, the poems of Homer would have remained long undiscovered. The story of the Trojan War was read in the celebrated romance called the History of Guido delle Colonne, from which also were derived many wild inventions and apocryphal records of Homeric times, and various dramas, like Shakespeare's *Troilus and Cressida,* containing not a single circumstance to be met with in the *Iliad* or *Odyssey.* Nor should it be forgotten, that undertakings like these demanded affluence, which Petrarch possessed; while Boccaccio's whole life was passed in the midst of difficulties and privations. He compensated for the want of pecuniary resources by indefatigable industry; he submitted to mechanical labours, wholly unsuited to the bent of his character and genius, and copied manuscripts with his own hand. Leonardo Bruni, who was born before the death of Boccaccio, was astonished when he saw the multitude of authors' copies transcribed by him. Benvenuto da Imola, who was a disciple of Boccaccio, relates a curious anecdote on this subject, which as we do not recollect that it is anywhere to be met with, except in the great collection of the writers of the Middle Ages, by Muratori, a work inaccessible to the greater number of our readers, we shall insert. Going once to the abbey of Monte Cassino, celebrated for the number of manuscripts which lay there, unknown and neglected, Boccaccio humbly requested to be shown into the library of the monastery. A monk dryly replied, 'Go, it stands open', and pointed to a very high staircase. The good Boccaccio found every book he opened torn and mutilated; lamenting that all these fruits of the labours of the great men of antiquity had fallen into the hands of such masters, he went away weeping. Coming down the staircase he met another monk, and asked him 'How those books could possibly have been so mutilated?' —'We make covers for little Prayer-books out of the parchment leaves of those volumes', said he, coolly, 'and sell them for twopence, threepence and sometimes fivepence each'. —'And now go', concludes the pupil of Boccaccio, 'go, you unfortunate author, and distract your brain in composing more books.' Such were the obstacles [imposed] by the imperfect civilisation of his age which this admirable man, together with Petrarch, had to surmount; and it is an act of tardy and religious justice to show that the tribute of grateful recollection which they were both entitled to receive from posterity was almost [only] awarded to his more fortunate contemporary. We cannot conclude our remarks, without paying another debt to the memory of Boccaccio. The indecency of the *Novelle,* and their immoral tendency, can neither be justified nor extenuated; but from the herd of writers in England, who confidently repeat this merited censure of Boccaccio, year after year, it appears but too much as if the study of the language and of the style had been made a pretext for feeding the imaginations of the readers with ideas which all are prone to indulge, but compelled to conceal; and that the tales of Boccaccio would not have predominated so much over all other literature, if they had been more chaste. The art of suggesting thoughts, at once desired and forbidden, flatters while it irritates the passions, and is an efficacious instrument for governing the consciences of boys, and of the most discreet old men. The Jesuits, therefore, no sooner made themselves masters of the schools of Italy, than they adopted this book, mutilated in the same manner as some of the licentious Latin poets, well knowing that the expunged passages are the most coveted, precisely because they *are* expunged, and that the imaginations of youth supply ideas worse than they would have formed had the books been left entire.

In order to excuse the use they made of the *Decameron* in their colleges, the Jesuits succeeded in persuading Bellarmine to justify, in his controversies, the intentions of the author. Perhaps, indeed, they interpolated these arguments as they did soon many others, in the edition of Bellarmine, wherever the doctrines did not accord with the interests of their order. It is, moreover, probable that they favoured a book famous for its invectives against the rules of the cloister, and written long before their order had arisen to acquire a jurisdiction over all. Bellarmine was much less indulgent than Boccaccio to the reputations of the old congregations; and although some writers who have undertaken their defence have called his *Gemitus Columbae* apocryphal, it was, at all events, printed among his works during his life. To return to Boccaccio. Before he died he had atoned for his want of respect for decorum; he felt that men thought him culpable, and he expiated his tales by a punishment heavier, perhaps, than the offence. There is some reason to believe that he wrote them when under the influence of a lady whom he abjured just before, and whom he defames in his *Laberinto d'Amore.* However this may be, he conjured fathers of families not to suffer the *Decameron* to go into the hands of any who had not already lost the modesty of youth. —'Do not let that book be read; and if it is true that you love me, and weep for my afflictions, have pity, were it only for my honour's sake.'

With remorse of conscience which does more honour to the excellence of his intentions than to the strength of his mind, he even tried to atone for the ridicule he had poured upon the priests and their infamous superstitions. No writer, perhaps, since Aristophanes, has so bitterly satirised the effrontery of ignorant preachers, and the credulity of their ignorant hearers, as Boccaccio in the *Novelle,* which are written in a spirit of implacable hostility to monks. In one of them [VI, 10] he introduces one of these vagabonds boasting from the pulpit, that he had wandered through all the countries in the terraqueous globe, and even beyond it, in search of relics of saints, and making the people in the church pay to adore them. And yet, in spite of this, he said, on his death-bed, that he had been long in search of holy relics through various parts of the world, and he left them, for the devotion of the people, to a convent of friars. This desire was found expressed in a will, written in Italian in his own hand; and in another in Latin, drawn up many years afterwards by a notary, and signed and approved by Boccaccio a short time before he died. In both these wills he bequeathed all his books and manuscripts to his confessor and to the convent of Santo Spirito, in order that the monks might pray to God for his soul, and

that his fellowcitizens might read and copy them for their instruction. It is therefore more than probable, that there was among these books no copy of the *Decameron;* and from the following anecdote, which being found in books which are read by very few is little known, it appears that the original manuscript of the *Novelle* was destroyed long before by the author; it is, in fact, as we have already remarked, impossible to find it.

Towards the end of his life, poverty, which is rendered more grievous by old age, and the turbulent state of Florence, made social life a burden to him, so that he fled to solitude; but his generous and amiable soul was debased and depressed by religious terrors. There lived at that time two Sienese, who were afterwards canonised. One of them was a man of letters and a Carthusian monk, mentioned by Fabricius as Sanctus Petrus Petronus; the other was Giovanni Colombini, who founded another order of monks, and wrote the life of St Pietro Petroni by divine inspiration. The Bollandists allege that the manuscript of the new saint, after having been lost for two centuries and a half, miraculously fell into the hands of a Carthusian, who translated it from Italian into Latin, and in 1619 dedicated it to a Cardinal de Medici. It is possible that Colombini never wrote, and that the biographer of the saints, who wrote in the seventeenth century, drew his descriptions of miracles from those recorded in the chronicles and other documents of the fourteenth century; and in order to exaggerate the miraculous conversion of Boccaccio, he perverted a letter of Petrarch, entitled 'De Vaticinio Morientium', which is to be found in his Latin works. The blessed Petroni, at his death, which happened about the year 1360, charged a monk to advise Boccaccio to desist from his studies and to prepare for death. Boccaccio wrote in terror to Petrarch, who replied [in June 1362]:

> My brother, your letter filled my mind with horrible fantasies, and I read it assailed by great wonder and great affliction. And how could I, without fearful eyes, behold you weeping and calling to mind your near-approaching death; whilst I, not well informed of the fact, most anxiously explored the meaning of your words? But now that I have discovered the cause of your terrors, and have reflected somewhat upon them, I have no longer either sadness or surprise. You write that an—I know not what—Pietro di Siena, celebrated for his piety, and also for his miracles, predicted to us two, many future occurrences; and in the witness of the truth of them, sent to signify to us certain past things which you and I have kept secret from all men, and which he, who never knew us, nor was known by us, knew as if he had seen them with his mind's eye. This is a great thing, if indeed it be true. But the art of covering and adorning impostures with the veil of religion and of sanctity, is most common and old. Those who use it explore the age, the countenance, the eyes, the manners of the man; his daily customs, his motions, his standing, his sitting, his voice, his speech, and above all, his intentions and affections; and draw predictions which they ascribe to divine inspiration. Now if he, dying, foretold your death, so also did Hector in former times to Achilles; and Orodes to Mezentius, in Virgil;

and Cheramenes to Eritia, in Cicero; and Calamus to Alexander; and Posidonius, the illustrious philosopher, when dying, named six of his contemporaries who were soon to follow him, and told who should die first, and who afterwards. It matters not to dispute now concerning the truth or the origin of such-like predictions; nor to you, if even this your alarmer [*terrificator hic tuus*] had told the truth, would it avail any thing to afflict yourself. How then? If this man had not sent to let you know, would you have been ignorant that there remains not to you a long space of life? and even if you were young, is death any respector of age?

But neither these, nor all the other arguments in Petrarch's letter, which is very long, nor the eloquence with which he combines the consolations of the Christian religion with the manly philosophy of the ancients, could deliver his friend from superstitious terrors.

Boccaccio survived the prediction more than twelve years, and the older he grew the more did he feel the seeds scattered in his mind by his grandmother and his nurse, spring up like thorns. He died in 1375, aged sixty-two, and not more than twelve or fourteen months after Petrarch. Nor did Petrarch himself always contemplate death with a steadfast eye. Such was the character of those times; and such, under varied appearances, will always be the nature of man.

Boccaccio on the purpose of the *Decameron* (1348-53):

In these tales will be found a variety of love adventures, bitter as well as pleasing, and other exciting incidents, which took place in both ancient and modern times. In reading them, the . . . ladies will be able to derive, not only pleasure from the entertaining matters therein set forth, but also some useful advice. For they will learn to recognize what should be avoided and likewise what should be pursued, and these things can only lead, in my opinion, to the removal of their affliction. If this should happen (and may God grant that it should), let them give thanks to Love, which, in freeing me from its bonds, has granted me the power of making provision for their pleasures.

Giovanni Boccaccio, in his preface to the Decameron, *translated by G. H. McWilliams, Penguin, 1972.*

Francesco De Sanctis　(essay date 1870)

SOURCE: *History of Italian Literature, Vol. 1,* translated by Joan Redfern, Harcourt Brace Jovanovich, 1931, pp. 290-359.

[*De Sanctis was a nineteenth-century Italian critic who is regarded as the founder of modern Italian literary criticism. He is best known for his* Storia della letteratura italiana *(1870;* History of Italian Literature*), a collection widely viewed as a classic in Italian literary history. In the following excerpt from this work, De Sanctis provides one of* the first scholarly analyses of the Decameron *and explains how it profoundly influenced subsequent Italian literature.*]

[If] we open the **Decameron,** hardly have we read the first tale when we seem to have fallen from the clouds and be asking with Petrarch, "How came I here, and when?" It is not an evolution; it is a cataclysm, a revolution—one of those sudden revolutions that from one day to another show us a changed world. Here we have the Middle Ages not only denied, but made fun of.

[The character] Ser Cepperello is a Tartuffe some centuries before his time, with the difference, however, that where Molière aims at rousing us to hatred and disgust for the hypocrisy of Tartuffe, Boccaccio gets fun out of Cepperello's, and is less concerned with our feelings towards the hypocrite than with making us laugh at the expense of his good confessor and the credulous friars and the credulous people. So the weapon of Molière is sarcastic irony, whereas the weapon of Boccaccio is merry caricature. To meet again with Boccaccio's forms and aims we must go as far as Voltaire; Giovanni Boccaccio, in certain aspects, is the Voltaire of the fourteenth century.

Many people complain of Boccaccio, saying that he spoiled the Italian spirit. And he himself, in his old age, was overcome with remorse and ended his life as a cleric, inveighing against his own book. But it is evident that his book would never have been possible if the Italian spirit had not already begun to be spoiled—if "spoiled" is the correct word for it. If the things Boccaccio laughed at had been venerated (granting for the sake of argument that then he could have laughed at them) the people of his day would have been indignant. But the very opposite was the case. The book seemed to respond to something in people's souls that for a long time had been wanting to come out, and to be saying boldly what all were saying in their secret hearts. It was applauded so loudly, and met with such great success, that the good Passavanti took fright at it and set up his *Specchio di vera penitenza* as an antidote. Boccaccio, then, was the literary voice of a world that men were already confusedly aware of. A secret was about: Boccaccio guessed this secret, and every one applauded him. This fact, instead of being cursed, deserves to be studied.

The character of the Middle Ages was transcendence: an ultra-human and ultra-natural "beyond" of Nature and man, the genus and the species outside of the individual, matter and form outside of their unity, the intellect outside of the soul, perfection and virtue outside of life, the law outside of the consciousness, the spirit outside of the body, and the aim of life outside of the world. This philosophical theology was based on the existence of universals. The world was populated by beings or intelligences, and there were endless disputes over their nature. Were they divine? Were they real genera and real species? Were they intelligible species? But the structure was already shaking under the blows of the Nominalists, the people who denied the existence of the genera and the species and declared that only the single, the individual, existed. Theirs was the motto which was afterwards to become so familiar, "Entities should not be multiplied unnecessarily."

The natural result of this exaggerated world of theocracy was asceticism. Earthly life had lost its seriousness and its value. Man lived on the earth with his spirit in the next life. And the acme of perfection was set in ecstasies, prayers, and contemplation. So literature too was theocratic, and the mysteries, visions, and allegories arose, so [Dante's] *Divine Comedy* was born, the poem of the other world.

[In the **Decameron** Boccaccio turns his back] on allegory and chivalry and mythology, on the world of Dante and the world of the classics, shuts himself up in his own society, and lives in it, and is happy, for at last he has found himself: the life he depicts is his own life. And we wonder that he took so long to find his genre and recognize that his strength as a writer lay precisely in the depiction of his own society, directly and naturally, as he knew and saw it at first hand. And yet . . . what a long gestation and difficult labour were necessary before that world of his spirit could come to birth.

But Boccaccio's world of the **Decameron** was not a new world: it had existed long before Boccaccio. The whole of Italy was filled with romances and stories and Latin canzoni, licentious songs. Women . . . were in the habit of reading these books to each other in the privacy of their rooms, and a continuous stream of amusing and licentious tales was provided for them by the writers of *novelle.* The romances as a rule were connected with the adventures of the knights of the Round Table and of Charlemagne. The *Amorosa visione* mentions a large number of these heroes and heroines of chivalry: Arthur, Lancelot, Galahad, Iseult the Fair, Chedino, Palomides, Lionel, Tristan, Orlando, Rinaldo, Guttifre, Robert Guiscard, Frederick Barbarossa, Frederick II. Boccaccio, like the others, wrote his romances for women. Having written a new version of the romance of Florio and Biancofiore, he had turned to the heroic and primitive times of Greek tradition as more compatible with his studies of the ancients. But of all the types of literature of that day the one that was to spread the quickest and be the most enjoyed was the *novella,* the tale or short story, for this was the type which was most in keeping with the spirit of the times. And the writers of tales furbished up or invented every sort and kind of them, serious and comic, moral and obscene, decking them out and varying them to suit their public. So the short story was alive—was a type of literature that was swayed and changed by the imagination. Men of culture despised the legend equally with the tale, and kept to their own sphere, high above both of them, leaving *The Little Flowers of St. Francis* and the *Life of the Blessed Columbine* to the friars, and the story of the simpleton Calandrino and the gallant adventures of Alatiel to the ordinary man who liked an amusing story.

And here is Boccaccio, walking into the middle of this profane and frivolous world of *novelle,* with no other aim than to turn out pleasant tales to suit the women who were his public. And lo! from that rough and illiterate and unformed material he created the harmonious world of art.

Learned researches have been made into the sources of Boccaccio's tales. And there are many people who are under the strange impression that one is taking away from

Boccaccio's glory by proving that the greater number of them were not invented by himself—as though the duty of an artist were to invent rather than to shape. As a matter of fact, the material of the **Decameron,** like the material of the *Divine Comedy* and of [Petrarch's] *Canzoniere,* was not the creation of a single brain, but was the growth of numberless minds in unconscious collaboration, and had passed through many and various forms before Boccaccio with his genius fixed it and made it eternal.

Tales under different names were extremely common among all the Latin peoples; there had been stories and story-tellers, but never as yet *the* story and *the* story-teller, especially not the latter. There had never yet been the single author in whom the separate tales had been brought together, unified, and made into an organic world. It was reserved for Boccaccio to take these separate stories, of different times, of different customs, of different tendencies, and fuse them into a single and complete picture of the living world of his time, of his own contemporary society, of which he himself had all the tendencies whether for good or for evil.

Boccaccio is not a superior soul, a writer who looks at society from a lofty height, sees the good and the bad in it, exposes it impartially, and is perfectly conscious of it all; he is an artist who feels himself one with the society in which he lives, and he writes with that sort of semiconsciousness of men who are swayed by the shifting impressions of life without stopping to analyze them. And this really is the quality that divides him substantially from the ecstatic Dante and the ecstatic Petrarch. Boccaccio is all on the surface of life, among the pleasures and idlenesses and vicissitudes of everyday existence, and these are enough for him, he is busy and satisfied. He is not the type to turn his soul into himself and think deeply with knitted brow and pensive gaze; it was not for nothing that they called him "Giovanni the Tranquil." Intimacy, raptness, ecstasy, the unquiet deeps of thought, the living in one's own spirit with phantasms and mysteries, disappear from Italian literature when Boccaccio enters it. Life rises to the surface, and is smoothed down, made attractive. The world of the spirit makes its exit; the world of Nature comes in.

This world of Nature, empty and superficial, devoid of all the inner powers of the spirit, has no seriousness at all of means or of end. The thing that moves it is instinct— natural inclination; no longer God nor science, and no longer the unifying love of intellect and act, the great basis of the Middle Ages: it is a real and violent reaction against mysticism. The author introduces us to a merry gathering of men and women who are trying to forget the ills and tedium of life by passing the warm hours of the day in pleasant story-telling. It was the time of the plague, and men faced by death on every side felt that all the restraints of life were loosened, and gave themselves up to the carnival of the imagination. Boccaccio had had experience of carnivals at the court where the happiest days of his life were spent, and his imagination had taken its colour from that dungheap on which the Muses and the Graces had lavished so many flowers. In the *Ameto,* the pastoral **Decameron,** we have a similar gathering of people. But the stories in the *Ameto* are allegorical, so are preordained to an abstract ending. Though the poem has nothing of the spirit of the *Divine Comedy,* it is built on its skeleton. Here, on the contrary, the sole aim of the stories is to make the time pass pleasantly; they are real panders to pleasure and to love, the Greek title of the book being only a modest veil of the author's Italian title, which was that of the Prince Galeotto. And the characters, evoked from so many different people and so many different epochs, here are all of the same world, the external world of tranquil thoughtlessness.

In this care-free world of the *Decameron* events are left to take care of themselves, the results being decided by chance. God and Providence are acknowledged by name, almost by a sort of tacit agreement, in the words of people who have sunk into complete religious, political, and moral indifference. Nor is there even that intimate force of things which endows the events with a sort of logic and necessity; the book, indeed, is charming for exactly the opposite quality; it is charming for its completely unexpected dénouements, which are utterly different from anything we could reasonably have foreseen, and this by the whim of chance. It is a new form of the marvellous, no longer caused by the penetration into human life of ultra-natural forces, such as visions and miracles, but by a curious conflux of fortuitous events that no one could possibly have foreseen or controlled. We are left with the feeling that the ruler of the world, the *deus ex machina,* is chance; we see it in the varied play of the inclinations of these people, all of them ruled by the changing chances of life.

Since the machinery, the moving force of the stories, is the marvellous, the fortuitous, the unexpected, it follows that their interest does not lie in the morality of the actions, but in the strangeness of their causes and effects. Not that Boccaccio rejects morality or alters the ordinary ideas of right and wrong; it is only that questions of morality do not happen to be the questions that interest him. But the thing that does interest him is his power to stimulate his readers' interest by strangeness of character and events. Virtue is used as a means of impressing the imagination, an instrument of the marvellous like the rest, so ceases to be simple and proportionate; in fact, it is exaggerated to such a degree as to show clearly the emptiness of the author's conscience and his want of moral feeling. A famous instance is the story of the patient Griselda, the most virtuous of all the characters of the book. To prove that she is a good and faithful wife she suffocates every natural feeling of a woman, and her own personality, and her free will. The author, in trying to show an extraordinary example of virtue that will strike the imagination of his readers, has fallen into the very mysticism he dislikes, and makes use of it by placing the ideal of feminine virtue in the abnegation of self, exactly like the theologians, who teach that flesh is absorbed by spirit, and spirit by God. It is a sort of sacrifice of Abraham, except that here it is the husband who puts Nature so cruelly to the test. And the virtue in the stories of Tito and of Gisippo is proved by such strange and out-of-the-way happenings that instead of charming us as an example it only amazes us as a miracle. But extraordinary and spectacular virtue is rare in the tales; the virtue is generally the traditional virtue of chivalric and

feudal times—a certain generosity and kindliness of kings and princes and marquises, reminiscences of chivalric and heroic tales in bourgeois times. A prince's virtue lies in his using his power to protect the people below him, and especially to protect the men of high intelligence and culture who happen to be poor, as did the Abbot of Cluny and Can Grande della Scala, who treated Primasso and Bergamino with magnificence. A much-praised person is Charles I of Anjou, who instead of seizing and raping two beautiful girls, daughters of a Ghibelline, who had fallen into his power, preferred to dower them magnificently and find them husbands. These powerful nobles were virtuous because they did not misuse their power, but behaved instead in a liberal and courteous manner. And already a class of literati was arising who lived at the expense of this virtue, feeding on its bounty and extolling it in fair exchange. The lofty soul of Dante had bent itself with difficulty to this patronage; not the least of his causes of bitterness was the begging of bread from strangers, crust by crust, and the treading of other people's stairs. But the heroic age was past. Petrarch allowed his Maecenas to provide for him and support him, and Boccaccio lived on the refuse of the court of Naples, comically enraged when the provision struck him as not up to standard, and disposed to panegyric or satire according to whether the food was good or bad. In Boccaccio's world "virtue" as a rule means liberality or courtesy of soul, which had spread from the castle to the city, and even into the woods where the outlaws had taken refuge—men like Natan, and Saladino, and Alfonso, and Ghino di Tacco, and the wizard of Ansaldo. Strictly speaking, of course this virtue is not morality; but at least it is a sense of nice behaviour, which makes the habits of the day more agreeable, takes from virtue that theological and mystical character connected with abstinence and suffering, and gives it a pleasing appearance, in keeping with a cultured and gay society. It is true that the chance which ruled the lives of these people played them many a trick, and the pervading gaiety, the charming serenity, were often disturbed by some sad event. But the clouds came suddenly, without warning, were soon scattered, and gave an added value to the sun when it shone again; in Fiammetta's words, sorrow was "a fine material for tempering gladness."

If we look more deeply into these questions of joy and sorrow, we shall see that the joy has very few chords; the joy would be level and dull, and no longer joyous (as is often the case with idyllic poems), except that pain pierces into it—pain with its richer and more varied harmonies, and its living passions of love, jealousy, contempt, indignation. Pain is here not for its own sake, but as a seasoner of joy; it is here to enliven the spirit, to keep it in suspense, to excite it—until kindly fortune, or chance, shall suddenly make the sun to shine again. And even when the story has a sad ending (as in all of the tales of the third day) the sadness is only superficial; it is relieved and softened by descriptions, dissertations, and musings, and is never so strong as to be torment, like Dante's proud suffering. In that world of Nature and love pain is a tragic apparition that flits past. It is not caused by a moral purpose, but by the "point of honour," the chivalric virtue—by honour in collusion with Nature and love. A case in point is the lovely story of Gerbino; and also the story of Tancredi, who is a witness to his daughter's shame, and kills the lover, and sends the lover's heart to his daughter in a golden cup; his daughter puts poison in the cup, and drinks it, and dies. The tragedy turns on the point of honour. Tancredi feels more dishonoured by his daughter's having loved a man beneath her in rank than by the fact that she has loved illicitly. But his daughter justifies her love by quoting the laws of Nature, and saying that true nobility comes from worth and not from blood. When we take leave of the father weeping vainly and remorsefully over his daughter's body, we see him not as a man who has avenged his tarnished honour, but as a traitor to the laws of Nature and of love. But indeed we pity the father and daughter equally—the high-souled father and the human and tender-hearted daughter; both are victims of the society they belong to, and neither has sinned. Our last impression is that Nature and Love have taken their revenge. So the tragic motive is in keeping with Boccaccio's world; and the fugitive, vanishing pain is shown most tenderly and gently, almost with compassion. Pain gives a flavour to joy, for joy would end by being insipid if pain were not there to season it. Tragedy is changed at its root. There is no longer the terror of a mysterious fate, shown in catastrophe, as with the Greeks, nor of a punishment falling on man for breaking the laws of a higher justice, as in Dante; tragedy here is the fact that the world is at the mercy of its own blind and natural forces, and the higher law in this struggle is love—whoever opposes love is in the wrong. With Dante Nature was sin; with Boccaccio Nature is law. And it is not opposed by religion or morality (of which nothing remains at all, though both are believed in theoretically, and quoted), but by society as arranged in that complex system of laws and customs called "honour." But the struggle is all external; it is shown in the events that arise from these various forces brought into conflict, and is ended by the kindness or the spite of chance or fortune. And the struggle stops short at that inner conflict which leads to passion and makes character. Boccaccio has no idea of rebelling against society, and certainly is nothing of a reformer; he takes life as he finds it. And though his sympathies are entirely with the victims of love, he is not biased for that reason against the characters who are driven to cruel actions through love; they too are worthy of respect, for they are victims of love like the others. Though he glorifies Gerbino, who breaks his pledge to the King, his grandfather, rather than break the laws of love and be thought a coward, he has no word of blame for the King, who orders the death of his grandson, "choosing to be without a grandson rather than be thought a king wanting in honour." In the midst of the outer conflict of events an inner calm, a sort of equilibrium, is born, an inner calm quite empty of emotion, except the degree of emotion that is necessary for varying its life. And so this bourgeois, indifferent world of tragedy, whose only ruler is Nature, is external and superficial, is a piece of wreckage adrift on the immensity of the ocean. The action is developed from strong passions provoked by the conflict of events, not by conscious thought; and it melts away into a game of the imagination, becomes an artistic contemplation of the different events of life that arrest our attention and surprise us. Virtue and vice are meaningless except in so far as they lead to "adventures," to strange events governed by the caprices of chance. To the audience they are only a means for making the time pass pleasantly; virtue and pain are procurers of pleasure.

A world ruled by pleasure and guided by chance is heedless and gay, but is comic too. This taking of events without seriousness, this capricious interweaving of chance happenings, this inner equilibrium undisturbed by the most cruel vicissitudes, are the natural breeding-ground of the comic. When laughter is empty and meaningless it is nothing but the mirth of fools; laughter to be intelligent and malicious must have a point and a meaning, must be comic. And the comic gives this world its physiognomy and its seriousness.

Boccaccio's world is material for comedy by its very nature; for nothing is more comic than a thoughtless and sensual society, which gives rise to types like Don Juan and Sancho Panza. But it represented the extreme of culture and intellect that was known at that time, and was aware of the fact. It had the advantage of being taken seriously by all the world, and at the same time of being able to make fun of the world. In fact, these tales have two sides to them that are serious: the glorification of intelligence (the most powerful nobles are shown as respecting it) and a certain pride of the burgher who is taking his due position in the world and is setting himself up as the equal of the barons and the counts. This bourgeois class was Boccaccio's own; it was a class of educated, intelligent people, who thought that they were the only people who were civilized, and that all the others were barbarians. And the comedy springs from the caricature by the intelligent man

Traditional portrait of Fiammetta, from the frescoe of the Spanish Chapel of S. Maria Novella, Florence.

of the things and people in a lower stratum of intellectual life than his own. Side by side with cultured society were the friars and priests, or, in Boccaccio's words, "the Catholic things"—prayers, confessions, sermons, fasts, mortifications of the flesh, visions, and miracles. And behind the Catholic things were the people, with their stupidity and their credulity. These are the two orders of things and people round whom he cracks his whip.

Prayers like the Lord's Prayer of St. Julian, the serving of God in the desert, the everyday life of the friars and priests and nuns, which belied their teachings, the art of sanctification taught to Fra Puccio, the miracles of saints and their visions, such as the apparition of the Angel Gabriel; and the stupidity of the people made game of by the clever—these are comic material. Most clear of all in the **Decameron** is the reaction of the flesh against the inordinate rigour of the clergy, who had forbidden the theatres and romances, and had preached that Paradise was only to be won through fasting and the wearing of hair shirts. The natural form of expression of the reaction is licence and cynicism. The flesh avenges its curse, turns on its enemies, and calls them "merchanists"—meaning people who judge stupidly, who follow vulgar opinion. So the exaggerated world of the spirit has become "vulgar." We can well picture all the voluptuousness of the flesh as it stretches itself after its long subjection; with what relish it unfolds its joys one by one, choosing just those ways and expressions which of all others have been most forbidden, and often giving obscene double meanings to holy words and sayings. The profane world is in open rebellion, has broken its bonds, and is mocking its former master. This is the basis of the comedy; a great variety of intertwined chance events are built on it. We have the two eternal protagonists of all comedies: the person who makes fun and the person made fun of, the clever man and the simpleton; and of all the simpletons the most cruelly treated and the most innocent, are the husbands. And amid the many fortuitous events are born a great variety of comic characters, of which some have remained as real types, such as the *cattivello,* the naughty one, of Calandrino and the revengeful scholar who knows where the Devil keeps his tail. The serious characters are rather singularities than types; individuals lost in the minute description and the eccentricity of their natures, like Griselda, Tito, the Count of Anguersa, Madama Beritola, Ginevra, Salvestra, Isabetta, and Tancredi's daughter. But the poignant and intimate part of the book is in the comic characters; these are the universal types which we meet with every day, like Compar Pietro, and Maestro Simone, and Fra Puccio, the friar who was sheep-like, and the judge who was *squasimodeo* (of no account), and Monna Belcolore, and Tofano, and Gianni Lotteringhi, and all the others, for "the number of the stupid is infinite." And this gay and thoughtless world unfolds itself, gains an outline and a character, and becomes the "human comedy."

And so, within a short distance of each other we get the comedy and the anti-comedy—we get the "divine comedy" and its parody, the "human comedy." On the same threshold and in the same times we have Passavanti, Cavalca, Catherine of Siena—voices of the other world—and Giovanni Boccaccio drowning them with his loud and profane laugh. The Gay Science has arisen from its grave with its laughter as fresh as ever; the troubadours and the story-tellers, whom the priests had silenced, have come back to life and are dancing as merrily as before and are singing their profane canzoni in the Florence of the Guelfs. The forbidden tale and romance are ruling in the realm of literature; they forbid in their turn, and are the absolute masters of literature. Naturally the change is not quite unannounced, does not come like an earthquake. As we have seen, the lay spirit has kept an unbroken tradition through the whole of literature, until in the *Divine Comedy* it takes its place with boldness, and declares that it too is sacred and of divine right, and Dante, a layman, speaks like a priest and an apostle. But Dante is so careful that his building shall stand, that its foundation shall be firm. Dante's *Divine Comedy* is a reformation; Boccaccio's is a revolution, which throws the whole edifice to the ground and erects another on its ruins.

The *Divine Comedy* ceased to be a living book; it was expounded as a classical work, but was little read or understood or enjoyed, though it was always admired. It was divine, but no longer alive. And sinking into its grave it drew along with it all those kinds of literature whose germs appear so strongly and vigorously in its immortal sketches: tragedy, drama, the hymn, the laud, the legend, the mystery. There feeling died with them for the family, for Nature, for country, the belief in a better world, rapture and ecstasy and inwardness, the pure joys of friendship and love, the seriousness of life, and ideality. Of all this immense world which collapsed before it came to fruition, all that remained was Malebolge, the realm of malice, the seat of the "human comedy"; Malebolge, which Dante had thrown into filth, the place where laughter was choked by disgust and indignation. Here is Malebolge, but on the earth, laughing infernally, adorned by the Graces, and announcing that it alone is truly Paradise—as Don Felice understood very well, but not poor Fra Puccio. The world in fact is upside down. To Dante the *Divine Comedy* is heavenly bliss; to Boccaccio the "comedy" is earthly bliss, and one of the pleasures of this earthly bliss is the driving away of sadness by making jokes about Heaven. The flesh is out to enjoy itself; the spirit is paying the bill.

The flesh was reacting against a spirituality that was overstrained and out of touch with real life. And if the reaction had taken the form of an active struggle in the lofty regions of the spirit, as happened in other countries, the change would have come more gradually or have been more opposed, but would have borne more fruit. Faith and conviction would have been strengthened by the struggle, and would have generated a literature full of vigour and substance, with something of the passion of Luther, the eloquence of Bossuet, the doubts of Pascal, and with those literary forms which are found only when the inner life is strong and healthy. The movement would have been at the same time negative and positive, destructive and constructive. But audacity of thought had been punished without mercy, the Ghibelline faction had been crushed with bloodshed, and the papacy was near at hand, watchful and suspicious. The world of religion, as corrupt in its habits as it was absolute in its doctrine and grotesque in its forms, collided with the new culture that had grown so fast, with the spirit that was so adult and so matured by the study of the classics. These cultured people were unable to take the religious world seriously, and so were cut off from the rest of society, from the greater part of the people, who remained as they were, passive and inert in the hands of the priest of Varlungo, of Donno Gianni, of Frate Rinaldo, of Frate Cipolla. Educated people came to look on that world as stupid and mechanical, and to laugh at it became the hallmark of a cultured person; even the priests themselves laughed at it, those priests who aspired to being cultured.

And so there were two separate and distinct societies, living side by side, and on the whole without bothering each other too much. Men were forbidden to think for themselves, or to question abstract doctrines, but their everyday lives were another thing entirely—they lived and let live, squeezed amusement out of everything, and eased their feelings by calling on the names of God and Mary. Even the preachers amused their congregations with mottoes, jokes, bantering, a habit which Dante thought obnoxious in the highest degree, but which drew a laugh from Boccaccio. At the end of his *Novelliere* he says: "If the sermons of the friars, preached to make men remorseful for their sins, are full of jokes and nonsense and mockery, it seemed to me that these same things would not be unbecoming in my tales, which are written to drive away melancholy from women." Dante's indignation has gone, and in its place has come laughter, as though at the expense of things become common. Anger is the sign of saints and of men of conscience everywhere; to be angry a man must first believe, must feel his beliefs to be outraged. But the cultured society of that day had no notion of losing its temper over the sinfulness of mankind. In the *Decameron* the "unblushing dames of Florence" are charmers and seducers of men and are grouped into "living pictures," as they would be called today. The traffic in holy things, which drove believing Germany to schism, which Dante in his noble wrath called "adultery," here is only a matter for amiable quibbling, without rancour or malice. The confessional is the centre of ambiguities that are very amusing; the laity, both men and women, play tricks on the priests—on "the round and fat men"—as we see from the confessor of Ser Ciappelletto and from Frate Bestia, excellent comic characters. Sham miracles, like that of Masetto, the market-gardener, or of Martellino in difficulty, or of Frate Alberto, or of Frate Cipolla, and the faking of saints and making them into miracle-workers, as in the tale of Ser Ciappelletto—these are shown with the gay sense of the comic of a cultured and sceptical people. Profanations like these make people laugh, because the things profaned no longer inspire any reverence.

This society was taken bodily, just as it was, warm, palpitating, vividly alive, and was put into the *Decameron.* The book is an immense picture of life in all its variety of the characters and the events most calculated to make people marvel. Here is Malebolge, the sensual and profligate world of cunning and ignorance, taken out of Hell and staged on the earth; and within Malebolge, but not amalgamating with it, is the cultured and civilized world, the world of courtesy, the echo of chivalric times—just a trifle bourgeois, perhaps, but witty, elegant, clever, pleasing; its

finest type is Federigo degli Alberighi. The priests and friars and peasants and artisans and lowly burghers and small merchants, with their women, are the natives of the country; and the loud plebeian laughter of these people in their perpetual carnival is all around the ladies and the knights of the world of spirit, culture, wit, and elegance, with its courtesies and habits of chivalry—a world gay like the other, but with a polite and measured gaiety, with a large way of doing things, pleasant modes of speaking, and decorum in its customs. These two worlds, different, but living cheek by jowl, are fused together in the background of the picture, producing an effect of harmony that is unique; they are fused into a single world that is thoughtless and superficial, living externally in the enjoyments of life, and led hither and thither just as fortune decrees.

This twofold world, whose varied notes are so excellently harmonized, takes its tone from the author and from the merry company he puts on the stage. The author and the characters who tell the tales belong to the cultured class: the name of God is often in their mouths, they speak respectfully of the Church, conform to the customs of religion, take a holiday on Friday, because Friday was the day on which Our Lord "died that we might live," sing allegorical and Platonic canzoni, and live a life of gaiety, but one arranged in a manner befitting civilized persons. This society had culture, wit, elegance, poetry, to make it pleasant—was, in fact, like the high society of today. It reflected the feudal world of courtesy, which the cultured and wealthy burgher-class was taking as its model, but dressing up with a new adornment of culture and wit. Just as the feudal world had had its buffoons and jugglers, this society had the people who made it merry; its buffoons and jugglers were the people about it—that numberless crowd of priests, friars, peasants, and artisans; amusement was drawn from everything, from the stupid as well as from the clever. The comedy is utterly lacking in any high or serious intention, either to break down prejudice, or to attack institutions, or to fight ignorance, or to moralize, or to reform—as was true with Rabelais or Montaigne, whose comic art is a reaction of good sense from the artificial and the conventional. The laughter of those writers is serious because it leaves something behind it in the consciousness. But Boccaccio's laughter is an end in itself. Its aim is to drive away melancholy and prevent tedium, and that is all. Boccaccio looks at that plebeian world with the eye of an artist studying his model; he is bent on mastering its curves and features and placing it in the light best calculated to please his noble company. From all the immense shipwreck of conscience there still survives a sense of literary integrity, of artistic feeling, strengthened by wit and culture. The masterpieces of the *Decameron* are the fruit of this literary conscience; types are idealized to suit and please the intelligent and sensual society of our genial artist, the idol of the young women to whom he dedicates his stories.

The special quality that makes these models immortal is the comic ideal of showing that society at close quarters and exactly as it is, with all its ignorance and malice, and as seen through the eyes of intelligent people who are there merely to enjoy the spectacle and clap their hands. The motive of the comedy does not come from the mortal world, but from the intellectual world; the intelligent people are making fun of the ignorant, who are much more numerous. What makes the picture so lively is chiefly a certain simplicity of mind that we find in uncultured people, thrown into relief by that cunning which is the basis of a fool's character; besides being stupid, the fool is often credulous, vain, boastful, vulgarly ambitious. So cunning gives vanity to character and throws its ridiculous side into relief. But cunning is comic too—not, of course, to the fool himself, but to the clever people who understand him. So the two types of actor play into each other's hands, each doing his best towards getting the laughs. And here we have the foundation of Boccaccio's "comedy": culture blossoming for the first time, and conscious of itself, and turning the ignorance and malice of the lower classes into a joke. And the comic element is most highly flavoured of all when it happens that the people made game of are those who have the habit of victimizing others—the cunning people who victimize the simpletons made game of in their turn by the intelligent, as when women make game of their confessors.

Then the comedy leaps out with a sudden movement that illumines the whole situation, and laughter breaks out, spontaneous, irresistible. The stories are short, and their flavour is all in their tail, as with the sonnet. Such, for example, is the story of the Jew who is converted to Christianity on seeing how corrupt the Christians are. The ending is so utterly unexpected, so surprising, in view of what has gone before, that the effect produced is very great. There are several stories of this type that are not so effective, because the author was working on a material that was already known, for instance, the tales of the Marchesana di Monferrato, of Guglielmo Borsiere, and of Maestro Alberto. These cross-fires of mottoes and subtleties, which shine so splendidly in high circles, and win for the author the title of a man of wit, are after all the most elementary part of his wit; these mottoes, jokes, epigrams, subtleties, belong to the school of the troubadours and the Gay Science. A great number had already passed into the Florentine dialect, among the many others invented by the acute and wide-awake Florentines. The *Decameron* is sprinkled with these sayings. But they had already passed into the language and had ceased to be anything but phrases and words. Burchiello's work of collecting and arranging them is unworthy of a man of intelligence. They are only the colouring of the comic, not the comic itself; they are already a national patrimony and so have lost the freshness and spontaneity that are needed for wit; they are only effective if the writer adds some new and unsuspected association. Burchiello's work is dull and uninteresting because to Boccaccio these mottoes were not ends in themselves, but were only methods of style, only colouring.

Wit, in its higher meaning, is an artistic faculty; it may be said to take the place in the comic that sentiment takes in the serious. And wit, like emotion, is a great condenser; it quickens our perceptions and gives us like and unlike in the same breath under contrary appearances. Cleverness travels to its goal by the road of thought, but wit makes a leap straight to the same goal by intuition. Ugolino's sons in their exaltation of emotion say, "Thou didst put upon us this miserable flesh, and do thou strip it off." Here emotion takes the place in drama that wit takes in comedy; it joins different ideas and images unexpectedly in one sentence. But wit must be feeling too, the feeling of the ridiculous. The writer must stand in the middle of his world feeling all its emotions, must live inside of it, be amused by it, and must take the same interest in it that others take in the more serious things of life. But at the same time his emotion must be that of an intelligent onlooker, rather than that of an actor taking part in the piece. He must have that calm and quickness of mind which hold him aloof from the events of the play. The man who is really witty does not laugh himself, but makes others laugh. He dominates his world by reason of the calm that makes him superior to it; and so he can fashion it as he chooses, can tie up the threads and develop the plot and describe the personages and distribute the colouring.

Wit in Boccaccio is more imagination than intellect; it shows itself more in producing comic forms than in looking for far-fetched connections. Where his predecessors had tried to spiritualize, Boccaccio tries to incorporate. And he makes his effects not through this or that characteristic, but through the whole, through the details taken together in a mass. His predecessors wrote sketches; he writes descriptions. They looked for impressions rather than for things; Boccaccio shuts himself up and entrenches himself in the thing itself and gets to know it inside out. So often we are given the thing rather than the impression it produces, its sensation rather than its emotion, imagination rather than fantasy, sensuality rather than voluptuousness. Too much density and repetition make his work opaque. This manner is intolerable when the subject is serious, as in the *Filocolo* and the *Ameto* with their endless orations, which make us feel that we are stuck fast in the mud and unable to budge. And even the *Decameron* is irritating at times, for instance, when Tito and the daughter of Tancredi make speeches according to all the rules of rhetoric and logic. But the comic form is one of the most natural in the whole of art, and was the first form to appear after the elementary eruption of mottoes and proverbs. Comedy is the realm of the finite and the senses, and its first impressions are centred in minute observation of habits, whereas in serious literature the first impressions give us the forms of allegories and personifications, forms generalized in the intellect. The first form of the comic is caricature.

Caricature means depicting the object directly in such a way as to put its defective and ridiculous side into evidence. No doubt it would have been enough just to show us the defect and leave us to guess the rest: a single ray is enough to light up the whole and show it to our imagination. But Boccaccio aims at more than this; he is like a painter who depicts the entire figure, choosing and distributing the accessories in such a way that more light is thrown on the defective parts than on the others. Therefore the element of the ridiculous is not isolated, but spreads to the whole picture; each part contributes to the effect produced; there is a kind of crescendo in the comic scale. He so prepares us and puts us in the right mood for the laugh that it rarely breaks out unexpectedly and irresistibly, as in those short passages which give us unexpected connections; instead of laughter we more often get a feeling of equable pleasure, are kept gently satisfied. We are appeased, not excited. Though we do not actually laugh, our faces are serene and happy; the laugh is there, but is latent; it is not an irresistible laugh that breaks out in spite of ourselves. And the reason is this: the author does not give us a series of related thoughts, the fruit of his intellect, but a series of forms made by his imagination. And the forms he gives us are ample, solid, fully clothed, and minutely described. He seems to be sunk in that world of the imagination, and at the same time to be its creator; he has the air of adding nothing at all of his own. And we look at it as though enchanted. His attention never strays, and he never turns his head with a grimace to make us laugh. He never treats his subject lightly, laying it down, going back to it; his mind is fixed on it, and his subject pursues him, catches hold of him, pins him down, and gives him no rest till it has all come out. And our minds do not wander any more than his; we seem to be rocked deliciously in our contemplation; though we laugh from time to time, we are still attentive, and plunge back at once into the subject and run with it; and when the race is finished we are still running, gently exhausted. It is not the Eastern world, in which the opium-drugged imagination springs tremblingly from the branch of love to fly away into the vast infinitude, giving us that feeling called voluptuousness, the infinite of the senses—that something which is vague, indefinite, and musical, which enfolds us and uplifts us and reveals God to us. Boccaccio's world is purely sensual, enclosed in precise, well-defined forms; there is nothing here to detach us and carry us off into exalted regions. And for the very reason that these flowers have no scent and these lights no rays, we get sensation instead of feeling, imagination instead of fantasy, sensuality instead of voluptuousness. Our eyes are no longer fixed on the sky in ecstasy; we have found our Paradise—in that full and delightful reality. The flesh, making its reappearance in the world, seems to have stripped itself naked for our enjoyment, and fills our Paradise with allurement and caresses. And so we get cynicism, more especially when an ironical sense of modesty is used to stir up the senses.

As the form of Boccaccio's world is caricature, the fruit of a rich imagination, we are shown the whole object complete in its finest shades—not merely its peaks and elevations. The author has very few preliminaries and sets about his work quickly; the curtain is raised, and the action already in full swing, with the characters moving and speaking. From the very first we get comedy, which develops little by little, step by step, each comic motive dovetailing into the others with increasing effect. Boccaccio develops that special quality which the French call *verve* when they try to imitate his force and facility, and the Italians call *brio* when they aim at lively wit. The tale of Alibech and that of Ser Ciappelletto are wonderful examples of this quality. To add pungency to the caricature he mixes it with irony, and irony here is not a primary form but an accessory. It is an apparent good-nature, an air of ingenuousness; the person telling the tale has an assumed air of being easily shocked and full of scruples, says a thing hesitatingly, but says it all the same, hesitates to believe a thing but believes it all the same, and crosses himself with a half-smile. This irony is like a kind of comic salt that gives pun-

gency to laughter at the expense of the paternoster of St. Julian and the miracles of Ser Ciappelletto.

The *Decameron,* being based entirely on description—that is, the object not with its rays of light and its scent, but isolated and individualized—requires a full and rich form of expression. And so we get the two forms of the new literature: in poetry the *ottava rima,* and in prose the "period."

The *ottava rima* was not invented by Boccaccio, any more than the period was his discovery. What he did was to give to both body and resonance. The *ottava rima* before his day had been a detached medley of objects thrown together at random, objects that could very well have stood separately—mere objects, not developed nor clothed: it was a mechanism, not yet an organism. Boccaccio in the *Decameron* made it into an organic whole, the thing developed little by little in all its shades. It is true that we find some very successful octaves in his poems, but as a rule they are complicated, badly put together, and falling away suddenly in their best moments. In his heroic poems they are forced and stretched; in the idyllic they are commonplace and redundant. The fact is, the *ottava rima* is the highest form in poetry, and requires a bright activity of the spirit that is wanting in Boccaccio, who wanders in artificialities and conventions. His fault is within him, in his very soul; whatever is coldly conceived comes to birth as a weakly and badly formed creature; and artifice does not help it.

But in the *Decameron* Boccaccio is at home, he is painting his own world, in which he lives with the greatest enjoyment, and as he is right in the very middle of it, he throws aside all artificial wrappings. He is more than a literato, he is the man who sinks into his world and swims in it, is proud of it, and revels in it like an epicure. The result is a form which is that very world itself, that world which excites our flesh and our imagination. And this is how the form arose that is known as the "Boccaccian period."

The great literary movement centred in Florence had of late been spreading beyond Tuscany. The rediscovery of antiquity had opened new horizons to the imagination; the world of Greece was just dawning, wrapped in those vague half-lights which heighten illusions; men were beginning to be aware of it. The language of Dante was not yet the Italian tongue; it was called the "Florentine idiom"; Latin was still the language of Italy, and the opinion still held good that only frivolous and amorous stories could be treated in *latino volgare,* as they called the dialect. Boccaccio says of himself that he wrote in the "Florentine idiom," and the writers who used the vulgar tongue said that they wrote in *latino volgare.* Latin was still the ideal, the perfect, language, and the erudite classes aimed at a vulgar tongue that would be noble and illustrious, modelled on Latin, and raised to the Latin perfection of form. This is what Dante aimed at in the *Convivio;* he was fully convinced that the most serious speculations of science could be expressed in the vulgar tongue as successfully as in Latin; he took the scholastic *latino volgare* or *volgare latino,* naked, all nerve and bone, and wrapped it magnificently, for the first time, in the large folds of the Roman toga. But the vice of scholasticism was rooted even in Dante, and these scholastic barbarians, dressed out in their rich clothes, seem ill at ease, like the villager out for a holiday dressed in his Sunday garments. There is no fusion, but only points and contrasts.

Boccaccio had not passed through the schools, and later in life, when he studied philosophy and a little theology, his spirit had already been formed in the experiences of ordinary life, in the use of the vulgar tongue, and in the study of the classics. Like Petrarch, he abominates the scholastics; he sees them as the very contrary of that elegant Greek and Roman culture; to him they are simply roughness and barbarism. His mind is ruled by Virgil, Ovid, Livy, and Cicero, and not by the Bible, and St. Thomas. When he wants to paint some serious side, moral or scientific, of his world, his imitation is an outer and mechanical artifice, since he has more imagination than feeling, more intellect than reasoning. His form is noble, decorous, often easy, but too equable and placid—and now and then he makes us sleepy. His period is like the monotonous sound of a wave, moved laboriously by a tired and sleepy sea. In the place of inspiration he gives us rhetoric and logic; for Boccaccio when separated from images and thrown into the vagueness of feeling loses his footing and goes under. He treats ideas as though they were solid things, analyzes them and dissects them to the point of exhaustion. The ideas are commonplace and diluted by a coming and going of little useless accessories with "ifs" and "buts" and "thoughs" and "becauses." He strives so much for exactness, and anatomizes every smallest thought so minutely, that he makes the emptiness and commonplaceness of the idea show all the more plainly. The form stands out visibly from the thing, and shows itself as an ingenious mechanism, accurately worked out, and always mechanical. What is underneath? The commonplace. This was later called "literary form." And there is nothing more contrary to science, which is word and not phrase, and is hardly recognizable amid the circumlocutions, the periphrases, the pleonasms. This artifice is certainly a progress in literature; we find in it an art of connections and shadings that was new to prose, and it shows a matured spirit educated in the classics. But there is the opposite fault— the wish to make every idea into a chain beginning and ending in itself; which is more like a puddle of stagnant water than a running stream. Though Boccaccio hates the scholastics, his period is nothing more than a disguised syllogism, or a generalized phrase, such as, "It is human to pity the afflicted." His formulae are well constructed, but the old foundation is still there; the scholastic has a new dress and one more fashionable. And if the "period" of Boccaccio in its ample circuit is an artificial chain in which science loses its simplicity and elasticity and freedom of movement, it is quite as absurd when it tries to express feeling, to show the freer and uncontrollable forces of the spirit, which break the ties of logic and leap out impetuously. The sudden and tragic movements of the soul seem here to be crystallized between conjunctions and parentheses and reasonings. There is nothing of the subjective and it is difficult to get into the inner life. The events are extraordinary, the action is interesting, and the situations are dramatic, but our tears refuse to come, because the soul is revealed in commonplace and contorted sentences. Take for instance the tale of Madonna Beritola and that other of the Count of Anguersa, where the form never

changes, but stays in its ceremonial dress and neatly gloved through all the most piteous calamities and changes of fortune. Yet here and there we do feel a certain—not excitement, exactly, but a certain emotion of warm imagination, and now and then there are movements of feeling, as in the last words of Tancredi's daughter, and in places in the story of Griselda.

This form of the "period," so little suited to science and feeling, in which it seems like a mere bit of machinery pretending to be Latin, takes a meaning and movement of its own when staged in the imagination, that is to say, when the author is in the midst of it, dealing with living actors, not with ideas and feelings, and is faced by welldetermined objects. Take for instance the description of the plague or the fight of Gerbino. The action is no longer single and simple, like an idea, but is an aggregate of circumstances and accessories. This is the "period," which in its evolution has become in literature what in painting is called a picture. To group circumstances, grade them, and coördinate them around a centre, is the supreme art of Boccaccio. When description stands alone, abstract and separated from action, it does not sufficiently warm the imagination, and it becomes overloaded, as often happens in the introductions. But when it contains something that moves and walks, and resembles an action, the imagination gets going too, joins in the action, and paints pictures, in those large forms which are called "periods." This way of telling a story by means of pictures is certainly not the natural gait of action, which loves impetus and attrition; the rapid movements of action are arrested by the quiet eye of the imagination that is painting it. So this manner is unsuited to history. Nor is it exactly prose: it is art in a prose form with poetical narration. These paintings and periods do not give us the successive movements, the order of the action, nor its connections, nor its meaning, but its movements and attitudes and degrees: the result is a form called "physiognomy" or "expression."

But where Boccaccio's period becomes a creation *sui generis,* a living and breathing thing, is when he is treating of the comic and sensual side of his world; and not because his art or finesse is greater, but for the reason that here he is the very soul of his world—which means that he gives us a whole subjective train of malice, sensuality, mordacity, the true feeling of comic and sensual art. And this is the only sentimentality that Nature had given to Boccaccio; it penetrates into these flexible turnings of the form, and makes of them its chords. This period curves and winds and glides and twists most wantonly, with sudden shrinkings and breakings off and languishings and swellings, with digressions and graces and coquetries of style, which show us not only the spectacle in its prosaic clearness, but also its sentimental and musical motive. Those resounding waves, those ample Latin folds, grave and decorous, that embodied the majesty and pomp of public life, have been removed from the Forum and put within the walls of an idle and sensuous private life, have become the lewd transports of pleasure, tickled by malice. In the mouth of Tito or of Gisippo, we feel the rhetorical imitation of a world that had ceased to exist in the consciousness; the tune was the same, but it was sung by a bourgeois class that did not feel it, and often missed its meaning. But here, on the contrary, in this erotic and malicious world, we have the same air with a different motive, one that conquers and assimilates it; those magniloquent forms which puffed out the orators' cheeks are used here to soften vice, to adorn it, and to provide its finishing touch of allurement. As a rule, when Latin authors want to express the comic they discard their heavy weapons and arm themselves lightly. Boccaccio conceives like Plautus and writes like Cicero, yet so alive and so true is his imagination that it turns Cicero into an enticing siren who bends and moves her body alluringly. But often when he is deep in his subject he throws away the wrappings and coverings and jumps out of it, alert, swift, direct, incisive; he is a master of shortcuts and the jumping of fences. When his imagination is warmed by true feeling, he roams like a master among ancient and modern forms and melts them into one; of them he makes his own world, and stamps it with his own personality. If it were not for the art that pervades it, this world would be unbearable, would be deeply disgusting, but art clothes its nudity in these ample Latin forms as in a veil blown by lascivious winds. Art is the only thing in life that Boccaccio feels seriously, the only thing that makes him pause in the orgies of his fancy, in his moments of greatest licence, and knit his brows in thought—as happened with Dante and Petrarch in their highest and purest inspirations. Boccaccio's style is a reflection of the different men who lived in him: the literato, the man of erudition, the artist, the courtier, the man of the study, and the man of the world. It is a style so personal, so intimately one with his nature, that no imitation of it is possible: it stands alone, a stupendous monument, among many counterfeits.

What is it that we miss in Boccaccio? What we miss in this world of Nature and the senses is that feeling for Nature and that voluptuous perfume which later were found in Politian. What we miss in this world of comedy is that other feeling for the comic in its humorous and capricious forms which later was found in Ariosto.

And what is this world? It is the cynical and malicious world of the flesh, left in the low regions of sensuality; it is caricature that is often buffoonery, charmingly clothed in the graces and allurements of a form full of coquetry. It is a plebeian world that snaps its fingers at spiritual things; a world that is gross in its feelings, but polished and adorned by the imagination. And within it moves elegantly the bourgeois world of wit and culture, with echoes of the chivalric life.

It is the new comedy—not the divine comedy but the earthly one. Dante wraps his Florentine robe around him and vanishes; and the period of the Middle Ages, with its visions, its legends, its terrors, its shadows, and its ecstasies, is banished from the temple of art. And into the temple Boccaccio comes with a clatter, drawing after him the whole of Italy for many years to come.

John Addington Symonds (essay date 1895)

SOURCE: *Giovanni Boccaccio: As Man and Author*, 1895. Reprint by AMS Press, Inc., 1968, 101 p.

[*Symonds was an English poet, historian, and critic who wrote extensively on Greek and Italian culture. In the following essay, he surveys several of Boccaccio's early compositions—*Filocopo, Amorous Vision, Ameto, *and others—finding them a unique blend of classical, medieval, and modern elements. Symonds also offers a mixed assessment of Boccaccio's poetry, stating that although his verse is inventive, "the style is never choice, and often simply vulgar."*]

Among the Italian works due to Fiammetta's inspiration, *Filocopo* takes the first place. This is the earliest composition by Boccaccio known to us, and it deserves to be called the earliest monument of genuine Renaissance literature. In it appears for the first time that fusion of mediæval and classical material under forms of a distinctly hybrid modern art, that marriage of Faust and Helen, with the bizarre resultant birth of a new genius, which constitutes the real note of the transitional period known to us as Renaissance. Boccaccio adopted for his groundwork a romance of possibly Byzantine origin, which had already been popularised in several languages of Europe, and was well known to the Italians of his day. His originality did not consist in the choice of subject—that was given him by Fiammetta—but in its handling. The main story became a framework for slightly connected episodes, for descriptions of landscape, for pictures of life, and for analyses of passion, interwoven with extraordinary luxuriance of fancy in a labyrinth of highly coloured scenes. Together with this addition of new motives and new sources of interest to the fable, an entirely new form is given to the manner of narration. The mythology of Greece and Rome makes sudden and imperious intrusion into the region of romance. Farfetched terms are invented in order to accommodate this scholarly Olympus to the elements of Christian thought and the conditions of mediæval experience. We find ourselves, so far as literary form goes, transported into a conventional wonder-world of imagery, allusion, and rhetorical periphrasis. This explanation renders the reading of *Filocopo* at the present day well-nigh intolerable. Yet it was precisely this which attracted contemporaries, not only by its novelty, but also by its adaptation to the taste of the Revival. Italian prose, again, which had hitherto been practised with the dove-like simplicity of the *Fioretti di S. Francesco,* or with the grave parsimony of the *Vita Nuova,* is now made to march in sonorous periods. The language, no less than the stuff and manner of *Filocopo,* proclaims the advent of Renaissance art. In Petrarch the two streams of literature, which were destined to coalesce, had flowed apart. He wrote Italian verse with exquisite purity; and he attempted to restore classical culture with conscientious thoroughness. Boccaccio in his earliest experiment as author mixed the two sources. But so vivid was the poet's natural genius that, while accomplishing this revolution in manner, while so rehandling matter, he introduced at the same time a spiritual element, partly sensuous, party sentimental, partly scientific, which was neither classical nor mediæval, but emphatically modern. We must remember that the people of Boccaccio's day were familiar with the story of *Filocopo.* We must remember that they delighted in those longdrawn romances, and were accustomed to follow their labyrinthine windings with facility.

We must also remember that what seems to us rococo and affected in Boccaccio's mythological rhetoric and masquerade machinery, had for them the charm of brilliant style and learning genially displayed. What gives us trouble and inflicts fatigue, was fascinating at that epoch. Having then transported ourselves, so far as this is possible, into their atmosphere of thought and feeling, we shall be able to comprehend the enthusiasm which that glowing delineation of natural existence, those ardent outpourings of passion, that pompous and yet liquid diction, those finished landscapes, that richly coloured tone conveyed by aptly chosen words, inspired in men and women accustomed to mediæval directness or dreaminess. Boccaccio's originality in the *Filocopo* is incontestable. We may condemn his work as artificial and its form as meretricious. We may deplore the direction which it gave to literature. But we shall be uncritical if we forget that such artificial work, such ornaments, such mixed species of art, were what the age of nascent humanism demanded, and that without them the Italians could not have arrived at the plastic perfection of Ariosto. The arraswork of this embroiderer, we say, is glittering, is splendid, is effective. But it is composed on radically false principles. It is not classical, it is not mediaeval, it is not modern. True; but its originality consists precisely in the fact that it satisfied an age which was not classical, which was not mediaeval, which was not modern. It fulfilled the needs of a transition-age, which had to reabsorb antiquity, to free itself from mediæval impediments, to appropriate the modern liberty of sense and intellect on lines of the least palpable resistance. To estimate the immediate influence of the *Filocopo* is difficult; to feel sure that it would have determined the course of Italian literature, if it had stood alone, is impossible. But it was only the first of many similar productions by the same author; and reviewing these in their totality, we are justified in asserting that Boccaccio created for his nation the style which culminated in the *Cinque Cento.* Men are more imitative than one commonly allows. But for this great writer's originality in perceiving that a hybrid form of art was adapted to his age, and expressive of its stirrings, but for the attractive examples which he gave of the mixed style, it is possible that Italian literature might have taken a very different course. Boccaccio intervened at a critical moment, and effected that junction between humanism and vernacular poetry which proved afterwards decisive for one of the world's most brilliant and fruitful epochs. Had he been suffered to pursue his own course of study unchecked in adolescence, this same result would not have been attained. We might have had a second Petrarch, of a somewhat diverse kind and calibre. We should certainly have had a more accomplished scholar than Boccaccio became. He would have left behind him eclogues and epistles marked by purer Latinity, erudite treatises displaying a more intimate acquaintance with the spirit of the classics, and probably some ambitious monuments of Italian verse in the allegorical or epic style. But we should not have possessed the *Filocopo,* and many other works of the same order, which were formative of modern literature. What is noticeable in this first essay, is that its learning, though scattered broadcast over every page, remains that of a dilettante rather than a scientific student. Boccaccio employs it for adornment and stylistic

purposes. He revels in it with the gusto of an epicure, for whom its antique flavour is delicious. Yet it has not penetrated his heart, or remade his intellect; nor has it moulded the inner substance of his art. On the other hand, the genial, the enduringly delightful elements in this romance—its feeling for nature, its experience of life, its keen appreciation of sensuous pleasure—could not have been acquired in the study of a scholar. Boccaccio owed these things to the fortune he bewailed at Virgil's tomb, to the hard necessity of wandering through many cities in pursuit of trade. We may pause to reflect upon the crooked ways whereby some men of genius are fashioned for their proper work. Had Boccaccio been free to follow his own bent in youth, he would have lost all this, which made him far more powerful in the future than his idol, Petrarch. Had his father succeeded in that cherished plan of shaping him into a merchant, he would have accumulated wealth, but the many aspects of the world would have been wasted on him. As it was, the idleness of those twelve years of misdirected energy, which he bewailed in middle life, and which was grief and sorrow to his parent, endowed the man, when he applied himself to literature, with special gifts and peculiar aptitudes. This idleness, while it precluded him from becoming a first-rate Latin and Greek scholar, fitted him to found the Italian style of the coming age, and prepared him for his masterpiece, the *Decameron.* . . .

While engaged upon the composition of *Filocopo* at Naples, Boccaccio was recalled by his father to Tuscany. That may have happened at the end of 1339, or perhaps in 1340. So far as we can see through the obscurity which involves his movements, Boccaccio remained at Florence or Certaldo until 1345, busily employed in literature. Those five years must certainly have formed the most productive period of his life. He was not happy in his native land. Florence, distracted by internal quarrels and enfeebled by commercial failures, had placed herself under the protection of the Duke of Athens. Instead of being a wise dictator, Walter of Brienne proved himself a rapacious tyrant, and had to be expelled by force. The city was plunged still deeper into trouble by these commotions. Though Boccaccio never allowed himself to withdraw from study by public events, yet the disturbance of society around him must have been irksome to one who had been basking in the ease and luxury of Naples under King Robert's paternal government. Deeper discomforts rendered his present life distasteful. These arose from the incompatibility of views and temper between him and the elder Boccaccio. At the close of *Ameto,* which must have been written soon after 1340, he draws a painful picture of their household. After reverting in strains of fervent enthusiasm to the delights which he had left behind at Naples, he proceeds to speak of his own Tuscan home: "Here one laughs but seldom. The dark silent melancholy house takes and retains me much against my will; for here the sour and horrible aspect of an old man, frozen, uncouth, and avaricious, adds continual affliction to my saddened mood." Nothing but extreme irritation and dejection of spirits can have justified this portrait of his father, who, if we may trust Villani, was dealing with him generously. Again, in the *Amorosa Visione,* composed at the same period, he describes the old Boccaccio among the misers, employed perpetually in scratching tiny morsels with his nails from a huge mountain of gold, his whole heart being set on money-making.

It was in such circumstances, then, that the poems and prose fictions, with which we have now to deal, were composed. The *Ameto* may be described as an idyllic romance, written partly in verse and partly in prose. The scene is laid in Italy, but the story carries us to that ideal Arcadia, which fascinated the imagination of the Renaissance. *Ameto* is indeed the first of a long series of romantic idylls which became fashionable throughout Europe by the industry of Sannazzaro, Montemayor and Sidney. Critics have suggested that its form may have been derived from Petronius, or Apuleius, or "Aucassin et Nicolette." But such inquiries are to little purpose. In his *Ameto* Boccaccio projected a new species of literature, the pedigree of which can be traced in the imitations of successors, but which owed little to any pre-existing work. The romance was intended to show in what way wild and rustic natures may be humanised by love—a theme which the author rehandled in his novel of *Cimone* [in the *Decameron*]. The main story served, however, also as a framework for introducing a variety of episodes and secondary tales. Boccaccio's genius delighted in what the Italians call *intrecciatura,* that is, the interweaving of tale with tale upon a large tapestry of invention, Here, again, he determined the course of Renaissance fiction, the special feature of which, especially in its finest poetry, is a luxuriant display of episodes, combined into a splendid whole by slender links of almost casual connection.

The *Amorosa Visione* was produced under the same conditions as *Ameto.* It shows that Boccaccio was still wandering, uncertain of his destination, in the fields of literature. Having created romance of a new species in *Filocopo* and *Ameto,* he reverted in this poem to the allegories of his predecessors. The *Amorosa Visione* is written in manifest rivalry with Dante, and with the *Trionfi* of Petrarch. It leads the soul through various contemplations of learning, fame, wealth, love, and fortune, to the supreme felicity of life. That, says the poet, is the union of intelligence and moral energy in an enthusiasm of the soul. Lower ambitions, on which the activities of men are usually spent, have to be abandoned in the search for happiness. We pursue the quest with some impatience to its long-deferred conclusion. But when Boccaccio reveals his secret, the conclusion is discovered to be lame and impotent. The enthusiasm of the soul, to which he brings us, turns out to be the union of two beings in a mutual passion; and the *Amorosa Visione* closes in a paradise of sensual beatitude. Unless Boccaccio intended to satirise the mystical allegories of a former age, which I do not believe, he appears before us in this poem as a Balaam who blesses what the Muse had summoned him to curse. The fact is that he had no other prophecy to utter, and what he did utter he regarded as a prophecy. Like all his compositions at this period, the *Amorosa Visione* reveals the closing of one era and the opening of another. The forms of mediæval idealism are pressed into the service of Renaissance realism. Natural instinct, against which Dante strove with all his might, and which Petrarch clothed in the subtlest drapery of sentiment, is defined in an impassioned apotheosis.

The future author of the *Decameron* betrays himself unconsciously and all against his inclination in the *Amorosa Visione.* The poem is furthermore remarkable, because it first exhibits an insincerity which became stereotyped in Renaissance literature. Time-honoured phrases and forms of art are used, which were adapted to obsolete modes of thinking and feeling about love. Chivalrous mysticism is no longer intelligible; but its symbols are retained for the expression of frank human appetite. This, at least, is how I read the *Amorosa Visione,* and why I think it has a special value for the understanding of Boccaccio and his relation to the age which followed. After innumerable modifications, the doctrine of the *Amorosa Visione* found its ultimate expression in Marino's *Adone.* Studying it, we are inclined to wonder how far the allegories of chivalry, upon which Boccaccio moulded his poem, had any correspondence to the truth of human feeling. It seems at first sight, if I may use two vulgar metaphors, to knock the bottom out of them, to let the cat out of their imposing bag. But further consideration of the changes which were being wrought at that time in society, delivers us from this apparent paradox. Woman, in the Middle Ages, was not yet known as the companion, but either as the goddess or the slave of man. The Renaissance effected her emancipation from this dilemma. She took a new position in the scheme of life, which rendered the allegorical language of metaphysical chivalry inapplicable. Yet this language had to be retained through the transition period which followed, because it was respectful and was sanctioned by the best associations of civility emergent from a phase of semi-barbarism. The insincerities of the *Amorosa Visione* and of Renaissance lyric poetry conducted literature in this way to modern freedom of expression, in which feeling finds its own appropriate and natural vent.

The *Ninfale Fiesolano* is a tale in verse, written certainly under Fiammetta's influence, which connects itself to some extent with the *Ameto.* Under the form of a pastoral, it shows how gentle emotions lead to culture. Affrico is a shepherd of the hill-region behind Fiesole; Mensola is a nymph of Diana, dedicated to chastity. They meet and love. When Mensola has been changed into a fountain by the virgin goddess, whose vows she broke, the poem winds up with a myth invented to explain the founding of Fiesole. Civil society succeeds to the savagery of the woodland, and love is treated as the vestibule to refinement. The two parts of the poem, the romantic and the mythological, are ill-connected; and except in the long episode of Mensola's seduction, Boccaccio displays less than his usual power of narration. That episode might be separated from the rest. It breaks the style adopted for the beginning and conclusion of the poem, lapsing more than once into obscenity but thinly veiled by innuendoes in vogue among the Tuscans at that period. It would not have been necessary to dwell upon this composition, except that we find in it another new species of art invented by Boccaccio—the versified novella—which afterwards proved so great a favourite with his successors. In the *Ninfale Fiesolano* he employed *ottava rima.* Critics for a long time believed that he was the creator of this stanza. But we know now that he borrowed it from the people and adapted it to the uses of polite literature.

Boccaccio made further use of the octave stanza in two epical poems of a more ambitious flight. Both have special interest for Englishmen, on account of their influence on our own literature. They are called *La Teseide* and *Filostrato*. From the dedications, without dates, it appears that both poems were composed in the neighbourhood of Fiammetta; the former at some time when her lover had some reason to complain of her unkindness; the latter in the town of Naples, on some occasion when Fiammetta had removed into the mountain region of the Abruzzi for change of air or other business.

The *Teseide* was founded on an ancient love-tale, which Boccaccio translated for the first time into modern language, decking it with rhyme and metre. It owes its title to the fact that the scene of the romance was laid at Athens in the reign of Theseus. The poem pretends to be an epic; but it is nothing really but an episode, capable of novelistic or dramatic treatment. From this point of view, the fable deserves our highest approbation, and the man who brought it into literary prominence must be acclaimed as an inventor. Palamon and Arcite, old friends and tried, are imprisoned in the same castle. Both see and love Emilia. It is arranged between them that they shall contend fairly with one another for the prize. Arcite, however, having been released from prison, treacherously employs his liberty in paying suit to Emilia. Finally, the two friends meet in the lists of chivalry. Arcite is wounded and dies; Palamon wins the hand of Emilia. That is the bare outline of the story. Chaucer rehandled it in the *Knighte's Tale.* Shakespeare and Fletcher dramatised it in *The Two Noble Kinsmen.* Dryden retouched it in his incomparable poem of *Palamon and Arcite.* And so the story has gone sounding on through the spacious times of English literature. But it was Boccaccio who first "fished the murex up," if I may use the metaphor of Robert Browning.

English literature owes a similar debt to *Filostrato.* Chaucer founded his *Troilus and Creseide* upon this poem, while Shakespeare dramatised it in *Troilus and Cressida,* Under the form of an epic, *Filostrato* is really a versified novel of the passions. In spite of Greek names and incidents borrowed from the tale of Troy, we feel ourselves to be studying some contemporary love-tale, narrated with the vigour of a master in the arts of story-telling and of psychological analysis. The dominant sentiments are as alien to the heroism of the Homeric age, as they are congenial with the customs of a corrupt Italian city. All interest centres upon the three chief personages, Troilo, Pandaro, and Griseida. In Troilo a feverish type of character, overmastered by passion which is rather a delirium of the senses than a mood of feeling, has been painted with a force and fulness that remind us of the *Fiammetta,* where the same disease of the soul is delineated in a woman. Pandaro exhibits an utterly depraved nature, revelling in seduction, glutting imagination with the spectacle of satiated lust. The portrait is ugly; but the execution is so masterly that we do not wonder at the name of this fictitious person having passed into common language to indicate the vilest of his sex. The frenzied appetite of Troilo, Pandaro's ruffian arts, and the gradual yieldings of Griseida to a voluptuous inclination reveal the hand of a great literary draughtsman. The second and third cantos of the poem are remarkable for their dramatic movement and wealth of sensuous fancy, not rising to sublimity, not refined with the poetry of sentiment, but welling copiously from a genuinely ardent nature. The love described is nakedly and unaffectedly luxurious; it is an over-mastering impulse, crowned at last with the joy of carnal fruition. Being only interested in the portrayal of his hero's love-languors, ecstasies, and disappointment, Boccaccio hurries the poem to a slovenly conclusion. In fact, *Filostrato* may be best described as the epic of the licentious and ephemeral amour.

The poems I have been reviewing are all of them distinguished by great qualities; by fecundity of invention, by originality of conception, by wealth of fancy and descriptive brilliance, by rapidity and vividness of narration. Yet, judged as poems, they leave much to be desired. The style is never choice, and often simply vulgar. In some parts the execution is unpardonably slovenly. Proportion is neglected. You feel that the author only sympathises with certain aspects of his work, mainly the emotional, and that he was indifferent to the rest, because it did not stimulate his fancy. He gives the expression of being always in a hurry. There is a want of self-control, an absence of loving care. In other words, Boccaccio fails to be an artist in these compositions. When the verse is good, it sounds like the outpouring of his own desires and passions in self-indulgent improvisation. He does not, in the spirit of a true poetic artist, view the object from outside, and feel the paramount necessity of giving every part its proper value. To tell the tale with brief and hasty energy, to dilate upon its voluptuous incidents and themes of passionate emotion with burning rhetoric, satisfied his sense of poetry. In fact, he was working with inappropriate materials. Nature had made him an artist; but verse was not the vehicle his genius demanded; when he quitted verse for prose, he became a poet. It seems paradoxical to say this, when we remember that he gave the octave stanza and the style of narrative poetry to Italian literature. Yet the imperfections of his efforts in verse composition cannot be otherwise explained.

Before quitting the Italian works of fiction which Boccaccio composed for Fiammetta, I must speak of the novel which bears her name. When, where, and whether Boccaccio wrote this novel, remains a puzzle. How far it is autobiographical, admits of grave doubt. Accepting *La Fiammetta* as a piece of Boccaccio's writing, are we to take it as the record of personal experience? It seems almost impossible to do so. How could a book of this sort about a married woman have been given to the public by her titular lover? The story can be briefly told. Panfilo, under which name Boccaccio used to indicate himself, is compelled to leave Fiammetta at Naples, while he goes, at his father's command, to Florence. She hears that he has transferred his affections to another woman. This throws her into an agony of despair and longing. She recalls the days of their past happiness together, upbraids him for his infidelity, and closes with a passionate prayer for his return. Panfilo is lost. But Panfilo might come again, and save her from the tomb. It is incredible that Boccaccio should have insulted Fiammetta and her husband by publishing these revelations, if they told the truth. It is equally incredible that he should have published confessions of that nature in her name, if they were fictitious. The brutality of the one course and the indelicacy of the other are alike inconceivable. No period of social corruption known to us, not even that of Naples under Queen Joanna, has been so abandoned as to accept scorching satire in lieu of compliment. Boccaccio could not have survived the husband's wrath, the wife's resentment, for one day, in Fiammetta's neighbourhood, after giving either this truth or this fiction to the world. The dilemma I have stated is so cogent that we are almost forced to choose one of two hypotheses: either that *La Fiammetta* did not see the light till long after the time of its composition, or else that its attribution to Boccaccio is incorrect.

After stating these critical difficulties, there remains no doubt that *La Fiammetta* is a very wonderful performance. It is the first attempt in modern literature to portray subjective emotion exterior to the writer. Since Virgil's *Dido,* since the *Heroidum Epistolae* of Ovid, nothing had been essayed in this region of psychological analysis. The picture of an unholy and unhappy passion, blessed with fruition for one brief moment, then cursed through months of illness and anxiety with the furies of vain desire, impotent jealousy, and poignant recollection, is executed with incomparable fulness of detail and inexhaustible wealth of fancy. The author of this extraordinary piece proved himself not only a consummate rhetorician by the skill with which he developed each motive furnished by the situation, but also a profound anatomist of feeling by the subtlety with which he dissected a woman's heart and laid bare the tortured nerves of anguish well-nigh unendurable. At the same time, *La Fiammetta* is full of poetry. The **"Vision of Venus,"** the invocation to Sleep, and the description of summer on the Bay of Baiæ relieve the sustained monologue of passionate complaining, which might otherwise have been monotonous. The romance exercised a wide and lasting influence over the narrative literature of the Renaissance. It is so rich in material that it furnished the motives of many tales, and the novelists of the sixteenth century availed themselves freely of its copious stores. If we are right in assigning *La Fiammetta* to Boccaccio, it is clear that he at last had found his proper instrument of art. The prose is no longer laboured and affected, as in *Filocopo* and *Ameto.* Yet it has not attained that sparkling variety, that alternative of stately periods with brief but pregnant touches, which reveals the perfect master of style in the *Decameron.*

Lucy Hardy   (essay date 1899)

SOURCE: "The Women of Boccaccio," in *Belgravia,* Vol. XCIX, No. 391, June, 1899, pp. 719-24.

[*In the essay below, Hardy discusses Boccaccio's depiction of Medieval women, finding that while the poet often portrayed them negatively, he also "preserved to us many noble types of womanhood, of which the nineteenth as well as the fourteenth century might justly be proud."*]

According to local tradition, the villa occupied some years ago by Queen Victoria at Florence stands upon the site of that "stately palace, around which were fine meadows and

The frontispiece of the 1492 Venetian edition of the Decameron.

delightful gardens," at which Boccaccio laid the scenes of his *Decameron*; indeed, portions of the original building are said to be still extant. We are aware that there are other claimants to the honour of being selected by the novelist for the site of his imaginary "ten days' entertainment"; but the villa Palmieri appears to have the best title to rank as the locality described by Boccaccio.

A wondrous contrast certainly exists between the imaginary occupants of the villa in the fourteenth century, and its real guests in the nineteenth. In nothing probably is the difference between mediæval and modern times more marked than in their types of womanhood. Like Molière, Boccaccio depicted the actual social life of his age in his works of fiction; and many of the novelist's tales are probably founded upon real contemporary incidents. The writer of the *Decameron* has left us a strange picture of that polished, yet corrupt, society of mediæval Florence—a picture which renders comprehensible the quaint exclamation of Roger Ascham, "who was wont to thank God that he was but nine days in Italy, yet he saw more liberty to sin in one city (Venice) than he ever heard of in London in nine years." It is his too faithful reproduction of the social life of his epoch which renders Boccaccio's chief work an impossible one for a "family library." Boccaccio is not an author (like Herrick or Shakespeare) who can be easily adapted for general perusal by the judicious excision of a few words and passages; which are never missed from the main action of the play or poem. It is the cheerful uncon-sciousness of wrong doing, the naiveté with which the worst actions are described as mere matters of course, which is the most singular feature of the *Decameron;* at least, to modern readers. It is not that the morals are bad; they are simply non-existent. Truth is a virtue too little practised by many of us; but it is hardihood to celebrate lying as a fine art, and select as "a most agreeable matter of discourse. . . . stratagems which are in daily practice from women to men, and from men to women, or from one man to another."

There is a curious survival of the ancient folk-lore teach-ings which applaud the "master thief" as a genius in the approval which Boccaccio bestows upon the most un-blushing falsehoods and the most shameless deceptions, when uttered and practised by his imaginary characters. Even the victims of these domestic treacheries appear to have been more than resigned to their fate, provided they were duped with sufficient cleverness. The blunderer *who was found out* deserved condign punishment; but the skil-ful trickster, male or female, who played his or her part with skill always excited admiration. It is only by reading works like the *Decameron* that one can fully understand the impulse which led pure-minded and noble men and women like Francis of Assisi, Angela de Foligni, Cather-ine of Siena, to forsake a world with which they had so lit-tle in common, and to find refuge in the cloister. Not that even convent walls always offered a safe asylum; some of Boccaccio's worst tales are laid in the precincts of the cloisters, and his nuns are assuredly not the purest of his heroines.

Yet it would be unfair to the fourteenth century Floren-tines to accept Boccaccio's odious creations as the univer-sal type of mediæval womanhood. Now and then, even amid his worst pages, we come upon the "tall white lily" (as Longfellow remarks) blooming amid the mire. Faithful Isabella, and her "pot of basil"—patient Griselda, with her unselfish hope that "you will not take the same heart-breaking measures with this lady as you did with your last wife"—Madonna Zincura (prototype of Shakespeare's Imogen) who is traduced by another Tachimo, but, after many vicissitudes, triumphantly vindicates herself to her husband, and (rare virtue in a mediæval woman) is mag-nanimous enough to forgive her would-be murderer—these are but a few of the noble and beautiful types of womanhood we find depicted in Boccaccio's pages. It is much to be regretted that he did not give us more of such pleasant portraitures. Chaucer, who has copied from the Italian novelist some of his least edifying tales, has at least amply compensated us for his "Carpenter's Wife," and the faithless consort of "The Merchant who dwelled at St. De-nise," by his abundant gallery of more attractive feminine portraits. *The Canterbury Tales* alone abound in examples of pure and noble womanhood, which far outnumber the low and coarser types of "The Wife of Batti," "May," "Al-ison," and "Fair Constance," persecuted, yet pure and

true; "Sweet Emelie," whose wedded life was so happy that

> There was never no word them between
> Of jealousy, or any other tene (*i.e.* vexa-
> tion).

"Canace," with her "very womanly benignitee" (a charac-ter so attractive that the stern Puritan, Milton, regretted that her story was left unfinished)—these are but a few of Chaucer's attractive heroines. The English and the Italian writers both described the manners of their day; but it must be confessed that the darker side of the picture is the one most dwelt upon by the foreign author. Chaucer lin-gers lovingly on his portraits of good women; Boccaccio reserves his fullest details for the lives of his questionable heroines. Griselda's story gains by the handling of the En-glish bard; and, in one of the least quotable of the tales which Chaucer has adapted from Boccaccio ["The Mil-ler's Tale"], our native poet has at least made a more "moral" ending than his Italian author, in that the wicked wife and her accomplices do not prosper as they do in Boc-caccio's pages.

But, as we have said, even the Italian author has described other women than Delilahs. He has drawn the brave and noble woman of the era, as in the case of the "gentlewom-an of Gascony," who arouses the King of Cyprus from sloth by a pointed reprimand. Having received injuries which this monarch was too indolent to redress, and, find-ing that "the King was so little of a man, and so careless of his honour, that he suffered an infinite number of af-fronts to himself and injuries to his subjects," this high-spirited woman knelt before him to ask, "not satisfaction for the injuries I have received, but that you, my lord, who can so patiently bear your own disgrace, may teach me to endure mine also with like resignation"—words which, like the address of Agnes Sorel to Charles the Seventh, ef-fectually aroused the monarch from his lethargy. "He avenged the lady's wrongs, and was afterwards most solic-itous in all that concerned his honour."

The faithful wife of the period, true to her husband during his absence amid all temptations, has been also depicted in the Italian novelist's sketch of the "lady of the Marquis of Montserrat, who, by wise speeches, cured the King of France of his dishonourable love."

Chaucer never drew a more attractive female character than Madonna Giovanna (heroine of the wellknown tale of "The Falcon"), who, when her lover so chivalrously sacrifices his treasured hawk for her sake, declares that she will marry him in spite of his poverty, "for I would sooner have a man without riches than riches without a man."

Madonna Beritola, who loves her husband and sons too well to return to the world without them, and refuses to leave the desert island where she has escaped after the sup-posed death by shipwreck of her beloved ones; Andre-veala, who retires to a convent after the death of her be-trothed, despite the most flattering offers from her other lovers—these are types of the loving and faithful women of the era.

To the patient reader, who will wade through much that is offensive for the sake of an occasional jewel, Boccaccio's pages will always possess a certain attraction. It is only by perusing works like his that we can thoroughly understand the condition of social life of his day. No grave historian has so fully set it before us; with its strange mixture of superstition and profanity, courtesy and coarseness, exaggerated sense of honour, and singular lack of morals.

Chaucer apologises for some of his tales, as related "by churles"; and one imagines that the knight, and the prioress, and the more respectable of the company, must have been riding out of earshot when "the miller" and "the reeve" related their histories. But Boccaccio's far more startling anecdotes are supposed to be spoken by, and addressed to, ladies of high rank and unsullied reputation. There is a record that one of these dames once checks a gentleman in an "unseemly song"—but it is difficult to understand how this fair moralist could have tolerated, even applauded, some of the preceding stories. Russian peasants turn their sacred pictures with their faces to the wall before proceeding to commit any bad action in their houses; but Boccaccio's heroes and heroines pray devoutly for success in committing all manner of breaches of the Decalogue; and are as piously thankful for prospering in an unlawful amour as if it had been the most innocent of undertakings. "He returned devout thanks to God and St. Julian" is recorded of one hero; after some adventures which could scarcely be supposed to have attracted the blessing of heaven.

The pious company at Pampinea's villa refuse to listen to tales on Friday, "it being fitter to pray on that day than to hearken to novels," though there is a more mundane reason hinted at by the hostess. "Friday and Saturday are inconvenient days, on account of laying in provisions, and making things clean." But the assemblage amply indemnify themselves for the temporary restraint laid upon their tongues at the end of the week, by the startling stories with which they beguile the hours of Sunday. Its graphic descriptions (as the well-known sketch of the plague at Florence in 1348), and its portraiture of the manners and customs of the time, will always make the **Decameron** a work of interest to the student; and amid much, very much, which the author might have been better advised to blot, he has preserved to us many noble types of womanhood, of which the nineteenth as well as the fourteenth century might justly be proud.

Walter Raleigh   (essay date 1913)

"Boccaccio," in *The English Review*, Vol. 14, May, 1913, pp. 209-29.

[A renowned lecturer and author, Raleigh was appointed the first professor of English literature at Oxford in 1904. In the following excerpt, he lauds Boccaccio's invention of varied literary genres and ranks the Decameron *as one of the greatest creations in European literature. As Raleigh states, Boccaccio "was as fine an artist as the best of them; his method was all his own; he cannot be superseded; and his work has aged less than the work of those who borrowed from him. He has the elixir of life; he is eternally joyous, and eternally young."]*

We know hardly anything of the intimate life of Boccaccio except what he has told us, and almost all that he has told

---

---

us is presented to us under the guise of fiction. Was he speaking of himself? Here enter the two eternal schools of literary criticism with their tedious controversy. The early romances and poems of Boccaccio—the **Filocolo**, the **Filostrato**, the **Teseide**, the **Ameto**, the **Amorosa Visione**, the **Fiammetta**, the **Ninfale Fiesolano**—are all romances, poems, and allegories dealing with love; all point to a loveaffair which reaches the summit of happiness and is then broken by desertion and separation. There was only one love-story, it seems, which interested Boccaccio; what wonder if it was his own? And his own, so far as we have independent knowledge of it, corresponds with the love-story of the romances and poems. The **Filostrato**, in its dedication to *Fiammetta*, asserts the identity:

You are gone suddenly to Samnium, and . . . I have sought in the old histories what personage I might choose as messenger of my secret and unhappy love, and have found Troilus, son of Priam, who loved Cressida. His miseries are my history. I have sung them in light rhymes and in my own Tuscan, and so when you read the lamentations of Troilus and his sorrow at the departure of his love, you shall know my tears, my sighs, my agonies; and if I vaunt the beauties and the charms of Cressida, you will know that I dream of yours.

Yet in these same works Boccaccio was inventing the various literary art-forms which he bequeathed to Europe. The *Filocolo* is a prose romance after the French fashion. The *Filostrato* and the *Teseide* are epics of love (*Troilus and Cressida* and *The Knight's Tale*) written in the *ottava rima;* the *Ameto* is a pastoral in prose and verse; the *Amorosa Visione* is a poem in *terza rima;* the *Fiammetta* is a psychological novel. In all that he does, Boccaccio shows the way to modern literature.

In his later life he was infected by the habits of the learned, and produced heavy compilations in Latin, encouraged thereto by his friend Petrarch. The *De Claris Mulieribus,* the *De Casibus Illustrium Virorum,* the *De Genealogiis Deorum,* the *De Montibus, Silvis, Lacubus, Fluminibus,* &c., were dictionaries of themes, mythological and geographical encyclopædias. They remind us how great a part of the business of the Renaissance was concerned with knowledge rather than art. Their influence has been enormous. The Legends of Good Women, the Falls of Princes, the Mirrors for Magistrates, the whole mythological apparatus of poetry—all have Boccaccio for a chief source. Indeed, his dull Latin works were in some ways more influential than his perfect Italian poems. They supplied poets with raw material.

Between these two groups of works there falls a greater thing than either: the hundred tales called the *Decameron.* If all the rest were lost and forgotten, we should lose many beautiful things, but the reputation of Boccaccio would be no lower than it is. I shall speak only of the *Decameron* and of its author. I believe that English readers sometimes find it difficult to understand how it is that the *Decameron* has placed its author in the highest seat along with the few great creators of modern literature. It is well to confront this difficulty at once, so that we may not take our own prejudices, and limitations, and modern conventions of sentiment as a measure of a wider world. Our taste must always be, more or less, the victim of our limitations, but we should beware of glorying in it, and, above all, we should beware of mistaking the aversions of timidity and sensibility for critical judgments.

Why has this writer of vain, light tales become an immortal? His success is not a success of scandal. Other writers have been as gay as he was, and less decent; yet they have gone down to the pit. What is his secret?

I must speak at large of the *Decameron,* but here, and at first, I will try to answer this question. The secret of Boccaccio is no hidden talisman; it is the secret of air and light. A brilliant sunshine inundates and glorifies his tales. The scene in which they are laid is as wide and well-ventilated as the world. The spirit which inspires them is an absolute humanity, unashamed and unafraid. He is willing to pass his time and cast in his lot with the brotherhood of men, whether they be in rags or fine linen. He is no lone thinker, living in those dark and fantastic recesses of the soul where ideas are generated. As soon as you open his book you are out of doors, subject to all the surprising chances of the world, blown upon by the wind and rain, carried hither and thither in our crowded life, to drinking parties and secret assignations and funerals. Shocked you may be, and incommoded by the diversity of your experience, but you are never melancholy and never outcast. The world, which is the touchstone of sanity, is always with you. Indeed, Boccaccio might be called the escape from Dante. The dreamer awakes, and tastes the air, and sees the colours of life, and feels the delight of moving his limbs. He is among men and women. He has touched ground after his dizzy flight of the spirit; he has come out of the prison-house of theological system, nobly and grimly architected, and is abroad again in the homely disorder of our familiar world. Small blame to him if he laughs.

The divine power, the highest wisdom, and the primal love made Hell, says Dante, very profoundly. But the world, which was also made by God, is a lighter thing, with less of the symmetry of an institution. It is like one of those suddenly conceived works (and this view has the warrant of orthodoxy) which are thrown off by the artist in happy moments of careless inspiration. Those who enter Hell, says Dante, must abandon hope. But the world is made of hope; and the *Decameron* is a portrait of the world.

There is more than this sense of relief from system in the *Decameron.* The world is wide; and its width supplies a kind of profundity in another dimension. In a confined place life can raise itself and be high; in a low-lying plain it can extend itself and be broad. The *Decameron* is so generous in its breadth, and so various, that no criticism from without is needed: it criticises itself. Experience cannot be criticised by our idea of what experience ought to be like; it can be criticised only by more experience. This is what is called the irony of life, which, in its literary reflection, is found in all the best drama. Life criticises itself. If any one of us desires to have a criticism of his own way of life, he will not find anything of worth in the ideas of a secluded student, who often enough is willing to tell his opinion of what such a life ought to be. When the secluded student is a passionate and eloquent creature, like Ruskin, his ideas often produce a great effect, and a whole generation of the weaker sort endeavours to conform itself, not to circumstances or the pressure of experience, but to the sentiments of a revered teacher. But this is only an echo, a prolongation of the murmur of applause that greeted the voice, and it soon dies. The life of, say, a professor or a resident fellow of a college is to be effectively criticised not by the ideas of another professor or another fellow of a college, but by the mere juxtaposition of other dissimilar lives—the life, say, of a soldier or a brewer's drayman. Boccaccio describes so many kinds of lives that each of them is seen in relation to all humanity; and this is the truest criticism; it gives the right perspective. He knows that the event of human actions is manifold and incomprehensible; he is very humble and very humane; so he accepts things as they are, and shows how dire effects spring from trivial causes, how a gay beginning may have a disgraceful and lamentable ending, and how a disgraceful beginning may be turned by the whim of Fate to laughter and ease. This is what is called the mixture of tragic and comic effects.

The best of Boccaccio's stories are so entirely like life that the strongest of the emotions awakened in the reader is not sympathy or antipathy, not moral approval or moral indignation, but a more primitive passion than these—the passion of curiosity. We want to see what happens. This is the passion of all watchers of life who are not pedantic or foolish. They know only that they are sure to be surprised. Life is an infinitely subtle game, delightful to watch, giving glimpses here and there of the underlying causes of things, luring on the gamesters who believe they have discovered a winning system, fortifying them in their folly by granting them a short run of luck, and then, by a turn of the wheel, overthrowing and mocking their calculations. The interest of the game and the joy of its uncertainty give millions of readers to the daily newspapers. Indeed, to suppress the gambling news, you would have to suppress the news. The same interest gave a large public also to Boccaccio and the novelists, his followers. Here is set down a lively record of the miseries and happiness that have fallen to the lot of those who lived before us. In the world we see only scraps and fragments of the lives of others; in the book we may see the whole extent of the good and bad fortune that falls to man in this life. Often there is a moral, clear enough; flightiness and folly are seen to work their own punishment. But not always; and the moral is a very small part of the story; Boccaccio cares very little about it; he knows only that pleasure and sorrow chase each other across the sky, that no one can be sure to escape from suffering some of the bitterest and most awful of life's chances except by escaping from life itself; and life is what he loves. . . .

The sources of Boccaccio's stories have been carefully investigated and catalogued. But this investigation does not belong to the study of Boccaccio, for he did not know the sources of his stories. He picked them up where he found them—the greater part, perhaps, in conversation. A man who buys wares and trinkets from a travelling pedlar does not generally concern himself much with the trade routes of Europe. But it is possible to make a rough classification of the stories—or of the plots, for the manner of telling them is Boccaccio's own. About a third of them are found among the *fabliaux* of the lower kind of minstrels in Northern France. Another group contains moral apologues, Oriental in origin and essence, but scattered through many countries. Last, and most important, there are the stories founded on real incidents of Italian life, some of them belonging to his own time. These are what I may call the newspaper stories; they have this enormous advantage over the others, that they were not invented to illustrate a moral lesson or to indulge a lewd fantasy; they are merely true. The *Hundred Merry Tales,* the *Seven Wise Masters:* these are famous examples of two kinds of popular anecdotes—the anecdotes of the tavern and of the pulpit. The one kind is commonly as extravagant as the other. Both are enormously popular, for they write their lessons

large. The coarse jest is quite clear and intelligible; the moral parable is seldom elusive or subtle. But the truth of life is a much more delicate affair; it cannot be advertised on hoardings or sandwich-boards. By far the most precious of Boccaccio's bequests are those stories which tell us what actually happened during his own time, or not long before, in Italy and the Mediterranean. These set the standard; and the strange thing is that he is not satisfied with the wooden framework of the other stories, he tries to make them lifelike too, so that the most elaborate art of modern portraiture is applied to traditional indecencies and traditional moralities. Punch and Judy come to life. Let me take one instance—the first story in the *Decameron,* it will serve as well as another. The first story of the first day gives a notable example of hypocrisy; the last story of the last day, the famous story of Griselda, celebrates the virtue of patience. Both are raised to a height almost heroic, and yet both are almost brought to the likeness of humanity. . . .

The dangers of passion, the dangers of folly and vanity, these certainly are morals to be found everywhere in the *Decameron.* Boccaccio has a singularly light and happy touch in his treatment of foolish persons. He has no acquaintance with the kind of foolishness that confounds the wisdom of this world; he is never metaphysical in his treatment. Shakespeare's fools are, many of them, also God's fools; they live in the deeper issues of things. But Boccaccio's fools and dunces are ordinary human creatures in whom the human faculty of prudence and discernment is quaintly and delightfully lacking. They are a numerous and amiable family. There is the poor simpleminded painter Calandrino, a troubled soul, who was sadly duped time and again by his fellows, Bruno and Buffalmaco, men of very recreative spirits. There is the foolish young gentlewoman of Venice, empty-headed and vain of her beauty, who was induced to believe that the god Cupid himself had fallen in love with her. There is the medical man, Doctor Simon, who took a house in Florence and watched the passers-by, in the hope that he might get them for patients. Unfortunately he chanced to fasten his attention on Bruno and Buffalmaco, and he noticed that they lived merrily and with less care than anyone else in the city. When he heard that they were poor men, and painters by profession, he wondered (knowing nothing of the artistic temperament) how it was possible for them to live so jocundly and in such poverty. So he asked them what hidden means of livelihood they had. They, perceiving him to be a loggerhead, plied him with tales of a secret club, founded by a necromancer, frequented by Kings and Empresses, and endowed with all the luxuries of the world. Then the Doctor had them daily for guests, and employed them to paint his dining-room and his street-door and all the parts of his house with suitable frescoes. And he besought them to admit him to their club—the Pirates' Club, as they were pleased to call it. All the time that Bruno was painting the Battle of the Rats and Cats in the gallery of the Doctor's garden, the Doctor would stand by and hold the candle for him, for he painted after dusk, and tease him to be allowed to join the club. "Hold the candle a little nearer," said Bruno, "till I have finished the tails of these rats, then I will answer you." The poor Doctor ransacked his head for everything that might tell in his favour. "I would do anything for you," he said;

> you might take me into your club. You can perfectly well see what a handsome man I am, and how well my legs are proportioned to my body, and I have a face like a rose, and, more than that, I am a Doctor of Medicine, and I think you have none of that profession in your club, and I have a great store of anecdote, and can sing a good song, and if you don't believe it, I will sing you one.

With that he began to sing. In the sequel Master Doctor was very shamefully treated by the high-spirited painters. Folly never triumphs in Boccaccio, and the practical jokes that are put upon it often transgress the limits of delicate taste.

If Boccaccio is the first of the moderns, the world that he paints is more than half mediæval. The nobility and beauty of that older world of chivalry shine out in the loftier tales. . . . [An example] is the ninth story of the fifth day, told by Fiammetta, who was elected Queen for that day's session. . . .

It would be difficult to over-praise the delicacy and beauty of that story. It is not tragic, yet it has a pathos as lofty as tragedy. It is not well adapted for the stage, as Tennyson's distortion of it shows; the actual crisis is dangerously trivial—a housekeeper's dilemma. It is perfectly adapted for Boccaccio's narrative method with interspersed speeches which take us into the confidence of the characters. It is only one proof out of many that he can take the stuff of daily life, stuff that would be rejected offhand by more ambitious writers, and can wring from it effects that poetry might well envy.

The prose style of Boccaccio was dominant in narrative literature for centuries, yet it will disappoint those who test it by modern standards, and it misled many imitators. It is not a simple style—rather it is curious and alembicated, but this was for a sufficient purpose. The stories he had to tell were many of them very plain broad folk-stories, but they were to be told in a courtly circle. Boccaccio never uses a coarse word. He is very sparing in his use of colloquial expressions, which, when they do occur, have the more effect from their rarity and their setting. In this matter he is like Malory, who also preserves a single atmosphere throughout all his tales. The atmosphere of the *Decameron* is the atmosphere of the polite garden; if the exploits of clowns and rascals are told, the language in which they are told sets the speaker aloof from them in the attitude of a curious student of human life. The reported speeches of the characters, especially the longer speeches, are not dramatic; they are written to reveal thought and motive. When Tancred, Prince of Salerno, finds that his daughter has a secret lover, he causes the lover, Guiscardo, to be seized, and reproaches Ghismonda with her crime. She replies in a long speech, not truly dramatic, but none the worse for that. It is a noble speech, full of faith and courage and defiance. She knew that Guiscardo was as good as dead, and she felt indescribable anguish; she could have wept and cried aloud, but the pride of her soul disdained tears and entreaty, for she intended not to sur-

vive him; wherefore, not in the least like a weeping woman, or one who accepts reproof for her sin, she answered her father in high, careless fashion, frankly and courageously, without a tear in her eyes, and without a sign of perturbation in her soul. "Tancred," she said,

> I am in no mind either to deny or to entreat; the one way would bring me no help, and I seek no help the other way; moreover, I do not intend by act or word to appeal to your love or mercy; I shall confess the truth, first vindicating my honour with sound reasons, and then resolutely following the dictates of my unconquered soul. It is true that I have loved Guiscardo, and I do love him, and so long as I live, which will not be long, I shall love him; and if there is love after death, I shall never cease to love him. But it was not the frailty of woman that led me to this, so much as the little care you had to marry me, and the virtues of Guiscardo himself. You ought to know, Tancred, since you are made of flesh and blood, that the daughter you begot is also flesh and blood, and not stone or iron; and you ought to remember, though now you are old, what are the laws of youth, and how powerfully they work their effect.

These are the opening sentences of this amazing speech, so exalted in its temper, so fearless in its humanity, so perfectly characteristic of Boccaccio. It could hardly have been spoken at a tragic crisis; it is too elaborate for that; but it sets forth the whole inward meaning of the crisis, and some part of the creed of the author. The story of Tancred and Ghismonda has been told a hundred times since first it was told in Tuscan prose, but the first telling has never been equalled.

We make too little of Boccaccio. The splendid palace that he built, with a hundred rooms, has not been neglected, it is true, but it has been used as a quarry by other builders. Chaucer, Shakespeare, and how many more, took what they wanted from it, so that we are sometimes tempted to regard Boccaccio as if his chief use were to lend material to greater men. It is not so; he was as fine an artist as the best of them; his method was all his own; he cannot be superseded; and his work has aged less than the work of those who borrowed from him. He has the elixir of life; he is eternally joyous, and eternally young.

Birger R. Headstrom (essay date 1928)

SOURCE: "The Humanism of Boccaccio," in *The Open Court*, Vol. LXII, No. 3, March, 1928, pp. 181-86.

[*In the essay below, Headstrom claims that Boccaccio's friendship with Petrarch and his devotion to Fiammetta significantly shaped the* Decameron, *a work that reveals, in the critic's estimation, Boccaccio's "sublime humanism."*]

In the two distinct periods that combined to give definition to Boccaccio's life, we find that each served to give expression, and to reveal, the sublimity and depth, not only of his genius, but of the quality which has earned him immortality—his humanism. Without the profound mysticism of Dante, or the extraordinary sweetness and perfection of Petrarch, he was more complete than either of them; in his passion, his love, his suffering which defines the first period of his life, he is full of laughter and humility and love,—that humanism which in him alone was really a part of his life; and which later, under profound grief and melancholy, developed into that noble friendship with Petrarch, —a friendship which has become one of the most beautiful things in literature, and in which Boccaccio saw the beauty and glory of an idealism that later became associated with Erasmus.

A poet by nature, sensitive to the influence of love, his passion for the unfaithful Fiammetta controlled his entire life. She had awakened in him the slumbering spark of genius; and years later her memory still continued to be his inspiration. Under the influence of his love for her, he gave expression to his happiness by the development of his creative genius. He wrote for her, first to please her, and then to regain her. Even when she betrayed and deserted him— even though his love affair was at an end, never to be renewed—his love for her gave him hope and inspiration, and found such beautiful expression in the work he wrote for her. Extraordinarily personal, his state of mind is visible in them. One simple thought seems to dominate his mind; he had loved a princess and had been loved in return; and though he had been forsaken by her she remained, in spite of all, the guiding star of his life. To regain her love, he enchants her with stories, he glorifies her, constantly telling her his own story; but what hopeless means to win back the love of a woman; what folly to suppose she will read his thousands of lines!

"You are gone suddenly to Sammium," he writes to her in the dedication to Filostrato,

> and . . . I have sought in the old histories what personage I might choose as messenger of my secret and unhappy love, and I have found Troilus, son of Priam, who loved Criseyde. His miseries are my history. I have sung them in light rhymes and in my own Tuscan, and so when you read the lamentations of Troilus and his sorrow at the departure of his love, you shall know my tears, my sighs, my agonies, and if I vaunt the beauties and the charms of Criseyde you will know that I dream of you.

It is an expression of his love. He wants her to know what he suffers, to tell her of his experiences, his pains, his joys. And though the story serves as a means of self-expression, it is, in its exquisite beauty of sentiment and verse, one of the loveliest of his works.

But his sufferings, his journeyings, were but the progress of preparation for the work which was to give perpetuity to his name. In his travels, he became familiar with the people of his country, their joys, their sorrows, their pleasures, their hardships; and in his own sufferings, he learned life, learned to recognize and appreciate its beauties, its crudities. And then suddenly all the bright world about Florence, among the woods of Vincigliata under Fiesole and the olive gardens and podere of Corbignano, on the banks of Affrico and Mensola, so full of voices for Boccaccio, was silenced. The end of the world had come, some said. In a sense it was true. For the Plague was the end of the Middle Age. And at Florence, the vengeance

of God, or an outraged nature, had deprived Boccaccio of all those for whom he had cared, or had lived, and now alone, he retired from the world to devote himself to the task of giving to posterity his great immortal work, which some have called the Human Comedy.

It is rather strange that the work which best represents his genius, his humour and his wide tolerance and love of mankind, should be so different to his other works which are so involved with his own affairs. It can probably be best explained by the transition and change that had taken place in his soul, and which was to serve as an indication to that later period when a nobler and graver bearing gave definition to his friendship for Petrarch, and his interest and zeal in reviving the learning of the ancients.

Even his style had undergone a strange change, a style which, for its beauty and simplicity of expression, was in a certain sense to mark the rise of Italian prose. It is true that Dante's *Vita Nuova* was written before, but its involved sentences, founded essentially on Latin construction, cannot be compared with the infinite suppleness and precision of Boccaccio's prose. For the first time, Boccaccio presents a new idiom, which, like the character of the nation, is flexible and tender, and capable of rendering all the shades of feeling, from the coarse laugh of cynicism to the sigh of hopeless love. Like most progressive movements in art and literature, his remodeling of Italian prose may be described as a "return to nature." Indeed, it is the nature of the Italian people itself which he has made articulate in the *Decameron;* we find southern grace and elegance, blending with the unveiled naivete of impluse which is such a striking and admirable quality of the Italian character. And though the descriptions of low life, with its coarseness and indecency, might seem incomprehensible to the northern mind because of the freedom with which the life of the Italian finds expression, they are so admirable, and the character of the popular parlance rendered with such humour, that one cannot help but feel he is one of them, even though their immorality might seem disgusting.

The *Decameron* is a world in itself, and the effect upon the reader is the effect of life itself, which includes for its own good, things moral and immoral. It is Italy in the fourteenth century, and though with all its looseness, it is a philosophy of the world, with its variety, and infinity of people, dealing with man as life does, never taking him very seriously, or without a certain indifference, a certain irony and laughter. Yet it is full, too, of a love of country, of luck, of all kinds of adventures, gallant and sad; a true and realistic mirror of life in all its forms, among all classes, filled with observations of those customs and types that made up the life of the time. Dramatic, comic, tragic, ironic, philosophic and ever lyrical; indulgent of human error, it is a human book, perfect in construction and in freedom, full of people, of living people—that is the secret of its immortality. They live forever. And yet it seems to lack a certain idealism—a certain moral sense—an idealism which would have given it balance, a sense of proportion.

It was inevitable that a style so concise and yet so pliable, so typical and yet so individual, as that of Boccaccio should exert an enormous influence upon the progress of the prose created by it. This influence has persisted down even to the present day, to an extent beneficial upon the whole although frequently fatal to individual writers. But it is rather by its humanism that it has earned its place in literature. Even Chaucer, who turned freely to it, is not so complete in his humanism, his love of all sorts and conditions of men; Goethe, Shakespeare, Tennyson and many others looked to it for inspiration but in the literature of the world it stands, for its humanism, alone. Even the Divine Comedy cannot rock it from its pedestal.

In this immortal work is revealed, without the slightest constraint, the width and depth of his humanism, that admirable quality, the richness and beauty of which testifies to the sublimity of his inspiration. For with its completion, Boccaccio is no longer the same man, human, loving and tranquil, but rather sad, melancholy and somewhat cynical, a cynicism that found such terrible expression in that savage and mysterious satire, *Il Corbaccio.* Fiammetta was dead; and with the realization of that stern fact, the passion that had given him inspiration and expression to his creative genius, expired. He had written for her alone; now that she was dead he was sad, and his grief, on which he brooded, served to offer room for imaginative fancies. He had been injured and treated shamefully, woman was an evil creature, a tool of the arch enemy, to torment and destroy mortal man; and he found an outlet for his emotions in that wild invective against Woman, laughable in its wildness and unmeasured malice. But it was merely the reflection of the change that was taking place in his soul; the change that marks the transition from his youth to his maturity; from the freedom and exuberance of the boy to the grave and dignified bearing of the man. And when the storm had subsided and he found comfort in Petrarch, he still continued to cherish her fond memory, for that vain shadow always haunted him, the emptiness in his heart never left him.

In Boccaccio's deep and intimate friendship for the great humanist, it was inevitable that he should become interested in the cause for which his friend was laboring. Partly to forget his grief, and partly to be able to follow in the footsteps of the man whom he so greatly admired, he plunged with energy and enthusiasm into the work of reviving the learning of the ancient masters. Boccaccio was no scholar who saw in the literature of antiquity wisdom and thought, which Petrarch sought to make more profound, but rather, as a humanist, something living and splendid. He was no longer able to create living men and women; but he could find in the vast literature of the past a wealth of material which by industry and spade-work could be restored and given to the world. His devotion to this task, and his success, can be measured by the indebtedness of posterity to the classics of antiquity.

By his industry and interest in reviving the learning of the past, as well as the influence of the austere Petrarch, Boccaccio's humanism gradually grew from the simple love of human nature to adopt a higher and an intellectual significance. Having been far from virtuous, he gradually recognized the need of spiritual enlightenment and comfort, and the preparation for a future life. His conversion was precipitated, or rather hastened by that strange incident of the Carthusian monk which produced such a deep reaction on his impressionable nature. Having often attacked the institutions and servants of the holy mother church, and terrified by the approach of immediate death, he resolved to abandon literature and devote the remainder of his life to penance and religious exercise. Writing to Petrarch to this effect, he is cautioned in words of tenderest friendship not to lose hold of himself.

"No monk is required to tell thee," Petrarch writes in part,

> of the shortness and precariousness of human life. Of the advice received accept what is good; abandon worldly cares, conquer thy passions, and reform thy soul and life of degraded habits. But do not give up the studies which are the true food of a healthy mind.

This advice and wisdom Boccaccio heeded; and learned more than ever to look to his friend for guidance and comfort. Their ties of friendship were strengthened; and Boccaccio, already ill and weighed by the grief which he could never throw off, felt strangely drawn to the great scholar. He survived his friend but a short time.

In summary, we can do no better in fitting tribute to Boccaccio's sublime humanism, than to quote the few lines engraved on his tombstone, an epitaph composed by himself shortly before his death. Calm and dignified, it is indeed worthy of a great life with a great purpose.

> Hac sub mole jacent cineres ac ossa Joannis;
> Mens sedet ante Deum, meritis ornata laborum
> Mortalis vitae; Genitor Baccaccius illi;
> Patria Certaldum; studium fuit alma poesis.

Charles G. Osgood   (essay date 1930)

SOURCE: An introduction to *Boccaccio on Poetry*, edited and translated by Charles G. Osgood, Princeton University Press, 1930, pp. xi-xlix.

[*Osgood was a distinguished American classicist. In the following excerpt, he summarizes Boccaccio's conception of poetry and lauds his use of ancient myth in the* Genealogy of the Gods, *stating that the work was "the first attempt on a large scale to assemble, arrange, incorporate, and explain the vast accumulation of legend, and reduce it, after the manner of his times, to convenient encyclopaedic form. It was the work of a generous and patriotic poet."*]

If at this moment Boccaccio were to inquire concerning his reputation, he would no doubt be disappointed. Fame is his, in measure such as he craved, but not in kind. To be generally famous as the author of the *Decameron,* a mere teller of tales, a "vulgar" poet, a novelist, when he had dreamed of so different a reputation, would seem to him the very irony of fame. One hears him protest: "It is my peculiar boast and glory—meum est hoc decus, mea est gloria—to cultivate Greek Poetry among the Tuscans." Clearly it was his passionate hope to survive as the scholarhumanist, rather than as the literary artist.

There are, then, two Boccaccios—poet and scholar—one famous, the other obscure. It is easy to dwell upon an imagined antinomy between poet and scholar, but in Boccaccio at least, if not in general, such antinomy is quite fictitious. One cannot remind oneself too often that Boccaccio's scholarship and his art were but projections of the same powers of his mind, and that his humanistic Latin prose works come unmistakably from the hand of a poet. To conceive them otherwise is to miss their meaning. The author of the *Decameron* and of the *Genealogy of the Gods* is one and the same man, employing in these achievements the same energies and enthusiasms.

The *Genealogy* is a huge encyclopaedic repository of classical mythology in fifteen books. Both in form and in plan it is a book of its times. It embodies the Aristotelian-Catholic idea of the cycle of learning, with pagan precedents such as the works of Pliny and Varro. More contracted times required more contracted epitomes; Augustine's *De Ordine*, Isidore's *Etymologiae*, Rabanus' *De Universo*, and many others, offered a whole conspectus of learning in small compass. As learning revived such works expanded. The twelfth century produces the *Metalogicus* and *Policraticus* of John of Salisbury, to be followed in time by the stupendous achievements of Albertus, Aquinas, and the four vast *specula* of Vincent of Beauvais and his imitator.

Boccaccio designed his book as a speculum of ancient myth. The design was exquisitely appropriate. It is easy for us to forget that a cultivated man of his time could learn from his reading of Latin classics almost as much about classic myth as most of us know today. Vergil, Ovid, Horace, Statius, Seneca, Claudian, such commentators as Servius on Vergil and Lactantius on Statius, Cicero on the Nature of the Gods, Pliny, the Fathers, Apuleius, Macrobius, Fulgentius, Boethius—all these authors were accessible, and contain most of the legends of mythology; but accessible as these writers were to the student, the tales were too scattered and confused for general knowledge and use. Boccaccio makes the first attempt on a large scale to assemble, arrange, incorporate, and explain the vast accumulation of legend, and reduce it, after the manner of his times, to convenient encyclopaedic form.

It was the work of a generous and patriotic poet. Warm enthusiasms and deep convictions quicken it throughout. Whether or no Boccaccio undertook the project at the request of King Hugo, as he avers in his Preface, his labor was never perfunctory. From the age of thirty or thereabouts to the end of his life he had the task by him. His endeavors were doubtless interrupted for long periods, or slackened under the very weight of the labor. But he was clearly in love with the work, and even when not closely engaged upon it, was ever alert for material, whether in his reading, in chat with scholar, or traveller, or connoisseur, or in observation of ruins and localities as he journeyed about. Even near the end of his life he was loth to part with it as a finished work. Revision and additions kept on. He writes to Pietro di Monteforte in high indignation that a friend, Count Hugo of San Severino, to whom he had lent the work not yet ready for publication, should have allowed it to be copied.

His love for the work no doubt grew in part out of his delight in the very material which he was handling. But in part it derived from his purpose in having assumed so oppressive a task. This purpose was definite and serious if not wholly single. In the Preface to his geographical dictionary, *De Montibus*, etc., he says that he has prepared this book especially for students of poetry and history, particularly of the works of pagan writers, to help in explaining geographical allusions. He must have been well aware that very similar would be one of the commonest uses of the *Genealogy of the Gods.*

But the book must prove useful to poets as well as to readers of poetry. Boccaccio, true to his critical tradition, insists upon learning as indispensable to the poet, and he was quite aware that he was making material of first importance available for future poets. At any rate for two or three subsequent centuries the book dispensed much of the material for poetic adornment most in fashion in the Renaissance. Many a poet and man of letters in cultivated Europe saved himself a deal of trouble by Boccaccio's very readable encyclopaedia, and incidentally achieved renown for wide reading of the Ancients which he did not wholly deserve. Altogether Boccaccio very likely conceived all his humanistic works—*De Claris Mulieribus, De Casibus Virorum Illustrium*, the *Genealogy, De Montibus, etc*, as constituting an encyclopaedic set of works useful to poets and students, and therefore an agent for the increase of poetry. Of these the *Genealogy* was the greatest.

But another intention—possibly more occasional, though none the less sincere—informs the book. This is the justification and defence of ancient classical literature. It is this purpose of the author which particularly concerns us, since it involves his convictions on the very nature of poetry itself.

It was not enough merely to rehearse the ancient myths, nor to arrange them genealogically in as articulate a system as the discrepant accounts would permit. As mere tales, however ingenious or strange, they have no lasting claim on our attention, no power or right to survive. But the poetic literature of the Ancients is charged with immutable truth that deserves, nay, insures immortality; and Boccaccio undertakes to discover this truth by the aid of many commentators and authorities, ancient and modern, at his disposal. Where they fail to inform or satisfy him, he relies upon his own poetic insight. Thus he reveals the glory and vitality of ancient poetry.

These various intentions Boccaccio summarizes in declaring the "usefulness, both public and private" in which the book's chief value lies:

> Some men have thought that the learned poet merely invents shallow tales, and is therefore not only useless, but a positive harm. This is because they read discursively and, of course, derive no profit from the story. Now this work of mine removes the veil from these inventions, shows that poets were really men of wisdom, and renders their compositions full of profit and pleasure to the reader. So if poets who seemed to have perished from want of appreciation are now brought back to life, as it were, and to a high

place in the state, while their usefulness to the individual, which was ignored because it was unrecognized, is now revealed by this work of mine, they thus rouse the reader's mind to higher feelings. Furthermore, I hope that men will rise up as they have done in the past who will devote themselves to the study of poetry. As they peruse the memorials and remains of the Ancients, they cannot fail to derive much help from this work of mine, which will prove valuable to them if not to others.

Boccaccio speaks, then, at once as poet, critic, and scholar. Nor does he from time to time exchange one function for another, but all three powers of his mind are coactive throughout his discussion, if indeed they are not really one and single. . . .

A summary of Boccaccio's ideas concerning poetry properly begins with his definition. Poetry is *"fervor quidam exquisite inveniendi, atque dicendi, seu scribendi quod inveneris"*—"fervid and exquisite invention, with fervid expression in speech or writing, of that which the mind has invented."

This is a practising poet's definition, not that of a speculative critic. It inclines rather to the act and experience of creation than to a description of a finished poem. Boccaccio agrees with his fellow poets in recognizing two necessary processes by which a great work of art comes into the world—first, "inspiration" or emotional excitement, then deliberate critical afterthought or revision—"nature" plus "art," to use more recent terms. "This fervor," he adds,

> impels the soul to a longing for utterance; it brings forth strange and unheard of creations of the mind; it arranges these meditations in a fixed order, adorns the whole composition with an unusual interweaving of words and thoughts, and thus it veils truth in a fair and fitting garment of fiction.

Poetry, then, is an art, not a mere craft or technique. Poetry differs from rhetoric in its rhythm and metre; its style is more exalted, its meaning far more subtle, its invention more free and spontaneous. Poetry differs from history in departing from the chronological order of events to gain more artistic effect; but particularly is it distinguished by its moral or secondary intention, for it may so alter historical fact by suppression or elevation as better to veil and convey the poet's ideas of truth in whatever field.

As for philosophy, while poetry and philosophy win towards one goal, the truth, they seek it by different ways—the philosopher by the slower pace of reason, the poet by contemplation. The philosopher is literal, scornful of embellishment; the poet "writes in metre, with an artist's most scrupulous care, and in a style distinguished by exquisite charm." A philosopher is a propagator, consorting to that end with his fellow men; a poet dwells apart. And if philosophy is the keener investigator, and poetry in this respect, is, as it were, ancillary to her, yet poetry more carefully protects the truth beneath her subtle veil.

But above all the poet is the creator who fashions a new world of nature and of man in all their phases and activities, and so manipulates the illusion of this new world as to capture and control the minds of his hearers.

But not all poetry is good. Poets and poetry there are also that corrupt the soul and pervert readers to vicious thought and action. Such poets Plato would have banished from the State, and only such; such it was that Boethius condemned. Ovid's *Art of Love* is a case in point, and the "comic" poets.

Good poetry and great is the product of more than mere technique; it is a high creative art, the gift of heaven to only a few rare souls. But we are not to suppose that even the "fervor," the divine afflatus, is enough for great poetry without instruments of learning—thorough schooling in the Liberal Arts, in science, both moral and natural, in history, in literature, archaeology, and geography; in short, the full cycle of knowledge as the mediaeval mind comprehended it.

Finally the poet's learning is not mere erudition, nor is it a mere assembling of raw materials for his work. It furnishes him thoughts and objects for long, careful, and high contemplation, from which genius derives its impulse to creation and its fertile ideas.

Small wonder then if poets have always seemed to the rest of men a little strange and egregious—if they have avoided the crowd and its acclaim, to meditate and sing in solitude. They are withal the true aristocrats, and find their natural kinship among men of highest genius in whatever field, even of war and state.

But the glory of poetry appears not only in its nature, its rarity, and the quality of its creators, but in its very ancient origin. For, while authorities cannot agree whether the Hebrews, the Babylonians, or the Greeks invented the art, two facts are clear: poetry is a primitive art; and its origin is religious. It arose from primitive wonder at the forces of nature, which to the unsophisticated man implied a God. To placate or honor him men consecrated temples and devised a ritual, and this worship required exalted and uncommon language—metrical and polished discourse. This demand brought forth the first poets, who, working under divine stimulus created the first poetry, in which they veiled the mystery. And this is what Aristotle means by calling the first poets theologians; for such they were. Yet Moses, composing much of the Pentateuch in heroic verse, and the holy Prophets, are distinguished by inspiration through the Holy Ghost from secular poets, whose inspiration is rather through sheer energy of genius. Wherefore these were called *vates*.

Lastly, poetry is distinguished by its effects and functions. Poetry is essentially a veil of fiction which clothes the naked truth. Such it is in the holy Prophets and the Apocalypse; such it is in secular masterpieces. This fair investure, far from defeating or impairing the truth, much enhances its power among men. It thus finds protection from weaklings who only misunderstand it, pervert and abuse it. Besides, truth made common and obvious suffers desecration through ordinary utterance into cant and platitude. It grows cheap and weak. But the outward poetic veil, while it gives mere sensuous pleasure to the unskilful, only allures and challenges the worthier intellect, which accordingly exercises itself by every effort and at length wins the priceless guerdon of truth itself.

This allegorical theory of poetry, deriving from the Ancients, and sustained from early mediaeval times by a naturally strong inclination to symbolism and allegory, supports the allegorical quality of literature and art from Prudentius to Spenser. Nor is it confined only to formal allegory such as the *Divine Comedy,* but suspects and seeks ulterior meaning in all art and poetry worthy of the name.

Yet is it a stumbling-block and foolishness to modern critics and historians, who remark its esoteric and aristocratic complexion. For such there is no room in these democratic days. Yet who that, like Boccaccio, has taken active part in the propagation of poetry at any time can believe that poetry belongs to everybody; and not rather only to such as are qualified in mind and heart to comprehend it—to pierce the veil? Such is his opinion. But he is not without serious concern for novices and tenderer minds, and excuses his prolixity on the ground that a fuller account appeals to the less educated and the young.

His great humanistic undertakings draw much of their energy from his conviction that the appreciation of poetry is something which can be imparted to others by instruction. Did not Petrarch teach King Robert to enjoy it in his old age? The study of poetry, however, has been grievously neglected as compared with that of philosophy, law, medicine, theology, and the arts both liberal and technical. Like the poet, the student of poetry needs learning and erudition, and these Boccaccio has done his part to supply. But even these are not enough.

> You must read, you must persevere, you must sit up nights, you must inquire, and exert to the utmost every power of your mind. If one way does not lead to the desired meaning, take another; if obstacles arise, still another, until, if your strength holds out, you will find that clear which at first looked dark.

Above all you must experience a kind of conversion before the qualities of poetry will reveal themselves unto you.

Then will you be capable of its twofold Horatian power, to delight and to teach: to delight with its music and its beauty of language, and with a delight that is not effeminate nor unworthy as some allege; to teach not by precept alone, but, by the very charm of its beauty and its music, to refine your emotions and make you susceptible unawares to impulses toward noble and upright action.

It will readily appear that Boccaccio offers his reader no new ideas. Even a well read man of the fourteenth century could hardly have thought his apology very original. The considerations of his defence of poetry are such as had been accessible and current during all or part of the millennium before him. Petrarch, Isidore—and through him Suetonius and Varro—Gregory, Macrobius, Lactantius, Augustine, Jerome, and Horace were Boccaccio's chief instructors. But he is also indebted in some measure, not always easy to define, to Dante, Rabanus, the pseudo-Dionysius, Fulgentius, Boethius, Apuleius, Quintilian, Vergil with Servius' commentary, Cicero, and perhaps indirectly to the *Poetics* of Aristotle. Virtually every objec-

A reproduction of Eduard Chmelarz's Eine Französiche Bilderhandschrift von Boccaccios Theseide, *in which Boccaccio presents the* Teseida *to Fiammetta.*

tion of his opponents had been revived from the Christian apologists, Augustine, Lactantius, and Jerome; and most of Boccaccio's replies derive from these men. He has furthermore made very good use of contemporary scholars, to whom he pays generous acknowledgment.

But single and peculiar among those who helped Boccaccio is Petrarch. In his works he assembled the stock objections to poetry rehearsed by Boccaccio: that poets are liars; that they are useless and unintelligible; that they are unsociable and poor; immoral and irreligious; condemned by Plato, Boethius, Jerome.

To meet these objections he either compiled from various sources the replies already in common use, or devised refutations which Boccaccio used after him.

If Boccaccio owes his chief debt for his ideas to Petrarch, yet in all fairness the credit for assembling these ideas may belong to Albertino Mussato.

What mark of distinction, then, what glow of originality, raises Boccaccio's performance as a critic to high significance?

If Petrarch was the more original, more enterprising, yet Boccaccio was the more generous, the more catholic of the two. As Zenatti observes, Petrarch wrote in effect to defend only his own performance in Latin verse, Boccaccio to defend all poetry. Boccaccio, to be sure, is content with certain traditions, definitions, conceptions, formulae; and the limitations in his more literal use of the words "poet" and "poetry" are obvious. Critics love to point them out. They seem, however, to forget that Boccaccio himself was primarily a poet, and that, however he may at moments lapse into literalism, his experiences, enthusiasms, intuitions, as a creative artist are bound to assert themselves, and subtly to qualify all that he has to say on the subject of mythology and poetry.

Above all theories and minor motives which actuated Boccaccio is his conception of poetry as an agency of regeneration in the State. He saw about him an Italy deplorably given over to war, rapine, intrigue, greed, selfish ambition. Yet he saw her giving birth to men—notably Dante and Petrarch—as great as those who had glorified the name of Rome. How, then, could her gifts be turned to her regeneration? By the moral and intellectual forces of poetry. For these would grow by what they fed upon. Poets would stir in statesmen a higher notion of fame; statesmen in turn would encourage poets; and the power of poetry thus increasing would permeate the imaginations and conduct of the whole state.

The propagation of poetry, then, was the object not only of the Fourteenth and Fifteenth Books, but of the whole of the *Genealogia,* and, indeed, of all Boccaccio's encyclopaedic works in Latin. No one could have been better fitted for the task. With the keen instinct of the journalist— and there is a journalistic element in his work—he seizes an occasion of controversy, knowing that contest most certainly engages the human attention. To refute his opponents, then, is after all an occasional and minor object. To get his book read was paramount. To this end his style is fluent, voluble, often diffuse, bad as Latin, excellent for its purpose, lively, saturated with the writer's charm. And he succeeded. Not in regenerating Italy, of course, but, as often happens, in something greater. He produced a book which was a powerful implement of literary cultivation for two or three hundred years. The large number of manuscripts and editions, especially in the sixteenth century, is only one sign of its popularity. As a mere handbook of mythology and interpretation of myth its traces are everywhere recurrent in the literature of the Renaissance. In English alone they appear in Chaucer, Spenser, Jonson, Greene, Milton, perhaps Dryden; and the figure of Demogorgon as employed by Shelley in his *Prometheus Unbound* is in the tradition that derives from the opening chapter of Boccaccio's work. It is not unlikely that Shelley may have picked up an old copy in Italy. They were numerous in some editions, and are still easy to find.

But as a propagator of ideas concerning the art of poetry the book was quite as effective. These ideas reappear early in the next century in the letters of Salutato, in reply to the stock objections, and thenceforward are current and recurrent in the flood of critical essays that abound for two hundred and fifty years.

No better example of their persistence is needed than Sidney's *Defence of Poesy,* based upon Italian tradition, particularly Minturno. In it we hear again of the ancient religious origin of poetry, of the *vates,* of the metrical and poetic quality of Holy Writ, especially the Pentateuch, the Psalms, the Prophets, the parables, and the Apocalypse. Sidney insists upon the moral values of poetry, admits that some poetry is vicious, and uses this distinction to refute the belief that Plato banished the poets. Like Boccaccio he meets the objections that poetry is a waste of time, a mother of lies, a breeder of license. As Boccaccio elevates poetry by comparison with rhetoric, history, and philosophy, Sidney to the same end cites history and philosophy, though his points of comparison, under the influence of

the recovered *Poetics* of Aristotle, naturally differ somewhat. Both critics insist upon the supreme function of the poet to create—Boccaccio, perhaps, less than Sidney, who had the advantage of Aristotle's help. Both, after Horace, urge the twofold function of poetry to teach and to delight. In Boccaccio is distinctly implied the subtle, unconscious edification through the beauty of poetry, which Sidney argues at length. It is not necessary to suppose that Sidney borrowed these notions directly from Boccaccio, though verbal echoes indicate first-hand acquaintance; they may have been more than once removed. But the translation and frequent reprinting of the *Genealogy* in the sixteenth century prove that it was still widely read. Common sources were also accessible. The discovery of the *Poetics* wrought a fundamental change in all critical ideas. But instead of superseding the old ideas, it only effected in them necessary adaptation for the time being, and the fact remains that they had the power to survive.

But Boccaccio's essay must not be weighed as a mere document in the history of criticism and scholarship. To look upon it only as such is to miss the very quality which made it a document, the power that gave it momentum in the minds of men. Into it passed a winsome personality, which permeated and quickened the old tradition. For all his polemics, he is no fanatic, trying to subvert the old culture by a new. Rather is his the greater way, to revive the old by infusing it with the energies of a new humanization. Therefore his defence of poetry and the classics is not, as often implied, a manifestation of his lower powers, a reflection of the lesser Boccaccio, with his creative imagination laid asleep. Into it he poured his entire self—his thirst for knowledge and his tireless industry; his skill in narrative and his lively imagination; his half-conscious drollery, his delight in beauty, his persuasive humanism, his moral sense, his love of Italy; his eagerness to share his enthusiasms with others; his sympathies, his warm and loyal adorations, and his irresistible charm.

Obsolete as his critical ideas may be in their literal sense, they show, under his handling, a constant tendency to transcend it and escape into larger implications, to become perennial. Boccaccio's book is a composite of elements which in the last five hundred years—for whatever reason—has dissolved. Scholarship has perforce become a specialty, and with increasing specialism scholars suffer increasing occupational deformity. Criticism too has warped and shrunk in an opposite direction towards impressionism, more or less ephemeral and journalized. Even poets now are specialists, in matter, manner, and form. I fancy this disintegration of function would have appalled Boccaccio, in whom, if I may repeat, artist, scholar, and critic were all one and united in action. The feebler scholar, he who is not essentially artist and critic, the feebler artist who is not scholar and critic, the feebler critic who is not artist and scholar.

As a student of literature he pays all heed to the necessity of concrete knowledge. One cannot know enough, he would say, his utmost scholarship cannot suffice to understand the full truth and value of poetry. But it is by no means wholly a matter of concrete knowledge. Give range too to the individual mind; let the warm imagination brood and hover until it provokes a meaning—*the* meaning—from the work of art, confirmable but unattainable by mere scientific scholarship. Withal the whole process must be subject to both stimulus and guidance of a God–given artistic sense that knows what is right and true as the artist knows it.

It would be vain to wish back the encyclopaedic days of Boccaccio, with all the limitations that made their success possible. It would be vain to try to imitate him. But there is something infectious and edifying to the student of these latter days in his fervor, his tense curiosity, his mustering and deploying of all his extraordinary powers in the humanizing of literature as a means of new life to his people.

W. P. Ker on Boccaccio's amalgamation of modern and classical learning:

Boccaccio, in adopting [a] popular stanza for his romantic and epic verse, was acknowledging his reliance on the genius of the popular poetry. This, together with his command of the vulgar idiom in his prose, gives him his authority in Italian literature at the beginning of the new age. It is the good fortune of Italian poetry that at a time when there was so much danger of pedantry and formalism, of mere classical imitation, Boccaccio was there to set the force of his example and influence against the encroachments of fanatic precisians. He had too much learning, too strong a faculty for design, too great variety and liveliness of elocution, to be ignored by any scholar. He could not be dismissed as a barbarian; and he was too ingenuous, too fond of the Tuscan earth, the Tuscan air, to admit the sterile blight of the false classicism. In his own way and degree he did what Catullus and Lucretius, Virgil and Ovid, had done before him—by taking all he could get from the universal sources of learning, while he kept his loyalty to the native genius of Italy. Thus he appears at the beginning of the Renaissance well protected against some of its most insidious vanities, —just as the great Latin poets were saved by the same Italian genius from the dangers of a too absolute subservience to Greece.

W. P. Ker, "Boccaccio," in his Essays on Medieval Literature, *Macmillan and Co., 1905.*

Burton Rascoe   (essay date 1932)

SOURCE: "Boccaccio and the Renaissance," in his *The Story of the World's Great Writers: Titans of Literature*, Blue Ribbon Books, 1932, pp. 154-61.

[*In the excerpt below, Rascoe contends that the* Decameron *is less an exploration of sexual love than a commentary on human nature.*]

My first acquaintance with The *Decameron* came in early adolescence. Curiosity, says Aristotle, is the strongest urge experienced by human beings, surpassing love and hunger in intensity and duration; and curiosity in an adolescent is particularly strong concerning the nature and functions

of male and female. Time has consecrated The *Decameron* as one of the textbooks for adolescents in such matters, and this is all the more interesting in that it is a tradition which has evidently been handed down by word of mouth through the ages. Just the other night I learned, by asking, that The *Decameron* had occupied precisely the same place, in the early education of seven men gathered together, as it had occupied in mine. And in Montaigne I discover that the books which gave him, in part, the particular information he sought in his boyhood were "Boccaccio's *Decameron,* Rabelais, and the *Kisses* of Johannes Secundus."

Frankly, I must say that, tradition or no tradition, The *Decameron* is disappointing as a textbook of information to the adolescent confronted with the mysteries of his early sexual promptings; for the information is of a nature such as he can only regard as academic and of very little practical use to him. A boy of fifteen in our day and country is not likely to find all the ruses and subterfuges, so ingeniously set forth in The *Decameron* to bring about the meeting of lovers, quite to his purpose; he has no difficulty in meeting whatever girl upon whom, however transiently, his interest is fixed; nor is he likely to avail himself of the knowledge of how to behave after taking refuge in a wine cask on the sudden return of the husband he has just cuckolded when the husband brings with him a man who wants to inspect and buy the cask at a certain price and the wife informs the husband that she has just been offered more money by a man who is now inside examining it: what he wants to know is how to comport himself if, by some remote chance, he should find himself in some situation similar to that in which the chap in Boccaccio found himself just before it was necessary to take refuge in the wine cask. In such information The *Decameron* is deficient. What the adolescent wants to know is this and that, specifically, very little light on which is thrown anywhere by The *Decameron.* And so he learns to avoid the tedious prologues to each story and reads through the hundred tales with the desperate hope of a bio-chemist seeking the meaning of life. In the end he has acquired, quite against his intention, and almost subconsciously, a perception of human nature to mitigate the awful seriousness of adolescence.

When one has lost one's innocence one can return to The *Decameron* with a new interest and a heightened pleasure. Here now are delightful and amusing tales, involving all sorts and specimens of humanity in situations grave and farcical, romantic and lecherous, natural, earthy and unregenerate; here is satire, whimsical or boisterous, directed against friars, monks and nuns of a type plentiful in the Middle Ages, and against women whose concupiscence balks at nothing and in whose "frailty" there is purpose and cunning; here are the plots of all the merry comedies ever written; here are pleasure and voluptuousness, adventure and joy in life, related with relish and gusto.

The *Decameron* is the highest type, the prose masterpiece, of a literary genre in which mankind has always taken delight and probably always will. It is the genre which produced the *Mimes* of Herondas, the comic episodes of *The Golden Ass* of Apuleius, the Milesian tales (one of which, the *Matron of Ephesus,* was incorporated into the *Satyri-*

con by Petronius), Rabelais' story of Hans Carvel's ring, the *Facetiæ* of Poggio and on down through Chaucer's *Canterbury Tales* to our own time. It is a genre that is humanizing and refreshing. Man is an aspiring animal and he is constantly glossing the facts of his nature with illusions of perfections toward the attainment of grace and, taking it all in all, he makes a fairly commendable effort to live up to his illusions; but, if there were nothing to remind us, when we see certain imperfections in our own nature, that there are any number of others in the same fix as we are, we should probably find life intolerable. It is a very fortunate thing for all of us that there is a *Decameron* to counter-poise The *Divine Comedy*.

Some one has pointed out that whereas The *Divine Comedy* was designed to prepare the reader for the life to come, The *Decameron* was designed to prepare the reader for the life on earth; and there you have, I think, the difference between the essence of the Middle Ages and the essence of the Renaissance. The *Divine Comedy* was the culmination of the dominant ideas of the Middle Ages, an epoch that came to an end with the Black Plague. After that wholesale devastation of Europe, in which three-fourths of the population died within a year, it was necessary to start life afresh and to give those who survived something to live for. Millions of people had been all too precipitately ushered out of this life into the life to come by a plague supposed to have been brought to Italy by Genoese galleys; and so it was necessary to bolster up the spirit of the survivors by creating a new interest in the life vouchsafed them. In The *Decameron,* ten fugitives, seven women and three men, turn their thoughts away from the plague with amusing tales involving strictly earthly concerns.

The *Decameron* is one of the greatest impersonal, disinterested and objective works of literature. Nowhere in it does the author's personality obtrude; nowhere is the author's private moral conviction allowed to color the narrative. This method, of course, precludes any depth or grandeur in the recital. Every episode is related with detachment and is therefore related from the outside; such and such occurred in such and such a manner, we are told, without any pity or censure, compassion or distaste for the principals. What would actually be tragedy for the participants becomes comedy to us. And that is precisely how things turn out in life. Some one you know, for instance, may be involved in a love entanglement which has a number of ramifications. You have observed that person and have known him or her to do strange and interesting things under the stress of his or her situation. To that person these actions are performed under compulsions of the most powerful sort, perhaps anguished in the extreme. But, as you relate the story of the affair to me it becomes, to both you and me, absurd or comical. So, too, a story of venery, if told simply as a story, is amusing or not, depending upon how it is told and whether, as a tale, it has point; and certainly, if it is a good story with application to human life, showing up in bold relief some trait of human nature, it is a story which would be ruined by moralizing, for its whole purpose is to evoke the response of the listener to a fact of common knowledge or common experience. The stories in The *Decameron* throw light upon almost every trait of human nature, including the traits of modesty, chastity and piety. . . .

E. M. W. Tillyard   (essay date 1954)

SOURCE: E. M. W. Tillyard, "The Renaissance: The Fourteenth Century in Italy," in his *The English Epic and Its Background*, Oxford University Press, 1954, pp. 181-200.

[*An English scholar specializing in Renaissance literature, Tillyard wrote widely respected studies of John Milton, William Shakespeare, and the epic form. In the following excerpt, he investigates the impact of Boccaccio's early works and his later Latin writings on the tragic and epic genres of the Renaissance.*]

If Petrarch balanced his extravagant claims for *Africa* by the doubts expressed in his *Secretum* concerning the spiritual safety of leading a life of letters, Boccaccio after a youth and early middle age given to vernacular verse and prose experienced some kind of religious conversion that caused a panic in his mind about the life he had hitherto led. It was Petrarch himself, the master he never ceased to look up to, who wrote him a letter of comfort that restored him to sanity. He had already imitated Petrarch by ceasing to write in the vernacular, and after his conversion he wrote long didactic works in Latin prose. One of these was the *Genealogia,* which includes the most important piece of literary criticism transitional from Middle Ages to Renaissance. The bulk of the *Genealogia* is a large handbook of classical mythology, resembling the handbook of Conti that was composed and much used in the later Renaissance. This bulk is appropriate as introducing Boccaccio's final portion, on poetry, because the accumulation of mythology was specifically intended to help the poet in his subject matter and rhetorical ornamentation. And very serious subject matter Boccaccio thought classical mythology to be, because it had multiple meaning after the familiar medieval manner. Multiple meaning had first been applied to Scripture, and Dante had expounded the four meanings of a scriptural passage in his letter to Can Grande. Boccaccio with equal seriousness expounds the four meanings of the Greek myth of Perseus killing the Gorgon. There is the literal meaning and then in addition the three hidden meanings; the moral meaning is the wise man's triumph over vice; the allegorical is the pious man's scorn of worldly delight; and the anagogical is Christ's victory over Satan and ascension. By making this claim for a Greek myth Boccaccio shows himself the transitional figure he is. The doctrine of the four meanings is a medieval inheritance; the passionate promotion of Greek mythology has the accent of the Renaissance. And what applies to this detail of Boccaccio's treatise on poetry applies to the whole. As Osgood points out, Boccaccio says nothing original about poetry; he defends it on grounds already familiar in medieval writers; yet there is an assurance about his utterance of old arguments that is new and looks forward to those defences of poetry which are so fine a part of Renaissance criticism. In reading Boccaccio we are often reminded of Sidney.

The most important passage for the criticism of the epic

concerns the *Aeneid* and especially the episode of Dido. Here too the sentiments are not original, but they are of very recent borrowing and echo Ennius's words in *Africa,* on the poet's duty. Boccaccio gives various reasons for justifying the Dido episode. First, through the portion of it that narrates earlier history, Virgil imitates the practice of Homer, his predecessor. Such imitation is good both because it is imitation and because the practice imitated is a right one. Poets are not like historians (Lucan, many think, was too much of one) and should begin their narrative in the middle or towards the end. Secondly, Virgil had a veiled purpose: through the Dido story he shows 'with what passions human frailty is infested, and the strength with which a steady man subdues them'. Thirdly, by praising Aeneas Virgil seeks to extol the *gens Julia.* Lastly, through the symbolism of Rome and Carthage he exalts the name of Rome. Here, very clearly, are the qualities Petrarch required in the most serious and ambitious poetry: the copying of a great model, a veiled as well as a literal sense, a subject largely political. No more than Petrarch does Boccaccio treat the epic as literary form; indeed, it is scarcely yet a heroic poem, for he makes out Aeneas more a repertory of virtues than a character. Nevertheless, he later calls Petrarch's *Africa* a divine poem written in heroic verse and recounting the great exploits of the first Scipio Africanus. Boccaccio's references to the formal epic entirely confirm the assumptions or assertions of Petrarch. . . .

To revert to Boccaccio's general critical tone, one of the finest passages and also the most prophetic of full Renaissance criticism comes near the end of the *Genealogia.* It describes the different aptitudes of mankind; how nature intended this man for a lawyer, that for a farmer. And ordinarily we should follow nature's intention. He believes that God intended him for a poet and he adds a charming piece of autobiography about his own struggles to escape being put to business. The passage is effective because it puts the poet and poetry into a larger context, into the context of the Chain of Being, where every diversity of existence has its proper and necessary place. That the poet and poetry are important parts of the Chain is their complete and sufficient justification and renders them immune from any attack by medieval puritanism. This assurance is in the true spirit of the Renaissance and very different from the heart-searching of Langland about his own justification as poet. And without this assurance men could never have dared to raise the noblest of the literary forms, the epic, to such a pinnacle among the possible achievements of man.

Boccaccio also reinforced Petrarch's belief in the patriotic virtue of great poetry, and especially in his Latin letter to Pizzinghe [in F. Corazzini, *Le Lettere edite ed inedite di Boccaccio,* 1877]. Here he says that Italy is being made illustrious by its new poets and especially by the *Divine Comedy* and *Africa* (Boccaccio never allowed Petrarch's contempt for the vernacular to influence his judgement of Dante). He hopes that God has decided to be merciful to Italy's good name by inspiring Italian hearts with the spirit of antiquity and making them ambitious to excel not in cunning or violence but, through their poetry, in the fame they will acquire after their death throughout distant ages.

Such is the nature of Boccaccio's explicit criticism, and I have upset the time order in speaking of it before his original works in Italian and the criticism implicit in them because it naturally follows on and confirms the assertions of Petrarch. W. P. Ker thinks that his criticism counts for little in the history of literature and that his original works count for much. He finds him little troubled about rhetorical principles and uninformative about his art beyond explaining his allegorical theories. In his lectures on Dante [in his *Essays on Medieval Literature,* 1905], he points out, Boccaccio brings in Virgil, but in so doing speaks of him as a magician and says nothing about the idea of the heroic poem:

> but while he neglected the theory of poetical composition he was making discoveries and inventions in literary form, and establishing literary principles in a practical way. He has no criticism in him but he does more than the work of criticism by the example he sets.

While thinking that Ker misses the importance of Boccaccio's *Genealogia* I agree with him generally in thinking Boccaccio important for the examples he sets in his original works; and some of these works have a bearing on the epic. These are three: the *Filocolo,* the *Teseida,* and the *Ameto.* They were all composed in the 1340's and before Boccaccio met Petrarch; and of them the *Teseida* is by far the most important, the other two having no more than an accidental relevance. That relevance is briefly the following. The *Filocolo* is a long and complicated romance about the loves of Biancofiore and Florio and it derives from the French romance of *Floire et Blanceflor.* Whether by accident or whether because the French original went back to a lost Greek romance, Boccaccio's story is quite in the vein of Heliodorus's *Aethiopica,* and in so doing is at the head of the long series of prose stories, of which *Arcadia* is the most prominent English example, aspiring in the full Renaissance and neo-classic ages to the status of epic. The *Ameto* is a pastoral romance with verses scattered in it and thus sets the model for this practice in Montemayor and Sidney.

The *Teseida* differs greatly from these other two, being in verse and having most features of the epic form. It tells the stories of Theseus and Hippolyta, of Palamon, Arcite, and Emilia in a classical not a medieval manner. There is no dream-introduction, and the poet invokes the Muses, introduces classical mythology, and follows Dante's lead in using the formal epic simile. But there is no narrative of past events and no council of the gods. It is long, in twelve books; and Chaucer greatly abbreviated it in his *Knight's Tale.* The *Teseida* has a special importance as being the first would-be epic on the classical model written in the vernacular; it is an example of what much later was the dominant epic form and is thus prophetic in one way the Latin of *Africa* is not. W. P. Ker goes further and says:

> *Paradise Lost* is one of the successors of Boccaccio's *Teseide. Paradise Lost* was written with the same kind of ambition, to show that the epic form of the ancients could be reproduced, and filled afresh, by a modern imagination using a modern tongue.

I think Ker goes much too far. There is no evidence that Boccaccio had any conception of the epic form or that he took his poem very seriously. The *Teseida* is less severely neo-classic than *Africa,* and he never mentions the two poems together. He probably grouped it with other romances, while thinking that his classicising made it pleasantly and even startlingly different. It is only part of the plot that comes from a classical source, namely Statius; the source of the Palamon and Arcite story is unknown, but is certainly medieval and not classical. And when in this supposed classicising epic Boccaccio calls Theseus 'magnifico barone' he is not departing from the spirit of his work. If the *Teseida* stands at the head of the classicising epics in the vernacular it does so rather by accident than by any intention of the author. Like the *Filocolo* and the *Ameto* it is there, half accidentally anticipating a common use of many years later but exercising no influence and founding no school; in the history of the epic much less important than *Africa.*

It is not easy for us to realise that the works of Petrarch and Boccaccio which have stood the test of time and which exercised the greatest influence a hundred and fifty years after their day were not those that had the highest repute in their authors' lifetimes. It was not till the sixteenth century that the sonnets to Laura and the *Decameron* came into their own. Petrarch's Latin pastorals and pseudo-Ciceronian letters were more highly regarded than his sonnets, and Boccaccio's moralisings in Latin prose than his *Decameron.* There was in fact something premature about much of their work, including their would-be epics. Europe was not yet ready to confirm Petrarch's effort to make an imitation of a classical epic the most serious thing a poet could undertake. When Chaucer rehandled Boccaccio's *Teseida* he (quite rightly) removed much of the classicising, the excess of rhetoric and much of the pomp, and put the clock back by making it entirely medieval. But Boccaccio's Latin moralisings were in a different category from all the works I have just mentioned. They really spoke for their age and they were *immediate* influences as these other works were not. Since they have their place in the history of the epic I must include them in this [essay].

Willard Farnham in his *Medieval Heritage of Elizabethan Tragedy* found that Boccaccio's *De Casibus Virorum Illustrium* was of prime importance in the history of tragedy: and I welcome this finding as making more probable the conclusion, independently reached, that this work was important for the history of the epic also. The *De Casibus* was Boccaccio's first book after his religious conversion and his renunciation of profane literature in the vernacular for moral prose in Latin. It recounts the falls of many eminent people throughout history, beginning with Adam and coming right up to date in the French King John who was captured by Edward III of England. In general, it is in the tone of the medieval works preaching the contempt of the world, but Boccaccio was the first writer to express the old sentiment not through the homily but through an elaborate series of biographies. Further, he treats the old material with a new humanist vitality and at times gets away from the pessimism of the 'contempt' literature with its despair of earthly conditions to a state of mind that ad-

mits of some connection between man's acts and his fate in this world. It may have been this new turn given to the old and familiar literature that made *De Casibus* extremely popular when it was published and very influential for years after.

But though the *De Casibus* was outstanding in its popularity and influence it should not be separated from Boccaccio's own *De Claris Mulieribus* and the work that suggested the second, if not both, of these, Petrarch's *De Viris Illustribus.* All three works are portents of certain fundamental changes in the thought of western Europe. They are all biographies and they all show how about this time biography began to take on a different character. (I must here remind the reader that they are all serious narratives and as such may have some bearing on another form of serious narrative, the epic.) In his note of explanation to his *De Claris Mulieribus* addressed *Altevillae Comitissae* Boccaccio explains that, except for Eve, he writes about pagan women because these have been less written of than saints; and this mention of hagiography points aptly enough to the nature of medieval biography. Dorothy Everett in her article, "A Characterization of the English Medieval Romances," [in *Essays and Studies of the English Association,* 1929], commenting on Saintsbury's idea that the legends or lives of the saints gave its origin to the romance, said that the two modes were different: 'the legend is written with didactic intent, the romance chiefly to give pleasure'. Of course, the lives of the saints were meant to instruct but in actual fact they were mainly recreational. Bede in the preface of his life of St Cuthbert addressed *ad Joannem Presbyterum* said he undertook the work to commemorate his own devotion and to lighten John's journey: *ad memoriam meae devotionis vel ad tuae peregrinationis levamentum.* He thus had no doubt about the recreational side of biography being legitimate. In most of the legends themselves a modern is struck by a note of what can only appear as frivolity. The marvels are presented with an airy levity out of keeping with the nominal holiness of the matter. Though the medieval mind would have noticed no incongruity, it would have admitted to gaining great entertainment from such narrative. And anything like heavy and earnest didacticism is generally absent from the legends. Indeed, Bede's remark to John is true of most medieval biography, whether secular or sacred. It served to record events worthy to be remembered, and to entertain. In so doing it did of course instruct, but the tone of the works themselves shows that this was not the chief thing. The first lines of Barbour's *Bruce,* in which the author speaks of his own narrative work, give us the state of affairs. Barbour begins with the recreational notion. Even fabulous stories are delightful, but true stories (like that of Bruce) much more so. And when stories are true they are also instructive. Further, brave deeds, like those of Bruce, are worthy of record so that their memory may be perpetuated.

At first sight it is strange that in the age of faith the legends of the saints should have received such light treatment. But there were a great many saints, and they were individuals; and in an age when an ideal of holiness was more important than the individual, however good, it was not natural to accord great solemnity or severe didactic emphasis to this or that saint. It was more natural to record and to amuse.

If such was the typical medieval state of affairs, it will be evident how great a change was shown in Petrarch's grim, selective statement in his preface to *De Viris Illustribus:*

> Apud me nisi ea requiruntur quae ad virtutes vel virtutum contraria trahi possunt: hic enim, nisi fallor, fructuosus historicorum finis est, illa persequi quae vel sectanda legentibus, vel fugienda sunt.

Mere record is not to be tolerated; pleasure does not enter in. Severe didacticism is now the rule. And the lives themselves of the illustrious Romans Petrarch recounts are long and scholarly and instructive in a manner alien to medieval practice. In this new kind of didacticism Petrarch was much in advance of his age; but he does also truly interpret a great change of conditions that was taking place at the time.

This change was partly religious and partly political. The dominance of an ideal of holiness over the homage to the great individual could only continue when effectively backed by the Church. When the Church began to weaken, and particularly when the Popes lived at Avignon, the balance began to shift the other way. And when it did begin to shift, some of the awe that had invested the spiritual ideal began to be transferred to the individual. There has always been great men, good and bad. But now they counted for more. Through the same processes the different nations of Europe began to count for more, and Europe itself, that is the area that accepted the Roman Catholic religion, counted for less. Politically, the fourteenth and fifteenth centuries were ages of pessimism. The papacy failed to abbreviate the long and exhausting wars between England and France. The Italy of Petrarch and Boccaccio was distracted by feuds and civil war, and Rome itself was half deserted and wholly corrupt. The character of the individual ruler appeared to count more than ever before in the gamble of whether a country was to be happy or wretched. When Petrarch wrote the lives of the eminent Romans, he had these new conditions in his mind. Roman history, he thought, provided an unsurpassed repertory of great men, good and bad; and if the princes or dictators of Italy could model themselves on the good Romans and learn what to avoid from the warning of the bad, the state of the land could be really bettered. Petrarch, it must be remembered, was hopeful of what the dictatorship of Rienzi could do for Rome, and he supported him. By moralising biography in the *De Viris Illustribus* Petrarch thought he was serving his country and advancing the general political good of mankind.

Boccaccio's two works did the same kind of thing but by less abrupt and more traditional means. Petrarch goes straight to antiquity: Boccaccio, as pointed out above, introduced the traditional motives of the medieval works *de contemptu mundi* into the composition of biography; at the same time he insinuated a conception of human responsibility absent from them. I say 'insinuated' because it is only in some stories that Boccaccio goes beyond the mere impact of fortune on any great man and relates that impact to the mind or acts of the victim. But these excep-

tional stories, in giving a more reasonable appearance to the events of this world, show man as more of a resident and less of a passenger on earth and mark a true change of centre: a change favourable to substituting the story of a hero for the pilgrimage as the epic theme. To give examples: Boccaccio made Agamemnon a good man who did not deserve his sufferings, but adds that if he had lacked ambition and been content with poverty he would have escaped. Hannibal was not the mere victim of fortune in a capricious world; he was partly responsible for his own decline because he failed to ride to Rome and take it when, after the battle of Cannae, he had the chance. Boccaccio's innovation was not that the introduced human cause and effect into unfortunate events; his gropings are feeble things compared with Dante's achieved sense of human responsibility. It is that by shifting the centre from which human events are seen he gave to the causes of those events a different value. Dante and Langland show the liveliest sense of human responsibility, but for them the ultimate human goal and home are heaven: Boccaccio has a fainter sense of human responsibility, but he combines it with the beginnings of a new orientation of man.

But Boccaccio's **De Casibus** and his *De Claris Mulieribus* also derive from (and very significantly modify) another medieval practice, the *exemplum*. The medieval *exemplum* was a story, usually quite short, serving to illustrate a moral in a longer work, whether homiletic or narrative. In a homiletic work like Gower's *Confessio Amantis* the moral comes first, and the story illustrates the moral; in biography an incident is seized on as exemplary, and a moral is added. In Barbour's *Bruce,* when Bruce was in his worst plight on the island of Arran, his hostess there prophesied a happy issue. Bruce was encouraged but did not altogether put faith in her words; whereupon Barbour inserts a little homily upon the virtues and vices of prognostication. Such a moral homily is not organic but decorative; and in general the *exemplum* was not independent but illustrative and subsidiary. The main point about Chaucer's *Monk's Tale* is that the Monk, nettled by the Host's impertinent request for a risky tale, does not give a tale at all but brings out of his clerical cold storage a great string of *exempla* which should never have been strung together at all but which should have served severally to illustrate morals already stated in the abstract. Now in his **De Casibus** Boccaccio did just what Chaucer's Monk did: he made the *exemplum* into an independent tale. But what for Chaucer was a joke was for Boccaccio serious, and an act destined to have an immense influence. The change from the medieval form of biography, till now dominant, to Boccaccio's form of the independent moral example is indeed great. In the first the subject was a man who did things worthy of record, diverting, and capable of illustrating incidental items of morality. In Boccaccio's biography the man or woman begins to be himself the embodiment of certain virtues and vices in such a way that he serves *in his own right* as a great example, a highly significant object-lesson, a figure of solemn and inspiring didacticism.

I was careful to say that Boccaccio *began* this process, because his narrative method is not consistent. Sometimes he narrates without comment, as if the mere story was self-justified. But there are quite enough men who explicitly embody a moral to make Boccaccio's intention plain. Thus in the first book of the *De Casibus* Adam and Eve embody the vice of disobedience, and Nimrod that of pride; and we are shown their reward. Theseus embodied excessive and sudden credulity; he ought to have been more suspicious about Phaedra and Hippolytus. And in the prefaces to both works under review he leaves no doubt about his didactic intent. He says in the preface to the *De Casibus* that he recognises the insensibility and the viciousness of men and wishes to correct them. But such insensibility is beyond the reach of straight argument and elegantly narrated history, and can only be reached by the awful example. In the preface to *De Claris Mulieribus* he tells the Countess that these lives are presented to her so that the example of these noble women may incite her already noble mind to higher nobility.

These two works of Boccaccio do really mark the beginnings of conceptions that came to dominate the tragic and the epic forms of the Renaissance. Tragedy, whatever else it was, was a concrete demonstration that evil motives brought ruin: and the line of its descent was destined to be from Boccaccio through Lydgate, the *Mirror for Magistrates* and *Gorboduc* into the main body of Elizabethan drama. Neo-classic epic was, on one side, a narrative showing exemplary men in action, and that side descends from Petrarch's *De Viris Illustribus* and the two works of Boccaccio that derive from it. The line of descent is not so clear as for tragedy, but there is no doubt that, by whatever devious means, Boccaccio's words to the Countess look right forward to Sidney when he says, 'If the Poet doe his part a-right, he will shew you in *Cyrus, Aeneas, Ulisses,* each thing to be followed.'

Giuseppe Petronio　(essay date 1957)

SOURCE: "The Place of the 'Decameron'," translated by Robert S. Dombroski, in *Critical Perspectives on the "Decameron,"* edited by Robert S. Dombroski, Hodder and Stoughton, 1976, 48-60.

[*A highly regarded Italian educator and scholar, Petronio has written several distinguished works on Enlightenment culture and Italian Romanticism. In the following excerpt, first published in 1957, Petronio argues that the society depicted in the* Decameron *is neither Medieval nor Renaissance; rather, it is a transitional community characterized by the secular ideals of the Florentine* popolo grasso, *or bourgeoisie.*]

Feudal society was founded on personal relationships. By restraining man with the bonds of subjection and vassallage, it shattered the social unity of the previous times into a myriad of small societies each built around a leader. In the small, self-contained world of the castle, a whole court lived around a count or a baron. Warriors, pages, unmarried vassals, nobles and indentured servants fulfilled their apprenticeship in arms and courtly manners, while into the castle came guests of every sort: pilgrims travelling to important holy places, merchants on their way to the seasonal fairs, monks, beggars, and minstrels. Every so often the lord threw open the gates of the castle and held 'open

court'. Everyone, the rich and the poor, the great and the humble, was able to spend several days there; the castle became a place for meetings and banquets, and, when it was over, no one was granted permission either 'to remain or to depart' without having received one or more gifts. Thus, feudal economy, entirely based on the indirect exploitation of land, assembled around a lord a mass of parasites who, together with him, derisively exploited the villein, the only one who actually produced goods. The life of these parasites was moreover conditioned by the generosity of the lord who needed their number and devotion as testimony of his power and nobility.

'Magnanimity', or 'liberality' as it was also called, was therefore, at a certain moment in feudal society, a necessary virtue, bound to the conditions of castle life as an essential part of courtesy (cf. *Convivio,* II, X, 7). It is natural that later, when art began to idealize this life, it also idealized the virtue, and prescribed it to the lords as an essential condition of valour or excellence. A liberal man is one who gives freely, without being asked or obliged, who gives to someone according to his merit, who avoids any sort of stinginess and actually squanders his money to display his unselfishness. Obviously, avarice is characteristic of a mean and common spirit, *villano:* 'Avaritiam sicut nocivam pestem effugias' instructs Andreas Capellanus (*Trattato d'amore,* S. Battaglia ed., Rome, 1947,). 'Be generous in spending and have beautiful houses without doors or keys' recommends a Provençal nobleman Arnaut Guilhem of Marsan in his *Ensenhamen;* and an Italian lord, the marquis Malaspina, having been reproached for acts of brigandage, replies that he stole in order to give, not to hoard, and the justification appeared to be good. The French chronicler Geoffroi de Vigeois tells us about a knight who had a piece of ploughed land sown with silver coins, and another who, 'out of vaingloriousness', had thirty of his own horses burned alive. . . .

Meanwhile, during the thirteenth and fourteenth centuries, the new social and political organisation of the Commune was being developed. The Commune, at least at the height of its development, was composed of bankers, merchants, and artisans who assembled in the city and made their living from small industries and trade, rather than from the exploitation of the land. Money takes on a new meaning: earned through work, it is used to make money. A self-subsistent economy, which aimed only at fiscal balance, is replaced by a barter economy whose goal is the creation of a surplus wealth. The change in the social structure brings about a change in the philosophy of life and in moral judgement. One still talks about and celebrates the ideals of liberality and courtesy, because when a new social class begins to rule, it tends to ennoble itself by taking on the customs and philosophy of life of the former ruling class. But the words acquire new connotations in their attempt to express a new way of perceiving reality; while at the same time, other concepts and words arise and become diffused. Hence the bourgeois writers of treatises begin to celebrate a new virtue: temperance (or moderation) which no longer complements the courtesy of old, but replaces it. . . .

It would be wrong, however, to think that the process I

have briefly described came about in a simple and linear way through a steady and continuous evolution. Reality is always complex, never simple and uniform, and the evolution of systems and ideologies is never steady or linear. We find in every moment of social reality an intermixture of at least three currents: institutions and philosophies that have been already superseded, yet whose spirit remains; the dominant institutions and philosophies that give an age its colour and tone; new institutions and philosophies that arise confusedly and toil along with difficulty. Social reality is thus riddled with contradictions, and the men of an historical epoch reflect the divergent institutions and philosophies in their own particular way; they too suffer internal conflicts of which they are not entirely aware and which they are not capable of solving.

In the thirteenth and fourteenth centuries, the flow of life and ideas in Florence was therefore divergent and complex. Writers emerging from the new merchant and artisan classes expressed, more or less consciously, the new social reality of the Commune; while other writers, belonging to the noble cliques and educated in the previous culture, cherished the antique ideals. Since they did not see these ideals as a part of the people and customs, they clothed them in a seductive light of regret; and being contemptuous of a vile present, they idolised a chivalric past of refinement and courtesy. Thus the life styles and the ideals of the nobility continued in part to inform society, even now that the social world in which they arose had disappeared. . . .

Boccaccio came from a family of merchants, but his refined humanistic culture had kindled in him a strong desire to set himself apart from the masses who were devoted only to trade and profit. He considered the vile 'mechanics' (men who, incapable of raising themselves to free and impartial cultural activity, were given to manual labour and mercenary work) with the same aristocratic contempt that Dante had for the 'genti nove'; while he yearned for the courtly times of Saladin and past generations. Boccaccio's cultural ideal was therefore chivalric and courtly; but living in the middle of the fourteenth century, he was forced to push his ideal back in time, for his age was truly 'mechanical'. The feudal courts were no longer in existence, and the great princely courts of the Renaissance had yet to be created. Like Dante's Romagna, all of Italy was divided between 'tyranny' and the 'Frankish state', between the Communes made up of proud, quarrelsome merchants and signorie of tyrants, preoccupied with the future, not yet softened by time and by the security of dominion. Patronage was a thing of the past and would rise again in the future: the magnanimous feudal barons were dead and the magnificent lords of the Renaissance had yet to be born. Contemporary knights were gross and tyrannical, like those who composed the 'courts' and the 'families' of the podestas, such as the judge of the Marches of *Decameron* VIII, 5, whose breeches are taken by three young men while he is on the bench. Thus the world of chivalry belongs to the past; but by celebrating chivalric times and men, Boccaccio naturally expresses an ideal present to him and sets in not so distant times the aspirations he would have liked to see realised in his own age. For this reason, he exalts with reverent wonder the knightly loyal-

ty of the Norman king William II, who in order to keep his word has his most beloved young nephew killed, and casts in such an ideal light the chivalric magnanimity of anyone who consumes all his wealth for love, while remaining faithful to the lady and her cult (V, 8, 9); for this reason, in the Tenth Day, he varies and repeats his praise for magnanimity and for all the aspects of courtesy, even up to the point of renouncing love and life itself; for this reason, when appropriate, he continually inveighs against the great enemy: avarice, the gross cupidity that extinguishes in man's spirit every spark of generosity; this is why he often rages against the 'corrupt and vile habits of those who today wish to be considered gentlemen and lords', but who instead should be called 'asses, bred in the filth of all the wickedness of the vilest men' (I, 8).

Nevertheless, Boccaccio does not limit himself to representing and exalting only the cultural ideals of the past, ignoring or not acknowledging the present. Like every great writer, he is capable of acutely observing and objectively representing the real world around him, and the representation of contemporary social reality is, in the *Decameron,* vaster and more animated than it would seem from the above quotations. The deep meaning of the communal revolution lies in its having given way to a new culture that has inserted lay and earthly themes into the context of the religious and clerical culture of the past, preparing the way for Humanism and the Renaissance. . . .

In its renewal of life and culture, the Commune had not only politically destroyed the old feudal nobility (in the sense of replacing it as a ruling class), but it had also destroyed a particular way of viewing man, his virtues, and his work. Money acquires a new value that derives from the activity of men, not from its intrinsic worth; nobility is no longer a matter of blood and heredity, but rather an individual matter based on intimate refinement and personal valour. . . .

Boccaccio is the poet of this new burgher communal aristocracy. It is true that he often assails the movement of people from the country to the city, which he feels is responsible for the introduction of base feelings and customs into Florence (cf. *Letter to Pino dei Rossi,* in *L'Ameto,* N. Bruscoli ed., Bari, 1940,). It is true that he seems to yearn for and regret the passing of the antique chivalric world; but in reality, he is the poet of the most elevated classes of the new fourteenth-century society, of those classes that, mercantile by interest and birth, tended to set themselves apart from the less wealthy and refined in order to institute an aristocracy of the intellect, of feeling, of taste. Thus we have Federigo degli Alberighi, 'renowned above all other *donzele* of Tuscany for his prowess in arms and in courtesy'. Here the word '*donzela*' appears somewhat abstract and literary, because if *donzela* in the sense of 'young aspiring knight' was common in Provençal literature, it was rare in Tuscany, where chivalric traditions were always rather weak. In fact, Federigo, of noble family and courtly manners, puts into practice his politeness according to traditional chivalric rules: in loving, in the handling of arms, and in giving beyond measure. Yet there is something more modern, more 'bourgeois' in his story, and the novella ends, in a bourgeois way, against all norms of courtly tradition, with marriage. Andreas Capellanus, the great theoretician of courtly love, had taught that love and marriage were mutually exclusive; in fact, the concept of marriage had been alien to all Italian and Provençal love poetry, as well as to all chivalric literature; but here Monna Giovanna marries Federigo in a bourgeois way and Federigo, instructed by his difficult experience, 'having become more prudent with his money', lives happily with her. The noble and courtly *donzela* is transformed into an advocate of economy and moderation, virtues characteristic of the merchant Paolo da Certaldo and of Leon Battista Alberti. An age has definitely ended and Boccaccio has faithfully registered its demise.

With the end of the world of old, Boccaccio documents the birth of the new, in the tale of Cisti the baker. Naturally, the story should be read together with the introduction that precedes it, because only in this way is it possible to view the contrast between Boccaccio's ideological convictions and his zest for realism. Boccaccio the ideologue cannot understand how Cisti, a man whose polite and courtly discretion he greatly admires, could only be a baker. For him, nobility of spirit should be bound, if not exactly to nobility of blood, at least to social rank, to economic independence which permits the education of the mind and the long practice of refined customs. But the new social reality is in contrast to these traditional biases which still persist. And there are many examples (. . .) of how Fortune gives 'a base occupation to a body endowed with a noble soul'. Boccaccio cannot help noticing this new social reality. Among the common people working in the minor trades who take part in the councils of the Commune, there are not only the base 'mechanics' seeking vile earnings, but courteous, unselfish men, endowed with minds sharpened through participation in the political process, and instinctively magnificent spirits. With frank realism, Boccaccio can only attribute to this strange phenomenon an imaginative and mythical explanation: 'And so the two ministers of this world—Nature and Fortune—often hide their most valuable possession under the shadow of the occupations reputed base, so that when they are drawn forth at the fitting moment, their splendour will be the more apparent.' (VI, 2) But it is precisely the mythical character of this explanation that reveals Boccaccio's embarrassment and clarifies the contradictions present in him while he writes and the triumph of his realism over the prejudices stemming from his upbringing and social class. . . .

Moreover, in order to understand the seriousness with which Boccaccio grasps and expresses the character of his age, let us reconstruct the picture that the ***Decameron*** gives us of fourteenth-century Florence. The novellas of courtesy and tragedy, the rhetorical and abstract novellas, are never set in Florence. The great (too great!) heroes of courtesy are sovereigns (King Charles and King Peter), who reside in the lands of Lombardy—understood in its widest medieval meaning—rich in feuds and in lords (Messer Torello, the Marquis of Saluzzo); they are foreigners, imaginary characters of old. The Florentines, even when they are noble, courteous, cultured, are always, so to speak, concrete, endowed with a courtesy that is realistically human and earthly: Federigo degli Alberighi, whose wholly fourteenth-century character we have underscored; Guido Cavalcanti, philosopher, logician, who as poet seems abstract, yet so brilliant a product of society, so typically Florentine; polite men and women gifted with sharp wit, so able to fling back witticisms and jibes; Chichibio's master, for example, so lordly, yet so realistically represented; quick-witted and clever minds, like Giotto and Messer Forese da Rabatta; artisans like Cisti, the baker, and artists of the populace, like Bruno, Buffalmacco, and Calandrino; burgher physicians like Maestro Simone; rich merchants like the characters in the tale of Gerlamo; plebeians like Simona and Pasquino, merry fellows like Scalza, half 'men of court', that is, outright parasites such as Ciacco and Biondello, empty heads such as the young men who take the breeches off the judge of the Marches. And surrounding these characters, there is the country with its 'earnest gentlemen' (the man who is playing court to Belcolore, or the accomplice to the practical jokes of Bruno and Buffalmacco), its innkeepers and their families, peasant women ready to lie in the hay, merry, open-minded monks, and crude farmers. All of fourteenth-century Florence is present with its diverse social levels, yet by now completely Guelf and burgher; and the ten young men and women of the graceful and honourable company of story-tellers, in whom Boccaccio has pictured himself, his ideals and taste, represent the new Florentine burgher aristocracy: rich, cultured, honourable, and free living, yet already idealised and stylised, as the symbol and idealisation of their class. They represent a new aristocracy of wealth which also seeks to be an aristocracy of the spirit, but which has nothing in common with the ancient feudal world. Yet it feels itself different from the vile customs of the 'mechanics' and is contemptuous of baseness and avarice, yearns for the courtly companies of old (VI, 9), and has nostalgia for the ladies and the knights, the troubles and the comforts of the past. But it does so in its own way, within the limits we have drawn—which are the same limits that set apart the new century from the preceding ones and made this second or third generation of fourteenth-century citizenry fundamentally different from the first generation of thirteenth-century citizenry.

Thus the ***Decameron*** appears conceived on the divide that sets apart two worlds and two ages, in years abundant in sharp contrasts that are reflected somewhat subtly and harmoniously in the work. They are the years in which the Commune, incapable of becoming a people's government, already anticipates the Signoria; years in which a new intellectual caste begins to separate itself from the populace with which it is unable to merge. On the surface, the courteous, liberal, magnanimous tales appear only as a weary continuation of feudal literature; and, in a certain sense, this is true. But there is more. If at times liberality and courtesy appear as literary themes, at other times they are vital elements of the fourteenth-century world that the ***Decameron*** reflects in all its complex structure. Moreover, we have evidence of this diversity in inspiration in the artistic diversity among the various tales: the abstract ones, even though great literature, are rhetorical, wholly literary, replete with superhuman heroes, unrelated to the fourteenth-century society; in the other tales we have great, powerful, realistic art filled with modern and practical courtesy. Having read the ***Decameron,*** one tends to remember Mitridanes and Natan or Tito and Gisippo, while forgetting Cisti the baker, or Federigo degli Alberighi and Monna Giovanna. The actuality of Boccaccio's art is an index of the actuality of his inspiration, which depends on the possibility of adhering to life: to real life and to the vital forces at work in it. . . .

It is very difficult to assign a place to Boccaccio and to the **Decameron** in the evolution of the concept of culture and art, because among his contemporaries the conceptions of the meaning and value of culture were varied, complex, and contrasting. The ideas of past epochs linger on, kept alive by tradition and by the schools, while newer ideas forge ahead with difficulty.

At the beginning of the thirteenth century a great cultural tradition was about to reach its fullest maturity. The culture is in the hands of clerics; it is learned and discussed in Latin, in a language no longer spoken or understood except by the *scholae*. Its object is the rational understanding and systematisation of revealed truths; it utilizes all of the cultural patrimony handed down from Greek and Roman antiquity, but evaluated against a rigorous criterion of judgement that establishes whether or not its assertions correspond to those of the Holy Scriptures. The 'masters of the sentences' had already promoted this culture, and soon the great authors of the *summae*, Albertus Magnus and Saint Thomas Aquinas, would brilliantly systematise it.

But at that very moment, a clamorous rebellion erupts alongside and against this orderly work of systematisation. The wave of mysticism moving from the Franciscan Umbria threatens to overthrow even the fortress of scholasticism, while the Friars Minor, in their impassioned reinterpretation of all human values, also give a new interpretation to learning. We have, in a certain sense, the return of the Christian position which countered the pagan

Illumination of Boccaccio and Petrarch, from a 1409 French manuscript.

docta sapientia with the *docta ignorantia* or the *indocta sapientia*. . . .

Thus Saint Francis and the Franciscan literature take a clear stand against all vacuous and worldly learning. For Saint Francis, as for his early followers, at least until 1230, the only learning accepted was Christian learning. The *scientia graeca,* the *quaestiones curiosae et aridae,* that is, liberal arts, philosophy, and law, were prohibited. And theological studies themselves, although necessary, were allowed only to those who had entered the order already skilled in them. . . .

Similar polemics recur in all of Franciscan literature, throughout the century and beyond. In the thirteenth and fourteenth centuries, while Saint Thomas was assembling his *Summa,* while Dante was composing the *Divine Comedy,* and Petrarch and Boccaccio were laying the foundations of Humanism, many friars, Franciscan and others, continued to contrast the wisdom of the faithful with the knowledge drawn from books . . . Jacopone da Todi was continually to contrast holy madness with systematic knowledge, stressing the antithesis between Assisi and Paris, between infused and acquired knowledge, and between the feeling for God and the knowledge of Him. . . .

The devaluation of learning, pursued in the middle of the fourteenth century, has no longer a positive historical significance, but is only the sign of the inert survival of old themes or the mystical withdrawal from the new values that in the meantime were being advanced. Attitudes like those of Jacopo Passavanti, Saint Catherine of Siena, Giovanni delle Celle, and Saint Bernadine, taken individually could have a highly positive value, as signs of religious experiences lived with absolute fullness; socially, however, they had a negative value, inasmuch as they were no longer in harmony with the course of social-cultural institutions already under way. Instead, the devaluation of learning in the early thirteenth century was a sign of that youthful fervour which animated the whole of Italian society in those years when the common people were deeply moved by a force that was at the same time political, social, and spiritual.

In that particular moment of Italian history, when the new Communes were being created everywhere, to deny scholastic and juridical learning, to evoke feeling and faith, meant to deny the culture on which the feudal society was structured, even if, as often happens, the ideals and the goals of the rising communal society presented themselves in the guise of a return to the past: to a mythical, apostolic, and evangelical age. . . .

But for this very reason the cultural revolution conquered only certain restricted circles. These were years of social, political, and economic development, years of intense cultural life; years, in Dante's words, that were followed not by etadi grosse, but by steadily more refined ages, and the new human values affirmed themselves not against the culture, but within it. . . .

Therefore soon even the new religious orders became learned. The following decades witnessed the fierce battle waged by the mendicant orders for the conquest of the Sorbonne, and the early ascetic spirit that celebrated the *docta ignorantia* remained alive only among the heretical groups, or among the Friars Minor and spiritual groups banished by the Church and persecuted as heretics. The Church recognized itself not in Fra Jacopone but in Saint Thomas Aquinas.

On the other hand, even though the Commune did not express the interests of the magnates, neither did it express those of the common people. It became more and more the organization of the bourgeoisie, of the *popolo grasso, the buoni popolani,* who, having immediately understood the value of learning as a powerful instrument of freedom and domination of civilization and progress, wanted to make it its own. The evolution of the schools in the thirteenth and fourteenth centuries, the development of lay schools in addition to the clerical schools, the ever increasing diffusion of learning, . . . the gradual predominance of technical over, say, humanistic studies are both the signs and the consequences of the transformation of thirteenth-century society.

We have thus a rapid development of learning and literature, and the intelligentsia of the new ruling class, the judges, and notaries, seek in many ways to adapt the old culture to the demands of a new public. . . .

The Commune had also become the social and political organization of the *popolo grasso,* that is, of a class that inserted itself between the feudal nobility, with which it eventually merged, and the common people. The *popolo grasso* (the 'good and dear citizens', as they were called), which quickly became a class in itself, were the true masters of the Commune and the protagonists of a new history. . . . For them, learning was the property of the public and not of a caste. They felt that it should be transmitted in the vernacular, because the new generation of merchants, financiers, and artisans were unacquainted with Latin; that it should be both popular and national and, besides restating old theses and theories, reflect—which in effect it did—the new social, economic, and spiritual interests of the new classes to which it addressed itself and from which came its writers. However, it was not a universally democratic culture that represented the spirit and the interests of all the citizens in the Commune. . . . Nevertheless, the literature of the thirteenth century within certain limits does have a national and popular character that perhaps is not equalled in Italian literature at least until the Risorgimento: Dante's *Divine Comedy* is the highest expression of this character. . . . But after the *Divine Comedy* the unity of culture with popular tradition, of personal inspiration and collective spirit, is shattered . . . [and] it becomes easy to distinguish clearly between a cultured and petty bourgeois literary tradition, between works that are intentionally 'rhetorical' such as Petrarch's *Canzoniere* and the *Decameron,* and those of medium tonality based on a more modest and less ambitious form of culture: this is a literature, created by base and crude men, that addresses itself to the common people. Thus we are headed towards Humanism, where literature and culture become once again the patrimony of a closed caste, a caste this time made up of the laity. . . .

During the fourteenth century a new type of intellectual was being formed. He was no longer a man among men,

citizen of the Commune: notary, judge, prior, merchant, magnate, dedicated to politics, one who worked and administered by day, and translated and composed by night. The new intellectual was on the contrary a man of letters who made a profession out of learning and an occupation out of poetry. The greatest example, almost the model and symbol, of this type of intellectual was Petrarch, who already in the fourteenth century anticipated better than anyone else the character of the humanist, completely dedicated to learning. . . .

Boccaccio, as a man, is halfway between the old and the new *literato;* but as a theoretician, at a certain point in his life, it is he who, along with Petrarch, depicts, in his ***Trattatello in lode di Dante,*** the figure of the new intellectual. No longer a *fabuloso parlare,* poetry is now theology. . . . and the poets and *literati* are the saints of this new secular theology, saints whose lives are to be narrated according to the hagiographic schemes of old. . . .

The ***Decameron*** is situated at the height of the parabola, at a halfway point between the two ages, when the cult of literature had assumed in Boccaccio a character that was no longer medieval; but, at the same time, not having met Petrarch, Boccaccio had yet to detach himself from literature and still shared Dante's hope in the maturity and in the expressive possibilities of the vernacular . . . . The ***Decameron,*** therefore, is written in the vernacular, in prose; and [its stories] 'bear no title' [and are written] in 'the most homely and unassuming style it is possible to imagine', dedicated to the gentlest and dearest ladies; that is to say, it is intentionally conceived and addressed not to the new caste of intellectuals then being formed, but to the middle class Florentine reading public. Thus, as Branca's studies have shown, the book circulated in mercantile and burgher circles, and Boccaccio later, when he was converted to Humanism, repudiated it together with all his other early works. In other words, for Boccaccio himself the ***Decameron*** belonged to the literature and the culture of the Communes; in it we find no trace—with respect to themes, style, and tonality—of any link with the poetics of Humanism of which the ***Trattatello in lode di Dante*** some years later draws the essential characteristics. On the other hand, the poetics of the ***Decameron*** are altogether different from those of the folk literature of the common people; it is a work pervaded by an aristocratic spirit and by a conscious desire to go beyond the naturalism of the subject matter through the medium of literary reelaboration, in an attempt to sublimate the crudeness of reality into literary schemes.

Whoever in fact picks up the ***Decameron,*** after reading the minor writers of the fourteenth century, is immediately aware of passing from one world to another. Those writers of prose were capable of reaching a certain degree of art, but the ***Decameron*** is something else. It not only contains a greater knowledge of man, and a greater power of art which is lacking in the others; but there is a different conception of art based on the faith that writing even in prose, in the common vernacular, recounting tales, is a task to which the Muses give assistance; the conviction that poetry is a world by itself, an *art* that independently of its content sustains itself by its own rules and aspires to its own effects.

Hence the character of the book, which is never the reproduction of the vocabulary or the syntax of the spoken idiom, but rather, even in the most earthy of situations, the transposition of the vocabulary and the syntax to another system, possessing its own rules and cadences, its own forms: the inversion of words and phrases so that they may answer the demands of rhetoric and music.

Thus the impression that the reader receives is one of a greater artfulness than that to which Boccaccio aspired. For upon careful examination and viewed within the perspective of the language of the times, the **Decameron** appears more vivid and 'modern' than we are generally accustomed to think; it issues from the emerging of two equally dominant tendencies in Boccaccio: the aspiration towards art understood as rhetoric and his propensity toward realism. . . . In a word, the vocabulary of the **Decameron** may be described as 'urbane', the Florentine idiom of the wealthy and cultured classes of the fourteenth century: the language which the seven young women and their three young knights would more or less have spoken if, having met during the plague, they really had fled to the country hills to tell each other stories in a refined manner.

Quintilian has defined 'urbanity' as a quality having nothing dissonant, rustic, or alien in meaning, expression, gesture, or sound, consisting not so much in the singular terms as in the general tone of the discourse. And earlier, he had even been more precise, calling it a discourse in which there is a flavour of the language of the cultured citizenry; in sum, the very opposite of a rustic tone. Now it is precisely this urbaneness, this flavour of the city and of its learning that makes up the linguistic fabric of the **Decameron,** in which are present words of diverse tonality: even rustic, base, or plebeian, but seen as such, employed from time to time in the service of particular artistic effects. . . .

The vocabulary that Boccaccio calls *volgare* and *umile* is cast in a sentence structure accurately studied and elaborated according to precise rules, belonging to a long tradition and subjected, when necessary, to the refined and complex norms of medieval and artistic prose and of the *cursus*. To be sure, the language of the **Decameron**—its words and its grammar—is not that of the models of Guido Faba or of Guittone d'Arezzo, nor of Dante's *Convivio,* nor even of Boccaccio's early romances. Having been the fruit of a long linguistic elaboration, it marks the moment in which the ideal of thirteenth-century artistic prose reaches its dignity as art, equally distant from naturalistic immediacy and academic composure.

Guido A. Guarino   (essay date 1963)

SOURCE: An introduction to *Concerning Famous Women* by Giovanni Boccaccio, translated by Guido A. Guarino, Rutgers University Press, 1963, pp. ix-xxxii.

[*In the following excerpt, Guarino depicts Boccaccio's writings as transitional works that incorporate the spiritualism of the Middle Ages and the humanism of the Renaissance. He also compares* Concerning Famous Women *with the* Decameron, *stating that in the latter "the author's first desire was to entertain, while in the biographies of women it was to teach."*]

Boccaccio's fame today rests on his masterpiece, the **Decameron.** From the moment it was published this work forced everyone to be aware of its existence but was not always praised by Boccaccio's contemporaries and the men of the Renaissance; at times it was attacked together with its author. To the men of the Renaissance Boccaccio was primarily a Latin scholar: the Humanist who had brought Tacitus back to life, the scholar who had embraced the wisdom and knowledge of the ancients, the lover of poetry who had been the first, after so many centuries, to commune with the divine Homer. The great artist had to give way to the learned scholar, whose fame rested on his Latin works. With his **De Casibus Virorum Illustrium, De Montibus, De Claris Mulieribus,** and other works, Boccaccio was the great propagator of classical history, literature, and mythology, and his **Genealogia Deorum Gentilium** in particular became the textbook and font of inspiration for generations of poets.

When these works had fulfilled their historical role and helped bring new life to the ancient world, they were slowly relegated to oblivion. The world had come a long way from the time when adventurous Humanists searched every corner of Europe for lost treasures. Men who could easily buy Latin and Greek classics in the original and in translation as they came off the Aldine and other presses no longer needed Boccaccio to synthesize the learning of antiquity for them. Thus, the Latin works of Boccaccio slowly went out of use, print and fashion, and are today condemned to live among cobwebs in the lowest stacks of libraries and in the minds of a few scholarly professors.

Boccaccio's **De Claris Mulieribus** is a remarkable treatise which contains the lives of one hundred and four women. It is the first collection of women's biographies ever written, as the author proudly points out in the preface. It is very fitting that this honor should belong to Boccaccio, who took such pains to please and entertain women, and whose answer to those who criticized him for it was that yes, he liked women indeed. He was also among the first men of his age to turn his attention seriously to biography, a genre which was to become so popular. Boccaccio looked for glory in this world, not in the next, and believed that it was here that man affirmed himself and achieved fame, and that it was the writer's duty to preserve the deeds and achievements of great men for posterity. It was for this reason that he turned to biography.

Boccaccio's **De Claris Mulieribus** follows in the tradition of the medieval didactic and moralizing works. It has many characteristics of the encyclopedia and the *speculum* which were very popular in the Middle Ages. It shares with them the concern to instruct and strengthen the reader. Yet, there are many differences. His moralizing is not always of the medieval type; his attitude toward women and the ideals he asks them to follow are quite different. Above all, we notice a change in his attitude toward the ancient world, and in his reasons for writing this work and the treatises on mythology and geography. His motive is not simply compiling facts to make them more easily available, nor is it a mere show of erudition. He is filled with the desire to accumulate new knowledge to be added to that of the Christian Middle Ages. He wants to show that the ancient myths, which the Middle Ages had misinterpreted, contain much truth, and that under the veil of poetry there are universal sentiments, ideals, and beliefs. He places the myths of the ancients on a par with Holy Writ as teachers of mankind. In the preface to the *Genealogy of the Gentile Gods,* the soldier Donino, speaking on behalf of King Hugo, asks Boccaccio to write about the ancient gods, and refuses to listen to his objections:

> I can well believe that those nations you mention are inaccessible, and that such records as they possess are wholly unknown to the Latins. But whatever has passed by way of Greek literature among the Latins, or whatever can be found in Latin writers themselves, who in early times won no little distinction and glory in literature, let it all be brought to light. . . .

Boccaccio, then, sees his mission in life as that of dispelling the gloom of centuries and restoring the knowledge of the ancient world. In accepting King Hugo's invitation, he stresses the difficulties that lie ahead and shows the awe and reverence with which he approaches his task:

> At your behest, then, I leave behind the mountain snails and barren soil of Certaldo, and, raw seaman that I am, embark in my frail little craft on a stormy sea all involved with reefs, little knowing whether my voyage will be worth the trouble. For I may trace every shore and traverse every mountain grove; I may, if need be, explore dyke and den afoot, descend even to hell, or, like another Daedalus, go winging to the ether. Everywhere, to your heart's desire, I will find and gather, like fragments of a mighty wreck strewn on some vast shore, the relics of the Gentile gods. These relics, scattered through almost infinite volumes, shrunk with age, half consumed, well-nigh a blank, I will bring into such single genealogical order as I can, to gratify your wish. . . . Who in our day can penetrate the hearts of the Ancients? Who can bring to light and life again minds long since removed in death? Who can elicit their meaning? A divine task that—not human! The Ancients departed in the way of all flesh, leaving posterity to interpret according to their own judgment. What wonder? There are the words of Holy Writ, clear, definite, charged with unalterable truth, though often thinly veiled in figurative language. Yet they are frequently distorted into as many meanings as there are readers. This makes me approach my own task with less misgiving. Where I do not perform it well, at least I shall arouse a wiser man to do it better.

> It is, therefore, my plan of interpretation first to write what I learn from the Ancients, and when they fail me, or I find them inexplicit, to set down my own opinion. This I shall do with perfect freedom of mind, so that men who are ignorant and fastidiously despise the poets whom they do not understand, may see that the poets, though not Catholics, were so gifted with intelligence that no product of human genius was ever more skillfully enveloped in fiction, nor more beautifully adorned with exquisite language, than theirs. Whence it is clear that they were richly imbued with secular wisdom not often found in their jealous accusers. And these interpretations will enable you to see not only the art of the ancient poets, and the consanguinity and relations of the false gods, but certain natural truths, hidden with an art that will surprise you, together with deeds and moral civilization of the Ancients that are not a matter of every-day information.

Boccaccio is concerned with the "human genius" of the ancients, their "secular wisdom," and the "natural truths" their works contain. This "moral civilization" of antiquity is definitely set apart from the Christian world. Boccaccio does not attempt to find Christian truths in the works of the ancients, as the men of the Middle Ages and Petrarch himself had done. He does not try to redeem the pagans by finding similarities with Christian thought and doctrine in their works. His work is a celebration of the ancient world for the human and secular values it contained, and for those "natural truths" which are part of every man's world, whether pagan or Christian.

In his defense of poetry in his *Vita di Dante* and in the *Genealogia Deorum Gentilium,* Boccaccio expresses his lifelong love for this art, which he places on the same level with theology. In his views on poetry we find the reason for his concern with ancient myths and his efforts to place all this material at the disposal of other poets. In his *Vita di Dante* he states that primitive men shared with us the natural desire for knowledge. Seeing the order which reigns in Nature, they thought there must be a power or force from which this order emanates. This they called "deity." They decided that this deity was to be venerated by other than ordinary means. They appointed priests for this purpose, built statues, and invented poetry in order to express their devotion in words different from their everyday speech. Poetry, then, finds its origins in theology. But poetry did not content itself with the deification of the sun, the moon, Jupiter and the other planets; it also showed that everything which was useful to man was a deity, no matter how earthly. It sang the praises of those men who rose above others through their intellect and strength, and who, because of their excellence, were deemed gods rather than men. Thus poetry celebrated battles and notable events in which both men and gods played a role. Boccaccio strives to give a rational explanation of religion and poetry, and at one point states that they are the same thing. Theology is the "poetry of God" and its purpose is to instruct men in divine mysteries so that one day they may reach the kingdom of heaven. With their myths, the ancient poets instruct men in the things of this world and show them the virtues they must pursue and the vices they must flee. The myths and the gods of the poets may be false, but under the veil of fiction they explain the world of man, or, as he says, the "natural truths."

In giving equal importance to the secular myths of the poets and to Holy Writ, Boccaccio does not intend to lessen the importance of the spiritual values of man; he was a believer like his contemporaries, although, unlike his friend Petrarch, he did not allow religion to torture him. He insists, however, that this earth is part of man's world. In re-telling the myths of the ancients and interpreting them, Boccaccio wishes to present a different concept of life on this earth. He sees man as having certain "natural" powers and capacities which he must develop fully in order to play an active role in this world. Man is not to abandon God, but he must no longer renounce the world. Like Petrarch, he believed that the ancients had found a way of life and certain values proper to man. This concept of life was to be found in the works of the poets. By collecting and interpreting their myths, Boccaccio was making this material available to future generations of poets, for in his view there could be no poetry without myths. But more important, he was undertaking the "divine task" of bringing "to light and life again minds long since removed in death"; he was taking a world which the Middle Ages had distorted and was attempting to restore it to its original state. In many works of the Middle Ages, the ancients appear as men who have the same ideas and feelings and speak in the same way as the author and his contemporaries. In the *Novellino,* Hercules, Socrates, Trajan and others do not differ at all from Christian heroes. Boccaccio knew they were different and tried to learn what they and their world were like. As an historian and as a critic Boccaccio did not equal Petrarch. His reconstruction of the ancient world is not very accurate or successful, and he lacks Petrarch's objectivity and critical resources. Yet in some ways he seems to approach it more closely through his love and admiration, which are evident in every line. It is a world peopled with heroes who, because of their "natural abilities," have become representatives of the civic and secular virtues which form the basis of Boccaccio's new world. They allow him to indulge in his love for the magnificent and the extraordinary, for the deed or word which symbolize man's greatness.

The stories and myths of the ancient world also give Boccaccio the opportunity to moralize, which was one of his favorite occupations. His moralizing is often highly conventional. At times, when he moves away from tradition, he shows doubt and even defends ideals which seem to clash. This is especially true of the ideals he proposes as models for women. An example of his ambivalent attitude is found in Chapter V, where he discusses the results of civilization. In itself civilization is good, for it has brought man from the condition of an animal to that of a human being; he has become refined and has acquired high spiritual values. Yet civilization is also evil. In his primeval state of bliss man knew no vice and lived without fear or wants, envy or greed. Civilization has changed him into a being who cannot live in peace with other men for he is never satisfied with his possessions. Boccaccio felt these questions very deeply and personally. If we know something about this man who was given the name of *Giovanni della tranquillità,* which he bitterly resented, we can easily see how serious and sincere he was even in his ambivalent attitude to civilization. His ideal life was one of peace and quiet, devoted to scholarly pursuits and to poetry, a simple life in which everyday necessities do not intrude. His personal life was quite different from this ideal, and we can easily understand his dreams of an age of gold. He loved

heroic deeds, but was not of heroic temper. All this appears in his moralizing and in his interpretation of ancient myths.

In all his works on classical poetry, Boccaccio uses the fourfold medieval system of interpretation. Any given myth has four meanings: literal, moral, allegorical, and anagogical. In his *Genealogy of the Gentile Gods,* he gives an explanation of this system:

> According to the poetic fiction, Perseus, son of Jupiter, killed the Gorgon, and flew away victorious into the air. Now, this may be understood superficially in its literal or historical sense. In the moral sense it shows a wise man's triumph over vice and his attainment of virtue. Allegorically it figures the pious man who scorns worldly delight and lifts his mind to heavenly things. It admits also an anagogical sense, since it symbolizes Christ's victory over the Prince of this World, and his Ascension . . . But it is not my intention to unfold all these meanings for each myth when I find one quite enough.

Usually Boccaccio resorts to the moral and allegorical interpretations. As for the literal or historical meaning of myths, Boccaccio adheres to the rationalistic system of Euhemerus, with which he was acquainted through Lactantius. An explanation of euhemerism is found in the *Life of Dante:*

> Afterwards, various men in various places began to rise above the ignorant multitudes in their regions through their excellence in different things. They judged disputes not according to written laws, for they still did not have them, but through a certain natural sense of justice, which some had more than others. They gave order to their lives and customs, for they had been enlightened by Nature itself. They resisted adverse events with bodily strength, and took precautions against those which might happen. They called themselves kings and appeared before the people followed by servants and wearing ornaments which men had not used until that time. They made others obey and finally worship them. This happened without difficulty, if they but dared demand it, for they seemed gods rather than men to these primitive people who saw them in that guise. These men did not put all their trust in their strength, but began to multiply the number of religions. Through them they cowed their subjects, and bound to obedience through sacraments those whom they could not have subjected through force. In addition, they began to deify their fathers, grandfathers, and ancestors so that they would be feared and revered more by the people. These things could not be done without the aid of the poets, who . . . with various masterly myths made the people believe what the princes wanted. In the service of these new gods and the men for whom they claimed divine origin, they used the same style which the first poets had reserved only for the worship of the true God.

Boccaccio was conscious of living in a new age. However, he was still in what may be called a transitional period in which new values were making themselves felt but had not yet displaced the old. Thus, as he moved in new directions, he carried along a number of medieval traditions and practices. One of these was *exemplarism,* that is, the use of the *exemplum* whereby the author expresses his ideas and discusses various topics. For instance, to demonstrate the power of Grace and to show that God's mercy is infinite, a writer presents the example of a man who has committed many offenses against God and men, repents and is then saved through God's Grace. This is one of the three basic patterns which are found in medieval sermons and the *Vitae Sanctorum.* Boccaccio uses this method, but his stories no longer demonstrate God's love, as was the case for the Christian *exemplum,* but the operation of Nature and the human intellect: the method is the same, but the purpose differs greatly.

Boccaccio makes use of this method in the **Decameron** as well as in **Concerning Famous Women.** Both these works can be divided into categories which exemplify vices and virtues, and celebrate man's ability to live in this world. For instance, in the **Decameron** lust is exemplified by Masetto da Lamporecchio (III, 1), Brother Puccio (III, 4), Rustico and Alibech (III, 10), and the village priest of Varlungo (VIII, 2). Fidelity in love is illustrated by Ghismonda (IV, 1), Isabetta (IV, 5), the wife of Guglielmo Rossiglione (IV, 9), and Federigo degli Alberighi (V, 9). For the power of love and its results there are Cimone (V, 1), Gerbino (IV, 4), and Federigo (V, 9). Adventure and the ways of Fortune are represented by Landolfo Ruffolo (II, 4), Madonna Beritola (II, 6), Andreuola (IV, 6), and Simona and Pasquino (IV, 7). Examples of intelligence and stupidity are don Felice and Brother Puccio (III, 4), Ferondo (III, 8), and Brother Alberto (IV, 2). Generosity and magnanimity may be found in Natan (X, 3), Ansaldo (X, 5), and King Charles (X, 6), and naive belief in saints and miracles in Ser Ciappelletto (I, 1), Brother Alberto (IV, 2), and Brother Cipolla (VI, 10), to cite only a few.

These same categories may be used for **Concerning Famous Women:** lust is exemplified by Venus (VII), Clytaemnestra (XXXIV), Helen (XXXV), and Faustina Augusta (XCVI); fidelity in love may be found in the chapters on Penelope (XXXVIII), Dido (XL), Nicaula (XLI), Artemisia (LV), and Portia (LXXX); the power of love and its results is shown by Iole (XXI), Aemilia (LXXII), and Triaria (XCIV); adventure and the ways of Fortune are illustrated by Polyxena (XXXI), Cassandra (XXXIII), Hypsipyle (XV), and Thisbe (XII); the chapters on Amalthea (XXIV), Thamyris (LIV), Irene (LVII), and Paulina (LXXXIX) contain examples of intelligence and stupidity; generosity and magnanimity are portrayed in Busa (LXVII), Aemilia (LXXII), and Camiola (CIII); naive belief in gods and miracles is shown in Minerva (VI), Isis (VIII), Flora (LXII), and Paulina (LXXXIX).

The similarities between the **Decameron** and **Concerning Famous Women** do not end here. Almost all the *novelle* of Boccaccio's masterpiece have their counterpart in his later volume on women, and the comments found in the latter work may well serve as an explanation of the author's thought in the **Decameron.** His handling of the subject is often similar in both works: the story of Ser Ciappelletto in the **Decameron** and Flora; Isabetta and Artemisia;

Cimone and Triaria. Perhaps the best illustration, however, can be found in the *novella* of Brother Alberto and Lisetta (IV, 2) and the story of Paulina (LXXXIX). Alberto was a scoundrel who was forced to leave his city when his crimes became public knowledge. He went to Venice, where, in order to cloak his hypocrisy more successfully, he became a friar, and then a priest. He played his role of a humble and devoted priest so well, even crying during the sacrifice of the Mass, that his fame as a holy man spread throughout the city. Now, it happened that among the many women who flocked to Alberto's church to be edified by his holiness there was a certain Lisetta, who was both beautiful and foolish. After she had confessed her sins, Brother Alberto asked her whether she had any lovers. She answered that she had a husband, and he was more than she needed. How could he think she had a lover? Did he not realize that she was too beautiful to let another mere mortal caress her? Alberto now thought that the occasion had arrived to start reaping the rewards of the saintliness he had shown during the Venetian interlude. He convinced the naive woman that the Angel Gabriel had come to him during the night and had asked him to let Lisetta know that he had been captivated by her extraordinary beauty and would like to spend a night with her. On receiving this message Lisetta's joy knew no bounds, and she told Alberto that she would be delighted to receive the Angel at night, if he promised he would never abandon her for the Virgin Mary. Then Alberto let her know that angels are not of the same substance as men; therefore, Gabriel would have to assume a man's body to visit her. She agreed to this. Now, Alberto had a favor to ask: could the angel assume Alberto's body for his visit with her so that Alberto's soul might dwell in heaven for a few hours? Thus the woman spent the night with Alberto's body, and the following day Alberto told her of the joys of heaven, which his soul had experienced.

Paulina's story is very similar to that of Lisetta. She was a Roman woman who had great devotion for the god Anubis, whose temple she visited every day. She too was beautiful, and a young man, Mundus, fell in love with her. His advances were harshly rejected by Paulina, who proclaimed her fidelity to her husband. Thus the young man was forced to resort to subterfuge. He gave a great deal of money to the priests of the temple of Anubis to secure their help. The following day, when she arrived at the temple, Paulina was met by the most venerable of Anubis' priests, who had a message for her from the god. He told her that Anubis was very pleased by her long devotion to him and wanted to reward her for it. That night she was to sleep in the temple, and Anubis would come to her. Paulina went home and told her husband, who expressed surprise and delight at so signal an honor and gave her his permission. That night Paulina slept in the temple, where Mundus came to her in the regalia of the god Anubis and shared her bed. Before leaving he told her that she could expect the birth of a son who would be a god.

The similarity in plot and technique in both these stories is striking. In both cases an outrageous and ridiculous fraud is perpetrated on a foolish and simple woman. Both these women are devout: one lights a candle before every image of the Angel Gabriel, and the other visits the temple of Anubis every day to honor him with sacrifices. Both women are beautiful; both are inordinately proud, one of her beauty, the other of her saintliness. It is because of this pride that they refuse to accept the attentions of mortal lovers. One, madonna Lisetta, believes and finds it most natural that she has been noticed by the Angel because of her most marvelous body, which was not to be defiled by the touch of common lovers: "I am not the sort to be loved by anyone who comes along! How many women can you quote me, who can hold a candle to me? Why, I'd be considered good-looking even in Heaven!" The other, Paulina, adores Anubis with great affection and thinks it only just that her saintliness be rewarded with his love. Both take great pride in being singled out among women by a divine being. Both are apprised of this divine love by hypocritical intermediaries of the gods. Blinded by their ridiculous vanity, both women fall prey to their lovers' wiles, and afterwards one waits impatiently for the return of her angel, and the other, together with her husband, awaits the birth of a god. Boccaccio delights in the foolishness of the women, the slyness of their deceivers, and the duplicity of the priests, whom everyone considered saintly. In both cases the perpetrators of the fraud are punished, but this is a minor detail. However, even in this there are similarities: the two women are ridiculed by everyone because of their credulity; the punishment meted out to the false Anubis is lighter and less cruel than that of Brother Alberto, but this is explained by the fact that Alberto belonged to a religious order, thus deserving harsher treatment, just as the deceitful priest of Anubis did. All the basic ingredients of the *novella* of the **Decameron** can be seen in Paulina's story, which could easily have found a worthy place in Boccaccio's masterpiece.

The story of Paulina is one of the very few in **Concerning Famous Women** where the spirit and humor of the **Decameron** retain some of their brilliance. But a significant relationship between these two works is to be found elsewhere. From an artistic point of view, or in respect to humor and satire, they are very different. **Concerning Famous Women** does not have the lightness of touch and the sparkle of the prose of the **Decameron.** It was not meant to have these qualities. Many chapters are somewhat dull because Boccaccio was more interested in moralizing than in telling a story. Yet, this concern for moralizing provides the strongest link with the **Decameron.** In the light tales of the latter work, Boccaccio is guided primarily by artistic, rather than pedagogical reasons. But beneath all his laughter he remains a moralist. This becomes very clear if we compare the *novella* of Masetto da Lamporecchio (III, 1) and the life of Rhea Ilia (XLIII). Artistically these two stories have nothing in common. The Masetto story is one of the most successful in the **Decameron;** Rhea is the mere retelling of an event without any artistic distinction, wit, or life. In both of these, however, we find the same moral.

Masetto was a shrewd young man, completely alive and full of animal vigor. He was a lustful man, whose only purpose in life was to gratify his senses. One day, an old man, who had been employed as general handyman in a convent, told him that he had left his job because there were too many young women in that place, who, having nothing else to do, spent their time devising ways and means of annoying him. Masetto said nothing, but immediately made his way to the convent. Once there, he pretended he was mute and was immediately hired, since the mother-superior felt that his handicap was a valuable asset in that he would not be able to reveal any of their secrets. Boccaccio portrays the young nuns who dwelt in this convent very skillfully. They were not in the cloister because of their overpowering love of God. Their convent was a prison for them, and their thoughts were not of God but of the pleasures of life which other women enjoyed in the outside world, and which were denied to them. Now, to these young women Masetto's arrival seemed a godsend, for here was the opportunity to enjoy the love they desired without any danger, since Masetto, being mute, could not reveal the secret. Thus Masetto's stratagem met with success, and the forces of Nature triumphed once more, for Masetto spent the rest of his life bringing little monks into the world, as Boccaccio puts it.

The story of Rhea Ilia is a well-known one. For political reasons, she was forced to become a Vestal Virgin, incurring the obligation of eternal chastity. Again the forces of Nature are too powerful, and she cannot fulfill her obligation. When this becomes known through the birth of Romulus and Remus, she is put to death. Boccaccio makes little or no effort to give this biography distinction of style or bring the tragic figure of Rhea to life. He uses her story simply as a framework on which to hang the moralistic comments he has to offer. He protests vehemently against the practice of forcing young girls to enter the cloister against their wishes, and at an age when they cannot know what life has to offer and what they are sacrificing. Those who force them to become nuns, thinking that they are dedicating them to a holy life, do not realize that the flesh will claim its own:

> So, when I consider this woman and see the sacred bands and vestments of nuns hiding furtive love, I cannot help laughing at the madness of some. . . . They say that they have dedicated those virgins to God so that with their prayers their own affairs will prosper more, and after death they will gain eternal life. This is ridiculous and foolish. They do not know that an idle woman serves Venus and that these nuns greatly envy public prostitutes, whose chambers they think preferable to their own cells. . . . Wretched are parents and other relatives if they think that others can endure what they themselves avoid and cannot bear.

Is this not the same theme that appears in the *novella* of Masetto? And is this *novella* not an *exemplum* of the power of Nature and of an injustice to women, according to Boccaccio? Of course, the shift in emphasis in the two works is clear. In the **Decameron** Boccaccio does not preach. We can read Masetto simply as a delightful and droll story. The author does not point out the moral of the story at length as he does in his other work. But in the **Decameron** too he cannot escape the temptation to make sure that his point is understood, as can be seen at the beginning of Masetto's story:

> Loveliest Ladies, there are many people foolish

enough to believe that, once a girl has a white band tied around her head, and a black cowl hanging down her back, she is no longer a woman, with a woman's desires! As though by becoming a nun, she had turned to stone! If those fools happen to hear anything contrary to their belief, they fly off the handle as though an execrable, unnatural sin had been committed, unmindful of their own personal experience— they whom even license cannot satisfy, and disregarding the great temptations of idleness and brooding.

Yet, some critics have found it difficult to believe that the *Decameron* and *Concerning Famous Women* could have been written by the same man. Their misconception of the author's masterpiece made them see a dichotomy which does not really exist. They saw a libertine in the author of the earlier work and a moralist in the biographer of women. Many attempted to find an explanation for this difference. For Hortis the solution lay in the fact that a period of ten years had passed between the writing of the *Decameron* and *Concerning Famous Women.* Boccaccio had become old, he could no longer enjoy the pleasures of life, and so he became a severe judge condemning them for others. Landau faced the same problem. He stated [in his *Giovanni Boccaccio Sein Leben und Seine Werke,* 1877] that the treatise on women was a "good" book, which could have been written by a pious monk who had never left his cell. The truth is that Boccaccio always remained a moralist. In all his works, including the *Decameron* and *Concerning Famous Women,* he places great stress on man's condition in this world, his freedom, his duties and obligations, and the bonds which enslave him. The difference between his *novelle* and his lives lies in a change of emphasis. In the *Decameron* the moral and the *exemplum* can be found just as well as in the later book, but the purpose of these works is different. In the *Decameron* the author's first desire was to entertain, while in the biographies of women it was to teach. The same moral, therefore, which in Boccaccio's *novelle* appears in a subtle fashion, to be found by the reader himself, is clearly stated in *Concerning Famous Women,* an historical and pedagogical work which presents the author with a greater opportunity for his comments. Thus even if we compare Rhea, one of the dullest chapters in the latter work, to Masetto, one of those stories which have caused a number of critics to call Boccaccio a libertine, we cannot escape the conclusion that both of these were indeed written by the same man. Both have the same basic morality.

It is clear that Boccaccio adopted the form which the *Vitae Sanctorum* and medieval legends offered him. However, while the Christian *exemplum* was focused on Grace, Boccaccio, as I have said, substituted "Nature" and the human intellect for it. Moreover, he used this same form to ridicule the Christian legends. We find instances of this in both the works we have been discussing, and again they show striking similarities. The first story of the *Decameron* fires the initial salvo against Christian legends. Boccaccio proceeds to create a "saint" out of Ser Ciappelletto, a worse scoundrel than any the world will ever see. As the story opens, Ciappelletto is on his death-bed in a strange city. His hosts are worried, for they find themselves in an

impossible situation: if Ciappelletto dies without having seen a priest, they will be accused of having harbored a heretic; if he does see a priest, they will suffer just the same, for no priest can give absolution to a man who has committed every crime conceivable and shows no repentance. Ciappelletto, however, comforts them; he will see a priest and no harm will come to them. The priest who finally comes to minister to him is a very old and holy man, who is revered by everyone in the neighborhood. Ciappelletto's confession consists in the very opposite of his sins: every vice becomes a virtue, and this master criminal seems to be as innocent as a child. The simple priest is moved by the rogue's false tears and by his professions of faith and repentance and believes he has finally encountered a really good man. Ciappelletto dies after having received absolution. At the funeral, the old priest extols the virtues of good Ciappelletto in a sermon to the assembled people, and offers his life as an "example" to follow. His enthusiasm and admiration are contagious; everyone rushes to kiss Ciappelletto's feet and secure a piece of his clothes as a relic. He is finally buried in a marble sepulcher, which became a shrine, and soon everyone begins to tell of the miracles performed by Saint Ciappelletto. Thus this scoundrel became a saint with a last sacrilegious act, when the flames of hell were already burning him.

One saint is not enough for Boccaccio; he also presents the goddess Flora (LXII) in similar fashion and for the same purpose. Flora was a prostitute who plied her trade and accumulated great wealth over the years. As death approached, a desire for glory and immortality seized her. To be remembered forever, she left her wealth to the Roman people, with the proviso that it be used for yearly games in her honor. The Romans were delighted to accept. They were a lusty lot and insisted on properly honoring Flora by hiring prostitutes to perform at her festival. As the years passed, Rome became ruler of the world, and dignified senators began to feel that to hold games in honor of a prostitute was a blot on their great city's name. They attempted to put an end to these games, but unsuccessfully, for the people clamored for them. The people's will could not be thwarted, and yet Rome's honor had to be safeguarded. What was to be done? Finally the senators found a solution. They foisted a legend upon the people: Chloris had once been a beautiful nymph loved by the god Zephyrus. He married her and as a wedding gift he made her an immortal goddess, whose duty it was to adorn the world with flowers in the spring. And he called her Flora. Now, since flowers are a harbinger of new life and the fruit which will follow, the ancient Romans had established a festival in her honor to propitiate her. At this festival prostitutes had been employed to symbolize fertility. The people believed this legend, and thus a prostitute was metamorphosed into a goddess.

Boccaccio, then, ridicules the Christian legends by creating saints and gods, and by using the very form of the legends to do so. He felt that the authors of the *Vitae Sanctorum* had lost their sense of proportion and that their fantastic claims were an insult to man's intelligence. He has very little patience with the miraculous or the supernatural and states his skepticism bluntly. He makes this quite clear when dealing with myths or with the pagans. He shows greater care in dealing with Christianity, but does manage to show his disbelief, as can be seen from some of the parenthetical remarks in the life of Eve. His reluctance to deal with the Middle Ages and the Christian era in general is quite apparent, for the vast majority of the figures treated in *Concerning Famous Women* belong to classical times. He tries to explain his neglect of the Christian era by affirming that he does not wish to offend Christians by placing them next to pagans. Some critics have accepted Boccaccio's statement, seeing in it a sign that the author still belonged to the Middle Ages, and stating that later in the Renaissance writers no longer showed such scruples. Boccaccio's affirmation, however, cannot be accepted at face value, and as for having scruples, he has amply expressed his ideas on the subject in all his works. He did not write of saints and martyrs simply because he was not drawn to them, while classical antiquity held him enthralled with its charms.

The condition and place allotted to women in the Middle Ages is well known. They and their beauty were seen as tools of Satan devoted to man's perdition. Their faults and weaknesses were many, and they were mercilessly reminded of them. They were inferior beings, incapable of understanding, and were to be restrained and ruled with an iron hand, not guided, by their fathers and brothers at first, and then by their husbands. They were chattels rather than individual human beings: a necessary evil for the continuation of the species. The knight's lady-love and the *donna angelicata* of the *Dolce Stil Novo* may have been placed on a pedestal, but were not granted independence of will and action. The fact that their love may have been idealized and exalted by the knights of the Age of Chivalry, by Andreas Capellanus, and by the poets of the *Dolce Stil Novo* does not alter the basic position of women in that period, for reality showed itself in everyday life with all its brutality in spite of the poetic allegory of love. In a theological encyclopedia of the thirteenth century by the Dominican Nicolas Byard we find the following assertion:

"A man may chastise his wife and beat her for her correction; for she is of his household, and therefore the lord may chastise his own, as it is written in Gratian's *Decretum,* under the gloss *judicari.*" And in a much later period, Thomas More states in his *Utopia:* "The husbandes chastice theire wyfes; and the parentes theire chyldren." And in speaking of the position of each member of the family he affirms: "The eldeste (as I sayde) rueleth the familie. The wyfes bee ministers to theyr husbandes, the chyldren to theyr parentes, and, to bee shorte, the yonger to theyr elders." Woman's condition was to change slowly during the Renaissance, and the beginning of her metamorphosis may be observed in Boccaccio's works.

In the preface to his *Concerning Famous Women,* the author stated that the biographies of illustrious men had been written often by a number of excellent writers, and he cited Petrarch as an example. No one, however, had ever done the same for women. Boccaccio's surprise at this lack, and the fact that he set about writing a book on women shows the author's different attitude towards them. He recognized that women can live and achieve glory just as men do. But once again he shows that he is

in a period of transition, where the new clashes with the old. Women can become great scholars, rulers, painters and poets, if they but put their minds to it. But this requires a greater effort on their part since Nature has not made them the equals of men. Nature has given them frail bodies and sluggish minds, and to achieve glory they must first overcome these handicaps. Many of them have done so, and therefore deserve greater praise than men, according to Boccaccio. This is a sort of left-handed compliment, which he uses repeatedly. To lavish praise on a woman, Boccaccio can think of no better adjective than "manly," and his greatest condemnation of sluggish and insignificant men is to call them women. Yet he has taken a step forward, for he grants them the right of independent will and action. In fact, he often exhorts them to lay aside the traditional tasks of women and turn their minds and energies towards greatness of thought and action. Indeed, the overt scope of his treatise is to inspire them to do so. Yet he also seems to fear that women may encroach on the rights of men. In speaking of the honors and rewards heaped by the Roman Senate on Veturia for having saved the country, he states in his inimitable fashion that the senators outdid themselves in generosity, their minds befuddled by gratitude. Veturia and the Roman women would have been satisfied with the temple erected in their honor. Why then did the Senate have to grant them so many other rewards and prerogatives, which women have tenaciously held on to over the centuries to the discomfort and inconvenience of men? As always, Boccaccio moves forward instinctively towards a new era, but his progress is hindered by the *impedimenta* of traditions and prejudices of a former age.

In *Concerning Famous Women,* Boccaccio's comments and digressions give a picture of the world as he saw it, and as he would have preferred it to be. There are few facets of life that he does not touch upon in his commentaries and in his comparison of the customs of his and previous ages, usually to the detriment of the former. He discusses education, monastic life, politics, and morals, as well as the temperament and clothing of women. In these comments we find many problems which were afterwards developed and discussed fully by the men of the later Renaissance: fame and earthly glory; Fortune's role in the affairs of men; the individual's duties and obligations towards his fellow men; the place of the Church in everyday life; Man and Nature. From these lives, which are a blend of mythology, history and fantasy, there emerges the picture of Man as Boccaccio saw him. He is basically good when in his natural state. Civilization has brought about many changes. Some of these are good in themselves, but have had a detrimental effect on his character. They have prevented the individual from attaining the utmost fulfillment of his powers. The idea of property has prevented both rich and poor from pursuing ideals worthy of a human being: the rich, to become wealthy, turn all the powers of their minds to the acquisition of wealth, and the poor have to struggle for the basic necessities for themselves and their families. Thus both lose their independence. Wars destroy Man's character. He is born good but becomes cruel and harms his fellow creatures. Envy makes friendship impossible. Some of the practices of the Church are against Nature and deprive human beings of their natural rights. These are the evils Boccaccio struggles against. He believes they are the bonds which have enslaved humanity and he strives to burst them because he believes that Man is good and worth saving. It is his environment and the society in which he lives that bring out evil in him. To these evils he opposes those qualities which we should hold dear, and which he himself admired and cherished: peace of mind, goodness, mercy, friendship, and love of Man. Yet, because his concern is often hidden by a smile, Boccaccio has been accused of superficiality, immorality, and selfishness. Being not only Italian but Tuscan, he smiles and is amused by the stupidity of others and by the spectacle they offer as they make themselves ridiculous while pursuing their folly. But beneath this there is a deep love for his fellow creatures and a desire to improve their lot. His smile cloaks his great concern for man's welfare and a love deeper, perhaps, than that of his accusers who were always ready to offer man fire and damnation.

For the sources of his lives Boccaccio depends mainly on Latin authors, with the exception of Flavius Josephus, whose work, however, had been translated into Latin, Eusebius in Jerome's translation, and Homer, whose poetry he struggled to read in Greek. Valerius Maximus, Livy, Hyginus, and Tacitus are his most frequent sources. The following authors are consulted with less frequency: Pliny, Vetruvius, Suetonius, Ovid, Sallust, Cicero, Virgil, Justinus, Servius, Annaeus Florus, Macrobius, Paulus Orosius, Lactantius, Pomponius Mela, and the Augustan Historians, Julius Capitolinus, Vulcatius Gallicanus, Aelius Lampridius, Trebellius Pollio, and Flavius Vopiscus.

To understand Boccaccio's way of handling his sources, we must not forget the nature of his work. He is interested in telling the story, of course, but even more interested in presenting an example of vice or virtue. When the source of his example is very brief, Boccaccio weaves out the story to a suitable length for a chapter. He does this by putting in details which help him create the atmosphere he desires. He provides a background, writes speeches for the characters and discusses their motivation. These additions fit in quite well with the stories or characters he presents. When historical sources do not come to his aid, Boccaccio feels justified in using his imagination, for after all he must write the story, give the example, and make it palatable. A good illustration of this technique is the chapter on Megullia Dotata. The author found only two or three lines on Megullia in Valerius Maximus, but expanded them into an entire chapter. Valerius Maximus states only that Megullia brought a large dowry to her husband, and was then given the name of Dotata (richly dowered). Boccaccio provides a background by discussing the simplicity and frugal life of the Romans at that time. He speaks of the results of her action. He then praises the simplicity of the Romans, compares it to the love of luxury of his own time and moralizes on the vices of his contemporaries.

At times Boccaccio reverses this procedure. If his source is lengthy and contains matters which are not essential to his purposes, he shortens it considerably. In the chapter on Niobe, Boccaccio wants to present an example of the foolishness of pride and the harm it can cause. He uses as his source Ovid's account of this queen in the *Metamor-*

phoses (vi. 146-312), but reduces the part devoted to the queen to about one-fifth the length of the original. He does this by deleting Ovid's description of the sacrifices to Latona, the description of the queen's robes, her speeches, Latona's complaints to the other gods, and the manner in which Niobe's children died. He does not speak of Niobe's continued defiance as some of her children died, and her ultimate despair and entreaties to the goddess to spare her youngest son at least. He gives just the bare outline of the story, and in this case his reasons are obvious. The essential part for him is the example and he does not want it to become lost in details. To make doubly sure of this, he allots about one-third of the chapter to comments of a moralistic nature.

At times Boccaccio uses more than one author as his sources for the same chapter. In the majority of cases he simply uses details given by one author in order to expand or complete the story he has taken from another. In the cases where his sources are at variance, the procedure is somewhat different. When he is able to determine critically which version is correct, he will invariably use it. When this cannot be determined, he uses the version which lends itself more to his moralistic purposes. He often mentions the fact that there are other versions of the story, and gives his reasons for choosing one over the other. His methods of criticism may seem very simple and unsophisticated to us; yet he does make an attempt at criticism, at times with excellent results. He has a very suspicious attitude towards his sources and constantly seeks confirmation for his facts. He is greatly annoyed by discrepancies in chronology or identity and does his best to arrive at the truth. He relies heavily on etymology but without a great degree of accuracy. Whenever possible he reads his sources in the original rather than in translations, which he regards with suspicion. He rejects supernatural explanations of events. Instead he makes an effort to find an explanation based on the psychology of the men he is discussing and in accordance with their times and culture. He does not accept blindly even the most respected authorities. Above all, he had a genuine love of poetry and scholarly studies. As Osgood observed, his methods were a little better than those of his day; we cannot ask more of anyone. . . .

R. Hastings (essay date 1975)

SOURCE: *Nature and Reason in the "Decameron,"* Manchester University Press, 1975, 116 p.

[*In the excerpt below, Hastings argues that the* Decameron *occupies an intermediate position between the Middle Ages and the Renaissance and suggests that Boccaccio's secular outlook and ethical ideals are "the natural reflection of attitudes prevalent among the more advanced, enterprising and forward-looking sections of the late medieval Italian society to which he himself belonged. If Boccaccio appears to us in the* Decameron *as a transitional figure it is because he lived in a transitional age."*]

In general terms, Boccaccio's secular outlook, his adherence to nature, his enlightened and liberal attitudes, his broadmindedness, sympathy and tolerance all present an appreciable contrast to the ascetic tenor of much medieval ethics, the artificiality of many existing moral conventions, the strictness and severity that frequently characterised their enforcement, and the narrowness and rigidity of outlook that often lay behind them. In this he clearly foreshadows the Renaissance (though he is not, of course, by any means alone in doing so). Similarly his recognition of the need for some reasonable restraint of natural instinct, to be achieved through the enlightened exercise of the intellect, can be said to anticipate the rationalism of later Renaissance writers like Ariosto and Montaigne, and to require a degree of self-consciousness and self-awareness that is another frequent feature of Renaissance activities. The conception of virtue that emerges from this discipline (positing as it does the individual's ability to determine his conduct through the exercise of his own free will, and arising out of the self-sufficiency and sense of personal responsibility of the fulfilled and contented man) similarly reflects the self-confidence of the Renaissance and its faith in the capacities of the individual.

In more specific terms, his permissive attitude to love represents a conscious departure from the repressive approach of the medieval Church. His comparatively enlightened attitude to marriage in the *Decameron,* and to the place of women in society as a whole, is a foretaste of the *Cortegiano* and the cultured ladies of the Renaissance who figure therein (though his advocacy of courtesy and consideration in the treatment of women is at the same time clearly influenced by the medieval code of chivalry and courtly love). His criticisms of the corruptions of the clergy are part of a long medieval tradition, but here too he displays an understanding of their predicament, and a recognition of the difficulty of keeping to their ascetic ideal, that sound a new note. His admiration of intelligence, education and culture derives largely from the humanist's faith in the powers of the individual human intellect and belief in the ennobling powers of scholarship (though once again there is an essential continuity here with medieval culture: compare, for example, the *dolce stil novo's* equation of nobility with scholarship and the intellect). His suggestion that human intelligence can be used constructively to minimise the perils of fortune, and to exploit promising opportunities to the full, is symptomatic of the spirit of enterprise and self-reliance that also characterises so much Renaissance thought and action. The celebration of courtesy is, at one and the same time, a development of the medieval code of chivalry and courtly love and an anticipation of the ideal of courtesy that finds expression in the *Cortegiano* and the *Galateo*. His conception of nobility, like his conception of intelligence, reflects the humanist idea of the nobility of the intellect and the ennobling effects of culture. It also reflects the democratic and republican sympathies of the Florentine bourgeoisie (though Boccaccio rejects the bourgeois association of nobility with wealth in favour of the humanist idea of the nobility of the intellect). There are again, however, recognisable medieval elements here: the chivalrous virtues of gallantry, gentility, courtesy and magnanimity are essential ingredients of nobility. And even the fundamental idea that nobility is a matter of character, rather than of rank or wealth, has a well established medieval precedent in Guittone d'Arezzo and in the *dolce stil novo*. This is because the values of Guittone, the *stilnovisti* and Boccaccio

were all influenced by the republicanism of the medieval communes of north and central Italy, a social and political system that had its origins far back in the tenth century but which was, right from its inception, an integral part of the developing Renaissance, for it was in these medieval communes that the Italian Renaissance was born.

Boccaccio's attitude to fortune, too, belongs in different ways both to the Middle Ages and to the Renaissance. Divine providence is still envisaged as a factor in the shaping of human affairs, and Boccaccio does not yet entirely rule out the influence of the stars either: the plague, he suggests, could have been due to the disposition of the heavens, or it may have been God's visitation upon the wicked. The religious and astrological explanations advanced in the Introduction to Day I still retain a marked medieval flavour, though the astrological hypothesis does at least imply natural causes of a sort. But, broadly speaking, Boccaccio's interpretation of fortune in the *Decameron* is closer to that of later Renaissance writers than to medieval theories of predestination and free will. It is not based primarily on transcendental, providential or astrological considerations. Generally, human life is neither determined by the movements of the heavens nor governed directly by the will of God. Fortune to Boccaccio is, for the most part, the classical and Renaissance *fortuna:* fate, the product of natural causes, of the forces of man's immediate environment, the physical world around him; and as such it is essentially arbitrary and undirected. And man's defence against fortune lies principally in himself, in his own intelligence, courage and resilience. Thus Boccaccio's interpretation throws the onus of responsibility for determining one's fate on the personal initiative of the individual, and

Laurent le Premierfait's rendering of the ladies and youths of the Decameron *leaving Florence, 1414.*

on his capacity for self-reliance. Man can already be seen in the *Decameron* to be striving to shape his own destiny, as far as prevailing circumstances will permit. He cannot *ensure* that things will work out well for him, no matter how hard he tries; but it is nevertheless up to him, and to no one else, to extricate himself from such misfortunes as he encounters, using his own God-given intelligence and native wit. Boccaccio here foreshadows both Alberti and Machiavelli; but it is with Machiavelli that he has most in common, for he too gives man only a fifty-fifty chance of success in his battle against fortune, whereas Alberti expresses the belief that man can actually dominate fate and rule his own destiny if he is strong enough.

The most obvious medieval feature in Boccaccio's values is the code of chivalry, as embodied in characters like Federigo degli Alberighi. This derives ultimately from the code of conduct of the feudal knight. But in Boccaccio it is no longer chivalry as it was originally conceived by the feudal barons of the early Middle Ages (a code of martial prowess and aristocratic honour). It is imbued with the culture, civilization and refinement, the courtesy and gallantry associated with the code of courtly love, as evolved in the courts of Provence, inherited by medieval and Renaissance Italy, and interpreted in the medieval literary traditions of lyric poetry and chivalrous romance. It is the code of chivalry in the refined, idealised form in which it was to survive all the way through the Renaissance: chivalry and courtesy as envisaged later at the Renaissance court of Ferrara, where it is reflected in the works of the court poets Boiardo, Ariosto and Tasso; and as interpreted in the courtesy books of Castiglione and Della Casa.

The picture that emerges from this somewhat cursory review tends to confirm the image of Boccaccio as a transitional figure. Medieval values still play a great part in the shaping of Boccaccio's standards in the *Decameron.* But there is nevertheless already discernible the nucleus of a new kind of morality, fundamentally different from the traditional standards of the past. The conventional moral values propagated by the medieval Church, and by the society of feudalism, both in their different ways exert an important formative influence on the development of the very attitudes that outgrow them: from medieval Christianity Boccaccio inherits his compassionate and charitable instincts, and the legacy of feudalism is apparent in his admiration of chivalry and courtesy, and in his love of courtly refinement. But in the *Decameron* this medieval inheritance is absorbed, assimilated and finally transcended: the emphasis changes, the centre of attention is transferred, and the new total is somehow greater than the sum of its constituent parts. Thus it is that the *Decameron,* written in the medieval literary convention of the *novella,* has paradoxically more of the attitudes and values of the Renaissance than Boccaccio's later works of humanist scholarship.

Such values did not, however, develop in a vacuum. Boccaccio is only reflecting the attitudes prevalent in the social milieux in which he moved, for, like everyone else, he too is a product of his background. There would appear to be two decisive influences here. The first is that of the courtly society of Naples, under Robert of Anjou, where

Boccaccio spent a great deal of his youth and early manhood: the civilised, sophisticated, cultured, worldly and pleasure-loving society that bequeathed the idealised code of chivalry and courtesy to Renaissance Italy. The second is that of the educated Florentine bourgeoisie, the *popolo grasso* or rich merchant classes, into which he was born and to which he returned from Naples in 1341. From his stay in Naples Boccaccio probably retained the pleasure-loving attitudes of the young courtiers and nobles (the men and women of the *gaie brigate* that Boccaccio is supposed to have frequented, and which are remembered in the *Filocolo*—Fiammetta's garden—and in the settings of the *Ninfale d'Ameto* and the *Decameron* itself); he retains also the medieval love of chivalry as it was cultivated in Naples (the courtly and chivalrous traditions having remained stronger there than in north and central Italy, partly because of the strong feudal culture imported into Naples from northern France under Angevin rule); and his love of education and culture, his admiration of intelligence and his idea of the nobility of letters owe much to the influence of early humanist scholars, with whom Boccaccio would have come into contact in Naples, and who must have played a significant part in his own education. Finally, the prominent function assigned to story-telling and discussion in the educative process suggested by the cultural activities of the narrators in the *cornice* of the *Decameron* is almost certainly due initially to the author's direct participation in such activities at the Neapolitan court, from which experience the germ of the *Decameron* probably emerged.

From the society of the educated Florentine middle classes, on the other hand, Boccaccio doubtless inherits much of his liberal, enlightened and tolerant attitude, and his secular and world outlook (in particular his sound common sense, which recalls the practical spirit and hardheaded commercial realism of the merchant). In addition, the qualities of decency (*onestà*) and moderation (*misura*) contained in his conception of virtue are recognisable bourgeois virtues that became increasingly valued as the Middle Ages developed into the Renaissance, and the rich merchant classes increased their dominance of civic society. This background also helps to explain his emphasis on individual intelligence and personal initiative, especially in dealing with fortune. The medieval merchants were among the first to develop, in response to the challenges and hazards of commerce, the spirit of enterprise and self-reliance, the self-confidence and faith in one's own judgement and ability, that are conventionally associated with Renaissance society as a whole. The Boccaccian protagonist pitting his wits against fate is strongly reminiscent of the medieval trader, risking goods and capital to sell his wares and make his profit, confronted by a formidable array of obstacles (the elements, pirates, brigands, taxes and levies, fluctuations in the market, bankruptcies and so forth), and with nothing but his own judgement and determination to see him through. Notice how many of the stories of fortune and intelligence concern merchants, and how many involve travel and adventure, often abroad and overseas, with all the hazards this entails. Similarly one may cite Boccaccio's conception of nobility and his republican sympathies as further attitudes inherited from his middle-class Florentine background; even the love of medieval chivalry and courtesy instilled in Naples seems likely to have been reinforced by the cultural enthusiasm of the educated and aspiring bourgeoisie for the old chivalrous ideal. Lastly, we should remember that his idea of the educative value of story-telling and discussion probably received a similar reinforcement from the popularity of such pursuits among the more leisured and cultivated members of the Florentine middle classes.

This consideration of the Florentine bourgeois origins of Boccaccio's values reveals one thing above all others: that the progressive outlook of the author of the **Decameron** is not that of a visionary or prophet, of a man born ahead of his time. Boccaccio remains very much a man of the fourteenth century, a typical product of his age, for even his most radical ideas are ultimately nothing more than the natural reflection of attitudes prevalent among the more advanced, enterprising and forward-looking sections of the late medieval Italian society to which he himself belonged. If Boccaccio appears to us in the **Decameron** as a transitional figure it is because he lived in a transitional age.

In the final analysis, however, it is not the discussion of the medieval or Renaissance nature of Boccaccio's views, or the question of their social provenance, that most commands our attention. It is simply the message of the author himself to his readers: the declaration that to be at ease with life and with oneself, to find fulfilment in the responsible exercise of one's natural functions, is the means to achieve the happy and virtuous life to which all men are entitled. It is an eminently sound and sensible conclusion, a supremely normal, wholesome and realistic attitude, a message that is infinitely refreshing, reassuring, sane and wise. And the **Decameron** reflects it at every turn. It is bursting with gaiety and mirth, vitality and vigour, gusto and enthusiasm. It radiates *joie de vivre,* cheerful, good-humoured optimism, exuberant high spirits, a rollicking, rumbustious sense of fun, a great appetite for experience and flair for living, and an immense capacity for enjoying life and all that it has to offer. There is in the **Decameron** a joyous acceptance of life in all its manifestations, but also, underlying it, a dignity and maturity of outlook born of a profound understanding of human nature and a proper appreciation of human needs.

Vittore Branca   (essay date 1976)

SOURCE: *Boccaccio: The Man and His Works,* edited by Dennis J. McAuliffe, translated by Richard Monges, New York University Press, 1976, 341 p.

[*A noted Italian literary critic, Branca has written numerous studies on Francesco Petrarch, Alessandro Manzoni, and Boccaccio. In the following excerpt, Branca discusses Boccaccio's literary career from 1334 to 1341—the Neapolitan period—highlighting his experimentation with genres like the prose romance, the narrative, the epic poem, and others.*]

In the decade between 1330 and 1340, Boccaccio progressed toward literary maturity. The childish and indiscriminate enthusiasm of the student at the Mazzuoli school was transformed by the stern experiences of life and

---

Willard Farnham on the English translation of the *Decameron:*

[The] *Decameron* made a more difficult entry into England than into any other country with literary pretensions. While France had its complete translation in 1414, England waited until 1566 and then got an incomplete group of the tales. It waited over fifty more years for an unmutilated book, first done into English in 1620. Along with this conclusion goes a strong feeling that the *Decameron* was hard to know because hard to possess. When we find literary men in England up to a hundred years after the death of Chaucer exhibiting unmistakeable ignorance that there was such a book, we cannot express pained surprise that he did not use it or carefully acknowledge a debt to it. There are good reasons why he should not have known it. He went to Italy and discovered books there, it is true, but so did literary men from other countries, who seem to have had the same fortune in missing that particular book until well into the fifteenth century. Just how much Boccaccio's sense of sin and his reformed literary philosophy had to do with holding back his most regretted book we should like to know. We can guess that these things had some effect.

Certainly a careful look at what England did with Boccaccio in the fifteenth century ought to keep editors from making so large a gesture as [Edward Hutton's, in his introduction to the *Decameron,* 1909]: "From the day the *Decameron* was finished its influence both in Italy and abroad was very great."

Willard Farnham, in his "England's Discovery of the Decameron," *PMLA (March 1924).*

---

the varied yet powerful cultural experiences in Naples, the crossroads of the oriental and occidental cultures. Already apparent is the characteristic bilingualism of the author who, throughout his long career, would constantly interweave Latin and the vernacular in his literary works. The enrichment and strengthening of this mixture grows from the **Elegia di Costanza** and the **Caccia** to the learned works, the **Esposizioni** and the final version of the **Decameron.** Even in this decade two equally important influences dominate his work: culture and imagination. Boccaccio had developed an impassioned and growing enthusiasm for erudition, for "summae," and for every shred of information. This enthusiasm pervaded, in different ways, the **Filocolo** and the **Genealogia**—works separated by a lapse of forty years. The second influence is characterized by a strength of imagination and narrative power that evolved from the **Filostrato** and **Filocolo** to the **Decameron** and the **Esposizioni.** This narrative power could combine elements from the most diverse sources with an utter disregard for repetitions, tracings, or plagiarisms. It had the strength to fuse the most disparate elements into the strictest unity, yet to make everything distinct through its expressive rhythm and its extraordinary representative vitality.

[Imagination] and culture characterize Boccaccio's writings of the Neapolitan period, which are difficult to date with precision, probably because of many successive editions. They have the flavor of early and laborious scholastic exercises based on texts proposed as models by the teachers of the time. Boccaccio himself, with smiling *pietas* for his apprenticeship, wanted to preserve two of the exercises in the *Zibaldone Laurenziano* (cc. 60-62). One was an example in poetry entitled the **Elegia di Costanza,** a paraphrase of the famous epitaph of Homonoeia, truly done "cum nondum novisset quibus seu quot pedibus carmen incederet" (**Gen.,** XV, 10) and the other in prose—the so-called **Allegoria mitologica,** in part an adroit cento drawn from the first two books of the *Metamorphoses* in a confused mingling of mythical allegory and history, of paganism and Christianism. Already, however, a surer style and a certain felicity in narration are visible in the two short narrative poems, **Caccia di Diana** (1334?) and **Filostrato** (1335?), which are considered early works of the Neapolitan period because the myth of Fiammetta and her *senhal* [sign, mark], which were to embellish all his other writings down to the **Fiammetta,** are not mentioned in these two.

The **Caccia di Diana,** a narrative poem in eighteen short cantos in tercets (terza rima), tells of a fantastic "hunt," where Diana herself leads the most noted Parthenopean beauties (almost always identified by name and surname), who on the initiative of the "fair lady whose name remains unspoken" rebel against the rule of Diana and turn instead to that of Venus. Actually, what little action there is serves as a pretext for rendering a gallant and courtly homage to the most famous beauties of the time, elegantly depicted against the enamelled and storied background of the Neapolitan landscape.

Probably written immediately afterwards (1335?), the **Filostrato**—in young Boccaccio's approximate Greek it means "the one overcome by Love"—is dedicated by its author to his beloved Filomena to make her feel his sufferings as a far-away lover. In its nine parts, in fluent octaves he narrates the loves of Troilus, son of Priam, and of Griselda (Cressida: Chryseis), Calcante's daughter (returned to her father, a fugitive among the Greeks besieging Troy), and later of Griselda's unfaithfulness with Diomed and the impassioned laments and utter despair of Troilus, who is finally slain by Achilles while searching vainly for Diomed in order to avenge his betrayal. The principal plot was used previously as a secondary episode in the medieval romances based on Trojan material, and in particular in the *Roman de Troie* of Benoît de Sainte-Maure and in the *Historia Troiana* of Guido delle Colonne.

[These] works reflect Boccaccio's use of a new poetical style, that of Dante and the "sweet new style." But the change in style and rhythms reveals the influence of other and more humble poetical traditions: that of the "sirventesi," which introduced coveys of ladies, and especially that of the "cantari," which in the first decades of the fourteenth century was gaining in strength and popularity. Thus from Venetia and Tuscany the "fabulationes suas . . . in sonorum cantum productas" were introduced in Naples to gladden even Giovanna and Luigi of Taranto thanks to the famous Giovanni de Firenze. Indeed, in re-

newing the Dantean "epistola in the form of a sirventese," in which were collected "the names of sixty of the most beautiful ladies of the city" (*Vita Nuova,* VI), the tradition of the "sirventesi" must have been strengthened and amplified, as is attested in those years by the "caudato semplice" *Deo alto pare* (1309) and the "gay sermintese full of love" composed by Antonio Pucci (1335). And in these very same decades the "cantari" (popular poems in octaves or ottava rima) won their most typical public, the landed and mercantile middle class with its yearnings for the days of chivalry and its new cultural aspirations.

With his awakened awareness of middle class taste and with his cultural ambitions, Boccaccio resolutely and decisively engaged in writing his narratives in octaves. He not only broadened the melodic turn of the strophe and made it more variously adequate for its material, but brought into the narration his own sorrowing and direct experience of love and that full and very human sentimental and psychological life which the popular singers, the canterini, who favored the adventurous and the fabulous, had rejected even when it was available to them, natural and abundant, in the French sources. Despite the ingenuous feudal and communal deformation of Trojan society, despite the various technical and syntactic uncertainties, and despite the considerable dallying and imbalance of narration and presentation—obvious weaknesses of a novice in writing—in the **Filostrato** Boccaccio succeeds in finding a voice and a style peculiarly his own, particularly evocative in its oblivious song of the joys of love and in its despairing laments and regrets. And with Griselda he succeeds in sketching the first of those penetrating feminine portraits, all womenly nobility and impassioned coquetry, which characteristically punctuate his later writings down to the vivid and unforgettable examples of the **Decameron.**

In these early works, Boccaccio seems to consecrate and renew those traditions of literature which were still current, but undergoing change. With a firm grasp of tradition, he ventured into the difficult field of the Italian prose romance (as in the **Filocolo**), and participated in the development of the Italian narrative. In the **Teseida,** he experimented with the octaves of the "cantari," and with the romance of chivalry; in the **Comedia delle Ninfe,** he worked with pastoral fables for the first time; in the **Elegia di Madonna Fiammetta,** he championed the purely psychological novel; and in the **Ninfale Fiesolano,** he attempted the pre-Renaissance transfiguration of etiological narration into a dreamy rustic fantasy. From the time of his very first works, Boccaccio intended to be a frank and courageous mediator between the most acclaimed literary traditions and the newer requirements of communication with a public by then very different from that of the feudal age. Thus, in the **Caccia,** mythological fantasy and moralistic "contrasto" [medieval poetic dialogue] are bent into a new meaning, that is, into the portrayal and the glorification of a refined society which arose between the court and the bourgeoisie, with a form of joyous and elegant living, visualized with the taste of a miniaturist of the late Middle Ages.

The random and weighty cultural baggage Boccaccio accumulated in the years following 1331, which also were the most romantic in the youthful experience of Boccaccio, is displayed in all its magnificence in the *Filocolo,* the work first born and fully developed under [the sign of] the myth of Fiammetta (she appears in the Introduction and asks her lover to write the beautiful story, removing it from the "legendary talk of ignorant people"). It is she whom Florio encounters in the "court of love" in the garden at Mergellina. It is she who in one shape or another recurs in the love stories of Galeone, of Fileno, and of Idalogo. The *Filocolo* (1336-1338?), which in the approximative Greek of Boccaccio is intended to mean something like "weariness of love," is a long romance divided into five books, which for the first time in Italian prose relates the adventures of Florio, son of the king of Marmorina, and Biancifiore, a poor girl received into that court without anyone knowing of her princely Roman origin. It tells of their love from childhood, their cruel separation, the romantic quest of Florio to find his beloved, their splendid joyful wedding, their conversion to Christianity in Rome, and their victorious and joyous return home. But the telling of the famous legend of Byzantine origin (reworked in French as early as the thirteenth century and later in an Italian "cantare") is continually ornamented by Boccaccio with learned digressions, with autobiographical allusions, more or less exact, and with narrative, indicative of the *Decameron* to come. In fact Florio, during his wandering search for Biancifiore, in a beautiful Neapolitan garden, takes part in the refined conversations of an aristocratic group of young men and girls who, in their elegant discussions of "questions of love," illustrate them with examples which are actually novellas (Book IV). Two of these were to be repeated in the *Decameron* (X, 4 and 5). Boccaccio's choice of a great love story is already indicative of a definite taste and poetics, of an art which attempts an escape from daily routine yet still concerns human beings, an art enwrapped in mythical sentiments and heroic adventures (Quaglio) and exalted by culture. The enthusiasm for erudition of the self-taught young man is first manifested in continual digressions, historical and mythological, geographical and geological, scientific and archeological, as well as literary. A cultural X-ray examination of the *Filocolo* reveals zones of direct and unbridled derivation from Paolino Veneto, Andalò del Negro, Paolo da Perugia, and Dionigi da Borgo San Sepolcro. Naturally it also reveals the influence of Valerius Maximus (in all probability still read in a vernacular version), as well as that . . . of the classical writers to whose works the student had most assiduously devoted himself: Virgil, Ovid, Statius, Lucan, and in whose company Dante was reverently placed.

In this first great original romance of Italian literature, set in the sixth century (following the chronology of Paolo and Paolino), the most striking feature is the thematics already so congenial to Boccaccio's imagination. He displays a prodigious narrative diversity in all aspects of his work: the epical and the courtly episodes, the adventures on land and sea, combats and love, the ever so varied human situation and other situations extraordinary to the point of the miraculous, the gallant conversations and solemn and even theological or hieratic discourses, the depiction of famous cities of west and east (Verona, Naples, Rome, Alexandria, Cairo) and of lonely stretches of country and seashores, and the delineation of human characters and backgrounds of the most varied kinds, from agricultural Tuscan society to harems, from the Papal court to that singular Neapolitan court of love in which the lyrical schema of Boccaccio's fancy just appears, and which he would repeat in the so-called "cornici" (frames) of the *Comedia* and the *Decameron.* In the romance, also, the amorous material is presented with a most original and felicitous expression, albeit stressing the writer's personal experiences too warmly and too directly. The material is overwhelming: from the sprouting of passion in Florio and Biancifiore as children and later in their ecstatic abandon and agitations, in their suspicions and anguish, in their anxious search for one another and in their ultimate joy; and in the outline of other loves, in which the sentimental experiences of young Boccaccio are involved. However, the quest of Florio is only the guiding thread of an extremely confusing narrative plot, and for this reason the *Filocolo* is not to be read like a modern novel nor with one eye fixed on the *Decameron.* As Quaglio says, "it [*Filocolo*] was born and remained a cento, a medley of a medieval type, of which the framework recalls either the structure of the thirteenth and fourteenth century epics of European extraction or the encyclopedias and anthologies of scholastic culture in which anecdotes, legends and proverbs of the Middle Ages are closely packed with classical sources."

Boccaccio first displays his erudition in this early work, in a great variety of styles and with a superabundance of sentiment, which work together to achieve a superior yet sometimes inharmonious general effect. Thus the style of Boccaccio and his particular doctrinal technique both appear at almost the same time. He experiments with adapting models taken from the Latin writers of the decadence (from Apuleius and Servius to Martianus Capella and Boethius), and he creates the first romance art prose by adapting Latin techniques of the *artes dictandi* to the requirements of the new language. They are daring experiments, resulting in aristocratic rigidities in the *cursus* and Alexandrine preciosities and complacent stylistic haughtiness in the rhymed prose. Above all else, Boccaccio pursues a militant culture prompted by the lofty examples of Dante and the poets of the *stil nuovo,* and by the laborious efforts of the *dictatores* of the new language: the popularizers, the narrators composing octaves.

This early experimental work and this diligence, both venturesome, are sustained by Boccaccio's overwhelming ambition to master rhetoric, an ambition which causes him to force rhetorical figures on a difficult milieu. It is precisely the ambition which inspires the rhetorical-literary debauches of the first four epistles (1339), preserved by Boccaccio together with the *Elegia* and the *Allegoria,* and written, perhaps, while he was still bound to his juridical studies. . . . Addressed paradigmatically, the first two epistles follow Dantean models: one to a great nobleman, another to an important author (perhaps Petrarch), still another to an unfaithful friend, and the last to a praiseworthy and consoling one. Recently revealed as obligatory exercises in style, these epistles are often "strangely glossomatic and enigmatic" (Parodi) in their Latin, and in their lofty themes based on models imitative of Ovid and Apuleius. They are very remote from that autobiographical confidence and abandon which until twenty years ago critics—first romantic, then positivist and finally impressionist—wanted to read into them. Even the historical notes and the precise references to some person are examples of Boccaccio's rhetorical art, rather than of his autobiographical interests. Boccaccio always tried to anchor his freest stylistic exercises to a hallucinative exactness and solidity. This is evident in the *Filocolo,* the *Comedia,* the *Decameron,* and in the famous letter written in the Neapolitan dialect and addressed to Franceschino dei Bardi (although in my opinion this letter is of doubtful authenticity). The very attestations on the letter, such as "sub monte Falerno," "apud busta Maronis Vergili," are, however, influenced by passion, as were many incidents in the *Filocolo.* Even his description of himself is "a development of formulary teaching." He describes himself as first humble and completely possessed by his devotion to his high correspondents, and finally as afflicted by poverty and misfortunes (IV), a condition typical of the "querule clausule" used to close a letter. As an appendix to the collections of *ars dictaminis* there constantly appeared one or more formulas with which the student, in prose or verse, bewailed his *questua* of money and aid. At the end of this epistle to Franceschino dei Bardi, the request for a commentary to the *Thebaïd* of Statius seems, therefore, to correspond to a typical theme for closing, that is, to the *petitio,* canonical precisely between the *narratio* and the *conclusio* in every *epistola fucata* and *phalerata* (ornate letter in fine language).

The very interesting and precious rhetorical precepts in the letters of this period, heretofore regarded as conventionally romantic, contradict the assumption that Boccaccio's request for a commentary on the *Thebaïd* of Statius supports the assertion that he wrote the *Teseida* at this time. Although the *Teseida* is written in the style of the school of Statius, it corresponds, in a way, to the prolepses of that high rhetoric which must have occupied Boccaccio at the end of his Neapolitan sojourn. This concern was previously expressed in the *De Vulgari Eloquentia* and reiterated in the conclusion of the *Teseida* ("arma vero nullo latium adhuc invenio poetasse," II, ii, 10, and "but thou, O book, the first to sing to them [the Muses] of Mars dost sustain the anguish, in vulgar Latin nevermore seen" XII, 84).

The dedicatory letter to Fiammetta, analogous in tone to that of the *Filostrato* and to the Introduction of the *Filocolo* but drafted in calm and nostalgic abandon, is clearly related to the Neapolitan period by its evident character of *dictamen* (precept). But the more extensive presence of the "canterina" tradition and especially some references to Florence in the glosses Boccaccio himself carefully appended to the poem make it probable that the completion of the *Teseida* and a good part of the commentary must be assigned a date following his return to Florence (where his poem appears to have been known prior to 1348; it was mentioned by Matteo Frescobaldi, who died in that year).

The *Teseida* (1339-1341?) is a poem in octaves divided into 12 cantos, the classical number for epic poetry (in fact, 9896 verses as in the *Aeneid*). Starting from the narra-

tion of Theseus' victorious wars against the Amazons and afterwards against Thebes, Boccaccio sings of the love of Arcita and Palemones—two faithful friends of Thebes held prisoner in Athens—for Emilia, the very young sister of Hippolita, queen of the Amazons and wife of Theseus. After various adventures, Theseus decides that the two rivals will establish by combat who will have Emilia: and in a grandiose tourney in which Greece's greatest heroes participate, Arcita is victorious. But, having been seriously wounded, he dies shortly thereafter: and Palemones obtains from Theseus the hand of Emilia. . . .

The *Teseida,* much more than the *Filostrato,* reveals a significant weight of culture and ambition, corroborated and developed in the glosses rich in an erudition, mythological and genealogical, literary and archeological, of a typically Angevin stamp. Indeed, Boccaccio, like Statius and perhaps the author of the *Roman de Thèbes,* probably took the *Teseida* from a Byzantine source, to which the author himself seems to allude when he states that the "ancient story" "has not been translated from the Greek into Latin" (1, 2 and glos.: Is it Digenes Akritas?). There is also a Hellenizing influence in evidence, which certainly favored the translation and success which the poem enjoyed in fourteenth-century Greece.

At the time he wrote the *Teseida,* Boccaccio, by then experienced in rhetoric and stylistic exercises and in the secrets of vernacular poetry, made a choice that would be decisive for Italian literature. In the *Caccia,* he turns the octave from the prevailingly lyrical trend of the *Filocolo* to one firmly narrative and epical. Notwithstanding the long digressions, he lays out the general design of the action with a sureness of development still unknown to the author of the *Filocolo.* The visualizations of the *Caccia* and certain of the poems seem to have initiated those very elegant descriptions of the Amazons and of Hippolitus and in particular the portrayal of the youthful little figure and the Pisanello-like profile of Emilia (very much a foreshadowing of Poliziano's Simonetta, in the opinion of some critics); the mournful lamentations Boccaccio conveyed through Troilus and some of the sonnets are renewed by Arcita in a more subdued register. In juxtaposing weapons, adventures and loves, characteristic of the *Filocolo,* Boccaccio is in the *Caccia* on his way to achieving a harmonious fusion. For the first time the turbulent, sentimental use of autobiography is bound up and restrained by art: by a literary, cultural, technical and rhetorical preparation and diligence which sometimes makes the expression of ideas heavy and arid, but which represents clear mastery on the part of the writer.

The many verses also bespeak Boccaccio's mastery of the *rime,* which presumably he wrote during his Neapolitan years (with the exception of some sonnets written between 1373 and 1375, no lyric can be dated with certainty). They are sonnets, felicitous and evocative, especially the nostalgic pictures of Neapolitan shores and countryside, the lively and mordant portraits of feminine coquetry and passion, the cries of a soul prostrated or uplifted by love. The influence of Dante—especially the Dante of the *Vita Nuova* or the poems to a certain Pietra—and of Guido and Cino, is always present and compelling in this lyrical exercise, whereas the new Petrarchan experience is barely touched. Perhaps in the revelation of those very refined utterances Boccaccio experienced one of his impulsive and excessive discouragements, one which led him to burn "vulgaria et profecto juvenilia nimis poemata," which thirty years later he would recall in a very ardent exchange of letters with Petrarch and would repeat later to Pietro Piccolo. . . .

With these cultural and literary achievements, at a date difficult to determine with any exactness, Boccaccio's critical, decisive Neapolitan experience came to an end. It would be pleasant to believe as some scholars still do that he was among the swarm of scholars of the University and the cultured men of the Court present at the public examination of Petrarch before King Robert in March and April 1341, prior to the latter's crowning with laurel on the Capitoline Hill and his weaving the praises of poetry and of poets. Dionigi, Barbato, Giovanni Barrili (later the king's representative at the Roman ceremony) were certainly present with the "proceres in facultatibus variis"; Boccaccio himself seems to recall the solemn "conventus," stressing the emotion and literary conversion of King Robert:

> Qui clarus olim phylosophus et medicine preceptor egregius, atque inter ceteros eius temporis insignis theologus, cum in sexagesimum sextum usque etatis sue annum parvi pendisset Virgilium . . . quam cito Franciscum Petrarcam arcanos poematum referentem sensus audivit, obstupefactum se ipsum redarguit, et, ut ego, eo dicente, meis auribus audivi, asseruit, se numquam ante arbitratum adeo egregios atque sublimes sensus sub tam ridiculo cortice, uti poetarum sunt fictiones, latere potuisse.

(Gen., XIV, 22)

Because no other meetings of Petrarch and King Robert are known to have occurred and because Boccaccio did not return to Naples before the king's death in January 1343, it has been thought that this testimony could refer only to that memorable occasion. To the contrary, however, an expert like Hauvette, a Latinist like Hecker, a Petrarchist like Wilkins—followed by a variety of other scholars—noted that the parenthetic *eo dicente* does not seem attributable to Robert (the *eo* would be redundant); more probably it refers to Petrarch, who might have recounted the episode to Boccaccio in one of their various meetings after 1350 (and, besides, he did mention it in the *Posteritati* and reported it in the *Rer. mem.,* I, 37). It may be added that, following a custom very common among the chroniclers and hagiographers of the time, Boccaccio frequently claims to have seen and heard, directly, persons and events of which he had sure and certain information but of which he had learned only indirectly (for example in the *De Casibus,* IX, 21 and 26 and in the ep. IV). We may also add that on none of the occasions on which Boccaccio spoke of his meetings with Petrarch or the Neapolitan examination or the coronation, nor even in the hagiographic biography, did he ever mention, as he was wont to do under similar circumstances, his own presence at the crowning, or his direct acquaintance with Petrarch during the month of the latter's sojourn in Naples close to a mutual friend like Dionigi. On the contrary, in 1350 Boccac-

cio went to greet Petrarch on the latter's arrival in Florence, "miro nondum visi hominis desiderio" (*Fam.,* XXI, xv), as Petrarch wrote later; surely Boccaccio, then, when he received Petrarch in his own house, would not have failed to mention having met or, at least, seen him in Naples. If not by the stately "conventus," certainly Boccaccio's Neapolitan sojourn and his enthusiastic devotion to Petrarch were crowned by the happy news that, for the awarding of the crown, the "magister et preceptor" had preferred Naples and Rome to Paris (*Fam.,* IV, iv and v, of September 1 and 10, 1340). Boccaccio's stay in Naples, instead, was darkened by the absence of the dearest friend of his worldy and courtly youth. Niccolò Acciaiuoli had departed in October 1338 on the mission to Morea from which would grow his power and greatness as a politician and statesman; but at that time the enterprise appeared to be beginning under difficult and worrisome circumstances. This was reflected in the anxieties and sadness Boccaccio expressed at the time ("Niccola, if any trust is due to the wretched, I swear to you on my suffering soul that your departure weighs on me no less heavily than did that of Trojan Aeneas on Carthaginian Dido": ep V; see p. 56).

The departure of Boccaccio from Naples, some time late in 1340 or early 1341, may be partly explained by the fact that, in the years immediately preceding his leaving Naples, the relations between Florence and Naples had been modified, which changed the situation of his father and his family. The political and economic ties which had bound the bankers and the government of Florence closely to the Angevins had slackened almost to the point of rupture. With his finances all in order, Robert was no longer as indulgent as in the past with the "companies." Furthermore, the companies were weakened by a lack of confidence which was creeping through Naples (and which led to the failure of the Bonaccorsi and other lesser companies). The break between Florence and Naples may have been due to the disappointments the Florentines encountered from their urgent requests to Naples for help in the long wars over Lucca. Filled with resentment and hoping for a change in the situation, the Florentines were not averse to overturning their traditional alliances. In these difficult circumstances, in this movement backwards following the period of the expansion of the "companies," Boccaccino appears no longer to have been connected with the Bardi after October 1338.

Since at least August 1333 Boccaccino had been domiciled in S. Felicita, the quarter most frequented by people from Valdelsa, and in which in that same year he had purchased a house for his son Francesco; then between 1336 and 1337 he had been bailor in important dealings and had traded in properties of considerable value, in the name and by the agency of his wife and son (with Biagio Pizzini of Certaldo as guarantor, one of those "merry fellows" portrayed in connection with Frate Cipolla!). But on November 5, 1339 he had to sell a house in S. Felicita (perhaps a part of his own dwelling?) in satisfaction of a debt of three hundred florins which he would have been unable to pay otherwise. In that same period he was obliged to borrow sizeable sums from his sister-in-law (who died prior to June 1340). Perhaps Boccaccino's difficulties had arisen from the general business situation and from his separation from the Bardi company (which, incidentally, passed through a series of difficulties between 1339 and 1340, carrying it to the crisis of 1345). Or they may have ensued on the death of his wife, Margherita, in 1338 or 1339, for she had belonged to a rich and powerful family. In this period, at least after January 1337, Boccaccino had taken a five-year lease "pro se ipso et suo nomine et vice et nomine Johannis ipsius Bocchaccii filii" on property belonging to the church of San Lorenzo a Croce in Capua, with the contracts executed in Florence. Customarily payment was due on the lease in November; however, Boccaccino delayed that of 1340, amounting to 23 florins, evidently because of financial difficulties, until January 1341. It is probable that Boccaccino, having returned to Florence, entrusted the responsibility of obtaining those Capuan leases to his son, still residing in Naples, if, contrary to other deals in which he acted alone or with other men, in this one he wanted him to be associated officially. (This would be another contradiction of the legend of the profound disagreement between father and son, and of that other legend about a Giovanni in a state of extreme indigence in those years and absolutely abhorrent of any business or administrative activity.) In the contract of January 11, 1341, repeating the formula quoted above, the notary added to the name "Johannis Bocchaccii filii," "dicti populi," that is to say, of the people of S. Felicita. This new detail has too easily given rise to the supposition that by that date Boccaccio had already returned to Florence and taken up real domicile in the paternal house, whereas the phrase alludes simply to the legal domicile. In any case it is certain that he was not in Florence during the terrible pestilence of 1340 (G. Villani, XI, 114), as he himself declares (*Esposizioni*, VI, i, 65: "because at that time I was not there, I hear that in this city [Florence] . . ."). However, he had already left Naples by the spring of 1341 because he was not present at the petrarchan "conventus" or at the triumphal return of Acciaiuoli to the Angevin capital in mid-June.

Even ignoring an account of the winter memories of a similar journey accomplished by Panfilo, who is probably a figuration of the writer himself to (*Fiammetta*), it seems in conclusion quite probable that Boccaccio returned from Naples to Florence in the winter of 1340-1341.

Robert Hollander   (essay date 1977)

SOURCE: *Boccaccio's Two Venuses*, Columbia University Press, 1977, 246 p.

[*An American poet and educator, Hollander is widely praised for his scholarly commentary on Dante and Boccaccio. In the excerpt below, he compares Boccaccio's first and last fictional narratives—the* Caccia di Diana *and the* Corbaccio—*observing that, although the works were composed twenty years apart, they manifest similarities in tone, theme, and structure.*]

If it can be demonstrated, or at least argued, that all of Boccaccio's vernacular fictions conform to the same matrix of meaning, we would do well to study two of his works that have generally been taken to have very different significances. The one vernacular fiction often seen as

incongruent with Boccaccio's usual fictional concerns is the last, the *Corbaccio.* Further, because it was written after the *Decameron* and because most treatments of the *opere minori* are pleased to move from good, to better, to best (or from mediocre, to surprisingly good, to best), and thus to neglect the work which follows the "best," or the *Decameron,* it is rarely given more than scant attention. In brief, the *fortuna Corbacci* has been a stunted one for these two major reasons: It fails to support the usual view most critics have of Boccaccio's status as *scriba Amoris,* and it has the misfortune to be the only vernacular fiction to follow the great *Decameron.* At the other end of Boccaccio's productive life in fiction lies, if not absolutely certainly, the *Caccia di Diana.* Here too we have a work which has received scant attention, first, because until recently it was not generally considered to be among Boccaccio's genuine works; second, because it seems to most of its readers (even to its rescuer and perhaps best reader, Vittore Branca) to be inferior stuff. This [essay] will offer analyses of what are at least likely to have been the first and the last of Boccaccio's vernacular fictions and will try to suggest that the gulf of time (roughly a quarter century) that separates them does not result in their being—at least insofar as it is their significance that interests us—as different from each other as has generally been supposed.

It is only recently that the *Caccia di Diana* has been widely accepted as Boccaccio's own work. It is, as is so often the case, Vittore Branca who must be given the credit for a major contribution to Boccaccio studies. In 1938, in a study which is in need of only slight *aggiornamenti* ["Profilo biografico," in *Tutte le opere di Giovanni Boccaccio,* Vol. 1, 1967], Branca demonstrated, against the majority of "authoritative" opinion, that the *opuscolo* is surely Boccaccio's. Once we are as sure as Branca has allowed us to be that the *Caccia* is by Boccaccio, we realize that the little work, which continues to receive the slightest of notice, whether we consider it particularly good, or even particularly good Boccaccio, at least ought to be studied seriously in order to see in what ways it does or does not conform to its better known and more highly regarded sisters. Probably written, as Branca has argued, around 1334, and thus by a would-be poet of barely more than twenty years of age, the *Caccia* is comparable to the lesser works of many an acclaimed author. Its technical insufficiencies seem shameful only to those who expect Shakespeare to have composed *King Lear* in his apprenticeship rather than *Venus and Adonis* or *The Rape of Lucrece* and help explain why those who denied authenticity felt moved to do so. Yet what we have to deal with here is more than likely Boccaccio's first work in the vernacular, a literary object, in other words, of more than passing interest.

In eighteen *canti* of *terza rima,* all but one of nineteen *terzine* and thus fifty-eight lines, Boccaccio describes a hunt led by Diana, and its happy (or perhaps, as I shall suggest, disastrous) conclusion in the disappearance of Diana and the triumphant advent of Venus. Let us begin at the beginning. As is always the case in Boccaccio's vernacular fiction, the first presence we confront is that of the narrator. In the fresh fields of spring we see a sad and solitary figure seeking relief from the pains of love. This is our "frame," and it is one familiar to Boccaccio's readers, who are probably accustomed to finding in that first framing element a sad lover who will shortly tell the tale of love that is Boccaccio's customary subject. The narrator is not here, nor is he elsewhere, with the single exception of the **Amorosa Visione,** named in the text. All that we can surely say of him is that he is in love, that he has written (at least that may be Boccaccio's and our own mutual pretense) the poetic narrative which follows. He is a poet of love for the simple reason that he is in love.

The action of the **Caccia di Diana** begins quickly—much more quickly than is usually the case in Boccaccio's fictions—with the verbal formula one usually associates with medieval dream visions: "when I *seemed to hear* [we usually find a visual rather than an auditory verb following the copulative] a gentle spirit come calling loudly in its flight." This spirit convokes by name those ladies of the court of Naples who have been chosen as consorts by none other than the lofty goddess Diana. Her name should probably strike us as something of a surprise, for the vernal setting, the love-struck narrator, the list of ladies—all of these would make Venus a more likely goddess to convoke this gathering. In her time, she will do so. For now she is totally absent from the scene and from the poem (she will not even be mentioned until she is summoned by our narrator's beloved in the seventeenth canto). Diana's *nuncio* calls to assembly thirty-three Neapolitan ladies, the first thirty-two of whom are named, and were actual presences in the Angevin court of Boccaccio's time. The thirty-third lady is not named. But for the narrator she is clearly the most important of them all, since she is his own, that is, the one in whose thrall he suffers the pain of love. She is not named here or later.

Line six of the first canto has given us the cause of the narrator's *duolo amaro: amor.* Line 46 introduces us to his lady, the last one summoned by *il messo di Diana.* The six lines which describe her quality would seem to be conventional enough: Amore honors her more than any other because of her *somma virtute* that has such a powerful effect upon the other ladies; for their *salute* (Boccaccio seems to be playing with Dante's high sense of the word, which includes "well-being" and "salvation" in its range of meanings, in the *Vita Nuova*) she acts as their leader and guardian. And the conventional anonymity of the beloved is maintained by the combined forces of Diana's messenger and the narrator: "and he did not call her by name, because higher praise would befit her name than I am here able to recount." The lady is thus associated with the Lord of Love, son of Venus. We may well wonder why she has been summoned by Diana, traditional rival of Venus, to be one of her consorts. The first canto of the **Caccia** has established the precondition for a struggle between the forces of chastity, marshalled in the hunt, and those of Venery, devoted to another kind of hunting, one that ends in the toils of carnal affection. The struggle is so long delayed in coming to a head (the rebellion of the ladies against Diana occupies the concluding lines of the sixteenth canto, and the triumphant advent of Venus will occur halfway through the penultimate canto) that readers tend to neglect its presence altogether, or, if they do perceive it, to underestimate its importance. Before examining the conclusion, we should look briefly at the intervening matter.

The second canto moves us from the fields of spring to a lovely valley, enclosed by four mountains (one for each major point on the compass), in which the requisite greenery and floral decoration is of course present. Nor do we do without an abundantly flowing fountain. The surrounding mountainsides are so thickly treed (and the trees are so thickly leafed) that the sun's rays can barely penetrate this pleasant place. Here birds sing their carols, breezes gently blow, and every kind of animal is to be found. The surrounding is, one might argue, morally charged but morally neutral; what you choose to do here will tell us what you are. It is here that Diana, "che 'l tiepido foco/ne' casti petti tien" (II. 22-23), receives her thirty-three recruits. She is the keeper of less than ardent flames. And while a Romantic reader may see fit to despise flames in ladies' breasts which burn less than hot, it is at least likely that Boccaccio expects us to admire the moderation that Diana urges in her followers. She commands the ladies to bathe in the waters of the fountain, to cleanse themselves with "freschi liquori." They do so, then put on purple vestments and garlands of olives and flowers. At this point the goddess divides the group into four platoons. The first, led by the "bella donna," the narrator's lady, is sent to climb the mountain to the south, the second, under Isabella degli Scrignar, is directed to the western peak; the third, led by Fior Curial, is sent north; Diana's own party moves to the smallest of the four mountains, the one lying to the east.

In the action that follows (III-VIII) we observe the four hunting parties at their effortful play, first Diana's, then that of the "bella donna," that of Isabella Scrignara, and finally Fior Curial's. In the ninth canto we return to the narrator, hidden among the green fronds of the base camp, who sees another group approach. He is at first afraid that it may be composed of evil folk, but is reassured to discover that it too is made up of pretty ladies. Their names occupy two cantos, and one must agree, following Vittore Branca, that Boccaccio, if not attempting to storm Olympus, is making an assault of some kind upon the Neapolitan court in his painstaking salute to fifty-eight of its ladies. The following cantos (XI-XV) recount the adventures in the hunt of this new group. It is with a certain relief that we find the sixteenth canto bringing us to noon, when, because of the increasing heat of the sun, Diana calls for a rest from their sport. She sends one of her party to call in all the others. Once they have all descended, Zizzola d'Anna, who alone had gone to hunt that day without being called by Diana's messenger, also joins the group, bringing her own numerous prey. As the fifty-nine ladies, returned to their starting point, sit around their mountain of prey ("un gran monte"—XVI. 32), Diana rises, her face joyful, to address them. It is the first and last time in the poem that she will say anything of moment. She makes appeal to the "donne gentili e donzelle" (in XVI. 12, the ladies, called back from the hunt, are referred to as "le donne e le pulcelle"), reminding us that the huntresses are either married ladies or virgins of the court: "It is my desire that you make sacrifice of your prey to Jove, king of the high kingdom, and to honor me, who should be worshipped by you in a fitting manner. This I beg of you, this I seek as earnestly as I am able; make haste so that you may assume your seats in my choir." This modest proposal causes the turning point in the work. For in response the narrator's lady, identified only as "la donna piacente," rises in her place, her face troubled, to say: "Nothing like this shall come to pass! Until this moment, as you have commanded, so have we, gathered here, in fact done. Now we have no further desire to follow your deity, since our breasts and souls are inflamed by a different fire." At this Diana, *turbata* in her turn (she and the "bella donna" share the same adjective at lines 47 and 57, thus underlining their roles as the primary antagonists of the first sixteen cantos), concludes the canto by leaving the *brigata* and returning to the heaven whence she had come.

Had the poem ended even here we would have beheld enough in the way of action (as fanciful as it may have been) to see at least a possible moral point to it all. Under the auspices of Diana, of the chaste life, the ladies of the court have spent a successful morning killing every kind of animal. The moral sense of such endeavor is, at least in one branch of medieval convention, evident: their ordered hunting of the beasts of nature corresponds to their ordering of their own carnal lives. They should all seek, in short, to be governed by Diana, "che 'l tiepido foco/ne' casti petti tien" (II. 22-23), whether they be *donne,* and thus chastely contented with their husbands, or *donzelle,* and thus virgins until they be wed. The dead bodies of their prey, in one sense approximate to the bodies of the men at court whom their beauties "kill," are to be sacrificed for the sake of chastity, not enjoyed. This solution is patently unwelcome to the "bella donna." She has been hunting, we can only surmise, for the pleasure of the prey. Her abrupt, even colloquial response ("E' non sarà così niente!") reveals that she is no friend of Diana or chastity. Rather than Diana's proposed sacrificial fire, she seeks the flames of lust. Against such opposition, Diana's sudden withdrawal should probably be seen not as the defeat of the goddess, but as her scornful response to the disloyal ladies. She deserts them, for they are not worthy. Their behavior, as Branca's note makes evident, is similar to that of the ashamed Dante in the Earthly Paradise. The action of Canto XVII continues with the urgings of "la donna gentile" (is the verbal formulation dependent on "la gentile donna" of the *Vita Nuova,* Dante's "wrong" lady?). She advises the assemblage to seek the aid of "Venus santa Dea, madre d'Amore" (XVII. 8) by sacrificing the prey in *her* honor. This direct contravention of Diana's wish— that the prey be sacrificed to Jove, or God, and for the sake of chastity—is surely not casually put. The new plan, nonetheless, pleases all the ladies. They set fire to their catch, and pray to Venus: "O holy Goddess, heeding the worth of our sacrifice, do not disdain our words, which express our desires; compassionate in your joyful office, receive us, in your beneficence, by merit of our humble prayers. Drive low thoughts out of our breasts and by your power make our minds sublime and our hearts liberal and gentle. Oh, allow us to feel the pleasure of your effects, and make our minds content in loving."

That is quite enough for Venus. She shortly descends, standing nude on a little cloud, and, suspended just above

them, speaks: "I am she of whom each of you seeks grace in her prayers; and I promise you, by the high gods, that each who is worthy of following me shall be granted what she seeks." Venus turns to the fire, says things which the narrator either cannot hear or cannot understand ("non so che disse"—XVII. 38), thus pointing to her skill and power in the casting of spells, and, presto, the burning beasts turn into handsome young men who run about upon the grasses and flowers. *They* now bathe in the *fiumicello* in which the ladies had bathed while they were under Diana's tutelage. But instead of a *purpurea veste* (II. 29) each of these now puts on a *vermiglio drappo* (XVII. 44-45). And then Venus addresses them: "Be subjects of these ladies, love them until you merit victory and pity by your effort." Venus has put them under the rule of the familiar "religion of love." Having delivered herself of this code of behavior, she too goes back to her heaven. Her visit, so different in purpose from that of Diana, has a strikingly dissimilar result. For where Diana disappeared without leaving any sign of her ministry in the hearts and minds of the fifty-nine ladies, Venus withdraws "lascinado a' petti/di tutti segno d'etterna memoria." In the ***Caccia di Diana*** it is Venus who triumphs, despite the title of the work, at least in the minds of the ladies.

The last canto begins by revealing the effect of her victory on the narrator. Summarizing the actions which he has observed since he last spoke to us (in Canto IX), he culminates his brief description of the events of the last eight cantos with "il sovrano/miracol. . . . maraviglioso ad intelletto umano" (XVIII. 4-6) that Venus's metamorphosis of the dead animals into living men represents to him. He wonders to find himself in the same *mantel* as that worn by the other men (see XVII. 44-45: "d'un vermiglio/e nobil drappo si facean mantello"). He sees himself offered to the "bella donna," and, most surprisingly, "di cervio mutato in creatura/umana e razional esser per certo" (XVIII. 11-12), changed from a stag into a human and rational being. Boccaccio would certainly seem to be playing with his Ovid here, for what we have is a reversal of the myth of Actaeon (*Metamorphoses* III, 138f.), the hunter who saw Diana plain and was turned into a stag for the pleasure and subsequently torn to death by his own dogs. The business is accomplished in so sophisticated a manner that the fairly obvious parallels have apparently hitherto gone unnoticed. If Diana turned a man into a stag, Venus turns this hiding stag into a man. The effect, comparable to that achieved by running a film backwards, is rather stunning—especially since it preserves the Diana/Venus antithesis so neatly. At this moment the reader, whether he is aware of the Ovidian parallel or not, should feel at least mildly uncomfortable: up to this point his narrator has been, he must reflect, a stag. If it does nothing else, this bizarre revelation forces the reader to attempt to penetrate Boccaccio's intention in the ***Caccia.*** And one of the first facts he can now grasp more clearly is that the animals who populate this allegorical vision from the first to the penultimate canto are what we have previously intuited. They are representations of men. And our forest glade is, *in senso allegorico,* no such place at all, but the court of Naples. The masque-like events we have witnessed recede in this perspective and make the triumph of Venus all the more important (and, some might conclude, dangerous), for she rules not merely in the fictive glade but in the very center of civilization, where men are governed, in one of the most compelling tropes of the middle ages, by their bestial, not by their rational, natures.

The narrator's response to his new human condition, that of hopeful lover, may or may not represent the thoughts and feelings of his creator, Giovanni Boccaccio. The rest of the final canto is devoted to what is a conventional (and certainly Boccaccian) check list of a *laus dominae: angelica bellezza. . . . discreta e saggia nel suo ragionare e signorevol donna nello aspetto, lieta e baldanzosa nello andare* (XVIII. 16-21). Even God (*l'etterno Signor*), the narrator believes, takes particular joy in having made her (XVIII. 26-27). Four of the seven capital sins (*superbia, accidia, avarizia, ira*—1.34) are banished from the narrator's mind when he sees her. (Does that leave *gola, invidia,* and, more importantly, *lussuria* still at work in him?) The praise, while unstinting, may not be above reproach. The narrator appeals to those of us who are, like him, lovers. His words are worth attending:

> For these reasons I devoutly pray that everyone who is, as am I, a subject of that lord who makes every ignoble mind gentle will pray on my behalf that I long remain in her affection, and that I be capable of honoring her. For I shall always make this same prayer for him who possesses his beloved in joy, or who desires to possess her, and also for those who are rebels to their ladies: that they have peace, with anguish no longer their scourge.

Does Boccaccio consent in these sentiments? Their ironic possibilities are several. Replacing "l'etterno Signor" (Himself more like a gallant than the Creator in his joy in the "bella donna") we find the lord of Love. Replacing prayers of penitence we have prayers for lovers. And perhaps in the last group of these, those who would escape the toils of love, we have another clue. Diana, who was rebelled against by the ladies, would certainly side with these. For the love of which the narrator speaks is the mere gross fulfillment of the carnal, dressed up in the finery of fraud. The last lines of Canto XVII show us the beasts-turned-into-men, "some taking various delights in the fields, some sighing and picking little flowers, all awaiting the promised gifts" (XVII. 55-58). Now we all know what these are: the sexual favors promised by Venus. (Since she has already promised the same to the ladies, we know that none or few will have too long to wait.) And our narrator, who congratulates himself on having turned from beast to man ("uom ritornai/di brutta belva"—XVIII. 23-24), is he really such a rational creature? In a nice touch, the tenses of the verbs in the last canto have turned from past to present, lending the entire process of lofty praise and carnal hope a sense of urgency. The poem concludes with the narrator gazing on the *pietate* he sees enacted on the green fields (are the others already receiving their "promised gifts"?), while he hopes for his own *salute* from the "bella donna," a *salute* that has little or nothing to do with anything but sexual gratification.

Whatever we make of the *Caccia di Diana* (and few have made very much of it at all), we ought to think either that it means something or that it means nothing. While the second hypothesis is of course logically possible, all that we know of literary efforts—at least until our own time, which may have produced some intentionally meaningless works—tends to make us doubt its validity. If we can agree that the *Caccia* means something we have only two likely possibilities. One is that the work is an ironic presentation of the lustful enthusiasm of those who are devoted to Amore, the other is that it is a positive celebration of the triumph of natural human urges. (Our views of Venus and Diana are essential in making a judgment between the two interpretations.) The reader need hardly be reminded that this second view is the most widely accepted view of *all* Boccaccio's vernacular fiction, with the exception of the *Corbaccio.* Without at this point developing a framework which might attempt to justify the choice of the other alternative, may I simply suggest that there might be some merit in the interpretive position that is sketched out in the foregoing presentation of the *Caccia?*

What is put forth here may not seem to constitute the rudiments of a convincing reading. It may at least seem a possible reading. Let us turn from what is likely the first to what is almost certainly the last of Boccaccio's vernacular fictions, one that has long been understood as revealing a frame of mind that has little good to say about carnal love. Although minor uncertainties concerning the *Corbaccio* continue to exist, the work is clearly, at least within the interpretive context of the present study, the vernacular work of Boccaccio that presents fewest problems. There are no or few ambiguities in the meaning of the piece, from the narrator's opening remarks to the long misogynist harangue that occupies roughly one-half of the text. We begin, as we always do in Boccaccio's fictions, with a "narrator's frame." Once again the narrator is not named. He begins obliquely, with a general proposition: The man who fails to acknowledge openly benefits he has received, unless he has some appropriate reason for not doing so, shows himself to be an ingrate. Therefore, so that he will not be accused of that failing, he will describe, in the following *trattato,* the special grace conceded him by the Virgin, who had interceded on his behalf with God. This narrator acknowledges openly the favor of Heaven. By telling of it, he continues, he will not only repay part of his debt, but will doubtless be of help to many readers. So that this may in fact be the result, he seeks, in devout prayer, divine aid in writing the work, solely that it may bring honor and glory to His most holy name, utility and consolation to the souls of those who may read it.

This paraphrase of the first paragraph of the *Corbaccio* shows, both in tone and expressed intent, antithetic desires to those we usually find in the statements of purpose made by Boccaccio's narrators. To suggest that the difference is polar in nature would not be to exaggerate. And if that is the correct characterization, it in turn suggests a reason for the difference: Boccaccio's earlier narrators were guilty of inverting the order of values which Boccaccio himself holds to in his works. . . . [There is an] enormous difference between what we have encountered here and what we find in the opening six lines of the *Caccia,* since we have just come from that work. Where the narrator of the *Caccia* is in love, the narrator of the *Corbaccio* has been favored by an intervention of the Virgin, the result of which is that (as we are shortly to be told) he has been freed from the chains of carnal love—the *duolo amaro* of *amor* no longer pains him. To be brief, we can say that the attitudes of the two narrators (if not of their single author) are utterly opposed, the first being "pro Amore," the second "contra Amorem." Whether we choose to believe that the latter narrator expresses Boccaccio's sentiments or not, he, even more clearly than the narrator of the *Decameron*, expresses overt and clear Christian purpose. If I have argued for an ironic reading of the narrator's view of the events of the *Caccia*, . . . I must certainly agree that such a reading is possible here also. That is, it is conceivable that in the *Corbaccio* Boccaccio is making fun of those who attack Love (since he is one of the praisers of Venus). Such a hypothesis does not seem immediately reasonable. And almost all of the limited number of critical responses to the work do in fact take the narrator's view as being the antivenereal product of Boccaccio's old age.

Let us examine the second framing element of the dream vision that constitutes the major element of the *Corbaccio*, the "situational frame," as it were. Turning from his purpose in writing the *trattato*, the narrator briefly describes the crisis in his personal life which led him to his "conversion." Alone in his room, weeping, sighing, regretful, he directs his thoughts to the "accidenti del carnale amore." A widow who has brutishly turned aside his epistolary protestations of love (the hilarious business will be recounted at length during the dream sequence) is the cause of his affliction. His own *bestialità* and her *crudeltà*, considered in pain, lead him to the conclusion that death must be preferable to a life such as his own has become. Having chosen a method of doing away with himself, he fears he may thereby go from bad to worse ("di malvagia vita a peggiore"). The choice he must make, between a life cursed by love and death in damnation, leave him in a "battaglia" of conflicting thoughts which only begins to be resolved when "uno pensiero" adds a striking new element to the internal drama.

"Deh, stolto," it begins, in a delightful parodistic joining

of the language of address of love poems to the jarring saltiness of *stolto*. The "thought," which delivers itself of sane advice for two pages, is described in the following glowing terms by the comforted narrator: "A wondrous thing in the minds of mortals is divine consolation: this thought, sent forth, in my opinion, by the most merciful Father of light, having lifted from my mind's eyes almost all darkness, made my sight sharp and clear. . . ." (47). The phrase *divina consolazione* and the function of the "thought" point clearly in the direction of Boethius. And a Boethian bourgeois, the sixty-year-old "guide" whom we shall shortly meet in the ensuing dream action, will continue the motif (he and the "thought" speak with similar unembellished, bone-crunching simplicity). This second frame is thus Boethian in character as well as message. The internalized "thought" presents a clear analysis of the narrator's present condition, making it plain that his unhappiness is not the lady's fault but his own, that his death would only give her pleasure, and that he should consequently give over "questo tuo folle appetito" (43)— his lust for the *donna*—and these thoughts of suicide. It is in these directions that his own best selfish interests are seen to lie.

The narrator, strengthened, leaves his lonely room, his face as serene as it can be after so much pain, and seeks the company of his fellows. One can almost smell the sweet air of Florence and sense the pleasant feeling of escape, of unilateral movement toward the pleasant and the good. He and his friends, like those tale-tellers in the *Decameron*, move away from the place of pain and death to gather in "dilettevole parte." There, also like those other speakers, they speak with order and discretion. The subjects which they discuss take the following arrangement: the changefulness of *fortuna* (one of the persistent topics of the *Decameron*, and certainly one that continues the Boethian strain initiated by the "thought"), the foolishness of those who embrace her eagerly and rest their hopes in her. From moral philosophy they move to natural philosophy, discussing the "perpetue cose della natura" (50), and thence to theology ("da queste passammo alle divine"—50), the outermost reaches of which are simply too

Pesellino's illustration depicting the story of Griselda.

exalted for human comprehension by less than the most sublime intelligences. Like the ravaged Boethius, the narrator turns from the world's deceits to the steadfastness of philosophy. Only the advent of evening brings their discussion to a halt; the narrator describes his condition: "as though I had fed on divine food, all my former unhappiness fled, now almost forgotten, I returned to my customary lodging, consoled" (52). The participle *consolato* reminds the reader once more of the role of a Boethian conception of philosophy in the entire "situational frame."

What follows is one of Boccaccio's triumphs. Those who love Dante will rarely or never observe their *poeta* being "sent up" in better or more loving ways. Boccaccio has inherited the dream vision from a long tradition in medieval literature, and he has inherited—it is by far his most precious inheritance from the recent past—Dante's *Commedia.* As various tales in the **Decameron** show his uneasiness with the otherworldly setting of the *Commedia,* here too Boccaccio returns to his Dante in a mildly corrective way, as though to say, "Dante, I know that you present your poem as a vision, but I also know that you made it up." In something like this frame of mind Boccaccio "redoes" the first two cantos of *Inferno.* Since it is not the purpose of this [essay] to consider Boccaccio's omnivorous use of the greater poet, I shall leave the reader to his own instruction and pleasure. The reconstructions of Dante are numerous, evident, and delightful to behold. And Boccaccio's own contribution to the craft of handling the literary dream is vastly underrated. The only present-day sensibility one thinks of easily as being competent to handle the Dantesque machinery of otherworldly procedures, the quick leaps in comprehension that reveal the gradual awakening of the dreaming character to his horrible situation, the completely Boccaccian awareness of the humor of that situation, based in a sure grasp of the relation of dream to life, is Fellini's. Let a moment suffice. The narrator is certain that he knows his "Virgilio" from somewhere. And then, with a blinding shock of recognition, he realizes that he "knew" him indeed—he is the shade of a dead Florentine acquaintance. He wants to run but, "siccome sovente avviene a chi sogna, che gli pare ne' maggiori bisogni per niuna condizione del mondo potersi muovere," he cannot move a muscle (84). It is difficult to think of a more "modern" dream vision in all of medieval literature, or of a funnier one.

The narrator's dream leads him along a lovely path into a *locus amoenus* which quickly turns into an infernal landscape. The place is densely Dantesque ("una solitudine diserta, aspra e fiera, piena di salvatiche piante, di pruni e di bronchi, senza sentiere o via alcuna, e intorniata di montagne asprissime"—61). Horrid sounds assault his ears ("mi pareva . . . sentire mugghi, urli e strida di diversi e ferocissimi animali"—63). He is terror-stricken, and must be content either with grieving at his own condition or calling on God's aid. At this moment a man who looks sixty or more, wearing a vermilion garment that seems even brighter than garments painted by "i nostri maestri," appears to him (67). Calling the narrator by name, he speaks: "What evil fortune or destiny has brought you to this desert? Where has your good sense flown?. . . . Can't you understand that here one finds physical death, that

here one loses one's soul, which is much worse?" (74). The narrator, weeping and shamefaced, replies that he has been brought to this low estate by "il falso piacere delle caduche cose." It is an admission worthy of the errant narrator of the **Amorosa Visione,** but he is much too happy with the corruptible things of this world to make such an admission or (it is probably the better word) confession. Where we are is becoming clear enough. We are in hell on earth. All the borrowings from the *Inferno* are underlined by a colloquial version of Virgil's "facilis descensus Averno" to make this point clear. And the particular hell in which the narrator finds himself has particular affinity with the fifth canto of the *Inferno* (for obvious reasons it seems to have been Boccaccio's favorite *locus* in Dante). Its various names, which are supplied by the guide, make that clear enough. It is known variously, he explains, as "il laberinto d'Amore" (appropriated by Boccaccio as the subtitle of the work), "il porcile di Venere," "la valle de' sospiri e della miseria." The labyrinth of Love is not a pleasant place. You cannot leave it, the guide tells him, unless a heavenly light lead you out (95). Something like this has been his own fortunate fate, it appears, since he now purges himself in Purgatory (101). The narrator begins to understand his own good fortune in being offered such a light. In a passage that helps to clarify Boccaccio's earlier uses of the language of the religion of love, he expresses his nascent gratitude to God for sending the *guida* to him to help bring about his *salute* (not the carnal gratification so often implied by the word in its uses by lovers). His words remind us of that other religion by negating it. He speaks of (109) "la benignità del mandatore" (God, not Amore), his "umiltà" (before God, not a *donna*), "l'altezza e la potenzia del mio Signore" (God, not the Lord of Love), "la mia viltà" (not a lover's hopeful protest but a believer's penitence), "Colui che . . . mi si mostrava pietoso e liberale" (not a prayer to a lady to be so, but thanksgiving to God for His grace). The words constitute not only a litany of sorts, but also a "counter-litany" to the "litany" of the religion of love. Yet the narrator is only beginning to come round. Within a page he makes a serious and indicative error when he believes that the inhabitants of the *valle* must be those who have been exiled by Amore from his court. As for the noises that he hears, he supposes them to be made by the beasts who inhabit this place. That is enough for our *guida,* who offers the foolish narrator some unvarnished home truths in what can be treated as a commentary on this hellish place, or, to speak more to the point, on the religion of love. Although its message is obvious, it is worth having in full.

> Truly I understand that the ray of the true light has not yet reached your intellect, that you, as do many fools, consider this thing, which is the worst of miseries, to be the greatest happiness. You believe that in your concupiscent and carnal love there is some good; therefore, open your ears to what I now will tell you. This miserable valley *is* the court that you call "Love's"; those beasts, which you say you have heard and still hear bellowing, *are* those miserable creatures—of whom you are one—who are ensnared by false love; their voices, insofar as they speak of such love as that, have no other sound in the ears of sane and educated men than that which they

> now have in yours. And thus a little while ago
> I called this valley "the labyrinth" because in it
> men, as they used to of yore, become trapped,
> without knowing how they may ever escape.

His meaning is clear enough: Carnal love is hell. The rest of the activities described in the *trattato* may be judged against this clear statement. Thus, when the narrator describes the awakening in himself of the flame in the heart he felt for the sexually attractive widow, he is different from Boccaccio's other love-sick protagonists only in that he is learning and will eventually have learned the way in which he should consider such emotions. All of his description of the birth of lust in himself sounds exactly as it sounds in the mouth of the narrator of the *Caccia,* of Troiolo, of Fiammetta (in the *Elegia*). There is a single and pivotal difference: His account begins with the phrase "da falsa opinione vinto" (150). And we thus have a way of disapproving, and of experiencing his own growing disapproval, of lust.

The *guida* knows full well the attractions of love. But the narrator is rebuked because at least his age (something past forty) and his studies should have been proof against "questa matta passione" (180). He is, after all, a poet, and poetry,

> no less than the other sciences, should have
> shown you the nature of love and the nature of
> women. . . . Consider ancient as well as mod-
> ern tales and behold how many evils, fires,
> deaths, undoings, ruinations, murders this dam-
> nable passion has caused. And yet crowds of you
> miserable mortals—among whom yourself—
> having thrown aside your intelligence, call him
> 'god,' and as though to the highest granter of
> aid, sacrifice your minds to him in your need and
> pray to him with utter devotion (195-96).

That poetry, both ancient and modern, should have shown the narrator the falseness of love and of the religion of love may not seem, to many, a Boccaccian sentiment. But what if it had always been Boccaccio's sentiment? Let us at least admit the possibility. The *guida* concludes this part of the *somnium* with a mocking picture of the Lord whom lovers worship. His effigy, as it was made by the ancients—if philosophy or experience had not been warning enough—should have been sufficient admonition in itself. Look at him. He is young, nude, has wings, veiled eyes, and a bow (198). He is dangerous, in short, if we put ourselves in range.

We shall not here consider the attack on women that fills, for some four dozen uninterrupted pages, or something more than half the text, the remainder of the *Corbaccio.* In his verbal assault upon his own former wife the *guida* means to warn us against all *femmine* who style themselves *donne*—of whom there are precious few. The venom of his diatribe, which takes its first image of disgust in the menstrual instruments of the fourteenth century and ends with the praise of true gentility (which is where we began and which is seen to consist in the positive use of the free will—hardly the position of the "court of love"), has long been noticed, if not universally admired. Its purpose, within the pretext of the fiction, was to turn the narrator's lust into hate. And certainly our narrator seems to have re-

quired something like this version of a sermon on Hell to amend his lustful ways. One positive image of womankind inserts itself into the tirade, as an *exemplum* of all the feminine virtues that the *guida* finds almost entirely lacking on this earth (indeed he says that virtuous women are more rare than phoenixes—268): the blessed Virgin.

The *somnium* ends with a Dantesque ascent. The *guida* moves easily to the summit of one of the surrounding mountains, drawing with him his charge (who makes the ascent only with the most painful difficulty). From Boccaccio's version of the Earthly Paradise the narrator, now in the veritable *locus amoenus,* looks down at the valley of Love and sees it for what it is—an inferno. Now his *guida* (as, in the same place, Virgilio had done for Dante) sets him free. As he wishes to throw himself down at the feet of the spirit in gratitude, his Macrobian dream concludes (551-54). We move back into the "situational frame." Having decided that his dream was a true one, he returns to the company of his friends. They expound the dream with him (clearly along the lines the guida has already laid down). In a few days the narrator is completely cured of his carnal affection for the widow and has regained the liberty he had lost by loving her. If he is given the time, he will punish her properly (a promise fulfilled in the book which we hold in our hands). The work ends with the usual *congedo* (except that in this one the amatory values which usually inform the narrator's final words are turned upside down). He hopes that the "piccola mia operetta" will be of use to the young and will bear witness to his "beneficio. . . ricevuto" of the Virgin (as Boccaccio closes his circle by returning to the first line of the work). But then he warns his book to avoid finding its way into the hands of bad women—especially the widow's—where it will be poorly received. This is a distinct reversal of the pattern of Boccaccio's usual *congedo,* in which the narrator prays that his work *will* find its way into the hands of his lady. And the work ends with the promise, repeating itself, of still harsher treatment of the widow.

If the meaning of the *Corbaccio* is clear enough to all of its readers, Boccaccio's intention in writing it is not. In attempting to confront the problem, one might reasonably conceptualize possible views of Boccaccio's career in vernacular fiction as follows: Either he was always a follower of Venus (and thus had undergone either a "conversion" of some sort before writing the *Corbaccio* or is ironizing the simple-minded Christianity of his narrator, whose dream is far from being a true one—the second possibility, though logically possible, has only recently been proposed by Cassell), or he was never a follower of Venus (and thus in the *Corbaccio* is only saying overtly what he had previously said ironically). A third possibility is that there is no consistent interest in saying anything at all to be found in Boccaccio's fiction—he was "just a writer," and thus may have played with some of the *topoi* literary critics like to deal in, but we make a mistake to take such behavior seriously. For certain readers (they are likely to be on good terms with the partisans of "Jolly Geoff Chaucer") the last formulation has its appeal. In actual fact the major view of the *Corbaccio* has been the first one. And the most enlightened views of its relationship to the earlier works stress its opposition to their values. Perhaps the most trenchant passage written in this vein was composed some thirty years ago by Giuseppe Billanovich [in his *Restauri boccacceschi,* 1945]. If he has led us to consider the *Corbaccio* in the light of the tradition of Ovid's *Remedia amoris* and its medieval sisters, his argument holds to the point of believing that Boccaccio (like Ovid and Andreas in this) is apologizing for the praise of sensuality which we find in his earlier works. While Billanovich is not ultimately clear (and thus ultimately most suggestive) on this point, a later *studioso,* Giorgio Padoan, one of Boccaccio's most schooled readers, has [in his "Mondo aristocratico e mondo comunale nell'ideologia e nell'arte di Giovanni Boccaccio," *Studi sul Boccaccio* (1964)] returned to Billanovich's interpretation and reinforced it, seeing the *Corbaccio* as the rejection of the amorous tradition of the earlier works. The "conversion theory," in whatever form it is advanced, has much to recommend it, insofar as we perceive that Boccaccio's intent, at least through the *Decameron,* is, if not lascivious, at least venereal, that is, that he holds carnal love to be a positive good—whether in relationship to higher goods or simply in itself. But it is at least possible that such an appreciation of Boccaccio's intent is itself at fault. Without doing more than repeat that suggestion, I might offer another way of seeing the difference between the *Caccia* (to which I shall limit myself for the moment) and the *Corbaccio.* Simply assume, for the purposes of experiment, that the *Caccia* is as ironically antivenereal as the *Corbaccio* is openly so. The fact remains that the early work (in this like most or all of the preceding vernacular fictions) *feels* like a very different sort of thing indeed. It seems light-hearted in tone, whatever its meaning. And certainly I could say at least as much (if not a great deal more) about the *Corbaccio*'s "neighbor," the *Decameron.* There is so much happy (along with a good deal of destructive and sad) sensuality found there. Hasn't the author of the *Corbaccio* moved away from that, if not to "a new moralizing attitude" (to use Padoan's words), then to a *more* moralizing one? And here the answer must be affirmative.

If so, what can I say, within the boundaries of my own hypothesis, to explain the change? Must I agree to the theory of a "crisis" or a "conversion"? Not necessarily. All that I must grant is a change in tone and method, brought about by the growing conviction that to treat moral matters convincingly, one must sound more like a cleric. This hypothesis, or explanation, takes its sense of the reason for the change in Boccaccio's tone from within and without the writer's own persuasions. That is to say that the tone of Boccaccio's late works—of the classicizing Latin works as well as of the *Corbaccio*—is more outwardly Christian both because the author himself felt the need to take such a position (either because he genuinely felt that need or because he felt pressed by his detractors, whose traces are already evident in the prologue to the Fourth Day and in the Conclusion of the *Decameron*—or, as is most likely to be the case, for both these reasons) and because the more sober audience which he now sought to address expected such literary behavior. To attempt to assay the varying weights of these considerations would be difficult, if not impossible. But to see them as all being present is probably just. However, to argue that the explicit Christianity of the *Corbaccio* is altogether a change from the position taken in the early works may simply be the result of our having misread these works. . . .

Thomas G. Bergin   (essay date 1981)

SOURCE: *Boccaccio,* The Viking Press, 1981, 392 p.

[*An American educator, editor, and translator, Bergin has written several scholarly studies on Dante, Petrarch, Cervantes, and Boccaccio. In the following essay, he elucidates the political and cultural history of Boccaccio's era.*]

Boccaccio's entire life span was cast in the fourteenth century. Since, like his contemporaries Dante and Petrarch, the author of the *Decameron* was not only a keen observer of events but an active participant in public matters, some acquaintance with the history of his times—political and cultural—is essential for a proper appreciation of his work.

Historians confront the fourteenth century with a certain uneasiness and, reluctant to pigeonhole it as either "medieval" or "Renaissance," commonly designate it as "a century of transition." Certainly the assurance, innocent or savage as it may seem to us, that characterized the High Middle Ages is gone. In the sphere of philosophy and faith the contrast between the thirteenth and fourteenth centuries may be illustrated by the works of the great doctors of the respective ages: the serenity—one might fairly say the optimism—of the great *Summa* of St. Thomas Aquinas was challenged by the scrutiny of Duns Scotus and William of Ockham, whose perceptions, however admirable in showing the way to a new world of intellectual emancipation, were *au fond* corrosive of traditional values.

In a humbler sector of human things too we may find not only the cause but also the justification for the troubled anxiety of fourteenth-century mankind. "Economic depression was to grip the age," [writes Charles T. Wood, in his *The Age of Chivalry,* 1970], "and the root of the difficulty lay in agriculture. Population had continued to rise since the eleventh century and by the end of the thirteenth it had clearly begun to exceed the available food supply . . . crop failures posed a constant threat and . . . from 1315 on bad harvests followed each other in rapid succession. Prices soared; disease reached epidemic proportions." Nor was economic distress in any way alleviated by political guidance; the century was devastated by the Hundred Years' War, fought between two Christian nations, unchallenged and unrestrained by the once supreme and now enfeebled world authorities of Church and Empire. Needless to say, the costs of the war added soaring inflation to the tribulations of society.

Henri Pirenne, whose chapter on this period is entitled "The European Crisis," sketches its profile [in his *A History of Europe from the Invasions to the XVI Century,* 1939]:

> Nothing more involved and bewildering and more full of contrasts can be imagined than the period extending from the beginning of the fourteenth to about the middle of the fifteenth century. The whole of European society, from the depth to the surface was as though in a state of

fermentation. . . . A spirit of restlessness was abroad; it was a restlessness that almost amounted to mental confusion. The world was suffering and struggling, but it was hardly advancing. . . . Though they were badly shaken, the old ideals still survived; one finds them everywhere, modified, no doubt, or impaired, but still unchanged in any essential. . . . What is really new about this period, what strikes one immediately upon a general survey, is its revolutionary tendencies. They were nowhere triumphant, but they were felt in every department of life. No previous epoch had ever furnished so many names of tribunes, demagogues, agitators and reformers. . . . But there was no coherence in all this unrest, and no continuity.

Petrarch, instinctively sensing the instability of his age—which matched and perhaps to some extent explained his own spiritual unease—did not hesitate to define it as the worst in all history, and if we recall that its chronicles are full of wars, endemic crime on a continental scale, to say nothing of recurrent famines and plagues, of which the Black Death is the most spectacular but not the only example, it is not hard to agree with him. Barbara Tuchman gives to her recent survey of the era the significant subtitle: "The Calamitous 14th Century" [in her *A Distant Mirror,* 1978]. There are, to be sure, colorful episodes that capture the imagination and still have about them an aura of glamor and romance: for those of the English-speaking family the battles of Crécy and Poitiers and the names of Edward and the Black Prince still glitter in memory, and the cometlike effulgence of Cola di Rienzi, "the last of the Tribunes," which fascinated Bulwer-Lytton and Wagner (whose *Rienzi* was Hitler's favorite opera) lingers on in Italy. Yet such shining names also aptly illustrate Pirenne's thesis. For in fact the Hundred Years' War had no victor; and Cola came to a sad end.

In terms of literary history, however, the contributions of the uneasy century are not to be scorned; out of its stress and turmoil emerged a number of writers without whom the realm of letters would be sadly impoverished: the great Italian trio, Dante (even though it may be argued that his formation must be credited to the thirteenth century), Petrarch, and Boccaccio; in England Chaucer and Langland; in Spain the ebullient Juan Ruiz and in Germany Meister Eckardt. For Italy especially the trecento holds an unrivaled preeminence. Not only did the *Divine Comedy,* the *Canzoniere,* and the **Decameron** bring the adolescent vernacular into assured maturity, but the perceptive industry of Petrarch and Boccaccio also brought about the reassessment of the Latin heritage and the appreciation of Greek literature, which are the components of humanism, a vital element in the Renaissance that lay ahead.

For Europe as a whole, politically and culturally, the century's instabilities derived in large part from the displacement of both of the main pillars of medieval life: the Empire and the Church. Dante, in the century's first decade, had placed all of his hopes for the renewed well-being of the Christian world on the success of the Emperor Henry VII. But Henry not only failed to bring imperial authority back to Italy, he died prematurely in 1313 (the year of Boccaccio's birth), and throughout the fourteenth century no emperor arose endowed with the personality and the competence to reassert his preeminence among the sovereigns of Europe. Ludwig of Bavaria, who dared to do battle with the Avignon papacy, was outmaneuvered, excommunicated, and eventually humiliated. When his successor Charles IV (who so graciously charmed Petrarch) went to Rome for his crowning in 1355 he took every care not to offend the pope. The old empire was dead.

The papacy to be sure lived on, but its universal pretensions were gravely flawed. It no longer spoke from Rome but from Avignon; to Italians in particular but in some degree to all good Christians, this dislocation seemed unnatural and made the authority of God's vicar suspect. The Babylonian Captivity lasted through most of the century (1309-1377); all of the popes during this period were French, the College of Cardinals (naturally enough, since its members were nominated by the pontiff) had a French majority; invariably the princes of the Church were sympathetic to the policies of the French monarchy.

It should be said, in all fairness, that the Avignon popes were not by any means the least able or the least worthy of the successors of St. Peter. Clement V (1305-1314) and John XXII (1314-1334; it was he who humbled Ludwig of Bavaria) were men of vision and political competence; Benedict XII (1334-1342) was a decent man of goodwill, famous for his charitable works and honestly eager to put an end to the Hundred Years' War; Clement VI (1342-1352) was an enlightened patron of the arts; Innocent VI (1352-1362) dealt boldly and efficiently with brigands—and his bishops; Urban V (1462-1470) was of such high character as to win subsequent beatification (he made an effort to bring the papacy back to Rome but, understandably, found the brawling anarchy of the Eternal City intolerable); Gregory XI (1370-1378), another well-intentioned pontiff, finally succeeded in bringing the Church back to its true home. (He did not long survive his translation, although only forty-five years old at the time of his death.)

But the damage had been done. No matter what might be the character of an individual pope, all of the Avignon succession was suspect; its claim to universality and impartiality was weakened. It must be said too that the court was consistently venal. The Avignon papacy scandalously commercialized religion by simony, the sale of indulgences, and similar practices. The source of the "Triple Schism" of the early fifteenth century was in the Babylonian Captivity—and the schism in its turn nurtured the seed of the Reformation. Indeed the Reformation had a kind of premature dawning in the emergence of such reformers as Wycliffe and Hus, and one aspect of Protestantism was clearly foreshadowed in the *De Monarchia* of Dante Alighieri, which would divest the pope of his temporal power, and the *Defensor pacis* of Marsilius of Padua, which would deny him his preeminence within the Church. And no follower of Luther or Calvin would ever write more scathingly on the subject of the venality and corruption of the Curia than Francis Petrarch; his sonnet (*Rhymes* 136), perhaps more forceful in the sixteenth-century English of an anonymous translator than in the original Italian, voices the scandalized indignation of honest Christians:

> Vengeaunce must fall on thee, thow filthy
>   whore
> Of Babilon, thow breaker of Christ's fold,
> That from achorns, and from the water colde,
> Art riche become with making many poore
> Thou treason's neste that in thie harte dost
>   holde
> Of cankard malice and of myschief more
> Than pen can wryte, or may with tongue be
>   tolde,
> Slave to delights that chastitie hath solde;
> For wyne and ease which settith all thie store
> Upon whoredome and none other lore,
> In thye pallais of strompetts yonge and olde
> Theare walks Plentie, and Belzebub thye
>   Lorde
> Guides thee and them, and doth thy raigne
>   upholde;
> It is but late, as wryting will recorde,
> That poore thow weart withouten lande or
>   goolde;
> Yet now hath golde and pryde, by one ac-
>   corde,
> In wichednesse so spreadde thie lyf abrode
> That it doth stincke before the face of God.

If the sonnet, as seems likely, may be dated as of about 1347 it was written only a year or less after Crécy, which brought to an end the first phase of the most memorable political phenomenon of the century, the Hundred Years' War. The struggle had begun in 1336 with Edward III's claim to the throne of France, motivated in part by characteristic medieval dynastic territorial greed and in part by the necessity to protect the English province of Aquitaine from being gradually absorbed by the dynamic French monarchy.

The great duel between the two best-armed and best-organized nations of the West fascinated and indirectly involved all of Europe. It was not to end until nearly eighty years after Boccaccio's death; it raged, with intervals of uneasy peace while the combatants paused to draw breath, throughout his mature lifetime and its repercussions were felt in Italy as indeed throughout Christendom. We may here summarize the pattern of hostilities during the fourteenth century. Topography as well as his posture as claimant obliged Edward to take the offensive. He began with a campaign in the North, making allies of Ludwig of Bavaria and the Flemish clothworkers, who were willing to accept him as the lawful king of France. This phase (1339-1340) was inconclusive, although the English won a notable naval victory at Sluys (1340). For two years the scene of combat then shifted to Brittany where each monarch supported his own candidate for the dukedom; this episode too yielded no decisive result. In 1345 Edward turned his attention to the South where his generals were successful in recovering the English possession won by the French from his father; thus encouraged he turned his attention again to the northern flank and after a brilliant campaign in Normandy soundly defeated the forces of Philip at Crécy, famed in history for the triumph of the English longbow over the armor-plated chivalry of France. This phase of the war closed a year later with the capture of Calais by the British; the onslaught of the plague cooled the belligerent ardor of both parties. Philip died in 1350; the English had won most of the battles and were comfortably lodged on the Channel but the fate of Aquitaine was still uncertain.

Taking advantage of tensions between Philip's successor John II and his cousin the king of Navarre, Edward reopened hostilities a few years later. In 1355 the Black Prince raided Languedoc and the following year pressed up to the Loire in a campaign that culminated with the battle of Maupertuis (Poitiers), a repetition of Crécy, where again English tactical skill and the efficiency of the archers completely routed the French; this time the French king was taken prisoner, leaving his country to be ravaged at will by bands of English and their auxiliaries. The peasantry, maddened by their misery and disillusioned by the ineptness of their betters as displayed at Crécy and Poitiers, rose in revolt in the first great proletarian manifestation of the Middle Ages. The "Jacquerie"— as the exasperated peasantry was called—burned and pillaged their masters' castles; they evoked the sympathy of some burghers as well, including Étienne Marcel, spokesman for the third estate and in effect ruler of Paris, but the rising was abortive and after a few short months the nobility restored order—with a savagery no less barbarous than that of the rebellious peasants.

In 1359 Edward renewed the war; this time his opponent was the canny Du Guesclin who, like Fabius of Rome, refused pitched battle but bled the English by constant harassment; at the Peace of Brétigny (1360) Edward renounced his claim to the French throne, settling for the uncontested suzerainty of Aquitaine and a substantial ransom payment for the prisoner King John. It was after this truce that the "free companies" of mercenaries reached their pestilential apogee, devastating France south of the Seine, threatening the pope at Avignon, and passing on to spread their infection into Italy. The war meanwhile, under the new French king Charles V ("the Wise"), entered into a Spanish phase; the Black Prince was drawn into an alliance with the bastard brother of Peter the Cruel of Castile and although he won his usual victories, Du Guesclin, Peter's ally, eventually triumphed. In Aquitaine the nobles, unhappy with the taxes levied under English rule, revolted; in three years the province was recovered by the French crown and the Treaty of Bruges (1375) preserved for the English only Calais and a small coastal strip of Gascony. The death of Edward two years later closed a long chapter in the interminable struggle; ahead lay many more years of strife including the epic of Agincourt and the romance of Jeanne d'Arc. But such matters take us beyond the span of Boccaccio's lifetime.

Unless he was born in Paris (which, as we shall see, seems unlikely to scholars today) Boccaccio never set foot in France and never had a chance (as Petrarch did) to observe the traces of the ravages of war. But the great duel had deep and significant repercussions in Italy. First, as we have noted, the "free companies," essentially armed and disciplined gangsters, spawned by the struggle and otherwise unemployed during its recurrent truces, crossed into Italy and, as the century wore on, became an endemic political pestilence south of the Alps, sometimes taking service under various princes, sometimes acting independently, sometimes blackmailing cities; it was not long before the natives followed the alien example; the "free companies" are in fact the forerunners of the *condottieri* who were to plague the peninsula until the early years of the sixteenth century.

Another effect of the Hundred Years' War was of a different nature but felt very keenly by Boccaccio and the Italians of his class of society. War is an expensive business, and to finance their efforts the kings of both France and England turned to Italian—usually Florentine—bankers. The interest demanded was ruinous and for some hard-pressed monarchs repudiation was inevitable. The most spectacular case was that of Edward III; after his first campaign in Flanders (where he had needed large sums to buy the assistance of his allies) Edward was obliged to renege on his debt to the Peruzzi (1339); this marked the beginning of the collapse of the Florentine banking houses; by the mid-forties they were all in trouble, with effects on the commune that we shall remark below.

Italy, politically speaking, was still what it had been since the fall of Rome and would remain until the time of Garibaldi, a geographical expression, divided into a number of separate states struggling for supremacy or in some cases for survival. The dream of a "garden of the empire" in peaceful union with the rest of Christendom under a benevolent monarch, which Dante hoped to see realized, had vanished with the death of Henry of Luxembourg following his unsuccessful siege of Florence in 1313. Yet in spite of the instability of its institutions and recurrent conflicts of its rival states, the presence of Italy loomed larger in the Europe of the fourteenth century than it does in our time. Since America was yet to be discovered and the window on the Atlantic was as yet, as it were, unopened, Italy occupied a central position on the continent. In population too it ranked much higher than it does today. Census figures for the Middle Ages are difficult to establish with precision but it has been said that in 1300 of the five cities in Europe with a population of 100,000 or more four were Italian: Milan, Florence, Genoa, and Venice. Their only rivals were Constantinople and Paris; such modern centers as Madrid and Berlin were mere villages or small towns.

The combined wealth of the peninsula's cities surpassed that of all Europe; the chivalry of the West had for some time looked to Italy for the financing of its enterprises (we have but to recall the role of Venice in the Fourth Crusade a century before Boccaccio's day) and, as the techniques of banking developed, Italians and particularly Florentines had a hand in all the major political events of Europe. The significance of their contribution was symbolized by the alliances between the wealthy families of the communes and the most ancient aristocratic houses of the continent. We do not have to wait until the Renaissance exports its Medici heiresses to France; in Boccaccio's time (1360) Galeazzo Visconti "bought" a princess of France as a bride for his son Gian Galeazzo by the payment of the ransom demanded by the English for the return of John II. (Gian Galeazzo's daughter, later in the century,

marrying the duke of Orleans, would be the mother of the graceful poet Charles d'Orléans, as much Visconti as Valois). The cultural preeminence of Italy was reinforced by the tradition of Rome, seat of Europe's only faith and rich also in its monuments and its classical memories. The splendor of the Renaissance was yet to come but the works of Giotto and Arnolfo di Cambio were its harbingers. Italian traders and merchants traveled to all corners of the world (Marco Polo even to far Cathay) and a countercurrent of pilgrims from every country in Europe flowed incessantly to the Holy City. Italy had been the mother of the oldest universities in Europe and although by the fourteenth century Paris and Oxford afforded healthy competition, Bologna, Pisa, and Padua still maintained their prestige, and Italian scholars—as well as churchmen—held prominent positions abroad.

Yet if the word "Italy" in the Middle Ages carried a connotation far richer than the purely topographical, it must be admitted that politically it was meaningless. "France" or "England" could convoke assemblies, make laws, or embark on wars but "Italy" could not speak with one voice. Since the defeat of the Lombards by Charlemagne there had been no power on the peninsula sufficiently dominant to serve as a nucleus for nationhood. The land had become the battleground for the claims of two worldwide authorities, the pope, defended by his ultimately victorious Guelphs, and the emperor, backed by his tenacious Ghibellines. Both were well entrenched and neither was able to unite the faction-ridden land under his own exclusive control—indeed for neither was the unity of Italy a primary objective. The result of the rivalry had been to exacerbate regional tensions and thwart every possibility of union. The South to be sure had been unified under the aggressive Normans who created the Kingdom of Naples and Sicily; coming into the hands of the Hohenstaufens under the able leadership of Frederick II it might have served as the Prussia or Piedmont of its time, but papal opposition frustrated Frederick's design and his successors were either ineffectual or, absorbed in problems of their own domains, not very much interested in the "garden" of their empire. Throughout Boccaccio's lifetime neither pope nor emperor was resident in Italy but the fragmented political condition of the land was a lasting legacy of the centuries of strife between the two institutions they represented.

An outline of political developments in fourteenth-century Italy must in the nature of the case require a survey of the fortunes of the more important independent states that had burgeoned, as it were, in the interstices of the papal-imperial pretensions. Although these states were all small when compared to such kingdoms as France and England, they were nevertheless centers of power and prestige, viable political units and significant in the councils of Europe. In Boccaccio's time the most powerful of these were the despotism of Milan, the republics of Venice and Florence, and the ancient feudal Kingdom of Naples (officially known as the Kingdom of Sicily). Of these the Milanese state was the richest and most aggressive.

In the early Middle Ages the Commune of Milan had earned fame and respect for its stalwart resistance to the

German emperors; it had been the moving spirit of the Lombard League and had defeated the great Barbarossa at Legnano (1176). In the course of the thirteenth century, in keeping with the pattern of all Italian communes, Milan had ceased to be a democracy and had become a signoria, under the lordship of the Della Torre family. But in the last years of the century the vigorous Archbishop Otto Visconti had displaced the older family and established a dynasty that was to dominate the city and its far-reaching domain for well over a hundred years. In 1294 the archbishop's nephew Azzo succeeded him; his loyal services to the Ghibelline cause were rewarded by Henry VII who, on coming to Italy in 1310, made him imperial vicar of Lombardy. Azzo's prowess on the field of battle was matched by his diplomatic skill; under his rule Piacenza, Pavia, Bergamo, and Cremona—among other lesser communities—were annexed by the Milanese state. Azzo was excommunicated by John XXII and abdicated in favor of his son Galeazzo I, famous for his defeat of the papal forces at the battle of Vaprio (1324).

A misunderstanding with the Emperor Ludwig of Bavaria led to Galeazzo's incarceration a few years later; he was, however, soon released and on his death his son Azzo II again secured the title of imperial vicar from the emperor. The seven-years' rule of the second Azzo was distinguished by yet further extension of the power of Milan through Lombardy and (perhaps more usefully for the security of the line) by Azzo's murder of his uncle (who had conquered Pisa and Lucca) and defeat of his cousin, thus doing away with any possibility of dynastic feuds. On Azzo's death he was succeeded by his two uncles, in turn, Lucchino and Giovanni. The former thrust the hand of the Visconti yet deeper into Italy; first making his peace with the Church he proceeded to purchase Parma from the house of Este and solidified the grasp already established on Pisa, to the disquiet of the Florentines. He died, poisoned by his wife, in 1349; his brother Giovanni, already archbishop of Milan, succeeded him.

Petrarch, who accepted the hospitality of the archbishop, professed great admiration for his host and the verdict of historians is no less favorable. Though Giovanni ruled for only five years (1349-1354), his prudent administration and considerable enlargement of his inheritance are credited with making the Milanese state a respected and enduring power in Northern Italy. Genoa was taken under his wing, Bologna was occupied, and at the time of his death most Northern Italian lands, with the exception of the smaller states of Mantua, Verona, and Ferrara, had come under the sway of the Visconti. So large had its domain become, in fact, that on the archibishop's death it was partitioned among the three sons of his brother Stefano. Such fractionalizing might have been fatal, but happily for Milan—if not her neighbors—it was not destined to be permanent. Matteo, something of a monster, was assassinated within a year by agents of his brothers, Galeazzo II and Bernabò.

Galeazzo II, who held court at Pavia, was already the typical Renaissance prince; he too extended his patronage to Petrarch, founded the University of Pavia, and was renowned for his charm and diplomatic skill. We have noted how he arranged the marriage of his son with a daughter of the House of France; later (1368) he gave his daughter's hand (with a dowry of 200,000 florins) to Lionel, duke of Clarence, the son of Edward III. The ceremony was marked by regal splendor. "Such was the profusion of the banquet," writes the chronicler Giovio [quoted in John A. Symonds's *The Renaissance in Italy,* 1881], "that the remnants taken from the table were enough and to spare for 10,000 men."

Meanwhile, for his brother, who had inherited Milan itself, things did not run so smoothly. Constant wars with both the Church and the emperor led to oppressive taxation of the citizens; nor did Bernabò have either the graces or the statesmanlike skills of his brother. He survived Galeazzo by seven years and plotted to make himself sole master of the state; but he was outmaneuvered by Galeazzo's son, the wily and somewhat enigmatic Gian Galeazzo, who had his uncle executed in 1385, thus bringing the archbishop's inheritance once more under single administration.

Gian Galeazzo was to be one of the ablest and most distinguished personages of his time; his death in 1402 was perhaps a misfortune for Italy—although a great relief to Venetians and Florentines; it is probable that he might have established a united kingdom of Northern Italy, anticipating the laborious and half-fortuitous achievement of the House of Savoy four and a half centuries later. Boccaccio did not live to see the high tide of the Visconti fortunes; it was, however, evident to him as to others that during his whole lifetime the state of Milan was on the march. It is significant that the chronicles of Milan during this period contain no such allusions to class warfare and economic contention as we find in Florence. Save for oppressive taxation and occasional wanton acts of tyranny the burghers and folk of Milan seem to have been content with their state.

West of Lombardy, already dominated by the Visconti, lay Piedmont, in the fourteenth century still feudal but well integrated and ably ruled by the House of Savoy. Destined five centuries later to play a leading role in the creation of the Italian nation, Piedmont, during the years of which we write here, could hardly be counted an Italian state; the contribution of the region to the cultural development of the Renaissance was minimal and its political intervention in peninsular matters relatively negligible. Looking eastward from the city of St. Ambrose, however, the inquisitive eyes of the aggressive Milanese could envisage potential fields for further conquests and, past the waterline, look upon the face of a rival, with whom in the quattrocento the rulers of the city would be locked in a grueling struggle. For close to the Adriatic shore lay the *Serenissima* Republic of Venice, rich, resourceful, and well disciplined.

The Republic of St. Mark, as it had come to take form in the Middle Ages, was politically and socially sui generis; indeed something of a paradox. It was a republic, yet ruled by an oligarchy; the people, regulated and regimented, had little to say about their destiny. It could be called a tyranny—but without a tyrant. Situated on a complex of tiny islands, Venice had had a unique history that set it apart from other Italian states. It had never been a monarchy, nor in fact, ever been a part of the medieval feudal order. It was thus spared the civil strife that sprang up—in the states of Romagna and Tuscany for example—between the old aristocracy and the new bourgeoisie. Venice had escaped too the contagion of the Guelph-Ghibelline rivalry and had shrewdly worked out a constitutional pattern that prevented prominent families from challenging the state. It never followed the sequence of feudal dependence to commune to signoria that characterized almost every other Northern Italian state. Almost from the beginning the affairs of the republic had been administered by an oligarchy of the wealthy trading families; the doge to be sure was the supreme magistrate but he was responsible to the grand council and his office was not hereditary. (In 1335 Marin Faliero, suspected of trying to make it such, was convicted and executed.) In effect Venice was a totalitarian state in which even the members of the patrician families were subject to the discipline they had imposed upon their fellow citizens. An island people, the Venetians were fiercely nationalistic; even the clergy of the city was required to be of Venetian blood. It would not be incorrect to call the state in some sense "communist," for the chief means of production, the great trading galleys, were state property and could be leased but not owned by the merchants who sailed them. Finally, it should be noted the Venetians were rich. From the time of the city's founding in the fifth century it had cultivated commercial relationships with the East, gradually coming to own "concessions" as we would call them in all the principal cities of the Levant; it had also profited enormously from the lucrative business of ferrying crusaders to the Holy Land.

In 1310, three years before Boccaccio's birth, two decisive events took place in the City of the Lagoons. The pages of the *Libro d'Oro* had been closed; that is to say, the number of the families eligible for membership in the grand council was fixed forever, and, as a result of a conspiracy against the state, the Council of Ten was instituted. This council, working in secret, was given absolute power in matters of state policy; originally it was set up on an ad hoc basis, but it soon became permanent. Drawn from the membership of the council and working in cooperation with the doge who was himself a member, this small and therefore effective group was to guide the republic through its triumphs in the embattled centuries that lay ahead. If it inspired terror, it also commanded respect. It need hardly be added that membership on the council was not for life nor was it hereditary. And if the decisions of the council were secret and its actions final and without appeal, it must be said that over the years its patriotism, its judgment, and its impartiality were above suspicion. "Against the decrees of the Council," J. A. Symonds writes,

> arbitrary though they might be, no one sought to rebel. The Venetian bowed in silence and obeyed, knowing that all his actions were watched, that his government had long arms in foreign lands, and that to arouse revolt in a body of burghers so thoroughly controlled by common interests, would be impossible. Further security the Venetians gained by their mild and beneficent administration of subject cities and by

the prosperity in which their population flourished. . . . At home, the inhabitants of the island city, who had never seen a hostile army at their gates, and whose taxes were light in comparison with those of the rest of Italy, regarded the nobles as the authors of their unexampled happiness. Meanwhile these nobles were merchants. Idleness was unknown in Venice. Instead of excogitating new constitutions or planned vengeance against hereditary foes the Venetian attended to his commerce on the sea, swayed distant provinces, watched the interests of the state in foreign cities, and fought the naval battles of the republic.

Thus the political history of the *Serenissima* during the fourteenth century hinges on foreign policy. The overriding objective of the Venetians during the life span of Boccaccio was the attainment of supremacy in the Mediterranean; this meant, in effect, the destruction of the sea power of Genoa, its only rival. The long struggle ended, after many vicissitudes, with the Peace of Turin some years after Boccaccio's death; the war had bled both republics dry, but while Venice soon recovered Genoa never did. A portent of the final decision could be seen in the Venetian naval victory of Alghero (1352); it was their defeat on this occasion that threw the Genoese into the arms of the Visconti; although they survived to carry on the war, their vulnerability was apparent and the Visconti had only to bide their time.

A corollary of the century-long duel was a major change in Venetian policy. Until the fourteenth century the sons of St. Mark had, generally speaking, turned their backs on mainland Italy and sought their conquests in the East. The specter of a siege by the Genoese (which in fact the *Serenissima* underwent toward the end of the struggle in the War of Chioggia) compelled them to seek some convenient granary on the mainland; the island state could not grow its own food supply. Taking advantage of its role as a partner in an alliance against the tyrant Mastino della Scala of Verona in 1339, the republic occupied Treviso. It was the first step in a *Drang nach Westen* that would, in the succeeding century, see the banner of the lion floating triumphantly over Padua and Verona. These two states, independent signorie under the lordship respectively of the Scaligeri and the Carrara, led an uneasy existence during the fourteenth century; on the death of Mastino the Signoria of Verona disintegrated and was promptly annexed by the Visconti and a similar fate overtook Padua which, in effect, lost its independence at the time of Mastino's defeat in 1339. These once powerful centers did not have the wealth or the manpower to survive, placed as they were between the two great powers of the North. Both were annexed by the *Serenissima* in the early quattrocento (1404-1405) and remained a part of the Venetian Republic until its extinction in 1797.

As the Milanese thrust to the East moved the Visconti nearer to confrontation with the *Serenissima,* so their expansion southward seemed, during the years of the fourteenth century, to endanger the liberty of yet another vigorous Italian state, the Commune of Florence. The history of the Tuscan capital during the lifetime of Boccaccio reflects, in fact, both the struggle within the walls among the various social classes for political power and a share in the new wealth growing out of the wool trade and the successful banking and commercial enterprises and, concurrently, the efforts of all classes to maintain their independence against the pressures of foreign neighbors in a permanently unstable political situation. The story of Florence, chronicled by writers of rare talent from Dante to Guicciardini, is of particular interest because of the city's unique contributions to arts and letters; considering its bountiful gifts to mankind, as well as the contentious vivacity of its citizens, Florence may fairly be compared to classical Athens.

During the period we are here surveying Florentine foreign policy (with its inevitable repercussions on events within the walls) was in the main defensive and to a great degree shaped by an underlying legal disability. In the feudal chain of command during the Middle Ages Florence had been simply a part of the patrimony of the rulers of Tuscany, in theory dependent on the emperor but, by a legacy of Matilda of Tuscany (the humbler of Henry IV at Canossa), it had been put under the protection of the pope. Hence, recurrently, the city was obliged to appeal to one "protector" or another within the traditional feudal framework. It became the charge of magistrates as the years passed and Guelph and Ghibelline battled for supremacy, to preserve the city's independence against those who sought to destroy it and simultaneously to keep a wary eye on those who, under the guise of protecting its integrity, would hope to dominate it.

In 1313, the year of Boccaccio's birth, the Black Guelphs, who for a decade had been supreme in the city, had special cause to rejoice. Henry VII, beloved of Dante, died of a fever at Buonconvento, having failed in his effort to restore imperial power on the peninsula and, incidentally, to displace the Guelphs and put his own Ghibellines (and schismatic White Guelphs of which Dante was one) back into power. In their time of danger (1310) when Henry came to Lombardy, the rulers of Florence had invited Robert of Anjou, king of the Two Sicilies (i. e., Naples) and champion of the papal cause, to be their defender for a five-year period. After the death of Henry, the aggressive campaign of Uguccione della Faggiuola, another Ghibelline leader, posed yet another threat. Following Uguccione's capture at Lucca the Florentines urged Robert to send his brother, Piero, to lead their armies; he was, however, defeated and slain at the Val di Nivole. His successor, Count Novello d'Adria, was extremely unpopular and the anti-Neapolitan faction (even in crisis the Florentines were rarely at one in their sympathies) displaced him and put in his stead Lando d'Agobbio, who immediately abused the power vested in him and made himself a tyrant; he maintained himself until 1321 when a Neapolitan intervention in its turn overthrew him. It should be stressed that the parade of dictators within the city was occasioned by the constant menace from without, first from Uguccione, later from the even more aggressive Castruccio Castracani, self-made despot of Lucca (1281-1328), who at his death held Pistoia and Pisa, too close to Florence for comfort.

It was immediately after the downfall of Lando d'Agobbio

that Castruccio made his thrust toward the city, putting nearby Prato under siege. The Florentines, now free from Neapolitan "protection," had reorganized their government and were striving to unite the factions, even promising to invite the exiles to return. A large army was sent to the relief of Prato; Castruccio withdrew and the victors fell to quarreling over the advisability of pursuing him. According to Machiavelli the people favored pursuit but the "signori" wished to retire to Florence. So not only did Castruccio escape, but he left in his train a rancorous division between the people and the magnates of Florence. The promise of reinstatement of the exiles was withdrawn and a new charter of the city was drawn up providing for a somewhat broader base of representation and longer terms in office.

The familiar pattern was repeated a few years later when Castruccio seized Pistoia and once more alarmed the Florentines. Their defeat at Altopascio obliged them once more to turn to the House of Naples for a protector; this time it was the young prince, Charles of Calabria. Happily for the freedom of the city, in 1328 both Castruccio and Charles died; so for a dozen years the commune was spared the dangers of invasion and benevolent intervention and was relatively free of factionalism as well. (These were, roughly speaking, the years of Boccaccio's residence in Naples; Machiavelli notes that during these years too Giotto's campanile was finished and the Arno overflowed its banks in a vast inundation [1333]).

Dissension between the classes arose again in 1341 when the people, enraged at the ineptitude of the administration, which had let slip a golden opportunity to occupy Lucca, called for the overthrow of the government. Manipulated by the nobles and a few of the powerful merchants, the mob proclaimed Walter of Brienne, so-called duke of Athens, in the service of Naples, ruler for life. Within a year however Walter had managed to antagonize all classes and was compelled to flee the city. Again the commune was reinstated with a new charter, this time to the advantage of the merchant class over the nobles. The latter took to arms in protest and were so completely defeated that, says Machiavelli [in his *Le istorie Fiorentine, Tutte le opere*], "never afterward did they dare to take up arms against the people." A decade of tranquility ensued, marred by the great famine of 1343 and the Black Death, which came to the city in the spring of 1348 and carried off, according to Machiavelli, some 96,000 souls—probably an exaggerated figure but indicative of its impact.

It must be remembered as we follow the affairs of the city through these years that behind the official framework of government, the council, the priors, and the various elected officers (frequently reorganized and reshuffled as the humbler elements of the citizenry, the lesser guilds, and the *popolo minuto* pressed their claims for representation) there was another body, extralegal but often the true arbiter of the commune's destinies from the time of Dante: the *Parte Guelfa*. The function of the party, something like that of the Communist party in Russia or the Fascist party under Mussolini's regime, was, in effect, to see that the commune remained loyal to its traditions; in this case opposition to the emperor and close association with the pope. To be sure, in moments of emergency political expediency might be allowed to prevail over pious devotion to principle, but the *Parte Guelfa,* whose core was the wealthy merchant class, remained inviolate. In the years following the plague—marked by an uprising of the lower classes who had suffered greatly from the hardships attendant on the calamity—the party prevailed upon the commune to institute a policy of issuing "warnings" to citizens suspected of subversive plotting with Ghibellines. These "warnings" were in effect proscriptions and a "warned" citizen was usually fined or banished, with confiscation of his property by the state. According to Machiavelli the device was invented by a few powerful families as a useful method of ruining their potential rivals, but of course the security of the state was regularly invoked. The more liberal members of the merchant class who were not in sympathy with the policy of "warnings" were of course suspect and liable to be "warned" themselves. The issuance of "warnings" was first sanctioned by the magistrates in 1357; by 1366 the system had become generally unpalatable but in the intervening years "warnings" were recurrently given out, notably in 1359-1360, when some of Boccaccio's friends, conspiring to attack the ruling faction, were banished.

To follow the events that fill the chronicles of the "great town by the Arno" year by year during Boccaccio's lifetime would be to survey what seems to be an endless succession of factional quarrels within the walls and petty wars abroad. Yet through it all the commune flourished. It recovered not only from the devastation of the plague but, perhaps more surprisingly, also from the economic disaster caused by the collapse of the great banking houses in the forties. It was diplomatically and militarily strong enough to hold off the Visconti when they occupied Bologna fifty miles north in 1350. By the sixties the tenor of life had improved and the commune had prepared its defenses by annexation or dominance over the neighboring Tuscan towns, such as Pistoia, Prato, and San Gimignano. It withstood successfully the incursion of the Great Company in 1358-1359 and the even more alarming forays of the *condottiere* Hawkwood in alliance with the Pisans (1362-1364). (In 1379, four years after Boccaccio's death, "Giovanni Acuto" would bring his White Company into the service of the Florentines; his portrait, by Paolo Uccello, adorns the inner facade of the Duomo.) One rather surprising political shift may be noted. In 1375 the pope's legate in Romagna held up the city's grain supply and encouraged further ravages on the part of the doughty Hawkwood; there is reason to believe that the legate, if not his master, was thinking of adding Florence to the patrimony of Peter. Incensed by such behavior, the commune, hitherto proud of its fidelity to the pope, turned about and declared war on the papacy. The war, administered by a special council known as "the Eight Saints," was a popular one and was vigorously waged. It ended, however, in a stalemate, with the commune paying a fine for its contumacious action.

Beyond, as the century waned, lay the proletarian rising of the Ciompi, the conservative reaction, and the political climate that would prepare the way for the Medici. But all of this was after Boccaccio's time. So too were the great artistic and cultural triumphs of the Renaissance, but for all that the cultural life of fourteenth-century Florence, still free and undisciplined, is not to be despised. Giotto's tower was finished, the first doors were put on the Baptistery, the university was founded. And if Dante died in exile and Petrarch avoided the town of his ancestors, yet the roll call of Florentine men of letters is impressive: Pucci, Sacchetti, the succession of the chroniclers Villani, and more. And Giovanni Boccaccio.

A twentieth-century political scientist, reading the story of Florence in the years of which we are writing, would find the pattern of events easy to understand and in many ways surprisingly "modern." The struggle for power—and the economic opportunity that accompanies it—is a phenomenon familiar to all of us; it continues today. We can understand the aspirations of the Florentine *popolo minuto* and the uneasiness of the magnates in the face of their demands. We can sympathize with the ideal of liberty to which all Florentines (and the majority probably quite sincerely) professed devotion. In spite of the measures sometimes employed to suppress dissidents (and it is fair to remember that out of necessity the commune was a kind of garrison state during most of the turbulent century) it is undeniable that the burghers of the City of the Lily enjoyed a greater liberty of thought, of speech, and even of action, than prevailed in any other Italian state—greater by far than anything that the Visconti would tolerate or that could hope to flourish under the watchful eye of the Venetian Council of Ten.

To move from Florence to the Kingdom of the Two Sicilies (for so it was styled, though somewhat inaccurately since Sicily had broken away from the Angevin state in 1282; the twain would not be joined again until the eighteenth century) is to move into a completely different social order. The kingdom was the largest political unit on the peninsula and Naples, its capital, was a large and busy city. But the social structure of the realm was still feudal—indeed perhaps more so than a century earlier, for Charles of Anjou, who had displaced the Swabian line, had by his legislative measures augmented the privileges already enjoyed by the nobility and the clergy.

The economy was primarily agricultural; the kingdom possessed, as it does today, few exploitable natural resources. Trade was largely in the hands of foreigners among whom Florentines were prominent; Catalans, Genoese, Venetians, and Marseillais also plied their trades of banking and merchandising. The middle class, in Florence the seedbed of social progress and the cult of liberty, was in the kingdom relatively small and impotent. Underneath it the great mass of the peasantry lived in abject misery, relieved sporadically by savage uprisings, savagely repressed. In the kingdom too as in the North the mercenary "companies" were a scourge; veterans of the recurrent wars in Sicily as well as adventurers from the North ravaged the countryside, which indeed did not lack brigands of its own spawning; brigandage in fact became a tradition of the kingdom; in such regions as Lucania and Calabria specimens are still to be found. At the top of the ladder was the nobility, a large and parasitic element, arrogant, punctilious, and inept. During the reigns of Robert and Joan, foreigners, who as noted dominated the world of commerce, also rose high in the councils of the state; the native ruling class had as little talent for politics as for finance. The most able statesman in the service of the Angevin rulers during Boccaccio's lifetime was his fellow Florentine, Niccolò Acciaiuoli. Neapolitan history therefore is not the story of class rivalry or of a striving for social progress or liberty; it is hardly the history of a community at all; it is a dynastic chronicle. The story of the monarchy is the story of the monarch.

In Boccaccio's years there were but two rulers of the kingdom: Robert, surnamed the Wise, who reigned from 1309 to 1343, and his granddaughter Joan, who succeeded him and came to a wretched end, murdered by order of her cousin and successor six years after Boccaccio's death. Under both sovereigns the principal objective of foreign policy was to recover Sicily from the Aragonese who had been firmly entrenched on the island since the "Sicilian vespers" of 1282 had driven out the Angevins. As to internal policy, there was none to speak of save, perhaps, for Joan, survival on the throne.

In the early years of his reign Robert was an important figure in the affairs of the peninsula. On the occasion of Henry VII's invasion of Italy the pope had made Robert his vicar, Florence had put herself under his protection, and he became, in effect, the leader of all Italian Guelphs. The death of Henry spared Robert a confrontation with the imperial invaders, which may have been fortunate for him; two years later, in alliance with the Florentines at Montecatini he was badly beaten by the Ghibelline chieftain Uguccione della Faggiuola. Serving also as the pope's vicar against the aggressive Visconti, for a time he had some success promoting and controlling a Guelph rising in Genoa (1318), but in the end the Visconti came out on top. Since Robert was not only king of Naples but also count of Provence (a part of the Angevin patrimony) he had a legitimate interest in the affairs of Northern Italy. But his abiding concern was the reconquest of Sicily; perhaps his seven humiliating years as hostage in the Aragonese court during his adolescence added a personal incentive to his dynastic purpose. In any case between 1314 and 1342 he made no fewer than five attempts to recover the island; all were failures and all signified the even greater impoverishment of the kingdom and resulted in even more crushing taxes for its people.

History's verdict on Robert is somewhat ambivalent. In his own day, if Dante did not think much of him, Petrarch admired him greatly, seeing in him not only the perfect ruler but also the illuminated patron of arts and letters. Robert gave cordial welcome to Laura's liege man and was instrumental in his coronation as poet laureate. The king also embellished his capital, inviting Giotto to work in the city; the Royal Library flourished under his aegis if not direction; he even wrote a book (of devotional nature) himself. His court was notable for its splendor, and the city—at least the upper classes—prospered under him. Boccaccio, who knew Naples in the last decade of Robert's reign, compares the order and elegance of urban life in the

Angevin capital very favorably with the incessant restlessness and relative bourgeois shabbiness of Florence.

And in fact Boccaccio's sojourn coincided with a prosperous period in the life of the capital; Fausto Nicolini estimates that the population grew from 40,000 to 60,000 between 1280 and 1340, and though wars were waged abroad the city thrived untroubled by the factional disputes that seemed endemic in Boccaccio's Florence. But with the death of Robert in 1343 the years of tranquillity in glamorous Naples came to an end.

Both of Robert's sons predeceased him. In order, so he thought, to avoid dynastic rivalries (he was himself a descendant of a cadet branch and his kinsman, the king of Hungary, might have pressed a claim to the throne), he had his granddaughter Joan betrothed to his elder brother, Charles Martel's grandson Andrew of Hungary; both children were seven years old when the engagement took place (1333). The marriage was solemnized in 1342; it was a brief and unhappy alliance. In 1345, in circumstances that still remain mysterious after six centuries, the young prince was murdered; many suspected that the queen, said to be in love with her cousin Louis of Taranto, had a hand in the affair. It was the end of peace in Naples. The prince's brother, Louis, king of Hungary, twice invaded the kingdom (1348 and 1350-1352); on the second occasion his armies occupied the capital but in the face of general hostility could not hold it. Meanwhile Joan had been obliged to flee to her county of Provence; there, ably guided by Acciaiuoli, she managed to get the pope's absolution and also his blessing on her marriage to Louis of Taranto (although she had to cede Provence to the papacy as a part of the bargain). The royal pair returned in triumph and were crowned in the capital in 1352. A decade of relative serenity ensued, although the king and queen were each jealous of the other's prerogative. Inevitably the reconquest of Sicily was essayed; under Acciaiuoli's leadership it promised to be successful; a six-year campaign of attrition and negotiation with the slippery baronage of Sicily ended in failure however when Louis died (1362), leaving the kingdom once more unstable. Joan's third husband, James III of Mallorca, had little interest in the affairs of the kingdom, or, for that matter, in the queen. Acciaiuoli died three years later and the last years of Joan's unhappy reign were dedicated to keeping her throne secure against the intrigues of the rival branch of the family, the clan of Durazzo, destined to succeed her in the end. At long last a treaty in 1372 put an end to the ninety-year-old effort to recapture Sicily.

The foregoing survey may suffice to indicate the principal developments in the most prosperous and politically significant states of Italy; many of these events were witnessed at first hand by the author of the *Decameron*. Another large area of the peninsula with which he had frequent contact was the patrimony of Peter: the lands of Emilia, Romagna, and the Marches, over which the Holy Father was temporal lord. In these provinces, although there was plenty of activity, much of it violent, one cannot detect any special direction, nor do the congeries of petty signorie have any collective goal. The pope was, in the fourteenth century, an absentee landlord and in his absence disorder reigned. "Tyrants like the Malatesta of Rimini, the Ordelaffi of Forlì . . . and the Manfredi of Faenza pursued their schemes in defiance of the Papacy" [*The Shorter Cambridge Medieval History,* Vol. 2, 1952] and Bologna, as we have noted, fell for a while into the hands of the Visconti. Finally, in 1353, Innocent VI sent the Spanish Cardinal Albornoz to Rome and Romagna; Albornoz was both soldier and statesman and he soon brought the contentious despots to heel; he was obliged to make a second incursion (1358-1363), however, before his master's authority was firmly reestablished.

The Eternal City itself, during the Babylonian Captivity, had fallen to low estate. Its population shrank drastically—some historians say to a mere 20,000—and it was ineffectually administered by a papal vicar and a quarrelsome senate, composed of representatives of the Roman nobility who made the city and the surrounding countryside the scene of incessant feuding and brigandage. The monuments of antiquity—the Colosseum, the Theater of Marcellus, and the like—served as fortresses for the embattled clans.

> Vulture and serpent, lion, wolf and bear,
> on a high marble column work their will,
> Yet, gnawing it, likewise themselves devour,

as Petrarch poetically puts it. This dismal chaos provided the background and the motivation for one of the most spectacular events of the century, the seizure of power by Cola di Rienzi who, though of lowly origin, managed by a coup to dislodge the nobles and make himself master of Rome, assuming the ancient title of Tribune. For a few brief months in 1347 Cola ruled the city, applauded by Petrarch and doubtless by many other men of goodwill. His own vanity and the machinations of the great families brought him down; he returned briefly with Albornoz in 1354 but once more became too arrogant for the tolerance of the people on whom he depended, and was murdered by the mob at the foot of the Capitol. But his dream of restoring the glory and dominion of Rome and its people left its mark on men's memories; like Hus and the Jacquerie he seems—looking back—a portent of things to come. As far as pacifying the city was concerned, however, Cola's labors were fruitless; when Urban V returned he found the anarchy and violence as intolerable as ever.

As in political and social matters the fourteenth century was a time of agitated stagnation wherein it is difficult for the historian to trace any clear lines of development, much less "progress," so too in matters of technology it is a relatively barren age. Pirenne, granting that during the century "bigger ships were built and they made longer voyages," yet comments wryly [in his *History of Europe*] that the chief technological advance was the discovery of a method for salting herring. Perhaps this is a little harsh; there were improvements in papermaking and in bookkeeping; spectacles (though an invention of the thirteenth century) came into wider use and must have considerably enlarged the reading public. Arabic numerals replaced the clumsier Roman symbols. And it was "towards the beginning of the fourteenth century," Marc Bloch reminds us [in his *Feudal Society,* 1961], that "counterpoise clocks brought with them at last, not only the mechanization of

the instrument, but, so to speak, time itself." Gunpowder came to Europe in Boccaccio's day, too, portending the doom both of the French knight and the sturdy English bowman—but its triumph was some time in the future.

Boccaccio's imagination was stirred by reports of the rediscovery (in 1342) of the "Fortunate Isles" (the Canaries), but the age of the great explorers was still to come, even as the splendors of the Renaissance. Yet the contributions of the fourteenth century are not contemptible. Aside from the great creative writers in the various vernaculars that we have mentioned, the century also produced in music the great champions of the *ars nova:* Philippe de Vitry and Guillaume Machaud in France and Francesco Landini in Italy. And it is the century too of Giotto, Andrea Pisano, Duccio, and Simone Martini.

A survey, even capsular, of the technology of the fourteenth century may serve to remind a twentieth-century reader of what is so often forgotten or discounted as he follows a political or aesthetic thread through the tangled skein of the past: the day-to-day texture of medieval life. Yet, as we make our way through the **Decameron** or savor the tales of Chaucer's blithe companions, it may add a dimension to our appreciation if we call to mind what kind of world it was in which their great creators lived and wrote. If we can, that is—for in fact the conditions of life in the Middle Ages were certainly much closer in existential respects to those of the Homeric or even the biblical age than to anything we have known since the industrial revolution.

The gulf between our way of life and that of medieval men is so great as to call for some imagination to bridge it. It is not merely a matter of such recent amenities as airplanes, radio, or television. Boccaccio's time not only knew nothing of trains; it was likewise ignorant even of stagecoaches. There was in fact no public transportation. A journey was an exercise in private enterprise, calling for one's own horse or mule; impedimenta were carried on the back of sumpter animals, rarely and exceptionally on wagons. The traveler was not sheltered from the elements; he was furthermore exposed to the endemic brigandage of the times and, in Italy at least, also liable to run afoul of the soldiery of the warring communes. Travel by sea was perhaps more hazardous—Petrarch, after one narrow escape, permanently foreswore ships. The sailing craft of his day were powerless against head winds, vulnerable to storms—and, like brigandage ashore, piracy at sea was a recognized, quasi-respectable career, as several tales of the **Decameron** make evident. To take an example from another field: it was not simply that the Middle Ages had no telephones or telegraph; there was not even a postal service. Letters were carried by friends—and subject to all the risks of travel mentioned above. Or, to glance at another sector, it was not simply a matter of lack of central heating; for many a well-to-do household there was only a rudimentary kind of fireplace, imperfect in draft; even the halls of the great castles smoked and were warm only in the proximity of the fire itself. The man of the Middle Ages, even of the upper classes, shivered in winter even as he sweated in an insect-infested summer.

With regard to food, although we have many records of

sumptuous banquets, often with entrées of game that has become scarce or unavailable nowadays, the day-by-day fare of the overwhelming majority was limited in range. Bread was the staple for the masses; not the white bread we know but dark and coarse, made more often of rye, barley, or maslin (a mixture of rye and wheat) than of wheat. Lack of refrigeration made meat in some months unavailable, at all times potentially hazardous. Not only were such alleviating beverages as coffee, tea, and chocolate still unknown; medieval Europe had yet to know the sustaining and, as it now seems, basic bounties of the New World: tomatoes, potatoes, corn. (It is strange to think that Boccaccio never sat down to a plate of *polenta,* the daily fare of wide regions of Italy nowadays.)

Men had not yet learned how to control—or cooperate with—the forces of nature; famines, floods, and plagues are recorded with inexorable recurrence in the chronicles of all nations and communities. Matters of medicine and sanitation scarcely bear thinking about; it is doubtful that the average man of the twentieth century could survive a week of life in a medieval town. Save for the torches of festive occasions cities were dark at night; the streets were narrow, noisy, and carpeted with dung. Florence, to be sure, had more amenities than the average town of the times; it could offer paved streets, hospitals, and schools. Indeed Villani gives an impressive account of the educational facilities available—to the better classes. Even so the vast majority of Europeans could neither read nor write. Writing was indeed a specialized skill and a good copyist was highly prized. Nor did these specialists always write with a clear hand. And what they wrote was often read by flickering candlelight. Such considerations may increase our respect for the industry as well as the talents of such geniuses as Petrarch and Boccaccio who wrote voluminously—and for their circle of readers too. Whatever amenities the fourteenth century lacked, it need not apologize for its creative minds nor the intellectual level of the class that gave them a hearing.

Judith Powers Serafini-Sauli   (essay date 1982)

SOURCE: *Giovanni Boccaccio*, Twayne Publishers, 1982, 173 p.

[*Serafini-Sauli is an American linguist who specializes in Italian language and literature. In the following excerpt, she familiarizes the reader with the Europe and Italy of Boccaccio's time.*]

We know relatively little about Giovanni Boccaccio from his contemporaries. His earliest biographer, Filippo Villani (fl. 1364-1405), describes him as ". . . large and portly; round of face with large but attractive lips, a dimple in his chin that was lovely when he laughed; merry and jocund in aspect, pleasing and human in speech, and one who took great pleasure in conversation" [Angelo Solerti, *Le vite di Dante, Petrarca e Boccaccio scritte fino al secolo decimosettimo,* 1904]. For us of the twentieth century, familiar with Boccaccio as the author of the delightful stories of the *Decameron,* this portrait meets our expectations, for it depicts a jolly storyteller. Apparently he was also humble and modest. The humanist Coluccio Salutati,

a younger contemporary of Boccaccio, remarked upon this and, indeed, found his modesty so exaggerated, that he saw fit to rewrite the epitaph Boccaccio had prepared for himself. As we can still see today on his tomb in the church of Saints Michele and Jacopo in his hometown of Certaldo, Boccaccio had written simply: "Here lie the ashes and bones of Giovanni; his mind sits before God adorned with the works of his mortal life; Boccacius was his father, Certaldo his homeland, poetry his calling." Boccaccio speaks broadly of poetry as his calling. Coluccio, in noting his modesty, takes the trouble of specifying his works, but certain ones. He mentions only the scholarly Latin works Boccaccio wrote later in life. ". . . Why do you speak of yourself so humbly, bard? You have listed mountains and rivers, fortunes of men and women and ancient gods. Famous in a thousand things, no age will not speak of you."

The portrait of a pleasant, humane storyteller hailed by his contemporaries for erudite works in Latin creates a certain confusion. Is Boccaccio to be characterized as the bemused, unbridled narrator of the *Decameron,* first author of the Renaissance, or is he really more medieval, the stern moralist of his later, and even his earlier works? The question is confounding. If we look beyond the caprices of taste from age to age—Boccaccio was hailed throughout the fifteenth century for his scholarly works, whereas subsequently the *Decameron* has generally been considered his masterpiece—we find that this confusion is hardly dispelled by Boccaccio himself. In a moment of religious crisis he threatened to break up his library which was rich in classical works (Petrarch, *Sen.* I,5,1362). A few years later he may have commissioned an altarpiece for the church of Certaldo; and in one of his last letters (*Epist.* XXI, 1373) we find him exhorting his friend Mainardo Cavalcanti not to let the ladies of his house read the *Decameron* or his "domestic trifles," as he called them. It would seem, then, that if some of his works were indeed secular and pagan, he had repented. But as we contemplate the life and works of Boccaccio, the conflict between the sacred and the profane, the didactic and the delightful, is never quite resolved, for as recent scholarship has shown, at the end of his life this supposedly repentant Christian undertook the enormous task of recopying his least sacred work, the *Decameron.*

Any scheme applied to a personality or to the entire course of a lifetime is ultimately inconclusive. Reflecting the disquiet of his times, Boccaccio's works waver between the traditional hierarchy of old orders, expressed by means of established canons for moral teaching, and the flux and innovation of new cadres revealed through narrative autonomy. His works are often Christian allegories or moral treatises whose formal message is a rejection of terrestrial pleasures and profane passion in favor of holy rewards and sacred love. But the rejection is never quite total; a certain indulgence in earthly delights frequently creeps in to compromise the erudite plan or to color the message of moral and Christian enlightenment.

The life of Boccaccio (1313-75) spans most of the fourteenth century, and his activities and interests place him so much in the mainstream of events and ideas that his

Botticelli's 1483 rendering of the Nastagio story from the Decameron.

works could serve as a prism through which to study the currents of this complex period. Conversely, an understanding of the times is essential to the appreciation of his works. The fourteenth century was a period of profound upheaval and transformation in Western Europe. Italy, especially, was a land of contrasts and confusion. It was the stage for many of the conflicts of the waning Middle Ages—the contest between the Empire and the Papacy, Church and State, feudalism and mercantilism, aristocracy and bourgeoisie. Intellectuals and men of letters sensed the change and displayed both optimism and uneasiness.

For Italians there was the most dramatic and disturbing fact of the so-called Babylonian Captivity. This abduction of the Papacy to Avignon, reducing it to a secular entity to be manipulated by kings, seemed to confirm a breakdown in the traditional universal Church and created a feeling of disquiet which was accompanied by an ardent desire to return the Papacy to its rightful place in Rome. Boccaccio himself had his small role in this issue, for he was sent as Florentine ambassador to Avignon, and like most of the major writers and intellectuals of the age, he remarks upon the devastation and chaos that had overtaken the eternal city of Rome, home of both ancient and Christian glory. Against this backdrop was the everlasting contrast between North and South. The South was subsumed under the Kingdom of Naples, an impoverished land with a small and strong aristocracy, a large and oppressed peasantry and a meager middle class. This area had remained essentially feudal and was under the dynastic rule of the French family of Anjou. The great Angevin

leader in the fourteenth century was the famous King Robert, called The Wise. He was a generous patron of the arts and the center of an illustrious court whose enlightenment, however, did not extend beyond the city of Naples. Though a Tuscan, Boccaccio lived as a youth in Naples which was an important center for Florentine merchants and bankers in that period. The rest of his life—part of his childhood and all of his adult life—was spent in Tuscany and Florence.

In contrast with Neapolitan society, Florence was a dynamic city of merchants and bankers whose wealth was based primarily on cloth trade, and was dominated by the upper middle class. It is to this class, which was essentially practical in needs and outlook, that we owe many of the great civic monuments that characterize the city of Florence; their influence on taste and artistic canons probably could not be exaggerated. Likewise, the needs of this bourgeoisie had a lasting effect on language and letters where both the use of Italian and a new kind of interest in the classics began to emerge. The need to draw up contracts and bills led to a preeminence of law, and particularly of the work of notaries. It also led to an increased use of Italian alongside Latin, and these factors in turn had literary significance. The dawn of Italian literature is closely associated with notaries, many of whom were accomplished poets in Italian. And a more participatory and broadly based literate public created a demand for works and translations in Italian. The study of law, and especially of ecclesiastic canon law, led to greater contact with the *ars dictandi,* which was influential in the formation of Italian prose style. It also led to the study of Roman law, which in its turn contributed to a generally growing interest in ancient civilization and left an imprint of classical Latin on the developing Italian language as well. At the same time, the secular thrust of this upper bourgeoisie contributed to the emergence of an increasingly nationalistic spirit. Major figures such as Dante and Petrarch contemplated Italy as a nation, and Petrarch particularly was determined that this embryonic nationalism find expression in an appreciation of Italy's ancient heritage. This, too, further helped revive the cultivation of the classical world.

The painting of the period reflects a similar secularization. Subjects are primarily religious, but the divine is humanized. Representations of traditional religious themes become less symbolic and dogmatic, and are more literal, tranquil, and realistic. Narration becomes more important than allegory, and fidelity to nature and the human dimension predominate. With the bourgeoisie's emphasis on individuality, industriousness, and civic and social activity, traditional cult figures are personalized. They are presented as mediators for mankind and as people with real stories.

The painter who most completely represents this new spirit is Giotto. We need only call to mind the scenes he chose for the fresco cycles in the Scrovegni Chapel in Padua or in the chapels in Santa Croce in Florence to understand the emphasis on the individual and his personal relationships. Boccaccio knew Giotto and his work, and in a story in the **Decameron** in which Giotto is the protagonist, he proffers not only his admiration for the great painter, but the measure of what he considered significant in his art. Giotto, he says, had

> . . . genius of such excellence that there was nothing created by nature . . . that he, with stylus, pen or brush could not paint so like it that it seemed not a likeness but the thing itself, so that many times, when seeing things made by him, the visual sense of man was deceived, taking for real that which was painted. And therefore, having brought back to light that art which for many centuries had been buried, through the error of some who had painted more to delight the eyes of the ignorant than to please the intellect of the wise, he can justly be called one of the lights of Florentine glory. (VI, 5)

Nevertheless, bourgeois mercantilism, with its industriousness, optimism, and materialism, was also accompanied by feelings of doubt and guilt, and was contested, condemned, and qualified by a rejection of wealth, best characterized and voiced by the Franciscan Fraticelli, throughout most of the early part of the century. The ascetic Franciscan *paupertas,* combined with a classical Stoic spirituality, helped to foster an attitude prevalent in the early humanists—Petrarch and Boccaccio in particular—that one must eschew earthly goods and seek poverty and seclusion. The guilt and ambivalence with regard to wealth and earthly possessions, exacerbated by the preaching of the Franciscan followers in the minds of the bourgeoisie, came to a crisis in the middle of the fourteenth century through a series of disastrous events which affected Florence and its environs. Bank failures, the death

of Florence's ally King Robert of Naples, a year under dictatorial rule, and the Black Plague were some of the disasters that created a shift from the hegemony of the upper middle class—and the more rational, secular optimism that accompanied it—to a greater emphasis on the *popolo minuto,* on the Franciscan strain of poverty, and on a more hieratic, dogmatic, and emotional art. This latter period culminated in the popular uprising of the Ciompi, who were soon after suppressed by the urban patriciate.

Boccaccio was in touch with important centers of intellectual activity and, as he himself indicated in his epitaph, was passionately interested in all forms of literature. As a youth he became familiar with the aristocratic court of Naples, the feudal society upon which it was predicated, and the courtly French culture from which it derived. But in Naples he also knew the Florentine merchant world, studied poetry in Italian, canon law and the *ars dictandi,* and began his study of the ancients. His return to Florence brought renewed contact with Tuscan allegorical literature, which was essentially Christian and didactic, but at the same time he absorbed the earthly optimism of the bourgeoisie. With the crisis at midcentury he too underwent a change, turning to more systematic studies of the ancients, erudite Latin treatises, and a Franciscan kind of penury, and emerging, together with Petrarch, as one of the fathers of humanism.

The manifestations of these experiences in literary terms are considerable. Boccaccio's works embrace medieval and classical literature, prose and poetry, epic and lyric, Latin and Italian, popular and "high" culture. He revived the pastoral romance, attempted a modern epic, established the vernacular *ottava* as the epic stanza in Italian, and then, later in life, renewed the classical epistle and eclogue in Latin, wrote biography, helped revive the study of Greek, and began formal Dante criticism. He also affirmed in a manner unmatched by anyone before or after him the validity and variety of Italian prose. Yet what predominates in all Boccaccio's very different endeavors is the force of narration. He was a consummate storyteller. He turned his efforts in biography, literary criticism, and even the sonnet into narrative episodes; and he wrote short stories in the various guises of myth, history, and Christian allegory.

Because of the preeminence of narration, the culmination of Boccaccio's literary experience is the **Decameron,** which becomes perforce the touchstone for any consideration of his works. In it he proposes narration for its own sake, and, in advocating amusement as much as improvement, his point of view becomes earthbound. The **Decameron** is Boccaccio's human comedy, "the luminous and fully human epic," that stands next to Dante's *Divine Comedy* [V. Branca, in his *Boccaccio medievale,* 1956]. Passing human affairs under a lens of practical causality and uncompromising humor, he captures the realities of terrestrial existence with candor, tenderness, intelligence, and bemused indulgence. These qualities, and a passionate devotion to literature, infuse all the works of this great man of letters for whom poetry was, in the full sense, a calling.

Hubertis M. Cummings on Boccaccio's influence on Chaucer:

In the main, Chaucer's debt to Boccaccio is that of a borrower. The English poet served no apprenticeship to the Italian. He never became a literary disciple to him. He did not weakly imitate him as a master. What of Boccaccio he drew upon he drew as from a storehouse; and, like the materials he drew from numerous other literary storehouses, he fitted it deftly into the great mosaic of his own work. The two Italian poems [*Il Filostrato* and the *Teseida*] only furnished a few more strands of fiction and truth, of reality and phantasy, of comedy and tragedy for him to weave into the great pictorial tapestry of mediaeval life which Chaucer's complete works will ever represent.

The English poet's indebtedness to Boccaccio, not wholly an unacknowledged one and not wholly a conscious one, is yet a very great one. The fairest of the gardens and the temples in his tapestry, the most beautiful of his ladies, the most chivalrous of his knights, the most pathetic of his youthful characters, and the most human of his middle-aged ones, come many of them from Boccaccio. And from Boccaccio they bring the breath of old romance. But Boccaccio owes a great debt also to Chaucer. It was Chaucer who made him in *Troilus and Criseyde* and in the *Knight's Tale* part and parcel of English Literature. And admission to a share in such a realm, and through such a hand, is no slight privilege.

Hubertis M. Cummings, in his The Indebtedness of Chaucer's Works to the Italian Works of Boccaccio: A Review and Summary, *1916. Reprint. Haskell House, 1965.*

David Wallace (essay date 1985)

SOURCE: *Chaucer and the Early Writings of Boccaccio,* D. S. Brewer, 1985, 209 p.

[*An English-born American educator, Wallace has written extensively on Medieval British and Italian literature. Here, he briefly summarizes the relationship between the works of Boccaccio and those of Geoffrey Chaucer.*]

When visiting Florence in the spring of 1373, Chaucer may have heard Boccaccio referred to as the distinguished elder statesman of Tuscan culture who was to deliver a series of lectures on Dante's *Commedia* at the church of Santo Stefano di Badia. He may have associated Boccaccio with the performances of *cantari* which took place regularly at the Piazza San Martino. He may have associated him with both church and piazza and have formed a mental image of Boccaccio as a writer who gains inspiration from (and lends inspiration to) both illustrious and popular traditions of vernacular narrative. But even if Chaucer had never heard Boccaccio mentioned by name—which seems most unlikely—he was nevertheless capable of forming a comparable mental image simply through his reading of Boccaccio's works: for comparative study of the *Troilus* and the *Filostrato* suggests that Chaucer was a dil-

igent and discerning Italianist. His own willingness to draw inspiration from a generous range of literary forms and styles qualified him to recognise a similar willingness in the Italian poet. The remarkable variety of influences operative in Boccaccio's early writings (which proved so congenial to Chaucer) reflects the extraordinary circumstances of Boccaccio's upbringing and literary formation at Angevin Naples.

Chaucer's verse and Boccaccio's early writings hold the ancient Latin poets in the highest regard. Both poets are fascinated by the relationship of their Christian epoch to the world of pagan antiquity; and both are evidently convinced that their relationship to the *auctores* lends definition to their own enterprise as vernacular authors. Each writer is similarly conscious of the power and prestige of the French vernacular, for each grew to maturity in an environment in which French culture was deeply and firmly rooted. Each poet derives much material from French romances, and each is familiar with the frameworks and narrative procedures of French dream poetry and the *dits amoreux*. The *Roman de la Rose* was of fundamental importance to both writers. Boccaccio's **Amorosa Visione**—which prepared the way for the Petrarchan *Trionfi*—extends the enterprise of transitional works, such as Brunetto Latini's *Tesoretto,* which had prepared the way for the *Commedia* by adapting the lessons of the *Rose* to Italian conditions. Five generations of Italian poets participate in this Italianising of the *Rose:* Brunetto; Durante; Dante; Boccaccio; Petrarch. Chaucer's Englishing of the *Rose* begins with diligent, close translation and becomes ever more subtle as his poetic career progresses. The sheer, concentrated brilliance of Chaucer's single-handed achievement in fashioning a *vulgaris illustris* from the scant resources of a retarded native vernacular has no parallel in the history of European poetry.

For both Chaucer and Boccaccio, the *Commedia* stands as the supreme model of what a vernacular poet might achieve. Boccaccio was, from the first, a tireless champion of Dante's reputation, and he made extensive use of the *Commedia's* verse form. Chaucer was more wary of bringing the form and content of the *Commedia* within the bounds of his own *makinge:* but he outshines Boccaccio in furthering the aesthetic and poetic principles of the *Commedia.* Chaucer is the more convincing continuator of Dante's great example of vernacular eloquence.

Chaucer was evidently alert to Boccaccio's imperfect comprehension of aristocratic values and vocabulary. Although he shared Boccaccio's mercantile origins (and later worked in close collaboration with Italian merchants), Chaucer was distanced from such origins by his education in an aristocratic household. Boccaccio remained an outsider to the courtly world; his poetic evocations of *cortesia* actually furthered the debasement of courtly language that Petrarch found cause to complain of whilst lamenting the popular reception of Dante's *Commedia*. Perhaps this was why Chaucer was anxious to publicise his admiration for Petrarch and Dante whilst passing over Boccaccio in silence. It is quite evident that Chaucer, in completing his *Troilus,* is willing to countenance association with the greatest of poetic masters, ancient and modern. Had he acknowledged Boccaccio by name, this might have prompted comparisons that he was willing to avoid. And when, unsolicited, we make such comparisons, we discover that the literary strategy pursued throughout Boccaccio's early writings is essentially similar to that developed throughout Chaucer's career: the marriage of popular and illustrious traditions. It is, after all, this fruitful union which makes possible the variegated and densely-peopled worlds of the *Decameron* and *The Canterbury Tales.*

Robert Hollander   (essay date 1988)

SOURCE: *Boccaccio's Last Fiction: "Il Corbaccio,"* University of Pennsylvania Press, 1988, 86 p.

[*In the following excerpt, Hollander analyzes the fictional narrative structure and textual development of* Il Corbaccio, *finding Boccaccio's organization of the work highly sophisticated.*]

Boccaccio's final work in vernacular fiction [*Il Corbaccio*] has been for the most part an embarrassment, even to its admirers. It is almost universally understood as running counter to the spirit of the preceding masterwork, the *Decameron.* And few who are drawn to the study of this apparently shrill misogynist outburst find it possible to argue that it has, to borrow again from Montaigne, "come from the same shop." Yet, whether it was written in 1354-55 or in 1365-66, the fact remains that, for all our difficulty in giving secure dates to Boccaccio's works, no one who has studied the Boccaccian *oeuvre* with care has suggested that *Decameron* and *Corbaccio* are not "neighbors." While I argue for the traditional dating of the work (1354-55), which makes it a "next-door neighbor" to the hundred tales, even a later dating of the text would allow that, in whatever ways, the *Corbaccio* might profitably be dealt with as a work which manifests a continuation of the themes, subjects, and techniques of the *Decameron,* that it might in fact be in relation to the latter in the role of an "afterword" or *conclusione.* . . .

It is fair to say that little attention has been paid to the care with which Boccaccio has organized and articulated the relation among the parts of the *Corbaccio.* One is tempted to assert that most readers have not thought of its subdivisions at all, preferring to consider the work an unswerving and unpartitioned autobiographical outburst against the female sex. In any case, and perhaps understandably, since the text is presented without clear marginal or rubrical indications of its divisions, no one has paid public heed to the elaborate and balanced organizing principles of the work. The following tabular representations will offer some immediate sense of exactly how carefully structured the work is (the numbers in parentheses refer to Nurmela's numeration of the parts of the text [in his edition of *Il Corbaccio,* 1968]).

(1-5) *proemio*	thanksgiving, desire to be of use to others, and invocation of divine assistance in writing the book
(6-53) situational frame	Boethian consultation and sleep
(54-131) "little *Inferno*"	1) dream vision of Hell 2) dialogue with spirit-guide
(132-177) the lover's tale	autobiography: 1) his *innamoramento* 2) the fatal letter
(178-290) the guide's speech	particular: 1) the scholar's fault general: 2) *contra feminas* general: 3) *pro hominibus* particular: 4) the scholar's fault
(291-512) the guide's tale	biography: 1) his wife's behavior 2) her response to his letter
(513-554) "mini-*Purgatorio*"	1) dialogue with spirit-guide 2) dream vision of Purgatory
(555-559) situational frame	awakening and Boethian consultation
(560-562) *conclusione*	thanksgiving, hope to be of use to others, that God will punish widow

The chiasmic organization of the work may thus be displayed as follows:

> (1) narrator *in propria persona*
>   (2) narrative: his situation
>   (3) dream vision (Hell)
>   (4) lover's autobiography
>   (5) guide's oration
>   (6) guide's biography of wife
>   (7) dream vision (Purgatory)
>   (8) narrative: his situation
> (9) narrator *in propria persona*

That the work is effectively in nine parts is interesting for its resonances with Boccaccio's own earlier work, which is also in nine parts (*Filostrato, Elegia di madonna Fiammetta*), as well as for its probable reflection of Dante's favorite number. What seems to me most interesting, however, in the formal arrangement of the parts of the *Corbaccio* is the effect the presence of so highly wrought a design—a perfectly balanced chiasmic structure—has (or should have) on its reader. The misogynist diatribe, which most readers—often apparently characterizing the work from a memory of earlier unhappy encounters with the text—take as its virtually sole concern, occurs at its center, in its fifth and sixth parts. It issues, significantly, from the mouth of the guide, not even from that of the putative

"Boccaccio" who is telling us all this. Everything about the arrangement calls out for us to think of artifice, of a fictive narrative, as Nykrog has recently tried to tell us. And when we read the text sequentially, Boccaccio's strategies also seem more apparent than we have usually allowed ourselves to perceive (and here I point an accusing finger not only at others, but also at my younger self). With the exception of Barricelli and, to a certain degree, Cassell, students of Boccaccio who have dealt with the work have remained convinced that it must be taken "seriously." . . .

It is useful to imagine that we are mutually reading the *Corbaccio* for the first time, innocent of any knowledge about it or about its author, if perhaps possessing some acquaintance with earlier literature and some knowledge of its own literary conventions. In short, it would be helpful to take on the role of a contemporary reader of the text, one who has happened upon it in a friend's study and picks it up for perhaps two hours of reading. What are our likely reactions to this text if we come to it without being convinced that we know what it means to tell us before we begin reading?

1. The narrator's introduction (1-5). The proem seems to ask us to take the work very seriously indeed. We hear of benefits received that ought to be acknowledged with gratitude, of grace obtained from God by the intercession of Mary. This the narrator will now record, with God's illuminating aid, so that "per me quello si scriva che onore e gloria sia del suo santissimo nome e utilità e consolazione dell'anime di coloro li quali per avventura ciò leggeranno" [that I may write that which will be the honor and glory of His most Holy Name, and that this work may be of use and consolation to the souls of those who may chance to read it] (5). Hearing this much, what do we imagine the rest will reveal? Surely we confront a writer who wants to tell us of a soul-searing experience, one that nearly brought him to his death, perhaps, and that at the very least was marked by such sinful behavior on his part that we must rejoice along with him at the great and generous forgiveness of God. And while I would argue that even the *proemio,* like its predecessor in the *Decameron,* is far more "literary" in its gestures than has generally been supposed, it would not be proper to make that case in this context, which is posited on a more innocent reading. The narrator to whom we listen, given the nature of the words which he utters, seems almost necessarily to be taken as speaking in seriousness and in truth. Hearing his words, we have as yet no reason to interpret his speech in any other way, nor any indication of the need to assume an ironic distance from him.

2. Boethian consolation and sleep (6-53). As the *pars executiva* of the *Corbaccio* begins, we immediately learn the cause of the narrator's trouble: "gli accidenti del carnale amore" [the vicissitudes of carnal love] (6). These, then, will be his subject. Alone in his room, he reaches the following conclusion: ". . . giudicai che senza alcuna mia colpa io fossi fieramente trattato male da colei, la quale io mattamente per mia singulare donna eletta avea, e la quale io più assai che la mia propria vita amava e oltre ad ogni altra onorava e reveriva" [I concluded that through no

fault of mine I had been cruelly ill-treated by her whom I had chosen in my madness as my special lady and whom I honored and revered above all others and loved far more than life itself] (7). The speaker, while he does admit to some foolishness in loving this woman, immediately puts the entire blame for his unhappiness upon her. We will soon have grounds on which to question the validity of his view of the woman's culpability. At this point in our reading, however, all we can assert is that the question is an open one—our unhappy lover may be speaking the truth. Yet surely we are warned by the conclusion of this period that he is a flowery speaker, one who does not so much pay heed to the need to express truth as he yields to being tempted toward rhetorical exaggeration. His love for his lady is protested overmuch, or so our awareness of similar confessions is likely to suggest to us. However, if he blames his lady's cruelty, he simultaneously admits his own foolishness ("bestialità"—9). Then, . . . he records the crucial moment in his subsequent judgment: ". . . estimai che molto men grave dovesse essere la morte che cotal vita, e quella con sommo disidero cominciai a chiamare" [I decided that Death must be far easier to bear than such a life; and I began to cry out to him with the greatest longing] (9). The resulting battle of conflicting thoughts concerning suicide is resolved only by the ratiocination provided by his personified "thought," which comes to convince him to return to a desire for life.

The clearly Boethian framework of the ensuing monologue (13-46) offers us our first indication that the narrator's initial complaint is to be considered from another point of view than has as yet been made available. This projection of his inner voice, which he now believes to have been sent to him by heavenly light ("credo da celeste lume mandato"—12), is a fourteenth-century "municipal" version of Boethian wisdom. His opening sally, "Deh stolto!" [You silly fool!] (13), puts us on guard. If we are about to hear unvarnished home truths, delivered in hopes of putting a foolish lover back on the track, we hear them from a provocative source, one whose very diction undercuts the seriousness of the moment. His message, on the other hand, seems "orthodox" enough. Where the narrator has previously held his lady blameworthy, the "thought" puts the fault solely upon him: "tu, non ella, ti se' della tua noia cagione" [you, not she, are the cause of your torment] (17). And he continues by paraphrasing and then commenting upon the narrator's logical procedures in the following condemnatory way: "Ella, conoscendo che io l'amo, dovrebbe amar me; il che non faccendo, m'è di questa noia cagione; e con questo mi ci mena e con questo mi ci tiene. Questa non è ragione che abbia alcun valore: forse che non le piaci tu. Come vuoi tu che alcuno ami quello che non gli piace?" ["She should love me, knowing that I love her; and by not doing so, she is the cause of this grief of mine; with this she leads me here and with this she holds me." This is not a valid reason at all. Perhaps she finds you unpleasing. How do you expect anyone to love a person whom she does not find attractive?] (19-21). The unanswerable argument receives no answer.

The narrator's *noia* (and we should remember the importance of that word as it works its way from the *Proemio* through the rest of the **Decameron,** joining the twinned phenomena of plague and carnal appetite in its first appearances) is self-caused. The "thought" expounds, in a low-mimetic version of scholastic argument, the logical reasons which stand against his intention to do away with himself (25-46): if you love her and she loves you, your death will cause her pain; if she hates you, your misery will give her pleasure. Thus it is best to give over mad desire for sexual pleasure: "tuo folle amore" (42—see *Paradiso* VIII, 2), "questo tuo folle appetito" (43).

All this is conventional wisdom of a most familiar Boethian strain. In place of the narrator's first version of the "love affair," we now have a better one. However, even the *pensiero* seems to realize that, in order to convince his auditor to go on living, he must supply a positive reason for doing so. The conventions of his monologue lead us to expect a conventional conclusion, urging his auditor to turn aside from the vanities of such behavior to seek a better being in philosophy or religion, or at least in contented abnegation among those who have also been freed from the pangs of love. The conclusion of this first oration of the **Corbaccio,** however, is quite different from what we have been led to expect: If the narrator goes on living, no one can say with certitude that he will take pleasure from his lady; but if he dies he will certainly not achieve the joys of revenge (" . . . ogni speranza di vendetta od altra letizia di cosa che qui rimanga, fugge, nel morire, a ciascuno" [all hope of revenge, or any other joy in things which remain here below, flees everyone at his death]—45). Therefore, he should choose to live on, thereby making her unhappy by his very existence (44-46). It is a surprising resolution. In place of the concupiscible appetite, the narrator is enjoined to put himself under the sway of the irascible. If nearly everything else in the oration is conventional, with the exception of its comic tone, its ending is far from being so. Instead, it offers the narrator exactly the wrong advice, urging him to continue his passionate feelings in another and complementary form, exchanging hatred for lust. . . . [*Vendetta*] is perhaps the key word of the **Corbaccio.** We have seen it introduced in this passage. Our basic interpretation of the work depends on whether or not we consider the narrator's desire for vengeance as being presented as a praiseworthy form of behavior.

The effect of this admonition is enormous and immediate. As we begin the second segment of this section of the work, we hear the following gratified outburst from the narrator in response to the advice he has just been given:

> Maravigliosa cosa è quella della divina consolazione nelle menti de' mortali: questo pensiero, siccome io arbitro, dal piissimo Padre de' lumi mandato, quasi dagli occhi della mente ogni oscurità levatami, in tanto la vista di quegli aguzzò e rendé chiara, che a me stesso manifestandomi scoprendosi il mio errore, non solamente, riguardandolo, me ne vergognai, ma da compunzione debita mosso, ne lagrimai e me medesimo biasimai forte, e da meno che io non arbitrava d'essere mi reputai.

> [Divine consolation in the minds of mortals is a wondrous thing. This thought, sent, I believe, by the most holy Father of Lights, took away al-

most all the darkness from the eyes of my mind and at the same time sharpened and cleared their vision; so that finding my error so obvious, not only did I feel ashamed as I looked upon it, but, moved by due repentance, I wept about it bitterly, reproved myself, and felt less self-esteem than before]. (47)

Again, let us imagine that we are reading these words for the first time. Do we not seem to be hearing a *recusatio* of the most serious sort? Is not this man cured of his disease? Had the "thought" not finished his oration as he did, had not the promise of *vendetta* been the culminating point in his argument, and were not the narrator to spend the rest of his literary effort in search of this revenge, we might think—as so many readers have thought—that we are dealing with a genuine Christian conversion to the good, even one which might mirror such an occurrence in Boccaccio's own life. Boccaccio, playful as always, allows us to read past the promise of *vendetta* as though it were not there (there is, in fact, no reference to it in the lengthy expression of thanksgiving which we have just examined). He will exploit the power of this prolonged desire for revenge as the work progresses, for we will see that it is the sole motivation for all else that the narrator finally thinks and does, although it will take some time to resurface.

Indeed, the second Boethian scene of this part of the **Corbaccio** is also without reference to vengeance. Instead, we see the refreshed narrator, his face serene, leave his room to find a group of friends with whom he withdraws to a familiar pleasant surrounding for discourse of a philosophical kind. They speak of changeful Fortune (49), of abiding natural laws (50), and of Divinity, whose nature exceeds human comprehension (51). After a day spent with friends in such lofty pursuits, the narrator returns, *consolato,* to his chamber, where he recalls the day's conversations with pleasure and finally finds the ease of sleep (53).

If the **Corbaccio** had concluded here, we would be tempted to read it as most readers have read the work as a whole, believing that Boccaccio had left us a brief, Boethian homiletic treatment concerning the best ways to deal with the pangs of unrequited love for an unworthy woman. But the *pensiero,* who reveals to the lover the true nature of his love for the woman (in some respects resembling the "thought" [*pensero*] in *Vita Nuova* XLI, who reveals something of the true nature of Beatrice to her lover), has made available a single possibility for the furtherance of the plot. Instead of aiming for a philosophic acceptance of things as they are and for thoughts of a better directed future course, the narrator will be bent on vengeance. If he cannot get sexual pleasure, he will at least get even. We might reflect that the *pensiero* is, after all, a part of the narrator's own psyche, not an external agent of reform—despite what his own claims for its divine provenance may insist. The sheepish lover may be won back to life only by the hope for vengeance, no matter that only the Lord should be relied on to repay ("Non vosmetipsos defendentes charissimi, sed date locum irae. Scriptum est enim: Mihi vindicta: ego retribuam, dicit Dominus" [Dearly beloved, avenge not yourselves, but rather give place unto wrath: for it is written, Vengeance is mine; I will repay, saith the Lord]—Romans 12:19).

3. Dream vision and dialogue (54-131). The narrator's dream will occupy over nine-tenths of the work . . . and is divided into five parts, as I have already indicated. Its introduction shows how intent its author is upon warning his readers to be alert to the changes he has wrought upon our expectations. The narrator has been made healthy—or so it would appear—by the combined result of the intervention of his "thought" and the philosophical musings enjoyed with his friends. If he is now to dream (and *there's* the rub), we expect the vision presented to him to be the further agent of his recovery, reinforcing the message he has already had so clearly presented for his amelioration. Yet the dream will cause him to return to his dilemma, as his own words suggest: ". . . non parendo alla mia nemica fortuna che le bastassero le 'ngiurie fattemi nel mio vegghiare, ancora dormendo s'ingegnò di noiarmi" [my enemy Fortune, believing that she had not done me sufficient injuries during my waking hours, contrived to harm me even as I slept] (54). His complaint against Fortune, whom he has only recently presented as being expectably unstable (49), reveals how little Boethian advancement he has in fact accomplished. The dream offers a return to *noia,* a word, as I have suggested, that brings with it the context of the *Decameron's* conjoining of plague and carnal love. If the narrator was "consoled" after his conversations with himself and with his friends, the dream, apparently, has the function of making him once again a sick man, precisely by reminding him of the *noia* he has suffered from the widow's disdain.

The first segment of this part of the dream vision is pure narrative (54-73) and contains the most evidently Dantean elements of the *Corbaccio,* as has often been noted. This exercise in pastiche is put to amusing service. The dream landscape, which begins with visions of delight, ends with unmistakably Dantean reminiscences of Hell ("una solitudine diserta, aspra e fiera, piena di salvatiche piante, di pruni e di bronchi" [a desolate wilderness, rough and harsh, rankly overgrown with trees, thorns, and brambles]—61), where our narrator hears bestial cries that similarly derive from Dante ("mugghi, urli e strida" [roars, howls, and shrieks]—63). And, as the spirit-guide in the dream—Boccaccio's version of Dante's Virgil—will point out, what seems so foul is in reality what the narrator has always taken for fair: carnal affection for the opposite sex. This figure, perhaps the most realized presence in Boccaccio's cunning fiction, is an after-the-fact rigid moralist, a former lover himself who will prove almost pitiless in his castigation of present lovers.

The second segment of this first part of the dream vision (73-131) is devoted nearly entirely to dialogue. In the second section of the *Corbaccio* the *pensiero* had indeed spoken, delivering himself of a lengthy speech (13-46), but there was no verbal interaction between speaker and listener, as befitted that situation, in which a character was listening to his own inner voice. Now, however, what had been only first-person narrative, from opening prayer to ensuing relation of event to following dream, becomes a mixture of narrative and Dantesque otherworldly dialogue, which, paradoxically, soon begins to seem both more immediate and more "realistic" than what had preceded.

The guide's first word to his pupil is the (playfully unreported) name of the narrator (leaving us to supply the "Giovanni" if we are so minded), when he calls out to him, "per lo mio proprio nome chiamando" (73). The act of naming establishes links between *magister* and pupil, between both of them and their similarly unnamed city ("la comune patria"—78). We learn gradually of the tie that binds these two men, first only that the elder of them was once wrathful against the younger, but that his wrath is now turned (as is fitting in a purging spirit) to charity (82). That news comes in company with the notice that the speaker is no longer among the living, information which fills the narrator with the dread apprehension that he is addressing a ghost and which reminds us that we are witnessing an otherworldly scene. That the relation between them is their mutual woman, one who has often cuckolded her husband but who avoided at least one act of posthumous sexual betrayal because she did not respond to the advances of the middle-aged scholar, sets the encounter in a low-comedic atmosphere that dominates the rest of the work.

Our protagonists share a common negative attribute: neither of them is particularly successful with women. The first purpose of this guide is to reassure his charge; his second, to educate him concerning the nature of his desires for sexual pleasure. Both tasks are completed by the conclusion of this section of dialogue. The narrator comes to understand that the "hell" of lust punished is no more than the eventual condition of lust indulged. The "laberinto d'amore" (93), which had at first seemed to be the opposite of the "dilettevole e bel sentiero" [delightful and beautiful path] (54) which had led him there, turns out to be only its logically necessary destination: "Questa misera valle è quella corte che tu chiami 'Amore' e quelle bestie che tu di' che udite hai e odi mugghiare sono i miseri, de' quali tu se' uno, dal fallace amore inretiti" [This wretched valley is what you call "the Court of Love"; and these beasts, which you say you heard and hear growling, are the wretches—of whom you are one—who have been caught in the net of false love] (124).

4. The narrator's tale of his beloved (132-177). The next fictional mode assumed by the text is that of autobiography. This section of the *Corbaccio* is also in two parts, or movements. In the first, the narrator rehearses his *innamoramento* with his guide's widow. A male relative of the departed spirit had praised his widow to the narrator (135), with the inevitable result: the scholar decides to fall in love (141). He seeks out the widow. Once again, his good opinion of her is entirely due to the opinions of another, this time a lady who claims that the widow's mourning dress becomes her (145). The narrator still does not know the identity of his beloved and does not do so until the helpful lady points her out to other female onlookers ("La terza, che siede in su quella panca" [The third one seated on that bench]—147). It is enough, this first, literarily unpromising sight of his beloved. He burns with the fire of love (150). Her appearance, he claims, gives him hopes for future bliss (151). It is important to note that, even in the narrator's own version of this "primal scene" in any medieval love story, there is absolutely no indication of the widow's interest in him. (. . . [If] the widow is nothing else, she is constant precisely in her aversion to the narrator.)

At this point, the ghostly guide intervenes (154) to set the questions which will be answered in the second part of the narrator's love story, asking his pupil to explain how he revealed his affection to the widow and whether she ever encouraged him (certainly a valid question in light of the scant information we have previously been offered). The narrator confesses (and the scene is indeed reminiscent of a confessional encounter between priest and sinner) to having written a letter expressing his affection, to which the widow responded with limping epistolary verses alluding to the migration of souls between lovers and seeking to know his identity. The trap had been set. Not even the literary pretensions of the widow's letter are sufficient to cause the lover's retreat. He writes again, as she had requested. And therein, as he tells us at some length (167-175), lay his woe. The lady wanted him further to reveal himself only in order to be able to mock him; in fact, her own letter had been composed not by her but by her lover, the two of them conspiring to enjoy his discomfort. The guide's question which produces this response is worth pondering: "Se più avanti in questo amore non è stato, che cagione t'induceva, il dì trapassato, con tante lagrime e con tanto dolore sì ferventemente per questo a disiderare di morire?" [If there were no further developments in this love affair, what induced you when the day was over to desire death so fervently for this—with so many tears and so much grief?] (166) If we have not thought so previously, can we now avoid understanding that the lover's problem is not a broken heart but spite? He had wanted to kill himself from shame. The guide's response summarizes what we have learned in this section (177):" . . . come tu t'innamorasti e di cui, e il perché e la cagione della tua disperazione . . ." [how you became enamored, and of whom, and the reason and cause of your despair . . .].

5. The guide's misogynist diatribe (178-290).

The last three questions (how, with whom, and why did the narrator fall in love) are used to organize the central section of the work. The husband's outburst, presented as a single, developed rhetorical unit, an *oratio contra feminas,* is what most readers of the ***Corbaccio*** take to be the central point of the work, considering it as reflecting Boccaccio's own latter-day view of woman-kind. It is divided into four parts, the first of which is a brief presentation of the charge against the lover himself (179-194), and is thus concerned with the particular and not the general case, for he is portrayed as the source of his own incorrect behavior. Both his age (179-187) and his studies (188-194) should have served to quell such a desire.

This first segment ends with a peroration declaiming the blindness of love (193-194). The lengthy presentation (195-273) of the general case begins with the repeated assertion that the narrator's studies should have revealed the nature of women to him. Since they obviously did not, the guide makes up for this lack with a full-scale oration con-

tra feminas. This begins by claiming that women are like privies, to which one resorts out of necessity in order to deposit a necessary discharge but otherwise strives to avoid (201), and rapidly becomes still more wildly vituperative. The major topics which he chooses to address are as follows: women's use of cosmetics (207-208); their desire to assume *signoria* over their husbands as quickly as possible (209-221); their urge to take lovers once their husbands are made subject (222-233); their suspicious and wrathful nature (234-239); their avarice (240-244); their flightiness, with their only constant desire being lust itself (245-246); the vain wishes and vain knowledge revealed by their incessant garrulity (247-269). We are spared a recounting of still other defects when the guide tells the narrator that this would take too long and that enough has already been told to convince him of the flaws of womankind (270-273).

To this oration on a general theme is joined a second, a mad forerunner of Pico della Mirandola's oration on the dignity of man (274-278). The *oratio pro hominibus* would have it that males, made (unlike women) in the image of God, are born to lordship over women, not to be subject to them. The fourth part of the oration returns to the particular. Scholars are themselves superior to other men (279-280). How then, the guide wants to know, can the narrator desire so vile a woman (281-282)? Instead, he should consort with the Muses—so superior in beauty to *malvage femmine*—in deserted places, not seek pleasure under widows' cloaks (282-290). And it is with this piece of wisdom that the guide pauses before entering another avenue of attack.

6. The widower's revenge: Biography of a wife (291-512).

Moving from oratory to biography, the guide warms to his task with relish and at length. Where his first assault upon the heart and mind of the amatory scholar has primarily assumed the form of oratorical presentation of a *quaestio,* the worth of women, his concluding argument is less an oration *contra feminas* than it is spectacularly an argument *ad feminam.* A widower himself, he tells us he first knew his new and monstruous wife, herself a widow, when their marriage was arranged by relatives and friends (292). He then proceeds to reel off a list of her faults. . . . [Its] contents closely correspond to those which were produced in the *contra feminas* portion of his oration (207-269).

As soon as they were married, his new wife assumed *signoria* over him, making their home life more full of quarrels than the strife-torn city itself (293-301). The guide then details the result of her avaricious desire to gain control of his wealth: her expenditures on vestments and cosmetics to make herself more attractive (302-337). If asked, she would have insisted that her cosmetic extravagances (which the guide has displayed with venomous and compendious detail) were committed for his sake; in fact, she employed them in order to attract other men, of whom there were many, including one to whom she gave his goods (350) and with whom she shared her sexual favors (338-375). Next, he turns to her vain wishes to be admired for her noble lineage and to the empty folly revealed in her insistent and incessant talk (376-385).

The preceding four segments of his description correspond

to charges we have heard about women in general. Now the guide marshals his culminating evidence against his former wife: Since, he says, doctors must sometimes prescribe harsh medicines, he will now display her physical attributes as they actually are. Undressing her, at least in words, he describes first her undecorated face, then her pendulous breasts, her belly, her huge vaginal aperture, and finally her anus (386-422). The prosecution rests its case and now makes its final plea to the jury (423-452): In light of the above, the scholar-lover must acknowledge that his opinion of her virtues was wrongly based (was she steadfast? no, she delighted in his sudden death, brought on by the stress caused by her behavior, bought a house [in which her "paternosters" are French romances] near a church in order to seem pious, but actually to find paramours in that church). In the course of this penultimate harangue, the guide refers to the scholar's main rival, the "second Absalom" (443). He tells the narrator that, although his spirit is offended by his wife's infidelity with this younger lover, he will one day have his revenge (*vendetta*), since he himself had previously cuckolded "Absalom," whose son by his lawful wife is in fact the guide's (444).

While no further persuasions would seem necessary, the guide cannot resist a concluding thrust (453-512), thus adding a second element to this "biography" of his wife. It is perfectly calculated to be the most telling of all. He informs the narrator that spirits in Purgatory are at certain times vouchsafed visits to their loved ones and friends on earth (454). As a result, it happened that he was back in his own house, "tirato da una cotale caritevole affezione la quale non solamente gli amici, ma ancora i nimici ci fa amare" [drawn by a certain charitable affection, which makes us love not only our friends but also our enemies] (455). And there he sees his wife in bed with "Absalom," witnesses their mocking of the narrator's first letter, their plans for his further vilification (456-465). Had the narrator known of all this then as certainly as he knows it now, the guide suggests, he surely would have hanged himself (468). How could he have loved such a creature? His mind should have convinced him of her unworthiness (476-493). If not, then his natural advantages (maleness, physical comeliness at least as great as hers, relative youth) should have helped him to control himself. And if her noble lineage made him feel inferior, her behavior reveals that she is not noble in any true sense at all (501-511). And with that final demonstration the guide falls silent, awaiting the narrator's response (512).

7. The narrator's penitence (513-554). In chiasmic parallel with its corresponding section of the work (the third), in which an otherworldly dialogue is preceded by an otherworldly experience, this one begins with such a dialogue (514-544). The narrator has come round, has utterly changed his opinion of his beloved, but now fears that, after such sinfulness, he must despair of pardon (514-517). God's mercy, he is told, may extend even unto him if he is truly contrite and truly makes amends (518-520). The narrator proclaims his contrition and wants to know exactly how he can atone for his sin (521). The guide informs him (522-530): "Ciò che tu hai amato ti conviene avere in odio . . . ; voglio che della offesa fattati da lei tu

prenda vendetta; la quale ad un' ora sarà a te e a lei salutifera" [What you have loved you must hate . . . ; I wish you to avenge the offense she has done to you, for it is something which will bring salvation to both of you at the same time] (523, 526). As for the particular form this penitent hatred should take, a scholar like him,

> eziandio mentendo, sa cui gli piace tanto famoso e sì glorioso rendere negli orecchi degli uomini, che chiunque di quel cotale niuna cosa ascolta, lui e per virtù e per meriti sopra i cieli estiman tenere le piante de' piedi; e così in contrario, quantunque virtuoso, quantunque valoroso, quantunque da bene stato sia uno che nella vostra ira caggia, con parole che degne paiono di fede nel profondo di ninferno il tuffate e nascondete.

> [can render even by fiction whom he pleases so famous and so glorious to the ears of men, that whoever hears anything of that person, considers him to have the very soles of his feet above the heavens both because of his virtue and his merits; and so, on the contrary, however virtuous, however worthy and upstanding a person may be who enrages you, with words which seem believable, you cast and hide him in the depths of Hell] (527).

It is thus that the guide "commissions" *Il Corbaccio.* The narrator is quick to accept the charge. As long as skillfully crafted words maintain their power, he says, "a niuno mio successore lascerò a far delle ingiurie ricevute da me vendetta, solo che tanto tempo mi sia prestato che io possa o concordare le rime o distendere le prose" [I will leave none of my successors to avenge the outrage I have received, if only I am granted enough time either to tune my rhymes or to draft my prose] (532). The word *vendetta* has now passed from the *pensiero* (45) to the guide (444, 526) to the narrator himself. He at last has hold of his purpose. Continuing, he says that he will leave the *vendetta* of deeds ("la quale i più degli uomini giudicherebbono che fosse da far co' ferri" [which most men would judge should be taken with the sword]—533) to God. But then all writers think the pen is mightier than the sword—especially *their* pen. And his disclaimer in no way indicates that he hopes his literary effort will help to bring the widow to self-knowledge and thus perhaps eventual salvation, a possibility three times held out by the guide in his last speech. On the contrary, he hopes that God will indeed punish her.

This section is rounded off by a statement of the narrator's desire to know why the guide was chosen in heaven to come to his aid when they never knew one another (537). The guide replies that souls in Purgatory are moved by disinterested charity, and that, in any case, he knew the details of the case better than anyone (538-541). The narrator's response is to ask what he can do for his benefactor (542), who responds that, since he has no one to pray for him, he would appreciate the narrator's paying to have a few masses said in order to lessen his torment in Purgatory (543).

The concluding part of this section, balancing the Infernal descent of the third section of the *Corbaccio,* presents a Purgatorial ascent. The narrator feels the weight of sin lifted from his back and follows the guide along a shining path upward (545-550). The view from the mountaintop reveals both a lovely landscape and the hellish hole which represents earthly love and wherein he began. He turns to offer thanks to his guide only to find him gone, and his dream ended as well (551-554).

8. Awakening and Boethian consultation (555-559). Awakening from his dream, the narrator decides that it was a truthful one—as later consultation would affirm (555). He leaves the *misera valle* to rejoin his friends, who confirm his interpretation of the dream; he decides to cease loving the widow, within a few days regaining his lost *libertà* (556-558). His final remark in this section shows little concern for the soul of the widow: "E senza fallo, se tempo mi fia conceduto, io spero si con parole gastigare colei, che vilissima cosa essendo, altrui di schernire co' suoi amanti presume, che mai lettera non mostrerà che mandata le sia, che della mia e del mio nome con dolore e con vergogna non si ricordi" [Without fail, if time be granted to me, I hope with my words so to chastise that woman—who, though she is a contemptible thing, presumes to mock others with her lovers—that she will never show a letter sent to her without recalling mine and my name with grief and shame] (559). The entire energy of the former lover is now bent just as fiercely on hate as it was on love.

9. The narrator's conclusion: "Go, little book" (560-562). In his envoy the narrator, reversing the intention expressed in almost all of the concluding passages in Boccaccio's earlier vernacular works, wants his book to avoid his beloved, not to find and inflame her:

> Ma sopra ogni cosa ti guarda di non venire nelle mani delle malvage femmine, e massimamente di colei che ogni demonio di malvagità trapassa e che della presente tua fatica è stata cagione; per ciò che tu saresti là mal ricevuta; ed ella è da pugnere con più aguto stimolo che tu non porti teco. Il quale, concedendolo Colui che d'ogni grazia è donatore, tosto a pugnerla non temendo le si farà incontro.

> [But above all, see that you do not come into the hands of evil women, especially into those of her who surpasses every demon in wickedness and who has been the cause of your present toil, since you would be ill received. She is to be stung by a sharper goad than you bear with you; this will advance upon her swiftly and fearlessly to wound her, if the Giver of all Grace grants it.] (561-562)

The narrator is clearly referring to 533, where, in addition to his own literary vengeance, he hopes for the *vendetta di Dio* to strike his former lady. He has, once again, forgotten entirely about the guide's advice that his correction may bring the widow to self-knowledge and, eventually, to salvation. Instead, all the narrator really desires is revenge (and, if Cassell is correct [in his 1975 translation], he does so with a similarly "stony" envoy of Dante's in mind). It is worthy of note that Dante's poem ("Così nel mio parlar voglio esser aspro") ends with the very word which has had such an important role in revealing the motives of the narrator of the *Corbaccio:*

> Canzon, vattene dritto a quella donna
> che m'ha ferito il core e che m'invola
> quello ond'io ho più gola,
> a dàlle per lo cor d'una saetta;
> ché bell'onor s'acquista in far vendetta.

[My song, get yourself straight to that lady who has wounded my heart and who robs me of what I most hunger for, and shoot an arrow through her heart; for fair honor is won by taking revenge.]

The *Corbaccio* is not a work that is out of control, as so many have thought. It is a work about a man who is out of control.

David Wallace on Boccaccio's literary legacy:

The instant and enduring popularity of the *Decameron* is due to the energy and versatility of its style and the originality of its form. Boccaccio achieves a new kind of literary language, a prose that escapes the formative constraints of its Latin models and yet draws from them sufficient subtlety, rhythmic variety and complexity to map out new areas of human experience. He sometimes (most often in opening a new *novella*) writes with a constraint and balance reminiscent of Dante's *Convivio;* and sometimes (when a *novella* is in full flow) with a simulated abandon that suggests the spontaneity of colloquial speech rather than the discipline of writing, *parola* rather than *scrittura.* Boccaccio sometimes imitates and sometimes parodies the full range of medieval genres, from courtly lyric and *chanson de geste* to saint's life and fabliau. And yet (unlike Chaucer) he chooses to contain such encyclopaedic variety within the limits of a single, stabilized genre, the *novella.* These short prose narratives are set in sequence by an organizing frame or *cornice* which transforms a mixed bag of tales into a unitary work of art. Boccaccio's *novelle* sequence thus becomes the prototype of the modern novel; its literary line of descent extends beyond the Middle Ages and Renaissance to connect novelists as diverse as Manzoni, Lawrence and Faulkner.

David Wallace, in his Giovanni Boccaccio: Decameron, *Cambridge University Press, 1991.*

Anthony K. Cassell and Victoria Kirkham   (essay date 1991)

SOURCE: Introduction to *"Diana's Hunt—Caccia di Diana": Boccaccio's First Fiction,* edited and translated by Anthony K. Cassell and Victoria Kirkham, University of Pennsylvania Press, 1991, pp. 1-96.

[*In the excerpt below, Cassell and Kirkham discuss the background of* Diana's Hunt, *including the poem's dating and subject matter, its cultural and religious milieu, and its stature among medieval hunt literature.*]

Diana's Hunt is Giovanni Boccaccio's first work. A sylvan fantasy in terza rima, it has been dated by historical evidence and internal stylistic features to 1333-1334. The author, then barely twenty, would have been about midway through a five-year course on canon law at the University of Naples. In truancy from a curriculum imposed by his father, he penned this imaginative tribute to the high-born ladies of the circles surrounding King Robert's court. His fiction makes them nymphs-for-a-day, convened to a hunt by the goddess Diana. At the end, surprisingly, the tutelar of chastity must yield to Venus, who descends from heaven and turns a great heap of slain beasts into handsome young men. By such startling reversals set in a woodland alive with bestiary and religious symbolism, the novice poet created a witty conundrum: although Diana loses, virtue wins; pagan divinities rule by turn, but we are in Christian allegorical territory.

The story is set in springtime, "that fair season when the new grasses reclothe each meadow, and the bright air smiles for the sweetness that moves the heavens." While the poem's solitary narrator (whose identity we do not know) is wondering how to shield himself from Love's bitter blows, a "gentle spirit" comes flying down and thrice summons the women whom Diana has elected her companions in Parthenope. Their names are called out one by one, but the last of the chosen, "that Lady whom Love honors more than any other for her lofty virtue," remains anonymous because, according to the narrator, "praise more sovereign would suit her name than I could here set forth."

Diana bathes with her newfound nymphs in a rivulet, divides them into four groups, and sends each party to hunt in a separate direction. The narrator notes one by one their venatic triumphs over such beasts as the roebuck, boar, lion, and unicorn. Then, just when it seems all has been said, more ladies with limers come rushing loudly into the woods. They too are Neapolitan noblewomen, again named seriatim, who energetically renew the chase, fanning out in teams toward the cardinal points, their bravest conquest a seven-member family of snakes.

At last, with noon approaching, Diana calls an end to the hunt and reassembles her followers. But "the Fair Lady, whose name is not spoken," now incites her companions to rebel against the goddess. Her authority rejected, Diana storms back up to heaven. On the advice of the Mystery Lady, the huntresses make a sacrificial fire of their kill and dedicate it to Venus, whom they solemnly invoke. Venus drops down on a little white cloud, announcing, "I am she from whom each one of you through her prayers awaits grace; and I promise you by the gods above that each one who is worthy to follow in my footsteps shall have what she asks." Love's avatar keeps her promise by transforming the burning beasts into happy young men. Naked, they leap from the flames, run through the meadow into a river, and resurface mantled in vermilion. Venus commands them to be wise and keep faith with their huntress-mistresses.

What follows this mass metamorphosis is an even more amazing turn of events. The narrator himself, who, we at last discover, has actually been a stag all along, undergoes the same wondrous transfiguration:

> And I saw myself offered to the Fair Lady,
> changed beyond doubt from a stag into a human

being and a rational creature; and not unjustly, for nature never bestowed more worth or nobility than upon her, so chaste and pure.

The beauty and virtues of his Unnamed Lady are such that she seems to be an angelic creature from heaven, come to "extinguish" human vice and bring peace to the hearts of all troubled lovers. By serving her humbly, the narrator hopes to win "salvation" (Italian *salute*), the word that closes his remarks and the poem.

> It pleases me now to speak no further, because for a place more praise-worthy I reserve my words to praise more truthfully that beauty that her soul traces upon her, she through whom other women are honored and whom my heart ever contrives to serve. And I go back to contemplate in the green meadows that mercy and the other great virtue that adorns with beauty this Lady from whom I yet hope to have salvation.

Boccaccio was in his early teens when he left Florence, the city of his childhood, to go live in Naples with his father, a businessman who transferred there as principal agent for the Bardi Bank and became "Counsellor and Chamberlain" to King Robert the Wise. Newly arrived, probably in 1327, for a sojourn that would stretch into twelve years, the adolescent had to work the counters, or *banchi*, as a money changer. Still, his father's privileged relationship with the monarch was to give him entrée to the court and prominent local families. Their names are memorialized in **Diana's Hunt**, a Who's Who in the Kingdom of Naples that rosters clans like the Caracciola, Sighinolfi, Barrile, Coppoli, Carafa, Brancaccia, and Aldimaresca.

The city in that era was a capital of mixed cultures. At its court, the most brilliant on the European continent, an Angevin dynasty had ruled since 1266, and French was the official language. The nobility were a chivalric society, readers of romances imported from France and a public often visited by their own vernacular poets from north of the Alps. King Robert the Wise, who was acknowledged during his reign (1309-1343) as Italy's most powerful prince, followed his father and grandfather in a policy of close ties with the papacy, which was by then resident at Avignon, Robert's own city. High praise for that monarch came from the contemporary historian of Florence, Giovanni Villani, in whose estimation he is "the wisest of Christians for the last five hundred years, both in natural wisdom and learning, a very great master in theology and a consummate philosopher." This Second Solomon, as Boccaccio called him, was an amateur expert on medicine and became famous for the sermons he composed in Latin, of which 289 survive. Steeped in Aristotle, Averroës, and Scholastic thought, these pieces reflect a person of austere life, so much so that Dante rather sourly implied Robert should have stuck to kerystics instead of seeking the throne.

Scholasticism flourished at the Dominican *Studium*, a center of intellectual activity whose establishment dated from 1269. Thomas Aquinas visited in 1272, and San Domenico Maggiore continued to be a seat of theology where his students taught. A university was founded at Naples by Emperor Frederick II (d. 1250); law, medicine, and the natural sciences, including the field of zoology in which Frederick himself practiced, held places of honor. Italy's most outstanding jurist, Cino da Pistoia, taught there alongside Luca da Penne, author of a major commentary on the Justinian Code. Luca's compilation, which reveals vast learning, is a profile in scholarship that Boccaccio emulated: some Greek classics in Latin translation; Plautus, Terence, Sallust, Cicero, Livy, Quintilian, Seneca, Suetonius, the two Plinys, Valerius Maximus; Saint Jerome, Augustine, Cassiodorus, Boethius, Isidore of Seville, Papias, Saint Bernard, Saint Thomas Aquinas, Egidius Romanus, Cino da Pistoia, Barbato da Sulmona, Francesco Petrarca.

Boccaccio came to frequent one of the city's most celebrated cultural institutions, the royal library. Its holdings emphasized theology and medicine, classic and modern, works such as Gregory the Great's *Moralia in Job,* writings by Augustine and Boethius, Aquinas's *Summa contra Gentiles,* Hippocrates, Galen, and texts from the Salerno school of medicine. Curator for many years was Paolo da Perugia, whose formative influence on his intellectual development, especially the ***Genealogies of the Gentile Gods,*** Boccaccio remembers fondly in the last book of that encyclopedia of allegorized myths:

> Advanced in years, of great and varied learning, he was long the librarian of the famous King Robert of Sicily and Jerusalem. If there was ever a man possessed of the curiosity of research he was the one. A word from his prince was sufficient to send him hunting through a dozen books of history, fable, or poetry.

Paolo, with great knowledge of Greek lore, had made a compendium of mythography called the *Collectiones,* but as Boccaccio's anecdote goes, the librarian's shrewish widow prevented its survival:

> to the very serious inconvenience of this book of mine [the ***Genealogies***], I found that his saucy wife Biella, after his death, wilfully destroyed this and many other books of Paul's. . . . I am convinced that at the time when I knew him no one was his equal in studies of this sort.

The young Boccaccio was not limited to French and Latin literature; he also had access to the latest works of his homeland. By around 1330, among the ever-growing number of Florentine merchants and bankers present in the bustling city, Tuscan literature began to eclipse the old-fashioned courtly fiction favored by the French aristocracy. Before 1323, two years after Dante's death (1321), the *Divine Comedy* reached Naples, ordered by one of the city's Florentines, or carried there by the preacher Agostino d'Ancona. Graziolo de' Bambaglioli, one of its earliest commentators, was in Naples between 1334 and 1335, and there are at least six extant manuscripts of the poem copied by various scribes and commentators illuminated in Naples during the Trecento.

The plural cultures of its Neapolitan birthplace mingle in the poem. Despite its brevity, the *Hunt* vibrates with an amazing encyclopedic energy, reflecting the medieval passion for polyglot synthesis, a desire for ordered universal knowledge that promoted all manner of compendia and catalogs. Here, to give a list of women an artistic form, Boccaccio adapted from Dante a type of poetic form called a *sirventese,* then merged that inventory with a dictionary of animals, or bestiary. His narrative in Tuscan, fusing Italian, Galloromance, and Latin literary traditions, displays a stylistic predilection for startling *contaminatio*—juxtaposition of material and ideas from many sources widely dissimilar in subject, medium, and manner. By conservative reckoning, the authorities on which the young writer relied range from Ovid's *Metamorphoses;* through Apuleius's *Golden Ass;* a panegyric by Claudian; Boethius's *On the Consolation of Philosophy;* the Bible; patristic exegeses of the Psalms; Gregory's *Moralia in Job;* Rabanus Maurus (works genuine and spurious); Isidore of Seville's *Etymologies;* Gratian's *Decretum;* poets of the *dolce stil novo;* Dante's *Vita nuova* and *Divine Comedy;* Petrarch's earliest lyrics; Latin, French, and Italian bestiaries; medieval hunt manuals and allegories; the Roman Catholic and Byzantine liturgies of baptism; and baptismal iconology in the visual arts.

For purposes of ***Diana's Hunt,*** courtly Naples has reverted to a mythical "Parthenope," that Mediterranean promontory marked in antiquity by the name of the "virgin" whose tomb it kept. This woodland, timeless as its immortal visitants, is a preserve posted for women only. Diana, fifty-nine Angevin nymphs, and Venus define a fantasy sphere where there rules, with civilizing force, the feminine power of chastity and love. The allegorical meanings layered in the confrontation between ladies and beasts will presently unfold.

But first, another question: why did Boccaccio choose for his literary debut a poem dominated by women?

The idea clearly came to him from a youthful work of Dante's, one now lost, but known from a reference in the sixth chapter of the *Vita nuova.* There Dante mentions an epistolary *sirventese,* written to praise the sixty most beautiful ladies of Florence, among whom his most blessed Beatrice held ninth position:

> There came to me a wish to record the name of that most gentle one and to accompany it with many ladies' names. . . . And I took the names of sixty of the most beautiful ladies in the city where my lady was placed by the Lord most high, and I composed a letter in the form of a sirventese, which I shall not write here; and I should not have mentioned it were it not to say what happened, marvelously, as I was composing it, that is, that the name of my lady would not suffer to stand on any number other than on nine, among the names of these women.

The *sirventese,* a form that passed into Italy with the troubadours of Provence, could vary in versification as much as content, which was sometimes political, sometimes amorous. How, then, Dante would have devised his "letter" is hard to guess. Nor can we say whether Boccaccio knew it directly. In any event, secondhand information from the *Vita nuova,* our sole record, would have been sufficient. To answer his Tuscan model, Boccaccio prepared a Neapolitan counterpart, honoring by name fifty-eight noble women of Naples. With the narrator's anonymous Mystery Lady and Diana herself, the ladies Boccaccio assembles for his hunt come to the same total as those lauded on Dante's list.

Under the rubric of poetry in praise of women, a heading that broadly defines the *Hunt,* other medieval gynotypical conventions come into play. Notwithstanding social custom, which made hunting a pastime for males or mixed company, Diana's bands, by literary tradition, formed self-sufficient female communities. As Boccaccio would have it, these nymphs in "venery" are also servants of Venus, who comes at their behest to gladden all hearts. Women very properly take charge where love is at issue, for on that subject they are the experts: from Andreas Capellanus's twelfth-century manual, *On the Art of Courtly Love,* to Boccaccio's own *Filocolo,* when love was debated had not women always been the arbiters? Did not Guido Cavalcanti and Dante, puzzling over love's nature, address themselves to feminine interlocutors? "Ladies who have understanding of love" are precisely the audience of privilege whom Dante invokes to extol his "most blessed one" in the first canzone of the *Vita nuova.*

So Boccaccio, in accordance with convention, looks to the ladies. Like Dante, he has a chosen love object, the huntress who "for the other women's welfare [*salute*] . . . went much like a guardian to the head of the group to guide them safely" (1.49-51). As the stag-narrator's mistress, she is distanced and kept anonymous by the rule of secrecy in courtly romance. The stag, who evidently has committed to memory passages in both prose and poetry from the *Vita nuova,* claims that her name must be suppressed because he is unworthy of speaking it. Were Boccaccio to comment, he would adduce the custom of shielding milady's true identity with a *senhal,* or poetic sign. The sign behind which he chooses to screen his Mystery Lady in the *Hunt,* however, is not a false name, but a code number, a cipher that signals her symbolic character. Going by the qualities with which Boccaccio explicitly endows her, she can perform the same kind of miracles as Dante's Beatrice, who utterly dissipates evil, especially sensual thoughts in the men struck by her gaze: "When she goes walking, Love casts a frost into vile hearts from which their every thought freezes and perishes." Hers is a virtue contagious and irresistible, bringing salvation (*salute*) by guiding men to God.

In a wider sense, the power Dante attributes to Beatrice with his canzone in the nineteenth chapter of the *Vita nuova* applies to all the women in *Diana's Hunt.* The stag's mistress, with Medusan potential beneath her humanizing powers, has looks that kill unless they enkindle love: "Whoever gazes fixedly into her eyes becomes merciful or else must die" (18.29-30). Similarly, from the collective impact that the huntresses have on each creature they encounter, we can extrapolate the effect of any Angelic Lady on masculine admirers. Beatrice's eyes, like those of ancient forebearers and endless descendents in poetry, figuratively give forth "spirits kindled with love that strike the eyes of whoever then watches her, and passing inward, each one finds the heart." In witty parallel, the nymphs of Naples, armed with bows and arrows, actually shoot to death all the men/animals they find. Love's fatal glance

is delightfully literalized and, through happy operation, at once murders and turns its targets into "something noble," that is, changes them from beasts who die to men who come alive.

On one thematic level, then, *Diana's Hunt* capitalizes on a topos of the courtly and stilnovistic traditions, the ennobling power of women and love. It is a motif to which Boccaccio returned in later works—eventually, to the point of satirizing it. Those that repeat the pattern most obviously are the *Comedìa delle ninfe fiorentine,* or *Ameto,* which tells how seven nymphs "humanize" a young rustic; and, in sly mocking of a convention once so unquestioningly embraced, the first tale of the Fifth Day in the *Decameron:* "Cimone by loving becomes wise and kidnaps his lady Efigenia at sea."

Diana's Neapolitan nymphs, authorized by literary tradition, are women who act aggressively to achieve their goals. The preponderance and power of women in this early poem set a standard that held, one way and another, throughout Boccaccio's writing career. Many novelle of the *Decameron,* dedicated to women and mostly narrated by women, rely on resourceful female protagonists. In the *Elegia di madonna Fiammetta* (*Amorous Fiammetta*), Boccaccio produced the first psychological romance with a female heroine; in his *Corbaccio* he explored the rhetoric of misogyny. Some thirty years after *Diana's Hunt,* he would compose the first collection ever of female biographies, *De mulieribus claris* (*Concerning Famous Women*), to immortalize the daughters of Eve whose deeds, blameworthy or laudable, deserve remembrance. That book, as an author's preface explains, required a female dedicatee. Fearing the offering too poor for Queen Giovanna of Naples, he selected Andrea Acciaiuoli, countess of Altavilla. Her given name, from the Greek *andres* (men), proclaims of itself, the scholar points out, her superiority to her sex. But praise for her virile character masks Boccaccio's more practical motive for sending Andrea his volume of women's lives: it was her brother, Niccolò Acciaiuoli, who had risen in the Angevin realm to become Grand Seneschal of Naples, who was in a position to help Boccaccio financially. Unfortunately, the support Boccaccio needed and hoped to receive in his later years from Niccolò was never forthcoming; nevertheless, as a ploy to gain patronage, the dedication of *Concerning Famous Women* may tell us something about the ladies honored in his first work.

Diana's Hunt, we can assume, is dedicated to all whose names appear there. Not counting the stag's mistress, they are fifty-eight ladies of the Neapolitan aristocracy. Many are women otherwise lost to history. (What little is known of them we report in our Glossary.) Most are young, in their early teens, and still carry their patronymic. Of an age to marry, they may be humorously programmed for the poem as girls "hunting husbands" in the "virgin's territory," Parthenope.

At the same time, nomenclature suggests that Boccaccio had more in mind than a gallant tribute, sounded with nuptial overtones, to the fairest damsels of the land. The budding poet clearly delights in caressing their names, whose forms and variants serve not only the wonderful pleasure of a medieval list, but resonate in themselves with euphony and rhythm. How quaintly they echo through the verses of the *Hunt* struck Francesco Torraca, who observed that "not less than nine are called Caterina. Three are the Vanellas, three the Zizzolas, three the Jacopas—Jacopa, Giacovella, Covella—three the Ceccas or Ceccolas, two the Beritas or Beritolas." But sheer joy in words, girlish names reeled off with paronomastic verve, is only one side of Boccaccio's play. In his strategy, the family and its cognomen count for just as much, if not more, than given names and sweet diminutives. It is no accident that the lady summoned at the start of the messenger's list—she who stands on number one, as Dante would have liked to put it—happens to be Zizzola Barrile. Although Zizzola eludes fuller identification, her surname is significant. Highly esteemed by both community and court, the Barrile (or Barrili) were blue bloods in the Capuan See, a neighborhood that boasted the rich cream of Neapolitan aristocracy. Giovanni Barrile, Captain General of Calabria and Chamberlain to King Robert, was one of those "citizens of probity" whose opinion the sovereign sought in 1332, before promulgating a law "against ribalds and heinous men who kidnap virgins under the pretense of marriage." In 1341 he would have represented his king at Petrarch's coronation as poet laureate on the Campidoglio, had he not fallen among thieves on the way to Rome. Like Petrarch, Boccaccio was a friend of Giovanni, a gentleman whose culture he compliments in his facetious dialect letter to Franceschino de' Bardi—"isso sape quant'a lu demone" (that fellow knows as much as the Devil)—and whom he calls more reverently, in honor of conversations they used to have about Virgil, "magni spiritus homo, Iohannes Barillus" (a man of great spirit) in the *Genealogie* XIV, 19. *Diana's Hunt* honors not only noblewomen of Naples but their kinsfolk as well, and thus, indirectly, the leading men of the Kingdom. The author aimed, in other words, to attract attention in glamorous social quarters, as he would again when, dreaming of a triumphal return to Naples from Florence in the early 1360s, he dedicated *Concerning Famous Women* to Niccolò Acciaiuoli's sister. He hoped for patronage beyond the ladies' power to give, but well within the political reach of their fathers.

A classic mythological rivalry between Diana and Venus propels the poem's dynamics, keyed most obviously to Ovid. His *Metamorphoses* depict the quiver-bearing huntress in her forest retreats, shady grottoes with flowing streams that sealed the fates of Callisto, seduced to love by Jove (*Met.* 2.409ff.) and Actaeon after he glimpsed her bathing (*Met.* 3.155ff.). These settings return in the *locus amoenus* of Boccaccio's *Hunt,* where Diana leads her nymphs to bathe in a woodland spring before deploying them as a general would. The Calydonian boar hunt (*Met.* 8.271ff.) may have contributed to the fiercely aggressive rhythm of their chase overall, as well as some detail, such as descriptions of those marshlands on the plain where waterfowl are captured. The stag-narrator's final transformation amusingly inverts Actaeon's punishment in the same way that the climactic metamorphosis of beasts en masse overturns that Ovidian archetype.

Although important features of this Italian fiction depend

directly on Ovid, nowhere in the *Metamorphoses* is there a hunt that can account for the general pattern of Boccaccio's. Precedent for the structure in his strategy, previously unnoted, appears in the late-classical author Claudian, who in the Trecento ranked as a Florentine of fame. His panegyric *On Stilicho's Consulship* culminates with a global chase orchestrated by Diana to provide caged animals from every corner of the empire for spectacles in the Roman arena. Claudian's Diana, from dizzying Alpine heights, summons her companions seriatim by name, and those initially convened are then joined by a second band. On instructions from the goddess, they divide and hunt in every direction. Diana will go down to the Lybian desert; others, followed by dogs of various breeds, lead their parties east to Dalmatia and Mount Pindus; north to the lowlands of Gaul and Germany; they scour the Alps and Apennines at Europe's center, head west to the banks of the Iberian Tagus; and south to the islands of Corsica and Sicily. Claudian sums up the reach of their operation:

> Whatsoever inspires fear with its teeth, wonder with its mane, awe with its horns and bristling coat—all the beauty, all the terror of the forest is taken. Guile protects them not; neither strength nor weight avails them; their speed saves not the fleet of foot.

Both borrowings and calculated departures from the Latin source are evident. In each case Diana musters a hunt; she and her captains spread out in the cardinal directions to stalk quarry of every description, hunting with hounds high and low, from mountain peak to marshy bottom. Claudian's goddess makes her appearance at the top of Italy, in the Alps; Boccaccio's comes to the bay of Naples, in the boot's foot. Claudian counts his ladies out loud: Diana plus seven chieftans in the first wave, three parties of one hundred in the second. Boccaccio, too, arranges roll calls, but instead of recording how many were present in all, he leaves it for us to count and interpret the numbers at play in his lists.

Beyond any doubt, the authority most influential in Boccaccio's poetic debut was Dante, his "first guiding light." Many verses of the *Hunt* echo passages in the *Divine Comedy.* Particularly striking are parallels with the last cantos of *Purgatory,* where Dante enters Eden. Notable among them is the stag's description of his secret mistress as "that lady whose face seems always to burn with love" (4.11-12), an epithet that repeats almost verbatim Dante's allusion to Venus, "who seems always burning with the fire of love" in the third of his predawn dreams on the purgatorial mount (*Purg.* 27.96). The connection is appropriate, since it is that unnamed lady who at the end of the *Hunt* will be the one to summon Venus.

Precedent for the catalog of ladies that structures Diana's *Hunt* can also be found in Dante's *Commedia,* if one recalls his many lists of personae, such as those populating Limbo. Boccaccio's decision to compile a census of highborn Neapolitan women was prompted specifically, however, by Dante's "*sirventese* in the form of an epistle." If he did not have direct knowledge of it, his tribute to the women of Parthenope indicates the extensive borrowings he made from the *Vita nuova* itself. That small book contributed significantly to the **Hunt's** last cantos, in which Venus quite literally brings new life both to the burning beasts captured by Diana's companions and to the poem's unhappy cervine narrator. The marvelous effects of love, described there in the manner of the *dolce stil nuovo,* are revealed to the stag by his Mystery Lady, a figure with angelic attributes inspired by Beatrice. Her newly appointed servant praises her at the end of the **Hunt** in words that recall the *Vita nuova's* concluding promise, his final hopeful word, "salvation," being none other than Dante's focal signifier, *"salute."*

By metrical format, Boccaccio's *sirventese* is a *ternario,* that is, a composition in hendecasyllables of terza rima. Dante had invented this rhyme scheme (ABA, BCB, CDC) for his *Comedìa,* setting it into a sequence of one hundred cantos, 115 to 160 verses long, for a total of 14,233 lines. Boccaccio's small-scale poem contains eighteen cantos, all but one with fifty-eight verses (Canto 3 has sixty-one), the sum being 1,047 lines. The younger poet's appropriation of Dante's new terza rima is an important clue to the kind of poem he was writing. The **Hunt,** too, is an allegorical drama of conflicts between evil and virtue in man's soul.

Antagonists to the huntresses are a forestful of beasts. Over one hundred strong—the narrator tells us that they are actually too numerous for exact reckoning (Canto 8.56-57)—they number close to thirty distinct types: roebucks, hares, boars, stags, wolves, a leopard, foxes, bears, a lion cub, hedgehogs, tigers, rabbits, a unicorn, a crane, mallards, a cormorant, a *paolin* (8.55), a beaver, an elephant, seven serpents, a fallow deer, a panther, a bull, a porcupine, a hydra, two swans, and an ostrich. From the character of this list, it is clear that Boccaccio's acquaintance with most of these animals came neither from nature walks nor from outings with court hunting parties. On the contrary, he probably encountered almost all of them in the library through bestiaries and sundry florilegia of the church fathers.

Boccaccio at Naples had access to bestiaries from several of the many branches into which that popular genre had, from antiquity, been multiplied and cloned. Classical texts, such as Aristotle's *Historia Animalium* and Pliny's *Natural History,* had provided material for the ancestor of the European moralized bestiary, a curious Greek archetype dating from about A.D. 200. To the Middle Ages it was known as the work of "Physiologus," or alternatively, that name was considered its title, *Physiologus.* From that source there evolved the *Physiologus* family of texts, whose voices became a sort of "standard reference," although in a richly varied, complex tradition of versions, Latin and vernacular. Through the centuries *Physiologus* was transmitted by encyclopediasts who added to and adapted it as their contexts warranted: authorities such as Isidore of Seville, Rabanus Maurus, Peter of Beauvais, Thomas of Cantimpré, and Brunetto Latini were joined by the anonymous popular compilers of the Italian *Bestiario moralizzato, Il bestiario toscano,* and the *Tusco-Venetian Bestiary.* Never intended as works of natural history (the unaltered text of Pliny and later, Saint Albertus Magnus's *De animalibus* filled that need), the curious and fanciful "books

of beasts" were rather a source of exempla and ethical teaching and a rich font of poetic imagery throughout the Middle Ages, one from which the youthful Boccaccio eagerly drew for many of the adventures in the **Hunt.**

In Southern Italy, from the first half of the thirteenth century, when the Swabian house of Palermo began patronizing Greek and Arabic scholarship, the natural sciences had been subjects of special cultivation. Emperor Frederick II had personally encouraged a zoological tradition not only by establishing a private zoo but also by writing *De arte venandi cum avibus* (*The Art of Falconry*). His treatise, which became and remains a standard even for modern hawking enthusiasts, contains scrupulously detailed information about the life cycles, habits, training, and use of many birds of prey.

With the transition from Swabian to Angevin rule, bestiaries proper began to appear, bearing testimony to ties between the French court at Naples and culture in the mother country. At least two such works are known to survive from the second half of the thirteenth century, ascribed to the Neapolitan area. Exactly which texts Boccaccio may have consulted has not been established. But in spite of individual variations and occasional eccentricities, the bestiaries generally retain certain unchanging features, and these are reflected in **Diana's Hunt,** very much a product of the most traditional, enduring lore.

Typically, as *Physiologus* attests, the bestiary includes an admirable variety of animals, starting with the lion, King of Beasts. In his train come a parade of quadrupeds, bipeds, insects, various categories of birds and fish, and even fantastic composite species such as the giant hydra, the sirens, the griffin, the basilisk, the "lanzanus," and the man-eating manticore. As impressive as this range of types are the amazing habits (*naturae*) peculiar to each animal: the ferocious unicorn can only be subdued by a virgin; the elephant, with unjointed legs, topples helplessly when he leans to nap against a tree partly sawn through by the patient hunter; the beaver (*castor*), when pursued, obligingly castrates himself to give the hunters the medicinal prize they seek; the swan sings along in rhythm and harmony with the harpist; the "mild" panther attracts other animals by his sweet breath.

But wondrous species and behavior traits are only half of the Christian bestiary. To complete each entry in his zoological dictionary, or confront them in a Bible passage, an author had to moralize his animals. Sometimes the meaning was positive (*in bono* or *in bonam partem*), such as when the beast could be likened to Christ. This was true, for example, of the regal lion, who delighted in mountain heights, carefully brushed away its tracks with its tail, and gave birth to dead cubs animated by the breath of life from their sire on the third day. In allegory this signified the Lord Christ, who sought high places for proximity with God the Father; in the lion's deception of the hunters the moralizers glimpsed the theological "pious fraud" by which Christ's divinity was concealed from the Devil to enable mankind's salvation; in the quickening of the lion cubs they saw the resurrection of Christ on the Third Day after the Crucifixion. Far more often, the beast stood for diabolical powers (symbolism *in malo* or *in malam partem*): the lion could be Satan on watch to catch the unwary sinner; the wolf signified pride and the Devil; the leopard symbolized fraud; the fox, whose name (*vulpis*) was said to derive from "twisted foot" (*volupes*), was an emblem of heresy whose trickery made him kin to the Temptor.

On these symbolisms, both *in malo* and *in bono,* turned small but critical moral dramas. Christ, Man, and the Devil performed as their three main characters. What conflict they enacted came down quite simply to the eternal struggle involving the choice between God and Satan, between good and evil. Thus, when a lion challenged the hunter he was Christ, whom all good men should diligently pursue. The leopard, decorated with spots that implied treachery, should remind any devout Christian to shun deceptions practiced by the Devil.

We can see how elaborate these morality lessons could be by examining three cases from the **Hunt:** Covella d'Anna's maniacal pursuit and strangulation of an ostrich (Canto 15); the capture and killing of rabbits and hares (Cantos 3 and 6); and Berarda's gathering up of the hedgehogs in the lap of her dress (Canto 5).

In the first case—involving, actually, the last animal to be slaughtered in the poem—Covella's ferocity seems unmotivated and incomprehensible. The fleeing ostrich, oddly out of place in the environs of Naples, seems the barest threat to her, for its only belligerence is its occasional turn to flail its wings. She is, however, aflame to destroy it, lacerating her body and clothes in her obsessive chase. Clearly, on the literal level, we are to remark the inconsistency between the provocation and reaction; clearly, too, the author means that we note it as a jarring rupture.

A full explanation comes from the conventional reputation of the ostrich among the fathers of the church. The generally favorable moral view of the bird given in the bestiaries from the *Physiologus* tradition—it ignores its eggs after laying them as a good Christian should scorn the goods of this world—was given an opposite, negative interpretation in biblical exegesis following the wide wake cut by Saint Gregory the Great. Commenting on the bird's neglect of its eggs in Job 39:13-14, Gregory saw the ostrich as the type of the fraudulent dissembler or hypocrite neglecting all for its own pride, gain, and ambition. "It raises its wings as if to fly, but yet never raises itself from the earth by flight. Thus doubtless are all dissemblers, who, while they simulate the conduct of the good, possess a resemblance of holy appearance, but have no reality of holy conduct."

The widespread patristic "wings of fraud" topos springs from this passage in Gregory: compare the pseudo-Rabanus Maurus's *Allegoriae in Sacram Scripturam:* "By wings . . . is meant the purposes of the dissembler"; or Richard of St. Victor's *De eruditione* 3.12: "Do you still want to know more fully what sort of wings fraudulence has? . . . Let one be said of simulation, the second of dissimulation, the third of ostentation, the fourth of excuse." Thus, the one detail that Boccaccio gives us concerning the bird, its habit of beating its wings as if to fly, is the very behavior that church doctors saw as an analogy to fraud.

Fraud is the worst of sins, since it involves the misuse of man's divine mind; the huntress rips off the bird's head because the head is the seat of the intellect. Covella's fear of the flapping wings and the energy with which she decapitates this bird can be understood best in terms of the struggle between virtue and vice at the allegorical level. As the worst of sins and as the sin "peculiar to man" (as Dante had said in *Inferno* 11.25, "de l'uom proprio male"), the ostrich is fittingly last to be routed.

Similar moral situations can be seen in the capture and slaughter of the rabbits and hares. At first (Canto 3.26-27), they seem to appear simply as a realistic detail in a passing observation of the stag: "hares, headed toward the mountain." Not so, as we learn when we check the literary tradition. In Saint Albertus Magnus's *De animalibus,* and in amalgamated bestiary texts, such as that of Thomas of Cantimpré, we find the widespread item of lore that hares run uphill more easily than down: "Its back legs, by which it goes along, are longer, and therefore, it is easier for it to ascend a mountain than descend it." The hare, thus, was the conventional figure, *in malam partem,* of the learned philosopher, who would mount upward in pride, yet could not descend to humility. The writer of the *Allegoria in Sacram Scripturam,* believed in Boccaccio's time to be Rabanus Maurus and widely followed, informs us with his typical logic, "The hare [rabbit] is any wicked person, yet one who is learned in the law. 'The hare, for that too cheweth the cud' [Lev. 11:6]. Because, although they are wicked, they are nonetheless learned." *In bonam partem,* the creature could signify those who turned to the good in the "hind part" of their days and easily ascend to heaven!

Less arcane, perhaps, is leporine symbolism in the secular literary tradition. A mythological attribute of Venus, the prolific rabbit signified *lussuria,* or carnality. Thus, to show the Virgin Mary's victory over lust, medieval and Renaissance painters would depict a white hare at her feet. In **Diana's Hunt,** hares and rabbits are little creatures large with allusive possibilities: they point to Venus, to the sins of pride and lechery, and, more generally, to human sexuality, which chastity and reason must raise from sinful lapses to civilized levels of expression.

The case of the humble hedgehog (*ericius*) is again most telling. In Canto 5.55-58, Berarda makes a "novel" capture with her hounds: "She had caught six hedgehogs [*ricci*], no less, and fearful of being pricked, she was carrying them wrapped up in her lap." This episode, briefly mentioned at the close of a canto whose dominant event is the capture of two tough-hided bears, at first seems trivial, merely an addendum recounted from observation of the hedgehog's protective habit of rolling itself into a spiky ball when threatened. Religious tradition and the bestiaries, however, can again demonstrate satisfactorily how Boccaccio's *riccio* might be bound to a spiritual sense.

The spiny hedgehog habitually steals grapes by pilfering in vine-yards, snapping off clusters, and then rolling on the ground to impale the pieces of fruit on his spikes. These very spines—the prickles that threaten the huntress on the literal level of the poem and that are enclosed suggestively in her lap—are the devil's traps: they can make man as sterile and empty as the vineyard thus despoiled.

The Bible and its commentators reveal even more concerning the hedgehog. The creature appears in a wrathful prophecy in Isaiah 32:2-15:

> The indignation of the Lord is upon all nations, and his fury upon their armies: he hath killed them and delivered them to slaughter. . . . And the unicorns shall go down with them, and the bulls with the mighty; their land shall be soaked with blood. . . . it is the day of vengeance of the Lord, the year of recompense of the judgment of Sion. . . . The bittern and the ericius [the hedgehog] shall possess [the land]. . . . there hath the ericius had its hole and brought up its young ones, and hath dug about and cherished them in the shadow thereof.

Contrary to what we would expect to be the meaning of this hedgehog at its family burrow—perhaps some model for the parent who protects threatened offspring—Saint Gregory equates the animal's behavior upon being captured with the exacerbating sin of self-exculpation, "the defense of wicked minds." The fervor and choplogic, so typical of his analogical reasoning, make that Father's arguments from the *Moralia in Job* worth citing at length:

> Under the name of "hedgehog" is designated the defense of wicked minds; because, namely, when a hedgehog is being seized, his head is seen, and his feet appear, and all his body is beheld; but presently, as soon as he has been seized, he gathers himself up into a ball, draws his feet inward, hides his head; and the whole which was before seen at once, is lost at once in the hands of him that holds it. Thus, doubtless, are wicked minds, when they are caught in their own excesses. For the head of the hedgehog is seen, because it is seen with what beginnings the sinner made his approach to sin. The feet of the hedgehog are seen, because it is seen with what footsteps his wickedness has been perpetrated; and yet the wicked mind, by suddenly adducing its excuses, draws its feet inward, because it conceals all the footsteps of its iniquity. It withdraws its head, because, by its extraordinary defenses, it gives the impression that it has never even begun anything wicked; and it remains as a ball in the hand of him that holds it, because he who reproves a sinner involved within his conscience, and he who had before seen the whole, by detecting it being deceived by the evasion of the wicked defense, is equally ignorant of the whole. The hedgehog therefore has a "hole" in the reprobate, because the wicked mind, gathering itself within itself, hides in the darkness of its defense. But the Divine discourse shews us also how the sinner—in thus excusing himself, and in thus clouding over, by his defenses which serve to obscure, the eye of the reprover which is fastened upon him—is supported by those who are like him.

Other church authorities condemned hedgehogs as "duplices et dolosi" (duplicitous and crafty), figures of fraud, like the ostrich. These details of animal lore, so markedly specific, suggest that Boccaccio was well acquainted with Gregory's "arsenal" of figurative language. If he did not know the *Morals on the Book of Job* in their entirety by the time he wrote the *Hunt,* he had at least acquired good portions of them as a student of canon law through excerpts, epitomes, or through uncredited patristic citations. Gregory's voluminous corpus was, along with the works of Saint Augustine, the richest source of ecclesiastical imagery in the later Middle Ages. His *Morals,* not merely the standard authority on Job, but a towering column of biblical commentary that gave theologians a common discourse, was still basic for Boccaccio when he wrote the *Trattatello in laude di Dante (Short Treatise in Praise of Dante)* (begun ca. 1350); there he was to adapt the fundamental Gregorian definition of allegory in Scripture to his own cornerstone discussion of allegory in poetry. Gregory's *Moralia in Job,* and the exegetical tradition that had grown around them for eight centuries, may help explain how these episodes in the *Hunt* form an integral part of the psychomachic allegoresis in which the youthful Boccaccio was working.

What most strikes us is how greatly the weighty patristic interpretations, particularly of the hedgehog and hare, contrast with the light-hearted innocence of the literal level in the poem. Yet, in the light of Boccaccio's aesthetics such daring tension between letter and spirit was a poetic ideal.

Medieval hunt literature, a broad category of writings to which the *Hunt* belongs, has come down to us in many branches. The oldest, offshoots of prototypes composed in antiquity by Xenophon and Oppian, are cynegetic manuals. Treatises on coursing the stag, such as the Middle Eastern *Moamin et Ghatrif,* were transmitted to the Latin West around mid-thirteenth century through the Sicilian court of Emperor Frederick II, who was a published expert on hawking. Bookish advice, if not the sport itself, was evidently familiar to Boccaccio, since his huntswomen owe moments of success to techniques advocated by the manuals. They know, for instance, how to gauge a bird to down a chosen quarry and how to reward it, how to snare prey by spreading nets or baiting a pitfall, and how to flush fowl with beaters.

During the fourteenth century, practical and scientific texts of this sort were to evolve into a popular genre with an aesthetic and ethical intent. Most famous was Henri de Ferrières's lavishly illustrated *Livres du roy Modus et de la royne Ratio,* or *Book of King Modus and Queen Ratio* (ca. 1354-1376), a French etiquette of temperance whose embellishments include allegories of the stag and boar. A prologue tells how "Measure," or "Method," the symbolic ruler of its title, "organized all the sports of hunting to save us from laziness." That idea, as old as Ovid's *Remedies of Love (Remedia amoris,* 199-210), had become a commonplace among notions associated with the hunt. Thus the *Livre de chasse (Book of the Hunt)* written in 1387 by Gaston Phébus, count of Foix, could stress the salubrious effects of hunting on the soul because it forestalled the sin of sloth: we should hunt eagerly "to remove cause for idleness, which is at the root of all evils." Although these texts postdate Boccaccio's, they reflect the courtly and aristocratic climate, hospitable to "spiritual-ized" hunting, in which his poem was conceived. The art of venery was an easy rhetorical vehicle for allegory; hunting had parallel physical and moral benefits.

Yet not quite everyone agreed on its salubrious qualities. Danger could lie in its potential for arousing the passions, a problem attested by the sad case of Dido: the thunderstorm that disrupted her day in the forest with Aeneas (*Aeneid* 4.117ff.) drove the couple to a cave for shelter, and the queen's honor was lost. Mindful of this sensual pitfall, John of Salisbury attacked the sport as immoral, and he supposed that the ancients appointed a goddess rather than a god to preside over it because they would not have wanted to debase one of their more important immortals by assigning him a province ridden with self-indulgence and vice.

Although hunting was a universal human activity, and many medieval heroes such as Saint Eustace, Siegfried, and Sir Gawain reflected its acceptance in circles both pious and courtly, John of Salisbury speaks from a long history of poetic fictions that associated the "venery" of the hunt with the "venery" of love. Ovid, who counted the chase an antidote to love in *Remedies of Love,* had by contrast in the *Art of Love* played upon the metaphor of the hunt as amatory pursuit. Similar vocabulary, casting the lover as hunter, returns in the preface to *The Art of Courtly Love* by Ovid's late twelfth-century admirer, Andreas Capellanus. The popularity of coupling the two sorts of pursuit, widely exploited in the language of lyric and narrative poetry, was reinforced by possibilities for punning in both Latin and the Romance languages alike on words such as *"venerie," "venatio," "venison," "Venus,"* and "venereal." In this tradition, since both Cupid and the hunter are bowmen, it is the lover who is stalker and his lady the quarry. That relationship structures the earliest French allegory of the love chase, *Li dis dou cerf amoreus* (*The Tale of the Amorous Stag*), composed in 326 verses around mid-thirteenth century. There the hart represents the woman, forced to her knees and acceptance of love by Amours, the hunter. The image may ultimately descend from a Virgilian *locus classicus,* verses in which Dido, love-stricken for Aeneas, is likened to a helpless, wounded hind:

> Unhappy Dido burns, and through the city wanders in frenzy—even as a hind, smitten by an arrow, which, all unwary, amid the Cretan woods, a shepherd hunting with darts has pierced from afar, leaving in her the winged steel, unknowing: she in flight ranges Dictaean woods and glades, but fast to her side clings the deadly shaft.

Medieval allegories of the "sanguinary stag," as Marcelle Thiébaux labels this bloodied, love-struck figure [in his *Stag,* 1974], sometimes reverse the roles of lover and beloved. Love's victim, then, is the male stag-lover. *La prise amoureuse* (*Love's Capture*), dated April 1332, by the French court poet Jean Acart (or Acars) de Hesdin, presents just such a fiction. Could Acart's piece, written one year before the biennium to which *Diana's Hunt* is assigned (1333-1334), have traveled from the court of France to the French Angevin court of Naples and reached Boccaccio? Whatever the answer, Acart speaks

"par mistère"—"mysteriously," that is, allegorically—to bring his readers more pleasure. His protagonist and narrator is a stag who wanders in springtime through "a forest of youth." Four routes traverse it where Love often hunts with his hounds. Most of the hounds are allegories of the lady's qualities (Beauty, Courtesy, Sweetness, and so on), the attractions that will wound and ambush the stag-narrator. His death signifies his complete surrender to her; the portions of the eviscerated quarry (in Old French, *curée*) she receives are his heart and will. The lover ends his poem with a plea for the lady to have pity and care for him.

Whether Boccaccio knew Acart or not, the stag-narrators they each created are literary cousins. In *Diana's Hunt,* however, the love-wounded stag does not suffer capture and evisceration. He is rescued from love's blows and raised to a better state, changed, as if by magic, from beast into man. That moment is both a reversal and a renewal. As reversal, it may parry Acart's picture of a passion destructive unto death. It certainly counters, by the technique of narrative antithesis, Ovid's Actaeon, the man degraded to a brute hounded and doomed. [The] stag is a symbol also of renewal, and the transformation of Boccaccio's stag alludes to that animal's legendary capacity for rejuvenation. His attainment of a "new life," based on lore in the bestiaries, reenacts allegorically the sacrament of Christian baptism.

James H. McGregor   (essay date 1991)

SOURCE: *The Shades of Aeneas: The Imitation of Vergil and the History of Paganism in Boccaccio's "Filostrato," "Filocolo," and "Teseida,"* The University of Georgia Press, 1991, 133 p.

[*McGregor is an American classicist who has examined the impact of the literature of antiquity on Boccaccio's writings. In the excerpt below, he studies how in the* Teseida *Boccaccio addresses the differences between the classical past and his own Christian era, focusing on the poet's understanding of Vergil's judgment of pre-Christian culture. McGregor also scrutinizes the* Tesida's *major characters, stating that while the poem is based on Statius's* Thebaid, *its protagonists are more closely identified with the leading figures of Vergil's* Aeneid.]

Like the *Filostrato* or *Filocolo, Teseida* is a work in which an event in the history of the pagan world is depicted in terms of the fundamental forces in human nature and human history that Christianity identifies. *Filostrato* shows how one kind of love and a disobedience to divine suggestion lead to personal and civic disaster. *Filocolo* shows the opposite: how a love that does not set itself apart from the divine leads to miraculous results, not just for individuals but for nations as well. *Teseida,* too, focuses on a great historical situation, the conquest of Thebes by Athens. In *Teseida,* Thebes comes to represent the libidinous aspect of man, and Athens, the human capacity for self-control, but the poem demonstrates the impossibility of such control in the absence of divine collaboration. In *Filostrato,* Troilus refuses to collaborate with deities closely linked to Christian Providence. In *Teseida,* however, pagan divinities are represented not as veiled figures of God's Providence but as demons. *Teseida* therefore shows the failure of human virtue, when it is not aided by grace, to exert control over human passions. It shows, in effect, the failure of pagan efforts to rule the irrational side of human nature and argues implicitly, therefore, for the necessity of Christian faith.

The story of Palemone and Arcita, two of the major protagonists in *Teseida,* is like that of Troilus. These men suffer the consequences of a dominating and ultimately destructive love. The *Teseida,* however, adds a further dimension to their story when it places Theseus over these men as ruler and as one who attempts to exert over them a control that they cannot manage. Theseus is a great man, relatively unmoved by passion, and willing to obey the gods, yet he fails to impose effective control on the lovers' behavior. His failure is not personal but lies in forces beyond his control. They are, as we will see, historical ones. Theseus's failure represents the failure of pagan men, even at their best, to impose control on man's fallen nature.

Neither *Filostrato* nor *Filocolo* hesitates to describe the behavior of pagan men and pagan communities in terms of Christian virtues. In these texts, Boccaccio treats such virtues as universally valid and sees them as at least potentially within the reach of men unenlightened by Christian revelation. In *Teseida* he turns away from this optimistic view, and, while he continues to maintain the universal validity of Christian truth, he depicts the inability of a pagan community, which is not itself vicious, to achieve the control of human passion. The reason for this failure is probably found in the historical situation of Athens. Both *Filostrato* and *Filocolo* depict events in the history of Rome that are linked by Vergil and Orosius to divinely sponsored destinies. The Athens of Theseus, however, is not part of this providential scheme. The face of divinity that Theseus encounters is not crypto-Christian and providential but ultimately satanic. Divorced from great actions in which God's Providence is at work, Theseus experiences the demonic dominance of human fate that governed the majority of mankind before the Incarnation. Theseus is a pagan whose individual efforts at goodness are thwarted by the historical and religious situation of the world in his era.

This more pessimistic theme is accompanied by a significant development in the way the ancient world is presented. It centers in Boccaccio's darker vision of the nature of pagan divinity. . . . [Boccaccio] represented the contact between men and gods primarily through dreams and epiphanies. In the *Teseida* contact with the gods, almost without exception, takes place within temples and is part of the normal course of pagan worship. Temples become the meeting place of men and gods, and that pattern, so characteristic of the heroic life, both in Boccaccio's earlier works and in Vergil's works, of direct and personal contact between men and gods, is for the most part absent in *Teseida.* Temples and related monuments embody the formal contact between worshiper and deity. Moreover, these structures are so placed in *Teseida* that they symbolize the development of Boccaccio's social and theological argument there. In effect, then, Boccaccio has made artifacts

of the ancient world, which he has constructed with all the verisimilar skill at his command, the bearers of the thematic structure of his work. Ancient monuments serving their pagan religious purpose act as thematic signposts in the structure of a work about paganism. This is an extraordinarily successful means of connecting the larger historical situation with the conduct of individual life, for temples serve as the meeting points of cosmic and individual action. Not only the historical situation, then, but also the classicizing details of scene and setting carry out Boccaccio's argument in *Teseida.*

In this [essay] . . . I will describe the shape of Boccaccio's argument in *Teseida* and the temples that punctuate his argument. I will describe the wilderness that occupies the middle of the poem and then sketch out the sequence of civic monuments that represent Athens's attempt to impose reason on savage men, the limited success of that attempt, and the divine settlement the city must finally accept. In the process I hope to reveal in *Teseida* a level of organization and sophistication that has not been observed and an integration . . . of classical setting and action to produce a coherent argument about the limitations of historical paganism.

Critics have seen Boccaccio's *Teseida delle nozze d'Emilia* as the closest the poet ever came to harnessing the two forces always at play in his Neapolitan works. On the one hand, the work is seen as classicizing, and Boccaccio is credited with a degree of erudition, especially in the glosses he composed to accompany the poem, that looks forward to his mature work of this type, the *Genealogies of the Pagan Gods.* On the other hand, the work is clearly a romance, and, like *Filostrato* and *Filocolo,* it is patterned on French examples. Critics have generally agreed that, while these two aspects of *Teseida* are both more skillfully carried off and more successfully integrated than in the other poems of this period, the blending of the love story of Palemone and Arcita with the martial themes of Theseus's success in battle and his clemency is, finally, imperfect. The poem's own claim that it is "the first to sing of Mars in the Italian vernacular" (*Tes.* 12.84) and, as such, is entitled to membership in the epic tradition is generally not granted.

Teseida is unified, however. From beginning to end it is, as the title suggests, a Thesead. Theseus is its central character, and the episodes in the poem represent a series of problems presented to him. In book 1, he faces the cruel and pitiless Amazons, whom he conquers. In the second book, he conquers the impious Creon. His motives in both cases are good ones, and his actions are effective. From each of these foreign campaigns he brings home prizes. From Scythia, the land of the Amazons, he brings his bride, Hippolyta, and her younger sister, Emilia. After conquering Creon, he leads in triumph the last survivors of the Theban royal house, Palemone and Arcita. These living spoils of war, Emilia, Palemone, and Arcita, once they return to Athens, soon begin to interact: both Thebans fall in love with Emilia and so become increasingly savage rivals. Their interaction presents Theseus with a complex domestic crisis that is in effect an internalization of the conflicts he has resolved abroad by war. His efforts to control and direct at home the passions he has subordinated abroad, his failure to achieve this control, and his response as well as Athens's response to this failure make up the climax of the *Teseida.*

The plot of the poem is unified, then, although a combination or *contaminatio* of classical sources is recognizable in it. The imitative core of the poem is not the structure of Statius's *Thebaid* but its theme, the resolution by the godlike Theseus (with the collaboration of the gods and fate) of the civil and fratricidal war of the Seven against Thebes. Statius's poem is an indirect model, however; the last event in *Thebaid,* Theseus's decisive intervention against Creon, occurs very early in *Teseida.* Boccaccio's poem is partly a continuation of the *Thebaid,* then, but it is also a response to it. He distances *Teseida* from Statius's poem by inverting the order of episodes in *Thebaid* and by inserting into it a partially disguised version of the second half of the *Aeneid.* From the moment Palemone and Arcita agree to fight for the love of Emilia, Boccaccio characterizes them, as I will show, as Aeneas and Turnus. Thus there are two Aeneases in the poem—the furious Palemone and the pious, self-controlled Theseus. Emilia, whose Latinate name recalls an Italian place-name, plays the part, both logically and explicitly, of Lavinia, Aeneas's Italian bride-to-be. For the single combat Emilia's rivals have sworn, Theseus substitutes a more restricted form of combat. This duel breaks down, as does that between Aeneas and Turnus, and gives rise to a war in Theseus's amphitheater which is frequently punctuated with explicit references to the Italian warfare described in *Aeneid* 9-12. The gods finally intervene in the Athenian contest, as they do in the duel with Turnus, and force a result. This ends the Vergilian portion of the narrative, since the *Aeneid* itself ends with the death of Turnus. That much of the poem is described in this [essay]. . . .

The actions of these complexly intertwined Christian, Vergilian, and Statian plots take place within a landscape punctuated by a series of pagan monuments. Through the integration of these actions, rich in their reminiscences of Latin epic, and the monumental architecture of *Teseida,* a complex and far-reaching unity is achieved.

In the first book of *Teseida,* Theseus sets out to avenge the Amazons' murder of their husbands. Apparently fed up with masculine control, these women have rebelled and now rule themselves. Boccaccio's opinion of their action is unmistakable: it reveals them as "crude e dispietate" ["savage and without *pietas*"] (*Tes.* 1.6.2). By invoking the term "dispietate," Boccaccio seems to reflect its double sense, as lacking compassion on the one hand and negligent or irresponsible on the other. Theseus, who opposes them, is portrayed with increasing insistence as *pius.* Such a characterization, of course, suggests Aeneas, the "man outstanding for *pietas,*" as Vergil describes him (*Aen.* 1.10). Thus the confrontation between Theseus and the Amazons emerges as an essentially Vergilian conflict of almost emblematic quality, pitting cruelty and barbarism against Theseus's civilized virtues of compassion and responsibility.

The Amazons defend themselves with great strength and skill, and Theseus has the greatest difficulty making headway against them. Besieging them, he undermines their walls, and they at last recognize the impossibility of further resistance. They recognize at the same moment that their position is untenable not only physically but spiritually as well. Hippolyta sees the gods and not just Theseus opposing them (*Tes.* 1.116). Venus in particular, she believes, is their opponent; and the goddess has recruited Mars to aid Theseus (*Tes.* 1.117). When Theseus emerges as the victor, Hippolyta senses that he is not a cruel man. Indeed, he has the reputation of being "humble and easy to one who humbles himself" (*Tes.* 1.121, 4).

Moreover, in these portrayals by Hippolyta, Theseus comes to resemble Aeneas. He is supported by Venus, as Aeneas is. She sees him as one who also responds gently to those who are humble. This characteristic is one Aeneas is urged to adopt, although he cannot always achieve it. Anchises, as part of the procession of Roman descendants he shows his son, urges him "to impose the habit of peace, to spare the humble and to make war against the proud" (*Aen.* 6.852-53). There is no reason to be ashamed of submission to this man, as Hippolyta recognizes. Since the Amazons *are* women, there can be no shame in *acting* as women do (*Tes.* 1.121).

It is this recognition that finally makes the "natural" solution to the war possible. Theseus is a man, Hippolyta a woman; they can end their strife by marriage as well as by treaty, and this is what they both agree and desire to do. For their wedding, the temple of Venus, which the Amazon women had "serrato ne' lor primi mutamenti" ["barred up in their first rebellion"] (*Tes.* 1.134.3), is reopened, and a mass wedding ensues (*Tes.* 1.135). All the conditions of the Amazons' rebellion are reconciled by this wedding.

In this solution Theseus has emerged as a kind of Aeneas. He enforces the habit of peace by making war. He makes war to subdue the women who are *dispietate,* but he responds humbly to them when they humble themselves. He is championed by Mars for Venus's sake. As Aeneas aims to do but does not actually achieve in the *Aeneid,* he consolidates his victory by marrying his opponent. This marriage, like that projected for Aeneas, is carried out under the sponsorship of Venus. She is represented not in person but by means of her Scythian temple. This temple becomes the first in the series of monuments that define the underlying argument of *Teseida.*

The victory over the Amazons is completed by a triumph not described until book 2. I anticipate the careful plotting of *Teseida* by describing the triumph here, but it is important to recognize that Venus does not stand alone. Her conquest of the Amazons is completed by and shared with the goddess Pallas, in whose honor the triumph is held. Immediately upon his return to Athens, Theseus

> diritto andò al tempio di Pallade
> a reverir di lei la deitade.
> Quivi con reverenza offerse molto,
> e le sue armi e l'altre conquistate
>
> [went straight to the temple of Pallas to worship her divinity. And there with reverence he offered

much, both his own arms and conquered ones] (*Tes.* 2.23.7-24.2).

This donation of his own arms along with captured ones diminishes any sense of this as a triumph over the Amazons. Theseus triumphs with Hippolyta over the cruelty and pitilessness the Amazons had displayed. Similarly, the triumphant dedication to Pallas binds that goddess with Venus. It does not distinguish the two, and the reader may think of the whole triumph as one embracing Venus and Pallas. Such a fusion of deities has already occurred in **Filocolo.** The image it suggests is wisdom in marriage or, in other common medieval terms, a union of reason and sensuality. It is essential to realize, however, that despite their emblematic meaning, the goddesses are also to be understood as sponsoring divinities. The solution worked out through the collaboration of Theseus, Venus, Pallas, and ultimately Hippolyta is one that will prove impossible for men alone or for men in collaboration with the destructive face of pagan divinity to achieve.

Present at this triumph is Hippolyta's "sorella picciolina," Emilia (*Tes.* 1.128.6). She is too young for marriage, but Theseus reserves her in his mind for Achates (*Tes.* 1.137). Emilia has not taken part in the settlement by marriage of the Amazon problem. When she comes to Athens with Theseus, she remains a vestige of Scythia that will return to plague and ultimately defeat Theseus in the poem's crisis.

Palemone and Arcita, the men destined to be Emilia's suitors, are acquired by Theseus much as Emilia is. If anything, they are even more clearly spoils of war than she since they are captives; but all three become Theseus's responsibilities as a result of successful warfare. Their story begins in Scythia, where Theseus lingers after his marriage to Hippolyta. In a scene recalling the descent of Mercury to urge Aeneas's departure from Carthage, Theseus is confronted by a ghostly image of his friend Perithoos. The image demands:

> Che fai tu ozioso
> con Ipolita in Scizia dimorando,
> sotto amore offuscando il tuo famoso nome?

> [What are you doing lazily staying with
> Hippolyta in Scythia, obscuring your
> famous name with love?] (*Tes.* 2.4.4-7).

While the apparition recalls the epiphany of Mercury in *Aeneid* 4, here, as is typically the case in *Teseida,* there is only indirect contact between man and god. When Theseus recovers from his fear of this sudden apparition, he realizes that

> dal cielo,
> da qualche deità la qual provede
> al suo onor con caritevol zelo,
> era venuto cotal ragionare
> [from the sky, from some deity
> who watches over his honor
> with loving zeal, this speech
> had come] (*Tes.* 2.7.5-7).

At the spur of this divine suggestion, Theseus, like Aeneas but unlike Troilus, obeys: he returns to Athens. In his absence the war of the Seven against Thebes has been completed. That war, which is the subject of Statius's *Thebaid,* begins when Oedipus's twin sons contest their father's legacy. Each wishes to rule Thebes, and Polynices eventually raises an army incorporating seven Greek champions to fight for his rights. In a climactic duel, the brothers kill each other, and Jocasta's brother, Creon, assumes the Theban kingship. Creon, however, as Sophocles' *Antigone* describes, refuses burial to Polynices and the champions who fought at his side against Thebes. Their corpses are left to litter the ground outside the "liberated" city.

In this refusal of burial, Boccaccio sees evidence of "fiera crudeltà" ["savage cruelty"] (*Tes.* 2.12.7), worse even than that which characterized the Amazons. Also at issue in this war is behavior lacking in *pietas,* parallel to the Amazons *dispietate.* This aspect of Creon's behavior is reflected most clearly through those who enlist Theseus's help in fighting against him. These are Greek or Argive queens, the wives of the seven champions who fought alongside Polynices and to whom Creon also denies burial. As Theseus passes them on his triumphal entry into Athens, they urge him in the name of *pietas* to oppose Creon and ensure their husbands' burial.

The spot these women pick as vantage point while they wait to approach Theseus is significant. They choose the temple of Clementia, the deified personification of clemency. In placing the queens here, Boccaccio is following Statius, whose epic celebrates Theseus's triumphant exercise of this virtue. Boccaccio's point would seem to be a different one, however. He means to distinguish between the actions of Theseus's virtue that are in collaboration with divinity and those that are not. In book 2, as in book 1, Theseus opposes cruelty and impiety, and he does so under the tutelage of a divinity. In book 1, that divinity is represented by a combination of Venus and Pallas. Here it is represented by the divine Clementia. Like Venus's temple in Scythia, Clementia's temple stands for the collaboration between men and gods that makes Theseus's *pietas* effective.

The Argive queens see this virtue as primary, both in their own motivation and in Theseus's. "Pietose," they address Theseus as "pio signore" and ask that he be "pietoso" (*Tes.* 2.32.1, 2.32.5, 2.33.2). They define burial as the "pio oficio" (*Tes.* 2.34.3). Theseus himself identifies *pietas* as a motive for action. He is

> nella miseria delle sconsolate,
> da intima pietà nel cor trafitto

> [stricken to the heart with
> deepest compassion at the
> misery of the unconsoled]
> (*Tes.* 2.43.3-4).

He tells his soldiers,

> Certo ciascun ne dovrebbe esser pio,
> e al vengiar dovreste esser ferventi

> [Surely everyone must be compassionate, you must be eager to
> avenge] (*Tes.* 2.46.3-4).

Theseus's *pietas* is thus well established. His exhortation to his troops reaffirms his imitation of Aeneas's imperial responsibility:

> Andiamo adunque, e lui, fiero Creonte,
> umil facciàn con le spade tornare

> [Let us go there and make proud
> Creon humble with our swords] (*Tes.*
> 2.47.1-2).

Theseus is successful. His army overcomes Theban opposition, and he himself defeats Creon. Boccaccio's description of Creon's death directly recalls the death of Turnus. Here that death is seen as justified, in contrast to the way it is viewed in *Filostrato,* and by it Theseus, like Aeneas, consolidates his victory over cruelty and lack of *pietas.*

Theseus clearly represents Aeneas throughout this book, and here he represents him at his most dutiful and successful: turning away from the distractions of Carthage and resuming his heroic responsibility; asserting his *pietas;* subduing cruelty in accordance with the Roman imperial mission. Every episode in the life of Aeneas that Theseus's career recalls is a divinely sanctioned one of great importance, and Theseus's assumption of the perfected career of Aeneas is plainly established in books 1 and 2 of *Teseida.* In the remainder of the poem this Aeneas will confront himself in another guise, for, as I have already suggested, the trio of lovers and rivals who emerge from the first two books take on the roles of Aeneas, Turnus, and Lavinia. In effect, then, the poem pits a completed Aeneas against an incompleted one and lets the one attempt to set the other to rights. Before this can be achieved, however, two essential characters must be acquired at Theseus's charge.

At the death of Creon, Theseus gives Thebes into the hands of his men; they are to sack it at their pleasure, but the temples of the gods must remain inviolate (*Tes.* 2.73.6-7). Then follow the funerals of Creon and the Argive kings (*Tes.* 2.74-77). In a final act of vengeance, the Argive women burn Thebes itself (*Tes.* 2.81-88). Despite the multiple disasters and the repeated attempts by Thebes's enemies to kill its leaders and destroy its fabric—the last vestige of the crime of Oedipus—some spark of Thebes still remains. Theseus's men are ordered to search the battlefield, and there they discover

> due giovani feriti dolorando
>
> . . . . .
>
> e ciaschedun la morte domandava,
> tanto dolor del lor mal gli agravava

> [two wounded and sorrowful
> young men . . . and each asked
> for death, so much did sorrow for
> their misfortune afflict them] (*Tes.*
> 2.85.5.7-8).

When these two are led before Theseus, he asks them if they are members of the royal house of Cadmus.

> E l'un di loro altiero al suo dimando
> rispose: "In casa sua nati e cresciuti
> fummo, e de' suo' nepoti semo; e quando
> Creon contra di te l'empie arme prese,
> fummo con lui, co' nostri, a sue difese."

> [And one of them haughtily replied to

his question: "In his house we were born and raised, and we are his grandchildren; and when Creon took up impious arms against you, we were with him, and with our own men in his defense"] (*Tes.* 2.88.5-8).

While Theseus is "aware of their disdain,"

> non seguio
> però l'effetto a cotale ira degno;
> ma verso lor più ne divenne pio.

> [the effect, however, appropri-
> ate to so much wrath did not
> follow, but he became more
> compassionate towards them]
> (*Tes.* 2.89.1-4).

Theseus and the Theban knights are thus strongly contrasted in this brief scene. The Thebans emerge from the most sweeping catastrophe almost as if by a miracle, and yet they retain the disdain and the wrath that first led to Thebes's disaster. Theseus does not respond to their wrath as he did to that of Creon but is merciful and keeps them alive for his triumph (*Tes.* 2.92.1-2). So he brings them into Athens before his chariot (*Tes.* 2.94-95), just as, in the triumph that begins book 2, he has brought Emilia to Athens. Theseus's second triumph in book 2 is a triumph of Mars: Creon's armor is dedicated in Mars's temple (*Tes.* 2.95).

Four monuments, then, focus and summarize the themes of the first two books of *Teseida:* the temple of Venus in Scythia and the temples of Pallas, Clementia, and Mars in Athens. Each is associated with a particular action, and each embodies significant themes in the poem. Each represents an aspect of Theseus's heroic character and, more significantly, an aspect of his successful imitation of Aeneas. The temple of Venus, where the marriage of Theseus and Hippolyta takes place, represents Theseus as Venus's champion and as one who responds to humility with gentleness. It represents the triumph of Anchises' formula for Roman imperialism and suggests the peace to be anticipated from the marriage of Aeneas and Lavinia. The temple of Pallas, the Athenian temple par excellence, complements the temple of Venus and characterizes the marriage of Theseus and Hippolyta as one in which sensuality and reason are blended. The temple of Clementia continues the imperial theme announced by Anchises, for clemency is both a private and an imperial virtue. Here Theseus is presented with a task associated with *pietas* and is himself characterized as *pius.* He sets out to make war against the proud, and, like Aeneas, he is victorious. That wrathful victory is rightly celebrated in the temple of Mars. This triumph, however, like that preceding it, is one combining the virtues of contrasting gods. Venus associated with Pallas blends reason and sensuality. Mars associated with Clementia suggests wrath tempered by compassion. While Theseus defers his virtue to these paired divinities, his success is unparalleled.

This is the pinnacle of Theseus's achievement and the high point of his imitation of Aeneas. After this point in the poem, Theseus is no longer alone in representing Vergil's hero. At the moment of their enamorment, both Palemone and Arcita reflect elements of Aeneas's character, and later in the poem they assume Vergilian roles that overlap those Theseus continues to play. From a window of the prison where Theseus perpetually guards them, Arcita one morning sees the Amazon Emilia. In wonder, he exclaims, "Quest' è di paradiso!" ["She is from Paradise!"] (*Tes.* 3.12.8). He invites Palemone to join him at the window and tells him, "Vener è qui discesa veramente" ["Venus has in truth descended here"] (*Tes.* 3.13.3). Palemone is equally certain that this vision is celestial, and he identifies the unknown girl with the same goddess: "Per certo questa è Citerea" ["Certainly this is Venus"] (*Tes.* 3.14.6).

The Thebans thus mistake Emilia for Venus. While there are no direct verbal resemblances, the scene in many of its themes reflects Aeneas's meeting with his mother in Carthage and the work the goddess and Cupid carry out there. When Aeneas first sees Venus in disguise he recognizes her divinity but cannot identify her. This scene at first glance seems an odd model for an enamorment, but its main motif, the identification of the girl with a goddess, reflects both its Vergilian origin and a major theme in Boccaccio's notion of love. Boccaccio often represents the act of falling in or out of love as one in which divinity plays a part. Typically, enamorment involves the recognition of a divinity—usually Cupid or Amor—in some earthly woman. To the extent that the earthly woman is seen in terms of divinity, the love remains exalted. When divinity is ignored and the woman is loved for herself alone, the love then becomes problematical. Troilus experiences this debasement of a love that is divine in its origins. Here the love of Palemone and Arcita for Emilia begins on the same exalted level.

The Venus who appears in Emilia certainly has her origin in the *Aeneid;* but, unlike the Venus who aided Theseus against the Amazons, she is revealed in the end as a destructive force. Robert Hollander [in his *Boccaccio's Two Venuses,* 1977] has argued for a substitution of Venuses at the beginning of book 3 of *Teseida.* In his view, whereas the Venus who sponsors Theseus's war against the Amazons may be thought of as the celestial Venus, as her association with Hymen and Pallas argues, here a furious and predatory Venus has appeared. It is true that Theseus reacts differently to Venus's suggestion than these Thebans do. Nonetheless, it is not so much their desire that distinguishes them as the way they respond to their own passion. Theseus has some discipline and self-control; the Thebans have demonstrated none. When an impulse as strong as love strikes such different people, the results are bound to be different.

While the way love affects them is exceedingly important, Theseus's eventual inability to control the passion of the Thebans reflects the fact that love is, in Boccaccio's view, always divine in origin. In their fury, Palemone and Arcita are still collaborating with an aspect of Venus. Theseus, in opposing them, is not collaborating with any god or goddess. Instead, he sets himself and his own virtue against the will of the gods. Even though this may seem to be a confrontation between his good and the gods' evil, what emerges is not a victory for the good but a demonstration of Theseus's impotence in the face of divine opposition. Theseus's impotence, moreover, is shared by all

men unaided by divinity in their struggle against the irrational forces in human nature. This, as I will argue, is the underlying theme of *Teseida.*

The sparks of love first struck by the celestial image of Emilia quickly become threatening when the freed Arcita, who has assumed the name of Penteo (Pentheus) and returned to Athens, encounters his former cellmate, Palemone, who is newly escaped from prison. The two meet not far from Athens in a grove, or bosk (*bosco* or *boschetto*), where Penteo has often gone:

> E era sì rimoto da l'andare
> di ciaschedun, che ben poteva il foco
> d'amor con voci fuor lasciare andare[And it was
>   so remote from the path
> of anyone that the fire of love could
> be released in words] (*Tes.* 4.64.3-5).

The grove is a little paradise, and Boccaccio describes it in the conventional terms appropriate to a *locus amoenus* (*Tes.* 4.65). It serves as the scene of the decisive actions in the middle books of *Teseida.* Its fate becomes tied more and more closely to that of the lovers, and, as their passions become less restrained, they cause it increasing damage. Finally, at the death of Arcita, it is felled to make space for his funeral pyre. Thus its fate is like the fate of paradise, from which it conventionally descends. It is gradually involved in the destructive play of human passions and suffers death as a consequence of human actions.

The bosk is the complement to the monuments that dominate the enclosing portions of the poem. It reflects the opposition between Theseus's civilizing virtue, *pietas,* and the cruel, even bestial opponents who resist him. While its biblical resonances are manifest, it recalls with equal insistence the involvement of the Italian landscape in the fury of the war in Italy described in *Aeneid* 7-12.

The first encounter of the lovers in the bosk is distinctly onesided. Arcita is asleep, and Palemone, the eventual winner of Emilia, the man who will soon be figured as Aeneas, and the aggressor in this encounter, addresses his sleeping cousin in imagination:

> O bello amico molto da lodare,
> se al presente tu ti risentisse,
> tosto fra noi credo si finirebbe
> qual di noi due per donna Emilia avrebbe
>
> [O lovely friend greatly to be praised,
> if at present you were to awaken I think
> that soon between us would be de-
> cided which of the two of us would have
> Emilia for his lady] (*Tes.* 5.36.5-8).

Arcita awakens:

> E'nsieme si fer festa di buon core
> e i loro accidenti si narraro
> [And they greeted each other
> wholeheartedly and told each
> other their adventures] (*Tes.*
> 5.39.1-2).

This good spirit remains until Palemone asks Arcita to give up his love for Emilia and let her be his alone (*Tes.* 5.40.3-4). Arcita is enraged at this, and Palemone expresses surprise that his cousin will not yield (*Tes.* 5.41.1-4). It is Palemone, however, who presses for battle and Arcita who resists (*Tes.* 5.43.1-3). Palemone swears a battle oath:

> Io ti giuro, per l'onipotente
> Giove del cielo e per Venere dea,
> che prima ch'io di qui faccia partenza,
> co' ferri partirén tal differenza

> [I swear to you by the omnipo-
> tent Jove of the heavens and by the
> goddess Venus, that before I leave
> here this dispute will be settled with
> swords] (*Tes.* 5.43.5-8).

This oath is based on one Aeneas makes at a critical point in the *Aeneid.* In the second half of that poem, Aeneas, although he has reached Italy, must fight to secure his foothold in that country and to win his promised bride. His opponent, Turnus, who thinks of Lavinia as pledged to him, raises Italian tribes against Aeneas and his Greek ally. After heavy losses on both sides, Aeneas and Turnus agree to end the war by single combat. To give their decision the force of law, representatives of the two contending forces meet and swear treaty oaths. Palemone's oath reflects that sworn by Aeneas. Arcita eventually swears an oath as well, but first he acknowledges that this battle is not their own entirely but is brought about by the will of the gods:

> Omè, ch'io sento l'ira dell'iddii,
> li quali ancor ne vanno minacciando
> contrarii tutti alli nostri disii;
> e la fortuna ci ha qui lusingando
> menati con effetti lieti e pii,
> e non Amore, a voler che moiamo
> per le man nostre, come noi sogliamo.
> Omè, che m'era assai maravigliosa
> cosa a pensar che Iunon ci lasciasse
> nostra vita menare in tanta posa,
> e come i nostri noi non stimolasse

> [O how I feel the wrath of the gods
> who still threaten us, all of them con-
> trary to our wishes; and deceptive
> Fortune has led us here and not Love,
> with happy and pious results, wishing
> that we would die at our own hands,
> as we are accustomed to do. O how
> marvelous a thing it appeared to me
> that Juno would let us live our lives in
> such quiet, and would not goad us as
> she did our fathers] (*Tes.* 5.55.2-56.4).

Arcita's complaint, then, widens the context of the lovers' rivalry. It is not entirely of their own making but bears with it the heavy weight of Thebes's heritage, the divine wrath of Juno and the fratricide that often springs from it. This Theban theme emerges parenthetically, however, from an essentially Vergilian scene, and the goddess it identifies as the enemy of Thebes is a vindictive presence in the *Aeneid,* too. While Palemone has called on Jove and Venus in his oath, Arcita refers to Juno, not as his patron but as his destroyer. Turnus, the champion Arcita will soon recall, is the favorite of Juno. She stirs the Italian champion to resist the invading army led by Aeneas, knowing full well that Aeneas is supported not only by her

rival Venus but also by omnipotent Jove and the will of fate. Her action in stirring Turnus to futile and ultimately fatal resistance is thus an irresponsible and cruel one. It only delays the fated victory of Aeneas, but it leads to Turnus's death. When Arcita recalls Juno, then, not as his patroness but as his destroyer, he is telling a truth about himself as Turnus, which Turnus never realizes. Juno destroys both Arcita and Turnus, one through "friendship," the other through enmity, but when the gods are involved (as Dido and Aeneas learn to their cost), contact itself is often fatal.

As political leader, Latinus, the father of Aeneas's eventual bride, swears an oath that will govern Turnus in his fight with the Trojan. Arcita's vow, like this Vergilian counterpart, is a moving pastoral lament. He uses his oath, in fact, to express not his animosity but his unwillingness to do battle. He calls on all the elements of nature, the sky, the rising sun, the unnamed sylvan deities, and Priapus, not as a god of lust but of orchards, as Boccaccio's own gloss makes clear. Like Turnus, Arcita is closely bound to the earth and to the natural world, and his oath reflects this. Arcita and Turnus are natural men; here, before battle, at their most dignified and restrained, they speak for a compelling sympathy among men and between man and nature. When this sympathy is overcome by wrath, they become victims, and so too does the pastoral world they represent.

Battle soon begins, but not before the knights are offered an opportunity to reconsider their violent course of action. No sooner has the fight begun than

> il valoroso Arcita
> su l'elmo con la spada a Palemone
> diede un tal colpo ch'appena la vita
> li rimanesse fu sua oppinione

> [the valorous Arcita gave such a
> strong blow with his sword to
> the helmet of Palemone that he
> thought life could hardly remain in
> him] (*Tes.* 5.66.1-4).

Arcita's reaction fits his earlier reluctance; he "wept in sorrow" ("piangeva doloroso"); he regrets his blow and the love that led to it (*Tes.* 5.70.2, 5.70.8). Meanwhile, Palemone comes to. He realizes that Arcita is weeping for him (*Tes.* 5.72.7-8), but he nevertheless insists that battle resume:

> Non creder però aver perdono
> da me, perché pietoso t'ho veduto

> [But do not think to be excused
> by me because I have seen you
> compassionate] (*Tes.* 5.73.5-6).

These are the familiar Vergilian terms that have distinguished opponents in previous confrontations in the *Teseida.* Arcita, like Theseus, is *pius,* but this virtue, in strong contrast to its effectiveness in the earlier books of the poem, is here both short-lived and impotent. Bestial wrath soon overwhelms it, and both Thebans begin to "ferir come draconi" ["wound each other like dragons"] (*Tes.* 5.75.8). The simile recalls the origin of the Thebans, who were sown from the dragon's teeth "sanza aver più l'un dell'altro pietate" ["without having any more pity for each other"] (*Tes.* 5.76.3).

While the Theban rivals are hard at their destructive task, Emilia, who has become separated from a hunting party led by Theseus, happens into the bosk. She is the very image of Diana.

> Ell'era sopra d'un bel pallafreno
> co' can dintorno, e un corno dallato
> avea e dalla man contraria al freno,
> dietro alle spalle, un arco avea legato
> e un turcasso di saette pieno,
> che era d'oro tratto lavorato;
> e ghirlandetta di frondi novelle
> copriva le sue treccie bionde e belle
>
> [She was on a beautiful palfrey with
> dogs around her, and she had a
> horn, and at the side opposite her
> bridle hand, behind her back, she
> had a bow tied and a quiver full of
> arrows which was embroidered with
> gold threads; and a garland of new
> branches covered her blonde and
> beautiful tresses] (*Tes.* 5.79).

Though the scene has medieval elements, it also recalls the hunt in *Aeneid* 4; and the description of Emilia has a great deal in common with the description of Dido before the hunt that leads to her false "marriage" with Aeneas and to her eventual death (*Aen.* 4.129-39). Her effect on the two combatants is most Dido-like. She inspires them not to virginal coldness but to an increased ardor. At the sight of her, both warriors become "più forti e più fieri" ["stronger and more fierce"] (*Tes.* 5.80.6). For them this becomes a second enamorment. It is not so much a falling into love as a falling into *furor* that expresses itself in combat. Because their wrath is now fed by the very vision that established love and mutuality before, from this moment on, the love of Palemone and Arcita for the same woman is an impossibility.

Theseus soon follows Emilia into the bosk, and, once there, he parts the combatants. Learning who they are, he acknowledges, as they do, their violations of his law, but he determines to pardon them. This pardon is superficially like the role the more formal virtue of pardon, clemency, has already played in the poem. Clementia, from whose temple precincts the Argive queens appeal to Theseus for their husbands' burial, is a divinized, imperial virtue. Theseus's march against Creon, which begins in her temple, enjoys the sponsorship of that divinity. His success in overcoming the bestial cruelty of Creon is at least partially attributable to the goddess. Here, Theseus's action in pardoning the Thebans is different in motivation and in kind. It is based on the recollection of his own experiences: Theseus was once in love, and it led him to acts as risky and extreme as those the Thebans have carried out. As Boccaccio's gloss explains, "In his youth Theseus abducted Helen, daughter of Tindarus, who was later stolen away by Paris; but Theseus's mother returned her to Castor and Pollux, her brothers, without her ever having been touched by Theseus: for this reason his offense was pardoned."

Acting on the basis of his own experience, Theseus gladly pardons the errant Thebans. This is not an official act but a personal one, not a divinely instigated act of clemency but an example of individual mercy. There is nothing wrong with such an act, as long as its limitations are understood. However, Theseus appears to disregard these limitations, and his merciful act runs counter to those divinities whose interest in the love and combat of the Thebans has already been manifested. In effect, then, Theseus's intention to be merciful runs counter to fate and to the divine will. We cannot expect it to succeed in the way his earlier, divinely sponsored actions did.

Theseus asserts more than mercy in this scene. He declares, as the lovers have earlier declared themselves, that *pietas* will be opposed to their fury. This, too, is a familiar opposition in the poem, but once again, the opposition is made in terms that do not fully correspond to the pattern of *Teseida* 1 and 2. There, *pietas* embraced Theseus's devotion and duty to the gods. Here, it is an individual, perhaps civic, characteristic or virtue. Although it is not wrong to assert *pietas,* then, the virtue is impotent without divine response. We saw it quickly evaporate when Arcita tried to assert it single-handedly early in the duel with Palemone. It is not immediately set aside or overpowered in the poem's final books, but it nevertheless fails.

Theseus sets his *pietas* against the lover's passion in a single, highly important statement. He asserts, "Vincerà il fallo la mia gran pietate" ["My great *pietas* will overcome their fault"] (*Tes.* 5.92.8). Theseus's assertion that his *pietas* will overcome not only the *furor* of the knights but also their *fallo* is an extremely bold one. In the poem's climax it will prove to be impossible. No man, not even Theseus, can set his will against love. Love is a god who collaborates with human will; he is not to be overturned by a man alone, even a man whose *pietas* is as great as that of Theseus. Moreover, the love of these men and their Theban fate has a demonic dimension that will become clear in the poem's denouement. Theseus unaided by grace has no power to oppose its force.

Theseus's method for overcoming this "fault" is to remove the combatants from the wilderness and to impose order on their combat. He sees regulated battle as the only way to settle their dispute. He regards that as a rather pleasant and amicable thing, calling it "amorosa battaglia" (*Tes.* 7.8.1), and relies on a monumental amphitheater in Athens as the proper setting for imposing order on the unregulated *furor* of the Theban barons.

This theater eventually replaces the grove and signals the reemergence in the poem of urban monuments like those that governed in books 1 and 2. It represents the imposition of civilized Athenian control on the unregulated practices of the wilderness. It represents, too, the monument by which Theseus proposes to exert the control of his *pietas* over the lovers' fault. In book 6 of the *Teseida,* however, we hear little of this monument, and it does not yet serve as a scene for the action of the poem, a role in which it will dominate for much of the second half of *Teseida.*

Book 6, instead, is entirely occupied with an extensive description of the champions each Theban assembles in his behalf. Far from being an intrusion into the structure of the poem, the book carries on the poem's themes of *furor* and *pietas*. It anticipates the contest in the theater when it introduces those who will take part in it. More significantly, it introduces an analogy, which is also present in Vergil and Statius, between war and games. This analogy, like the identities of the warriors who take part in the contest, suggests the impossibility of controlling *furor* in the way that Theseus intends to do. Just as the amorous battle at Troy leads to massive destruction, destruction that is recalled in the war in Italy, and just as Thebes itself has been decimated by the Argive army, so Theseus's theater is about to be overthrown by the combined fury of the champions of these past and future battles.

The proximate source of book 6 is the description in *Thebaid* 2 of the Argive champions, but the combatants in Theseus's theater include heroes who play prominent roles in the war in Italy, whose coming together is described in *Aeneid* 7, and others clearly associated with the Trojan War. This is a rather ominous beginning to a game, accenting as it does both the martial and fratricidal elements of two of the struggles it recalls and the libidinous cause of the third. It also serves as a prelude to the particular nature of the bloody contest in Theseus's theater. There . . . the wilderness reemerges not as a physical setting but in similes describing the savagery of the combatants and more particularly in a series of scenes directly recalling significant battle deaths in *Aeneid* 9-12 and *Thebaid* 7-10.

The list of champions begins with Lycurgus, "ancora lagrimoso / per la morte d'Ofelte, a ner vestito" ["still weeping for the death of Opheltes, dressed in black"] (*Tes.* 6.14.1-2). His appearance as the first of the champions epitomizes the themes I have already described, but with an ominous emphasis. Opheltes' death is the occasion for the games that, in *Thebaid* 6, stand before and forecast the war of the Seven against Thebes. In the *Teseida* Opheltes' funeral is systematically recalled in the funeral of Arcita. Lycurgus's entrance as Arcita's champion, then, foreshadows the doom that will befall that hero.

The champions Agamemnon and Menelaus (*Tes.* 6.21-24) recall the Trojan War. Their companions in arms, Castor and Pollux, are described in relation to their sisters, Helen and Clytemnaestra, the one responsible for the destruction of Troy and the other, of Argos (*Tes.* 6.25). All four champions thus recall the war that serves as the very model of *amorosa battaglia*. The war to avenge Helen's rape by Paris symbolizes, both in Latin poetry and in Boccaccio's *Filostrato*, the martial *furor* love can produce. Boccaccio blends these champions with those described in the second half of the *Aeneid*. The systematic reference to the *Iliad* in the second half of that poem anticipates this conflation.

Other Greek champions include Pelleus, Chromis, Hippodamus, Nestor (who takes no part in the war against Thebes), Perithoos, Ulysses and Diomedes, Admetus, Anchelados, and several others. Of these, Admetus, Chromis, and Hippodamus participate not only in the war but in the funeral games for Opheltes as well. Pelleus is a famous though unscrupulous racer himself. Ulysses and Diomedes, who have no place in the *Thebaid*, are champions of

the Trojan War and two who stand in Vergil's poem for the worst of Greek treachery and cruelty. At the time of the Theban War, Nestor, although he was of appropriate age, "refused to take part in a doomed campaign." As Vessey points out [in his *Statius and Thebaid*, 1973], this "traditional exemplum of wisdom has no part in folly." Despite his wisdom, however, Nestor plays a role in Theseus's game. Evander is similar. His age, wisdom, and *pietas* mark him off and make his participation in the war in Italy inappropriate. Nevertheless, he enters this tragic contest.

Perhaps the most interesting and surprising champions to enter the theater are Pygmalion and Sychaeus. Sychaeus is the husband of Dido, and she had vowed to him her eternal chastity. He is thus a reminder of the violation of her vow and her chastity which love for Aeneas represents. Pygmalion is the murderer of Sychaeus. The appearance of Pygmalion and Sychaeus together here naturally recalls what happened between them. The two are united by bonds of kinship, yet Pygmalion, in *furor* and *impietas*, disregarding his sister's affection and moved by a lust for gold, destroys his companion. The story has some of the dimensions of the story of Palemone and Arcita, of course. Their tie is blood and not marriage, yet *furor* divides them, too, and the killing of one by the other would be a kind of fratricide, the Theban crime par excellence and an example of horrid *impietas*. That Dido stands between Pygmalion and Sychaeus as Emilia, a Dido figure, stands between Palemone and Arcita is also suggested by their presence here.. . . .

It is Theseus's monumental response to the unregulated *furor* of the Theban barons, who meet in fratricidal battle in the bosk outside Athens. Theseus himself emphasizes the benign nature of the contest in the theater: there is, he says, no kingdom at stake here, no disputed heritage (*Tes.* 7.7.3-5). He emphasizes, too, the consanguinity of the Argive people and the inappropriateness of bloodshed among father, son, and other close relatives (*Tes.* 7.10.4 7). To avoid the consequences of such actions and given what he believes to be the benign nature of the strife between Palemone and Arcita, he imposes a number of conditions on the battle. These conditions justify, he feels, his belief that the contest will be not like a war but "com'un palestral gioco" ["like a wrestling match"] (*Tes.* 7.4.8). This game, moreover, will not win, as a fratricidal war would do, the hatred of the gods (*Tes.* 7.10.5); instead,

> Questo sarà come un giuoco a Marte,
> li sacrifici del qual celebriamo
> il giorno dato; e vederassi l'arte
> di menar l'armi in che c'esercitiamo
>
> [This will be like a game to Mars,
> whose sacrifices we celebrate on the
> given day; and the art of bearing
> arms, in which we exert ourselves,
> will be displayed] (*Tes.* 7.13.1-4).

In at least two matters Theseus is seriously deluding himself. As the catalog of champions has already shown, the strife provoked by love is no less than that provoked by lost kingdoms or inheritances. Agamemnon and Menelaus fight to regain Helen; Paris and his nation fight to keep her. Theseus has seen these very champions "d'affanno d'ira e d'amor pieni assai" ["filled with fatigue, wrath, and love"] (*Tes.* 7.11.8). Yet, despite what he has seen, he believes that the "amorosa . . . battaglia" in his theater will be relatively harmless. He believes, too, in the efficacy of his own *pietas* and of his own capacity to regulate so much *furor*.

Theseus recognizes the presence of another force in the theater as well, and just as he misunderstands the fury of the human combatants there, he also misapprehends the power and malevolence of this second presence. Mars acts in the theater; his sacrifices are celebrated on the appointed day of battle, and in effect this game will be dedicated to him . . . [Boccaccio] was familiar with Roman games dedicated to Mars. Like the contest in the theater, they are far from benign or bloodless. Mars, too, of course, is the god of war, and his presence in the theater as dedicatee of the games is another reminder of the analogy between game and war. When the game escapes Theseus's control, two factors will combine to make it do so. The *furor* of the lovers, which he underestimates, and the power of the god, which he appears to regard benignly, will combine to overthrow his *pietas* and sabotage his plans.

In addition to the theater, three significant monuments emerge in the seventh book of *Teseida.* These are the temples of Mars, Venus, and Diana, where the lovers and Emilia express their devotion to patron gods and make the prayers that determine their fates. Arcita expresses his devotion first, and it is directed primarily toward Mars. Palemone's prayer to Venus is in keeping with his portrayal in the earlier oath-swearing scene as Aeneas, another hero championed by the goddess. Emilia, as a former Amazon and still a virgin, prays to Diana. There has been considerable discussion of the temples, the deities they enshrine, and the elaborate glosses Boccaccio provides to their mythographical and allegorical significance. My aim is to establish the notion that these temples, like the theater and like the temples of *Teseida* 1 and 2, are monuments that center and embody the meaning of Boccaccio's poem. All the participants in the conflict leading up to Arcita's death are represented by these monuments: Venus and Mars, who oversee the contest, are each represented by a temple; Diana, too, has a shrine. Theseus's *pietas* is represented by the theater itself. This configuration of monuments recalls the similar configuration in books 1 and 2. There, temples of Mars and Venus were also present, but no human institution was set against or among them. The temple of Clementia and the temple of Pallas, instead, stood as monuments that supported Theseus's *pietas* and his assumption of the imperial task of Aeneas. Here that *pietas* is unsupported by divinity, as the solitary theater suggests.

In its imagery and in many of its details, the battle in Theseus's theater is, as the catalog of heroes has forecast, not a game but a war. Its civilized setting, moreover, is transformed by *furor* into a wilderness. In it the gods participate, as they regularly do in battles, and in the end the outcome there is determined by their choice in collaboration with the fallen will of men.

The human savagery that transforms the game into war

and the theater into a wilderness is apparent in the similes introducing the major combatants. Arcita enters first:

> Tale a veder qual tra giovenchi giunge
> non armati di corna il fier leone
> libico, e affamato i denti munge
> con la sua lingua e aguzza l'unghione,
> e col capo alto, quale innanzi punge,
> l'occhio girando, fa dilibrazione;
> e sì negli atti si mostra rabbioso,
> ch'ogni giovenco fa di sé dottoso
>
> [In appearance like the savage Libyan
> lion when it comes among heifers not
> yet armed with horns, and famished,
> licks [lit., milks] its teeth with its
> tongue and sharpens its claws; and
> with its head high and rolling its eyes,
> it deliberates which to strike first,
> and it shows itself by its acts to be so
> enraged that each heifer is terrified of
> it] (*Tes.* 7.115).

The savagery of the lion, his predatory deliberation, the contrast between his strength and the weakness of his domesticated prey, even the implied Libyan setting, all combine to show that Arcita is far from embodying the constraints of the civilized contest he has entered.

Palemone is described in similar terms, but the epic simile following his entrance into the theater refers specifically to the bosk where the lovers first did battle. In the simile it has been transformed from a *locus amoenus* into a wild and savage place:

> Qual per lo bosco il cinghiar ruvinoso,
> poi c'ha di dietro a sé sentiti i cani,
> con le sete levate e isquamoso,
> or qual or là per viottoli strani
> rugghiando va fuggendo furioso,
> rami rompendo e schiantando silvani,
> cotale entrò mirabilmente armato
> Palemone
>
> [As through the bosk the destructive
> boar, when it has heard the hounds
> behind it, with its bristles raised and
> shaggy, wandering this way and that
> runs through strange paths fleeing,
> furiously breaking branches and destroying the woods, so Palemone
> entered wonderfully armed] (*Tes.*
> 7.119).

The simile clearly suggests that the bosk, a place where hares and rabbits were hunted with dogs and snare, is now the scene of a savage boar hunt and that in fleeing the hounds the boar causes it considerable harm. The savagery of the boar, which represents the savagery of Palemone, continues the process of destruction which his wrath began. It is significant, too, that, as Limentani recognizes, this simile is at least loosely based on *Aeneid* 10.707-13. There it is applied to the savage Mezentius as he stands in for Turnus. In Palemone's career as Aeneas, this is a surprising substitution. However, it is characteristic of the *furor* of battle in the second half of the *Aeneid* that men of such different natures as the civilized Aeneas and the barbarous Mezentius act in similar ways. The simile thus reflects again the relationship between the games in the theater and the war in Italy.

Deaths occur in the games as they do in the war, and their very existence gives evidence of the failure of *pietas* to control the action there. Some of these deaths are modeled on death scenes in the *Aeneid* and *Thebaid,* and such recollections reinforce the already well established deterioration of the game into a war. Two scenes in particular recall a climactic moment in the career of Aeneas when his own *pietas* is overcome by *furor.* When Turnus kills Pallas, whose father, Evander, has placed the young hero under Aeneas's protection, the Trojan hero appears to go berserk. Possessed by unmatchable *furor,* he rages through the battlefield and slaughters every enemy in his path. He single-handedly chases the Latin forces from the field (*Aen.* 10.510-605). He kills violently and without mercy. His fury is first recalled in **Teseida** when the champion Artifilo Itoneo kills Cremiso:

> E mentre lui lo suo fratel pio
> volea levar, li sopragiunse il forte
> Eleno, e orgoglioso il perseguio
> e lui uccise ancor similemente
> allato al frate dolorosamente
>
> [And while in compassion he
> tries to lift his brother, thestrong Helenus came
> up to him
> and arrogantly attacked and
> killed him, too, miserably at
> the side of his brother] (*Tes.*
> 8.15.4-8).

The details recall Aeneas's brutal killing of two brothers as they fight to protect each other (*Aen.* 10.335-41). A similarly poignant battle death from *Aeneid* 10 is recalled later in book 8. This time, Arcita is the killer, and his victim, his face clotted with blood, calls out:

> Se te padre raspetasse,
> Quale hai me concio qui ti ritrovasse
>
> [If indeed a father waits for you,
> may that which you have done to me
> find you out] (*Tes.* 8.84.7-8).

This scene, as Limentani notes, is loosely based on one in which a Latin soldier begs Aeneas for mercy (*Aen.* 10.597-98). The plea is unsuccessful.

A savagery like that Aeneas shows in his rage at Pallas's death transforms Theseus's urban theater into a war zone. This process is further abetted by the gods. Mars and Venus, unlike the human spectators in the theater, look on at this scene of human violence and are dissatisfied. Mars especially senses "intiepidire il foco / che facea prima gli animi ferventi" ["that the fires were cooling that earlier had made hearts burn"] (*Tes.* 8.112.3-4). To rekindle this ardor, Mars, taking the form of Theseus, appears in the theater and berates Arcita (*Tes.* 8.112). The effect of the god's appearance is decisive. Their wrath rekindled, Arcita and his companions move against Palemone and his men, who "alquanto nel cor paurosi / divenner" ["became somewhat fearful at heart"] (*Tes.* 8.117.3-4). Shortly after this intervention, Arcita's faction is victorious when Palemone is seized by the man-eating horse of Cromis.

Theseus, the constant emblem of *pietas* in the first two books of **Teseida** and the man who asserts the dominance of that virtue in this very struggle, does not actually take part in the fighting. Nevertheless, even he is not immune to the *furor* manifested in the theater. Although Theseus remains in his seat, he is nonetheless

> tutto nel viso rosso come foco,
> tanto 'l disio del combatter poteo,
> di che più volte si tenne per poco
>
> [all red as fire in the face, so
> powerful was the desire for combat from which several times he
> barely restrained himself] (*Tes.*
> 8.89.3-6).

As a spectator, Theseus, too, capitulates in the triumph of *furor* over *pietas.*

Every factor, then combines to transform the theater of Theseus into a scene of savagery and furor. Although it is urban and manmade, it is transformed by human passions into a wilderness of violence. By the same process, the game Theseus designs for it becomes a war. The gods themselves aid this process, entering the theater and enflaming one group of champions against the other. Even Theseus succumbs to the pull of rage. Finally, it is the gods who determine the outcome of what Theseus expected to control himself. Their conclusion is the final and most blatant triumph of fury over *pietas.*

From above the acropolis, the gods look down on the scene in the theater (*Tes.* 9.2). They are content with the way events have worked out so far, they see a chance to fulfill the prayers of their worshipers. Arcita, the worshiper of Mars, has won the military victory for which he had prayed. Palemone has prayed to Venus not for victory but for Emilia to be his, and now the goddess prepares to reward her worshiper, as she explains to the war god:

> Bene hai d'Arcita piena l'orazione,
> che, come vedi, va vittorioso;
> or resta a me quella di Palemone,
> il qual perdente vedi star doglioso,
> a mio poter mandare a secuzione
>
> [You have completely fulfilled
> Arcita's prayer; he is, as you see,
> victorious; now that of Palemone,
> the loser, who is miserable, as
> you see, remains for me to bring
> to completion as best I can] (*Tes.*
> 9.3.1-5).

The particular method Venus chooses to achieve her goal confirms the triumph of *furor* over *pietas,* already evident in so many ways. Venus has already visited hell, where she has chosen one of the Furies, here called Erinis, for her purpose. The Fury, whose terrible form is described at length (*Tes.* 9.6), appears in the theater in the poem's only epiphany and causes great horror. The Fury's appearance, which is strongly reminiscent of manifestations of the divine in **Filostrato** and especially in **Filocolo,** shocks even the elements and the building itself (*Tes.* 9.6.5-8). The terrifying figure causes Arcita's horse to rear, and the beast falls on its rider. In this fall Arcita is mortally wounded (*Tes.* 9.8).

Arcita's fall from his horse completes the ordering of events that Venus and Mars have worked out between them to fulfill their worshipers' prayers. Arcita has the victory he prayed for, and the way is now cleared, after his lingering death, for Palemone to have Emilia. With the intervention of the Fury, too, the work of *furor* itself is completed. Theseus's *pietas* could not prevent the death of Arcita or, as it quickly appears, the deaths of fourteen other champions in the theater game. Theseus was indeed wrong when he asserted, "Vincerà il fallo la mia gran pietate." The *furor* of man's nature and the gods' collaboration with it have overcome Theseus's unaided virtue.

In his death fall, Arcita resembles Mezentius, as Limentani notes. At the conclusion of the contest in the theater, this identification of Arcita with one of Turnus's strongest and most furious companions in arms is significant. The confusion in the theater, which was reflected in the identification of both champions with Mezentius and Aeneas, appears to have resolved itself. In his fall, Arcita again resembles the furious Latin opponents of Aeneas. This general identification is given extra weight and extra significance by an event that quickly follows. Seeing the fall of the man she has immediately regarded as her fiancé, Emilia laments:

> Ora conosco ciò che volea dire
> Bellona sanguinosa, che davanti
> oggi m'è stata
>
> [Now I understand the significance of Bellona who has stood before me all day covered with blood] (*Tes.* 9.12.1-3).

This description recalls the angry prediction of Juno as she surveys the effects of Aeneas's campaign in Italy. She promises Lavinia, the presumed fiancée of Turnus who will eventually be won by Aeneas, that the goddess of war will be her bridesmaid:

> Sanguine Troiana et Rutulo dotabere, virgo
> et Bellona manet te pronuba
>
> [You will be dowered with the blood of the Trojans and Rutulians, virgin, and Bellona will go before you as bridesmaid] (*Aen.* 7.318-19).

By identifying Emilia with Lavinia, the equation between the contending suitors, Palemone and Arcita, and their Vergilian equivalents, Turnus and Aeneas, is reinforced.

The dying Arcita is identified with yet another Vergilian hero. After he is pulled from under his horse and laid in the theater, he soon regains consciousness. He cannot speak,

> ma gli occhi erranti in qua e 'n là voltava
> or questo or quello con sembianza pia
> mirando
>
> [but he turned his wandering eyes here and there, looking now
> at this one, now at that with a pitiful gaze] (*Tes.* 9.17.3-5).

Boccaccio's specification that Arcita's gaze went "here and there" ties the passage directly to a significant moment in the *Aeneid.* When Dido becomes convinced that Aeneas will indeed abandon her, her tender mood and expression change:

> Talia dicentem iamdudum aversa tuetur
> huc illuc volvens oculos totumque pererrat
> luminibus tacitis et sic accensa profatur
>
> [She had been looking at him distractedly while he spoke; then turning her gaze here and there, and looking him up and down, with empty eyes, and altogether enraged she spoke] (*Aen.* 4.362-64).

It is this empty look of incomprehension, not the rage that follows, that Arcita shares with Dido. He shares her tragic fate as well. She is as much a victim of her passion and the treachery of Venus, which aroused it, as she is Aeneas's victim. With this final portrayal of Arcita, his characterization becomes comprehensible and complete. He represents Turnus, Mezentius, and Dido, victims of Aeneas and of their own *furor* and victims of the gods as well. Dido, the victim of Venus, Mezentius, the victim of Jupiter, and Turnus, the victim of his protector, Juno, are merged in Arcita, whose fall, like theirs, is caused by *furor* in collaboration with an ultimately malevolent divine will.

In terms of the monuments of *Teseida,* then, it is clear that the temple of Venus, where Palemone makes his prayer, the temple of Mars, where Arcita prays, and the temple of Diana, where Emilia expresses her devotion, overpower the theater that stands for Theseus's unaided *pietas.* This is true, but the situation is more complex. I have suggested . . . that the theater is not a neutral structure or one that represents paganism in an unambiguous fashion. On the one hand, the theater is a monumental architectural achievement, and it testifies to the wealth and social organization of the ancient world. However, the theater also shows, as the Christian fathers asserted, the fundamental depravity of pagan culture. It is the theater, scene of bloody hunts, lewd plays, and violent gladiatorial contests, that shows most powerfully the uncontrollable passions of pre-Christian society. In a very real historical sense, the theater represents the *furor*—either lascivious or violent—that Roman culture, despite the civilizing mission Vergil announces, continued to reflect. The theater as the scene of Theseus's attempt to calm the *furor* of Palemone and Arcita is therefore a prejudiced choice. Christian, indeed, Stoic, polemic has paved the way for the notion that theatrical shows represent not *pietas* by any means but massive inducements to every sort of libidinous excess.

It is equally significant that the ancient theater was not a secular institution. Theseus may presume to rule there and pretend to impose order on the events that occur there, but, as the Christian encyclopedist, Isidore of Seville, summarizing a long tradition, continually asserts, theaters and theatrical games were dedicated to the pagan gods, and simple attendance at their functions constituted idolatry and demon worship. The intervention of the gods is to be anticipated, then, for the theaters are dedicated to their cult. The particular form in which the divine enters the theater in *Teseida*—that is, through the infernal if not the blatantly demonic—is predicted by the encyclopedic tradition of the Christian Middle Ages, as it is by patristic literature.

Theseus's choice of the theater as the scene for the confrontation of Palemone and Arcita is thus not just a misfortune within the context of the poem; it is, in a very real sense, historically determined. The institution Theseus chooses for the resolution of his problem is fundamentally corrupt. It fosters *furor,* not *pietas,* and it invites the intervention of gods who are really demons. In essence, then, Theseus's failure is not merely a private one; it also has implications for the whole of paganism. In Boccaccio's view, neither Athens nor the pre-Christian world in general can assert the control of *pietas* over *furor.*

Boccaccio uses this theater not only to assert this failure of historical paganism but also to critique major themes of the *Aeneid* and *Thebaid* from a Christian point of view. Both of these poems concern themselves with the control of *furor* by *pietas.* Generally speaking, Boccaccio sees the *Aeneid* as the story of Aeneas's attempt to assert control over his own violent and libidinous nature and that of his antagonists. Such control is only ambiguously reflected by the final event of the poem, Aeneas's furious killing of Turnus. It is clear, however, that where such control does occur, it occurs with divine sanction, and it is continually aided by the pacification of furious divinity by Jupiter and fate. In the *Thebaid,* there is a clearer triumph of *pietas.* There, Theseus, aided by fate and divinity, achieves a final settlement of Theban *furor.* That settlement had eluded Adrastus, a hero who was good and *pius,* as Theseus is, but never found his efforts seconded by divinity. Adrastus was right in his views, but he was ineffectual because his will was out of touch with the gods. Theseus's *pietas* prevails not only because of his greater personal qualities but also because his intervention in the aftermath of the Theban War is divinely supported. It is the purpose of *Teseida,* too, to assert the importance of the divine in overcoming *furor.* When the divine cooperates with *pietas, furor* is put down. When divinity is contrary, human effort is unavailing. While these themes are implicit in both the *Aeneid* and the *Thebaid,* Boccaccio makes them explicit and uses them to make a statement about pre-Christian society.

It is essential to this argument that the pagan gods in the second half of *Teseida* are not figures for Christian Providence. As Orosius argues, certain actions of the pagan gods were indeed providential. . . . [In] the case of the *Filocolo,* Boccaccio sees Providence at work in many moments of history. He sees it principally in the historical events that led to the founding of Rome, which, in its appointed time, gave birth to and disseminated the gospel of Christ. Not every action of the pagan gods is providential, however. The majority, while not contrary to the will of God, will certainly serve the more immediate ends of those demons who have presented themselves, in the Christian polemical view, to the credulous as Venus, Mars, Juno, and the rest. This is precisely what Theseus experiences. The gods who intervene in his theater are demonic in their

manifestations and have little inclination for aiding his pious intentions.

We can ascribe to Boccaccio in *Teseida,* then, a critique of paganism. He asserts in general that *furor* cannot be controlled by *pietas,* not only because passion overcomes man's self-control but also because the divine that should aid man is, in the days before Christ, largely demonic. The pagan claim to control *furor* through *pietas* is contradicted here. Without Christian or providential divinity to second it, Boccaccio argues, *pietas* is insufficient. . . .

Steven Grossvogel   (essay date 1992)

SOURCE: *Ambiguity and Allusion in Boccaccio's "Filocolo,"* Leo S. Olschki Editore, 1992, 254 p.

[*Here, Grossvogel offers an overview of the critical reception of the* Filocolo *and identifies one of the work's more problematic aspects, namely its ambiguous treatment of courtly and Christian love.*]

Of all Giovanni Boccaccio's Italian works, the *Filocolo* is among the least read and least studied. Written when Boccaccio was in his late twenties and living in Naples (1336-1338), the *Filocolo* is his first and longest experiment in narrative prose prior to the *Decameron.* The plot is largely derived from the considerably shorter *cantari* of Fiorio and Biancofiore which in turn were derived from the Old French romances of Floire and Blanchefleur. It narrates the love of Florio, King Felice's sole heir, and Biancifiore, the daughter of two Roman nobles, Lelio Africano and Giulia Topazia. Born on the same day, the two protagonists are raised together at Felice's court in Verona. When they fall in love with each other, the king separates them out of fear that Florio's love for the socially inferior Biancifiore will diminish their family's nobility. After sending Florio to the neighboring town of Montoro, the king and his seneschal plot to kill Biancifiore in the hope that her death will bring an end to Florio's lovesickness. Upon hearing that his beloved has been falsely accused of treason and condemned to the stake, Florio returns to Verona and rescues her. Once liberated, Biancifiore is restored to her place in court, and Florio returns to Montoro. The king, however, continues to plot against Biancifiore and sells her as a slave to two Italian merchants who in turn sell her to the Admiral of Alexandria. In the meantime, the king and queen make their son believe that Biancifiore is dead. When Florio discovers that she is not, he sets off to find her. Florio's quest for Biancifiore brings him first to Naples, where he participates in Fiammetta's court of love, and finally to Alexandria where the two protagonists consummate their love. The two lovers are caught *in flagrante delicto* by the Admiral, and are sentenced to die at the stake. When Florio's friends hear about it, they come to the rescue and defeat the Admiral's forces with the help of Mars and Venus. After the lovers' liberation, the Admiral discovers that Florio is his nephew, and asks him to marry Biancifiore in public. The protagonists spend almost a year in Alexandria before beginning their long journey back to Felice's court. On their way home they stop in Rome where Biancifiore discovers her noble ancestry and where she and Florio convert to Christianity. The

Woodcut from the 1568 Florentine edition of Ninfale Fiesolano.

narrative concludes with a reconciliation scene on Felice's deathbed, and the subsequent coronation of the two protagonists.

Boccaccio added to this fairly simple plot a large number of digressions and amplifications which have made the *Filocolo* the object of considerable criticism. For well over a hundred years critics and scholars have pointed to the work's narrative and structural "weaknesses" without carefully considering the function Boccaccio intended them to have in the *Filocolo.* Such criticism has largely been due to the scholars' own embarrassment at the fact that the father of European narrative prose (as Boccaccio has often been called) should have written a work which fails to live up to the standards later set by the *Decameron.* Their criticism often reflects modern aesthetic and literary tastes, and is not responsive to the medieval qualities of this work, qualities which are harder to appreciate when juxtaposed to the "modernity" of the *Decameron.* The following overview of what critics and scholars have said about the *Filocolo* during the past fifty years will reveal some of the problems which this work has generated and which still need to be resolved.

One of the first scholars to devote serious attention to the *Filocolo* was Salvatore Battaglia. Besides his edition of this work, Battaglia also wrote one of the first important critical essays on the *Filocolo* [*Schemi lirici nell'arte del Boccaccio,* 1935]. Unlike the positivist scholars before him who attempted to interpret the *Filocolo* in autobiographical terms, Battaglio attempted to place some distance between the work and its author. Instead of an autobiographical text, Battaglia saw the *Filocolo* as a lyrical expression of a sentimental journey filled with psychological adventures. The sentimental tone and lyrically abstract atmosphere which permeate the *Filocolo* are a significant departure from the typical medieval romances on which this work is based. The numerous digressions, episodes, characters, and descriptions are, according to Battaglia, echoes of one voice—that of the author. They constitute the literary fiction into which his personal experiences are translated; but because they are given a lyrical and abstract mein, they are never purely empirical.

Speaking about the world of the protagonists, Battaglia says that it is a reflection of the courtly world Boccaccio had become acquainted with at the Angevin court in Naples. It is also an internalized world which, according to Battaglia, reflects the protagonist's solitude and, by extension, that of the author: it is an idyllic interlude that has been externalized. Battaglia claims that Boccaccio took this from Ovid's *Metamorphosis,* where myths are projections of human passions translated from illusory and unstable experiences to perennial and immobile ones. Similar transformations in the characters of the *Filocolo* celebrated these abstract and contemplative aspects of erotic passion; and in so doing, they translate the static nature of sentimental behavior into mythic and idyllic forms. These metamorphoses, concludes Battaglia, freeze the immobile solitude of amorous contemplation within the solitary and tacit forms of Nature.

Although Battaglia rarely cites examples from the *Filocolo* to support his generalizations, anyone familiar with Boccaccio's text will find his observations quite compelling. A closer reading of the *Filocolo,* however, reveals that there is more to the world of the protagonists than fantastic, idyllic, and solitary meditations on love. Contrary to what Battaglia claims, the fantastic is not used at the expense of human values and social customs. The world of the *Filocolo* may be far from the realism of the *Decameron,* as Battaglia states, but the "communal sentimental existence" of the characters is not divorced from reality. [The] *Filocolo* is actually a *speculum mundi* in the guise of a courtly romance.

With regard to the work's shortcomings, Battaglia states that it is too episodic, dispersive, and discordant in its tone and proportions. He attributes these "caratteri negativi" to the work's sources: Boccaccio's periphrases and linguistic elaborations accentuate the defects in the fluid and quick paced *cantari.* According to Battaglia, the byzantine qualities of the sources are deformed by Boccaccio's excessive use of additional literary and extra-literary material. By amplifying his meager sources, Boccaccio made each *amplificatio* a story in itself which often has no connection to the plot or the other stories in the *Filocolo:* it lacks the unity one would expect from a work which is meant to have the structure of a medieval romance. Battaglia concludes that the disorderly structure of the *Filocolo* is a reflection of the author's youthful exuberance and his inability to "discipline" his culture. Battaglia's overall impressions of the *Filocolo's* weaknesses seem justified after a cursory reading of this long and seemingly incongruous work. [But many] of the amplifications and digressions in the *Filocolo* are thematically connected to the plot: the apparent lack of unity of form, style, and narrative artistry does not necessarily preclude a thematic unity of content and meaning.

Several years after Battaglia's article, Natalino Sapegno wrote an essay on the *Filocolo* [*Il Trecento,* 1942] which shares some of the same views. Like Battaglia, Sapegno feels that Boccaccio's artistry lies in the young writer's linguistic and stylistic experiments: the oratorical, majestic, and analytical prose of the *Filocolo* will reappear in the *Decameron* in a pared and lightened form. Sapegno praises the precious sonority and hidden harmonies in this poetic prose, but claims that Boccaccio was unable to distinguish between eloquence and poetry, thereby giving rise to the prolix dialogues and "useless" descriptions which permeate the *Filocolo.*

Like Battaglia, Sapegno sees Boccaccio's elaborate narra-

tive as a vehicle for expressing psychological experiences within the fragmentary plot of a conventional romance. The narrative is adapted and transformed, according to Sapegno, to suit Boccaccio's minute psychological analyses, his understanding of human experience, and his dialectics of love. The love story itself, however, is tenuous and gets lost in the dispersive and unbalanced structure of the narrative. Sapegno recognizes the thematic and not purely autobiographical importance of love in the *Filocolo,* and states that this love is not Dante's Platonic and heaven-bound love, but rather a carnal and fragile love which never becomes coarse or vulgar. Although Sapegno's characterization of the protagonists' love is correct, he overlooks several of the thematic implications love has in the *Filocolo.*

Like Battaglia, Sapegno too sees a lack of unity in the *Filocolo,* particularly between the plot and the overwhelming "cultura" Boccaccio attempts to incorporate in it. His criticism of Boccaccio's seemingly disorganized use of literary and extra-literary sources is echoed by later critics. Vittore Branca, the dean of Boccaccio studies, makes a similar observation when he notes [in his *Giovanni Boccaccio: profilo biografico,* 1977] that Boccaccio's "disordinato e pesante bagaglio culturale" overwhelms the narrative of the *Filocolo.* Antonio Enzo Quaglio, the leading authority on the *Filocolo,* when confronting the apparent lack of unity in this work [in his *Tra fonti e testo del Fiocolo,* 1963], and the seemingly disproportionate importance Boccaccio gives to the various episodes, digressions, and addenda, concludes:

> esso è nato e resta un centone di tipo medievale, la cui ossatura ricorda sia l'impianto dei romanzi di avventura e d'amore dell'epica due e trecentesca di estrazione europea, sia le enciclopedie e i florilegi di cultura scolastica in cui si stipano con fonti classiche aneddoti, leggende, proverbi dell'età di mezzo.

If indeed Boccaccio can be accused of overburdening the *Filocolo* with cultural erudition, even at the expense of narrative form, we must assume that he had a reason for doing so. Is his use of erudition purely a rhetorical strategy (*imitatio, dilatio,* and *amplificatio*)? Or could it be that Boccaccio also used these and other rhetorical devices for reasons which critics have not taken into account? More than draw our attention to an inappropriate use of culture in the *Filocolo,* the criticism leveled against the *Filocolo* indicates the need to deal with this cultural erudition. Rather than regard it simply as rhetorical "baggage", we must see if Boccaccio's "cultura" has a more precise function in the narrative.

Similar criticism of the *Filocolo* was also expressed by Luigi Malagoli [in his *Timbro della prosa e motivi dell'arte del Boccaccio nel Fiocolo,* 1959]. For Malagoli the narrative moves rigidly within a rhetorical frame which consists largely of speeches and conventional divine interventions in human affairs, both of which break the action. The dialogues, which follow one another in a fairly rapid succession, break the narrative and make it languid. Malagoli also criticizes the schematic and predisposed order in which events take place within the protagonists' lives. ([However,] this is actually a deliberate authorial strategy:

the predisposed order of events is meant to reflect the providential plan at the heart of the plot itself.) Malagoli mitigates his criticism, however, by stating that the discursive parentheses in the narrative, with its repetitions and recapitulations, are another example of the work's prolonged rhythm and the author's partiality for delay and deferral, all of which have their own legitimacy in the narrative. Unfortunately, Malagoli does not tell us what this legitimacy consists of. A possible answer can be found in the classical rhetorical device of *dilatio* (delay and deferral) which, as Patricia Parker has shown [in her *Inescapable Romance: Studies in the Poetics of a Mode,* 1979], is a common attribute of the romance genre. Boccaccio's use of *dilatio,* as well as other narrative devices such as *amplificatio* and *imitatio,* reflect the young writer's deliberate choice of narrative techniques. Like critics before him, Malagoli did not recognize that many of these techniques serve to convey the narrative's thematic meaning.

Besides analyzing the rhetorical qualities of the *Filocolo,* Malagoli also analyzes Boccaccio's style. Malagoli takes into account Boccaccio's deliberate and, at times, innovative use of medieval stylistics, particularly the combination of various *cursus* (*planus, tardus,* and *trispondaicus*) with the rhythmic syntax of Boccaccio's long sentences. Malagoli sees elements of style, which became famous in the *Decameron,* already present in the *Filocolo.* Speaking about Boccaccio's early style, Malagoli indicates that the syntax and intonations are uniformly rhythmic and slow-moving, giving the *Filocolo* its fluid, musical, and at times monotonous style. The intricate interlacing of relative clauses, causative constructions, consecutive conjunctions, and gerundives within a single Ciceronian sentence are the trademark of Boccaccio's syntax. Malagoli adds that the subordination of clauses and the way these clauses are used in a sentence produce a cause and effect relation which serves to represent reality in a new and innovative manner: things are seen in terms of how they are connected to one another, but are not explored in depth. Everything is held together by a unifying chain of events, but no one thing is ever the object of particular attention. As a result, concludes Malagoli, everything represented in the *Filocolo* seems to be placed on the same narrative plane: no single event or idea stands out. This in turn makes the narrative fluid and circular in its representation of reality, uniform and constant in its dramatization of events; all of which anticipates, according to Malagoli, the dramatic elements in the *Decameron.*

Malagoli's analysis of how Boccaccio's style affects his narrative is compelling; but by viewing Boccaccio's choice of stylistic and rhetorical devices in purely aesthetic terms, he fails to take into account the manner in which these devices are related to the meaning of the text itself. In fact, Malagoli's interpretation of the plot of *Filocolo* is actually a projection of the characters' own inability to comprehend the importance of the events in their life. The fact that both the narrator and the protagonists fail to see the significance of their own experiences (an important theme in the *Filocolo*) should not be mistaken for the author's inability to highlight the most important episodes in his work.

Many of the "caratteri negativi" which critics found in the *Filocolo* were reevaluated for the first time by Guido Di Pino [in his *La polemica del Boccaccio,* 1953]. Di Pino was one of the first critics to suggest that Boccaccio's narrative and poetic strategies were an integral part of the tale's meaning. Analyzing key passages from the *Filocolo,* Di Pino illustrated the poetic devices Boccaccio adopted in the portrayal of the characters. Biancifiore is portrayed in dramatic terms: her character takes shape as a result of the dismal conditions she must live in, and her dramatic confrontation with her misfortune gives her nobility. As Di Pino astutely points out, Boccaccio plays with shade imagery and *chiaroscuro* descriptions of Biancifiore in order to heighten the dramatic clash between her nobility and her ignoble condition: her "turbata bellezza" becomes the poetic essence of her character. As the narrative progresses, her personality acquires greater autonomy and self-awareness. She accepts her adversity with the same constancy of Griselda (the heroine of the last novella in the *Decameron*), while displaying the same signs of anxiety that we find in the unhappy love stories of the fourth day of the *Decameron.*

The portrayal of Florio, on the other hand, is more lyrical and elegiac: his internal solitude is constantly juxtaposed to his actions. The dichotomy between action and elegy is accentuated by the divine interventions which often determine the nature of the protagonist's actions. As a result, the world of adventure recedes and gives way to Florio's melancholy which in turn becomes the dominant and most poetic note of the romance. It is unfortunate that Di Pino's brilliant insights into the portrayal of the characters in the *Filocolo* do not also take into account the thematic issues which are emblematized by the characters' conduct: the relationship between action and elegy, love and melancholy, drama and dramatic irony, all of which are thematically important because they govern the plot.

Looking at the poetic qualities at work in the plot itself, Di Pino states that by elevating the tale of Florio and Biancifiore above the level of the popular *cantari,* Boccaccio was not simply elevating the style but also the dramatic tone and cultural setting of the tale. Boccaccio accomplished this by using supernatural interventions and historical, mythological and geographic digressions, all of which give the *Filocolo* its solemn tone. The elevated tone of the tale is also created by the soliloquies and dialogues which embellish the expression of the characters' sentiments. According to Di Pino, the pomp and splendor of Boccaccio's writing have only one purpose, the creation of an atmosphere which ennobles the sensual and enlivens the inner quest of each character. Although Di Pino is correct in recognizing the deliberate attempt to elevate the narrative to a higher stylistic plane, one must take issue with his claim that this is the sole purpose for these digressions. [These] digressions are thematically connected to the plot itself, and play a significant role in the narrative's overall meaning.

Carlo Muscetta made a claim similar to Di Pino's several years later. Muscetta states that by choosing to write in prose rather than in poetry, Boccaccio adopted a stylistic means which would give a nobler quality to the popular tale of Florio and Biancifiore. Muscetta sees in Boccaccio's use of epithets, rhetoric, erudite insertions, and long sentences with several different verb tenses a deliberate attempt to obliterate the humble origins of this tale (much the same way Boccaccio attempted to cover up his illegitimate birth by claiming to be born of a French noblewoman). Having obliterated its humble origins, Boccaccio elevates the love story of Florio and Biancifiore by giving it a higher style and by amplifying the tenuous plot of the *cantari* with numerous digressions, new episodes, literary and extra-literary insertions, fables, and legends, all of which are set, according to Muscetta, in a "cornice" which is historic, realistic, and contemporary at the same time. Boccaccio's use of important authors, most notably Ovid, Lucan, Dante, and other acknowledged and unacknowledged writers, is, according to Muscetta, another example of Boccaccio's elevation of this tale to the dignity of the works he is using. Muscetta's observation suggests that Boccaccio is giving his work an importance which is comparable to that of his classical sources, a point Victoria Kirkham would make several years later [in her "Reckoning with Boccaccio's 'Questioni d'Amore'," *Modern Language Notes* LXXXIX (1974)]. If that is the case, it would only seem natural that the *Filocolo* should be read along the same lines these other works have been read. Instead, the biases which have plagued the *Filocolo* have also prevented it from even getting the kind of critical attention Boccaccio's other "minor" works have received.

Speaking about the "superfluous" descriptions and the "meandering" structure of the plot, Muscetta states (as Battaglia had done before him) that they are typical of Byzantine and Hellenistic narratives, but adds that Boccaccio goes to great lengths to reiterate and amplify his sources, and does so with a "youthful desire" to outdo himself. Muscetta also states that the action of the plot is revealed in monologues, epistles, dialogues, and innumerable descriptions which increase the pathos of the dramatic circumstances and give depth to the author's psychological analysis. It is hard to agree with Muscetta's assertion that these seemingly extraneous insertions in the narrative "sembrano scritti per sfoggio di bravura decorativa".

Muscetta's observations reflect the difficulty that even the best critics have in grasping the puzzling structure of the *Filocolo.* These difficulties may have been spawned, in part, by Fiammetta's own statement at the beginning of Book I: "ti priego che [. . .] tu affanni in comporre un picciolo libretto, volgarmente parlando, nel quale il nascimento, lo 'nnamoramento e gli accidenti de' detti due infino alla loro fine interamente si contenga" (I 1, 26). If we give any credence to the myth that Fiammetta (the *senhal* for Boccaccio's beloved) asked him to write "un picciolo libretto", then one could consider the more than six hundred pages which make up the *Filocolo* as the product of youthful exuberance and a lover's zeal. But in so doing we are also assuming that Boccaccio and the narrator are one. Whether Fiammetta's influence on the narrator is fact or fiction, the *senhal* should be regarded as a figure for poetic inspiration. The fact that she should have prompted the narrator to write over six hundred pages (everything but "un picciolo libretto") is part of the Boccaccio's use of

irony. This and other ironic remarks in the *Filocolo* could be seen as Boccaccio's way of mocking the narrator as lover, and lovers in general. Boccaccio's ironic voice is present at the beginning of the *Filocolo* to distinguish it from the narrator's persona. As in the case of Dante and other medieval writers who served as models for Boccaccio, the figure of the beloved as the writer's prime source of inspiration is a well-established topos, a literary device with a fiction of its own. If we deem the persona of the narrator as the prime means of expression in the *Filocolo,* then it is not surprising that critics from Battaglia to Muscetta consider this work a stylistic "failure". If, on the other hand, we distinguish the narrator from Boccaccio the author, we discover that the narrative is more profound and far less superficial than these critics have led us to believe.

It seems safe to conclude that most Italian criticism on the *Filocolo,* prior to Quaglio's critical edition of 1967, was more intent on giving "un giudizio critico complessivo sul valore dell'opera" (the words are Quaglio's) than on arriving at the kind of interpretations Vittore Branca, Luigi Russo, Giovanni Getto, et al. were proposing for the *Decameron.* Although many of these critical appraisals provide insight into the *Filocolo*'s historical, linguistic, stylistic, and inter-textual background, they seldom consider the work's thematic significance.

Quaglio's critical edition of 1967 did more to alter the way the *Filocolo* would be read than any previous work of scholarship. Quaglio's wealth of textual and critical annotations proved that Boccaccio's first work of narrative prose fiction was not nearly as simplistic as critics had claimed. As both Quaglio and Muscetta have shown, the bad fortune of the *Filocolo* was in part due to Gaetano Tizzone's Renaissance edition of this work. Tizzone revised the *Filocolo* so that its style would conform to Renaissance literary tastes: many archaic words and latinisms were expurgated, and the original syntax of Boccaccio's sentences was made less precious and laborious. Since Tizzone's edition served as the basis for practically all editions of the *Filocolo* (including Battaglia's) prior to Quaglio's, it is not surprising that some of the negative criticism directed at the style of the *Filocolo* was in part due to the lack of an unadulterated text.

After Quaglio's critical edition appeared, scholars and critics working on the *Filocolo* could no longer settle for broad generalizations. Quaglio's painstaking work of identifying sources, inter-textual allusions, and footnoting practically every difficult or puzzling line in the *Filocolo* forced scholars to look at this work more closely and analyze its key passages in greater detail. To cite just a few examples, Luigi Sasso reevaluated previous interpretations of the characters' names; Giuseppe Chiecchi looked at Boccaccio's use of epistolography as an extension of the Provençal "amor de lonh" motif; Luigi Surdich analyzed the quest motif in the protagonists' journey to and from Alexandria; and Francesco Bruni has reconsidered the way Boccaccio used his Latin sources. Although these studies have proven to be more accurate than the previous ones in their critical appraisal of the *Filocolo,* they still fall short of offering an overall interpretation of the text. This is best illustrated in Bruni's thought-provoking essay ["*Il Filocolo* e lo spazio della letteratura volgare," in *Miscellanea di studi in onore di Vittore Branca II: Boccaccio e din torni,* 1983].

Like critics before him, Bruni underscores the overabundant and disorderly narration in the *Filocolo,* but points out (as Victoria Kirkham and Janet Smarr had done before him) that the work has symmetrical correspondences and reference points whose purpose, according to Bruni, is to balance this excessive material. In addition to pointing out some of these symmetrical patterns, Bruni ascribes the importance of the allusions in the *Filocolo* to Boccaccio's desire to write in a middle style (as opposed to the higher style of Virgil, Statius, Lucan, and the other classical writers he uses in his work). By comparing the context in which Boccaccio's literary allusions are made with the context from which they are taken, Bruni concludes that Boccaccio was not attempting to say the same things his *auctores* were saying. Following a premise which is similar to Giuseppe Velli's, Bruni claims that Boccaccio used literary allusions for poetic *imitatio,* and concludes that there is no superior moral perspective that runs through the *Filocolo,* nor any connection between a source and the way it is used in this work. Boccaccio's choice of allusions and source material is strictly meant to convey a certain tone (dramatic, elegiac, etc.) and to elevate the tale of Florio and Biancifiore above the level of the *cantari,* but not high enough to deal with the same philosophical ideals or "sottigliezze" that his classical sources dealt with. Bruni claims that by detaching himself from the major classical works of Latin and early Italian literature, and by distancing himself from the committed ideology of medieval Latin culture, Boccaccio was able to delve further into the Ovidian tradition of elegiac comedy, the romance genre, and the culture of the early vernacularized editions of Latin classics, all of which acknowledged their inferiority vis-à-vis their major classical models. Bruni illustrates this by comparing the *Filocolo* to the Old French *Roman d'Eneas* which shifted its center of gravity from the *Aeneid*'s religious, political and historic concerns to Ovid's erotic concerns. By divorcing himself from the more elevated themes of the classics, Boccaccio is able to give the amorous aspects of his romance their own literary space.

Bruni's essay reflects an assumption which has persisted throughout the century among Italian critics of the *Filocolo:* the work's style matches its content—one is a reflection of the other. If we were to apply Bruni's method to Dante's *Commedia,* which, like the *Filocolo* was deliberately written in a middle style, then one would have to conclude that the *Commedia* does not deal with religious, political and historic concerns comparable to those found in the *Aeneid.* Unfortunately, Bruni's essay is symptomatic of the extent to which Boccaccio's style and narrative form have prejudiced many critics' views on the allusions, themes, issues, and "lofty" concerns which actually permeate the *Filocolo.* If we keep in mind the large number of allusions which Boccaccio makes to Dante's *Commedia* and *Vita Nuova,* we soon realize that the *Filocolo* is as much an *imitatio* of Dante as it is of the classical Latin authors Bruni cites. This in itself suggests that we should

read the *Filocolo* along the same lines that Boccaccio might have read the *Vita Nuova* and the *Commedia.*

In the United States, where the study of Dante has determined to a large extent the way Boccaccio is read, we find critical approaches to the *Filocolo* which give considerably greater importance to the ethical and moral issues raised in the text. Four critics in particular, Nicolas Perella, Victoria Kirkham, Robert Hollander, and Janet Smarr, have provided us with new insights into the *Filocolo* which have significantly contributed to our understanding of this work. Nicolas Perella, the first American critic to devote serious attention to the *Filocolo,* analyzed it in thematic terms [in his "The World of Boccaccio's *Filocolo, PMLA* CXXVI (1961)]. Perella states that the main theme is "the natural or instinctive love that attracts two young people of the opposite sex and the persistence of their love against the obstacles erected by an unsympathetic law or by class conscious relatives concerned with preserving the distinctions created by social and economic position". Other themes in the *Filocolo* (love, fortune, beauty, and courtliness) are essential to an understanding of Boccaccio's spiritual world, according to Perella, because they are part of the author's psychological portrayal of man's sentimental life.

Looking at the theme of love, Perella concurs with Italian critics who claim that it is far from animalism. Sexual love is made beautiful, not condemned, but the context in which it takes place is criticized. The most erotic moments, such as the near seduction of Florio by the two maidens, are free of "crude materialistic description" and are filled with the "tremulous yet passionate awe and desire for possession that accompany the awakening to the vision of beauty". Awe at feminine beauty is a motif in the *Filocolo* which, as Perella points out, Boccaccio has taken from the "dolce stil novo": Biancifiore has a celestial splendor and divine attributes which, however, do not diminish her physical attractions or "lift her into a sphere of impalpable spirituality". Furthermore, "it is beauty primarily as a physical quality that is made to have a refining or elevating effect". As Perella correctly points out, all these courtly elements can be found in the protagonists' conduct and reasoning, and serve to ennoble both the characters and the text. What Perella does not show, however, are the ambiguous aspects of the protagonists' courtliness: while at times it may ennoble the characters, at other times it also debases them.

Looking at those elements which make the *Filocolo* an "immature work", Perella, like Italian critics before him, criticizes Boccaccio's inability to fuse the diverse material he brings to his work, his arbitrary juxtaposition of differing traditions, tendencies, and episodes, his enthusiastic but inordinate outpouring of culture, and his use of numerous and diverse allusions and echoes, all of which, according to Perella, have no apparent connection to one another. In the words of Perella, much of this is "irrelevant material" which may have been intended as an integral part of the work, but is simply an ornamental device. For Perella, the classical gods are a case in point: they are principle actors and ruling agents of a world which Boccaccio studies with such psychological realism that their presence is "superfluous and bothersome". According to Perella, the gods are an expedient for Boccaccio to move action without having to give logical connections or additional psychological probing: they are one more example of how Boccaccio's culture could "tyrannize him and do violence to his own genius".

Despite the prominence of these "unsubstantial literary phantasms", the pagan deities are not the real antagonists in the *Filocolo,* Fortuna is, according to Perella. Fortuna is not conceived as a Dantean-Christian "handmaiden or administrator of God operating within an intelligible providential order of things", but rather a metaphorical expression, "a personification, a rhetorical device seeking to vitalize the abstract and neutral concept of the [. . .] unexpected happening". It is hard to agree with Perella that Fortuna has no relationship to a transcendent order of things. [Fortuna] is closely connected to the providential plan which permeates the plot of the *Filocolo.* This, however, does not preclude Fortuna from also functioning as a metaphor: many characters in the *Filocolo* in fact treat her as such, blaming her for their own shortcomings and failures. Perella is correct, however, when he says that the reality of Fortuna is completely contingent upon the given desires of human beings. [Fortuna] does not abate her ill will against the protagonists until they have brought their appetites fully under the control of reason.

Several years later Victoria Kirkham revealed the central importance of the thirteen *questioni d'amore* which are discussed at Fiammetta's court of love in Naples. As Kirkham has shown, the *questioni* have a symmetrical structure which centers around the debate between Fiammetta (the queen of this court of love) and Caleone, whom both Kirkham and Quaglio identify as Boccaccio the narrator. The debate centers around the relative merits of *amore onesto* and *amore per diletto,* with Fiammetta supporting the former and Caleone the latter. Fiammetta rejects *amore per diletto,* which Kirkham identifies with courtly love, in favor of *amore onesto,* which Kirkham associates with Christian love. Kirkham concludes that, "The *questioni d'amore* thus appear to be structured around a double perspective involving on the one hand the relative, or peripheral, supremacy of Cupid, and on the other the absolute and central supremacy of God".

Kirkham's analysis, however, is not limited to the *questioni d'amore.* She illustrates the way in which this "double perspective of courtly and Christian love" has both a structural and thematic importance in the plot itself. For example, the dream visions Florio has immediately before and after the court of love episode represent, according to Kirkham, courtly love and Christian love respectively. The concentric patterns Kirkham finds in the love court and in the dream visions that frame it also appear in the larger frame of the tale itself. As Kirkham has shown, the protagonists' movement from courtly love to Christian love (as witnessed by their conversion to Christianity) also brings them full circle when they complete the pilgrimage Lelio and Giulia had begun, and when they fulfill in Book V the numerous visions which appeared in the first four books. By proposing these thematic and structural patterns within the *Filocolo,* Kirkham rectifies earlier criti-

cism about the digressive and seemingly meaningless structure of the *Filocolo.* Kirkham's analysis proves that the innovative passages Boccaccio added to the rough material of the source tale play an integral part in both the meaning and the structure of the narrative.

A few years later, Robert Hollander [in his *Boccaccio's Two Venuses,* 1977] incorporated Kirkham's conclusions in his contention that there are two Venuses in the *Filocolo,* a terrestrial and a celestial Venus. Hollander concludes that "whatever the aesthetic merit of the *Filocolo,* [. . .] Boccaccio has constructed what we might call [. . .] a "Christian romance," in which the deity with whom we begin, the Venus of the *Ars amatoria,* is superseded by a better Venus, who in turn yields to the true God". Hollander's thesis thus rectifies Perella's claim that the classical gods are insignificant in the narrative.

More recently, Janet Smarr [in her *Boccaccio and Fiammetta: The Narrator as Lover,* 1986] has taken the theses of Kirkham and Hollander a step further. Since many of the issues and episodes discussed in her compelling study are also discussed in this book, a close look at her essay can serve as the point of departure for our analysis of the *Filocolo.* Smarr begins by reaffirming the literary fiction behind the name Fiammetta and the persona of the narrator. This means, according to Smarr, that Boccaccio's work must be read on several levels, not just the literal level (as earlier scholars and critics had done). In addition to proposing a moral and allegorical reading of Boccaccio's work, Smarr sees a polarity between the Ovidian and Dantean elements that appear throughout the *Filocolo.* Boccaccio's use of Ovid reflects a worldly love whose literature serves as a means of attracting the woman to the narrator, whereas his use of Dante reflects the holy love whose literature serves to move the lover to his lady, and in turn to God. According to Smarr, Boccaccio is writing "to seduce and to educate, to draw the soul toward pleasure and toward truth [. . .] to join the erotic with the moral".

Looking at the opening chapters, Smarr sees a mixture of religious and secular narratives which reflect two different writers: the narrator as lover "who writes as a labor of love at the request of his lady Maria", and Ilario "the original author of the history [. . .] who within the story converted Florio and his companions to Christianity". The existence of two fictional authors (besides the real Boccaccio) implies two different intentions for the same narration: the narrator's offer to educate lovers "in the art of "perfect" love exemplified by Florio and Biancifiore" and Ilario's story which is supposed to educate future readers in the same holy love he converted Florio and Biancifiore to. The *Filocolo,* therefore, is meant to inspire "two quite different kinds of love: human and divine".

As Smarr has shown, the doubleness of the text is reflected in similar dualities between the spiritual and erotic themes and allusions that appear in the tale itself: Priapus/Astrea, lover/monk, classic epic/Christian allegory, Florio's adventures/Christ's mission on earth, Florio and Biancifiore's love/Christ's incarnation and redemption of man, etc. This doubleness also appears in Florio's journey to Biancifiore and in his journey to God, as revealed by the double meaning of the word "salute": besides its Dantean meaning of salvation, the word also has sexual connotations, as seen in the expressions "porto di salute" and "nave in porto". Smarr's insight into the spiritual meaning of "salute" and its thematic importance in the *Filocolo* is very convincing. It is hard to agree, however, with her claim that Florio's "etterno esilio" (i. e. his journey to Biancifiore) is due to Eve's sin and is equated with the loss of Biancifiore. [Florio's] journey brings him close to the "etterno esilio" of Hell (like Ulysses's journey in *Inferno* XXVI) before it brings him to God. His journey to Bianci-fiore must end (along with his *amor per diletto*) before he and Biancifiore can find God and *caritas* (*amor onesto*).

Looking at Fiammetta, the queen of the court of love, Smarr states that she is the same lady the narrator addresses in the introduction to his book, whereas her admirer (Caleone) is a figure for the narrator. As Smarr has convincingly shown, both women are introduced with religious resonances. The queen of the court of love is given attributes reserved to the Virgin Mary, including the notion that her love "binds together both the cosmos and human society". This in turn is supported by the fact that it is Fiammetta who advocates *amore onesto* over *amore per diletto*. Fiammetta becomes for Smarr "a miracle sent from the heaven of the celestial Venus as a demonstration of divine love, the holy alternative of Cupid's 'dardi' ".

There is, however, a certain amount of ambiguity in the debate between Fiammetta and Caleone, as Smarr astutely points out: if *amore onesto* is the best kind of love and *amore utile* the worst, where does *amore per diletto* stand? "Fiammetta's argument with Caleone attempts to classify it on one side or the other, ignoring the idea of a middle ground. Is she, then, entirely correct in her assessment or is she failing to acknowledge the possibility that such love can lead to good?" Smarr looks for answers to these crucial questions in the amorous adventures of Florio and Biancifiore. Looking at the literary antecedents of the episode narrating the protagonists' falling in love (*Inferno* V and *Aeneid* I), Smarr claims that "the negative implications of both these models are transmuted by the innocence of Boccaccio's young couple". A closer look at the protagonists' conduct, however, suggests that they are not quite as innocent as Smarr and other critics have suggested. Smarr attempts to further support her claim by viewing the protagonists' secret marriage in the tower as a positive step: "The *Filocolo* celebrates their marriage as a relation that can reconcile virtue and chastity with sexual desire. Venus and Diana, the motivating deities of much of the *Filocolo*'s action, join forces for the marriage of Florio and Biancifiore". Marriage is indeed the only solution to the protagonists' amorous and social hardships; however, the fact that the two lovers secretly marry because of their *amor per diletto,* and the fact that this marriage brings about a massacre and almost kills them, suggest that there is a darker side to the protagonists' clandestine activities in the tower.

Smarr concludes that Boccaccio, like Dante, "is turning love stories to an ultimately Christian use, thus "saving" the pleasures of Ovid's poetry in both senses of the word: preserving them and transforming them for Christian

readers", and adds that "human love can actually lead to Christian love without our needing to reject the former". I believe, instead, that in the *Filocolo* Ovidian love gives way to Christian love: *amor per diletto* is one of several stumbling blocks the lovers must overcome in their quest for beatitude (*amor onesto*). [Ovidian] love is a false (i. e. pagan) image of Christian love, and must be renounced before *caritas* can be attained.

If we interpret the duality between *amor per diletto* and *amor onesto* as a clash between courtly love and Christian love, whereby the latter rejects the former (as suggested by Kirkham), are we overlooking the possibility that these two kinds of love have something in common? If, on the other hand, we interpret this duality as a contrast between Ovidian and Dantean love, whereby the former leads to the latter without rejecting it (as Smarr has suggested), are we ignoring the possibility that these two loves might be irreconcilable? Although it may be argued that Ovid's works were "moralized" in the Middle Ages in order to make them more acceptable to a Christian audience, it is hard to see how Dante's love for Beatrice, or even Christian love, can be reconciled with the love described in the *Ars amatoria*. By the same token, it is hard to see how Dante's repressed sexual desire for Beatrice (as revealed in the first dream of the *Vita Nuova*) can be placed at the same level as *caritas,* even though Dante feels Christian charity and beatitude whenever he sees Beatrice. Could it be that Boccaccio viewed Dante as someone who tried unsuccessfully to bridge the gap between "human love" and Christian love?

If, as Smarr claims, Dante and Ovid coexist in the *Filocolo,* it is because the narrator's Ovidian love story barely hides Ilario's Dantean tale on which it is based. Ilario's subtext and its Christian message are a palimpsest which lies just beneath the narrator's own superficial tale of Florio and Biancifiore. It is up to the reader to go beyond the narrator's story in order to reach Ilario's more meaningful source tale. The fact that the narrator as lover is oblivious to the spiritual message of Ilario's subtext suggests that the love he valorizes in his narrative (*amor per diletto*) has little spiritual significance other than the fact that it may eventually lead to or be superseded by *caritas.* Furthermore, the fact that the narrator believes, as do the characters in the *Filocolo,* that this kind of love will bring happiness (a point that is repeatedly disproven by the misadventures of Florio, Biancifiore, Fileno, Caleone and Idalogo) suggests that he, like Caleone, does not recognize that *amor per diletto* and beatitude ("true happiness") are two different things. Ultimately, it is the author, not the short-sighted narrator, who understands the moral implications of his Ovidian/classical and Dantean/Christian sources. Ilario's subtext and the narrator's own text are indeed polar opposites, representing two totally different concepts of love, as Smarr has pointed out. I believe, however, that Boccaccio's point of view is to be found in Fiammetta and Ilario's views of love, rather than in those of Caleone and the narrator. Ilario's subtext functions, therefore, as a theological objective correlative to the narrator's text: it shows the shortcomings of Florio and Biancifiore's love before their conversion.

In the *Filocolo* Christian love (*amor onesto*) is only attained after the protagonists have been converted to Christianity (almost a year after they have consummated their love in Alexandria). Their love prior to conversion undergoes three transformations: before their adventures in Alexandria, it is continent; during their adventures in Alexandria it is passionate; and after their adventures in Alexandria it attains the cardinal virtue of temperance. It is not surprising, therefore, that the protagonists' conversion to Christianity and *caritas* takes place almost a year after they have been married, a year during which their appetites have been brought under the control of reason. The only passionate love that we find in Book V of the *Filocolo* is that of the three unrequited lovers who still believe in *amor per diletto*—Fileno, Caleone, and Idalogo. Rejecting *amor per diletto* for *amore onesto* does not mean, however, that the two have nothing in common. The ambiguity that Smarr noticed in the debate between Fiammetta and Caleone can be seen as a subtle recognition on the part of Boccaccio that *amor onesto* and *amor per diletto* are neither reconcilable nor completely divorced from each other: they both share an innate desire for beatitude, but totally different views of what beatitude is and how it is attained.

Besides drawing our attention to the importance of love in the narrative, Fiammetta's court of love also alludes to the importance of interpretation. Each *questione d'amore* deals with an aspect of amorous conduct which Fiammetta is asked to judge. The person asking the *questione d'amore* invariably has an interpretation of his/her own which runs counter to that of the queen, and from these differing interpretations arise the debates between Fiammetta and her interlocutor. (Even the words and deeds of the characters within the *questioni d'amore* are often equivocal and must be interpreted.) By setting the court of love in a period of time that is disjointed from the actual setting of the plot (i. e. Boccaccio's fourteenth century Naples versus Florio's sixth century Italy), Boccaccio is holding a mirror to his fourteenth century readers—the very same people in Fiammetta's entourage. Boccaccio's intended audience would have probably discussed aspects of the *Filocolo* the same way Fiammetta's participants discuss the issues raised at the court of love. One can assume, therefore, that his readers are also expected to question and interpret the amorous conduct of the characters in the *Filocolo* in much the same way.

The importance of interpretation is further suggested by the two dream visions which immediately precede and follow the court of love: both visions beg to be interpreted. If they are not interpreted, they make no sense and have no purpose in the narrative. The same is true, to a certain extent, of many of the other episodes in the *Filocolo*. It is not surprising, therefore, that the *questioni d'amore* bear directly on the events in plot, as Kirkham, Smarr, Cherchi, and Surdich have shown. [The] acts of interpretation which begin at the center of the *Filocolo* (at Fiammetta's court of love) ripple to the work's furthest edges.

By illustrating how the court of love goes about interpreting the words and deeds of other lovers, Boccaccio is not simply telling his readers that they too should debate, discuss, and interpret the amorous conduct of the characters

in his work, he is also illustrating what happens when one is engaged in interpretation. Arguments which may be used to support one point, actually support the opposite point of view, as Smarr has shown in her analysis of the debate between Caleone and Fiammetta. Furthermore, many of the interpretations and much of the logic used at the court of love are quite arbitrary (this is true even of some of Fiammetta's rulings on the *questioni*). This arbitrariness is made more evident by the fact that Fiammetta always has the last word (since she is the queen) and is therefore always "right". Therefore, while Boccaccio is encouraging us to interpret and discuss his work, he is also showing us the pitfalls, limitations, and arbitrariness of interpretation. It is not surprising that, in the debate between Caleone and Fiammetta, the issue of *amore onesto* and *amore per diletto* is never fully resolved: any resolution would arbitrarily give more importance to one kind of love than to another. Ultimately, the *questioni d'amore* reveal the relative and arbitrary nature of interpretative judgments.

[There] is a certain amount of ambiguity throughout the *Filocolo,* making any interpretation of this work quite difficult. The ambiguity of the text, as Robert M. Durling has pointed out, is not only present when an overt meaning is contradicted by ironic implications, creating a tension between the two, but also when the text presents two conflicting possibilities without offering clues that permit decision, either because the author could not decide or for some other reason (confusion, an oversight on the part of the author, etc.). Sometimes the ambiguities in the *Filocolo* are simply Boccaccio's oversights, but in the majority of cases they are not. Boccaccio, in fact, uses irony (especially dramatic irony) to contradict the assumptions held by his characters and his audience. It is by analyzing these assumptions and the manner in which Boccaccio undercuts them that we can better understand the *Filocolo*.

Kirkham and Smarr have set us on the right path by showing the thematic importance of love in the narrative. The duality between *amor onesto* and *amor per diletto,* however, can be extended to include the larger duality between classical and Christian cultures. By applying this polarity to a broader range of themes and issues, we will be able to interpret in a more comprehensive fashion the plot of the *Filocolo.* The juxtaposition of two different, yet extremely important cultures also allows us to see the limitations of each. Hence our interpretation of the *Filocolo* becomes, as it were, a passing of judgment on the classical, courtly, and early Christian cultures of the protagonists, not unlike the judgments passed by Fiammetta and her interlocutors in their court of love.

Christopher Nissen (essay date 1993)

SOURCE: *Ethics of Retribution in the "Decameron" and the Late Medieval Italian Novella: Beyond the Circle*, Mellon University Press, 1993, 141 p.

[*In the following excerpt, Nissen analyzes the motif of retribution in four principal fourteenth- and early fifteenth-century novella collections—Libro dei sette savi, Gesta romanorum, Disciplina clericalis, and the Decameron—and*

An 1873 interpretation of Boccaccio's storytellers in the garden, by T. Stothard.

illustrates how moral "choices, embodying the basic ethical substance of the Decameron *novella, can be reduced to three fundamental patterns of behavior," models which the critic terms "ethical modes."]*

The prevailing interest in the novella as a vehicle for the literary portrayal of society has naturally been directed primarily at the **Decameron,** the collection which has received the most attention. **Decameron** studies reveal, in the main, a considerable tendency toward sociological analysis in their approach to the work. It is not difficult to see why: even to the casual glance, Boccaccio appears in his book to be principally concerned with the depiction of society and social values; it is in this depiction that most critics in the past century have sought clues to explain the **Decameron**'s overall meaning. This accent on sociology derives in part from Boccaccio's sustained interest in describing societal relationships, but also to a great extent from the **Decameron**'s clear evidence of kinship with older medieval traditions of exemplary and sententious literature. The text is pervaded with ethical language which appears to suggest that the reader is expected to appreciate the work for its didactic content. Inevitably, the various sociological studies have frequently centered on the problem of determining precisely how the **Decameron** is to be read ethically, and this problem has given rise to much controversy. A substantial critical school, inspired by Francesco de Sanctis' assertion over a century ago that Boccaccio was ideologically more dedicated to art than to morality, has found little didactic purpose in the **Decameron;** greatly impressed by Boccaccio's frequent assertions that his work is meant to give delight, these critics frequently portray him as an "anti-Dante," dedicated to art and entertainment for their own sakes. This trend has more recently been refuted by scholars who have sought instead to emphasize the **Decameron**'s morality, and to clarify the work's meaning through the identification of ethical or didactic notions within the text. **Decameron** critics have long been inclined toward somewhat polemical refutations of preceding notions in their search for *sovrasenso,* a single concept summing up the work's overall meaning. The **Decameron** has been assigned a dizzying array of concise "labels" over the years; few other works of medieval literature have inspired so much controversy.

Although it is by now traditional to begin a new study of the **Decameron** with a capsule history of earlier **Decameron** criticism, listing its distinguished canon of theorists, this will not be necessary here. My study will concern itself with ethics, and thus with literary manifestations of sociology, but it is not my intention to declare yet another formula for *sovrasenso,* to reveal some heretofore undiscovered totalization of meaning in the book. I propose rather to describe what I see as certain primary structures giving us a key to understanding Boccaccio's awareness of the role of ethics in the novellas he creates. The **Decameron** is generally seen to put forth a grand view of the human experience, a picture made large of man and society. If this is so, then is there a key to help us grasp a unified scheme for the ethics of Boccaccio's novellas? What moral system do they set forth and how does the reader, now or at any other time in history, "read" them ethically? Given the great influence Boccaccio had on subsequent generations of *novellieri,* how can we trace the wider impact of Boccaccio's ethical notions on the history of the novella genre?

Analysis of ethics necessitates analysis of culture: culture is the matrix within which ethical systems are formulated, and cultural considerations, as manifested in the text, must lie at the root of any examination of **Decameron** ethics. The hundred tales present a particularly intricate picture in this regard, for within the forest of individual narratives two different cultural worlds can clearly be distinguished, representing two contrasting sets of values.

The critical studies which first emphasized the **Decameron**'s relationship to Trecento culture and society in the 1950's and 1960's frequently stressed the idea that Boccaccio constructed his book around a commingling of aristocratic and bourgeois values. This approach produced a pair of studies, by Vittore Branca and Mario Baratto, which have provided much of the basis for my own analysis of ethics in terms of the **Decameron**'s cultural dichotomy. In his article "Registri narrativi e stilistici nel **Decameron**" Branca delineates the two social worlds of the work as they relate to Boccaccio's use of literary style: the real, corresponding to bourgeois values, and the ideal, corresponding to the aristocratic; that is to say the world as it is and the art of living well according to an ideal of virtue.

In Branca's view, Boccaccio epitomizes the division between these stylistic and social realms in his portrayal of two iconic novella characters, Ciappelletto in the first tale and Griselda in the last: Ciappelletto lives according to "ragion di virtù," akin to the "arte di ben vivere" which infuses the *Decameron*'s general moral message. Stylistically the first is comic and "low," the last is tragic and sublime, with all the tone of hagiographic narrative. These two stories are the "gothic pilasters" of Boccaccio's great building, and stand as points of reference for all that goes on between them. The two worlds are fluid, not rigidly delineated: they may share a single *topos* in many novellas, for example that of mistaken amorous encounters in the dark, and yet remain intact and distinct in terms of style. This *topos* appears in numerous tales as different as those of Frate Alberto and Tito and Gisippo; stylistically the tone of the stories varies from the low to the lofty yet the *topos* remains the same. Style is the key: word choice, portrayal of sentiments, use of *cursus* tell us which world, ideal or real, is being presented. Implicit in the ideal/real dichotomy is a sense of variability of ethical worlds, for the social values between the two are so at odds as to create opposing ethical systems. Branca does not, however, explore this idea systematically or at any great length. Overall Branca's view of the *Decameron* reveals a progression from vice to virtue, from "low" to "high," from Ciappelletto to Griselda: what Branca does not seek to describe are the ethical subcategories we may be able to identify in conjunction with his stylistic *registri*.

Style is also the subject of Mario Baratto's study *Realtà e stile nel Decameron,* and like Branca he searches for a breakdown into categories, a description of divisions into discrete stylistic tendencies, based primarily on considerations of genre type. Baratto's intent is to isolate and describe the stylistic patrimony that Boccaccio passes on to succeeding generations, and he acknowledges that Branca in his "Registri narrativi e stilistici" does much the same thing, although we are told Branca's biform structure does not fit exactly into Baratto's more complicated scheme. Baratto sees Branca's division between comic and tragic overcome and even nullified by a more complex internal dialectic between various narrative modes. Nonetheless he finds a place for Branca's biform scheme in his discussion of the *Decameron*'s moral content. Throughout the *Decameron,* says Baratto, mercantile ethics predominate but coexist uneasily with aristocratic ethics, as they are most plainly set forth in the Tenth Day; this we may regard as a manifestation of the crisis of the new bourgeoisie which required recourse to other ethical systems in its illustration of examples of high virtue. Mercantile morality is the overriding norm of the *Decameron,* but it is jarred by the intrusion of aristocratic ideals of magnanimity and self-sacrifice. Baratto resolves this confusion by calling Boccaccio's world view open-minded and intuitive, and his moral vision by necessity provisional, capable of shifting according to the situation confronting novella characters. There can be no totalizing morality, such as can be found in Dante's *Commedia.* Baratto regards the ethics of novella texts as separate from the moralizing commentary which appears in the *cornice;* for him such observations are marginal to the ethical world view revealed within the novellas themselves. The novella texts do not set out to

display established truths according to a programmatic, inviolate system: they only show us "situazioni da verificare". Man is judged by man, not by God or any other higher truth. According to Baratto, Boccaccio forges his sense of ethics out of the choices characters must make when confronted by the dominant forces of the *Decameron*'s world: nature, fortune and society. In terms of social structures Boccaccio's provisional sense of novella ethics manifests itself along the lines of the confrontation between bourgeois and aristocratic values: the resulting scheme for ethics resembles that which Branca would like to impose upon the *Decameron*'s stylistic diversity.

For all his dismissal of Branca's biform analysis of Boccaccio's style as too simplistic, Baratto cannot resist noting a similar tendency toward duality and polarization in his own discussion of the clash between different social realities in the *Decameron.* Boccaccio, the merchant's son who spent his young manhood in the Angevin court, could not help but aid in portraying the moral crisis of his age when he set out to write a book that he felt should be built of discrete cultural elements. Baratto recognizes the split between the ethical consciousness of the merchant class and that of the aristocracy as Boccaccio sets it forth, and indeed he must, for without such recognition the *Decameron*'s moral structure becomes very difficult to comprehend. Deprived of this awareness we would be baffled not only by the startling co-existence of novella characters such as Ciappelletto, Guglielmo Borsiere, Frate Cippolla and Griselda within a single work, but also by the differing moralistic observations that the tale-tellers themselves make concerning their novellas. To a great extent Branca's ideal/real scheme is of primary importance not only for understanding Boccaccio's use of style, but also for understanding his moral consciousness and how he applies it to his text. Different values are evoked according to the different worlds portrayed, and it is only in the unifying light of the *cornice,* which links the disparate parts and infuses them with wider meaning, that we are able to recognize the *Decameron* as an integral text and, indeed, a monument of world literature.

Branca, searching for the medieval elements in the work, finds patterns and thematic subdivisions in its structure and even has recourse, as we have already noted, to medieval architectonic metaphor when he calls the tales of Ciappelletto and Griselda "gothic pilasters" holding all the novellas together and giving them meaning within a scheme of linear progress toward a quasi transcendent goal. Branca's view of Boccaccio's "human comedy" reveals a world dominated by the three primary forces of *Fortuna, Amore* and *Ingegno,* which receive final summation in the apotheosis of *Virtù* in the Tenth Day. For Branca, a correct reading of the *Decameron* requires awareness not only of the stylistic and cultural dichotomy which distinguishes between real and ideal worlds, but also awareness of the schematic subdivisions that tell of different realms of human experience. In this study I intend to demonstrate further the *Decameron*'s susceptibility to such a paradigmatic approach by postulating a system of three ethical modes for Boccaccio's novellas. I do not set this system forth in order to refute Branca's reading or indeed to reduce *Decameron* exegesis to yet another facile definition of *sovrasenso,* but rather to provide a key, as yet un-described by others, to help us comprehend patterns of textual ethics as they are manifested within the work. I shall now proceed to an explanation of what I mean by ethical modes, beginning with an exposition of some of the general features of the ethical structures of the *Decameron* novellas.

Boccaccio's purpose in writing the *Decameron* is stated plainly enough in his *proemio*—he means to provide de-light and entertainment for women. The *brigata*'s purpose in recounting novellas, as Boccaccio has his character Pampinea inform us, is to find the most pleasant way to pass the hot hours of the afternoon during a self-imposed exile from a scene of iniquity, dissolution and death. Such emphasis on delight and entertainment should not, how-ever, lull us into forgetting that the 101 stories contained within the *Decameron* (100 tales recounted by the *brigata,* and one tale told by the author himself in the introduction to the Fourth Day) are derived from literary traditions substantially endowed with examplaristic or didactic characteristics. Boccaccio calls his stories "novelle, o favole, o parabole, o istorie;" in explaining these terms Branca reminds us that we may identify several literary traditions standing behind the *Decameron* stories, among them *exempla,* parables, *fabliaux* and tales of historical figures. In the mind of the medieval reader some of these traditions were primarily moralistic and indeed all of them had at least some didactic purpose. Even the *fabliau,* which differs ideologically from the *exemplum,* often ex-plicitly claims in its concluding verses that the reader may derive an edifying lesson from the humorous story it has set forth. In any case the medieval reader would have had ample cause to expect moralistic content in any collection of tales because so many previous collections, such as the well known *Libro dei sette savi, Gesta romanorum, Disci-plina clericalis,* etc. were primarily and explicitly exempla-ry. Indeed the *Decameron* provides, in the form of com-mentary on the novellas contained within it, constant ref-erences to the didactic potential of the tales. Each novella seeks to illustrate a certain human truth, and the tale teller often sets out in the opening commentary (or *cappello*) to explain what the novella reveals and what the hearer may learn from it. Let this example, drawn from the *cappello* to 3.3, be regarded as characteristic of a tendency which pervades the whole work:

> La quale (beffa), o piacevole donne, io raccon-
> terò non solamente per seguire l'ordine imposto,
> ma ancora per farvi accorte che eziandio che i
> religiosi, a' quali noi oltre modo credule troppa
> fede prestiamo, possono essere e sono alcuna
> volta, non che dagli uomini, ma da alcune di noi
> cautamente beffati.

Leaving aside the irreverent irony implicit in the lesson, as the tricking of priests is certainly not usually a feature of the *exemplum,* we can still note that Filomena's pur-pose here is to "farvi accorte," to instruct through an ex-ample. In numerous other cappelli a preferred term is "di-mostrare," or "mostrare": the terminology of didactic lit-erature.

It would nonetheless be a mistake to conclude from these observations that the *Decameron* is collection of *exempla*

in the same fashion as the *Disciplina clericalis* or the *Libro dei sette savi.* It clearly is not. The true *exemplum* is an aphorism expanded into narrative, ultimately a tool of the sermon wherein it aids the illustration of universal truths, external to the tale itself, which become crystallized in the form of a *sentenza.* Lucia Battaglia Ricci calls the *exem-plum* "la verifica narrativa di una tesi precedentemente en-unciata," distinguishing it from the novella as created by Boccaccio in that it does not employ "mimetic" narration based on the actual experiences of life. Unlike the *exem-plum,* the novella may advocate a clear-cut behavioral norm and at the same time consciously seek to entertain its audience without appearing to contradict itself. The primary purpose of the *Decameron* is not to educate its readers in the same way *exempla* collections do: we may note that the truths illustrated in the *Decameron* are not always oriented toward teaching correct behavior, toward helping the reader distinguish between right and wrong actions. We see this characteristic in the stories of the Sec-ond Day, which present by and large ethically neutral messages meant to reveal the effects of fortune on human affairs. These novellas show human truths without seeking to establish a norm for correct behavior or correct choices made by individuals. Nonetheless the *Decameron* novella frequently employs homiletic structures that ultimately derive from both the *exemplum* and the *fabliaux:* it does "demonstrate" truths rendered explicit by statements in the *cornice* structure (external to the narrative world of the novella itself, and thus akin to the *sentenza* of more specifically exemplaristic tale types), truths which give the story some additional purpose beyond mere entertain-ment. The medieval reader, accustomed to expect homilet-ic structures and content in most kinds of short tales and tale collections, would hardly be surprised to find them substantially present in the *Decameron.*

These homiletic structures, pertaining to individual novel-las, are set within the wider context of the *cornice*'s own value system, which in turn is enclosed by the *proemio*'s stated purpose, to undertake the kind and compassionate task of entertaining confined females. The *brigata* demon-strates proper conduct through words and behavior with-out resorting to blatant didacticism or indeed bothering to go far in analyzing the apparent ethical contradictions be-tween the various novellas. Baratto notes that the central stated exigency of the text, that of the need to seek recre-ation through delight, tends to overcome any tendencies of the *brigata* characters to make moralizing comments. The *brigata* derives its sense of manners and propriety from the nexus between two seemingly contradictory so-cial needs, those of discretion and delight, of "onestà" and "diletto": together they provide for a sort of ambiguity which precludes an overtly moralistic tone. The linking factor in the presentation of so many ethically varied no-vellas, so heterogenous in values, is the essential law of "diletto." Indeed it seems a law, set out for us repeatedly by the *brigata* and so pointedly that it attains something of a didactic tone:

> Amorose donne, se io ho bene la 'intenzione di
> tutte compresa, noi siamo qui per dovere a noi
> medesimi novellando piacere; e per ciò sola-
> mente che contro a questo non si faccia, estimo

a ciascuno dovere essere licito (e così ne disse la
nostra reina, poco avanti, che fosse) quella novella dire che piú crede che possa dilettare . . .

This didacticism is provisional, a characteristic of the exigencies of this particular group ("se io ho bene la 'ntenz-
ione di tutte compresa"); these people have made a point
all along of spending this brief interlude in their lives according to a provisional moral code, since plague-stricken
Florence has been temporarily deprived of morals. When
Dioneo repeats these sentiments later on in the *cappello* to
5.10, "diletto" is again a prime factor in justifying the
choice of action of the *brigata:*

> E per ciò che la fatica, la quale altra volta ho im-
> presa e ora son per pigliare, a niuno altro fine rig-
> uarda se non a dovervi torre malinconia, e riso
> e allegrezza porgervi, quantunque la materia
> della mia seguente novella, innamorate giovani,
> sia in parte men che onesta, però che diletto può
> porgere, ve la pur dirò.

Diletto and *onestà* here clash head on, and *diletto* has the
better part of the encounter. Ethically the *brigata* tends
more to distance itself from the novellas than to live according to their systems, all the while providing judgments in the *cappelli* which point up valuable lessons to
be derived from each novella. After paring away the *Decameron's* various textual layers, from the *proemio* to the
cornice, we arrive at the novellas and their own peculiar
moral world, infused with didactic content by their *cappelli* which most properly belong to the textual world of the
cornice. This brings us to the basic question which has
long been asked: what is the prevailing sense of ethics in
the *Decameron* novellas? How can we identify a moral
system which predominates in the exemplary actions of
their characters? The simple answer is that there is no single system. The dichotomy of values and cultural settings
in the *Decameron,* the clear distinction between "mondo
aristocratico" and "mondo comunale," provide us with a
pair of differing systems. As Branca speaks of "registri
stilistici," he might well have distinguished between corresponding "registri etici." Ethics in its most fundamental
sense constitutes the potential for an individual to make
correct choices of action in a social context. In the majority of *Decameron* novellas one or more characters are presented as making clear choices for right action; these are
the protagonists with whom the reader is expected to identify, whose moral choices are defensible according to a
moral system fully understood and accessible in terms of
reader expectations. The peculiarity of the *Decameron* is
that it has more than one such system; previous tale collections typically do not present so much variety in this regard. The *Decameron* is a document of the urban Italian
Trecento, representing a society in a state of flux and social change, with a concomitant shifting of values.

With the *Decameron* it becomes necessary to talk of opposing ethical systems, opposing modes of ethical discourse which, on the level of the text, embrace a wide variety of factors: elements of style mingle with presentation
of character type and sociological references to create an
overall tone of "propriety" for a given novella. Recognition of the ethical mode which predominates in a novella
involves awareness of the most fundamental goals of the
character whom the text presents as morally defensible, a
sense of which basic choices result in the presentation of
the moral good, of how a just end is achieved. To some extent this can be determined through the didactic statements of the frame characters in the *cappelli,* but the central element for establishing a tale's ethical content must
lie in choices, the choices that characters are shown to
make as the story unfolds. Boccaccio is the first European
tale teller to pay careful attention to this point; the characters he creates are imbued with a moral individuality
which allows them to break out of the flat iconic molds of
the *exemplum* tradition. The notion that action is the principal narrative element of the *Decameron* novella has been
made much of by formalist and structuralist students of
Boccaccio, and the observations of such critics as Tzvetan
Todorov and Marga Cottino-Jones in this regard show a
certain awareness of the ethical implications inherent in
characters' choices of action. I hope now to demonstrate
how these choices, embodying the basic ethical substance
of the *Decameron* novella, can be reduced to three fundamental patterns of behavior, patterns which we may conveniently term ethical modes.

The ethical mode which is perhaps most fundamental to
the *Decameron* is the one in which characters may be seen
to gain materially or hedonistically while remaining
praiseworthy; the example they set is one upholding the
propriety of gain. This mode is most readily associated
with Giorgio Padoan's "mondo comunale," with Branca's
"mondo reale" or "mondo comico": for the purposes of
this study I would like to call it Ethics of Acquisition. Opposite it, naturally enough, stands a contrary mode in
which material or hedonistic gains are foregone according
to another system of values: this is the mode corresponding to the "mondo ideale," to be associated with adherence
to aristocratic or feudal values of magnanimity, charity or
largesse. This mode I will call Ethics of Renunciation.
Ethics of Acquisition and Ethics of Renunciation are the
opposing moral poles of the novella characters; their correct choices in society frequently reflect clear identification with one or the other of these modes. Yet these two
are not sufficient in themselves to describe all motivation
for right behavior in Boccaccio's characters, and indeed
one more mode remains to be described. This is Ethics of
Retribution wherein "right" characters deliberately (or at
times, instead, almost unwittingly), set out to correct or
punish the behavior of "wrong" ones who are often clearly
labelled as such.

I must stress that these modes may go beyond considerations of novella type or stylistic mood. Ethical modes do
not always correspond exactly or uniformly to the social
status of characters or to the different narrative styles,
"high" and "low," to be found in the *Decameron,* despite
the clear tendency or Renunciation to be a characteristic
of the ideal world and Acquisition to be a characteristic
of the real, as we have noted. These modes reflect, in the
most direct way, the primary goals and choices of action
of ethically correct characters. Seen in these terms, such
characters are either acquiring, relinquishing or punishing: in their actions lies the essence of whatever moral
message the reader may extract from the tale. Reading the
tales in terms of ethical modes allows for some blurring

of the lines between various stylistic tale types, for Acquisition is not solely a motivation of lower class characters in the more comic situations of adultery and *beffa,* and Renunciation is not solely the domain of aristocratic or solemnly tragic figures, despite the fact that such modes derive ultimately from the spirit and mood of different, even opposing, social worlds. Ghismonda, an aristocrat, chooses a moral good in the name of personal gain while Cisti, a baker, chooses to do right in the name of virtuous renunciation. The values according to which Cisti lives his life derive ultimately from the *cortesia* of the feudal aristocracy and are therefore to be associated with the "mondo aristocratico"; the fact that here a baker lives by them merely reflects the intricate state of social consciousness in Trecento Florence, the confluence of societal norms as Boccaccio sees them. In his stylistic analysis ["Storicità e invenzione nel *Decameron*"] Baratto recognizes distinct variations of story type in the ***Decameron*** which he identifies according to a variety of criteria, so that ultimately he can identify in each tale categories he calls *racconto, romanzo, novella, contrasto,* etc. We may be inclined to recognize the validity of this approach and yet not feel we must reject the validity of a scheme of ethical modes, for the two systems can co-exist and even overlap without contradiction. The ***Decameron,*** as I have said, is highly susceptible to paradigmatic analysis, to division into categories reflecting variations in narrative type. On different planes different subdivisions, which are not necessarily mutually exclusive, suggest themselves. On one plane, the stylistic, we may follow Baratto's lead and identify tale types which, we may then find, cannot correspond to wholly different subdivisions on another plane, the ethical. We have noted how Branca recognizes the stylistic variability of certain ***Decameron*** *topoi,* such as confusion of identity in darkened beds: a *topos* is fluid, interchangeable, not fixed by a certain stylistic category. In a similar way an ethical mode may prevail to some extent in differing stylistic categories: the solemn, tragic tone of Ghismonda's tale does not preclude acquisition, so often to be associated with comic characters, as a factor in this particular character's choice of goals. Simple acquisition does not go far enough in describing the motivations of a protagonist as richly complex as Ghismonda, who in the end becomes a tragic heroine relinquishing her very life, but it is certainly a feature of her initial motivations in carefully choosing a lover to satisfy the longings of her body. This story can stand as an example of contamination of modes: acquisition is here glorified by an act of sublime renunciation, renunciation of life itself in the name of love. Boccaccio's ethical modes relate to his differing novella types in the same way his *topoi* do; they are capable of shifting somewhat between stylistic categories.

Through examination of various structural features in and around a given novella we may form a kind of ethical "portrait" of it, a portrait which leads us to conclusive identification of the ethical mode which predominates in it. The two novellas I have chosen as introductory models for analysis show us traits of acquisition (Agilulf and the groom) and renunciation (Federigo degli Alberighi and the falcon).

The novella of Agilulf provides us with some intriguing moral material because its presentation of didactic content is not simplistic or linear: the king and his groom each present different, parallel moral lessons. It is a novella about which a great deal can be said with regard to the subject of ethics.

The first line of approach in determining the ethical content of this novella (or indeed that of any ***Decameron*** novella) is to take note of certain external factors belonging more properly to the *cornice* than to the text of the novella itself, but which provide the initial orientation for the study of novella ethics. Of primary importance is awareness of the day in which the novella is recounted: here we are in the Third Day, wherein we read of novella protagonists who gain things they want or regain lost things through their own cleverness, through human intelligence which can defeat the machinations of Fortune. Given this awareness, we can readily identify the protagonist of this tale and recognize in him those qualities of wit which, in the context of this day's theme, are set forth for our admiration. He is the *pallafreniere,* or groom, and the choices of action he makes are those which are ethically correct for this particular narrative moment in the ***Decameron.*** We are clearly expected to find him praiseworthy, for he gains something he has long desired, and gains it through cleverness.

Still within the realm of the *cornice* lies the next element we must consider, i. e. the *cappello,* placed in this case in the mouth of Pampinea:

> Sono alcuni sí poco discreti nel voler pur mostrare di conoscere e di sentire quello che per loro non fa di sapere, che alcuna volta per questo, riprendendo i disaveduti difetti, in altrui, si credono la lor vergogna scemare là dove essi l'acrescono in infinito: e che ciò sia vero nel suo contrario, mostrandovi l'astuzia d'un forse di minor valore tenuto che Masetto, nel senno d'un valoroso re, vaghe donne, intendo che per me vi sia dimostrato.

There is a sort of contradiction here, which makes this story so interesting. Boccaccio means the protagonist to be the groom but a major part of the story's moral lesson will derive from the right actions of the king, his antagonist. The first will be acclaimed for his *astuzia* while the second will appear to be no less admired for his *senno.* Boccaccio stresses the king's discretion and wisdom in the *cappello,* and as it turns out, these will be characteristics which will apply as well to the groom, who is so careful to hide his love. Boccaccio's language tells us about his characters' motivations—they act in their own best interests, for personal gain. The two main characters stand in conflict, but each has a reward of sorts. The groom outwits the king but the king makes the best of things by displaying a discretion uncommon to men in his position: his *senno* provides a contrast for the groom's *astuzia.* In the wider context of the ***Decameron,*** wit and discretion emerge as essential components of Ethics of Acquisition—they recur constantly when characters are to be praised for gain. Traditional "high" virtue, as it appears in Boccaccio's world, is exemplified best by acts of renunciation and liberality, and can frequently be a public act designed to attract attention and general praise. On the other hand acquisition, for all that it may be a good thing and an ethically correct goal, is best sought away from the public eye, in the margins of social awareness. In this novella all is done in secret: the king discovers something it behooves men in his position never to know ("che per loro non fa di sapere"). Having discovered it he shows great wisdom in staying discreet and maintaining appearances, gaining thereby the avoidance of shame and tarnished honor. Likewise the groom acts secretly and to his consistent advantage, first in assuaging his love desire, second in employing his *astuzia* to outwit the king.

Curiously, Pampinea mentions "i disaveduti difetti" with reference to acts like those of the groom. Branca's footnote [to *Boccaccio medievale,* 1956] calls these "le colpe non conosciute, non evidenti, nascoste." This term "difetti" reminds us that Boccaccio's Ethics of Acquisition treads a narrow line between sin and virtue (unlike Ethics of Renunciation, the type of traditional, aristocratic "high" virtue which is closer to Christian ethics) and that acquisition for personal gain, even in the context of a didactic lesson, still occurs at someone else's expense. Boccaccio was very aware of how controversial his tendency to uphold Ethics of Acquisition would become, as we realize in reading those passages in the *Decameron* which defend the work against critical reproach for moral content. Throughout the *Decameron,* what may seem a "difetto" to one person may become another's ethical right, the right to acquire what he or she wants, the more so since it is "disaveduto," i. e. done discreetly.

The creation of the ethical portrait continues in the presentation of the natures and deeds of the characters. About Agilulf we read standardized, positive things: he is a good king, whose *vertù* and *senno* make his kingdom prosper. Similar terminology may be found in exemplary portraits of good potentates throughout medieval literature, in the historical tales of the *Novellino* and the *Fiori e vita dei filosafi* to cite examples near in time and tone to the *Decameron.* Agilulf's "goodness" as a positive character is given great emphasis in his initial description and this becomes a basic premise of the tale. The portrait of the groom reflects instead certain ideals of the medieval love lyric. He is proud to love far beyond his station ("pur seco si gloriava che in alta parte avesse allogati i suoi pensieri") and in any case his "vilissima condizione" does not preclude greatness of soul capable of the highest and most worthy passions. In the fashion of the love ideal of the *dolce stil novo,* we are reminded here that social rank has nothing to do with ability to feel such stirrings and to dedicate oneself to faithful service in love. Boccaccio takes pains to sanctify the *pallafreniere's* bizarre passion, to ennoble it, by describing him in such terms. His love is rendered proper, even solemn, by these reference to codes of amorous behavior; there are echoes here of certain doctrinal pronouncements of Andreas Cappellanus. In his own humble way the groom provides the requisite courtly service to his lady, becoming her most loyal attendant. He associates himself all the more to the culture of the high love ethic when he contemplates suicide, the ultimate sacrifice of the desperate courtly lover. Boccaccio feeds the reader a steady stream of such specific references designed to arouse feelings of sympathy for the groom's state and ad-

miration for his behavior, yet we can detect elements here of Boccaccio's typical merging of social and ethical currents, in keeping with his recognition of the peculiar state of Trecento culture. The groom's sexual conquest of a completely unaware love object by means of a clever trick is not typical of the more exalted love traditions, and is certainly far from the ideals of *fin' amors.* It is, in fact, the *amor naturale* which is so often manifested in Boccaccio's tales of middle class sexual adventures, reworked with the trappings of that *amor cortese* which pervades the *Decameron,* even in untraditional contexts. The groom may be moved by the highest feelings of love, and he may be inclined to conceive of that love in highflown terms, but the fact remains that he can never reveal even the slightest hint of his desire to his lady nor to anyone else, because of the stark social realities which are the essence of this tale. His love is not so much unrequited as completely unknown to anyone. The groom, faced with the choice between lyric anguish in the face of utter deprivation and cunning action in the name of acquisition, chooses the latter, rendering his lady an absolutely passive object to be gained by skill, instead of a lofty *domna* whose mercy must be sought through heartfelt pleas.

Thus we see that the groom reflects not only ideals of service and sacrifice, but also the shrewdness of the realist, as befits a protagonist of the Third Day. He is intelligent enough to know that revelation of his desire will gain him nothing, so he says nothing and makes no gesture that might betray him. He comes to his choice of action through rational reflection and assessment of his condition: "E pensando seco del modo, prese per partito di volere questa morte per la quale apparisse lui morire per l'amore che alla reina aveva portato e portava: e questa cosa propose di voler che tal fosse, che egli in essa tentasse la sua fortuna in potere o tutto o parte aver del suo desidero". His situation is so hopeless that death must be his prime course of action, and yet it is a kind of rational death, oriented towards a challenge of fortune that might give him all or part of his desire and thereby infuse his act with purpose and significance. He commits this deed in the name of acquisition, an acquisition which we are clearly to perceive as righteous. After he takes his brief possession of the queen's body he resolves not to lose the bliss he has acquired ("pur temendo non la troppo stanza gli fosse cagione di volgere l'avuto diletto in tristizia"), so he discreetly withdraws and preserves his life. Against all odds, through intelligence, he achieves his goal.

The most overtly didactic message of the tale arises from the example of the king's discretion, as indicated by the *cappello* and borne out by repeated assertions made in the narrator's own voice. But the tale resolves itself in a battle of wits between the groom and the king, with repeated references to the intelligence of both. Each makes the best of a bad situation and is content with the outcome. The king acts not only to preserve his own honor but also that of his queen, whose innocence he is shrewd enough (and merciful enough) to recognize. The portraits of the deeds and natures of these men stress both their intelligence and competence in acting in their own best interests. The groom gained as much as fortune would ever concede him, and as he is wise enough to recognize this fact, he never again will so tempt fate ("né piú la sua vita in sì fatto atto commise alla fortuna"). Ethics of Acquisition is the ethics of rational choice, of the intellect and the process of intellection, of the wise recognition of the scope and limits of the gifts of fortune. All of these characteristics are well reflected in this novella, and recur frequently in many others throughout the **Decameron.**

The novella of Federigo, which we shall use as a model for the mode of Renunciation, is told in the Fifth Day, wherein love stories have happy endings. For most of the tales of this day the predominant mode tends to be Acquisition, so Federigo's stands as something of an exception. And indeed, Fiammetta's *cappello* gives no clear indication of which mode will come to the fore, since she only alludes in passing to Federigo's great sacrifice by telling the ladies that this story will show how deep an influence they have on men of noble hearts (". . . quanto la vostra vaghezza possa ne' cuor gentili . . ."). Fiammetta leaves the question of characters' choices of action out of her preamble, concentrating instead on a didactic message for the discerning reader: the tale should inspire ladies to bestow their amorous gifts as they themselves choose, not as Fortune, the fickle arbiter, would decide. We must therefore establish the dominant ethical mode of this tale through the presentation of characters within the novella text itself, through the portrayal of their choices and deeds, most notably Federigo's.

Of Federigo we hear that he is a nobleman distinguished in arms and *cortesia*. The word *cortesia* immediately channels us into a moral atmosphere that differs significantly from that of the tale of Agilulf, despite Agilulf 's regality and kingly virtue. Specific mention of *cortesia* evokes an ideal, in which desire for gain is submerged by the need for magnanimity and self-sacrifice; avarice has no place in the *corte d'amore*, the poetic realm of the courtly lover. We have shifted ethical worlds and expectations. Various *topoi* consonant with the world of *cortesia* and the feudal aristocracy now begin to present themselves: for example, we see now a *topos* not uncommon in the novella tradition, that of the lovesick knight who jousts to win his love and is left impoverished. Despite his ultimate motivation, which is that of desire to possess a woman, his acts are those of feudal service, which take the form of sacrifice and adherence to a sense of duty. Left poor, we hear that he endures his lot with patience, as befits a man who has dedicated himself to chivalric ideals of dignity in the face of defeat. Throughout this novella Boccaccio sounds the note of *cortesia* with the kinds of characters he presents, their activities (jousting, falconry), their humble and decorous ways of addressing one another, etc. In tales of this sort, Boccaccio tempers his characters' naked desire for gain with the solemnity of aristocratic ritual (as we see in Federigo's dedication to knightly service for love) or with the stylized and quasi-surreal *topoi* of the romance tradition (as in the case of the boy who falls grievously ill and can only be cured by gaining the object of his desire.) Humility, honorable deeds and self-sacrifice predominate over the gross motivations of acquisition. Boccaccio balances his portrait of the gentle nobleman Federigo with those of the other characters who, nonetheless, belong to the class of the *borghesia*. Giovanna has the principal

qualities of faithful devotion to her husband and tender love for her son, while the husband himself is honorable and generous.

Boccaccio employs elements of *cortesia* in constructing his tale and characters, but allows these elements to mingle with certain traits more typical of the middle class: for example, Federigo's love has no regard for those tenets of aristocratic love doctrine which demand a man choose for a love object a woman higher born than himself. Moreover, when Giovanna finds herself dealing with her brothers' objections in her choice of a new husband, we must recognize a motif more typical of the world of the *borghesia*, one which would naturally appear out of place in the *cortesia* ambience. But all this hardly puts the novella on a different track. A melancholy tone of lofty renunciation has been sustained throughout the tale, and this tone is not substantially jarred by the addition of the brothers' concerns. Boccaccio wants to resolve his tale in terms of the Fifth Day's overall theme of love tales with happy endings, and the device of marriage allows him to do this even though it runs counter to the tale's primary narrative focus. The brothers' role and the marriage stand as a sort of detached element in the novella, added to help us recognize the benefits the *borghese* Giovanna has derived from her lesson in aristocratic virtues. By her appreciation of Federigo's gesture, Giovanna can be "promoted" into the ranks of the aristocracy—we can regard her as an *exemplum* of manners for her class. Marriage is the social mechanism which, in effect, creates this "promotion."

Boccaccio builds his tale around a central act of pathetically ironic renunciation: the confused Federigo, challenged to commit a great act of self-sacrifice in the name of hospitality and courtly largesse, unwittingly eliminates his chance to earn his lady's favor through bestowing the falcon to her alive—in effect, one act of renunciation precludes the other, leaving him profoundly distressed ("m'è sì gran duolo che servire non ve ne posso, che mai pace non me ne credo dare"). This tragic sense of irony is heightened by the lady's grief at what she has brought about and by the eventual death of the boy. But sacrifice, for the faithful knight no less than for the pious Christian, has its reward in final acquisition, and Federigo gains both the woman and material wealth at the tale's conclusion. This resolution in marriage and material gain shows how completely Boccaccio allows his tale to be pervaded by elements of the *borghese-comunale* world, and yet we must still note that Federigo is motivated not so much by *borghese* intelligence as by dogged adherence, in the face of all rejection and adversity, to the ideals of *cortesia*. His moral lesson is one of the value of renunciation.

In both of these novellas, the prime substance of plot lies in the protagonist's central choice of action. The groom chooses his secret conquest of the queen, and Federigo chooses to sacrifice his falcon. Each choice reflects a completely separate moral ideal. Character choice combines with lesser factors such as style, character type, *topoi*, etc. to produce varying moral moods, which is to say (in terms of the present study) varying ethical modes. These moods reflect patterns of character behavior and plot which in time become familiar to the reader of the **Decameron** novellas, resolving themselves into predictable and recurring conclusions for the different tales. Exposition of the system of ethical modes helps us analyze and systematize the varying moral atmospheres that infuse different novellas in turn, allowing us to understand characteristics which otherwise can appear vague and even contradictory.

Although all *Decameron* novellas tend toward a certain specific and readily identifiable cultural orientation, some of them may still resist easy categorization according to ethical modes: these are for the most part the stories in which human choice of action is not an important factor. This is especially true of the tales of the Second Day; here the driving force shaping human affairs is not so much free will as the machinations of *fortuna,* or adverse circumstance. Nevertheless this day can be said to play an indirect role in the presentation of ethical modes, for the illustration of the effects of *fortuna,* as introduced here, attains its true culmination in the eventual triumph of Ethics of Acquisition in the Third Day, wherein characters achieve their desires and defeat *fortuna* through their own intelligence. Thus the tales of the Second Day ultimately make a contribution to Boccaccio's general apotheosis of the power of human intelligence and the capacity of individuals to control the world around them.

The figure of Ciappelletto is also quite problematic, not because he makes no choice, but because the choice he makes defies easy interpretation in terms of ethics. This tale of a profoundly evil man who becomes a saint through a false deathbed confession appears as a tissue of ironies, ironies no less apparent in the tale-teller's commentary than in the story itself. The narrator Panfilo presents the novella as an illustration of the notion that God, through his infinite mercy, will grant sincere prayers even if they are mistakenly directed at false saints. But the reader finds this tone of exemplary righteousness attenuated by the comic portrayals of both the overly naive confessor and the simple-minded Burgundians who are all too quick to venerate the supposed saint. Even though the topic is serious, and Panfilo's pronouncements are quite solemn, the story comes across as something of an amusing parody of that most solemn of genres, the saint's life.

Nor does the text make completely clear Ciappelletto's motivations for choosing to make his outrageous confession. His hosts, expatriate Italian businessmen, are afraid their affairs will suffer if Ciappelletto dies without confession in their house, and yet they imagine that any true confession of his iniquities will surely lead to an equally detrimental denial of absolution. Ciappelletto reassures them that he will arrange things to their advantage if they will but fetch a confessor. He says he has done so much to offend God that one more sin could make no difference, but we are left wondering about his real motivations for this uncharacteristic altruism. Boccaccio allows him to speak, but does not reveal his innermost thoughts, nor permit us to follow the interior deliberations which lead to his act of perverse generosity. We see him choose, but we are not made to understand his choice.

If we examine Ciappelletto in terms of ethical modes, we can almost trace a hint of Ethics of Renunciation in his willingness to sacrifice his chances for salvation, however

remote, for the good of his compatriots, while the wily trick he plays on the monk shows some parallels with the actions of Boccaccio's many heroes of ethically correct acquisition. But we cannot acribe the overall tone of this novella to either of these modes. No matter how much some of his deeds may resemble those of Boccaccio's many morally justified characters, it is well not to forget what a monster he has deliberately been made out to be. He cannot play the role of the ethically correct protagonist, for this story is not meant to have such a protagonist. Like Frate Alberto, Ciappelletto as a central character amuses us, but does not gain our admiration. The ethical substance of this story is not transmitted through the characters' actions within the narrative, but rather through the external "application," which appears as the narrator's final commentary. This is not Boccaccio's usual pattern; he rarely has the *brigata* pronounce anything more than the sketchiest of concluding comments at the end of a novella. We are close here, in a certain sense, to the world of the traditional *exemplum,* wherein characters' choices are not especially relevant, and the story in and of itself is neither moral nor immoral—what matters ultimately is the extra-textual final statement, which serves to define the story's *a priori* ethical message. Having read the events of this tale, we are at a loss as to how to appreciate them ethically until Panfilo speaks up and gives us an exemplary interpretation:

> . . . grandissima si può la benignità di Dio cognoscere verso noi, la quale non al nostro errore ma alla purità della fé riguardando, così faccendo noi nostro mezzano un suo nemico, amico credendolo, ci essaudisce, come se a uno veramente santo per mezzano della sua grazia ricorressimo.

There has been controversy about the degree to which we are to accept this application at face value, and indeed there is far more irony implicit in the relationship between this conclusion and the tone of the tale itself than we should ever expect to find in the traditional *exemplum.* Nonetheless Boccaccio's conclusion is the only aid he provides, in the absence of clear adherence to any ethical mode, to help us resolve the moral vacuum which the tale creates.

Modes of Acquisition and Renunciation ought not to be difficult for a reader to grasp as concepts, since **Decameron** criticism has long been accustomed to the idea of a socio-stylistic dichotomy between real and ideal worlds; recognition of these two modes springs ultimately from continued awareness of at least the bare outlines of this dichotomy. Retribution, which will be the major emphasis of this study, is another matter: it seems less likely to suggest itself as a cohesive unit in the scheme of the **Decameron**'s ethical structure, even if it is so frequently a central element of plot. This is due in part to the fact that it does not fall neatly into one or the other of the two categories of the dichotomy. But it must also be acknowledged that there has been little critical attention paid to Boccaccio's treatment of morally sanctioned punishment, even though it is a phenomenon pervading a great many of his novellas.

It must continually be remembered that Boccaccio allows so much of the burden of his novella ethics to fall on the shoulders of his free-thinking characters: Ciappelletto aside, the ability of these characters to choose correct courses of action is consistently held up for our admiration in the vast majority of **Decameron** stories. If retribution is so frequently an element of plot, a type of "transformational action" (in Cottino-Jones' terms) which carries the narrative to its proper conclusion, it is because characters are repeatedly shown to be choosing it as the best means to bring that proper conclusion about. Character choice, oriented toward acquisition, renunciation or retribution, remains a central dynamic in the ethical system of the **Decameron** novella.

FURTHER READING

Biography

Carswell, Catherine. *The Tranquil Heart: Portrait of Giovanni Boccaccio.* New York: Harcourt, Brace and Co., 1937, 352 p.

Traces Boccaccio's life within a cultural and political context. Includes brief critical bibliography.

Chubb, Thomas Caldecot. *The Life of Giovanni Boccaccio.* Port Washington, N. Y.: Kennikat Press, 1930, 286 p.

Traditional biography wherein Chubb describes fourteenth-century Florentine society and recreates "the complex personality of an extremely interesting and extremely human man."

Krutch, Joseph Wood. "Giovanni Boccaccio." In his *Five Masters: A Study in the Mutations of the Novel,* pp. 3-60. 1930. Reprint. New York: Jonathan Cape & Harrison Smith, 1931.

Overview of Boccaccio's life and career, noting "how the curve of his life anticipated that of the Renaissance as a whole."

MacManus, Francis. *Great Writers of the World: Boccaccio.* New York: Sheed & Ward, 1947, 306 p.

Portrays Boccaccio as a transitional figure between the Middle Ages and the Renaissance. Contains illustrations and brief critical bibliography.

Criticism

Bergin, Thomas. "An Introduction to Boccaccio." In Boccaccio's *The Decameron: A New Translation,* translated and edited by Mark Musa and Peter E. Bondanella, pp. 151-71. New York: W. W. Norton & Co., 1977.

Surveys Boccaccio's tales and offers background information on their composition.

Boitani, Piero. *Chaucer and Boccaccio.* Oxford: Society for the Study of Medieval Languages and Literature, 1977, 210 p.

Examines the impact of Boccaccio's *Teseida* on Chaucer's *Knight's Tale,* focusing on similarities in plot, style, and characterization.

Cole, Howard C. *The All's Well Story from Boccaccio to Shakespeare.* Chicago: University of Illinois Press, 1981, 145 p.

Comparative analysis of Boccaccio's story of Giletta and William Shakespeare's *All's Well that Ends Well.*

Cottino-Jones, Marga. *Order from Chaos: Social and Aesthetic Harmonies in Boccaccio's "Decameron."* Washington, D.C.: University Press of America, 1982, 200 p.

Maintains that Boccaccio's tales represent society's progression from confusion to stability. Linking the *Decameron*'s narrative complexity to the tumultuous environment in which it was written, Cottino-Jones suggests that Boccaccio offered the *Decameron* as a solution to the societal problems of his time.

Deligiorgis, Stavros. *Narrative Intellection in the "Decameron."* Iowa City: University of Iowa Press, 1975, 233 p.

Analyzes the "patterns of internal dependence" in the *Decameron* and identifies the work's major and minor themes.

Dole, Nathan Haskell. "Boccaccio and the Novella." In his *A Teacher of Dante and Other Studies in Italian Literature,* pp. 142-200. New York: Moffat, Yard, and Co., 1908.

Highlights Boccaccio's contribution to the development of the novella, heralding him as "the story-teller of the Renaissance."

Dombroski, Robert S., ed. *Critical Perspectives on the "Decameron."* London: Hodder and Stoughton, 1976, 146 p.

Collection of essays on various aspects of the *Decameron* by such critics as Ugo Foscolo, Francesco De Sanctis, and Alberto Moravia.

"The *Decameron* of Boccaccio." *Edinburgh Review,* Vol. CLXXVIII, No. CCCLXVI (October 1893): 500-29.

Discusses the influence of pagan and medieval Christian cultures on the *Decameron,* stating that the work "is the true literary exponent of the worldly life of the fourteenth century."

Lee, A. C. *The "Decameron": Its Sources and Analogues.* London: David Nutt, 1909, 363 p.

Scrutinizes the various stories in the *Decameron* to identify their historical and literary sources.

Lewis, C. S. "What Chaucer Really Did to *Il Filostrato.*" In *Chaucer: The Critical Heritage,* Vol. 2: 1837-1933, edited by Derek Brewer, pp. 468-86. Boston: Routledge & Kegan Paul, 1978.

Important study (first published in 1932) wherein Lewis discerns how the *Filostrato* underwent a process of "medievalization" at the hands of Geoffrey Chaucer.

Lipari, Angelo. "The Structure and Real Significance of the *Decameron.*" In *Essays in Honor of Albert Feuillerat,* edited by Henri M. Peyre, pp. 43-83. New Haven, Conn.: Yale University Press, 1943.

Opposes the traditional critical view that the stories in the *Decameron* are primarily literal, concluding that it is "unfair to assume [that Boccaccio's novellas] were meant to be allegorical in character."

Mazzotta, Giuseppe. *The World at Play in Boccaccio's "Decameron."* Princeton, N.J.: Princeton University Press, 1986, 280 p.

Discusses the role of the imagination and desire, as well as various intellectual traditions—courtly love, medical texts, scientific and legal discourse, among others—evoked by the *Decameron* "in order to define the cultural frame of reference for the narrative."

Moore, Edward. "The Lives Attributed to Boccaccio." In his

Dante and His Early Biographers, pp. 4-57. London: Riving-tons, 1890.

> Pays tribute to Boccaccio's preservation of Dante for fu-ture generations in his *Life of Dante* and *Short Treatise in Praise of Dante*. As the critic states: "Most grateful should we be to Boccaccio for this precious heritage; for not only is it recorded in his own delicious and inimita-ble prose, not only is the portrait traced with a loving and skilful hand, but without it we should not have pos-sessed any such portraiture at all."

Moravia, Alberto. "Boccaccio." In his *Man as an End: A De-fense of Humanism*, translated by Bernard Wall, pp. 134-55. New York: Farrar, Straus & Giroux, 1965.

> Asserts that the eroticism which pervades the *Decamer-on* is not of primary importance, but rather only a means by which Boccaccio advances his characters' actions.

Noakes, Susan. "From Dante to Boccaccio." In her *Timely Reading: Between Exegesis and Interpretation*, pp. 68-97. London: Cornell University Press, 1988.

> Suggests that in the *Decameron* Boccaccio served as an editor, theorist, and commentator.

Ó Cuilleanáin, Cormac. *Religion and the Clergy in Boccac-cio's "Decameron."* Rome: Edizioni di Storia e Letteratura, 1984, 305 p.

> Investigates the religious element in the *Decameron*, contending that although Boccaccio employed religious forms, he was little concerned with spiritual matters or contemporary Christianity.

Scaglione, Aldo D. *Nature and Love in the Late Middle Ages.* Berkeley: University of California Press, 1963, 250 p.

> Elucidates the relationship between nature and love in medieval Italian and French literature, with particular attention to the *Decameron*.

Smarr, Janet Levarie. *Boccaccio and Fiammetta: The Narra-tor as Lover.* Urbana: University of Illinois Press, 1986, 284 p.

> Studies "Boccaccio's technique as a writer of fiction: chiefly, his introduction of readers and narrators within the text, the narrator's recurrent pose as a lover, and the reappearance from work to work of the beloved Fiam-metta in changing roles."

Wood, Chauncey. *The Elements of Chaucer's "Troilus."* Durham, N.C.: Duke University Press, 1984, 204 p.

> Discerns the impact of Boccaccio's *Filostrato* on Chau-cer's *Troilus*, concluding that the former was the major source for the latter.

Wright, Herbert G. *The First English Translation of the "De-cameron."* Cambridge, Mass.: Harvard University Press, 1953.

> Explores the textual transmission of the *Decameron*, with special attention to John Florio's disputed 1620 En-glish translation.

Additional coverage of Boccaccio's life and career is contained in the following source published by Gale Research: *Short Story Criticism*, **Vol. 10.**

Demosthenes

384 B.C. -322 B.C.

Greek orator.

INTRODUCTION

Demosthenes is considered the greatest orator in history and one of the preeminent prose stylists in the Greek language. He was a master of the skills and techniques of oratory, an art form devoted to the use of words for purposes of persuasion which developed in the democracy of fifth-century B.C. Athens. Contemporaries and subsequent critics have praised Demosthenes for such qualities as a lucid and convincing presentation of argument; a compositional style that is at once clear and elaborate; variety in both style and tone; an expert handling of metaphor; and a sophisticated use of narrative that combines the appearance of spontaneity with a sensitivity toward the circumstances of the audience. Through his major political speeches Demosthenes exerted enormous influence on fourth-century B.C. politics, and his eloquence and commitment to the cause of Athenian liberty have inspired numerous statesmen, including Cicero, William Pitt, and Winston Churchill.

Biographical Information

Demosthenes was born in Athens into a moderately wealthy family. Upon the death of his father, a successful armorer, the seven-year-old boy's estate was managed by three guardians. At the age of eighteen, Demosthenes discovered that his property had been badly mismanaged, and it is believed that he studied rhetoric and legal procedure at this time under the famous orator Isaeus in order to bring legal action against his father's trustees. Three years later, Demosthenes successfully prosecuted the latter in his first speeches, *Against Aphobus* and *Against Onetor*. He thereby became known as a skilled orator, and in the 350s B.C. he was frequently employed as a speech-writer for both private cases and public trials. Toward the end of this decade, Demosthenes became increasingly involved in the political issues of his day. Beginning with *Philippic I*, he aggressively attacked the expansionist policies of Philip II of Macedon. In 346 B.C. Demosthenes served on two controversial embassies to Macedon which succeeded in securing peace. In the following years, however, he advocated that the peace be discarded and that anti-Macedonian alliances be forged with other states. Following the decisive defeat of Athenian forces at Chaeronea in 338 B.C., Demosthenes quickly organized his city's defences against invasion. Nevertheless, Philip's successor, Alexander the Great, annexed Athens in 336 B.C. Toward the close of the decade, Demosthenes's political actions were attacked in court by his oratorical opponent, Aeschines. Demosthenes defended his career in his masterpiece, *On the Crown*, which was considered so con-

clusive that Aeschines was fined and deprived of the right to prosecute. In 323 B.C., however, Demosthenes was successfully prosecuted for misappropriation of funds—an issue that still remains obscure to scholars. He left Athens the following year, was condemned to death, and committed suicide on the island of Caularia.

Major Works

Approximately forty-five authentic speeches by Demosthenes have survived, and all have been translated into English. They have been divided by scholars into three main categories: speeches of political deliberation; speeches of private litigation; and public speeches of praise or blame for great occasions. Demosthenes is best known for his political speeches, especially the four *Philippics* and the three *Olynthiacs*, as well as the personal speech *On the Crown*. In the *Philippics* and *Olynthiacs* Demosthenes passionately urges his fellow Athenians to combat the military aggression of Philip of Macedon. *Philippic I*, for example, focuses its argument on the contrast between the apathy of Athens and the dynamism of the Macedonian king, who "is always adding to his conquests, and casts his snare around us while we sit at home postponing." In the *Olyn-*

thiacs Demosthenes advocates a bold pro-war policy, arguing that Athens should devote her civic funds entirely to military purposes. *On the Crown* is considered the greatest of all Greek speeches and the apex of Demosthenes's rhetorical art. This large and dramatic work provides a retrospective account and justification of Demosthenes's policies. In lucid and passionate language he vindicates his actions in the years prior to the Macedonian victory over the Greek city-states, asserting: "Everyone, everywhere, lets the past go, and no one offers advice about it. It is the future or the present that requires the adviser to perform his function."

Critical Reception

Since ancient times, Demosthenes has been regarded, together with Plato, as one of the supreme prose writers of Greek literature. In the Greek world his influence was pervasive throughout the Byzantine era; in western Europe his impact on Cicero ensured that his reputation survived during the Middle Ages, despite the fact that his works were not available. In the fourteenth and fifteenth centuries, however, manuscripts of his speeches were brought by Byzantine scholars to Italy, where they became the subject of humanist study. Numerous editions, translations, and commentaries on the Demosthenic corpus were published throughout Europe in the sixteenth and seventeenth centuries. At this time, Demosthenes was studied for practical as well as aesthetic reasons. The Elizabethan scholar and civil servant Thomas Wilson, for example, translated several of Demosthenes's speeches into English and advocated that they be studied by those intent on serving the State. The rhetorical style of the great political speeches of Demosthenes became a model for British parliamentary speakers in the eighteenth and nineteenth centuries. Moreover, the British saw Demosthenes as the embodiment of their democratic ideal. In Germany, by contrast, the orator's reputation declined in the nineteenth century, when scholars criticized his anti-imperialist policy as short-sighted and suicidal. Twentieth-century commentators have reasserted Demosthenes's importance. While modern historians have unanimously praised his artistic achievement, some have suggested that his advocacy of war against Macedon resulted from a flawed, if heroic, assessment of the political realities of his age.

PRINCIPAL WORKS

SPEECHES

Against Aphobus 364 B.C.
Against Onetor 364 B.C.
Against Androtion 355 B.C.
Against Leptines 354 B.C.
On the Symmories 354 B.C.
Against Timocrates 353 B.C.
For the Megapolitans 353 B.C.
Against Aristocrates 352 B.C.
On the Liberty of the Rhodians 351 B.C.
Philippic I 351 B.C.

For Phormio c. 350 B.C.
Olynthiacs I-III 349 B.C.
Against Meidias 348 B.C.
On the Peace 346 B.C.
Philippic II 344 B.C.
On the False Embassy 343 B.C.
On the Chersonese 341 B.C.
Philippic III 341 B.C.
Philippic IV 340 B.C.
On the Crown 330 B.C.

PRINCIPAL ENGLISH TRANSLATIONS

Demosthenes: The Orations (translated by Charles Rann Kennedy). 5 vols. 1852
Demosthenes (translated by J. H. and C. A. Vince, and various hands). 9 vols. 1926-49
Greek Political Oratory (translated by A. N. W. Saunders) 1970

CRITICISM

Pseudo-Longinus (essay date first century)

SOURCE: A chapter, translated by H. L. Havell, in *Aristotle's Poetics, Demetrius on Style, Longinus on the Sublime*, Dent, 1963, pp. 184-86.

[*The Greek literary treatise* On the Sublime *has in the past been erroneously attributed to the third-century writer Cassius Longinus. Modern scholarship has demonstrated that the authorship and exact date of this work are unknown, though it was probably written in the first century; nevertheless, as an analysis of sublimity in literature, it has exerted a powerful influence in the history of aesthetics. In the following excerpt from* On the Sublime, *Demosthenes's rhetorical skills are compared with those of his contemporary, Hyperides.*]

If the number and not the loftiness of an author's merits is to be our standard of success, judged by this test we must admit that Hyperides is a far superior orator to Demosthenes. For in Hyperides there is a richer modulation, a greater variety of excellence. He is, we may say, in everything second-best, like the champion of the *pentathlon,* who, though in every contest he has to yield the prize to some other combatant, is superior to the unpractised in all five. Not only has he rivalled the success of Demosthenes in everything but his manner of composition, but, as though that were not enough, he has taken in all the excellences and graces of Lysias as well. He knows when it is proper to speak with simplicity, and does not, like Demosthenes, continue the same key throughout. His touches of character are racy and sparkling, and full of a delicate flavour. Then how admirable is his wit, how polished his raillery! How well bred he is, how dexterous in the use of irony! His jests are pointed, but without any of the grossness and vulgarity of the old Attic comedy. He is skilled in making light of an opponent's argument, full of a well-aimed satire which amuses while it stings; and through all this there runs a pervading, may we not say, a matchless charm. He is most apt in moving compassion; his mythical digressions show a fluent ease, and he is perfect in bending his course and finding a way out of them without violence or effort. Thus when he tells the story of Leto he is really almost a poet; and his funeral oration shows a declamatory magnificence to which I hardly know a parallel. Demosthenes, on the other hand, has no touches of character, none of the versatility, fluency, or declamatory skill of Hyperides. He is, in fact, almost entirely destitute of all those excellences which I have just enumerated. When he makes violent efforts to be humorous and witty, the only laughter he arouses is against himself; and the nearer he tries to get to the winning grace of Hyperides, the farther he recedes from it. Had he, for instance, attempted such a task as the little speech in defence of Phryne or Athenagoras, he would only have added to the reputation of his rival. Nevertheless all the beauties of Hyperides, however numerous, cannot make him sublime. He never exhibits strong feeling, has little energy, rouses no emotion; certainly he never kindless terror in the breast of his readers. But Demosthenes followed a great master [Thucydides], and drew his consummate excellences, his high-pitched eloquence, his living passion, his copiousness, his sagacity, his speed—that mastery and power which can never be approached—from the highest of sources. These mighty, these heaven-sent gifts (I dare not call them human), he made his own both one and all. Therefore, I say, by the noble qualities which he does possess he remains supreme above all rivals, and throws a cloud over his failings, silencing by his thunders and blinding by his lightnings the orators of all ages. Yes, it would be easier to meet the lightning-stroke with steady eye than to gaze unmoved when his impassioned eloquence is sending out flash after flash.

Herbert Henry Asquith   (essay date 1877)

SOURCE: "The Age of Demosthenes," in *Studies and Sketches*, 1924. Reprint by Books for Libraries Press, 1968, pp. 173-82.

[*Asquith was a prominent English politician and man of letters. In the following essay, originally published in the* Spectator *in 1877, he discusses Demosthenes's role in fourth-century B.C. politics, asserting that, "had his counsels been followed, the era of free Greece might have closed not in ignominy and disgrace, but in the noble spectacle of a heroic death."*]

It is not easy to realize distinctly the nature of the political problems which presented themselves to an Athenian statesman of the fourth century before Christ, and yet, complex as they are, they must be clearly conceived and steadily kept in view, if we would do justice either to Demosthenes or to his leading opponents. Over and above the difficulty which besets every attempt to express ancient ideas in modern terms, there is in this case need for additional caution, arising, in part, from the character of our chief authorities for the period, and still more from our own prepossessions. Contemporary rhetoric is in some respects the worst material for history, and as we try to balance the conflicting statements of the rival orators, and to evolve out of the chaos of contradictions and recrimina-

tions the actual form and body of the time, we sigh in vain for a Thucydides, or even a Xenophon. There is, unfortunately, no reason to suppose that Demosthenes himself, high as he towers above all his contemporaries, was at all superior to the rhetorical vice of over-colouring for party purposes, and there are obvious inconsistencies in the accounts which he gives at different times of the same persons and events. But the task of getting at the truth is rendered still more arduous by our constant liability to be misled through associations derived from an earlier and more splendid epoch in Grecian history. The memories which naturally suggest themselves at the mention of names like Athens, Sparta, and Thebes are the memories of the Persian invasion, of the age of Pericles, and of the Peloponnesian War. The fact is that, whether we regard its external dangers or its inner civic life, the Greece of the fourth century B.C. was as unlike the Greece of the fifth century as the England of to-day is unlike the England of Mr. Pitt and the French war. Fear of the Great King and his designs of ambition or revenge was no longer a powerful factor in Greek politics. A doctrinaire politician like Isocrates might still preach a Pan-Hellenic crusade against the traditional enemy, but the spasmodic Persophobia (if we may use the phrase) which his pamphlets aroused, and which the interested agents of Philip probably kept alive, had no more influence with the practical statesmen of the time, than the occasional outbursts of a like sentiment in reference to France have had in our own country within our own memory. Persia, the only Power whose aggression could have aroused the imaginative side of Greek patriotism, and absorbed in a national movement of self-defence the petty jealousies of the States, was no longer a formidable foe, and the liberties of Greece were menaced from a quarter which seemed at once too familiar and too insignificant to justify suspicion or alarm.

The semi-barbarous kingdom of Macedonia, after several fitful attempts to take a place and play a part in the Hellenic economy, had, under Amyntas, the father, and Perdiccas, the brother of Philip, become a prey to its savage neighbours, and all but ceased to exist. When Philip himself ascended the throne, there was nothing either in the past history or the present condition of the disorganized tribe over which he exercised an almost nominal supremacy, to excite the fears of the cultured and well-ordered cities which had for more than a century competed for the hegemony of Greece. The early years of Philip's reign were employed in establishing his authority at home, and in perfecting the "military instrument," to which, like the Prussian statesmen of the present century, he looked for the accomplishment of his far-reaching schemes. It is true that almost from the first he set to work to gain a footing for himself in Thrace, and to undermine the traditional influence of Athens in the outlying quarters of the Hellenic world, but it was not till, after seven years of cautious encroachment, he boldly intervened in the Sacred War, and made himself master of Thessaly, that even Demosthenes began to suspect the ultimate aims of his ambitious policy. From this point onwards the nature of his designs is so clear to the modern student of history, that it is hard to understand how they could have been hidden from the eyes of his contemporaries. The next twelve years are occupied with the gradual development of a scheme of patient, consistent and continuous aggression. The conquest of Olynthus and Chalcidice is rapidly succeeded by the ruin of Phocis, and at last the fatal blindness of the Amphictyonic Council, and the decisive victory of Chæronea, only hastened a consummation which had long been inevitable.

Throughout this period, Demosthenes stands out among the men of his day as the one steady opponent of Macedonian policy, and our estimate of his statesmanship must therefore depend upon the answer which we give to two questions—first, were the liberties of Greece, as he conceived them, and as they existed in his time, worth preserving? and second, was their preservation possible?

The first of these questions appears to us by no means so superfluous as it is generally assumed to be. "Freedom" is a misleading and often a question-begging term, and nowhere is it used to cover so large a variety of confused and contradictory meanings as in the pages of Greek historians and orators. The simple enthusiasm for liberty which brightens the narrative of Herodotus is a very different sentiment from the spirit of democratic propagandism with which it is often confounded in the rhetorical utterances ascribed by Thucydides to the Athenian speakers of the era of the Peloponnesian War. But in the age of Demosthenes the word, and the thing which it represents, had reached a further stage of degradation, which cannot be properly understood except by reference to the altered circumstances of the time. Free institutions are only valuable as means to an end, and in the celebrated oration which Thucydides puts into the mouth of Pericles, this truth is clearly grasped by the speaker, who finds the peculiar glory of the Athenian Constitution in the many-sided type of character which it developed, and in the generous and imperial policy which it encouraged. Nor was this a mere rhetorical boast. At the outbreak of the Peloponnesian War, Athens had passed her prime, and already began to exhibit some of the symptoms of degeneracy. The self-forgetful enthusiasm, which had led her people to dare and suffer so much for Greece half a century before, had given place to an aggressive and overbearing temper, and the new culture, if it had summoned into life the latent powers of the Athenian mind, had at the same time corrupted its simplicity. Nevertheless, when we compare Athens at this period with her rivals, we cannot hesitate to declare that the principles of free government, as understood and practised by her statesmen, were justified by their results. The Athenian citizen lived in a more enervating atmosphere than that in which the heroes of Marathon were reared, but culture and prosperity had not destroyed in him the springs of action, and he was neither too effeminate for the rough work of the assembly and the battlefield, nor too absorbed in his own city to be indifferent to the larger claims of his country and his race.

But three-quarters of a century later a change had taken place, of the nature and extent of which we have the best evidence in the speeches of Demosthenes himself. The occasional sketches of the Athens of his day with which he points his invectives against the ignominious lethargy of his fellow-countrymen seem like a malicious caricature of the glowing picture of Pericles. They show us a people among whom free institutions have run to seed, and who have reached that state of settled insensibility to the duties and responsibilities of corporate life which is perhaps more perilous, because less curable, than one of actual anarchy. Politics are handed over to a professional class of experts, and are no more the common interest of all. Public life itself is specialized into a number of separate departments—one set of men do the fighting, another set the talking, others, again, intrigue and pull the wires in the interest of foreign Powers; while the mass of the people sit by, and are bored or amused, applaud or hiss, like the spectators in a theatre whom the play occasionally excites to an artificial and disinterested sympathy. It is no longer the fashion to contribute freely and splendidly to the service of the State; the duties of the trierarchy, which used to arouse an honourable rivalry among the rich, are habitually evaded or jobbed; the humbler ranks in the army and navy, which were once composed of the less wealthy citizens, are now filled up with mercenaries; and every attempt to add to the effective resources of the city, whether by the imposition of a property-tax or by the diversion of the Theoric Fund, is sure to encounter the opposition of either the rich or the poor, or both, in the exact proportion in which their respective comforts or luxuries are menaced. In short, to the contemporaries and fellow-citizens of Demosthenes, patriotism was unintelligible and public spirit unknown, and the rival cliques who made a profit out of the game of politics were so notoriously and systematically venal, that even the name of the great orator himself—by universal admission, the purest and most unselfish statesman of the age—cannot be cleared from a dark shadow of suspicion. If this is, as we believe it to be, a substantially accurate account of the state of Athens in the fourth century, and if, as we also believe, Athens was not only the freest State in Greece, but the most energetic in its opposition to Philip, may it not be that many unnecessary tears have been wept, and many superfluous sighs have been sighed, over "that dishonest victory at Chæronea, fatal to liberty?"

But even assuming, as Demosthenes assumed, that Greek freedom was yet worth fighting for, and that a system of small, autonomous States was in any case preferable to the paralysing supremacy of a universal monarchy, we have still to meet the further question—where were the materials for an organized resistance? The Peloponnesian War destroyed the Athenian Empire, without substituting for it any new centre of authority or bond of union. Sparta was, of all the leading Greek cities, the least fitted by her traditions and her political principles for the duties of hegemony, and during the twenty years of her disastrous ascendancy she left nothing undone that the fatuity of the most wrong-headed statesman could have devised to hasten the decay of the Panhellenic sentiment. The battle of Leuctra gave a death-blow to the power of Sparta, which fell beyond hope of recovery, and for a time it seemed as though the genius of Epaminondas would unite the northern and southern States in a compact confederacy, with Thebes for its centre. But the life-work of this great statesman hardly survived its creator, and the temporary rejuvenescence of Athens which followed was from the beginning hollow and unreal, and was soon cut short by the Social War. Thus at the moment when Philip began his active career, the States of Greece were never more impotent as individuals, or more disunited as a whole.

It is to the credit of Demosthenes that he perceived from the first this fatal flaw, and that throughout his career he lost no opportunity of insisting on the necessity of union. Again and again, on behalf of Megalopolis, of Olynthus, of Phocis, he urged his short-sighted fellow-citizens to submit, in the interest of Athens itself, to the temporary sacrifices involved in a generous and self-forgetful policy. Had his counsels been followed, the era of free Greece might have closed not in ignominy and disgrace, but in the noble spectacle of a heroic death. But the end, though it might have been dignified, and even delayed, could not have been averted. The policy of Demosthenes was, after all, a policy of expedients, and when he recalled the inspiring memories of the Persian invasion and the Peloponnesian War, he exhausted all the resources of his matchless eloquence in appeals to a sentiment which, if it were not altogether dead, had at best but an artificial life. It was vain to urge this combination or that, when the absence of any possible head and of any durable basis of union doomed all imaginable combinations to ultimate futility. It was equally vain to preach a crusade in the ears of men who had no faith in the cause for which they were called upon to sacrifice what they really valued and enjoyed, and whose degenerate ideas of liberty were in nowise outraged by the considerate rule of a Macedonian governor. There are few figures in history which have a better title to our respectful sympathy than that of Demosthenes, "fallen on evil days and evil tongues," and confronting with a noble enthusiasm which nothing could damp or dim the indifference of an age which was not worthy of him. That he was the apostle of a cause already lost is no derogation from his greatness, and need not qualify our admiration of his character and purposes, for the failures of such men are more instructive than the petty triumphs of successful ambition.

Gilbert Murray (essay date 1897)

SOURCE: "Demosthenes and His Contemporaries," in *A History of Ancient Greek Literature*, 1897. Reprint by Frederick Ungar Publishing Co., 1966, pp. 353-69.

[*An English educator, humanitarian, translator, author, and classical scholar, Murray is considered one of the most influential twentieth-century commentators on Greek literature. In the following excerpt, he provides an assessment of Demosthenes's career, concluding that "he is a man of genius and something of a hero; a fanatic, too, no doubt, and always a politician."*]

Demosthenes lost his father when a boy of seven. His three guardians made away with his property and failed to provide for his mother. It was she that brought him up, a delicate, awkward, and passionate boy, industrious and unathletic. Doubtless the two brooded on their wrongs; and as soon as Demosthenes was legally competent he brought actions against the guardians. They were men of position, connected with the moderate party then in power. They may possibly have had some real defence, but, instead of using it, they tried to browbeat and puzzle the boy by

counter-actions and chicanery. When at last he won his case, there was not much property left to recover. The chief results to him were a certain practical skill in law and in speaking, enhanced, it is said, by the lessons of Isaeus; a certain mistrust of dignitaries, and a contempt for etiquette. The sordidness, also, of the long quarrel about money offended him. He was by nature lavish; he always gave largely in charity, helped poor citizens to dower their daughters, and ransomed prisoners of war. On this occasion he spent his damages on fitting out a trireme—one of the costliest public services that Athens demanded of her rich citizens; then he settled down to poverty as a speechwriter, and perhaps as a teacher. He succeeded at once in his profession, though his hesitating and awkward delivery interfered with his own speaking. His practice was of the highest kind. He did not deal with 'hetaira' suits like Hyperídes, and he steadily avoided 'sykophantic' prosecutions, though he both wrote and spoke for the Opposition in cases of political interest.

His first personal appearance was perhaps in 355, *Against Leptînes*, who had proposed to abolish public grants of immunity from taxation. It was a prudent financial step, and hard to attack; but these grants were generally rewards for exceptional diplomatic services, and formed an important element in the forward policy advocated by the Opposition.

Eubûlus had taken office after the Social War in 357, when the time called for retrenchment and retreat. His financial policy was an unexampled success; but it meant the resignation of the Empire, and perhaps worse. He had inherited a desultory war with Philip, in which Athens had everything against her. Philip was step by step seizing the Athenian possessions on the shores of Thrace. Eubûlus, since public opinion did not allow him to make peace, replied by a weak blockade of the Macedonian coast and occasional incursions. The hotter heads among the Opposition demanded an army of 30,000 mercenaries to march upon Pella forthwith. This was folly. Demosthenes's own policy was to press the war vigorously until some marked advantage could be gained on which to make a favourable treaty.

But Philip did not yet fill the whole horizon. In the speech *For the Rhodians* (? 351 or 353 B.C.) Demosthenes urges Athens to help a democratic rising in Rhodes, in the hope of recovering part of her lost influence in the Ægean. Eubûlus was against intervention. In the speech *For Megalopolis* (? 353 B.C.) Demosthenes merely objects to taking a definite side in favour of Sparta. It would have been impossible at the time to give active help to Megalopolis; though perhaps it would have prevented one of the most fatal combinations of the ensuing years, the reliance of the anti-Spartan parts of the Peloponnese upon Philip's support. In 352 Philip had attempted to pass Thermopylae into Lower Greece; Eubûlus, for once vigorous, had checked him. But the danger had become obvious and acute, and Demosthenes presses it in the *First Philippic*. The king retired northwards and laid siege to Olynthus. Athens knew the immense value of that place, and acted energetically; but the great diplomat paralysed her by stirring up a revolt in Eubœa at the critical moment. Demosthenes, in his three **Olynthiacs**, presses unhesitatingly for the relief of Olynthus. The government took the common-sense or unsanguine view, that Eubœa, being nearer, must be saved first. Euboea was saved; but Olynthus fell, and Athens was unable to continue the war. When Philocrates introduced proposals of peace, Demosthenes supported him, and was given a place on the commission of ten sent to treat with Philip for terms. He was isolated among the commissioners. The most important of these, after Philocrates, was ÆSCHINES of Kothôkidæ (389-314 B.C.). He was a man of high culture and birth, though the distresses of the war compelled all his family to earn their own livelihood. His father turned schoolmaster; his mother did religious work in connection with some Mysteries. Æschines himself had been an actor, a profession which carried no slur, and a clerk in the public service. He was a hater of demagogues and a follower of Eubûlus. The three speeches of his which we possess are all connected with Demosthenes and with this embassy.

The negotiations were long. Eventually a treaty was agreed to, containing at least two dangerous ambiguities: it included Athens *and her allies*, and it left each party in possession of what it actually held *at the time*. Now Athens was anxious about two powers, which were allies in a sense, but not subject allies—Kersobleptes, king of a buffer state in Thrace, and the Phokians, any attack on whom would bring Philip into the heart of Greece. Philip's envoys refused to allow any specific mention of these allies in the treaty; the Athenian commissioners were left to use their diplomacy upon the king himself. And as to the time of the conclusion of the treaty, Athens was bound to peace from the day she took the oaths. Would Philip admit that he was equally bound, or would he go on with his operations till he had taken the oaths himself? Philocrates and Æschines considered it best to assume the king's good faith as a matter of course, and to conduct their mission according to the ordinary diplomatic routine. Demosthenes pressed for extreme haste. He insisted that they should not wait for Philip at his capital, but seek him out wherever he might be. When the commissioners' passports did not arrive, he dragged them into Macedonia without passports. However, do what he might, long delays occurred; and, by the time Philip met the ambassadors, he had crushed Kersobleptes and satisfactorily rounded his eastern frontier. Demosthenes made an open breach both with his colleagues and with the king: he refused the customary diplomatic presents, which Philip gave on an exceptionally gorgeous scale; he absented himself from the official banquet; he attempted to return home separately. When he reached Athens he moved that the usual ambassador's crown should be withheld from himself and his colleagues.

Before the end of the month Philip had passed Thermopylæ, conquered Phokis, and got himself recognised as a member of the Amphictyonic League with a right to interfere in the politics of Central Greece. The same year (346) he presided at the Pythian Games. The first impulse at Athens was to declare the peace broken; but that would have been suicidal, as Demosthenes shows in his speech **On the Peace** after the settlement. Still indignation was hot against the ambassadors, and their oppo-

nents became active in the law-courts. Demosthenes associated himself with one Timarchus in prosecuting Æschines for misconduct as ambassador. Æschines was in great danger, and retorted by a sharp counter-action against Timarchus, who, though now a leading and tolerably respected politician, had passed an immoral youth. In modern times it would perhaps only have caused a damaging scandal. In Athens it deprived him of all public rights. The unfortunate man collapsed without a word, and Æschines was safe, though it went less well with his friends. Philocrates fled from trial and was condemned. His accuser was Hyperides, son of Glaukippus, an orator considered only second to Demosthenes in power and superior to him in charm. He was an extremist in politics. In private life his wit and his loose ways made him a favourite topic for comedy. The traditional *Life* is a mere hash of hostile anecdotes, and a current jest accused him of trying to influence a jury by partially undressing a certain Phrynê in court. His works were absolutely lost till this century, when large parts of five speeches—not eloquent, but surpassing even Lysias in coolness and humour, and a frank dislike of humbug—have been recovered in papyri from Upper Egypt.

Demosthenes himself was engaged in preparing for the future war and trying to counteract Philip's intrigues in the Peloponnese (**Phil. II.**). It was a pity that in 344 he revived the old action against Æschines (**On Misconduct of Ambassadors**). The speeches of both orators are preserved. Æschines appears at his best in them, Demosthenes perhaps at his worst. His attack was intemperate, and his prejudice led him to combine and colour his facts unfairly. He could have shown that Æschines was a poor diplomat; but, in spite of his political ascendency, he could not make the jury believe that he was a corrupt one. Æschines was acquitted, and Demosthenes was not yet secure enough of his power to dispense with publishing his speeches.

We possess one (**On the Chersonnese**) in which he defends the irregularities of his general Diopeithes on Philip's frontier; and another (**Phil. III.**) in which he issues to all Greece an arraignment of Philip's treacherous diplomacy. Most of Demosthenes's public speeches have the same absence of what we call rhetoric, the same great self-forgetfulness. But something that was once narrow in his patriotism is now gone, and there is a sense of imminent tragedy and a stern music of diction which makes the **Third Philippic** unlike anything else in literature. War was declared in 340, and at first Athens was successful. It was a stroke of religious intrigue that turned the day. The Locrians were induced to accuse Athens of impiety before the Amphictyonic council. Impiety was in Greece, like heresy afterwards, an offence of which most people were guilty if you pressed the inquiry. The Athenians had irregularly consecrated some Theban shields. But the Locrians themselves had profanely occupied the sacred territory of Kirrha. Æschines, who was the Athenian representative, contrived to divert the warlike bigotry of the council against the Locrians. He is very proud of his achievement. But either turn served Philip equally well: he only desired a sacred war of some sort, in order that the Amphictyons, who were without an army, might summon him into Greece as defender of religion. Once inside Thermopylæ, he threw off the mask. Demosthenes obtained at the last moment what he had so long sought, an alliance between Athens and Thebes; but the Macedonian generalship was too good, and the coalition of Greece lay under Philip's feet at Chæronea in 338.

Athens received the blow with her usual heroism. Lycurgus the treasurer was overwhelmed with voluntary offerings for the defence fund, and the walls were manned for a fight to the death. But that was not Philip's wish. He sent Demâdes the orator, who had been made captive in the battle, to say that he would receive proposals for peace. The friends of Macedon, Phokion, Æschines, and Demâdes, were the ambassadors, and Athens was admitted on easy terms into the alliance which Philip formed as the basis of his march against Persia. Then came a war of the law-courts, the Macedonian party straining every nerve to get rid of the war element. Hyperîdes had proposed, in the first excitement of the defeat, to arm and liberate all slaves. This was unconstitutional, and he was prosecuted by Aristogeiton. His simple confession: *"It was the battle of Chæronea that spoke, not I . . . The arms of Macedon took away my sight"*—was enough to secure his acquittal. A desperate onslaught was made against Demosthenes; Aristogeiton, Sosicles, Philocrates, Diondas, and Melanthus, among others, prosecuted him. But the city was true to him. Some of the accusers failed to get a fifth of the votes, and he was chosen to make the funeral speech over those slain at Chæronea. Then came the strange counter-campaign of Lycurgus against the Macedonian party. The man was a kind of Cato. Of unassailable reputation himself, he had a fury for extirpating all that was corrupt and unpatriotic, and his standard was intolerably high. The only speech of his preserved to us is *Against Leocrates*, a person whose crime was that he had left the city after Chæronea, instead of staying to fight and suffer. The penalty demanded for this slight lack of patriotism was death, and the votes were actually equal.

This shows the temper of the city; but resistance to Macedon was for the time impossible. Athens was content with an opportunist coalition directed by Demosthenes and Demâdes. On Philip's murder a rising was contemplated, but checked by Alexander's promptitude. Soon after, on a rumour that Alexander had been slain in Illyria, Thebes rebelled, and Demosthenes carried a motion for joining her. Army and fleet were prepared, money despatched to Thebes, and an embassy sent to the Great King for Persian aid, when Alexander returned, razed Thebes to the ground, and demanded the persons of ten leaders of the war party at Athens, Demosthenes among them. Demâdes, the mediator after Chæronea, acted the same part now. Alexander was appeased by the condemnation of the general Charidêmus; the other proclaimed persons were spared (335 B.C.).

These repeated failures made Demosthenes cautious. He drew closer to the patient opportunism of Demâdes and gradually alienated the extreme war party. This gave his old enemies the opening for their most elaborate attack. It was indirect and insidious in more ways than one. A certain Ctesiphon—celebrated, according to Æschines, as being the only man who laughed at Demosthenes's

jokes—had proposed soon after Chæronea to crown Demosthenes in the theatre of Dionysus in recognition of his public services. Æschines had in the same year indicted Ctesiphon for illegality, but for some reason the trial did not take place till 330. The speech *Against Ctesiphon* rests on three charges: it was illegal to crown an official during his term of office, and Demosthenes held two offices at the time; secondly, it was against precedent to give crowns in the theatre; thirdly, Demosthenes was a bad citizen and ought not to be crowned. Obviously, if the third point was to be considered at all, the other two sank into insignificance. The action was a set challenge to Demosthenes, and he came forward as counsel for Ctesiphon (*On the Crown*), to meet it by a full exposition of his political life.

But here comes the insidiousness of Æschines's attack. In the real points at issue between the two policies the country was overwhelmingly on the side of Demosthenes. The burning question was whether the Demosthenes of the last eight years was true to the Demosthenes of the *Philippics*. Æschines knows that the issue of the trial lies with Hyperîdes and the radical war party, and he plays openly for their support. He emphasises Demosthenes's connection with the Peace in the first part of his life. He has the audacity to accuse him of having neglected three opportunities of rising against Alexander in the last part! It was well enough for Alexander's personal friend and tried supporter to use such accusations. Demosthenes could only answer them by an open profession of treason, which would doubtless have won his case, and have sent him prisoner to Macedon. He does not answer them. He leaves the war party to make its judgment in silence on the question whether he can have been false to the cause of his whole life, whether the tone in which he speaks of Chæronea is like that of a repentant rebel. It was enough. Æschines failed to get a fifth of the votes, and left Athens permanently discredited. He set up a school in Rhodes, and it is said that Demosthenes supplied him with money when he was in distress.

But the hostile coalition was not long delayed. In 324 Harpalus, Alexander's treasurer, decamped with a fleet and 720 talents—full materials for an effective rebellion. He sought admission at Athens, and the extremists were eager to receive him. But the time was in other ways inopportune, and Demosthenes preferred a subtler game. He carefully avoided any open breach of allegiance to Alexander. He insisted that Harpalus should dismiss his fleet, and only agreed to receive him as a private refugee. When Alexander demanded his surrender, Demosthenes was able to refuse as a matter of personal honour, without seriously compromising his relations with the king. The Macedonians insisted that Harpalus should be detained, and the treasure stored in the Parthenon in trust for Alexander. Demosthenes agreed to both proposals, and moved them in the Assembly himself. What happened next is not known, but Harpalus suddenly escaped, and the Macedonians insisted on having the treasure counted. It was found to be less than half the original sum. That it was going in secret preparations for war, they could have little doubt. They would have liked a state trial and some instant executions. Demosthenes managed to get the question entrusted to the Areopagus, and the report deferred.

It had to come at last. The Areopagus made no statement of the uses to which the money was applied, but gave a list of the persons guilty of appropriating it, Demosthenes at the head. His intrigue had failed, and he had given the friends of Macedon their chance. He was prosecuted by Hyperîdes on the one side, Deinarchus on the other. The latter, a Corinthian by birth, rose into fame by this process, and nothing has survived of him except the three speeches relating to it. Dionysius calls him a 'barley Demosthenes,' whatever that may mean—the suggestion is probably 'beer' as opposed to 'wine'—and his tone in this speech is one of brutal exultation. Very different, suspiciously different, is Hyperîdes, who not only says nothing to make a permanent breach, but even calls attention to Demosthenes's great position, to the unsolved problem of what he meant to do with the money, to the possibility that his lips are in some way sealed. For his own part, Hyperîdes talks frank treason with a coolness which well bears out the stories of his courage. Demosthenes was convicted, and condemned to a fine of fifty talents. Unable to pay such an enormous sum, he withdrew to Troizên.

Nine months after, Alexander died and Greece rose. Demosthenes joined his accuser Hyperîdes in a mission to rouse the Peloponnese, and was reinstated at Athens amid the wildest enthusiasm. The war opened well. The extant *Funeral Speech* of Hyperîdes was pronounced after the first year of it. In 322 came the defeat at Crannon. The Macedonian general Antipater demanded the persons of Demosthenes and Hyperîdes. Old Demâdes, unable to mediate any more, now found himself drawing up the decree sentencing his colleague to death. Demosthenes had taken refuge in the temple of Poseidon at Calauría, where he was arrested, and took poison. Hyperîdes is said to have been tortured, a statement which would be incredible but for the flood of crime and cruelty which the abolition of liberty, and the introduction of Northern and Asiatic barbarism, let loose upon the Greek world in the next centuries.

Demosthenes has never quite escaped from the stormy atmosphere in which he lived. The man's own intensity is infectious, and he has a way of forcing himself into living politics. The Alexandrian schools were monarchical, and thought ill of him. To Grote he was the champion of freedom and democracy. To Niebuhr (1804), Philip was Napoleon, and Demosthenes the ideal protest against him. Since 1870, now that monarchical militarism has changed its quarters, German scholars seem oppressed by the likeness between Demosthenes and Gambetta, and denounce the policy of *'la revanche'*; one of them is reminded also of 'the agitator Gladstone.' In another way the technical critics have injured the orator's reputation by analysing his methods of arrangement and rhythm, and showing that he avoids the concourse of more than two short syllables. There is a *naïf* barbarism in many of us which holds that great pains taken over the details of a literary work imply insincerity.

It is not for us to discuss the worth of his policy. It depends partly on historical problems, partly on the value we attach to liberty and culture, and the exact point of weakness at which we hold a man bound to accept and make the best of servitude to a moral inferior. Athens, when she had suffered the utmost, and when the case for submission had been stated most strongly, decided that it was well to have fought and failed.

As for his methods, the foolish tendency to take his political speeches as statements of historical fact, has produced a natural reaction, in which critics pounce fiercely upon the most venial inaccuracies. Holm, for instance, finds "three signal falsehoods" in "that masterpiece of sophistry, the third *Philippic*": viz., the statement that when Philip took certain towns he had already sworn the truce—whereas really he had only made the other side swear it; the suggestion that Philip's rapid movements were due to his using light-armed troops—which is true, but seems to ignore his heavy phalanx; and the charge that he came to the Phokians 'as an ally,' when in truth he had left his intentions designedly ambiguous. The critic who complains of such misstatements as these, must have somewhat Arcadian notions of political controversy.

Demosthenes is guilty, without doubt, of breaches of etiquette and convention. He prosecuted his fellow-ambassadors. He appeared in festal attire on hearing of Philip's assassination, though he had just lost his only daughter. In the prelude to the last war, Philip's action was often the more correct, as was that of another Philip in dealing with William of Orange. In Demosthenes's private speech-writing we are struck by one odd change of front. In 350 he wrote for Phormio against Apollodôrus in a matter of the great Bank with which they were both connected, and won his case. Next year he wrote for Apollodôrus, prosecuting one of his own previous witnesses, Stephanus, for perjury, and making a violent attack on Phormio's character. The probability is that Demosthenes had made discoveries about his previous client which caused him to regret that he had ever supported him—among them, perhaps, the discovery that Stephanus was giving false evidence. The only external fact bearing on the problem is the coincidence that in the same year Apollodôrus, at some personal risk, proposed the measure on which Demosthenes had set his heart—the use of the Festival Fund for war purposes—and that he remained afterwards attached to Demosthenes. The Mîdias case is a clear instance of the subordination of private dignity to public interest. Mîdias was a close friend of Eubûlus, and had both persecuted and assaulted Demosthenes when he was Chorêgus at the great Dionysia. Demosthenes prepared to take action, and wrote the vehement speech which we possess (*Against Mîdias*), in which he declares that nothing will satisfy him but the utmost rigour of the law. But meantime there arose the negotiations for the peace of 346, and Demosthenes had to act in concert with Eubûlus. He accepted an apology and compensation, and let the matter drop.

We must never forget in reading Demosthenes and Æschines, that we are dealing with an impetuous Southern nation in the agony of its last struggle. The politenesses and small generosities of politics are not there. There is no ornamental duelling. The men fight with naked swords, and mean business. Demosthenes thought of his opponents, not as statesmen who made bad blunders, but as perjured traitors who were selling Greece to a barbarian. They thought him, not, indeed, a traitor—that was impossible—but a malignant and insane person who prevented a peaceful settlement of any issue. The words 'treason' and 'bribe' were bandied freely about; but there is hardly any proved case of treason, and none of bribery, unless the Harpalus case can by a stretch of language be called so. There are no treasury scandals in Athens at this time. There is no legal disorder. There is a singular absence of municipal corruption. The Athenians whom Demosthenes reproaches with self-indulgence, were living at a strain of self-sacrifice and effort which few civilised communities could bear. The wide suspicion of bribery was caused chiefly by the bewilderment of Athens at finding herself in the presence of an enemy far her superior both in material force and in diplomacy. Why was she so incomprehensibly worsted in wars, where she won most of the battles? Why were her acutest statesmen invariably outwitted by a semi-barbarous king? Somebody must be betraying her! Demosthenes on this point loses all his balance of mind. He lives in a world peopled by imaginary traitors. We hear how he rushed at one Antiphon in the streets, and seized him with his own hands. Happily the jurors did not lose their sanity. There were almost no convictions. It was very similar in Italy before and after 1848. People whose patriotism was heroic went about accusing one another of treason. The men of 404, 338, and even 262, will not easily find their superiors in devotion and self-sacrifice.

Another unpleasant result of this suspicion and hatred is the virulence of abuse with which the speakers of the time attack their enemies. Not, indeed, in public speeches. In those of Demosthenes no opponent is even mentioned. But in the law-courts, which sometimes gave the *coup de grace* to a political campaign, the attacks on character are savage. The modern analogue is the raking up of more or less irrelevant scandals against both witnesses and principals in cases at law, which custom allows to barristers of the highest character. The attack on Æschines in the **De Corona** is exceptional. Demosthenes had a real and natural hatred for the man. But he would never have dragged in his father and mother and his education, if Æschines had not always prided himself on these particular things—he was distinctly the social superior of Demosthenes, and a man of high culture—and treated Demosthenes as the vulgar demagogue. Even thus, probably Demosthenes repented of his witticisms about the old lady's private initiations and 'revivals.' It is to be wished that scholars would repent of their habit of reading unsavoury meanings into words which do not possess them.

Demosthenes can never be judged apart from his circumstances. He is no saint and no correct mediocrity. He is a man of genius and something of a hero; a fanatic, too, no doubt, and always a politician. He represents his country in that combination of intellectual subtlety and practical driving power with fervid idealism, that union of passion with art, and that invariable insistence on the moral side of actions, on the Just and the Noble, that characterises most of the great spirits of Greek literature. To say with Quintilian that Demosthenes was a 'bad man,' is like saying the same of Burke or even of Isaiah. It implies either that noble words and thoughts are not nobility, or

else, what is hardly more plausible, that the greatest expressions of soul in literature can be produced artificially by a dodge. Two sentences of Demosthenes ring in the ears of those who care for him, as typical of the man:

> Never, never, Athenians, can injustice and oath-breaking and falsehood make a strong power. They hold out for once and for a little; they blossom largely in hopes, belike; but time finds them out and they wither where they stand. As a house and a ship must be strongest at the lowest parts, so must the bases and foundations of a policy be true and honest; which they are not in the diplomatic gains of Macedon.
>
> [Olynth. 2.10.]

> It cannot be, Athenians, that you did wrong when you took upon you the battle for the freedom and safety of all. No, by our fathers who first met the Mede at Marathon, by the footmen of Platæa, by the sailors of Salamis and Artemisium, by all the brave men lying in our national sepulchres—whom the city has interred with honour, Æschines, all alike, not only the successful or the victorious!
>
> [Crown, 208]

J. F. Dobson   (essay date 1919)

SOURCE: "Demosthenes," in *The Greek Orators*, Methuen & Co. Ltd., 1919, pp. 199-267.

[*In the following excerpt, Dobson examines Demosthenes's literary reputation and the style and structure of his speeches.*]

The art of rhetoric could go no further after Isocrates, who, in addition to possessing a style which was as perfect as technical dexterity could make it, had imparted to his numerous disciples the art of composing sonorous phrases and linking them together in elaborate periods. Any young aspirant to literary fame might now learn from him to write fluent easy prose, which would have been impossible to Thucydides or Antiphon. If the style seems on some occasions to have been so over-elaborated that the subject-matter takes a secondary place, that was the fault not so much of the artist as of the man. Isocrates never wrote at fever-heat; his greatest works come from the study; he is too reflective and dispassionate to be a really vital force.

With Demosthenes and his contemporaries it is otherwise; they are men actively engaged in politics, actuated by strong party-feeling, and swayed by personal passion. This was the outcome of the political situation: just as feeling was strong in the generation immediately succeeding the reign of the oligarchical Thirty at Athens, so now, when Athens and the whole of Greece were fighting not against oligarchy but the empire of a sovereign ruler, the depths were stirred.

A new feature in this period is the publication of political speeches. From the time of the earliest orator—Antiphon—the professional *logographoi* had preserved their speeches in writing. The majority of these were delivered in minor cases of only personal importance, though some orations by Lysias and others have reference indirectly to political questions.

Another class of speeches which were usually preserved is the *epideictic*—orations prepared for delivery at some great gathering, such as a religious festival or a public funeral. Isocrates was an innovator to the extent of writing in the form of speeches what were really political treatises; but these were only composed for the reader, and were never intended to be delivered.

Among the contemporaries of Demosthenes we find some diversity of practice. Some orators, such as Demades and Phocion, never published any speeches, and seem, indeed, hardly to have prepared them before delivery. They relied upon their skill at improvisation.

Others, for instance Aeschines, Lycurgus, and Dinarchus, revised and published their judicial speeches, especially those which had a political bearing. Hyperides and Demosthenes, in addition to this, in some cases gave to the world an amended version of their public harangues. Demosthenes did not always publish such speeches; there are considerable periods of his political life which are not represented by any written work; but he seems to have wished to make a permanent record of certain utterances containing an explanation of his policy, in order that those who had not heard him speak, or not fully grasped his import, might have an opportunity for further study of his views after the ephemeral effect of his eloquence had passed away. It is probable that most of the speeches so published belong to times when his party was not predominant in the State, and the opposition had to reinforce its speech by writing. The result is of importance in two ways, for the speeches are a serious contribution to literature, of great value for the study of the development of Greek prose; and they are of still greater historical value; for, though untrustworthy in some details, they provide excellent material for the understanding of the political situation, and the aims and principles of the anti-Macedonian party. . . .

The verdict of antiquity, which has generally been accepted in modern times, ranked Demosthenes as the greatest of orators. In his own age he had rivals; Aeschines, as we have seen already, is in many respects worthy of comparison with him; of his other contemporaries Phocion was impressive by his dignity, sincerity, and brevity—'he could say more in fewer words'; the vigorous extemporizations of Demades were sometimes more effective than the polished subtleties of Demosthenes; Aeschines claims to prefer the speaking of Leodamas of Acharnae, but the tone in which he says so is almost apologetic, and the laboured criticism to which Aeschines constantly subjects his rival practically takes it for granted that the latter was reckoned the foremost speaker of the time.

Later Greek authorities, who are far enough removed to see in proper perspective the orators of the pre-Macedonian times, have an ungrudging admiration for Demosthenes. The author of *The Sublime* saw in him many faults, and admitted that in many details Hyperides excelled him. Nevertheless he finds in Demosthenes certain divine gifts which put him apart from the others in a class by himself; he surpasses the orators of all genera-

tions; his thunders and lightnings shake down and scorch up all opposition; it is impossible to face his dazzling brilliancy without flinching. But Hyperides never made anybody tremble.

In later times we find Demosthenes styled 'The Orator,' just as Homer is 'The Poet.' Lucian, whose literary appreciations are always worthy of attention, wrote an *Encomium of Demosthenes*, containing an imaginary dialogue, in which Antipater is the chief speaker. He pays a generous tribute to his dead enemy, who 'woke his compatriots from their drugged sleep'; the ***Philippics*** are compared to battering-rams and catapults, and Philip is reported to have rejoiced that Demosthenes was never elected general, for the orator's speeches shook the king's throne, and his actions, if he had been given the opportunity, would have overturned it.

Of Roman critics, Cicero in many passages in the *Brutus* and *Orator* expresses extreme admiration for the excellence of Demosthenes in every style of oratory; he regards him as far outstripping all others, though failing in some details to attain perfection. Quintilian's praise is discriminating but sincere; in fact we may say that the Greek and Roman worlds were practically unanimous about the orator's merits.

It is difficult to take a general view of the style of Demosthenes, from the mere fact that it is extremely varied; the three classes of speeches—the forensic speeches in private and public suits, and the public harangues addressed to the assembly, all have their particular features: nevertheless there are certain characteristics which may be distinguished in all classes.

First of these is his great care in composition. Isocrates is known to have spent years in polishing the essays which he intended as permanent contributions to the science of politics; Plato wrote and erased and wrote again before he was satisfied with the form in which his philosophy was to be given to the world; Demosthenes, without years of toil, could produce for definite occasions speeches whose finished brilliancy made them worthy to be ranked as great literature quite apart from their merits as contributions to practical policy.

It is a well-known jest against him that his speeches smelt of midnight oil, but he must have had a remarkable natural fluency to be able to compose so many speeches so well. It is quite possible, on the other hand, that the speeches which survive are not altogether in the form in which they were delivered. It seems to have been a habit among orators of this time to edit for publication their speeches delivered in important cases, in order that a larger audience might have an opportunity of reading a permanent record of the speakers' views on political or legal questions which had more than a transitory interest.

We have indirect evidence that Demosthenes was in the habit of introducing corrections into his text. Aeschines quotes and derides certain expressions, mostly exaggerated metaphors, which do not occur in the speeches as extant to us, though some of them evidently should, if the text had not been submitted to a recension. We may note the remark of Eratosthenes [in Plutarch's *Demosthenes*] that while speaking he sometimes lost control of himself, and talked like a man possessed, and that of Demetrius of Phaleron, that on one occasion he offended against good taste by quoting a metrical oath which bears the stamp of comedy:

> By earth and fountains, rivulets and streams.

This quotation is not to be found in any extant speech, but it is noticeable that formulae of the kind, typically represented by the familiar 'Ye Earth and Gods'—are commonly affected by Demosthenes, as indeed they are to be found in his contemporary Aeschines.

Evidently the Attic taste was undergoing a modification; such expressions are foreign to the dignified harmonies of Isocrates and of rare occurrence in the restrained style of Lysias; but they begin to appear more frequently in Isaeus, whose style was the model for the early speeches of Demosthenes. Certain other expressions belonging to the popular speech, and probably avoided by Isocrates as being too colloquial, are found in Demosthenes' public speeches—e. g. ο δεινα and ω ταν.

Under the same heading must come the use of coarse expressions and terms of personal abuse. In many of the speeches relating to public law-suits Demosthenes allows himself all the latitude which was sanctioned by the taste of his times. In the actual use of abusive epithets . . . he does not go beyond the common practice of Aeschines, and is even outstripped by Dinarchus; but in the accumulation of offensive references to the supposed private character of his political opponents he condescends to such excesses that we wonder how a decent audience can ever have tolerated him. Evidently an Athenian audience loved vulgarity for its own sake, apart from humour.

In the private speeches there is at times a certain coarseness—inevitably, since police-court cases are often concerned with sordid details. Offensive actions sometimes have to be described; but this is a very different matter from the irrelevant introduction of offensive matter.

In the speeches delivered before the ecclesia Demosthenes set himself a higher ideal. Into questions of public policy, private animosities should not be allowed to intrude, and throughout the *Philippics* and *Olynthiacs* Demosthenes observes this rule. Under no stress of excitement does he sink to personalities; his political opponents for the time being are not abused, not even mentioned by name. The courtesies of debate are fully and justly maintained.

Though Demosthenes wrote in pure Attic Greek, it is to Lysias and Isocrates rather than to him that Dionysius assigns praise for the most perfect purity of language. It is probable that Demosthenes was nearer to the living speech.

Demosthenes seems to discard metaphor in his most solemn moments. [In] an outburst of indignation he can speak of rival politicians as 'Fiends, who have mutilated the corpses of their fatherlands, and made a birthday present of their liberty first to Philip, and now again to Alexander; who measure happiness by their belly and their basest pleasures' [*On the Crown*]; but on grave occasions, wheth-

er in narrative or in counsel, he reverts to a simplicity equal to that of Lysias. The plainness of the language in which he describes the excitement caused by the news of Philip's occupation of Elatea is proverbial; and the closing sentences of the *Third Philippic* afford another good example:

> If everybody is going to sit still, hoping to get what he wants, and seeking to do nothing for it himself, in the first place he will never find anybody to do it for him, and secondly, I am afraid that we shall be forced to do everything that we do not want. This is what I tell you, this is what I propose; and I believe that if this is done our affairs may even yet be set straight again. If anybody can offer anything better, let him name it and urge it; and whatever you decide, I pray to heaven it may be for the best.

The simplicity of the language is only equalled by the sobriety of tone. The simplest words, if properly used, can produce a great effect, which is sometimes heightened by repetition, a device which Demosthenes finds useful on occasion—αλλ ουκ εστιν, ουκ εστιν οπωσ ημαρτετε—'But surely, *surely* you were not wrong.' We realize a slight raising of the voice as the word comes in for the second time. Dinarchus, an imitator of Demosthenes, copies him in the use of this 'figure,' but uses it too much and inappropriately. In this, as in other details, his style is an unsuccessful parody of the great orator.

Dionysius compares Demosthenes to several other writers in turn. He finds passages, for instance, which recall the style of Thucydides. He quotes the first section from the *Third Philippic,* and by an ingenious analysis shows the points of resemblance. The chief characteristic noticed by the critic is that the writer does not introduce his thoughts in any natural or conventional sequence, but employs an affected order of words which arrests the attention by its avoidance of simplicity.

Thus, a parenthetical relative clause intrudes between the subject and the verb of the chief relative clause, while we are kept in long suspense as to what the verbs are to be, both in relative clauses and in the main clause itself. The peculiar effects which he notices cannot be reproduced in a non-inflexional language such as English.

At other times, especially in narrative, Demosthenes emulates the lucidity of Lysias at his best. Dionysius quotes [Dionysius of Halicarnassus in his *de Demos.*] with well-deserved approval the vivid presentment of the story on which the accusation against Conon is based. As the speech gives us an excellent picture of the camp life of an undisciplined militia, it will be worth while here to quote some extracts:

> Two years ago, having been detailed for garrison-duty, we went out to Panactum. Conon's sons occupied a tent near us; I wish it had been otherwise, for this was the primary cause of our enmity and the collisions between us. You shall hear how it arose. They used to drink every day and all day long, beginning immediately after breakfast, and this custom they maintained all the time that we were in garrison. My brothers and I, on the contrary, lived out there just as we

were in the habit of living at home. So by the time which the rest of us had fixed for dinner, they were invariably playing drunken tricks, first on our servants, and finally on ourselves. For because they said that the servants sent the smoke in their faces while cooking, or were uncivil to them, or what not, they used to beat them and empty the slops over their heads . . . and in every way behaved brutally and disgustingly. We saw this and took offence, and first of all remonstrated with them; but as they jeered at us and would not stop, we all went and reported the occurrence to the general—not I alone, but the whole of the mess. He reprimanded them severely, not only for their offensive behaviour to us, but for their general conduct in camp; however, they were so far from stopping or feeling any shame that, as soon as it was dark that evening, they made a rush on us, and first abused us and then beat me, and made such a disturbance and uproar round the tent that the general and his staff and some of the other soldiers came out, and prevented them from doing us any serious harm, and us from retaliating on their drunken violence.

Another passage quoted from the same speech [*Against Conon*] gives a companion picture of the defendant's behaviour in civil life:

When we met them, one of the party, whom I cannot identify, fell upon Phanostratus and held him tight, while the defendant Conon and his son and the son of Andromenes fell upon me, and first stripped me, and then tripped me up, and dashed me down in the mud. There they jumped upon me and beat me, and so mishandled me that they cut my lip right through, and closed up both my eyes. They left me in such a weak state that I could neither get up nor speak, and as I lay on the ground I heard them uttering floods of abominable language. What they said was vilely slanderous, and some of it I should shrink from repeating, but I will mention one thing which is an example of Conon's brutality, and proves that he was responsible for the whole incident—he began to crow like a game-cock after a victory, and the others told him to flap his arms against his sides in triumph. After this I was carried home naked by some passers-by, while the defendants made off with my coat.

Dionysius observes that the ecclesia and the courts were composed of mixed elements; not all were clever and subtle in intellect; the majority were farmers, merchants, and artisans, who were more likely to be pleased by simple speech; anything of an unusual flavour would turn their stomachs: a smaller number, a mere fraction of the whole, were men of high education, to whom you could not speak as you would to the multitude; and the orator could not afford to neglect either section. He must therefore aim at satisfying both, and consequently he should steer a middle course, avoiding extremes in either direction.

In the opinion of Dionysius both Isocrates and Plato give good examples of this middle style, attaining a seeming simplicity intelligible to all, combined with a subtlety which could be appreciated only by the expert; but De-

mosthenes surpassed them both in the perfection of this art. To prove his case he quotes first the passage from *The Peace* which Isocrates himself selected for quotation, as a favourable example of his own style, in the speech on the *Antidosis*. With this extract a passage from the **Third Olynthiac** is contrasted, greatly to the advantage of Demosthenes, who is found to be nobler, more majestic, more forcible, and to have avoided the frigidity of excessive refinement with which Isocrates is charged.

The criticism professes to be based on an accumulation of small details, but there is no doubt that Dionysius depended, in the main, not upon analysis, but upon subjective impressions. After enumerating the points in which either of the writers excels or falls short, he describes his own feelings:

When I read a speech of Isocrates, I become sober and serious, as if I were listening to solemn music; but when I take up a speech of Demosthenes, I am beside myself, I am led this way and that, I am moved by one passion after another: suspicion, distress, fear, contempt, hate, pity, kindliness, anger, envy—passing successively through all the passions which can obtain a mastery over the human mind; . . . and I have sometimes thought to myself, what must have been the impression which he made on those who were fortunate enough to hear him? For where we, who are so far removed in time, and in no way interested in the actual events, are led away and overpowered, and made to follow wherever the speech leads us, how must the Athenians and other Greeks have been led by the speaker himself when the cases in which he spoke had a living interest and concerned them nearly? . . .

Dionysius, as we know from many of his criticisms, had a remarkably acute sense of style; he had also a strong imagination. In this same treatise he recounts how the forms of the sentences themselves suggest to him the tone in which the words were uttered, the very gestures with which they were accompanied.

Though we modern students cannot expect to rival him in these peculiar gifts, it is still possible for us to sympathize with his feelings. We cannot fail, in reading a speech like the **Third Philippic,** for instance, to appreciate how fully Demosthenes realizes the Platonic ideal, expressed in the *Gorgias,* that rhetoric is the art of persuasion. We need not pause to analyse the means by which he attains his end; he may resemble Lysias at one moment in a simple piece of narrative, at another he may be as involved and antithetical as Thucydides, or even florid like Gorgias; he can be a very Proteus, as Dionysius says, in his changes of form; but in whatever shape he appears, naïve, subtle, pathetic, indignant, sarcastic, he is convincing. The reason is simple: he has a single purpose always present to his mind, namely, to make his audience feel as he feels. Readers of Isocrates were expected, while they followed the exposition of the subject-matter, to regard the beauties of the form in which it was expressed; in Demosthenes there is no idea of such display. A good speech was to him a successful speech, not one which might be admired by critics as a piece of literature. It is only incidental that his speeches have a literary quality which ranks him among the foremost writers of Attic prose; as an orator he was independent of this quality.

The strong practical sense of Demosthenes refused to be confined by any theoretical rules of scholastic rhetoricians. He does not aspire to the complexity of periods which makes the style of Isocrates monotonous in spite of the writer's wonderful ingenuity. Long and short, complex and simple sentences, are used in turn, and with no systematic order, so that we cannot call any one kind characteristic; the form of the sentence, like the language, is subordinate to its purpose.

He was moderately careful in the avoidance of hiatus between words, but in this matter he modified the rule of Isocrates to suit the requirements of speech; he was guided by ear, not by eye; thus we find that hiatus is frequently omitted between the *cola* or sections of a period; in fact any pause in the utterance is enough to justify the non-elision of an open vowel before the pause. Isocrates, on the contrary, usually avoids even the appearance of hiatus in such cases.

There is one other formal rule of composition which Demosthenes follows with some strictness; this is the avoidance of a succession of short syllables. It is notable that he very seldom admits a tribrach (three short syllables) where a little care can avoid it, while instances of more than three short vowels in succession are very exceptional. An unusual order of words may often be explained by reference to this practice.

We know from Aristotle and other critics that earlier writers of artistic prose, from Thrasymachus onwards, had paid some attention to the metrical form of words and certain combinations of long and short syllables. Thrasymachus in particular studied the use of the *paeonius . . .* at the beginning and end of a sentence.

The effect of increasing the number of short syllables, whether in verse or prose, is to make the movement of the line or period more rapid. The frequent use of tribrachs by Euripides constantly produces this impression, and an extreme case is the structure of the Galliambic metre, as seen, for instance, in the *Attis* of Catullus. Conversely the multiplication of long syllables makes the movement slow, and produces an effect of solemnity.

Demosthenes seems to have been the first prose-writer to pay attention to the avoidance of the tribrach; Plato seems to have consciously preferred a succession of short syllables where it was possible. The difference between the two points of view is probably this—that Plato aimed at reproducing the natural rapidity of conversation, Demosthenes aimed at a more solemn and dignified style appropriate to impressive utterance before a large assembly.

This is the only metrical rule which Demosthenes ever observed, and one of the soundest of modern critics believes that even this observance was instinctive rather than conscious. He never affected any metrical formula for the end of sentences comparable to Cicero's famous *esse videatur,* or the double trochee . . . at the beginning of a sentence, approved by later writers. An examination shows that he

has an almost infinite variety both in the opening and the close of his sentences. He seems never to follow any mechanical system.

Much labour has been expended, especially in Germany, on the analysis of the rhythmical element in Demosthenes' style. There is no doubt that many orators, from Gorgias onwards, laboured to produce approximate correspondence between parallel or contrasted sections of their periods. In some cases we find an equal number of syllables in two clauses, and even a more or less complete rhythmical correspondence. Such devices serve to emphasize the peculiar figures of speech in which Gorgias delighted, and may have been appropriate to the class of oratory intended primarily for display, but it is hard to believe that such elaboration was ever consciously carried through a long forensic speech.

The appendix to the third volume of Blass' Attic oratory is a monumental piece of work. It consists of an analysis of the first seventeen sections of the **de Corona**, and the whole of the **First Olynthiac** and **Third Philippic** speeches, and conveys the impression that this Demosthenic prose may be scanned with almost as much certainty as a comparatively simple form of composition like a Pindaric ode. It is hard to pronounce on such a matter without a very long and careful study of this difficult subject; but the theory of rhythmical correspondence seems to have been worked out far too minutely. In many cases emendation is required; we have to divide words in the middle, and clauses are split up in an arbitrary and unnatural way. I am far from believing that analysis can justifiably be carried to this extent; it is more reasonable to suppose that Demosthenes had a naturally acute ear, and that practice so developed his faculty that a certain rhythm was natural to all his speech. I am not convinced that all his effects were designed.

Isaeus, the teacher of Demosthenes, was a master of reasoning and demonstration; Demosthenes in his earliest speeches shows strong traces of the influence of Isaeus, but in his later work he has developed varied gifts which enable him to surpass his master. Realizing the insufficiency, for a popular audience, of mere reasoning, he reinforced his logic by adventitious aids, appealing in numerous indirect ways to feeling and prejudice. One valuable method of awakening interest was his striking use of paradox [in **On the Symmories**]:

> On the question of resources of money at present at our disposal, what I have to say will, I know, appear paradoxical, but I must say it; for I am confident that, considered in the proper light, my proposal will appear to be the only true and right one. I tell you that we need not raise the question of money at all: we have great resources which we may fairly and honourably use if we need them. If we look for them now, we shall imagine that they never will be at our disposal, so far shall we be from willingness to dispose of them at present; but if we let matters wait, we shall have them. What, then, are these resources which do not exist at present, but will be to hand later on? It looks like a riddle. I will explain. Consider this city of ours as a whole. It contains

almost as much money as all other cities taken together; but those individuals who possess it are so apathetic that if all the orators tried to terrify them by saying that the king is coming, that he is near, that invasion is inevitable, and even if the orators were reinforced by an equal number of soothsayers, they would not only refuse to contribute; they would refuse even to declare or admit the possession of their wealth. But suppose that the horrors which we now talk about were actually realized, they are none of them so foolish that they would not readily offer and make contributions. . . . So I tell you that we have money ready for the time of urgent need, but not before.

Similarly in the **Third Olynthiac** he rouses the curiosity of the audience by propounding a riddle, of which, after some suspense, he himself gives the answer. The matter under discussion is the necessity of sending help to Olynthus. There is, as usual, a difficulty about money.

> "Very well," you may say; "we have all decided that we must send help; and send help we will; but how are we to do it; tell me that?" Now, Gentlemen, do not be astonished if what I say comes as a surprise to most of you. *Appoint a legislative board.* Instruct this board not to pass any law (you have enough already), but to repeal the laws which are injurious under present conditions. I refer to the laws about the Theoric Fund.

This mention of the Festival Fund suggests some reflections on the orator's tenacity and perseverance. He is not content to say once what he has to propose, and leave his words to sink in by their own weight. Like a careful lecturer he repeats his statement, emphasizing it in various ways, until he perceives that his audience has really grasped its importance. The walls which he is attacking will not fall flat at the sound of the trumpet; his persistent battering-rams must make a breach, his catapults must drive the defenders from their positions. Such is the meaning of Lucian's comment in the words attributed to Philip.

The speech **On the Chersonese,** for instance, may be divided into three parts, dealing successively with the treatment of Diopeithes, the supineness of Athens, and the guilt of the partisans of Philip; but in all parts we find emphatically stated the need for energetic action. This is really the theme of the speech; the rest is important only in so far as it substantiates the main thesis.

The extract last given shows with what adroitness he introduces dialogues, in which he questions or answers an imaginary critic. This is a device frequently employed with considerable effect. The following shows a rather different type:

> If Philip captures Olynthus, who will prevent him from marching on us? The Thebans? It is an unpleasant thing to say, but they will eagerly join him in the invasion. Or the Phocians? —when they cannot even protect their own land, unless you help them. Can you think of any one else? —"My dear fellow, he won't want to attack us." It would indeed be the greatest surprise in the world if he did not do it when he got the

chance; since even now he is fool enough to declare his intentions.

Narrative, too, can take the place of argument; a recital of Philip's misdeeds during the last few years may do far more to convince the Athenians of the necessity for action than any argument about the case of a particular ally who chances to be threatened at the moment.

Demosthenes' knowledge of history was deep and broad. The superiority of his attainments to those of Aeschines is shown in the more philosophic use which he makes of his appeals to precedent; his examples are apposite and not far-fetched; he can illuminate the present not only by references to ancient facts, but by a keen insight into the spirit which animated the men of old times.

The examples already quoted of rhetorical dialogue with imaginary opponents will have given some idea of his use of a sarcastic tone. Sarcasm thinly concealed may at times run through a passage of considerable length, as in the anecdote which follows. We may note in passing that he is usually sparing in the use of anecdote, which is never employed without good reason. Here it may be excused by the fact that it figures as an historical precedent of a procedure which he ironically recommends to his contemporaries.

Inveighing against the reckless procedure of the Athenian politicians, who propose laws for their own benefit almost every month, he recounts [in **Against Timocrates**] the customs of the Locrians, and, with an assumption of seriousness, implies a wish that similar restrictions could be imposed at Athens:

> I should like to tell you, Gentlemen, how legislation is conducted among the Locrians. It will do you no harm to have an example before you, especially the example of a well-governed State. There men are so convinced that they ought to keep to the established laws and cherish their traditions, and not legislate to suit their fancy, or to help a criminal to escape, that any man who wishes to pass a new law must have a rope round his neck while he proposes it. If they think that the law is a good and useful one, the proposer lives and goes on his way; if not, they pull the rope and there is an end of him. For they cannot bear to pass new laws, but they rigorously observe the old ones. We are told that only one new law has been enacted in very many years. Whereas there was a law that if a man knocked out another man's eye, he should submit to having his own knocked out in return, and no monetary compensation was provided, a certain man threatened his enemy, who had already lost an eye, to knock out the one eye he had left. The one-eyed man, alarmed by the threat, and thinking that life would not be worth living if it were put into execution, ventured to propose a law that if a man knocks out the eye of a man who has only one, he shall submit to having both his own knocked out in return, so that both may suffer alike. We are told that this is the only law which the Locrians have passed in upwards of two hundred years.

This, however, occurs in a speech before the law-courts;

it is excellent in its place, but would have been unsuitable to the more dignified and solemn style in which he addresses the assembly. Equally unsuitable to his public harangues would be anything like the virulent satire which he admits into the *de Corona*, the vulgar personalities of abuse and gross caricatures of Aeschines and his antecedents. For these the only excuse is that, though meant maliciously, they are so exaggerated as to be quite incredible. They may be compared to Aristophanes' satire of Cleon in the *Knights*, which was coarse enough, but cannot have done Cleon any serious harm. Demosthenes indeed becomes truly Aristophanic [in *On the Crown*] when he talks about Aeschines' acting:

> When in the course of time you were relieved of these duties, having yourself committed all the offences of which you accuse others, I vow that your subsequent life did not fall short of your earlier promise. You engaged yourself to the players Simylus and Socrates, the "Bellowers," as they were called, to play minor parts, and gathered a harvest of figs, grapes, and olives, like a fruiterer getting his stock from other people's orchards; and you made more from this source than from your plays, which you played in dead earnest at the risk of your lives; for there was a truceless and merciless war between you and the spectators, from whom you received so many wounds that you naturally mock at the cowardice of those who have never had that great experience.

He is generally described as deficient in wit, and he seems in this point to have been inferior to Aeschines, though on one or two occasions he could make a neat repartee. As Dionysius says:

> Not on all men is every gift bestowed.

If, as his critic affirms [in *On the Sublime*], he was in danger of turning the laugh against himself, he had serious gifts which more than compensated this deficiency.

It must not be supposed that he was entirely free from sophistry. Like many good orators in good or bad causes he laboured from time to time to make a weak case appear strong, and in this effort was often absolutely disingenuous. The whole of the *de Corona* is an attempt to throw the judges off the scent by leading them on to false trails. It may be urged in his defence that on this occasion he had justice really on his side, but finding that Aeschines on legal ground was occupying an impregnable position, he practically threw over the discussion of legality and turned the course of the trial towards different issues altogether. In this case, admittedly, the technical points were merely an excuse for the bringing of the case, and were probably of little importance to the court. The trial was really concerned with the political principles and actions of the two great opponents, while Ctesiphon was only a catspaw. But a study of other speeches results in the discovery of many minor points in which, accurately gauging the intelligence of his audience, he has intentionally misled them. Thus, his own knowledge of history was profound; but experience has proved that the knowledge possessed by any audience of the history of its own generation is likely to be sketchy and inaccurate. Events have not settled

down into their proper perspective; we must rely either on our own memories, which may be distorted by prejudice, or on the statements of historians who stand too near in time to be able to get a fair view. This gives the politician his opportunity of so grouping or misrepresenting facts as to give a wrong impression.

Instances of such bad faith on the part of Demosthenes are probably numerous, even if unimportant.

In the speech on the *Embassy* he asserts that Aeschines, far from opposing Philip's pretension to be recognized as an Amphictyon, was the only man who spoke in favour of it; yet Demosthenes himself had counselled submission. In the speech *Against Timocrates* there are obvious exaggerations to the detriment of the defendant. Timocrates had proposed that certain debtors should be given time to pay their debts; Demosthenes asserts that he restored them to their full civic rights without payment. Towards the end of the speech a statement is made which conflicts with one on the same subject in the exordium.

But such rhetorical devices are only trivial faults to which most politicians are liable. The orator himself would probably feel that even more doubtful actions were justifiable for the sake of the cause which he championed. We must remember that all the really important cases in which he took part had their origin on political grounds, and during his public career he never relaxed his efforts for the maintenance of those principles which he expounded in his public harangues. Until the end he had hopes for Greek freedom, freedom for Athens, not based on any unworthy compromise, but dependent on a new birth of the old Athenian spirit. The regeneration which he pictured would be due to a revival of the spirit of personal self-sacrifice. Every man must be made to realize first that the city had a glorious mission, being destined to fulfil an ideal of liberty based on principles of justice; secondly that, to attain this end, each must live not for himself or his party but wholly for the city. It is the consciousness that Demosthenes has these enlightened ideas always present in his mind which makes us set him apart from other orators. Lycurgus, a second-rate orator, becomes impressive through his sincerity and incorruptibility; Demosthenes, great among orators, stands out from the crowd still more eminently by the nobleness of his aspirations.

The structure of the speeches will give us a last example of the versatility of the composer and his freedom from conventional form.

We find, indeed, that he regularly has some kind of exordium and epilogue, but in the arrangement of other divisions of the speech he allows himself perfect freedom; we cannot reckon on finding a statement of the case in one place, followed regularly by evidence, by refutation of the opponent's arguments, and so forth. All elements may be interspersed, since he marshals his arguments not in chronological nor even, necessarily, in logical order, but in such an arrangement as seems to him most decisive. He is bound by no conventional rules of warfare, and may leave his flanks unprotected while he delivers a crushing attack on the centre. In some cases it is almost impossible to make regular divisions by technical rule; thus, in the *de*

Corona there is matter for dispute as to where the epilogue really begins.

The majority of the speeches actually end, according to the Attic convention which governed both Tragedy and Oratory, in a few sentences of moderate tone contrasting with the previous excitement; a calm succeeds to the storm of passions. In the forensic speeches there is usually at the very end some appeal for a just verdict, or a statement of the speaker's conviction that the case may now be safely left to the court's decision; thus the *Leptines* ends with a simplicity worthy of Lysias:

'I cannot see that I need say any more; for I conceive there is no point on which you are not sufficiently instructed'; the *Midias* more solemnly, 'On account of all that I have laid before you, and particularly to show respect to the god whose festival Midias is proved to have profaned, punish him by rendering a verdict in accordance with piety and justice.'

In the *de Falsa Legatione* there is more personal feeling: 'You must not let him go, but make his punishment an example to all Athens and all Greece.' The *Timocrates* is rather similar: 'Mercy under these circumstances is out of place; to pass a light sentence means to habituate and educate in wrong-doing as many of you as possible.' The *Androtion* ends with a personal opinion on the aspect of the offence, and the *Aristocrates* is in a similar tone. The (first) speech against Aristogiton appeals directly to the personal interests of all the jurors: 'His offence touches every one, every one of you: and all of you desire to be quit of his wickedness and see him punished.'

The *de Corona* is remarkable in every way; this great speech, which, arising from causes almost trivial, abandons the slighter issues, and is transformed into a magnificent defence of the patriotic policy, begins with a solemn invocation: 'I begin, men of Athens, with a prayer to all the gods and goddesses that you may show me in this case as much good-will as I have shown and still show to Athens and to all of you.' It ends in an unique way with an appeal, not to the court but to a higher tribunal, an appeal which is all the more impressive as its language recalls the sacred formulas of religious utterance. 'Never, ye gods of heaven, never may you give their conduct your sanction; but, if it be possible, may you impart even to my enemies a sounder mind and heart. But if they are beyond remedy, hurl them to utter and absolute destruction by land and sea; and to the rest of us grant, as quickly as may be, release from the terrors which hang over us, and salvation unshakable.'

The speeches before the assembly are naturally different in their endings from the judicial speeches; there is no criminal to attack, and no crime to stigmatize; the hearers themselves are, as it were, on their defence, and Demosthenes freely points out their faults, but, as has been noticed, individual opponents escape; if there have been evil counsellors, the responsibility for following bad advice rests with the public, and they can only be exhorted to follow a better course. The speeches on the *Symmories* and on *Megalopolis* end with a summary of the speaker's advice. So, too, does that *On the Freedom of Rhodes*, the last

words containing a fine appeal to the lesson of antiquity. 'Consider that your forefathers dedicated these trophies not in order that you might gaze in admiration upon them, but in the hope that you might imitate the virtues of those who dedicated them.'

Several of the speeches dealing with the Macedonian question end with a short prayer for guidance: thus, the *First Philippic*, 'May that counsel prevail which is likely to be to the advantage of all'; the *First Olynthiac*, 'May your decision be a sound one, for all your sakes'; the *Third Philippic*, 'Whatever you decide, I pray to heaven it may be to your advantage'; the *Third Olynthiac*, 'I have told you what I think is to your advantage, and I pray that you may choose what is likely to be of advantage to the State and all yourselves.'

Sometimes there is a greater show of confidence, as in the *Second Olynthiac*: 'If you act thus, you will not only commend your present counsellor, but you will have cause to commend your own conduct later on, when you find a general improvement in your prospects.'

The *Second Philippic* ends with a prayer rather similar to that in the *de Corona*, though less emphatic; the speech *On the Chersonese* with a reproof and a warning. *The Peace* contains no epilogue at all, but breaks off with a sarcasm . . .

Plutarch on Demosthenes's training (c. 105-15):

Demetrius, the Phalerian, tells us that he was informed by Demosthenes himself, now grown old, that the ways he made use of to remedy his natural bodily infirmities and defects were such as these; his inarticulate and stammering pronunciation he overcame and rendered more distinct by speaking with pebbles in his mouth; his voice he disciplined by declaiming and reciting speeches or verses when he was out of breath, while running or going up steep places; and that in his house he had a large looking-glass, before which he would stand and go through his exercises.

Plutarch, in his "Demosthenes" in The Lives of the Noble Grecians and Romans, *translated by John Dryden, 1683-86.*

Charles Darwin Adams   (essay date 1927)

SOURCE: *Demosthenes and His Influence*, Longmans, Green and Co., 1927, 184 p.

[*In the following essay, Adams explores the influence of Demosthenes and the transmission of his texts in western Europe from the fourteenth to the twentieth centuries.*]

The study of Demosthenes in the western world of the Renaissance began with the lectures of Chrysoloras, a Greek scholar who came to Italy from Constantinople in 1396, and taught in Florence, Venice, Padua, Milan, and Rome. He was the first professor of Greek in the West, the first to lecture on Demosthenes, and perhaps the first to bring a manuscript of the speeches from the East. His transcript of the Greek text is in the Vatican, and we have a letter of his on the meaning of technical terms involved in certain of the speeches.

In 1423 nearly all the speeches of Demosthenes came to Italy among the 238 Greek manuscripts brought over by Aurispa. Leonardo Bruni (1369-1444), a pupil of Chrysoloras at Florence, translated into Latin Demosthenes' ***Third Olynthiac***, the speech ***On the Chersonese***, and the speeches of Demosthenes and Aeschines ***On the Crown***. This Latin version of the two speeches ***On the Crown*** was printed in Venice in 1485. In the middle of the fifteenth century Vittorino established at Mantua the first great humanistic school of Italy. Nowhere in the West at this time was Greek so well taught, and here Demosthenes had a large place in the curriculum, not only with mature students, but with boys and girls as well. "Whole orations of Cicero or Demosthenes, books of Livy and Sallust besides large portions of Virgil and Homer, were recited with accuracy and taste by boys or girls of less than fourteen years of age."

In the middle of the century Theodorus Gaza, a Greek from Thessalonica and the ablest classical scholar of his time, was lecturing on Demosthenes at Ferrara, and in the last quarter of the century Janus Lascaris, a Greek from Constantinople, was lecturing at Florence on the same orator.

When in the last quarter of that century the Turks were pressing upon Christendom, Bessarion, Patriarch of Constantinople, earnestly giving himself to the attempt to unite the Eastern and Western churches, used as a part of his propaganda for union against the barbarians a Latin translation of the ***First Olynthiac***, which he had caused to be printed at Paris. In his comments on the ancient fight for freedom Bessarion summoned the Christian princes to the impending struggle.

In France, England, and Germany Greek studies were making their way very slowly. Individual students from those countries were studying in Italy, and were bringing back Greek manuscripts. Many other Greek manuscripts were brought directly from the Greek cities, and were widely copied; and certain wandering Greeks were giving something of Greek instruction, but we have no mention of the teaching of Demosthenes until late in this century.

The *Editio Princeps* of the Greek text of Demosthenes came from the press of Aldus Manutius at Venice in 1504. This text, based on three Greek manuscripts, was the joint work of Aldus and Scipio Fortiguerra (Carteromachos), Secretary of the New Academy of Hellenists. The volume contained all the speeches ascribed by manuscript tradition to Demosthenes, the Introductions and 'Life' by Libanius, the 'Life' by Plutarch, and an index of variant readings.

In 1543 another complete and carefully edited edition of the speeches was published in Venice by Felicianus. Between 1550 and 1557 Italian scholars published Latin translations of the speeches ***On the Peace*** and ***On the Chersonese***, and translation into Italian was well begun in versions of the ***Olynthiacs*** and ***Philippics***, the speeches ***On***

the Embassy and ***On the Crown***, the ***Midiana***, the ***Leptinea***, and the speech ***Against Androtion***.

Meanwhile the study of Greek had made sufficient progress in Northern Europe to make possible the study of Demosthenes in France, Switzerland, Germany, and England. From the press of the Basel publisher, Johannes Hervagius, a text of all the speeches appeared in 1532, and to the Lives and Introductions were added Ulpian's *Scholia* and notes from the studies of Erasmus, Budaeus, and others, with a table of variant readings. Erasmus contributed a preface to this volume. French scholarship was represented by the edition of Benenatus, Paris, 1570.

In 1572 the publication at Basel of the great edition of Hieronymus Wolf of Augsburg marked a new stage in the study of Demosthenes. Wolf had published a complete Latin translation of the speeches twenty-two years earlier; he now added to this a revised Greek text, and with the Lives and Introductions, together with ancient and modern notes and variant readings, he gave to the student a generous apparatus for Demosthenic studies. In the volume he included the speeches of Aeschines, in Greek and Latin.

In Germany the study of Demosthenes was already flourishing before the publication of Wolf's great Graeco-Latin edition. In the last quarter of the fifteenth century Reuchlin, one of the "two eyes" of humanistic Germany, was lecturing on Demosthenes, and the earliest definitely dated German translation of any Greek work is a German version of the ***First Olynthiac***, which Reuchlin sent in manuscript to Count Eberhard of Würtemberg, who was then attending the famous Diet of Worms of 1495. Some have thought that in the mind of Reuchlin the Demosthenic summons was to the Emperor Maximilian to resist the pretensions of the French Emperor. Reuchlin translated also the ***First*** and ***Second Philippics***, and one of the last acts of his life was to urge the hasty printing of an edition of Demosthenes and Aeschines ***On the Crown***, to be used by his students at Tübingen. The volume came from the press in 1521, after Reuchlin's death, and was the first edition of the great speech to be printed separately. Reuchlin passed on the Demosthenic tradition to his nephew, Philip Melanchthon, scholar of the German Reformation. Melanchthon began the publication of Latin translations in 1524 with the ***First Olynthiac***. The other ***Olynthiacs*** and the ***First Philippic*** followed, and the speech ***Against Aristogiton*** was added. These translations were again and again reprinted, two of them fourteen times. His Latin translation of Aeschines and Demosthenes ***On the Crown*** was printed in 1562, two years after his death. In his introduction to the ***First Olynthiac***, Melanchthon says we cannot hope for a translation which shall completely reproduce the combined strength and beauty of this surpassing oratory until Nature shall have produced another Demosthenes. In the speech ***Against Aristogiton*** Demosthenes describes the defendant as a man who creeps through the Agora like a viper or a scorpion with uplifted sting, a man without friends or associates, his only companions those whom the painters portray as attending the wicked in Hades—Malediction, Defamation, Envy, Discord, Strife. Of this tremendous indictment Melanchthon says: "No writer of tragedy was ever able to say anything more brilliant." Melanchthon closes the introduction to the same speech with words which show how far he was from thinking of studies in Demosthenes as purely linguistic or literary:

> Would that there were no Aristogitons in the States of today! But whereas at Athens there was one solitary Aristogiton, now many are in power everywhere, and worse they are than Aristogiton of Athens, in that they cloak private greed with the pretext of religion. When their image shall be seen depicted here, may good youths perceive therein an admonition to themselves, that they may study to show themselves better men than they, and to bring modesty and other virtues to the service of the State.

While Melanchthon was spreading the knowledge of Demosthenes throughout Germany by his Latin translations of the speeches, the other maker of the school system of Protestant Germany, Johannes Sturm, was giving the study of Cicero and Demosthenes the central place in the curriculum of the new Gymnasium at Strassburg. The study of Cicero was a part of the course from the very first reading in Latin to the beginning of professional studies, and in the higher classes Demosthenes had an important place. Even in his student days in Paris, Sturm had been lecturing, as privat docent, on Demosthenes, and the very great emphasis which he always placed on the study of ancient rhetoric as embodied in classical oratory gave impetus to Demosthenic studies.

In the sixteenth century we hear of only one translation of the speeches of Demosthenes into German, a version of the four *Philippics*, made from the Latin, and published at Augsburg in 1543.

The first translation of Demosthenes into the French language was that of the three *Olynthiacs* by Louis Le Roy, Paris, 1541. Guillaume du Vair, ecclesiastic and publicist, added to his treatise on French eloquence (1592-93) a French translation of Demosthenes' and Aeschines' speeches *On the Crown*. A half-dozen other French translations of selected speeches of Demosthenes appeared before the close of the sixteenth century.

We know that the study of Greek began in England soon after the middle of the fifteenth century, but it is doubtful whether anything of Demosthenes was read in this earliest period. Individual Englishmen may have learned something of his oratory in their studies in Italy. But in 1540 Sir John Cheke became first Regius Professor of Greek at Cambridge, and afterward Public Orator of the University. Shortly after Cheke's appointment, Roger Ascham in a private letter, writing of the progress of Greek studies in St. John's College, says, probably with something of exaggeration, that now Demosthenes is as well known there as Cicero was at an earlier time. We have the testimony of Thomas Wylson, the first English translator of Demosthenes, to Cheke's devotion to the orator. Wylson, in the introductory epistle of his translation, speaks of Cheke as having "traveled in Demosthenes as much as any one of them all," and he recalls his own experience at Padua, when all the English students there were inspired by

Cheke "to go to their booke," and he tells us how Cheke read gladly to himself and others certain orations of Demosthenes in Greek, and interpreted them. Of Cheke's command of Demosthenes he says:

> Such acquaintance had he with this notable orator, so gladly did he read him, and so often: that I thinke there was neuer olde Priest more perfite in his Portreise, nor supersticious Monke in our Ladies Psalter as they call it, nor yet good preacher in the Bible or testament, than this man was in Demosthenes. . . . He was moued greatly to like Demosthenes aboue all others, for that he saw him so familiarly applying himselfe to the sense and vnderstanding of the common people, that he sticked not to say, that none euer was more fitte to make an English man tell his tale praise worthily in an open hearing, either in Parlament or in Pulpit, or otherwise, than this onely orator was.

Among the works of Cheke were Latin translations of the *Philippics* and *Olynthiacs*, together with the *Leptinea* and "the orations of Demosthenes and Aeschines on the two opposite sides."

Roger Ascham says in the *Scholemaster:*

> Yea, I haue heard worthie M. Cheke many tymes say: I would haue a good student passe and journey through all authors both Greeke and Latin: but he that will dwell in these few bookes onelie: first, in Gods holie Bible, and then ioyne with it, *Tullie* in *Latin, Plato, Aristotle: Xenophon: Isocrates:* and *Demosthenes* in Greeke: must nedes proue an excellent man.

Ascham further says that Redman, Cheke, Smith, and their scholars brought Aristotle, Plato, Cicero, and Demosthenes

> to florishe as notable in Cambridge, as euer they did in Grece and in Italie: and for the doctrine of those fowre, the fowre pillars of learning, Cambridge then geuing place to no vniuersitie, neither in France, Spaine, Germanie, nor Italie.

Ascham, who calls Sir John Cheke "my dearest frend, and teacher of all the little poor learning I haue," had the privilege of bringing Demosthenes to Queen Elizabeth herself. Her tutor before her accession to the throne and director of her studies afterward, he tells us how, after a dinner at Windsor Castle, where the discussion had turned on school discipline, he

> went vp to read with the Queenes Maiestie. We red then togither in the Greke tonge as I well remember, that noble oration of Demosthenes against Aeschines for his false dealing in his ambassage to king Philip of Macedonie.

In the *Scholemaster* he tells of the progress in Greek which Elizabeth has made by daily exercise for a year or two in 'double translation' from Isocrates and Demosthenes. For perfecting style he gives this advice:

> If a Master woulde haue a perfite example to folow, how, in *Genere sublimi*, to auoide *Nimium*, or in *Mediocri* to atteyne *Satis*, or in *Humili*, to exchew *Parum*, let him read diligently for the

first, **Secundam Philippicam**, for the meane, *De Natura Deorum*, and for the lowest, *Partitiones*. Or, if in an other tong, ye looke for like example, in like perfection, for all those three degrees, read *Pro Ctesiphonte*, **Ad Leptinem**, et *Contra Olympiodorum*, and, what witte, Arte, and diligence is hable to affourde, ye shall plainely see.

He adds that in his opinion no man of his time is perfect in all three styles save his friend Iohannes Sturm (the Strassburg student of Cicero and Demosthenes). In 1550 we find Ascham reading Herodotus, Sophocles, and Demosthenes to Sir Richard Morisine, whom he was serving as secretary on an embassy to Germany. Possibly the suggestion which Ascham gives for the improvement of a controversialist of his own day might not have been without value to certain silver-tongued men of our own time:

> If *Osorius* would leaue of his lustiness in striuing against *S. Austen,* and his ouer rancke rayling against poore *Luther*, and the troth of Gods doctrine, and giue his whole studie, not to write any thing of his own for a while, but to translate *Demosthenes*, with so straite, fast, and temperate a style in Latine, as he is in Greeke, he would become so perfit and pure a writer, I beleue, as hath beene fewe or none sence *Ciceroes* dayes: And so, by doing himself and all learned moch good, do others lesse harme, and Christes doctrine lesse injury, than he doth.

At Cambridge, Nicholas Carr, who became Regius Professor of Greek in 1547, carried on the Demosthenic tradition. Francis Bacon says of him that he "almost deified Demosthenes." In 1571 he published a Latin translation of the **Olynthiacs** and **Philippics**.

The first English version of Demosthenes is of peculiar interest, for it is believed to have been made at the solicitation of Queen Elizabeth, at a time when she was facing her desperate struggle against a modern Philip, and had need of every appeal to the English love of liberty. The title-page reads: The three Orations of Demosthenes, chiefe Orator among the Grecians, in fauour of the Olynthians, a people in Thracia, novv called Romania: vvith those his fovver Orations titled expressely & by name against King Philip of Macedonie: moqt nedefull to be redde in these daungerous dayes, of all them that loue their Countries libertie, and desire to take vvarning for their better auayle, by example of others. Englished out of the Greeke By Thomas Wylson Doctor of the ciuill lavves. After these orations ended, Demosthenes lyfe is set foorth, and gathered out of Plutarch, Lucian, Suidas, and others, with a large table, declaring all the principall matters contayned in euerye part of this booke. Seene and allowed according to the Queenes Maiesties Iniunctions. *Imprinted at London by Henrie Denham.*

The book is dedicated "To the right Honorable Sir William Cecill, Knight, principall Secretarie to the Queens Maiestie." It is to be regretted that English orators of the later period did not profit more by Wylson's comparison of Cicero with Demosthenes:

> Demosthenes hath more matter couched in a small roume, than Tullie hath in a large discourse, and Demosthenes writing is more binding, more fast, firme, and more agreable to our common manner of speach, than Tullies Orations are. And who so speaketh now as Demosthenes doth, I doe thynke he should be counted the wiser, the more temperate, and the more graue man a great deale, than if he wholly followed Tullie, and used his large veyne and vehement manner of eloquence.

Wylson alludes to the charge that Demosthenes was not brave on the battlefield, saying that he "had the stomacke of a Lion, to speake boldly although not to fight manfully." He concludes the *Testimonia* with these words: "Thus much of this worthy and famous Demosthenes, whose name as it is by interpretation the strength and force of the people: so was he in very deede and by nature, the strong bulwarke, and mighty defence of his most deare natiue Countrie."

Wylson's translation was issued in 1570. He had already published his *Rule of Reason, conteyning the Arte of Logike*, and his *Arte of Rhetorique*. A member of the inner circle of English Hellenists, student and friend of Cheke, and friend of Ascham, and in his later years holding important civil office, Wylson gave a distinct impulse to the study of Demosthenes in England as bearing on the service of the State.

The seventeenth century saw no new volumes of the Demosthenic corpus, but we find a score of editions of selected speeches, chiefly the **Olynthiacs** and **Philippics**, and the **Crown Speech**. Nearly all of these were by German and French scholars: none were of great importance, and no noteworthy translations into the modern languages were made. It would seem that the great edition of Wolf, reprinted in 1604, 1607, and 1642, met the needs of the more advanced students throughout the century.

The eighteenth century was a time of marked progress both in editing and expounding the text, and in translation. Two great text editions appeared, with introductions, notes and indices: Taylor, Cambridge, 1748-1774, and Reiske, Leipzig, 1770-1775. Some twenty-five editions of selected speeches were published, eleven of them in Great Britain. Translations were numerous, both in Latin and in the modern languages. The English translation of Leland, London, 1756-1777, became a standard; it included the public speeches, and Aeschines and Demosthenes **On the Crown**. Auger's French translation of all the speeches of Aeschines and Demosthenes (1777) was equally valuable. The geographical range of the texts and translations shows how widely the study of Demosthenes was extending in the eighteenth century—from Rome to Moscow, from Paris to Dublin. It is interesting to find among the English editions a translation of the **Second** and **Third Olynthiacs** by the Right Honourable George Granville, written in 1702, the year of his entering Parliament. Johnson says that Granville published this translation "with the design of turning the thunder of Demosthenes upon the head of Lewis."

While much that is best in Demosthenic style is inevitably lost in translation—the emphasis of words and phrases, and the artistic periodic structure—yet the translation when it is well done can bring over much that is characteristic both in thought and expression, and it can reproduce fully the splendid political aims and principles of his career. The widespread translations of the eighteenth century were therefore a powerful means of extending his influence in the States of Europe. Leland writes as follows in his preface:

> To animate a public renowned for justice, humanity, and valour, yet in many instances degenerate and corrupted; to warn them of the dangers of luxury, treachery, and bribery, of the ambition of a powerful foreign enemy; to recall the glory of their ancestors to their thoughts and to inspire them with resolution, vigour, and unanimity; to correct abuses, to restore discipline, to revive and enforce the generous sentiments of patriotism and public spirit—these were the great purposes for which the following orations were originally pronounced. The subject therefore may possibly recommend them to a British reader, even under the disadvantages of a translation by no means worthy of the famous original.

Throughout the nineteenth century Demosthenic studies received their full share of the more critical historical and philological investigations, especially in Germany, France, and England. New editions of the whole corpus, based on better knowledge of the whole manuscript tradition, prepared the way for a host of annotated editions of separate speeches. Among the latter, editions of the public speeches by Henri Weil are preëminent. Among the numerous translations, Jacobs' German translation of the **Philippics** (1805) is noteworthy both for the text and the explanatory material. It is interesting to learn that Jacobs in his work, and Niebuhr, then an unknown young man, in a German translation of the **First Philippic** published the year after, both treated Demosthenes' struggle against Philip as a stimulating example to the German peoples in their desperate war with Napoleon. Niebuhr dedicated his little volume to the Czar Alexander, with an adaptation of Virgil's words:

> Hic rem Romanam, magno turbante tumultu,
> Sistet, eques sternet Poenos Gallumque rebellem.

A translation of the whole corpus by Charles Rann Kennedy (1848) was of especial value to English readers.

Comprehensive works on political and legal antiquities made the speeches more intelligible. Most important of all were two great works, Arnold Schaefer's *Demosthenes und seine Zeit*, and the volume *Demosthenes* in Friedrich Blass' *Die Attische Beredsamkeit*. Schaefer, in his three volumes, treats in the utmost detail every step of Demosthenes' political career, writing from the standpoint of an outspoken admirer. Blass, bringing to the study of Demosthenes' speeches a critical knowledge of all Greek oratory, gives the most minute criticism of the argument and style of every speech. Another powerful influence toward the appreciation of Demosthenes came from Grote's *History of Greece* (1846-1856). Grote, a man active in the ranks of the extreme Liberals of his own time, brought to his study of the career of Demosthenes a profound faith in democracy, and a real enthusiasm for Demosthenes' struggle

to maintain democracy against the Macedonian imperial monarchy. Mitford's *History of Greece* (1784-1810) had treated the period from the standpoint of an ultra Tory; Grote carried English opinion to the opposite view, as Schaefer was doing at the same time in Germany. Lord Brougham also was lending his great influence to the honor of Demosthenes in his essays, *Demosthenes, The Eloquence of the Ancients*, the *Glasgow Inaugural Discourse*, and his translations of the speeches **On the Chersonese** and **On the Crown**. Brougham, with his practical experience both in politics and oratory, made an indispensable addition to the studies of historians and philologians. But even in a period in which Demosthenes was so generally admired, occasional protests were made, and very near the close of the nineteenth century a movement began among some of the ablest German scholars which at the first threatened Demosthenes' reputation for political sagacity, and finally would discredit his integrity altogether. As German scholars looked back upon the Greek states as they were in the time of Demosthenes, helpless in their separative disorganization, and apparently in a position to secure strength and prosperity by union under the monarch of Macedon, they could not fail to be impressed by the analogy of the one-time situation of the states of Germany, at the mercy of one another and of their powerful neighbors, until the Prussian monarchs brought them unity and power. If a Grote and a Brougham saw in Demosthenes the champion of their own ideal democracy, certainly men who were enjoying the marvelous prosperity of imperial Germany could not fail to see in a Frederick the Great or a Wilhelm I another Philip of Macedon, and in the opposition to the Macedonian Empire they saw only a suicidal attempt to maintain the system of petty states. Beloch, in Vol. II of his *Griechische Geschichte* (1897), so interpreted the struggle of Demosthenes against Philip. Eduard Meyer added his commanding influence to this view, and Paul Wendland followed. Finally, in 1916, when German imperialism seemed to be on the point of sweeping French and English democracy before its resistless military power, Engelbert Drerup, in his little volume, *Aus einer alten Advokatenrepublik*, rewrote the story of Demosthenes' public life, upon the assumption that Demosthenes was a typical demagogue, with an eye single to his own advancement, leader of a party 'from the streets,' and the forerunner of those modern lawyer-politicians, Asquith, Lloyd George, Poincaré, and their like, who were hastening England and France to their ruin. And now, the World War over, and the modern democracies triumphant, Georges Clemenceau seeks to bring Demosthenes back to his own. In the little volume *Démosthène*, with no pretension to critical study of the sources, in language more dithyrambic than sober, Clemenceau, out of the vicissitudes of his own experience, pays homage to the man who knew how to hold up to its own best ideals a democratic people, fickle in time of peace, gloriously united and heroic in the face of danger.

Werner Jaeger   (essay date 1944)

SOURCE: "Demosthenes: The Death-Struggle and Transfiguration of the City-State," in *Paideia: The Ideals of Greek Culture, the Conflict of Cultural Ideals in the Age*

Copy of a third-century B.C. statue of Demosthenes that originally stood in the marketplace of Athens.

of Plato, Vol. III, translated by Gilbert Highet, Oxford University Press, Inc., 1944, pp. 263-89.

[*Jaeger was a German scholar best known for his* Paideia: The Ideals of Greek Culture *(1939-44). In the following excerpt from that work, he considers Demosthenes as a tragic figure attempting to stem the decline of the Greek city-state.*]

Ever since he returned to life in the Renaissance, Demosthenes has been held to be what his first modern editor called him: the awakener of the Greeks to liberty, and their eloquent champion against oppression. When the hand of Napoleon lay heavy on Europe, Demosthenes' works were translated by the German philologist and humanist Friedrich Jacobs, in order to strengthen the spirit of national independence. Soon after the First World War, the French statesman Clémenceau wrote a hasty book on him [*Démosthène*, 1926], full of glowing French rhetoric against the German Macedonians, warning the Athenians of Paris not to allow their refinement to make them a nerveless people of artists and *rentiers*, without enough will to life and enough vital energy to resist their barbarous enemy. In a Latin civilization, with all the oratorical devices of Demosthenes himself, that book founded a new cult of the long-dead patriot, on whose altars the old fire of classicism blazed up once again, for the last time. But not long before, a German scholar [Engelbert Drerup] had written another book with the contemptuous title *Aus einer alten Advokatenrepublik*—'An Ancient Lawyers' Republic'. After a century of sharp reaction against the classicist admiration for the powerful orator and the great agitator, who had been wrongly canonized by academic rhetoric, this work now summed up the whole case, and was meant to destroy Demosthenes' reputation for good and all. Of course, it was a war book; it was highly inflammatory, and it put the harshest construction on every fact, so as to distort the truth into a caricature. Yet it was only the lowest point on the line down which the historians' estimate of Demosthenes had travelled since the new attitude to history had come into being, a hundred years earlier.

The first great representative of the new historical attitude in the sphere of classics, Niebuhr, was one of Demosthenes' most devoted admirers. But violent criticism of Demosthenes' career and policy began with Droysen [*Geschichte des Hellenismus*, 1836]. It was initiated by the epoch-making discovery of the Hellenistic world. Hitherto, Greek history had always come to a dramatic conclusion with the loss of the political liberty of the city-states at Chaeronea. Demosthenes had been presented as the last Greek statesman, standing above the grave of Hellas and delivering her funeral oration. But now the curtain suddenly opened, to reveal a great new drama—the age when Greece dominated the world politically and spiritually, the age that began with Alexander's conquest of the Persian empire. The perspective shifted, to disclose a continuous external and internal development of Greek civilization into something cosmopolitan, something universal. With the change of proportion, Demosthenes' greatness came to seem very small and limited. He appeared to belong to a world which was foolishly deceived about its own importance, and which was living on an anachronism—the rhetorical memory of its glorious ancestors. He and his contemporaries, it seemed, were trying to revive the deeds of their fathers in their own day, although they themselves belonged to the past. His critics became increasingly bitter. They started by discarding his political standards, which historians had hitherto willingly accepted, because there was no connected account of the history of his age by one of his contemporaries. Then, after doubting his statesmanship, they went on to examine, and to condemn, his character. At the same time his opponents, Isocrates and Aeschines, began to rise in estimation because they had given up hope for the future of Athens at the right time, and advised their countrymen to abandon the fight. As often, success became the standard of historical achievement, and scholars were reassured to find that Demosthenes had had opponents during his lifetime who were just as far-sighted as modern professors.

The critics have gone too far. It is time for the general picture of Demosthenes to be revised. The radical revaluation in the customary estimate of the characters of Demosthenes, Aeschines, and Isocrates was so improbable, psychologically, as to offend common sense and natural feeling.

Apart from that, there has been a marked advance in our knowledge of the fourth century since Droysen's discovery of the Hellenistic world. This advance did not begin with politics, but with new light cast on the intellectual movements of that critical epoch, which revealed how closely political movements were connected with the general trend of Greek thought and Greek culture. Worlds which had formerly appeared to be, so to speak, in watertight compartments—such as political history and philosophy, journalism and rhetoric—are now all seen to be living members of one single organism, each with its share in the process of the nation's life. We are now able to give to the idea of historical necessity discovered by Thucydides a broader interpretation than has been usual, particularly in political history. Nowadays it looks like coarse rationalism to judge the appearance of a historical phenomenon like Demosthenes in the decline of the Greek city-state simply by his own personal character and his success in practical politics. His resistance to the forces moving his age was a fulfilment of a supra-personal law—the law by which every nation tries doggedly to maintain the pattern of life moulded by itself, founded on its own natural disposition, and responsible for the highest achievements in its history.

Throughout the centuries from Homer to Alexander, the fundamental fact in Greek history was the city-state, the form of political and spiritual life which was fixed very early, and never wholly abandoned. In forms as manifold as the ever-varying Greek landscape, it had unfolded all those rich potentialities of internal and external life which the Greek race possessed. Even after the Greeks awoke to spiritual nationhood, in the fifth century, and smaller political units began to group themselves into confederations of larger size, the independent existence of the city-state still remained the frontier which was bound, sooner or later, to stop the new trend to nationalism. The problem of how far the several city-states could be independent had found no satisfactory solution since it had first been rudely thrust on one side by the imperialist Athenians under Pericles, who crushed the allies of Athens into subjection. When the Spartans succeeded to the leadership of Greece after the close of the Peloponnesian war, they were compelled to base their hegemony on a formal recognition of the autonomy of individual states. After the first great revolt of the Greek cities against their Spartan overlords in the Corinthian war, their independence was solemnly recognized in the peace of Antalcidas. However, the formula that all the Greek city-states should be independent was useful to Sparta too. It meant that it would be difficult for a league to be formed against her under the leadership of another state. But when she herself tightened the reins, and invaded the liberty of the separate cities, the result was the fall of the Spartan hegemony. Never afterwards did any single one of the Greek city-states manage to assert a decisive domination over the others. In other words: the Greeks were not able to think of giving up the independence of their city-states, any more than to-day we have been able to think *in practice* of giving up our own national states in favour of any more comprehensive form of state.

Demosthenes' youth fell in the period when Athens was recovering from her catastrophic defeat in the Peloponnesian war. While the philosophical thought of the age, embodied in Plato, was concentrating all its energy on solving the problem of the state and its moral reconstruction, the contemporary Athenian state was making its way step by step out of its weakness to a liberty of movement which allowed it to plan the gradual repair of its strength. Thucydides' prophecy that a change of power would produce a shift in sympathy was all too promptly fulfilled. With the support of Thebes and Corinth, the former allies of Sparta, Athens slowly regained her position among the Greek states, and, with the help of Persian money, rebuilt the fortifications she had been compelled to destroy after the war. Then followed the second stage in her recovery. The defection of Thebes from Sparta gave Athens the opportunity to found the second naval confederacy; and she was astute enough to bind her allies closely to her by avoiding the domineering policy that had broken up her first league. Its leaders were distinguished soldiers and statesmen like Timotheus, Chabrias, Iphicrates, and Callistratus. Soon after it was founded, Athens fought bravely and devotedly beside Thebes against Sparta in the seven-year war which ended successfully in the peace of 371. Thus her undisputed domination at sea was ensured, and the new confederacy was finally legalized by international agreement.

The young men of Athens, absorbed in philosophical study or vainly dissipating their time on adventure and sport, were swept into the great current of history which seemed to be carrying Athens forward once again to play a leading part in the political life of Greece. They belonged to a different generation from the youths who had struggled under the problems of the Peloponnesian war, the defeat, and the collapse. Plato had written *Gorgias* to be a call to battle for them. In the first decade of the fourth century they had felt themselves to be the founders of a new society. Later, in *Theaetetus*, Plato described the wise man as retreating further and further into remote speculations about mathematics and astronomy, and sceptically turning his back on all kinds of political activity. But the younger generation was drawn into the whirl of politics, and left it to immigrants from the small towns and frontier states—men like Aristotle, Xenocrates, Heracleides, and Philip of Opus—to take up the Platonic life of pure research. Isocrates' school was not like Plato's Academy. It produced a group of active politicians, most notably Isocrates' friend and prize pupil, Timotheus, the soldier and statesman who directed the new naval league. Yet the younger generation got its real training from party politics, from speaking in the law-courts, and from addressing the public assembly. Demosthenes was taken to court secretly by his tutor, when he was a boy, and heard Callistratus' great speech in his own defence in the Oropian case, the speech which saved him from ruin once again.

That historical anecdote, which is probable enough, shows the spirit of the new generation. It reveals where Demosthenes' true interests lay: apart from the harassing anxieties about his stolen home and inheritance, which fill his first speeches, delivered when he was only twenty. His character was destined by the trend of events to be moulded into a statesman's. The course of his life was set by the great men on whom he modelled himself, the makers of the second naval league. It was aimed at reviving for the present age the greatness Athens had possessed in the century of her highest political glory (somewhat dulled, now, by Plato's philosophical criticisms), and at rejuvenating the present by the ideals of the past. But the agony of watching that glory break into dust had not been fruitless. Struggling through the gloom to understand the reasons for the collapse, the post-war generation had found a certain knowledge which must not be lost, if the past was not to repeat itself. It was the task of the young men to pour some of this cold and pure knowledge into the old intoxicating wine of Athenian imperialism. That was the only way for them to cope with the new era. The difference between it and the fifth century, between the ages of the second and the first naval leagues, was the new spirit of wary moral and political reflection. It was perfectly natural that the fourth-century movement for political restoration should be so idealistic and so literary. There had been none of that spirit in the unquestioning energy of the previous century. It was only in the Indian summer of Athens, the Demosthenic age, that political oratory developed into a great form of literary art. The tradition that Demosthenes eagerly studied Thucydides while training himself as an orator fits the facts very well. He could not model his style on the political speeches of Pericles as actually delivered—for they had not been formally published as works of literature, and did not survive. In fact, the speeches of Thucydides were the sole surviving echo of Athenian political oratory from the great age. In the artistic and intellectual perfection of their form, and the richness of their thought, they stood far above all actual contemporary political eloquence. It was Demosthenes alone who was to create a literary form that combined the energy and suppleness of the spoken word with the dialectic profundity and aesthetic elegance of Thucydides' speeches, and to re-create in literature that most essential element in rhetorical persuasion, the interplay of living emotion between speaker and audience.

When Demosthenes himself stepped upon the platform, twelve years after he had heard the great Callistratus speak, the political situation had entirely changed. The Social War had ended. Athens had once more lost the most important of her allies. The second naval confederacy, founded with such splendid hopes, was broken. Most of its members held that its function had been fulfilled with the overthrow of Spartan domination. That done, it had no inward bond of union to hold it together. Although it had reached its greatest extent only after Athens' victorious peace with Sparta, it was soon evident that it had no positive community of interests to ensure its continuance; and when financial stringency compelled Athens, its leading power, to resume her old imperialistic policy of force against her allies, the rebellious spirit which had once before overthrown Athenian naval supremacy arose again. But the most important new positive factor in Greek politics since the peace of 371 was the unexpected rise of Thebes under the leadership of Epaminondas. This brought about an entirely new grouping of forces. At first Athens had stood at the side of Thebes against Sparta, but in the peace of 371 she had parted company with Thebes in order to take the profits of the war. However, immediately after she had made an independent peace, and by this concession to Sparta secured her recognition of the naval

confederacy, the Spartan land forces were conclusively defeated by the Thebans under Epaminondas at Leuctra. This victory raised Thebes to unprecedented new heights, and forced Sparta down to the second place in Greece. At this juncture, Callistratus, the leading politician of Athens, sharply changed the policy of the state, and entered an open alliance with Sparta so as to counterbalance the new power of Thebes, the erstwhile ally of Athens. A new idea now came into being: *the balance of power*. It was an idea that dominated Athenian politics for the next ten years, and went some way towards stabilizing a new sort of relation among the Greek states. It was the creation of Callistratus, the statesman who had proposed the break with Thebes even during the peace negotiations, and had forced it through in spite of strong pro-Theban feeling in Athens. On the other side, Epaminondas, the only great statesman Thebes ever produced, proceeded to dissolve the Peloponnesian League after defeating Sparta. He liberated the Messenian and Arcadian peoples from Spartan oppression, making them independent states, each with a central government. They now became, like other small states, vassals of Thebes. This broke Sparta's hegemony even in the Peloponnese. It was only the military support of Athens that saved her from complete destruction. It is impossible to tell what would have been the course of Greek politics now that Athens had swung into opposition to Thebes, if Epaminondas had not been killed in the battle of Mantinea, the last Theban victory over Sparta, and if his powerful Athenian opponent Callistratus had not soon afterwards been overthrown. Thereafter the two rival states were led by less competent men. Their power quickly diminished. The conflict between them quieted down. Both Thebes and Athens had to fight hard to maintain their authority over their allies, Thebes in central Greece and Thessaly, Athens on the sea. Still, their hostility was still active in the age of Demosthenes, and came out in every minor question. However, in Athens it was naturally obscured by the internal difficulties she had to face during the next few years, when the naval confederacy was falling irretrievably into ruin. This was the inheritance which came to Demosthenes and his generation in 355.

The fall of the naval league forced to the front again, and for the last time, the question of the political future of Athens. It looked as if Isocrates had given the only possible answer to it, in the bold proposal he made in one of the war's dark hours, in his speech *On peace*. He had publicly proposed that Athens should finally abandon all her imperialist policy, all attempts to revive the former Attic empire, all power-politics of the type which the second naval confederacy had inevitably reintroduced. He supported this proposal by a highly utilitarian type of political morality. It was more advantageous, he said, to gather laurels in peace, than to incur the hatred of the entire world by the pleonexia, the greed for more, which is implicit in all imperialist policy; and to expose the state to frightful danger under the leadership of universally despised political agitators and military gangsters. At the same period the same change of policy was being recommended on economic grounds by the talented economist who wrote the essay *On the Revenues*. But whether Athens adopted the new policy because of a fundamental change of principle, or because she was merely bowing to the inevitable, she was bound to start her reforms by concentrating on the reconstruction of her financial stability and the restoration of her credit (in every sense of the word) in the eyes of the world. The propertied classes must have been discussing even more comprehensive plans for reconstructing the constitution of the state which had fallen, during the last ten years, into the hands of the radically minded masses. Otherwise Isocrates could not have dared to suggest publicly that a more authoritative government should be instituted, as he did in his pamphlet, the *Areopagiticus.* Athens was very far from taking such a step; but the fact that the proposal could be made shows how powerful and how combative the upper classes felt in that desperate period when only they could help the state. They now produced an opposition leader of great prestige. This was Eubulus, whose principal interest was economic and financial reform. He was followed by the best brains of the younger generation, including Demosthenes himself. Demosthenes belonged to a rich Athenian family; and it was only natural for him to join those of similar birth, education, and outlook. These young men had first turned to politics when the renaissance of Athenian power was at its height. Their highest ambition had been to give all their strength to the service of the state. Now they were forced to begin the career to which they had been looking forward so eagerly, just when the Athenian state was at the nadir of its historical career. Inspired by the loftiest of ideals, they were thrust into the gloomiest of realities. It was clear from the very outset that their efforts to mould the future of Athens must end in acknowledging and resolving this enormous conflict between ideal and reality.

Demosthenes' private life brought him into contact with the law at an early age. His father left him a great deal of money, which was misappropriated by his guardians. After making his first appearance before a jury as a speaker in his own behalf, he chose to follow the profession of legal consultant and 'logographer' or speech-writer. In Athens a regular connexion between politics and the law-courts had grown up, so that it was perfectly normal to start one's public life by taking part in political prosecutions. The first documents we have for Demosthenes' political activity are therefore speeches made in great state trials during the years of the depression. He did not deliver them himself, but wrote them for others. The three orations **Against Androtion, Against Timocrates,** and **Against Leptines** are all expressions of the same policy. They are aimed against the most vulnerable personalities of the political party which had governed Athens during the disastrous Social War, and which had managed to maintain itself in power even after the defeat. At once it was clear that Demosthenes was one of the cleverest and most dangerous of the opposition's shocktroops. The savagery of the dispute shows the bitterness with which the opposition was struggling for power. Even here we can see how much of Demosthenes' strength lay in the fact that he followed up his aims logically, systematically, and resolutely—although he was then working chiefly for others and under the guidance of others. But he soon came forward as an orator in his own right. Significantly, his interest was directed to foreign affairs, from the very beginning. It is thrilling to watch the development of the future statesman in these first utterances. We can see him taking

up the decisive problems of Athenian foreign policy one after another with remarkable power and firmness: so that the comparatively few early speeches display a complete picture of the position of Athens in international politics.

During that period of slow and laborious internal reconstruction, it was difficult for Athens to develop an energetic and productive foreign policy. This makes it all the more remarkable that the young Demosthenes should have approached each political problem as it appeared, with such independence of mind and such lively initiative. Defeated and depressed, Athens was condemned to complete inactivity in international politics. Demosthenes could therefore intervene only when the occasion presented itself—and the times were so busy, so full of conflicting interests, that such occasions did occur now and then. Here a gulf was inevitably bound to open, and to grow wider and deeper with the years. One school of thought, represented in literature by Isocrates and in politics by Eubulus, the leader of the well-to-do opposition party, firmly maintained that Athens in her weakened condition should have nothing to do with any foreign affairs whatever; the only possible future for her, they believed, lay in concentrating upon careful economic and internal policy. In his first speech on foreign affairs, Demosthenes showed some sympathy for that isolationist attitude. There were many calls for a preventive war against the threat, real or imaginary, of a Persian invasion. On this question Demosthenes attacked the warmongers, with a well-judged violence of language and a sureness of touch that pleased the party of Eubulus. His courage in voicing an unpopular view must have been sympathetically noted by the reformers who had taken it as their watchword to oppose vulgar sentiment and pupular clichés. But although he judged the political risks with sober caution, at heart he believed that Athens must work her way out of her present impotence, to take an active part in international politics. He must therefore have welcomed every opportunity for Athens to move beyond her miserable isolation, and to regain her prestige and power by a moderate and just, but watchful, attitude in foreign politics. However cautiously he might advance towards this aim, it was impossible to follow this policy, and use the chances that presented themselves, without taking *some* risks. Meanwhile, the partisans of complete isolationism were playing for complete safety. Even during this period of passivity, Demosthenes was intellectually active. He followed the struggles of the combatants in the political arena like an eager spectator who is waiting for the moment to leap into the ring and take a leading part in the contest.

The next stages in his development are his great speeches **For the Megalopolitans** and **For the Liberty of the Rhodians**: along with the legal speech **Against Aristocrates,** which is largely concerned with foreign politics. He had explained his view of the relations between Athens and the Persian empire in his first public speech. Now, in these orations, he attacks the other three main problems of Athenian foreign policy: the Peloponnesian question; the question of the relations between Athens and her seceding partners in the naval league; and the problem of northern Greece. Thereby he completed for the first time a bold sketch of the future foreign policy of Athens, as he conceives it. The aim of his endeavour is always the same. Demosthenes keeps his gaze fixed firmly upon it. It is to lift Athens out of her crippling isolation, and to lay the foundations for a practical policy of forming alliances, so that, if the opportunity comes, it may be seized. It was inevitable that any Athenian politician concerned with foreign affairs should adopt the constructive plan which had been outlined by Callistratus with his original idea of the balance of power. Ever since the amazing rise of Thebes to a place beside Sparta and Athens that idea was bound to look like the classical inheritance from the most successful period of Attic policy since Pericles. As long as the factors of Greek international politics remained the same as they had been when the maxim of equilibrium was formulated fifteen years before, a rising politician could only adapt and develop it; it could not be challenged. Demosthenes' speech *For the Megalopolitans* is a proof of the suppleness of his mind. Like all other Athenian politicians, he adopts Callistratus' principle; and he does his best to interpret it anew to suit the changed times, without losing the spirit of the statesman who laid it down. The idea that Sparta and Thebes should counterpoise each other in the scales, while Athens swung like the tongue of the balance between them, had once before brilliantly illuminated the situation, when the predominance of Thebes and her allies had compelled Athens to come to an understanding with her old enemy Sparta. But soon Thebes found her level. Then she was weakened by the disastrous beginning of the war against the Phocians in central Greece; and it became essential for Athens to keep the new states of Messenia and Arcadia, which Thebes had created in the Peloponnese to oppose Sparta, from being crushed once more by the renewed power of Sparta. Otherwise Athens would have become a Spartan vassal, and Thebes would have been irrevocably weakened. The new states were defenceless. They had to ask for Athenian support. Demosthenes believed this was the right moment to shift the balance, which had stood still for some time, and to counterbalance the power of Sparta (allied to Athens since Leuctra) by a new alliance with Arcadia and Messenia.

This highly independent idea is followed, in the speech *For the Liberty of the Rhodians*, by another which is no less interesting. The Rhodians, who had been tampered with by the king of Caria, were one of the first states to secede from the Athenian naval league. They had not reckoned with the fact that Athens was the only state which could really help a democratic country to defend its independence. When the king of Caria drove the democratic politicoes out of Rhodes, they ran to Athens, full of remorse, and anxious to sign a new alliance. In the case of the Arcadians, the Athenian isolationists, who had the public ear, pled that they could not help, because of the Spartan alliance. And so now, they made full use of the popular feeling of well-earned rancour against the Rhodians: having betrayed Athens, they were welcome to the consequences. Demosthenes sharply attacked this superficial emotionalism. He said it was merely a cloak for passivity and indecisiveness on the part of the government. In both cases he acted quite independently, and risked his growing reputation on his words. In both cases he was defeated. Rejected, the suppliants joined the enemies of Athens. The Arcadians and Messenians later sided with Philip

of Macedon. Athens lost not only the Rhodians but the other small states which would certainly soon have come back to Athens, if the Rhodian alliance had matured, just as Rhodes had led their secession in the Social War.

With his speech *Against Aristocrates* Demosthenes turns for the first time to the politics of northern Greece. The question at stake was the security of the Dardanelles. The last stronghold of Athens at sea was her command of the Hellespont Straits, upon which her grain supply depended, and which also assured her predominance in the waters of northern Greece. Demosthenes knew the importance of this region from personal experience, having toured the coasts as trierarch of a battleship. The Thracians near by had been threatening the Dardanelles for many years, and for some time actually seized them. Now that several brothers had divided up the kingship, Demosthenes proposed to take advantage of the temporary disunity of the Thracians, so as to prevent the recurrence of this peril, and weaken, as far as possible, the dangerous neighbours of the strategic Straits. Meanwhile, however, another factor had entered northern Greek politics. This was Philip, the brilliant new king of Macedonia. In the short time since his accession he had contrived to make his country (which was formerly mutilated and dependent now on this state, now on that) into the dominant power throughout the whole region. Even before this, in his speech *For the Liberty of the Rhodians*, Demosthenes had mentioned the danger threatening Athens from that side. Philip had been at war with Athens ever since annexing the long-disputed Macedonian port of Amphipolis, which Athens claimed as an old-established base for her commerce and fleet. After he united his country, he made himself ruler of its neighbour, Thessaly, which had long been torn by political turmoil, and was ready for some foreigner to solve its problems. Then he entered the war between Thebes and Phocis, beat the Phocians, and was about to invade central Greece through Thermopylae in order to appear as arbitrator of the many disputes outstanding there, when the Athenians, with a sudden effort, threw an army corps into that easily defended pass, blocking his way. He did not try to force the pass. He turned north again, marched practically unopposed through Thrace, and suddenly threatened Athens at the Dardanelles, where no one expected him. All Demosthenes' plans for protecting the strait against the Thracians were suddenly ruined; the entire picture changed. The Macedonian danger was revealed in a flash, enormous and terrible.

The news caused a panic in Athens. It soon changed, however, to careless gaiety when it was reported that Philip had fallen ill and abandoned the expedition. Still, that was the moment when Demosthenes finally determined to abandon the passive isolationist policy which the administration was following. It had thwarted all his efforts to improve the position of Athens by grasping at favourable opportunities as they offered. Now it was no longer merely a question of principle, a choice between intervention and isolation. The country was in danger. Doing nothing would not now be interpreted as trying to 'save Athens first'. It meant surrendering the most vital interests of the state. The blockade-war against Philip, which no one had really taken seriously, had suddenly forced Athens onto the defensive. The country's entire strategy had to be changed.

Philip's rapid advance called out all Demosthenes' energies. At last he had found the dangerous assailant who was needed to justify Athens in taking a bold stand in foreign policy at this moment. It is difficult to say whether, in more fortunate circumstances, Demosthenes might not have become one of those statesmen who are born in a rising country, and help to build it up and make it stronger. Certainly, in fourth-century Athens, he could not have existed without an opponent like Philip to bring out all his determination, his far-sightedness, and his bulldog grasp of the essentials. The moral scruples which had long obstructed any attempt at an active foreign policy, in that most moral age, among men so deeply concerned with philosophical problems of conscience, were now blown away. That made it easier for Demosthenes to by-pass the leading appeasers and appeal directly to the people, from whom he had been very remote in his earliest speeches. In his speech on behalf of the Rhodian democrats he had already advanced some political arguments which were aimed at convincing the masses—something very different from the lofty, didactic, ironical tone of his first speech, which had been meant to cool down their excitement. The speech *Against Aristocrates* contains some violent attacks on the politicians in power: Demosthenes says they enrich themselves and live at ease in fine houses, while they do nothing more to help the country than plastering a wall here and repairing a road there. In his speech *On Armaments* he drew a critical comparison between the Athenian people of his own day, living off the state as if they had independent incomes, and the battle-scarred empire-builders of the past; and he closed with the idea that since the appeal to the politicians had been useless, *the people must be educated to a new mentality*—for politicians always said what the public wanted to hear anyhow.

That sentence contains a great programme. Hitherto it has not been taken seriously, because the speech has, until recently, been considered spurious. Nineteenth-century scholars often pushed their scepticism beyond the limits of probability, as here. But it was hardly necessary to prove the speech genuine to show that the next speeches of Demosthenes form a homogeneous spiritual unity. The ancients put them into a separate group and called them the *Philippics*: but it is not only the fact that they are all against Philip that distinguishes them from Demosthenes' earlier speeches. They are held together by *the great ideal of educating the Athenian people*, which is formulated briefly and impressively in the sentence quoted above. That sentence is the plainest commentary on the change which has been wrongly described as Demosthenes' move towards the 'democratic party', and which is really his transformation into a great popular leader. We can see it happening in the *Philippics*. Of course the speeches have a great deal of the conscious art with which the Athenian orators used to diagnose the future reactions of the public, and dominate them. They had more than a century's experience to go upon; and since many of them were not commoners, they had worked out a special language to appeal to the mob's instincts. But no one who has any intellectual discrimination can confuse the tone of the ordinary demagogue with Demosthenes' ability to use that language on occasion. The emotions which led him to appeal directly to the people were fundamentally different from those of the demagogue; they were the result of his accurate political knowledge, which made it necessary for him to overcome the limitations imposed on him by his youth and his gentle character, and come forward as a critic. And similarly the influence which his remarkable character had on Athenian politics was worlds apart from that not only of the loud-mouthed demagogues, but of the ordinary, hard-working, file-reading, respectable career-politicians like Eubulus. It is obvious that a spiritually mature statesman, such as Demosthenes is shown to be in his first speeches on foreign policy, does not suddenly change his nature, and become a mere tub-thumper, as some serious scholars have had the temerity to suggest. No one capable of realizing how new and how great is the language used in Demosthenes' *Philippics* could ever be guilty of such a misapprehension.

To understand the statesmanlike quality of these speeches it is not enough to study the practical measures proposed in them. They show that Demosthenes had a profound historical sense of the destiny of Athens and himself, and a profound determination to meet it. It is more than mere politics. Or perhaps we should say that it is politics as Solon and Pericles understood the word. He stands face to face with the people, and consoles them for their misfortunes, which are indeed great enough. But they have done nothing to let them expect anything better! That is the only really cheerful aspect of all their misery. Just as Solon once arose to warn the Athenians, so now Demosthenes admonishes them: 'Do not blame the gods for having given up your cause. You yourselves are to blame if Philip pushes you back step by step, and if he has now gained such power that many of you think it irresistible'. Solon brought in tyché, chance or fate, in discussing the part played by the gods in the misfortunes of the state. The same idea comes back, transformed once more, in Demosthenes' warning speeches against Philip. It is one of the basic themes in his profound analysis of the fate and future of Athens. It was an age of greatly increased individualism; men craved for freedom, but they felt all the more keenly how dependent everyone really is upon the outward course of world events. The century which began with the tragedies of Euripides was more alive to the idea of tyché than any other era; and the men of that age tended more and more to resign themselves to fate. Demosthenes boldly takes up Solon's old and bitter fight against the fatalism which is the worst enemy of resolute action. He places the historical responsibility for the fate of Athens squarely on the shoulders of his own generation. Their task, he declares, is the same as that of the generation which lived through the dark period after the loss of the Peloponnesian war, and which, against the opposition of all Greece, exalted Athens once more to great power and prestige. To do this, they used only one thing: the alert and energetic assistance of the people's whole strength. Nowadays, he adds bitterly, Athens is like a barbarian in a boxing-match, who can only clap his hands to the place where his opponent hit him last, instead of looking out for a place to punch.

These are the simple and striking ideas with which Demosthenes begins his work of educating the Athenian people in the first *Philippic*. The preliminary proposals for a new strategy which he makes, before Philip has delivered a new attack on Athens, prove that the speech (which is often dated too late) was made in the period when Philip's unexpected threat to the Dardanelles had opened Demosthenes' eyes to the danger for the first time. The military and financial measures which he proposed Athens should adopt so as to be ready at the next attack were not accepted by the Athenian people. He had to propose them anew, when Philip recovered from his illness, attacked Olynthus, the powerful commercial state in northern Greece, and provided a last opportunity for Athens to join with the Olynthians and stop the forward pressure of the Macedonians. Once again, with redoubled earnestness, Demosthenes asked whether Athens was to be responsible for its own destiny or to surrender to fate. He endeavoured to bring back the courage she needed for independent action. He bitterly attacked the false teachers who were trying to create alarm and distress, so as to convince the public—too late—that the time had really come to act. His own analysis of the enemy's power is not the kind of thing which a 'practical politician' would offer. It is a discussion and criticism of the moral foundations on which it is built. We ought not to read these speeches as if they were the considered report of a statesman to a cabinet meeting. They are efforts to guide a public which is intelligent, but vacillating and selfish. They are intended to mould the masses, like raw material which must be shaped to suit the statesman's ends. That is what gives particular importance to the ethical element in the speeches Demosthenes delivered at this time. There is nothing like it in any other speech on foreign policy throughout Greek literature. Demosthenes well knows what a great man Philip is, and what a magical, demoniac personality he has—a character not to be measured by purely moral standards. But he is Solon's pupil, and he refuses to believe any power built on such a basis can long endure. Despite all his admiration for Philip's mysterious tyché, he still clings to his belief in the tyché of Athens, whose light pinion is touched by a glory shed from the splendid historical mission of the Athenian state.

No one who has traced the development of the ideal of the statesman's character down through the various changes of the Greek spirit can follow Demosthenes' struggle to make the Athenian people understand its own destiny, without being reminded of the first grand personifications of the responsible political leader, which appear in Attic tragedy. They too breathe the spirit of Solon, but they are caught in the tragic dilemma of decision. In the speeches of Demosthenes, the tragic dilemma has become a reality, and the consciousness of this, not merely subjective excitement, is the source of the overwhelming emotion, the 'pathos', which men of succeeding ages felt in Demosthenes—although they were interested only in aesthetics, and stirred only by the wish to imitate his style, which they rightly felt to be the foundation of a new era in the history of oratory. That was the style which expressed the tragedy of his age. Its deep and moving shadows appear again on the faces carved by Scopas, greatest of contemporary sculptors; and a direct line can be traced from these two

great harbingers of a new feeling for life, to the magnificent Pergamene altar, a rich and powerful rush of emotion in which the new style reaches its loftiest expression. How could Demosthenes have become the greatest classic of the Hellenistic age, which had so little sympathy for his political ideal, if he had not uttered, fully and perfectly, all the characteristic emotions which it felt? But the emotions and the style in which they are expressed are, for him, inseparable from his struggle to achieve his political ideal. Orator and statesman, in Demosthenes, are one. His eloquence alone would have been nothing without the power and weight of the political thoughts striving to express themselves through it. They give the passionate creations of his mind the firmness, depth, and solidity which have never been rivalled by his myriad imitators, and which anchor them fast to the place, the time, and the historical crisis which are immortalized in them.

I do not intend to give a complete exposition of Demosthenes' policy in itself. The material his speeches provide for a reconstruction of the actual events, and, even more, of his development into a statesman, is discontinuous, but (compared with the historical evidence we have for most periods) extremely rich. What we shall do here is to trace how he grew to his full stature as the guide of his nation, until the final battle for the independent existence of the Athenian state.

The fall of Olynthus, and the destruction of the flourishing towns on the Chalcidic peninsula, which belonged to the Olynthian alliance, compelled Athens to make peace with Philip of Macedon. The treaty was signed in 346, and even Demosthenes supported the wish for peace wholeheartedly. But he opposed the acceptance of Philip's terms, because they handed over central Greece defenceless to the enemy, and tightened the encircling ring around Athens. However, he could not prevent peace from being signed on these terms. In his speech *On the Peace* he was compelled to advise the Athenians most strongly not to offer armed resistance after Philip had occupied Phocis and Thermopylae, which were essential bases for commanding central Greece. Like his earliest orations in the period before the fight against Philip became his lifework, this speech shows what a realistic politician he was: he did not strive for impossibilities, and he dared to oppose the rule of irrational emotion in politics. No one attacks his enemy at the enemy's strongest point. These highly practical speeches show an aspect of Demosthenes which is essential for any clear judgment of his worth. Here, as elsewhere, he is essentially a teacher. He does not simply want to convince the masses, and overpower them with oratory. He compels them to move onto a higher plane, and, after leading them up step by step, to judge the facts for themselves. A good example of this is the speech *For the Megalopolitans*, with its discussion of the policy of the balance of power, as applied to the case under discussion. The speeches *On the Symmories*, and *For the Liberty of the Rhodians* are classical examples of his steadily increasing ability to quell and dominate loud-mouthed jingoistic emotions. They reveal with perfect clarity Demosthenes' conception of politics as a wholly objective art; and his speech after the unfavourable peace of 346 shows that his struggle with Philip did nothing to change his attitude.

The first *Philippics* and the three speeches on Olynthus, full of wise counsels, confirm the view that he was now a statesman who saw far into the future, and planned for it, who knew when it was right to hold fast a decision once made, and who knew how much depends on favourable chances in this world ruled by tyché. His acts always show that he knows how much depends on chance: that is the explanation of his remarkable reserve after the peace of 346. Neither his critics nor his more emotional supporters have realized this, even yet. They both think that, when his strictly logical reasoning makes him change his attitude to suit circumstances, they have detected vacillation and weakness of character.

But even when Demosthenes was delivering his speech *On the Peace* he knew what he wanted. His eye was on the target. He never believed in the permanence of the peace, which was only a tool to dominate Athens; and he chose to allow its practical usefulness to Philip to be defended by politicians who shut their eyes to the facts because their will to resist was broken (like Aeschines) or who were (like Isocrates) ready to go further, to make a virtue of necessity, and to proclaim Philip as the Führer of all Greece. It is impossible to understand Isocrates' peculiar position in the spiritual war against the threat of Macedonian domination, without remembering how he gradually became the chief herald of Greek political unity. Greece was incapable of achieving unity by dissolving the independent city-states into a single nation-state, even if the several states were as weak as was then the case. Greek unity could come only from outside. Nothing could unite the Hellenes into a nation, except the fight against a common enemy. But why did Isocrates think the enemy was Persia, whose attack a hundred and fifty years earlier had made the Greeks forget their quarrels, and not Macedonia, which was the really imminent danger of the moment? The only real reason is the force of inertia. Isocrates was not blessed with a flow of original ideas, and he had been preaching the crusade against Persia for many, many years. But his idea of evading the Macedonian danger by making Philip—enemy of the liberty of Athens and of all Greece—the predestined leader of the national war against Persia, was an unforgivable political blunder. It handed over Greece to her enemy with her hands tied. It elevated Philip to a position he was only too glad to assume, because it would do away with the moral objections some of the Greeks might have to his plans for dominating them. From this altitude, Isocrates could cry 'warmonger' against everyone who was reluctant to accept the encroachments of Macedonian power; and the pro-Macedonians found it easy to make systematic propaganda out of Isocrates' Panhellenic slogan.

We must always remember the enormous part played by political warfare as preparation for Philip's military attacks on the Greeks. Of course, his policy was always to disguise it as self-defence. The actual military decision was meant to come as suddenly as possible, and finish everything with one stroke. The democracies, unprepared for war, were to have no time to improvise a stronger armament. Therefore, the work of undermining their strength and morale by agitation was long and well organized. Philip was sharp-sighted enough to see that a nation like the

Greeks might very well allow itself to be conquered: for culture and liberty always entail disunity on the solution of vital questions. The masses were too short-sighted to look ahead to the correct answer. Demosthenes says a great deal about pro-Macedonian agitation in all the Greek cities. This systematic propaganda was the really new and subtle thing in Philip's military technique. Its outcome usually was that one of the quarrelling parties called in Philip to make peace. When we see how carefully Demosthenes chooses his point of attack in his speeches, we must realize that the main problem for him was this propaganda within Athens, cleverly and energetically carried on by his opponent in such a way as to twist all the threads and blur all the issues. Demosthenes' task was to convince not a small cabinet, but an apathetic and misguided people, whom blind or false leaders were trying to drug into insensibility with the soporific belief that it depended solely upon their own honest love of peace whether or not they would have to fight for their liberty and their life.

Demosthenes was not the sort of man to shrink from this new battle within his own lines. He now struck boldly out against the pundits of pacifism; and resumed his old efforts to break down first of all the isolationism of Athens. Philip had disguised himself as the leader who would unify Greece. Demosthenes set out to unify the Greeks *against* Philip, and to summon them to defend their national independence. The speeches he made during the peace are a series of urgent efforts to set up his own Panhellenism against that of Isocrates, and to organize it as a real political force. After the battle for the soul of Athens, he started to fight the battle for the soul of Hellas. The only way for Athens to escape being encircled, he cried, was to draw Philip's Greek allies away from him, and to step to the head of all the Greek states. That and no less is Demosthenes' ideal. In the second *Philippic* he himself describes his efforts to detach the Peloponnesian states from Philip. At first he was unsuccessful. They might have been won over to the Athenian side when they came and asked for an alliance. That was years before the struggle against Philip had grown so fierce: Demosthenes had openly supported the policy of gaining allies wherever possible, and advised the people not to repel all the other Peloponnesian states in order to maintain the almost worthless alliance with Sparta—which was the only reason for doing so. Now, Athens had thrown them all into Philip's welcoming arms. Even Thebes, which would have been a weightier ally than Sparta, had been driven close to Philip by the Spartan and Athenian support of her enemies, the Phocians—closer even than her own interests dictated. As he says later, Demosthenes always thought it was poor policy to support the Phocians simply out of dislike for Thebes. Now the Phocian war had given Philip the opportunity to intervene in the politics of central Greece. The Phocians were crushed; and Athens could not, for many years, resume her friendship with Thebes. It looked like the labour of Sisyphus to build up a Panhellenic front against Philip out of so many Greeks divided by such enmities. And yet, after years of effort, Demosthenes did it. His growth into the champion of Greek liberty is all the more astounding in that the Panhellenic ideal, even after it was proclaimed in rhetoric, sounded like a fairy tale. The man who carried this through was the same Demosthenes who, in his first speech on foreign policy, laid down the axiom, 'The interests of Athens are for me the basis of every decision on foreign policy'. Then he had been a politician of the school of that clear-headed and strong-willed imperialist Callistratus. Now, by the time he had delivered the third *Philippic*, he had become a Panhellenic statesman. He thought it was Athens' greatest task to take over the leadership of the Greeks against Philip, mindful of the great national tradition of her previous policy. His success in uniting most of the Greeks under this banner was described even by classical historians as an achievement of the highest statesmanship.

In those great speeches, ***On the Chersonese*** and the third ***Philippic***, delivered shortly before the war began, Demosthenes grapples with the forces of doubt and despair, and reveals himself once again as a popular leader—just as he had been in the earlier ***Philippics***, delivered before the peace of 346. But now the whole scene has changed. Then he was a solitary warrior, fighting for his own hand. Now he is the leading spirit of a movement which is sweeping all Greece. Then he was trying to arouse the Athenians. Now he is calling to all the Greeks to throw off their lethargy and fight for their lives. Philip's power spreads with overwhelming speed, while they stand inactive as if in a storm or some natural catastrophe which men only watch passively, feeling absolutely helpless, and hoping that the approaching hail will strike their neighbour's house instead of their own. It is the task of the true leader to free the people's will from this crippling passivity and to save it from its evil counsellors, who are glad to betray it to the enemy, and serve the interests of Philip alone. The public likes listening to them, because they make no demands on it. Demosthenes counts up the cities which Philip's fifth column has already handed over to him. Olynthus, Eretria, and Oreus now admit, 'If we had known this before, we should not have fallen. Now, it is too late'. The ship must be saved while it is sound. When the waves have overpowered it, all effort is useless. The Athenians themselves must *act*. Even if everyone else gives way, they must fight for freedom. They must provide money, ships, and men, and by their self-sacrifice carry the other Greeks along with them. The petty greed of the masses and the corruption of the professional politicians must and shall give ways to the heroic spirit of Greece, which once struck down the Persian invader.

Many years before, Demosthenes had raised the question, which this comparison drives home again, whether the modern Athenians were not a degenerate race, unworthy to be named in the same breath as their great ancestors. But he was not a historian or an ethnologist, interested solely in facts. Here as elsewhere he was, naturally and necessarily, a *teacher*, conscious of the educational duty he had to perform. He did not believe that the Athenian character was degenerating, although most of the symptoms looked unfavourable. He could never have borne to do what Plato did—to turn his back on the Athenian state, and close the door on it, as on a patient dying of an incurable disease. Yet its conduct had become mean and petty. Surely its spirit must be petty too? How could it rise to finer thoughts and higher daring? When Isocrates com-

pared the present and the past, he came to only one conclusion—that the past was dead for ever. But Demosthenes as an active statesman could not take that view, so long as a single wall of his fortress still stood and could still be defended. He simply used the early greatness of Athens as a spur to get every ounce of strength out of his contemporaries. But when he compared past and present, he did not merely conclude that the Athenians of his own day *ought to* rival their ancestors. He thought that they *must*. However broad and deep the gulf that separated today and yesterday, Athens could not break away from her history without abandoning her own self. The greater the history of a people, the more surely it becomes their destiny in their decline, and the more tragic is their inability to escape their obligations even if it is impossible to fulfil them. Of course Demosthenes did not deceive himself purposely, and irresponsibly lead the Athenians into a perilous venture. Yet we must ask ourselves whether the urgency of the moment, which he saw better than any other politician, really allowed him or anyone to practise that type of politics which has been called 'the art of the possible'. He was much more of a practical politician than most modern historians have realized. But there must have been a very earnest debate in his soul between the practical politician and the idealistic statesman concerned with justice and moral obligation, on the fundamental question whether it was right to risk the whole existence of Athens and to ask her, with her limited strength, to do the impossible. When he did ask her to give so much, he was not making a wild romantic plea for a forlorn hope. He knew very well that a nation, no less than an individual, can make enormous and unimaginable efforts in a crisis of mortal danger; and that the extent of its effort depends on how far it is aware of its danger, and how much it really wishes to live. This is a mystery of nature which not even the wisest statesman can prognosticate. It is easy enough after the event to say that the real statesmen were those who treated this problem as one of simple arithmetic, and found it perfectly easy to refuse a gamble which they were not impelled to undertake by faith in their country, belief in its powers, and realization of the inevitability of fate. At that critical moment it was Demosthenes who gave urgent and splendid expression to the heroism of the city-state ideal. Look at the face of his statue, anxious, meditative, and furrowed with care. It is easy to see that he was not born to be a stalwart like Diomede or a paladin like Achilles; he was a man of his age. Surely that makes his fight all the more noble, because he made greater demands on his more sensitive nature and more subtle individuality.

Demosthenes could not refuse the challenge. He accepted it, fully aware of all it would mean. Thucydides had said that the Athenians could face danger only if they understood it, whereas others often rushed into dangers they did not comprehend. Demosthenes followed that principle. He warned the Athenians that the war would not be like the Peloponnesian war, in which Athens confined herself to admitting the invading enemy to Attica, and watching him from behind the walls. The technique of war had improved since then. Athens would waste her effort if she waited till the enemy crossed her frontiers. That is one of the main reasons why Demosthenes refused to 'wait and see'. He appealed not only to the Greeks but to the Persians; and since, directly after conquering Greece, the Macedonians went straight on to overthrow the Persian empire, the Persian indifference to the fate of Greece was crass blindness. Demosthenes thought his statesmanlike reasoning would be strong enough to make the Persian king realize what was in store for Persia if Philip beat the Greeks. Perhaps it might have been, if he had visited Asia in person. But his envoys were unable to break down the Persian inertia.

Another of the problems which Demosthenes had to face was the social problem. Throughout his career, the gulf between rich and poor had been widening. He understood quite clearly that this division must not be allowed to interfere with the war for survival, for if it did, it would seriously diminish the efforts which could be made by every section of society. The fourth *Philippic* is his endeavour to bridge the gap, at least by finding some compromise to neutralize some of the ill-feeling that existed. It asks for sacrifices from both sides. It shows how closely the solution of the social question depends on the people's will to defend itself against the aggressor. Perhaps the best evidence of Demosthenes' success is the self-sacrificing spirit which all the Athenians showed in the subsequent war.

The conflict went against the united Greeks. After the battle of Chaeronea in 338 the independence of the Greek city-states was destroyed. Even when they joined in an alliance to fight the last fight for liberty, the old states were unable to resist the organized military power of the king of Macedon. Their history now merged with that of the Macedonian empire, founded by Alexander on the ruins of the Persian dominion, by a fierce march of conquest through Asia after the sudden and violent death of Philip. A new and undreamt-of future opened up to Greek colonization, Greek science, and Greek commerce; and remained open even after Alexander's early death, when the empire broke up into the large monarchies of the Diadochoi, the Successors. But the old Greece was politically dead. Isocrates' dream of uniting all the Greeks under Macedonian leadership in a national war against the hereditary foe, Persia, actually came true. Death spared him the grief of realizing that the victory of a nation which had lost its independence, over an imaginary enemy, did not really mean an improvement in national morale; and that union imposed from without does not solve political disunity. During Alexander's expedition every true Greek would have far preferred to hear of the death of the new Achilles, than to pray to him, by supreme command, like a god. It is tragic to read how feverishly all the Greek patriots waited for that news to come through, how often they were disappointed, and how they raised premature revolts on false information. The Macedonian troops thrust down their rebellions in blood; and Demosthenes, believing that he and the Greeks had nothing left to hope for, found liberty in death.

But what would have happened if the Greeks had really succeeded in throwing off the Macedonian chains after Alexander's death? Even if they had won, they had no political future, either within or without foreign domination. The historical life of the city-state had come to an end, and no new artificial organization could replace it. It would be a mistake to judge its development by the standard of the modern nation-state. The fact is that the Greeks were unable to develop the feeling of nationhood, in the *political* sense, which would have enabled them to build up a nation-state—although in other senses they had plenty of national consciousness. In his *Politics* Aristotle declares that if the Greeks were united they could rule the world. But that idea entered the Greek mind only as an abstract philosophical problem. Once, and once only after the Persian wars, in Demosthenes' final struggle for independence, did Greek national feeling rise up and take real political action, in common resistance to a foreign enemy. In that moment, when it was gathering its failing strength for the last time to defend its life and its ideal, the city-state was immortalized in the speeches of Demosthenes. The much admired and much abused power of political oratory, which is inseparable from the ideal it is put to uphold, rose once again in those speeches to the highest significance and value; and then fell away into nothing. Its last great fight was Demosthenes' wonderful speech *On the Crown*. That oration is not concerned with practical politics, but with the judgment of history on the personal character of the man who had led Athens throughout the critical years. It is wonderful to see Demosthenes still fighting for his ideals, almost with his last breath. It would be wrong to think of the speech as an effort to have the last word after the finger of history had written, and moved on. But his old enemies had crept out of their ratholes and had tried to pass a final verdict on him in the name of history. He was forced to rise for the last time, and tell the Athenian people what he had tried to do, from the very outset, and what he had done. The struggle which we have witnessed in reading the *Philippics*—that heavy past, that growing danger, those hard decisions—all comes before us now once more as history, complete with its fateful end. Demosthenes is a tragic figure as he defends his own career; but he exhorts the Athenians not to wish that they had made any other decision except that which their history demanded of them. The glory of Athens shines forth once more in his words, and ends in a music which, for all its bitterness, is harmonious.

Albin Lesky   (essay date 1963)

SOURCE: "The Flowering of the Greek City State: The Art of Rhetoric," in *A History of Greek Literature*, translated by James Willis and Cornelis de Heer, second edition, Thomas Y. Crowell Company, 1966, pp. 582-615.

[*An Austrian classicist and educator, Lesky is the author of numerous works on ancient Greek literature. His* Geschichte der Griechischen Literatur (*second edition, 1963; A* History of Greek Literature, *1966) is considered an authoritative text. In the following excerpt from that work, he surveys Demosthenes's life and times and assesses his rhetorical art.*]

In the same way in which the Greeks meant Homer when speaking of 'the poet', so Demosthenes was simply 'the orator' for later antiquity. At that time his fame had been an established fact for a long time, and it remained associated with his name until in this century modern scholarship made him a controversial problem. As a result of the

---

Plutarch on the presentation of Demosthenes's speeches (c. 105-15):

The action which [Demosthenes] used himself was wonderfully pleasing to the common people, but by well-educated people, as, for example, by Demetrius, the Phalerian, it was looked upon as mean, humiliating, and unmanly. And Hermippus says of Æsion, that, being asked his opinion concerning the ancient orators, and those of his own time, he answered that it was admirable to see with what composure and in what high style they addressed themselves to the people; but that the orations of Demosthenes, when they are read, certainly appear to be superior in point of construction, and more effective. His written speeches, beyond all question, are characterised by austere tone and by their severity. In his extempore retorts and rejoinders, he allowed himself the use of jest and mockery. When Demades said, "Demosthenes teach me! So might the sow teach Minerva!" he replied, "Was it this Minerva, that was lately found playing the harlot in Collytus?" When a thief, who had the nickname of the Brazen, was attempting to upbraid him for sitting up late, and writing by candle-light, "I know very well," said he, "that you had rather have all lights out; and wonder not, O ye men of Athens, at the many robberies which are committed, since we have thieves of brass and walls of clay."

Plutarch, in his "Demosthenes", in The Lives of the Noble Grecians and Romans, *translated by John Dryden, 1683-86.*

---

fame which Demosthenes enjoyed in antiquity, there are fairly abundant sources available for him. Apart from Ps.-Plutarch's *Vitae or.* and the two treatises of Dionysius of Halicarnassus (Περι τησ Δημοσθενουσ λεξεωσ and Επιστολησ προσ Αμμαιον) there is Plutarch's biography of Demosthenes which also contains polemical features; another of the same kind by the orator Libanius, with hypotheses to the individual speeches; one by Zosimus; an anonymous one; and finally three articles in Suidas. Since most of Demosthenes' speeches provided a great deal of biographical information, they are of great importance, like the speeches of his opponents Aeschines, Hyperides and Dinarchus, for our knowledge of his life.

Demosthenes, the son of Demosthenes of the deme Paeania, born in Athens in 384, belonged, like Isocrates and the metic Lysias, to the class of the well-to-do entrepreneurs. His father had a weapon-workshop and also possessed other property. His mother Cleobule is supposed to have had Scythian blood, which caused his opponents (Dinarchus, *Against Dem.* 15. cf. Aeschines, 3. 172) to turn him derisively into a Scythian. Still it may be fairly asked if the sombre passion which, together with a very acute feeling for form, moulded him into the greatest orator of antiquity, should not be understood as a maternal legacy.

When the boy was 7 years old he lost his father. The three guardians, Aphobus, Demophon and Therippides, proved

to be untrustworthy trustees of the property, and immediately upon reaching manhood Demosthenes was involved in important lawsuits to save at least something of his previous wealth. So at an early stage he had to test in earnest what he had learned from Isaeus, whom tradition mentions as his teacher. Already during his training he gave evidence of the rigour of his will-power which later ensured his influence over the masses, when he successfully struggled with several physical handicaps. He formed his mind with the same care. According to Cicero [in his *Brutus*] he read and even heard Plato. Thucydides had a particularly strong influence on him and the picture of Athenian greatness which he found there remained a controlling influence in his life; Plutarch's story of how he became interested in rhetoric (*Dem.* 5) sounds like an anecdote; his pedagogue smuggled him into the session of the law-court at which Callimachus defended himself brilliantly against the accusation that the loss of the frontier place Oropus was his fault, and there the young Demosthenes received the decisive impression of the power of speech. The veracity of the story cannot be proved, but it should not be rejected out of hand.

Demosthenes' speech of indictment in the legal battle he had to wage against his dishonest guardians, *Against Aphobus*, and his answer to the latter's defence, have been preserved. A third speech, *Against Aphobus*, in which Demosthenes defended the witness against the accusation of perjury, was often suspected, but increasingly serious grounds for its authenticity have been produced. At first Demosthenes had some success in his action, which lasted for years and was held up for various reasons, such as his service as an ephebe. But Onetor, the brother of Aphobus' divorced wife, disputed this success by laying hands on a piece of land which Demosthenes wanted to mortgage. And so the battle was carried on, of which two speeches *Against Onetor* provide us with evidence. We do not know its result but suspect that Demosthenes incurred heavy losses.

The art which he had practised for his own ends was now put at the disposal of others against payment. He is supposed to have given classes in rhetoric as well, but there is nothing to tell of the extent of this activity; he certainly did not run a school.

Demosthenes' entry into Athenian politics is announced by four of his speeches, three of them in lawsuits concerning domestic politics (*Against Androtion, Against Timocrates, Against Leptines*), while the speech *On the Symmories* was his first policy speech. It is important that we can date the first of the speeches mentioned with sufficient confidence at 355/354. At the time the War of the Allies (357-355) and with it the dream of the restoration of Athenian naval power had just come to its conclusion. The prevailing mood was one of resignation, as reflected in the peace oration of the ageing Isocrates. But Demosthenes was of a different opinion; for him the failure of the naval alliance could not mean the end of a glowing faith, nourished by tradition, in the greatness of Athens. In those years an opposition had formed which wanted to make a clean sweep of the leaders of the régime that had failed, in order to raise up Athens again economically through prudent limitation to what was feasible and with a careful maintenance of peace. The faction which advocated this sober economic programme, which is also reflected in Xenophon's *Poroe*, was headed by Eubulus, who since 354 had held a key-position as the administrator of the fund for theatre moneys (theoricon). Recent research has brought to light the important information that Demosthenes, though his later path inevitably deviated from Eubulus', took his first steps in politics as the latter's follower.

The speech *Against Androtion* is directed against the pupil of Isocrates who is known as the complier of an *Atthis* which is often referred to and who played a political role in the circles against which the representatives of the new political trend had declared war. Formally it deals with an indictment for illegal motion . . . ; Androtion had moved the crowning of the council, although they had not completed the construction of new ships to the number prescribed. Its actual aim, however, was the political elimination of Androtion, who had also made himself unpopular through the collection of taxes. The speech *Against Timocrates* points in the same direction. It attacks a law which had helped state debtors, amongst them Androtion, to escape impending imprisonment for debt. An extensive section of the *Timocratea* (160-168 and 172-186) has been lifted almost verbally from the speech *Against Androtion* (47-56 and 65-78), a circumstance which strongly stresses the similar direction of the attack just indicated. Occasionally doublets of this kind are also found elsewhere in Demosthenes.

While the two speeches just mentioned were written for personally insignificant speakers who were to lead the way for the attack, Demosthenes himself is supposed by the tradition (Dion. *Ep. ad Amm.* I.4) to have spoken the speech *Against Leptines* as Ctesippus' attorney. The latter was a son of Chabrias' who fell in 357 off Chios as trierarch and who had been one of the greatest hopes for Athens' new rise. The speech opposed Leptines' motion to repeal all freedom from taxes . . . and to permit exceptions only for descendants of the tyrant-slayers. If Demosthenes really wrote it to be read by himself, the precise solemn tone, which stands in strong contrast with the vehemence of the later political speeches, deserves special attention.

Demosthenes' first political speech, *On the Symmories*, is of the same time as the three forensic speeches just discussed. The expression symmories means tax-fellowships which had to equip naval units. Demosthenes appeared before the popular assembly in order to increase the number of citizens liable to this duty from 1200 to 2000. The proposal for the increase in armament is connected with the Persian question in that it opposes all frivolous war-mongering against the old enemy with the consideration that at the time Athens did not command the resources for such an undertaking.

Conjointly with this oration there are two political speeches which each deal with a current problem of foreign policy. The speech *For the Megalopolites* of the year 352 throws a light on the unutterable confusion of Greek politics. While Thebes held its position of hegemony, it had taken under its protection the federal state of the Arcadi-

ans founded in 370 and Messene which gained its independence in 369 as a bastion against Sparta. But when Thebes was past its heyday and got into difficulties through its troubles with the Phocians, the position of the new Peloponnesian states with relation to Sparta became highly critical. At the time the Arcadians asked Athens for an alliance and although they were still tied to Sparta by treaty, Demosthenes favoured this request. We emphasized the confusion of the situation to make it understandable that a criticism of the correctness of this attitude is not easy. At any rate, according to Eubulus' interpretation, Athenian intervention in the Peloponnesus meant reembarking upon the adventure of power politics, and so the paths of the two politicians separated. In the speech *For the Liberty of the Rhodians*, which possibly dates from the same year 352, Demosthenes recommended support for the democrats whom the Carian despot Mausolus had ejected. Such a recommendation was neither easy nor promising, since the same democrats had allowed themselves to be persuaded by Mausolus to defect from Athens and so bore a share of the guilt in the failure of the second naval league.

Against Aristocrates, though delivered before the lawcourt, is also one of the speeches on foreign politics. Demosthenes wrote it for Euthycles of Thria, with whom he had been trierarch at the Hellespont. The speech deals with conditions in the Thracian region, which was so important for Athens. At the time—the speech was delivered in 352 or 351—Philip had already undertaken his first advance into Thrace, but as yet the danger which Philip meant to Athens is not emphasized. The indictment for illegality is directed against the motion of Aristocrates for a vote of special protection for the person of Charidemus, the brother-in-law and minister of the Thracian king Cersobleptes; whoever killed him was to be outlawed. In opposition to the group for whom Aristocrates spoke, Demosthenes favoured support for the Thracian joint ruler Amadocus, Cersobleptes' brother.

Very soon after this speech, Philip of Macedon decisively intervened in Thracian affairs. His intervention forced the Thracian kings to ally themselves to him by treaty and brought him before the walls of Heraeum Tichus north of the Propontis and in dangerous proximity to Byzantium. At the time the Athenians had been in a state of war with Philip for several years; he had provided the cause for this in the year 357 by occupying Amphipolis and there were enough other occurrences which indicated who was going to make history in the future. Pydna had been occupied by Philip, Potidaea destroyed; in the summer of 354 he took the Greek city of Methone on the Gulf of Therme opposite Chalcidice; then the 'sacred war' against the Phocians about the hegemony in the Delphian amphictyony, which divided all Greece in two camps, gave him an opportunity to intervene and to find a footing in Thessaly in 352. But beforehand he had had to accept two defeats at the hands of the Phocian Onomarchus, and in the summer of 352 he had been forced to retire by a demonstration of Greek power at Thermopylae. And finally Macedon did not possess a fleet which could constitute a real danger. So far there had been other worries to occupy the Athenians, but the siege of Heraeum Tichus, the attempt on the

Black Sea approaches, was the storm-signal. In the *Third Olynthiac Speech* Demosthenes reminds the Athenians of the alarm and activity which the report of Philip's undertaking had evoked in the city, though this had soon abated again. It must also have been the moment of understanding for himself, for from now on we see his political leadership directed only against one single country and enemy: Macedon and Philip.

The earliest evidence of this understanding and its consequences is the *First Philippic*, a vigorous call to the Athenian citizenry, which links criticism of past failures with cheering encouragement. He makes a concrete proposal for equipping two battle-groups in order to harass Philip incessantly on land and to be able to attack him with a naval force in his territory. Demosthenes also gave a detailed plan for the procurement of the means for these forces, but in our text we read only the key-word 'indication of financial measures', valuable evidence that the speeches, which were actually delivered, were meant to exert their influence also as pamphlets in which some details had been altered by the author.

The dating of the speech poses a difficult problem. Dionysius (*Ep. ad Amm.* 4) indicates the archontic year of 352/1. The time immediately after the attack on Heraeum Tichus and the relief caused by Philip's illness would provide an excellent background to the speech. But it mentions an attempt by Philip against Olynthus (17), and this can hardly refer to any other but the one of 349. On this basis Eduard Schwartz [*Festschr. F. Th. Mommsen*, 1893] established the date in this year and this has found general acceptance.

Wilamowitz and others wanted to deny that the speech *On the Reorganisation* was by Demosthenes, taking into account the correspondence of numerous passages with other speeches, but recently there has been a tendency to admit it as genuine. The tenor of the speech, which demands financial reforms and calls for exertion in the interest of the city, indicates the year 350.

An illness had deprived Philip of success before Heraeum Tichus; for Athens it only meant a pause for breath. The next Macedonian thrust was aimed at the Greek cities in Chalcidice, especially Olynthus. In the year 348 the city fell and was completely destroyed; Chalcidice was in Philip's hands. At the last minute Athens had concluded an alliance with the Chalcidians and sent auxiliary forces, but everything came too late. Demosthenes' three *Olynthiac Speeches* occurred in the period of the impending catastrophe, i. e. between the spring of 349 and the early part of 348. It is no longer possible to connect them in detail with concrete causes and especially in this case it is difficult to decide what part belongs to the spoken oration and what was originally political publication. The first of the speeches generally continues the tone and suggestions of the *First Philippic*. This applies also to the second which attacks the habits of making Philip into a bogyman in order to overawe the people; he argues that what is required is rather the strengthening of their inner attitude. Philip's power is shown to be a structure erected on falsehood and deceit; this moral fervour is nourished by the ancient Greek conviction that hybris cannot escape its 'dike'.

The *Third Olynthiac* goes particularly far; though taking the existing laws into consideration, it moots the subject of utilizing the theoric fund for munitions. What a *crimen laesae maiestatis*—Demades called the theoric fund the glue of democracy (Plut. *Plat. Quaest.* 1011 b)—any attempt on these moneys was considered is demonstrated by the reaction to a motion of Apollodorus, (Ps.- Dem. *Against Neaera* 3-5).

The speech *Against Midias* also falls in the period of the battle of Olynthus. Midias, one of the wealthiest Athenians, had long pursued Demosthenes with his enmity until, at a festival of Dionysus, this unpredictable bully attacked the orator openly. Demosthenes reacted immediately with a provisional complaint . . . , but probably did not proceed to sue him, powerful as he was. Since Midias belonged to Eubulus' party which Demosthenes was opposing more and more vigorously with his policy of action, this affair, which originally was entirely a private matter, now also acquired political colouring.

Philip's successes had created a situation in which only a united Greece could have any chance of effective action. But this was still a very remote goal, and so Demosthenes joined the Athenian embassy which went to Pella in 346 for negotiations with Philip. In the same year the peace of Philocrates was concluded which forced the Athenians to abandon the Phocians and permitted Philip to find a firm footing in central Greece. It was evident that this situation would produce a host of new conflicts, but also that at the time Athens had no prospect of success and so Demosthenes advocated the preservation of peace in his speech *On the Peace*. It was the time in which Isocrates in his *Philip* called on the Macedonian to be the leader of Greece.

In the following years of a hollow truce Demosthenes succeeded in gaining control of Athenian politics in an increasing degree. In foreign affairs it was necessary to win allies in order to form the most united possible Greek front against Philip; at home the pro-Macedonian party had to be suppressed. The *Second Philippic* of the year 344 warns against Philip, deals with Argos and Messene, which complain about Athens's pro-Spartan policy, and in its final section sharply attacks Aeschines. Demosthenes had had the latter indicted for bribery and fraud soon after the return of the embassy of 346. But Timarchus was an unfortunate choice as the formal accuser and Aeschines managed to make him impossible with a morals action of which his speech has been preserved. Not until 343 did matters come to a head between Aeschines and Demosthenes, who this time had to conduct his own prosecution. The two speeches *On the Fraudulent Embassy* have been preserved, the one by Demosthenes in a revised form meant for publication; consequently Aeschines' defence does not correspond in individual points with the accusation preserved. Aeschines was acquitted with a slight majority. The party of the pro-Macedonians lost ground, but Hyperides managed to have Philocrates sentenced to death, whereupon he fled abroad.

To this period (342) belongs the speech *On Halonnesus*, which defends Athens' title to the little island south of Lemnos. In antiquity, however, some authors such as Libanius in his *Hypotheses* thought that Hegesippus of Suni-um rather than Demosthenes was the writer.

When in 342 Philip had firmly incorporated Thrace in his realm and the direction of his thrust to the sea approaches began again to become distinct, tension, and with it Demosthenes' activity, rose to its highest pitch. Three speeches of the year 341 bear this out. In the one *On the Affairs in the Chersonese* he adopts a protective attitude against Philip's complaints about Diopithes, the mercenary commander whose operations from this territory had become an annoyance to Philip. Demosthenes reached the climax in his career as a political orator with the *Third Philippic*. It blazes with the passion which Eratosthenes compares with the emotion of one possessed by Bacchus (Plut. *Dem.* 9). He stresses that the need of the moment is to speed up the manufacture of munitions and to work towards the union of all Greeks against Philip; nothing else counts more than this. The speech is preserved both in a shorter and a longer form. It is difficult to determine whether Demosthenes wrote them both or the second has been interpolated. The authenticity of the *Fourth Philippic* used to be disputed, but Alfred Körte restored it to Demosthenes. The speech strongly stresses that attempts were being made to reach agreement in domestic politics; in public opposition to Isocrates, Demosthenes (32-34) underlines the hope of collaboration with Persia more strongly than elsewhere.

These years were the climax of Demosthenes' career. Philip's attacks on Perinthus and Byzantium were unsuccessful, but under the impression of this danger the greater part of the Greek states united in one league under Athens's leadership. Thebes, which still held aloof, did not join until directly before the decision. At home the new law of the symmories demonstrated an increased readiness to sacrifice self-interest. Twice, in the years 340 and 339, the people, who now recognized Demosthenes as their political leader, honoured him with a golden wreath.

Since 340 Athens had again been in open warfare with Philip. Battles in the north of his realm caused a delay of the decision, which fell eventually in the year 338 at Chaeronea. It meant the end of Greek freedom, but at the same time the beginning of a new era, for the Philip who in the very year of Chaeronea united the Greek states except Sparta under one 'general peace' and in one alliance under his leadership, proved himself to be one of the few men in history who can think of peace after winning a war.

The Athenians did not make Demosthenes suffer for the defeat; he was commissioned to deliver the funeral oration for the fallen. The preserved *Epitaphios* is quite remote both in style and emotion from the assembly speeches, but the difference of the situation and the genre should be borne in mind. Those who defend its authenticity are probably right. Years later Demosthenes delivered the real and lofty *Epitaphios* to Athens' fight for freedom under unusual conditions. In 336 Ctesiphon moved his solemn crowning in the theatre during the Great Dionysia for his merits in improving the walls and for his sacrifices of personal property in the service of the state. Aeschines objected with a complaint of illegality, but the trial was postponed and the case was not tried until 330. Aeschines' for-

mal objection merely offered a pretext to fight once more, in a way typically Greek and typically Athenian, the great battle of the years before Chaeronea whose outcome had long ago been decided by history, this time on the field of rhetoric. We possess both speeches, Aeschines' *Against Ctesiphon* and Demosthenes' *On the Crown* in which he elaborated his defence of Ctesiphon into a tremendous retrospect of the ends aimed at and a justification of the course taken at the time. Demosthenes was victorious, Aeschines did not even obtain a fifth of the votes and had to leave Athens.

It is not difficult to imagine that Demosthenes shared the hope of Athens which blazed up at Philip's death (336), but the speech *On the Treaties with Alexander* handed down under his name, which opposes the Macedonians, is not his.

A dark shadow fell over his old age when he became involved in the Harpalus affair. This faithless treasurer had deposited in Athens some money with which he had defected from Alexander and had passed part of it on to Athenian politicians. Demosthenes was one of them; we do not know the motives which made him accept the money. The court imposed (324) a fine of fifty talents on him; he avoided imprisonment for debt by fleeing to Troezen. When Athens rose together with Argos and Corinth at the death of Alexander, he returned home in triumph. But the rebels' dream of freedom soon ended with the defeat of the fleet at Amorgos and of the army at Crannon. Again Demosthenes had to flee; in the late autumn of 322 he committed suicide with poison on the island of Calauria when he saw himself surrounded by Antipater's myrmidons.

Demosthenes' work was surveyed in connection with his life and political activity. It has become clear that the collection of sixty-one speeches is interspersed with an abundance of spurious material. Among the latter is also the *Eroticus* (61), a letter which praises a beautiful boy. Another six letters have been preserved, all of which, except the fifth, have his exile as a background. For the second and the third the question of authenticity may be considered, but is by no means settled. On the other hand many of the fifty-six prefaces to political speeches are genuine, for several of them reappear in the surviving speeches. It may be supposed that a collection of Demosthenes' works was later enriched with imitations.

The changes to which the image of Demosthenes was subject in the course of time form in themselves a chapter of history. Cardinal Bessarion published in 1470 the *First Olynthiac Speech* in Latin in order to incite enthusiasm for the struggle against the Turks; Friedrich Jacob translated Demosthenes in the days of Napoleon; time and again attempts were made to kindle new flames with the glow of his ardour. The latest member in this series is Clemenceau's *Démosthène* [1924] of the period after the first world war. During the same war appeared Engelbert Drerup's book *Aus einem alten Advokatenrepublik* [1916] which represents an extreme opposite viewpoint. Since our picture of Greek history has tremendously changed through Droysen's discovery of the Hellenistic era, judgment of Demosthenes' political activity has been made from a different aspect. The Greeks' last struggle for freedom became a period without interest compared with the world-wide influence which Alexander's deeds opened up for the Hellenes, and Demosthenes withdrew in the shadows of those who welcomed Philip as the bringer of a new development. He necessarily fared badly by such a judgment passed *ex eventu* and he had to pay heavily for the classical halo which he still wears in Arnold Schäfer's great work. At present the pendulum may have stopped swinging between the two extremes and the time may be ripe for a formulation of questions which result from another point of view. We have some comprehension of the interplay of the forces which prepared for the end of the polis of the classical era and which blazed a trail for new developments and we can evaluate what was lost and what gained. As for Demosthenes, our questions are whether his life and struggles are of a truly tragic character or were a mere shadow-play. Our answer will depend on two further questions: did the issues for which he fought belong to the rank of great historical reality or were they illusions? did he fight his battle for these issues for the sake of a conviction or did he use legal quibbles for personal renown and gain? These two questions answer themselves in the asking. And this means that Demosthenes, whose task it was to bear witness to the proud tradition of his polis in the very hour of its downfall, becomes a great tragic figure in the history of the Greek people.

The art of his rhetoric endures independent of the appreciation of his political activity. Especially in Britain, but in other European countries as well, he has long been esteemed and utilized as the unrivalled teacher of political eloquence. Earlier, in connection with Isocrates, we spoke of the dangers of rhetoric for Greek intellect and Greek art. Therefore it should be emphasized all the more strongly that in Demosthenes true passion and power of conviction pervade the perfected form to such an extent that his strongest speeches are inspired with real life. In the beginning of his rhetorical career Demosthenes still shows here and there that he is influenced by the example of the Isocratic period with its calculated balance and cool smoothness, but he soon acquires a personal style which draws even in the most elaborate sentence constructions on the actuality of situations and permeates them with the temperament of the speaker. The uniformity of Isocratic speech is contrasted in Demosthenes by an incomparably greater richness of variety, just as the broad sweep of the political speeches is in clear contrast with the simpler period construction of the forensic speeches. He is moderate in the use of figures of speech and sound; he avoids hiatus, though not with the same strictness as Isocrates, and in his choice of words he exerts the same discipline, although occasionally he does not shrink from using a strong expression. Already in antiquity it was noticed that the effect of Demosthenes' speeches depended largely on their rhythm. It is difficult to ascertain the laws of this rhythmical construction. Blass [F. Blass in *Att. Beredsamkeit*, 1893] discovered one important detail when he observed that Demosthenes avoids the sequence of more than two short syllables. The effect of Demosthenes' style rests largely on the moderate utilization, controlled by a very subtle sense of rhythm, of the freedom of word-order which gave to writers of Greek such an abundance of possibilities to create an effect. Like other masters of prose, Demosthenes devoted careful attention to the rhythmical structure of his sentence conclusions. The study of this technique of clause construction has not yet achieved any definite results and has lately stagnated somewhat.

George Kennedy   (essay date 1963)

SOURCE: "The Attic Orators," in *The Art of Persuasion in Greece*, Princeton University Press, 1963, pp. 125-263.

[*Kennedy is an American scholar who has written extensively on classical rhetoric. In the following essay, he charts Demosthenes's development as an orator, concluding that "he alone of Greek orators shaped, perhaps without much realizing it, Plato's belief in absolute goals and rejection of rhetorical relativism."*]

The antithesis of Isocrates as an educator is Plato, as an orator Demosthenes. This is true not only in the specific historical sense that Demosthenes' energies were directed against Macedon but in the attitude of the two orators toward speech and policy. To Isocrates oratory is a thing in itself; artistic creativity is his goal; he looks for what is literarily expedient. Demosthenes, though he begins as a rhetorician and logographer, subdues his art and constrains it to be his tool in the defense of his country. Once his political instincts are fully awakened they establish absolute standards: he can be inconsistent about all things except patriotism, and to that end his oratory is the single greatest means.

There is a very weak tradition (*Lives of the ten orators* 844b) that makes Demosthenes a pupil of Isocrates, and attempts have been made to point out specific influences of one on the other. But Demosthenes' whole concept of the function of the orator, of art, of style, and of politics is so essentially different that occasional verbal similarities need only mean that Demosthenes had read and occasionally picked up a phrase from Isocrates. [He] may have studied some kind of judicial handbook circulated in Isocrates' school, for he was to a great extent self-taught. When he was still a boy the oratory of Callistratus first roused in him a desire to be a great speaker (Plutarch, *Demosthenes* 5). He definitely learned something from Isaeus when preparing his prosecution of his guardians, and the story (Plutarch, *Demosthenes* 7) that his delivery was criticized and improved by the actor Satyrus may well be true. Although they have not always admired him, all critics, ancient and modern, have felt the uniqueness of Demosthenes: it is seen in his Periclean isolation, his disinterest in the gymnasium, his water-drinking among the wine bibbers, his autodidacticism, his ability to draw something from everyone.

In the oratorical career of Demosthenes certain speeches illustrate critical steps in his development. The following discussion will deal with them in an attempt to outline the most satisfactory critical approach to his rhetoric. Any greater discussion covering all the speeches would be out of proportion to this work.

Demosthenes' earliest speech, his prosecution of his guardian Aphobus, is a remarkable product, as much a piece of accounting as of rhetoric. Despite the attested influence of Isaeus, the character of the speech is much more open than is usual in Isaeus. The direct evidence is relevant and extensive: statement and substantiation, statement and substantiation, again and again. Argument from probability finds only a limited use (e. g. 55). There is no indulgence of love of speech, no unnecessary word. The shamelessness of Aphobus is shown repeatedly (e. g. 38), but there is no scurpility. Though the speech falls into the standard formal parts: prooemium 1-3 (with the usual attack on the intractability of the opponent, expression of inexperience—justified for once—and request for a fair hearing), narrative 4-6, proof 7-48 (with 47-8 as a recapitulation), refutation 49-59, and peroration 60-69 (with indirect recapitulation and effective pathos), the impression of the speech is entirely narrative, as though the orator were telling his story and proving every word. Except for the increase in pathos at the end the parts do not show the stylistic differences found in parts of other such speeches. Nothing is probably more reassuring and convincing to a jury than this candid technique. An orator can only use it if he has a very good case with many documents and witnesses and is himself the complete master of the material.

The second speech against Aphobus is a reply in the same trial to Aphobus' charge that Demosthenes' father was a public debtor. It is less successful, less thought out. Direct evidence was not procurable, for the attack had come unexpectedly, and Demosthenes apparently delivered the first part of the speech extempore. There is no formal narration, which is not unusual in "second" speeches; however, one is really needed here to explain the basis of the charge, and the orator fills up the void with a representation of facts from the first speech and a proportionally larger peroration, perhaps to be expected since this is the conclusion of his case. The speech is not a poor one. Demosthenes did what he could at the time, he does not allow himself to be led into any wild statements, and the impression of the case which the jury had from the first speech was doubtless confirmed.

The third speech against Aphobus was delivered some time later, after Aphobus had brought a suit of false witness against Phanus, who had testified for Demosthenes. It was necessary to discuss the earlier trial, and the nature of the attack meant that little direct evidence was available; thus, the use of argument from probability (e. g. 22 ff.) makes the speech seem more regular than the two earlier works, though at the end of the narration (10) the speaker makes a distinction between probabilities and argument from what seems just to all. The speech has great versatility not only in argument but also in style, for example in the liveliness of the imaginary debate between Demosthenes and Aphobus in 40-41. The speech ends abruptly, but perhaps the peroration was not published or has been lost.

Although Demosthenes continued to have difficulties with his guardians and soon afterward delivered the first and second speeches *Against Onetor*, it must have been the prosecution of Aphobus which gave him a limited fame as a writer of courtroom speeches. For the rest of his life he was a logographer; we cannot say with what frequency

since many of the works he wrote probably were not preserved or published. His clients seem to have been carefully chosen from among friends and equals: he was not the defender of the downtrodden, but of the affluent, of the creditor against the debtor. Birth was not important to him, as his defense of Phormio shows, but money was. Even when his clients claim poverty one finds it difficult to believe them. In the speech *Against Callicles* the client says that he has small means, but he does not care about the money (35) and has recently paid something over a thousand drachmae in fines (2). Of all the clients the most modest in circumstances was perhaps Euxitheus, who prosecutes Eubulides in the fifty-seventh oration. His opponents claimed that he was rich, but he denies this (52) and there are indications of poverty in the speech (25 and 31). If Euxitheus was indeed poor, it is tempting to see a political significance in Demosthenes' acceptance of the case, for the speech was delivered in the mid 340's during the great campaign against Philip, when Demosthenes wanted to arouse popular sentiment.

The surviving private orations of Demosthenes show him to be a business-like logographer. He can portray the character of a client with conviction, he can narrate with clarity and vigor, and he can construct a logical proof without an impression of slyness. He usually follows standard rhetorical structure and employs many of the commonplaces of prooemium, proof, and peroration. But for all Demosthenes' technical skill there is virtually no evidence in the private speeches of that point of view, seen in Lysias, Isaeus, and Isocrates, which regarded rhetoric as a joy in itself. Demosthenes accepted cases, it would seem, not to find occasions to prove his cleverness, but to gratify his friends and make money. He did not seek sensationalism, did not deal with adulterers and courtesans, did not introduce spectacular pathetic effects.

There is perhaps only one instance in which a charge of questionable practice could be brought against Demosthenes. In the thirty-sixth speech he ably defended the banker Phormio in a suit brought by Apollodorus for recovery of twenty talents. Phormio had been an employee of Apollodorus' father, and after the latter's death became the trustee of his estate. Releases were given for all claims, but after many years had passed Apollodorus again insisted that money was owed to him. Phormio, with Demosthenes' speech, won more than four-fifths of the jurors' votes and Apollodorus had to pay a fine. Soon afterward Apollodorus brought suit for false witness against a minor witness in Phormio's defense, one Stephanus. We have a speech (45) apparently written by Demosthenes on behalf of Apollodorus which contains a virulent attack on Phormio (71 ff.). The orator's change of clients has been much discussed. Was he simply available to the higher bidder without himself feeling any involvement in the cases? This would seem more probable in the case of other orators than Demosthenes, who apparently picked his clients with care. Aeschines (*On the embassy* 328) criticizes Demosthenes for showing the speech for Phormio to Apollodorus before the trial, not for writing a speech for him. Several hundred years later Plutarch criticized the action and regarded it as clearly morally wrong, but Plutarch may not have understood the conventional standards of logography. Blass [Friedrich Blass in *Die attische Beredsamkeit*, 1887] suggested and others have agreed that Demosthenes' change of sides was influenced by political consideration, since Apollodorus took the personal risk about this time of proposing transference of the theoric fund to the war chest (*Against Neaera* 4), a motion consistent with Demosthenes' recommendations in the *Olynthiacs*. A political trade of this kind is probably no more admirable than a lack of involvement and purely literary attitude toward a client's case, but it does show that Demosthenes' actions were based on what he thought to be patriotic principles. The personal attack on Phormio is, however, an acceptance of rhetorical convention, maybe insisted upon by Apollodorus, but regrettable.

Among the private orations is one (51) which does not belong to that category, a claim for a trierarchic crown, delivered some time after 361 by a speaker who was supported by Cephisodotus. We know that Demosthenes as a trierarch carried Cephisodotus as general on board his ship to the Chersonese in 360/359 (Aeschines, *Against Ctesiphon* 51 f.), an occasion vividly described by Demosthenes later (*Against Aristocrates* 163 ff.). The facts fit well enough to make it probable that Demosthenes is speaking in his own person and the speech is, therefore, evidence that he was wealthy enough to be required to furnish a warship at this time, not indeed the only occasion on which he did so (*Against Midias* 78 and 161). It is also evidence of a difference of opinion between Demosthenes and certain supporters of Aristophon (16), then the first man in the city. The speech is not impressive rhetorically; it is querulous in tone and has none of the breadth of vision which Demosthenes later develops: no mention is made, for example, of what the ships did or were intended to do.

As a result of his success in private cases (*dikai*) Demosthenes gained an opportunity to write speeches in suits involving an offense against the state (*graphai*), where there was usually an underlying political rivalry. Greater public interest was aroused by these, and the speeches are often two or three times as long as speeches in private cases. Since Athens had no public prosecutor, individuals had to bring charges in the public suits, and the actual speeches delivered might be written for the prosecutors by logographers, just as in private suits. Demosthenes' function has not changed, therefore, in his speeches *Against Androtion* (355), *Against Timocrates* (353), and *Against Aristocrates* (352), but opportunity for imaginative treatment and fame are much greater. The speech *Against Leptines* (355) is not essentially different from the private speeches, though Plutarch (*Demosthenes* 15) reports that Demosthenes spoke it in public himself, which would be a further step toward an active public career. Nor has Demosthenes' economic view altered. *Against Androtion, Against Timocrates*, and *Against Leptines* are all directed against a taxation policy that had been especially hard on Demosthenes' prosperous friends and clients. All these works may be regarded as support for the conservative, peaceminded Eubulus. This does not, of course, mean that Demosthenes' views are in any way oligarchic. Eubulus was not an oligarch nor was his supporter Aeschines, nor, in fact, was oligarchy an important ideology in fourth-century Athenian politics. The democratic sentiments of

Demosthenes' early speeches can be quite sincere and yet his sympathies can be with the wealthy. The Athenian system of relying on the rich for large capital expenses meant that the state's finances were only as sound as the finances of wealthy individuals. Demosthenes' bias for wealth was to him a bias in favor of financial order.

Since the speeches are consistent in function and social viewpoint with what Demosthenes had been doing, it seems appropriate to ask whether there is any rhetorical difference between these speeches and the private orations, taking *Against Androtion* and *Against Leptines* as examples.

In the public orations of Demosthenes it is often necessary to distinguish the object of a speech from its subject, or, to put it another way, the real from the ostensible and legal issue. The real objective of the speech against Androtion is to discredit a political faction which had been hard upon the wealthier class of society. Androtion as a tax gatherer had especially won the ill will of many. We do not know whether his motives were patriotic or demagogic. An excuse for prosecuting him was found in his proposal to crown the members of the outgoing council, a traditional mark of honor, although in this year (356/355) they had not fulfilled the technical requirement of building new ships because the treasurer had absconded with the money. The charge of illegality was, in other words, a legal technicality. The two prosecutors, coming from the same humble class as the jury, were personal enemies of Androtion, which was satisfactory since personal enmity was a tolerable ground for litigation in Athens and could effectively mask more complicated motives. We do not know who wrote the first speech for the prosecution, perhaps Euctemon, who delivered it. Demosthenes composed the second speech, delivered by Diodorus.

The rhetorical problem involved was to make the action of Androtion seem sufficiently grave to justify condemnation. Demosthenes had to convert a legal technicality into a threat to Athens. He no doubt believed in his cause, and he was aided by Androtion's arbitrary methods and the fact that, as a former pupil of Isocrates he could be presented as a tricky sophist. Demosthenes' chief technique, and the striking feature of the speech, is the interweaving of three themes: Androtion is vicious, Androtion's crimes are a public concern, Androtion is a sophist. There is a systematic generalization of the charge, or elevation of it from the immediate and legalistic to the symbolic and patriotic. These techniques, first used here, become permanent features of Demosthenes' art.

The three themes are stated in the prooemium (1-4). Androtion has done dreadful things to Euctimon, but worse things to Diodorus. Worse than that, he has attacked Diodorus' uncle. Worse than that, he now has harmed the entire state. But the judges must be careful and not misled, for Androtion is a clever sophist. The themes are rhetorical commonplaces, but usually they are restricted to the prooemium. The distinctive feature of Demosthenes' treatment is that throughout the systematic discussion that follows these threads are never dropped; perhaps the first is the most prominent, but the others continually appear.

The generalization of the charge begins with the first words of the speech, where Euctemon is said to have come to the aid of the city as well as of himself. Androtion's assertion that the council was not responsible for the loss of the funds and its consequent inability to build ships presents an opportunity for amplification of the importance of the navy (12 ff.) with examples from Persian, Peloponnesian, and fourth-century wars, all leaving the clear impression that Androtion is undermining national defense. Androtion must be convicted as a warning to future councils that they must build ships to be honored (19-20). The charge that Androtion was technically incompetent to take part in the assembly is likewise made the occasion for amplification of the wisdom of Solon in guarding Athens against immoral leaders (31-32). Gradually Demosthenes builds up a picture of Androtion as a would-be oligarch: his conviction will make the council more democratic and Athens a better place (37). Are the constitution, the laws, the oaths of the jurymen to be bartered away for the small amount of overdue taxes collected by the plaintiff (45)? The methods of Androtion are oligarchic and exceed the violence of the Thirty Tyrants (47 ff.). The citizens are in fact being treated as slaves (55). Thus Androtion becomes a symbol: whatever kind of man is honored in the state will be imitated (64); the golden crowns which he destroyed are a symbol of merit and honor, qualities held highest by Athenians (75); the bowls dedicated by Androtion are only symbols of wealth. What impiety for Androtion to be conducting the sacred rites of Athens (78)!

By the time Demosthenes has finished speaking Androtion seems a monster and the charge a crucial one in the preservation of the state. The problem of social prejudice is cleverly avoided by granting that rich men were wrong to fail to pay their taxes (42) and subsequently speaking as though Androtion were mainly exacting taxes from the poor (65). Demosthenes has likewise avoided attacking the council members of the past year and asserts that no disgrace will be brought upon them by condemning the actions of these few culprits (36). The speech was heard but once, and in once hearing or once reading today the logical fallacies and exaggerations are not easily perceived. It is possible that some of the facts were more adequately dealt with in the speech given by Euctemon. Demosthenes does not *prove* that the methods of Androtion were oligarchic, nor that he had been a prostitute, nor that his father had been a state debtor—a charge which had been used against Demosthenes himself by Aphobus—certainly not that he had defrauded the treasury as is implied toward the end of the speech (76). It is highly unlikely that Androtion's methods were worse than those of the Thirty Tyrants: Demosthenes produces nothing to equal the experience of Lysias and his family. Demosthenes objects to the use of alternative defenses by Androtion (18) but introduces alternatives himself later on (e. g. 37 and 44). He is also unfair in denying the right of a defendant to dispute the method by which he is brought to trial (28). In other words, there are sophisms and tricks to be found and Demosthenes is clearly a rhetorician. But his motives, unlike those of Lysias, Isocrates, and Isaeus, are not rhetorical, they are political or economic. The end, the discrediting of Androtion, is what is really important and personally important to Demosthenes, though he does not personally

deliver the speech. If unfair and tricky, he is yet personally consistent and sincere.

The speech *Against Androtion* has regularity of form and clear structural members. There is a prooemium (1-4) dealing with plaintiff, defendant, motive, and significance as usual. A narration is strictly unnecessary, since this is a second speech for the prosecution; but sections five through seven function as a narration in making a statement of the case, and the usual word introducing the narration (γαρ) is found. The proof extends from section eight to sixty-eight. It is divided into a demonstration, with enthymemes and examples, of the illegality of Androtion's action (8-20), of his immorality (21-24), of the legality of the prosecution (25-34), then a refutation of the points made by Androtion (35-46) and an attack on Androtion's character (47-68). The peroration is introduced as though it was a further discussion of the faults and errors of the defendant. There is no recapitulation, but the pathos increases in the presentation of the crowns and bowls as symbols and in the introduction of the religious motif at the very end.

Against Leptines is part of the same political program and is an attempt to repeal a law invalidating grants of immunities to the ordinary recurring liturgies or financial burdens imposed upon the rich. Some wealthy citizens, Chabrias for example, had at one time been exempted because of unusual services to the state. Leptines had abolished the exemptions ostensibly to equalize the financial burden on other citizens. Demosthenes is no doubt sincere in believing that these honorable grants served an important function in encouraging public responsibility, but it is nevertheless true that the class with which he has been identified benefited most from the immunities. The speech contains (24-25) a spirited defense of the existence of private wealth in the state in which Demosthenes' viewpoint is clearly seen. Furthermore, the law of Leptines abolishing the immunities was clearly a part of the same political program as Androtion's tax gathering activities. Aristophon, the statesman in power at the time, was one of the commissioners defending the changes made by Leptines (148), and Eubulus, the leader of the opposite group and soon to become the leading Athenian statesman, was one of those who had been granted an immunity (137). According to Plutarch (*Demosthenes* 15) Demosthenes spoke in person, perhaps in hopes of marrying the widow of Chabrias, whose son, deprived of his father's immunity, nominally was bringing the charge against the new law. The speech is unique in being a prosecution of a law rather than an individual. Since the statue of limitations prevented prosecution of Leptines himself, Demosthenes attacked his law instead and proposed a substitute for it. Commissioners were appointed to defend Leptines' law.

If Demosthenes did speak in person we can see his image in the ethos of the speech. Jaeger [Werner Jaeger, in his *Demosthenes; The Origin and Growth of His Policy*, 1963] drew a picture of a restrained, dignified, somewhat aristocratic advisor—in a word a humanist. Critics have admired the polished tone and assured elegance of the speech, but its conservatism is equally striking. The laws and constitution are viewed as a political framework evolved with care throughout the past, unexcelled in wisdom. Change is most to be distrusted. What has made Athens great once will do so again (e. g. 88 ff.).

The rhetorical problem of *Against Leptines* is a simpler one than in the case of *Against Androtion*. Obviously the matter is not just a technicality; the speaker must show that the benefits of granting immunities more than balance the immediate financial advantages of abolishing immunities. His theme invites a wide discussion of national self-interest and public service. This is the earliest speech in which Demosthenes begins to formulate his vision of a national character, and he uses that actual phrase a couple of times (11 and 64). He also (61) views Philip of Macedon with some alarm.

Rhetorically the most interesting feature of the speech is its structure. This at first appears loose in the extreme, merely a series of points strung together and introduced by an almost unvarying τοίνυν, "well then." Such a technique contributed to the ethos of the speaker, who seems no slick and ranting professional, but a respectable citizen saying what he has to say. On closer inspection, however, the structure turns out to be somewhat more complex. Demosthenes' proposal for a substitute law is set in the very center of the speech (88-104) and framed by two attacks upon the law of Leptines, each divided into two parts. Thus, after a very brief prooemium (1) there comes first (2-28) the general objections against Leptines' law based on the topics of justice, expediency, honor, profit—the typical topics of fourth-century deliberative oratory—rather artlessly woven together. Then follows (29-35) a section devoted to historical examples of those who deserved and received immunities, what Blass called the "positive" side of the case. Such examples are relevant to the issue, unlike those introduced by Isocrates in the *Philip*. After the discussion of the substitute law comes the negative side of the case, the refutation of claims made in support of Leptines' law (105-133), and finally a section which returns to the general considerations of the beginning: justice, honor, and expediency (134-156). The speech ends with a not unemotional peroration of recapitulation. A modern Belgian school of critics has stressed Demosthenes' use in many speeches of a "psychological" structure rather than the traditional rhetorical arrangement; certainly it can be agreed that he shows no signs of being the docile follower of rhetorical rules. He carries along simultaneously a number of different themes, all of which are repeatedly illustrated and each of which is repeatedly brought to the surface. The symmetry which the speech contains may seem rather artificial, but Demosthenes' artistic independence and ability to synthesize standard topics into a whole which will effect a practical end, and not simply stand as a monument of words, are already evident.

In 354 Demosthenes delivered his earliest surviving deliberative speech, *On the symmories*. It is much more compressed than any of the works we have been discussing, too compressed, perhaps, for oral presentation; therefore, we may well have a revision of what was actually said. The topics are more systematically treated than in *Against Leptines*, but the structure is again symmetrical: after a

brief prooemium attacking impractical orators Demosthenes deals first with the proposed Persian war, which he opposes (3-13); expediency (3), honor (6), justice (7), and possibility (9) are the topics touched upon. This takes us about a third of the way through the speech. At the center is the discussion of ways and means for war: Demosthenes does not oppose preparations, but money must be allowed to remain in the hands of its owners (24 ff.), a course which is possible, honorable, and expedient. Roughly the last third of the speech is devoted to a refutation of the need to fight Persia, a peroration emphasizing justice, and the concluding, matter-of-fact recapitulation. This topical approach can also be seen in the early speech *On the liberty of the Rhodians* (351): practicality, expediency, and honor all point in one direction (2, 8 and 28).

About this time two changes take place in Demosthenes' work. One is political. After supporting the program of Eubulus, which was based on financial security at home and peace abroad, Demosthenes rather suddenly turns against Eubulus in alarm at the continued growth of the power of Philip. The change can be attributed largely to Philip's unexpected successes in Thessaly and Thrace. The first fruit of the new point of view is the *First Philippic*. Since such a change must have alienated many of Demosthenes' friends he could only have had a sincere and patriotic belief that a determined opposition to Philip was best for Athens. The personal concerns of Demosthenes' wealthy associates are swept aside as trivial.

Corresponding to this political change is a rhetorical change. New vigor appears in the *First Philippic*, unlike anything in Greek oratory since the sharply focused speeches in Thucydides. There is no question of weighing the relative expediency of courses of action and of attributing to them justice and honor. It is assumed that Philip acts in his own interest, and Athens must act in hers. Territory in the north is the prize of war. The property of the careless belongs to those willing to run a risk (5). Demosthenes so focuses Athenian interests that the question seems not one of advantage, but of necessity, not the choice of a course of action, but the pursuit of the only possibility. His major point is that success is possible (2-12). All other rhetorical arguments are only accessory: Athens' failure to act will bring on her the deepest disgrace and will allow Philip to go unpunished (42-43), but no honor is promised Athens for action, and disinterested justice is not involved. It seems that Demosthenes' patience has been suddenly exhausted; the futility of expecting right to triumph in the course of nature has overwhelmed him.

Succeeding speeches show a similar intensity. The *First Olynthiac*, for example, makes no mention of the honor or justice to be observed in helping Olynthus, only of the fact that it is to Athens' interest to seize the opportunity presented to fight Philip near his own home (11). Finally, in the *Second* and *Third Philippics* Demosthenes takes a further step. His idea of expediency had never been that of the speakers in Thucydides. Perhaps expedient policy was not so evident in the bewildering fourth century as it had been a hundred years before. The ugly principle that might makes right was no longer acceptable: the fourth century demanded at least an appearance of justice, morality, and rectitude, which is no doubt at the bottom of the common synthesis of topics. Beginning with the *Second Philippic* Demosthenes finds a basis for his argumentation in a higher principle than self-interest, and one which combines ethical nobility with rhetorical force. This is the concept of the national character. Philip looks only to the immediately expedient, and most other Greek states are as bad, Demosthenes says, but Athens has the tradition of her past to demand her loyalty (7-10). Self-interest and expediency for her are thus primarily the maintenance of this tradition. The *Third Philippic*, Demosthenes' most forceful speech, carries on this same spirit. Justice in the old sense is not discussed and expediency is coupled with the possibility of preserving Athens (4). There are none of the self-conscious topics of the professional rhetoricians, yet the whole speech is concerned with the necessity of action in Athens' interest. Failure to act will inevitably bring disgrace for all that Athens has been, and the orator's vision of the national character is the point on which the whole speech focuses and under which all arguments are subsumed. It is also the physical center of the speech (36 ff.) framed symmetrically by considerations of practical concerns of the moment. A battle for Athens, decadent and fond of flattery, forgetful of her past, is fought out between Demosthenes the unpopular patriot (2) and Philip, the violent foreign king, compared successively to a fever (29) and a hailstorm (33).

Surely this viewpoint, like Demosthenes' political position, is one of stubborn, unselfcentered patriotism. The normal goals of the rhetorician and politician are equally rejected for the faith of the prophet. There appears to have been an austerity and loftiness in Demosthenes even in his early career; perhaps this finds expression in his deliberate self-devotion to a cause which, it must have been increasingly clear, was impossible. A splendid passage of *On the crown* (190 ff.) betrays the instinct of the martyr. It must be read with recognition of Demosthenes' assumption that no fundamental change could be admitted into the Athenian constitution and traditional way of life, an assumption which others did not accept and which could not permanently be maintained. In his lonely radicalism, Demosthenes was a pure conservative.

Patriotism, to one who does not share an enthusiasm for a particular cause, can be very distressing, for the patriot is capable of ignoring details of specific and inconvenient facts, social conventions, or even ordinary responsibility. The more he believes in his goal, the more it seems to justify all means of attainment. His cloak is his sincerity and his shield the fact that he defends others who cannot or will not defend themselves; but his position can become absurd. In responding to a purely rhetorical challenge the rhetorician, perhaps with tongue in cheek, colors and molds his case within the limits of probability; the patriot, in pursuit of what seems essential, is occasionally blinded to probability. The unattractive aspect of Demosthenes' oratory is mostly the result of the purity of his patriotism; it can best be seen in the prosecutions which arose from the Peace of Philocrates.

After the fall of Olynthus Demosthenes apparently became convinced that at least a temporary truce with Macedon was necessary, because Athens was not making any progress in the war. Negotiations were conducted in 346 and Demosthenes took part, together with Philocrates, Aeschines, and others. Aeschines describes (*On the embassy* 21 ff.) Demosthenes' conduct during the trip to see Philip: he had promised fountains of words and boasted that he would sew up Philip's mouth with an unsoaked rush. His speech was to be the climax of the interview, but, when the moment came, Demosthenes collapsed completely. He fumbled his prooemium and finally stopped, helpless. Philip, Aeschines relates, was rather condescending and encouraged Demosthenes, but that just aggravated the orator. Finally the herald imperiously commanded the withdrawal of the ambassadors. Various inferences can be drawn from the story: one is that Demosthenes did not have the instinct for replying to a sudden rhetorical challenge, which Aeschines shows; another is that his collapse represents his painful horror at speaking, more or less as an inferior, before a barbarian; in other words, it was a result of the greatness of his love of Athens. It may well also be true that this incident is the source of his great hatred of Aeschines, who claims to have distinguished himself oratorically, perhaps for the very reason that he was less emotionally involved in the situation. It was to Aeschines that Philip addressed his reply.

The peace was achieved, though Philip dallied and secured more territory before swearing to it. Contrary to Athenian expectations, which had been encouraged by Aeschines, Philip then advanced into central Greece and reduced the cities of Phocis, which he had prevented from being expressly included in the treaty. Inevitably those responsible for the peace found themselves attacked. Demosthenes, no doubt anxious to show that he had played no active role in making the peace (*On the false embassy* 223), turned his guns on Aeschines. But he showed the irresponsibility of the frenzied patriot in so doing, for the hatchet man he chose to oppose the hated Aeschines was one Timarchus, a man long active against Philip (*On the false embassy* 286), but whose private life was notorious. Aeschines immediately charged that Timarchus' crimes made it illegal for him to participate in public deliberations and to bring actions. Aeschines prevailed, but Demosthenes remembered.

Three years later, encouraged by Hyperides' successful prosecution of Philocrates, Demosthenes personally pressed the prosecution of Aeschines. The speech, known as *On the false embassy*, attempts to achieve on a very large scale (three hundred and three sections) the passion of the *Philippics*, the clarity of Demosthenes' earlier prosecutions, and the subtlety of interwoven themes, especially the vision of Athenian national character, which underlies all of Demosthenes' work. All in all the speech is a failure. Despite some fine bursts of rhetoric, it is unpersuasive and misleading. Demosthenes is most interested in an opportunity to discredit Aeschines generally. As in the prosecution of Androtion he wishes to amplify a charge into a sweeping denunciation, though here the specific indictment is no legal technicality, but the grave accusation of receiving bribes from Philip. This Demosthenes does not come near to proving: there was in fact no evidence for what Demosthenes had talked himself into believing. His secondary charges are also in some cases equally unsubstantial and flatly denied by Aeschines. The allegation, for example, that Aeschines had mistreated a freeborn woman of Olynthus (196) is sheer spite; Aeschines says in reply (4) that the audience shouted down the charge as it was made. Among the more serious indictments are, first, that Aeschines and the other ambassadors, this time not including Demosthenes, deliberately tarried on the trip to exact the oath to the treaty from Philip, although it was desirable to ratify the treaty as soon as possible; second, that Aeschines promised the Athenians that Philip would respect Phocis and move against Thebes, when in fact he did just the opposite. The first charge is easier to answer: it had no doubt been perfectly clear to the ambassadors and many other Athenians that Philip simply was not going to swear until he had accomplished certain preliminaries. This is shown by the slowness with which he took the oaths when the ambassadors did meet him. The ambassadors need not have been bribed to realize that following Philip around when he was not minded to see them would not increase their influence. Aeschines says (97 f.) that a journey straight to Philip in Thrace was not part of the instructions and that the ambassadors could not have reached Philip before he left Thrace. To the second charge, that he made the assembly promises on behalf of Philip, Aeschines replies with a flat denial. It seems unlikely that a seasoned diplomat would have promised anything on behalf of a foreign king, but Aeschines on other occasions was carried away with himself and he may have said more than he intended or have been deceived by Philip. It is as possible that Demosthenes regarded Aeschines' unofficial explanation of Philip's probable intentions as a "promise" and felt that the assembly had been hoodwinked.

Another unattractive feature of the speech, and of several speeches of Demosthenes, is the personal attack on the background, private life, or appearance of an opponent. Aeschines' mother and father and his career as an actor are frequently mentioned to discredit him. Aeschines, of course, makes similar attacks on Demosthenes. These techniques reflect the fourth-century interest in personality and are a kind of perverted ethos. To Demosthenes some explanation of the wickedness of Aeschines must be found, and it seems probable to associate it with his background and upbringing.

Aeschines made a very creditable reply to Demosthenes' attack and was acquitted, quite rightly. The bad blood between the two continued, however, and produced years later (330) the most celebrated oratorical duel of antiquity, Aeschines' *Against Ctesiphon* answered by Demosthenes' **On the crown.** The latter of the two has traditionally been venerated as the masterpiece not only of its author but of ancient eloquence and perhaps of the spoken word. Such a judgment, of course, cannot be proved, though it may possibly be true. Twentieth-century students on first reading the speech often are not greatly moved, but then they are rarely conditioned to respond to any oratory. The critic who reads and rereads frequently ends by embracing the verdict of the centuries. In any event, **On the crown** is a splendid compendium of all those features which in other speeches seem most characteristic of Demosthenes.

In 337, a little over a year after the battle of Chaeronea at which Philip had decisively defeated the Athenians and their allies, Ctesiphon proposed in the assembly that Demosthenes should be honored with a crown at the Great Dionysia of the following spring because "he continues to speak and do what is best for the people." We have seen that the Athenians voted crowns to the council regularly and crowns were often used to honor individuals (*Lives of the ten orators* 843c). There was not, therefore, anything necessarily remarkable about the award of a crown, but the circumstances made this particular motion a question of confidence in the policies of Demosthenes and a tribute to him in the period of Athens' discouragement and defeat. Aeschines, continuing his personal feud with Demosthenes and opposing any expression of confidence in his leadership, immediately introduced a charge of illegal motion against Ctesiphon. This made the award of the crown impossible until the trial had been held, an event which did not take place until 330, perhaps because Philip's assassination in the summer of 336 strengthened Demosthenes' position. Strictly speaking, Ctesiphon, not Demosthenes, was on trial, but Demosthenes appeared as an advocate with him and delivered the major speech for the defense. Ctesiphon probably did little more than introduce Demosthenes.

Aeschines' able speech for the prosecution has survived. It is most successful in the clarity with which it presents the technical argument against the legality of Ctesiphon's motion. Broader issues are raised, but they are rather a second string to the orator's bow. Aeschines calls upon Demosthenes to reply in the same order. The first rhetorical problem of the defense is, therefore, to avoid this, for it would mean putting weak arguments in a conspicuous place early in the speech. Ctesiphon's motion probably had not been made at the legal time and place. Yet this avoidance must not be evident either. The cleverness with which Demosthenes solves this problem has long been recognized: he denounces Aeschines for making charges foreign to the indictment and insists upon his right to answer these first. What he means are the charges relating to his part in the Peace of Philocrates, foreign to the indictment only in the sense that the events were more remote in time from the date of Ctesiphon's motion. Since the basis of awarding the crown was Demosthenes' statesmanship in general, there was no reason why Aeschines should not discuss any period of the orator's activity. Presumably he omitted the very earliest events either because Demosthenes had then been cooperating with Eubulus or because they antedated his own public career. Actually Demosthenes is well satisfied to be able to discuss his services to Athens over a long period. This preliminary issue extends as far as section fifty-two, after which comes the main refutation of Aeschines' charges; but even here the substantive issue of Demosthenes' statesmanship is dealt with first and at great length. Only when he feels that the audience has begun to appreciate his viewpoint does the orator venture to deal, and then but briefly, with the technical charges (110-125). An invective against Aeschines is next introduced, and the great torrent of abuse which pours forth effectively removes any attention the audience might have paid to weakness in Demosthenes' replies to the technical charges. In other words, what Aeschines wished to be the main issue of the trial becomes a kind of overlooked valley of detail, lost between the enormous cliffs of Demosthenes' statesmanship and Aeschines' crimes.

A second rhetorical problem which Demosthenes faced was occasioned by the fact that his policies had been unsuccessful. Aeschines made much of Demosthenes' ill fortune and tried to identify Athens' troubles with the person of his enemy. Even without Aeschines' vilification Demosthenes had to plead in the dark shadow of the Battle of Chaeronea. This challenge he meets head on, and from it achieves great pathos. The most striking passage is that beginning at section 199 which contains the great oath by those who fell at Marathon, much admired by the author of *On the sublime* (16.2). As in the ***Philippics***, Demosthenes insists upon loyalty to Athenian traditions; that is the only true expediency. Success or failure are of secondary interest. Athens has won a moral victory:

> If what was going to be had been clear to all, and if all had known ahead of time, and you, Aeschines, had foretold and prophesied with cries and shouts, though in fact you said not a word, not even in that case should the city have abandoned her traditions. . . . (199)

Again and again he hammers at the theme "what else could I have done?" (e. g. 28, 62, 66, 69, 101, 188, 190 ff., 301) meaning by "could," within the framework of Athenian traditions. The possibility of shutting eyes at what seemed inevitable he expressly rejects as impossible (63). This loyalty to national traditions is the foundation on which Demosthenes builds his defense. Neither blunt expediency nor justice to individuals nor honor in the narrow sense play any separate role, but all are synthesized into the single obsession.

Three ways, then, in which ***On the crown*** resembles earlier speeches of Demosthenes are its attempt to concentrate attention on wider issues rather than on legal technicalities, its presentation of the need for loyalty to Athenian traditions as the central issue logically and the central topic rhetorically of the trial, and its effective use of recurring themes. A fourth way is in the structure of the speech, which shows the tendency to symmetry already noticed in other speeches and an ability to adapt rhetorical conventions to specific occasions. Formally speaking, ***On the crown*** has all the traditional parts of a courtroom speech: there is a prooemium that performs the usual functions (1-17) including (9-17) a preliminary consideration of the procedure which Aeschines has demanded and which Demosthenes knows he cannot successfully follow. Then comes a narration, introduced by the narrative word γαρ (18-52), though it does not deal with the entire circumstances, only with what Demosthenes labels as outside the present case. Because these are earlier events it is possible for Demosthenes to give here an excellent background for the subsequent body of the speech. When the background is set (52) he can break off the narrative abruptly and return to it whenever he wishes later. Thus he gains several advantages at the same time: he disposes of some of Aes-

chines' arguments, he gives the impression of logical order and clear narration, he does not tire his audience with an excessively long narrative account, and finally he does not run any danger of repeating himself when he takes up later events further on in the speech. The proof also shows the two usual parts, a logical one, which here is a refutation of Aeschines' charges (53-125), and an ethical one (126-296), largely a contrast between the character of Demosthenes and that of Aeschines. The central point of the speech in terms of bulk comes around section 160, and significantly there appears here a turning point in the thought too, for Demosthenes, having made his shattering charges that Aeschines brought on the war and lost Greek freedom (142-159), turns to his own measures to counteract these deeds and to his noble expression of Athenian traditions. A symmetry is noticeable in the passage as a whole:

> 126-140 attack on Aeschines
> 141 invocation to the gods, echoing that at the beginning of the speech
> 142-159 deeds of Aeschines
>
> 160-198 deeds of Demosthenes
> 199-210 Athenian traditions, beginning with oath by the gods
> 210-250 deeds of Demosthenes

The contrast between the fortunes of the two orators is then made specific in the following sections. The speech ends with a peroration (297 ff.) which is decidedly recapitulatory. Demosthenes asks again the question "what ought the loyal citizen to have done?" (301) and again (315) demands a comparison between himself and Aeschines.

Just as the structure of the speech follows the traditional pattern, but is free from any constraint which this might have imposed, so the style of Demosthenes is his own delicate instrument. Neither clarity and austerity nor rhetorical fullness occupies his entire attention. The context determines the style, and the orator is the master of all styles: he can narrate vividly, argue with precision, and especially he can mount to moving pathos. One of the greatest passages of ***On the crown*** shows well his versatility. It comes at that crucial moment, the hinge of the speech, when, after Aeschines has ruined everything, Demosthenes comes forward to save what can be saved. The tension of the scene in Athens is conveyed by the narration, in short sentences, of each step as the assembly is summoned (169): evening, the messenger, his disastrous news, the meal of the prytanes interrupted. The market place is closed, the generals are summoned, and the assembly meets. The herald cries "who wishes to address the assembly?" "But no one came forward." All of this is in a sense irrelevant, but the details of the scene are burned into the mind. The tragic pause comes. Demosthenes looks around at the assembly: there are the generals, there the orators, there Aeschines. None speak. The next touch is typically Demosthenic: the voice of the herald who called for speakers becomes the voice of the fatherland pleading for deliverance. All the qualities of patriotism and tragic suffering are imposed upon the dramatic narrative scene. Thunderous parallel contrary-to-fact conditions roll in to demonstrate the gap between desire to act and ability to advise, then like a red flag the name of Philip, and, finally, Demosthenes stands forward in a sentence remarkable for its emphatic word order: "I showed myself, then, this one, on that day, I." In what follows the tone rapidly changes to one of competent comprehension and logical argument.

The greatness of *On the crown* consists in part of this command of style, in part of the success with which the contrast of Aeschines and Demosthenes is everywhere developed into black and white portraits of evil and of good, and in part of the magnificent moral tone, intense, noble, sincere, transcendent. Demosthenes' defense is by no means all true—some of the unproven arguments of the embassy speech recur, Aeschines' character is slandered, and some questions are unsatisfactorily dealt with—but the orator is, in his own view, dealing with matters of principle which transcend facts. His sophisms are not uttered for the sake of making a good speech, but for the sake of his country. The attitude is very much like that of Plato in the *Menexenus*, where truth is not equated with historical fact, but with a moral absolute like that of myth. In contrast Aeschines' speech seems tricky, gaudy, and superficial. Demosthenes himself was not unaware of the

---

Pseudo-Longinus on the rhetorical qualities of Plato, Demosthenes, and Cicero (first century):

Plato, like the sea, pours forth his riches in a copious and expansive flood. Hence the style of the orator, who is the greater master of our emotions, is often, as it were, red-hot and ablaze with passion, whereas Plato, whose strength lay in a sort of weighty and sober magnificence, though never frigid, does not rival the thunders of Demosthenes. And, if a Greek may be allowed to express an opinion on the subject of Latin literature, I think the same difference may be discerned in the grandeur of Cicero as compared with that of his Grecian rival. The sublimity of Demosthenes is generally sudden and abrupt: that of Cicero is equally diffused. Demosthenes is vehement, rapid, vigorous, terrible; he burns and sweeps away all before him; and hence we may liken him to a whirlwind or a thunderbolt: Cicero is like a widespread conflagration, which rolls over and feeds on all around it, whose fire is extensive and burns long, breaking out successively in different places, and finding its fuel now here, now there. . . .

To resume, then, the high-strung sublimity of Demosthenes is appropriate to all cases where it is desired to exaggerate, or to rouse some vehement emotion, and generally when we want to carry away our audience with us. We must employ the diffusive style, on the other hand, when we wish to overpower them with a flood of language. It is suitable, for example, to familiar topics, and to perorations in most cases, and to digressions, and to all descriptive and declamatory passages, and in dealing with history or natural science, and in numerous other cases.

Pseudo-Longinus, in Aristotle's Poetics, Demetrius on style, Longinus on the Sublime, *translated by H.L. Havell, 1963.*

---

contrast and accused Aeschines (280) of producing a show-piece, of answering a rhetorical challenge and caring nothing about the punishment of wrong-doing. The theme is taken up again in the peroration (308). Against Demosthenes that charge cannot be made. He knew all the tricks and rules of rhetoric, but they were to him only means to a far more important end. As his career developed he made that end the preservation of Athenian democracy and institutions as he knew them and the recovery of the spirit that had made them. He alone of Greek orators shared, perhaps without much realizing it, Plato's belief in absolute goals and rejection of rhetorical relativism.

A. N. W. Saunders   (essay date 1970)

SOURCE: An introduction to *Greek Political Oratory*, edited and translated by A. N. W. Saunders, Penguin Books, 1970, pp. 7-29.

[*In the following essay, Saunders discusses the emergence of oratory in fifth-century B.C. Athens, the styles of the major orators, and the relationship between oratory and politics.*]

1. THE GROWTH OF ATTIC ORATORY

When we speak of political oratory, we think first in terms of the great British orators of the eighteenth and later centuries, and of speeches in the House of Lords or House of Commons rather than of speeches in a court of law. It is therefore important to begin a discussion of Greek political oratory by emphasizing the fact that only a small proportion of the extant work of ancient orators was of this kind, consisting, that is, of speeches made in a constituent assembly and intended directly to influence political policy. In fact almost the only speeches of this kind which we still possess in Greek are the shorter speeches of Demosthenes, most of which are included in this volume, and a few ascribed to him, but now regarded as of doubtful authenticity. The great majority of extant Greek speeches are not deliberative, but forensic, that is to say that they were delivered in a court of law and aimed to secure the condemnation or the acquittal of an individual, as were Lysias' prosecution of Eratosthenes and Andocides' defence of himself against prosecution for impiety, which are both included here. This selection also includes two discourses of Isocrates, 'speeches' which were never actually delivered, but were published pamphlets employing an oratorical form and style. Greek prose literature sometimes adopted a convention of appearing in the form of speeches, like those of Isocrates, or of dialogues, like those of Plato. Finally, the speeches in this selection are preceded by a translation of the celebrated Funeral Speech, nominally of Pericles, which serves to represent a further division of Greek oratory, the epideictic, speeches made for public occasions. It is most unlikely ever to have been delivered at all as it stands, since it is part of the *History* of Thucydides. All these, however, share a markedly political content, and are closely associated with important political events or trends, and provide matter of importance for understanding political history.

All Greek oratory known to us is in the Attic dialect and was delivered or published in Athens. This of course is true of the great majority of Greek literature of the fifth and fourth centuries B.C. and is a fact which inevitably colours the views we hold of Greek life and politics. That oratory, like poetry, flourished in Athens can readily be understood. Athenian quickness of wit and tongue ensured it. It is not only in art, but in philosophy that Athens excelled. Nonetheless, there must have been speeches made by Spartans, Thebans or Argives, which are not preserved except for one or two which are given, changed, if not improvised, in the pages of Thucydides. But it must be remembered also that Athenian pre-eminence in speech must have been reflected in the choice of passages for reproduction by later centuries. The actual selection may have depended a lot on chance, or the requirements of rhetorical teaching, but it constitutes a judgement of posterity which, while it may have allowed some things of value to perish, did not preserve much of what was worthless. And the speeches which were so selected are entirely Athenian.

Nor is any Greek speech extant which belongs to an earlier date than about 417 B.C., the probable date of Antiphon's speech *On the Murder of Herodes*. This is in part due to the circumstances regarding publication, which will be mentioned below. Addicted as they were to self-expression, the Greeks seem not to have begun till then to write and record the speeches which were made, despite the enormous importance attached to the power to speak well. This is manifest from the Homeric poems onwards. Not only do we find speeches given to historical persons in the work of Herodotus and Thucydides, but they appear as forensic, not merely dramatic, as early as the *Eumenides* of Aeschylus (458 B.C.), while the tragedies of Euripides show frequent signs of familiarity with speech-making both as a habit and as an organized art. Herodotus and Thucydides, indeed, used speeches in an original fashion, but it is unlikely that any of their readers supposed that the speeches in question had been delivered as they stood. They do, however, presuppose the habit of speech-making. The Herodotean speech, and after it the Thucydidean, presented ideas dramatically, in the words of an orator who made or might have made such a speech on such an occasion. Such is Thucydides' *Funeral Speech*. Of a similar kind, too, is Plato's *Apology*, which purports to be Socrates' defence at his trial. Plato was probably present on that occasion, and in any case the general lines of Socrates' defence were no doubt well known. But Plato, as the great dramatizer of Socrates, may with equal certainty be supposed to have worded his defence in keeping with the rest of the picture he painted of him.

This last instance at any rate belongs to the fourth century B.C., but the true beginnings of Greek oratory are earlier. Prose is always later in the field than verse, but the rise of political freedom, especially in Athens, in the fifth century led to the realization that prose as well as verse could be developed as a literary form, and that human needs of expression covered wider ground in the pursuit of knowledge and the maintenance of civic rights. From this need arose what is called the Sophistic movement: the intellectual ferment of the fifth century had by the latter half of it been systematized in the hands of professional men of learning. They were in a sense successors of the early philosophers, such as Heracleitus or Pythagoras, and they met in the eager intellectual *milieu* of Athens. Men like Protagoras, Hippias, Prodicus and Gorgias professed among other things to teach and stimulate the art of speaking, both as one of a number of cultural subjects (Plato [in his *Protagoras*] makes Socrates discuss with Protagoras whether virtue can be taught) and as a practical technique of its own. Either part of this programme was expected to be of value both in politics and in litigation, to which Greeks were prone, and also to offer an inherent value in the improvement of education. It was perhaps most desired for its utility in a litigious community, and it is in this context that there arose the claim parodied by Aristophanes in the *Clouds* that the Sophistic training would 'make the weaker argument the stronger', while Gorgias in Plato's dialogue of that name is made to contend that the subject which he professes is the 'greatest and best of human concerns'. These statements involve a claim to improve the citizen's ability to plead a case and win it, but they were used as material for detractors, and can be seen behind Aristophanes' satire in the *Clouds*, and in Plato's many dialogues criticizing the Sophistic movement. The Sophists took fees for the tuition they gave, and in due course began to specialize in speech training. Some formed schools and composed a *'techne'*, a rhetorical handbook, as Antiphon did. Jebb declares [R.C. Jebb in his *The Attic Orators*, 1876] that Greek oratory begins with Gorgias, Attic oratory with Antiphon.

Gorgias of Leontini in Sicily was born, like Protagoras, about 485 B.C., and is known not simply as a rhetorician. He led an important delegation to Athens in 427 to ask for Athenian assistance for his city. But it was probably his fame as a speaker which led to his nomination as a leader, as in the case of Teisias, who accompanied him. He is also known to have been chosen to speak at the Olympic festival of 408. He is in the sequence of Sicilian rhetoricians together with Teisias, the teacher of Lysias, and the reputed head of the movement, a certain Korax. Gorgias' claim to fame as an orator seems to have rested on skill in expression rather than on exposition or treatment of his matter. His influence is said to have extended in particular to Thucydides and Isocrates. The only continuous passage of his which survives is itself part of a funeral oration. It must be granted that it is tiresomely overloaded with symmetrical anti-theses, and does not suggest great oratory. Nonetheless it can readily be understood that this style explains some of the peculiarities of the speeches which Thucydides includes in his narrative, and also the smoother antithetical method of Isocrates. And it was to Gorgias more than to any other, as we see in Plato's dialogue, that most early Greek orators of whatever origin looked up.

Born a little after Gorgias, Antiphon played a prominent part in the oligarchic revolution of the Four Hundred in Athens in 411 B.C., which is his claim to political fame (a fame, like that of Gorgias, due to rhetorical skill) and to which he owed his execution. But his extant speeches are not political in this sense. He was perhaps the first to do in Athens what Gorgias had not done (though Teisias did in Syracuse): that is, to organize a school and compose a manual of oratory. He was also the first professional writer of speeches, and thus the precursor of all the great Athenian orators. Greek orators did not deliver speeches for others, as Cicero did, but wrote them for others to deliver. Thucydides says that Antiphon never appeared in court except in his own defence in 411, with a speech extolled for its excellence, but in the event unsuccessful. His extant work is confined to cases of homicide, in which he seems to have specialized, and includes his four *Tetralogies*, sets of speeches in imaginary cases, two each for the prosecution and the defence. These bridge the gap between theoretical accounts of the needs of oratory and actual speeches in court. He was a pioneer in the practice and in the style of Attic oratory, writing, as did Thucydides, at a time which lacked a prose tradition. He is credited with many of the same characteristics of style as Gorgias, but his work seldom reminds one of Gorgias' existing remnants. Both are said to have played a part in the teaching of Thucydides, but except for occasional phrases Antiphon does not provide a strong resemblance to the speeches in Thucydides' history, though he too is given to brevity, symmetry and antithesis. These are characteristics which probably seemed to both writers to offer a method of bringing prose to the literary level of poetry.

From these beginnings, social and stylistic, Attic oratory rose and soon flourished. Of course Athenians had made speeches earlier than this, but they were probably extemporized. It is said that Pericles was the first to deliver a written speech in court, and it must be assumed that written speeches in the Assembly were a later habit. Pericles is described by the comic poets, Eupolis and Aristophanes, who refer to his lightning speed and persuasiveness. But we have no record of his speeches except Thucydides' versions, nor of speeches by the famous demagogues, Cleon, Hyperbolus and Cleophon. In the extant speeches forensic oratory appears first, and most of the early examples were written for delivery in court. Two of these which are particularly concerned with political events are translated here, those of Lysias, *Against Eratosthenes*, and Andocides, *On the Mysteries*. The oratorical antecedents of these two orators are very different. Lysias learnt oratory from Teisias of Syracuse before coming to Athens. As an alien, however, he was not entitled to speak in court except during the brief amnesty after the fall of the Thirty in 404, when he delivered the speech against Eratosthenes. Most of the rest of his work consisted of speeches written for others. He was, however, distinguished enough to be chosen to deliver the Funeral Oration at Athens (probably 392 B.C.) and a Panegyric Oration at Olympia (388 B.C.). Andocides, on the other hand, spent much of his life in exile, and there are but three of his known works of oratory, two delivered in his own behalf, and one in the Assembly after his acquittal. Jebb calls him an amateur, which is not surprising since we know nothing of professional study in his instance. It is the occasion of his most important speech which makes it noteworthy. Indeed it concerns an earlier event than that of Lysias, though it was delivered later. Both, though politically important, are forensic in form. But the majority of speeches by Greek orators were on narrower and more personal subjects, like those of Isaeus, who enjoyed a special reputation as an expert in the composition of law-court speeches, particularly in cases of inheritance. Perhaps it is partly because of such narrow and individual aims that Plato regards [in his *Phaedrus*] oratory with such evident distaste and dispar-

ages it in a number of places. He calls it an art of spellbinding, and criticized its lengthy irrelevance, naming Pericles the greatest of orators, because he learnt from Anaxagoras, and could fortify his art with philosophy.

There are also examples of epideictic speeches (the Greek word means speeches of display) delivered for particular occasions of importance. Mention has already been made of funeral speeches by Pericles, by Gorgias and by Lysias. The *Panegyricus* of Isocrates is in form of this kind. But with the exception of Andocides' speech *On the Peace with Sparta* we have no deliberative speeches from the Assembly till those of Demosthenes, the earliest of which was delivered in 354 B.C. It may be in part his eminence that secured his speeches from oblivion, but in fact the practice of publishing deliberative speeches does not seem to have begun much before his time and that of Isocrates. The speeches of litigants were commonly written from the later years of the fifth century B.C., when oratory developed in theory and practice owing to the habit of making handbooks of rhetorical theory, and the habit of 'speechwriters' composing speeches for clients to deliver. The publication of political speeches may, it is suggested, have been begun by aliens, like Lysias, who were interested in politics, but not admitted to the Assembly, or due to private circumstances like those of Andocides, who seems to have published his *On the Peace with Sparta* by way of self-justification. These and the like may have led to the practice of Isocrates and Demosthenes. Demosthenes, indeed, may well have been the first to publish deliberative speeches already delivered in the Assembly. Such speeches may on occasion have been subject to alteration in the interval. This is suggested, for instance, by some passages in **Philippic III** whose genuineness has been doubted as well as by the statement of Plutarch that comparisons were drawn between Demosthenes' extempore speeches and his written ones. In any case it appears that Demosthenes did publish speeches in his lifetime, perhaps to substantiate their political importance.

2. ISOCRATES AND DEMOSTHENES

Within these limits stand most of the Greek orators of whom we have knowledge, the Ten Orators, known to the first century A.D. in a list which became an established canon and thus ensured its survival. The list includes Antiphon, Andocides, Lysias and Isaeus, whom we have mentioned, the two great names to whom we now go, and in addition Aeschines, the great opponent of Demosthenes, Hypereides, Lycurgus and Deinarchus.

One, however, Isocrates, made still another use of oratory. He was full of talent, as Plato makes Socrates describe him in a celebrated passage at the end of the *Phaedrus*, and had wide views about the Greek world and particularly his native Athens. But he lacked the voice and the robust temperament needed for active oratory. He therefore found his own niche as a teacher, and communicated his ideas as written pamphlets. But he did not practise either activity on the same lines as his predecessors. He was a teacher of rhetoric, yet one who was neither a mere theorist nor a mere exponent of technique, and therefore departed from the practice of writing speeches for imaginary situations, like Antiphon, because he regarded contact with real and vital questions as important. Yet he did not seek to achieve it by speaking. He was a sophist, as a man who took fees for teaching oratory. But in an early discourse [*Against the Sophists*] he makes a strong protest against Sophists for making extravagant claims which they can never fulfil, for being oblivious of practical aims and for bringing discredit on genuine teachers—charges little different from Plato's. What he sought to instil into his pupils he called 'philosophy'; but it was not what Plato meant by the word. He regarded the Platonic pursuit of truth as too unpractical, indeed as humanly unattainable, while Plato grouped him with the Sophists, regarding them as tamperers with the truth rather than seekers of it. Finally he was a passionate admirer of Athens, but took no narrowly partisan view of her position in Greece, desiring to see her lead a united Greece against the Persian enemy whose attack had united her before. Isocrates was in fact a great liberal when liberalism was not the language of the day, and his political ideas were in advance of those of his contemporaries. As such he may be called doctrinaire or idealistic, and as such he differs from the great speaker of the day, Demosthenes.

Isocrates' pursuit of rhetoric made it into a general culture, almost a liberal education. He did not go quite as far as Cicero was to do [in *De Oratore*] in depicting the orator as the ideally cultivated individual. But he did regard rhetoric not solely as a means to a practical end, success at law, but as a development of human powers by the study of the written or spoken word, the *logos*, which would enable learners to improve their judgement of all kinds of activities, specialized or otherwise. This was an educational system very different from Plato's and it is not wholly surprising if the two men were alienated from each other. Whether the tale of their enmity is true cannot be certainly determined. Opposite views are entertained. In any case we may imagine that they differed considerably in temperament, as they did in outlook. Plato scorned rhetoric, Isocrates believed in it, and hoped to find in it a means to recover for Athens and for Greece some of their old life and vigour. This was to be achieved by teaching, and, no doubt, inspiring the young with the feelings which he wanted to disseminate. This is the purpose which the *Panegyricus* in particular was designed to serve, and in some degree achieved. At least it greatly enhanced his reputation, increased the demand for his services as a teacher, and launched, if unsuccessfully, his campaign for the sinking of differences and the solidarity of Greece.

This was not a theme which was due to his unaided invention. In particular it had been put forward by his master, Gorgias, on the occasion of his Olympic speech in 408 B.C., which has been mentioned. But this Pan-Hellenism was suited to Isocrates' outlook and to the aims he was setting himself, to bring his pupils to the highest attainments by means of the *logos*, and to affect the trend of politics by exerting an influence on the leading men. In the aim of Pan-Hellenism he showed an exceptional insight into the needs of the age. It may seem to have needed no unusual penetration to realize the difference between the atmosphere and the attitude maintained by the Greeks in the defeat of Persia in 490 and 480 B.C. and after the collapse of Athens during the Spartan hegemony. But in times of

declining community of spirit it is easier to confine attention to narrow aims and the securing of narrow gains, than to go against the common view and seek a genuine broadening of outlook. To have a real effect on public opinion and alter the attitude of the Greek states proved more than Isocrates could achieve. In the *Panegyricus* he had realized the need to unite them in attack on a common enemy, the same enemy, Persia, whose attack had united them in the great days of the past. With the stimulus of that aim he hopes that they will overcome jealousies about leadership and agree to accept that of Athens. This may have seemed somewhat naïve. If so, the feeling—that it was naïve—was part of the spirit which needed to be overcome. But it was not overcome. And whether or not he made overtures to other rulers (it is said that he approached both Dionysius of Syracuse and Jason of Pherae, but this is disputed) the *Philip* shows him sufficiently disappointed of his previous hopes to feel that the only chance lay in finding a single champion who could rally the Greek states round his standard. For this purpose he saw a suitable figure in Philip of Macedon, clearly the leading single ruler in the Greek world after 350 B.C., and sufficiently integrated in it to appear acceptable.

Yet never, or never until it was too late, do Isocrates' aspirations appear to have been taken seriously. This was not principally because they did not appeal enough to Philip, nor because of the rise of Demosthenes, who took a different view. Better to say that it was due to the political state of fourth-century Greece, to which we shall revert, and to something in the character of Isocrates himself, which must have been partly realized by his contemporaries, and which makes us temper praise of a man who was ahead of his time, by calling him too little of a realist. The philosophers, according to Plato, must be the rulers, but they will never wish to rule. This applied to his ideal state. In the real world it seems doubtful whether they *can* ever rule, not merely through unwillingness, but through inability to make sufficient compromise with the actual. It is a charge made by Isocrates against the sophistic philosophers, and perhaps against Plato himself, as we have seen. Now it rebounds—on Isocrates; and we may speculate why exactly we feel it to be just, not only in relation to his ideas, but to his smooth, unvarying style, so that we prefer Demosthenes, sensing that greatness depends in part upon success.

Not that Demosthenes was greatly successful. Indeed he is generally regarded as the patriot who could never induce a declining state to surmount self-seeking and revert to action. This is not wholly true. He was too great an orator to be always unsuccessful, even though the times were against him too. He is the culmination of this line of orators, the exponent of political oratory in our original sense, using his powers to sway a political assembly and influence actual legislation. He saw the truth, perhaps with a limited view, but without distortion or wishful thinking, unless it was indeed unrealistic to hope for any Athenian revival. If so, he was optimistic, where Isocrates was doctrinaire or academic. In one sense the two men were at one, in another far apart. Isocrates, like Demosthenes, had been prepared to castigate Athens for her unwillingness to face unpleasant facts. Demosthenes, like Isocrates, was inspired by the past greatness of Athens, but he longed for her to recover it in the world as it actually was, not as it might become. To Demosthenes, Isocrates (strangely enough we seem to have no record of contact between them) must have seemed to lack all common sense in expecting concord among Greek states without a strong motive for it, or Philip's unselfish abandonment of the quest for power in Greece. But we can hardly fail to answer the question which of them was right, and it will be asked again at a later point.

Meanwhile we may make some assessment of Demosthenes himself and of the claim of greatness that is made for him by later Greek and Latin writers. Great oratory is not solely a matter of style, but also of character. Whatever else Demosthenes was, he was a man of courage. He must have felt at his best when he was wrestling with difficulty: with his own temperament and physique, with his financial troubles after the early death of his father, with acquaintances who found him tiresome, pompous and self-righteous (which he probably was) as well as with an inert and complacent Assembly. What qualities has his oratory which are lacking in the others of his day? Critics of the time of Cicero and later credit him with numerous stylistic features. Cicero himself dwells [in his *Orator*] on his variety, subtlety, dignity. But we have to wait for the writer wrongly known as Longinus to come nearer [in *On the Sublime*], with 'rugged sublimity', 'intensity', and finally 'stature'. He was single-minded in his foreign policy, however double-minded he may have been called by his opponent, Aeschines, and showed, as perhaps no one else among the ancients could, the ability both to give lofty expression to a high cause and to make that contact with his audience which is the essence of practical oratory, and which Cicero describes under the word *'flectere'*, the power to influence hearers. We are not here much concerned with his private habits, except as they affect our view of him as an orator and a statesman. He may be accused of disingenuous, even dishonourable dealing on occasion; the personal rivalries which coloured his public relations with, for example, Aeschines, were sometimes sordid and his expression of them, worded in the normal fashion of the time, displeasing. We shall find this tendency in a personal speech, such as **On the Crown**, a forensic speech, but political in that it includes Demosthenes' assessment of his own career. It is too long for inclusion here, but it will reinforce the impression given by his speeches to the Assembly of an orator who can be called great for discarding popularity in a lofty cause. On the issue of success we must, in his case too, look more closely at the history of his time.

3. STYLE OF THE ATTIC ORATORS

In introducing a translation not much need be said of style. But some attempt has been made in this one to differentiate between individual characteristics, though it cannot be hoped that a translation will by itself make style or manner clear. Nor can style be entirely detached from character and conduct. Some mention has already been made of it in discussing the authors referred to. And style was of great moment to the ancients, particularly in the Ciceronian period and later, when analysis of the great

treasure of Greek literature was prevalent. But, as with other critical study, the first to systematize it was Aristotle, and Cicero's own works on oratory and later the treatises *On the Sublime* and *On Style* can still be reckoned as indebted to him.

The Ciceronian age made much of a controversy on the relative merits of the Attic style as represented by the best Athenian orators of the fifth and fourth centuries B.C., and the more florid Asian style, so called, which had developed since that time. We need not spend time in considering this, though Cicero devotes a little space to it. But it is to Attic that he pays most attention, and to the differences within it. In this connexion Thucydides is mentioned, to distinguish his style from that of Lysias. Cicero specifically says that Thucydides has no part in oratory, but that the speeches he includes 'contain so many remote and obscure passages as to make them barely intelligible'. The translator can only attempt a faint suggestion of this Thucydidean style, which is perhaps due to intense feeling packed into an antithetical style derived from Gorgias. It is as far as possible removed from the manner of Lysias. Ancient criticism of Lysias was no doubt based largely on the speeches he wrote for others to use in court, so that Cicero, for instance, denies him full grandeur of style, and Dionysius [of Halicarnassus] comments on his power of character-drawing. The speech **Against Eratosthenes** is in fact fuller than most of Lysias, and shows that his plain and natural narrative could give place on occasion to more swelling oratory. But his most marked characteristic is his straightforward ease of statement, and the essay *On Style* follows Cicero in stressing his 'charm'. The earlier orators were more practical in aim than Gorgias, and found that such an easy flow met their largely forensic needs. Andocides has it too, but his style suggests what is in fact true, that he was not at first a professional speaker; the present version has been composed with the feeling that ordinary speech touched with the colloquial might be nearest to the manner of the amateur.

Isocrates is a different matter. His methods were much more self-conscious. The author of *On the Sublime*, who was apparently no strong admirer of Isocrates, quotes Caecilius' reference to Alexander as 'one who subdued the whole of Asia in fewer years than Isocrates took to write his *Panegyric* urging war on Persia', and later criticizes the *Panegyricus* itself for a long-winded passage sufficient to spoil Isocrates' point. But Cicero points out [in *Orator*], and we should remember, that Isocrates wrote with a view not to the 'thrust and parry of the courts, but to give pleasure to the ear'. It is a polished style in which the antithesis he had learnt from Gorgias is ironed out, though it is still at times perceptible, and in which period succeeds period 'with no less regularity than the hexameters in the poetry of Homer', avoiding even hiatus as an undesirable roughness. It is thus a style of more beauty than strength, reflecting perhaps Isocrates' personality and his own praise of a style which is as artistic as that of poetry.

Demosthenes was universally upheld by Greco-Roman authors as the prince of orators, and has maintained that reputation since. Cicero [in *Orator*] speaks of 'one man's astonishing eminence in oratory', and though he finds some deficiency when he compares Demosthenes to his imagined ideal ('he does not always fill the measure my ear demands') he finds in him 'all the subtlety of Lysias, the brilliance of Hypereides and the vivid vocabulary of Aeschines', noting whole speeches that are marked by subtlety, others by weightiness like some of the *Philippics*, others by variety. Cicero follows well-known stories like that referred to in the introduction to Demosthenes (1) below, when he speaks of Demosthenes' stress on delivery, and though he too avoided hiatus as harsh, his is not the smoothness of Isocrates, but that of a practised and practising speaker. Preeminently this is what Demosthenes is, and even if there are passages in his work which are no more than practical and may even have dissatisfied Cicero, he can rise to oratorical heights, for instance in parts of *Olynthiac II* or in the *Philippic III*, which justify the language of the writer on *The Sublime*.

4. ORATORY AND POLITICS

Though oratory is an art particularly connected with politics, its rise in Greece coincides with a political decline. And this is no mere coincidence. The same factors at least contributed to both. To say this makes it necessary to attempt some assessment of the nature of this political decline and to justify the phrase, if we are to understand our orators themselves and to estimate them in the context to which they belong. We can therefore hardly avoid some brief historical summary. Here reference is made from time to time to the sectional introductions below, but inevitably there is some overlapping.

The Periclean age of the greatness of Greek, especially of Athenian, civilization ended with the outbreak of war between Athens and the Spartan alliance in 431 B.C. Pericles himself did not long survive. And, though there was an interval in the fighting, war continued till the collapse of Athens after the battle of Aegospotami in 405. This war, which in Gilbert Murray's words [in *Journal of Hellenic Studies*, LXIV], 'destroyed the hope of Hellenism', was fought to prevent the commercial expansion and imperialism of Athens from having full scope and leading to the enlargement of Athenian power. Ever since the Athenian assumption of the leading role after the defeat of Persia in 479 B.C. the power of Athens had shown this tendency to expand, when she changed a Confederacy of Aegean states, organized for defence against Persia, into an Empire geared to her own advancement—a gradual change which coincided with her development as a democratic and maritime community. During the war Athens' resources and Athenian popularity underwent serious vicissitudes, but she did not refrain from further imperialism, notably in the attack on Sicily between 415 and 413. This grandiose scheme ended in disaster, and the superstitious could look back on the sacrilege committed as it sailed. . . . Signs of strain began to appear, when a *coup d'état* put the city for a time in the hands of an oligarchic *régime*, in which the orator, Antiphon, took a leading part. But Athens was not brought down till 404. By then Persia, almost forgotten for over forty years, had been invited back into Greek affairs by Sparta to combat the Athenian fleet. With her resources now at an end Athens had to submit to Sparta and to oligarchic control. There

was a reign of terror under the so-called Thirty Tyrants, . . . and though it was not long before Athens reverted to democratic ways, she did not regain her old wealth.

Then began the supremacy of Sparta, as the liberator of Greece from Athens. The Spartans inspired even deeper hatred than most liberators. The extraordinary Spartan community did not know how to govern except by rigid control. Within a few years Sparta was again at enmity with Persia and at war with an alliance in which Athens, now recovered, though not financially, was joined by Thebes, Corinth and Argos. Having brought Athens down less than twenty years before, Persia now helped her to a naval revival, and then, growing nervous, in 386 agreed to the much vilified 'King's Peace', whereby, with Spartan assistance, she dictated terms to the Greek states. After it Spartan exploitation continued, and resentment against Sparta increased. It was vain at this time for Isocrates to write of unity, to praise the greatness of Athens and urge her leadership, even in partnership with Sparta. It was just at this time, in 379, that Sparta caused the disruption of the rising confederacy of Olynthus, an act subversive of unity. However, dislike of Sparta did stimulate Athens, perhaps influenced by Isocrates, to form a new confederacy of her own, with altruistic intentions. Eventually in 371 a conference of the Greek states took place at Sparta, by which Athens and Sparta agreed to abandon empire in a pact of non-aggression. But Thebes, in the person of Epaminondas, claimed to sign on behalf of Boeotia. To this Sparta took exception and, in contravention of the treaty just made, attacked Thebes and, against the military genius of Epaminondas, suffered a severe defeat at Leuctra.

Now it was the turn of Thebes to liberate the world from Sparta. The process continued for nine years—just so long as Epaminondas remained alive to conduct it. It included attacks on the Peloponnese, the reconstitution of Messene, which was 'liberated', and, as a further counterpoise to Sparta, the foundation of Megalopolis as a new city in the heart of Arcadia. But Theban self-seeking and intransigence alienated Arcadia as well as other states, and brought Athens into the arms of Sparta. They were allies in the campaign of Mantinea (362), when they met the force of Thebes. Although successful in the battle, Epaminondas lost his own life; this was fatal for Thebes, and the Theban supremacy collapsed.

If we cannot quite talk of liberation from Thebes, whose dominance was less complete and more short-lived than Sparta's, yet she raised numerous opponents among the Greek states, two in particular at different times. Athenian power had been regained in part, as has been seen, first in reaction to Sparta, when Persia allowed the repair of the fortifications (the Long Walls of Athens) and Conon revived her naval strength. Then, after the King's Peace, Athens returned to vigour in the Second Confederacy of 378, which started as a genuine attempt to avoid the exploitation of her fifth-century Empire. After 370 this confederacy was directed against Theban power in alliance with Sparta. But Athens suffered from continual lack of funds, and could not long maintain power in the Aegean without resorting to some methods which did not live up to the aims of the Second Confederacy. The reappearance of cleruchies and the exactions of the mercenary forces which fought for Athens, but subsisted on plunder, caused alarm and discontent. In 357 the important islands of Chios, Cos and Rhodes revolted under the influence of the ambitious tyrant of Caria, Mausolus . . . . Peace was made in 354, but by then Athens had lost several valued possessions to the rising power of Philip of Macedon.

The other, and later, opponent of Thebes was Phocis. Her rise in response to Theban attempts to use the weapon of the Amphictyonic League against her, and the onset of the Sacred War, are referred to in the introduction to Isocrates' *Philip* and the rise of Philip of Macedon in that to Demosthenes. . . . These need not be described in detail here. Peace between Philip and the Athenian alliance (excluding Phocis) was made in 346 and known as the Peace of Philocrates. For the last time Isocrates hoped to secure a leader and general support for his campaign for unity, and to induce Philip to assume this role. But the peace, which began with Philip's destruction of Phocis, only lasted as long as it suited him, and ended in 340, when the insistence of Demosthenes raised an alliance against him. In 338 Demosthenes' fears were realized, and Philip, himself making use of an Amphictyonic dispute, marched south through the pass of Thermopylae, and overwhelmed the Greek forces at Chaeronea. At last there had been a rally in support of the view Demosthenes had voiced since 351, but the Greeks could not match Philip's trained troops and superior tactics.

Philip turned on Thebes, but spared Athens. Not for the last time the past greatness of Athens saved her from destruction by a conqueror who appreciated it, and saw a chance to gain her assistance by leniency. By the terms of peace Athens was compelled to abandon her existing confederacy and join the new Pan-Hellenic union proposed by Philip. The hegemony of Greece now rested with Macedon, a monarchy outside the circle of the Greek states of the past. The first assembly of the new congress was summoned at Corinth, though it was not till a year later, 337, that Philip announced a new campaign against Persia, and the arrangements for it were organized. Isocrates wrote to Philip to express his delight that his aim had at last been accomplished. One enactment, however, the establishment of three Macedonian garrisons at strategic points in southern Greece to maintain control of it, might have made him wonder if he was right.

5. THE DECLINE OF GREECE

Having made our summary, we must return to the suggestion that in the fourth century in Greece the rise of oratory is connected with a political decline, and to the question of whether the orators could make any contribution to combat it. We may see this decline in several different ways; we may regard it as a political failure of the city state, the failure of the Greeks to achieve the unity which might have preserved their continued development in a political world to match their economic development. We may see it as a social failure of the middle class to maintain and extend democracy because it sought to remain exclusive; or as the cultural failure of a community which kept

to slave labour instead of pursuing the curiosity which leads to fresh scientific developments. Finally we may think of it as a psychological failure, a loss of confidence on the part of a world clinging to its own past. In any case it involves, as two interacting factors, a tendency to particularism in which narrower interests are preferred to broader ones, and a tendency to the static in which the enjoyment of what already exists takes the place of the pursuit of what is new. In a discussion of political oratory we shall be more concerned with the breakdown of the city state than with the other factors, though all are facets of a single situation.

This political disruption or particularization is due to individual or sectional self-seeking, which wished to establish its own desires at no matter what cost to the community. The grimmest chapters of Thucydides describe the spread of this evil, which he calls by the name of '*stasis*', division in the state pursued with violence in quest of sectional ends, usually of a kind which we should call ideological. Thucydides specifies the symptoms in a horrifying analysis. This is the positive side of the disease, the virulent pursuit of private aims. The negative side is the reluctance to be active for public ones. This can be seen in lighter, but no less telling lines in the comedies of Aristophanes, in the *Ecclesiazusae* (393 B.C.), or earlier in the *Acharnians* (425 B.C.), in the picture of an Assembly reluctantly giving itself to public business, or in the *Clouds* in that of the effect of Sophistic teaching in reversing traditional moral ideas. Such changes of feeling, connected by common opinion, if that is what Aristophanes represents, with Sophistic teaching, were changes in the direction of individual self-seeking. And common opinion certainly took oratory, like Sophistic training, as detrimental in tendency to the sound outlook of conservatism. It is true at any rate that the practice of oratory arose in direct connexion with the Sophistic movement, and was obviously conducive to exploiting private advantage.

The Greeks themselves were not oblivious of the disease in its political aspect. Attempts were made to break new ground and achieve a new basis for the organization of society either by means of alliance on new terms or by actual federation. But the new was undermined or obliterated by the final efforts of the old. The Olynthian or Chalcidic Confederacy, for instance, dates back to the fifth century. In 432 B.C. Olynthus, together with other states, seceded from the Athenian Empire, largely because the old Confederacy of Delos, as it was originally called, had been turned by Athenian exploitation into an empire over unwilling subjects. During the great struggle of the Peloponnesian War and after it the Chalcidic Confederacy began to rival Macedon as a fringe power of the Greek world. Macedon was largely disordered and inefficient between 400 and 359 B.C., when Philip rose to power, and the Chalcidic Confederacy seemed to promise better than others. One new feature of note appeared in it, a principle of dual citizenship, by which citizens of each member state were citizens also of the Confederacy as a whole, and all laws and rights were to be shared equally. Olynthus was the nominal head of the Confederacy, but assumed no privileges apart from the others. At first confined to a single promontory, the movement gathered adherents fast, but two cities which were unwilling to be brought in appealed to Sparta, who forcibly dissolved the League in 379 B.C. The new growth had proved inadequate to resist the old.

Two other instances show the contemporary tendency to try the confederate principle to secure ends which were out of reach of single cities. The Second Athenian Confederacy was conceived in a spirit of altruism and of unity against the detested power of Sparta. The confederate states were to have their own assembly distinct from that of Athens, and no measure affecting both was to be valid till passed by both. There were to be no cleruchies, no 'tribute', none of the hated features of the old Empire of the fifth century. Yet perhaps this was a negative approach with a limited aim. It failed eventually, as has been said, because Athens, perpetually short of funds, failed to avoid exploitation; cleruchies and the old abuses began to reappear, and in the Social War she was again involved against her allies. The Arcadian League, which was virtually created by Thebes after Leuctra to curb Spartan power, and involved the foundation of the new city of Megalopolis as a federal capital to replace villages in the neighbourhood, is a third instance, however specialized, of the attempt to supersede small units of organization in favour of larger ones.

These attempts to do what was necessary for Greek civilization by broadening its basis were altogether too weak for their purpose. They had not enough support to convince a world accustomed to warfare within itself. Thinkers and orators alike failed to see a solution, even if they envisaged a need for it. Plato, if he may represent the thinkers, exemplifies two opposed reactions to the problem, that of withdrawal and that of compulsion. To imagine a Utopia (as he did) is to make too little contact with the actual. This is a withdrawal into the spiritual realm different from, but comparable with the later withdrawal of Stoicism. But the *Republic* also suggests the way of compulsion with its arbitrary division of classes and its strong flavour of Spartan control. Compulsion is often enough used to end disagreement. The orators, too, had little to offer except to revert to the past and urge its virtues on the present. Isocrates alone had a sense of the needs of the time and an idea, however inadequate, of a remedy for them. In the letter to Archidamus he enlarges on the disorders of Greece as he does in the *Philip*, and urges co-operation and unity. In the *Peace* he had urged the abandonment of empire and the making of a peace which should not merely rest on *ad hoc* principles to end the Social War, but should be permanent and embrace all the Greeks. Seventeen years later in the *Philip* he had decided, whether or not for the first time, that unity could only be achieved under the leadership of a single king or general. But throughout he saw the need of good will and some compelling principle of unity. When Pan-Hellenism came with Philip, and when the Stoic *homonoia* (concord) was prefigured by the ideas of Alexander, both father and son might have been conscious of a debt to Isocrates. Yet he failed for lack of a principle that was compelling enough. By the majority he went unheeded. It was easier to stimulate an unwilling community to energy than to concord. The stirring oratory of Demosthenes could animate a last stand for the aspirations of an ear-

lier century, even if his hopes did not survive Chaeronea. By this achievement he rendered Isocrates' hopes as vain as his own. After that any peace or agreement was one imposed on the Greek world, not generated by it, and any new deal would not arise from a settlement of differences, but from the enactment of a conqueror. So the splendid patriotism of Demosthenes reduced to ineffectiveness the ideals of Isocrates. It becomes vain to speculate whether either could ultimately have succeeded. We must probably agree that the Greek civilization which rose at last to the support of Demosthenes' efforts against Philip could never have risen to the pleas of Isocrates for concord and agreement with him.

Lionel Pearson   (essay date 1976)

SOURCE: *The Art of Demosthenes*, Verlag Anton Hain, 1976, 207 p.

[*In the following excerpt, Pearson elucidates the characteristics of Demosthenes's speeches, paying particular attention to their narrative style and presentation of argument.*]

Ancient critics do not explain very successfully why they considered Demosthenes the greatest of the orators. Their admiration seems genuine enough, particularly when it is based on careful reading of the speeches, but they do not describe his artistic supremacy in terms that satisfy a modern reader. They are not very helpful to the critic who is trying to analyze it. They show how well his speeches exemplified the rules and principles of rhetoric and how he was master of rhetorical technique. But their highest praise is reserved for the power of his oratory and its emotional impact on an audience. Dionysius of Halicarnassus [in his *Demosthenes*] says: "When I pick up a speech of Demosthenes, I feel like a person possessed, carried in this direction and that, as one emotion after another takes possession of me—distrust, agonized uncertainty, terror, contempt, hate, pity, admiration, anger, envy—all the different feelings to which the human heart is subject." And yet none of these critics had heard him speak. They were dependent for information on the traditional praise handed down from one generation to another. Any comparison that they make between their own contemporaries and "the great orators of old" is artificial so far as the effect on an audience is concerned. They are using their romantic imagination, like people who try to describe how great singers of the past held their audiences spellbound—without any records to guide them.

Writers of modern times have been quick to notice how highly practising orators admired him—Lord Brougham as well as Cicero. Cicero knew how much he could learn from him, and a search for Demosthenic imitation or influence in his speeches is a rewarding occupation. His observable debt to Demosthenes is a better testimonial than any formal acknowledgment in his rhetorical works. It is more difficult to guess how much he owed to earlier Roman orators or even to men like Hortensius. His critical remarks in the *Brutus* about orators before his time must be largely repetition of what others had told him, traditional criticism handed down from men who had actually heard them speak.

A silver coin issued by Philip of Macedon depicting Zeus on the left and a horse and jockey on the right.

He is more interesting when he writes about his own apprenticeship, telling us what he learned from his eminent elders and how Apollonius Molo in Rhodes taught him to change his style. It is useful to be reminded that distinguished orators recognized their debt to their teachers. Demosthenes is supposed to have received instruction from Isaeus. It would be a pity to discredit or reject this tradition, but the few passages in Demosthenes which appear to be modelled on parallel passages in Isaeus or to use the kind of arguments that Isaeus preferred prove only that he was familiar with the older man's written work. They do not oblige us to believe that the two men knew one another personally. Nor does the tradition tell us what Isaeus taught him, as Cicero describes his experience with Molo. All the tales of Demosthenes' private training and rigid self-discipline—the pebbles in the mouth and so on—are concerned with the technique of delivery and emphasize his difficulty in mastering it. The proof that he did master it can be found in the *Olynthiacs* and the *Philippics*, where there are passages that no one would write for himself unless he had confidence in his advanced technique; but the ancient critics do not think it worth while to cite these passages as illustration of his virtuosity or artistic mastery.

Demosthenes delivered his *Philippics* with an eye to the prevailing opinion in the assembly and the effect on the audience of remarks made by previous speakers; that setting is part of his speeches. It might be argued that the Areopagus crisis is part of the *Eumenides* or the memory of the plague in Athens part of the *Oedipus Tyrannus*, or that we cannot appreciate the *Trojan Women* properly unless we recreate the political setting of 415 B.C., with the memory of the Melian massacre fresh in our minds. But the setting is not so essential for our appreciation of a play's dramatic quality, unless we believe its principal value lies in its po-

litical message; and in that case we are treating the play as though it was the work of an orator, an attempt to influence public opinion.

In order to appreciate the quality of a speech we must determine how well its argument and its style suit the occasion. A play may come to be regarded as a masterpiece though it was not well received at its first performance. When a fine play is poorly received, we can blame the poor taste of the audience or the poor performance of the actors, and remind ourselves that it was not the duty of the playwright to write for this particular audience or this particular theatrical company. But when a speaker, who has written his own speech, makes a poor impression on his audience, it is not easy to absolve him of all blame, since his task was to meet that particular occasion. There can be extenuating circumstances. The task that he faces may be very difficult, even impossible. No one would call the *First Philippic* a poor speech because it failed to make the Athenians take appropriate action, or think that Aeschines' reply to Demosthenes' speech *On the Embassy* was the better speech just because he was acquitted; and there are other reasons besides the acquittal of Ctesiphon for thinking that *On the Crown* is a better speech than [Aeschines'] *Against Ctesiphon*.

It is not a simple task to set down the principles by which the forensic or political speeches of an Attic orator should be judged. We must take account of the setting, but it is not strictly our business to inquire if he is recommending the best policy to the Assembly or if the client whom he represents in court is in the right. The historian cannot ignore the first question, and it must be answered if we are to pass judgment on Demosthenes as a politician. The jurist cannot resist attempting to answer the second, but the answer does not affect Demosthenes' merits as a legal counsel. Sometimes, when he seems to have a hard case, we have too little information to be quite sure that he has handled it wisely. If we had the speech of the opposing party, we might be in a better position to pass judgment. And yet, when we have the opposing speech in the contest with Aeschines, we are easily able to decide that Demosthenes' speech is the better of the two, although (especially in the *Embassy* case) this decision does not help us to decide judicially how we should have cast our vote if we had been on the jury.

If we are to pass judgment on a forensic speech, we must first master the relevant facts of the case as well as we can and decide what are the points at issue; then we must ask if a strong and convincing case has been presented and how difficult it would be to counter (we can only guess when it would be tactically possible to protest that the speaker is lying or misrepresenting facts). The procedure will be similar for a political speech, though we must remember that here the audience may be much better informed about the relevant facts than the members of a jury before the trial starts. But we cannot with any confidence estimate the actual emotional impact of a speech when delivered. We cannot even be sure how closely the written version resembles the original spoken version. We must be content to pass judgment on the written version that we have.

Demosthenes had ten years' experience in civil cases before he started on his political career, "leaping from the law-courts to the bema," as Aeschines says (3.171), and the private speeches will be examined first, since they provide evidence of the stages by which he learned his craft. He started very young, as soon as he came of age, at eighteen; either because of poverty or from independence of spirit he decided to handle his own case against his guardians. His speeches as they are preserved show that his self-confidence was amply justified. Already in these first attempts we find characteristics that he retains throughout his career. His narrative is economical and he avoids unnecessary or irrelevant detail; he knows what can be left out and what must be included. Also, more noticeably in the speeches *Against Onetor* than in those *Against Aphobus*, he shows his ability to pick out the weak points in his opponent's story which give him the best chance of discrediting his claim.

In Athenian litigation the plaintiff frequently wants to do more than establish the fact that he has been treated unjustly or that the defendant has committed certain acts. He wants to establish the worst possible motive on the defendant's part, so as to convince the jury that his guilt is even more serious than the evidence seems to demand. The argument is essentially the same when directed against Aphobus as when directed against Aeschines. A criminal intention on the defendant's part is presented as the only explanation of his behaviour.

This was the method of attack that was used against Socrates at his trial. Socrates might have tried to save his life by offering the jury a penitent explanation that would cause them to modify their sentence, if not their verdict. The accusers had insisted on his criminal intentions, and he might have attempted (though it would not have been

easy) to convince people that he was unaware of what he was doing and was not as intelligent as they said. But he refused to play the game that was expected of him; he declined to propose an acceptable alternative to the death sentence or give an explanation that might make his "guilt" seem less serious, and the jury supposed themselves forced to pass the severe sentence.

Just as a prosecutor presented the guilt of the defendant in the blackest terms, so he regularly asked for a severer penalty than he expected the jury to vote; and in civil cases a plaintiff asked for a larger sum of money than he expected to receive, because he would be lucky if he succeeded in collecting even half of the sum to which the jury's verdict entitled him. Demosthenes asked for and obtained a judgment of ten talents against Aphobus, but he did not expect to recover more than half that amount, and with a less severe sentence his chances would have been further decreased. It is not necessarily foolish to demand more money than the other party can produce. A political opponent, who is unwilling or unable to pay more than a fraction of what the court orders, can be forced into exile, and this should satisfy his prosecutor, whose real aim is to drive him out of politics.

In the cases *Against Aphobus* and *For Phormio* we are able to follow developments after the trial and to see what difficulties a litigant faced in actually securing the object for which he went to court. All these considerations should have some bearing on our judgment of the speeches of Demosthenes. He must be well aware that he often overstates his case, and his object will then be to force his opponents to suggest to the jury the kind of judgment that they will be willing to pass. Recognition of his tactics may lead us to a fairer appreciation and interpretation than any attempt to discover the true facts and the strict demands of the law.

The case against Meidias is supposed never to have come into court. Demosthenes is reported to have accepted an offer of money and to have settled the matter privately, and he has been criticized for doing so in both ancient and modern times. The object in bringing suit was, of course, to ruin the public career of Meidias and eliminate him from politics. But if Demosthenes failed to secure a favourable verdict, it would ruin his own career. With strong feelings on both sides the result was very uncertain, and Meidias was likely to be no less brutal in his defence than Demosthenes in his attack. And since we never hear of Meidias causing him trouble afterwards, this may be an instance when the threat of prosecution was effective. The threat of prosecution evidently meant the careful preparation of a prosecutor's speech, perhaps also a deliberate "leaking" of information about its contents.

It is easier to pass judgment on a speech when one is in no doubt about the object that it has in view. In political trials, when one politician is trying to discredit the character of another and to wreck his good name, the technique may not be the same as in a regular civil suit, where he will be content to prove his opponent in the wrong and recover money from him. When Demosthenes wrote his first speech for a political prosecution, *Against Androtion*, he had nearly ten years' successful experience in civil suits behind him, and it must have been on the basis of that experience that Diodorus engaged him to write a speech for him. In this kind of case (as the speech *On the Crown* makes very clear), though the formal basis for prosecution is a legal technicality, it is not so important to prove that the proposal made by the defendant in the Assembly was unconstitutional as to present evidence or supposed evidence of the defendant's character. The precise legal issue becomes less important in a struggle for power between rival politicians, and the jury's verdict may depend, in great part, on larger and not strictly relevant questions. Furthermore, the greater length of time allowed for speaking does not enforce the same kind of economy that is required in private cases. A different manner of introduction and a different style of narrative can be used.

In private cases, when certain facts are in dispute and there is conflict between the evidence offered by plaintiff and defendant, Demosthenes may begin the plaintiff's speech by presenting the defendant as a dishonest and unsavoury character, as the kind of man likely to have wronged the plaintiff and with no scruples about prejuring himself in the story that he tells. He will present the man's alleged bad character as though it were evidence of his wrongdoing, as though his character were known and only his particular acts in dispute. In political trials the situation is different. The jury will be more familiar with the defendant's career, and some of his acts will be beyond dispute—his activities in the Assembly, the results of a diplomatic mission or military expedition when he has been in charge. This supposedly familiar material can be used as the basis for conclusions about his general character and his eligibility for public office; if an unfavourable conclusion can be sustained, the jury can be invited to remove him from public life by their verdict and the actual legal question at issue loses most of its importance.

In a political trial the current version of his opponent's career may be so firmly established that the speaker cannot call it into question, even though it is unfavourable to him. Or he may decide that these "facts" will be favourable or damaging to his case according to the manner in which they are presented. The first point of view seems to be reflected in Cicero's youthful treatise *De Inventione*. A narrative, he says, will not help your case if the facts have been set forth by your opponents and there is nothing to be gained by telling the story again or in a different way. In his later practice it is doubtful whether Cicero thought such a situation ever occurred. He certainly did not think he could do without narrative in *Pro Milone*, though the Greek treatises which he had studied may have recommended a very scanty use of narrative in such a situation.

Demosthenes certainly seems to have recognized that narrative was the heart of any speech in the courts and that no inconvenient version of the "facts," the current version or his opponent's version, need ever be accepted. He clearly believes that the "facts" can and must be presented in such a way that the desired conclusion will seem to follow naturally from his narrative. Quintilian puts this point of view very well when he says that the purpose of narrative is not merely to put the judge in possession of the facts, but to make him share our opinion.

Plutarch on Demosthenes (c. 105-15):

It is told that some one once came to request [Demosthenes's] assistance as a pleader, and related how he had been assaulted and beaten. "Certainly," said Demosthenes, "nothing of the kind can have happened to you." Upon which the other, raising his voice, exclaimed loudly, "What, Demosthenes, nothing has been done to me?" "Ah," replied Demosthenes, "now I hear the voice of one that has been injured and beaten." Of so great consequence towards the gaining of belief did he esteem the tone and action of the speaker.

Plutarch, in his "Demosthenes," in The Lives of the Noble Grecians and Romans, *translated by John Dryden, 1683-86.*

K. J. Dover   (essay date 1980)

SOURCE: "Classical Oratory," in *Ancient Greek Literature*, edited by K. J. Dover & others, Oxford University Press, Oxford, 1980, pp. 122-33.

[*Considered one of Britain's most eminent classical scholars, Dover is best known for the studies* Aristophanic Comedy *(1972),* Greek Popular Morality in the Time of Plato and Aristotle *(1974), and* Greek Homosexuality *(1975). In the following essay, he places Greek oratory in its social and political context and examines the salient features of the major orators' styles. The critic maintains that "Demosthenes often conveys an impression of spontaneity which it is fair to suppose he achieved by spending twice as much time on achieving it as lesser men spent on displaying a more obvious virtuosity of style."*]

I

Of all the genres of Greek literature, oratory is the least appreciated in our own time; many of us who have read a great deal of Greek epic, drama, history, and philosophy have yet to read a Greek speech. Yet we cannot expect to understand the Greeks' view of their own literature and culture unless we come to terms with their respect for the good orator. Some societies in which the art of writing is unknown develop a very sensitive ear for the spoken word, enjoying the inventiveness, ingenuity, colourful imagery, pathos, and histrionic skill of a man pleading for justice or exhorting an assembly, and there is little doubt that the Greeks of the archaic period were such a society. Homer portrays some Trojan elders (*Iliad* iii 204ff.) as recalling how the Greek envoys who had come to demand the return of Helen differed in stance, gesture, voice, and fluency, and it is noteworthy that they say nothing of the validity of the arguments used; it is the art of the speech as a performance that they remember.

Throughout the history of the Greek city-state decisions which affected the fate of the whole community were taken not by a committee after the digestion of written reports but by an assembly under the immediate impact of speeches. The historians show themselves well aware of this fact in the amount of space which they devote to the presentation of direct speech, and Thucydides (i 22.1f.) treats the discovery of 'what was said' and of 'what was done' as being equally important. Though the outcome of a debate was less predictable in a democratic assembly than in a small oligarchy, deliberative bodies in oligarchies might still be large by modern standards, and political alignments within such a body might be governed by unstable alliances between individuals and groups rather than by the predetermined policies of tightly organized parties. The Athenian democracy, moreover, assigned the task of deciding private lawsuits and criminal prosecutions to large juries (sometimes as many as 501), which, unlike a modern jury, received no technical guidance on points of law. The concept of relevant evidence was acknowledged, but irrelevance was not easily controlled, the techniques available for the investigation of crime were rudimentary, and cross-examination was not employed. Skill in manipulating the thoughts and feelings of a crowd was required by politicians, but not only by them; a man could lose his fortune, his citizen status, even his life, if a jury found him less persuasive than his adversary in court. Litigants could be supported by the speeches of more articulate friends, and they could also seek the advice of men who had devoted much time and thought to the art of pleading, but they had to speak themselves, and they usually made a better impression if they carried the main burden. Since prosecution for offences which would incur punishment by the state was undertaken not by the state itself but by individuals acting out of political zeal or personal enmity, and political, administrative, and military malpractice (or even misjudgment) could be severely punished, the career of a man seeking high standing in the community might well entail both speaking on questions of policy in the assembly and fighting actions in the courts on the widest variety of civil and criminal issues. In court, in order to establish himself in the jury's eyes as trustworthy, he needed to boast of his political career, while his adversary tried to present it in the opposite light, and in the assembly the respect with which he was heard depended on how he had fared in the courts. It could therefore become necessary for the same man to apply himself to 'forensic' and to 'political' oratory, but it was naturally open to the skilled consultant without political ambitions of his own to specialize.

A speaker would have made a deplorable impression if he had read his speech from a written text, and even if he used notes he would suffer by comparison with an adversary who did not; in law and politics, as in war, no standard is satisfactory save that which ensures victory. A speaker therefore had to give a great deal of thought in advance to what he was going to say, and if he was the defendant in a court case he knew that he would have to improvise a rebuttal of unforeseen allegations of bad character and misconduct which might have only marginal relevance to the point at issue. What we read in a Greek speech is not a transcript of the words uttered in court, and its relationship to the speech prepared in advance is hard to determine. There are some reasons to believe that before the written version of a speech was put into circulation it was revised to take account of matter which the composer had not foreseen and to omit matter which had

gone down badly. The written speech therefore assumed the character of a political pamphlet, a weapon wielded in the prosecution of a feud, and it endeavours to make us not only respect the composer as a citizen but also fear him as an adversary and admire him as a man of intellectual acumen and artistic sensibility. Few modern readers accord the orator the admiration which he sought. We tend to mistrust technical skill in the service of persuasion; so, indeed, did the Greeks—such mistrust is often expressed in their literature—but the need to win made it indispensable, and the Greeks differed very significantly from us in the sensitivity of their response to the choice, arrangement, and delivery of words. This sensitivity has been dulled to the point of extinction in our own culture by the quick production and consumption of the printed word in immense quantities, the development of pictorial communication, and the importance now assumed by studies and activities which find their most efficient expression in figures and diagrams. Awareness of this difference between our culture and the Greeks' helps us to understand why the functions of oratory were not limited to political deliberation and litigation; great occasions such as international festivals or the burial of the war-dead could be enhanced, on a much greater scale than is acceptable nowadays, by what the Greeks called 'epideictic' oratory, the oratory of display, in which the speaker's concern was to articulate and fortify the sentiments of his audience. Arguments on any topic, designed to stimulate thought by their novelty, were often cast in the form of a speech (the modern equivalent would be an article or essay, perhaps a pamphlet), and by being read aloud at private gatherings they were disseminated far beyond the possessors of the written texts. Compositions of this kind included 'prosecutions' and 'defences' of legendary characters or of persons involved in hypothetical cases, as well as the 'praise' or 'blame' of creatures, inventions, commodities or abstractions; in Plato's *Symposium* the guests take it in turn to extemporize speeches in praise of Eros, the deity who personifies the experiences of falling in love and being in love.

It was undoubtedly the importance of the spoken word in politics and law—that is to say, in the life of the community—which diverted so much intellectual energy in the second half of the fifth century B.C. into the analysis and systematization of the techniques of persuasion, and away from scientific activity. The 'sophists', who in their way performed the function now performed for a very much larger section of society by tertiary education, interested themselves in a great range of subjects, from physics and biology to logic and ethics, but their pupils were commonly motivated by an ambition to attain high standing in the community, through skill in persuasive speaking. In Aristophanes' *Clouds*, where Socrates is caricatured as a sophist, the old man who tries to learn from him wants above all to know how to defeat his creditors in court, for Socrates knows how to 'make wrong appear right'. However great the misunderstanding of Socrates' interests and priorities, the comic poet's notion of sophistic teaching is not wholly mistaken; a chain of affinities links the practical techniques of persuasive speech with intellectual exercises in 'praising and blaming the same thing' (an educational practice ascribed to the sophist Protagoras) and philosophical enquiry into the fragility of inference from the evidence of one's senses.

II

It seems to have been between 430 and 420 B.C. that the practice of circulating speeches in writing began at Athens; it may possibly have begun a little earlier in Sicily. Tradition, founded in the first place on experience and memory and thereafter sustained by reference to the available allusions and representations in comedy and history, regarded Pericles as the supreme political orator. He died in 429, and no Periclean speech was transmitted in written form; the relation between what he actually said on certain occasions and the highly condensed, sophisticated speeches put into his mouth by Thucydides is controversial. The earliest orator whose speeches could be read by posterity was Antiphon, active in Athenian anti-democratic circles as a political consultant but unobtrusive in public life until he took part in the revolution of 411 and was executed for treason in the following year. What we have of his work all concerns homicide, and it includes three quarters of speeches on imaginary cases—two by the prosecution, and two for the defence, in each case. These oratorical exercises may not be by Antiphon himself, but there is no reason to dismiss them as late forgeries, and some reason to think that they may be a little earlier than Antiphon; theoretical works on oratory, accompanied by the construction of models and exercises, may perhaps antedate the publication of written versions of speeches composed for actual occasions. It is also necessary to remember that Athenian booksellers in the fourth century B.C. liked to ascribe to one or another of a small number of famous orators many speeches actually composed by little-known individuals, very much as London music-publishers in the late eighteenth century sold under the name of Haydn a great deal of music which was not his. The Greeks themselves took it for granted, and did not think it pedantic or over-ingenious to suspect, that a speech which bore the name of X might not be by X. These uncertainties frustrate attempts to write the biography of an individual orator or to characterize his personal range of styles, but they do not prevent us from studying the history of oratory as a genre, for the speeches sold under the name of X in the fourth century and catalogued as his in the Alexandrian Library a century later were normally the products of his period and ambience.

The language of oratory in the late fifth century seems to have been exuberant and inventive. Antiphon, like Thucydides, had a penchant for rare words, and perhaps coined some (though before speaking with assurance of the coining of words we would need much more evidence than we have). Gorgias, a Sicilian teacher of oratory well known at Athens, interested more in artistic and intellectual display than in the practicalities of law and politics, exploited to an exaggerated degree the potential of the Greek language for assonance and symmetry, as, for example, in his *Praise of Helen* (he calls it a *paignion*, 'conceit' or 'entertainment'), where he argues that Helen of Troy is not to be blamed for going off with Paris.

> It was either by the wishes (*boulēmata*) of Fortune and the counsels (*bouleumata*) of the gods

and the decrees (*psēphismata*) of Necessity that she did what she did, or carried off by force, or persuaded by argument, or seized by Love. In the first case, her accuser merits accusation; for it is impossible by human forethought (*promēthiā*) to thwart the determination (*prothūmiā*) of a god. For it is the law of nature not that the stronger should be thwarted by the weaker, but that the weaker should be ruled (*arkhesthai*) and led (*agesthai*) by the stronger. (Gorgias, *Helen* 6)

Gorgias's style had enduring influence, though in forms much more refined and subtle than the example displays, on epideictic oratory, which from the beginning of the fourth century was clearly differentiated in style from forensic and political oratory. At the same time a sharper demarcation between prose and poetry established itself rapidly. There are still poetic constructions and expressions in the long speech *On the Mysteries* composed in his own defence by the politician Andocides in 400/399, but by that time a style in touch with the spoken language, but invested with a force and dignity lacking in everyday speech, was already establishing itself as the appropriate medium for the courts and the assembly.

III

Among the orators whose reputations have best stood the test of time is Lysias, the son of a wealthy Syracusan arms-manufacturer long resident at Athens; as an alien, he was debarred from exercising the rights of an Athenian citizen, but after the 'Thirty Tyrants', imposed on Athens by the enemy at the end of the Peloponnesian War, had killed his brother, he joined the democratic forces in exile and was able to contribute to their restoration through his business connections. His work for a variety of litigants displays an ability to match the style and argument of a speech to individual personalities, as the following three examples show. The first speaker is a husband who has trapped and killed his wife's lover; the second, a cripple whose right to a state subsidy has been questioned; and the third, a man whose qualification to serve on the Council is in dispute.

> So off went the old woman, and straight away I was in a great turmoil, and everything came into my mind, and I was full of suspicion, when I thought how I'd been locked in the bedroom and I remembered how that night the courtyard door creaked, and the outer door too, which had never happened before, and I got the impression that my wife had had make-up on. All this came into my mind, and I was full of suspicion. (Lysias, *On the Murder of Eratosthenes* 17)

> About my riding horses—to which he had the audacity to refer, with no fear of Fortune and no shame in front of you—there's not much I need say. It seems to me that all those who labour under a misfortune use their wits above all in looking for some way to cope with the suffering inflicted on them, some way that will most save them distress. I'm one of them, and, given the plight I'm in, riding is the most comfortable way I've found of going on any journey that's more than the minimum. (Lysias, *Defence of the Cripple* 10)

Now, first, you must realize that no man is by
nature either oligarchic or democratic; whatever
constitution is to the advantage of an individual,
that is the one which he wants to see established
. . . It is not, therefore, difficult to see that the
subject of conflicts is not the constitution, but
the personal advantage of the individual. So you
should assess the loyalty of citizens by looking
at their political conduct under the democracy
and asking whether they stood to gain anything
by revolution. (Lysias, *Defence on a charge of
anti-democratic activity* 8, 10)

One of the surviving speeches of Lysias is the accusation
which he himself made against a member of the Thirty Tyrants, Eratosthenes (unconnected with the adulterer in the
excerpt above); it is a speech of great lucidity and force,
and ends with seven Greek words which require some amplification to pass muster as English, literally, 'I-shall-stop
accusing.   You-have-heard,   you-have-seen,   you-have-
undergone, you-have. Judge.' That is to say, 'Here I end
my speech. You have heard my words. You have seen
him. You have suffered under him. You have him. Now
judge him!' (Lysias, *Prosecution of Eratosthenes* 100).

IV

From the period 403-390 we possess half a dozen forensic
speeches composed by Isocrates, who grew up during the
Peloponnesian War and lived to see the decisive victory
of Philip over the Greek city-states, dying in 338 at the age
of ninety-eight. He was never an active politician, and in
middle age he abandoned the practice of writing for litigants; instead, he established a school of oratory. As a
teacher of oratory he inevitably incurred much the same
odium as the sophists of the previous generation, being
vulnerable to the allegation that in return for payment he
taught people who were in the wrong how to persuade a
jury that they were in the right. His teaching, however,
had little bearing on the practice of the lawcourts; it assumed and gave expression to generally acceptable moral
values, aligned itself with conservative sentiment on political and economic issues, and adopted a notion of the Athenian past which was patriotic, moralistic, and altogether
lacking in the precision and discrimination demanded by
genuine historical curiosity. During the second half of his
life he published a number of essays, cast in the form of
speeches, on major political issues. They preach the need
for a reform of attitudes but avoid detailed discussion of
the relation between ends and means in political and administrative procedures. Like Xenophon and no doubt
many others who looked at the mid-fourth century with
eyes which had seen the endless shifts of the balance of
power between the city-states, he was preoccupied with
the problem of Greek disunity, and he saw in Philip of
Macedon a potential leader of Greeks and Macedonians
in a long and profitable war against the Persian Empire.

At eighty-two Isocrates wrote a work, *On the Exchange*
(the title is derived from a certain procedure in the Athenian system of taxation), in which he explains and defends
his own concept of culture and his own system of education through oratory. His attitude to serious intellectual
activity is strikingly patronizing and philistine. Mathematics and astronomy, for example, he regards as studies

which attract the ingenious young and perform a useful
function in sharpening their wits, as well as keeping them
away from more sensual pastimes, but do not merit the attention of mature men. And the fact that philosophers disagree fundamentally on metaphysical questions seems to
him a good reason for wasting no time on metaphysics.
When he praises orginality, he does not mean the radical
originality which exposes the weakness of traditional belief, but inventiveness in the service of traditional virtues.
For him, the articulation of argument and exhortation fortifies the character of the speaker as father, citizen, soldier,
and Greek and enhances the solidarity and endurance of
the family, the city, and the civilized world. He devoted
immense care to the architecture of language, and the
complexity of a typical Isocratean sentence contrasts with
the simple symmetries and assonances of Gorgias. The following examples is set out in print in a way designed to
display its structure.

> I assert
> that to acquire the requisite knowledge of the
> modes of utterance
> on which all composition and delivery of dis-
> course is founded
> is not among the most difficult of tasks,
> provided that one puts oneself in the hands
> not of those who make easy promises
> but of those who have real understanding of the
> subject,
> but to choose the elements appropriate for any
> given occasion
> and to combine them one with another
> and to order them suitably
> and moreover to make no misjudgment of the
> occasion
> but to elaborate the thought of the whole speech
> becomingly
> and to attain harmony and art in language
> requires great preparation
> and is a task for a vigorous and inventive mind;
> and that it is necessary
> that the pupil,
> in addition to the natural endowment which is
> indispensable,
> should learn the different kinds of speech
> and be practised in their use,
> while the teacher
> should be able to expound some lessons with
> such thoroughness
> as to omit nothing of what can be transmitted in
> teaching,
> and for the rest should make himself an example
> of such a kind
> that those who are modelled on him
>   and capable of imitating him
> should be recognized unquestionably as speak-
> ing
> more artistically and more acceptably than all
> others.
>
> (Isocrates, *Against the Sophists* 16-18)

V

There is a striking contrast between Isocrates and the
greatest of the fourth-century orators, Demosthenes. Demosthenes came into prominence in Athenian politics in
the 350s; by that time he had already proved himself a fo-

rensic speaker of considerable power and elegance and a tenacious adversary, for he had brought actions against the guardians who had handled his inheritance from his father during his adolescence, and through that he had been caught up in a nexus of long-standing feuds. A set of massive speeches written in the period 355-352 displays his deep involvement with an influential group in political life. These speeches are rarely read in translation nowadays; to disentangle their intricate and allusive arguments requires patience and much technical knowledge. It is easier for the modern reader to appreciate the shorter speeches, the **Philippics** and **Olynthiacs**, charged with passion and scorn, in which Demosthenes sought to encourage Athenian resistance to Philip of Macedon. After Philip's victory in 338, positive attempts to organize opposition to the Macedonians became imprudent and pointless. When Philip's son, Alexander the Great, died in 323, revolt flared up; Demosthenes played a part in this revolt, but it failed, and he killed himself in 322 to avoid arrest and execution. He is commonly admired as a champion of democracy against absolute monarchy and of the small, proud city-state against the military might of an alien conqueror. He was that among other things; but two centuries later Polybius (xviii 14) made the point that Demosthenes was too free in branding as 'traitors' men in many parts of Greece who sided with Philip as a refuge from Spartan aggression and were not unreasonably cool towards the maintenance of Athenian power.

Like Isocrates, Demosthenes took great artistic trouble; they both avoided 'hiatus' (the placing of a word which begins with a vowel immediately after a word ending with a vowel), and Demosthenes introduced a further refinement, avoiding any combination of words which would create a succession of more than two syllables scanned 'short' by the rules of Greek metre. Greek commonly admits of alternative orderings of the words in a clause, and though the principles governing a writer's choice between the alternatives are reasonably well understood, we cannot expect to assess the subtleties with confidence; hence we cannot easily pass judgement on the 'naturalness' of Demosthenes' language. We can, however, observe that whereas the elaborate structuring of Isocrates' prose distracts our attention from the content, Demosthenes often conveys an impression of spontaneity which it is fair to suppose he achieved by spending twice as much time on achieving it as lesser men spent on displaying a more obvious virtuosity of style. In the following passage he introduces a long argument to the effect that a decree proposed by a certain Aristocrates is illegal.

> It is only right, I think, that having promised to demonstrate three points—one, that the decree proposed is contrary to law; secondly, that it is disadvantageous to our city; and thirdly, that the beneficiary of the proposal does not merit what he is offered—I should give you, who will hear my argument, the freedom to choose what you wish to hear first, what second, and what last. Consider your performance, so that I may deal with that first. You prefer the argument about illegality? Very well, I will speak about that. (Demosthenes, *Prosecution of Aristocrates* 18f.)

We do not normally expect to find, in the small fraction of Greek oratory which has survived, two speeches which are concerned with the same case—indeed, we do not as a rule know whether the speech which we read was a successful or unsuccessful plea—but two famous occasions on which Demosthenes found himself in opposition to Aeschines furnish exceptions. In 343 Demosthenes prosecuted Aeschines for betraying Athenian interests on an embassy (in which they both participated) to Philip of Macedon, and his speech **On the Misconduct of the Embassy** may be read in conjunction with Aeschines' defence; and Aeschines' *Prosecution of Ctesiphon*, delivered in 330, is answered by Demosthenes' **On the Crown**, the most famous of Greek speeches, in which Demosthenes presents a justification of his own policies in the years which culminated in Philip's final victory. The speech is massive, but charged throughout with vigour, pathos and drama; a random sample may convey its qualities.

> Everyone, everywhere, lets the past go, and no one offers advice about it. It is the future or the present that requires the adviser to perform his function. On that occasion it was apparent that some of our perils lay ahead, while others were already upon us; look at the policy I chose *then*, don't carp at me for the outcome. All things turn out in the end as God wills; it is choice of policy, and that alone, which reveals the mind of the adviser . . . If the hurricane was too strong, not just for us, but for all the Greek world, what can be done? As if a ship-owner, who had done everything for the safety of his ship and equipped it in a way which, to the best of his belief, would bring it through safely, and then met a storm, and the tackle were damaged, or even completely smashed, and someone blamed him for the wreck! 'It wasn't my hand on the tiller', he would say—just as I wasn't a general—'and I was not the master of Fate; she is the mistress of everything.' (Demosthenes, **On the Crown** 192-4)

Nothing illustrates the Greeks' interest in oratory more vividly than the fact that side by side with political speeches on issues of the greatest magnitude, such as **On the Crown**, ancient critics valued and transmitted speeches written for unimportant litigants involved in petty squabbles. Granted that we may err in assessing the importance of a man about whom we may by chance know nothing else, we can at least be sure that the erosion of a field by a neighbour's blocking of a stream was not an event upon which the fortunes of Athens turned; but it is precisely on cases of such a kind that Demosthenes on occasion employed his most sensitive craftsmanship. These 'private' speeches, together with the surviving speeches of an orator, Isaeus, of the generation before Demosthenes (all concerned with disputed wills, though we know that Isaeus handled other types of case too), have a peculiar value in that they illustrate the social attitudes and values of classical Athens in the fourth century B.C., and the best of them bring Athens vividly to life.

Cecil W. Wooten　　(essay date 1983)

SOURCE: *Cicero's "Philippics" and Their Demosthenic*

Model: The Rhetoric of Crisis, The University of North Carolina Press, 1983, 199 p.

[*In the following excerpt, Wooten examines the essential features of Demosthenes's style and argumentation, maintaining that "the hallmark of Demosthenic oratory is variety, both in style and in the modulation of tone."*]

The hallmark of Demosthenic oratory is variety, both in style and in the modulation of tone, which is clearly related to style. Dionysius of Halicarnassus points out at the end of his essay on Demosthenes (*On Demosthenes* 43):

> Now that I have shown the qualities of Demosthenes' chosen style, the reader may examine his speeches for himself. He will observe that they are composed as I have described, now serious, austere and dignified, now pleasant and agreeable. And if he still feels in need of illustration, let him take in his hand any of the speeches, beginning at any point he wishes, and read on, analysing every sentence and seeing whether the structure is sometimes halting and broken up, sometimes coherent and compact; sometimes harshly grating on the ear, sometimes gently soothing; sometimes impelling hearers to emotion, sometimes leading gently on to moral seriousness; and producing different effects in the actual composition.

Closely related to this variety of style is Demosthenes' keen sense of propriety, his ability to choose the form that will most vividly convey the content that he wants to express. Style in his speeches is always functional, it is never merely decoration, it always clarifies a point that he wants to make or reinforces an idea that he wants to convey to his audience. In many ways, what is most striking about Demosthenes' oratory is the firm control, the ability to deal in a direct way with what is most important, which he consistently shows. His oratory is flesh and bones and muscle; there is no fat. This gives to his speeches vigor, directness, and immediacy in a way that was rarely equaled in ancient oratory.

The best analysis of Demosthenes' style, and the one that brings out most clearly its variety, is that found in Hermogenes' *On Ideas* [edited by H. Rabe]. This is not the place for a detailed analysis of the system of Hermogenes, which is quite complicated; and that is not my intention here. However, a general discussion of Hermogenes' analysis, with illustrations from Demosthenes' speeches, is the best way to bring out the point that I want to make, that is, the variety of styles and the rapid change of tone that one finds in Demosthenes' speeches.

Hermogenes sees in Demosthenes' oratory seven "types" or forms of style that he calls clarity, grandeur, beauty, rapidity, character, sincerity, and force (*saphēneia, megethos, kallos, gorgotēs, ēthos, alētheia,* and *deinotēs*). What is distinctive about Demosthenes' style is the way in which all of these types, as well as delicately nuanced variations on them, are combined in his oratory. As Hermogenes says:

> All these are, as it were, woven together and interpenetrating. For such is the style of Demosthenes . . . and thus [by diversifying his style]

he has made all things fit together in his style, which forms a unity because all the types interpenetrate in it. And so, from all the beauties of style the one most beautiful, the Demosthenic, has been created.

Therefore, let us look more closely at the various types from which, according to Hermogenes, Demosthenes' style was created. Hermogenes divides his discussion of clarity into two parts, purity (*katharotēs*) and distinctness (*eukrineia*). Purity is concerned with the sentence itself; distinctness is concerned with the clarity of the speech as a whole.

A clear sentence expresses a thought that is familiar to most people, a thought that is not esoteric. It will be expressed as a direct statement of fact, having the appearance of conversation. The structure will usually consist of a subject, in the nominative case, and a main verb; and the clauses will be short and complete in themselves. The rhythm will be the loose rhythms of conversation, especially iambs.

Demosthenes is very fond of the direct style described above, a style that depends more on statement than elaboration or embellishment, and consequently shows a preference for simple or compound sentences over periodic sentences. Most of his sentences are fairly brief and simple in their structure, using no uncommon words, no figurative language, and clauses that are short and concise; the elaborate sentence is used only to create a special emphasis or a special effect.

Distinctness demands that the orator state clearly what is going to be said and how it is going to be developed and that the transitions from one thought to the next be clear and smooth. In other words, the points that the orator wants to make must be obvious to his audience.

Demosthenes employs many devices that make clear to his audience the points that he wants to make. What really holds his speeches together is the repetition of certain themes or motifs, sometimes called Demosthenic commonplaces, that appear throughout the argumentation. This repetition of certain ideas, sometimes of certain words that sum up those ideas, images, types of argument, or patterns of action makes the import of the whole speech more emphatic. This recurrence, however, is not a "heavy repetition of ideas, but a subtle process of elaboration and development bringing to light new dimensions of meaning and sensation" [quoted from Galen Rowe, "Demosthenes' **First Philippic**: The Satiric Mode," *Transactions of the American Philological Association* 99 (1968)]. **Philippic I**, for example, is primarily a call to action, an effort to arouse the Athenians from their inertia to take the action that Demosthenes felt had to be taken. The repetition of verbs expressing necessity or obligation throughout this speech underlines that idea. They run like a leitmotiv throughout the speech. Although, as Hermogenes points out, Demosthenes frequently states explicitly what points he will develop at the outset of an argument, he often passes almost imperceptibly from motif to motif; there are quick but almost unnoticeable changes in thought and tone. However, since there is no effort to make more than one point at a time, it is easy for the hearer or reader to keep his bearings in the speech; and these imperceptible transitions from one thought to the next contribute to the directness of the speech by removing any appearance of hesitation. Moreover, to make his ideas more effective, he usually limits the number of points that he wants to make to a few only.

Another principle of argumentation of which Demosthenes was fond is the scheme whereby the orator makes a seemingly paradoxical statement and then has an imaginary interlocutor ask him to explain. This is a clever practice, for it gains the audience's attention and stimulates the hearer to follow the rest of the speech more closely. It also gives the orator an effective means for leading into his argumentation. The beginning of the argumentation of *Philippic I* is a good example. Demosthenes tells the Athenians that they must not be disheartened because "what is worst from days gone by is best as regards the future." Then the question is asked, "What then is this?" To this Demosthenes replies that the situation of Athens is bad because the Athenians have enacted none of the measures that would have ameliorated their position, which leaves hope that things will improve if they do what must be done.

The clarity of Demosthenes' style and of the organization of his speeches is indicative of the simplicity with which he viewed Athens' struggle with Philip, the advocate's tendency to see the situation in terms of black and white. It is also indicative of his tendency to stake out a firm, clearcut, and unqualified position, to which he holds tenaciously and without compromise.

Demosthenes realized that the first requirement of any speech was that it be clear, and this accounts for the importance of *saphēneia* in his speeches. He also realized, however, that clarity can appear trite or commonplace. In his discussion of grandeur (*megethos*), Hermogenes deals with the various ways in which Demosthenes prevents the clear from seeming mundane. Hermogenes divides grandeur into six subtypes that for our purposes here can be divided into three groups: solemnity and brilliance; abundance; and asperity, vehemence, and florescence.

Solemnity (*semnotēs*) is used for universal and general statements about elevated topics such as the soul, justice, and temperance or for descriptions of glorious human deeds. These thoughts are directly stated, without hesitation of any sort, using clauses that are short and complete and relying on the use of nouns more than verbs. To increase the dignity of the sentence, the orator uses words with broad sounds, that is, which have many long syllables and diphthongs. In other words, passages that are conversational employ the loose iambic rhythm into which speech most naturally falls. More oratorical and less commonplace passages should employ more artificial, more stately rhythms. In his speech *On the Crown*, for example, Demosthenes opens the sentence that describes Philip's taking of Elateia in a dactylic hexameter, the stately meter of epic poetry (*On the Crown* 143). Epic meter is appropriate for an event of this magnitude, for Elateia commanded the entrance into Attica. In general, rhythms in which there is a predominance of heavy syllables produce a slow, somber, majestic, and sententious effect since they take longer to pronounce, and such rhythms should be used in passages of great gravity and importance. Light syllables produce a more rapid effect, and rhythms in which short vowels (or light syllables) predominate should be used in more conversational passages. Blass has pointed out that Demosthenes generally avoids more than two light syllables in succession, which gives a more dignified, manly, and solemn tone to his prose.

There are many examples of solemnity in Demosthenes. The most famous is the oath by those Athenians who had fought the Persians:

> But it is not possible, it is not possible, men of Athens, that you acted wrongly when you chose to fight for the liberty and safety of all the Greeks, no, I swear it by your ancestors who fought at Marathon, by those who drew up in battle array at Plataea, by those who fought in the sea battles at Salamis and Artemisium, and by many other brave men who lie in the public sepulchers, all of whom the city buried at its own expense, thinking them worthy of the same honor, Aeschines, not just those who were successful and victorious. And justly so. For all performed the duty of brave men. Their fortune was such as heaven granted to them. (*On the Crown* 208)

One sees here the use of epanadiplosis, the repetition of a phrase to emphasize and drive home a point; the first time it is expressed in a moderate tone, then is repeated in a much more forceful tone with added vocal stress. Demosthenes especially uses this figure with negatives when he wants to insist upon the negation. One sees in this passage as well the appeal to the finest traditions of the city of Athens, which is so typical of Demosthenes.

Hermogenes recommends the use of metaphor as a device that is characteristic of solemnity, although strong metaphors are more typical of asperity. . . . Demosthenes uses metaphors to make an abstract idea or complicated concept clearer to his listeners and to arouse their attention. The metaphor makes his thought more vivid and puts him into closer contact with his audience. Many of his metaphors, reflecting his combative nature, are dominated by the idea of struggling, and many of them are taken from warfare. There are also metaphors from hunting, another form of combat. One sees this obsession with struggling in his metaphors taken from physical life as well, especially in metaphors concerning sickness and health. He also prefers images of the weather, a natural phenomenon against which man struggles for survival, just as, according to Demosthenes, the Athenians were struggling against Philip and just as Demosthenes himself was struggling for his own political survival. Demosthenes' similes are thematically very similar to his metaphors. They also deal primarily with struggle and combat, activity and movement, sickness and health, reflecting once again Demosthenes' own psychological makeup.

The most striking characteristics of Demosthenes' metaphors and similes are their simplicity and the fact that they are never added just to adorn the speech, never purely ornamental. Demosthenes' figures are always natural and appear to be spontaneous. They always have a persuasive function and are closely related to the point that the orator is making. In fact, this repetition of certain images is typical of Demosthenes' emphatic style and is intended to plant certain concepts deeply in the minds of his listeners through a recurrence of certain motifs, which often contributes significantly to holding the speech together.

Brilliance (*lamprotēs*) is closely related to solemnity. Again the speaker uses this type of style when he has confidence in what he is saying, that is, when he is saying what is generally approved by or what will please the audience. The difference between solemnity and brilliance is related to content. The orator uses brilliance when he is describing a noble act of less universal import than those glorious deeds that would be described by solemnity, when he is discussing, for example, his own acts as opposed to those of his ancestors. The style is basically the same as the solemn except that the clauses are often rather long and use amplification:

> I did not fortify the city with stones or with bricks, nor do I pride myself especially on these works. But if you want to consider my fortifications justly, you will find weapons and cities and outposts and seaports and ships and horses and many ready to fight for them. (*On the Crown* 299)

As Hermogenes points out, it is amplification or abundance (*peribolē*), the second major element of grandeur, that Demosthenes uses most often to give emphasis to a thought and to lift it above the commonplace. Many of the techniques that make the style full are seen in the following passage:

> What Philip took and held before I became a politician and a public speaker, I will pass over. (1) For I think that none of these gains concerns me. (2) But what he was prevented from doing from the day when I turned my mind to political affairs, I will remind you of and give an account of them, premising only the following. (3) A great advantage, men of Athens, existed for Philip. (4) For among the Greeks, not some, but all alike, it happened that there was a crop of traitors and venal politicians and men hateful to the gods such as no one ever remembers having existed before. (5) Having taken these as assistants and accomplices, he made the Greeks, who even before had been badly disposed to one another and quarrelsome, even more so, deceiving some, and bribing others, and corrupting others in every way, and he split them into many factions, although one thing was beneficial to them all, to prevent him from becoming greater. (*On the Crown* 60-61)

Many elements in this passage amplify the thought. There is antithesis and parallelism in the first sentence and the third; however, as usual, Demosthenes avoids the strict, obvious antitheses of the Gorgianic style. He never allows the desire for contrast or parallels to control his thought. He often purposely disturbs a perfect balance to make the expression seem more natural while still retaining the emphatic contrast achieved by the use of an antithetical structure. Antithesis for Demosthenes was a much more flexible means of expression that it was for Gorgias or

Isocrates. He controls the style; the style does not control him. Demosthenes' antitheses, moreover, all grow out of the thought. He usually prefers equivalence, or antithesis of ideas, to detailed antithesis in structure, for this shows more sincerity and appears to be more natural and truthful than strict antithesis. He uses antithesis and parallelism only when it fits his design, when it heightens, say, the irony of a contrast, such as "from small and humble Philip has grown great" (*Philippic III* 21).

In this passage, too, is seen Demosthenes' fondness for the figure of speech called synonymity, the repetition of nearly synonymous words to allow the speaker to emphasize and dwell upon an idea. These synonyms give the passage more weight and majesty and the sort of repetition that contributes to the clarity of the speech. They force the attention of the hearer on an idea that he might pass over otherwise and fix the idea in his mind. There is generally no real difference between the synonyms except that the first is often more general. The synonyms, moreover, are often arranged in groups of three and become more intense or more general as they progress (climax); and Demosthenes quite often uses polysyndeton to allow him to linger even longer on each component that makes up the group, as he does in the fifth sentence quoted above.

The goal of abundance is to make the thought clear, vivid, and emphatic; and its importance in the speeches of Demosthenes is another indication of the clarity and directness with which he viewed Athens' conflict with Philip. There is no hesitation, no doubt; the issue to him is clearcut and obvious.

The third group comprising grandeur is composed of asperity (*trachutēs*), vehemence (*sphodrotēs*), and florescence (*akmē*). These three share a common feature: they all involve criticism or reproach.

Asperity is the style to be used when the orator is making an open reproach of someone or some group more important than himself. The style is often figurative, usually uses very short clauses and often simple phrases, and takes no notice of sounds that clash. Indeed, by means of this style, the orator attempts to produce a harsh effect in order to convey anger or impatience:

> When, therefore, Athenians, will you do at last what must be done? What are you waiting for? Until, by Zeus, it is necessary. But now how should one consider what has happened? For I think that for free men shame because of their position is the greatest compulsion. Or, tell me, do you want to run around and ask one another, "Is there some news?" For what could be more shocking news than that a Macedonian is making war on the Athenians and managing the affairs of the Greeks? "Has Philip died?" "No, by Zeus, but he is sick." And what does it matter to you? For indeed, if he dies, swiftly you would create another Philip, if this is the way you manage your affairs.(*Philippic I* 10)

The rhetorical questions and the exclamations give the impression that Demosthenes' anger and impatience have spontaneously burst forth and are intended to provoke the same reaction from his audience. By being angry himself, he attempts to make his audience angry. Questions, direct forms of address, and parenthetical expressions such as "tell me" give an air of spontaneity and liveliness to the passage and put the orator in closer contact with his audience. The imaginary dialogue that Demosthenes uses here is intended to have the same effect on the auditor as the rhetorical question, to strike him with the foolishness of the situation as the orator presents it and to arouse his indignation. Demosthenes' own answers to the imaginary questions of the Athenian populace underline the seriousness of the situation and the naiveté of the Athenian people. The short sentences, spoken one right after the other with no connectives, also create an air of passion and rapidity of proof. The irony and sarcasm of the last sentence are intended to shame, even to anger, the people into taking some action. The whole passage is a call to action, an attempt to provoke the people by means of a passionate appeal to do what Demosthenes felt had to be done. The passage has great force. It is intended to shock and arouse. Through the use of the dramatic imaginary scene, the orator causes the reader or audience to feel what he feels. One can only imagine how forceful it must have been when delivered by an orator as consummate at delivery as Demosthenes is supposed to have been.

Vehemence should be used for reproach or abuse directed against people who are considered inferior to the orator. The charges are made very openly, and there is no mitigation of the criticism since the audience would receive it gladly. The best examples of vehemence in Demosthenes are those passages that he directs against Aeschines in the speech *On the Crown* (cf. 121, 127, 209), but there are also examples in the speeches against Philip:

> Although he is not only not a Greek, nor related to the Greeks in any way, but not even a barbarian from a place that is respectable, but a wretched Macedonian, from an area from which it was not even possible to buy a decent slave before. (*Philippic III* 31)

Florescence is like vehemence or asperity in that it is appropriate for criticism. However, just as the vehement style makes criticisms more openly and more harshly than asperity, florescence is used when the orator wants to make reproaches in a gentler manner; it is "expansive where the others are concise" [quoted from Annabel Patterson, *Hermogenes and the Renaissance*, 1970]. In other words, by using longer clauses, with amplification and figures of speech, such as the anaphora which one sees in the following passage, he mitigates the element of anger in the reproach and makes the criticism in a less accusatory fashion:

> It would not have been safe to plead Philip's cause in Olynthus unless the people of Olynthus were being benefited by sharing the revenues from Potidaea. It would not have been safe to plead his cause in Thessaly unless the majority of the Thessalians had benefited by his driving out the tyrants and giving them back the right of sending deputies to the Amphictyonic Council. It would not have been safe in Thebes until he had given back Boeotia and destroyed the Phocians. But at Athens, although Philip not

only has snatched from you Amphipolis and Cardia, but also is preparing Euboea as a seat of operations against you and is now proceeding on the way to attack Byzantium, it is safe to speak on his behalf. (*On the Chersonese* 65–66)

These three subtypes, asperity, vehemence, and florescence, inject an element of passion into the speech. They lift it above the commonplace by giving certain passages an air of the sort of spontaneity that is provoked by anger. The frequency with which Demosthenes uses such passages is another indication of the vehemence with which he waged the battle against Philip.

Just as anaphora and other figures of speech often associated with poetry can be used to mitigate passages of criticism or reproach, such figures can be used throughout the speech to give it some ornamentation, which charms and delights the audience with carefully chosen and meticulously wrought language. This aspect of the speech Hermogenes deals with under beauty (*kallos*). This style, which is usually associated with Isocrates, is relatively rare in Demosthenes, who generally avoided apparent artificiality in his style; but there are examples. Demosthenes sometimes uses climax, for instance, the repetition of the last word of a clause at the beginning of the following clause:

> I did not speak without making proposals, nor did I make proposals without serving as an ambassador, nor did I serve as an ambassador without persuading the Thebans. (*On the Crown* 179).

This passage also uses antithesis; and all of these figures create a pleasing and charming effect, which also impresses the thought on the audience.

Hermogenes associates beauty with the oratory of Isocrates, whose hallmark is the periodic style. Something should be said, therefore, about Demosthenes' use of this style. The period is a full combination of several thoughts into one independent sentence. Its hallmark is subordination. The period is so constructed that the various ideas that make up the sentence are "rounded off " at the end into a complete thought. All the clauses in the sentence are subordinated to and directed toward the completion of a single thought that is expressed in the principal clause. The period, therefore, expresses in one sentence a whole situation, that is, an action with the attendant circumstances that produced it and the consequences that followed upon it.

The period is composed of thought elements or clauses that are called *membra*. (There is here an analogy to the human body, the source of much critical terminology in antiquity, where the limbs make up the whole.) The *membra* are composed of smaller elements, such as prepositional phrases, which are called *incisa*. The classical period was thought of as having four *membra* or clauses, each of approximately sixteen syllables, the normal breath span; however, the best stylists vary the length of the clauses to avoid monotony. Demosthenes quite often alternates long and short clauses within the period, and in his speeches one often finds long periods alternating with shorter sentences that sum up the idea in the period.

Sometimes variety is achieved by the insertion of long sentences between periods that use coordination rather than subordination to unite the thoughts. He uses this coordinate construction when dealing with disparate ideas that in themselves lack unity and organization. Demosthenes realized that it was more effective to blend his well-constructed periods with sentences of a looser and freer construction. Even his periods are sometimes spacious and sometimes compact, and his spacious periods are always flowing and unartificial. He combined the elaborate and the simple, the periodic and the unperiodic, the strained and the relaxed.

There are three types of period. There is first what one might call the analytical period, a type of sentence in which the principal thought is stated first in an independent clause and then all the ramifications and consequences of that thought are expressed in subordinate clauses. The sentence opens up successively to different aspects of one single idea that is expressed in the main clause. It often progresses from the particular to the general and from the real to the ideal, especially in Demosthenes:

> What language should have been used, what proposal made by an adviser of the people of Athens (for indeed this makes a great difference), when I was conscious that from all time up until the day when I myself ascended the speaker's platform our country had always struggled for renown and honor and glory and that she had expended both more money and more lives in behalf of her honor and the common welfare of all than the other Greeks had spent only on their own behalf, and since I knew that Philip himself, against whom we were struggling, for the sake of empire and power had had an eye knocked out, fractured his collar bone, broken his hand and his leg, was willing to lose any part of his body fortune demanded, provided that there should be a life of honor and glory for the rest? (*On the Crown* 66–67)

This is the most direct type of period since it states the main thought at the very beginning, thus putting the audience in possession at the outset of what is most important, and then spins out the ramifications and consequences of it. Demosthenes, a basically direct and analytical man, preferred this type and it could appropriately be called the Demosthenic period.

The second type, the suspenseful period, is just the opposite of the first since the full meaning is kept suspended until the end. In this type of period, the thought grows through subordinate clauses but is not completed until it reaches the end of the period, where the principal clause is located. This type of period builds up; the former works down. Although Demosthenes really prefers the first type, he does sometimes use this sort of periodic structure:

> If all the results of the peace that were promised to you have happened, and if you confess that you are filled with such cowardice and wickedness that although there were no enemy troops in your land and you were not being besieged by sea and the city was in no other danger, but you were buying grain at a low price and other con-

ditions were no worse than now, knowing in advance and hearing assurances from these men both that your allies would be destroyed and the Thebans would grow strong and that Philip would gain control of the affairs in Thrace and would set up in Euboea bases of attack against you and that all things that have been done would happen, if then you cheerfully made the peace, acquit Aeschines and do not add perjury also to such serious disgraces. (*On the False Embassy* 218–19)

After such a long and elaborate period, Demosthenes often uses a very short sentence that sums up his thought: "For he has done you no wrong but I am mad and I was full of folly to accuse him."

The third type is the logical period, in which the clauses that set the stage for the principal verb of the sentence, such as cause and attendant circumstance, come before the main clause and those clauses that express actions or ideas that logically follow the main idea in the sentence, such as result, come after the main clause:

> When Philip had sworn to the peace and had secured Thrace because of these men who did not obey my decree, he bribed them to prevent our leaving Macedonia until he had made ready the preparations for his campaign against the Phocians, in order that, if we should announce to you here that he was intending and making preparations to march, you might not set out and sailing with your fleet to Thermopylae block the passage as you did before but that you might hear us reporting these things when he was already on this side of Thermopylae and you could do nothing. (*On the Crown* 32)

Demosthenes uses this logical period more often than he does the suspenseful period discussed above, especially in relating the unified nature of a series of historical events.

The period is a vertical expression. It builds up to or works down from a central point, which is the main clause. The other ways of joining thoughts together are horizontal expressions; they lack the unity and organization of the period. Placing thoughts side by side in simple independent sentences or joining them together by coordinate conjunctions expresses a series of ideas that are not closely united. A series of actions or thoughts that are essentially unified are best expressed by means of the periodic structure.

Beautiful language tends to distend the speech, to relax and soften its intensity. This style can be used to beguile members of the audience when the orator does not want them to examine his thoughts too closely. Often, however, it is appropriate to compress the argument, to sketch out a situation or point as rapidly as possible, to give energy and vivacity to the speech, again in an attempt to convey the impatience or excitement of the orator. Hermogenes deals with this style under the heading of rapidity or *gorgotēs*. It is characterized by very short, choppy sentences that are often composed of short questions, quick replies, and sharp antitheses, and it often involves the use of trochaic rhythms:

> But this is not possible, it is not. For why would you have summoned them at this crisis? For

peace? But all enjoyed peace. For war? But you yourselves were discussing terms of peace. (*On the Crown* 24)

"By Zeus, the men are wretched and exceedingly stupid." To be sure, but still it is necessary that they be saved. For it is beneficial to Athens. (*On the Chersonese* 16)

Demosthenes, who was a nervous and excitable man, is very fond of this style; and the frequency with which one finds it in his speeches is indicative of the intensity and impatience with which he carried on his struggle against Philip.

Hermogenes' fifth type of style, *ēthos* or character, is somewhat more difficult to comprehend than the others since it does not seem to be a style so much as a type of argument. It is a collection of several types of style, most of them similar to those that have been discussed before, whose purpose is somehow to express the orator's character in an attempt to win the goodwill of the audience. In other words, it is a collection of various approaches whose purpose is to accomplish what Aristotle had called the ethical appeal.

The first of these approaches is simplicity or *apheleia*, a style similar to clarity but whose purpose is to convince the audience that the orator is the sort of man who can perceive and explain complex issues in a simple and comprehensible way. By this means the orator attempts to win their goodwill and their trust. A remarkable example is found in the *Third Philippic* when Demosthenes has been discussing why the affairs of Greece were in such a sorry state in the fourth century:

What then is the cause of this? For not without reason and a just cause were either the Greeks then so disposed toward liberty or those now so ready for slavery. There was something, men of Athens, something in the attitudes of the masses that does not exist now, something that triumphed over the wealth of the Persians and that kept Greece free and that was never defeated by sea or land, but now the fact that it has been lost has ruined everything and has thrown our affairs into confusion. What then was this? Nothing recondite or subtle, but that all hated those who took bribes from men who wanted to rule or to destroy Greece, and it was very serious to be convicted of taking bribes, and they punished the bribe taker with the greatest severity and there was no appeal and no pardon. (36–37)

Here Demosthenes has explained a very complex phenomenon in a very simple way, using language that is clear and straightforward, in an attempt to convince his audience that he is the sort of man who should be believed because of his clear insight into difficult situations and his ability to explain complex matters in a direct way.

There are three other approaches that can contribute to winning the goodwill of the audience: sweetness or *glukutēs*, subtlety or *drimutēs*, and modesty or *epieikeia*. Sweetness charms and delights the audience by injecting poetic elements into the speech, elements similar to those discussed under beauty but of a more poetical rather than

oratorical nature, such as the phrase "made the danger pass away like a cloud" (*On the Crown* 188), so admired by Longinus (*On the Sublime* 34.4). Subtlety impresses the audience with the orator's intelligence by showing his ability to express his thoughts in a striking and clever way: "But I do not fear that Philip is alive but that in Athens the spirit that hates and punishes wrongdoers is dead" (*On the False Embassy* 289). Finally, modesty tries to convince the audience that the speaker is a naturally humble and unpretentious person, so that the audience will sympathize with him more readily. This approach is seen most clearly in the speech *On the Crown:*

But if I address myself to what I have accomplished in politics, I will often be forced to speak about myself. I will try to do so as modestly as possible, and he who has started this controversy is the one to blame for the fact that the situation necessitates this. (4)

Here Demosthenes wins the audience's goodwill by convincing them that he will praise his own accomplishments only against his will.

The ethical appeal is extremely important in the speeches of Demosthenes, especially in his greatest speech, *On the Crown*. He can convince the audience that only he has a clear insight into the situation at hand and can explain it precisely, only he can sweep the audience away with the beauty of his language and the cleverness of his expression, and he alone can win their goodwill by convincing it that he is basically a humble and modest man who speaks out only because he must (cf. *Philippic I* 1).

Hermogenes' next type, verity or sincerity (*alētheia*), is closely related to *ēthos* in that its effect on the audience is to project an image of [what Annabel Patterson has described as] "one plain-dealing man addressing another in whose judgment he has perfect confidence." Sincerity is reflected in passages such as prayers, oaths, and exclamations of surprise that appear to be spontaneous outbursts on the part of the speaker. Such passages must be introduced without connectives or transitions and without any sort of preparation so that they will appear to have burst forth from the soul of the orator without having been thought out in advance:

And in your presence, men of Athens, I call on all the gods and goddesses who protect the land of Attica, and Pythian Apollo, who is the city's ancestral god, and I pray to them all. (*On the Crown* 141)

Anacolutha and sudden reproaches, which give the impression that the orator has suddenly been carried away by emotion or is composing his speech extemporaneously, also convey sincerity:

Therefore, since a righteous and just verdict has been indicated to all—but it is necessary that I, although I am not a slanderer. . . . (*On the Crown* 126)

To give an impression of spontaneity, the orator will also use figures of speech such as apostrophe, diaporesis, correctio, unfinished enumerations, and parentheses that seem to occur to him on the spot:

Why you, you—calling you what would anyone address you aptly—was there any occasion when you were present. . . . (*On the Crown* 22)

And to convey his emotion he will use short clauses and broken rhythms that Hermogenes has already associated with vehemence. Finally, there is a minor subdivision of sincerity, weightiness or *barutēs,* that basically involves the use of irony, which also reflects a candid relationship between the orator and his audience.

There are many examples of the sincere style in Demosthenes. Indeed, the first impression that the reader gets from his speeches is one of extreme earnestness. Prayers and oaths especially, such as the famous oath by those who died at Marathon, appear at points in the speech when the orator seems carried away by emotion; and there are many passages in which he seems to lose track of his train of thought or to be incapable of expressing what he feels because of the intensity of emotion that he experiences. These passages bring out once again the fervor and vehemence with which he combated Philip.

Hermogenes' seventh type, gravity, force, or *deinotēs,* is simply the correct use of all the previously discussed types of style at the proper time and in the proper place. As I indicated earlier in this essay, he considers this the hallmark of Demosthenic oratory and the real secret of his power. It is responsible for the extreme modulation of tone in Demosthenes' speeches. As Dionysius of Halicarnassus says: "Whenever I pick up any of the speeches of Demosthenes, I am filled with emotion and I am driven in this direction and that, feeling one emotion after another, disbelief, anguish, fear, scorn, hatred, pity, goodwill, anger, envy, all the emotions that can move the mind of man" (*On Demosthenes* 22). Hermogenes points out, however, in spite of his frequent declaration that all the types are found comingled in the style of Demosthenes, that clarity, character, sincerity, and rapidity are most characteristic of Demosthenes' style.

The system of Hermogenes was devised to describe the style of Demosthenes, and it brings out very well the variety and flexibility of his oratory:

> The aim of Clarity is that the audience should understand what is said, whereas Grandeur is designed to impress them with what is said. Beauty is designed to give pleasure, Speed to avoid boredom, Ethos helps to win over the audience by allying them with the speaker's customs and character, and Verity persuades them he is speaking the truth. Finally Gravity . . . stirs up the audience, and they are carried away by the completeness of the performance, not only to accept what they have heard, but to act upon it. [Annabel Patterson, *Hermogenes and the Renaissance*]

This stylistic versatility is one of the most characteristic features of Demosthenes' eloquence. His use of argumentation was also unique in many ways, and something should now be said about that.

In the fifth century, orators tended to focus on a single argument, especially the argument from expediency. In the fourth century, however, Isocrates, probably under the influence of Plato, tried to make oratory appear more moral. He popularized the practice of combining several arguments, honor, justice, and expediency, in a single speech. The early speeches of Demosthenes follow this practice; thus, *On the Symmories* and *On the Rhodians* employ appeals to expediency, honor, and justice. In the *Philippics,* Demosthenes returns to the fifth-century practice, seen most clearly in the speeches in Thucydides, of focusing on a single argument, especially the argument from expediency. To regain the vigor and directness of using a single argument and maintain the ethical and moral qualities of a synthesis of arguments, Demosthenes identified expediency, Athens' self-interest, with the preservation of Athenian national tradition. He appeals to Athenian patriotism in an effort to persuade the populace that the course of action that he proposes is the only course worthy of them. He is constantly holding up to the Athenians events in their earlier history, such as the Persian Wars, of which they would be extremely proud, in an attempt to rouse them to action through shame at the contrast between how they were acting and how their ancestors had acted.

In the arrangement of his speeches, both deliberative and judicial, Demosthenes abandoned the traditional rhetorical schema of proemium, narration, confirmation, refutation, and epilogue that was most typical of judicial speeches, except that his proemia and epilogues are usually distinct. The latter are quiet in tone, often containing prayers or wishes for the future. The main function of his epilogues is generally to recapitulate his major points and repeat his concrete proposals. Although some rhetoricians recommended an emotional close to the speech, Demosthenes preferred a calm, quiet ending, as did most Attic orators, which leaves the impression that his advice has been reasonable and based on facts.

What comes between is ordered in various ways and usually combines narration, confirmation, and refutation, a versatile arrangement that Demosthenes probably took from Isaeus. Demosthenes was quite clever at using narration as a means of argumentation and at keeping the attention of his audience by combining passages of narrative, confirmation, and refutation. In some ways, a formal narration is not necessary in a deliberative speech. Demosthenes, however, like Cicero, realized how effective narration could be, not only in proving a point but also in evoking a desired emotional reaction, or in drawing historical parallels or contrasts; both were aware that in giving advice on a particular problem it was necessary to describe clearly the situation that produced the problem.

In arranging the argumentation of his speeches, Demosthenes quite often places his specific proposal in the very center, flanked on either side by a general discussion of the situation that has made the proposal necessary. In the third section of the speech, which follows the nucleus of the argumentation, he often returns to points that were made in the general discussion preceding the specific proposal. What he wants to do is to prepare his audience to receive his proposal by showing them that the general situation makes such action necessary and then, having made the proposal, to return to a discussion of the general situation to show how the specific proposal can alleviate the difficulty.

In *Olynthiac I*, the section preceding the concrete proposal contains several Demosthenic commonplaces: all democracies are opposed to a monarchial form of government (2–7); Athens must seize the opportunity that the gods, who have always been on the side of the city, have offered to her in making possible an alliance with Olynthus (8); Philip has grown great because Athens has neglected her interests (9–15); Demosthenes will propose what he thinks is best for the state, whether he thinks that it will be popular or not, since this is really what is wrong in the state, that orators have spoken only to please for thirty years (16). Then there is the specific proposal that Athens send out two expeditionary forces and levy a war tax. In the third section, he returns to the general motifs of the first: just as the situation is most opportune for Athens, it is most difficult for Philip (21–24); Athens must act quickly to keep the war from Attica herself (25–27). *Olynthiac II* and *Philippic I* show this same sort of symmetry, in which general discussion of the situation is framed around a specific proposal (the *cardo* or hinge of the speech).

Even the earlier political speeches show a preference for this sort of arrangement. In the speech *For the Megalopolitans*, Demosthenes arranges his arguments almost in a circle around his main idea that Athens should keep both Sparta and Thebes weak rather than allying with either one (23). Likewise, in the speech *On the Symmories*, Demosthenes' specific proposal for reorganizing the naval boards stands in the middle of the argumentation (14–28), flanked on either side by more general discussions of Athens' relationship with the Persian king. Even the speech *Against Leptines*, which is loosely composed and in which the arguments seem to be lined up one right after the other, all introduced by the same transitional particle, shows this sort of symmetry in a sense. The considerations at the beginning (5–57) and end (88–162) of the argumentation are of a more general nature than those in the center, where Demosthenes discusses the honors granted to Chabrias and Ctesippus, in whose favor he was speaking. *On the Crown* shows the same sort of arrangement. Here

Demosthenes deals with the technical charges involved only after he has focused the jury's attention on the larger issues, identified himself with Athens, and thus obtained the jury's goodwill.

FURTHER READING

Cawkwell, George. *Philip of Macedon*. London: Faber & Faber, 1978, 215 p.
  Political biography of the Macedonian king in which Demosthenes's speeches are placed in the context of contemporary events.

Goldstein, Jonathan A. *The Letters of Demosthenes*. New York: Columbia University Press, 1968, 320 p.
  Study of Demosthenes's surviving letters that combines textual history and analysis with translations of four of the letters.

Jaeger, Werner. *Demosthenes: The Origin and Growth of His Policy*. New York: Octagon Books Inc., 1963, 273 p.
  Authoritative study of Demosthenes's political ideas.

Jebb, R. C. *The Attic Orators*. 2 vols. London: Macmillan and Co., 1893.
  Classic study of Athenian oratory, containing numerous references to Demosthenes.

MacDowell, Douglas M. "Introduction." In *Demosthenes: Against Medias (Oration 21)*, edited with introduction, translation, and commentary by Douglas M. MacDowell, pp. 1-85. Oxford: Clarendon Press, 1990.
  Analyzes the issues surrounding Demosthenes's prosecution of Medias.

Pearson, Lionel. "Introduction." In *Demosthenes: Six Private Speeches*, pp. 3-22. Norman: University of Oklahoma Press, 1972.
  Examination of Demosthenes's early litigation speeches.

Sealey, Raphael. *Demosthenes and His Time: A Study in Defeat*. New York: Oxford University Press, 1993, 340 p.
  Political history of fourth-century B.C. Athens that focuses on Demosthenes's role in opposing Philip of Macedon.

Usher, Stephen. "Demosthenes: Statesman and Patriot." *History Today* XXVI, No. 3 (March 1976): pp. 164-71.
  Sympathetic account of Demosthenes's career.

Flavius Josephus

c. 37-100

(Also known as Yoseph ben Matatyahu) Jewish historian.

INTRODUCTION

Josephus was a first-century Jewish historian known for his comprehensive post-biblical history of the Jews. His *Bellum Judaicum (Jewish War)* and *Antiquitates Judaicae (Jewish Antiquities)* reverently present the history of the Jewish people from the time of Adam and Eve to the fall of Masada in the year 73. His writings also shed light on Roman-Jewish relations, with a particular emphasis on the reigns of the emperors Vespasian, Titus, and Domitian. Since he lived under the patronage and protection of the Roman emperors, however, scholars are divided as to the credibility of Josephus's historiography.

Biographical Information

Born Yoseph ben Matatyahu around the year 37 or 38, Josephus was the son of a wealthy priestly family of Jerusalem, and was distantly related to the Hasmonean (Maccabbees) royal house. He was well educated and a devout Pharisee. Following his defense of a Jewish priest in a case before Nero at Rome, Josephus returned to Galilee, the northernmost region of Israel, where he commanded the Jewish forces in their revolt against the Romans which began around the year 66. Captured and jailed, Josephus was released after rightly predicting Vespasian's rise to the emperorship of Rome. Josephus instantly became a favorite of Roman royalty, but a traitor in the eyes of the Jews; for this reason, he habitually defends himself in his account of the Jewish war. Later, he was accused of treachery against Rome by anti-semitic Greeks and Romans, and, in response, Josephus wrote an autobiography and a short work explaining his actions and defending himself and his religion. It appears that Josephus died sometime after the year 93 (many scholars believe in the year 100), after the publication of *Jewish Antiquities*.

Major Works

Written in Rome during the final decades of the first century, Josephus's works focus on Jewish history, Judaism, the goodness and greatness of Rome, and his own personal history. His first work, *Jewish War*, presents the history of the Jewish war with the Romans and Josephus's role in it. Using various Gentile sources and his own recollections, Josephus suggests that radical Jewish groups were responsible for the war, and that Rome tried to restrain itself in order to avoid a war and the destruction of Jerusalem. *Jewish War* concludes with the fall of Masada, where nearly one thousand Jews refused to surrender to the Romans, committing mass suicide in the spring of 73. *Jewish Antiquities* follows as a survey of Jewish history from the

An eighteenth-century rendering of Josephus.

time of creation to the Jewish war years. The work is dedicated to the Greek grammarian Epaphroditus, and was meant to convey to Gentiles the integrity and antiquity of Jewish religion, laws, and customs. However, the work has become most famous for its "Testamonium Flavium" passage, which is the most complete reference to Jesus of Nazareth outside of the *Bible*.

Vita (*Life*) and *Contra Apionem* (*Against Apion*) are two lesser works in which Josephus defends his honor and that of his religion. The autobiographical *Life* counters Justus of Tiberias's claim that Josephus had favored the Galilean extremists, and had therefore instigated the revolt and the subsequent war with Rome in Galilee. Josephus's defense includes the observation that Justus conveniently made these accusations after the emperors and the Jewish kings in question were dead. *Against Apion*, on the other hand, responds to the Alexandrian Greek scholar's attack on the Jews and Judaism, and presents Josephus's eloquent and sensitive explanation of aspects of the Jewish religion.

Textual History

Although *Jewish War* was originally written in Aramaic because Josephus was not comfortable writing in Greek, the earliest extant editions of his works are Greek. After the fourth century, three Latin translations appeared, and, later, an Old Slavonic text with expanded passages on Christianity. By the eleventh century a Hebrew paraphrasing of Josephus's works called *Yosippon* was published, and in 1470 the first printed Latin text appeared at Augsburg, Germany. A printed Greek edition appeared at Basel in 1533. Although there were French and Spanish editions of Josephus's writings by the sixteenth century, it was not until the eighteenth century that William Whiston's English translation was published (in 1693 a revised English translation of Robert Arnauld d'Andilly's French edition had appeared). Over the next two centuries, however, Whiston's edition emerged as the principal English source for the works of Josephus, and was revised by Arthur Richard Shileto in 1889-90. The translation of *Jewish War* by G. A. Williamson and the nine-volume English-Greek edition of the complete works of Josephus in the Loeb Classical Library series are the standard English translations utilized by scholars today. But many post-biblical experts, such as Heinz Schreckenberg, have questioned the authenticity of the earliest extant Greek editions of Josephus's works. These scholars cite the numerous Christian intrusions found in *Jewish Antiquities* and suggest that they were the additions of early Christian apologists who tried to provide an historical basis for the emerging Christian church.

Critical Reception

Critics generally agree that Josephus is a significant first-century historiographer, but disagree regarding his accuracy and veracity. Because of his favorable treatment by the Roman emperors, his descriptions of and conclusions about leaders and events are often considered biased. For example, Zvi Yavetz has questioned Josephus's picture of Titus, and has contrasted it with information gleaned from other sources. Furthermore, some scholars have questioned the accuracy of Josephus's handling of the physical elements and circumstances of events: though Yigael Yadin has found his own archeological conclusions regarding the fall of Masada basically consistent with Josephus's account, J. D. Cohen, using the same archeological data and other sources, has concluded that there are many discrepancies in Josephus's version. Then, too, scholars refer to Josephus's consistent preoccupation with the Gentiles, pointing out his reinterpretation of Jewish scripture stories for the edification of Gentile readers, among them the Roman emperors. Nevertheless, other critics focus on Josephus's insightfully personal explanation of the grandeur of Judaism in *Against Apion* as an example of his total dedication to Judaism and his people. Finally, the controversial "Testamonium Flavium" in *Jewish Antiquities,* dealing with the person of Jesus of Nazareth, has received much attention. Many Christian scholars, from Eusebius to the present, have regarded Josephus's record of history as an important tool in understanding the foundations of the Christian church, while others have remarked that the

Christian emphasis in *Jewish Antiquities* is antithetical to the author's self-described Jewish religious devotion. Consequently, Josephus remains an enigmatic historiographer whose works are valued as the primary source of our knowledge of post-biblical Jewish history.

---

*PRINCIPAL WORKS

Bellum Judaicum [*Jewish War*]   (history)
Antiquitates Judaicae [*Jewish Antiquities*]   (history)
Vita [*Life*]   (autobiography)
Contra Apionem [*Against Apion*]   (essay)

---

*These works are generally thought to have been written in this order and before the year 100.

PRINCIPAL ENGLISH TRANSLATIONS

†*The Works of Flavius Josephus* (translated by William Whiston) 1752?
Josephus   (translated by H. St. John Thackeray, Ralph Marcus, Allen Paul Wikgren, and Louis H. Feldman). 9 vols. 1926-65
The Jewish War (translated by G. A. Williamson) 1959
Josephus, the Jewish War (translated by Gaalya Cornfeld) 1982

---

†1752 marks the date of Whiston's death. His translation includes *Jewish War*, *Jewish Antiquities*, and the *Vita*.

CRITICISM

Norman Bentwich   (essay date 1914)

SOURCE: *Josephus*, The Jewish Publication Society of America, 1914, 266 p.

[*In the essay below, Bentwich examines the extensive use of Gentile sources in* Jewish Antiquities, *contending that, while he preserves Jewish national pride, Josephus severely neglects the spiritual development of the Jewish people.*]

Josephus is the sole writer of the ancient world who has left a connected account of the Jewish people during the post-Biblical period, and the meagerness of his historical information is not due so much to his own deficiencies as to the difficulty of the material. From the period when the Scriptures closed, the affairs of the Jews had to be extracted, for the most part, out of works dealing with the annals of the whole of civilized humanity. With the conquest of Alexander the Great, the Jewish people enter into the Hellenistic world, and begin to command the attention of Hellenistic historians. They are an element in the cosmopolis which was the ideal of the world-conqueror. At the same time the nature of the history of their affairs vitally changes. The continuous chronicle of their doings, which had been kept from the Exodus out of Egypt to the Restoration from Babylon, and which was designed to impress a religious lesson and illustrate God's working, comes to an end; and their scribes are concerned to draw fresh lessons from that chronicle. The religious philosophy of history is not extended to the present. The Jews, on the other hand, chiefly engage the interest of the Gentiles when they come into violent collision with the governing power, or when they are involved in some war between rival Hellenistic sovereigns. Hence their history during the two centuries following Alexander's conquests, *i.e.* until the time when we again have adequate Jewish sources, is singularly shadowy and incoherent.

Josephus was not the man to pierce the obscurity by his intuition or by his research. Yet we must not be too critical of the want of proportion in his writing when we remember that he was a pioneer; for it was an original idea to piece together the stray fragments of history that referred to his people. It has been shown that in his attempt to stretch out the Biblical history till it can join on to the Hellenistic sources, Josephus interposes between the account of Esther and the fall of the Persian Empire a story of intrigue among the high priests. He there describes the crime of the high priest John in killing his brother in the Temple as more cruel and impious than anything done by the Greeks or Barbarians—an expression which must have originated in a Jewish, probably a Palestinian, authority, to whom Greek connoted cruelty. And in the next chapter Josephus inserts the story of the Samaritan Sanballat and the building of the Samaritan Temple on Mount Gerizim, as though these events happened at the time of Alexander's invasion of Persia. Rabbinical chronology interposes only one generation between Cyrus and Alexander. The Sanballat who appears in the Book of Nehemiah is represented as anticipating the part played by the Hellenists of a later century, and calling in the foreign invader against Judea and Jerusalem in order to set up his own son-in-law Manasseh as high priest. Probably, in the fashion of Jewish history, the events of a later time were placed in the popular Midrash a few generations back and repeated. Jewish legendary tradition is more certainly the basis of the account of Alexander's treatment of the Jews. The Talmud has preserved similar stories. According to both records, the Macedonian conqueror did obeisance before the high priest, who came out to ask for mercy, because he recognized in the Jewish dignitary a figure that had appeared to him in a dream. And when Alexander is made to revere the prophecies of Daniel and to prefer the Jews to the Samaritans and bestow on them equal rights with the Macedonians, the historian is simply crystallizing the floating stories of his nation, which are parallel with those invented by every other nation of antiquity about the Greek hero.

Passing on to Alexander's successors, he has scarcely fuller or more reliable sources. For Ptolemy's capture of Jerusalem on the Sabbath day, when the Jews would not resist, he calls in the confirmation of a Greek authority, Agatharchides of Cnidus. But he has to gloss over a period of nearly a hundred years, till he can introduce the story of the translation of the Scriptures into Greek, for which he found a copious source in the romantic history, or rather the historical romance, now known as the Letter of Aristeas. This Hellenistic production has come down to us intact, and therefore we can gather how closely Josephus paraphrases his authorities. Not that he refrained altogether from embellishment and improvement. The Aristeas of his version, as of the original, professes that he is not a Jew, but he adds that nevertheless he desires favor to be done to the Jews, because all men are the work of God, and "I am sensible that He is well pleased with all those that do good." Josephus states a large part of the story as if it were his own narrative, but in fact it is a paraphrase throughout. He reproduces less than half of the Letter, omitting the account of the visit of the royal envoy to Jerusalem and the discourse of Eleazar the high priest. For the seventy-two questions and answers, which form the last part, he refers curious readers to his source. But he sets out at length the description of the presents which Ptolemy sent to Jerusalem, rejoicing in the opportunity of showing at once the splendor of the Temple vessels and the honor paid by a Hellenistic monarch to his people.

From his own knowledge also, he adds a glowing eulogy, which Menedemus, the Greek philosopher, passed on the Jewish faith. The Letter of Aristeas says that the authors of the Septuagint translation uttered an imprecation on any one who should alter a word of their work; Josephus makes them invite correction, adding inconsequently—if our text is correct—that this was a wise action, "so that, when the thing was judged to have been well done, it might continue forever."

Having disposed of the Aristeas incident, Josephus has to fill in the blank between the time of Ptolemy Philadelphus (250 B. C. E. [Before the Christian Era]) and the Maccabean revolt against Antiochus Epiphanes, nearly one hundred years later, which was the next period for which he had Jewish authority. He returns then to his Hellenistic guides and extracts the few scattered incidents which he could find there referring to the Jewish people. But until he comes to the reign of Antiochus, he can only snatch up some "unconsidered trifles" of doubtful validity. Seleucus Nicator, he says, made the Jews citizens of the cities which he built in Asia, and gave them equal rights with the Macedonians and Greeks in Antioch. This information he would seem to have derived from the petition which the Jews of Antioch presented to Titus when, after the fall of Jerusalem, the victor made his progress through Syria. The people of Antioch then sought to obtain the curtailment of Jewish rights in the town, but Titus refused their suit. Josephus takes this opportunity of extolling the magnanimity of the Roman conqueror, and likewise of inserting a reference to the friendliness of Marcus Agrippa, who, on his progress through Asia a hundred years before, had upheld the Jewish privileges. He derived this incident from Nicholas' history, and thus contrived to eke out the obscurity of the third century B. C. E. with a few irrelevancies.

His material becomes a little ampler from the reign of Antiochus the Great, because from this point the Greek historians serve him better. Several of the modern commentators of Josephus have thought that his authorities were Polybius and Posidonius, who wrote in Greek on the events of the period. He cites Polybius explicitly as the author of the statement about Ptolemy's conquest of Judea, and then reproduces two letters of Antiochus to his generals, directing them to grant certain privileges to his Jewish subjects as a reward for their loyal service. We know that Polybius gave in his history an account of Jerusalem and its Temple, and his character-sketch of Antiochus Epiphanes has been preserved in an epitome. Josephus, however, be it noted, has only these scanty extracts from his work. The letters are clearly derived, not from him, but from some Hellenistic-Jewish apologist, and the passages from Polybius, it is very probable, are extracted from some larger work. Here, as elsewhere, both facts and authorities were found in Nicholas of Damascus.

We know from Josephus himself that Nicholas had included a history of the Seleucid Empire in his *magnum opus*. He is quoted in reference to the sacking of the Temple by Antiochus Epiphanes and the victory of Ptolemy Lathyrus over Alexander Jannaeus. Josephus, indeed, several times appends to his paragraphs about the general history a note, "as we have elsewhere described." Some have inferred from this that he had himself written a general history of the Seleucid epoch, but a more critical study has shown that the tag belongs to the note of his authority, which he embodied carelessly in his paraphrase.

Josephus supplements the Jewish references in the Seleucid history of Nicholas by an account of the intrigues of the Tobiades and Oniades, which reveals a Hellenistic-Jewish origin. Possibly he found it in a special chronicle of the high-priestly family, which was written by one friendly to it, for Joseph ben Tobias is praised as "a good man and of great magnanimity, who brought the Jews out of poverty and low condition to one that was more splendid." The chronology here is at fault, since at the time at which the incidents are placed both Syria and Palestine were included in the dominion of the Seleucids; yet Tobias is represented at the court of the Ptolemies. Josephus follows the story of these exploits with the letters which passed between Areas, king of the Lacedemonians, and the high priest Onias, as recorded in the *First Book of the Maccabees* (ch. 12). The letters are taken out of their true place, in order to bridge the gap between the fall of the Tobiad house and the Maccabean rising. Areas reigned from 307-265, so that he must have corresponded to Onias I, but Josephus places him in the time of Onias III.

For his account of the Maccabean struggle he depends here primarily upon the *First Book of the Maccabees,* which in many parts he does little more than paraphrase. Neither the *Second Book of the Maccabees* nor the larger work of Jason of Cyrene, of which it is an epitome, appears to have been known to him. It is well-nigh certain that in writing the *Wars* he had no acquaintance with the Jewish historical book, but was dependent on the less accurate and complete statement of a Hellenistic chronicle; and in the later work, though he bases his narrative on the Greek version of the Maccabees, and says he will give a fresh account with great accuracy, he yet incorporates pieces of non-Jewish history from the Greek guide without much art or skill or consistency. Thus, in the *Wars* he says that Antiochus Epiphanes captured Jerusalem by assault,

while in the *Antiquities* he speaks of two captures: the first time the city fell without fighting, the second by treachery. And while in the *Book of the Maccabees* the year given for the fall of the city is 143 of the Seleucid era, in the *Antiquities* the final capture is dated 145 of the era. He no doubt found this date in the Greek authority he was following for the general history of Antiochus—he gives the corresponding Greek Olympiad—and applied it to the pillage of Jerusalem. For the story of Mattathias at Modin, which is much more detailed than in the *Wars*, he closely follows the *Book of the Maccabees,* though in the speeches he takes certain liberties, inserting, for example, an appeal to the hope of immortality in Mattathias' address to his sons. He turns to his Greek authority for the death of Antiochus, and controverts Polybius, who ascribes the king's distemper to his sacrilegious desire to plunder a temple of Diana in Persia. Josephus, with a touch of patriotism and an unusual disregard of the feelings of his patrons, who can hardly have liked the implied parallel, says it is surely more probable that he lost his life because of his pillage of the Jewish Temple. In confirmation of his theory he appeals to the materialistic morality of his audience, arguing that the king surely would not be punished for a wicked intention that was not successful. He states also that Judas was high priest for three years, which is not supported by the Jewish record; and he passes over the miracle of the oil at the dedication of the Temple, and ascribes the name of the feast to the fact that light appeared to the Jews. The celebration of Hanukkah as the feast of lights is of Babylonian-Jewish origin, and was only instituted shortly before the destruction of the Temple.

His use of the *Books of the Maccabees* stops short at the end of chapter xii. He presumably did not know of the last two chapters of our text, which contain the history of Simon, and probably were translated later. Otherwise we cannot explain his dismissal, in one line, of the league that Simon made with the Romans. The incident is dwelt on in the extant version of the *First Book of the Maccabees,* and Josephus would surely not have omitted a syllable of so propitious an event, had he possessed knowledge of it. On the other hand, he inserts into the history of the Maccabean brothers an account of the foundation of a Temple by Onias V in Leontopolis, in the Delta of Egypt, and describes at length the negotiations that led up to it; and in the same connection he narrates a feud between the Jewish and Samaritan communities at Alexandria in the days of Ptolemy Philometor. From these indications it has been inferred that he had before him the work of a Hellenistic-Jewish historian interested in Egypt—the collection of Alexander Polyhistor suggests that there were several such at the time—while for the exploits of the later Maccabees he relied on the chronicle of John Hyrcanus the son of Simon, which is referred to in the *Book of the Maccabees,* but has not come down to us.

From this period onwards till the end of the *Antiquities*, Josephus had no longer any considerable Jewish document to guide him, nor have we any Jewish history by which to check him. For an era of two hundred years he was more completely dependent on Greek sources, and it is just in this part of the work where he is most valuable or, we should rather say, indispensable. Save for a few scattered references in pagan historians, orators, and poets, he is our only authority for Jewish history at the time. It is, therefore, the more unfortunate that he makes no independent research, and takes up no independent attitude. For the most part he transcribes the pagan writer before him, unable or unwilling to look any deeper. And he tells us only of the outward events of Jewish history, of the court intrigues and murders, of the wars against the tottering empires of Egypt and Syria, of the ignoble feuds within the palace. Of the more vital and, did we but know it, the profoundly interesting social and religious history of the time, of the development of the Pharisee and Sadducee sects, we hear little, and that little is unreliable and superficial. Josephus reproduces the deficiencies of his sources in their dealings with Jewish events. He brings no original virtue compensating for the careful study which they made of the larger history in which the affairs of Judea were a small incident.

The foundation of his work in the latter half of book xiii and throughout books xiv-xvii is Nicholas, who had devoted two special books to the life of Herod, and by way of introduction to this had dealt more fully with the preceding Jewish princes. We must therefore be wary of imputing to Josephus the opinions he expresses upon the different Jewish sects in this part of the *Antiquities*. He introduces them first during the reign of Jonathan, with the classification which had already been made in the *Wars*: the Pharisees as the upholders of Providence or fate and freewill, the Essenes as absolute determinists, the Sadducees as absolute deniers of the influence of fate on human affairs. The next mention of the Pharisees occurs in the reign of Hyrcanus, when he states that they were the king's worst enemies.

> They are one of the sects of the Jews, and they have so great a power over the multitude that, when they say anything against the king or against the high priest, they are presently believed . . . . Hyrcanus had been a disciple of their teaching; but he was angered when one of them, Eleazar, a man of ill temper and prone to seditious practices, reproached him for holding the priesthood, because, it was alleged, his mother had been a captive in the reign of Antiochus Epiphanes, and he, therefore, was disqualified.

This account is taken from a source unfriendly to the Pharisees. Though the story is based apparently on an old Jewish tradition, since we find it told of Alexander Jannaeus in the Talmud, it looks as if Josephus obtained his version from some author that shared the aristocratic prejudices against the democratic leaders. The reign of Hyrcanus had been described by a Hellenistic-Jewish chronicler or a non-Jewish Hellenist, from whom Josephus borrowed a glowing eulogy, with which he sums it up: "He lived happily, administered the government in an excellent way for thirty-one years, and was esteemed by God worthy of the three greatest privileges, the principate, the high priesthood, and prophecy." To the account of the Pharisees is appended a paragraph, seemingly the historian's own work, where he explains that "the Pharisees have delivered to the people the tradition of the fathers, while the Sadducees have rejected it and claim that only the written

word is binding. And concerning these things great disputes have arisen among them; the Sadducees are able to persuade none but the rich, while the Pharisees have the multitude on their side." Again, in the account of the reign of Queen Alexandra, he represents the Pharisees as powerful but seditious, and causing constant friction, and ascribes the fall of the royal house to the queen's compliance with those who bore ill-will to the family.

Whenever the opportunity offers, Josephus brings in references to Jewish history from pagan sources. He quotes Timagenes' estimate of Aristobulus as a good man who was of great service to the Jews and gained them the country of Iturea; and he notes Strabo's agreement with Nicholas upon the invasion of Judea by Ptolemy Lathyrus. General history takes an increasingly larger part in the account of the warlike Alexander Jannaeus and the queen Alexandra, and reference is made to the consuls of Rome contemporary with the reigns of Aristobulus and Hyrcanus, in order to bring Jewish affairs into relation with those of the Power which henceforth played a critical part in them.

Josephus marks the new era on which he was entering by a fresh preface to book xiv. His aim, he says, is "to omit no facts either through ignorance or laziness, because we are dealing with a history of events with which most people are unacquainted on account of their distance from our times; and we purpose to do it with appropriate beauty of style, so that our readers may entertain the knowledge of what we write with some agreeable satisfaction and pleasure. But the principal thing to aim at is to speak truly." It is not impossible that the prelude is based on something in Nicholas; but it is turned against him; for in the same chapter Josephus controverts his predecessor for the statement that "the Idumean Antipater [the father of Herod] was sprung from the principal Jews who returned to Judea from Babylon." The assertion, he says, was made to gratify Herod, who by the revolution of fortune came to be king of the Jews. He shows here some national feeling, but in general he accepts Nicholas, and borrows doubtless from him the details of Pompey's invasion of Judea and of the siege of Jerusalem. He appeals as well to Strabo and the Latin historian Titus Livius. But though it is likely that he had made an independent study of parts of Strabo, since he drags in several extracts from his history that are not quite in place, there is no reason to think he read Livy or any other Latin author. He would have found reference to the work in the diligent Nicholas. We may discern the hand of Nicholas, too, in the praise of Pompey for his piety in not spoiling the Temple of the holy vessels. Josephus writes altogether in the tone of an admirer of Rome's occupation, attributing the misery which came upon Jerusalem to Hyrcanus and Aristobulus.

Thanks to his copious sources, he is able to give a detailed account of the relation of the Jews to Julius Caesar and of the decrees which were made in their favor at his instance. It has been conjectured with much probability that Josephus obtained his series of documents from Nicholas, who had collected them for the purpose of defending the Jews of Asia Minor in the inquiry which Marcus Agrippa conducted during the reign of Herod. He says that he will set down the decrees that are treasured in the public places of the cities, and those which are still extant in the Capitol of Rome, "so that all the rest of mankind may know what regard the kings of Asia and Europe have had for the Jewish people." In a subsequent book, when he is recounting the events of Herod's reign, Josephus sets forth a further series of decrees in favor of the Jews, issued by Caesar Augustus and his lieutenant Marcus Agrippa. These likewise he probably derived from Nicholas, who was the court advocate and court chronicler at the time they were promulgated. But he enlarges on his motive for giving them at length, pointing to them with pride as a proof of the high respect in which the Jews were held by the heads of the Roman Empire before the disaster of the war. Though in his own day they were fallen to a low estate, at one time they had enjoyed special favor:

> And I frequently mention these decrees in order to reconcile other peoples to us and to take away the causes of that hatred which unreasonable men bear us. As for our customs, he continues, each nation has its own, and in almost every city we meet with differences; but natural justice is most agreeable to the advantage of all men equally, and to this our laws have the greatest regard, and thereby render us benevolent and friendly to all men, so that we may expect the like return from others, and we may remind them that they should not esteem difference of institutions a sufficient cause of alienation, but join with us in the pursuit of virtue and righteousness, for this belongs to all men in common.

The Jewish rising and defeat had increased the odium of the Greco-Roman world towards the peculiar people, and the captive in the gilded prison was fain to dwell on their past glory in order to cover the wretchedness of their present.

Josephus claims to have copied some of the decrees from the archives in the Roman Capitol. The library was destroyed with the Capitol itself during the civil war in 69. It was restored, it is true, during the reign of Vespasian, and it is not impossible that the old decrees were saved. But Josephus might have collected from the Jewish communities those documents which he did not find ready to hand in Nicholas, if they formed part of an apology for the Jews of Antioch in 70 C. E. [Christian Era]. At least there is no good reason to doubt their authenticity, and they are in quite a different class from the letters and decrees attributed to the Hellenistic sovereigns, which lack all authority.

The story of Herod's life, which is set out in great detail in these books, has more dramatic unity than any other part of the *Antiquities*. It bears to the whole work the relation which the story of the siege of Jerusalem bears to the rest of the *Wars*. Josephus seems to manifest suddenly a power of vivid narrative and psychological analysis, to which he is elsewhere a stranger. But at the same time, where the story is most vivid and dramatic, its framework is most pagan. The Greco-Roman ideas of fate and nemesis, which dominate the shorter account of the king's life in the *Wars*, are still the underlying motives. The reason for the dramatic power and the pagan frame are one and

the same: Josephus uses here a full source, and that source is a pagan writer.

It is apparent at the same time that Josephus had a better acquaintance with the historical literature about Herod than when he wrote the *Wars*, and that he compared his various authorities and exercised some judgment in composing his picture. For example, in relating the murder of the Hasmonean Hyrcanus, he first gives the account which he found in Herod's memoirs, designed of course to exculpate the king, and then sets out the version of other historians, who allege that Herod laid a snare for the last of the Maccabean princes. Josephus proudly contrasts his own critical attitude towards Herod with the studied partisanship of Nicholas, who wrote in Herod's lifetime, and in order to please him and his courtiers,

> touching on nothing but what tended to his glory, and openly excusing many of his notorious crimes and diligently concealing them. We may, indeed, say much by way of excuse for Nicholas, because he was not so much writing a history for others as doing a service for the king. But we, who come of a family closely connected with the Hasmonean kings, and have an honorable rank, think it unbecoming to say anything that is false about them, and have described their actions in an upright and unvarnished manner. And though we reverence many of Herod's descendants, who still bear rule, yet we pay greater regard to truth, though we may incur their displeasure by so doing.

It was not so difficult for the historian to write impartially of Herod as to write impartially of Vespasian and Titus. At the same time Josephus, though in these books more critical, seldom escapes the yoke of facts, and says little of the inner conditions of the people. Of Hillel we do not hear the name, and Shammai is only mentioned, if indeed he, and not Shemaya, is disguised under the name of Sameas, as the member of the Sanhedrin who denounced Herod.

The speeches, which are put into the mouth of the king on various occasions, are rhetorical declamations in the Greek style, which must be derived either from Nicholas or from Herod's Memoirs, to which the historian had access through his intimacy with the royal family. Yet, prosaic as the treatment is, it has provided the picture of the "magnificent barbarian" which has inspired many writers and artists of later ages. It is from the Jewish point of view that it is most wanting. He does indeed say that Herod transgressed the laws of his country, and violated the ancient tradition by the introduction of foreign practices, which fostered great sins, through the neglect of the observances that used to lead the multitude to piety. By the games, the theater, and the amphitheater, which he instituted at Jerusalem, he offended Jewish sentiment; "for while foreigners were amazed and delighted at the vastness of his displays, to the native Jews all this amounted to a dissolution of the traditions for which they had so great a veneration." And he points out that the Jewish conspiracy against him in the middle of his reign arose because "in the eyes of the Jewish leaders, he merely pretended to be their king, but was in fact the manifest enemy of their nation." It has been suggested that Justus of Tiberias supplied him with this Jewish view of Herod, which is unparalleled in the *Wars*. But in another passage, where he must be following an Herodian and anti-Pharisaic source, he makes some remarks in quite an opposite spirit, as if the Pharisees were in the wrong, and provoked the king. He says of them: "They were prone to offend princes; they claimed to foresee things, and were suddenly elated to break out into open war." He calls them also Sophists, the scornful name which the Greeks gave to their popular lecturers of morality.

In dealing with Herod's character, Josephus is more discriminating than in the *Wars*. He sums him up as "cruel towards all men equally, a slave to his passions, and claiming to be above the righteous law: yet was he favored by fortune more than any man, for from a private station he was raised to be a king." One piece of characterization may be quoted, which is not the less interesting because we may suspect that it is stolen:

> But this magnificent temper and that submissive behavior and liberality which he exercised towards Caesar and the most powerful men at Rome, obliged him to transgress the customs of his nation and to set aside many of their laws, by building cities after an extravagant manner, and erecting Temples, not in Judea indeed, for that would not have been borne, since it is forbidden to pay any honors to images or representations of animals after the manner of the Greeks, but in the country beyond our boundaries and in the cities thereof. The apology which he made to the Jews was this, that all was done not of his own inclination, but at the bidding of others, in order to please Caesar and the Romans, as though he set more store on the honor of the Romans than the Jewish customs; while in fact he was considering his own glory, and was very ambitious to leave great monuments of his government to posterity: whence he was so zealous in building such splendid cities, and spent vast sums of money in them. [*Antiquities* XV. 9, 5]

He bursts out, too, with unusual passion against Herod for his law condemning thieves to exile, because it was a violation of the Biblical law, "and involved the dissolution of our ancestral traditions."

If the account of the Jewish spiritual movement at a time of great spiritual awakening is meager, the picture of Herod's great buildings, despite occasional confusion and vagueness, is full and valuable. He gives us an excellent description of Caesarea and Sebaste, the two cities which the king established as a compliment to the Roman Emperor, and an account of the Temple and the fortress of Antonia, which he himself knew so well. Of the Temple we have another description, in the Mishnah, which in the main agrees with Josephus. Where the two differ, however, the preference cannot be given to the writer who had grown up in the shadow of the building, and might have been expected to know its every corner. As we have seen in the *Wars*, he was in topography as in other things under the influence of Greco-Roman models.

Josephus did not enjoy the advantage of a full chronicle to guide him much beyond the death of Herod. Nicholas died, or ceased to write, in the reign of Antipater, who succeeded his father. Apparently he had no successor who devoted himself to recording the affairs of the Jewish court. Hence, though the events of the troubled beginning of Antipater's reign are dealt with at the same length as those of Herod, and we have a vivid story of the Jewish embassy that went to Rome to petition for the deposition of the king, the history afterwards becomes fragmentary. Such as it is, it manifests a Roman flavor. The nationalists are termed robbers, and the pseudo-Messiahs are branded as self-seeking impostors. After an enumeration of various pretenders that sought to make themselves independent rulers, there is a sudden jump from the first to the tenth year of Archelaus, who was accused of barbarous and tyrannical practices and banished by the Roman Emperor to Gaul. His kingdom was then added to the province of Syria. Josephus dwells on the story of two dreams which occurred to the king and his wife Glaphyra, and justifies himself because his discourse is concerning kings, and also because of the advantage to be drawn from it for the assurance both of the immortality of the soul and the Providence of God in human affairs. "And if anybody does not believe such stories, let him keep his own opinion, but let him not stand in the way of another who finds in them an encouragement to virtue."

The last three books of the *Antiquities* reveal the weaknesses of Josephus as an historian: his disregard of accuracy, his tendency to exaggeration, his lack of proportion, and his mental subservience. He had no longer either the Scriptures or a Greek chronicler to guide him. He depended in large part for his material on oral sources and scattered memoirs, and he is not very successful in eking it out so as to produce the semblance of a connected narrative. His chapters are in part a miscellany of notes, and the construction is clumsy. The writer confesses that he was weary of his task, but felt impelled to wind it up. Yet, just because we are so ignorant of the events of Jewish history at the period, and because the period itself is so critical and momentous, these books (xviii-xx) are among the most important which he has left, and on the whole they deal rather more closely than their predecessors with the affairs of the Jewish people. The palace intrigues do not fill the stage so exclusively, and some of the digressions carry us into byways of Jewish history.

At the very outset Josephus devotes a chapter to a fuller delineation than he has given in any other place of the various sects that flourished at the time. The account, ampler though it is than the others, does not reveal the true inwardness of the different religious positions. He repeats here what he says elsewhere about the Pharisaic doctrine of predestination tempered by freewill, but he enlarges especially on the difference between the parties in their ideas about the future life. The Pharisees believe that souls have an immortal vigor, and that they will be rewarded or punished in the next world accordingly as they have lived virtuously or wickedly in this life; the wicked being bound in everlasting prisons, while the good have power to live again. The Sadducees, on the other hand, assert that the souls die with the bodies, and the Essenes teach the immortality of souls and set great store on the rewards of righteousness. Their various ideas are wrapped up in Greco-Roman dress, to suit his readers, and the doctrine of resurrection ascribed to the Pharisees is almost identical with that held by the neo-Pythagoreans of Rome. But Josephus' account is more reliable when he refers to the divergent attitudes of the sects to the tradition.

> The Pharisees strive to observe reason's dictates in their conduct, and at the same time they pay great respect to their ancestors; and they have such influence over the people because of their virtuous lives and their discourses that they are their friends in divine worship, prayers, and sacrifice. The Sadducees do not regard the observance of anything beyond what the law enjoins them, but since their doctrine is held by the few, when they hold the judicial office, they are compelled to addict themselves to the notions of the Pharisees, because the mass would not otherwise tolerate them. The Essenes live apart from the people in communistic groups, and exceed all other men in virtue and righteousness. They send gifts to the Temple, but do not sacrifice, on which account they are excluded from the common court of the Temple.

Lastly, Josephus turns to the fourth sect, the Zealots, whose founder was Judas the Galilean:

> These men agree in all other things with the Pharisees, but they have an inviolable attachment to liberty, and they say that God is to be their only Ruler and Lord. Moreover they do not fear any kind of death, nor do they heed the death of their kinsmen and friends, nor can any fear of the kind make them acknowledge anybody as sovereign.

Josephus, however, cannot refrain from imputing low motives to those who belonged to the party opposed to himself and hated of the Romans. "They planned robberies and murders of our principal men," he says, "in pretense for the public welfare, but in reality in hopes of gain for themselves." And he saddles them with the responsibility for all the calamities that were to come. About the Messianic hope, which appears to have inspired them, he is compulsorily silent.

The historical record that follows is very sketchy. We have a bare list of procurators and high priests down to the time of Pontius Pilate, a notice of the foundation of Tiberias by the tetrarch Herod, and an irrelevant account of the death of Phraates, the king of the Parthians, and of Antiochus of Commagene, who was connected by marriage with the Herodian house. Still there is rather more detail than in the corresponding summary in the second book of the *Wars*, and Josephus must in the interval have lighted on a fuller source than he had possessed in his first historical essay. It is not impossible that the new authority was again Justus of Tiberias. Of the unrest in the governorship of Pontius Pilate he has more to say, but the genuineness of the passage referring to the trial and death of Jesus, which is dealt with elsewhere, has been doubted by modern critics. It is followed in the text by a long account of a scandal connected with the Isis worship at Rome, which led to the expulsion of Jews from the capital. In this way the chronicler wanders on between bare chronology and digression,

until he reaches the reign of Agrippa, when he again finds written sources to help him. The romance of Agrippa's rise from a bankrupt courtier to the ruler of a kingdom is treated with something of the same full detail as the events of Herod's career, and probably the historian enjoyed here the use of royal memoirs. He may have obtained material also from the historical works of Philo of Alexandria, which were partly concerned with the same epoch. He refers explicitly to the embassy which the Alexandrian Jews sent to the Roman Emperor to appeal for the rescission of the order to set up in the synagogue the Imperial image, at the head of which went Philo, "a man eminent on all accounts, brother to Alexander the Alabarch, and not unskilled in philosophy." Bloch [in *Die Quellen des Flavius Josephus*] indeed is of the opinion that the later historian did not use his Alexandrian predecessor, either in this or any other part of his writings, and points out certain differences of fact between the two accounts; but in view of the references to Philo and the fact that Josephus subsequently wrote two books of apology, one of which was expressly directed in answer to Philo's bitter opponent Apion, it is at least probable that he was acquainted with Philo's narrative. He may, however, have used it only to supplement the memoirs of the Herodian house, which served him as a chief source. Josephus devotes less attention to the Alexandrian embassy than to the efforts of the Palestinian Jews to obtain a rescission of the similar decree which Petronius, the governor of Syria, was sent to enforce in Jerusalem. His account is devised to glorify the part which Agrippa played. The prince appears as a kind of male Esther, endangering his own life to save his people; and indeed higher critics have been found to suggest that the Biblical book of Esther was written around the events of the reign of Gaius.

The story of Agrippa is interrupted by a chapter about the Jews of Babylon, which has the air of a moral tale on the evils of intermarriage, and may have formed part of the popular Jewish literature of the day. Another long digression marks the beginning of the nineteenth book of the *Antiquities*, where Josephus leaves Jewish scenes and inserts an account of Caligula's murder and the election of Claudius as Emperor. This narrative, while of great interest for students of the Roman constitution, is out of all proportion to its place in the Jewish chronicle. Josephus, it has been surmised, based it on the work of one Cluvius (referred to in the book as an intimate friend of Claudius), who wrote a history about 70 C. E.; he may besides have received hitherto unpublished information from Agrippa II, whose father had been an important actor in the drama, or from his friend Aliturius, the actor at Rome, who had mixed in affairs of state. Anyhow, he took advantage of this chance of making a literary sensation. Doubtless also, the recital, which threw not a little discredit on the house of the earlier Caesars, was for that reason not unwelcome to the upstart Flavians, and may have been inserted at the Imperial wish.

Agrippa I is the most attractive figure in the second part of the *Antiquities*. He is contrasted with Herod,

> who was cruel and severe in his punishments, and had no mercy on those he hated, and everyone perceived that he had more love for the

Greeks than for the Jews. . . . But Agrippa's temper was mild and equally liberal to all men. He was kind to foreigners and was of agreeable and compassionate feeling. He loved to reside at Jerusalem, and was scrupulously careful in his observance of the Law of his people. On his death he expressed his submission to Providence; for that he had by no means lived ill, but in a splendid and happy manner.

His peaceful reign, however, was only the lull before the storm, and the last book of the *Antiquities* is mainly taken up with the succession of wicked procurators, who, by their extortions and cruelties and flagrant disregard of the Jewish Law and Jewish feeling, goaded the Jews into the final rebellion. It contains, however, a digression on the conversion of the royal house of Adiabene to Judaism, which is tricked out with examples of God's Providence. Yet another digression records the villainies of Nero (which no doubt was pleasing to his patrons) and the amours of Drusilla, the daughter of Agrippa I. But of the rising discontent of the Jewish people in Palestine we have no clear picture. Josephus fails as in the *Wars* to bring out the inner incompatibility of the Roman and the Jewish outlook, and represents, in an unimaginative, matter-of-fact, Romanizing way, that it was simply particular excesses—the rapacity of a Felix, the knavery of a Florus—which were the cause of the Rebellion. This is just what a Roman would have said, and when the Jewish writer deals at all with the Jewish position, it is usually to drag in his political feud. He especially singles out the sacrilege of the Zealots in assassinating their opponents within the Temple precincts as the reason of God's rejecting the city; "and as for the Temple, He no longer deemed it sufficiently pure to be His habitation, but brought the Romans upon us and threw a fire on the city to purge it, and brought slavery on us, our wives, and our children, to make us wiser by our calamities." Thus the priestly apologist, accepting Roman canons, finds in the ritual offense of a section of the people the ground for the destruction of the national center. He is torn, indeed, between two conflicting views about the origin of the rebellion: whether he shall lay the whole blame on the Jewish irreconcilables, or whether he shall divide it between them and the wicked Roman governors; and in the end he exaggerates both these motives, and leaves out the deeper causes.

The penultimate chapter contains a list of the high priests, about whom the historian had throughout made great pretensions of accuracy. He enumerates but eighty-three from the time of Aaron to the end of the line, of whom no less than twenty-eight were appointed after Herod's accession to his kingdom; whereas the Talmud records that three hundred held office during the existence of the second Temple alone. That number is probably hyperbolical, but the statement in other parts of the Rabbinical literature, that there were eighty high priests in that period, throws doubt on this list, which besides is manifestly patched in several places.

With the procuratorship of Florus, Josephus brings his chronicle to an end, the later events having been treated in detail in the *Wars*; and in conclusion he commends

himself for his accuracy in giving the succession of priests and kings and political administrators:

> And I make bold to say, now I have so completely perfected the work which I set out to do, that no other person, be he Jew or foreigner, and had he ever so great an inclination to it, could so accurately deliver these accounts to the Greeks as is done in these books. For members of my own people acknowledge that I far exceed them in Jewish learning, and I have taken great pains to obtain the learning of the Greeks and understand the elements of the Greek language, though I have so long accustomed myself to speak our own tongue that I cannot speak Greek with exactness.

He makes explicit his standpoint with this *envoi,* which shows that he was writing for a Greek-speaking public and in competition with Greeks, and this helps to explain why he sets special store on the record of priests and kings and political changes, and why he so often disguises the genuine Jewish outlook. As an account of the Jewish people for the prejudiced society of Rome, the *Antiquities* undoubtedly possessed merit. History, indeed, at the time, was far from being an exact science, nor was accuracy esteemed necessary to it. Cicero had said a hundred years earlier, that it was legitimate to lie in narratives; and this was the characteristic outlook of the Greco-Roman writers. The most brilliant literary documents of the age, the *Annals* and *Histories* of Tacitus, are rather pieces of sparkling journalism than sober and philosophical records of facts; and therefore we must not judge Josephus by too high a standard.

Weighed in his own balance, he had done a great service to his people by setting out the main heads of their history over three thousand years, so that it should be intelligible to the cultured Roman society; and had he been reproached with misrepresenting and distorting many of their religious ideas, he would have replied, with some justice, that it was necessary to do so in order to make the Romans understand. On the same ground he would have justified the omission of much that was characteristic and the exaggeration of much that was normal. He shows throughout some measure of national pride. To-day, however, we cannot but regret that he weakly adopted much of the spiritual outlook of his Gentile contemporaries, and that he did not seek to convey to his readers the fundamental spiritual conceptions of the Jews, which might have endowed his history with an unique distinction. His record of two thousand years of Israel's history gives but the shadow of the glory of his people.

H. St. John Thackeray   (lecture date 1928)

SOURCE: *Josephus: The Man and the Historian*, KTAV Publishing House, Inc., 1967, 160 p.

[*In the following excerpts from the texts of lectures originally given in 1928, Thackeray examines Josephus's biblical sources, demonstrating that he utilized the Greek Lucianic edition of the Jewish scriptures. The critic then attempts to identify various literary styles evident in Josephus's writ-*

ings, contending that they represent the work of Josephus's Greek assistants.]

The world in which he [Josephus] moved comprised three classes: his Jewish countrymen, the wider Greek-speaking community which he addressed (including his Roman patrons), and the little body of Christians just emerging from obscurity. I propose in this and subsequent lectures to offer some observations on the historian's relationship respectively to Judaism, to Hellenism and to Christianity. On the first and last of these heads I speak with diffidence. I am conscious that my present audience are far better qualified than I am to appraise our author's Hebraic affinities; while his relation to Christianity is, on more grounds than one, a highly controversial subject, the difficulty of which is increased by the fact that the latest evidence has not as yet been subjected to searching criticism, nor even been fully presented in an accessible form.

I am indeed aware of my temerity in attempting to criticize Josephus the Jew—to estimate the extent of his acquaintance with Rabbinical thought and the contributions of permanent importance to our knowledge of Judaism which we owe to this Hebrew of Jerusalem, priest and descendant of priests, proud of his connexion on his father's side with the first of the twenty-four priestly courses, on his mother's with the royal Hasmonaean house, and, if we may believe him, acknowledged by his compatriots to outstrip them all in the learning of his race. This last proud boast is, indeed, immediately followed by a modest admission that he never succeeded in mastering the pronunciation of Greek; and here I am happy to follow his example, knowing that I lay myself open to the charge of a defective grounding, not only in Hebrew pronunciation, but in Rabbinical lore.

Yet, it must, I think, be granted, that these high pretensions lead us to expect something more than we receive: the author's contribution to our knowledge not only of the deeper religious aspects of Judaism, but even of its ritual, customs and antiquities, is somewhat disappointing. We are conscious of a certain superficiality, partly attributable, no doubt, to the Greek audience which he addresses, but largely also to character and training. He excels as a popularizer of the external history of his nation and, in his latest work, as an apologist. But as profound theologian and religious devotee he is wanting, or at least rarely betrays such deeper knowledge and emotions in his works. He lacks the erudition and piety of the Palestinian Rabbi, the rapt mysticism of the Alexandrian Philo. As has been recently been said by Professor Moore [in his *Judaism* i], "it may be fairly inferred that Josephus, like most of the aristocratic priesthood to which he belonged, had little interest in religion for its own sake, and that his natural antipathy to all excess of zeal was deepened by the catastrophe which religious fanatics had brought upon his people." His fine apology for Judaism, the ***Contra Apionem***, must not, however, be forgotten, where he does rise to a higher level and display a sincere and impassioned zeal for his country's religion. Apart from that noble legacy, probably the most important contributions which we owe to him are the information which he indirectly supplies on the Biblical texts current in the first century, and, to a less de-

gree, a miscellaneous mass of traditional lore of *Haggadah*. I propose to concentrate on the author's Bible and his Biblical traditions; but, before I pass to those matters, a few words must be said on the subject of language and some strange explanations which he incidentally gives of some Hebrew proper names.

The "language of his forefathers" in which Josephus composed the first draft of his ***Jewish War*** was doubtless Aramaic, of which he must have had a thorough mastery. Was his knowledge of Hebrew equally profound? It seems impertinent to question the proficiency of the learned priest in the language of Scripture. Yet others more competent to express an opinion have concluded that his knowledge was "superficial." The test to which he lays himself open is his translation of proper names. Many of these are correct enough according to the standards of his time; some were taken over from his Bible, whether Hebrew or Greek. But others are, to say the least, slipshod or actually inaccurate. It is true, as Professor Moore reminds us, that such "interpretations of names were not put forth for the satisfaction of modern philologists but for the edification of . . . contemporaries," and must not be overstressed. The Professor is speaking of etymologies, even worse, perpetrated by the Alexandrian Philo. Josephus knew better than to suggest, as Philo does, *Greek* derivations for Semitic words, *e.g.* to connect *Pascha* with the verb $\pi\alpha\sigma\chi\epsilon\iota\nu$ "to suffer" or "Euphrates" with $\epsilon\upsilon\phi\rho\alpha\iota\nu\epsilon\iota\nu$. Still we have a right to expect from the Palestinian priest greater exactitude than in the following instances. Eve . . . , he says, signifies . . . "mother of all"; his Bible (Gen. iii. 20) told him that Adam called his wife *Hawwah* ("Living" or "Life") "because she was the mother of all"; but that is not what Josephus states. However, this may be attributed rather to indolence than to ignorance: "that is good enough for my Greek readers." On the year of Jubilee he states that the word $\iota\omega\beta\eta\lambda o\sigma$ signifies "freedom"; this he takes from the LXX rendering "year of release" . . . , ignoring the traditional Hebrew meaning "ram" or "ram's horn." With this may be linked his explanation of Gilgal or Galgala, "this word means 'free' "; the only freedom discoverable here is the liberty taken by the author in this loose paraphrase of the correct Biblical explanation, the *rolling away* of the reproach of Egypt. The interpretation of Samson, "the name means strong" is probably guesswork, the connexion with *Shemesh* "Sun" being practically certain. Philology clearly cannot be regarded as the historian's *forte*. Yet, as already said, these instances must not be overemphasized, and it is perhaps precarious to draw inferences from them as to his comparative knowledge of the two Semitic languages, since this looseness of interpretation extends even to Aramaic forms. With reference to Pentecost, the Hebrew *'atzereth*, he writes "the feast which the Hebrews call $\alpha\sigma\alpha\rho\theta\alpha$ means 'fiftieth' "; had he said "is called Pentecost by the Greeks," he would have been correct, but no etymology of the Semitic word can, I imagine, support this alleged numerical sense. In one curious instance, the name of Reuben, he deserts the Hebrew text and significantly adopts the Syriac and possibly older form, writing $Po\upsilon\beta\eta\lambda o\sigma$, which he interprets as "by the mercy of God." How he extracted the meaning "mercy" out of the first syllable is uncertain; but this agreement with the Syriac, and the use of Aramaic forms like $\alpha\sigma\alpha\rho\theta\alpha$ and others, suggest that he was perhaps more conversant with Aramaic than with Hebrew, and, when not using a Greek Bible, would turn more naturally to a Targum than to the original text.

Passing to another subject, we find a similar departure from normal Rabbinical practice in a well-known passage in the *Contra Apionem*, on the canon of Scripture, where Josephus contrasts the 22 "accredited" books of his race with the "myriads of inconsistent and conflicting books" of other nations. I must not linger on the notorious difficulties of this passage. Josephus implies that the canon had long been closed; whereas we know that almost at the time when he was writing the canonicity of two books, Song of Songs and Ecclesiastes, was being debated by Palestinian Rabbis. Again, though he gives a tripartite arrangement of Scripture, it is not the normal division—Law, Prophets, Writings; four books only remain in his third category, the historical books outside the Pentateuch being all placed in the second; and the total number is not the normal 24, but 22. We cannot adopt the view suggested by Grätz that Josephus rejected the two disputed books; for we find this same total of 22 in lists, which enumerate the several books and are given by Christian writers (Origen and Jerome) who were in touch with and derived their information from Palestinian tradition, and who moreover associate the number 22 with the number of letters in the Hebrew alphabet. The constituent books intended, but not named, by Josephus were doubtless the same as those enumerated by these writers, the total being reduced from 24 to 22 by uniting Ruth with Judges and Lamentations with Jeremiah. When we find Origen giving a list which includes the Hebrew titles and states "Judges, Ruth, with them (i. e. with the Hebrews) in one," "Jeremiah with Lamentations and the Epistle in one," we are led to infer that this strange division of the Bible attested by Josephus was not peculiar to himself or to the Alexandrian school but had support in some Palestinian circles.

I pass on to consider the *Biblical* text of Josephus, a matter which, in view of the historian's date, is of considerable importance. First century witnesses to the letter of Scripture are few: indeed we can name only one earlier writer who quotes it freely, viz. Philo, and Philo's quotations are practically confined to the Pentateuch. In the large use which he makes of the later historical books Josephus stands alone, and his evidence antedates our earliest complete MS in any language, the Greek Codex Vaticanus, by nearly three centuries—a period during which the text did not remain unaltered. Widening divergence between local varieties of text led to various revisions on the part of both Jewish and Christian scholars, with a view to establishing the *Hebraica veritas* and checking the progress of corruption. A witness who takes us far back behind the three local recensions of the Greek Bible known to Jerome in the 4th century, behind the Hexapla of Origen in the 3rd, and even behind or at least to the opening days of the great Rabbinical school of Jamnia at the end of the first, carries therefore considerable weight.

What was the nature of the text, or texts, which Josephus employed? Whence did they emanate and what is their precise worth? What part did he himself take in the task of translation, and how much does he owe to the labours of predecessors? Those are some of the questions which arise, and the results which seem to emerge are not without interest and importance.

The historian himself would lead us to suppose that he translated the Hebrew Scriptures himself. "This work which I have undertaken," he writes in the proem to the *Antiquities*, ". . . will contain the complete account of our ancient history and constitution translated . . . from the Hebrew Scriptures"; elsewhere he states, less equivocally, "At the outset of my work . . . I remarked that I was merely translating (or "paraphrasing," . . .) the books of the Hebrews into the Greek language and promised to repent the more without omission or addition on my own part."

These statements, like others of their author, are not to be taken at their face value without reservations. The broad result revealed by a careful study of his use of Scripture is that he employed at least two texts, one in a Semitic language, the other in Greek. Sometimes one was used almost to the exclusion of the other: sometimes both were consulted and amalgamated. I speak of a Semitic language, because the adjective which he uses, $E\beta\rho\alpha\iota\sigma\tau\iota$, might, like the adverb $E\beta\rho\alpha\iota\sigma\tau\iota$ in the N. T., include Aramaic, and, while it is probable that he has sometimes gone back to the original Hebrew, there are also indications in places that he is dependent on a Targum. As regards the respective use made of his two Bibles, a clear line of demarcation can be drawn at the close of the Octateuch: perhaps I should rather say at the close of the Pentateuch, for his text of the three books which immediately follow it in the Greek Bible (Joshua, Judges, Ruth) stands a little apart. Throughout the Pentateuch his main authority is a Semitic text, and the use made of the so-called "Septuagint" is slight; here he is presumably justified in claiming that the translation is his own. From Samuel onwards to the end of the historical books the position is reversed: the basis of his text is a Greek Bible, and the Semitic text is only a subsidiary source. Here he found a large part of his work already done for him, his own share being confined to polishing the style and removing what he considered the vulgarisms of the existing translation. For the three intervening books (Joshua, Judges, Ruth) I find no certain evidence for the use of a Greek text; as between Hebrew and Aramaic, I suspect, in Judges at least, dependence on a Targum.

[It] is the Greek Bible of Josephus which is of main interest. Dependence on the Greek is obvious in the use made of whole books, Alexandrian paraphrases of Scripture, such as the so called 1st Esdras, including the fable, of purely Greek origin, of the three pages of Darius, the Greek Esther with similar interpolations, or the 1st book of Maccabees, drawn from the extant Greek and not from the lost Hebrew original. It is evident again in the acquaintance shown with isolated Greek glosses in the earlier books, as when Josephus takes over from the LXX that vapid reply of David to Goliath's question "Am I a dog?" —"No but even worse than a dog."

Not only, however, can we confidently state in general

terms that Josephus used a Greek Bible. We can go further and identify the particular type of Greek text which lay before him. This text was not one of those contained in our oldest uncial MSS, the codex Vaticanus or Alexandrinus, on which our modern printed editions of the Septuagint are based. It was a text allied to one preserved only in a small group of MSS, written not in uncial but in cursive script at a much later date, between the 10th and the 14th centuries, and known by the figures assigned to them by the eighteenth century editors, Holmes and Parsons, as 19, 82, 93 and 108. This type of text, which has survived only in these late and, as might be thought, insignificant MSS, was in the nineteenth century identified with a particular recension of the Greek Bible current in Syria and adjacent countries in the fourth century and commonly designated "Lucianic" after its supposed author, the Christian Lucian of Antioch, who suffered martyrdom under the emperor Maximin in the year 311 or 312. And now that we have in our hands fuller and more accurate editions both of the Septuagint and of Josephus, we discover that this "Syrian" text in an older form was in existence more than two centuries earlier, and can be carried back from the age of the Christian Lucian to that of the Jewish historian.

Lucian's Antiochene text, current throughout Northern Syria and Asia Minor in the fourth century, is based on an older text current, apparently in the same region, before the end of the first. Josephus is not the only person who has built on and been given the credit for other men's labours; we are forced to postulate an *ur-Lucian*. Before Origen's time the Greek Bible apparently existed in two main types of text, a pre-Lucianic or Syrian form used by Josephus on the one hand, and an Alexandrian on the other.

The Josephan Biblical text is *uniformly* of this Lucianic type from 1 Samuel to 1 Maccabees. He has, for this large portion of Scripture, used a single Bible, not two or more; and, were it not that in his day the codex form of book was hardly in existence, and that the papyrus scrolls are believed to have been small and confined to not more than a book or two, I should be tempted to think that he has used a single MS, mutilated at the beginning and end. Take the last historical book which he uses, 1 Maccabees. Here, in the first place, the persistence of the "Lucianic" type of text militates, as I said, against the theory that he knows the book only at second hand through some anonymous writer who has already incorporated the bulk of it; it is improbable that his predecessor should here have employed precisely the same recension as Josephus uses throughout. Again, he shows no knowledge of the last three chapters of that book. Here it is maintained that he knew the work in a shorter edition. I should rather suggest that his MS was defective at the close; and it is perhaps significant that there is a similar indication of loss of leaves at the beginning. In 1 Samuel the "Lucianic" element does not make its appearance for the first six or seven chapters.

Where did the historian obtain his Greek Bible? He shows no acquaintance with it in that short sketch of Maccabaean history in the *Jewish War*, and this ignorance of it in his earlier work, together with the fact that the old Latin version of the Greek Bible, the *Vetus Itala*, has affin-

ities with the "Lucianic" text, might suggest that his Greek Bible was not among the books which he brought with him from Palestine, but was found in Rome. However this may be, I have no doubt that its ultimate place of origin was northern Syria. Next to "Lucian," the Biblical text most nearly allied to the historian's is that of Symmachus, and Symmachus was an Asiatic; the only recorded incident in his life is placed in Cappadocia. The text of Lucian in the fourth century was current from Constantinople to Antioch, i. e. throughout Asia Minor and N. Syria; and it is probable that the parent text used by Josephus had much the same range. We can hardly suppose that this Greek version was wholly indigenous to Syria; but who was the real author of this Antiochene recension of the Alexandrian Bible, and how much older it may be than Josephus, we do not know.

A few instances of "Lucianic" readings of Josephus must suffice. I draw my examples again from the books of Samuel. In 2 Sam. xxiii. 11, in the narrative of the exploits of David's mighty men, we read in the Masoretic text that "the Philistines were gathered together . . . ," which yields no tolerable sense. The English and American revised versions render "into a troop," as from . . . "a clan." The majority of the Greek MSS seem correctly to recognise that the word is a place-name, rendering εισ θηρια; but we cannot identify any place bearing the strange name of "Wild beasts." The correct name appears only in Josephus, in the MSS representing the "Lucianic" text and in the Armenian version, which have "to (a place called) Jawbone"; we recognise at once Lehi, a name which the Philistines had good cause to remember as the scene of a famous exploit of Samson. In the next chapter, 2 Sam. xxiv. 22, the various Greek renderings of an agricultural instrument seem to preserve local distinctions, suggestive of their place of origin. Araunah the Jebusite offers David the oxen at work on the threshing-floor for a burnt offering and the threshing-instruments for fuel. For "threshing-instruments" most Greek MSS have "the wheels" . . . ., meaning the threshing-*waggon* on rollers "not used in Palestine . . . rare in Syria (except in the north) but . . . the usual instrument in Egypt" [in Driver, *Joel and Amos*, 1915]. Here evidently we have the Alexandrian rendering. The Lucianic text, as often, has two words for one, "the boards and the ploughs" . . . ; Josephus (*Ant.* vii. 331) has "the ploughs" alone. The "boards" doubtless mean the threshing-board or drag usual in Syria and Palestine; the "ploughs" possibly indicate Arabic influence, . . . being a loan-word in Arabic, with the meaning "ploughshare." Here the Biblical text of Josephus is in partial agreement with Lucian, and, whether emanating from Syria or from Arabia in the larger sense, clearly does not come from Egypt.

Another curious case of approximation of the Josephan and Lucianic texts occurs in 1 Sam. xxiii. 25, where we read in the M. T. [Masoretic Text] of David's taking refuge from Saul "in the wilderness of Ma'on." The geography in this context shows that Ma'on is right; but both in Josephus and in Lucian an intrusive initial *shin* has converted the proper name into *Shim'on*. The two texts differ, however, in one respect: Josephus (*Ant.* [*Jewish Antiquities*] vi. 280) retains the Semitic name unaltered, "in the wilderness of Simon;" Lucian translates it by Επηκοοσ, "into the listening wilderness," as in fact Josephus does elsewhere. As is suggested by Mez [in his *Die Bibel des Josephus*, 1895] the exemplar of Josephus is probably not Semitic, but an earlier form of the Lucianic text which left *Shim'on* untranslated.

A final minor coincidence may be mentioned. Josephus, in common with Lucian, places David's death at the close of a book. A natural arrangement, indeed, but it is not that adopted either by the Masoretes or by the bulk of the Greek MSS, which attach David's old age to the reign of his successor narrated in the first book of Kings. I believe that curious arrangement to be attributable to an attempt to make Samuel and Kings into volumes of more equal dimensions, and that the more natural division of books in Lucian and Josephus is also the older.

So much for our author's text of the historical books. Of the prophetical books naturally little use is made, apart from the narrative chapters of Jeremiah, and, if we may include it under this category, as Josephus would have done, the Book of Daniel. He appears to have used a Greek Daniel combining the peculiarities of the two known versions; in Jeremiah and in the slight allusions to the other *Nebiim* I find no certain evidence of acquaintance with a Greek text. We have a strange allusion to predictions of the calamities of Jerusalem, including its capture by the Romans, attributed to Jeremiah and Ezekiel, the latter of whom is said to have written *two* books on the subject; but the text is doubtful and the last clause may originally have referred to two books of Jeremiah, viz. the prophecy and the Lamentations. The only definite prediction of Isaiah mentioned is quoted at second hand, namely the prophecy of the erection of an altar to the Lord in the land of Egypt, on which Onias relied in building the schismatic temple at Leontopolis. The story of Jonah is told somewhat apologetically "as I found it recorded"; and we are given a paraphrase of Nahum's prediction of the fall of Nineveh, the only prophetical passage showing possible dependence on a Greek text.

Apart from Law and Prophets, using the latter term in the wider sense to include the historical books, I should be inclined to assign a separate place to certain "writings deposited in the temple" which Josephus expressly mentions on three occasions, and to which he possibly alludes more vaguely elsewhere. As these passages, with one doubtful exception, all refer to lyrical portions of Scripture, I venture to regard them as references, not to the sacred scrolls of the Law and the Prophets, but to a separate collection of chants, taken mainly from the Bible, for the use of the temple singers. The first, which is the doubtful instance, runs: "A writing deposited in the temple shows that God predicted to Moses that water would thus spring from the rock." Here I think the reference is to the little song to the well in Numbers, with the preceding promise to Moses of a miraculous gift of water: "From thence to Beer—that is the well whereof the Lord said unto Moses, Gather the people together and I will give them water." And then, rather inconsequently, because it refers to water produced by human exertion, follows the song, once probably included in the old book of Jashar, "Then sang Israel this

song, Spring up O well," and so on. If my suggestion here is not wholly erroneous, the temple hymn-book must have included beside the song the prefatory prediction. Again, we are told of Moses' song that "he read them a poem in hexameter verse, which he has also left in a book in the temple, containing a prediction of things to come"; and again, of Joshua, "that the length of the day was then increased and surpassed its usual measure is attested by writings deposited in the temple." Here we have an allusion to Joshua's incantation to the sun, which in the extant text includes a statement of its fulfilment, and which, as we are there told, stood in the old national song-book known as the book of Jashar. To these three passages I should be inclined to add two others relating to dirges, one extant and one lost, which, though the temple is unnamed, are here stated to have been preserved until the writer's time. "(David) wrote also lamentations and funeral eulogies on Saul and Jonathan, which have survived to my day," and, we may add, were also included in the book of Jashar; elsewhere we read that "Jeremiah the prophet composed a funeral elegy on (Josiah) which survives even until now." This last may be drawn from a similar statement in Chronicles, but should rather, I think, be ranked with the other passages as resting on personal knowledge. Lastly the statement that Moses' song at the Red Sea was composed "in hexameter rhythm" connects it with his other song in Deuteronomy and suggests possible adaptation for a temple choir.

Josephus more than once asserts that he has added nothing, or nothing of his own, to the Biblical narrative. We need not scrutinize his meaning too closely, or ask whether, as a Pharisee, he regarded the rich store of tradition which he has incorporated as part and parcel of Scripture. Anyhow, he has, to attract his Greek readers, diversified the record with a mass of legendary matter, which is of considerable interest to us. He has culled from all quarters: Alexandria and even the *Sibylline Oracles* have contributed their quota. But a large proportion find parallels, or partial parallels, in the Rabbinic works, which were not compiled until a century or more later, and these, with other traditions for which no parallel can be traced, may be regarded as a valuable collection of first century *Midrash*. Here it is but possible to touch on a large theme, which has been fully, I do not know whether exhaustively, dealt with by Rabbinic scholars.

As illustrations of what should, I suppose, be described as *Haggadah*, we may take a few instances where Josephus agrees with the *Book of Jubilees*, one of the earliest works of this class, dating from a century before our era. In common with *Jubilees*, he tells us that the beasts in Paradise spoke with human tongue; that Adam and Eve had daughters; of the inscriptions on pillars made by the antediluvians to ensure the preservation of their discoveries; that the name of Pharaoh's daughter, the foster-mother of Moses, was Thermuthis.

The identification of persons or dates and other inferences deduced from a comparison of Biblical passages are characteristically Rabbinic. It was Nimrod, the city-builder, who designed the Tower of Babel; one anonymous prophet who denounced Jeroboam was named Ιασων, another who foretold Ahab's death because he spared Benhadad was Micaiah; the man who drew a bow at a venture and slew him was Aμανοσ , possibly meaning Naaman; the woman who besought Elisha to save her from her creditors was the widow of Obadiah, who, in order to support the prophets in hiding, had resorted to money-lenders. Moses, according to Josephus, died on the first of the month Adar, according to Rabbinical tradition on the seventh; and so on.

Around the lawgiver in particular there grew up a rich crop of legend, both among friends and foes. The **Contra Apionem** gives us the inventions of the enemies of Judaism, representing Moses as the leper expelled with his band of lepers from Egypt: in the **Antiquities** we have the reverse picture. Tales here given of the infant prodigy find partial parallels in Alexandrian literature. The allusion in Numbers to "the Cushite woman whom he had married" gave rise to stories of his leadership in an Ethiopian campaign, which take various forms in Josephus, the Alexandrian Artapanus and Rabbinical writers. In the account of his end, as I have mentioned, the author has not scrupled to draw upon descriptions of the "passing" of the founders of the Roman race, Aeneas and Romulus.

In his interpretation of the laws—the sphere of *Halakah*, . . . Josephus has points of contact with the Palestinians on which I cannot dwell. But the most striking of such interpretations is purely Alexandrian and alien to the spirit of the O. T.: "Our legislator has expressly forbidden us to deride or blaspheme the gods recognised by others, out of respect for the very word 'God'." This is based on the LXX use of the plural θεουσ in Ex. xxii. 28 "Thou shalt not revile Elohim"; or perhaps drawn directly from Philo who gives the same interpretation and the same reason for the injunction—the hallowing of the Name.

This brings me to some other indications which have been traced of an acquaintance of Josephus with the writings of the great Alexandrian. He mentions Philo but once, in a brief notice of the embassy to Caligula which was led by that philosopher to defend the maligned Jews of his native city against the accusations of Apion. But Josephus himself has devoted a large part of his apology for Judaism to the refutation of the slanders of that same opponent; and this bond of union in attacking a common enemy might lead the historian to consult the works of his predecessor. The perusal was probably slight, the deeper philosophy of Philo being beyond his grasp; but there is enough to show that he had looked into the work *On the Creation* (*De opificio mundi*) and perhaps the *Life of Moses*. The projected work on *Customs and Causes* would probably have revealed further points of contact.

The preface to the **Antiquities** and the opening of the *De opificio mundi* run on parallel lines. Both works raise the question why the Mosaic code is preceded by an account of the Creation. Josephus expects that his readers will ask why his work, intended as a record of laws and events, has so large an element of what he calls "physiology." He explains that Moses, unlike other legislators, whose codes begin with contracts and the rights of man, held it necessary, before laying down his code, to elevate men's minds by setting the highest of examples before them and induc-

ing them to contemplate the nature and actions of God, especially as exhibited in the creation. Philo has a similar exordium, contrasting the procedure of Moses and that of other legislators. Moses did not begin by laying down commands and prohibitions, but opened with a marvellous account of the creation, in order to show the harmony existing between the universe and the law and that the law-abiding man is a true citizen of the world. . . . This unanimity between the law and the universe is also emphasized by Josephus. Josephus and Philo both refer to the mythical stories which disfigure the codes of other legislators.

In the same context Josephus admits that allegory, which in Philo plays so large a part, has a place in the interpretation of Scripture, reserving details for his projected work. Of such allegorical explanation he gives us elsewhere one striking instance, in which the tabernacle and its furniture and the various articles in the high priest's dress are explained as symbolical of the universe and its constituent elements. Philo gives a similar interpretation of the materials used for the hangings of the tabernacle and the high priest's vestments in the *Life of Moses*. The details are not all identical in the two writers, and this particular form of allegorical explanation appears to have been more widespread, parallels being quoted from the *Midrashim* and even from the Samaritan liturgy; so that direct dependence on Philo is here not definitely established.

Again, Josephus remarks on the strange use of the cardinal number "one" instead of the ordinal in the account of the first day of creation in Gen. i. 5, "And there was evening and there was morning, one day," and again reserves his explanation for his future work. Philo had previously commented on the fact and given his own mystical interpretation in the *De opificio mundi*.

To that same work there is another curious parallel in the **Contra Apionem**, both writers being apparently influenced by Greek philosophy. Plato in the *Timaeus* had represented God as employing collaborators in the work of creation. And Philo partially followed him, deducing from the plural in Gen. i. 26 ("Let *us* make man") that man, being of a mixed nature, both good and bad, required a plurality of δημιουργοι, whereas for the rest of creation—heaven, earth, sea, the beasts and plants—God needed no assistant. Josephus does not venture expressly to countenance this heretical doctrine of the "two powers," so firmly rejected by the Rabbis, and indeed he may be intending to combat both Plato and Philo; but he significantly omits to mention man in the passage in question. "We behold His works," he writes, "the light, the heaven, the earth, the sun, the waters, the reproductive creatures . . . , the sprouting crops. These God created, not with hands, not with toil, *not with assistants of whom He had no need*; He willed it so, and forthwith they were made in all their beauty" [**Contra Apionem** ii].

In these passages, then, Josephus comes to some extent under the influence of Alexandrian thought. It is impossible here to review his theology as a whole and to estimate the various factors that have gone to the making of it; and indeed his historical works are not the place in which to look for any connected statement of doctrinal beliefs.

Writing in Greek and for Greeks, he naturally and almost necessarily adapts himself to their terminology and modes of thought, as when he employs the impersonal phrase "the Divinity" or writes of Fate or Destiny. But, in large measure, he is in harmony with orthodox Rabbinical Judaism. I can but touch on a few points.

He never published his projected work on the being of God, but here is his brief statement, a sort of paraphrase of the first two commandments, immediately preceding the last passage which I quoted: "The universe is in God's hands; perfect and blessed, self-sufficing and sufficing for all, He is the beginning, the middle, and the end of all things. By His works and bounties He is plainly seen, indeed more manifest than ought else; but His form and magnitude surpass our powers of description. No materials, however costly, are fit to make an image of Him; no art has skill to conceive and represent it. The like of Him we have never seen, we do not imagine, and it is impious to conjecture" [*Contra Apionem* ii]. Elsewhere, he writes [in *Contra Apionem*] that the lawgiver "persuaded all to look to Him as the author of all blessings . . . He convinced them that no single action, no secret thought could be hid from Him. He represented Him as One, uncreated and immutable to all eternity; in beauty surpassing all mortal form, made known to us by His power, although the nature of His real being passes knowledge."

On a future life, the historian, as a Pharisee, believes in a return to bodily existence of the souls of the good. The Pharisaic belief he expresses thus: "All souls are imperishable, but the soul of the good alone passes into another body, while the souls of the wicked suffer eternal punishment" [*Jewish War* ii], and elsewhere, "Their belief is that souls have a deathless vigour, and that beneath the earth there are punishments and rewards for those who have been devoted in life to vice or virtue: for the former is prescribed everlasting imprisonment, for the latter facility for return to life" [*Jewish Antiquities* xviii]. In keeping with this is his statement of general Jewish belief in the *Contra Apionem*: "Each individual, relying on the witness of his own conscience and the lawgiver's prophecy, confirmed by the sure testimony of God, is firmly persuaded that to those who observe the laws and, if they must needs die for them, willingly meet death, God has granted to be born again and to receive a better life in turn." Similarly in the speech at Jotapata on the iniquity of suicide, "Know you not that they who depart this life in accordance with the law of nature and repay the loan which they received from God, when He who lent it is pleased to reclaim it, win eternal renown . . . that their souls, remaining spotless and obedient, are allotted the most holy place in heaven, whence in the revolution of the ages . . . they return to find in chaste bodies a new habitation? But, as for those who have laid mad hands upon themselves, the darker regions of Hades receive their souls." [*Jewish War* iii].

Of any Messianic beliefs Josephus gives no sign. The sentence, of very doubtful authenticity, in the well-known *testimonium* in the *Antiquities*, "This was the Christ" must be reserved for another lecture. Apart from that, he is silent on a subject, associated by him with risings which had brought his country to ruin and to which it was dangerous

to allude. But there are two passages, darkly hinting at the fulfilment of prophecy, which seem to suggest that the author had his private opinions and a presentiment of the downfall of the Roman power and of a possible amelioration of his nation's lot. In one, he writes that from the fulfilment even within his own memory, of many of Balaam's prophecies, one may conjecture that the remainder also will come true. In the other, he refuses to deal with a prophecy of Daniel concerning the stone in Nebuchadnezzar's vision, which is to break the kingdoms in pieces, and refers the curious reader to the text of Scripture.

He is careful to note the fulfilment of prophecy and shows something of Rabbinic casuistry in reconciling predictions seemingly inconsistent. And, although as he says in his statement on the Canon of Scripture, the succession of the old prophets has failed, the gift of prophecy was still in his opinion bestowed on favoured individuals. It was possessed by John Hyrcanus, the Essene Judas, the Pharisee Pollio (or Abtalion) and by the historian himself. For miraculous events in the O. T. narrative he constantly suggests rationalistic explanations; he is here accommodating himself to incredulous heathen readers and to a contemporary canon of historical writing on the treatment of "myth," but seems quite ready to accept such explanations himself. In common with most of his contemporaries he shared the belief in the reality of demoniacal possession.

But it is as apologist, rather than as theologian, that Josephus excels, and I will conclude with a reference to that fine apology for Judaism, from which I have often quoted, the *Contra Apionem*. Here, at the close, we have something approaching a connected statement of the writer's religious beliefs, and a glowing defence of the lawgiver and his code, expressed with a sincerity and a zeal for his country's religion unmatched in his other works. In the earlier portion of the treatise he challenges the alleged antiquity of the Greeks, accounts for their silence on Jewish history, adduces an array of external evidence for the antiquity of his own race, and crushes the malignant and absurd fictions circulated by their enemies. But he considers the best defence against these false accusations is to be found in the laws themselves, which he proceeds to summarise. He describes the constitution of Moses as a "theocracy," coining the Greek word apparently himself. The religion of Moses was for the many, not, like Greek philosophy, for a select few. His system of education combined precept and practice; through the weekly lessons all Jews know their Law, under which they live as under a father and master. Their unity of creed results in admirable harmony. "Could God," he writes [in *Contra Apionem* ii], "be more worthily honoured than by such a scheme, under which religion is the end and aim of the training of the entire community, the priests are entrusted with the special charge of it, and the whole administration of the state resembles some sacred rite of initiation?" Then he passes in review the various laws, the temple cult (strangely spoken of as if still in being), the equitable treatment of aliens, the humanity of the Law. "We put into practice," he says, "what Greeks regard as visionary ideals, and our discipline which leaves no room for freak or individual caprice in matters of everyday life results in the heroism which we display in face of death. Our Laws have stood the test of time and been widely imitated. Without any seductive bait, the Law has found its way among all mankind. Let each (he adds) reflect on his own country and his own household and he will not disbelieve what I say. Were we not ourselves aware of the excellence of our laws, we should have been impelled to pride ourselves upon them by the multitude of their admirers."

[In this essay] I turn to consider [Josephus] in another aspect, as the Hellenist, trained in all the riches of Greek learning. But with him I would here associate others to whom he is immensely indebted. We hear much from our author of his own achievements: we hear little of those skilled and assiduous helpers in the background, who were no mere amanuenses, but polished his periods, occasionally took over the composition of large portions of the narrative, and hunted up, made extracts from, and translated into elegant Greek, edicts, acts, and other relevant records written in crabbed Latin characters and deposited in the imperial archives in the Roman Capitol. These anonymous menials deserve recognition for their invaluable services, and, in considering our author as Hellenist, instead of leaving him in solitary grandeur, we should do them justice by speaking of "Josephus and Co."

The historian's literary career opened with a narrative of the Jewish War written in his native Aramaic or, as some think, Hebrew, for an Eastern audience. But that medium was soon discarded. His extant works are all addressed to Graeco-Roman readers, and for that wider circle a thorough mastery of Greek was essential. His life in Palestine in that period of turmoil, culminating in the Great War, would afford little opportunity for such study. True, it was a bilingual country, but the vernacular Greek there spoken was ill suited for works addressed to cultivated and fastidious readers. Our author's "hard training and laborious exercises" in his student days were devoted to the investigation of the tenets of the rival sects of his nation, nor, we may be sure, did his three years residence in the hermitage of Bannus include a course in Thucydides. The mastery of Greek displayed in his writings must have been wholly acquired in Rome.

The Jewish Dispersion at all times produced accomplished linguists, though the foreign tongue was by some assimilated with difficulty and their native Aramaic left an occasional mark on their Greek syntax. The pioneers who produced the first Greek version of the Scriptures at Alexandria performed a remarkable feat; it is true they wrote for the people in the vernacular, not the literary, Greek, and were moreover hampered by their task as translators and by their reverence for the letter of the inspired original, which accounts for their retention of some Hebrew phraseology. The thorough command of the language of which Alexandrian writers, free from such restrictions, were capable, is seen to perfection in the book of Wisdom or the works of Philo.

But Alexandria was the university of Greek learning, and the Alexandrian Jew, who had forgotten his Aramaic, was acquainted with a smattering of Greek from his infancy. At Rome the Palestinian Josephus had almost to start from the beginning and to master the grammar, before im-

mersing himself in those masses of literature which were to serve alike as the materials for his history and as his models of style. He clearly took immense pains to acquire a good style and, though his work is very unequal, portions of it attain a remarkably high level. No trace of his native Aramaic is allowed to sully the pages of the Greek version of his *Jewish War*, and the one trace of Semitism thought to have been discovered elsewhere proves illusory. He must further endeavour fastidiously to abjure the "vulgarisms" of the later Alexandrian speech, which were not disdained even by such a writer as Polybius.

This command of the language was, however, as I said, not wholly his own, and I propose to go in quest of some of his assistants. It will be a study in diversities of style. Such a study, taking us back as it were into the scriptorium of an ancient writer and disclosing something of his methods, is not without its human interest. I have elsewhere shown how variations in style may be detected in the Greek Bible, and how the different renderings of such a common phrase as "Thus saith the Lord" and other changes of style, which make their appearance after the middle of a book of the LXX suggest that the Alexandrian translators of some of the prophetical books worked in pairs, and, to expedite their labours, bisected the particular book upon which they were engaged and alternately dictated and translated the Hebrew. In the New Testament we know the name of one of S. Paul's amanuenses, and the names of others have been plausibly conjectured; variations in the style of some of the Pauline Epistles have been thought to be traceable to the employment of various amanuenses. But in the case of Josephus we are not left merely to conjecture: we have his own admission that he employed assistants.

Two passages may first be quoted, in which the author alludes to his literary qualifications and his appreciation of the value of style. Here is his estimate of his own attainments which he makes at the close of the *Antiquities*. There is little modesty about it, though it does contain one significant admission about his pronunciation of Greek, in apology it would seem to those who had heard his attempts to speak the language. "I make bold to say that no one else, whether Jew or alien, could with the best will in the world have produced a work of such accuracy as this for Greek readers. For my countrymen admit that I am easily pre-eminent among them in the lore of my native land; and I have moreover striven to acquaint myself with Greek literature (some MSS add 'including poetry') and am proficient in the grammar, although long habituation to my native tongue has prevented me from acquiring the correct pronunciation." That little addition in some MSS, "and poetical learning," is intriguing. It is quite possible to account for the accidental omission of the words by what is called *homoioteleuton* ("like-ending"); on the other hand, as will appear, one of the author's assistants was a keen lover of the Greek dramatists, and my friend Dr. Eisler suggests that it is he who, knowing the truth about these boasted achievements of his master, has deliberately erased the words from a later edition. Here again is a passage on the virtue of style at the opening of Book xiv, written when the author was wearying of his task and was soon to entrust it to other hands: "Among other qualifications the historian and reporter of events, which owing to their antiquity are unfamiliar to most men, needs the charm of style, in so far as this is attainable by the choice and nice adjustment of words and by whatever else may serve to embellish the narrative, in order that the reader, along with instruction, may find a certain fascination and delight." By the "nice adjustment" or "harmony" of words he refers to the avoidance of hiatus (or clashing of vowels): the rule that a word ending with a vowel must not collide with an initial vowel of the next is studiously observed throughout a large portion of his work—a very exacting requirement.

Turning to our author's earliest and greatest work, we find, as I have said, that the *Jewish War* possesses extraordinary merits. The style is an excellent specimen of the Atticistic Greek of the first century, modelled on, if not quite on a level with, that of the great masters of the age of Pericles. A choice vocabulary, well knit sentences and paragraphs, niceties in the use of particles and the order of words, a uniformly classical style without slavish imitation of classical models—these and other excellences combine to give the work high rank in Greek literature.

This thorough command of the intricacies and niceties of the Greek language in an author who had hitherto written

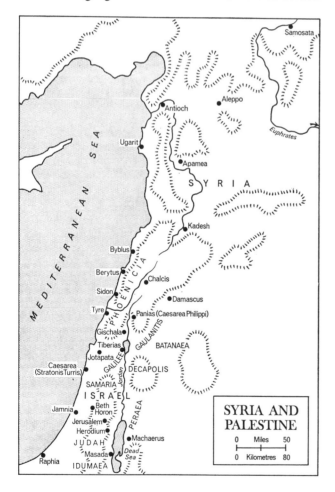

Map of the cities and towns of Palestine and Syria, which figured prominently in Josephus's Jewish War *and* Jewish Antiquities.

only in Aramaic would be astounding, were it not for an *obiter dictum* in a later work. In the *Contra Apionem* written about a quarter of a century after the *War*, the historian makes a tardy acknowledgment of the help received by him in the composition of the earlier work. He employed, he tells us, certain collaborators for the sake of the Greek.

The modern editor is grateful for this illuminating acknowledgment and can afford to forgive its tardiness. The assistants concerned may well have complained that it was not made before, and indeed it is possible that, like other admissions in his later works ("matters about which I have hitherto kept silence" as he says [in *Life* 338]), it was extorted from him by expostulation. It is true that ancient works had no exact counterpart to the modern preface, that convenient receptacle for due acknowledgment of indebtedness and other personal matters. But the *Jewish War* does include a full proem, in which the author has said a good deal about himself. A word of graceful and timely acknowledgment would not have been out of place here; instead of this the only allusion there made to "erudite Greeks" is a severe censure for their disregard of historical accuracy. The assistants indeed had a thankless taskmaster. That they were at least well remunerated out of the author's pension may, I hope, be inferred from a remark in his proem: "For myself, at a vast expenditure of *money* and pains, I, a foreigner, present to Greeks and Romans this memorial of great achievements." Their names and social status are unrecorded. Their culture and recondite knowledge of Greek literature led me at first to think of them as the author's "literary friends in Rome"; but we should perhaps be more correct in regarding them as his slaves, like that eunuch slave who was tutor to the historian's son and was punished by Domitian's orders for defaming his master. Josephus had foes in his own household.

At any rate the immense debt which the author of the *Jewish War* owes to these admirable assistants is apparent on almost every page. Among other excellences, the work contains a large and choice vocabulary—not confined to military terms—peculiar to itself, or but rarely represented in certain parts of the *Antiquities*. The last book (vii) stands apart: here another vocabulary, characteristic of the *Antiquities*, makes its appearance. It would seem that the author at the close of his task has been thrown more upon his own resources, though here too indications of assistance are not wanting. The last book of a literary work was liable to escape revision, and, though different causes probably came into play, it is curious to recall that the last book of Thucydides similarly stands apart from the rest: as has often been remarked it seems to have lacked the author's final touches. Some marks of the author's own style also appear at an earlier point, in the narrative of his youthful career in Galilee at the end of Book ii.

Josephus mentions $\sigma\upsilon\nu\epsilon\rho\gamma\omega\iota$ in the plural. I have not so far succeeded in discriminating the respective contributions of the two or more members of his literary staff employed on the *War*. The detection of two of his main assistants comes only in the later work, the *Antiquities*, to which I now turn. There is no allusion to any help having been obtained here, but the collaborators have left their own indelible impress upon the text.

The short proem to the *Antiquities* contains an interesting personal statement concerning the genesis of the author's *magnum opus*, with some human touches on his shrinking from the formidable task which he had undertaken and the encouragement of his patrons which alone enabled him to carry it to completion. He tells us how originally, when he wrote the *Jewish War*, he had contemplated a single comprehensive work, to embrace in addition to the narrative of the recent campaign the whole history of his nation, but how, realizing the unwieldy compass of such a work, he decided to divide it into two. Yet even so the writing of the *Archaeology*, the complete history of the race, proved an appalling task. "As time went on," he writes, and historians of all ages would sympathize with his feelings, "as is wont to happen to those who design to handle large themes, I was beset by hesitation and delay in presenting so vast a subject in a foreign and strange tongue. However, there were certain persons who wished for the history and instigated me to pursue it, and above all Epaphroditus," &c.

"There was hesitation and delay." The phrase, like so many, is reminiscent of a favourite model, Thucydides, and of the most well-thumbed portion of his work, the Syracusan expedition, but expresses a verifiable fact. It is possible, I think, to lay a finger on one point where the work was laid down and probably abandoned for a season. That point is the end of Book xiv, where the narrative has just reached the capture of Jerusalem by Herod and Sossius in the year 37 B.C. and Herod the Great has just come into the kingdom conferred on him three years earlier in Rome.

At this point the narrative undergoes a marked transformation. Just before it we may detect, if I am not mistaken, an indication of weariness; just after it begins a new manner of dealing with the author's materials, accompanied by a change of style. These changes persist for nearly five books. I infer that the work has been entrusted to other hands. The "weariness" of which I spoke betrays itself in the repeated use of old materials. The author has now reached a period which he has previously covered: the story of the rise of Antipater and Herod, which is the subject of Book xiv of the *Antiquities*, has already been graphically told in the *Jewish War*. He has some new materials at his disposal, but is mainly still dependent on his old source, Nicolas of Damascus. Now, while it was customary for ancient historians to make free and unacknowledged use of the published work of their predecessors, without any sense of what we should call "plagiarism," it was almost a point of honour with them to vary the phraseology. Still more did this rule apply where the writer was twice covering the same ground: he must not "plagiarise" from himself. Even a speech delivered on a particular occasion must, if reduplicated, be reported in different language. Now, Josephus, who is usually scrupulous in this matter, at the end of book xiv of the *Antiquities*, contrary to his wont, gives us an account of Herod's capture of Jerusalem which is almost a *verbatim* repetition of that already given in the *Jewish War*. He is beginning

to repeat himself or rather to transcribe afresh his old authority, Nicolas. For some time the two narratives have been running so closely parallel as to make the minor changes significant and purposeful; and it is not accidental that Laqueur selects just this fourteenth book for a detailed analysis and comparison of the different points of view presented. He could not have done the same for Book xv. Here the narrative has been completely recast and amplified by recourse to Nicolas and by the incorporation of new matter, and whereas in the *War* the external history of Herod's reign has been kept distinct from the domestic tragedies, in the *Antiquities* the events are presented in chronological order.

This change of treatment is, as I said, accompanied by a change, or rather changes, of style, extending from the opening of Book xv to near the end of Book xix. Towards the end of Book xix there is a return to what may be called the "normal" style, which continues to the end of the work (Book xx) and on into its appendix, the *curriculum vitae*. The author, approaching the end of his task, apparently once more takes the pen into his own hands.

This long section, compiled largely or wholly by others, occupies some five books or about a quarter of the whole work, and covers a period of 78 years from the establishment on his throne of Herod the Great in the year 37 B.C. to the confirmation of Agrippa I in his kingdom by Claudius in the year 41 A.D. It is the period which to some of us appears the greatest in the world's history, that immediately preceding and following the opening of the Christian era; and it is remarkable that the extraneous composition includes the famous *testimonium Flavianum* on Jesus Christ.

The peculiarities of this portion cannot be referred to the author himself. Some variation in an author's style might not be unnatural in a work laid by for a considerable time. But a writer does not change his style two or three times over, nor suddenly lapse for a time into patent and unmistakable mannerisms such as we find in three of these books. For the extraneous section in which these abnormalities occur falls into two smaller portions. Books xv and xvi bear the marks of an able assistant, such as those employed in the *War*; while Books xvii-xix betray the idiosyncrasies and pedantic tricks of a hack, an imitator of Thucydides.

Nor again, as might be thought are the peculiarities attributable to the author's use of different authorities. For the long narrative of Herod's reign begins in Book xiv in the "normal" style, extends right through the more elegantly written books xv and xvi, and ends in the extravagant phraseology of xvii. The main source throughout is doubtless Nicolas; yet the variation in style cuts this connected episode into three, and one pen after another takes up the poignant tale. Again, the work of Nicolas ceases with the accession of Archelaus in the middle of Book xvii; and while the second assistant begins with Herod the Great and his successor, he ends in xix with Roman history and the assassination of Caligula, obviously drawn from quite a different (Latin) source. Yet the same blatant mannerisms pervade this whole section (xvii-xix) from beginning to end.

We may speculate on the reasons which induced Josephus to seek such liberal aid at this particular point. A main cause was doubtless that weariness, hesitation and difficulty of coping with an acquired tongue, to which he alludes in his proem. But we can imagine others. He had reached a period already partially covered, also with assistance, in the *War*: he was content to leave the reproduction of the sequel to others, with instructions to reshape the materials and vary the phraseology. But, over and above the old documents, he had now found fresh matter to incorporate and much of it was in *Latin*. For a large part of Book xviii and nearly the whole of xix the scene shifts the narrative from Palestine to Rome, and, though much of the narrative has but a remote bearing on Jewish history, it becomes an authority of the first rank for the court history of the successors of Augustus. The varying fortunes of Agrippa I in Rome are the peg on which is hung an interesting disquisition on the dilatory policy of Tiberius and the fullest extant account of the murder of Caligula and the accession of Claudius. Here the author is doubtless dependent on Latin sources, and, if Greek always remained to him a foreign tongue, his proficiency in Latin was even slighter. He needed a helper to translate those documents in cursive Roman characters in the imperial archives or other Latin literary works.

We are then, I think, justified in regarding these two contiguous portions, books xv-xvi and xvii-xix, as the work of a pair of assistants, whom, for lack of names, I will call respectively α and β.

I will consider the latter first, because the characteristics of his style are patent and cannot fail to strike a reader's eye. A student who happened to make his first acquaintance with Josephus in this portion would pronounce him a difficult writer and perhaps be deterred by the involved and turgid language, whereas he would find the *Life* absurdly easy and crude. The distinctive features of the writer of xvii-xix are (1) free plagiarism from Thucydides and (2) certain mannerisms of his own, in which he seems to be trying his hand at imitating, without actually copying, his great model. He may be called the Thucydidean hack.

Thucydides was the natural standard of historical style, and a restrained use of his phraseology—an occasional reminiscence, such as we find in the *Jewish War*—was quite legitimate. When we turn to the *Antiquities* the parallels become more abundant and reach their climax in these books xvii-xix, where the writer in every paragraph quarries freely from this mine. He may also, as I hope to show, be held responsible for some of the parallels in the earlier books.

The "Thucydideans," as they are called, were a notorious tribe in the days of Josephus. A generation or two before his time we find them ridiculed by Cicero, a generation after him by Lucian. Cicero's satire is directed against the rhetoricians who frame their speeches on the model of the great Athenian. "See," he says, "there are some who profess themselves Thucydideans, a new and unheard of class of ignoramuses . . . Their speeches have so many obscure and recondite sentences that they can scarce be understood," and so on. Lucian in his excellent little treatise on "How history should be written," containing sound advice

not only for the historian but for the modern lecturer, makes sport of the imitators of the Athenian, who pompously open their works with their own outlandish names— "Crepereus Calpurnianus the Pompeiopolitan wrote the history of the war in which the Parthians and the Romans fought against one another, beginning to write when they first took up arms"—and who fill their pages with "little rags" from their model. After listening to one of these ranters declaiming his work, he says "I left him burying the unfortunate Athenians in Nisibis, knowing exactly what he would say on my departure."

Just so it may be said that in portions of the *Antiquities*, and in these three books in particular, the old Grecian battles are refought, the orations of Pericles redelivered, on Palestinian or Italian soil. The whole history of the Peloponnesian war is at the writer's finger ends, but the retreat from Syracuse, the siege of Plataea and the speeches of Pericles provide the most numerous reminiscences.

A few instances of "Thucydideanisms" and other tricks of style must suffice. This journalistic hack is verbose and prefers two or more words to one. Periphrasis is frequent and the double negative—"not incapable of," "not averse from"—a special favourite. Thucydides had once used the former phrase in a character sketch of Themistocles "who even in matters in which he had no experience was not incapable of forming a sufficient judgment." The writer of [*Jewish Antiquities*] xvii-xix uses the phrase, found nowhere else in Josephus, some 15 times, once with obvious dependence on the Thucydides passage. After the assassination of Caligula in the underground passage still shown to visitors to the Palatine in Rome, Claudius was found in hiding and carried off by the Roman troops as their emperor. "One of the soldiers," I translate literally, "being unskilled to make sure of the features because of the darkness, but not incapable of being a judge that the skulking figure was a man." That illustrates the cumbrous pedantry of the scribe: "being unskilled" for "unable," "not incapable" and the resolution of the simple verb . . . ("judge") of Thucydides into . . . ("be a judge").

The cult of Thucydides was, as I said, in fashion: his devotees formed a clique like the Browningites or the Meredithians of modern days. If we seek for further reasons for this writer's whimsicalities, we may perhaps name two. In the earlier portion of his work, the account of the latter days of Herod the Great in Book xvii, we have merely a verbose paraphrase of the previous narrative in the *War*: there has been no such recourse to the original authority, Nicolas, as we find in Books xv-xvi. The amanuensis here must have received instructions from his "boss" (if that colloquialism may be used of the great historian) "Take the *War* as your authority, but be careful to vary the phraseology." This gave the scribe free rein to indulge his natural propensities. But I cannot help thinking that there may have been another more malicious incentive. Invited to become a partner in an important literary undertaking, for which his employer was to take the sole credit, and given a free hand in the phraseology, he was determined to leave his own mark, if not his name, upon his handiwork, and he has successfully done so.

That this Thucydidean is thus responsible for writing

practically the whole of Books xvii-xix appears unquestionable: his speech betrays him. But, as I said, imitation of Thucydides is not confined to this portion, though here it reaches a climax. The question then arises, did this secretary lend occasional aid elsewhere? I think he did, and that where we find in earlier portions of the *Antiquities* an accumulation of Thucydidean phrases, especially if they are among the favourite phrases in Books xvii-xix and moreover occur in conjunction with some known mannerism, there the same hand has been at work. He has not yet fully developed those later mannerisms, but we can already detect one or two of them in embryo. I have mentioned his cumbrous seven-word periphrasis of "forthwith," repeated a dozen times in *Ant.* xvii-xix. To this we find one parallel in an earlier book, in the description of the despatch of messengers from Jerusalem to report Absalom's plans to David outside the city, where we read (in a literal translation) "and they deferred nothing to delays and procrastination," i. e. "they departed post-haste." Here we may well suspect the hand of the hack. Still more significant is the account of the destruction by fire of Korah and all his company, because here we find not only express imitation of Thucydides, but also one of this scribe's most distinctive marks, the use of the pronoun οποσοσ for οσοσ, of which there are 100 instances in *Ant.* xvii-xix and only four elsewhere. You may remember how in the Peloponnesian War the besiegers of Plataea attempted to destroy the city by a huge bonfire. "A flame arose," writes Thucydides, "of which the like had never before been made by the hand of man"; and then, with characteristic avoidance of exaggeration and an allusion to an ancient belief, he adds "I am not speaking of fires in the mountains, when the woods have spontaneously blazed up from the action of the wind and mutual attrition." The Plataean bonfire fell short of those mighty forest-fires. Well, our writer can better that: he must have a blaze that will "lick creation." Here is his picture: "And Aaron and Korah, with his 250 followers, came forth, and they all offered incense in the censers which they had brought. And suddenly there blazed up a fire, the like of which had never in the records of history been made by the hand of man, nor was ever ejected from the earth through subterranean current of heat, nor yet spontaneously broke out in the woods from the violence of the wind and mutual attrition."

From these and a few similar passages we may infer that, besides taking over the large portion towards the close, the Thucydidean has been requisitioned to impart some purple patches to the earlier narrative.

The pilferer of whom I have been speaking has thus left his indelible impression. The thumb-marks are there and it needs no Sherlock Holmes to detect them. The handiwork of his fellow, a man of a distinctly superior type, was not so easily discoverable, and a personal allusion to the circumstances which brought me upon his tracks will, I hope, be forgiven.

Many years ago, I began collecting materials for a *Josephus Lexicon*, which, thanks to the munificence of the *Kohut Memorial Foundation*, is now on the way to publication. I began with a limited portion, the last five books

of the *Antiquities*. My immediate object was to collect and classify all peculiarities of the Thucydidean assistant and to fix the precise limits of his work. I knew the approximate limits (Books xvii-xix), but it was necessary to include, as a contrast, some portions of what I regarded as the "normal" style on either side of this, viz. Book xvi on the one side and Book xx on the other. I was not, I think, mistaken in regarding Book xx as written in the "normal" style of our author; here and in the appended *Life* we get as near as we can anywhere to the *ipsissima verba* of Josephus. But I was, as it proved, mistaken in regarding Book xvi as also in the "normal" style. I had unwittingly started my investigation in the middle of the work of a second assistant. It was not until I extended my researches to the whole of the *Antiquities* that I became aware of this. I then found that Books xv and xvi were linked by a special vocabulary and numerous small niceties of style, which were either peculiar to these books or only to be paralleled in certain parts of the *Jewish War*: I was on the track of a second associate. Josephus had wearily laid down his pen at the end of Book xiv, and for the next five books employed successive assistants, responsible for two and for three books respectively.

This first assistant ("α") excelled the other ("β"), and Josephus was fortunate in securing his services. As before, the criteria are two: certain distinctive characteristics of style, and an affinity to a particular class of Greek literature. But here instead of "mannerisms" I should speak of "niceties" and instead of "plagiarism" of "felicitous reminiscences" of a cultivated mind. I need not trouble you with the various subtle delicacies of style and vocabulary which first put me on the track of this assistant, and will confine myself to his echoes of classical masterpieces. He was evidently well-versed in Greek literature as a whole and does not disdain an incidental reminiscence of Thucydides: but his distinctive characteristic is a love of Greek poetry, Sophocles in particular. Now Thucydides was a natural quarry for the hack historian, but Sophocles is perhaps the last model to which one would expect a Jewish annalist to turn. The occasional, unsought echoes of that most charming of Greek poets, which we here find, bespeak an instinctive literary taste. Whether the plays of Sophocles were acted in the Roman theatres I do not know; but this writer had clearly read them, especially the *Ajax* and the *Electra, con amore.* It is hard to believe that he was a slave. It is but a word or phrase inserted unobtrusively here and there, but their source is unmistakable. In Book xv of the *Antiquities* we find parallels to the *Ajax*, in the phrase απο του στεγουσ διοπτενειν of the dizzy spectacle from the roof of Herod's palace into the ravine below (after *Aj.* 307), a little below... "towards the sunbeams" i. e. "on the east" (after *Aj.* 877) and higher up the word ενωμοτοσ. From the Electra we find in *Ant.* xvi the phrases . . . , "Whither have your wits gone?" in the mouth of the old soldier Tiro expostulating with Herod (after *El.* 390) and μισοσ εντετηκεναι of hatred melting or sinking deep into the soul (after *El.* 1311). In all we find about a dozen echoes of the Athenian tragedian concentrated into these two books.

It is true that the parallels are not wholly confined to these books. But these Sophoclean reminiscences, taken in connexion with certain niceties of style, are the clue which reveal the activity of this assistant in other parts of the work. The results which emerge are, first, that the poet-lover, like the Thucydidean, has, besides taking over the composition of one large section of the *Antiquities*, lent occasional aid elsewhere, and, secondly, that he was one of the first-rate assistants employed on the earlier work, the *Jewish War*. When we find in the *War* reminiscences of the *same plays* of Sophocles as those from which the phrases in the *Antiquities* are derived, we may be sure that the same hand has been at work. No such parallels occur in *Ant.* xvii-xix, nor did the Thucydidean take any part in the writing of the *Jewish War*; his services were only employed for the historian's later work.

Reminiscences of Sophocles are specially frequent in the third book of the *War*. From the writer's favourite play, the *Electra*, we have the phrases . . . "armed by recklessness," . . . "to be prodigal of life" and what I take to be a paraphrase of a familiar line in the same context of that play put into the mouth of Titus, as a delicate compliment to his classical taste. From the *Philoctetes* we have ουδεν υγιεζ μρονειν, from the *Trachiniae* ουδεν υγιεζ μρονειν "afford confidence" and . . . "live and flourish."

From the same hand doubtless come some sporadic allusions to Euripides. I will mention but two which occur in earlier portions of the *Antiquities*. Hagar fleeing from Sarah with the infant Ishmael, when water fails, lays the child at his last gasp under a pine tree and wanders further on that he may not expire in her presence. . . . Here we have an obvious reminiscence of the *Hercules Furens* 324 f., where Amphitryon says, "Kill me and my wife first, that we may not see those children . . . at their last gasp and calling upon their mother. Josephus is not the place where we should look for an allusion to a *lost* play of Euripides; yet such may be found. Stobaeus has preserved a fragment of the *Ino* of that poet: —

> When blest by fortune slack not every rein:
> When faring ill hold fast to kindly hope. . . .

Of this we have a clear echo when we read of Aristobulus, after his defeat by Pompey, that "though faring ill he none the less held fast to good hope."

Beside these parallels with Greek poetry, there are not wanting echoes of Virgil and other Latin authors. Josephus, we may be sure, had but a slight acquaintance with Latin literature, and these reminiscences doubtless come from an assistant, probably from the poet-lover already mentioned. At any rate two of them occur in the same third book of the *War* which contains the Sophoclean phrases. The sack of Jotapata recalls the siege of Troy. In consequence of the information of a Jewish deserter that "about the last watch of the night, at an hour when . . . jaded men easily succumb to morning slumber, the sentinels used to drop asleep . . . the Romans advanced in silence to the walls. Titus was first to mount . . . They cut down the sentries and entered the city" [*Jewish War* III, 319]. So in a famous passage in the second Aeneid, where the Greeks issue from the wooden horse, "Machaon (came) first . . . They enter the city buried in sleep and

wine, the sentries are cut down . . . It was the time when the first rest steals over wearied mortals." Later on the tale of the fall of Jotapata is carried to Jerusalem by Rumour personified. Embroidering facts with fiction, where there is a reminiscence of the Virgilian picture of Fama, who "flew with rumors mixed of false and true."

I would add one more curious instance where Josephus, or rather his assistant, has apparently gone to a Latin prose writer, the historian Sallust, for a picture of a villain. If I am not mistaken, the black portrait drawn of John of Gischala is partly based on the character-sketch of that arch-villain and conspirator in the last days of the Roman republic, Lucius Catiline. Here is the description of John: "While Josephus was thus directing affairs in Galilee, there appeared upon the scene an intriguer, a native of Gischala, named John, son of Levi, the most unscrupulous and crafty of all who have ever gained notoriety by such infamous means. *Poor at the opening of his career*, his penury had long thwarted his malicious designs; a ready liar and clever in obtaining credit for his lies, he made a merit of deceit . . . Ever full of high ambitions, his hopes were fed on the basest of knaveries . . . He was already aspiring to the command and had yet higher ambitions, but *was checked by impecuniosity*." And here is a slighter sketch of the man elsewhere. "The people of Gischala had been incited to rebel . . . by John, son of Levi, a charlatan of an extremely subtle character, always ready to indulge great expectations and an adept in realizing them; all knew that he had set his heart on war in order to attain supreme power." Beside these passages I would set the portrait of the Roman conspirator or the main features of it: "Lucius Catiline was of noble birth, of great vigour both of body and mind, but of a depraved genius. From his youth up he revelled in intestine war, murder, rapine, civil discord . . . An audacious spirit, crafty, subtle, a ready hypocrite and dissimulator on any matter . . . His monstrous spirit . . . was ever ambitious of things too high for him (*nimis alta semper cupiebat*). . . . A burning passion had possessed him to capture the republic, and while seeking a kingdom for himself, he cared not by what means he pursued his ends. His fierce spirit was daily more and more agitated by *lack of money* (*inopia rei familiaris*) and by consciousness of his crimes." There are several minor parallels here, but the allusion to impecuniosity as the barrier to the criminal's nefarious designs clinches, to my mind, the connexion between the two portraits.

If John was in our author's eyes the villain of the tragedy of his nation, the hero was the high-priest Ananus; and the encomium upon him remotely recalls, though it is not a copy of, that of Thucydides on Pericles. "A man on every ground revered and of the highest integrity, Ananus, with all the distinction of his birth, his rank and the honours to which he had attained, yet delighted to treat the very humblest as his equals. Unique in his love of liberty and an enthusiast for democracy, he on all occasions put the public welfare above his private interests. To maintain peace was his supreme object" and so on. Thus while Athens has coloured the picture of the virtuous hero, Rome has provided a model of vice.

I have attempted to show how the relation of portions of

the historian's work to Greek literature—lavish imitation of Thucydides on the one hand, stray echoes of the poets on the other—enables us to detect and isolate the respective contributions of two of his assistants. Elsewhere it is not easy to distinguish how much of the wide acquaintance shown with that literature is due to the author's own reading, how much to the prompting of his subordinates. But between them, besides consulting the necessary pagan sources, they have ransacked, as models of style, historians such as Herodotus, Xenophon, Polybius and Dionysius of Halicarnassus, and, for the speeches interspersed throughout the narrative, Demosthenes and the orators. They have diligently followed the maxim of Horace, "Vos exemplaria Graeca Nocturna versate manu, versate diurna"; and an English translator of Josephus is grateful for the relief afforded to the tedium of his task by being sent back so often to the great masters.

But there is another side to the picture. With all this indebtedness to the wisdom of the Greeks, all this borrowed plumage and saturation in Greek phraseology, Greek modes of thought and Greek lore, the author has a profound contempt for the race, especially for the contemporary Greek historian. "As for the native Greeks," he writes in the proem to the *Jewish War*, "where personal profit or a lawsuit is concerned, their mouths are at once agape and their tongues loosed; but in the matter of history, where veracity and laborious collection of the facts are essential, they are mute, leaving to inferior and ill-informed writers the task of describing the exploits of their rulers. Let us at least hold historical truth in honour, since by Greeks it is disregarded." Here undoubtedly speaks the historian himself, and not his obsequious Greek assistant. Pro-Roman, in war days at least, our author was; phil-Hellene, never. One seeming exception to this is interesting. The allusion in Agrippa's great speech to "Greeks who, though *noblest of all races under the sun . . .* are yet subservient to six rods of a Roman magistrate" comes from the pen not of the author but of the assistant whom I call "α"; and here there are significant diversities of reading, suggesting a conflict of opinion between the two. I follow Niese's MS "preeminent in nobility", but the majority of the MSS have "reputed to be preeminent", while one of them reads "who are reputed and are preeminent," as if the assistant had protested and reasserted his proud opinion of his race. In other cases, where the rival claims of style and accuracy are contrasted, we seem to hear two voices speaking in the grudging admission, "Yes, you Greeks are excellent stylists, but style is not everything." Thus in the *Contra Apionem*, "While, then, for eloquence and literary ability we must yield the palm to the Greek historians, we have no reason to do so for veracity in the history of antiquity." . . .

[In *Contra Apionem*] as nowhere else in our author's works, we find the learning of Judaism and of Hellenism side by side, blended and contrasted in a volume of small compass. The writer's patriotic zeal for Judaism dominates the writing, but that zeal leads him to contrast his own religion with the beliefs of other nations and so carries him into some strange by-paths of Greek literature. The work is at once a defence of Judaism, a repository of recondite Greek lore, and an attack on the morality and

pretensions of the Greeks, combining just criticism of their faults with an appreciation of the merits of their great philosophers. It matters not how much of this learning the author owes to others: it is sufficient that he has produced an admirable book. His principal opponent, Apion, was an erudite grammarian, and he needed to be well-armed.

I spoke of the work as a repository of Greek lore, and the abstruse knowledge displayed is indeed astonishing. We seem to be moving in the literary circles of Apion's own Alexandria, in which antiquarian problems and questions of doubtful authorship are discussed and the merits of the great masters criticised.

We have at the beginning and close of the work a reasoned criticism of the pretensions and religion of the Greeks. They are untrustworthy as antiquarians, being, in comparison with Egyptians and eastern nations, but a people of yesterday. Their land "has experienced countless catastrophes, which have obliterated the memory of the past; and as one civilization succeeded another the men of each epoch believed that the world began with them. They were late in learning the alphabet and found the lesson difficult" and so on. The discrepancies between their historians are attributed partly to their neglect to keep public records, partly to their regard for style rather than accuracy. Their records are "mere stories improvised according to the fancy of their authors." And then at the close, introduced with apologies for the comparison of the rival religions to which opponents have driven him, we have a

---

Eusebius (c. 264 - c. 339) on Josephus:

[It] is well that the origin and ancestry of Josephus himself, who has provided so much material for this present history, should be generally known. He furnishes this information himself:

> I, Josephus, son of Matthias, am a priest from Jerusalem; in the early stages I myself fought against the Romans, and of the later events I was an unwilling witness.

Of the Jews at that time he was the most famous, not only among his fellow-countrymen but among the Romans too, so that he was honoured with the erection of a statue in the city of Rome, and the labours of his pen found a place in the Library. He has set out the whole of Ancient Jewish History in twenty books, and the story of the Roman war of his own day in seven. The latter work he committed not only to Greek but also to his native language, as he himself testifies—and in view of his general truthfulness, we may accept this. Two other worth-while books of his are extant, entitled The Antiquity of the Jews, his reply to Apion the grammarian, who had recently published an attack on the Jews, and to others who had made similar attempts to misrepresent the ancestral customs of the Jewish people.

Eusebius, in his The History of the Church from Christ to Constantine, *translated by G. A. Williamson, Penguin Books, 1965.*

scathing denunciation of the gross and immoral Hellenic ideas about their gods, showing acquaintance with the whole range of Greek mythology. The cause of these erroneous conceptions is traced to the neglect of religion by their legislators and to the licence given to poets and artists; while it is claimed, as had been claimed by Philo and others before him, that Plato and the great philosophers derived their higher ideas from Judaism and were in reality Moses' disciples.

The argument is well reasoned and sustained; the attack is as able as the defence; and the sentiments, if not all the language, are undoubtedly the author's own. If I began by putting in a plea on behalf of his assistants, I must end by admitting that Josephus here makes good his claim to have immersed himself in Greek literature, and has given us a vivid picture of the merits and defects of Hellenism.

Martin Percival Charlesworth   (essay date 1936)

SOURCE: "The Adventurer," in *Five Men: Character Studies from the Roman Empire,* Cambridge, Mass.: Harvard University Press, 1936, pp. 63-93.

[*In the following excerpt, Charlesworth explores Josephus's autobiographical writings, in particular some of his observations about Judaism, the Roman Empire, and Christianity.*]

In the year A.D. 69 any man whose business took him to Egypt or Syria would have found strange and stirring events taking place. The Roman Empire, after nearly a hundred years of tranquillity, had fallen upon troublous times: civil war had broken out, different armies each supported their own candidate for the palace of the Caesars, the Batavians and the Jews were in revolt, and to many provincials it looked as though the end of Roman rule might be at hand. One of the strangest events of that strange year must have been the proclamation of Vespasian, whom Nero had sent out as general to suppress the rising in Judaea, as *princeps* and *imperator.* For he was not a noble, not a man of high birth or education, but a plain country farmer (what some history books incorrectly term a peasant), with a record of good service in Britain and Africa, but with nothing else to forward his claim. Yet this was the man who was greeted as Emperor by the legions stationed at Alexandria on July 1, and acknowledged two days later by the army in Syria. It was the strangest, the most unpredictable of chances that this slow and stolid farmer should be raised to occupy the throne of an Augustus, to become ruler of the Roman world. Even so, strange as it was, his biographer Suetonius is careful to note that many omens and signs had already shown clearly what was destined to come, and he instances twelve of them. They are a miscellaneous lot, and not very convincing.

For instance, when Vespasian was an aedile, the Emperor Gaius, enraged one day at the filthy state of the roads, ordered his soldiers to fill Vespasian's gown with mud; we are assured that the sages (by a process hidden from us) interpreted this to mean that one day the State would come under Vespasian's protection. Others are similar and a little grotesque: an ox once burst into Vespasian's din-

ing-room and then knelt humbly before him; a stray dog brought in a human hand and dropped it under his table; Vespasian dreamt that good luck would begin for him when one of Nero's teeth had been extracted, and the next day the dentist showed him a tooth of Nero's freshly drawn.

So far, this is merely the kind of stuff which was told about any emperor, and believed by the credulous. But there is another omen related by Suetonius which is far more noteworthy. "In Judaea," he says, "one of the noble prisoners of war, Josephus, when he was being put in irons, asserted in the most positive terms that he would soon be released by Vespasian, but that Vespasian would then be Emperor." This is the only mention, as far as I know, in a classical author of a remarkable man, Josephus, the Jewish soldier and historian, and of a remarkable feat—the prophesying of something extremely improbable that yet came true. The career of Josephus is a striking example of what can be done in stirring times by self-confidence and small belief in scruple, and it throws an interesting light upon a corner of the Roman Empire at that period.

Apart from the notice in Suetonius, just quoted, and a few later scraps, Josephus is the only authority for his own life, and it is well to bear this in mind from the start. There is something rather engaging about his frankness; of many of the incidents in his career he can scarcely have been proud, yet he gives them with complete candor and rarely attempts concealment. Let me first outline briefly when he lived and what he wrote, so as to get our framework right. He was born in A.D. 37 and died (probably) during the reign of Trajan, that is, before A.D. 117. He took a prominent part in the great Jewish revolt of A.D. 66-73, and was captured and ultimately taken to Rome, where he was held in high esteem by Vespasian and his family. Here he wrote several works. The first is *The Jewish War*, which, as its name implies, gives an account of the revolt of the Jews and of the siege and capture of Jerusalem, of which Josephus was an eyewitness. The second is a more ambitious project, *The Jewish Antiquities*, a work in twenty books, giving a combined history and defence of the Jewish nation from the Creation down to A.D. 66. The third is usually called *Against Apion*, and is an attack upon those who could not believe his history, or who had abused him—there were many of both. Finally therd is the *Life*, a curious *apologia pro vita sua*, directed against another Jew, Justus from Tiberias, who had thrown doubts upon his patriotism, and jeered at his imperfect Greek. Thus most of his writings are defensive in their object, and it must be admitted that some of the defence is needed.

The very year of his birth, 37, the first year of the reign of the Emperor Gaius, was an ominous date for Jewry, for it was Gaius' insane desire to have his image set up for worship in the Temple at Jerusalem that embittered Jewish feeling, and caused a rapid increase in the desperate sect of the Zealots, with whom Josephus was to have dealings later. He came of a noble and priestly family, and on his mother's side was connected with the royal house of the Hasmoneans. Thus he received a good education and thorough training in Jewish literature, history, and lore, but not (be it noted) in Greek: unlike the Jews of Alexandria, such as the philosopher Philo, who could speak and write Greek with ease and fluency, the Palestinian Jews rather prided themselves upon not knowing the Gentile tongues too well. He soon showed himself a quick and apt pupil, especially in the Law, so that at the tender age of fourteen he began to be consulted by the chief priests upon knotty points (I must remind you from time to time that Josephus is our *only* authority for Josephus). As he grew older he had to decide to which of the great sects of Judaism he would ally himself; at sixteen he had determined to be an ascetic and so spent three years under the leadership of one Bannus, who wore no other clothing than what grew upon trees, ate nothing which did not grow of itself, and bathed frequently in cold water, night and day, in order to attain purity. A cynic might suggest that it gradually dawned upon Josephus that even purity could be purchased at too high a price, for after three years of this cheerless existence he returned to civilization and attached himself to the sect of the Pharisees. But the cynic is not always justified: granted that Josephus was ill fitted for the life of a hermit, and that his masterful, energetic, and intriguing brain must have demanded some wider field, yet no man can spend three years in the desert without learning certain lessons. We cannot question his bravery, or his powers of endurance, and both these qualities would have been confirmed by his stay there.

On his return to Jerusalem he was soon able to prove himself. The procurator of Judaea, Felix, had sent a party of priests, arraigned upon some trivial charge, in chains to Rome. Josephus heard of this, and struck with admiration for their piety and constancy in their misfortunes, decided he must work to save them. He was socially influential, and easily secured a mission to Rome. But he had an exciting voyage: the ship carrying him sank "in mid Adria"; through the night some six hundred of the passengers managed to keep afloat upon spars or planks, until at daybreak, "by God's providence" (a phrase we shall encounter again), a vessel from Cyrene hove in sight: Josephus and some eighty others managed to outstrip the rest (there seems a grim tale lurking in that casual phrase) and got themselves taken safely on board. Arrived in Rome, he was able to gain an interview with the wife of Nero, the Empress Poppaea, who was interested in Judaism; he secured the speedy release of his friends and returned home laden with gifts and glowing with the gratification of duty done.

But he returned to find his native land in a disturbing condition. The administration of Judaea under the procurators was not one of the bright spots in Roman rule; the last two procurators sent out were a disgrace, and succeeded only in bringing to a head the suspicion and indignation that Gaius had first aroused. There had grown up a band of men who termed themselves Zealots (defenders of the old faith); Josephus calls them frankly "bandits," and the Roman title for them was "men of the knife"—and these three names probably represent the position accurately enough. They were a motley lot, composed of the poor and needy, the debt-ridden and desperate, and the fanatical believers in a Messiah, filled with an explosive mixture of national and religious fervor, and with hatred for most things, hating the Romans as Gentiles and masters, hating

their own priests for their worldly subservience to the Romans, hating the rich for their riches. They were working principally in the hilly region round about the Sea of Galilee, robbing, killing, and converting,

> Fightin' like divils for conciliation,
> An' hatin' each other for the love of God.

But they were a serious problem for the Sanhedrin: what should it do with them? Put them down like brigands? In that event it would be accused of lack of national spirit. Support them? That meant inevitably collision with Rome. Surely here was an opportunity of using the tact and diplomacy of the young Josephus, who had been so successful in Italy. So he, with two other priests, was sent into Galilee to persuade the Zealots to lay down their arms. What actually happened was rather different.

On arrival, Josephus and his companions found the country around Galilee in complete confusion. The Zealots had chosen their ground well: hills and ravines provided admirable spots both for concealment and for ambushes, and from here they could easily sally out to raid the scattered cities and take their toll. In the cities opinion was not unanimous against the brigands: some were for armed opposition to them and keeping allegiance to Rome, others felt that it was only patriotic to throw in their lot with the Zealots, others counseled sitting on the fence. Josephus says he did what he could (and that means a good deal), but his two colleagues despaired and went back to Jerusalem and safety, and Josephus discovered that sweet reason and diplomacy and all his speeches (he was inordinately fond of making speeches) would not avail with fanatics. Eventually he reached a compromise: what he *says* is that he persuaded the cities to hire the fanatics as mercenaries by representing to the citizens that it was better to give a little voluntarily than to lose a lot involuntarily; what that apparently *means* is that Josephus promised the Zealots a monthly tribute from the cities, and to the cities a respite from attack; *he* acted as intermediary, and from what the cities reluctantly gave him, a fair percentage found its way into the pockets of the Zealots—but not all. In fact, he had become a sort of "boss" in Galilee, and indispensable to both parties; well indeed might he feel, as he himself notes, that God never neglects "those who do the right thing"!

Naturally he made many enemies, who envied him his simple and easy solution of the problem; the worst of these was John of Gischala, a bandit-leader who found his monopoly threatened, and to whom Josephus paid the truest tribute that one rogue can to another, that of blackening his character. Between John of Gischala, the cities, and various bandits, Josephus steered a tortuous course with amazing skill; his own life was continually in peril, but he declares that the providence of God constantly put into his mind certain "stratagems" which brought him through safely. He certainly had need of them all, for the dangers that beset him were many. His headquarters were at Taricheia, at the south end of the Sea of Galilee. On one occasion some young robbers from the town of Tiberias (the deadly rival of Taricheia) had successfully looted a caravan belonging to the royal house and brought the spoil to Josephus. Josephus did not distribute it; he intended, probably, to return it to King Agrippa as a sort of insurance. But the young robbers, disappointed in not getting any share of the loot, went about stirring up suspicion and strife, calling Josephus a traitor, spreading rumors, until the combined population of the two towns rushed upon his house with the intent to set it on fire. With his garments rent, and with ashes upon his head, Josephus came out and addressed them: "I have no intention of keeping the money," he declared. "No; rather what I am reserving it for is this. I have noticed how poorly defended our own city of Taricheia is, and how aggressive the men of Tiberias; I mean to present my fellow-citizens with a wall to guard them against all possible attack, and will spend every penny on that wall." Thus he went on, skilfully fanning the rivalry and suspicion between the men of the two towns; they began to quarrel with one another, words came to blows, blows to bloodshed, and in the resulting turmoil Josephus discreetly withdrew. The wall was not, apparently, built. But there remained malcontents still, and some two thousand of them surrounded his house with shouts and threats; against them Josephus employed, as he records with obvious pleasure, "another form of deceit." He went up on the roof, and standing there he calmed the mob into silence with his gestures, and then spoke: "I am unable to understand," he protested, "exactly what it is that you want, for the confusion and shouting make it hard for me to hear. I will do all you wish if you will only send some men to parley with me inside." This was agreed, the leaders and notables walked in, the great door was closed, and Josephus, sweeping them to the back of the house, had them flogged within an inch of their lives; then suddenly the door was thrown open and the bleeding and broken bodies staggered out upon their adherents, who were so panic-stricken that they dropped their arms and ran.

Indeed, he was master of every form of deceit, bluff, and cajolery, and these, coupled with his commanding presence and dramatic gifts, always stood him in good stead. His *Life* is full of examples, though space does not allow the recital of more than one or two. Take this: a riot had taken place at Tiberias, and the ringleader Cleitus had been caught; Josephus had no desire to execute a fellow-countryman, and determined he should be punished by having one of his hands cut off. The time came, but the executioner faltered and shrank at the thought of carrying out this punishment before a sullen crowd, containing so many of Cleitus' followers. This would never do, and so Josephus called Cleitus before him and exclaimed: "Since you have merited the loss of both your hands for your ungrateful conduct towards me, be your own executioner, lest a worse punishment befall you." Cleitus, overawed, begged hard to be allowed *one* of his hands, and at last Josephus yielded. (Doubtless he had realized a certain practical difficulty: that it is very hard for a man with only one hand left to cut that hand off.) Thereupon Cleitus, overjoyed at preserving one of his hands, seized the sword and cut off his left. "That," comments Josephus drily, "stopped the sedition."

But by now his enemies were united in their effort to get rid of him, and began to take elaborate measures. They despatched him a letter suggesting a friendly conference and meeting. The messenger strode in and interrupted Jo-

sephus at dinner; without appearing to do so, Josephus somehow managed to get a glimpse at the contents of the letter, and so had time to think of an answer. Meanwhile, he bade the messenger wait until dinner was finished, and offered him 20 drachmae for his pains. The man thanked him effusively, and Josephus at once perceived a weakness he could turn to good account—greed. Assuming an air of *camaraderie*, he cried, "Well, if you will only drink with me, you shall have a drachma for every glass," to which the fellow indicated that he didn't mind if he did. The natural result followed: drinking glasses at a drachma a time, the man got very drunk; he could not conceal the truth any longer, and told Josephus that the friendly meeting was really to be an ambush. Josephus dismissed the man graciously and the suggested interview did not take place. Well, indeed, might Josephus say, as he does of another successful "stratagem," "I was filled with pleasant satisfaction on beholding the folly of my opponents." No one but a man of considerable bravery and subtlety could have emerged unharmed from such a whirlpool of strife, and it was an admirable training for the serious warfare against the Romans which Josephus was now to undertake. For at last the pent-up fury and hatred of the Jews broke into open revolt against Rome in 66, and early in 67 Nero appointed Vespasian to suppress it; he was put in command of a force of three legions, a large number of auxiliary troops, and militia supplied by the client-kings; his headquarters at first were at Ptolemais (Acre). The appearance of this army dismayed some of the Jewish cities, who hastened to surrender; but hoping to stir up some resistance, Josephus, at the beginning of June 67, flung himself into the fortified town of Jotapata, lying in the hills roughly half-way between Ptolemais and the Sea of Galilee. At once Vespasian turned against Jotapata, for he judged Josephus to be of all the Jewish leaders the most intelligent (this is again Josephus' own account), and hoped that his capture might bring over all Galilee.

Jotapata lay upon a precipitous rock; on most sides the descent (according to Josephus) was sheer into bottomless ravines, "so that those who try to peer down find their sight growing weak at the depth." Only on the northern side was it approachable. Here naturally Vespasian determined to attack it, and brought up a formidable array of siege-engines; these attacks had to be countered by Josephus somehow, and he displayed a resourcefulness in devices which he narrates with obvious satisfaction. Reading through the third book of *The Jewish War*, one feels how much Josephus' efforts would have been appreciated by Aeneas Tacticus, the Greek writer on tactics. Aeneas' resourcefulness, too, is great; he knows the proper use of wasps in warfare, the importance of inspecting gates and defences before dinner and not after, and the limitations of the usefulness of women in defence. "You may dress them up as soldiers and line them along the wall, but don't let them throw; for you can tell a woman, by her throwing, from a long way off."

The situation was desperate enough, but (as our hero notes) "there's nothing like desperation for making men fight," and he succeeded in inspiriting the defenders to an amazing degree. The Romans soon built a mound as high as the city wall, and Josephus saw the wall must be raised, but no masons could work upon it under the shower of arrows and other missiles that the Romans hurled at them; to protect the masons Josephus devised wicker frames on which he stretched freshly skinned ox-hides. These hides gave way to the stones, while arrows and javelins slipped off them, and their damp surface quenched fire-darts. So the wall was successfully heightened, and now Vespasian thought of turning the siege into a blockade, and so starving out the defenders. This would never do; the shortage of water in the city was serious, but the Romans must not suspect it. Josephus bade his men dip their clothes in water and hang them over the ramparts, so that the wall streamed with moisture. Convinced by this display that the Jews had ample supplies of water, Vespasian again turned to assault. Meanwhile, in order to get messages in and out, and also to secure certain supplies, Josephus equipped his men with the skins of dogs: in these they used to sally out in the dark on all fours down one of the western ravines, until at last some brighter Roman sentry discovered the trick.

Still the assault continued relentlessly; a great ram was brought up to batter the walls, and they began to give way under its blows. Josephus promptly hung bags full of chaff against the parts attacked, which blunted the shock, and the wall suffered no hurt; and a heroic Jew, Eleazar, in a sally, hacked off the head of the ram and brought it back to the city, then, and not till then, collapsing under his wounds. When the Romans advanced to the assault in close order, shield locked to shield, Josephus replied by pouring burning olive oil down upon them, which penetrated under their armor and made them desist in agony; if they tried gangways and scaling-ladders, the Jews poured on to them melted fenugreek, which made them so slippery that the attackers could no longer keep their foothold.

Even so, after some forty-seven days, one dawn the end came. All the bravery and all the trickery in the world could not forever hold out against the combined pressure of starvation, exhaustion, and three legions, and at last the Romans broke into Jotapata. But Josephus was not there: he had discovered, in the last moments, a deep cave, well hidden, where he and forty other notables hid themselves with a small stock of provisions. But the exhaustion of this small supply soon turned the thoughts of Josephus to surrender, though his decision was met with a howl of rage from his companions. They abused him as a coward and a knave, clamored that he was disgracing the God of Israel and His law, and threatened to set upon him. The situation was hazardous in the extreme, yet this extraordinary young man (remember he was only thirty) proved equal to it. His comrades insisted that all should commit suicide; for some ten minutes Josephus harangued them on the evil of it, but without effect, until finally, "trusting in the favor of God," he conceived a brilliant plan. "Since you are determined on death," he cried, "let us draw lots for *who* shall kill *whom*, and thus Fortune shall deal with all impartially." In their heroic frenzy they consented; lots were drawn and twenty fell; lots were drawn again, and—but I prefer to conclude the story in his own words: "Finally Josephus was left with one other man, whether this should be ascribed to Fortune or to God's providence; and since

neither had any wish to be doomed by the lot, nor if he should survive to have kindred blood upon his hands, Josephus persuaded the other to live."

So, now, he was a prisoner of the Romans, but he had a purpose and a mission to fulfil. God had revealed to him in dreams a message, and that message he must deliver soon, for though young Titus pitied him, Vespasian ordered the rebel leader to be manacled and sent to Nero. Thereupon Josephus demanded and obtained a private interview; Vespasian and Titus, with two friends, and the prisoner alone remained in the tent. And now Josephus spoke out: he prophesied not only Nero's death, but also the coming elevation of Vespasian, telling him in plainest terms that he would shortly be Emperor. It was an astonishing prediction; it was in the highest degree unlikely— but Vespasian listened, and Josephus was removed in custody, but not sent to Nero—it would have been too dangerous. A few more months passed by, and one day in the summer of 68 there came the news of Nero's suicide—of civil war—and then, less than a year later, came the acknowledgement of Vespasian as Emperor.

Thus the prophecy of Josephus had come true, true in every detail. Vespasian now recollected with shame that the man who had made the prophecy was still in bonds; he sent for him and had the chains struck off. Henceforward he was to be in high esteem with the Emperor and his son Titus, for they planned to besiege Jerusalem in the next year, and Josephus could be very useful from his knowledge both of the locality and of the language. He was taken onto the staff, and Vespasian gave him one of the captive Jewesses from Caesarea as his wife. Next year, 70, saw the siege and fall of Jerusalem, and Josephus had to witness from the Roman camp the death-agonies of his countrymen. It was no enviable position: he was often in danger of death, for the Jews loathed him as a traitor, howled him down if he was sent to parley, and made every effort to capture him, while the Roman soldiery, if ever they suffered a reverse, were convinced that it must be due to double-dealing on his part, and shouted for him to be punished. His own conscience too may have given him uneasy moments occasionally. But we, looking upon the siege from a distance of nineteen centuries, dispassionately, can be grateful to him for his account of the last days of Jerusalem; as he says himself, "I knew everything that was going on in the Roman camp, and I alone understood what deserters said," and the picture he paints is authoritative and convincing.

After the fall of Jerusalem we hear little more of him, though it should be recorded to his credit that he saved the life of his brother and of over two hundred friends and did all he could to lighten the lot of the captives. But Judaea could be no place for him in the future, and he probably deemed it more prudent in the end to accept Titus' offer and accompany him to Rome, rather than remain in Judaea and live on the estates which the Romans, with clumsy kindness, had bestowed on him. The Imperial house, the Flavians, showed great favor to him: he was made a Roman citizen, given supplies of money, and housed in Vespasian's family mansion. To these benefactions later on the Emperor Domitian added the exemption of his estate from taxation. In Rome too Josephus found a remarkable patron in one of the Flavian freedmen, Epaphroditus by name; according to Suidas, Epaphroditus was "in form black and vast, resembling an elephant." *À bon chat bon rat*: this was a fitting patron for an extraordinary man. Josephus worked hard at the writing of his books, all attacks made upon him he evaded "by the providence of God," he was still alive in 93, and though there are some slight traces discernible of an uneasiness he felt then, we do not know how or when he died.

But his written works remain, and it is worth while spending some minutes on them and considering their purpose and effect. A hundred years ago in most households Whiston's translation of Josephus would have been found side by side with the family Bible: he was read and appreciated; his narrative style won for him the title "the Greek Livy." Now fewer read him and his works have fallen into an undeserved neglect. Probably the most interesting and important is *The Jewish War*. In this Josephus himself had, as we have seen, played a large part, and it certainly does not suffer in the telling; indeed M. Croiset (in the voluminous *History of Greek Literature* which he shares with his brother) delivers himself of the verdict that Josephus was "a very worthy man, whose conduct in the main seems to have been prudent and correct"—a verdict which makes me wonder if he had ever read the whole of *The Jewish War*. It must be remembered that we do not possess the work in its original form, for it was composed first in Aramaic, and only later translated into Greek. This fact gives us a clue to its purpose: it was written, says Josephus, to tell the truth to the Parthians and Babylonians, to the Jews beyond the Euphrates, and to the people of Adiabene. But what truth? The truth, it would appear, that Roman power was in the end invincible, invincible even by a patriotic and desperate nation, and the book in Aramaic served a very useful purpose, to warn peoples beyond the frontier to think twice before they challenged the might of Rome. In Book II, King Agrippa II is made to deliver a harangue to his turbulent people, and the whole burden of his speech is the hopelessness of a struggle against Rome—Athens, Sparta, Macedon, and Syria have all, one by one, fallen before her, and even the wild western barbarians have been subdued: "Are you richer," he asks, "than the Gauls, stronger than the Germans, more subtle than the Greeks, or more in number than the whole world?" Such a rhetorical appeal obviously expects the answer "No," and the moral Agrippa draws is that Judaea must keep the peace and be content. The publication of such a thesis, convincingly demonstrated in the *lingua franca* of the East, would have been very acceptable to the emperors, and there is no lack of indication that *The Jewish War* embodied the official pro-Roman view. The war with all its miseries was the punishment of God upon the Jews for their sins; in the details of the siege we can recognize something from Titus' own note-books; moreover Josephus is careful to depict Titus as a generous conqueror, pitying the Jews and willing to spare the Temple (whereas there can be little doubt that its firing and destruction was a deliberate act of policy). Indeed, we know that Titus gave the book his imprimatur; "he signed the work with his own hand," says Josephus, "and ordered it to be published." King Agrippa's enthusiasm went even further: he wrote no less than sixty-two letters of approval, testifying to the accuracy of the narrative, and Josephus gives copies of two of them. One is so perfect a model of how to reply to an author who has sent you his book, that I must give a translation. It is brief but gracious: "King Agrippa to his dear Josephus, greeting. I have gone through the book with great pleasure, and you appear to me to have attained far greater accuracy and precision than other writers on the subject. Please send me your other books. Best wishes." What could be better?

The Jewish War was undoubtedly a success, and for some years Josephus lived on, secure from attack, thanks to his powerful patrons; he was now engaged on a great history of the Jewish nation (*The Jewish Antiquities*, in twenty books), and this eventually appeared in the year A.D. 93, when its author was fifty-six years old. Yet it is a disappointing performance compared with *The Jewish War*, which was so full of his own resourceful and vigorous personality; for now Josephus was to some extent attempting to make Judaism acceptable to the Greek or Roman mind, and the results might be expected. The religion of the Hebrews becomes a respectable law-abiding affair, with all enthusiasm and feeling drained out of it; Josephus emphasizes the role of Moses as a law-giver, and dilates upon the excellent institutions that Judaism has secured. Anything miraculous, anything approaching religious fervor, has to be omitted or treated with great circumspection, in order not to arouse the mockery or suspicion of sophisticated Gentiles; magnificent episodes, such as Elijah's visit to Horeb, or his translation, are related in the flattest of flat prose as the most ordinary occurrences.

Moreover, since it is difficult to gain a reader's goodwill and interest for an account of "excellent institutions" spread over so many books, Josephus has to have recourse to other means of exciting attention. The famous tale of Joseph and Potiphar's wife is worked up with all the resources and color of a Hellenistic love-romance, and many familiar Old Testament stories are spoilt in the telling by a puerile rhetoric. Let one example suffice: Abraham, before sacrificing Isaac, first inflicts upon him a long harangue, more or less assuring his son that the sacrifice will hurt *him* far more than it will hurt Isaac, and Isaac at once retorts with a few noble sentiments. At this point a horrid fear grips the reader that the ram caught in a thicket may be made to contribute "a few words," but fortunately Josephus controls himself. True, once the narrative approaches Josephus' own time things become more lively, but in spite of a vivid sketch of the splendors and intrigues of the court of Herod the Great (it includes a delightful encounter between Herod and Cleopatra, and it gives fully the tragic story of Mariamme), in spite of a very suggestive picture of Tiberius upon the island of Capri—suggestive precisely because it represents him as living and working in a normal manner instead of amid the debaucheries upon which Tacitus and Suetonius descant—in spite of some scandalous and much useful information, the work as a whole is dull and diffuse, and no one who possesses an Old Testament need have recourse to the earlier books. Nobody would ever guess, from the pages of Josephus, the spiritual heights to which the great prophets of Israel had risen; apart from his desire to represent Judaism as a code of "excellent institutions," his other thesis appears to be that God *does* reward materially those who believe in Him, and punishes those who neglect Him—in fact, that it pays to be pious. Perhaps it is scarcely fair to blame him for this; it had been for long the orthodox way of writing Jewish history. Even Philo, the Neo-Platonist philosopher of Alexandria, shows a like spirit; in telling of the end of Flaccus, a Roman governor who had persecuted the Jews, he dilates with evident relish not only upon the unpleasant sea-passage which his journey to Rome involved, but also upon his agonizing death, remarking finally, "such were the sufferings of Flaccus, which afforded the most incontrovertible proof that the Jewish nation is never deprived of help from God." Elsewhere he suggests that wealth stored up in heaven through piety and wisdom can produce a sort of overflow of wealth in the world below, a hint that at least one Christian bishop has developed into the comfortable guarantee:

> Whatever, Lord, we lend to Thee
> Repaid a thousandfold will be;
> Then gladly will we give to Thee,
>   Who givest all.

If this was received doctrine (that God does reward and punish materially in this world), Josephus would surely find some confirmation in the amazing successfulness of his own career, where his faith, never wavering, had brought him triumphantly through what might have seemed unsurmountable difficulties. For that his faith was real and fervent cannot for a moment be doubted—whatever curious forms it occasionally took—and it would be the more confirmed by the fate that overtook his enemies or the way in which their attacks were foiled "by God's providence". . . .

In much the same way Josephus can relate the fate of persecutors of the Jews as awful examples and warnings. For there were plenty of scoffers. We hear that towards the end of the reign of Domitian (say about A.D. 95) four of the greatest Jewish sages visited Rome, perhaps to plead before the Emperor the cause of their religion. One mocking Roman put to them the question: "If your God finished making the world in seven days, what is he doing now?" Back came the answer: "He is making Hell hotter for the unbelievers."

Against mockery and against incredulity Josephus, supported by the knowledge of his own amazing career, could at any rate reply: "You may jeer, but my religion *does* work, and my God can deliver, yea and with a mighty hand!" This lengthy history of his, on which he must have spent some ten or twelve years, might vindicate the claim of Jewish religion and of Jewish history to respect, and perhaps to some sympathy, from the Gentile. Romans and Greeks should learn that Judaism was a religion for a reasonable man, that it was mainly a code, a code inculcating "excellent institutions." If something of this nature was his object, then it must be acknowledged that he failed. Neither the fanatical patriotism of the Zealots nor the time-serving of Josephus did anything for the future of Judaism: the future of Judaism was not to lie with those who took the sword in hand, whether those who rebelled in 66 or those who rebelled again, heroically but in vain, under Hadrian. The task of re-creating Judaism fell to a sage and

to his disciples, to the famous Johanan ben Zakkai. Escaping from Jerusalem before the encirclement was complete, he made his abode at Jamneia, and there in quiet and retirement he meditated and taught, and began the new development of an ancient faith.

This consideration, however, must not blind us to the very real merits of Josephus: every student of the Roman Empire owes a great debt to him. His writings are a mine of information upon social, religious, and political conditions prevailing in the countries of the East during the century before Christ and the hundred years after. It is not only about Judaea and Syria that he is so instructive; not only does he often quote edicts or rescripts of the Roman emperors concerning the Jews, but (curiously enough) he is one of our most valuable sources for the organization of the Roman legions. All this, and much more, we get in his books; in addition, there is the living picture of the man himself, unscrupulous maybe, playing sometimes a double game to further the cause which he has at heart, but resolute, never at a loss in the most urgent moment, prompt and clever, unshaken in his religious faith, and with a courage such as few men can have possessed. An adventurous career indeed amid troublous times; but before closing our account of it there is one other matter that claims attention.

It might have been expected that Josephus, keenly alive to the controversies of the time in which he was living, would have found something to say about Christianity. He did not: twice only does he make any reference to the founder of this new sect. The first reference is a short but notorious passage, obscure in itself and complicated by variant readings. Josephus has mentioned the procuratorship of Pontius Pilate, and then proceeds:

> About this time occurs the life of Jesus, a wise man [if one can call him a man]. For he was [a worker of extraordinary deeds], a teacher to men who received his truths [v. l., moral sayings], with pleasure, and he won over many Jews and many Greeks. [He was the Christ.] When Pilate, upon information laid against him by our chief men, had punished him with crucifixion, those who had at first loved him did not cease doing so. For he appeared to them on the third day alive again, as divine prophets had foretold this of him, and a hundred other marvels. And up to this date, the sect of Christians, called after him, has not failed.

In this celebrated passage, there is scarcely a word that has not been fought over, and in its present form it is a clumsy conglomeration of sentences. It has been attacked as a pious Christian interpolation; if so, it is a skilful one, for it has been shown by a Dutch scholar, L. van Liempt, that in words, phrasing, and structure it has a perfectly Josephan ring. Yet there has been some meddling somewhere. Origen, writing in the middle of the third century, says definitely that Josephus did not believe in Jesus as the Christ; on the other hand Eusebius, writing about a century later, is just as definite the other way, for he quotes the passage practically as I have given it. It looks, therefore, as though some zealous Christian hand had manipulated the passage in the interim. I say "manipulated" and not "interpolated," because it appears to me probable that Josephus made some mention of Jesus Christ, though not necessarily a favorable one. And that brings us to the second reference. In another part of *The Antiquities* (XX, 200) he refers to the apostle James as "the brother of the so-called Christ." The word he uses there, *legomenou*, might mean either "so-called" or "self-styled" or "alleged," but can hardly have been complimentary. Now suppose that Josephus had had in the first passage a fairly long paragraph, giving an account of Jesus but denying his Messiahship; for example, suppose that in it he had used phrases like "He was the so-called Christ," or "For his followers actually claimed that he appeared to them on the third day alive again"—it would not be difficult for a later Christian writer, by omitting a few inconvenient phrases or an occasional awkward adjective, to produce the shortened and mutilated version which we now have, which could be accepted as the testimony of a Jew to the Founder of Christianity. It is a procedure even nowadays adopted by some publishers in dealing with a slightly adverse review of a book that they want to push: the omission of a few words can do so much. We can well imagine a pious Christian to whom the temptation would prove irresistible.

But this is the mere suggestion of an amateur; a more ingenious explanation was offered about fifteen years ago by a German scholar, R. Laqueur (based to some extent upon a previous article by Professor Burkitt of Cambridge), which is worth reproducing. He imagines that Josephus in his old age was impoverished (there is no evidence for this); perhaps *The Jewish Antiquities* has not been selling as well as he wished (there is no evidence for this, either); so, casting around for a means of increasing sales, he recollects that there is a growing body of these people called Christians, and so summons some poor Christian to him and asks: "What is all this that you say about a Christ? Tell me what you claim," notes down the answer, inserts a few hasty sentences in the body of the narrative, and so gains a renewed popularity for the book. I give this suggestion here, not because I believe in it (rather the reverse), but because, though it is merely a pleasant fancy, it would be a final ruse, in fact a "stratagem," not unworthy of this Jewish Ulysses, whose adventurous career we have been considering.

F. J. Foakes Jackson   (essay date 1939)

SOURCE: *Josephus and the Jews*, Society for Promoting Christian Knowledge, 1930, 299 p.

[*In the essay below, Jackson examines Josephus's* Jewish Antiquities, *focusing on its Greek and Roman sources. He also addresses the contention that Luke's gospel borrowed from Josephus's* Jewish Antiquities, *and asserts that there are major discrepancies between the two documents.*]

Points of contact between the Jew and the Roman. —Josephus did not inaugurate a new idea when he compiled his *Antiquities*. His great work was designed to appeal to Roman readers; and was qualified to do so since the Romans as a practical people had an interest in their past. Although, therefore, the Jews in the days of Josephus were bitterly opposed to Rome, hating its methods of administration, which restrained their ambition, and contending against its armies with all the fury of fanaticism and despair, yet in some respects the two peoples were in sympathy, and even displayed a certain mutual respect for one another. One reason for this lies in the fact that the Roman, like the Jew, has always been temperamentally a legalist; and the tendency of the lawyer is to seek for precedent in the past, and to look upon the institutions of his country with respect. To him, what is ancient is not only honourable but of practical importance, because it is the foundation of the law under which he lives. It is true the Jew believed he possessed an unchangeable law, given by God Himself; but even herein he did not differ materially from the Roman, who looked on ancestral custom with religious veneration. The Romans also had a certain respect for Judaism as an institution based on law; and, if they hated the Jews, even the provocation of the war did not prevent them recognising the legal rights of Judaism. Subsequently, the Church in Rome so far carried on the traditions of the Empire, that at least in the papal city the Jews had the right to worship God in their own way.

Dionysius of Halicarnassus and Livy. —The Roman was, therefore, naturally interested in the origin and early history of his nation; and before Josephus there were two great works concerning the beginnings of the city, one by Dionysius of Halicarnassus in Greek, and the other by Livy in Latin. Josephus gave to Rome the story of the Hebrew nation to show that it was in all respects worthy to be compared with that of the Roman people, and also that its records were more ancient and better authenticated. According to his own statement, Dionysius of Halicarnassus came to Rome about 29 B.C., just after the conclusion of the Civil War, and remained there for twenty-two years, completing his historical work by 7 B.C. He wrote in Greek; but says that he took pains to study Latin and to consult the best historical works in that language. He had probably been a teacher of rhetoric at his native city, and his chief title to fame is as a critic and man of letters. To the student of Josephus, Dionysius is of peculiar interest in that his book is entitled *Roman Archaeology, or Antiquity*, whilst Josephus' work bears the same heading with 'Jewish' substituted for 'Roman.' The object of both writers is the same, namely, to show that Romans and Jews alike owe their fame to the excellence of their institutions. Both Dionysius and Josephus divide their work into twenty books, indulge in rhetorical disquisitions, and put imaginary speeches into the mouths of their leading characters. In fact, these 'Archaeologies' are written for cultured Romans to whom Greek was a second language, with a view of providing reading adapted to the taste of the public of the day. Another point in common to the themes of these two writers is that the founders of both Rome and Israel are represented primarily as legislators. Romulus, like Moses, is admitted to be the wisest of political leaders, whose institutions secured civil harmony, at least till the tribunate of Tiberius Gracchus. The religion and polity of the Greeks are unfavourably contrasted with those of Rome. Josephus naturally makes no mention of Dionysius, because his history only takes us as far as the beginning of the first Punic War, 264 B.C., and therefore could not be consulted for the later history of the Jews. But whether Josephus read Dionysius or not is immaterial; the important fact is that the design of their *Antiquities* is similar, the one to show that the civil constitution of Rome, and the other the religious ordinances of the Jews, were destined to endure because of their inherent excellence.

Dislike of the miraculous. —A tendency to rationalise the miracles recorded in primitive history has already been noticed in the *Antiquities* of Josephus; and the same is apparent in those of Dionysius. We have seen how careful Josephus is to call as little attention as possible to the miraculous ascension of Elijah; and Dionysius is equally solicitous to show that the legend that Romulus was carried up by his father Mars in the midst of a violent storm is capable of a perfectly natural explanation. Some, he tells us, say that the founder of Rome became in his later days a ferocious tyrant, punishing even patricians for robbery by hurling them down the Rock, and that they conspired and killed him, dismembering the body so that it could not be found, while some give another story. Others account for the tale of the mysterious disappearance of Romulus by the fact that both his birth and his death occurred during an eclipse of the sun. It, however, seems clear that there was a strong feeling that the credibility of early history was lessened by any record of miracles which might tend to reduce it to the level of myth. Thus, although both Dionysius and Josephus are by no means free from superstition, yet both, having a common object of proving the respective claims of Romans and Jews to great antiquity, desire to make the early story of these nations as free from the supernatural as possible.

Popular history. —The late Professor Bury in his 'Harvard lectures on the Greek historians' has some very suggestive remarks on the prevailing taste in historical literature, which throw light on the method of Josephus when treating the Hebrew Bible as his source. The orator Isocrates, the rival of Demosthenes in the fourth century B.C., had an immense influence on historical composition. Thucydides, the master historian of Greece, wrote with the object of recording such facts as came under his personal knowledge, or were based on the best information he could procure. His genius has rescued his history from the charge of dullness; but it cannot be said that he wrote to satisfy the taste of a large circle of readers. But those who studied under, or were influenced by, Isocrates deliberately strove to popularise their subject by employing the art of rhetoric, and indulging in philosophical disquisitions, both of which people demanded to satisfy their passion for eloquence and style, requiring to be charmed by the language of what they read rather than be instructed as to the facts.

Did Josephus read Latin? —It is doubtful whether Josephus had, like Dionysius, attempted to learn Latin. Probably the circle in which he moved in Rome was entirely Greek speaking; and, as he confesses, it took him no little trouble to acquire that language. He may, of course, have read the *Commentaries* of Vespasian and Titus in Latin, but it is quite conceivable that these emperors wrote in Greek, or, if not, that Josephus employed translators. At any rate we look in vain for references to Latin authors. Even the voluminous history of Livy is not mentioned by him except in one passage about Pompey's siege of Jerusa-

lem in the Fourteenth Book of the *Antiquities* to confirm statements possibly derived from Nicolaus of Damascus.

Josephus and the Greek historians. —It may safely be assumed that Josephus had made a careful study of the history of the Greeks, from the earliest prose sources. At the beginning of his treatise ***Against Apion***, for example, he gives indications that he has studied historical works written before the Persian expeditions against Greece. He declares that the historian Acusilaus corrects the statements of the poet Hesiod; and that he disagrees with Hellanicus of Lesbos on the subject of genealogies. Josephus also mentions Cadmus of Miletus and Pherecydes of Syros, who with the others wrote before Herodotus. In the *Antiquities* he gives extracts from several very early historians, as supporting the biblical statement that in ancient times men lived for a thousand years. How far he was acquainted with the works he cites we are unable to decide, but that he knew of them is certain.

The later books of the ***Antiquities***. —Hitherto we have considered Josephus and primitive history, where we are on the confines of myth, fable, and uncertain tradition, at any rate so far as the history of the Greeks is concerned. In the last books of the *Antiquities*, when the Hebrew Scriptures cease to supply information Josephus enters upon what was to him modern history and treats of events after Alexander the Great, the authorities for which stand in much the same relation to him as those of the seventeenth century and onward do to us. Here it must be borne in mind that Josephus has received less justice than he deserves from some modern scholars. Because he is a semi-ecclesiastical writer his testimony is regarded as of less value than that of certain so-called 'classical' authorities who in some instances lived centuries later than when he wrote his authorities.

Long period of silence in Jewish history. —One cannot but be struck with the fact that from the time of Nehemiah to the persecution of Antiochus Epiphanes, Josephus has virtually nothing to relate. He tells us of the rivalry about the Jewish High Priesthood, and of the visit of Alexander the Great to Jerusalem. Of the first Ptolemy (Soter, d. 283) he records nothing save that he captured Jerusalem on the Sabbath, and made a settlement of Jews and Samaritans in Egypt. Of the second Ptolemy (Philadelphus, 283-247) we have the long account of the translation of the Septuagint taken from the letter of Aristeas. In the days of Ptolemy III (Euergetes 247-221) Josephus tells about the rise of the Tobiades, who became the tax gatherers of Coele-Syria, and continued their activities down to the death of his successor Ptolemy IV (Philometer) in 205. In 198 the Ptolemies lost Syria, which came under the dominion of Antiochus III. In 190 the Romans defeated Antiochus III at Magnesia, and from that time became the real, if not the nominal, rulers of Asia. Of these important events—the loss of Syria to Egypt, and the coming of the Romans—Josephus has little or nothing to say. When we reach the days of Antiochus Epiphanes and his attempt to coerce the Jews, the history for many years seems to be entirely derived from our First Book of the Maccabees.

Materials for history of Egypt and Syria covered in the ***Antiquities***. —We have not to enquire what the materials for

Model of the city of Jerusalem during the first century, with the Temple complex and Fortress Antonia in the background.

the history of the great days of the Ptolemies and Seleucidae really are, since the Hellenistic period is one of the most important in antiquity; for, not only did the East and West come into contact and mutually influence one another as they have scarcely ever done before or since, but, in the eventful years which followed the break-up of the empire of Alexander the Great, a bridge was built to unite Greece and Rome. Greek civilisation also pushed its way into what was then the remote East; and Indian and Persian ideas, especially in the sphere of religion, found their way into the West. Then it was that Rome appeared as the future mistress of the known world, and in the hour of victory yielded to the culture of the vanquished Greeks. The strange cults of Egypt alternately repelled and fascinated the Western world, and the influence of Judaism began to be felt far beyond the bounds of Palestine. The various races of mankind began to mingle; and common languages, like Greek, Aramaic, and Latin, tended to unite them. As a time of transition the third century B.C. is alike interesting and eventful, and yet we have scarcely any definite information about it, which is the more remarkable because the Hellenistic period was not like those in which our historical knowledge is ordinarily at fault. At Alexandria, at any rate, it was an age of intense mental activity.

The first of the Ptolemies was the author of an account of the campaigns of Alexander in which he had himself taken part. Most of his successors, whether they ruled well or ill, took an interest in literature and science, and attracted men of learning to their court. Alexandria was the seat of a species of university, and scholars, critics, men of letters, antiquaries, mathematicians (in our sense of the word), abounded. Nor was this all: the social conditions of Greek life in Hellenistic Egypt are known better to us than they are in any other part of the ancient world. The papyri reveal how men bought and sold, paid their taxes, and wrote to their friends and relatives. The age so far resembled our own that in it, if culture was deficient, education was widespread. This makes us regret the more that in the days of the early Ptolemies there is no contemporary historian. The best authority whose works have survived is Polybius, a very honest and able writer belonging to the next century, having been born about 204 B.C. But even of the memorable expedition and career of Alexander the Great no account by anyone who took part in it has survived, except the narrative of Ptolemy I, which would have perished but for it having been utilised by Arrian, who lived towards the close of the second century A.D. It is the same throughout the period. Of the writers mentioned by Josephus or quoted by modern historians of the period between Alexander the Great and Antiochus Epiphanes, none records contemporary events, and many lived centuries after the Christian era. It is hardly too much to say that to-day we, who have access to the papyri and other documents to which so much modern information is due, have more knowledge about Ptolemaic Egypt and Seleucid Syria than Josephus.

Authors mentioned by Josephus. —The first author mentioned by Josephus is Agatharchides of Cnidus, who relates how Ptolemy I took Jerusalem on the Sabbath day owing to the 'superstitious' fears of the Jews, who refused to violate it by fighting. Agatharchides lived at the court of the later Ptolemies, i. e. after 146 B.C., and was a geographer interested in the natural sciences, especially zoology and botany. He is chiefly known to us from that indefatigable bibliophile Photius, Patriarch of Constantinople (A.D. 858, died c. 891), and he is mentioned by Athenaeus, a great collector of miscellaneous information who lived late in the second century of our era. It is a remarkable example of the unjust contempt for Josephus as an 'ecclesiastical' writer, that though he is eight centuries earlier than Photius, and lived a century before Athenaeus, the information he gives in the *Apion* and *Antiquities* is often ignored by the writers of most of the articles in the *Dictionary of Greek and Roman Biography* which appeared in 1844. In his allusion to the transference of Palestine from the control of Egypt to that of Syria (203-198 B.C.), Josephus quotes the sixteenth book of the historian Polybius, who was born late in the third century B.C. and died B.C. 128. Only the first five books of this author have survived in their integrity; the rest has been collected from a variety of sources. Diodorus Siculus is constantly referred to as an important authority on the history of Egypt, but strangely enough he is never mentioned by Josephus, although there are allusions to the Jews and Palestine in his writings, and a considerable portion of his works have survived. His contributions to history are said to be a compilation of other writers, and chiefly valuable for that reason. The other authors from whom historians have had to draw their information are all later than Josephus, with the exception of Livy who flourished in the days of Augustus and, as we have seen, is only once mentioned by our author. The geographer Strabo, who wrote in Greek, is freely used; but, as Dr. Thackeray [in his *Josephus, the Man and the Historian*, 1929] remarks: 'Beyond these authors it cannot be said that he has used others except at second hand.'

Writers later than Josephus. —Of the later writers those most frequently referred to by modern scholars are Justin, who apparently flourished in the fourth century and made an epitome of an earlier writer, Trogus Pompeianus, a man of Gallic origin who had acted as secretary to Julius Caesar and wrote a universal history in forty-four books; Plutarch at the end of the first century; Appian who flourished under Hadrian (A.D. 117-135); Dexippus late in the third century, fragments of whom are preserved by Photius; Orosius, a Christian writer belonging to the early part of the fifth century; and St. Jerome who commented on the Book of Daniel about the same time. But special reliance is rightly placed on Dio Cassius, a great Roman official at the close of the second century.

Josephus and I Maccabees. —Enough, however, has been said to explain the comparative silence of Josephus except for his long extract about the translation of the Scriptures in the days of Ptolemy Philadelphus as told in the letter of Aristeas, which, though obviously fictitious, was probably composed as early as 100 B.C. When we reach the persecution of Antiochus Epiphanes, Josephus follows the Jewish narrative of *I Maccabees*, which he treats in much the same fashion as he does the Scriptural history. This takes us down to the death of Simon the last of the heroic Maccabees in 139 B.C., before which event, however, Josephus ceases to use it. It is remarkable that Josephus evidently knew nothing about the *Second Book of the Maccabees*, nor of the history of the Jews by Jason of Cyrene of which it purports to be an epitome. In telling the story covered by *I Maccabees* Josephus at times abandons this source in order to relate incidents not contained in it. Thus, in the third chapter of his Thirteenth Book he introduces an account of how, in the days of Ptolemy Philometer and his wife Cleopatra, Onias, the son of the High Priest Onias, petitioned the sovereigns of Egypt for leave to build a temple at Leontopolis, and he gives the letter of Onias, and the reply of Ptolemy and Cleopatra authorising its erection. He then relates a dispute between two representatives of the Samaritans, Sabbaeus and Theodosius, and the Jew Andronicus on the relative merits of the rival temples of Gerizim and Jerusalem in which the Jew is naturally victorious, and the Samaritans pay for their defeat, as had been previously agreed, with their lives.

Nicolaus of Damascus. —When we reach the days of John Hyrcanus we are able to check what Josephus has previously related in his *War* by comparing it with the account in the *Antiquities*, and to note where the two narratives of the same period differ. In the *War*, no sources are mentioned, and rarely any in the *Antiquities*; but in the section comprising Books XIV-XVII, Josephus has fuller information and almost certainly follows Nicolaus of Damascus, the partial friend and historian of Herod the Great.

In his preface to the Fourteenth Book Josephus evidently realises that he has come to the most interesting part of his narrative, which demands an opening worthy of the events he is about to describe:

> In our previous book we have related the reign of Queen Alexandra, and how she died. Now we will tell of the events which followed and their connection with our story, making it our principal object to omit nothing owing to ignorance or defective memory. For we are relating the history and explanation of facts which because of their remoteness are unknown to most people. And although these demand to be told in an attractive way in well chosen language, so as to please our readers, in order that they may peruse our narrative with enjoyment, we must before all things aim at relating the exact truth for the benefit of those who are ignorant of our subject, and therefore must trust to what we are going to state to them.

Nicolaus of Damascus was indeed a remarkable man, and is mentioned by Plutarch and many later writers. The work Josephus had before him was his Life of Herod, which is the basis of this part of the *Antiquities*. It is generally agreed that the most brilliant historical work in the *Antiquities* is taken from Nicolaus.

Josephus on Christian times. —When he loses the guidance of Nicolaus and approaches the period of greatest interest to the Christian reader, Josephus as an historian becomes frequently unsatisfactory. Like many people to-day, Josephus knew little about what happened just before his own birth. In the Eighteenth Book he has nothing to say about the early procurators; even Pontius Pilate, as has been noted, is dismissed in a few paragraphs. Then follows some objectionable Roman gossip, an excellent account of the not too reputable youth of Herod Agrippa I, and the attempt of Caligula to place his statue in the Temple. Most of this information Josephus may have obtained from Agrippa II. There is no hint as to whence the historian derived the adventures of the Babylonian Jews Asineus and Anileus, which occupy a large part of this book. Book Nineteen is devoted to Roman history, the murder of Caligula, the accession of Claudius, and the rise, reign, and death of Agrippa I. The Twentieth Book is a summary of the history of the Jews from the death of Agrippa to the outbreak of the 'War' (A.D. 44-66). Two out of eleven chapters are given up to the story of the conversion of Izates of Adiabene. Evidently Josephus was tired of his task and anxious to bring the *Antiquities* to a close; or, if he had more to say, he does not wish to say it.

Josephus and official documents. —Josephus is careful to insert into his history several documents bearing on Jewish affairs, treaties, rescripts, concessions to his nation by Macedonian kings, Greek cities, and the Roman people. The genuineness of some of these, or, at any rate, their absolute integrity, may be open to suspicion, but they are of importance as showing the extent of the Dispersion and the legal position of the Jews in the Roman world.

Our debt to Josephus. —The debt the world owes to Josephus cannot be overlooked. But for him the bridge between the Old and New Testament, broken as it is, would be almost annihilated, and the life of Christ and His Apostles would have no background. To discover what Judaism actually was in the days of His ministry would have been wellnigh an insoluble problem. The books of the Maccabees would have given us some notion of the national uprising in defence of the Law, but very little idea of its results. Even secular history would have been the poorer had the works of Josephus perished. The Herods would have been mere names. Among other things we should not have known how Caligula died and how Claudius became Emperor, and the events of the Wars of Titus and Vespasian would have been forgotten. We may criticise Josephus but we cannot ignore him.

Josephus as a raconteur. —The *Antiquities* is a compilation, and perhaps inevitably an uneven work, nor is it always easy to say how much is actually due to the author. It is perhaps justifiable to surmise that, as he approached his own time, Josephus, if he fails as an historian, excels as a *raconteur*. His intimacy with Herod Agrippa II, with

whom he could claim remote relationship, may have furnished him with material for the very vivid description of how the Emperor Tiberius commanded the arrest of Agrippa I. In the story of the Parthian Jews, Asineus and Anileus, there appear to be signs that Josephus had heard of their adventures by word of mouth. But our author, even as a compiler, cannot be called in modern parlance a 'paste and scissors man.' As we saw in his treatment of biblical sources, his individuality, for both good and ill, appears in everything he touches; and in this he follows the tradition of Greek historical writing established by Isocrates. Indeed, unless one is permitted to question Josephus' statement that his education was Rabbinic rather than Hellenistic, the *Antiquities* is a remarkable example of his literary adaptability and versatility. Without doubt he possesses the Oriental gift of brilliant narration, in which imagination plays no small part. Most critics seem agreed that Josephus copied Nicolaus of Damascus in his dramatic account of Herod the Great; but from what we know of his use of the Bible and *I Maccabees*, we may legitimately assume that in some parts, at least, in this narrative, there may be additions and perhaps improvements by Josephus.

Josephus' lack of patriotism. —Mr. H. G. Wells in his brilliant *Outline of History* calls Josephus 'a maddeningly patriotic writer.' An even superficial perusal of his works will reveal that, unless patriotism consist in an interest in the past history, and an admiration for the institutions of one's nation, Josephus was conspicuously lacking in that quality. To a Jew he must always be painful reading. Hardly anything he relates justifies the assumption that the Judaism of Palestine in its death struggle with Rome deserved to succeed. The only good qualities he seems to credit his countrymen with are a readiness to die for the Law, and desperate courage against overwhelming odds in warfare. Even, however, the bravery of the Jews enhances the credit of Vespasian and Titus in subduing them. Of the better side of Judaism, except in the reply to 'Apion,' Josephus has little to say. At any rate, the last part of the *Antiquities* is invaluable for the history of an obscure period of the history of Israel; but for all our gratitude due to Josephus for composing it, it is hard to feel admiration for the man himself.

Did Luke borrow from Josephus? —It is somewhat rashly assumed that, until the books of Josephus appeared, a Christian writer could have had little or no records of the events of his time, and must have owed his information to the Jewish historian. Consequently it is confidently maintained that the Third Gospel and the Acts must be later than the writings of Josephus; and imaginary scenes have been depicted of Josephus reading his productions at Rome with the Evangelist as an interested auditor. But generally Josephus seems to have been, like other historians, original as far as his personal experience went, but otherwise a most industrious compiler and copyist of earlier works. It is not unreasonable to suppose that others had access to the same books as Josephus has employed. The assumption that Luke came after Josephus, whom he used as an authority, may be justifiable on other grounds, but it is legitimately open to question if the view is meant wholly to depend on the necessity of the *War* and *Antiqui-*

ties being anterior to the Gospels and Acts. The New Testament is singularly reticent as to contemporary history. But for the mention of Herod the Great, Archelaus, Herod Antipas, and Pontius Pilate, no names of public characters are found in Matthew, Mark or John's Gospels, and very few names of places mentioned by Josephus. In all the Pauline epistles there is no single name of any historical personage by which the letters could be dated. We are thus reduced to the Third Gospel and Acts as the only documents which bring us in touch with contemporary history, and are the only subject for our consideration.

The Enrolment. —The first passage in Josephus in which he touches on the story as related in the New Testament, is about the taxing or enrolment. The Gospel relates that Caesar Augustus decreed that the whole Empire should be assessed, and that the assessment was first made when Cyrenius was governor of Syria. Josephus, on the other hand, says that, when Archelaus was deposed for his misgovernment as tetrarch of Judaea, Augustus ordered Cyrenius (Quirinus) to assess his property, and, as Judaea was now Roman, to make a general valuation of the country. According to Josephus, therefore, the taxation was only a local matter, confined to the province of Judaea; for nothing is said by him of Quirinus having included the dominions of Philip and Antipas in his survey. The governorship, moreover, of Quirinus occurred about A.D. 6, whereas, if our Lord was born before the death of Herod, the first enrolment must have been about 5 B.C. Much ingenuity has been displayed by scholars in their endeavour to defend the accuracy of the Gospels in this matter; but here it is not necessary to enter the controversy as the question before us is merely the dependence of Luke upon Josephus, which in this instance is scarcely conceivable.

Rebellion of Judas of Galilee. —In connection with Quirinus and the enrolment is a rebellion by Judas of Galilee, alluded to in *Acts* in the advice given by Gamaliel to leave the Christians alone:

> For before these days rose up Theudas, giving himself out to be somebody; to whom a number of men, about four hundred, joined themselves: who was slain; and all, as many as obeyed him, were dispersed and came to nought. After this man rose up Judas of Galilee in the days of the enrolment, and drew away some of the people after him; he also perished; and all, even as many as obeyed him, were scattered abroad.

Nothing can save these words, put into the mouth of Gamaliel, from an obvious anachronism. In the very early days of the Church of Jerusalem the apostles are accused of inciting the people to sedition against the unpopular priests by declaring them responsible for the death of Jesus. The Sadducean party, represented by the High Priest, are all for enforcing the penalty of death. Before pronouncing sentence, a highly respected rabbi named Gamaliel ordered the Apostles to retire while he addressed the Sanhedrin. He advises that the case should be allowed to drop and they are dismissed with a caution and the comparatively mild penalty of a Jewish, as contrasted with the terrible Roman, scourging.

So far the proceedings are in accord with what Josephus

consistently tells us in regard to the two great Jewish sects, the Sadducees being generally on the side of severity, and the Pharisees on that of leniency. As for the speech it was delivered in a private session, and the author of Acts, who wrote many years later, may well have recorded what he considers Gamaliel ought to have said rather than his actual words. In this he follows the example of many ancient historians; and, except that he avoids his occasional prolixity, of Josephus himself.

Theudas. —The examples of the abortive disturbances of Theudas and Judas of Galilee are almost certainly anachronistic; as, according to Josephus, Theudas caused a fanatical outburst in the days of Cuspius Fadus, the procurator, in A.D. 44-46, at least ten years after the trial of the Apostles. But, as has been acutely observed, these instances are chosen with no little skill. Theudas had pretended to be a miraculous deliverer; and Judas of Galilee was the founder of a sect which was already giving trouble. Of course 'the days of the taxing' were long before Theudas, but the sons of Judas of Galilee were executed after his outbreak. The argument put into the mouth of Gamaliel is briefly this. Two other pretenders to a sort of Messiahship were put to death, and their followers came to nothing. Jesus had, in like manner, been executed; and why should not His few disciples similarly disappear?

The chapter in Josephus' ***Antiquities*** in which mention is made of Theudas and the sons of Judas is one of those summaries of a period on which the historian had obviously little material to work upon, though the events are near his own lifetime. He has related at some length the story of Izates, King of Adiabene, and his conversion to Judaism, in company with that of his mother Queen Helena. In some seventy lines he then proceeds to record the following:

> Fadus became procurator of Judaea; and in his time a deceiver . . . , named Theudas, persuaded a considerable multitude to follow him across the Jordan—for he declared himself a prophet. He promised, like Joshua, to stay the course of the river that the people might cross on dry land. Fadus sent a troop of cavalry and killed and captured many; and the head of Theudas was brought to Jerusalem.

> The next procurator was Tiberius Alexander, son of the pious alabarch of Alexandria, but an apostate. In his days there was a great scarcity in Judaea, relieved by the liberality of Queen Helena. At the same time James and Simon, the sons of Judas of Galilee, were captured and crucified by order of Tiberius Alexander. Judas of Galilee had withdrawn the people from their allegiance to Rome in the days of Quirinus, "as we related above." The King of Chalcis changed the High Priest. Cumanus succeeded Tiberius Alexander. Herod the brother of Agrippa the Great died in the eighth year of Claudius (A.D. 48) and Claudius gave his government to Agrippa II.

It is quite possible that the compiler of Acts may have composed Gamaliel's speech after reading this unsatisfactorily brief chapter of Josephus; but surely he might have heard of Theudas and Judas of Galilee and his sons long before Josephus' book appeared. It is worth noting that neither rebellion alluded to in Acts seems to have been of importance. As a matter of fact, every procurator had been constantly engaged suppressing petty insurrections, which were of almost everyday occurrence and so numerous that it would have been tedious to record them. Josephus says nothing of Pilate 'mingling the blood of the Galileans with their sacrifices,' mentioned by Luke, nor of the rebellion of Barabbas, which, if we may trust Mark, was a formidable one, and not unattended by bloodshed.

Was there a rebellion under Judas of Galilee? —But was the rebellion of Judas of Galilee in itself a serious outbreak? Here we must consider the statements of Josephus.

The chief passage in reference to this Judas is in *Antiquities*, xviii. I, where the property of Archelaus was assessed by order of Augustus, when he was banished by the emperor for his misgovernment of Judaea. Archelaus had been given Idumaea, Judaea, the country of Samaria, and the towns of Strato's Tower (Caesarea), Sebaste, Joppa, and Jerusalem. This part of Palestine was subject to the assessment; but not the dominions of Archelaus' brothers, Antipas of Galilee and Philip of Ituraea. Therefore, if there was a rebellion about the assessment it must have been confined to the Jewish parts of Archelaus' inheritance; presumably Judaea and Idumaea. And though Judas is described as a Gaulonite, and is elsewhere called 'of Galilee,' his activities seem to to have been confined to Judaea, as were the rebellions of his sons. Of this assessment of the domain of Archelaus, Josephus says that the Jews were horrified at the report that they were about to be taxed, and were persuaded by Joazar, the son of Boethus, who was High Priest, to submit; and they gave an account of their estates. But one Judas, a Gaulonite, of a city called Gamala associated himself with a Pharisee, named Sadduc, and tried to make the people revolt. In this they failed, but Judas founded a fourth sect of Judaism, professing the doctrines of the Pharisees, and in addition he displayed a readiness to suffer anything sooner than surrender the civil liberty of Israel. But the principles of this new sect did not become really dangerous till the very end of the Jewish state, when the Jews revolted in the days of Gessius Florus. In the twentieth book of the *Antiquities* Josephus says that he has elsewhere related how Judas of Galilee raised a rebellion against Rome, but his words may only imply that some of the people were persuaded to withdraw their allegiance. In the *War* Josephus states much the same. Dr. Thackeray rightly renders the words 'incited his countrymen to revolt,' as Josephus at the conclusion of his brief remarks says that Judas was not a warrior but a sophist. At the beginning of the outbreak against Rome, Menahem, the son of Judas the sophist, seized Masada.

The general conclusion to be drawn from what has been said above is that there never was a rebellion of Judas of Galilee, though it is generally assumed that shortly after the birth of the Christ Galilee was distracted by civil war. Josephus never calls Judas of Galilee . . . a brigand, but a . . . a philosopher, or rabbi. He was one of those dangerous persons who use their position as teachers to incite discontent and revolution. Himself probably a rabbi in Jeru-

salem, known as 'the Galilean,' he preached a dangerous nationalism uhich led to the rebellion long after his death. In his own days his efforts seem to have been practically abortive, in so far as there was no great rebellion; but he sowed the seeds of the ruin of his people in their two great wars with the Romans.

There does not, to return to the subject under discussion, appear any reason for supposing that the Acts of the Apostles in this instance need have borrowed from Josephus or that the author or compilers of the book necessarily waited for the appearance of the *Antiquities* or even of the *War*. Everybody must have heard of Judas of Galilee, whose sons were certainly leaders of the revolutionary party, and the little outbreak of Theudas may have been connected with it.

Chronological notice of the Baptist. —We now come to the elaborate chronological note by which the Evangelist dates the beginning of the preaching of John the Baptist.

> Now in the fifteenth year of the reign of Tiberius Caesar, Pontius Pilate being governor of Judaea, and Herod being tetrarch of Galilee, and his brother Philip tetrarch of the region of Ituraea and Trachonitis, and Lysanias tetrarch of Abilene, in the high priesthood of Annas and Caiaphas, the word of God came to John the son of Zacharias in the wilderness (Luke 3, 1-2).

This is a curious geographical description of Palestine, and would appear to be taken from some document which relates the preaching of the Baptist, with the same sort of introduction as we find at the head of some of the prophets of the Old Testament. Amos, for example, is dated 'In the days of Uzziah, King of Judah, and of Jeroboam son of Joash, king of Israel, two years before the earthquake.' The four governments mentioned by Luke are Judaea, including Samaria and Idumaea, Galilee, Ituraea and Trachonitis, and also Abilene, which lay quite outside the territory of Israel. 'Lysanias the tetrarch of Abilene' presents a perfectly insoluble problem if the historical accuracy of Luke has at all costs to be saved.

Josephus and the political divisions of Palestine. —The first subject for enquiry concerns what Josephus relates of these districts.

Pontius Pilate administered the domain which had been assigned by Augustus to Herod's son Archelaus. In the New Testament Pilate is always called as in Luke by the general term . . . (governor), whereas Josephus more correctly styles him . . . (steward or *procurator*). Herod, never called Antipas in the New Testament, had for his tetrarchy Peraea and Galilee. To Philip were assigned Batanaea, Auranitis and Trachonitis, with a portion of the domain of Zeno (*War*, elsewhere Zenodorus), in the neighbourhood of Caesarea Philippi.

Lysanias of Abilene. —This brings us to Lysanias and Abilene. Lysanias was the son of Ptolemy, son of Mennaeus, and when Palestine was invaded by Pacorus and the Parthians (40 B.C.) espoused the cause of Antigonus the pretender to the Jewish throne. This Lysanias was later put to death by Antony at the instigation of Cleopatra. In the enumeration of the grants made to Herod the Great, Philip, and Agrippa II, Abila of Lysanias or 'the kingdom of Lysanias' occurs. It was, therefore, customary to call the district by the name of Lysanias; and the statement Lysanias, tetrarch of Abilene, is a pardonable error. Neither he nor his kingdom occurs again in St. Luke's narratives in the Gospels and Acts.

Annas and Caiaphas. —That the statement in the chronological note could be taken from the extant works of Josephus is hard to believe. The Lucan and Johannine writings are in agreement that Annas was intimately associated with Caiaphas, the High Priest. Mark mentions neither, but Luke couples them twice together; and once calls Annas, and not Caiaphas, the High Priest. John says that Jesus was sent first to Annas and then to Caiaphas, and calls Annas 'the father-in-law of Caiaphas.' This evangelist speaks of Caiaphas as High Priest for the year of the Passion. Matthew speaks of Caiaphas only.

It is hard to imagine that, if the Evangelist had read Josephus, he would have described Annas and Caiaphas as joint High Priests. Annas or Ananus was deprived of the High-Priesthood by Valerius Gratus in A.D. 14. He was succeeded by Ishmael-ben-Phabi, then came Annas' son Eleazar, who was followed by Simon, son of Camithus. Finally, Joseph Caiaphas was appointed under Gratus, and held office during the procuratorship of Pilate. Yet Josephus says later that 'the elder Ananus was a most fortunate man; for he had five sons, who had all performed the office of high priest to God, and he himself had enjoyed that dignity a long time formerly . . .' [Antiquities XVIII, 2]. The usual explanation of the association of Annas and Caiaphas, that Annas was *de jure* High Priest, would not assist the theory that Luke and John had read Josephus.

Herod the tetrarch and the death of the Baptist. —'Herod the tetrarch' is only mentioned by Matthew and Mark in connection with the death of the Baptist; but Luke has allusions to him and his household. It is quite obvious that the story of the feast, the dancing of Herodias and the beheading of John is not derived from Josephus. But Luke, though markedly interested in the Baptist, omits entirely the narrative in the two first Gospels, giving at the same time a fuller account of John's prophetic address and advice to the people. All he says afterwards is as follows:

> But Herod the tetrarch, being reproved by him for Herodias his brother Philip's wife, and for all the evil things which Herod had done, added yet this above all that he shut up John in prison. [Luke 3, 19-20]

That Herod put John to death is naturally known to Luke.

> Now Herod the tetrarch heard of all that was done (by Jesus): and he was much perplexed, because it was said by some, that John was risen from the dead . . . and Herod said, John I beheaded: but who is this of whom I hear such things? And he sought to see him. [Luke 9, 7 and 9]

Josephus says nothing about the death of the Baptist in the *War*; but in the *Antiquities* he connects it with the war with Aretas, king of Arabia, which seems to be his reason

for introducing the subject. The famous passage informs us:

> But to some of the Jews it appeared that Herod's army was destroyed, and that he received a just penalty for his treatment of John called "the Baptist." For Herod killed him, though he was a good man and used to exhort the Jews to display justice to one another and piety towards God, and to unite in baptism. For this washing appeared to be acceptable to God, not if used with a view of obtaining pardon for sins; but to purify the body, if the soul were already cleansed by righteousness. And when the rest of the people were assembling (for they were greatly pleased to hear John), Herod was afraid that his persuasive eloquence might lead people to revolt, as they seemed to do whatever he advised. And therefore Herod considered it best to take time by the forelock and put John to death, before he could cause a revolution which might be regretted when it was too late. So John was sent by the suspicious Herod to Machaerus, the castle I mentioned before, and there killed. Now the Jews thought that Herod had provoked God to punish him by the destruction of his army for the death of John. [*Antiquities* XVIII, 5]

There appear, therefore, to have been several versions of the death of John, two, or perhaps three, of which have survived. The first is that of Mark abbreviated by Matthew.

The Baptist is imprisoned because he has told Herod that his marriage with Herodias, his brother Philip's wife, was contrary to the Law. Herodias resolves to kill John, who nevertheless obtains an influence over Herod, owing to frequent interviews in which Herod is at a loss to decide what it is best for him to do, *i.e.* whether or not to put away Herodias. At a birthday dinner Herodias' daughter dances, and pleases Herod. Instigated by her mother, she asks the head of John. Herod is grieved at her request; nevertheless he sends his executioner and beheads John. The scene of the imprisonment is evidently Galilee, and Herod is represented as feasting in the palace or castle where John was. The only obvious historic blunder in this account is that Mark calls Herod a king. Luke's account is in some respects more like that of Josephus. Certainly there is an agreement between the two writers as to the character of Herod Antipas, whom Jesus calls 'a fox.' Josephus regards the motive for John's execution, which he does not connect with the affair of Herodias, as a precautionary measure. Luke represents Herod fearing the influence of Jesus, as of a 'John risen from the dead.' At one time he wishes to kill Him, at another to see Him; and Herod was evidently not desirous, when the opportunity occurred, to be responsible for the death of Jesus. His long tenure of his tetrarchy, and the regard of Tiberius for him, prove that Antipas was considered what we should now term a *safe* man. But this agreement as to Herod's character does not necessitate dependence of one writer upon the other. Further, it may be urged that Josephus does relate a story of a Herod being rebuked for marrying his brother's widow. He tells earlier how Archelaus married Glaphyra, the wife of his brother Alexander. It might also be maintained that Josephus knew the Gospel view that the baptism of John was for remission of sin; and that he tried to refute this. Luke seems also to have had some information about Herod the tetrarch which cannot be derived from Josephus. Joanna, the wife of Chuza, Herod's steward, was one of the women who ministered to the Lord; and Manaen or Menahem, foster brother of Herod the tetrarch, was one of the five Christian prophets at Antioch. The mention of these persons may explain the anxiety of Herod to see Jesus. . . .

Herod Agrippa I. —Herod Agrippa I, the 'Herod the king' of Acts, occupies much space in the *Antiquities*, and in Acts appears as the first royal persecutor of the Christian Church. By Josephus he is said to have been in the days of his prosperity a most devout observer of the Law, and a strenuous upholder of the religion of his people. The words of Acts, 'When he saw it pleased the Jews,' might be taken as the motto of his brief reign. His death is told at some length in both Josephus and Acts and there is a certain similarity in the broad outlines of the story.

> Josephus says: 'Herod Agrippa came to Caesarea, and exhibited shows in honour of Caesar's (Claudius) birthday. On the second day he put on a garment made wholly of silver, and came into the theatre early in the morning. As the sun shone upon the king's garment it made him look so resplendent that his flatterers cried "Be thou merciful to us; for although we have hitherto reverenced thee only as man, yet we shall henceforth own thee as superior to mortal nature." He did not rebuke this flattery; and seeing an owl perched on a rope he regarded it as an omen of death. He was seized with violent pains and exclaimed "I, whom you call a god am commanded presently to depart this life." Five days later he expired in great agony.'

When we remember that Herod Agrippa was the one Herod, perhaps the one Asmonaean also, who was really beloved by the entire Jewish people, and that under him the nation had enjoyed a brief spell of liberty and prosperity, it did not need the appearance of Josephus' *Antiquities* to make an evangelist aware of the fact of his sudden seizure and death. That the famous Jewish King who had slain one of the close companions of Jesus, and had intended to kill His chief apostle, should be stricken down in the midst of his glory was not likely to be overlooked. In language more Hebraic and in accordance with the literary tradition of the Old Testament, Luke, or his source, informs us that Herod had quarrelled with Tyre and Sidon, whose inhabitants, as in the days of Solomon, looked for their supply of wheat to the fertile lands of Galilee. On the occasion of a reconciliation, due to Blastus the royal chamberlain, Herod addressed the delegates of the two cities. He had arrayed himself in royal apparel, and his flatterers shouted when he began to speak, "Tis a god's voice, not a man's.' For accepting such adulation unreproved an angel smote him and he died. Curiously enough the additional information that the assembly was occasioned by the composure of a dispute with the people on the seacoast, and that Caesarea was the place chosen to confirm the treaty, supplements the information, given elsewhere, both by Josephus and Philo, that Agrippa was exceedingly unpopular with the Greeks of both Syria and Egypt. Yet

so determined are the scholars of to-day to make Luke dependent upon Josephus that the very 'royal robe' in which Herod is made to appear in Acts has to be substituted for the robe of silver of the *Antiquities*.

The Egyptian and the sicarii. —There is one passage in Acts which at first appears a reminiscence of Josephus. When St. Paul was rescued from the furious mob in the Temple courts, he asked the chief captain for permission to address the people. The reply was:

> Dost thou know Greek? Art thou not then that Egyptian, which before these days stirred up to sedition and led out into the wilderness the four thousand men of the Assassins (*sicarii*)? [Acts 21, 37-38]

In the *War* Josephus says that an Egyptian false prophet got together thirty thousand deluded men and led them from the wilderness to the Mount of Olives, from whence he threatened to break into Jerusalem. However, Felix, aided by the inhabitants, prepared to resist. A battle was fought, and many were slain; but the Egyptian managed to escape. The story in the *Antiquities* is virtually the same, only the killed and captured do not seem sufficient for the defeat of the 30,000 men in the account in the *War*.

Acts does not seem to owe information to Josephus. —A plausible case could be made out for the Acts here being dependent on Josephus. It would be very natural for the chief captain to suppose that the infuriated mob had captured the Egyptian who had caused such trouble, and was presumably being eagerly sought. But one instance of this description is not sufficient to prove that the author of the Acts drew upon the historian. Standing as it does by itself the remark about the revolt of the Egyptian might be used as evidence in favour of Josephus having derived his information from Acts.

It is not necessary to assume that the writer of Acts knew the long histories of Josephus because he represents Agrippa II being accompanied by Berenice, or Porcius Festus being the successor of Felix. It is, however, worth noticing that Luke says that Felix sent for Paul, and he allowed the Apostle to address him and his wife Drusilla, 'who was a Jewess.' Josephus relates that Drusilla, the sister of Agrippa II and Berenice, had married Aziz, king of Emesa. She was very beautiful and Felix desired her as his wife. He used as an intermediary a Jewish sorcerer (*Magus*) of Cyprus called Simon, who persuaded Drusilla to leave her husband for Felix. It may be said in conclusion that the correspondences between Josephus and the last chapters of Acts is due to the fact that both writers were actually in Judaea during the procuratorship of Felix.

On the whole it is difficult to see what the New Testament owes to Josephus as an historian unless we assume that, as in our own day, he was then the only source of information; and also that a man like the author of the Third Gospel and Acts was ignorant of all that was going on in the world outside. Whoever wrote the 'Travel Diary' or 'We sections' had visited Jerusalem, spent some time in Palestine and shared in the Roman captivity of Paul, whose companion he was on the voyage. He must, therefore, have had as good opportunity as Josephus himself of knowing about Felix and Festus, Herod Agrippa II, Berenice, and Drusilla, or for that matter such events as the census in the days of Quirinus or the various rebellions in Judaea. The author of the Lucan documents may have made mistakes, as when he speaks of Lysanias as a tetrarch when Christ began his ministry, or places Theudas before Judas of Galilee. But he never committed a blunder comparable to that of Tacitus, who makes out that the procurator Felix married Drusilla, the granddaughter of Antony and Cleopatra, the more so that the Roman historian makes this statement in order to asperse the memory of the Emperor Claudius. Luke's mistake about Lysanias, if he consulted Josephus, would have implied that the evangelist had turned over many pages of his authority to obtain the information he had misunderstood.

An excerpt from Josephus's *Life*

The treatment which I received from the Emperors continued unaltered [after attacks on my views]. On Vespasian's decease Titus, who succeeded to the empire, showed the same esteem for me as did his father, and never credited the accusations to which I was constantly subjected. Domitian succeeded Titus and added to my honours. He punished my Jewish accusers, and for a similar offence gave orders for the chastisement of a slave, a eunuch and my son's tutor. He also exempted my property in Judaea from taxation—a mark of the highest honour to the privileged individual. Moreover, Domitia, Caesar's wife, never ceased conferring favours upon me.

Flavius Josephus, in Josephus: The Life, Against Apion, Vol. I, *translated by H. St. John Thackeray, William Heinemann, 1926.*

R. J. H. Shutt   (essay date 1961)

SOURCE: *Studies in Josephus*, S. P. C. K., 1961, 132 p.

[*In the essay below, Shutt discusses Josephus's* Against Apion, *focusing on his defense of Judaism.*]

"It may be fairly inferred", wrote Professor Moore [in his *Judaism* I] "that Josephus, like most of the aristocratic priesthood to which he belonged, had little interest in religion for its own sake, and that his natural antipathy to all excess of zeal was deepened by the catastrophe which religious fanatics had brought upon his people." This statement might be interpreted as meaning that Josephus did not possess sufficient interest to write on the subject of religion: such an interpretation would not be borne out by the facts. At the end of the *Jewish Antiquities*, Josephus mentioned his intention to write "three books concerning our Jewish opinions about God and his essence, and about our laws; why, according to them, some things are permitted us to do, and others are prohibited".

It would appear that Josephus did not write this book, for we have no evidence of its existence nor any reference to it. We possess the work known as the *Contra Apionem*.

Whether this is the originally planned work, slightly altered in scope, we have now no means of determining precisely; on the whole, perhaps it is not. Probably the original intention was never carried out, but only something on the same sort of general lines. The attacks of the opponents of Judaism may have stung Josephus into writing the *Contra Apionem* instead of the projected work.

The *Contra Apionem* was composed after the *Antiquities*, to which reference is made, and was dedicated, like the *Antiquities*, to Epaphroditus, the patron of Josephus and publisher of his works. It was the last major work of Josephus. The *Life* alludes to the death of Agrippa II, and was therefore written after A.D. 100. Epaphroditus is presumed to have died in A.D. 96, so that the *Contra Apionem* can be supposed to have been written between that date and the first publication of the *Antiquities* in A.D. 94.

The title of the work is not that originally given to it by Josephus; it appears for the first time in Jerome. It is convenient, because Apion is one of the opponents of Judaism who is referred to in the work; it might be misleading, if allowed to give the impression that the work is something in the nature of a mere pamphlet, the purpose of which is more destructive of the opponent's case than constructive in the presentation of Judaism. Earlier titles by which the work was referred to are, *Against the Gentiles,* and *Concerning the Antiquity of the Jews*.

The contents of the work are the best guide to the author's purpose and treatment of his theme. It is divided into two books, the first of which is concerned with the question of the antiquity of the Jews. This is precisely the sort of question which may have arisen when the *Antiquities* was published, so that Josephus takes an opportunity in the *Contra Apionem* to consider it at length. He promises to cite authors considered trustworthy by the Greeks, and to show why few Greek historians mentioned the Jewish people in their histories. His general thesis at this stage is that the Greeks are untrustworthy on matters of antiquity because they themselves are of comparatively recent origin. The oldest Greek writing is Homer, which was clearly composed after the Trojan war. (It is note-worthy that this reference to Homer and oral tradition was vital to Wolf's *Prolegomena*, which opened up a new chapter in Homeric criticism and study.) The Greek historians contradict themselves, and even Thucydides is accused of error. This is due principally to lack of official accounts, Josephus alleges, and also to lack of concern for truth among their historians. By contrast, the Jews took pains to compile official accounts, and showed a great concern for truth. This leads Josephus to speak of the Old Testament, the five books of Moses, the thirteen books of the prophets, and four containing hymns to God and moral precepts for man. A digression on the *Jewish War* follows, in which he declares again his concern for truth and accuracy, not only in that work, but also in the *Antiquities*.

Apparently great stress was laid on the allegation that the Greek historians did not mention the Jews, in support of the argument that the Jews were not an ancient people: Josephus declares his purpose of rebutting that allegation, and of producing evidence from writers of other nations in contradiction of it. His plan is now clear.

The Greek historians, he says, did not mention the Jews because they did not know them, not because they did not then exist. Of the non-Greek historians who testify to the existence (and antiquity) of the Jews he quotes Manetho, the Phoenician annals, and Dios the historian of Phoenicia and Menander of Ephesus, the Chaldaean annals and Berosus the Chaldaean historian. References to the Jews do, however, exist in the Greek historians, Pythagoras of Samos, Herodotus, Choerilus, Clearobus, Hecataeus, Agatharchides, and others.

How did these calumnies arise? Originally, Josephus asserts, from the Egyptians, who hated the Jews. As an example of this attitude, he first quotes Manetho again, and criticizes his statements at length; next Chaeremon, and Lysimachus. After criticizing their statements too, he breaks off, since his book has already reached a suitable length.

The second book opens with a brief resumé of the first, and proceeds straightway to further consideration of "the authors who wrote against us". Here the grammarian Apion is mentioned for the first time, but Josephus refutes his allegations at greater length; for example, the statement that the Jews were of Egyptian origin. There were, apparently, similar accusations against the Jews in Alexandria which Josephus rebuts. A new note is now struck in this work, for after mentioning the esteem in which some of the kings of Egypt held the Jews, he states that the Emperor Augustus acknowledged their services. Apion's calumnies are next rebutted that the Jews worship the head of an ass, and practise ritual murder, and such like. There the treatment of Apion ends, and Josephus proceeds to refute the errors of Apollonius Molon and Lysimachus, declaring that, compared with Moses, men like Lycurgus and Solon and Zaleucus are only recent. This leads him to an appreciation of the Jewish law-giver, with comments on the Jewish way of life under the influence of the Mosaic law and its theocratic constitution. Examples follow, which are intended clearly to inform his readers as well as to illustrate his thesis, and then the religion of the Greeks is compared and contrasted with that of the Jews. After a brief resumé of the whole work, it ends with a final dedication to Epaphroditus, and to all those who through his efforts may wish to know about the Jewish race.

There is no doubt that in this work Josephus feels strongly and shows his sentiments fearlessly and resolutely: his exposure of some of the accusations brought against the Jews and his vigorous counter-attack leave no doubt of his fearlessness, while his exposition of the meaning of the Law shows conviction and resolution. In evidence of the latter, one passage is especially noteworthy. Speaking of Judaism he writes: "What form of government then can be more holy than this? What more worthy kind of worship can be paid to God than we pay, where the entire body of the people are prepared for religion, where an extraordinary degree of care is required in the priests, and where the whole polity is so ordered as if it were a certain religious solemnity? . . . All men ought to follow this Being, and to worship him in the exercise of virtue; for this way of worship of God is the most holy of all others."

This is a fine piece of writing, and shows Josephus at his best. Perhaps he would have wished to be remembered as an apologist for Judaism first and foremost. In the Law he found an "everlasting possession"; Thucydides hoped that his history of the Peloponnesian War would merit that title. Therein lies a fundamental and ultimate difference of outlook, which is most significant.

Having now briefly considered the *Contra Apionem*, with special reference to its contents, we are in a position to examine some of the major problems raised in that work:

> 1. The nature of the opposition to Judaism as illustrated in the *Contra Apionem*.
> 2. The nature of the exposition of Judaism.

Anti-semitism existed in the first century A.D., and was sometimes manifested in dangerous forms: at the same time there existed the Jewish apologetic, which was designed to counter anti-semitism. It would be a mistake to magnify these two contending forces, and to compress all the problems of those days under that one issue, but it cannot be ignored as irrelevant or insignificant. The consideration of these problems will raise questions of particular methods used by the individuals mentioned in the *Contra Apionem*, including Josephus himself.

The *Contra Apionem* is of special value for its treatment of the literary opposition to Judaism, and the references made to the opponents illustrate the nature of the opposition not only in the first century A.D., but from about the second century before Christ.

(a) Manetho wrote an Egyptian history in Greek, between 270 and 250 B.C., "translated from the sacred tablets". Josephus has two long references to this work, the first of which includes a lengthy quotation from the second book of his history of Egypt, about the Hyksos. This quotation is impressive for its detail. The second reference is of a different kind, because there Manetho admits that he is narrating current legends concerning the Jews, which Josephus has no difficulty in demonstrating to be false. Bearing in mind the fact that Manetho states that he is only narrating popular tales concerning the Jews, one may wonder why Josephus goes to such length in disproving them, while attacking Manetho himself violently. Presumably such tales died hard, and formed part of the anti-semitic propaganda of Josephus' day. The question has been raised of the authenticity of the quotations. Reinach declared that it was of small importance whether the first quotation was first or second-hand; the second reference has been thought to be a later insertion, but in the absence of any considerable portions of Manetho large enough to permit an assessment to be carefully made, such a hypothesis seems very laboured and hardly justified.

(b) Apollonius Molon is mentioned several times as an opponent of Judaism. "Moreover, since this Apollonius does not do like Apion, and lay a continued accusation against us, but does it only by starts, and up and down his discourse, while he sometimes reproaches us as atheists, and man-haters, and sometimes hits us in the teeth with our want of courage, and yet sometimes, on the contrary, accuses us of too great boldness, and madness in our conduct. . . ." No quotations or exact references are given from this author, and, to judge from Josephus' statements about him, it would seem that his attacks on the Jews were particularly ill-informed.

Sometimes he is referred to as Apollonius Molon, sometimes as Molon, sometimes as Apollonius. He was a teacher of rhetoric, born at Alabanda in Caria, who afterwards lived at Rhodes. Cicero as a young man first heard the lectures of an Apollonius Molon at Rhodes in 87 B.C., and continued as his pupil nine years later. This tutor of Cicero was often known as Molon, and is to be distinguished from the other Apollonius Molon to whom Josephus refers. The Apollonius mentioned by Josephus was older than his name-sake and fellow-countryman; he was teaching in Rhodes when Scaevola went there as praetor in 121 B.C. His work was an attack on the Jews, including allegations against Moses and the Law. Josephus, in reply, decided to show that the Jewish laws contained very often ordinances quite different from the allegations of Apollonius, and in turn heaped upon Apollonius accusations of foolishness and blindness.

(c) Lysimachus is referred to by Josephus as an opponent of the Jews. Little is known of him, and he may be identical with the Lysimachus who wrote . . . (of Greek heroes from Troy). Perhaps he was an Egyptian. His accusations seem absurd, e. g. that the Jews were lepers, and that they were expelled under Bocchoris, king of Egypt, their leader being Moses. Josephus does not give the exact quotation from Lysimachus, but uses *oratio obliqua*. The date of the Exodus, and Lysimachus' reference to it, is mentioned again later, and Lysimachus is coupled with Apollonius Molon "and certain others" as a writer of "unjust and untrue" statements about Moses and the laws. Judging from Josephus his history was not of a high standard, and it was not difficult to rebut his statements.

(d) Chaeremon is mentioned once only. According to Josephus, he wrote a history of Egypt, which is quoted, as in the case of Lysimachus, in *oratio obliqua*. It seems that the work of Chaeremon was similar, in tone and outlook, to that of Manetho. Porphyry refers to the work of Chaeremon the Stoic: this is apparently the same person. The fact that he is called a Stoic is interesting, especially as he was an Egyptian priest himself. He may also be the Chaeremon who was tutor to the Emperor Nero. His work would represent the antisemitic views held in Josephus' own day, especially in an important centre such as Alexandria.

(e) Apion's attacks upon Judaism were singled out for special treatment; hence the title now ascribed to this work of Josephus. Apion the grammarian was born in Egypt, came to Alexandria, and became famous as a grammarian. Suidas states that he taught in Rome in the time of Tiberius and Claudius, and delivered lectures in Greece during the principate of Gaius. According to Josephus, Apion visited Rome under Gaius as spokesman of the Alexandrians against the Jews. There is no doubt of his hostility to the Jews. Pliny says that "Apion wrote that those to whom he dedicated a composition had his gift of immortality bestowed upon them". If that is true, how absurd! And, moreover, how vain! Pliny in the same passage also says, in a revealing parenthesis, that Tiberius called Apion the "world's cymbal", i. e. "as making the world ring with his

ostentatious disputations". Josephus' statement that Apion congratulated Alexandria on having such a citizen as himself is consistent with such a character.

He wrote much, and gained a considerable reputation for his work on Homer, but Josephus was only concerned with his *History of Egypt*, of which he mentions specifically the third book, and gives a quotation. It is hardly necessary to suppose that he wrote a book entitled *Against the Jews*, for that is an inference from the **Contra Apionem** of Josephus, which, incidentally, mentions no such work, but only the *History of Egypt*. This inference was first drawn by Clement of Alexandria.

According to Josephus, the grounds of Apion's attack on the Jews were threefold:

> (i) The departure of the Jews from Egypt.
> (ii) That the Alexandrine Jews disturbed the peace.
> (iii) The Jewish laws and worship.

So he refutes these accusations one by one. It seems that Apion's attack was connected with a deep-seated enmity for the Jews, to whom he appears willing to give no credit whatsoever. Josephus in turn attacked Apion without mercy, and saw a fitting and ironical retribution for his blasphemies in the fact that he died in terrible agony, having been circumcised in an attempt to save his life. "This", he says, "was the end of Apion's life, and this shall be the conclusion of our discourse about him."

These writers, to whom Josephus refers in detail, afford an opportunity to assess the nature of the opposition to Judaism. It appears to have been trivial and superficial, perpetuating similar if not identical accusations (e. g., about the Jews' worship of the head of an ass); it was focused upon the origin of the Jewish people, and upon the allegation, with variations, that they were expelled from Egypt as undesirable (e. g., the accusations that they were cast out because they were lepers). Such calumnies could be refuted without much difficulty, but the picture of anti-semitism which Josephus paints in the **Contra Apionem** contains an additional important element, which brought it up to date: this was the accusation that the Jews, by virtue of their religion, were anti-social, and more concerned in the affairs of the "clan" than in the interests of the community in which they lived. (This factor is significant, because if accepted as an explanation of the Jewish way of life, it justifies suspicion of them as citizens, and creates readiness to make them scapegoats as trouble-makers.)

Especially in the case of Apion, all this prejudice against the Jews is seen as a contemporary problem, not simply as something past and gone. This problem was most urgent in Alexandria where Apion lived, and, no doubt, was accepted as an exponent of these anti-semitic views. In Alexandria, the situation was complicated by the privileged position of the Jews who were given a status equivalent to that of "Macedonians".

Feelings against the Jews in the Greek cities began to run high and find expression in the middle of the second century B.C. the advantages, spiritually and philosophically, of monotheism, contrasted with polytheism. The same charge of contempt for the gods leads Josephus to answer the associated charge of Apion that the Jews refused to worship the Roman emperor, and were therefore dangerous. He replies that a sacrifice was daily offered for the emperor in the Temple at Jerusalem.

Through all this exposition there runs, like a thread, his respect for the Jewish Law, of which he writes in glowing terms. Here is a feature which he shares with Jewish apologists, but, even if the reader of the *Contra Apionem* agrees in general with Josephus in respecting the Jewish Law, there remains the difficulty of expounding satisfactorily the justification for such an attitude. For Josephus it is, on the whole, sufficient to say that such and such an observance is enjoined in the Jewish Law; no further need for its defence and support in his view exists, because the Law is for him the criterion. Logically, his attitude amounts to this: such and such an observance is enjoined in the Law, and therein lies its authority; if asked why the Law possesses that final authority, he would reply, because it is the Law, given to Moses for the Jews by God. That is sufficient and final. But for those like the Hellenists who did not accept a monotheism, nor even necessarily a theism in the strict sense of the word, this was unsatisfactory. And so the argument went on. Moreover, throughout his exposition of Judaism, there runs a view of the divine inspiration of the Jewish Scriptures. One can imagine the Hellenists requiring further information about the manner of this divine inspiration, and the evidence for the Mosaic authorship of some of the books, but Josephus does not deal with any such matters. He was content to dilate on the Law, or to resort to a vigorous attack upon his opponents, which was one of the chief weapons of Jewish apologetics. In this respect also, Josephus is typical of Jewish apologists. But it did not help to bridge the gap between Judaism and Hellenism. The attitude and work of Philo were likely to make a contribution of greater value than that of Josephus towards this end, and in this sense Hellenistic Judaism held a key position. "When after the fall of Jerusalem Judaism all over the world became Hebrew and Rabbinic, Hellenistic Judaism, as such, withered away. The Synagogue casts its works upon the scrapheap. . . ."

That was the end of Jewish apologetics. Josephus' *Contra Apionem* is one of its most note-worthy productions, which does credit to its author and the cause on behalf of which he wrote.

In contrast to the countless "divergent and contradictory" books of the non-Jews, Josephus claims with pride that the Jews have only "twenty-two books containing a record of all time and deservedly trusted":

> (i) *Five* of these are the books of Moses, i. e. the Pentateuch.
> (ii) *Thirteen* prophetical books.
> (iii) *Four* containing hymns to God and moral precepts for men. I. e., Psalms and Song of Songs; Proverbs and Ecclesiastes.

Thus, he arranged the Canon of Scripture into three parts, the law, the prophets, and the sacred writings, which he calls "hymns" because the Psalms were the first in this section. It is not quite the normal arrangement. His list contains a total of twenty-two books, whereas the Septuagint and the Talmud contain twenty-four.

It is clear, therefore, that this passage is important not only for the Canon with which Josephus himself was familiar, but it also raises further matters, such as Josephus' connection with Palestinian or Alexandrian Judaism: the fixing of the Jewish Old Testament Canon was more or less contemporaneous with the *Contra Apionem*, i.e., the end of the first century A.D.

Origen and Jerome enumerate twenty-two books, which indicates that Josephus is not alone in his view, and that he did not accept the Septuagint number, which is twenty-four. The probable reason for this is that the twenty-two books were commonly accepted in the Palestinian tradition, in which Josephus was brought up, and from which also Origen and Jerome derived their information.

The five books of Moses, known as the Pentateuch, are easy to identify and present no difficulty (Genesis, Exodus, Leviticus, Numbers, Deuteronomy): the four "containing hymns" are generally agreed to be Psalms and Song of Songs, Proverbs and Ecclesiastes. The thirteen prophetical books cannot be identified with the same certainty. They are probably as follows:

> 1. Joshua
> 2. Judges and Ruth (counted as one book)
> 3. 1 and 2 Samuel (counted as one book)
> 4. 1 and 2 Kings (counted as one book)
> 5. 1 and 2 Chronicles (counted as one book)
> 6. Ezra and Nehemiah (counted as one book)
> 7. Esther
> 8. Isaiah
> 9. Jeremiah and Lamentations (counted as one book)
> 10. Ezekiel
> 11. Daniel
> 12. 12 minor prophets (counted as one book)
> 13. Job

The twenty-four books of the Septuagint and Talmudic Canon are not different from those in Josephus and the Palestinian Canon: the smaller number was reached by counting two sets of two books, probably Judges with Ruth, and Jeremiah with Lamentations as two instead of four.

This reference in Josephus to twenty-two books of the Jewish Scriptures is important also because it gives his views on the essential marks needful in such books:

> 1. They contain divine doctrines; hence their absolute authority.
> 2. Because they contain divine doctrines, they are deemed holy, and therefore are to be distinguished as comprising in themselves a special category.
> 3. Nothing has been added nor taken away from them because they belong to this special category; that is not permitted.
> 4. They must have been written within the period from the death of Moses to the reign of Artaxerxes, King of Persia.

1. The first of these essential marks of canonicity is propounded in the opening sentence of the passage referred

Relief of the emperor Domitian's departure from Rome.

to (***Contra Apionem*** 1. 37) . . . "we have only twenty-two books, which contain the record of all the past times, and which are rightly believed in". Eusebius, referring to this passage (*Hist. Eccl.* 3. 10) apparently added the word Θεια (i. e. "believed to be divine"), which does not occur in the Greek or Latin texts of Josephus. Eusebius probably had in mind the statement of Josephus later in this passage, "it is become natural to all Jews . . . to esteem these books to contain divine doctrines".

2. The view that these books are distinct is amplified in the description of the Scriptures as "the holy books" (in ***Jewish War***, ***Jewish Antiquities***, ***Life***, and ***Contra Apionem***). Hence, in the very use of the adjective "holy", which implies being set apart for a particular purpose, Josephus makes clear the distinctness of the category to which in his view the canonical scriptures belong.

3. "For during so many ages which have already passed, no one has been so bold as either to add anything to them, to take anything from them, or to make any change in them." Hence we have another characteristic of these books.

4. Josephus also states that all the canonical books were written within a given period of time: the Pentateuch, belonging to Moses, contains the laws and the history of man from his origin until the death of Moses (traditionally about 3,000 years); from the death of Moses until the reign of Artaxerxes, King of Persia, the prophets who came after Moses wrote in thirteen books (i. e. a period of about 600 or 700 years). Then follows a very significant statement: "But from Artaxerxes to our times all things have indeed been written down, but are not esteemed worthy of a like authority because the exact succession of the prophets was wanting." No book therefore which was not written within the period from Moses to Artaxerxes could qualify for canonicity. This is consistent with the official Jewish teaching, which ultimately found expression in the Talmud.

Yigael Yadin　(essay date 1966)

SOURCE: "Masada's History in the Light of the Finds," in *Masada: Herod's Fortress and the Zealots' Last Stand*, translated by Moshe Pearlman, 1966. Reprint by Random House, 1966, pp. 204-07.

[*Yadin was one of Israel's eminent archeologists, particularly known for his excavation of the Jewish fortress Masada. In the following essay, Yadin compares his archeological findings with Josephus's account of the fall of Masada.*]

In the course of our [Yigael Yadin and associates'] two-season, eleven months' dig, we excavated 97 per cent of the built-on area of Masada. Though this does not mean that we now know all there is to know of the secrets of Masada, we have learned enough from the archaeological discoveries to present the main events in its history.

The earliest known occupants of the site, as revealed by our dig, belonged to the Chalcolithic period—fourth millennium BC. We unearthed their remains in a small cave on the lower part of the southern cliff, remains of plants, cloth, mats and sherds of Chalcolithic pottery found in 'cup-marks' on the floor. It is not to be concluded from these remains that their owners were a settled community established on Masada. They were one of the scores of typical cave-dwelling communities who lived in the Judean desert in that period.

In several places, including the middle terrace of the northern palace villa, we found a few scattered sherds from the time of the Israelite monarchy. We found no building which could be ascribed to this period, and it may therefore be assumed that these sherds simply show that from time to time during this era a few isolated individuals sojourned there.

One of the purposes of our expedition was to find the buildings erected, according to Josephus, by 'Jonathan the High Priest'—to find them, determine their date and identify the 'Jonathan'. We were only partially successful in our search for the solution. We discovered no structure which could with certainty be attributed to any period before that of Herod. Moreover, none of our pottery finds could be said to match the pre-Herodian types. On the other hand, we discovered scores of coins struck by Alexander Janneus (among them the most ancient of all the coins found at Masada). We can therefore now say, perhaps, that any buildings and cisterns, which were constructed on this site in the period before King Herod, were the work of King Alexander Janneus, and he is probably the 'Jonathan the High Priest' mentioned by Josephus.

If we were partially unsuccessful, however, in unravelling this problem, we were highly successful in unearthing every building erected by Herod: his palaces, his service structures and his fortifications. It is now definitely established that the Masada of King Herod was basically a citadel bounded by a casemate wall. In its western section stood his large palace with its residential, ceremonial and administrative functions; at its northern edge, just beneath the wall, perched his private palace-villa. In addition to these, Herod built several small palaces for members of his family and for his high officials. Most of the northern sector of the summit is taken up with the long and narrow storerooms, the large public baths, the administration building and the 'apartment' building.

To complete this Herodian picture, mention should be made of the amazing water system, whereby flash-flood water from the wadis was channelled through aqueducts to two series of huge cisterns which had been scooped out of the rock on the north-western slope of Masada. These cisterns were not among the sites excavated by our expedition.

Between the period of Herod and that of the great revolt of the Jews against the Romans, Masada had been a site of continuous settlement. This was known from Josephus who reported that the Roman garrison there was destroyed when Masada was captured by Menahem at the beginning of the Jewish revolt. Although we were unable to find any buildings which could definitely be ascribed to this period, our excavations confirmed such settlement, the most convincing of our finds being the hundreds of coins from the reign of Archilaus and of Agrippa, and particularly from the rule of the various Procurators (Roman governors).

As for the Masada of the Zealots, we can summarise our findings by stating that their main dwellings were in the chambers of the casemate wall, in which partition walls, stoves and cupboards had been installed. When these proved inadequate to meet the housing needs of the newcomers, additional dwellings were built, most of them close to the casemate wall. Several of the palaces also served as living quarters, possibly for the commanders. During this period, almost no additional public buildings were erected: to house their workshops and bakeries they used the wall towers. However, they did add some structures for special functions, mostly religious, such as ritual baths, a religious school and synagogue, but even there for the most part they utilised earlier buildings. Some Herodian structures, like the storehouses, were used by the Zealots as they were, without alteration, for they suited their needs. Some, like the palace-villa and the purely decorative parts of other buildings, such as ornamental columns, were not needed for their original functions, and so for example, sections of these columns were utilised for buildings they did need—the southern *mikve*, the synagogue benches, tables, and so forth—and as general building material. And fancy wooden floors were pulled up and used as fuel, particularly in the final phase of the siege before the Roman breach. It appears that parts of the palace-villa were already in a state of disrepair when the Zealots occupied Masada.

The large collection of 'pennies' (*prutot*)—bronze coins—of the period of the revolt, which we found mainly in the buildings used by the public, such as the southern *mikve*, the northern storehouses, the western palace, and the bakeries, suggests that life on Masada at this time was organised on a communal basis with centralised planning and control. These coins and the ostraca may therefore have been used as coupons or chits for a system of food rationing and the administration of services for the whole community.

All the public buildings which we excavated bore signs of having been burned in a formidable conflagration, matching the description in Josephus. Similar signs were evident in some of the Zealotian dwellings, where we found heaps of ashes in corners of the rooms with remains of humble family possessions.

On the Roman occupation of Masada after the revolt, Josephus observes that General Silva left a garrison there, but he does not give details of its size nor of its length of stay. Today we can say that Masada was garrisoned by the Romans for at least forty years. This we know from the coins we found both on the summit and in the large Roman camp at its western foot. This was Silva's camp, whose inner section was built after the conquest, as our dig revealed.

Of the Byzantine period, our excavations show that the monks who established themselves on Masada did so after the powerful earthquake which shook the area and caused great destruction to many of the buildings on the summit. The foundations of cells and other structures built by the Byzantine monks were found high up, resting on mounds of rubble and stones which covered the remains of the Roman garrison and the last defenders of Masada. To the future archaeologist is left the excavation of the Roman camps and clearance of the huge water cisterns. This may be done one day.

Michael Grant   (essay date 1970)

SOURCE: "Josephus," in *The Ancient Historians*, Charles Scribner's Sons, 1970, pp. 243-68.

[*Grant is a distinguished English classical scholar, translator, and editor known for his eminently readable studies of the classical world, especially Rome. His numerous writings, which encompass a large variety of topics, include* The Ancient Mediterranean *(1969),* The Jews in the Roman World *(1973),* Caesar *(1974),* Jesus: An Historian's Review of the Gospels *(1977), and* The History of Rome *(1978). In the essay below, Grant presents an overview of*

An excerpt from *Against Apion*

Unity and identity of religious belief, perfect uniformity in habits and customs, produce a very beautiful concord in human character. Among us [Jews] alone will be heard no contradictory statements about God, such as are common among other nations, not only on the lips of ordinary individuals under the impulse of some passing mood, but even boldly propounded by philosophers; some putting forward crushing arguments against the very existence of God, others depriving Him of His providential care for mankind. Among us alone will be seen no difference in the conduct of our lives. With us all act alike, all profess the same doctrine about God, one which is in harmony with our Law and affirms that all things are under His eye. Even our women-folk and dependents would tell you that piety must be the motive of all our occupations in life.

Flavius Josephus, in Josephus: The Life, Against Apion, Vol. I, *translated by H. St. John Thackeray, William Heinemann, 1926.*

the Jewish and Roman influences directly affecting the life and writings of Josephus.]

. . . [Josephus] takes us from Latin back to Greek, from the conquerors to the conquered, from a chair-borne view of events to a position on the stage. We also move from the capital of the Empire to a point at its eastern periphery; namely Judaea, roughly corresponding with the modern Israel.

Persia had allowed the Jews to rebuild Jerusalem in the fifth century BC, and the country remained subject to the Persians until their empire was destroyed and taken over by Alexander the Great (332). After the death of Alexander, Judaea formed part of the dominions of the Ptolemies of Egypt. Then it passed, after various vicissitudes, to the Seleucids who were based on Syria and Mesopotamia (202). They tried harder than the Ptolemies to assimilate this border province to the Greek or Hellenised regions of their empire, and found support among sections of the Jewish ruling class.

But when the Seleucid Antiochus IV Epiphanes dedicated Jehovah's Temple to Olympian Zeus (167), a nationalist and religious rebellion broke out. Priests-kings of the house of Hasmon, notably Judas Maccabaeus, created the Hasmonaean (Maccabee) line which won independence for Judaea for the first time for over four hundred years, and for the last time until the twentieth century AD. In the years around 100 BC there was, for a short time, a Greater Judaea, comprising a wide surrounding region. In 63, however, the whole country fell to the Roman armies of Pompey, who stormed Jerusalem and slew the priests at their altar.

Rome did not annex the country, but established its Jewish nucleus as a minor dependent state under the Hasmonaean John Hyrcanus II. He was subsequently stripped of his temporal powers, but recovered them after sending help to Caesar in Alexandria. The contingent was commanded by his vizier Antipater, a man from Idumaea (Edom), where the people had been forcibly converted to Judaism in the previous century. After a brief interval of Parthian suzerainty, Antipater's son Herod the Great ruled as king of the Jews, with the support first of Antony and then of Augustus (40-4 BC). A monarch of ruthless efficiency, and a munificent builder and patron, Herod was keen on Greek culture, yet he also championed the Jews of the Dispersion. At home, he was the mass murderer of his own family. After his death, ten years of squabbling between Herod's sons were followed by the annexation of Judaea, which became a minor Roman province. (This took place in the fifth year after the date which has been officially associated with the birth of Jesus. But the Christian era was only fixed in the sixth century, and the actual date when he was born is disputed.) The governors of the new province, who were loosely supervised by the governors of Syria, only ranked as procurators—Romans not of senatorial but of knightly rank. Under Augustus' successor Tiberius, one of these procurators was Pontius Pilate (AD 26-30), under whom Jesus was crucified.

Tension between the Jews and their rulers, already high because of numerous grievances, reached boiling-point when the next emperor Caligula (37-41) ordered his own statue to be set up in the Temple. At this juncture, however, Caligula was murdered, and Claudius (41-54) reconverted Judaea from a Roman province into a dependent kingdom. Its prince was now Herod's grandson Agrippa I (Herod Agrippa), who had intervened to avert Caligula's proposed desecration. When Agrippa I died in 44, his son Agrippa II was given a client state between that country and Syria-Phoenicia. But in Judaea the provincial régime of the procurators was restored, and during the remaining years of Claudius and under Nero (54-68) relations between ruler and ruled went from bad to worse. Finally, in 66, open revolt broke out. The governor of Syria, Gaius Cestius Gallus, intervened but failed to capture Jerusalem, suffering a reverse at Beth-Horon. Then Nero sent his general Vespasian to crush the revolt. Accompanied by his son Titus, Vespasian entered Galilee, north of Jerusalem, but operations were twice delayed owing to the convulsions of the Year of the Four Emperors (69), which culminated in Vespasian gaining the throne. Titus stayed behind to reduce Jerusalem in the following year, though a few other fortresses still resisted.

The revolt, and particularly the capture of Jerusalem, had been accompanied by appalling hardship, brutality and loss of life. The Temple was burnt down and its worship abolished, and the tax which every Jew had paid to its funds was transferred to Jupiter Capitolinus. The rebellion continues to this day to exert a profound influence on the politics of the middle east.

Its story is told us in Greek by the man who had commanded the Jewish rebel forces in Galilee, Josephus the son of Matthias (Yoseph ben Matatyahu). He was born in AD 37/8 and died at an uncertain date after AD 94/5. His *Jewish War* is divided into seven books and 110 chapters, though these divisions are not necessarily the author's own. The work was the offshoot of a larger project: 'I had, when writing the history of the war, already contemplated describing the origins of the Jews and the fortunes that befell them. . . . However, since the compass of such a theme was excessive, I made the War into a separate volume.' [*Jewish Antiquities* I, 2] According to the tradition established by the earliest Greek historians, the preface describes the war he has chosen to deal with as the greatest upheaval of all time. The rest of the first book is introductory, surveying Jewish history from the time of Judas Maccabaeus, with a long survey of the reign of Herod the Great. In the second book the introduction continues with an account of Herod's sons and the two periods of Roman annexation which finally led to the open hostilities of AD 66. We are also told how, after their outbreak, the Jewish authorities appointed Josephus governor of Galilee, the northern frontier-province of Judaea. Book III records the arrival of the future emperor Vespasian and his son Titus, and their southward advance. Compelled to surrender to the Romans, Josephus tells how he became their prisoner—and subsequently their favoured collaborator. The book also contains geographical descriptions of the various regions of Palestine, and an analysis of the Roman army.

Book IV describes the Jewish factions in Jerusalem and their alleged atrocities against one another. The accession of Vespasian to the imperial throne is then reported. The next two books give a detailed account of the siege and capture of the city by Titus, followed by the burning of the Temple (70). The last book contains the story of the subsequent mopping-up operations, including the heroic defence of Masada which did not fall for another three years.

Josephus was very proud of the eminence of his Jewish family. His father was a well-known member of the highest priestly aristocracy, and his mother possessed royal Hasmonaean blood. His native tongue, like Jesus Christ's, was Aramaic, the Semitic language which had become the official speech of the Persian Empire and had expanded enormously throughout the middle east. Josephus received the best education a priest's son could obtain, and claims, without undue modesty, to have been a child prodigy. When he was sixteen, he had to decide which Jewish sect he should belong to. He tried all the three principal groups (Pharisees, Sadducees and monastic Essenes), and then joined the Pharisees and became a priest at Jerusalem. In about AD 64 (shortly before the traditional dates for the martyrdoms of Peter and Paul) he went to Rome in order to intercede for some fellow-priest who had been arrested. His mission was successful, owing to the good offices of Alityrus, a Jewish actor who belonged to the entourage of Nero. Assistance was also received from the emperor's wife Poppaea, whom he reported to be favourably inclined towards Judaism. She presented him with liberal gifts, and he left the capital with friendly feelings towards the Romans.

He returned to Judaea to find the rebellion was already gathering force.

> To the ordinary Jew [says Arnaldo Momigliano] the duty of paying tribute to the Romans, the sight of the Temple commanded by the Roman garrison in the neighbouring Tower of Antonia,

the thought that the vestments of the High Priest were in Roman hands, and the knowledge that the traditional administration of justice was limited by the intervention of the Roman governor, which was inevitable in spite of the large share left to Jewish courts—all these things were a continual offence. The complete lack of understanding and consequently of tolerance that most of the Jews evinced for the Romans was matched on the Roman side. . . . It was a conflict between the Jewish ideal of a state subordinated to the national religion, and the cosmopolitanism of Imperial Rome in which religion itself was subordinated to the State.

The Jewish cause, however, was far from united. The Pharisees had split into right and left wings. The first of these groups, to which Josephus had decided to belong, differed at this time from its former rivals, the Sadducees, on certain doctrinal matters only, and had abandoned its political role. The left wing of the Pharisees, on the other hand, became the secret revolutionary network of the Zealots. They possessed a considerable following inside the cities, and an outlawed underground movement in the countryside. They were also assisted by a large number of more lukewarm anti-Romans, who did not dare to refuse to help. Declaring that there was no ruler but God, and, on a more practical level, that the tax-collectors of the Romans must be expelled from the country, this secret organisation was stimulated by Messianic beliefs. Josephus says nothing of these, because he refuses to allow the Zealots any theological significance. He assails them with every sort of abuse, blaming them savagely for the ruin of Israel.

For Josephus was convinced that going to war had never done the Jews the smallest good. 'Warfare has never been allowed our nation. Our fighting is always followed by defeat.' Instead, paraphrasing the Old Testament, he adhered to the anti-Zionist, supernationalist, cosmopolitan belief 'that the whole world is proposed to be your place of habitation for ever.' He did not, therefore, feel that the faith of Israel was irrevocably associated with its soil.

Passing from the general to the particular, he saw that the present revolt was doomed to failure.

> All over the city they were forging missiles and suits of armour, most of the young men were receiving haphazard training, and there was tumult everywhere. Among the more stable, however, there was utter dejection; many saw only too well the approaching calamity and openly lamented . . . . The whole condition of the city before the arrival of the Romans proclaimed the coming destruction. [*Jewish War* II, 17]

By airing these defeatist views, Josephus courted extreme peril. He was compelled to take refuge in the Temple. Other leading priests, who agreed with his policy, were equally powerless. It was believed by these people that the intervention of the Roman governor of Syria, Cestius Gallus, would bring the rebellion to an end; and clearly that is what they hoped. But instead Gallus was unexpectedly repulsed from the gates of Jerusalem and defeated at Beth-Horon. This success over one of the highest Roman officials enormously encouraged the war party among the Jews, and was therefore, according to Josephus, a catastrophe: 'This reverse of Cestius proved disastrous for our whole nation, for the advocates of the war were so elated with this success that they entertained hopes of remaining victorious to the end.' This elation, however, was soon modified by two developments: a murderous wave of anti-Semitism which spread through Syria, and the unmistakable imminence of Vespasian's penetration into Galilee. In Jerusalem, the temporary ascendancy of a moderate group enabled Josephus to emerge from hiding, and the Jewish leaders who were now in charge of the city sent him to take command of troops in Galilee. In the *Jewish War* he implied that his mission was to organise resistance against the Romans, although later, as a Roman pensioner, he preferred to say that his aim had been to deceive and pacify Jewish 'robbers' or extremists. The dispatch of a pro-Roman to hold this post shows that the authorities now in power at Jerusalem felt little desire for an all-out war against Rome.

The towns of Galilee were split into many different parties, and Josephus met with much opposition from his fellow-Jews. This was especially notable at the fortress of Gischala, where a chaotic situation prevailed: Josephus made a ferocious enemy of a local leader named John, whom he describes in terms of unmeasured abuse (borrowed from Sallust's attacks against Catiline). On the approach of Vespasian, Josephus' large army melted away, and he took refuge in the fortified town of Jotapata. This withdrawal by Josephus into what the Roman commander called 'this prison' does not look as if he intended to offer a very determined resistance. However, he stresses the efficiency with which he conducted the defence of the town, using boiling oil, covering his messengers with sheep-skins to disguise them as dogs, and plastering the enemy's gangways with a boiled mash of the clover-like herb fenugreek, on which the attackers slithered helplessly.

And so Jotapata held out. As the siege tightened, however, Josephus became convinced it was no use carrying on. And so, together with certain fellow-members of the upper class, he decided to desert his post, and to leave the rest of the defence force to its fate. As he himself put it with that devastating, self-revealing frankness which is one of his special characteristics, he discussed with the leading fellow-Jews how they could escape, because 'he realised that the town could not hold out long and that his own survival was doubtful if he stayed'. However, he manages to tell even this discreditable story with the usual abundant pats on his own back.

> Josephus concealed his anxiety for his own safety and declared it was for their sakes he was arranging to leave. . . . He did not see how by staying with them he could be of any use to them in the present conditions. . . .
>
> This appeal fell on deaf ears; it simply made the people more determined to hold on to him. Children, old men, women with infants in arms wept and fell down before him. They all grasped him by the feet and held him fast, imploring him with sobs to remain and share their lot—not through envy of his escape, I think, but in the hope of

their own; for they felt perfectly safe so long as he remained. [*Jewish War* III, 14]

The effect of this self-praise is a little spoilt by the very honest admission that follows: 'Josephus realised that, if he yielded, these appeals would be the end of the matter, but if he refused he would be watched.' So he stayed.

Finally, after the siege had lasted for nearly seven weeks and the situation was desperate, the defenders agreed to die together in a mass suicide-pact: and Josephus agreed to be one of those who would die. He had been against this plan, but was coerced into participation at the point of the sword—'although', he says, 'the others felt unable to press their weapons home against their beloved general. Even when he was at his last gasp they still respected their commander. Their arms were enfeebled, their blades glanced off him, and many while thrusting at him with their swords spontaneously lowered their points.' Be that as it may, he was compelled to associate himself with the terrible project. However, he succeeded in deceiving the others, and survived.

> Putting his trust in divine protection he staked his life on one last throw. 'You have chosen to die', he exclaimed. 'Well then, let's draw lots and kill each other in turn. Whoever draws the first lot shall be dispatched by number two, and so on down the whole line as luck decides. In this way no one will die by his own hand—it would be unfair when the rest were gone if one man changed his mind and saved his life.' The audience swallowed the bait, and getting his way Josephus drew lots with the rest. Without hesitation each man in turn offered his throat for the next man to cut, in the belief that a moment later his commander would die. Life was sweet, but not so sweet as death if Josephus died with them.
>
> But Josephus—shall we put it down to divine providence or just to luck? —was left with one other man. He did not relish the thought either of being condemned by the lot or, if he was left till last, of staining his hand with the blood of a fellow Jew. So he used persuasion, they made a pact, and both remained alive. [*Jewish War* III, 26]

Self-preservation is a natural instinct. But no one else has ever told so openly and complacently how, in tragic circumstances, he tricked his own courageous people in order to save himself. It would indeed be difficult, as Heinrich Graetz said in his *History of the Jews*, to believe all the instances of craft and duplicity on the part of Josephus, 'had he not himself dwelt upon them with unexampled shamelessness.' Or, to quote his own words, 'In this predicament, his resourcefulness did not fail him.'

He was taken to the Roman camp as a captive. Soon afterwards, however, he was set free, visiting Alexandria in the company of Vespasian and witnessing Titus' siege of Jerusalem as an observer. When, finally, the Romans closed round the walls, the Jews within were rent by internal disunity. Josephus, eager at every point to vilify the defenders, is at pains to stress these dissensions, emphasising also the ferocity which accompanied them. According to him, this compared unfavourably with the 'clemency' of the

Romans. Inside the city, the moderates were no longer in charge, and two rival resistance movements were fighting against each other for control. One was led by Josephus' enemy John of Gischala, and the other by Simon bar Gioura ('son of a proselyte') who had gained a reputation by the capture of Hebron and other commando actions against the Romans. However, in face of the final menace, the two groups finally came to an agreement.

Many times Josephus went round the walls, urging the population to surrender; 'pleading with them,' records G.A. Williamson, 'while the tears ran down his face, to yield to the merciful Roman whose one desire was to end their agony.' And so the greatest of Jewish historians became a traitor to his people at its most critical hour. Or, to say the least, he was unheroic in seeing the advantages of collaboration so clearly—though it would be much harder to say, in the light of cold reason, that he was wrong in supposing that the insurrection had no chance whatever of success.

At last the city fell to Titus, in circumstances of unrelieved horror.

> Those who perished in the long siege totalled 1,000,000. . . . Every man who showed himself was either killed or captured by the Romans, and then those in the sewers were ferreted out, the ground was torn up, and all who were trapped were killed. There too were found the bodies of more than 2,000, some killed by their own hand, some by one another's, but most by starvation. So foul a stench of human flesh greeted those who charged in that many turned back at once. Others were so avaricious that they pushed on, climbing over the piles of corpses; for many valuables were found in the passages and all scruples were silenced by the prospect of gain.
>
> Many prisoners of the party chiefs were brought up; for not even at their last gasp had they abandoned their brutality. But God rewarded them both as they deserved. John, starving to death with his brothers in the sewers, after many scornful refusals at last appealed to the Romans for mercy, while Simon, after battling long against the inevitable, gave himself up. John was sentenced to life-imprisonment, but Simon was kept for the triumphal procession and ultimate execution.
>
> The Romans now fired the outlying districts of the town and demolished the walls. So fell Jerusalem in the second year of Vespasian's reign, on the 8th September—captured five times before and now for the second time laid utterly waste. [*Jewish War* VI, 45 ff.]

The conquerors officially treated the war as over, and Vespasian and Titus returned to Rome and celebrated a magnificent Triumph (71). Simon, we saw, was executed, John condemned to imprisonment. Reliefs on the Arch of Titus at Rome still display the spoils: the table of the shewbread, the trumpets and the great seven-branched candlestick, the Menorah, which, despite varied rumours, has never been seen since. Yet the war was not, in fact, finished, since three of the powerful fortresses built by Herod were

still unconquered. The resistance of Herodium, south of Jerusalem, was brief. Machaerus in Transjordan held out longer. Masada above the Dead Sea's western bank, towering above a sheer drop of more than 1300 feet, endured under Eleazar ben Yair until April of the year 73. Josephus gives a harrowing account of how the last 960 survivors of Masada destroyed one another; only two women and five small children hid themselves and survived. It is astonishing that he could write with such uninhibited eloquence about this suicide pact after he had evaded another and let his comrades die. Some of his descriptions of what happened at Masada, including Eleazar's lengthy exhortations, are exaggerated or invented, even if one of the survivors, his informant, was a relative of Eleazar, 'superior to most women in intelligence and education.' But the basic facts are probably as Josephus told them. Recent excavations have revealed the charred sandals of small children, and a potsherd bearing Eleazar's name. This may have been one of the lots drawn at the final moment of catastrophe to appoint ten of the defenders who would put the rest to death.

Meanwhile, however, Josephus was safely out of the way. After the capture of Jerusalem he was given a piece of land outside the city, and he persuaded the Romans to release some of his friends. Then he proceeded to Rome, where he was awarded Roman citizenship, taking the imperial family name, Flavius, in the same way as an ex-slave might assume the name of his master. He was also given a pension and a residence. After the siege of Jotapata he had married a prisoner of war from Caesarea ('at the command of Vespasian'), but while he was at Alexandria with Vespasian he divorced her in favour of a woman of that city. In Rome, he wedded an aristocratic Jewish heiress from Crete. His Alexandrian and Cretan wives presented him with three and two sons respectively. What happened to his parents we do not know. They may have perished in the siege of Jerusalem.

Safely established in Rome, Josephus spent the last five years of Vespasian's reign writing the *Jewish War* (c. 74-9). However, the Greek text which has come down to us was not the original edition. As he indicates in the preface, that had been in Aramaic. It was intended for Parthians, Babylonians, southern Arabians, Mesopotamians and Assyrians. That is to say, the work was originally written for the numerous eastern Jews, ancestors of their communities today, who had remained scattered abroad in the Dispersion and had never returned to Palestine, becoming augmented meanwhile by local converts to Judaism. The Mesopotamian brethren, Josephus indicated, had been suspected of wanting to join the insurrection, and his work was intended to inform them accurately of its causes, the sufferings it entailed and its disastrous conclusion. He wrote, then, in the Roman interest, to ensure that these people should accept the *fait accompli* of the destruction of the Temple without fomenting discontents along the borders of the Empire.

The version that has survived, however, is a second, Greek edition, which he prepared 'for the sake of such as live under the government of the Romans.' It was designed for the educated, Hellenised Jewish upper class—and he also specifically names important Romans among his readers.

Josephus was aware that his Greek was shaky. Nearly twenty years later, he remarked that he had taken great pains with the literature and grammar of the language, though he admitted that his pronunciation was still imperfect. At any rate, he employed helpers to assist him with the *Jewish War*: 'In the leisure which Rome afforded me, with all my materials in readiness, and with the aid of some assistants for the sake of the Greek, at last I committed to writing my narrative of the events.' He himself gives us to understand that this new version was a *translation* of the Aramaic original. But numerous references to classical literature, including echoes of Thucydides and Sophocles and others (not to speak of Sallust, Virgil and Livy, whom he certainly cannot have read), necessitate the conclusion that his collaborators modified and amplified the Aramaic edition. If Josephus composed a complete first Greek draft (as may be doubted), they must have polished it up and radically altered and improved it. His Greek, or rather theirs, is a vigorous literary Attic, usually but not always clear, with an enormous vocabulary, and much adroit antithetical argument in the speeches.

What the Aramaic book was called we do not know. But the title *The Jewish War*, which Josephus gave the Greek edition, is what a Roman but not a Jew would have been likely to call the war. It shows the pro-Roman bias of the work. In his preface he attempts to grapple with this question of bias. While laying due emphasis on Roman power, genius and glory, he does not propose, he says, 'like other writers who claim to be writing history,' to disparage the actions of the Jews. For that, surely, would be no sort of compliment to the grandeur of Rome. Conversely, he stresses the might of the Roman army, not only to deter those who may be tempted to revolt, but to console the people who have been vanquished by so great a force. This is a more explicit version of Polybius' explanation to the Greeks that Rome was irresistible. Josephus also proclaims the harsher conviction that the tragic fate of the Jews was no more than they had deserved. From outside the walls of Jerusalem he harangued the besieged population with the words: 'I know that the Almighty has abandoned the holy places and stands now on the side of your enemies!' Looking back, he took the same view of Pompey's destruction of the Temple in 63 BC. The Jews who had then been subjected were people who did not deserve to be free. Then and now, the Roman conquests were providential, for 'without God's aid it would not have been possible to consolidate so great an empire.'

This eulogy of Rome was inseparably blended with praise of the Flavian dynasty which had welcomed and financed his own collaboration. Josephus reports (and the story is confirmed from Roman sources) that he was originally spared by his captors because, immediately after falling into their hands, he had declared to Vespasian that he was destined to become emperor of Rome. There were many current prophecies, in the Biblical tradition, indicating that rulers of the world were destined to come out of Judaea. The Messianic Zealot movement took over these forecasts for its own purposes. But they were also applied

to Vespasian and his sons. The Rabbi of Jerusalem Johanan ben Zakkai, who managed to leave the besieged city and come to Vespasian, made pronouncements on similar lines.

Josephus' piece of intelligent anticipation stood him in good stead with Vespasian and Titus. He refers, in his later works, to his utilisation of their official reports or commentaries, and it is likely enough that these were employed for the *Jewish War*. At all events his many items of precise information about the military affairs of the Romans evidently came from an official source. Not unnaturally, he adopts Vespasian's interpretation of events against his enemy Vitellius in the Year of the Four Emperors. Then, when we come to the Jewish War, Josephus has no criticisms to offer when Vespasian ties men up and throws them into the Dead Sea alive as an experiment, or lures 38,000 Jews to the town of Tiberias to be sold as slaves or butchered.

But he reserved the fullest resources of his adulation for Titus, who employed him as interpreter and intermediary during the siege of Jerusalem. Josephus depicts Titus as a paragon in every possible respect. This involves a good deal of special pleading, indeed lying. Not only is the most improbably pseudo-Jewish, monotheistic language put into Titus' mouth, but his alleged unwillingness to destroy the Temple appears to be quite untrue. And Josephus' assertion that, in contrast to the savagery of the Jews towards each other, the Romans showed them clemency is contradicted by his own account.

> While he remained at Caesarea Titus celebrated the birthday of his brother in the grand style, reserving much of his vengeance on the Jews for this notable occasion. The number of those who perished with wild beasts or in fighting each other or by being burnt alive exceeded 2,500. Yet all this seemed to the Romans, though their victims were dying a thousand different deaths, to be too light a penalty. . . . At Berytus [Beirut] vast numbers of prisoners perished in the same way as before. [*Jewish War* I, 8]

Josephus' indifference to this brutality need cause no surprise, because he himself was revoltingly cruel. When there was trouble at Tiberias, and a young man named Clitus became known as an extremist leader, Josephus had ordered both his hands to be cut off. But then, he flattered himself, he showed great generosity in permitting the youth to keep one of his hands, and allowing him to cut the other one off himself. (In a later publication he inserts an improving address that he delivered to Clitus on this occasion.) So the savagery of Vespasian and Titus did not worry him. Indeed, Titus is invariably depicted as an irreproachable fairy prince.

And Titus reciprocated by associating himself with the favours which his father extended to the historian. He gave the *Jewish War* his imprimatur, and issued instructions that it should be published: 'So anxious was Titus that my volumes should be the sole authority from which the world should learn the facts, that he affixed his own signature to them and gave orders for their publication.' Many Roman participants in the campaign received presentation copies of the *Jewish War*, but the first recipients were Vespasian and Titus. Josephus also showed forethought by praising Titus' younger brother Domitian, who in due course, after he had succeeded Titus on the throne, awarded him further honours.

Although the *Jewish War*, as it has come down to us, was detached from what would have been a larger work, it nevertheless contains an introductory survey of more than two hundred years of Jewish history. Through this tangle Josephus, after the embarrassments of his own career, wends his way with some discretion, but also with a certain degree of frankness. For example the Hasmonaeans (Maccabees) might well have been adversely regarded as the prototypes of the rebels. Yet, being related to them by marriage, he finds it possible to speak of them with approval. Herod is treated unevenly, but at considerable length—proportionally far greater length than is devoted to later periods, because there was more written material about his career. It was desirable, in this connection, not to say anything that would offend Herod's great-grandson Agrippa II whose domains bordered on Judaea. The goodwill of this prince was important to Josephus, because Agrippa was habitually treated as a spokesman of Jewish interests at the Roman court. Besides, his sister Berenice (with whom he was said to have an incestuous relationship) was for a long time the highly favoured mistress of Titus. She lived with him openly during her stay in Rome in 75, though he was more evasive when she paid a further visit to the capital four years later.

Agrippa, whose ancestors had been idumaean converts, was eager to be regarded as a true Jew, and stood in particular need of such justification because the rebellion had seen him on the side of Rome. He must have been pleased with Josephus' desire to be helpful because he wrote the historian 'sixty-two letters testifying to the truth of the record'. In one of these letters, Agrippa remarked that he had read the book with great pleasure. 'You seem to me', he added, 'to have written with much greater care and accuracy than any who have dealt with the subject before. Send me the remaining volumes.' In another letter he offered what sounds like a more equivocal compliment: 'From what you have written you appear to stand in no need of instruction, to enable us all to learn everything from you from the beginning. But when you meet me, I will myself by word of mouth inform you of much that is not generally known [*Life* 65]. If that contains a veiled criticism, Josephus evidently did not notice it. He tells us that copies of the *Jewish War* went not only to Romans but to 'many of our own men who understood Greek learning, including the admirable King Agrippa.' Elsewhere he remarks, 'I sold copies to a large number of my compatriots.' It is not known whether Agrippa got his copy free or not.

Examples have already been quoted to indicate how Josephus' various political preoccupations, as well as a relentless taste for self- praise, got in the way of telling a truthful story. Such instances could easily be multiplied. His villains are more than black, and his heroes are paste-board saints, very different from some of the flesh-and-blood personages of the antique Jewish historical tradition.

On factual matters he is variable. Though siege tactics are well described, his battles tend to be melodramatic set pieces of the kind that have so often been encountered in the pages of his Greco-Roman predecessors. Moreover, even when politics are not involved, Josephus is a great exaggerator, especially of figures and statistics. Mount Tabor is a plateau nearly two miles long, 1800 feet above the sea. In Josephus, these totals become three miles and 20,000 feet respectively.

He is also an inventor. It was traditional to fabricate speeches, but he does so with particular lavishness. The horrors of Jerusalem and Masada were no doubt dreadful enough to stand in no need of exaggeration. And yet his details still manage to have a conventional literary ring. Was it true that messengers covered themselves with sheepskins to look like dogs? Or that a missile hit a pregnant woman and shot her child out of her body for a hundred yards? Did a stone used as a projectile really knock a man's head off and fling it like a pebble more than six times that distance?

And yet to leave the matter there would be misleading. Josephus' numerous digressions, though often irrelevant except as background in the very widest sense, bear the stamp of personal and often accurate knowledge. Some of his topographical descriptions, for instance at Masada, have been confirmed by excavations. His account of the Temple at Jerusalem, too, even if it cannot be squared completely with archaeological conclusions, is both earlier and more reliable than any Hebrew authority.

Indeed Josephus is virtually our only source for a profoundly important chapter of history. He adds enormously to our information. Where his personal prestige was not involved and his taste for hyperbole not enlisted, he tells a knowledgeable, exact and comprehensive story, and tells it conscientiously and fascinatingly. Indeed, even his impregnable opinion of himself has an advantageous effect on his truthfulness, for it makes him confess freely to courses of action which a less complacent and more squeamish historian would have hesitated to record. Assisted by this powerful vein of frankness, which goes far to counterbalance his other aberrations, Josephus' narratives are, for the most part, both illuminating and reliable. They had to be, since they would be read by important people who had actually played a leading part in events. What he says about earlier writers of contemporary history applied to himself: 'it was impossible to depart from the truth without being detected'.

Undeterred by the shortcomings imposed by his own political necessities, he goes on to enlarge with some passion upon the conventional assurance that a historian has got to be truthful. 'I am determined to respect the truth of history, though it has been neglected by the Greeks. . . . To those who took part in the war or have ascertained the facts I have left no ground for complaint or criticism. It is for those who love the truth, not those who seek entertainment, that I have written' [*Jewish War* I, preface]. His stress on the search for truth is emphatic and repeated.

As we have seen, these assurances clash with blatant falsifications. Yet they are also to some extent warranted by his unusually workmanlike approach. Josephus' strongest card is the fact that he had participated himself. Like Thucydides and Xenophon and Polybius before him, he is able to claim the great advantage of having played a prominent role in so much of what happened. And like Polybius, he castigates those who write without ever having stirred from their own homes.

> We have actually had so-called histories even of our recent war published by persons who never visited the sites nor were anywhere near the actions described, but, having put together a few hearsay reports, have, with the gross impudence of drunken revellers, miscalled their productions by the name of history. I, on the contrary, have written a veracious account, at once comprehensive and detailed, of the war, having been present in person at all the events. I was in command of those whom we call Galileans, so long as resistance was possible; after my capture I was a prisoner in the Roman camp. Vespasian and Titus, keeping me under surveillance, required my constant attendance upon them, at first in chains. Subsequently I was liberated and sent from Alexandria with Titus to the siege of Jerusalem.
>
> During that time no incident escaped my knowledge. I kept a careful record of all that went on under my eyes in the Roman camp, and was alone in a position to understand the information brought by deserters. . . . [*Against Apion* 19]

These unusual opportunities gave Josephus some justification for claiming that he not only sought to pursue the truth, but was able to produce something truly valuable in the process. 'The real worker is not the man who merely changes the order and arrangement of another man's work, but the one who has something new to say and constructs a historical edifice of his own. I myself have gone to great trouble and expense, though an alien. . . .'

And yet, because of the deep flaws in his personality, we find ourselves reluctant to believe what he says. But is this fair or right? 'Dislike of an author as a person,' as Moses Finley points out,

> no matter how extreme, need not carry over to his work, at least not in the same measure. . . . Josephus was a good writer, sometimes almost a great one, after all. Even if his books are judged most harshly as accurate historical writing, they remain valid as testimonies. . . . Josephus has surely captured the tensions, the brutality, the religious fanaticism, and the intense horror of the war—he has that right even when his 'facts' are most fictitious and distorted. For obvious reasons, that particular struggle retains an interest, nearly two thousand years later, unique among the many wars fought by and against the Romans. And so Josephus had greatness thrust upon him.

Jerome saw him as the Greek Livy. That did both historians an injustice. The prejudices and distortions of Livy, though powerful, are less urgent and shocking than those of Josephus. But that is because Livy was a historian who

stayed at home, whereas Josephus stood right in the middle of one of the most terrible wars of repression that the world has ever seen.

The much wider project of which the *Jewish War* was an offshoot took shape as his second major work (*c.* 93-4). It is known to us as the *Jewish Antiquities*, though he himself called it the Archaeologia. This work is in fact a history of the Jewish race, right from the Creation up to AD 66, the year in which the rebellion began. Altogether this account had taken Josephus eighteen years to write. It fills twenty books of Greek—as long as the entire canon of the Jewish scriptures put together.

The first ten books more or less follow the Old Testament narrative. The story of Moses is given in Books II-IV, VII is devoted to David, and the three books that follow carry the story to the death of Ahab, the captivity of the Ten Tribes of Israel, and the conquest of Babylon and Assyria by the Persian king Cyrus (539). Then the next three-and-a-quarter centuries, down to the death of Judas Maccabaeus, are compressed into only two books. Books XIV and XV recount Pompey's sack of Jerusalem, Antipater's assistance to Caesar, and the rise of his son Herod. The next two books continue to dwell on the reign of Herod, which is described in much greater detail than had been devoted to it in the *Jewish War*. Book XVIII opens with the conversion of Judaea into a Roman province, and the final pair of books describes the fortunes and policies of successive Roman governors, down to the fatal deterioration.

The *Jewish Antiquities* are dedicated to a certain Epaphroditus, perhaps identifiable with a learned Greek grammarian and freedman, Marcus Mettius Epaphroditus of Chaeronea, who possessed a library of 30,000 volumes and died in the later nineties. The *Antiquities* were a work of piety to the Jews. Even if Josephus had deserted their political cause, he did not feel himself a renegade. His main purpose, therefore, was to assert the antiquity of Israel, and its lofty religious and ethical standards, and its place among the nations. In the same spirit, for centuries, men had written in Greek to praise their own peoples, Mesopotamians, Egyptians and Romans. And so Josephus, too, following up certain earlier Jewish writers in Greek, now sought

> 'to reconcile other people to us and to remove any reasons for that hatred which unreasonable men bear towards us. As for our customs, no nation observes the same practice as another; in nearly every city we encounter different ones. But Justice is a universally admired practice and advantageous to all men equally, whether Greek or barbarian. And for justice our laws have the greatest regard. These laws, therefore, if we observe them rightly, make us charitable and friendly towards all men. For this reason we have a right to expect similar treatment from others. . . .' [*Jewish Antiquities* XVI, 7]

And Josephus asserted the superior antiquity not only of the Jews themselves, but of their historiography. Although Hebrew writers had rarely, except in minor matters, attempted a secular approach, something could be said in favour of this claim. But there had not, hitherto, been any such continuous account available to the Greek-speaking neighbours of the Jews. That is what Josephus now sought to supply. Grounding the authenticity of the Hebrew tradition on the descent of the Biblical text through many centuries, he makes it his task to retell the Bible story. But he supplements it by numerous small deviations, due to alternative traditions or glosses derived from earlier Jewish historians and theologians and Pharisaic scholars. Moreover, the Bible is patriotically doctored; awkward features such as the Golden Calf are omitted.

Roman opinion is also borne in mind. Although the *Antiquities* are less aggressively pro-Roman than the *Jewish War*, some adjustments have been made with an eye on possible Roman reactions. For example, Daniel, interpreting Nebuchadnezzar's dream, had spoken of the fourth kingdom of 'iron mixed with miry clay'—which would be destroyed by another monarchy. But Josephus prudently omits the point, because this and similar stories were being currently echoed as prognostications of the fate of Rome.

His standard of Biblical interpretation is poor. So is his grasp of comparative religion. It is interesting, however, to see Greek doctrines of Fate and human responsibility blended with the Hebrew tradition of free will. Indeed, they are tacitly treated as part of Jewish doctrine.

> We must indeed assume that man's actions are predetermined by some inevitable necessity, which we call Fate, because nothing is done without it. This view, however, should be weighed against the one which attributes events in part to ourselves and holds man reponsible for the conduct of their lives—which is the teaching of our ancient law. . . . [*Jewish Antiquities* XVI, II]

In many such allusions to the Greek concepts of Fate, Fortune, and Nemesis, Josephus shows a paganised outlook. But there is little merit or accuracy in his comparisons between Jewish sects and Greek philosophical schools. Serious efforts to give his religion an underpinning of Greek philosophy (notably by Philo Judaeus of Alexandria, who also described his mission to the emperor Caligula) made no impression on him. Nor, indeed, was his Judaism at all profound: in the *Jewish War* the Synagogue only obtains a single mention. For Josephus as for many Romans, religion was all on the surface, a matter not of emotional excess but of accurate ceremonial. The lesson of history was that 'those who follow the will of God *and do not venture to break his excellent laws* are offered felicity for their reward' [*Jewish Antiquities* I, preface].

The post-Biblical sections of the *Antiquities* form the most valuable part of the work, because they deal with many events that are elsewhere recorded inadequately or not at all. But they also contain a number of fabrications. Among these is a long, anachronistic story of an alleged visit to Jerusalem by Alexander the Great, presented as a supporter of Judaism and an enemy of the Samaritans, whom Josephus like other Jews deplored. The two centuries preceding the Hasmonaeans are skimped, because there were no proper sources. The treatment of Herod contains strange inconsistencies, and notable contradictions of what had been said in the *Jewish War*. These anomalies are based on the imperfect assimilation of two schools of thought, one comprising servile flattery of Herod and the other incorporating a hostile tradition. At times, Josephus still mirrors the eulogistic attitude, since he makes great use of a *Universal History* by Nicolaus of Damascus, who had been Herod's court-historian. Yet, on other occasions, we find a more detached or even hostile point of view than had been apparent in the *Jewish War*. He also regrets the supersession of his kinsmen the Hasmonaeans by the family of Herod. Possibly a number of these more critical points date from a second edition of the *Antiquities*, published after the death of Herod's descendant Agrippa II.

The work also contains references to Jesus Christ, John the Baptist and James the brother of Jesus. Although these allusions have naturally attracted keen interest, they are disappointingly uninformative, considering that Josephus lived in the homeland of Christianity throughout its formative years. Besides, the remarks about Jesus, and probably portions of the other passages as well, do not in fact go back to Josephus at all, but are insertions by a later hand.

The *Antiquities* also allude to specifically Roman events. In particular, there is a long account of the murder of Caligula and the accession of Claudius, events missing from our surviving texts of Tacitus. The character of the secretive Tiberius, too, is illustrated by many private talks, emotions, prayers and thoughts which Josephus either invented himself or derived from an over-imaginative Roman source. It is also difficult to see how he can have known what King Monobazus of Adiabene did in the darkness with his sister-wife. 'As he was in bed with her one night he laid his hand upon his wife's belly and fell asleep, and seemed to hear a voice, which bade him take his hand off his wife's belly, and not to hurt the infant that was therein.'

Nevertheless, Josephus continued to profess a stern regard for the truth. He foreshadows Tacitus in his equal severity towards both types of imperial historian, the flattering sort 'who, as a result of being well-treated by Nero, neglected to tell the truth', and the opposite category 'who detested the emperors and, from sheer hatred, behaved so outrageously with their falsehoods that they deserve severe criticism'.

During the years between the *Jewish War* and the *Antiquities*, his life at Rome had not gone smoothly. In 73, on the occasion of a Jewish insurrection in Cyrene, a weaver there named Jonathan, one of many co-religionists who had a grudge against Josephus, denounced him to Vespasian as an instigator of this revolt. However, the historian was cleared by the intervention of Titus, and was even granted another estate in Judaea, while Jonathan was tortured and burnt alive. From time to time there followed other similar denunciations of Josephus, again brought forward by Jews alienated and shocked by his record. These attacks were all successfully warded off. Nevertheless, very soon after the publication of the *Antiquities*, or as an actual appendage, he decided to supplement it by a further work. This addition or epilogue, written in a somewhat unpolished style and apparently without the aid of helpers, is described as his *Life*, though it is not, in fact, a balanced autobiography since nearly nine-tenths of the contents consist of a defence of his conduct in Galilee in AD 67 which had led to his change of allegiance.

Josephus makes it clear that there was a special reason why he felt the need to produce a new account of this phase of the war. It was because another writer had now published a version hostile to Josephus, evidently charging him with being partly responsible for the rebellion of 66-70. In the oppressive last years of Domitian (81-96), when these accusations were launched, they could be extremely perilous. Fortunately, Josephus had flattered Domitian and enrolled him among his patrons. But the emperor had become a very violent and suspicious man, and now that his father and elder brother, Josephus' principal protectors, were dead, it was particularly necessary to argue that he had really been on the Roman side from the very beginning.

The unfriendly book which caused him so much anxiety was the work of a certain Justus of Tiberias in Galilee. His emergence to undertake this task was particularly awkward because Justus, like Josephus, had actually been present at the events he was describing. During the period of Josephus' Galilean command Justus had acted as the leader, in his home-town, of a party which, although not extremist in tendency, brought him into acute collision with Josephus. The grudge had persisted. Justus' work, which was another *Jewish Antiquities* from Moses to his own day, has not survived. But it was still extant in the ninth century, when it was known to Photius of Byzantium. He quoted a view that it was pure invention. Yet that idea may have originated from Josephus, and Justus evidently ranked with him as one of the leading Greco-Jewish historical authors.

Explaining the reasons for his own counterblast, Josephus claims that it is virtuous of him to write again 'while there are still living such as can either prove what I say to be false, or can attest that it is true' [*Jewish Antiquities* XX, 11]. Yet the holocaust of leading Jews during and after the war—including the victims of the suicide pact from which Josephus had made his escape—meant that, in fact, there were very few survivors who were in a position to contradict anything that he said. So he must have felt that the survival of this isolated observer was really bad luck. Whether Justus was still alive when the refutation was published we do not know. At all events Josephus unleashed a torrent of abuse upon his head, calling him a spiteful ignorant liar on a par with people who were forgers of contracts—a nasty dig since Justus, after enjoying the protection of Agrippa II on charges of rebellion, had subsequently been dismissed by the monarch for forgery.

Josephus goes on to say that it was not himself but Justus who, as far as Tiberias was concerned, had fomented the revolt.

> How then, Justus—if I may address him as though he were present—how, most clever of historians, as you boast yourself to be, can I and the Galilaeans be held responsible for the insurrection of your native city against the Romans and against King Agrippa, seeing that, before I

was elected by the general assembly at Jerusalem to the command of Galilee, you and all the citizens of Tiberias had not only resorted to arms, but were actually at war with the towns of the Syrian Decapolis? It was you who burnt their villages. And your servant fell in the engagement on that occasion. [*Life* 65]

Besides, he points out, Justus had lacked his own opportunities to discover the true facts—opportunities provided him by the Romans: 'The facts are recorded in the Commentaries of the Emperor Vespasian . . . you were neither a combatant nor had you perused the *Commentaries* of [Titus] Caesar, as is abundantly proved by your contradictory account.' Whereas Josephus himself, on the other hand, in order to refute the calumnies of Justus, now claimed to be bringing forward hitherto unpublished information. Why then, people would ask, had he not produced this information before? The explanation, he says, lies in his sheer niceness of character.

> Being therefore now compelled to defend myself against these false allegations, I shall allude to matters about which I have hitherto kept silent. My omission to make such a statement at an earlier date should not occasion surprise. For, while veracity is incumbent upon a historian, he is none the less at liberty to refrain from the harsh scrutiny of the misdeeds of individuals, not from any partiality for the offenders, but because of his own moderation.

In effect, what Josephus was now doing, at great length, was to explain that he had not really been an anti-Roman commander in Galilee at all. He had been sent by the Jerusalem Assembly (Sanhedrin) as one of three commissioners to pacify and disarm Jewish extremists. His mission was to wait and see what the Romans were going to do, keeping his arms in reserve against any emergency. Then, however, he was suspected of treachery by his fellow-Jews, and four commanders were actually sent to try to supersede him. This meant that he had to commit himself to an anti-Roman position, and was obliged to stand siege from Vespasian at Jotapata. Before that, as we are told with renewed emphasis, he had continually protested against the madness of the insurrection. And the wickedness of the arch-rebel John of Gischala is brought home to us in even more virulent terms than before.

In one way Josephus' account of his Galilean command in the *Life* may be more accurate than what he had said in the *Jewish War*. For he is at least forced to abandon the role of the great general: since Justus had been there to see, or at least near enough to know. On the other hand, the *Life* is evidently disingenuous in its interpretation of the official duties that had been assigned to him in Galilee. It is probable enough that he had undertaken the job more or less under compulsion and that his execution of his functions was lukewarm even before he turned traitor. The appointment of a man with his sympathies showed that the Jewish authorities in power at that particular time were not very keen on the idea of a war against the Romans. But the purpose of his command was surely to stave off and stop their invasion.

The *Life* was followed, perhaps almost immediately, by

another work answering further attacks. This time they had been directed not against his personal conduct, but against his literary work, with the *Jewish Antiquities* as a particular target. The hastily but skilfully written pamphlet which now emerged is known to us by the title *Against Apion*, because the second of its two books contains refutations of a long-dead Greco-Egyptian grammarian of that name. In the reign of Caligula (37-41), Apion had led a deputation from Alexandria to Rome to protest against the Jews. He had also published anti-Semitic writings which circulated widely at Rome; and Josephus is happy to report that he came to a miserable end. Manuscripts call the work *Concerning the Antiquities of the Jews: against Apion*, but the Alexandrian theologian Origen gave it the shorter name *Concerning the Antiquities of the Jews.* This is a more appropriate title, since the critics (now lost) whom Josephus is rebutting evidently included some who were a good deal more recent than Apion. For the wide range of unfriendly writers whom he sets out to contradict not only went back to Egyptians of earliest Alexandria, but included 'authors of scurrilous and mendacious statements' who were evidently his contemporaries.

This most famous of all justifications of Judaism, constituting a passionate expression of pride in Josephus' ancestry and beliefs, seems to be directed towards Jews of the Dispersion (rather than Palestinian Jewry) whose faith, subjected to the hostile barrages of Apion and his like, might become lukewarm. His arguments bring the controversy up to date by refuting current charges of anti-social, unpatriotic behaviour. But the main purpose of the work is to emphasise the timeless, universal validity of the Hebrew moral and legal codes. Particular stress, too, is laid on the venerable antiquity of Judaism, in comparison with the Greeks. It is also pointed out that a direct consequence of this antiquity is the greater seniority of Jewish historical writings

> My first thought is one of intense astonishment at the current opinion that, in the study of primeval history, the Greeks alone deserve serious attention, that the truth should be sought from them, and that neither we nor any others in the world are to be trusted. In my view the very reverse of this is the case. . . .
>
> In the Greek world everything will be found to be modern and dating, so to speak, from yesterday or the day before. Surely, then, it is absurd that the Greeks should be so conceited as to think themselves the sole possessors of a knowledge of antiquity and the only accurate reporters of its history. . . . While, then, for eloquence and literary ability we must yield the palm to the Greek historians, we have no reason to do so for veracity in the history of antiquity, least of all where the particular history of each separate foreign nation is concerned. . . . Our records contain the names of our high priests, with the succession from father to son, for the last two thousand years. . . .
>
> We have given practical proof of our reverence for our own Scriptures. For, although such long ages have now passed, no one has ventured ei-

ther to add, to to remove, or to alter a syllable. And it is an instinct with every Jew, from the day of his birth, to regard them as the decrees of God, to abide by them and if need be, cheerfully to die for them. Time and again ere now the sight has been witnessed of prisoners enduring tortures and death in every form in the theatres, rather than utter a single word against the Laws and allied documents.

> What Greek would endure as much for the same cause? [*Against Apion* I, 3]

Zvi Yavetz   (essay date 1975)

SOURCE: "Reflections on Titus and Josephus," in *Greek, Roman and Byzantine Studies*, Vol. 16, No. 4, Winter, 1975, pp. 411-32.

[*In the excerpt below, Yavetz examines the historical credibility of the description of Titus in* Jewish War, *contending that the favorable portrait of the emperor is the result of the his generosity toward Josephus.*]

Three major qualities of Titus are in the limelight as long as he was under the command of his father in Judaea *political astuteness and diplomatic skill* are stressed in connection with his mission to Galba and in his dealings with Mucianus; *remarkable organizational talent* and *distinction in military operations* are continuously emphasized. [All references from Josephus, unless otherwise stated, are to *Bellum Judaicum.*]

Titus' personality as commander-in-chief of the forces in Judaea after Vespasian left for Rome (5.39) could be described in one sentence: He was above all always and everywhere present at the side of all (5.310). His courage was in no dispute and his personal example made his troops follow him without hesitation. He is described as an ideal army commander who plans carefully all his operations, leaving no detail unchecked. Titus is an extremely severe and demanding officer. His frequent exhortations to his soldiers—free compositions of Josephus as they may be—appear natural against this background (*e.g.* 3.472-84).

Titus is not a tyrannical commander who endears himself to the *gregarius miles* by neglecting his fellow officers. On the contrary, he consults rather often with the high commanders in his army (5.491; 6.132; 6.237). They are loyal to him just as the common soldiers are and do not try to snatch victory from him (3.298-300).

It is perhaps to Josephus' credit that nowhere does he make an effort to hide Titus' ruthlessness, but he almost invariably tries to attenuate the harsh impression by means of an indulgent sentence: He spared no male in Galilean Japho, but women and infants were spared, though sold into slavery (3.304). In Jotapata the Romans gave no quarter to anyone and thrust the inhabitants down the steep slopes of the citadel in a general massacre (3.329). In Tarichaea there was a great slaughter without discrimination, but at the last moment Titus stopped the massacre (3.501). And in front of the walls of Jerusalem Titus ordered the crucifixion of prisoners of war. But he did it only hoping that the spectacle might lead others to surrender in dismay (5.289-450).

Syrians disembowelled two thousand Jews who escaped after having swallowed gold coins to prevent discovery by the Zealots. Titus stopped the massacre (5.421, 552, 556). He did not oppose the killing of more than 2,500 Jews by wild beasts in Caesarea Philippi after the destruction of the Temple (7.23, 37-39). But when prisoners were scourged and subjected to torture of every description before being killed, he felt pity for them (5.450). He did not, however, stop the cruelties.

Josephus' story of the burning of the Temple is well known. According to him (6.165) the Jews and not Titus started to burn the Temple. In the well-known war council Titus explicitly opposed the idea of burning the sanctuary (6.236-43). But things went out of control, and one of the soldiers, not waiting for orders but moved by some supernatural impulse . . . , snatched a branch from the burning timber and flung the fiery missile through the door. After having achieved the victory and before returning to Italy Titus revisited the ruins of Jerusalem. He contrasted the sorry scene of desolation before his eyes with the former splendour of the city, and calling to mind the grandeur of its ruined buildings and their pristine beauty, he commiserated its destruction (7.111).

No wonder that some scholars can discern only hypocrisy in Titus' behaviour. And indeed examples of hypocrisy are not missing in Josephus' writings. The soldier who set the temple on fire against the explicit wish of the commander was never punished. To mention just another minor case: when Arabs, Syrians and some Roman soldiers cut open suppliant Jews in order to search their intestines for gold coins, Titus reprimanded them but inflicted no capital punishment for disobedience; but when some Jews stole horses from Roman soldiers, he put a soldier to death for negligence (6.155). Massacring Jews (without having been ordered to do so) was not crime enough to receive the death penalty.

But Titus' hypocrisy is a minor issue; the major problem is whether Josephus should be believed at all. Bernays [in the article "Ueber die Chronik des Sulpicius Severus," in *Gesammelte Abhandlungen*, edited by H. Usener, II, 1885] analysing the story of the destruction of the Temple (6.237-66), reached the conclusion that Sulpicius Severus' version (*Chron.* [*Chronicles*] 2.30.6) should be accepted. Some members of Titus' staff suggested sparing the Temple, but Titus himself ordered the sanctuary to be burned down:

> Etenim nonnullis videbatur aedem sacratam ultra omnia mortalia illustrem, non oportere deleri, quae servata, modestiae Romanae testimonium, diruta, perennem crudelitatis notam praeberet. At contra alii, et Titus ipse, evertendum templum, in primis censebant . . .

This passage is believed to depend on Tacitus and should therefore be accepted as truthful. Tacitus, according to Bernays, had no obligations towards the Flavians, did not have to flatter them, and told things as they were. Bernays compared this passage with other Latin sources (Val.

Flac. 1.13; Sil. Ital. 3.600, 605, 607, 629; Suet. *Tit.* 5) and confirmed his view that it was Titus personally who should be blamed for the destruction of the Temple. Many others followed Bernays in principle but added new arguments. Montefiore [in his article "Sulpicius Severus and Titus' Council of War," *Historia* II (1962)] does not think that Sulpicius Severus necessarily depended on Tacitus and suggested Marcus Antonius—a former procurator of Judaea known to have written of the Jews—as a more plausible source. On the other hand he believes that Titus might have given orders for the Temple to remain intact in the knowledge that they could not be carried out. The officers must have smiled at Titus' orders.

Alon [in his *Studies in Jewish History* I, 1967] approaches the problem differently. First of all Josephus seems to contradict himself: in 7.1 he says explicitly that it was Titus who ordered the whole city and the Temple to be razed to the ground. Moreover, at ***Antiquitates Judaicae*** 20.250 he says that Titus captured and set fire to the city and the Temple. The story in ***Bellum Judaicum*** 6.254 that Titus ran to the burning Temple in order to arrest the conflagration is pure invention. Alon believes that there is enough internal evidence in Josephus to prove that Titus intended to destroy not only the Temple but the Jews as a nation. He executed deliberately all the priests (6.322), gave his troops permission to burn and sack the city of Jerusalem (6.353), and did not punish any of his soldiers who killed indiscriminately whomever they encountered (6.404). Eventually he stopped the massacre, but there was hardly anyone left to be worth killing (6.414); and last but not least, Vespasian ordered the destruction of the Temple of Onias in Egypt three years later (7.421).

In short, one is easily convinced that Josephus was capable of lying. His lies are innumerable. But in this case Bernays' and Alon's arguments, some of which are debatable, still fail to disclose Josephus' motive for not telling the truth. Did he try to endear Titus to the Jews by telling them that the Temple was destroyed against the professed wish and order of Titus? This can hardly be the case, because all other cruelties of Titus are known mainly from the same opus; and even if Josephus had proved that Titus was not to be blamed for the destruction of the Temple, his general image could hardly improve.

I doubt whether Josephus ever intended to depict Titus as the friend of the Jewish nation. On the other hand, did he seek to glorify Titus in the eyes of Romans or other gentiles? It was hardly necessary to wait till the downfall of the Flavians to disclose a well-kept 'state secret' that Titus ordered the destruction of the Temple. Cruelty towards barbarians was never considered to be a vice in Rome: *jus apud cives, modestiam apud socios* (Tac. *Ann.* 1.9) was the general rule of behaviour in Rome; *parcere subiectis et debellare superbos* was a virtue. This is precisely how Josephus would have liked to depict Titus: a true Roman who would punish the rebels without pity but would do his utmost to spare the peace-loving population, agricultural labourers whose only concern was the prospects of the crops (4.84-92). In a well-known passage Josephus admits that he intended first of all to impress Vespasian and Titus, then many Romans who had taken part in the campaign, and eventually Jews versed in Greek learning (*Contra Apionem,* 1.51).

This leads us towards an answer to another question. Who did Josephus expect to accept this characterization of Titus? Baer [in his *Israel Baamin,* 1955, and in "The Mishna and History," in *Molad,* 1964] refutes by means of an exacting critical analysis many of Josephus' stories. We need not recount each of them individually, but Baer's most convincing argument is worth repeating.

Josephus reduced the extent of the internal conflict in Judaea to one between peace-lovers and warmongers and ignored its much deeper significance, namely that it was a clash between two fundamentally different approaches to Roman domination: the readiness to compromise and submit in order to preserve peace at all costs *versus* the determination to protect social and religious traditions. Writing for gentiles, he suppressed any religious problems which he thought might be unintelligible for his readers. Instead, he described the constitution of Jerusalem in terms of a democracy tempered with aristocratic elements after the pattern of Isocrates and Aristotle and referred to the nomination of the High Priest by lot in Greek terms only, disregarding the true Jewish ancestral practices. In Baer's view, any attempt to depict the conflict between High Priests and rural priests as merely a struggle between social classes and to divorce it from its profound religious milieu is a gross over-simplification of the truth. In this direction his elaborations are illuminating. It seems to me, however, that Baer overdoes his search for *topoi* taken from Greek literature in Josephus' historical writing; *e.g.* while rejecting Thackeray's contention [in his *Josephus the Man and the Historian,* 1929] that John of Gischala's figure is modelled on Sallust's Catilina he maintains that the real prototype is the Cleon of Thucydides and of Aristophanes' comedies. The Idumeans of Jerusalem bear a striking resemblance to Thracians in Greek literature; the struggle between the wealthy and the poor in the besieged Jerusalem echoes Lysias' account of the reign of the Thirty Tyrants in Athens; and the situation in Jerusalem after the fall of the Galilee reflects that in Athens after the disaster.

It is not impossible to apply Baer's method even to the character of Titus himself, and to show that its delineation by Josephus is but the outcome of a Graeco-Roman literary commonplace concerning a successful military commander. There are many points of similarity between what Josephus said about him with respect to relations between soldier and commander and what Livy and Cornelius Nepos say about great generals. And the scene in which he surveys the ruins of Jerusalem is strongly reminiscent of Scipio Aemilianus' inspection of Carthage which he had razed to the ground.

Such a method, however, may sometime reduce history to the utmost absurdities. Some tyrants in various Greek cities seem to have borne similar features. This may be accepted as a plain historical fact, and it would be a waste of time to seek an *Urquelle* of all the stories about them. There were likewise similar phenomena in the stasis of 411 B.C. in Athens and the one of A.D. 69 in Rome. But just for this reason one is not justified in tracing back all accounts of stasis in our sources to a *topos.* It would be much sounder to assume that similar circumstances in different places and in different periods engender similar phenomena.

It is a fact that Josephus misleads his readers by using Greek terminology for Jewish problems. For this his Greek assistants may be partly blamed. The Aramaic version being lost, the truth will never be known, but not all the facts related in Josephus are to be disbelieved.

I do not intend to defend Josephus' overall veracity. On the contrary, I believe that he belongs among those historians whose procedure was well described by Churchill: "Give me the facts, Ashley, and I will twist them the way I want to suit my argument." He did so especially when he tried to defend himself. It is possible for a modern historian to find out which argument suited Josephus best and hence disclose why and in which direction he twisted some basic facts. This cannot be achieved by analysing literary *topoi* and using rigid philological methods. It is possible to analyse whether the description of Titus in Josephus' writings fits into his general framework and purpose. This method will certainly not disclose the whole truth, but it may help to clarify some obscure points. And this leads to a second question: Is Titus' character in keeping with the general tendency of Josephus' works?

After having dealt at some length with the Roman army (3.70ff) Josephus states that it was not his major intention to extol the Romans. Nevertheless, he makes it clear now and again that there was nothing greater than the Roman army (3.70), that God was on the Roman side (5.369, 412), and to scorn meaner masters might be indeed legitimate, but not those to whom the universe was subject (5.365-66).

It seems that Josephus did not reach the firm conclusion—that war against Rome was futile—only in his old age when he wrote his *Vita* (17-20) in order to defend himself against Justus of Tiberias. This must have been his genuine view from the days of his early manhood, when at the age of 26 he visited Rome and was impressed by her grandeur. He never believed in Rome's collapse, not even during the year of the four emperors, and never wagered on the Parthians (7.78, 79, *cf.* Tac. *Hist.* 4.54). His attitude to the war was ambivalent from the very beginning. When he accepted the command in the Galilee he hardly believed in a Jewish victory. This must have been his biggest fault: to lead people in a cause in which he never believed without serious doubts. And I think that his split personality should be interpreted against this background.

In 3.108 he declares the purposes of his work: (a) to console those who were conquered by the Romans (*i.e.* the Jews); (b) to deter others who may be tempted to revolt. By 'others' he could have had in mind not only other Jews but also gentiles in Asia Minor who might have hoped for Parthian help (*e.g.* 1.6, 2.388 etc.).

But the real undercurrent in his whole work is that Jews and Romans are two great nations. War between these two nations was not inevitable and peaceful co-existence was a real possibility, if wild extremists on both sides—Zealots on one hand and greedy procurators on the other—had not dragged the two nations into an unnecessary clash.

There were good and bad people on both sides (*e.g.* 3.335, 4.60 etc.). But the strongest strictures are reserved for those Jews who insisted on fighting against the Romans to the bitter end.

Jews were plauged by war, tyranny and faction (4.397). Titus himself asserted that the Jewish people owed its ruin to civil strife, and that the Jewish tyrants brought down upon the holy Temple the unwilling hands of the Romans (1.10). The Romans may well be found to have been the upholders of our laws. The real enemy was within the walls of besieged Jerusalem (4.184). Civil war paved the way to famine. The city was converted into a desolate no-man's-land for domestic warfare, and almost all the corn which might have sufficed for many years of siege was destroyed (5.25, 26). Dreary and famine-stricken, the city was exposed to daily atrocities (5.429ff). Jews suffered nothing worse at the hands of the Romans than what they inflicted upon each other. It was sedition that subdued the city, and all the tragedy may be ascribed to her own people (5.527). Such explanations were not alien to Jewish minds. Talmudic legends (*e.g.*, Gittin, 55b-56a) may illustrate the point.

But of course not all Jews were seditious. There were some excellent people too, who were not allowed to handle the difficult situation. Such a man was Ananus, the senior of the chief priests, a man of profound sanity, who might have possibly saved the city of Jerusalem had he escaped the hands of the extremists (4.151). Josephus would have liked to appear in Jewish history as another Ananus who unfortunately recognized the hopeless circumstances at an early stage. He knew that no one would listen to his advice, and had he remained in Jerusalem and fought for his ideas, his fate could have been similar to that of Ananus.

Josephus was aware of the fact that after his defection some people accused him as a coward, others as a traitor, and throughout the city there was general indignation and curses heaped upon "his devoted head" (3.432-39). He could not hope to be compared with a Jeremiah (5.391) or a Jehohachim (6.105). Jews were never prepared to compare a renegade who acted as an adviser of moderation in Titus' headquarters with a Jeremiah who preached for moderation within the besieged walls of Jerusalem. Josephus had to resign himself to the hatred of his people whenever he appeared outside the walls (5.547), but he would have loved to be remembered as another Ananus who did everything for the public welfare and not for his private interests (4.320). Had gentle men like Josephus and Ananus survived to lead the Jewish nation in the tragic days of 66-70, an understanding between Jews and Romans would certainly have been reached. They would have found a congenial counterpart in the Roman camp—Titus.

Josephus is convinced by the clemency of the Romans towards alien races, by Titus' anxiety to save the Temple (1.27), and by the fact that the burning of the Temple happened contrary to Caesar's wishes (1.28). In 1.10 we read that throughout the war Titus commiserated the populace who were at the mercy of the revolutionaries and often of his own accord deferred the capture of the city by protracting the siege to give the culprits time for repentance.

It is this conception that made Josephus describe Titus as he did. Personal ties, of course, should not be underestimated. Titus was his benefactor, and Josephus owed him a great deal. He was given Roman citizenship, and with a pension assigned to him he could start to write the *History of the Jewish War*, . . . a title clearly showing his original point of view. Roman official sources were put at his disposal, and the general purpose of a book written in such an atmosphere is obvious. Titus could expect little less than a panegyric (4.597).

Josephus' description of Titus' cruelty and ruthlessness, however, must be taken up again. According to Josephus, these were forced upon him and he committed them reluctantly (5.442-44, 455; 6.118-124, 128, 215-16). The real villains were the Jewish extremists. They divorced soul from body, and all remorse from evil was extinct (5.526). There is no word of understanding for the rebels. The fact that many of them had already been defeated once (in the Galilee) and that they might have known the Roman custom to treat more ruthlessly those who had been defeated twice did not occur to him. On the contrary, he believed that they left Titus no other choice and many times mistook his humanity for weakness (5.335: *cf.* 6.324; 5.340; 5.419; 6.356). They regarded Titus' overtures as due to his inability to be really harsh, and indeed Titus razes to the ground enemy fortifications only after long and stubborn fighting and only then when he can show no mercy (5.347). Only after having been double-crossed by the ruses of his enemy, he loses his patience and exerts his tremendous power to its fullest extent (5.319-30, 333). But even then he does it reluctantly, and the *topos* . . . appears *ad nauseam* in the ***Bellum Judaicum***. All that because Titus was a man with innate love for human beings . . .

Such a characterization of Titus could hardly convince a Jew between the years A.D. 70-80. But Josephus never intended to convince them and—as said before—he did not hope to be able to do so. He read Titus' memoirs (***Vita*** 358) and keeping in mind his potential readers (***Contra Apionem***, 1.51) decided out of personal gratitude to delineate his saviour as a man imbued with ἐπιείκεια and μεγαλοφροσύνη (*Jewish Antiquities* 12.128).

It is difficult to assess exact Latin equivalents for Greek philosophical terms. It is doubtful whether Josephus or his assistants knew exactly the differences and nuances of ἐπιείκεια, πραοτησ, φιλανθρωπια, but it is plausible to assume that they would have hoped a Roman reader would translate το φιλανθρωπον φυσει by *natura clemens*.

Clementia was a typical *Herrschertugend*, a virtue of rulers and an important one: *maxime tamen decora imperatoribus* (Sen. *De Clem.* 1.5.2), for in rulers it has an especial comeliness inasmuch as with them it finds more to save. *Clementia* is that which restrains the mind from vengeance when it has the power to take it, or leniency of a superior towards an inferior in fixing a punishment (*De Clem.* 2.3.1)—*lenitas superioris adversus inferiorem in constituendis poenis*.

A decree of an emperor in those days could decide what nations should utterly be destroyed, which banished, which should receive the gift of liberty, which have it taken from them, what kings should becomes slaves and whose heads should be adorned with royal honour, what cities should fall and which should rise (*De Clem.* 1.1.2). *Clementia* and *misericordia* are by no means identical. Pity is a vice: *misericordia vitium est animorum nimis miseria paventium* (*De Clem.* 2.6.4). Pity is a weakness of the mind that is overmuch perturbed by suffering, and if anyone requires it from a *sapiens,* that is very much like requiring him to wail and moan at the funeral of strangers.

One should not remit a punishment one ought to exact (2.7.3). To pardon (*ignoscere*) is to fail to punish one whom you judge worthy of punishment that is due (2.7.3). *Clementia* has also freedom in decision (*liberum arbitrium habet*), but pardoning should not be too common. When distinction between the good and the bad is removed the result is confusion and epidemic vice (1.2.2). Therefore *clementia* should not be indiscriminate or general. It is as much cruelty to pardon all as to pardon none. *Nec promiscuam habere ac vulgarem clementiam oportet nec abscissam. Nam tam omnibus ignoscere crudelitas quam nulli.*

As a matter of fact, *clementia* rather corresponds to *severitas* just as *misericordia* corresponds to *crudelitas.* A tyrant punishes because he finds pleasure in torturing in-nocent people. This is *saevitia.* Kings punish only for a reason and by necessity (1.11.4).

Seneca's *De Clementia* is dedicated to a young Nero, reluctant to sign a death sentence for two brigands and exclaiming, *Vellem litteras nescirem* (2.1.2). Vespasian was anxious to save Helvidius' life, although he banished him and later ordered his death. This is what Suetonius tells us, and he adds that Vespasian never took pleasure in the death of anyone but even wept and sighed over those who suffered merited punishment (Suet. *Vesp.* [*Vespasion*] 15).

This is precisely how Titus behaved in Judaea. He punished the rebels because he had to do so, but he did it reluctantly. He tried to make them surrender; they refused and made it impossible for Titus to say like Augustus (*Res Gestae* 3), *Externas gentes, quibus tuto ignosci potuit, conservare quam excidere malui.* The Jewish rebels never asked for *venia,* and Titus had to act like a true Roman: prove that *severitas* and *clementia* are both virtues. Having dealt elsewhere at some length with the strong concern of Roman politicians and emperors about their public reputation, I need not repeat the details here. Suffice it to say that highest and lowest admired rulers for their *clementia* (*De Clem.* 1.1.9). Augustus' merciful behaviour towards Lepidus made him popular and beloved, and he preserved his reputation for many years after his death (1.10.1).

Titus probably did not know the Stoic theory concerning *clementia.* But it was commonplace in those days in Rome that *clementia* makes rulers not only more honoured but also safer (*De Clem.* 1.11.4). And it was impossible to imagine anything more seemly for a ruler than the quality of *clementia* (1.19.1): *Excogitare nemo quicquam poterit quod magis decorum regenti sit, quam clementia.*

Josephus must have understood that it would do no harm to his benefactor Titus, designated to succeed Vespasian, if he should build up his public reputation as a man imbued with *clementia* even towards an enemy like the Jews. As a matter of fact it was precisely during the years when the **Bellum Judaicum** was written and published that Titus badly needed a trumpeter for his *clementia.* Bad tongues spread malicious rumours in Rome which might have incriminated Titus even with his father's death (Cass. [Cassius] Dio 66.17.1). This leads to our last question.

A literary analysis of Titus' biography by Suetonius may lead to the conclusion that it is the sort of panegyric to be encountered in the fragment of the Germanicus *vita* incorporated in the Caligula *vita* (1-7). There are, however, some passages in the biography which are far from being panegyric. It is even stated that Titus incurred such odium that hardly anyone ever came to the throne with so evil a reputation or so much against the desires of all.

Rumour was a decisive factor in forming public opinion, and it hardly mattered whether it was based on truth or not. Titus' case is a good example. Before he came to the throne he was blamed for his cruelty (*saevitia,* Suet. *Tit.* 7.1), which is a typical quality of tyrants. He was secondly suspected of *luxuria* since he protracted his revels until the middle of the night with the most prodigal of his friends. His *libido* was notorious because of his passion for Berenice, and it was said (*ferebatur*) that he promised her mar-

Bust of the emperor Vespasian.

riage. He was also suspected of greed (*rapacitas*), and it was well known that in cases which came before his father he put a price on his influence and accepted bribes. In short, people not only thought but openly declared that he would be a second Nero: *Denique propalam alium Neronem et opinabatur et praedicabant* (Suet. *Tit.* [*Titus*] 7.1).

Chronologically this description fits the period A.D. 71-79. After Titus' return from the East he became Vespasian's partner and protector: *Neque ex eo destitit participem atque etiam tutorem imperii agere* (Suet. *Tit.* 6.1). He took part in his father's triumph, became his colleague in tribunician power, assumed command of the praetorian guard, became censor in 73 and held seven consulships. It was during this period that he had to take upon himself the discharge of almost all the duties. And as usual, all his good deeds went to the credit of his father, while the dirty jobs which were assigned to him harmed his own reputation. Suetonius had to admit, however, that eventually his reputation turned to the highest praise, no fault was discovered in him any more, and people had good things to say about him. *At illi fama pro bono cessit conversaque est in maximas laudes* (Suet. *Tit.* 7.1).

It would not be wise to scorn Suetonius' chronology in all his biographies. True, he once confessed to write *neque per tempora sed per species* (Suet. *Aug.* 9.1). But in the biography of Titus this principle does not work, and Tacitus' testimony is decisive: *Laetam voluptatibus adulescentiam egit, suo quam patris imperio moderatior* (Tac. *Hist.* [*Histories*] 2.2).

Our sources are unanimous in telling us that after Titus' accession to the throne he made an immense effort to change his image. Reappearance of Augustan types on Titus' coinage is conspicuous. The new emperor would try to imitate the behaviour of the founder of the Principate. He would endeavour to gain the good will of the masses without humiliating the members of the upper classes. He would attend gladiatorial games and public baths—however preserving his dignity as well as observing justice: *Verum maiestate salva necminus aequitate* (Suet. *Tit.* 8.2). Indeed his whole behaviour changed. His banquets were pleasant rather than extravagant (Suet. *Tit.* 7.2, *iucunda magis quam profusa*), and Dio emphasizes that he was frugal in money matters and made no unnecessary expenditures (66.19.3a; Zon. 11.18.16-18, p. 55 Dindorf). No more *luxuria* and no more *libido* either. He sent Berenice away from Rome at once, against her will and against his own. He ceased to cherish dancers, put an end to his *rapacitas* and became famous for his *munificentia*. He took away nothing from any citizen, respected other people's property and, although many kept offering and promising him large sums, he accepted nothing from any citizen, city or king (Cass. Dio 66.24.4). After the eruption of Vesuvius he sent two ex-consuls to Campania to support the restoration of the region (Cass. Dio 66.23.5); the property of those who had lost their lives and had no heirs he applied to the rebuilding of the buried cities (Suet. *Tit.* 8.4). During the fire in Rome (in A.D. 80) he set aside all the ornaments of his villas for the public buildings and temples and put several men of the equestrian order in charge of the work. During the plague which affected Rome after the

fire he made great efforts to diminish the force of the epidemic. He gave most magnificent shows, and Dio gives a detailed description of some remarkable spectacles (66.25). He granted favours to many people, and when his officials warned him that he was promising more than he could perform, he said that it was not right for anyone to go away from an interview sorrowful (Suet. *Tit.* 8.1). And most important of all, no more *saevitia*: he banished the informers from Rome (Cass. Dio 66.19.3; cf. Suet. *Tit.* 8.5); never entertained cases on the charge of *maiestas* (Cass. Dio 66.19.1); put no senator to death, nor was anyone slain during his rule; and he was said to have sworn that he would rather be killed than kill, *sed periturum se potius perditurum adiurans* (Suet. *Tit.* 9.1). These points need no further elaboration. They have been exhaustively treated in various works by modern historians.

Whether his personality went through a deep change remains a matter of conjecture. Psychologists should not be let loose on the dead. What is certain is that he succeeded in changing his public image and in a short time endeared himself to all. Dio (66.18.4) doubts whether Titus would have remained as popular had he lived longer, and following him Syme remarks sardonically, "The favourites of the Roman People died young." Popularity and long life were hardly compatible. Indeed, after his death people heaped such praise on him as they had never done when he was alive (Suet. *Tit.* 11).

One should accept without any doubt the fact that Titus' popularity with the soldiers aroused suspicions in various quarters in Rome (Suet. *Tit.* 5.2; Tac. *Hist.* 5.1). And many a senator might have remarked "*mihi caligae eius non placent*" (Cic. *ad Att.* 2.3.1). Stories about his savageries in Judaea were added to his successes as a *praefectus praetorio* of his father, and his enemies did not find it difficult to brand him as *saevus*. Before ascending the throne, Titus might have welcomed any effort to change his image into *clemens*. Josephus must have known the situation and as a faithful client understood the hint. He described Titus as a man imbued with *clementia* and hence his terminology το φιλανθρωπον φυσει (6.324). Titus' picture as it emerges from this work reflects much more prevalent attitudes in the society in which Josephus moved when writing it than any real historical person acting in Judaea.

But is it really true that Titus was so anxious to see Josephus' book become the sole authority from which the world should learn the facts about the Jewish War? As a matter of fact, Titus affixed his own signature to them and ordered their publication (*Vit.* [*Vita*] 361). It is of course true that Rome perpetuated Josephus' memory. His statue was erected in the city and his works placed in public libraries (Eus. *Hist. Eccl.* [Eusebius, *Historia Ecclesiastica*] 3.9).

But some skepticism is warranted. History books, even if they appear to be works of propaganda, are taken less seriously by emperors or politicians in whose favour they have been written than by students or professors of history. Luce seems to exaggerate when he sums up an (in all other respects) excellent article on Livy with the words, "Instead of searching for Augustan allusions in Livian history, it might be more profitable to investigate to what extent Augustan policy was influenced by the Livian concept of the past."

History books were never a major means of propaganda. The Roman masses never read books, and it is doubtful whether Roman senators considered the opus of the Jewish historian a best seller. It seems that Josephus genuinely respected Titus and praised his benefactor on his own initiative. In the days of the republic Lucceius had to be reminded by Cicero (in a letter which did not blush) that the orator could not praise himself. He needed the services of another herald so as not to proclaim himself victor with his own voice. But Titus was not Cicero. Neither was Josephus a Lucceius. It would be oversimplification to believe that Titus asked for a panegyric. Of course, he did not mind, just as Augustus may not have been totally indifferent to Livy's history. But Livy and Augustus were never intimate friends, and the relationship between Josephus and the upper classes in Rome still remains to be studied.

It seems that Titus' simulatory gifts must have made it easy for him to act as a genuinely *clemens princeps*, and Josephus' panegyric was only of secondary importance. It is doubtful whether a Roman emperor considered friendship with Josephus to be an asset. He was never awarded the official title of *amicus Caesaris*. He was not among his *comites*. He must have been a member of the lower entourage, in the same category as doctors and magicians, philosophers and buffoons.

In spite of his victory Titus never became 'Judaicus'—perhaps because of the religious connotation of the term; and Tacitus in sketching the history of the Jews preferred other sources to Josephus. He might have read him but never quoted him. In Jewish tradition, his fate was similar. His name was never mentioned by Tanaim or Amoraim, and only Christian historians enhanced his reputation. For Hieronymus he was a *Graecus Livius*, for Cassiodorus a *paene secundus Livius*. For his Jewish redemption he had

to wait for the Middle Ages. In spite of his efforts Josephus must have been a very lonely man in his old age.

Louis H. Feldman   (essay date 1976)

SOURCE: "Josephus as an Apologist of the Greco-Roman World: His Portrait of a Solomon," in *Aspects of Religious Propaganda in Judaism and Early Christianity*, edited by Elisabeth Schüssler Fiorenza, University of Notre Dame Press, 1976, pp. 68-98.

[*In the following excerpt, Feldman examines Josephus's description of King Solomon in* Jewish Antiquities, *contending that this and other scriptural references are given new interpretations because Josephus wrote for a Gentile audience.*]

The *Antiquities* is, indeed, as we read in the proem, directed not merely toward Greek-speaking Jews but toward the entire Greek-speaking world. That it is a non-Jewish audience he has in mind is apparent from the fact that Josephus at the beginning seeks to establish that there is a precedent for communicating information about Jewish history to non-Jews, and that the Greeks had, indeed, been curious to learn about Jewish history, as seen in the fact that Ptolemy Philadelphus had commissioned the translation of the Torah into Greek in the third century B.C.E. There are still today, asserts Josephus, many lovers of learning ... like the king. He notes that only the first five books of the Scriptures were translated for the king, whereas Josephus proclaims it his intention to make available to his audience all the scriptural books.

At first sight Josephus' portrayal of Solomon appears to have fewer divergences from the biblical text than is the case with his depiction of other biblical characters, such as Abraham, Joseph, Moses, Samson, or Esther. But here too he has hardly adhered to his promise to set forth the precise details of the biblical records, "neither adding nor omitting anything." Perhaps Josephus is taking for himself the same liberty that was assumed by the translators of the Torah into Greek, who, despite the injunction in Deut. 12:32, did make certain deliberate changes, which are approved of by the rabbis (Talmud, *Megillah* 9a), while Philo says that the Greek is a precise, indeed divinely inspired, translation of the original (*De Vita Mosis* 2.38). And perhaps, when he says that he has translated his work from the Hebrew records, he means that his source is Jewish tradition generally and not merely the Bible. Some of this tradition had been committed to writing by Josephus' time, as we see from the Dead Sea *Genesis Apocryphon* and Pseudo-Philo's *Biblical Antiquities*, both dating probably from the first century C.E.

If we examine the portrait of Solomon that emerges in Josephus, we find that it is distinctly Hellenized, and that it is intended to appeal to the Hellenized Jew and educated Greek in his audience. He uses his paraphrase of Solomon to present certain apologetic motifs such as are found elsewhere in the *Antiquities* and especially in the *Contra Apionem*.

In particular, there are indications that Josephus may have had the character of Oedipus in mind in adapting the

---

An excerpt from *Against Apion*

We [Jews] have but one temple for the one God (for like ever loveth like), common to all as God is common to all. The priests are continually engaged in His worship, under the leadership of him who for the time is head of the line. With his colleagues he will sacrifice to God, safeguard the laws, adjudicate in cases of dispute, punish those convicted of crime. Any who disobey him will pay the penalty as for impiety towards God Himself. Our sacrifices are not occasions for drunken self-indulgence—such practices are abhorrent to God—but for sobriety. At these sacrifices prayers for the welfare of the community must take precedence of those for ourselves; for we are born for fellowship, and he who sets its claims above his private interests is specially acceptable to God.

Flavius Josephus, in Josephus: The Life, Against Apion, Vol. I, *translated by H. St. John Thackeray, William Heinemann, 1926.*

biblical character of Solomon. Thackeray has contended, on the basis of a close study of Josephus' vocabulary and style, that books 15 and 16 of the *Antiquities* are the work of one of Josephus' Greek assistants who was especially steeped in Sophocles. While most critics since then have for good reasons declined to accept this hypothesis, there are many marks of Sophoclean style in these books, as well as in the other books of the *Antiquities*. We here suggest that it is not merely in vocabulary and style that the influence of Sophocles is to be felt, but also in the coloring of the character. Furthermore, Josephus consciously colors his narrative with Stoic phraseology to make it more intelligible and attractive to his readers.

Overall, Josephus heightens the importance of Solomon and endeavors to defend him and to raise his stature. In Josephus, the place of Solomon is highlighted by G-d's prediction that after David's death the Temple would be brought into being "by his son, and successor to the kingdom, whose name would be Solomon" [*Jewish Antiquities*]. Although neither 2 Sam. 7:12 nor 1 Chron. 17:11 names Solomon there.

In 1 Chron. 22:11 it is David who prays that G-d may send his prosperity, while in Josephus the statement has greater force since David tells Solomon that G-d Himself has promised to bring prosperity to the country of the Hebrews during his reign [*Jewish Antiquities*].

In [*Jewish Antiquities*] David's statement to Solomon that G-d chose Solomon to be king even before his birth, raises the stature of Solomon. 1 Chron. 22:9 reads merely that a son is to be born to David. Likewise the omission by Josephus of the name of David in his version of Solomon's prayer to G-d (cp. 1 Kings 3:6-7) serves to keep attention focused on Solomon. Similarly, the anointing of Solomon is more vividly colored in Josephus than in 1 Kings.

Solomon's greatness is increased in Josephus' version by his stress on the fact, not mentioned in 1 Kings 2:12, that he was a mere youth upon ascending the throne (according to [*Jewish Antiquities*] he was fourteen upon accession to the throne). Josephus adds that despite this handicap of youth, Solomon performed all his tasks with as great scrupulousness ... as those of advanced age and mature wisdom. The youth of Solomon is likewise stressed in Josephus' account of Solomon's judgment in the case of the two women; in addition to what is said in Scripture, after he orders the two children cut in half, all the people secretly make fun of Solomon as a mere lad.

Josephus makes effective use of G-d's prediction, even before Solomon's birth, that David would have a son by that name who would build the Temple (2 Sam. 7:12; 1 Chron. 17:11; [*Jewish Antiquities*]), repeating it at the time of the dedication of the Temple. Solomon's stature is further magnified by G-d's promise, after the completion of the Temple, that He will, in Josephus' words, raise Solomon "to a height and greatness of happiness beyond measure" [*Jewish Antiquities*]—a promise that has no parallel in 1 Kings 9:4-5 or 1 Chron. 7:17-18.

The focus in Josephus' narrative is to an even greater degree on Solomon than in the Bible. Thus, in G-d's appear-

ance to Solomon after the completion of the Temple, He warns him in 1 Kings 9:6 that "if ye [i. e., the Jews] should turn away from following Me," He will cut off Israel from the land which He has given them. In Josephus' account, it is Solomon himself who is warned that if he should prove to be faithless G-d will cut him off root and branch.

The fact that Josephus assigns to Solomon a reign twice as long as that given to him in both of the accounts of the Bible (1 Kings 11:42 and 2 Chron. 9:30) and in the Septuagint, adds to the stature of the king. He is depicted as having reigned for eighty years, a period exceeded by no Greek, Roman, or Oriental sovereign, and as having lived to the age of ninety-four.

Josephus praises the character of Solomon by a number of touches not found in the biblical narrative. Thus, whereas 1 Kings 1:52 does not mention Solomon's qualities of mildness and moderation, Josephus does so, knowing that this was one of the four cardinal virtues of the Greeks and that *singularis moderatio* was particularly prominent in the emperor Tiberius, according to Velleius Paterculus. This mildness, shown in granting an amnesty to Adonijah, is stressed in Josephus' version of 1 Kings 1:53, for whereas the Bible reports that Solomon told Adonijah to go to his house, Josephus' version has Solomon bidding him to go to his own without any fear or suspicion.

Solomon is portrayed by Josephus as distinguished particularly for his piety toward his parents. 1 Kings 2:10 states merely that David was buried in the city of David, whereas Josephus adds that it was Solomon who arranged a splendid funeral and buried him with great abundance of wealth. Similarly, when his mother Bathsheba comes to him with Adonijah's request for Abishag, he is quoted in 1 Kings 2:20 as saying: "Ask on, my mother, for I will not deny thee." In [*Jewish Antiquities*], however, he dilates on "the sacred duty to do everything for a mother," and chides her for not speaking in complete confidence of obtaining her request. In the list of virtues which David exhorts Solomon to cultivate in [*Jewish Antiquities*], we find in fact, that he is urged to be pious, just, and brave. It is, in fact, the same virtues of piety, justice, and fortitude which, together with obedience, are set forth by G-d Himself to Samuel as the virtues which comprise beauty of soul and which He seeks in a king. In contrast, 1 Chron. 22:13 is more diffuse and hardly reduces to three such adjectives: "Then shalt thou prosper, if thou observe to do the statutes and the judgments which the L-rd charged Moses with, concerning Israel; be strong and of good courage; fear not, neither be dismayed." The first two of these epithets are repeated in a passage in Josephus which has no biblical parallel in 1 Kings 1:35, which it paraphrases. David, according to Josephus, gives instructions to Solomon that he rule with piety and justice over the Hebrew nation. Again, in an extra-biblical extension of David's exhortation to Solomon in 1 Chron. 28:9, Solomon is urged to be pious and just. And whereas David, in his dying charge to Solomon in 1 Kings 2:3 stresses piety alone, in Josephus' version there is equal stress that he be just toward his subjects and pious toward G-d. The attribute of piety is stressed throughout Josephus' treatment of Solomon.

Another quality of Solomon stressed by Josephus is his sense of gratitude. 1 Kings 5:25 reports that in return for Hiram of Tyre's gifts, Solomon gave Hiram 20,000 measures of wheat for food. Josephus prefaces this gift with the statement that Solomon commended Hiram's zeal and good will. Solomon's gratefulness is likewise stressed in Josephus' paraphrase of Solomon's prayer at the dedication of the Temple in 1 Kings 8:23-24. In the Bible, Solomon says that there is no G-d comparable to the G-d who has kept his promise to David. In Josephus, Solomon renders thanks to G-d "first for my father's sake whom Thou didst raise from obscurity to such great glory, and next on my own behalf, for whom unto the present day Thou hast done all that Thou didst foretell."

Solomon is depicted as a man of faith in G-d. Whereas 1 Kings 8:15 speaks sweepingly of the fulfillment of G-d's promises to David, Josephus has Solomon assert that some of the prophecies had been fulfilled and that others would likewise come to pass. He thus proceeds to exhort the people not to despair of anything that G-d had promised but, on the contrary, to have faith because of what they had already seen.

Solomon's modesty is stressed in a passage cited by Josephus from Menander's Greek translation of Tyrian records stating that a certain young lad named Abdemonos was always able to solve the problems submitted to him by Solomon. Josephus even quotes the statement of Dios, the historian of Phoenicia, that this Abdemon(os) not only solved Solomon's riddles but himself proposed riddles which Solomon was unable to solve and that on account of this failure Solomon had to pay large sums to Hiram.

1 Kings 10:13 notes that Solomon gave the Queen of Sheba all that she asked for in addition to gifts of his own, but in Josephus' account, Solomon's generosity is stressed still more by the statement that he showed his magnanimity by giving what she desired far more rapidly than he gave her the gifts of his own choice.

In summarizing Solomon's character, Josephus remarks that he was the most illustrious of all kings, the most beloved by G-d, and more outstanding in wisdom and wealth than any of those who had ruled the Hebrews before him.

Still, Josephus realized that Solomon's vengeful slaying of Joab required apology. The only reason David himself did not do so, according to Josephus' addition to 1 Kings 2:5, was that Joab had hitherto been stronger and more powerful than David. It was out of envy, says Josephus in another addition to 1 Kings 2:5, that Joab killed Abner and Amasa, and this again helps to justify Solomon's action. It was Solomon's piety toward G-d, according to Josephus' addition, that led Joab to flee for refuge to an altar (1 Kings 2:28). Lest Solomon be thought to have killed him in cold blood, Josephus remarks that he sent Beniah "with orders to remove him and bring him to the judgment hall to make his defense," contrary to 1 Kings 2:29 where Solomon gives orders to Beniah to "go fall upon him."

Similarly, Solomon's seemingly harsh action in punishing Shimei is more clearly justified in Josephus' version, for whereas 1 Kings 2:8 says merely that Shimei cursed David, Josephus reports that he did so repeatedly. Again, whereas 1 Kings 2:43 has Solomon ask simply why Shimei had not kept "the oath of the L-rd, and the commandment that I have charged thee with," Josephus builds up Solomon's defense by stressing that Shimei "had made light of his commands and—what was worse—had shown no regard for the oaths sworn to G-d". Further, Josephus has Solomon emphasize to Shimei that he is punishing him so that he may know that transgressors gain nothing through a postponement of their punishments.

Although Solomon had earlier, in a Josephan addition [in *Jewish Antiquities*], shown mildness and moderation toward Adonijah, we later find him arranging to have him slain in an apparently ruthless fashion. Josephus consequently feels the need for an apology, though 1 Kings 2:13 does not, and this he does with his reminder that Adonijah had even in David's lifetime attempted to seize the royal power. In 1 Kings 2:15 Adonijah merely notes that the kingdom had been taken from him and given to Solomon. Josephus adds Adonijah's reaction, namely, that he was "willing and happy to serve under him and was satisfied with the present state of affairs" Hence the reader has less sympathy for Adonijah's request to change the *status quo* by marrying David's widow Abishag. The request would indeed appear to be outrageous were it not for Josephus' addition to 1 Kings 2:17 which makes it clear that David, by reason of his age, had not had intercourse with her and that she still remained a virgin. Josephus builds up to Solomon's seemingly harsh action toward Adonijah by having Solomon note (a fact not found in 1 Kings 2:22) that Adonijah had powerful friends in Joab and Abiathar and implying therefore that his marriage to David's widow could make him a real threat to Solomon's rule.

The worst charge that could be made against Solomon was that he worshipped foreign gods. Josephus seeks, wherever possible to omit data on Solomon's contributions to such worship or to other direct violations of Jewish law (Halachah). Although Theophilus, a first century B.C.E. Hellenistic Jewish historian, mentions that Solomon sent some gold to the Tyrian king out of which the latter constructed the pedestal for a life-sized statue of his daughter (*ap.* Eusebius, *Praeparatio Evangelica* 9.34), Josephus tones the story down. Mindful of the prohibition against making images of human beings in Exod. 20:4, Josephus did not want to present Solomon as contributing to such a violation, and so, though he does mention a golden column in the temple of Zeus he does not indicate that it was Solomon who sent it.

The rabbis are divided in their opinions as to Solomon's marriages; but on the whole they berate him. For example, they record that after his wedding to Pharaoh's daughter he overslept the morning sacrifice the following day, and that to please another of his foreign wives, he crushed five locusts in his hands in the name of Molech, whereupon he was deprived of the Divine Spirit and of his wisdom and strength. Josephus, however, omits the reference in 1 Kings 11:7 to Solomon's building of high places for Chemosh the Moabite god, and for Molech, the Ammonite god, Solomon's grossest misdeeds in the worship of foreign deities. In place of these incidents, Josephus refers to a much slighter sin, namely, of setting up images of bronze bulls in the Temple and lions in his palace.

Josephus is sympathetic to Solomon even after he has sinned in building altars to alien gods, for when G-d rebukes him for doing so, he shows contrition by feeling pain, in Josephus' report, and by being especially confounded at the thought "that almost all the good things for which he was envied were changing for the worse."

Solomon's virtues appear all the greater when they are praised by others, particularly non-Jews. Hiram praises Solomon's wisdom in 1 Kings 5:21; in Josephus he praises him as a wise man endowed with every virtue. The friendship of Hiram for Solomon is an important part of Josephus' defense of the Jewish people against anti-Semites such as Apion, who charged that the Jews lacked fame in antiquity. Indeed, in the **Contra Apionem**, Josephus is careful to record the fact that the Temple is mentioned in a source external to the Bible, namely, the records of the Tyrians. These chronicles likewise show, according to Josephus, that Hiram was a friend of Solomon and that he contributed a great deal toward the construction of the Temple. To supply still further evidence for Hiram's relations with Solomon, Josephus twice cites Menander, who had translated the Tyrian records into Greek [**Jewish Antiquities** and **Contra Apionem**], as well as Dios, the author of a history of Phoenicia.

The fact that the Queen of Sheba bestows even higher praise on Solomon in Josephus' account than she does in 1 Kings 10:7 adds to the picture of Solomon's magnificence [in **Jewish Antiquities**]. Josephus tells us that she admired beyond measure what she saw "and was not able to contain her amazement." Furthermore, Josephus' account exaggerates Solomon's prosperity, for the Queen remarks that the reports about Solomon failed to convey the dignity of his state to its full extent ([**Jewish Antiquities** and **Contra Apionem**], 1 Kings 10:7). She says that she could not believe what she had heard because of its multitude and greatness, but that now she has witnessed things far greater than these. In an effort to present Solomon and the Queen as rulers of equal importance, Josephus reduces the gift of gold that the Queen gives Solomon from 120 talents (1 Kings 10:10; 2 Chron. 9:9) to 20 talents in order that it not seem a tribute.

Since the Jews in antiquity were often accused of hatred of humanity, *odium generis humani*, as Tacitus puts it (*Histories*), Josephus is constantly concerned to answer this charge (e. g., [**Contra Apionem**]). In connection with Apion's statement that the Jews "swear by the G-d who made heaven and earth and sea to show no goodwill to a single alien, above all to Greeks," Josephus not only repeats Solomon's prayer to G-d that He listen to non-Jews when they come to pray in His temple, but he adds his hope that G-d will do so in order to prove that Jews are "not inhumane by nature nor unfriendly to those who are not of our country but wish that all men equally should receive aid from Thee and enjoy Thy blessings."

Inasmuch as Apollonius Molo and Apion had accused the Jews of failing to make any useful contribution in the arts and sciences, Josephus stresses the greatness of the Temple, which had been acknowledged even by Polybius [mentioned in **Jewish Antiquities**] and which was Solomon's supreme achievement. Whereas 1 Chron. 22:14 ff. enumerates what David had prepared for Solomon, Josephus leads up to Solomon's great achievement by having David reassure Solomon: "Do not be dismayed at the magnitude of the labor, nor shrink from it." According to both the Hebrew text and the Septuagint of 1 Chron. 22:14, David had already prepared no less than a hundred thousand talents of gold and a million talents of silver. These are huge sums, and would have made David a wealthier king than Solomon, for the latter, according to 1 Kings 10:14, received in one year only 666 talents of gold and would have required 150 years to accumulate an equivalent sum. Josephus modifies the mention of this apparently fantastic sum, and in the process accomplishes his purpose of diminishing David's role and magnifying Solomon's in the building of the Temple by changing the figures to ten thousand talents of gold and one hundred thousand talents of silver. Similarly, whereas 1 Chron. 29:3-4 reports that David gave an additional gift of three thousand talents of gold and seven thousand talents of refined silver, Josephus omits the mention of the silver.

Josephus adds to the elaborate description of the Temple in the Bible a number of details calculated to enhance Solomon's prestige. Whereas 1 Kings 6:2 ff. contents itself with giving the dimensions of the Temple, Josephus adds that the foundations of the Temple consisted of strong stones capable of resisting the wear of time, and he refers to its massive height, graceful beauty, and magnificence. Relying perhaps on his recollections of the Temple that Herod built, he adds that it was built up to the roof of white marble; he doubles the height of the lower story, and states that it had a second story, details not found in 2 Chron. 3:4. Again, whereas Kings 6:5 says that Solomon made side chambers round about, Josephus gives the actual number, and exact dimensions of each chamber, perhaps on the basis of the passage in Ezek. 40:17, which speaks of thirty chambers in Ezekiel's version of the Temple. In general, Josephus emphasizes the sheer size of items in the Temple; thus he explains that the bronze sea in 1 Kings 7:23 was so called because of its size. He likewise exaggerates numbers by remarking that Solomon set up a great number of tables in the Temple, whereas 1 Kings 7:48 mentions only one table, and even 2 Chron. 4:8 mentions only ten. Again, whereas the Bible leaves the number of vessels in the Temple unclear and simply asserts that they were exceedingly many, (so 1 Kings 7:47), Josephus records precise numbers, stating that there were 20,000 of gold and 40,000 of silver. Both the Hebrew text and the Septuagint of 1 Kings 7:49 state that there were ten candlesticks in the Sanctuary; Josephus has expanded this to no less than 10,000 lampstands. Similarly, in other places, Josephus' precise numbers for items, such as the 80,000 pitchers, 100,000 golden bowls, 200,000 silver bowls are his own invention, not paralleled in 1 Kings 7:50, but based perhaps on traditions available to him as one of the leading priests.

Josephus likewise adds to 1 Kings 6:22 in describing the dazzling effect of the Temple created by the radiance of gold which met the visitor on every side. He also praises the workmanship of the Temple by remarking that one would marvel to see how cunningly the drums of the wheels of the lavers were fitted into the rims. In an unscriptural summary of his description of the vessels in the Temple, Josephus states that Solomon made all these things at much expense and with great magnificence to the honor of G-d, sparing no cost and acting with utmost munificence. In describing the Temple courts, Josephus adds to 1 Kings 7:51 the statement that the third court was so wonderful as to be beyond all words and even, so to speak, beyond all sight, since he filled up with earth great valleys into which one could not look without difficulty since they were of such great depth. He likewise adds details concerning the arrangement of the furniture in the Temple. Josephus particularly praises the naturalism in the art work of the Temple. Thus he adds to the account in 1 Kings 7:36 the statement that the animals on which the laver rested were so well fitted together "that to one looking at them they seemed to be one natural growth."

Josephus emphasizes the fact that the Temple, despite its magnitude, was completed in a very short time, whereas 1 Kings 7:38 merely notes that it took Solomon seven years to build it. Josephus remarks, in addition, that Solomon made such a display both of wealth and of zeal that any viewer would have thought that the work could not have been completed in the whole course of time.

The ceremony at the dedication of the Temple is considerably enhanced by Josephus' additions, and thus reflects still greater glory on Solomon. Whereas 1 Kings 8:5 speaks of the sacrifices performed then, Josephus also adds that the ground was drenched with libations and that so vast a quantity of incense was burned that its sweetness penetrated even to people who were at a great distance. Not only was there singing, as described in 2 Chron. 5:12-13, but Josephus adds dancing as well, and notes that the people did not weary of this singing or dancing until they had reached the Temple.

Although rabbinic agada tells of help from spirits and angel servants, Josephus does not mention this aspect, as is his custom with reference to the supernatural. He does, however, remark that G-d approved of and assisted in the work, as a way of adding to the stature of Solomon's achievement.

By deferring the account of the building of Solomon's palace until after the completion of his description of the dedication of the Temple, Josephus tends to stress the importance of the Temple and to diminish that of the palace. Indeed, seeking to emphasize Solomon's piety in devoting greater attention to G-d's house than to his own, Josephus says explicitly that the palace was much inferior in dignity to the Temple and took longer to complete because the materials had not been prepared so long in advance nor at the same expense and because it was intended as a dwelling place for a king and not for G-d. Yet, adds Josephus, it was worthy of note and was in accordance with the prosperity of the land and of its king. Although 1 Kings 7:2-5 simply gives the dimensions of the palace, Jo-

sephus describes the great and beautiful judgment hall, the chambers for eating and resting, the hall for feasts. He describes the materials used for building, and the painting and decorations, as well as as their variety. Josephus likewise notes the admiration of the Queen of Sheba for the palace.

Josephus also adds to Solomon's stature by noting that in addition to those cities mentioned in 1 Kings 9:17-19, Solomon built still others for enjoyment and pleasure, which enjoyed a mild climate and produced fruits in irrigated lands.

It is interesting that, aside from a brief mention—in accordance with the Bible—of Solomon's conquest of those Canaanites who were still unsubmissive, Josephus has nothing to say of Solomon the conqueror except in the treatise **Contra Apionem**, where he is answering Apion's argument that proof of the injustice of the Jewish laws is to be seen in the fact that they are not masters of an empire. In his reply Josephus contrasts the Egyptian kings, who suffered many disasters, with David and Solomon, who subjugated many nations. He further proudly states that Solomon governed his kingdom in perfect peace.

As was mentioned earlier, Josephus appears to have modeled Solomon's character on Oedipus. Support for the equation of Solomon and Oedipus appears at the very beginning of Josephus' account of Solomon. In 2 Sam. 7:14, G-d warns Nathan that if Solomon should sin, He will punish him "with the rod of men and with the stripes of the children of men." In Josephus' narrative G-d says that He will punish Solomon with sickness and barrenness of the soil if he should sin. It is true that the nature of the threatened punishment may have come to Josephus through the Bible itself, notably the curses enumerated in Deut. 28:15-68, but when viewed in conjunction with other Sophoclean elements in Josephus' narrative, the analogy with the opening scene of Sophocles' *Oedipus Tyrannus* is more striking. In [*Jewish Antiquities*], another passage reminiscent of Thucydides, he notes the effect of famine in the days of Joseph on the minds of the Egyptians in that it drove them to degrading means of subsistence. Again, in Solomon's prayer at the dedication of the Temple, he speaks in 1 Kings 8:33 of the time when "Thy people Israel are smitten down before the enemy, when they do sin against Thee." Josephus specifies, as the evils by which the Jews will be smitten "unfruitfulness of the soil or a destructive pestilence" [in *Jewish Antiquities*]. This picture is reminiscent of the plague from which Thebes is wasting away at the beginning of Sophocles' *Oedipus Tyrannus*. The plague has afflicted the blossom of the land and its herds, and it is manifest in the barren pangs of women. The word νοσος used by Josephus in [*Jewish Antiquities*] is a leitmotif throughout the play. Apollo is appealed to as a deliverer from the sickness which has afflicted the city [*Oedipus Tyrannus*]. The word likewise occurs in lines 217 and 303 with reference to the plague. Its central place in the play is shown by the fact that when the messenger comes to Oedipus with the news of the death of King Polybus, his first reaction is to ask whether he died through treachery or disease. Two lines later he repeats: "Ah, he died, it seems of disease?" A major theme of the play, as Knox remarks [in his *Oedipus at Thebes*, 1957] is Oedipus' περιπετεια from fame and honor to utter uncleanliness, so that we find him at last a pollution that must be covered up. And at the end of the play the thought of disease (by implication, the plague) recurs, when Oedipus, blind and miserable though he is, asserts that neither disease nor anything else can destroy him. One is reminded likewise of the picture drawn by Hesiod in *Works and Days* of nature responding to man's sins, where the guilt of a single man can bring failure of harvests, pestilence, and miscarriages.

When Josephus summarizes Solomon's character, he singles out his good fortune, wealth, and wisdom as the respects in which he surpassed all other kings. Hiram congratulates Solomon on his present good fortune [in *Jewish Antiquities*] when Solomon is anointed as king. The theme of good and bad fortune is, of course, a commonplace in literature generally, but it is perhaps more distinctive of Sophocles' Oedipus because of the ironic element than it is of any other ancient literary character. Thus, when Oedipus is one step from knowing the terrible truth about his identity, he reaches the highest point of hope and confidence and proclaims (most ironically from the point of view of the audience), "I hold myself the son of Fortune, that gives good" ([*Oedipus Tyrannus*]). The chorus exclaims after Oedipus discovers his identity, "Where, where is the mortal who wins more of good fortune than just the seeming?"

Josephus exaggerates Solomon's wealth in a number of places. Thus, while 1 Kings 5:3 declares that his provisions for a single day were a hundred sheep, [*Jewish Antiquities*] states this as a hundred fatted lambs. Similarly, Oedipus is presented as a wealthy king, and part of the effectiveness of the play is the great irony in Tiresias' statement that the man whom Oedipus is seeking (namely, Oedipus himself, as it turns out) as the murderer of Laius is in reality a blind man, though he now has sight, and a beggar, though he now has riches. Of course, wealth is hardly a trait restricted to Solomon and Oedipus, but in the context of all other parallels, it acquires added significance.

In Josephus' account of 1 Chron. 29:19, David's prayer is that Solomon may be given a sound and just *mind* [*Jewish Antiquities*]. And again, in contrast to Solomon's own request in 1 Kings 3:9 for an understanding heart (*lev*), Josephus' Solomon requests a sound mind ... and good practical wisdom .... One of the outstanding characteristics of Oedipus, as Knox has so well illustrated, is the use of intelligence. Just as Solomon gains a great reputation through the ingenuity he shows in solving riddles, so Oedipus gained his through solving the riddle of the Sphinx by his intelligence. Oedipus remarks in [lines] 396-398 that he used only his intelligence, unlike Tiresias, who might have used the birds to find his information. Again, the intellectual rivalry between Oedipus and Tiresias culminates in Oedipus' taunting Tiresias with failure of his νουσ: "You are blind in ears and mind and eyes." As Knox [*Oedipus at Thebes*] following a suggestion of Jebb, has remarked in a pregnant note, the first part of the very name of Oedipus is close in sound to, and thus reminiscent of, οισα, "to know," a word that is constantly on Oedipus' lips. In-

deed, as Knox continues, it is his knowledge that makes Oedipus the decisive and confident τυραννοσ. Similarly, Josephus remarks of Solomon, "It was not gold or silver or other form of wealth that he asked to be bestowed upon him, as a man and a young one might have done—such are considered by most men as almost the only things worthy of regard and as gifts of G-d," but wisdom that he chose ([*Jewish Antiquities*]; cf. 1 Kings 3:6, 11).

The primary example of Solomon's wisdom, cited in 1 Kings 3:16-28, is his adjudication of the case of the two harlots. In an addition to 1 Kings 3:16, Josephus stresses the difficulty of the case and notes that it was troublesome to find a solution, adding "I have thought it necessary to explain the matter about which the suit happened to be, in order that my readers may have an idea of how difficult the case was" [*Jewish Antiquities*]. He is presenting the case, continues Josephus, as a lesson in sagacity for his readers, so that if a similar situation occurs, his readers may be able to give a ready solution.

To magnify Solomon's wisdom by increasing the difficulty of the problem, Josephus, unlike 1 Kings 3:18, asserts that it was in the same room, on the same day, and at the very same hour that the two women gave birth to their respective sons, whereas 1 Kings states the second woman gave birth in the same house to her child on the third day after the first. The tale is dramatized further by Josephus, for whereas 1 Kings 3:18 states in a factual way that there was no one but the two women in the house at the time, in Josephus' version one of the women bitterly complains that the other "contemptuously relying on the fact that we were alone and that she had no one to fear who can convict her . . . stubbornly persists in her denial." Likewise, 1 Kings gives no indication that Solomon waited for others to resolve the case, but Josephus exaggerates Solomon's wisdom by asserting that when all others had failed to give a judgment but were mentally blinded as by a riddle, Solomon alone was able to devise a plan to determine the true mother. Now it is true that wisdom is a common trait for heroes to possess, but it is this striking addition which makes the story parallel to that of Oedipus, who likewise succeeded after all others had failed to solve the Sphinx's riddle and who, though mentally alert at that time, is blind to his own identity and at the end of the play puts out his own eyes.

Again, there is added drama when, after Solomon orders the children cut in half, all the people secretly make fun of the king as a mere boy, an incident not recorded in 1 Kings 3:25. Finally, Josephus expands the statement in 1 Kings 3:28 of the impression made by the case upon Solomon's subjects; in Josephus' narrative they regard the judgment as a great sign and proof of Solomon's prudence and wisdom. It is interesting to note that while the Midrash elaborates on the wisdom shown by Solomon in this judgment, it emphasizes G-d's role in bringing on the case and the heavenly voice ratifying the verdict, whereas in Josephus the focus of attention is on Solomon and on his human wisdom. Moreover, in the Midrash the litigants are said to have been not women but spirits; in Josephus the women are more human than ever, and the drama is consequently heightened. Moreover, in the midrashic literature, Solomon emerges as a prototype of the talmudic sage, for he is able to analyze the laws revealed to Moses and to give reasons for the commandments. It is Solomon's great mastery of the Torah that is praised, unlike Josephus, who shows Solomon's wisdom as a king and judge.

Solomon's wisdom is further exaggerated by Josephus' expansion of the 3,000 proverbs and the 1,005 songs that he composed to 3,000 *books* of parables and similitudes and 1,005 *books* of odes.

In particular, appealing to his educated Greek audience, trained in philosophy, Josephus stresses philosophical study of nature. According to Josephus' addition to 1 Kings 5:13, there was no form of nature with which Solomon was not acquainted or which he passed over without examination. It is this knowledge of the world of nature that had been stressed by Josephus' predecessor who had composed the Book of Wisdom and who had put into the mouth of his alleged author Solomon the statement that G-d had given him "an unerring knowledge of the things that be, to know the ordering of the world and the working of the elements," (presumably the four elements basic to Greek philosophy).

In view of the popularity of charms and amulets, as indicated in the magical papyri, it is not surprising that Josephus emphasizes this aspect of Solomon's wisdom. Conybeare [in "The Testament of Solomon," *Jewish Quarterly Review* 11 (1898-99)] conjectures that the *Testament of the Twelve Patriarchs* in its original form may have been the very collection of incantations which, according to Josephus, was composed by Solomon. But, on the whole, Josephus emphasizes the human wisdom of Solomon.

Josephus elaborates considerably on the account in 1 Kings 9-10 of Solomon's wisdom. He notes that Hiram, the king of Tyre, sent Solomon tricky problems and enigmatic sayings, requesting to be relieved of his difficulties. Because Solomon was clever and keen-witted, he solved them all through the force of reason, and discovering their meaning, he brought them to light. Their passion for learning is, indeed, said to have been the main bond of friendship between Hiram and Solomon [in *Contra Apionem*].

Solomon's wisdom is considerably magnified in Josephus' retelling of Solomon's meeting with the Queen of Sheba. Josephus avoids emphasizing the magical element, such as the tale in the Midrash's account of the hoopoe who reported to King Solomon (who understood the languages of birds and beasts) that there existed a land ruled by the Queen of Sheba which was not yet subject to him. Instead we read in what Ullendorff [in "The Queen of Sheba," *Bulletin of the John Rylands Library* 45 (1962-63)] calls Josephus' "smartened up" version of the biblical story, that the Queen of Sheba, who ruled over Egypt and Ethiopia, and who was thoroughly trained in wisdom and worthy of wonder in other respects, conceived a strong desire to meet Solomon because she had heard reports about his excellence and understanding every day. Josephus expands the account in 1 Kings 10:3 of how Solomon answered all her questions and wins her admiration by mentally grasping with ease the ingenious problems which she set before him and by solving them more quickly than anyone could have expected. In a further build-up of Solomon's wisdom, Josephus says that it was because kings everywhere could not believe that what was told about Solomon's virtue and wisdom was accurate because of its extravagance, they desired to see him with their own eyes (1 Kings 10:24, [*Jewish Antiquities*]).

The speed with which the wise man works is a commonplace, but it is particularly important to the effectiveness of Sophocles' Oedipus. As Knox has noted [*Oedipus at Thebes*], the characteristic action of Oedipus is the fait accompli; the characteristic word used to describe him in the play is ταχυσ, "swift"; even after his identity is revealed it is still characteristic of Oedipus, as we see in such statements of his as "Take me away from this place as quickly as possible;" "hide me away as quickly as possible" ..., and "throw me out of this land as quickly as may be." Indeed, one of the themes of the play is the danger of speed; for those who, like Oedipus, are quick to think things out are not infallible. Knox has rightly remarked that the swift action of Oedipus is founded on reflection, which, in turn, is the working of a great intelligence. Again, as Knox has remarked, the bitterest word of condemnation which Oedipus can hurl at both Creon and Tiresias is "stupid".

Beyond the seeming parallels between Oedipus and Solomon, Josephus has Hellenized his portrait of Solomon in yet other ways. Thus, whereas in 1 Chron. 22:9, G-d promises David that He will give Solomon "rest from all his enemies round about," in Josephus this promise is put in terms familiar to the student of Thucydides, Xenophon, and Lysias, namely, peace and freedom from war and civil dissension. Adonijah's request in 1 Kings 1:51 that Solomon swear that he will not slay him is Hellenized by Josephus, so that Solomon is asked to pledge to bear him no malice. This phrase, meaning not to remember past injuries, to pass an act of amnesty, is used by Thucydides, one of Josephus' favorite authors, in his description of the Megarians, who recall their exiles, first binding them by the most solemn oaths to bear no malice.

Thackeray has noted the Homeric echo in Josephus' addition to the prayer in 1 Kings 2:12 for Solomon at the beginning of his reign. In Josephus' version, the people pray that his affairs end well and that he may complete his reign at a sleek and utterly happy old age. This is highly reminiscent of the famous scene in the Odyssey in which Tiresias foretells to Odysseus that his death will come from the sea, "a death so gentle that shall lay thee low when thou art overcome with sleek old age." The same words are found when Odysseus repeats Tiresias' prediction to Penelope: "And death shall come to me myself from the sea, a death so gentle that shall lay me low, when I am overcome with sleek old age."

Since much of Josephus' projected audience was sympathetic to Stoicism, it is not surprising that there are a number of Stoic touches in his narrative. The incense which, according to Josephus' addition to the biblical narrative, was burned at the dedication of the Temple, was a sign of G-d's presence in His newly consecrated home. Norden [in *Agnostos Theos*, 1923] remarks that the phrase used by

Josephus in Solomon's dedicatory prayer for the Temple, that G-d was now present and not far removed, shows Stoic influence. Similarly in Josephus' version of Solomon's prayer at the dedication of the Temple, he asks that if the Jews should in the future gather in the Temple praying to be saved, G-d should listen to them as though He were within. Again, whereas 2 Chron. 7:3 reports that when the fire from heaven consumed the sacrifice at the dedication, the people bowed down at the sight and gave thanks to G-d, Josephus adds that the people interpreted the divine manifestation as a sign that G-d would thereafter dwell in His temple and consequently fell to the ground and prayed. Finally, in dedicating the sanctuary at Bethel, King Jeroboam uses Stoic terminology in telling his people that every place has G-d in it, that there is no place set apart for Him, but He hears and watches over His worshippers everywhere. Likewise, as Norden remarks, the phrase that G-d sees all things and hears all things is reminiscent of Homer, *Iliad.*

The Stoics, who, as Norden remarks, were so fond of calling their wise men in need of naught. . . . and self-sufficient. . . . Predicated these qualities also for G-d. Josephus also uses the word as an attribute of G-d, for he has Solomon say in his prayer at the dedication that the Deity stands in need of nothing and hence does not require gratitude [*Jewish Antiquities*].

One finds Stoic overtones also in the non-biblical addition in Solomon's prayer when he says that there is no more fitting way to appease G-d than through the voice (ωνη) "which we have from the air and know to ascend again through this element". Zeno the founder of Stoicism, and Chrysippus, his follower, define sound as smitten air or a smiting of the air.

The terminology which Josephus adopts, even in religious matters, is calculated to be intelligible to his pagan Greek readers. Thus in Solomon's prayer he says that he has built the Temple to G-d's name so that when sacrificing and seeking good omens the Jews may pray to Him. The word used for obtaining good omens is, as Schorr in his commentary has noted, completely strange to Judaism, since it is the pagan practice of obtaining favorable signs in a sacrifice.

In general, Josephus attempts to tone down the miraculous and supernatural element in his narrative, since he apparently thought that such details might appear incredible to the Greek reader. Thus, whereas 1 Kings 8:10 states with emphatic simplicity that "the cloud filled the house of the L-rd," Josephus gives a more precise and rationalized description of the cloud in [*Jewish Antiquities*]. It was not, he says, like a swollen rain-cloud but diffused and temperate. Josephus carefully avoids categorically equating the cloud with G-d but noted instead that it produced in the minds of the people an impression and belief that G-d had taken up residence in the Temple. The Midrash remarks that at the dedication of the Temple a heavenly voice was heard to proclaim: "You all shall have a share in the world to come," but Josephus avoids such an account of supernatural intervention.

N.G. Cohen, in ["Josephus and Scripture: Is Josephus's

Treatment of the Scriptural Narrative Similar throughout the *Antiquities* I-XI?" *Jewish Quarterly Review* 54 (1963-64)], argues that Josephus takes considerably greater liberty with his biblical material in the part of the ***Antiquities*** which parallels the five books of Moses than he does in the later books. Perhaps this is so because the midrashic traditions for these books were more highly developed, since these were the portions of the Bible that were constantly read and expounded in the synagogue from week to week. But the present study of Solomon shows that Josephus, here as elsewhere, in his eagerness to appeal to his Greek-speaking and Greek-educated audience, made very considerable changes in his version. These modifications are, in fact, generally paralleled by modifications found elsewhere in his Midrash-like paraphrase of the Bible.

Shaye J. D. Cohen   (essay date 1979)

SOURCE: *Josephus in Galilee and Rome: His Vita and Development as a Historian*, E. J. Brill, 1979, 277 p.

[*In the excerpt below, Cohen discusses* Jewish War, *asserting that Josephus manipulated the facts to explain and justify his own involvement in the war and to ensure his social position in Rome.*]

Since the literary relationship of ***BJ*** [***Bellum Judaicum***] to *V* [*Vita*] is not entirely clear, and since we depend almost exclusively on ***BJ*** and *V* for our knowledge of the early stages of the war, the only way we shall be able to separate historical fact from Josephan fiction is by historiographic inquiry. What are the aims and methods of both works? In this chapter we restrict our discussion to the relevant features of ***BJ***.

A. *Date*

Since we are interested in the variations between ***BJ*** and *V*, we need to know the date of each work. For ***BJ*** two views are encountered. The *communis opinio* places ***BJ*** between 75 and 79 CE [Christian Era]. Evidence: ***BJ*** 7.158-161 mentions the dedication of the *Templum Pacis* which took place in 75 (Dio Cassius 66.15.1). Vespasian himself, who died 23 June 79, received copies of ***BJ*** from the obsequious author (*V* 361 and *CA* [*Contra Apionem*] 1.50-51). Hence book seven, at least, is later than 75 and no part of ***BJ*** is later than mid-79. Laqueur and Eisler introduce a new factor, re-edition, which allows them, in spite of this evidence, to propose a broader time span. Eisler determines that the first Greek version of ***BJ*** was finished in 71 but the work gradually expanded until, by 79, it reached its present dimensions, although Eisler agrees with Laqueur that even after 79 ***BJ*** was frequently revised. Let us examine the evidence for these views.

Was Vespasian presented with the entire ***BJ***? At first sight *V* 361 and *CA* 1.51 suggest he was, but "the books" ... does not necessarily refer to all seven books of ***BJ***. Agrippa's letter (*V* 365) shows that Josephus circulated books (or sections) of ***BJ*** separately (probably one book per roll) and that Agrippa had to request future installments. . . . Only in *V* 367 does Josephus clearly refer to a completed product ("when my history was polished off "...), but there he does not mention presentation or dedication. Our *terminus ante quem* is not so unambiguous after all. Furthermore, a date of publication under Titus seems rather attractive. Only Titus gave *BJ* the royal *imprimatur* and only he appears in the proem to *BJ*. It was Titus who rescued Josephus at Jotapata. Vespasian is certainly not treated badly by *BJ* but Titus fares much better. The son's speeches are more numerous and more magnificent. Josephus never tires of lauding this *amor ac deliciae generis humani*, a great warrior who does not delight in slaughter but pities the surviving populace of Jerusalem. He wants to save the city and does not boast of its capture. He is not responsible for the barbarities committed by the Jews and he condemns those committed by the Romans. He has no desire to destroy the temple and even tries to save it. Vespasian receives this treatment only occasionally (3.127, he allows the Jews of Galilee to repent; 4.412, he pities the misfortunes of Jerusalem). His treachery towards the Jews, based on the advice of his friends, "there is nothing impious when fighting against the Jews," receives no apology. Titus would never have pursued such a policy. The contrast is best explained by the view that *BJ* was completed under Titus.

Another observation confirms. Aulus Caecina Alienus was an enthusiastic Vitellian in the troubles of 69 until he deserted to the Flavians before the battle of Cremona. Tacitus analyzes Caecina's motives:

> The historians, who, after the Flavian house rose to power, have narrated the memorable features of this war, have reported that Caecina and Bassus were motivated by concern for peace and love of the state (*cura pacis et amor rei publicae*), but the desire for adulation has corrupted their report; it seems to me that Caecina and Bassus destroyed Vitellius through their innate fickleness and because, after Galba had been betrayed, loyalty soon lost its value through the competition and jealousy among Vitellius' followers to be the first to cross over to Vespasian. (an elucidatory paraphrase of *Historiae* 2.101.1)

If any historian was a Flavian lackey, it was Josephus. And yet, *BJ*'s account of Caecina's activities stresses his treachery. Nowhere do we encounter *cura pacis et amor rei publicae*. Caecina plotted treason, deserted to Antonius, and, viewed as a traitor, was bound by the soldiers. Even Vespasian's gifts barely covered the disgrace of his treason (644). Josephus' hostility to Caecina is surely explained by the events of 79 when, just before the death of Vespasian, Caecina was executed by Titus for an alleged plot against the emperor (Dio 66.16.3; Suetonius *Titus* 6). Titus' favorite explained in his history that Caecina had always been treacherous and unfaithful. The earlier Flavian propaganda, castigated by the Roman consular, had to yield to the political exigencies of a later period. Thus *BJ* 4.634ff clearly obtained its present form no earlier than mid-79. We have no reason to regard it as an insertion into an earlier text, since the narrative, coherent, direct, and concise, is the last of a series of passages in *BJ* 4 about the dynastic wars of 69. A post-Vespasianic date for *BJ* 4 seems assured.

If *BJ* 1-6 was completed under Titus, *BJ* 7 is Domitianic. Its style, markedly inferior, is rather close to *AJ* [*Antiqui-*

tates Judaicae] and *V*. The literary assistants have not been at work here. A telling indication of date is the attitude towards Domitian. The first six books mention Domitian only three times and only in the continuation of the passage of Flavian propaganda discussed above (on Caecina). The references are bald statements with only moderate adulation ("the greatest portion of the hopes for victory" rested upon Domitian, 646). Perhaps Josephus is hiding Domitian's cowardice and incompetence, gleefully recounted by Tacitus, but *BJ* 1-6 knows no royal heroics or royal victories. Contrast *BJ* 7.85-88 which extols Domitian's prowess. The Germans are terrified merely by the rumor of his approach. Domitian single-handedly subdues rebellious Gaul. The Domitian of book seven is much more forceful than the Domitian of book four. Nor does Josephus neglect to mention that Domitian, who took no part in the destruction of Jerusalem, rode in the triumphal procession, magnificently attired and astride a great horse. Comparable details are lacking for Vespasian and Titus. Since *BJ* 6 forms an admirable close for the entire work, *BJ* 7 is presumably a Domitianic addition.

This view is supported by the characterization of John in *BJ* 7.264. *BJ* 4-6 frequently accuses the revolutionaries of lawless behavior and impiety. Which particular crimes are intended by theses words? Some of the accusations are general condemnations, but some have contexts specific enough to show that the crimes are of two sorts: capital crimes, notably murder, and interference with the temple cult. The laws which the brigands violate and the Romans defend are the universal norms of society and cult. No reference here to Jewish Halachah, e. g. the laws of purity, food taboos, festivals, prayer, etc. The two crimes are combined when Josephus charges the revolutionaries with polluting the temple. The temple is defiled not by a violation of Halachah (ritual impurity) but by a violation of universally held principles (the crimes of murder, etc.). Only once (*BJ* 5.100) does Josephus state that the temple was invaded by impure men but there—even if the word is used in its literal cultic sense—he forgets to mention that the temple was polluted by the ritual impurity. John is guilty of impiety for using the sacred timber, of sacrilege for using the sacred wine and oil, but not of a violation of the laws of purity. Contrast *BJ* 7.264 which defines John's impiety as the violation of the traditional laws of purity. He is accused too of serving improper food. This Halachic formulation of the crimes of the revolutionaries is not found in *BJ* 4-6 but typifies the attitude of *AJ*. Food taboos and laws of purity were prominent subjects in the Rabbinic discussions at Yavneh (and, indeed, in all varieties of sectarian Judaism). *BJ* 7.264 tells the Rabbis that John, a long time friend of Simon ben Gamaliel, was really a wicked Jew who violated the most important canons of Rabbinic Judaism. Cf. *V* 74-75 which describes John's ostensible concern that the Jews of Caesarea Philippi use only pure oil and not violate the traditional laws. *V* labels John's concern a sham, while the parallel passage in *BJ* 2.591 omits the religious polemic. The outlook and concerns of *BJ* 7 seem closer to those of *AJ* and *V* than *BJ* 1-6.

No matter what date we adopt for *BJ* 1-7, Laqueur's idea, frequent re-edition, may be correct since ancient book production afforded ample opportunity for changes and corrections. But *BJ* provides not a single convincing example of an interpolated passage and is Josephus' most polished work. Its tone and style are maintained at a uniformly high level at least through book six. The central tendentious elements appear quite consistently and the narrative is almost free of explicit contradictions (implicit contradictions are, of course, another matter). In all these respects *V* and *AJ* compare unfavorably, and all these make extensive revision or re-edition of *BJ* 1-6, after its initial publication, unlikely. Had Josephus rewritten, he would not have rewritten so well nor so consistently. So in *BJ* 1-6 we have a relatively coherent uniform work finished as a whole before 81.

B. *Literary Technique*

BJ is a good representative of rhetorical historiography. Everywhere *BJ* evinces a fondness for colorful detail, anecdotes, exaggerations, drama, and pathos. A few examples of these features from books two and three will suffice. 100,000 Galileans congregate against Josephus at Taricheae. The force of the catapault is illustrated by some rather amusing anecdotes. Corpses are hurled about, women shriek, the earth streams with blood. What could be more dramatic than the scene in the stadium of Tiberias? While Josephus is addressing the crowd, he hears some shouts and turns around—a knife at his throat! He jumps down and escapes.

One of the major motives of *BJ* is to blacken John. Josephus employs both direct pronouncements, which stop the narrative and describe John's character (occasionally on the basis of rhetorical common-places), and indirect charaaterization, the deft arrangement of material so as to produce a desired impression. Thus, the Galileans themselves, not Josephus call John "the conspirator against the community." The masses gladly denounce John's followers. The Jerusalemites do not believe John's charges and attack those who accepted them. In these passages it is not Josephus the narrator but the actors of history who give the desired effect.

We have already discussed (in chapters two and three) *BJ*'s fondness for thematic structure. The description of the Galilean war in *BJ* 2 is arranged not chronologically but thematically. The lists of those cities which attacked the Jews or were attacked by them combine data from different periods and render impossible an exact reconstruction of the events of 66. The catalogue of fortified cities (*BJ* 2.573-575) is an obvious parallel. A fourth passage too, the list of generals selected after the victory over Cestius (2.562-568), may be thematic. We shall return to this point in chapter six below.

C. *Aims*

In true Thucydidean fashion the proem to *BJ* claims that the Jewish war was the greatest of all time. It is no surprise that Josephus presents himself as one of the greatest generals of this war, hence of all time. His vanity is notorious. Vespasian muses before Jotapata that if he could only capture Josephus, "the most sagacious of his enemies", the fall of Judaea (sic!) would be swift and inevitable. The Jews too realize Josephus' greatness. They can suffer no

ill when he is present. All Jerusalem bewails his reported death. The rebels want to kill him more than anyone else.

Josephus displays his greatness by portraying himself as the ideal general. Here is Cicero's description (*De Imperio Cn. Pompei* 13 (36)):

> Non enim bellandi virtus solum in summo ac perfecto imperatore quaerenda est, sed multae sunt artes eximiae huius administrae comitesque virtutis. Ac primum quanta innocentia debent esse imperatores! quanta deinde in omnibus rebus temperantia! quanta fide, quanta felicitate, quanto ingenio, quanta humanitate!

This list of qualities is elucidated and explained by the orator. A general is free of avarice and ignoble passions, always self-controlled, never cruel to the conquered, readily approachable by the citizens, a fine speaker, endowed with great *auctoritas* and *felicitas*. Onasander, an author of the first half of the first century CE, has a similar description. I excerpt those terms (from 1.1 and 2.2) which correspond to the dominant elements of the Ciceronian passage. The origin and development of this tradition are of no concern here, but it is clear that Josephus was familiar with this conception. His Vespasian is an ideal figure and he, like Cicero, calls Pompey a "good general" because of the general's preference for goodwill to terror.

Josephus' greatness is demonstrated by *BJ* 2.568-584, the first part of his description of his own actions in Galilee. He and other nobles are chosen as generals by an assembly. To enhance his prestige he omits any mention of his two colleagues. His policy in Galilee has two aims: domestic support and military preparedness. To fulfill his first objective he strives for the goodwill of the natives, more specifically, of the well-to-do. He sets up a pan-Galilean judicial system with a supreme council of seventy and local courts of seven judges in every *polis*. In the military sphere he fortifies cities, recruits a large army, and trains it in Roman fashion. Josephus is concerned about the moral probity of his men. He cautions them to refrain from plunder and rapine; a clean conscience is the best ally. His forces do not rely on compulsion to obtain their supplies since one half of the recruits provision the other half. Here we see Josephus not only as a commander of a mighty army but also as a man concerned for *innocentia* and goodwill.

BJ 2.585-646 describes Josephus' encounter with John of Gischala and the rebellious cities. This section has two motives. The first is to disassociate Josephus from John. The two are generals in the same war fighting against the same enemy in the same province. But since John is the villain, the chief object of Josephus' hatred, *BJ* insists that John was Josephus' enemy from the very beginning and was thwarted only by the brilliant strategems of his rival. Further, in contrast to Josephus, the ideal general, John is mean and despicable. He lacks *fides*. He is a brigand who cheats the wealthy and corners the olive oil market to alleviate his poverty John knows how to pretend to be what he is not. He commands only a small band of Tyrian refugees.

The second motive is to continue the portraiture of the

ideal general. Josephus no longer pretends that he commands a large and well trained army. He emphasizes instead two aspects of his own character: *humanitas* and *ingenium*. He restrains his soldiers and the whole body of Galileans from beginning a civil war against John. He would rather not kill his opponents, not even a conspirator. He returns booty to the lawful owners. Josephus is very popular because he courts the goodwill of the Galileans. His enemies are motivated by jealousy. The *demos* of Jerusalem knows that John's charges are false. The loss of four cities is a testimony not to Josephus' unpopularity but to the delegation's secrecy. We also see Josephus' skill at escaping from dangerous situations. Onasander would say that Josephus is alert and prompt. He eludes the wrath of the Taricheaens by a stratagem, the adoption of a contrite pose which provokes the sympathy of the crowd and allows him to deliver a speech precisely calculated to enable him to escape. The vestiges of the disorder are removed by a second trick. Josephus boasts that he captured an entire city with but "empty ships and seven bodyguards". The two themes, humanity and ingenuity, are united in 630 where Josephus proudly proclaims that he won back four recalcitrant cities without recourse to arms and captured the delegates from Jerusalem by his schemes.

The final section of Josephus' account of his own actions is the extensive narrative of *BJ* 3. Both Vespasian and the Jews recognize his greatness. Here we see *virtus bellandi*. Josephus describes with particular pride the six tricks he employed while defending Jotapata against the Romans. He speaks as if he invented these techniques although at least four can be illustrated from independent sources. Whether Josephus actually used these tricks or not, is impossible to determine, but he considered it worthwhile to recount them all in *BJ* because they prove him a great general endowed with *ingenium*. Here are the tricks:

1. Josephus raises the height of the walls to counter the Roman earthworks. He protects the workmen by an awning of fresh oxhide which catches the Roman projectiles and extinguishes the fire brands. Everyone, especially Vespasian, marveled at his cunning. . . . Perhaps they marveled, but they should have known that all this is standard procedure in siege warfare. A writer of the Hadrianic period, who apparently does not know Josephus, mentions this use of raw hide as a routine matter. The same techniques were employed five hundred years earlier in the defense of Plataea in the Peloponnesian War, and were then made famous by Thucydides. Against the Spartan earthworks the townsmen raised the height of their wall while working under a covering of skins to protect them from missiles and fire brands.

2. The Romans know that the Jews are short of water and therefore decide to refrain from storming the fortress while famine and thirst waste the defenders. When, in response to this plan, Josephus hangs out garments dripping with water, the Romans think that the Jews have plenty of water and prepare to attack. This too is an old trick. Herodotus ascribes a similar stratagem to Thrasybulus of Miletus. Reinach appositely cites Florus 1.7.15 who draws from Livy 5.48.4 (Manlius hurls loaves of bread from the walls so that the besiegers will not suspect a shortage of food). Other examples are adduced by Frontinus Strategemata.

3. Josephus obtains supplies through unwatched gullies by covering the couriers with fleece so that they will be mistaken for dogs.

4. To blunt the effect of the battering rams, Josephus lowers sacks filled with chaff. The Romans retaliate by cutting the ropes which hold the sacks. Josephus boasts of his inventiveness but this technique is known already to Aeneas Tacticus 32.3 and others.

5. Josephus pours boiling oil on the Romans when they invade the fortress through the broken portions of the wall. The Romans suffer terribly. Josephus again boasts of this stratagem but it is well documented from many periods of siege warfare.

6. After recovering from the effects of the boiling oil the Romans press their attack. The Jews pour boiled fenugreek on the gang-planks which render them dangerously slippery. When the Romans stumble the Jews have an easy shot and the attack is foiled. This use of fenugreek is unattested elsewhere and may be Josephus' invention.

Like other ideal Roman generals Josephus enjoys *felicitas*. When the Romans capture Jotapata, Josephus receives aid from some supernatural force and escapes. In the cave he is nearly killed or forced to commit suicide but, having faith in God's protection, he emerges unscathed. Should he speak of chance or of divine providence? His prophetic visions, in which God forecast the approaching disasters, his priesthood, his prediction to Vespasian, his prophecy that the siege of Jotapata would last forty-seven days, all testify to his special relationship with the divine. Josephus thus possesses almost all the characteristics demanded by Cicero.

Josephus' description of his own actions does not fit one of the main motives of *BJ* as a whole. It is well known that *BJ* apologizes to the Romans for the Jews. Not all Jews revolted, only small bands of mad fanatics. These were in no way representative of the Jewish people or bearers of Jewish tradition. Those of them who finally maintained the revolt in Jerusalem and made it necessary for Titus (regretfully) to destroy the city, were a gang formed mainly of refugees who entered Jerusalem from the countryside and Galilee, established a tyranny, and forced the defenseless populace to fight against the Romans. Their motive was the selfish satisfaction of their lust for power, their deeds were execrable and beyond condemnation. They and not the Romans were responsible for the destruction of the temple (thus Josephus apologizes to the Jews for the Romans). Josephus is especially eager to exculpate the members of his own class, the priestly aristocracy and rich nobility. Even in the early stages of the war they opposed the revolutionaries.

But *BJ* also shows that these reconstructions are false. The masses often fight with gusto and abandon. Many members of the upper classes—including Josephus himself—participate in the war, at least until the winter of 67-68. Josephus realized that he had to separate himself from the process which led to the destruction of the temple and therefore claimed that he was an enemy, not an associate, of John of Gischala, his fellow general in Galilee and one of the most pernicious figures of the entire war. Josephus' conduct, unlike that of almost every other revolutionary leader, was above reproach. He was popular, respected, just, estimable, widely admired, and divinely guided. He was not a tyrant but an ideal general. He was loyal to his cause (thus demonstrating the quality of *fides*) although he knew that with the arrival of the Romans it was doomed to failure. His surrender was not betrayal—he would rather die than desert his people. He, a latter day Jeremiah, had divine authorization to cease the struggle. Inspired by his dreams he knew that he had to cross over to the Romans; Tyche herself already had done so. Josephus went not as a traitor but as God's prophet.

Josephus does not justify his surrender by appealing to the heinous character of the revolt. The tyranny theme is adumbrated in *BJ* 2.73 where, in 4 BCE [Before the Christian Era], the Jerusalemites disclaim any responsibility for an insurrection and blame a mob which entered the city and attacked the city populace as well as the Romans. *BJ* 2 emphasizes that the revolutionaries formed small bands separate from, and often opposed by, the *demos*. By the arrival of Albinus tyranny was everywhere. When the hostilities actually began, the apology becomes more frequent. Menahem was an "insufferable tyrant". The *demos* was helpless in the hands of the revolutionaries. Temple and city were polluted, God abandoned his sanctuary, the ancestral religion was polluted by illegitimate innovations. The priests and aristocrats opposed the war. The last occurrence of this motif in *BJ* 2 is 562a, which says that, immediately after the defeat of Cestius, the revolutionaries won over the peace party, some by force, some by persuasion. But with 562b the situation changes. In an orderly process, generals were chosen, only one of whom (Eleazar ben Ananias) had been involved in the previous action. Josephus points out that Eleazar ben Simon, who, he says, had been prominent in the war against Cestius (although not previously mentioned) and who would later lead the Zealots, received no recognition from the new regime. From this point until the fall of Jotapata we hear nothing of tyranny, pollution, and coercion. In Galilee Josephus was valiant and popular, an ideal figure. Only after Josephus was in the hands of the Romans does *BJ* claim that the inhabitants of the Galilean cities were basically pro-Roman but were forced by John and his ilk to participate in the war. Jerusalem was led by Ananus and some aristocrats who were anti-Roman but would oppose the fanaticism of the Zealots. Ananus prevented Simon bar Giora from tyrannizing over Akrabatene. The Jewish attack on Ascalon was obviously popular and no compulsion is mentioned. It is significant that even the leaders of Jerusalem who attempted to depose Josephus are not characterized as tyrants although they were opposed by the *demos*. The tyranny theme of the first part of *BJ* 2 returns again at the end of *BJ* 3 and especially in *BJ* 4 which graphically describes the overthrow of the government of Ananus by John and the Zealots.

Thus to explain his own participation in the war, Josephus has created a period of moderation and legitimacy sandwiched between periods of terror and anarchy. It is this

apology which has caused so much difficulty for modern historians. Why after the defeat of Cestius, when the revolutionaries were strongest, were generals selected who apparently had not been involved in earlier revolutionary activity? It seems clear that Josephus has intentionally obscured the early course of the rebellion. Ananus et al. must have been prominent in the revolutionary movement even before the defeat of Cestius. But by dividing the early history of the war into two parts, by severing almost all links between the two parts—and we remind the reader that the device used for separation, the list of generals, may be an invention of Josephan literary technique—, by characterizing the first period as tyrannical and the second as legitimate, Josephus was able simultaneously to condemn the fomentors of war and to justify his own involvement. When he needed an excuse for surrender, he invented divine authorization.

BJ explains why Josephus *stopped* fighting the Romans. A crucial issue it never faces is why Josephus *began* fighting the Romans. Why was he chosen as general? Why was he, a priestly aristocrat, a revolutionary? *V* attempts to provide the answer.

An excerpt from *Against Apion*

Those [historians] who rushed into writing were concerned not so much to discover the truth, notwithstanding the profession which always comes readily to their pen, as to display their literary ability; and their choice of a subject was determined by the prospect which it offered them of outshining their rivals. Some turned to mythology, others sought popularity by encomiums upon cities or monarchs; others, again, set out to criticize the facts or the historians as the road to a reputation. In short, their invariable method is the very reverse of historical. For the proof of historical veracity is universal agreement in the description, oral or written, of the same events. On the contrary, each of these writers, in giving his divergent account of the same incidents, hoped thereby to be thought the most veracious of all. While, then, for eloquence and literary ability we must yield the palm to the Greek historians, we have no reason to do so for veracity in the history of antiquity, least of all where the particular history of each separate foreign nation is concerned.

Flavius Josephus, in Josephus: The Life, Against Apion, Vol. I, *translated by H. St. John Thackeray, William Heinemann, 1926.*

R. J. H. Shutt (essay date 1980)

SOURCE: "The Concept of God in the Works of Flavius Josephus," in *Journal of Jewish Studies*, Vol. XXXI, No. 2, Autumn, 1980, pp. 171-89.

[*In the following excerpt, Shutt examines religious and Hellenistic cultural influences found in Josephus's sources and reflected in his writings.*]

By investigating the words, terms, and phrases used by Josephus of God, A. Schlatter [in his *Wie sprach Josephus von Gott?* Gütersloh, 1910] compiled an account of the nature of God in Josephus' writings, and concluded that Josephus' religious convictions influenced the nature of his writings, their contents, and the sources which he used. He noted particularly that Josephus held these views in the *Jewish Antiquities* and the *Contra Apionem*, which were written at least twenty years after the fall of Jerusalem and the destruction of the Temple in 70 A.D.

This article takes another look at Schlatter's theme.

The attitude of Josephus to the Jewish religion is important for the understanding of the man—and vice-versa—for he was of a priestly family, and proud of it; he was also a Pharisee, and writes with obvious knowledge of the sects in Judaism. It is also true that in the course of events leading up to the siege of Jerusalem he was captured by the Romans at Jotapata, and transferred his allegiance to his captors. During the siege he exhorted his fellow countrymen to surrender to the superior military strength of the Romans. After the war, he went to Rome, settled there, became a Roman citizen, and received a pension for his services. To some of the Jews, especially the Zealots, Flavius Josephus was a self-confessed traitor and renegade, and was denounced as such by Justus of Tiberias some twenty years afterwards. On the other hand, so-called Hellenizing Jews may have hailed him. The events of Josephus' career alone were sufficient to make his Jewish origin preeminently significant for him, highlighting his adherences to the Jewish religion and the Roman Empire; were these adherences mutually compatible, or completely contradictory?

He was closely involved personally in two cultures, and was bound to be rejected by the extreme wings of both. His involvement included familiarity with the customs and ways of life of them both. As to languages and communication, Josephus wrote in Aramaic the first edition of the *Jewish War*, which was later, with the aid of assistants, translated into Greek. He most probably knew also at least a smattering of Latin, and had some insight into the expressions, idioms and vocabulary of the Gentile culture represented by Rome and her Empire.

Against this background Schlatter's question 'How Josephus spoke of God?' is relevant. The aim of this article is to enquire whether the terms, words, and phrases used by Josephus to indicate and describe God and his nature show any appreciable influence of Greek language and culture. How did his life in Rome affect his Jewish background and upbringing? Did he experience any conflict? And if he did, how did he reconcile it?

Josephus' concept of God reflects and is influenced by Judaism which he professed, and by the Jewish Scriptures which were his main source in the early part of the *Jewish Antiquities*. The brief outline which follows indicates how closely he adheres to his source and shows sympathy with its contents.

Next the question also arises whether Josephus with his links with Rome and the non-Jewish world reflects also that Hellenistic environment and culture. Or, perhaps it may be so expressed, would it be fair to describe Josephus as a 'liberal' rather than a 'strict' Jew, judging from any other evidence which he provides?

God is addressed as Lord (*Despotēs*) by Moses and Joshua; also by Solomon, Izates (where *Kurie* is added), and by Nehemaiah. God is Father and Lord. (*Kurios* is often used in the Septuagint as a title of God.) God's Lordship is shown in and by the Creation, which Josephus describes with close reference to his Old Testament source, so that as Creator God is Lord, and vice-versa. Josephus also uses *Demiourgos as a synonym.* Consistently with this, God is the 'beginning and the end of everything' [*Jewish Antiquities* viii; *Contra Apionem* ii], to whom power, strength, and might are ascribed. As Judge, God dispenses justice; 'God's strength is justice'. This justice is that of the just judge, and is to be trusted. As Josephus indicates in the concluding sentences of the *Jewish War*, God indeed punishes wicked men and exerts a divine providence, but his anger is due to man's wickedness, not to God's cruelty.

Mighty as God is, creator, Judge, and Lord of all, he is also gracious and kind, and well-disposed towards the creatures of his creation. This is expressed and underlined by the use of various adjectives and nouns which convey the same thought. God is, for example, kindly, and gracious; he shows compassion and grants favours undeserved by the recipients, so that man can seek acceptance and find reconciliation with him. In almost every book of each of Josephus' works words occur expressing these themes: typical words used are *eumeneia, eunoia, pistis, gnomē,* and *pronoia.* The widespread examples are not the result of close literal adherence to either the Scriptural source or to the general outlook which these Scriptures display, in spite of the fact that Josephus states as his own opinion and belief, "For my part, I have recounted each detail here told just as I have found it in the sacred books. Nor let anyone marvel at the astonishing nature of the narrative or doubt that it was given to men of old . . . to find a road of salvation through the sea itself [*Jewish Antiquities* ii]." Josephus gives another instance in the story of Alexander of Macedon and the crossing of the Pamphylian sea, when "it pleased God to overthrow the Persian empire; and on that all are agreed who have recorded Alexander's exploits" [*Jewish Antiquities*]. Nevertheless, he admits characteristically that everyone is entitled to his own opinion. Similarly he concludes his narrative of Daniel with remarks on God's providence, and says "they are very far from holding a true opinion who declare that God takes no thought for human affairs" [*Jewish Antiquities* x]. Then again he adds, characteristically, that everyone is entitled to his own opinion. This emphasis on God's providence, expressed by Josephus frequently and in a variety of words, is consistent with his birth, upbringing, and religion as a Jew, and even if he cannot be absolved from the charge of being a renegade and traitor (which he indignantly rebuts in the *Life*), he comes in his final extant work to the spirited defence of Judaism in the *Contra Apionem*. According to the religion of the Jews God's providence includes his special relationship and covenant with his people, as their history claims to show and their religious observances reflect. Examples of this attitude can be further seen in his emphasis on the need for 'piety' and obedience to God's will, which if followed will gain his favour, and if neglected will earn his just displeasure. God indeed rules over all, omnipotent, yet gracious and merciful. "It was God, however," he writes, "who contrived that Chusis's counsel should seem better to his way of thinking." [*Jewish Antiquities* vii]. In this way he sums up the narrative of Ahithophel and Hushai, following his Scriptural source, and adding his own implicit approval.

The nature of God is indeed, according to Josephus, as he says in a revealing passage "varied and manifold". He does not exclude divine prophecy, and insists later in that passage that the previous narrative corroborates this view, while ascribing inability to foresee events to human ignorance and disbelief. He is content to state his view emphatically and without elaboration, and it is relevant to remember in this connection his own "prophecy" to Vespasian that he would become Emperor of Rome. In a somewhat similar way he comments on the completion of the Temple reconstruction by Herod, and the story that during the reconstruction no rain fell by day but only by night, so that the work was not interrupted, "and this story which our fathers handed down to us is not at all incredible if, that is, one considers the other manifestations of power by God" [*Jewish Antiquities* xv].

From the nature of God follow important conclusions and consequences for man and his conduct. Since man is God's creature, he should respond to God as his obedient creature. Hence the theme appears very frequently in Josephus of man's need to practise piety towards God, which is conducive to real happiness and prosperity. Conversely, impiety and disobedience incur the divine wrath and man's punishment, for God is judge of all. In recounting the slaughter of the Amalekites by Saul, for example, Josephus says that an important consideration was "the commandment of God, whom it was dangerous to disobey" [*Jewish Antiquities* vi]. He then goes on to add a detail and speculation of his own, that Saul spared Agag "for his beauty and his stature". Similarly, on the death of Nabal, Josephus says that David learned "that the wicked are pursued by God who overlooks no act of man but repays the good in kind, while he inflicts swift punishment upon the wicked".

So far, the nature of God and man's attitude towards him are mostly consistent with those of the Jewish Scriptures, which are Josephus' main source for the early part of the *Jewish Antiquities*. Examples have been noted of small additions and comments by Josephus, but he does not fail to give prominence to the view of his Scriptural source. He himself was a Jew, and a Pharisee of noble family, so that in general the picture which has so far emerged is as could be expected.

But, as was noted earlier, Josephus' career, and particularly his association with Vespasian and the Roman Empire, brought him in direct contact with Hellenism and non-Jewish thought and religion. It is therefore a relevant question whether these outside influences had any effect on his views and the expression of his beliefs. His attitude to the Jewish scriptures, and his exposition of their meaning, are of crucial importance in this matter.

Josephus' exegesis of Scripture is not always exact, and may not always be entirely dependable. Sometimes he adds, for no apparent reason and with no explanation, an unscriptural detail, such as e. g. "toward evening" [in *Jewish Antiquities* vii]. Marcus suggests that it may be due to a misunderstanding of 2 Sam xvii, 12. Similarly there may be underlying confusion in the statement "as impossible as it is for God to rain down from heaven torrents of barley or fine flour . . ." [*Jewish Antiquities* ix]. The Hebrew says "if the Lord made windows in heaven". The confusion may be between *kataraktas* 'windows' (LXX) and *katarraktas* 'torrents', as Marcus suggests. In fact, the accuracy which Josephus set himself as an ideal may not for him have involved meticulous attention to minute detail. Nevertheless, he shows some independence of thought in some of the conclusions which he draws. For example, in his comments upon Abraham he remarks, "It was Fate, I suppose, that prevailed and made the false prophets seem more convincing than the true one, in order to hasten Ahab's end" [*Jewish Antiquities* viii]. This is his own view, not found in Scripture. In the Esther story also, he gives it as his opinion that it was in accordance with God's will that the king accepted Esther's plea: his source states categorically that it was God's doing. In another place he gives it as his opinion that God urged Amaziah to war. This is not an independent view for it echoes the Scriptural source. The same formula occurs in the description of Josiah's death in battle against Necho king of Egypt, but here *pepromenē* is not found alone in all manuscripts, some of which (ROM) have *aladsoneias* also, i. e. 'and false boasting'.

The concept of 'Fate' and 'Fortune' and their possible connection with God are significant in Josephus. In addition to the references noted above, there are the following:— [*Jewish War* i] "Fate (*to chreōn*) laughed at his hopes." [*Jewish War* ii] The Pharisees "ascribe everything to Fate and to God". (*heimarmenē te kai theō.*) The close juxtaposition of Fate and God here could be taken to indicate that they are very close in meaning. But elsewhere he says that "the Pharisees say that certain events are the work of Fate (*heimarmenē*), but not all", whereas according to the Essenes "Fate is mistress of all things," but the Sadducees "do away with Fate" (the phrase used is almost identical with that in [*Jewish War* ii]).

In the account of the destruction of the Temple by fire in 70 A.D. the concept of Fate emerges rather strongly: [*Jewish War* vi] (Josephus' exhortation to the besieged to surrender) "In opposition to Fate (*heimarmenē*) I advise you and bring pressure to bear to save those condemned by God." In spite of Josephus' efforts, Fate and God prevailed.

[*Jewish War* vi] "God had long ago doomed the Temple to the fire, and now the fated circuit of the times was at hand, the tenth day" (*periodos* is here added to *heimarmenē*).

[*Jewish War* vi] The mourner for the conflagration of the Temple can "take comfort in *heimarmenē* which is unavoidable for living creatures, as well as for works and places." In a later comment [*Jewish War* vi] he says "it is impossible for men to avoid Fate (*to chreōn*), even when they foresee it." [*Jewish Antiquities* viii] "It was *to chreōn*, I suppose, that prevailed." This comment is given as Josephus' own opinion.

[*Jewish Antiquities* x] "It was Destiny (*tēs pepromenēs*), I believe, that urged him (Josiah) on to this course." Josephus again gives this as his own opinion. [*Jewish Antiquities* xvi] "For which reason we are persuaded that human actions are dedicated by her (i. e. *tuchē* or Fortune) beforehand to the necessity of taking place inevitably, and we call her Fate (*heimarmenē*) on the ground that there is nothing that is not brought about by her." Here, Fortune is said to be invincible, and is called Fate. Josephus is reflecting upon Herod's domestic tragedies. The passage . . . is wanting in the Latin version, and may possibly be an addition to the second edition of the *Jewish Antiquities*, prepared but not completed by Josephus. In any case, it represents a reflection made towards the end of his life when he wrote this work.

There are two other references to *tuchē*:

[*Jewish War* xvii] When men saw that he (Antipater) was vulnerable to the charges brought by the first witnesses and that *tuchē*, who had greatly favoured him before, was now openly delivering him to his enemies, they gave full rein to their implacable hatred of him. Also, [*Jewish War* xvi]. Was Herod attacked by *tuchē*?

When we ask whether any difference or development in Josephus' concept of Fate and Fortune can be detected between the *Jewish War* and the *Jewish Antiquities*, the references in both seem to indicate that Josephus himself thought that Fate is somehow operative in human affairs; he links it, in the *Jewish War*, with God. Three words *heimarmenē*, *pepromenē*, and *to chreōn* are used, in addition to *tuchē*. In the earlier part of the *Jewish Antiquities* the same applies, but in narrating events nearer his own time he introduces Fortune, which he then links with Fate, rather than, as previously, linking Fate with God. This would be consistent with Josephus' aim to write in terms understandable by non-Jewish readers, such as those Romans who expressed belief in the invincible Fortuna Romana favouring the Roman Empire.

But there are occasions when Josephus seems to have some misgivings about his narrative. For example, he seems almost apologetic about the inclusion of the story of Jonah [in *Jewish Antiquities* ix], prefacing it thus: "Since I have promised to give an exact account of our history, I have thought it necessary to recount what I have found written in the Hebrew books concerning this prophet." So Josephus only includes it, apparently grudgingly, because of the paramount needs of accuracy. At the end of his abbreviated summary he says, "And I have recounted this story as I have found it written down". With this statement he seems to breathe a sigh of relief, and proceeds with his narrative, omitting to mention the need for repentance which, as Marcus points out, is the main theme of the book of Jonah. Similarly, he might be thought to have misgivings about Elisha, and the blindness with which God struck the Syrians. He says that God was asked by Elisha "to blind the eyes of the enemy and throw a mist about them through which they would be unable to see

him." Marcus calls this mist "a rationalistic detail added by Josephus." It is not found in the Scriptural source.

What conclusions then can be drawn from the above evidence regarding Josephus' own views and attitude towards God?

It is certain that he remained deeply and inescapably influenced by his birth, background, and training as a Jew, and a Pharisee. His career brought all this into question; in particular his connection with Vespasian, Rome, and Agrippa. Attacks were made upon his personal character, according to the account in the *Life*, and upon his religion, so that he was represented as a political traitor and a renegade Jew. He was therefore obliged, by sheer force of events in his career if by nothing else, to consider these attacks seriously and to defend himself against them. His final work *Contra Apionem* is a spirited defence of Judaism as such. So he was born a Jew, and remained a Jew throughout his life, and was moreover not a little proud of his birth, upbringing, and religion.

Josephus asserts certain fundamental theological principles of Judaism, such as God's lordship, providence, creatorship, and overruling will. The understanding of these principles, and their expression in the religious life and conduct resulted in some tension within Judaism, and for Josephus, especially in the realm of politics, in conflict. This is borne out in the 'sects' of Judaism, to which Josephus refers at length, and in the political strife leading up to the siege and capture of Jerusalem in 70 A.D., in which Josephus took part.

In the course of his writings he provides important personal statements. His considered opinion is given, for example, in connection with the disobedience and punishment of the prophet whom he names as Jadon. (This is an addition to the Scriptural source.) "This came about, I think, in accordance with the will of God, in order that Jeroboam might not give heed to the words of Jadon, who had been convicted of lying." Josephus underlines in his comment his own belief in God's omnipotent will, which no lying can gainsay. This is consistent with a main theme of Judaism. Similarly, he ascribes "apparently to divine providence" Vespasian's despatch of a letter.

The similarity and the apparent divergences in the Scriptural language about God, and the statements and comments by Josephus on his Scriptural source are consistent with his steadfast adherence to the Jewish religion, in spite of everything.

As a result of his contact with the Gentile cultures, and partly also because he sought to express his Judaism in terms of that Greek culture, he used expressions and language which are neither Jewish nor Scriptural, in order to convey his meaning, e. g. God is present and "not far removed" [*Jewish Antiquities* viii], and "the Deity stands in need of nothing" [*Jewish Antiquities* viii]. Here we have reminders of some of the Stoic expressions and language about God.

Josephus would have been in modern terms a liberal Jew. This is the general conclusion which this article supports.

His references to Fate and Fortune, which were mentioned above, provide further examples. The Greek would be familiar with, and understand, the idea of Fate: similarly the Roman with the concept of Fortune. Josephus approximates them with God. So too with the Greek concept of 'insolence'. He refers to the madness of Gaius' insolence, and gives his reasons for recounting his death in full. Concluding his narrative of that event, he reverts to more familiar Jewish terms . . . "the story provides good evidence of God's power . . . It will teach a lesson in sobriety to those who think that good fortune is eternal, and do not know that it ends in catastrophe unless it goes hand in hand with virtue" [*Jewish Antiquities* xix]. His liberal attitude to his religion was reflected in his dealings with two influential leaders from Agrippa's jurisdiction who joined Josephus from Trachonitis. "The Jews", he says, "sought to compel them to be circumcised" [*Life*]. Josephus refused to permit compulsion, "saying that each man must worship God in accordance with the dictates of his own conscience and not under constraint". His view prevailed. His personal domestic life also reflected his liberal attitude. He was married three times. Divorce terminated one of these marriages. Thus Josephus was in some respects in harmony with the School of the more tolerant Rabbi Hillel, rather than that of the more rigid Shammai.

The circumstances of Josephus' career, if nothing else, forced him to come to terms with problems which confront most religions regarding Scriptures, their interpretation and exposition, the relationship with those of the same religion whose views are not identically the same, and the attitude towards others not of the same persuasion.

Magen Broshi   (essay date 1982)

SOURCE: "The Credibility of Josephus," in *Journal of Jewish Studies*, Vol. XXXIII, Nos. 1-2, Spring-Autumn, 1982, pp. 379-84.

[*In the following essay, Broshi discusses the credibility of Josephus's histories, comparing their data with that found in various Roman documents and battle commentaries.*]

Our knowledge of the last two centuries of the Second Commonwealth depends very substantially on the writings of Josephus. Matters such as his credibility, accuracy and sources are therefore foremost among the topics which should occupy scholarship.

The most obvious data for examination, it would seem to us, is 'archaeological' material. In many instances, numerous details provided by Josephus can be checked, including architectural data, and their accuracy confirmed. Such precision, where it can be established, is surprising, especially since the information was set down in writing years after Josephus had left Palestine. In addition, it is clear that in some cases he is describing objects that he cannot possibly have seen, let alone measured. Thus he probably never visited Masada or set foot on its summit, so he cannot himself have measured its walls. For sixty years preceding the Great Revolt, the desert fortress was occupied by a Roman garrison and civilians were not normally allowed entry. Even so, he writes in *War* (VII) that the walls of Masada were seven stadia, i. e., about 1300 m. long.

And so indeed they were. Similarly, he describes in *War* (I) the walls of Samaria-Sebaste, built by Herod, as being twenty stadia long (3720 m.). This figure also approximates to their length as unearthed.

The perimeter of the walls of Jerusalem is said by Josephus (*War* V) to extend to thirty-three stadia (6138 m.), whereas in Avi-Yonah's reckoning they were 5550 m. long; but this is a difference of merely 10%.

Again, the harbour of Caesarea built by Herod has been studied meticulously by A. Raban and he finds that Josephus's account of it is by and large correct. At Masada, too, the description of the northern palace (which Josephus calls the western palace, *War* VII) matches the remains as discovered. The same may be said of the width of the wall, eight cubits, which is close to 4 m. (*War* VII). On the other hand, the historian alludes to thirty-seven towers on the walls of Masada (*War* VII), whereas only twenty-seven were identified during the excavations. Either the excavators were unable to recognize all the towers, or Josephus's work contains a textual error, which may possibly be the fault of a copyist.

Further perusal of Josephus would undoubtedly reveal additional instances of similar archaeological data.

In Josephus' *War*, much of the data can be proved accurate and much of the rest reliably assumed to be so. They cannot always be ascribed simply to keen observation (cf. Masada) or to an exemplary memory (cf. the dates of minor military events). Thus in regard to geographical data, which can be checked exactly, the distances he gives are very often quite right. Jerusalem is said to lie 150 stadia from Jericho (about 30 km), and Jericho 60 stadia (some 12 km) from the Jordan (*War* IV). The distance between Jerusalem and Herodium is described as 60 stadia (about 12 km, *War* I); from Jerusalem to Gibeon, 50 stadia (10 km, *War* II); and to Gibeah of Saul, 30 stadia (about 6 km, *War* V). All these figures are reasonably accurate.

Another type of data concerning numbers of people cannot readily be verified but seems nevertheless reliable. Josephus' tendency grossly to exaggerate population figures is well known. Thus the inhabitants of Galilee are reckoned at more than three million (*War* VI). Josephus himself sensed that these numbers were incredible. Yet he outdoes even himself in his estimate, in the last cited passage, that in the census carried out under Cestius celebrants at the Passover sacrifices amounted to more than two million seven hundred thousand. At the same time this very same Josephus also gives modest round numbers likely to be quite correct. His information relating to the defenders of Jerusalem (*War* V) is an example of such reasonableness, namely that Simon son of Giora led ten thousand warriors and five thousand Idumeans, that John of Gischala commanded six thousand warriors, and that two thousand four hundred Zealots also joined him, and that the total involved was twenty-three thousand four hundred men. Another seemingly reliable figure is that of the ninety-seven thousand captives taken by the Romans in Jerusalem (*War* VI). These numbers stand out among inflated figures such as that of the corpses removed through one of the gates during the fifty days between May 1 and June

Stone relief from the Arch of Titus, depicting Titus's triumphant return to Rome with the spoils of the Jewish Temple following the fall of Jerusalem and the dismantling of the temple in 70 A.D.

A.D. 20, viz., one hundred and fifteen thousand eight hundred and eighty (*War* V; dates according to Niese). This precise number may appear credible but is in fact quite impossible.

Undoubtedly, the source of much of Josephus's accurate data was the Roman imperial commentaries, the *hupomnēmata*, specifically mentioned by him three times in his later works. Thus he answers Justus' accusations with the words: "Neither were you a combatant nor have you perused the *commentaries* of Caesar, as is abundantly proved by your contradictory account" (*Life*). Similarly against Justus he maintains: "This is no unsupported assertion of my own. The facts are recorded in the *commentaries* of the Emperor Vespasian" (*Life*). Finally, we read: "Even if, as they (Josephus' critics) assert, they have read the *commentaries* of the imperial commanders, they at any rate had no first-hand acquaintance with our position in the opposite camp" (*Against Apion*). Josephus does not actually state that he has read the Commentaries but he clearly made direct use of them. Moreover, as will be seen later, he drew material from them for his own writings, especially *War*, his earliest book.

What were these *commentaries*? According to one of the two principal schools of thought concerning them, the latest proponent of which is Bardon, they were memoirs written by Vespasian. Bardon admits that no such work is mentioned by the Roman historians, and expresses surprise that Vespasian should have shown any inclination for writing or found the time for it; but almost every emperor between Augustus and Nero did write memoirs. The other school is of the opinion that the *commentaries* were field reports of military commanders, in draft form or slightly edited.

The second view seems preferable, primarily because, as already noted by von Gutschmid, in the proemium to *War* Josephus castigates the available history books, an action unthinkable if a work by his patron, Vespasian, had figured among them.

Those who subscribe to the first theory suggest as another solution that the emperor's books was not published until after Josephus had completed writing *War*. But on the basis of the evidence already given here, there can be little doubt that he had them before him whilst working on the book. Moreover, the *commentaries* appear to have been used mainly during the composition of *War*; he seems to have resorted to them much less frequently, and possibly not at all, in his later works. But why does he not mention the *commentaries* in *War*? We share the opinion of those who believe that he avoided referring to them because he wished to emphasize his own status as an eye-witness. He wished to impress on his readers that he was no mere compiler relying on the evidence of others. "The industrious writer is not one who merely remodels the scheme and arrangement of another's work, but one who uses fresh materials and makes the framework of the history his own" (*War* I). He can hardly be expected to have admitted using the works of others after a statement such as this. It should be noted also that it is in his later writings that Josephus mentions the assistance he received in composing his Greek text, although it would surely have been in his first book that he would have most needed such help.

Having noted archaeological data drawn from the *commentaries*, and data which should probably be ascribed to military reports, geographical details and population statistics, two further types of evidence ascribed to the *commentaries* have now to be discussed, namely information relating to Roman military deployment throughout the empire and to military exploits and their dates.

The speech of Agrippa II (*War* II) has been studied thoroughly and von Domaszewski has found confirmation of the account it provides of the disposition of the Roman army. Recently, it has been claimed that this text does not reflect the situation in A.D. 66 but rather that of around A.D. 75, which would indicate—as we would in any case have assumed—that Josephus relied on *commentaries* dating not only from the period of the Great War but also on later *commentaries* found by him in the imperial archives.

Detailed reports on the activities of the Roman army and its various units appear at several other points in Josephus' works, for instance in his description of Titus's march from Alexandria to Caesarea (*War* IV), and in the listing, which bears the stamp of an actual military document, of Cestius' forces and their composition (*War* II). Josephus can scarcely have invented such matters or recorded them from memory, his own or another's. But the *commentaries* were not the source for "great" events alone. Many of the battle annals, even their minor details, smack of military field reports. An example is the account of the physique, looks, etc., of Sabinus the Syrian soldier who scaled the wall (*War* VI). It has the sound of a story told by military scribes, a tale on the basis of which medals were awarded.

Was Josephus always correct? Certainly not. His inaccuracies range from vagueness to blatant exaggeration. Shaye Cohen accuses him of "inveterate sloppiness". The index to Cohen's book [*Josephus in Galilee and Rome, his "Vita" and Development as a Historian*, 1979] goes so far as actually to include entries for "exaggerations", "inconsistency and sloppiness" and "corrupt transmission of names and numbers". Indeed, even if it is accepted that copyists were responsible for not a few of his mistakes (some of which have been hinted at already), it still cannot be denied that he was by nature somewhat negligent. The list of scholars who have deprecated his errors is long but suffice it to mention here the accusations of two eminent

archaeologists alone, since archaeology is the central theme of the present discussion. Albright remarks on "how inaccurate Josephus generally was in details . . ." [in the *Jewish Quarterly Review* 22 (1931-32)]. Vincent goes even further. "Il serait superflu", he maintains, "d'accentuer de nouveau la futilité de toute évaluation fondée sur les chiffres de Josèphe" [in his *Jerusalem de l'Ancien Testament* I, 1954]. However, a remark on the previous page, to the effect that a particular item of information is an "excellente approximation", reflects the reaction typical of scholars investigating Josephus' data.

This duality of sharp criticism alongside fulsome appreciation has consistently accompanied the scholarly treatment of Josephus' works. It has not been our intention here to prove that he is always exact or correct in every statement, but to show that his data are in many instances accurate, and that they stem from reliable sources to which he had access from the very beginning of his literary career.

Shaye J. D. Cohen   (essay date 1982)

SOURCE: "Masada: Literary Tradition, Archaeological Remains, and the Credibility of Josephus," in *Journal of Jewish Studies*, Vol. XXXIII, Nos. 1-2, Spring-Autumn, 1982, pp. 385-405.

[*Below, Cohen explores Josephus's account of the fall of Masada, contending that it does not square with accepted archeological facts.*]

Of all the numerous and distinguished accomplishments of Professor Yigael Yadin, none is so well known as his excavation of Masada. His popular book, *Masada: Herod's Fortress and the Zealots' Last Stand* (1966), found an appreciative audience in five languages and stirred up intense discussion among Jewish intellectuals. Unfortunately, perhaps because Professor Yadin has not yet published a complete report of his excavations, the scholarly world has not paid sufficient attention to his discoveries and their relationship to the narrative of Josephus. His book spawned numerous articles which sought to identify the occupants of Masada (the Sicarii) and to analyze the magnificent speeches placed by Josephus in the mouth of Eleazar ben Yair, the commander of the Sicarii, but these essays treat neither the archaeological remains nor the central historical problem, the credibility of Josephus. The precise identification of the Sicarii—were they a distinct revolutionary group, or were they, as Professor Yadin assumes, identical with the Zealots? —cannot help us to assess the reliability of Josephus' report that the Sicarii committed collective suicide. In his second speech to his followers Eleazar alludes to Plato, invokes the example of Indian philosophers, and declaims a philosophic essay on the immortality of the soul, but this wonderfully incongruous speech does not detract from the historicity of the narrative as a whole any more than an appropriate speech would have confirmed it. Professor Yadin's claim that his archaeological discoveries vindicate the Josephan account still awaits detailed discussion.

The incident at Masada shares many features with the other incidents [of mass suicide recorded in ancient history]. After a siege, the attackers breach the wall. Like the citizens of Abydus [in their war with Philip of Macedonia] the men of Masada build an inner wall. When it is clear that this wall too will fall, they assemble, again like the Abydenes, to deliberate their course of action. Eleazar advocates collective suicide because it guarantees the Jews their freedom and saves them from slavery. It also prevents the enemy from enjoying his victory. Eleazar tells his men that suicide will be a deed of "prowess and courage." They are convinced. They view the deed they are about to commit as an act of "manliness and good counsel." After each man has killed his wife and children, they gather all their possessions in one pile and set it ablaze. . . . Finally they kill themselves (in a fashion which accords with neither pattern), the last man alive also setting ablaze the building which contained the corpses. . . . Similarly Josephus accepts the prevailing attitude towards collective suicide. He does not explicitly praise the Sicarii, but the general tone of the narrative is favourable to them. Eleazar assures his followers that the Romans will be astonished and amazed at the manner of their death, and according to Josephus the Romans really were amazed, scarcely believing what they saw. The murder-suicide is an act of daring, an act of nobility. Even the references to "possession by a daimon" and "murder", which sound Livian, cannot change the impression that the historian, like the Romans, was amazed at the steadfastness of those who met a wilful death.

Some of the sixteen cases which parallel the episode at Masada are exaggerated or embellished products of the literary imagination. If any ancient historian loved exaggerations and embellishments, it was Josephus; we may therefore suppose that his Masada narrative is not an unalloyed version of the truth. This supposition is corroborated by Professor Yadin's archaeological discoveries and by analysis of the narrative itself.

According to Josephus, the death of the 960 inhabitants of Masada and the destruction of the palace and the possessions were the premeditated acts of all the people acting in unison. But the archaeological remains cannot be reconciled with this view. Josephus says that all the possessions were gathered together in one large pile and set on fire but archaeology shows many piles and many fires (in various rooms of the casemate wall, in some of the storerooms, in the western palace, etc.) . Josephus says that Eleazar ordered his men to destroy everything except the foodstuffs but archaeology shows that many storerooms which contained provisions were burnt. (In addition, Josephus reports that the Romans found arms sufficient for ten thousand men, as well as iron, brass, and lead—why weren't these valuable commodities destroyed?) Josephus says that the last surviving Jew set fire to the palace but archaeology shows that all the public buildings had been set ablaze. Josephus implies that all the murders took place in the palace (unless the women and children, after being killed, obliged their menfolk and the narrator by marching to the palace) but the northern palace is too small for an assembly of almost a thousand people.

Professor Yadin discovered three skeletons in the lower terrace of the northern palace and twenty-five in a cave on the southern slope of the cliff. He suggests that the twenty-five skeletons were tossed there "irreverently" by the Romans, but this suggestion will not do. If, as Josephus says, the Romans found 960 corpses in the palace, they would not have dragged twenty-five of them across the plateau in order to lower them carefully into a cave located on a slope where one false step meant death. This is not irreverence, this is foolishness. The obvious and simple procedure for the Romans was to take the corpses out of the palace and toss them over the nearest cliff. No, the twenty-five skeletons in the cave must be the remains of Jews who attempted to hide from the Romans but were discovered and killed. (Or did they commit suicide?) At the very least, then, archaeology reveals that Josephus' narrative is incomplete and inaccurate. The skeletons in the cave and the numerous separate fires cast doubt on Josephus' theory of unanimity of purpose and unity of action among the Sicarii in their final hours. Perhaps archaeology confirms other aspects of Josephus' narrative, especially his description of the site, but on these important points it contradicts him.

But even without the benefit of the archaeological discoveries we would know that something is wrong with Josephus' story. According to the historian, when the Jews saw that the Roman ram was about to breach the wall, they hurriedly built an inner wall out of wood and earth which could absorb the force of the ram. When they broke through the outer wall, the Romans tried the ram on the inner wall but without success. Therefore they set it on fire. So far, the narrative is plausible and probably true. The use of soft pliable material to blunt the effects of a ram, and the construction of an inner wall to replace an outer one which is about to be destroyed, were standard techniques in ancient siege warfare. The fact that the combination of these two techniques (the construction of an inner wall out of pliable material) is not readily paralleled elsewhere is double testimony to its veracity. Josephus cannot be accused of enriching his narrative with a tactic cribbed from a poliorketic manual, and the Sicarii are credited with a manoeuvre which befits their inexperience in siege warfare—who builds a wall out of wood? Further confirmation *may* come from archaeology. Some large wooden beams were stripped from the Herodian palace before its destruction by fire, perhaps to be used in the construction of this futile gesture. Confirmed or not, the story is at least credible.

But the story soon loses its plausibility. After being blown about by the wind, the fire takes hold of the inner wall. At this point the Roman assault should have begun. The wall was breached, the inner wall was rapidly being consumed, the army was ready. Instead, the Romans withdraw, postponing the assault until the following morning. Their only activity that night was to maintain a careful watch lest any of the Jews escape. This is incredible. Why withdraw when victory was so close? Even if it was late afternoon or evening when the fire finally took to the wall, a point which Josephus does not make clear, Silva could have stormed the fortress by night, just as Vespasian did at Jotapata. Why wait? Furthermore, since the wall was breached, the Romans will have had to maintain a careful guard not only in their camps but especially on the ramp, in order to prevent the Jews from attacking the tower and the other siege machines. And yet, according to Josephus, the Roman soldiers positioned both on the ramp and on the tower, the former only a few feet from the inside of the fortress, the latter able to survey all of Masada, were oblivious to the activities of that eventful night. They did not notice that 960 men, women, and children were slain, and that at least two large fires were set, one destroying the accumulated possessions of the Sicarii, the other destroying the palace and cremating the corpses. They did not hear the shrieks of the women and children or see that the plateau was ablaze or sense that anything unusual was afoot. When the Romans stormed the fortress the next morning, they suspected nothing. They expected a battle but found silence. Very dramatic but utterly incredible.

Drama was not the only reason for Josephus' invention of a premature Roman withdrawal and a careful Roman watch which saw and heard nothing. Josephus wanted Eleazar, the leader of the Sicarii, to make a speech in which he would publicly confess that he and his followers, those who had fomented the war, had erred and were now receiving condign punishment from God for their sins. Josephus even has Eleazar declare that God has condemned the "tribe of the Jews" to destruction because he wants the Jewish readers of the *Jewish War* to realize that the way of the Sicarii is the way of death and that the theology of the Sicarii leads to a renunciation of one of the core doctrines of Judaism, the eternal election of Israel. In order to allow Eleazar to confess his guilt and to display his rhetorical skills, and in order to allow the Sicarii to follow Eleazar's instructions and to destroy themselves in an orderly fashion, Josephus inserted a crucial but inexplicable pause in the Roman assault.

Eleazar made a second speech too. Entitled "On the Immortality of the Soul," it had for its major themes not Israel, God, and sin, but soul, death, and suicide. Its purpose was purely literary, to correspond to the speech which Josephus himself allegedly delivered at Jotapata under similar circumstances. Josephus gives us a *logos* and an *antilogos*, a speech in book III condemning suicide and a speech in book VII lauding it. The parallel between the incidents at Jotapata and Masada was developed further by the transference of the lottery motif from the former to the latter. If, as I have attempted to show, the occasion, content, and impact of Eleazar's speeches are fictitious, then the use of lots as described by Josephus must be fictitious too. Perhaps some of the Sicarii slew themselves in accordance with a lottery, but it is most unlikely that all of them did so. They had neither the opportunity nor the unanimity required for such an action. The idea that all of them did so was derived by the historian from his (very suspect) account of the episode at Jotapata.

Josephus needs no apology for these inventions and embellishments since practically all the historians of antiquity did such things. But if an apology were demanded, Josephus could respond that his narrative required inventiveness. If, upon storming the fortress, the Romans had discovered that the Sicarii had slain themselves, neither Josephus nor Flavius Silva nor anyone else could have known exactly what had transpired, since all the participants in the event were dead. Even the seven survivors, who are said to have reported to the Romans "everything that was said and done," could have known little. They were not present (though some might have been eavesdropping) when Eleazar exhibited his oratory—only the "manliest of his comrades" were invited. Before or during the actual killing they hid. Who could have told the Romans about the ten men drawn by lot and about the actions of the last man who set fire to the palace? Certainly not the women, safely ensconced in their cistern. If the Sicarii committed suicide according to Josephus' description, then that description must be a combination of fiction (inspired by literary and polemical motives) and conjecture. Surveying the corpses on the plateau, the Romans deduced that the Sicarii had killed themselves. Josephus, or his Roman informant, advanced more adventurous conjectures too. These conjectures may be true or false—ancient conjectures have no greater likelihood of being true than their modern counterparts—and we have seen already that some of them, at least, are false. The food supplies laid up by Herod the Great were discovered intact. Somebody, perhaps Josephus, believing that the food was still edible, conjectured that the Sicarii had intentionally spared their food from the destruction. Noticing a large pile of destroyed possessions and remembering some of the cases discussed above, someone conjectured that the Sicarii had gathered all their belongings in one place, oblivious to the fact that the fires and the smoke hid the remains of many such piles. The other conjectures can be neither verified nor refuted. Perhaps the Romans, like Professor Yadin, saw lots scattered about and deduced that a sortition played a role in the process of death. In addition to these motivated fictions and historical conjectures, Josephus' account also contains simple mistakes.

Is there any truth at all in this Josephan farrago of fiction, conjecture, and error? Did the Sicarii commit suicide? Did the Romans discover corpses when they arrived at the summit? The twenty-five skeletons in the cave show that Josephus' account is incomplete at best, but our question is whether *any* of the Sicarii preferred a self-inflicted death to flight, battle, or surrender. We might suggest that the Sicarii were captured by the Romans and massacred, or that they fought the Romans and were killed, and that Josephus, whose fondness for literary commonplaces and types is well known, substituted a collective suicide story for the truth. Perhaps. These conjectures, like those of Josephus himself, can be neither verified nor refuted, but we may readily believe that the Josephan story has a basis in fact. First, it is plausible. Many Jews committed suicide during the crucial moments of the war of 66-70, and, as we have seen above, many non-Jews also committed suicide rather than face their enemies. Second, the Masada story is too complex to be dismissed as a literary *topos*. It combines motifs from the two major patterns of collective suicide stories with motifs from the Jotapata episode. The whole is enriched with Josephus' own inventions. Finally, why should Josephus have invented such a story? He wished to show that the way of the Sicarii is the way of death, but death comes in many forms, and the Sicarii did not have to commit suicide to make this point clear. Death in battle would have served just as well. Had the Romans massacred the Sicarii, Josephus would have had no reason to disguise this fact. From the Roman point of view, the

Sicarii deserved death, since they had participated in the siege of the royal palace in Jerusalem in 66 CE, killing some Roman soldiers. And if Silva refused to take any prisoners, no one could have argued with his wisdom, for who would want a slave who could not be trusted with the kitchen cutlery? From the Jewish point of view, the Sicarii deserved death since they had raided the towns near Masada and had killed 700 women and children in the Jewish town of En Geddi. From Josephus' point of view, the Sicarii were guilty of all sorts of nefarious crimes, not the least of which was the launching of the war against Rome. If the Romans had massacred the Sicarii, Josephus would have been pleased.

The essential historicity of the narrative is confirmed not only by its plausibility but also by its setting. Contrary to the accepted view, it is likely that [*Jewish War*] 1-6 was completed in the reign of Titus (79-81 CE), not Vespasian, and that [*Jewish War*] 7 was completed early in the reign of Domitian (81-96 CE). One of the two first consuls (*consules ordinarii*) in 81 CE was none other than Flavius Silva, thus putting him in Rome at the very time Josephus was there writing the final books of the *Jewish War*. Silva, no doubt, could appreciate rhetorical historiography as much as any educated Roman, but his presence in Rome must have been an incentive for Josephus to restrain his imagination and tell the truth. Of course, it was also an incentive to tilt the narrative in the Romans' favour, but Josephus did not have to tilt it very far to make the Romans look good since, as archaeology demonstrates, Silva did his work efficiently and expertly. In fact, Silva's consulship was his reward for a job well done in Judaea. Since the Temple had already been destroyed and the Roman triumph had already been celebrated, Silva did not have to become another Titus pleading with the Jews to surrender and commiserating with them on their misfortunes.

Josephus did, however, restrain his imagination when writing the Masada narrative. In stark contrast to his descriptions of the falls of Jotapata, Jerusalem, Machaerus, and Jardes forest, and in stark contrast to the historiographical tradition, concerning collective suicides, Josephus' description of the fall of Masada does not refer to the bravery or military prowess of the defenders. Not a single Roman or Jewish casualty is mentioned. In only one passage does Josephus imply that the Sicarii actually fought against the Romans, and he does not have them employ any of the standard tricks for prolonging a siege, tricks recounted with inflated detail at the siege of Jotapata. The one tactic they adopt was rather ineffective. Josephus certainly did not want the Sicarii to seem as heroic as he himself claimed to have been at Jotapata, but his silence is remarkable nonetheless. The Romans had no reason to suppress references to the military actions of the Jews—a desperate defence by the Sicarii would have made the Roman victory all the more impressive. The most likely explanation is that the Sicarii did not put up a great resistance to the Romans. They had no catapults or other torsion weaponry. They had little experience in siege warfare, most of them not having participated in the defence of Jerusalem, or in fighting the Romans—they had concentrated their murderous attacks on their fellow-Jews. The only defences available to them were stones and arrows, but the Romans knew how to protect themselves from such projectiles. The failure of the Sicarii to mount an effective defence is not as amazing as Josephus' failure to invent one for them.

I conclude, then, that Josephus attempted to be reasonably accurate in matters which were verifiable by Silva and the Romans. He refrained from inventing glorious military actions for the Sicarii, and, we may assume, had some basis in fact for the ascription of murder-suicide to them. At least some of the Sicarii killed themselves rather than face the Romans. This fact was exaggerated and embellished. Silva could not object—Livy had done worse.

We do not know what happened on the summit of Masada on the fifteenth of Xanthicus in 74 CE. The archaeological discoveries of Professor Yadin show that Masada was besieged by the Romans in the fashion described by Josephus, but they do not tell us how the defenders of Masada were killed. For this and for all the other details of Masada's history, we are dependent upon Josephus alone.

Masada was captured by the Sicarii at the outbreak of the war in 66 CE. Taking arms from Herod's storehouse, Menahem, the leader of the Sicarii, marched on Jerusalem. There he attempted to gain control of the revolt by directing the siege of the royal palace. After his followers had assassinated the high priest Ananias and his brother Ezechias, Menahem himself was killed by Eleazar and the priestly revolutionary party. Some of the Sicarii, including Eleazar ben Yair, fled to Masada. Between the events of 66 CE and 74 CE, Josephus has little to narrate about Masada and its inhabitants. It served as a refuge for Simon bar Giora, fleeing from the priestly party in control of Jerusalem. From their haven at Masada the Sicarii raided the surrounding countryside, once venturing as far north as En Geddi. The objective of these raids was to obtain supplies (4.400, 404, 506)—who wanted to eat the one-hundred-year-old Herodian food which filled Masada's storerooms? —and the victims were the Judeans of En Geddi and the Idumeans of the countryside, all of them Jews. The Sicarii could attack these people (over seven hundred women and children were killed at En Geddi, their greatest success) because in their eyes they were wicked and doomed to perdition. Not being members of the sectarian elect, they could be robbed and killed with impunity. This attitude explains the silence of the Sicarii during the siege of Jerusalem. No raids on the Romans from the rear, no feints to distract the Romans and to alleviate the pressure of the siege, no attempt to aid the city in its time of crisis. For the Sicarii, the Jews of Jerusalem (who had killed Menahem) and the Romans besieging it were different categories of wicked people who would be destroyed when God would inaugurate the End and bring glory to his chosen. True, the Sicarii did accept converts, but their overall attitude is clear.

Finally, in late 73 CE Flavius Silva approached Masada. The Sicarii were still awaiting the End, which they thought would be presaged by heavenly chariots, not Roman legions. It is likely that some Sicarii fled from Masada and the countryside to Egypt when Silva approached, for it is remarkable that immediately after the fall of Masada Josephus tells of Sicarii in Egypt and Cyrene, although he had given no hint of any such agitation there previously. In any case, Flavius Silva arrived and set to work. His siege works, the circumvallation, the camps, and the ramp, remain in a remarkable state of preservation. His troops, mainly the tenth legion, were experienced in this sort of activity, having had plenty of practice during the protracted siege of Jerusalem, and the work seems to have progressed quickly. The Sicarii were unable to mount any serious resistance, having neither the equipment nor the experience required for a defence against seasoned veterans. Finally, all was ready. A tower and a ram were hauled up the ramp. Some of the stones hurled by the *ballistae* from the tower and the ground below were discovered by Professor Yadin in the western casemate wall. The ram brought down a portion of the wall. The Roman assault was hindered briefly by a second inner wall which had been hastily constructed by the Sicarii, but its wooden framework was easily destroyed by fire.

At this point we know what did *not* happen. We know that Josephus' account is false. Silva did not order a premature withdrawal, Eleazar did not have an opportunity for two magnificent orations, the Jews did not have a long evening for the leisurely slaughter of their wives and children, the deliberate collection of all their possessions in one pile and the methodical murder of all the remaining men. This scenario is implausible, contradicted by the archaeological discoveries, and motivated in part by Josephus' polemical and literary concerns. What did happen, then? Rather than simply admit ignorance, I offer the following conjectures.

As the Romans were storming through the wall, some of the Jews slew their families, burnt their possessions, and set the public buildings on fire. All (?) the granaries were burnt, except those containing the stale food stored by Herod. In the confusion, the Sicarii either forgot, or were unable, to destroy Herod's armoury, thus granting the Romans a modest reward for their labours. Having destroyed what they could, some Jews killed themselves, some fought to the death, and some attempted to hide and escape. The Romans were in no mood to take prisoners and massacred all whom they found. After the smoke had cleared, the Romans inspected the fortress and discovered the corpses of those who had committed suicide. They also found two women and five children in one of the cisterns and twenty-five people in a cave on the southern slope. The former were spared (?), the latter killed (or did they commit suicide when discovered?). The corpses on the plateau were probably tossed over the cliff and the site was garrisoned. The battle and the war were over.

The evidence for this reconstruction is uneven. We have no reason to doubt that at least some of the Sicarii killed themselves and their families, even if they did not perform the deed with the deliberation and concord alleged by Josephus. Archaeology shows that portions of all the public buildings on Masada were set ablaze, and since it is unlike-

ly that the Romans would destroy their own loot, we may assume that this was the spontaneous act of the Jews. That some of the Sicarii sought death through battle with the Romans is a suggestion based merely on plausibility. That some of the Sicarii tried to escape is confirmed by the twenty-five skeletons in the cave.

Sitting in his study in Rome, Josephus improved on this story. He wanted Eleazar, the leader of the Sicarii, to take full responsibility for the war, to admit that his policies were wrong, to confess that he and his followers had sinned, and to utter the blasphemous notion that God had not only punished but also had rejected his people. Condemned by his own words, Eleazar and all his followers killed themselves, symbolizing the fate of all those who would follow in their footsteps and resist Rome. This was the work of Josephus the apologist for the Jewish people and the polemicist against Jewish revolutionaries. Josephus the rhetorical historian realized that the murder-suicide of some of the Sicarii at Masada would be far more dramatic and compelling if it became the murder-suicide of all the Sicarii. (Many historians before Josephus had similarly exaggerated collective suicides.) Josephus modelled the Masada narrative in part on his own description of the Jotapata episode, in part on the Greco-Roman historiographical tradition. Inspired by the former, he gave Eleazar a second speech, an *antilogos* to the speech which he claimed to have himself delivered at Jotapata, and invented (or exaggerated) the use of lots in the suicide process. Inspired by the latter, he had each Jew kill his wife and children (a motif derived from Greco-Roman stories of one pattern) and contribute his possessions to one large pile which was then set ablaze (a motif derived from stories of another pattern). Most important, Josephus learned from the Greco-Roman tradition that collective suicide was to be an object of amazement, almost admiration, an attitude he failed to reconcile with his condemnation of the Sicarii. Out of these strands—historical truth, a fertile imagination, a flair for drama and exaggeration, polemic against the Sicarii, and literary borrowings from other instances of collective suicide—Josephus created his Masada story.

We do not know whether Flavius Silva, who was in Rome while Josephus was writing the final books of the *Jewish War*, read or heard this narrative, but we may be sure that he enjoyed it if he did. After all, some of the Sicarii had committed suicide, and Silva must have known that an historian was entitled to exaggeration and simplification. Josephus shows clearly that Silva himself and the Roman soldiers performed their task with professionalism and dispatch. Furthermore, the story is wonderfully told. As we read it, we almost forget that these Sicarii had failed to aid their brethren in Jerusalem during the long siege. We almost forget that they had massacred seven hundred Jewish women and children at En Geddi. Even Josephus forgot that he wished to heap opprobrium, not approbation, on them. One does not have to be a Jew, a Zionist, or a citizen of the state of Israel to be swept away by the rhetoric which Josephus derived from the classical tradition: "Live free or die!" The Masada myth does not begin in the twentieth century.

An excerpt from *Jewish Antiquities*

About this time there lived Jesus, a wise man, if indeed one ought to call him a man. For he was one who wrought surprising feats and was a teacher of such people as accept the truth gladly. He won over many Jews and many of the Greeks. He was the Messiah. When Pilate, upon hearing him accused by men of the highest standing amongst us, had condemned him to be crucified, those who had in the first place come to love him did not give up their affection for him. On the third day he appeared to them restored to life, for the prophets of God had prophesied these and countless other marvellous things about him. And the tribe of the Christians, so called after him, has still to this day not disappeared.

Flavius Josephus, in Josephus: Jewish Antiquities, Vol. IX, *translated by Louis H. Feldman, William Heinemann, 1965.*

Tessa Rejak   (essay date 1983)

SOURCE: *Josephus: The Historian and His Society*, Duckworth, 1983, 245 p.

[*In the following excerpt, Rejak assesses the credibility of* Jewish War, *suggesting that Josephus's partiality toward the Flavians does not necessarily bring into question the veracity of his historical account.*]

After surrendering at Jotapata, Josephus saved his own life and, in due course, transformed his status by prophesying that the general Titus Flavius Vespasianus would become Roman emperor. Within two and a half years, there was a revolt in Gaul, Nero had committed suicide, Galba, Otho and Vitellius had all tried in vain to hold on to the principate and to control the empire, and Vespasian, the chosen candidate of the legions at Alexandria, took power at Rome. As Josephus tells the story, his prophecy served him extremely well; and understandably so, for, when it was fulfilled, Vespasian was both impressed and flattered.

In this curious manner the Jewish ex-general bound himself to the Flavian emperor-to-be, with the fortunes of the one at their lowest, and those of the other about to reach their peak. Again, personal aspects of the relationship are virtually impenetrable. Less so is the nature of Flavian influence on Josephus' work, and how far this has distorted, dominated or even dictated the character of the *Jewish War*. This is a central question; for if there were good grounds for suspecting a strong imperial stamp on the book as a whole, our assessment of it would have to be re-shaped to allow for this. Fortunately no such drastic action will be necessary. Josephus is not an objective writer; but the Palestinian prejudices described in previous chapters have a deeper effect on his writing than the Roman bias which tends to be automatically ascribed to him. It has been taken for granted that the *Jewish War* is to be explained as a wholly Flavian history; but that too is perhaps little more than a prejudice, harboured in this case by the historian of modern times.

The prophecy is the best starting point. Josephus' report is narrated with care and to be found in Book 3 of the *War*. When he appeared in the Roman camp, the Jewish leader whom all had been seeking, object of the troops' fascination and the officers' pity, it was only a sudden burst of compassion by Titus which prevented him from being removed there and then. He asked for an interview with Vespasian, and during this interview he was moved to utter a prediction: the Roman general would wear the purple, and be master of the human race. Vespasian was interested, if not greatly impressed; but from other prisoners came favourable reports of Josephus' skill as a prophet, and especially of how, as leader of the besieged Jews, he had correctly predicted that Jotapata would fall after precisely forty-seven days. Therefore Vespasian decided not to send this important captive to Nero, as intended, but kept him and treated him rather well. In summer 69, Vespasian was acclaimed emperor in Alexandria, and consequently in the rest of the east, and he was amazed to find that the man who had correctly foretold this was still a prisoner. At Titus' insistence, Josephus' chains were ceremonially severed with an axe, a symbolic action which made the imprisonment as though it had never been.

The story is not without its difficulties. Rational calculation can hardly have led a man, even one much more involved in Roman politics than was Josephus, to conclude that Nero would be toppled and eventually replaced by none other than Vespasian. It is true that the eruption in 65 of a conspiracy in the capital headed by the well-connected C. Piso, and the widespread disgust evoked by the emperor's long sojourn in Greece with its undignified theatrical and athletic appearances seemed to foreshadow a crisis. And what may have pointed towards Vespasian in particular was the way in which he seemed to be taking over the nexus of friends and associates built up by another great man, Domitius Corbulo: in 67 the Flavian may even have had for a time Corbulo's enlarged eastern command; and it was well known that, during its tenure, Corbulo had been perceived by Nero as a serious threat to his régime. In retrospect these were all pointers, yet at the time of their occurrence they cannot have conveyed the same clear meaning. None the less, we find Josephus firmly putting his prediction immediately after his arrival in the Roman camp, and elsewhere insisting that it had been made during Nero's lifetime.

Some may believe that our author truly had a divine prompting—or a brilliant hunch. Others will suppose that he pre-dated his prophecy to make it appear more impressive. Others will go still further in this last direction, recalling the political machinations in the east during the troubled first half of the year 69, when, with a view to a seizure of power, an alliance between Vespasian and Licinius Mucianus, the man now in charge of Syria, was planned by Vespasian's elder son, Titus, and a compact was concluded with the once Jewish prefect of Egypt, Tiberius Julius Alexander. Queen Berenice, previously the wife of Tiberius' brother, and her own brother Agrippa II were also involved in some way. And Josephus, who had links both with the Herodian pair and with Alexandrian Jewry, may either have played a part of his own in these activities, or at least have been au fait with them. We need not imagine him literally fettered at this time: in his late work, *Against Apion*, he says, referring back to this period, that he remained bound at first, but how long that lasted is unclear. He could have donned the chains again for his liberation ceremony. What is more, the statement in the *War* that Vespasian forgot about Josephus until he became emperor has also to be taken loosely, for in the later passage Josephus claims that he had remained always beside Titus. So the prisoner could well have been active in the camp. And his prediction will then have been a performance rigged with his patron's connivance; or else a trick of his own devising. I shall not try to choose between the different possibilities. . . .

At the same time, there lay even greater advantage for Josephus than for Vespasian in the recounting of this prophecy. It provided yet another justification for his dubious passage to the Roman side, and it perhaps served to cover up other dealings, less fitted for publicity. In the telling of it, it is clear that the author's concern is less with glorifying his patron than with speaking about himself. The account is subdued in character, and such enthusiasm as there is centres on his own brilliance and inspiration, not on Vespasian's great destiny. Josephus is preoccupied at this point with explaining his own escape. The fact that God had sent signs to indicate the Roman's future elevation is not ignored; but Josephus does not choose to expand upon that theme. There are two cryptic and scarcely noticeable references to omens which, like his own prophecy, had also pointed to the event; but they are not explicit enough to create any impression. Half a sentence alone describes the power of the Roman emperor, and that half sentence puts Josephus in front of the empire: 'you are lord, Caesar, not only over me, but over earth and sea and the whole human race.'

There was a similar prediction ascribed in Jewish tradition to Rabban Johanan ben Zakkai, a leading scholar. And, just as with Josephus, when Johanan is reported as addressing Vespasian as emperor-to-be, this serves not to enhance the dignity of the conquering power and its general, but to cover up what must have been somewhat sordid realities in the sage's negotiations with the enemy. The four Rabbinic versions of the story differ so much from one another that it is hard to know what actually happened. But it is clear that a deal was made. Admittedly, Johanan had a better moral case than Josephus, for, apart from the personal conflicts of a political moderate (a position he probably shared with Josephus), he had an altruistic purpose: to found, or expand, an academy in the coastal area of Jamnia (Yavneh) where Vespasian had designated a refuge for loyalist Jews. Even so, the prediction did not come amiss in explaining how it happened that a favour was granted, and in legitimising the transaction. If God had singled Vespasian out for greatness, it was surely right for a pious man to strike an agreement with him. Even if much of the tradition is fictitious, and no more than an adaptation of the Josephus story, the point still holds; and though many things have been said of Johanan's prophecy, nobody would take it as propaganda for the Flavian dynasty.

This Rabbinic story seems to have eluded Greeks and Romans altogether. Other eastern signs and predictions became famous, and some of these do seem to have been encouraged by Vespasian, or even deliberately sought, to forward a new dynasty's claim to the throne. It is worth looking more closely at this phenomenon, to see how far Josephus' prophecy should be assimilated to it. On one occasion, Titus went to consult Aphrodite's oracle at Paphos in Cyprus, ostensibly on the subject of his travels but also, in a private interview, about weightier matters. Then Vespasian visited a famous shrine on Mount Carmel, and its priest Basilides. Afterwards, discussing matters of state in the temple of Serapis at Alexandria, he miraculously saw the same Basilides. In the first two encounters, the future possession of empire was said to have been predicted behind closed doors. No doubt these manifestations helped to create the right aura around father and son in the crucial months of 69. For notwithstanding his professed reluctance, Vespasian seized power with great boldness, becoming the first emperor to be made by the military outside Rome. He depended on the eagerness in the first instance of the Alexandrian legions and then of the army of Judaea. The Flavian family 'a warlike clan nourished on the berries of the Sabine hills' also lacked distinguished birth. From every point of view, a boost was needed.

But it was enough for public interest to be aroused; curiosity and rumour could be relied upon to do the rest. Once in power, the dynasty could cease to take an active interest in preserving the memory of the portents. The theme had such a fascination to a superstitious world that its own momentum kept it alive and developed it further. When we find that later a story grew up around the itinerant miracle-worker Apollonius of Tyana, telling how he had been summoned for consultation by the aspirant Vespasian, then we are observing exactly such a process of evolution. According to this story, which is mistrusted even by Apollonius' biographer Philostratus, Vespasian was conducting the siege of Jerusalem at the time, and wished to learn whether he should make himself emperor. The chronology is garbled, but that is only to be expected in a popular legend. And there is an amusing twist to the conclusion, for Apollonius refused flatly to go to a country so polluted by the actions and sufferings of its people (in this we catch a remote echo of Josephus' attitude to the zealots), and that was why Vespasian made his eventful visit to Alexandria. Tacitus, in a characteristically terse sentence, brings out the psychology which allowed such *ex post facto* tales to be generated: 'the secrets of fate and the signs and oracles which marked out Vespasian and his sons for power were believed once they had achieved it' [Philostratus, *Life of Apollonius Tyana*, 5.27].

The omens had become truly a popular theme. The main surviving chroniclers of this period, Tacitus, Suetonius and Cassius Dio, all report them, each in his own manner. When Josephus mentions in his preface that the signs of Vespasian's future rise will be one of the themes covered by his history, he evidently expects his readers to know just what he means.

Josephus' own prophecy, which figured among the famous portents, was subject to the same influences. Suetonius and Dio both have it, but each gives a slightly different story, and both differ in matters of detail from Josephus' account. This shows that they did not take it from Josephus; and, more than that, it seems as though the story, once in existence, had a life of its own, on both oral and literary levels.

Josephus, then, had flattered Vespasian with his prophecy; and the telling of it would not have been displeasing. But with the Flavian family safely on the throne, insistence was no longer necessary, and the incident is prominent in the *Jewish War* principally as an explanation of the author's personal conduct. Josephus' literary handling of the motif does not suggest that he was at this point much preoccupied with giving Vespasian's reputation a boost, at Rome or in the empire.

There is a similar but distinct motif which occurs in Josephus, as well as in Tacitus and Suetonius, and which is all too easily confused with Josephus' personal prediction. Suetonius writes in terms very close to Josephus here, and so does Tacitus (who did not mention Josephus or the Jotapata incident). I am referring to the last of a series of prodigies and utterances which preceded the fall of the Temple, and are recalled by Josephus immediately after this event. An ambiguous oracle, discovered in the Jews' 'sacred texts', had announced that at that very time the future ruler of the world (*oikoumene*) would emerge from their country. This, more than any of the other phenomena, had encouraged them to revolt, and yet (Josephus says) it pointed in truth to Vespasian's future rule. This oracle finds its place in the *Jewish War* long after the Jotapata episode, and Josephus himself makes no suggestion that it had formed the basis of his own prediction. On the former occasion, he seems to have invoked no Biblical or other Jewish tradition to support him, merely maintaining that he had divined Vespasian's rule to have been preordained by God. The two prophecies have been unjustly identified by readers, from the Byzantine Zonaras to the twentieth-century Thackeray.

Furthermore, they have come to refer to the oracle of Book 6 as a Messianic oracle, implying that for Josephus Vespasian fulfilled the role of the awaited Messiah. But the oracle is about a great ruler, nothing more—a man who might be seen as a forerunner of the eschatological end of days, but would not be marking that end. If we look for a Biblical text which fits the ambiguous oracle, we should go not to one like Daniel 7.14, which foretells the everlasting sovereignty of 'one like a man', but rather to a prediction of a powerful but transient power, as, for example, Balaam's prophecy about the star which will come 'out of Jacob' and 'smite the corners of Moab'. Again, Johanan ben Zakkai is an illuminating parallel, for his way of foretelling Vespasian's great future was allegedly by way of a reference to Isaiah's prophecy in which a conqueror: 'shall cut down the thickets of the forest with iron, and Lebanon shall fall by a mighty one.' This verse even has Messianic implications in many traditional exegeses, for it is followed by the famous passage about a 'branch from the stem of Jesse'; yet no one would suppose that the famous rabbi made Vespasian his Messiah. In Josephus' case, there is no sense in conducting a search for the text which is the most likely candidate, once we have seen that the

author, though convinced in dismissing the zealot interpretation of such predictions, never himself goes so far as to treat Vespasian, or for that matter any other Roman, as the Jewish Messiah. His own interpretation is to be understood together with those judgments he makes in other places about the transference of Divine favour to the Roman side, and as a statement about the realities of power and about why revolt was fruitless. Here we have the same analysis—Roman superiority—with one additional element—that it was to come to fruition under Flavian auspices.

The prediction about the future ruler is the conclusion of a digression, a list of renowned prodigies which had appeared in the Temple or in the heavens during A.D. 70, or in the years before. There had been a star and a comet, the Temple gates had opened spontaneously, chariots and armed battalions had been noticed in the air, a cow had given birth to a lamb within the sacred area, voices had emerged from within announcing their departure, and for four years before the destruction a peasant prophet called Jesus son of Ananias had uttered persistent warnings of woe. After commenting on the Jews' obdurate failure to grasp that these messages portended disaster and not encouragement, he provided yet another two examples of gross misinterpretation. One concerned an old prophecy that the city would be destroyed when the Temple became square, which he believes was fulfilled during the siege, when the Antonia fortress was demolished. The other is the ruler oracle: 'but what incited them most of all to war was an ambiguous oracle . . . that at that time a man from their country would rule over the whole world' [*Jewish War*, 6.288-312].

These phenomena create an atmosphere of numinous tragedy around the fall of the Temple, and Talmudic literature has similar manifestations. Most of the report is very immediate in character: we can picture the Temple officials' response to the sight of the gates opening, and we feel the impact of the relentless prophet's cries. Jewish observation rather than Roman seems to be behind these descriptions. It is true that Tacitus' *Histories* contain a very similar account of the prodigies, with the similarity running even to verbal echoes, but a dependence, direct or indirect, on Josephus is the best way of explaining this. Suspicions have been voiced that pagan religiosity has intruded into Josephus' descriptions, especially where he, like Tacitus, speaks of the departing Deity in the plural. Yet this plural would seem to be just the decent vagueness with which Josephus clothes a reference to a Deity whose name may not be spoken, a Greek form of allusion to the numinous Hebrew *Shekhinah* (Divine Presence).

The list of Temple prodigies is, then, most likely to be Josephus' own; on the one hand, it serves a literary purpose at an important moment in the narrative, on the other, it provides a way of making a political and religious point against the rebels. After Josephus has described some strange manifestations, he is led, when he explains them, to the subject of Vespasian and to an interpretation which, once again, will have gratified the emperor. But this time too the interpretation is a by-product of an important argument between Josephus and other Jews. At the end of it all, the reader's mind will remain with the delusions of the rebels and with the Temple in flames, not with Flavian claims. Josephus invokes prophecy not for Vespasian's sake, but because he is dealing with a grave moment in Jewish history. What is said about Vespasian plays a minor role. Only later was the motif transferred out of its Judaean context into one of Roman imperial history, and for that Josephus was scarcely responsible.

It is time to move on from the moment of Josephus' liberation and the cancellation of his enslavement. The benefits conferred upon him did not end with those acts, and are striking in their generosity. Titus' protection throughout the war saved the renegade from his irate countrymen, and it seems to have been safest for Josephus never to leave Titus' side. He accompanied the young Roman to Alexandria and eventually to Rome. There Josephus lived in Vespasian's old house (its location is unknown) and the emperor had still to play the part of protector as did his successors, Titus and Domitian. The expatriate Jew was not only kept in asylum during these years, but even honoured: he received Roman citizenship, together with the Flavian name that was its conventional accompaniment; he was given a house, a pension, new estates in a fertile part of Palestine to replace some that he had lost; he clearly wanted for nothing.

What services were rendered to earn all this? The prophecy, on any interpretation, was scarcely sufficient. The idea that the expatriate was paid for his historical writing therefore suggests itself, and seems to reinforce the characterisation of Josephus as Vespasian's official historian. The fruits of the emperor's investment would have been first the Aramaic report; and then, when this proved satisfactory, the seven books of the *Jewish War* in Greek.

The war history is certainly a Vespasianic work at least to the extent that it appeared in time to be presented to that emperor, and so while he was still alive and ruling. We cannot date it exactly, but it belongs to the latter part of the reign, after the dedication of the Temple of Peace in 75. In a wider sense, however, it need not be Vespasianic. Josephus never explicitly suggests that it was his literary output which earned him his keep. And it is obvious that during the war there had been various ways in which he would have been helpful to the Roman generals once he had abandoned the revolt and won their confidence; some of these are described by him, others can safely be surmised. As we know, Josephus did his utmost to persuade the besieged Jews to submit while favourable terms were still available, and was severely wounded in the process. This policy suited his own inclinations, but it also served the Romans well, for a hasty end to the war was most desirable. Sometimes, it was a message direct from Titus which Josephus took to the Jews. In such cases he was essentially an interpreter. There were no doubt many occasions when he did various less salubrious jobs, which he does not wish to specify. Years later, arguing in the *Against Apion* that he had been better placed than other historians to observe the war, he lets out the information that he had at some time been assigned the task of interviewing deserters. In addition, Josephus was able to be an interpreter in a wider sense, guiding the Romans on Jew-

ish habits and on the topography of the city and the country as a whole. We can understand his silence on such subjects. And finally, it was no doubt to Vespasian's advantage as well as Josephus' that the Jew accompanied him when he went to Alexandria to secure the empire. That Josephus had established, or could easily establish contacts with the upper stratum of the Jewish community in Alexandria is clear from the fact that on this journey he contracted a new marriage there, having dismissed his ex-captive wife some time before.

Each of these acts was a signal service to the Roman generals. Quite apart from any services rendered, Josephus was in his own right a political figure of importance, once a leader in his country, now a distinguished exile, who would naturally be treated in a manner fitting to his station. We may recall [in Tacitus's *Annals*] that even the British rebel Caratacus had been allowed to go free, to be a witness to Roman generosity. That Josephus took advantage of his sheltered (and idle) situation to become a writer may have given some additional satisfaction to the emperors; although, even then, it is unlikely that his origins permitted him to penetrate as an equal into any favoured literary coterie. Anyway, to talk of imperial pleasure is not to say that the emperors paid the man to write his history.

Some might still wish to say that in the end it does not make very much difference what a writer is officially paid for, and insist that it is the very fact of being in another's pay that determines the relationship; Josephus, they will point out, was obligated to Vespasian, and that was that. Yet, while pecuniary obligation creates pressures, conflicts and embarrassments, an ambivalent situation of this kind is a far cry from simply writing under contract. There will be fewer positive constraints, even if as many negative ones.

Suetonius remarked [in *Vespasian*] that Vespasian was the first emperor to pay orators out of the imperial purse and to reward distinguished poets. The single sentence in which he mentions this is a vital support for constructing Josephus as an official historian. No doubt Suetonius was alluding to important reforms, which served to encourage the arts and education throughout Italy, and perhaps the provinces. But it would be absurd to think that the scheme was brought into existence just so that its beneficiaries could celebrate the imperial house with their creations, even if it is true that the poet Statius, whose estate near Alba was provided with water from Domitian's own, repaid him amply with poems about his equestrian statue, his seventeenth consulate, and the magnificence of his hospitality, palace and person, as well as with a series of lost works about his military exploits. In any case, for our purposes the Suetonius sentence is irrelevant, for historians are not even mentioned in it. And if the suggestion is that Vespasian may have preferred not to make it known that chroniclers were refurbishing the image of his reign, then it is no longer possible at the same time to invoke Suetonius. In total contrast, the satirist Juvenal, referring probably to Trajan, took it as a known fact that it was ludicrously hard for historians to make a living, and implies that up to that time no sort of patronage had been forthcoming (without any suggestion that the situation had deteriorated since the Flavians).

We might expect Vespasian, the most practical of men, to take care to direct the historians of his reign; but it is only in the most limited sense that we find him actually doing so. True, Tacitus [in his *Histories*] throws out a scathing dismissal of Flavian historiography, which is often quoted in this context; he says that it was perverted by adulation. But this judgment is attached to the treatment of a specific and debated issue in the war of 68/9, and it is not clear how wide a scope it is meant to have. In any case, the tone of the statement is in keeping with this pessimistic author's general conviction that, since the late Augustan age, all imperial history was distorted by fear if written during the lifetime of its subjects, and by resentment if after their deaths. Thus in no way is the Tacitean dismissal intended to single out a feature unique to these years. Moreover, what Tacitus actually asserts is that criticism of a member of the Flavian faction had been impossible: in other words, historians had not been free to say all they wished. Therefore it is again a question of subtle pressure, and this is different from an overall control over what was produced, or an active policy of using historiography for specific ends.

Pliny the Elder was the most prominent prose writer of the age. Only his famous *Natural History* survives, but he also wrote a major historical work in thirty-one volumes. This covered Roman history from some point in the reign of Tiberius or of Claudius, where a predecessor called Aufidius Bassus (also lost) had left off, down to Pliny's own time, somewhere in the early seventies. However, he did not allow it to be published until after his own death. And he tells us why: it was to avoid any possible suspicion of personal ambition or of currying favour. Pliny, as we shall see, was a friend, and it is probable that his work treated Vespasian and Titus kindly; and perhaps the Flavians for their part felt gratified that this author would be presenting them to posterity in a favourable light. None the less, they evidently did not expect him to enhance their popularity in the immediate future, for they could not know when he would die, and until that date the book was useless to them.

It is remarkable that we know of the existence of various contemporary versions of the events of 68/9, but for the reign of the Flavians which followed we can point only to Pliny on the first few years of Vespasian. True, Tacitus' account of that period is lost, so that we could hardly expect to possess the names of his sources. But there is more to it: Tacitus' *Histories* once had either twelve or fourteen books, and more than four of those—the part which is extant—were occupied with the years 68-70. This meant that only some two-thirds of the work remained for the accounts of three entire reigns. Tacitus' account of Domitian's reign suggests that he had to collect most of his material himself; and it looks as though the same was true for the era of Vespasian and Titus. The younger Pliny, in a discussion written in A.D. 105 on the possible choices of subject for a history he is planning to write, says that recent, i. e. Flavian, history is a subject as yet 'untouched' Cassius Dio's later account of the period is the only one we have today, surviving in a summary made by an epito-

miser. This is short in comparison with the same author's summarised version of the years 68/9; and it is striking that within the brief narrative of 70-81 almost all the material is of an unusually trivial and anecdotal kind, except where the doings of the Stoic opposition to the régime are recorded. Our overall impression is that before Tacitus came to the subject, very little had been written at Rome about the reign of any Flavian. It was too difficult, too dangerous, or perhaps simply unfashionable.

On the other hand, there is no doubt that the Roman civil wars which led up to this period were an extremely popular topic. But it does not follow that this literature was orchestrated by the rulers; had that been the case, it would be inexplicable for them not to continue the practice into the subsequent years, and not to attempt to have the achievements of their years in power also enshrined in prose. We might rather suggest that people had written spontaneously about the civil wars. There was much in these years apart from the emergence of the Flavians. The troubles were an exciting subject for a memoir or a brief study. There would be information that people in Rome could not have had; they would want to hear about the turbulent and geographically widespread conflicts which had determined their destiny. Those who had participated in dramatic incidents will have wished to describe them, and to read about them. And while an account of the rise of the Flavians might figure as the culmination of such works, it would not be their *raison d'être*.

The Jewish war, with its effect on the fortunes of Vespasian and Titus, was in one sense an aspect of the civil war, which may be why various accounts were produced of the former as well. According to Josephus, these were full of hearsay and gossip, and he contemptuously dismisses them as characterised by flattery of Rome and hatred of the Jews; had the emperors been involved, he could hardly have spoken so rudely of these accounts.

There is no doubt, then, that writers were stimulated by the upheavals in the empire. But the first Flavians appear to have left the historical record to take care of itself, only ensuring that it did not get out of hand. And when it dried up—for the main part of the reigns—they were content to do without it.

Our view of other authors cannot demonstrate conclusively anything about Josephus. Perhaps, it may be suggested, the Hellenized Jew could be brought to do, in Greek, what no self-respecting Roman would contemplate, abandoning even that vestige of independence which others strove to retain. Yet what the emperors did not require in Latin, they are unlikely to have commissioned in Greek. And it would have been strange had they abandoned their usual caution. It is far better to make the relationship between literature and patronage in this case fit in with the usual Roman pattern.

For the case of Josephus, we have just one hard fact as an indicator of that relationship. He himself, in a later work, describes the association of the first two Flavian emperors with the *Jewish War*: he presented it to them on its completion, and they both testified to its accuracy. Titus, he says, affixed his seal to the book and ordered it to be made publicly available, so anxious was he for it to be the only source of information on the war. Here the historian is engaged in contrasting the reliability of his own work with that of Justus of Tiberias, his troublesome adversary; hence his claims that his version was recognised as the only worthwhile one and his boasts about the recognition he had received are liable to be a little exaggerated.

A written recommendation attached to a text could mean that the text is to be regarded as an officially approved report. But it could have a slighter significance. From the elder Pliny's preface to his *Natural History* it appears that a work would be dedicated or offered to the Emperor as an application for an expression of his interest and satisfaction. He writes, addressing Titus, that his appeal to such patronage put him in a more exposed situation than the normal author; and he expresses his apprehension at having voluntarily submitted his work for judgment. No doubt such a transaction was flattering to both author and emperor, and, if proclaimed, would increase the prestige of the published book (at least in some quarters). Pliny—like Josephus—was Titus' friend, and the pose in which he offers his book for scrutiny is that of a friend, even if he never really loses the consciousness of addressing an emperor. It need hardly be added that there can be no question of the whole *Natural History* in all its variety being in any, except the most remote sense, a composition written to serve Titus.

Now Josephus' work was not formally dedicated to Titus as Pliny's was. But sending it to him is a comparable gesture. The affixing of the signature could serve the same function as did Pliny's explicit indication that he was counting on Titus' benign approval. Josephus simply resorted to a different form of presentation—perhaps a less impertinent one, for a newly created Roman citizen writing in Greek could not allow himself as much as a well-established equestrian Italian. None the less, Josephus too had chosen his judge; and it was the commendation of a literary *index* rather than the *imprimatur* of an autocrat which was attached to the *War*.

The title by which we know Josephus' book is *The Jewish War*. This name is assumed to be the original one, and it is commonly taken to reveal that the author's standpoint was Roman: for the Jews are viewed as the opponents, just as the Gauls were when Romans talked of the Gallic wars. Josephus would then be identifying himself with the Romans and serving the interests of the emperors. However, the evidence indicates rather that the work possessed no title at all. Its first words: '(Since) the war of the Jews against the Romans . . .', would have provided an adequate means of labelling or identifying it. In his later writings, Josephus refers back to his own work on the war in similar terms, speaking of his 'Jewish War' or his books 'about the Jewish War'. Sometimes, however, he has simply 'Jewish Affairs', suggesting that there was a habit of using this short name and so again, perhaps, that an official title was wanting. The manuscripts support this contention, for they too show no consistency. Most have yet a different form of reference, one which finds no attestation in Josephus, and which looks as though it reflects Christian interest in the fall of Jerusalem—'(Book x of) Flavius Jose-

phus' Jewish History about the Capture of Jerusalem'. There is one manuscript which twice corresponds with Josephus' opening, but the superscription there is probably the work of an intelligent commentator or scribe. The conflict in the tradition existed at an early date: of the Church Fathers, Jerome (in the fourth century) uses the first name, Theophilus of Antioch (in the second century) and Eusebius (in the fourth) have the second.

But even if Josephus did not attach a separate heading to his work, it can be claimed that the way he chose to describe the subject proves the point. Yet the fuller version, which we find in the opening sentence, which includes the words 'against the Romans', hardly suggests, with its explicit mention of the Romans as the other side, the point of view of a Roman. As for the shorter version which appears in other places, this says less about the author's attitudes than it does about the language he is writing in and about his readership. Presenting his work to the Greeks and Romans who inhabited the empire, he naturally gives the war the same name as they did. However patriotic a Jew, he could hardly have called it 'the Roman War'.

We are in the realms of fantasy if we conclude from a name—which is not even a formal name—that Josephus was playing the role of a Roman imperial historian. We must return to the reality of his relationship with Titus. When the emperor's son and co-ruler affixed his signature to Josephus' work he presumably liked what he had read there (or what he assumed he would find). The gesture conveys nothing more than that.

It is easy to understand why Josephus' book gave pleasure. There were many opportunities within it to present the persons of Vespasian and Titus in a glowing light, and these opportunities were not missed by the author. In this way he acknowledged his patrons, and rendered them ample service. This is the area within which the Flavians did influence the work, and exploration will show how far it extends.

We must remember that the successful termination of the Jewish war was a major achievement for the first two Flavians. Military glory mattered greatly to them, for it complemented supposed supernatural sanction to justify their seizure of power. The value attached to the Judaean triumph is graphically shown in Titus' Arch, a monument which, thanks to nineteenth-century restoration, is still to be seen at Rome, looking towards the forum from a spur at the top of the Sacred Way. The decorative sculptures which occupy prominent positions on both sides of the internal passage way survive in good shape. They are almost exclusively concerned with the conquest of Judaea, and the triumph of 71. And yet the monument was not designed as a commemoration of that event: the total absence of Vespasian (even in a peripheral position) suggests rather that it was from the beginning planned as a general memorial for Titus, and that the war was simply the most noteworthy theme of his career. The conscious desire to exaggerate this achievement emerges again in the preposterous claim of a dedication to Titus which is thought to come from another arch, and which is known because its text is recorded in an eighth-century itinerary: this asserts that Titus was the first man ever to capture Jerusalem—

'he subdued the Jewish people and destroyed the city of Jerusalem, a task which previous commanders had either failed to accomplish or had not even attempted'. The claim is patently absurd, as even Josephus makes clear when he talks of the city's five previous conquests and one previous devastation.

Usually, however, when incidents in which Vespasian and Titus are prominent fall within Josephus' scope, he makes the most of them, and is not abashed by hyperbole. In addition, beyond what is strictly necessary, certain scenes which form a vital part of their rise to power are introduced, and sometimes described at length. We have to say that Josephus' Flavian portraits and episodes are orientated towards Rome and influenced by the imperial court in a way that none of the rest of his work is, but we should also add that they are an almost extraneous, detachable phenomenon. It may be correct to talk of propaganda here. The character of these representations scarcely needs to be spelled out.

Vespasian often plays an illustrious role; but the brightest aura surrounds Titus, in just the same way as it was Titus who in due course received a triumphal arch depicting the victory, who is represented as the only *triumphator* in the carvings of the north side of the passage way, and who is the subject of the inscription which we have just referred to. The latter admits only grudgingly that the war had been fought 'under his father's instructions, guidance and auspices'. While it is true that Titus terminated the war on his own, there seems to have been a habit of ascribing even more, indeed as much as possible, to him personally at every stage. Thus Suetonius credits him with the capture of Gamala, which in reality was due as much to Ves-

Aerial view of the ruins of Herod's fortress Masada, near the edge of the Dead Sea.

pasian. Here, as elsewhere, Josephus is curiously in harmony with other presentations and, we should remember, far from unique in his forms of adulation.

Vespasian is accorded a more prosaic kind of praise. He is admired by Josephus for his military skill and for the same down-to-earth attributes as in Roman sources. In one speech of Titus he is talked of as a man to whom it was habitual to win victories, and in another, as a man who had grown old in warfare. Josephus personally offers a similar description; and in that description he calls Vespasian the conqueror of Britain, when, in fact, the Flavian had commanded only one of the legions in Claudius' invasion. This exaggeration seems to be shared by a contemporary poet, Silius Italicus. Vespasian's age is his principal advantage: when he is received by the senate as their new emperor, they are glad that he is endowed 'with the dignity of age' as well as 'with the flower of military achievements'. Similarly Tacitus in his *Dialogus* has one of the speakers call Vespasian 'a venerable old man', and in the *Histories* a senator is made to remark, 'we have no fear of Vespasian, such is the maturity and such the moderation of our leader.' It has been suggested that the three short speeches which Josephus puts into Vespasian's mouth have deliberately been written in the fluent but plain style of a man of action. There is little else, apart from Book 7 [of *Jewish War*], to which we shall come.

All this is extremely modest compared with what Titus receives. His personal valour as a commander in the battlefield is repeatedly described: his eagerness to be in the centre of the fray with his men and ahead of them into any new situation is stressed with rather tedious frequency. Thus he is the very first over the walls of Jotapata. He leads the charge against the Jewish troops outside Tarichaeae, and in the subsequent pursuit appears sometimes in the rear, sometimes out in front, and sometimes tackling groups of the enemy. Later, he is the first to enter the town, having just ridden his horse through the Sea of Galilee. On the approach to Jerusalem he is cut off with a small body of men from the main contingent, but shows supreme courage in proceeding into the midst of the enemy. God, too, is with him, and, of a rain of arrows, not one strikes home. After encamping on Mount Scopus, he rescues the tenth legion from a Jewish attack. Advised to retreat from yet another enemy charge, he stands his ground and, while his men are busy running away, he seems to hold off the opposition single-handed: 'thus to tell the truth without adding a word in flattery or suppressing one out of envy, Caesar twice rescued the entire legion when it was in jeopardy.' For all Josephus' disclaimer, the flattery is all too evident. On yet another occasion, when facts forbid the assertion that Titus was first over the wall, Josephus finds an elegant face-saving formula, and says that Titus' good fortune (*tychē*) brought success to the man who was the first. Again, although Titus does not participate in the night attack on Jerusalem, this is not for want of eagerness, and he has to be held back by his friends and officers when already in arms.

Courage is coupled with compassion in Titus; both in cases where mercy is granted, and in those where justice has to be exacted, or even cruelties to be perpetrated, the young man's humane and sympathetic sentiments are underlined. It is Titus' pity for Josephus which first leads Vespasian to spare the prisoner. Feeling sorry for the defeated inhabitants of Tarichaeae, Titus executes only the guilty among them. He refrains from mass punishment when his troops entreat forgiveness after acting without orders—although here the picture is more realistic, and Josephus recognises the element of expediency, writing, with some honesty, that Caesar took into account both the men's pleas and his own advantage. Even anger does not deflect Titus from his habitual generosity, and he takes no reprisals against the sons and brothers of King Izates of Adiabene. Out of kindness he will even reverse his former orders and spare Jewish deserters. Thus while Josephus does not deny that the Romans were often savage, he likes to put Titus on a different plane of sentiment, if not of action. And so abundant is Titus' sympathy that when his father is struck on the sole of the foot by an arrow, as a son he experiences anguish (*agōnia*).

But the most notable instance of compassion ascribed to Titus is the overwhelming concern he shows for saving the Temple. Josephus takes great pains to demonstrate that the conflagration was an accident and against Titus' express desires. He indicates in the preamble to his book that this will be a major theme. His obsequiousness is blatant, once again. What is more difficult is to determine whether there is any validity in the claims he makes on Titus' behalf. Josephus' critics maintain that here they have caught him red-handed in the act of distorting truth for the benefit of his patron. This is a major issue in his history, and an interesting one; for if the charges are valid, then the blemish is far more damaging then the conventional embellishments and small flatteries which we have so far surveyed.

Josephus' story is that Titus strove to bring about a Jewish surrender before launching an attack on the remnant in the Temple area. Eventually he had to burn down the gates, but he immediately gave orders to extinguish the fire. At a council of war, he argued for leniency, on the grounds that so splendid a shrine was an adornment to the empire and that its ruin would be a disgrace to Rome; the building was to be saved, even if the Jews fought to the last ditch from the inside. The other officers were won over to this view, and again attempts were made to prevent a general conflagration. But the fire spread and was eventually brought into the edifice itself by excited Roman soldiers, who tossed in firebrands and rushed after them, mainly in the expectation of plunder. It was one of them who started the final and fateful blaze.

This account is full of circumstantial detail and quite acceptable. The only ground for suspicion is the author's somewhat excessive insistence on Titus' goodwill: as we have seen, the point is already made in his preface—and there more than once—and later too the writer seems to protest too much. But this is, after all, in keeping with the rest of his treatment of Titus; and it is improbable that it would have occurred to anyone to disbelieve Josephus, were it not for the existence of a rival account. A complicated set of hypotheses has been built upon this account.

In his Latin *Chronicle*, a universal history written in the late fourth century A.D., the Christian historian Sulpicius Severus describes Titus deliberating with his council about what should be done with the Temple, in similar terms to those of Josephus. But this time it is some of the other council members who feel that the building should be saved, and Titus who argues for its destruction. The key question, from which all else follows, is whether this narrative contains real information, deriving from a good source other than Josephus, or whether it is simply Sulpicius' (or someone else's) imaginative adaptation of the Jewish author.

The German-Jewish philologist, J. Bernays [in "Ueber die Chronik des Sulpicius Severus," *Gesammelte Abhandlungen* (ed. H. Usener), 2 (1885)], to whom we owe the development in 1861 of the 'sensational conjecture' that so greatly discredits Josephus, held that the character of Sulpicius' account suggests a well-informed source. Bernays thought that it did not accord well with Sulpicius' general argument to make Titus the instrument of destruction, and that therefore he would have had no motive for inventing the story. The exact opposite seems nearer the truth. Although Severus, like most early Christians, is convinced that the destruction of the Temple and the dispersion were punishments of the Jews, brought about by their rejection of Christ, he at the same time holds that the Romans' actual purpose was a different one: they had really been attacking the Jews in order to destroy the roots of Christianity, and that is what he says in the passage quoted. In other words, this was just another in a line of persecutions. In recounting persecutions, the habit of Severus and other Christian writers is to ascribe each to the wickedness of an individual emperor. In the very next chapter of Severus we read of the (supposed) persecutions of Domitian and Trajan. More than that: Hadrian is there represented as doing just what Titus had done, taking action against Judaism in an attempt to liquidate the daughter religion, this time by turning the Temple into a pagan shrine and banning Jews from Jerusalem. Here too, the emperor's personal thinking is made responsible. What could be more natural, therefore, than to adapt Josephus' dramatic setting for Titus' decision about the Temple, but to stand the situation on its head? Josephus will have been familiar to Severus in the famous Latin version which was known to the monk Cassiodorus and attributed to Rufinus, Ambrose or Jerome; that Severus *had* read the Jewish historian is shown by the fact that his figures for total losses in the siege and capture of Jerusalem derive from Josephus' figures, not from those of Tacitus. So Josephus' account must have precedence over Severus'.

Bernays held that Sulpicius had as a source the now lost narrative of the fall of Jerusalem from Tacitus' *Histories*. His proof was that elsewhere Severus had patently borrowed from Tacitus' account of Nero in the *Annals*. But use of the *Annals* does not prove knowledge of the same author's *Histories*. An additional claim made in favour of Tacitus as the source, that the *Histories* display a predilection for depicting councils of war, is worthless, when so many historians, from Herodotus on, have used the same device.

Even if Bernays is right, and the story in Severus is Tacitean, such origins would not endow it with authority, as Tacitus' sources may well have been inferior ones. To counter this weakness, Bernays made another proposal: Tacitus, he conjectured, used an eye-witness account of Titus' council of war. We find a mention in the *Octavius*, a third-century dialogue of Minucius Felix, of one Antonius Julianus, said there to be a Roman writer on the Jews, and we are referred to this writer for further proof of the familiar punishment-doctrine, that the Jews had deserved whatever misfortunes had befallen them, and that they had ignored earlier warnings. Who was Antonius Julianus? The solution, adopted by Bernays, but propounded already in Tillemont's great history of 1698, is that this was the procurator M. Antonius Julianus, whom Josephus mentions as having been present at the crucial council of war. This man *might* have written an account of the fall of Jerusalem, and is conjectured to have been Tacitus' source.

In fact, of course, we must remain tentative about the identity of Antonius Julianus. There was a rhetorician of that name in Hadrian's period, contemporary with Aulus Gellius; but we may well be dealing with a figure who is otherwise totally unknown to us. Yet it is only the pure supposition that the procurator's account, through the mediation of Tacitus, underlies Sulpicius Severus' story about the destruction of the Temple which gives the latter author any claim to be taken more seriously than Josephus.

Apart from the literary construction, other types of argument have been used against our author in the wake of Bernays. There are deductions from other passages in the *Jewish War*, such as the various warnings expressed there that the outcome of continued Jewish resistance would be the loss of city and Temple. There is the Roman decision (not, be it noted, ascribed to Titus) to burn all the remaining outbuildings once the Temple was gone. There are imprecise phrases in other authors, and above all, Valerius Flaccus' description of Titus as 'blackened with the dust of Jerusalem, as he scatters firebrands and wreaks confusion over all its towers'. This poetic passage from the opening of a mythological epic is taken to show that Titus himself, through the mouth of a compliant poet, exulted in the deed of destruction. But neither the portrayal of the Jews and of Josephus himself as fully aware that they risked their Temple by their obduracy, nor Titus' attempt to subdue them with threats, nor the effusive congratulations bestowed upon the conqueror after the events, serve to demonstrate that Titus had not aimed to keep the Temple standing.

Rabbinic literature and Jewish folk memory persistently represent Titus as the wicked agent of destruction, and stories have clustered around the theme of his punishment. These are emotionally compelling, and they may even have had an influence on Bernays (who had been taught the Talmud by his father, the chief Rabbi of Hamburg). But they arose from imagination, not knowledge. The Jews could have had no idea how the Roman decision was reached. Ironically, the same process of personalisation is at work here as in the anti-Jewish Sulpicius Severus. Its unhistorical nature will be apparent from one example:

there is a Rabbinic text which tells that Vespasian was present at the siege of Jerusalem (in fact he had left for Rome), and that he attached messages to arrows and sent them to the Jews. Such fictions are characteristic of Aggadic (non-legal) literature. And it is after all, in no way surprising that Jews and non-Jews alike should in retrospect regard the Roman commander as individually responsible for the destruction: for many purposes, it was what happened that mattered, not what nearly happened.

A wider view of Roman policy and interests can show us what is possible, but cannot resolve this problem. In 73, Titus himself did order the demolition of the sectarian Jewish Temple of Onias at Leontopolis; but then, after the main Temple had gone, there was naturally less incentive for concern. Again it could be said that there was evident advantage to Rome in eliminating the focus of Judaism. But equally it would have been in Titus' interest to obtain a Jewish surrender early in the siege rather than to have to fight to the bitter end for city and Temple. And at a later stage, a concession to the high priests and other aristocrats (many of them by now deserters) could ensure their cooperation in the future administration of the country. It is perhaps partly the disappearance of this opportunity for his class (and himself?) which Josephus regrets when he harps upon what might have been. In any case, the balance of probabilities is an even one.

Therefore, as long as it cannot be convincingly impugned, Josephus' story, the best we have, is the one that should stand. We do not have to believe that he knew all that was in Titus' mind nor all that went on at the private council of war. The description of the latter has a flavour of literary convention. Yet it is clear that Josephus would have had ample opportunity to discover the general direction of Titus' thinking—and might, indeed, have been consulted on some points. It is reasonable to follow him.

The theme of Titus' concern for the Temple is perhaps in the end less interesting for the light it sheds on the historical situation, or on Titus, than for what it reveals of Josephus. In his concern with demonstrating that Titus wished to save the Temple, he displays as much preoccupation with the vanished shrine as with Titus' reputation. Wilful destruction would, in Josephus' eyes, have been a great abomination: hence the kind of desperation with which he pleads Titus' innocence. This reflects an attitude which runs right through his work: he has an attachment to the Temple which is striking and constant, and which survives long after its fall. His respect for the cult as it had been and his distress at its disappearance are perceptible in many places in his writing. He evidently felt it still when he wrote the ***Antiquities***—even if not to such an extent that we would class him with those mourners who are castigated in the Talmud for excessive grief. For there is a notable moment in Josephus' rendering of Moses' last instructions to the Israelites, where the author makes a telling addition of his own: the Temple would be destroyed not once, but many times, yet God would restore it in the end (***Jewish Antiquities*** 4.311-14, deriving from Deut. 28). This lies in the future. But here what must be recognised is that Josephus' own brand of national feeling, one centred on that established order of which the Temple had been a part, was not diminished by his commitment to the Flavians. And it is with justice that the unusually powerful and controlled description with which he concluded Book 6 of the *Jewish War* and which told of the holy city's final hours became one of the most celebrated in all his work.

We shall return to the loyalist sentiments of Josephus the Jew. Here it should be noted that the theme of Titus' anxiety about the Temple united Josephus' different interests in a rather convenient way. Looking again from the Roman angle, we observe that (irrespective of the truth about the incident), by making compassion (tempered with firmness) into one of Titus' principal attributes, Josephus was ascribing to him what was the monarch's virtue *par excellence*. A philosophical tract on clemency was composed under Nero by the philosopher and politician Seneca; there *misericordia*, perhaps the nearest Latin equivalent to Josephus' *oiktos* (pity) is repeatedly linked with *clementia*. And nobody, at this time, would fail to realise that the display of both these attributes implied absolute power. Thus Josephus depicts Titus just as a fledgling emperor should be depicted. It is easy to exaggerate this point, and the portrait we are discussing is neither a philosophical manifesto, nor the ideal pattern for a *princeps*. Such characterisations are probably no more than an instinctive echo of themes heard by Josephus, at court or elsewhere. None the less, the nature of the compliment which he pays to Titus is unmistakable and characteristic of the literature of the period.

We are on more slippery ground if we seek the precise reason why Josephus (and others too) made the son and not the father emerge as the monarchical figure. That Josephus' history was published while Vespasian was still in power cannot be doubted. Did those who moved in imperial circles understand that it was politic to direct towards Titus that adulation in which the plain man, Vespasian, professed little interest? On Titus' position, after all, rested the dynasty's hope of continuance; and this was a matter of such importance to Vespasian that he was said to have burst into tears when his elder son's succession was challenged. Or was it that in this case Josephus was influenced by his own personal relationship with the young man? The two explanations are not, of course, incompatible.

The *Jewish War* was not simply the scene of Vespasian's and Titus' great military triumph; it was also the spark which fired their ascent to power. Josephus had to decide whether to tell that story too, and how much space to give to it. One thing is clear. His work does not centre on the emergence of the new dynasty. The historian announces that he is summarising the upheavals in Rome and the successive seizures of power which followed Nero's death only so as to avoid breaking up his story; and that is on the whole a fair description of the situation. He does this by keeping track of Flavian movements; Titus is first sent by his father to acclaim Nero's successor Galba, but when news reaches him in Greece that Otho has taken over, he decides to go back to Palestine. The subject is taken up again a little later, when Vespasian, having reduced the surroundings of Jerusalem, hears that yet another emperor rules, Vitellius this time. This is the point at which Jose-

phus puts the beginning of Flavian progress. The final eighth of Book 4 has Vespasian acclaimed emperor by the legions of Alexandria and Judaea, his first appointments and his journey back to Rome, as well as some major military and political developments in Italy. We read about Vespasian's departure from Alexandria, with Titus left behind to finish off the Jewish war; and about the return march, and the many festivities which punctuated the new ruler's progress. Not until the last of Josephus' seven books do we pick up Vespasian again, still on his journey; and there we find Titus at Caesarea Philippi, where he has been throwing spectacles for the people in which Jewish captives played a prominent part, to celebrate an imperial birthday.

A historian whose angle was narrowly Jewish would not have recounted these events, or, at any rate, not in this way. Yet, while peripheral, they do offer information which the reader naturally seeks, for there is something remarkable and perplexing about the sudden elevation of the leading Roman in the war, and his consequent removal from the scene. Moreover, the story of Josephus' prophecy and its fulfilment has established a link between the fate of the emperor and that of the Jews. At the same time, Josephus could expect such non-Jewish readers as he had to find matter of such public importance a welcome diversion from Judaea and its problems. Josephus' access to Roman events is thus in some respects an asset to his narrative.

As for the detail of his account, it clearly represents a version of the story which is highly favourable to the Flavians, and sometimes untrue. Their seizure of power is described as a direct response to the state's needs: the inadequacies manifested by Vitellius during the few months of his rule had greatly distressed Vespasian; the rest was due to the troops. They felt that they had as much right as the German legions to choose an emperor, and would have killed their leader had he resisted. He himself would have preferred to remain a private citizen. Alexandria followed Judaea, for when Tiberius Julius Alexander heard the news, he induced his two legions to take the oath of allegiance to the new emperor. We do not need Tacitus' rather different version to make us realise that the accession must have been designed with more forethought and deliberation than Josephus' account allows; and it emerges from between the lines that Titus' return to the east after Galba's death was a public declaration of Flavian ambitions. Tacitus makes this a turning point; and even Suetonius perceives that Vespasian's aspirations must have taken shape straight after the death of Galba. Tiberius Julius Alexander's understanding with Vespasian is shown by these authors to have made such aspirations feasible, and Tiberius' troops are rightly said to have declared their will not after, but two days before the three Judaean legions. Tacitus agrees with Josephus on only one point: that the declaration of the latter was spontaneous, and required no prearrangement.

Josephus' version of these political machinations is more pro-Flavian than any other which survives. But its twists and details are due as much to the author's source as to any deliberate argument on his part, and I do not think that Josephus personally had any concern with the finer points of the Flavian case or that he consciously contradicted other, less favourable accounts. The effect has come through his dependence at such points on source material of a pure Flavian character, and that material was probably the imperial records.

Josephus speaks once of the *commentarii* (notebooks) of Vespasian, citing them as authority for his own claim that his antagonist Justus of Tiberias had been implicated in a raid on the Decapolis region. He refers once to the 'notebooks of Caesar', as an authority which Justus had not consulted on the subject of the siege of Jerusalem. And on one occasion there is talk of the 'notebooks of the emperors' (*tōn autokratorōn*), described as a work which had been read by some of his detractors. This last reference suggests that the first part of the war had been covered by Vespasian, the second by Titus. The emperors' reports must have been available for consultation, even if not issued to the public. Although they are never mentioned in the *War*, it is more than likely that they were produced soon after the events with which they deal, and that our author had easy access to them because of his privileged position.

He did not, however, over-use this source. His criticism of Justus for ignorance of the notebooks does not mean that he himself was slavishly dependent. Unlike Justus, he was either an eye-witness or close to the crucial events almost all the time, and he was the last person to need to plunder another account. He confined his debt to specific kinds of material. The Flavian passages are among the most obvious, but military records could also provide exact information associated with the Roman campaign—measurements of distance, dates, topographical descriptions, the names of Roman soldiers (and perhaps even of Jews) who performed distinguished feats of valour. Then there are Josephus' topographical excurses, descriptions of the Jordan Valley and the Dead Sea, Egypt and the port of Alexandria, Jerusalem and the Temple, Herod's palaces on Masada, the fortress of Machaerus. Their level of accuracy is rather high; and since, given the circumstances of composition, he can hardly have surveyed the sites himself, these probably come out of the Roman account. All this was valuable, lending variety to Josephus' composition, and giving it the air of a proper war history. But, whereas the *commentarii* were once thought to be the key to understanding Josephus, it is now clear that such a key cannot unlock so involved an author.

It is only when Josephus reaches the seventh and final portion of his history that the Flavian material acquires a greater role in the economy of his writing. One reason for this springs to mind. Book 7 opens with the razing to the ground of the holy city's defences. Josephus' story is all but told. Book 6 has concluded with a solemn epilogue, a retrospect on the history of Jerusalem from its foundation by Melchizedek. And now he has to cast about for more material. He needs to plug the surprisingly long gap between the fall of Jerusalem and the subjugation of Masada in 73. Reports of the doings of Vespasian and Titus and members of their party, incidental to Josephus' main theme, come in very usefully for this purpose. And Josephus manages to provide a satisfactory link by making the events a reminder that Judaea was not at this time the world's only trouble spot: every part of the Roman empire was in a state of turmoil and panic. So, after the capture of Simon bar Giora, we read about the Flavian family birthdays; the revolts of Classicus and Civilis in Gaul and Germany; and the Sarmatian attack on the empire, with the successful resistance of Domitian and of Q. Petilius Cerealis who was his relative. We also learn how Titus preserved the privileges of the Jews of Antioch, a theme rather more germane to the history and to its author. However, there were also more acute and sensitive problems attached to framing a concluding book for the *Jewish War*. How was the Roman victory to be handled? There could be no evasion here. However free his patrons usually left him, Josephus could be sure that they would look for an account of the triumph in which *Judaea Capta* was the leading motif. This he did not deny them. The first part of Book 7 has two big set-pieces of description which make an important contribution to the total effect of his work. The first is the enthusiastic reception of the victorious Vespasian in Italy, the second and longer price is the triumph itself, at which Josephus may even have been present. Of these two scenes Vespasian and (in the second one) Titus are the resplendent centre-pieces, and we find in them an intensification of the aura which has throughout invested the imperial figures.

The Roman populace is overjoyed at Vespasian's return, and the whole of Italy begins to exult before he is anywhere to be seen. Senate, people and army are delighted with the *dignitas* and military distinction of their new ruler. The roads and the city are thronged with people. Vespasian is hailed as benefactor and saviour. There is feasting, libations are poured and prayers offered; we learn that this was the beginning of a new prosperity for Rome. The description is extravagant. It is echoed in briefer compass on Titus' return when, according to Josephus, a similar welcome was offered, better this time in that Vespasian could participate in it, and, since Domitian was present as well, all three Flavians were now reunited.

The scene of a formal entrance (*adventus*) closely akin to these is depicted for us in another medium. It is to be found in stone, in one of the marble panels (B) discovered at Rome in the Palazzo della Cancelleria in 1938. The subject has been identified as Vespasian's return, and the contents are a fusion of Josephus' two scenes. As in Josephus, senate and people—here in the form of figures representing the *genius senatus* and the *genius populi Romani*—are there to great him. At the same time, the theme stressed by Josephus in connection with Titus' arrival, that of a family harmoniously reunited, is illustrated here too, with Domitian doing his filial duty and responding to a greeting of his father—albeit, as some would have it, a little coldly. The suggestion that the two men were represented together in order to refute rumours of rivalry and hostility between them is an attractive one; and the same might be said of Josephus' insistence on the closeness of the three. Whether both Josephus and the sculptor were influenced by passages in the imperial notebooks, or whether the idea percolated to them in some other way does not matter: it is clear that each is presenting things the way the dynasty wanted.

Titus' return was followed by preparations for his military triumph, and then by the triumph itself. Josephus portrays it vividly and elaborately, moment by moment and gesture by gesture, and envisages it as a reflection of the empire's greatness. This triumph was another prominent motif in Flavian propaganda. Perhaps inspired by Titus' arch, art and poetry in the Flavian period shows a fondness for triumphal scenes and victory processions, both real and mythological. Furthermore, the great day could be taken as a celebration of the end of Rome's civil wars and the inauguration of an era of peace. So, as we might expect, Josephus does not neglect this implication, but looks forward to the year 75 and the dedication of the Flavian Temple of Pax. It was this Peace Temple which was to house, among its trophies, the Menorah from Jerusalem and the other ritual objects represented on the arch and previously described by Josephus as part of the procession. Thus the writer coolly depicts the symbolic expressions of his country's ruin. The Jews are now referred to as 'the enemy'. And it is as though the sufferings which they had endured and over which he had expressed his grief, now exist only as tableaux, themes figured in golden tapestries and framed in ivory, contributions to the triumphal pomp.

Here, the balance of Josephus' writing has shifted. The splendour of the Roman generals' display cannot be appropriate to a Jew's account of his nation's downfall; Josephus' admiration must be admitted as out of keeping with the reactions he had previously evinced, and only the triumph's conclusion, the execution of Simon bar Giora as the token enemy leader, can have given him any personal pleasure in the relating. Certainly, as a subject, the Roman triumph offered fine opportunities to the literary artist to exhibit his talent, and to Greeks to read about a famous Roman custom, with its religious and topographical associations; but that does not reduce the dissonance. Here Josephus can for the first time be said to glorify his patrons at the expense of his people.

Yet the historian evidently sought to redress the balance, at least to an extent; and Book 7 is noteworthy also for an increased intensity of Jewish patriotism. The triumph is followed by yet another great set-piece, the fall of Masada, with the courageous exploits and final suicides of its defenders.

It seems clear that Josephus had no direct information about the last stand of Eleazar's *sicarii* against the siege of Flavius Silva. Military activities are described entirely from the Roman sources—presumably the imperial notebooks again. Information about the defenders, and the way in which the last 959 committed suicide, must have been given to the Romans by the two women of whose escape Josephus tells us; this perhaps then circulated among Romans by word of mouth. But the organisation of the Jews and the conduct of their resistance remains a closed book even after this century's excavations. None the less, Josephus took an unexpected step: with an act of imagination he put himself among the defenders, and transformed that final scene into an extended dramatic narrative.

The framework of the story can safely be accepted as true. This we can say, not because archaeology has been able to confirm the events themselves—we could hardly expect this—but rather because the creation of so elaborate a fiction, either by Josephus or by a predecessor, is too hard to credit. The twenty-five skeletons found by the excavators on a lower terrace of Herod's northern palace may or may not be those of survivors. The eleven *ostraka* which they unearthed and one of which appears to say ben Yair may or may not be the lots drawn by those designated to kill their comrades and families. Josephus' narrative does not stand or fall with these identifications. And the over-ingenious theory that the suicide was an apologetic invention designed to assuage Josephus' unconscious guilt, to conceal a Roman massacre or for some similar purpose, is best left to bury itself.

Josephus did not invent the Masada incident, though he did embody it in a form which has given it lasting resonance, a continuing power both to inspire and to annoy. And he did create two important speeches for Eleazar. For all their debt to Greek philosophy, these speeches, in so vivid a context, stand out as designed to evoke in the reader respect for the man who is made to utter them. Eleazar and his companions are at the last made into virtual heroes by Josephus, and it is as though the author has forgotten his former abhorrence of such people and their ideals.

While the Roman scene of the triumph has been conspicuous for its external glitter, the Jewish episode is the more powerful. As a literary contrast, this is well-contrived. For all that, we may fancy that it was not aesthetic considerations but a serious uneasiness on Josephus' part about his handling of the triumph which drew him to provide a counterweight. That he allocates a prominent position in his final book to the fate of the Masada remnant, when he could well have closed with the end of the war proper and the triumph of 71, reveals as much about his commitments as does the portrayal of the procession at Rome. And even Masada is not the very end. The ***Jewish War*** terminates in the death of a persecutor; there is a lurid description of the disease which afflicted the Roman governor of Libya after he had executed perhaps 3,000 (wealthy) Jews on a false charge of revolutionary activity, and had dragged others in chains to Rome. That, too, does not seem accidental.

It is characteristic of Josephus to seek to reconcile different allegiances, just as it had been the hallmark of the social group to which he had belonged. There are, of course, times when conflicting claims simply cannot be made compatible, and in Josephus the occasion of the Roman triumph is one such. But he does not give up. The pull of the Flavians is not made to supersede earlier loyalties, and adulation of the emperors is rarely close to the heart of his work. Though we cannot altogether eliminate that disturbing figure, Josephus the flatterer of the conquering emperors, this Josephus must be put in his place.

There is no doubt that his multiple-responsiveness created for Josephus problems which were ultimately insoluble, in his writing as much as in his short-lived political career. The very act of redressing with a sequel of praise for his compatriots the pro-Flavian balance which he had produced by dwelling on the triumph brings with it its own inconsistencies. For the Jews of Masada, whose story he exploits for this purpose and whom he holds up momentarily for our admiration, are among those whom he most hates. Even in Book 7 we can still find harsh condemnation of the *sicarii*, as part of the author's retrospective castigation of all the rebel groups. But when the year 73 is reached, and the war contains no other Jewish protagonists, animosity has to be suspended. We might see this as yet another effect of the disappearance among Jews of a political middle ground; now there was really no other position which a moderate could take. This has a counterpart: after the war, Romans too perceived Jews as of one kind only, and this emerges clearly from a grotesque incident recorded by Josephus. It was probably still in A.D. 73 that the revolt of *sicarii* from Palestine, led by a weaver named Jonathan, was suppressed at Cyrene by the local Roman governor; apart from 3,000 wealthy local Jews, notables from Alexandria and Rome were incriminated, and among them Josephus himself. Such an attack is astonishing, even if our author was later cleared, and not, like Jonathan, tortured and burned alive. Still, a vestige of the old divisions among Jews survives, emerging in the fact that, while Josephus reserves his greatest enthusiasm for the governor's appropriately gruesome end, he expresses also some satisfaction at the rebel Jonathan's punishment: his old eagerness to dissociate himself from undesirable Jews has not entirely gone.

Masada, then, eases one difficulty, but makes another for its narrator. And the last book of the ***Jewish War***, like its predecessors, originates not in detached observation, but in intense involvement, and strong, if not particularly deep reactions. No longer, however, is the historian writing from a firm standpoint, with a clear set of political prejudices. Now contemplating the aftermath of the revolt, he is tossed to and fro, extending emotion in various directions. Along with his homeland, he has for a time lost his firm mental anchorage, and here his writing shows it. In this way it continues to be an immediate product of pressing circumstances, and to illuminate them through the strong responses expressed in it, and even through its weaknesses as history and literature.

Morton Smith   (essay date 1987)

SOURCE: "The Occult in Josephus," in *Josephus, Judaism, and Christianity*, edited by Louis H. Feldman and Gohei Hata, Wayne State University Press, 1987, pp. 236-56.

[*In the essay below, Smith discusses the role of the occult in the thought of Josephus, contending that he merges Greco-Roman polytheism with his own inherited Jewish monotheism.*]

I think that hitherto there has been no scholarly study of the occult in Josephus. First, the occult, although popular, is not fashionable in academic, rationalistic circles. Second, it is not prominent in Josephus' work, where military and political history and court intrigue hold the center of the stage, while religion, in the background, figures mainly as a cause and condition of actions and as a matter of legal observances and historical claims, anything but occult. Moreover, "the occult" is a vague concept—literally "the hidden," but now, in common usage, something mysteri-

ous, usually thought supernatural, something not a matter of socially accepted teaching or practice, a shadowy entity in the twilight zone of popular beliefs, where no precise line can be drawn around the shadow.

The ancient world, even more than the modern, lies mostly in that twilight. The intellectuals, the authors and readers of literary and scientific texts, are a tiny upper class, the thin, brilliant skin of a soap bubble filled with smoke. Flavius Josephus, Roman citizen, member of the hereditary priesthood of Jerusalem (a considerable civic honor), a well-known *sophistes* ("literary man"), who distinguished himself in imperial service, appears as a representative of that upper class. Though his native language is Aramaic, he writes in Greek for Romans and wealthy pagan provincials, in defense of his own people, and for wealthy Greek-speaking Jews, in defense of his own position: that cooperation with the Romans is necessary for Jewish survival. The surface of the soap bubble reflects the brilliant scene of the Roman Empire—consuls, armies and client kings, cities, temples, and theaters. Through these reflections we catch only glimpses of the dark cloud behind them. What is there?

To daimonion, "the demonic," a complex of supernatural powers.

Greatest among these powers is "the god," i. e., the god of the Jews. Josephus' Judaism and several schools of Greek philosophy had in common the teaching that the cosmos had only one cause, a god. Many Jews and a few pagans maintained that this god was the only—that is, the only "true"—one, and that all others were either inferior or totally false. Part of Josephus' religious tradition was an aggressive, monotheistic rhetoric, mainly derived from Isaiah 40-55, which declared all gods of all other peoples (sc. "the Gentiles") mere sticks and stones; more important were the Ten Commandments and other legal passages, which prohibited Israelites to worship any image at all, or any god but their own. Because of these, many Jews had made themselves conspicuous by refusing to join in Gentiles' worship, but others had proved more adjustable, some of them merely in order to get on with their neighbors, others in recognition of the many elements in the world which seem to have supernatural powers.

One common form of adjustment was to take advantage of the pagan and Old Testament practice of speaking of "god" without indicating which god was meant, as we say "God willing," in which the original (pagan) reference was to any god concerned. Since Hebrew, Aramaic, Greek, and Latin all lack an indefinite article, Jews and Christians found this anarthrous use of "god" a convenient way of referring to their god without making the reference explicit. Josephus' works are full of such references, which pagans would read as referring to "a god," but which Josephus expected his Jewish readers to understand as references to the Jewish god. For such references we shall use "a god," to indicate the absence of the definite article, sometimes important.

Almost equally convenient for Jewish adjustment to life in the pagan world was the belief then spreading among Jews that the true, personal name of their god should not be mentioned. It had not yet become unknown (as it since has—the form Yahweh, usually employed, is only a learned guess). Common people still knew it and used it in times of stress, but the upper class held to a (nonbiblical) law by which its use was, with rare exceptions, prohibited. When speaking Greek, they commonly referred to Yahweh as "the god"; pagans could take the reference as one to any god they chose. We shall try to preserve the effect by translating exactly, "the god."

Josephus was acutely aware of the necessity of getting on with the Romans—attempts to resist them had brought his city to ruin and him to the verge of death. However, he held to the traditional Jewish laws and monotheistic rhetoric. However, again, he was not a philosophic thinker, but shared the common notion of the world as full of supernatural beings. Consequently, he both repeated the rhetoric of monotheism and peopled his histories with a multitude of angels, spirits, *daimones*, and unspecified powers—an omnipresent, but usually inconspicuous, overworld of the occult. Here are some of the denizens:

Gods: Though Josephus usually reserves the Greek word *theos*, "god," for the Jewish god, he occasionally uses it for others. Vespasian, on first arriving as emperor at the imperial palace in Rome, sacrificed to "the gods within;" "the god" of the people of Akkaron was called *Myia*. These are mere concessions to popular usage, but Josephus' own usage sometimes approached the popular. Retelling the story of David and Jonathan [in *Jewish Antiquities*], instead of having Jonathan swear, as in I Samuel 20:12, by "Yahweh, the god of Israel," he made him take David outdoors and swear by "this god whom you see to be immense and extended everywhere," i. e., the sky. Did he identify Yahweh with "the god of the heavens" (Neh. 1:4) and so with Zeus? In spite of the Old Testament's prohibition of images and its occasional insistence that Yahweh never appeared in any form (Deut. 4:12-24), it contained a lot of reports of his appearance in various forms to various individuals; most of these Josephus took over with unabashed literalism. Worse, when he had no Old Testament model, he continued to write stories of "the god" and "the deity" appearing to men. Which god? We should suppose Yahweh, of course. But other gods were being worshiped. The Essenes evidently thought the sun a subordinate deity; Josephus says [in *Jewish War*] they prayed to it before sunrise and covered themselves when excreting "so as not to offend the rays of the god" (this must be the sun god).

Josephus himself, indeed, went further than the Essenes. In describing their teaching about immortality he says they think souls are "composed of the finest ether" and "pulled down into bodies, as if into prisons, by some physical magic" (II, 154). He emphasizes the similarity of their teachings to those of the Greeks. Therefore, we should probably understand "ether" in the Stoic sense, as the material of the highest god. This understanding is confirmed by Josephus' repetition of the theme, both in a speech he attributes to Titus and in the final speech that he puts into the mouth of Eleazar ben Jair in Masada. Urging the Sicarii to commit suicide, Eleazar tells them that life, not death, is man's misfortune, for the "connection between

the divine (soul) and the dying (body) is unseemly" and death frees the soul to return to its natural purity. Here the soul is unmistakably "divine." This cannot be thought of as a theory repudiated by Josephus. As a good *sophistes*, he uses the same argument for the opposite purpose in his own equally imaginary speech to his companions in the cave of Jotapata, urging them not to commit suicide, but to surrender. There he says flatly that the soul "is a part of a god housed in our bodies."

This recognition of divinity in men opens the door for all sorts of occult developments, not only efforts to recognize, reverence, and exploit the present god, but also cults of the souls of the dead and necromancy. Josephus makes both Eleazar and Titus point out that after death the souls have "divine strength and wholly unlimited power, although they remain invisible to human eyes as is the god himself." Nevertheless (though he does not point this out), it would seem that if they can be "pulled down into bodies . . . by some physical magic," they might also be compelled or persuaded by magic or worship to use their power as the magician or worshiper wished. Living in ancient society, where necromancy was common, Josephus presumably thought of this possibility. He certainly knew of necromancy from I Samuel 28:11ff., which he retells, without changing the basic events, in *Jewish Antiquities* VI, 332-336.

The belief that souls are parts of a god has taken us from "the (Jewish) god" (*ho theos*) to "the deity" or "the divine" (*to theion* means both). Josephus himself makes the transition often, and often without seeming to notice the difference; on many occasions he uses first one term, then the other, obviously with the same reference, to avoid monotony. On the other hand, the adjective *theios* ("divine") has a much wider field of reference than the noun *theos* ("god"). Josephus uses "divine" to describe the god's nature, spirit, power, voice, anger, help, gifts—whether in man (understanding, strength, etc.) or in the external world (rain, the manna, and the like)—will, providence, appearances, miracles, laws, angels, prophets, scriptures, Temple, territory, and so on and on. The way in which each of these things was thought to participate in divinity, or belong to the sphere of the divine, has to be decided separately for each case.

An especially important class of cases is that of certain men with whom "the divine" or "the divine spirit" consorts in such a way that they become "divine men" in contrast to the rest of mankind. Moses is the outstanding example; anyone who considers his legislation "will find him a divine man" (*Jewish Antiquities* III, 180). Even the Egyptians recognized this. Isaiah, too, was "admittedly divine" and Daniel, to whom "the deity became visible," enjoyed "a reputation of divinity" among the people. Such "divine men" were prominent in contemporary paganism, and Josephus seems a bit uneasy about the possibility of their being worshiped. This is understandable, since Christianity was growing up around him. He therefore insists that Moses "in the holy books declared himself mortal, fearing lest someone, because of his virtue's excess [of human limits?], might dare to say that he had gone to the divine." Yet of Enoch, on scriptural authority, Josephus himself said just that.

This notion of the special divinity of a few individuals does not contradict that of the divinity of all human souls. The difference may have been conceived as one of the adequacy and obedience of the different bodies. However he reconciled them, Josephus held both beliefs, and they alike proved that, for him, the deity was not wholly separate from the world; divine power penetrated creation and was manifest in many of its elements.

Some of these elements, however, had minds of their own and might, or might not, do as the god wished. His "messengers" (*angeloi*, "angels") appear mainly in Josephus' retellings of biblical stories and, as in the biblical texts, are sometimes called "gods", but Josephus, departing from his sources, also calls them *phantasmata*, "visionary beings." His references to angels, outside the biblical passages, are rare, but the angels were not. The Essenes knew (and kept secret?) their names; and Herod Agrippa II, when trying his utmost to persuade the people of Jerusalem not to revolt, called on "the Temple cult, and the holy angels of the god, and our native land" as witnesses that he had done all he could to save them. Herod's speech was, of course, written by Josephus long after the event, but it shows what Josephus thought would have been effective in the situation. Consequently, when he speaks of Israel's receiving the holiest laws "from the god, through *angelōn*" it is hard to tell whether he thought these "messengers" were the angels or the prophets. The distinction may not have been sharp to him because, as already shown, he thought the prophets, filled with the divine spirit, were themselves divine beings. He himself, when he had become "full of god" (*enthous*) and had, like Jacob, "laid hold of the dreadful *phantasmata*" of his prophetic dreams, went to Vespasian and declared himself "an *angelos . . .* sent forth by a god."

Whether gods or mere messengers, angels belong to the larger class of "spirits" (*pneumata*), which are likewise inconspicuous but important in Josephus' works. He once uses "the divine spirit" to translate "the angel of Yahweh" and twice to translate "the spirit of *'Elohim*" or "of Yahweh." Three times, to fill out biblical narratives, he makes up passages in Old Testament style, using "the divine spirit" or "the spirit of the god," in Old Testament fashion, for the power that enters men and causes prophecy. Similarly, he explains the vehemence of the Roman soldiers declaring themselves ready for war by saying that they are filled with some spirit like that of (the god) Ares. In man the spirit and the psyche cause life, because "a part of" a god's spirit was put into man, just as (Josephus suggests) it was into the Temple, As cause of life, spirit and psyche are somehow identified with the blood, but the identification must be only temporary because "the spirits of evil men," presumably after death, become "the so-called *daimonia*" and get into the living and kill them. The *daimonia* are distinguished from "the evil spirit" (both possessed Saul) in *Antiquities* VI, 211, another passage Josephus made up. Perhaps the distinction was dictated by I Samuel 19:9, which refers to Saul's tormenter as "the evil spirit of Yahweh," not to be explained as that of a dead

man. In *Antiquities* VI, 214 it becomes simply the "demonic pneuma."

This terminological muddle reflects the fact that Josephus' thoughts about *daimones* (and *daimonia*, a diminutive, but commonly equivalent) were, like those of most men of his time and ours, confused. He was clearer as to what could be done about them. Solomon had left directions for driving them out, and these directions were still effective. Josephus himself had seen an exorcist display his skill before Vespasian, using Solomon's method (*technē*), a ring with Solomon's seal, and a plant Solomon had prescribed; the plant was probably *baaras*, which was said to have many magical properties. The witch of Endor's ability to call up souls (*psychas*, not *daimonia* nor *pneumata*) of the dead was also described as a *technē*. Josephus thinks well of such skills; Solomon's method, in particular, commonly practiced by Jews, is part of the heritage of the Jewish people, and Josephus is proud of it, but he is little concerned about such matters. The wider range of his thought about the demonic appears more clearly when he uses the term for good powers. Even spirits of the dead might be beneficent. In Titus' account of immortality, the souls of brave men fallen in battle are said to become "good *daimones* and beneficent heroes" helpful to their people. Josephus wrote the speech, but its pagan terminology is not used in the parallels he also wrote. However, he told many stories of the demonic powers of the dead working on the side of justice. He even says that the *daimones* of the sons Herod had executed went through all the palace, searching out and exposing those who had participated in the plot against them, and silencing those who would have warned their enemy, Antipater, that his guilt was being exposed. Seth Schwartz remarks that the explicit demonology of these last two passages was not copied into *Antiquities*. Perhaps Josephus came to disapprove of it.

Securing justice is a rather grim beneficence, but Josephus often credits *daimones/daimonia* with more amiable activities. When the unfortunate Alexander did something right, his father, Herod, thought he must have fallen in with good *daimones*. The *daimonion* used to talk with John Hyrcanus and told him everything that was going to happen; thus he enjoyed one of the three greatest gifts that are given to men: prophecy. By contrast, Socrates' claim to have been advised by a *daimonion* cannot be taken seriously; he was just joking.

These examples have taken us from *daimon* to the cognate adjective, *daimonios*. This adjective covers the whole range of the supernatural, including both "the divine" and what we should call "the Satanic," as well as the morally indefinite powers. Consequently, there is no adequate English translation for it, and I must use the term "demonic" with this explanation. Sometimes it seems to be trivialized: it can be used to describe an amazing escape, a devastating earthquake, or a violent wind, but even in such contexts we must hesitate before dismissing it as merely rhetorical. The escape in question was, for Josephus, a *teras*, a prodigy which made people think Herod "a man peculiarly dear to the gods" and so hastened his victory. When the earthquake came Herod argued that it was a natural event, not a sign of divine displeasure—but Josephus' summary of his argument is probably ironical. Josephus himself says that the demonic wind "arose for the destruction of" the defenders of Gamala; and when describing the capture of Masada he also uses a wind, this time reversed, "as if by demonic providence," to give the Romans the victor. To prove his point he makes Eleazar, the leader of the Sicarii, drive it home: "Clearly our hope of escape has been taken away by the god himself; for the fire [blown by the wind] . . . did not turn back naturally against the wall we built, but these things show (the god's) anger" (*Bellum* VII, 331f.).

This expresses what was, in *Bellum*, Josephus' major theme: it was not the Romans who conquered the Jews and destroyed Jerusalem, but the god himself who used them as his agents for his own purposes and repeatedly intervened to make sure that these purposes were carried through. Most adjectival uses of *daimonios* in *Bellum* can and should be taken as expressive of this theme and therefore equivalent to "divine"/"godsent," while the noun, *to daimonion* ("the demonic"), is often equivalent to "the god." *Daimonios* appears repeatedly in descriptions of critical elements in the course of events: the means by which Josephus' life was saved at Jotapata, Vespasian's courage and his decision to seize the throne, and so on. The climax comes with the burning of the Temple, when a Roman soldier, "not waiting for an order, . . . moved by some demonic impulse, snatches up some of the burning wood and . . . hurls the fire inside a golden door" (*Jewish War* VI, 252).

The god of the Temple was not there to put it out. Months (or years) before, the priests, entering the Temple for their nightly service, had heard the sounds of movement "and then of (many) speaking in unison, 'We are departing hence'." Josephus reported the plural. He also referred indirectly to this omen in the speech he claims to have delivered to the defenders of Jerusalem. In this he reviews Jewish history and comes to the conclusion, "I think the divine has fled from the holy things" (i. e., from the sanctuary and the cult). One copyist changed "the divine" to "the god," but "the divine," with its range of meaning, probably reflects not only the plural in the reported omen, but also the plurality in Josephus' mind. He was thinking, probably, of the account in Ezekiel 11:22f., which described the departure from the Temple of the throne of Yahweh with its entourage of lightning and beasts and wheels and cherubim and all the multiplicity of the divine.

Yet even if this be granted, the story of the omen is not wholly explained. For Josephus also knows and accepts the belief that the Place of the Jerusalem Temple had or was a supernatural power. (Not the Temple itself, though Josephus thought the Herodian one the most marvelous building in the world and accordingly lamented its loss.) His belief in the supernatural power of the Place appears most clearly in the historical section of his speech to the rebels (*Bellum* V, 376-419), from which we quoted the climax. The speech is placed just before the final stage of the Roman attack; it urges the defenders to spare the Place from capture, by timely surrender. Addressed to Jewish nationalists, it appropriately appeals to the history of the people. Consequently, it is the fullest treatment in *Bellum*

of subjects from Old Testament times. Unlike the Old Testament, however, its central power is not Yahweh, but "this holy Place." It is from this Place that the rebels are fighting; this is the great ally, which they have polluted (Yahweh they could not). When Sarah was carried off by Pharaoh, Abraham, "raising his hands (in prayer) to the Place which you have now polluted, brought into battle on his side its invincible power." After one night, Sarah was restored and Pharaoh, "worshiping the Place now polluted by you," fled. God brought our fathers out of Egypt to be guardians of this shrine (not "this temple"; though the word is *neōkoros*, there was no temple and would be none for four hundred years). After the ark was stolen, the Philistines, smitten with plagues, restored it, propitiating "the holy" (Place, understand *chōrion*). Sennacherib was killed when he besieged this city. When the people were released from the Babylonian captivity they again became shrine guardians of their ally (the Temple had not yet been rebuilt). The Hasmonaeans brought down on us the Romans by sinning against "the holy things [the Place, Temple, and cult] and the laws." Therefore, "those who inhabit a holy Place should leave everything to the god" (of the Place). But under you "the Temple has become a receptacle of all [sins] and the divine Place has been polluted. . . . After these things do you look for the dishonored [Place] as an ally?" On the contrary, the Place has made its springs flow more freely for Titus, as it did of old for the Babylonians. From all this we come to the amazing conclusion quoted above: "Therefore, I think the divine has fled from the holy things [the Place, the sanctuary, and the cult] and is now with those you are fighting."

The one sort of god who cannot leave his sanctuary is a holy Place, and the preceding speech has shown that Josephus thought the Place a supernatural power. This notion is not likely to have come from his supposed Greek secretaries. The speaker is Joseph ben Matityahu, the priest of Jerusalem, who traced the sanctity of the site back to Melchizedek and for whom it was "the Place worshiped by the whole civilized world" (spoken by a chief priest). But Josephus also claimed to be a prophet. In this same speech he compared himself to Jeremiah, and in claiming that the divine had departed he followed Ezekiel 11:22f. The god of the prophets, the god of Israel who could take the country or leave it, was not committed to its holy sites. Josephus was a divided man. The fission in his sacred books between the prophetic and the priestly traditions, the fission in his own and his people's life between the demands of religion and the requirements for survival, emerge in this contradictory conclusion that the divine has fled from itself. And this split in his world will be perpetuated by the split in Judaism between the worship of a universal god and the devotion to a holy place.

A surprising proof of Josephus' occasional independence from his environment is the fact that among these supernatural powers there are no stars, except the sun, and no planets. Cosmic speculation had been active in the Jerusalem of his youth; it is clearly reflected in his accounts of the tabernacle and the Temple, but the only trace of an astral cult is the Essenes' sun worship. When the day destined for the destruction of the Temple came, it was determined not by astral configurations, but by its historical relation to the date of the burning by the Babylonians. The role of the luminaries is merely that of a cosmic clock—unless the practices that went with the Jerusalem speculation were part of what Josephus chose not to tell.

Since the demonic is multiplex, it deals with men and material objects in many ways. Josephus' favorite word for "providence," whether human, demonic, or divine, "of a god," or "of the god" is the strictly descriptive one, "forethought" (*pronoia*). Mythological terms—"fate," "the lot," "the given," etc., —he almost never uses, but he is fond of impersonal expressions meaning "it was/is necessary," some of which have strong moral overtones ("it is right"), but none of which, by itself, indicates a personal agent. *Nemesis* ("envy," "grudge," "anger") is occasionally attributed to a *daimon* or to the god (it can be induced in him by prayer and sacrifice), or to *Tyche* ("chance" personified), and sometimes it is an impersonal power; but it rarely figures in Josephus' accounts and is more likely a literary reminiscence and dramatic device than one of the supernatural powers he commonly reckoned with.

Tyche, by contrast, was not only a popular pagan goddess, but also, in Josephus' mind, a complex of powers, everywhere active, and especially complex because every individual had his own set, what we should call his "luck" or "fortune." So does every people. The Tyche of the Romans was famous, and Josephus, like everybody else, believed in her; her power and that of "the god" act together. Josephus was aware of, but rejected, the theory that identified a man's Tyche with his fate ("the allotted"). Tyche was more personal than fate, therefore more capricious, and more likely to be affected by men's actions, literally a supernatural femme fatale. Like women, Tyche was jealous, particularly of human virtues, and was apt to destroy those who excelled in them. She belongs in the world of the demonic, but her status there is never defined.

Besides the indirect governance of providence and the eccentric interference of Tyche, the various demonic beings intervened in human affairs in various ways, and men had been given or found out ways of foretelling and influencing the course of future events. The books of the Old Testament are mostly concerned with accounts of divine intervention in the past, prophecies of the future, and directions for observances—ritual, legal, and moral—said to please Yahweh and get desired results, while their neglect angers him and leads to predicted punishments. Implementation of these teachings and the observance of additional customs—the elements of an "unwritten law"—made up the recognized, legally authorized practice of Judaism and, therefore, do not belong to "the occult." Josephus was capable, when writing against Apion, of claiming that the mysteries of Judaism—which he defines as the teachings that the creator god is clearly known from his works and is to be served by moral behavior, but cannot be represented by any image—were well known and had been taught by Moses, not to a small circle of initiates, but to his many companions and all their descendants Van Unnik was capable of taking this at face value and deriving from it the conclusion "that revelation in Moses' law had no hidden truth and was open to all" ["Flavius Josephus

and the Mysteries," in *Studies in Helenistic Religions*, ed. M. Vermaseren, 1979].

Nonsense. Josephus himself mentions a few secrets not to be written—Yahweh's true name, the ten words on the tablets written on Sinai, the locations of the graves of the kings—and he says that he prefers to keep secret Daniel's explanation of the stone destined to fill the world, and that nobody can declare or even conceive what the cherubim of Solomon's Temple looked like. But these are trivia. Except for Daniel, Josephus says almost nothing of the apocalyptic literature flourishing in his time; he refers to the traditions about ascent to the heavens and the divine throne, but only with remarks (in *Jewish Antiquities* XVIII, 18) so cryptic that their meaning has rarely been recognized. He never faces the extent to which Judaism seemed to outsiders a mystery religion, as Plutarch described it in *Quaestiones Conviviales* 4.6.1, where Jewish doctrines and ceremonies are described as "things not to be declared," and the question discussed is the identity of the unknown Jewish god. What actually did go on in that great Temple in Jerusalem, of which only the outermost court was open to Gentiles? Even ordinary Jews could not enter the innermost court, and the adyton was closed to all but the high priest. Speculations were widespread and wild. And what of their holy books? Legends told of divine punishments of men who had even thought of revealing their content. Where could one get copies? We do not know. The usual ignorance of ancient authors, down to the third century A.D., about the content of the Old Testament is puzzling. Were its texts commonly kept secret? From the pagan point of view, Judaism itself might be described as an occult religion. Philo did so describe it. Josephus, however, tried to refute this notion, and we are concerned with what is represented in his work as occult.

First, Josephus regards knowledge of the future as occult. The various demonic beings reveal their intentions by signs and portents, which can be understood by those skilled in interpreting them, but not by common people or the wicked. These warnings occur, like the Northern Lights, from time to time throughout the course of history. The greatest display was that which preceded the destruction of the Temple: a stationary comet; an abnormal light; a cow that gave birth to a lamb; a Temple gate that opened automatically; chariots and armed men flying through the sky; the *daimones*' departure, which the priests heard. In addition, a peasant for some years prophesied disaster, yet people did not understand. This collection is remarkably close to those found in the works of pagan authors. Josephus' beliefs about these matters seem to be those of the surrounding world. But he also quotes a patently Jewish story to prove that birds are worthless for divining the future.

Besides omens, signs, and portents, the demonic communicated with men through dreams and prophecy. These are closely related in Josephus' thought, as they were in that of the ancients generally. Pagan prophets (*manteis*, as opposed to Jewish *prophētai*) and *soi disant* "Chaldeans," were supposed to be expert in interpreting dreams, and were consulted even by Jewish kings, but in vain. Jewish prophets were of course better, and among them Josephus himself was outstanding. The god chose him to foretell the future and revealed to him the course of the war. The revelations were given in dreams, which, although obscure, he was able to understand because of his knowledge of the sacred books and his priestly background. The god also entered him, so that he prayed and prophesied. His most famous prophecy was that Vespasian would become emperor, but he also prophesied the exact length of the siege of Jotapata and his own imprisonment, and when these prophesies came true he continued to be consulted about the future.

Besides himself, Josephus mentions a good number of prophets from postbiblical times, but only one other whose prophecy explicitly involved dreams. The god appeared to John Hyrcanus in a dream, and John took the opportunity to ask which of his sons would succeed him. (When told, he did what he could to make the god a false prophet, but, of course, failed). The Pharisees were also believed to prophesy, "because the god frequented" them, but of their three reported prophecies, two were disastrously wrong, while the third was perhaps no more than a shrewd, albeit moral, prediction. Perhaps the Pharisees are also meant by "those who prophesy" or those "who refer things to divine causes" and who said (truly) that Herod's colitis was a god-sent punishment. Prophets were expected to declare past causes as well as future results; the verb used in the passage just cited means "to prophesy" as well as "to ascribe things to the gods," and the Pharisees were said to do both. However, the reference is uncertain. John Hyrcanus not only saw the god in dreams, but "the daimonion"/"the divine" talked with him so that he foreknew everything. The peasant who prophesied "Woe to Jerusalem" is said to have suffered from "somewhat demonic" inspiration. Antipater had forebodings that dissuaded him from coming home "because his soul was already prophesying about its [fate]."

Apart from these we find a surprisingly mixed lot [in Josephus's *Jewish Antiquities*]. The pagan *manteis* and necromancers have their peculiar techniques, which sometimes work. The witch of Endor, incidentally, was a model of morality, and Balaam was the best *mantis* of his time. Israelite prophets are also said to have had a *technē*, and the Essene prophet Judas is called a *mantis*. King Aretas of the Nabateans learned, from omens given by birds, that an impending Roman attack would fail. A German prisoner, knowing the significance of birds, prophesied accurately the fate of Agrippa I. The emperor Tiberius had great skill in divining from omens and birth dates. Such examples are just what we should expect to find in any pagan historian's work of Josephus' time.

Besides these individuals, a good many anonymous authors had launched prophecies that circulated among the credulous. Josephus, though usually incredulous, thought some of these ambiguous and commonly misunderstood, but essentially true, for example: *Bellum* IV, 388 and its variant VI, 109, when factionalism arises, the Temple will be destroyed; *Bellum* IV, 311, the Temple will be destroyed when it becomes a square; and *Bellum* VI, 312, a world ruler will arise from Judea (this Josephus thought fulfilled by Vespasian). The last two, Josephus says, were

"written in the [sacred] scriptures/sayings." If so, they were all he was willing to publish, besides Daniel, of the enormous eschatological literature of his time, some of which he evidently accepted as inspired and, perhaps for that reason, thought should not be revealed. He says that most of these prophecies were either disbelieved or misinterpreted, and not only by his opponents, for "many of the wise erred." This is partly apologetic; he had been one of the errant. However, it expresses also a conclusion to which he had been brought by his error: "The god's nature . . . is complex and works in many ways" (*Jewish Antiquities* X, 142). Therefore, although his prophecies will come true, men, because of their ignorance and disbelief, are unable to profit from his ambiguous utterances. Such prophecies must be interpreted by exegesis both learned and inspired, like his own. Thus the root of occultism is the nature of the god.

In the material Josephus did choose to publish, the true prophets most prominent during his own time are the Essenes. We are not here concerned with the actual Dead Sea sect or sects, but with what Josephus says of the groups for which this peculiar name was used. He represents them as an occult sect within Judaism, closed by its special purity laws not only to Gentiles but also to all Jews except its own initiates. The initiates had to undergo probation, requiring years of candidacy before full initiation, and take "frightful" oaths not only to maintain good behavior, but also "to conceal nothing from fellow members, nor betray anything of theirs to others," to hand over the teachings and rules (*dogmata*) exactly, and to preserve the books of the sect and the names of the angels (as secrets?). This basic structure is supported by many traits common in occult groups: asceticism, communal economy, nocturnal silence, prayers at dawn to a special deity, peculiar ablutions, linen ritual garments, ritualized meals with common prayers (in ritual garments, to be put away afterwards), taciturnity, sobriety, subjection to superiors, and the study of ancient writings and the secret medical properties of plants and stones. Disputes and discipline are handled within this sect by its own courts, and the ultimate punishment is expulsion. Their doctrine of the natural immortality of the soul as an ethereal being magically imprisoned in the body is to be reconciled with the report in *Antiquities* XVIII, 18, that they "immortalize" the soul, by supposing the immortalization to be a restoration of the soul's original condition, freeing it from carnal corruption; compare this with the famous rite for "immortalization" in the Paris Magical Papyrus. "The access of the righteous man [to the heavens] is contested on all sides" (by demons, jealous angels, and heavenly guards); therefore, this secret rite is needed. Hence, too, their need to preserve the names of the angels, whom they would meet on the way—angels, like watchdogs, are quieted when called by their proper names.

Stories of ascents to the heavens pullulated in Palestine at this time; the Pseudepigrapha are full of them. The notion seems to have been a common dream which impressive, hypnotic ceremonies or powerful individual suggestion could transform into experiences the initiates would believe actual. Such experiences probably led to prophecies, hence Josephus' reports of Essenes "who profess to foresee

Ruins of a synagogue in Upper Galilee.

the future, having been brought up from childhood on holy books and extraordinary purifications and pronouncements of prophets" (notice that these pronouncements are distinguished from the holy books). Nor is it surprising that with all this sanctimonious secrecy the Essenes were widely revered and credited. Herod honored them as supernatural beings. (Had they not been immortalized and gone up to heaven?) One of them declared that Herod was chosen by a god for a happy reign of at least thirty years (*Jewish Antiquities* XV, 371-374, 377-379, and 375-376 are a correction by some enemy of Herod, probably Josephus).

Magically induced prophecies are also said to have been mentioned by Nicholas of Damascus in his speech against Antipater; he satirized the "female foolishness" of Antipater's harem allies, "prophecies and sacrifices to harm the king," and assorted scandals that helped enliven his deadly denunciation. These goings on, however, are less likely to have been connected with the Essenes, most of whom avoided women, than with the Pharisees, whom we have already seen practicing prophecy, and who also were protégés of the wife of Herod's brother, Pheroras. She was a leading lady in Antipater's circle.

The Essenes' study of the medicinal properties of plants and stones would make them a likely source for some of the philtres and poisons that turned up so often in Herod's court, were it not that other sources seem even more likely. Poisoning is usually secret; the Greek word *pharmakon*

means "drug, medicine, poison, magical material, spell" and, in the plural, "magic." Medicine and occultism were so closely connected that there is no telling how much of the latter was involved in the poison plots; some pretty certainly was. But many circles had some knowledge of such drugs, so we must look at the persons directly implicated, and these again belong mainly to the circle of Pheroras and his womenfolk, whose connections were with the Pharisees rather than the Essenes. (To judge from the Dead Sea documents, the two sects were not friendly.) Josephus himself shows a little knowledge of magical pharmacology (*Jewish Antiquities* I, 93: tar from Noah's ark is an apotropaic; *Jewish Antiquities* VIII, 47 and *Bellum* VII, 180ff.: the herb *baaras* has many magical properties and is sovereign for exorcism; *Jewish War* IV, 465, 476-481: the powers of Jericho spring water and of Lake Asphaltitis bitumen). He probably knew more.

The Essenes may have been the cause of many, and the source of some, of the traditions linking Judaism with other occult societies and mysterious peoples. Josephus states as a fact that they "use the way of life taught among the Greeks by Pythagoras." In *Against Apion* I, 163-165 Hermippus is said to have remarked that Pythagoras borrowed from Judaism several observances; but these were mostly ones that the Jews never observed. By contrast, Josephus' statement is almost plausible, if reversed. Essene practices do resemble Pythagorean teachings so often and so closely that some Pythagorean influence (indirectly, through Egypt?) seems likely. Elsewhere in *Against Apion*

(I, 179) Josephus quotes from "Clearchus" a report that Aristotle said the Jews are descended from some Indian philosophers called "Calani." No such Indian philosophers are known, but an Indian named Calanus greatly impressed Alexander's companions by burning himself alive. Josephus' report shows how the story had ramified in the intervening four hundred years. The cornered Eleazar's appeal to his men in Masada to "imitate the Indian philosophers", though in a composition surely by Josephus, may possibly, if Josephus observed dramatic propriety, be evidence for occultism among the Sicarii, and this might show Essene influence, since it is coupled with the Platonic account of the afterlife, which Josephus attributes to the Essenes. By contrast, the Cypriot Jew who claimed to be a *magos* and was used by the procurator Felix to seduce Queen Drusilla [recorded in *Jewish Antiquities* xx, 142] is completely credible as a historical figure, but quite inadequate as evidence either of Persian or of Essene connections. *Magos*, in the usage of the time, was often merely a polite term for *goēs*, "magician." Elsewhere in Josephus *magoi* appear only in the Daniel stories, as Babylonian court magicians, to be disgraced, and in the story of Darius' accession, to be massacred.

Although Josephus says that an Essene (perhaps an ex-Essene?) was appointed to one of the six military commands set up at the beginning of the official Jewish revolt, the course of events indicates that the most influential prophets of antebellum Palestine were neither the Essenes, nor the Pharisees, nor any of the upper class and their hangers-on whom we have thus far reviewed, but the many popular prophets, who talked mostly of political deliverance by supernatural aid and who constantly encouraged the revolutionists. Josephus is consistently hostile to them. They were lower-class, possessed by demons, and made up at will all sorts of bogus oracles; many were hired by the revolutionary leaders (i. e. "tyrants") to keep the people from surrendering; the one who told the people to go to the Temple "to receive the signs of salvation" became thus responsible for the great slaughter of civilians that occurred when the Temple was captured. In a word, they were the opponents' forecasters.

Except for the claims—doubtless often sincere—to divine possession and inspiration, there was nothing occult about such prophecies; they were produced for, and often during, public proclamation. However, by their general theme, and especially, in this last instance, by the teaching that the people must all go to some place where the divine power will be revealed, they are allied to the utterances of a class of false prophets, most of whom Josephus calls *goētes* (singular *goēs*), a term of which the meanings range from "magician" to "fraud." Basic is "magician" or, at least, "wonder worker," so Josephus' frequent choice of the term, with its occult connotation, when he might have used something merely descriptive, e. g., "false prophet," suggests that there was more in their teaching than appears in his accounts. Here is a list of incidents involving these "false prophets":

> In Pilate's time (ca. 26-36) the Samaritans were persuaded, by a lying demagogue (*not* called a *goēs*), to assemble on Mount Gerizim where he

would reveal the vessels hidden by Moses (*Jewish Antiquities* XVIII, 85).

Under Fadus (ca. 44-46) one Theudas, a *goēs* who claimed to be a prophet, called the masses to the Jordan, which he said he would divide (*Jewish Antiquities* XX, 97).

Under Felix (ca. 52-60) appeared a swarm of "*goētes* and deceivers" who, pretending to prophesy, set the crowd mad and persuaded them to take to the desert where the god would show them signs of freedom. Josephus specifically distinguished these from the Sicarii, a terrorist organization (*Bellum* II, 258ff.; *Jewish Antiquities* XX, 167f.).

Worse was an Egyptian *goēs* and prophet who led thirty thousand to the Mount of Olives, promising to take Jerusalem (by making the walls fall) (*Bellum* 261ff.; *Jewish Antiquities* XX, 169ff.).

Goētes and bandits joined forces and pillaged the countryside (*Bellum* II, 264f.; the parallel in *Antiquities* does not mention the *goētes*).

Under Festus (ca. 60-62) a *goēs* promised salvation and an end of evils to those who would follow him to the desert (*Jewish Antiquities* XX, 188).

Just before the capture of the Temple (August 70) a false prophet urged the people of Jerusalem to go to the Temple, where the god would show them signs of salvation (*Jewish War* VI, 285).

After the fall of Jerusalem, in Cyrene, ca. 72, a "most wicked man" led many of the poor into the wilderness, promising to show them signs and apparitions (*Jewish War* VII, 437f.; V 424).

All these gatherings the Romans put down by military force, but this tells us nothing of the teachings involved; it was merely the Roman method of discouraging illegal assembly. That Josephus does not call all these men *goētes*, and does use the term occasionally for mere deceivers, should not conceal the pattern common to this group. All these men promised miracles; the use of *goēs* to differentiate them from the rest of the revolutionists suggests that they were thought to do miracles. It may also reflect claims they made to be Moses *redivivus*, who was expected by many. Moses had often been described as a *goēs* because of his miracles, a description Josephus vigorously combats. Besides rebutting the charge, he tried to suppress the evidence for it; he made God, not Moses, bring the plagues, and he removed the magical details—smiting with the rod, scattering ashes in the air, invocations, etc. To justify Josephus' use of *goēs* for his contemporaries, we should like some such details about the methods they used; but for these, in Josephus' brief references, there was no space.

Consequently, such evidence is available only for Jesus, and Josephus' mention of Jesus (*Jewish Antiquities* XVIII, 63f.) has been so much corrupted that no attempted reconstruction of the original can be relied on. At most the description, "a doer of amazing works," can be salvaged—it means "wonder worker"—and it not only accords with the gospel accounts of Jesus' public appearances, but also, in Josephus' work, connects him with the other *goëtes*, although some differences deserve notice: he came a little before the others; the first of the above list, the Samaritan (who is not called a *goës*) came at the end of Pilate's governorship, while Jesus was executed about the middle of it. Although crowds are said to have followed Jesus into the wilderness (Mk. 6:32ff., 8:1ff.), he is not said to have called them out, or promised signs of salvation if they would come. Of course, Christian tradition would have forgotten, not to say suppressed, evidence of illegal activity and failed promises. The crowds following him were not broken up by military force because he was not in Roman territory but in that of Herod Antipas, and the Roman government frowned on the use of violence by its subordinate rulers against their subjects; Antipas' younger brother had been deposed for that, and the lesson had not been lost. If only we knew a little more about Josephus' original notice, we could probably argue with more confidence from his silence. As things stand, we can only say that Josephus seems to have mentioned Jesus partly because of his miracles (he liked wonder stories) and partly because he had been the founder of a sect which, by the time Josephus wrote, was probably becoming important, though Josephus hoped it would not last: "The tribe of the 'Christians,' named for him, has not yet died out." With these words Josephus dismissed the most important occult movement of his time.

In a society on the verge of revolution, as Palestine was throughout Josephus' youth, prophecies are important. The concentration of Josephus' narrative on political events further exaggerated their importance. In everyday life, most people were often more concerned about their health, their jobs, and their families than about revolution. So if we had a social history of the time, we should probably find the Essenes most prominent for their magical cures, and the importance of other groups explained by other functions. As it is, we find in Josephus a mixed bag of different sorts of details reported in different connections. Most of these details have already been mentioned or belong to types of which examples have been given. To review them under the different headings by which they might be classed seems needless, but a few concluding notes are called for.

Josephus seems to share the common belief of his time in the efficacy of oaths, prayers, and curses, particularly dying men's curses, and adjurations using the secret name of the god. In spite of the secrecy of the name, it was still used. Foragers who sneaked out by night from Jerusalem during its last weeks to find a little food, and were caught by the revolutionists, begged in the name of the god to be allowed to keep a part of what they had found, and were refused; propaganda, of course, but certainly intended for his Jewish readers, and therefore an indication of what they would find credible.

Of other magical means to ends, Josephus believed in the power of the spells left by Solomon to alleviate diseases. His belief in demonic avengers has already been mentioned; his statement that Antipater used the demonic vengeance for his brothers to destroy his father may refer

to some sort of black magic, of which the women of his circle were often accused. Accusations of magic were evidently common in the society. When a couple of Agrippa's Gentile officers deserted to Josephus in Caesarea the opposition accused them of being magicians, and the charge found much acceptance. Nevertheless, Simon's attempt to escape from the ruins of Jerusalem by passing himself off as a demon succeeded only for a moment.

Similar notions of the world are introduced by Josephus in a few passages of his retelling of biblical stories. Sinai was haunted by the god. The god, by giving his true name to Moses, gave him the power to invoke him effectively; consequently, the god came to meet the Israelites "in response to Moses' wishes" and came to the tent and the Temple "in response to our prayers". The gems of the high priest's garments lit up to signal the god's presence and also to foretell victory in war.

In II Kings 2:19-21 Josephus found a brief biblical report that Elisha "healed" a spring at Jericho, which had formerly blighted crops and caused miscarriages, by throwing into it salt from a new pot and saying, "Thus saith Yahweh, I have healed these waters; there will be no more death and miscarriage from that place"—a nice little miracle, but too simple for the Roman carriage trade. Therefore, Josephus retold it, or preferred a source which had retold it, as follows:

> Elisha, . . . having been hospitably received by the people at Jericho, since they treated him with particular kindness, rewarded them and the whole district with an eternal favor. Going out to the [pestilential] spring and throwing into the stream a pottery vessel full of salt, then raising his righteous right hand to Heaven and pouring out on Earth propitiatory libations, he besought Earth to soften the stream and open sweeter veins [of waters], Heaven to mix with the stream more fertile airs and to grant the people of the land both proper production of crops and children to succeed them, and [he asked that] the waters which would cause these [blessings] should never fail so long as the people remained just. With these prayers, and with the performance of many additional rites [known to him] from his art, he changed the spring, and the water which had formerly been a cause of their childlessness and famine was thenceforth made a source of healthy children and plentiful food. (***Bellum*** IV, 461-464)

Here is a Palestinian example of the Graeco-Roman "divine man" in action, his right hand raised to heaven, like that of a Hellenistic statue, pouring out his libations and prayers, not to Yahweh, but to Earth and Heaven, and uttering, not Yahweh's commands, but moralizing Hellenistic rhetoric, backed up by rituals from his (secret) knowledge. Josephus may have found all this in some source, but he found the source congenial to his taste and useful for his purpose, to re-do Judaism in Roman imperial style, of which an important decorative element was the occult.

For him, however, the occult was more than a decorative element. It was a constituent part of the Graeco-Roman world, a part made particularly important by the conflict between that world and his inherited Israelite monotheism. For the multifarious Graeco-Roman religious life, that monotheism, to which he was loyal, left no place. But that life was present and triumphant. Some place had to be found for it. If it was somehow to be made compatible with the henotheism of biblical law and the monotheism of Isaiah, their relationship could only be occult. He had to adopt the Septuagint's solution of the problem: "All the gods of the Gentiles are *daimonia*" (like Yahweh), "but the Lord" (Yahweh, as distinct from the others) "made the heavens." (Ps. 96:5, Septuagint 95:5).

An excerpt from *Jewish War*

Finally, then, the nine [last people at the Masada] bared their throats, and the last solitary survivor, after surveying the prostrate multitude, to see whether haply amid the shambles there were yet one left who needed his hand, and finding that all were salin, set the palace ablaze, and then collecting his strength drove his sword clean through his body and fell beside his family. They had died in the belief that they had left not a soul of them alive to fall into Roman hands; but an old woman and another, a relative of Eleazar, superior in sagacity and training to most of her sex, with five children, escaped by concealing themselves in the subterranean aqueducts, while the rest were absorbed in the slaughter. The victims numbered nine hundred and sixty, including women and children; and the tragedy occurred on the fifteenth of the month Xanthicus.

Flavius Josephus, in Joseph: Jewish War, *Vol. III, translated by H. St. John Thackeray, William Heinemann, 1928.*

Heinz Schreckenberg   (essay date 1987)

SOURCE: "The Works of Josephus and the Early Christian Church," in *Josephus, Judaism, and Christianity,* edited by Louis H. Feldman and Gohei Hata, Wayne State University Press, 1987, pp. 315-24.

[*In the essay below, Schreckenberg examines Josephus's histories against the works of some early Christian writers, contending that Christian apologists deliberately reinterpreted his writings in order to make the foundations of Christianity more credible.*]

It is apparent in the case of Josephus that an author's work and its impact are inseparable and that literary-sociological aspects must complete the purely literary-historical view. Indeed, the reception of Josephus' writings produces, among others, spiritual responses that arise more from the subjective bias or motivation of his readers than from the works themselves. This Jewish historian was for a long time paid little or no attention by his countrymen while, on the other hand, he was esteemed highly in Christian circles of the early church. In fact, Josephus placed a great abundance of information at the disposal of the young church's early developing historical, historical-

theological, and apologetic interests. His works, created in the style of Greek historiography, offered (in *Jewish Antiquities*) a colorful recapitulation of the Old Testament, rich in detail and arranged with skill, and (in the *Jewish War*) the tragic fate of the city of Jerusalem, a shocking and moving drama that appeared to be the continuation and culmination of the reports of the New Testament in which, to be sure, the prophecies of misfortune regarding Jerusalem play an important part (Mark 13:2; Matt. 23:38, 24:2; Luke 19:40-44, 21:6, 20-24). Beyond these accounts one soon saw during this time of early Christianity that there was, throughout the works of Josephus, the mention of numerous persons, places, and occurrences that either were known from the New Testament or whose stories completed the biblical accounts. In all cases, the works of Josephus furnished background information for the Bible in a welcome and impressive manner. Due to this strong affinity between Josephus and the Bible, the Jewish historian's great future as a famous author in Christian circles was determined almost in advance. One may assume that the theologians of the early Christian church at first reached for the works of Josephus with hesitation and astonishment, then, as they read, with a greater and greater joy of discovery.

The development of the early Christian church had already begun at the time of the New Testament; indeed, the New Testament reflects the first stages of its history. Hence, the relevance of our theme does not begin with the reception of Josephus by the church fathers but earlier, with the New Testament. In this connection, first and foremost, it is important to note that some parts of the New Testament, such as the Gospel of Luke, probably attained their final edited form only after A.D. 70; accordingly, one expects here and there, an echo of the Roman conquest of Jerusalem. This, indeed, occurs, and we have to realize this fact. The prophecies of misfortune, which, in the mouth of Jesus of Nazareth, were at first meant eschatologically, obtained their historical color in part from flashbacks to the fall of Jerusalem, that is from *ex eventu* presentations. These prophecies became the point of departure for the later reception of Josephus. The affinity between the historical depiction by Josephus and the reports given in the New Testament were destined to become the crucial factor of reception and impact. Besides this affinity, there were numerous points of contact so apparent that modern theologians did not discover them at first—namely the reports by Josephus about Jesus (*Jewish Antiquities* XVIII, 63-64; XX, 200), John the Baptist (*Jewish Antiquities* XVIII, 116-119), and James, the brother of Jesus (*Jewish Antiquities* XX, 200-203). In addition to these accounts about early Christianity, reports, for example, about the house of Herod, the Jewish sects, and the death of Herod Agrippa stimulated much interest among the church fathers. The church fathers did not yet perceive the full extent of the areas of contact and anticipated only partially what the current scientific exegesis partly confirms and partly ascertains, namely, that there are almost surely structural and formal correspondences between the actions of Jesus of Nazareth and the actions of the prophets and miracle workers of the period of the New Testament described by Josephus. Note, for instance, the actions of Theudas, Judah the Galilaean, the Egyptian, and the Samaritan who wished to lead his followers to Mount Gerizim. The connections perhaps help us to understand better the entrance and the messianic activities of Jesus. As Jesus was a Galilaean, an investigation of the connotations of the concept "Galilaean" in Josephus can also help to disclose certain characteristics of Jesus of Nazareth. The descriptions of the Zealots by Josephus and in relevant passages in the New Testament probably also illuminate each other. Even as complex a subject as the friendship for Rome by the Jew Josephus may perhaps allow one to understand better some pertinent features of the New Testament.

Because the publication of the works of Josephus (ca. A.D. 75-96) as well as the editing of the New Testament partially overlapped and in each case extended over a long period of time, an interaction of some sort between Josephus and the early Christian church of the first century is not to be discounted. In other words, the influence or dependence of one text upon the other is quite possible; and this problem presents itself, above all, in the case of parallel reports. It has often been assumed that Luke made use of Josephus. On the other hand, P. Fornaro [in "Il Cristianesimo oggetto di polemica indiretta in Flavio Giuseppe *Ant. Jud.* IV 326," *Revista di Studi Crociani* 27 (1979)] has presented the view that Josephus, with his representations of the passing of Moses and of Enoch and Elijah, created an indirect polemic against the views of the early church about the death and resurrection of Jesus of Nazareth. P. W. Barnett concludes, from the affinities between the reports of Josephus about the prophetic miracle workers of the first century and the figure of Jesus, that Josephus in his description was influenced by the Jesus tradition.

Neither Fornaro nor Barnett ["The Jewish Prophets— A.D. 40-70—Their Intentions and Origins," *New Testament Studies* 27 (1981)] is convincing in his hypothesis. It is more likely that the New Testament authors and the historian wrote independently of each other. To be sure, it is inevitable that the similarity in content between Josephus' report about the destruction of Jerusalem and the relevant assertions in the Gospel of Luke should lead us to draw conclusions regarding the dating of Luke. One cannot contest the legitimacy of such attempts, though the results are not certain, partially because varying premises must be taken into account. However, investigations regarding coincidences of literary peculiarity, as, for instance, between Luke and Josephus, move on a relatively secure terrain; and this area of research will, in the future, prove to be fruitful.

Since the work of Origen and of Eusebius of Caesarea, the judgment that Josephus is of incalculable value as source material forced its way increasingly into the Christian church, so that eventually one hears of Josephus as "a kind of fifth gospel" and as a "little Bible." Certainly the extant works of the Jewish author were valued for the most diverse reasons as an authoritative source regarding Judaica of all kinds. The *Jewish War* dominated the tastes of the Christian reading public so much that, in the tradition of the early church regarding Josephus' works, the *Jewish War*, the earliest chronologically, was transmitted

under the title *Halosis* (i. e. conquest [of Jerusalem in the year 70]) and placed in manuscripts after the *Jewish Antiquities*. In this way, Jewish history, as seen from a Christian point of view, ended chronologically in a catastrophe that took place as a result of the Jews' rejection of Jesus. Even B. Niese adheres to this order of the works in his major critical edition (Berlin, 1885-1895).

Origen was the first to make use of the Jewish historian with apologetic zeal. On the basis of a reinterpretation of suitable passages, he develops an anti-Jewish interpretation of the fall of Jerusalem, according to which the Jews lost their homeland and their Temple in the year 70 on account of their crimes and their rejection of Jesus. Eusebius goes even further. In his case, the anti-Jewish apologetic attains a surpassing importance. The tragic fate of the Jews in the year 70 and afterwards, as described in detail by Josephus, becomes for him a historical proof of the truth of Christianity. He does not shrink from falsifying the report of Josephus and speaks about a collective *servitus Judaeorum* ("servitude of the Jews") since the year 70. This collective servitude of the Jews is an unhistoric, apologetically motivated assertion; for the Jews of the Roman Empire, while they suffered in the course of late antiquity various legal disadvantages, remained, even under Christian emperors, free citizens in principle, and their cult remained a *religio licita*.

Quite similarly, the church father Jerome utilizes the reports of Josephus. It is characteristic of the Christian appropriation of Josephus that Jerome includes him in his Christian history of literature, *De Viris Illustribus*. This chapter (cols. 629-631) was often selected, moreover, in the Christian Latin tradition of Josephus, as a substitute for the *Vita* of Josephus, which is the one work of Josephus that was not translated into Latin in antiquity. For before the Western world became acquainted with Josephus' autobiography, preserved only in Greek and edited by Arlenius as the editio princeps of the Greek text (Basel, 1544), this was the only comprehensive information about the life of the Jewish historian. How much Jerome himself esteems him one may glean from the way in which he refers to him in connection with exegetic problems as if to a manual of high rank: "Read the history of Josephus". Isidor of Pelusium and Frechulf of Lisieux refer to Josephus in a similar manner. An ambivalent posture of early Christianity toward Josephus becomes especially clear in *Hegesippus*, a Latin revision of the Greek *Jewish War* that originated about 370. The Christian translator praises, on the one hand, the valuable deposition of the truth-loving Jew whose testimonial in favor of Jesus actually ought to oblige his fellow believers to turn to the Christian belief; but, on the other hand, he reproaches Josephus for his hardness of heart (*duritia cordis*) and for his stubborn disbelief (*perfidia*).

The example of the Venerable Bede allows one to recognize the extent of the Christian reception of Josephus in the early Middle Ages; for, as to Josephus' value as a faithful bearer of biblical Hebrew tradition, Bede places him side by side with Origen, Jerome, and Augustine. From that time on, the Jew Josephus often achieves almost the authority of a church father.

After our look at the significance of Josephus for some important authors of early Christianity, there are still some general aspects to be noted that are significant for the developing and forever more intensive relationship between the church and the Jewish historian. The foremost guiding theme and the dominant characteristic of the reception and appropriation of Josephus by Christian writers become apparent. From the third century on, the writings of Josephus, above all, the *Jewish War*, appeared to Christian theologians to be a commentary or a historic appendix to the New Testament, like the welcomed documentation of the *veritas christiana*, and to be evidence of the substitution of the disinherited Jewish people by God's new people, the Christians, in the history of salvation. Partially because of the reception of Josephus, a consciousness of the superiority of Christianity, based not only on theology, but also on history, developed.

The victory of the Romans over the rebellious Zealots in the year 70 was considered, in a certain sense, almost as a victory of Christianity over Judaism, as the *Vindicta Salvatoris* ("the Revenge of the Savior") and as God's punishment of the stubborn Jews for their misdeeds against the redeemer. This was already present in a preliminary way, so to speak, in the description and the theology of Josephus, above all in the *Jewish War*. As especially H. Lindner [in his *Die Geschichtsauffassung des Flavius Josephus im Bellum Judaicum: Gleischzeitig ein Beitrag zur Quellenfrage*, 1972] has shown, the historian introduces reflections about the history of salvation relative to the contrast of Rome with the Zealots (the Jews). This happens in such a way that there could easily result an anti-Jewish debate among the theologians of the early church as soon as the arguments were taken out of their context and were transplanted to the Christian realm of thought. Indeed, it lay only too close at hand to regard the lack of repentance on the part of the stubborn Zealots, who had been reprimanded by Josephus, as stage scenery for viewing Christian ways of thinking. The reader was probably scarcely aware of the distortion on the part of the Jewish author or took it into account because the color of historic authenticity borrowed from Josephus gave a great power of conviction to the new Christian picture of history. Thus, at least partially, a model of the later anti-Judaism of Christian theologians could develop out of the anti-Zealotism, leads the Jewish historian to the conclusion that God had turned away from his disloyal, sinful people for an indefinite time and stood now on the side of the Romans and, indeed, even wished that the Jews be subject to Rome.

It cannot come as a surprise that in this connection the events before the fall of Jerusalem in the year 70 play a certain role. These omens and miracles were snatched up with special eagerness by the Christian theologians since the time of the early church because their evidence seemed almost to be situated on the same plateau as the corresponding prophecies of destruction in the New Testament. They are arranged dramatically in the work of Josephus and were, therefore, far more impressive than the parallel account in Tacitus. On the whole, Josephus awakened, especially with his *Jewish War*, the emotions of his Christian readers; indeed, his depiction of the destruction of Je-

rusalem was in individual scenes composed almost like a tragedy and, especially at certain climaxes of the story, was perceived in just this way by Christian readers. They felt horror and fright in the face of the Jewish catastrophe; they felt, at the same time, on account of the frequently moralizing historical view of Josephus, a certain edification and satisfaction in stationing themselves on the side favored by God. Historical dependability mattered little in this; and, so, in the case of the Christian appropriation of the Jewish historian, distortions and misrepresentations appear that are not unimportant and that are motivated apologetically. For instance, the artificial coincidence of the timing of the crime (the crucifixion of Jesus) and of the punishment (the destruction of Jerusalem) on Passover, which Eusebius contrives and which numerous later Christian authors copy, is startling. In fact, the fall of Jerusalem did not take place in spring but, on the contrary, in midsummer.

Several elements of the pre-Christian anti-Judaism probably entered into the early Christian church. Josephus reports often about these matters; and so, possibly, elements of this hostility toward Jews could also become known to the early church through the reports of the Jewish author and intensify or confirm Christian prejudices that were already present. The church likewise learned from the manner in which Josephus carried on a discussion with the non-Jewish contemporary world and with non-Jewish Greek authors, above all, in *Against Apion*. This, however, is yet to be investigated.

The strong attraction, even fascination, which the works of Josephus held for the early church has various causes. As a kind of exegetic textbook they made more understandable many details of the Old and New Testaments. They also filled gaps of reporting or offered complete information and confirmation for the increasingly historically interested Christian theologians. Josephus' reports were all the more desirable since they came, so to speak, from the side of the antagonist. The detailed reports, for example, about the family of Herod and the Jewish sects, in addition to his often dramatic style and his treatment of the Jewish tradition according to the rules of Greek historiography, met the interests and tendencies of early Christianity obligingly—though Josephus had not really intended that—and he partially advanced these interests. The already tendentious development of historical material in the *Jewish War* favored a Christian-apologetic interpretation of the year 70 as the end of the history of the Jewish people, whose remnants must live in perpetual servitude as an atonement for the crimes that they had committed.

Thus, Christian theologians utilized Josephus to account for an anti-Jewish interpretation of the history of salvation, in which the Jewish historian's real intentions were distorted. In sum, the reception of Josephus is of great importance for the intellectual history of the early Christian church. Current interests bring about a new formulation of problems, for instance the question concerning the similar and different ways of viewing biblical tradition in the New Testament and Josephus. Moreover, the history of the early reception of Josephus can continue to lead to new exegetic knowledge, when, even more than hitherto, Josephus, as well as Philo, is read as a commentary on the New Testament.

Per Bilde   (essay date 1988)

SOURCE: *Flavius Josephus between Jerusalem and Rome: His Life, His Works, and Their Importance*, Journal for the Study of the Pseudepigrapha, 1988, 273 p.

[*In the following excerpt, Bilde gives an overview of Josephus's extant works, discussing their genre, content, and purpose.*]

In Rome, a new phase of Josephus' life history began. In reality, he was in exile from his native country, presumably never to return. He was cut off from active participation in the religious and political life of Judaea and he was no longer able to participate in the life of Jerusalem. Instead, he was set up in the 'capital of Edom', as Rome was customarily referred to in Talmudic literature. He owed his life, as well as his privileged position in Rome, to the new rulers of the Empire, the Flavians. Can there be any doubt as to what kind of writing would be possible in a situation like this? It is this fundamental question we shall now take up in the light of a close examination of each of Josephus' writings. Before undertaking this task, we shall briefly outline Josephus' own comments about his general qualifications as a writer of history in Rome. To this we shall add a brief survey of the transmission of his writings.

Josephus had a solid basis for writing about the history of the Jewish people, both from his own experience and from his general knowledge. As a priest in Jerusalem, as an aristocrat and a sometime politician and general, he had the best qualifications to deliver reliable information. But had he the necessary material at his disposal? Was he able to treat it and transform it into historical literature? In other words, did he in fact possess the skill of a writer of history? With regard to these questions we find a few pieces of information in *Ant.* [*Jewish Antiquities*] 1.6-7; 20.259-268; *Vita* 357-367; *Ap.* [*Against Apion*] 1.47-56. In the first place, these texts bear witness to the fundamental truism that as a Jewish priest Josephus was well acquainted with the holy scriptures, and having participated in the War he was an eye-witness. Therefore, he obviously possessed the fundamental qualifications to write about the history of the Jewish people and about the War which had just come to an end. In the second place, we learn, as already mentioned above, that during the siege of Jerusalem, Josephus claims to have made thorough records of all that happened on the Roman as well as the Jewish fronts. In the third place, according to *Vita* 342, 358 and *Ap.* 1.56, his own records were supplemented by written material. In these places, Josephus actually mentions Vespasian's and Titus' 'hypomnemata' or 'commentarii', i. e. their own records, or those of the Roman high command, concerning the campaign in Judaea, presumably a kind of unedited counterpart to Caesar's works about the wars in Gaul. Josephus' statements in the texts mentioned can be interpreted so as to testify that, in contrast to Justus from Tiberias, he himself had also utilized this material as a basis for his account of the Jewish War. If we extend our interest to include *Ant.* in our survey, we find that in several places in

this work, Josephus refers to documentary material from Roman and other archives. Furthermore, as a fourth factor, the style and literary expression came in addition to the material and contents. According to *Ant.* 1.7-8 and especially 20.263, Josephus had taken great pains to learn the Greek language and literature. He was therefore able to write in Greek and his knowledge of Greek literature, especially Greek historiographical literature, made it easier for him to compose his works in Greek.

We have now described the conditions under which Josephus was able to commence his work as a Jewish historiographer. Personal experiences, the fundamental material and the literary expertise, according to his own information, were at hand. Moreover, Josephus had time at his disposal to organize and formulate the material. Nevertheless, the task was overwhelming and full of difficulties, as indicated in *Ant.* 1.6-7. Not least, the presentation of the material in attractive and clear Greek seems to have caused Josephus some difficulty (cf. *Ant.* 1.7; 20.363). So, the first edition of *Bell.* [*Bellum* or *Jewish War*] took shape in Josephus' native language—presumably Aramaic. And for the final Greek edition of *Bell.*, he was compelled to seek help from some other writers or assistants who were able to offer the necessary literary and stylistic assistance.

The next phase was the matter of publishing, first that of *Bell.* We shall return to this topic in our next section, but already at this point it should be mentioned that copies of *Bell.* were first submitted to Vespasian and Titus, and thereafter to prominent Romans and Jews who had participated in the War in Judaea, i. e. persons who were competent to verify the account.

The transmission of Josephus' writings is comparable to that of Greco-Roman literature other than the Bible. For obvious reasons, the Old and the New Testaments—especially the latter—are richly attested and handed down. As far as the Old Testament is concerned, we are now in possession of Qumran manuscripts of several of the books, and with regard to the New Testament, there are papyrus fragments, some of which are as early as the second century CE, whereas the oldest complete manuscripts are from the fourth century CE (Codex Sinaiticus and Codex Vaticanus). In addition, there is an abundance of more recent manuscripts of the Old and especially of the New Testament. As for Josephus, we possess a single papyrus fragment from the end of the third century CE (papyrus P. Graec. Vindob. 29810, which contains *Bell.* 2.576-579, 582-584), but apart from that it is not until the 9th-11th centuries CE that we find the oldest Greek manuscripts containing Josephus' collected works or a few of his writings. Several other manuscripts belong to the 11th-14th centuries, but most of them are even later. However, the total number of Josephus manuscripts, particularly the Greek, is far smaller than that of the biblical manuscripts. With regard to *Ap.*, we are in an even worse position in that all existing Greek manuscripts are clearly dependent on one single, incomplete 11th-century manuscript, Codex L, from which 2.52-113 is missing.

In support of the direct transmission of Josephus' Greek texts, we have the Latin translations. The earliest of these translations is that of Hegesippus from c. 370. However, it is not of any particular significance because it represents a free Jewish-Christian treatment of *Bell.* only. Cassiodor's translation from about 570 is of far greater importance and it comprises Josephus' complete works. Cassiodor is of particular significance with regard to *Ap.* because we are completely dependent on this Latin translation for the text of 2.52-113.

Finally, we have the indirect transmission. Several of the earliest Church Fathers such as Justin, Irenaeus, Clement of Alexandria, Tertullian, Hippolytus, Origen and Eusebius quote or refer to passages in Josephus and may therefore be considered to attest the texts in his writings. First and foremost, Eusebius quotes long passages from Josephus in his church history, and thus he is a main witness to the text, although he often makes changes in it as he sees fit. Otherwise, the Church Fathers are particularly interested in *Testimonium Flavium* and the passages concerning Jesus' brother James and John the Baptist. We do, however, also find a great deal of interest in texts like *Bell.* 2.119-166 (concerning the three Jewish schools) This indirect transmission leads us back to the third and second centuries (Origen, Hippolytus, Clement, Tertullian, Irenaeus and Justin), i. e. to about the same time as we dated our earliest direct testimony to Josephus' text.

At the beginning of the present century, scholars such as Behrendts-Grass and especially Eisler launched the famous hypothesis that the existing Old Russian translation of *Bell.* could be traced back to its original Aramaic edition (*Bell.* 1.3). After a long and thorough discussion during the following decades, the majority of scholars arrived at the conclusion that—on the contrary—this translation is a free, paraphrasing translation from the 11th century, a translation which was made on the basis of a Greek edition of which essentially corresponds to some of the Greek handwritten manuscripts known today, and these belong to the less rather than the more reliable ones. The notorious hypothesis must now be said to have been invalidated, and Josephus' texts cannot be dated further back in time than the end of the second century and the beginning of the third century.

The scholarly editions of Josephus' works are based upon the material described here, but primarily on the complete Greek manuscripts from the Middle Ages. Niese's edition from 1885-1895 remains the best edition in existence. In addition there is the bilingual Greek/English Loeb Edition from 1926-1965 and the likewise bilingual Greek/German edition of *Bell.* by Michel-Bauernfeind from 1959-1969.

The Jewish War

. . . Josephus lived in Rome under favourable external circumstances, and under constant Jewish accusations and attack, when in the summer of 71 he began to compose his works. The first and best known of these is *The Jewish War*. This, however, contains much more than the account of the first Jewish revolt against Rome in 66-70(74). A closer analysis of the contents of the seven books of this work shows this clearly. Moreover, this analysis

will serve as a point of departure for our endeavour to penetrate further into *Bell.*, its topic, purpose and goal.

Bell. 1 begins with a lengthy introduction. Thereafter, the actual narrative takes its point of departure in the crisis which the Jewish people experienced under Antiochus IV Epiphanes (175-164 BCE). Here, Josephus describes Antiochus' conquest of Jerusalem and his persecution of the Jews and Judaism. Next, he tells us about Matthias' and his sons' resistance actions, victory and establishment of an independent Jewish state under Hasmonaean leadership. The following passages describe the strife among the Hasmonaeans which led to the intervention by the Romans, Pompey's conquest of Jerusalem in 63 BCE and his and Gabinius' reorganization of Palestine. There follows an account of Antipater's and his sons' rise to power during the reigns of Caesar, Anthony and Octavian in Rome. In these passages, Josephus tells us about Herod's appointment in the Roman senate as King of Judaea, about his conquest of the country with the assistance of Rome, his wars, building constructions and family tragedy. *Bell.* 1 concludes with an account of Herod's death in Jericho and his stately funeral procession to the city and fortress Herodion east of Bethlehem.

Bell. 2 begins with a detailed description of the disturbances which broke out in all parts of the country after Herod's death. This is followed by a less lengthy account of the strife between Herod's sons concerning the division of the country, Archelaus' short-lived reign, the transformation of Judaea to a Roman province after the demise of Archelaus and the revolt by Judas the Galilean, in this connection. This account is followed by the classical presentation of the three Jewish schools, the Pharisees, the Sadducees and the Essenes, of which the Essenes are given very thorough attention. There follows a chronologically arranged account of the reigns of Philip and Herod Antipas, Pilate's period as procurator (governor) to Judaea, of the Gaius Caligula crisis in 41-44, of Agrippa I and II and of the procurators in Judaea in the 40s, 50s and the beginning of the 60s. The rendering of this period is strongly marked by the increasing tensions between the Jews and the Romans, and we hear about the 'bandits', the Sicarii and the 'prophets', and their ever growing importance and influence in Judaea. At the same time, the accelerated conflicts between the Jews and the non-Jews, especially in Caesarea, are described. There is an imperceptible transition from this account into the description of an actual state of war which, according to Josephus, gradually develops in the course of the spring and early summer of the year 66. We hear about the Jewish rebels who drove the Roman garrison from Jerusalem, about Cestius Gallus' campaign against Jerusalem, his abortive attack on the city and his unexpected defeat during the retreat from Judaea. Moreover, we hear about the appointment of a proper Jewish rebellious government in Jerusalem, and *Bell.* 2 ends with a description of Josephus' preparations for war in Galilee and of corresponding preparations in Jerusalem during the winter of the year 66-67.

In *Bell.* 3, our attention is first called to the Romans. We are informed about Nero receiving the news from Judaea and about his appointment of Vespasian. Thereupon, we follow the latter during his preparations for the War and his advance from Antioch, where the army is assembled, to Ptolemais which is his base in the first phase of the War, the reconquest of Galilee. As a part of this prelude, in a famous passage, Josephus gives us a detailed description of the structure, discipline and tactics of the Roman army. Another well-known passage is his description of the scene of the War, Palestine and its Jewish provinces, Galilee, Peraea, Samaria, Judaea and the domain of Agrippa II in the north-eastern part of the country. The War in Galilee itself is depicted in the remaining part of *Bell.* 3 and in the beginning of *Bell.* 4. Here, we find the account of the conquests made by Vespasian and Titus: Gabara, Jotapata, Tiberias, Tarichaea, Gamala and Gischala.

Thus, *Bell.* 3 continues into 4 without any distinct transition. But, with 4.121ff., our attention is once again called to the situation in Jerusalem. We are now told about the dissension and the strife, indeed the open state of war, which in consequence of the discrepancies during the prelude to the War develops between the varying groups of the rebels, first and foremost the 'Zealots', John of Gischala's party, and the Idumaeans. There follows a brief reference to Vespasian's plans with regard to Jerusalem, which, precisely due to the internal strife among the rebels, he decides to let fall. This brief transitional reference leads to a new version of the internal strife among the rebels. Next, we are informed about a revolutionary group which was not present in Jerusalem, namely, the Sicarii, who, after the 'Zealots' had murdered Menahem in the Temple had isolated themselves on Masada. Josephus tells us about these and other groups of rebels who ravaged in Judaea. This Jewish offensive causes Vespasian to change plans, and he decides to attack Jerusalem after all. Therefore, he takes measures to subjugate systematically the rural districts outside the capital city. In the spring of the year 68, he conquers East Jordan (Peraea), the Valley of Jordan, Judaea and Idumaea, leaving Jerusalem to stand alone with Masada and a few other fortifications.

However, at the same time, decisive political events take place in Rome. Adhering to the maxim which Polybius, 200 years before Josephus, had practised in his universal history and which Lucian of Samosata, 100 years after him, established in his work on how history should be written (Chapter 50), Josephus begins to write concurrent accounts of synchronous events. The events described are those which end with the death of Nero on 9th June, in the year 68, and Galba's subsequent coming to rule. The result of these events is that Vespasian's campaign actually comes to a standstill just before it could have ended with the siege and conquest of Jerusalem. Owing to this, the rebels gain a new opportunity to take over the initiative, and now we hear about the coming leader in Jerusalem, Simon bar Giora. He is said to have joined the Sicarii on Masada, to have mustered a 'proletarian' army of slaves and oppressed people, and to have attacked the 'Zealots' and conquered Idumaea. When the Romans are able to regain the initiative, Simon advances against Jerusalem, and Josephus is able to give us a new account of the disruption within the Jewish rebels in the capital city. The conflict comes to an end in May 69 when Simon becomes ruler in Jerusalem. The remaining part of *Bell.* 4 describes the

brief reigns of Otho and Vitellius and Vespasian's own rise to power. When his power has been secured, Vespasian sends Titus from Alexandria to Jerusalem to complete the campaign (4.657-663). Thus, *Bell.* 4 describes a sort of stagnation in the War.

Bell. 5 is devoted to the battle for Jerusalem. All of the preparatory and delaying phases have now come to an end. It seems as if the conflicts on both sides have been settled, and that these two sides face each other, each having its own new leader, Simon on the Jewish side and Titus (Vespasian) on the Roman side. However, in reality this applies only to the Romans because the conflicts in Jerusalem continue. Therefore, *Bell.* 5 begins with a renewed account concerning this main topic and goes on to describe Titus' army and its march against Jerusalem. There follows an account of the preliminary siege and the first battles for the city. Not until then do we have the famous narrative describing Jerusalem and the Temple, the arena of the dramatic encounter. Attention thereafter reverts to the situation within the besieged city. A description of the first outright battles follows. With this the narrative gathers speed. In rapid succession, we hear about the Roman conquest of Jerusalem's first wall (25th May), and second wall (30th May), about Josephus' (first) great speech to the rebels in which he advises them to surrender, about the suffering and hunger in the isolated city, about new sallies and battles and about Titus' (first) council of war in which the decision is made to build a proper siege wall around Jerusalem. *Bell.* 5 ends with a new description of the increasing distress in the city.

Thus, the scene is prepared for the account of the conquest of Jerusalem, the burning of the Temple, the destruction of the city and the fate of its inhabitants during and after the catastrophe. This story is told in *Bell.* 6, and it is the highlight of the narrative. This book begins with violent battle scenes and leads into a description of Antonia's conquest and the end of the sacrificial offerings in August 70. A rendering of Josephus' (second) speech to the besieged people follows. This speech also serves as a delaying feature, after which we hear about the final struggle for the Temple which culminates with the burning of the porticoes around the Temple court (12th August). For the last time, we hear about the horrible famine in Jerusalem which drove some of its inhabitants to the madness of cannibalism. As the account continues, we are told about Titus' (second) council of war which this time debated the fate of the Temple. In spite of the fact that the council decided to spare the sanctuary, by an accident the inner court of the Temple was set on fire (30th August), and Josephus tells us how thousands were lost in the flames because they had sought security in God's own house. The climax of the work has been reached, the profound depth of the catastrophe has been described and all that follows merely serves to embellish what actually happened here. In the section following, Josephus describes several supernatural omens which preceded and thus gave warning of the impending catastrophe. This feature is seen in numerous other accounts which describe the conquest and ruin of a city or country, e. g. from Livy's account of the fall of Veii (Hist. [*Histories*] 5.15-23). Thus, the disaster was the will of God and predicted by him. Furthermore, we hear that the Roman troops bring offerings to their standards in the temple court itself, and they hail Titus as imperator. We read about the devastation of the conquered lower town and about the attack on the upper (western) part of the city, the rapid conquest of it, and thereby the final fall and subsequent systematic conflagration and destruction of the city.

Josephus explicitly compares this to earlier occasions when the city was conquered, in particular when the Babylonians sacked it under Nebuchadnezzar in the year 586 BCE.

Bell. 7 continues the theme of *Bell.* 6, by giving an account of the consequences and aftermath of the War. We learn about the military occupation of the country, Vespasian's acclamation as victor in Rome, and Titus' departure from Judaea and arrival in Italy. Thereupon, there is the classic account of the triumphal march. Our attention is thereafter drawn back to Palestine. Here, there were clean-up actions, particularly in connection with the siege and conquest of Machaerus and Masada. According to the results of the most recent research, the last fortification was taken as late as May 74. Thereby, all of Judaea was subjugated and was once more under the control of Rome. One consequence of the War is that all Jewish land in Palestine is taken over as imperial property and thereafter farmed out. Another consequence is that a new tax, the Fiscus Judaicus, is levied on all Jews in the Roman empire. This tax was no longer a tax to be paid to the Temple as was formerly the custom, but to Jupiter Capitolinus. *Bell.* 7 concludes with a brief account of the offshoots of the War in Egypt and Cyrene where the refugee Sicarii inspired Jewish revolts which were, however, also subdued. . . .

The review of the contents of *Bell.*, book by book, shows us how the whole work has been planned. Clearly, it reaches its highlight in the description of the siege and fall of Jerusalem in 5 and 6. The last part of the 6th and all of the 7th book describe the aftermath and the consequences of the War. Correspondingly, 1-4 must be understood as a prelude to *Bell.* 5-6. *Bell.* 3 provides us with an account of the War in Galilee, and *Bell.* 4 describes the period from the spring of 67 to the spring of 69. Here, we are told a great deal about the situation on both sides, but from the literary point of view the 4th book delays the account. We have to pause a while before undertaking our reading about the crux of the War. Whereas in 3 and 4 the introductory phases of the War are depicted in this way, in *Bell.* 1 and 2 a picture of its preliminaries is drawn, partly in a longer and partly in a shorter perspective. 1 describes how the Romans came to Judaea the first time and established their power there, although initially, during the client rule of Herod they were satisfied with ruling indirectly. 2 describes the collapse of this indirect rule, first, starting with the death of Herod, and then completely after the banishment of Archelaus. Thereafter, 2 goes on to explain how the conflicts between Rome and Judaea increase under the direct Roman rule during the first century. Thus, *Bell.* 2 traces and clarifies the immediate causes of the aggravation and the gradual development into an outright revolt. 1, however, can be said to treat the more profound causes of the War.

Thus, although *Bell.* contains much more than the direct account of the war between the Jews in Palestine and the Romans during the years 66-70(74), this other material has also been selected and determined by the main purpose of the work. Consequently, *Bell.* may be said to describe: (1) The siege and fall of Jerusalem, (2) the causes, outbreak and preliminary events of the War, (3) the consequences of the fall of Jerusalem, i. e. the ramifications and end of the War, and (4) the deeper causes of the War. . . .

Thus, the theme of *Bell.* is the fall of Jerusalem. The title, *On the Conquest* (*peri halôseôs*), as given in most of the manuscripts, is appropriate. We also find this title given by Origen and Hieronymus, and one cannot exclude the possibility that, as asserted by Hieronymus (*Comm. in Isaiam* [*Commentary on Isaiah*] 64), it is the title which Josephus himself gave his work. However, against this assertion are *Ant.* 20.258, *Vita* 412 and other references where Josephus names his books *The Jewish War* (*ho ioudaikos polemos*), or merely *The War* (*ho polemos*) (*Ant.* 1.6; *Ap.* 1.47 etc.). Moreover, the title *On the Conquest* can be said to reflect more clearly than the other titles the interests of the Christian tradition in this work by Josephus. Therefore, there is good reason to retain the title *The Jewish War*.

But the theme of *Bell.* is not only the War, the fall of Jerusalem and the Temple. The review of its contents, book by book, and the study of its disposition indicate that it is the catastrophe which dominates the work. Josephus is writing about an indescribable disaster. The fall of Jerusalem and the burning of the Temple are in reality incomprehensible and inconceivable events, and *Bell.* can and must be regarded as an endeavour to understand and describe how things could have come to this end. In this respect, *Bell.* is a work of tragic historiographical interpretation.

But *Bell.* is not just a narrative of the catastrophe, disaster and tragedy, because as these words in themselves imply it concerns the Jewish people to whom the War and its consequences were disasters. Not only does *Bell.* give an account of an important historical event, and not only is *Bell.* a piece of literature on a significant and dramatic topic, but the work renders a tragedy which struck the author's own people. Thus, the theme of *Bell.* also concerns Josephus himself. Naturally, Josephus plays a role in the War and in this respect he is a part of the theme of the book. He is also part of the theme in a deeper sense, because as a Jew he shares the tragedy as it is unfolded here in this work. Both of these features, the fall of Jerusalem as a tragedy for the Jewish people and thus as a tragedy for Josephus, are expressed explicitly in two places in *Bell.*, namely, in the Preface and in the 5th Book:

> I have no intention of rivalling those who extol the Roman power by exaggerating the deeds of my compatriots. I shall faithfully recount the actions of both combatants; but in my reflections on the events I cannot conceal my private sentiments, nor refuse to give my personal sympathies scope to bewail my country's misfortunes. For, that it owed its ruin to civil strife, and that it was the Jewish tyrants who drew down upon the holy temple the unwilling hands of the Romans and the conflagration, is attested by Titus

Caesar himself, who sacked the city; throughout the war he commiserated the populace who were at the mercy of the revolutionaries, and often of his own accord deferred the capture of the city and by protracting the siege gave the culprits time for repentance. Should, however, any critic censure me for my strictures upon the tyrants or their bands of marauders or for my lamentations over my country's misfortunes, I ask his indulgence for a compassion which falls outside an historian's province. For of all the cities under Roman rule it was the lot of ours to attain to the highest felicity and to fall to the lowest depths of calamity. Indeed, in my opinion, the misfortunes of all nations since the world began fall short of those of the Jews; and, since the blame lay with no foreign nation, it was impossible to restrain one's grief. Should, however, any critic be too austere for pity, let him credit the history with the facts, the historian with the lamentations (**Bell.** 1.9-12). . . .

However, the laws of history compel one to restrain even one's emotions, since this is not the place for personal lamentations but for a narrative of events (**Bell.** 5.20).

According to these important texts, Josephus naturally intends to be objective and write an impartial and realistic account of the facts of the War. But, at the same time, he is aware of the truth that it is impossible for him to suppress his personal feelings. Therefore, he tries to be objective and subjective at the same time. His intention is to represent the facts, 'the actions of both combatants' as they took place, but at the same time—as he emphasizes in advance—he wants to express his own emotions on what took place. For the War could have been avoided. It was caused by the 'civil strife'. The possibility for 'repentance' was there and thereby the disaster could have been prevented. Josephus is well aware of the laws of history which demand that a historian remains aloof and impartial, and he intends to abide by these laws. However, in the preface to **Bell.**, he employs a new and eccentric manner to tell that he will respect these laws, while at the same time he will allow himself to express his grief on the tragedy which has befallen his fatherland, his people and consequently himself. Thus, Josephus writes with grief for the misfortunes of the Jewish people, while at the same time, he endeavours to write accurately, painstakingly and impartially. An impossible task? Yes, but a good pursuit!

So, **Bell.**'s theme is a very personal matter for Josephus, and in order to write this work at all, Josephus, as already implied in the preface, had to work towards a thorough understanding of the War, its background, causes and consequences. . . .

Josephus perceives the War as a tragedy, and therefore he is greatly concerned about the decisive factors of its causes as well as its effects on the Jewish people.

As seen in **Bell.** 7, after the War the situation of the Jewish people was most precarious, and there are many indications to show that as far as Josephus and his literary activities were concerned, it was his main purpose to alleviate this situation. The manner in which he presents the conflict seems to indicate that he has attempted to do this. For he describes the role of the Jewish people in the War as the innocent, defenceless tool of those who were actually guilty, the Jewish 'tyrants', 'bandits' and rebels, in brief, the Jewish war party. By placing all of the blame of the War on these groups, which are marginalized beyond all historical probability in Josephus' account, it was his intention to exonerate the people as a whole. Therefore, not only does Josephus emphasize the pro-Roman and fundamentally peaceful attitude of the Jewish upper-class, but also the same attitude of the common masses of the people. This is done to such an extent that an anti-Roman rebellion in Jewish Palestine becomes nearly incomprehensible. The purpose of this method of presentation is obviously of a political-apologetic nature. By describing the Jewish people as a whole as being an innocent party to the Revolt, Josephus attempted to sway the Romans to a more lenient attitude and to persuade them to revert to the friendly attitude towards the Jews, which Rome had practised before the War. All of Josephus' presentation of the Jewish side of the conflict is influenced by this political-apologetic aim, which of course must be taken into consideration in every attempt to use **Bell.** in history writing.

The causes of the War concern Josephus to an even greater extent than its consequences. . . . Josephus considered the immediate cause of the outbreak of the Revolt to be the ever poorer administration by the Romans in the Jewish sector of Palestine, because it led to the growth of the Jewish war party, to the weakening of the party for peace and to increased tensions between Jews and non-Jews in Palestine. Thus, Josephus places the responsibility and guilt on all parties of the conflict.

If we turn our attention to the question of the deeper reasons for the War, we have already established that Josephus places a great deal of importance on the internal strife among the Jewish people. In his opinion, this is the reason why, under the command of Pompey, the Romans took over power in Palestine in the year 63 BCE, and in the year 66 CE it resulted in a revolt and war. But Josephus places the greatest stress on several Jewish transgressions of the law. He combines this factor with the dissension among the Jewish people as just mentioned. Thus, Josephus appears to believe that the unity of the Jewish people happens precisely as a result of the observance of the law, i. e. the righteousness of the people and its obedience to God (see esp. Agrippa II's and Josephus' orations in **Bell.** 2.345-401; 5.362-419; cf. **Ap.** 2.179-181). On the other hand, the dissension is an essential result of the fact that some of the Jewish people neglect to observe the law. And, according to Josephus, this is precisely what the Jews who support the War have done.

Most profoundly, Josephus sees the War from a theological i. e. 'prophetic' or 'Deuteronomic' point of view, because he interprets the arrival of the Romans, the fall of Jerusalem, the burning of the Temple and all of the disasters of the War suffered by the Jewish people as God's punishment for the sins of the people. Thus, Rome is perceived as a tool in the hand of God, by which he chastises his disobedient people, precisely in the same manner as—according to the Old Testament—he did through the Assyrians and the Babylonians. As Josephus sees it, the only way to avoid the catastrophe is a change of attitude by the people. This indicates that *Bell.* is also a work of theological historical writing related to the historical accounts in the Old Testament. This goes to show that only by a religious interpretation was Josephus able to accept what took place. . . .

We have now found an adequate basis on which to discuss the purpose and aim of *Bell.*, and consequently the circle of readers to whom the work is addressed. Obviously, Josephus had several objectives in mind when he wrote about the Jewish War. Already in the preface, he states his intention to write the historical truth about the war which had been waged, and thereby correct other, earlier accounts, which, according to him, could not live up to this aim. Undoubtedly, Josephus also intended to draw an appreciative and favourable picture of his benefactors, the Flavian emperors, Vespasian and Titus. This is done already in the Preface, which emphasizes the patience and lenience of Titus during the War, but we also find this expressed in the account of Titus' consideration for the Temple in Jerusalem, which he tries to spare and later to save when it had already been set on fire. According to several scholars (esp. Hölscher, Laqueur and Weber), here, we are faced with the primary, indeed the only purpose of *Bell.* But it was also Josephus' intention to depict his own person in a favourable light, and we can point out other purposes for the writing of *Bell.*

However, the fundamental and predominant aim of *Bell.* is of a different nature. It has to do with the understanding of the War which is the main theme of the work. We know now that the War was a disaster for the Jewish people, and the primary aim of *Bell.* is to overcome this disaster. Josephus is concerned to prevent a repetition of the catastrophe, and therefore he tries to convince his people that they chose the wrong solution. This runs like a red thread through the entire account, but Josephus also makes a direct warning against renewed attempts at rebellion:

> If I have dwelt at some length on this topic [the passages concerning the Roman army], my intention was not so much to extol the Romans as to console those whom they have vanquished and to deter others who may be tempted to revolt (*Bell.* 3.108).

Perhaps, this intention was even more pronounced in the first edition of *Bell.* which, according to *Bell.* 1.3 and 6, was written in his mother tongue, presumably Aramaic, and was certainly addressed primarily to Josephus' fellow countrymen. That such a warning was not unconnected with actual events is confirmed by the fact that revolts continued to occur in Cyrene in the early 70s, and were later followed by the confrontation under Trajan in 115-117, not to mention the great revolt of Bar Kokhba in 132-135. In the light of this, *Bell.* may be understood to be a contribution to the internal Jewish discussion about the attitude to the Roman state and the interpretation of the Messianic prophecies. Josephus' position in the matter is that in order to survive, the Jewish people must reject the militant nationalism and Messianism as it was maintained and practised by the rebellious groups before, during and after the War. Owing to political reasons, and especially

theological reasons, Josephus rejects these movements. Rome is too strong. This is demonstrated in many ways in *Bell.*, first and foremost in the speech by Agrippa II (2.345-401). However, the decisive factor is that Rome has her power from God and by his will. Accordingly, a revolt against Rome is a revolt against God. Josephus' admonition to the Jewish people is that they should repent. The people should thereafter content themselves with Roman supremacy as long as it is the will of God to uphold it. Actually, it is only for a limited length of time that Rome is in power. Therefore, the Jews should wait patiently until this situation changes and this will come to pass in God's own time. Thus, *Bell.* has a clear message to bring to Josephus' Jewish countrymen.

As seen in the Preface, however, *Bell.* addresses itself primarily to the Roman readers. *Bell.* 1.3 refers to the 'subjects of the Roman empire' and 1.6 to the 'Greeks' and 'Romans' as Josephus' audience. These general expressions are confirmed and defined by a few remarks in *Vita* 361-362 and *Ap.* 1.50-51. In these references, we find that the Greek *Bell.* was first presented to the Flavians and then to others, including several participants in the War, Romans as well as Greek-speaking Jews. This information corresponds with the purpose of *Bell.* as pointed out above, namely, that Josephus' intention was to mend the relationship between the Jews and Rome and to restore the Roman policy of tolerance towards the Jewish people. Therefore, as we have seen, Josephus places all of the responsibility on the part of the Jews onto the marginal groups—the 'bandits' and the 'tyrants'—as well as irresponsible individuals such as John of Gischala and Simon bar Giora, whereas he attempts to exonerate the Jewish people as a whole for responsbility and guilt with regard to the War.

Thus, the aim of *Bell.* is complex and the readers of the work diverse. First and foremost, *Bell.* is addressed to the ruling class in Rome in a political-apologetic attempt to mend the broken relationship and to restore the favourable situation the Jewish people enjoyed before the year 66. Next, *Bell.* addressed itself to Josephus' own people with a political and theological interpretation of the War and the disaster which occurred. This interpretation forms the basis of a concrete political programme which is an alternative to the policy of the party which supported the War. . . .

Bell.'s often extremely accurate and impartial rendering of the history of the War has frequently led scholars to consider whether in these and possibly other parts of this work, Josephus might have built upon an earlier, but now lost, Roman account of the Jewish-Roman war. Weber argued that *Bell.* was essentially dependent upon a now lost Flavian work of history based on the imperial, Flavian 'commentari' or *hupomnēmata* which are mentioned in *Vita* 342, 358; *Ap.* 1.56. Schlatter, on the other hand, was of the opinion that *Bell.* was based upon a work by Antonius Julianus, who according to Minucius Felix (*Octavius* 33.4) had written an account of the history of the War. The entire matter is very uncertain, because we are dealing with unknown quantities and with very brief time limits. In more recent years, Lindner has taken this theory up for reconsideration, but with far greater caution than that taken by Weber and Schlatter. . . .

The Jewish Antiquities

According to *Ant.* 1.6-7, already at the time he wrote *Bell.*, Josephus was contemplating writing the complete history of the Jews from the creation to his own time. It is, however, implied that at this early date the project was considered to be a far too overwhelming task, and instead he decided to write *Bell.* as an independent work (*Ant.* 1.7). In *Bell.* 1.17-18, Josephus touches upon the same idea, but here he expresses himself in a different manner. He writes that he refrains from relating the early history of the Jews, because this has already been done adequately by other Jewish authors. Therefore, he begins *Bell.* where these authors conclude their accounts. All the same, Josephus did not give up the great task he originally considered; alternatively, with the passing of time, he may have changed his mind and at a later date, when the thought of writing an all-comprehensive work occurred to him, he anachronistically, in his preface to *Ant.*, moved this thought back to an earlier stage in his life. According to *Ant.* 1.7, at any rate Josephus made early attempts at this task, but he encountered several difficulties owing to the magnitude and difficulty of it, not least linguistically. While he was faced with these difficulties, he received encouragement and support from his 'editor', patron or Maecenas, Epaphroditus to whom *Ant.*, *Vita* and *Ap.* are dedicated. With the assistance of Epaphroditus, Josephus finally succeeded in completing his great project. In the following, we shall attempt to elucidate *Ant.*, Josephus' most comprehensive work.

Ant. is truly a voluminous work. It is nearly three times as long as *Bell.*, and divided into twenty books. *Ant.* 1 is introduced by the Proem (1.1-26) in which Josephus states the background and purpose of this work. Here, he emphasizes that the Greek translation of the Old Testament, probably the Septuagint (LXX), is a parallel to his own work. He presents a résumé of *Ant.*'s moral and briefly compares the lawgiver of the Jewish people, Moses, with other lawgivers. This is followed, more or less closely connected with the Old Testament (either the Hebrew Bible or a Greek translation similar to the Septuagint, or based on both together), by a rendering of the contents of Genesis from the creation to the deaths of Isaac and Rebecca (Gen. 1-35). However, from the beginning in *Ant.* 1, it will be noted that Josephus does not follow the biblical text exactly or literally, neither with regard to the phraseology nor the sequence of the narratives. On the other hand, he does follow it to a high degree with regard to content and substance, so actually there are rather narrow limits to Josephus' deviations. Furthermore, one finds that here and there he introduces new material, not least references to the ancient historical writings. Thus, for example in *Ant.* 1.93-95, where Josephus refers to the accounts of Berosus, Hieronymus and Nicolas of Damascus concerning the flood.

Ant. 2 covers the material from Genesis 36 to Exodus 15, i. e. the period from the time of the controversy between Jacob and Esau up until the delivery of the Israelites from Egypt and their miraculous crossing of the Red Sea. In ad-

dition to the features mentioned above, we may add that in *Ant.* 2 Josephus takes particular interest in his namesake Joseph. His version of the story of Joseph as found in Genesis 37-50 takes up more than half of *Ant.*'s second book. Not only is the story of Joseph enlarged upon, it is also recreated. The dramatic, pathetic and erotic features are intensified. The interest in the individual persons and their emotions are emphasized and in crucial points in the story Josephus places long speeches in the mouths of Joseph and other important characters. Thus, the story of Joseph as related by Josephus becomes similar to a Hellenistic short story or a novel.

Ant. 3 describes Israel's sojourn in the desert and renders the remaining part of Exodus, as well as a considerable amount of material from Leviticus and Numbers. First, the miracles in the desert, and thereafter a narrative of the events at Sinai, having its highlight in the lawgiving. Here, it may be observed that Josephus places the Mosaic Laws into a system. In *Ant.* 3 (and 4), he combines material from Exodus, Leviticus and Numbers. For instance, he describes in an orderly sequence and with considerable interpretative additions, the scattered regulations from the Pentateuch concerning the tabernacle, the ark, the showbread table, the candelabra, the incense altar, the burnt-offering altar and the robes of the priests and the high-priests and other accoutrements. In like manner, the material on the laws concerning the sacrifices, the festivals, ritual cleanliness, etc., is systematized.

Ant. 4 covers the 40 years in the desert from the revolt of the people against Moses (Num. 14) until his death (Deut. 34). Here, Josephus renders the narrative material of Numbers and Deuteronomy concerning the people's resistance to Moses as well as that which remains to be told about the laws described in Leviticus, Numbers and Deuteronomy. However, the predominant feature is the narrative about the arrival of the Israelites in the East Jordan country and Jericho, Moses' farewell speech and, above all, a résumé of the Mosaic Law as a state constitution (*politeia*). Thereafter, a few other laws follow and we have the account of the death of Moses and Josephus' own eulogy to the great Jewish lawgiver.

Ant. 5 comprises the immigration under the leadership of Joshua and the time of Judges. By and large, in *Ant.* 5, Josephus follows the narrative material which dominates the book of Joshua and the book of Judges fairly accurately. In the rendering of the story of Samson, however, we find the same features which were characteristic of his treatment of the story of Joseph, and which are also observed in Josephus' rendering of the stories of Abraham (*Ant.*) and other famous characters in the Old Testament. However, the most interesting feature of *Ant.* 5 is that, apparently for chronological reasons, towards the end of the book Josephus places the book of Ruth (5.318-337) between material from the book of Judges and 1 Samuel.

Ant. 6 describes Israel's fights against the Philistines under Samuel and Saul. Here again, Josephus follows the Old Testament original fairly accurately (1 Sam. 5-31), and we encounter Josephus' usual parallel references, oratories, interpretations and reflections, e. g. on the harmful influence of power. At the same time, the account is characterized by a very particular interest in Saul, who dominates in *Ant.* 6. But special interest is also given to David, who plays an increasingly important role in the second half of the book. Nevertheless, let us note that in *Ant.* 6, to a higher degree than in the other parts of his work, Josephus follows his biblical model.

Ant. 7, in continuation of *Ant.* 6.156-378, is concentrated on David, who together with Moses and Herod is one of the most prominent characters in *Ant.* Here again, Josephus follows his sources in 2 Samuel and 1 Kings fairly accurately. But in *Ant.* 7, one can observe that he systematically combines the books of Samuel (2 Sam. 1-24) and the books of Kings (1 Kgs 1-2) with the books of Chronicles (1 Chron. 11; 16; 20-29; 2 Chron. 2), e. g. in *Ant.* 7.46-129, 301-342.

Ant. 8 concentrates on the reign of Solomon, but it also comprises the division of the kingdom and the history of the Southern and Northern Kingdoms until the time of Ahab. To a high degree, the account corresponds to that of *Ant.* 7 in that 1 Kings 2-22 is coordinated with the versions in 2 Chronicles 1-18 and the Septuagint. In the account of Solomon's reign, Josephus can substantiate the biblical account of the relationship between Solomon and King Hiram of Tyre with a reference to a preserved correspondence between these two kings and references to parallels in ancient accounts. Otherwise, *Ant.* 8 is of course dominated by the description of Solomon's building of the Temple. For this account, Josephus utilizes all of the above mentioned sources (2 Kgs 6; 2 Chron. 3-4 and 2 Kgs 6-7 [LXX]), and he adds a considerable amount of material. The actual rendering of Solomon is influenced by Josephus' by now well-known Hellenistic interpretation. He particularly describes Solomon as being a philosopher and a man dedicated to peace.

Ant. 9 deals with the period from the death of Ahab till the fall of the Northern Kingdom by the Assyrian conquest of Samaria in 722 and the corresponding period in the Southern Kingdom. The basic sources are 1 Kings 22, 2 Kings 1-18 and 2 Chronicles 19-31. In rendering these sources, Josephus makes use of both the Hebrew Bible and Septuagint. As observed in the previous books of *Ant.*, Josephus combines material from these sources, but in *Ant.* 9 he also incorporates material from the book of Jonah and the book of Nahum. *Ant.* 9 concludes with an allusion by Josephus to the testimony from Tyre which attests the Old Testament account of the Assyrian invasion, and a brief description of the Samaritans who appear on the historical scene at this time.

Ant. 10 is even more complex than *Ant.* 9, This book covers the period from the time of the Assyrian attack on Jersusalem in 701 to the fall of the city to the Babylonians in 586. The basic sources are 2 Kings 18-25 and 2 Chronicles 32-36, but in addition to these sources there is some other material which in particular includes significant contributions from the prophetic literature. Josephus incorporates material about Josiah from the apocryphal Ezra literature, information about Sennacherib as told by Herodotus and about Nebuchadnezzar's death given by Berosus, Megasthenes and other Hellenistic writers of history. The prophetic literature which Josephus uses is as

follows: the book of Isaiah 38-39, the book of Ezekiel 12 and above all, the book of Jeremiah, namely, chs. 22, 26, 29, 33-34, 37-43 and 52 and the book of Daniel, namely, chs. 1-6 and 8. Actually, the most interesting feature in *Ant.* 10 is the role which the prophets Jeremiah and Daniel play in this book. Jeremiah plays the leading role in the second third of the book and Daniel in the last third. Thus, *Ant.* 10 is predominantly a book of the prophets, and especially a book of the prophets of judgment.

Ant. 11 concerns the period from the time when Cyrus put an end to the Babylonian Exile (about 540) until the time when Alexander the Great conquered Jerusalem and Palestine in 332. The basic sources for this rendering are numerous and complex. The first third of the book builds on the books of Ezra and Nehemiah, supplemented by material from Isaiah 44, the apocryphal Ezra literature as well as an unknown letter from Cyrus. The last part of *Ant.* 11 builds on the book of Esther and the apocryphal Esther literature. In addition, there is some information about Alexander the Great for which the sources are unknown. In *Ant.* 11, there are two predominant themes which are of a brighter nature: the return of the Jews of Jerusalem from their exile in Babylon and the rescue of the Persian Jews on the intervention of Esther. The story of Esther is given special attention by Josephus. He embellishes this story in a way similar to his rendering of the stories of Abraham, Joseph, Moses, Samson, Saul, David and Solomon.

Ant. 12 covers the period from the death of Alexander (323) to the Hasmonaeans' deliverance of Judaea and the death of Judas Maccabaeus (161). Aristeas' letter, an otherwise unknown Tobiad chronicle and 1 Maccabees 1-9 are the main sources. These sources are supplemented by a few documents by Antiochus III and others, plus a number of references to Hellenistic historical writers such as Agatharchides, Nicolas of Damascus and Polybius. Again, we observe Josephus' predilection towards focusing his historical writings on significant persons such as Ptolemy Soter, the Tobiads, Joseph and Hyrcanus, and the Hasmonaeans, Matthias and Judas.

Ant. 13 covers the time when Judas' brother, Jonathan, assumed power (161) until the death of Queen Salome Alexandra (67), i. e. the history of the development of the Hasmonaean state. In the first part of the book, *Ant.* 13.1-217, the source material is still 1 Maccabees, namely, chs. 9-13, but beginning with *Ant.* 13.218 we are no longer able to trace Josephus' rendering back to any other known ancient Jewish sources. Already in *Ant.* 13.1-217, it can be established that 1 Maccabees is supplemented by other material, e. g. in 13.35-36, 58-80 and 106-121, but we cannot determine with certainty the source from which this material is derived. As far as *Ant.* 13.218-432 is concerned, we must be content to ascertain that Josephus quotes from or refers to Nicolas, Strabo, Timagenes and 'others'. Moreover, documentary material is cited consisting of a letter from the Roman Senate to Hyrcanus I (134-104). But we cannot determine the main basis for Josephus' account. Or, to state it more precisely, in these passages, Josephus follows the account previously rendered in *Bell.*, which is continually corrected and supplemented.

Nevertheless, we have no certain knowledge of the basis for this account, although most scholars tend to support the theory that in these passages Josephus' rendering is based on Nicolas from Damascus. Moreover, the account in *Ant.* 13 is quite naturally dominated by the Hasmonaean leaders and kings, Jonathan (161-142), Simon (142-134), John Hyrcanus I (134-104), Alexander Jannaeus (103-76) and Salome Alexandra (76-67).

Ant. 14 describes the time from the death of Salome Alexandra until Herod the Great conquers Jerusalem in 37, i. e. the troubled interim period between the Hasmonaean polity and the founding of the Herodian client rule. During this period, Pompey conquers Jerusalem in 63 and in reality subjugates the entire area under Roman rule. The basic source of *Ant.* 14, and the parallel rendering in *Bell.* 1.117-353, exactly as found in the second half of *Ant.* 13, is less obvious than that of the preceding books. However, a more thorough analysis indicates that here too, in addition to *Bell.*, which must be taken to be the underlying basis for the composition of this part of *Ant.*, Josephus either quotes from or makes reference to a number of nonbiblical sources. This applies to Nicolas, Strabo, Livy 'and many others'. Primarily, however, *Ant.* 14 is influenced by the numerous official documents which mention various forms of honours and privileges bestowed on the Jewish community throughout the world as it was known at the time. . . . Whereas on the basis of 14.185-189, it can probably be assumed that Josephus himself collected this material from Roman and other archives, we are not in a position to form an opinion with regard to his main source for *Ant.* 14. Most scholars, however, assume that in these books he has primarily relied on Nicolas. Apart from that, with regard to its contents, *Ant.* 14 is mostly concerned with the devastating conflict in the Hasmonaean House as the background and the reason, partly for the Roman penetration of the region, and partly for the rise of the Herodian Idumaean family and their consequent usurpation of power.

Ant. 15 renders the period from the conquest of Jerusalem by Herod (37) until his dedication of the Temple as it had been rebuilt in the year 18. It concerns the first reign of Herod during which he consolidates his own supremacy as against the Hasmonaeans, Cleopatra, the Nabataeans and the changing Roman rulers, first and foremost Anthony and Octavian. This is the period in which he gradually acquires considerable extensions of his realm. But at the same time, *Ant.* 15 tells us about the tragic strife within Herod's family, particularly with his wife, Mariamme. Finally, in this book, we find the important descriptions of Herod's building constructions, especially the Royal Palace in Jerusalem, Herodion, Caesarea and the extensive rebuilding of the Temple. With regard to the sources, in *Ant.* 15 we find only a few references, namely, to Strabo and to Herod's own 'Memoirs' and other 'sources'. In 15.425, however, we find an interesting reference: 'And this story, which our fathers have handed down to us', a wording which is probably to be understood as pointing to Jewish religious oral tradition. Nevertheless, the problem of sources in *Ant.* 15 is basically the same as in *Ant.* 14.

Ant. 16 covers the relatively brief period from the dedica-

Coins current in Palestine (34 B.C. to 98 A.D.): 1. and 2.—Coins of Herod the Great. 3.—Coin of Herod Agrippa I. 4.—Coin of Vespasian. 5. and 6.—Coins of Herod Archelaus. 7.—Coin of Pontius Pilate.

tion of the Temple until the year 7-6 when Herod executed his two sons born by Mariamme. In outward circumstances, Herod is described as being at the height of his power. His realm extends over an area as large as that of Israel under the time of David. He is a 'friend' of Augustus and Marcus Agrippa. He is in a position to give powerful support to the Jews in the Diaspora. He inaugurates the great sea port in Caesarea in the year 10. He is able to defeat the Nabataeans again. But at the same time, Herod's house and family are occupied with his perpetual strife with his own children and his brothers and sisters. Moreover, there is an increasing dissension between the king and his Jewish subjects. It is this tension between Herod's outward strength and his internal disintegration which dominates the account in 16. With regard to the sources for this book, Josephus makes a single reference to Nicolas in a passage in which he criticizes him for being partial and favourable in his presentation of Herod. In another passage, Josephus refers to and quotes from a number of official Roman documents of the same type as those which are listed in *Ant.* 14. Otherwise, the source situation of *Ant.* 16 is the same as we have in *Ant.* 14 and 15.

Ant. 17 contains an account of the events in Judaea from the execution of Mariamme's sons till Archelaus was deposed in the year 6 CE, when Judaea was reorganized as a Roman province, i. e. a period which is just as brief as the period which is described in *Ant.* 16. Thus, the period described is partly the last years of Herod and partly the reign of Archelaus. The part concerning Herod is a continuation of the account in *Ant.* 16. Herod's tragedy is consummated with his execution of a third son, Antipater, the increasing opposition to the people and with Herod's illness, suicidal attempt, death and burial. The part of the book which concerns the reign of Archelaus depicts the contest for power between Herod's heirs, and the increasing unrest and direct revolt in Judaea. In *Ant.* 17, Josephus makes no reference whatsoever to his sources, and therefore, with regard to this problem, we must assume that the remarks made on the same question in *Ant.* 14-15 apply here as well.

Thus, *Ant.* 14-17 present a chronological and very detailed account of Herod the Great as a person, his reign and his family life from the 40s till his death in 4 BCE. These books comprise the most comprehensive narrative cycle in *Ant.* In all probability, it is a narrative which builds on the historical works of Nicolas of Damascus. However, the rendering also has parallels earlier in *Ant.*, formally in the narrative cycles concerning Abraham, Joseph, Moses, Samson, David, Esther and Agrippa I, and with regard to the content in the story of Saul.

Ant. 18 comprises the period from the deposal of Archelaus to the death of Gaius Caligula (41). By and large, the account follows the parallel version in *Bell.* 2.117-203, but it has been greatly expanded, partly in the rendering of the same events and partly by the addition of a great deal of new material, e. g. the founding of Tiberias, *Testimonium Flavianum*, the passages on John the Baptist and the information concerning the Babylonian Jews. Besides, as mentioned above, some material, already seen in *Bell.*, has been expanded. This applies, for example, to the narrative cycle concerning Agrippa I. As for the question of sources, in *Ant.* 18 Josephus gives no references. In reality, therefore, we are completely at a loss. However, we must assume that aside from *Bell.* which he evidently draws on, Josephus has had several Roman sources at his disposal.

Ant. 19 covers a very brief period, namely, Agrippa I's reign as 'Great King' (41-44). The major part of the book is, however, devoted to a highly dramatic rendering of the intrigues which ensued around the murder of Gaius Caligula in Rome. This account is clearly based on an otherwise very valuable contemporary Roman source which Mommsen believes to be Cluvius Rufus. Josephus incorporates this source in his text. The story about the murder of Caligula is linked together with the other material about Caligula in *Ant.* 18 and 19. In a similar manner, Josephus combines the account of Claudius' election as the new emperor, by the intervention of Agrippa I, with the other narratives concerning this king. Again in *Ant.* 19, we find that Josephus has cited a few official documents.

Ant. 20, the final book, covers the time from the death of Agrippa I in 44 till the outbreak of the Revolt under Gessius Florus in 66. Here again, we encounter a largely expanded parallel to *Bell.* One of the largest expansions is found in *Ant.* 20.17-96, which describes the conversion of the royal family of Adiabene to Judaism. One of the most famous passages is the brief note about Jesus' brother James being executed by the high priest Ananus. Otherwise, it is characteristic of *Ant.* 20, that like *Ant.* 14-19, we learn nothing about the source material, and that in *Ant.*, the account paralleled in *Bell.* seems to be rendered in an edited and largely expanded version. . . .

Ant. can readily be divided into two main parts, 1-10 and 11-20. These parts differ from each other in three important factors, which are, however, interrelated. The first factor is the Temple. Its destruction in 586 BCE is described in *Ant.* 10, whereas *Ant.* 20 anticipates the second destruction in the year 70 CE. Yet, the latter is predicted already at the end of *Ant.* 10 (10.79, 276). Thus, *Ant.* 10 and 20 clearly refer to each other and may therefore be looked upon as fundamental in the structure and disposition of *Ant.* 1-10 may be regarded as the account of the history of the first Temple, and *Ant.* 11-20 as a parallel account of the period of the second Temple.

In the second place, *Ant.* 1-10 and 11-20 are at variance with regard to the sources. Whereas in *Ant.* 1-10, Josephus can be said to build on the 'law and the prophets', in *Ant.* 11-20, he can only rely on the least esteemed group of the texts in the Jewish canon, the so-called 'scriptures'. In *Ap.* 1.37-41, Josephus reviews the canonical scriptures perceived of as being historical sources. Here, in a manner which corresponds to the account in *Ant.*, he makes a clear-cut distinction between Moses and the prophets on one side and postprophetic literature on the other, albeit in *Ap.*, it is not made clear precisely which of the scriptures belong to the 'rest'. Nevertheless, it is obvious that *Ant.* 1-10, which renders Moses and the prophets, has a status which differs from that of *Ant.* 11-20, where the sources are of a different and secondary nature. Thus, from, *Ant.* 11 and onward, Josephus must rely on his use of the 'scriptures' to a greater extent, and beyond this source, he must incorporate non-canonical books and other material, especially official documents and the testimony of other historians. Therefore, from and including the 11th book, *Ant.* becomes increasingly reminiscent of *Bell.*, with which the great work does in fact run parallel in *Ant.* 13-20.

Thirdly, *Ant.* 1-10 and 11-20 are separated by the Babylonian Exile. To Josephus, this is important as a historical juncture, and therefore, it also influences his presentation of the work, corresponding to that dividing line which Mt. 1.1-17 sets up between the twenty-eight generations before the Exile and the fourteen generations after it. Naturally, this factor is very closely related to the first, because the Babylonian Exile may be looked upon as a consequence of the fall of Jerusalem and the Temple in 586. In Josephus' view, the Babylonian Exile, like the destruction of the Temple in 586, may be said to anticipate, predict and describe that exile which for Josephus himself and thousands of other Jews turned out to be a decisive result of the fall of the second Temple in the year 70.

If we have a closer look at *Ant.* 1-10, once again, we may say that this part of the work consists of two sections, 1-5 describing the foundation of Israel, and 6-10 describing its (first) realization. This dividing line may be interpreted in more ways than one. As far as the people are concerned, *Ant.* 1-5 deals with its coming into being and its formation outside of the country Canaan, whereas 6-10 gives us the account of its existence inside the country. As far as the state is concerned, its institutions and power are founded in the period covered by *Ant.* 1-5, whereas 6-10 give us an account of its realization, expansion and demise in the promised land. With regard to the Temple, we recognize the same pattern. These dispositional considerations may be summed up so as to show that Moses, the lawgiver of the people, dominates *Ant.* 1-5, whereas the Great Kings, first and foremost David, are prevalent in *Ant.* 6-10.

The arrangement of *Ant.* 11-20 is less clear, but several different divisions may be attempted. Thus, it may be argued that *Ant.* 11-13 comprise the Persian and Greek period, whereas 14-20 cover the Roman. Likewise, it may be said that *Ant.* 11-13 has its central theme in the Hasmonaean monarchy, 14-17 in the reign of Herod the Great and 18-20 in the rules of Agrippa I and Agrippa II. But these and corresponding attempts are not satisfactory, neither by virtue of the divisions proposed nor by the criteria by means of which they are undertaken. So far, I have not yet found the key to the arrangement of *Ant.* 11-20, but I am confident that the following reflections which continue the structural analysis of *Ant.* 1-20 should be taken into consideration.

Ant. 11-20, it seems to me, falls into three parts, each of which depicts three phases of restoration and fall from the time of the destruction of the first Temple to that of the second Temple. The restoration at the time of the return from the Babylonian Exile, the re-establishing of the Temple, the society and the state culminating with the Hasmonaean monarchy are described in vivid colours in *Ant.* 11-13. Thereafter, *Ant.* 14-17 unfolds the controversy which was hinted at already at the end of 11-13. The Hasmonaean monarchy, and with it the Jewish people and the country itself, was disrupted during the course of the controversy between Alexandra's sons, Aristobulus and Hyrcanus. Therefore, the country and the people fall an easy prey, first to Pompey and then to Antipater and his 'Herodian' family. Now, Israel is under the domination of Rome and her Herodian clients, and the splendid kingdom of Herod the Great is only a wretched cover over internal strife and disintegration. *Ant.* 18-20 narrates the last (and last but one) phase in this process of disintegration: the revolts after the death of Herod and the deposal of Archelaus; the transformation of Judaea into a proper Roman province; and the accelerating confrontations under the direct Roman administration. Viewed in this manner, *Ant.* 11-20, especially 18-20, set the stage for *Bell.* and the new work about the War and the time after the War, both of which are mentioned in the postscript to *Ant.* (20.259, 267).

In his introduction to and elsewhere, Josephus emphasizes that his 'archaeology' is 'translated from the Hebrew scriptures'. At the same time, he stresses the point that in the course of this 'translation', as he says, he is 'neither adding nor omitting anything' from the details of the scriptures. Or he may write that in:

> I have recounted each detail here told just as I found it in the sacred books.

The readers of *Ant.* are astonished by these statements. While going through the contents of *Ant.*, we noted partly that Josephus adduces a considerable amount of other material, and partly that in many places *Ant.* is very far removed from what we today would normally understand as a translation.

By presenting the problem in this way we are once again hurled into one of the classic discussions in research on Josephus. Does he write completely thoughtlessly? Or, is it possible to understand and explain the problem in some other way? We shall begin by considering the fact that *Ant.* especially *Ant.* 12-20, contains a great deal of material aside from the biblical scriptures. Thereafter, we shall discuss the question as to what Josephus might have meant by writing that *Ant.*, especially *Ant.* 1-11, is a 'translation' of the Bible.

From the outset, it is obvious that *Ant.* is not to be taken literally as a translation of the canonical Jewish scriptures, which according to *Ap.* 1.38 comprise only twenty-two books, and which, by and large, are probably the same books as are today recognized as belonging to the Jewish canon. *Ant.* 1-11 might possibly be accepted as being such a 'translation', but as we have just observed, *Ant.* 12-20 is largely based on non-biblical sources. Why does Josephus not call our attention to this circumstance in his Preface (1.1-26) and conclusion (20.259-268)? Could it possibly be an oversight in *Ant.* 1.5? One might consider this possibility because we have indeed observed that Josephus, throughout the twenty books of *Ant.*, often cites by name and refers to the many non-biblical sources he uses. Nevertheless, this possibility must be excluded because in his résumé of the contents of *Ant.* in 20.261, Josephus explicitly repeats that he rendered 'all as recorded by the Holy Scriptures'. . . .

Therefore, it is necessary for us to consider whether it is possible that there are good reasons why Josephus—contrary to the truth—so strongly emphasizes that he relies solely on the ancient Jewish scriptures. In my opinion, this is the case, because undoubtedly Josephus' main purpose with *Ant.* was to present the *ancient* history of the Jews, their 'archaeology', as it is called in the title of *Ant.*, to the Greco-Roman public. This is stated outright in *Ap.* 1.1, where Josephus tells us:

> I have, I think, made sufficiently clear to any who may peruse that work the extreme antiquity of our Jewish race, the purity of the original stock, and the manner in which it established itself in the country we occupy today.

Moreover, it appears from the entire argumentation in *Ap.*, especially 1.1-56, that it is the age of the Jewish people (their dignity) which is at stake and in this connection the 'ancient' books are the decisive criteria and proof. Since it is necessary for us to anticipate the following paragraphs concerning the purpose of *Ant.*, there is reason to assert that *Ant.*, at least in part, has the same aim as *Ap.*, and this aim is to prove the age and dignity of the Jewish people apologetically to the Greco-Roman world. With this as his purpose, in *Ant.*, Josephus attempts to present the history of the Jews from the beginning, and he places emphasis on its establishment and antiquity, precisely as Dionysus from Halicarnassus and Livy have done with regard to Rome. And for the earliest phase of this history, the biblical books were naturally the fundamental source. This is probably the basic reason why Josephus refers only to them in the passages cited.

The following observations are consistent with the reasons stated above. In the Greco-Roman period it was also fashionable to admire and respect the Orient and its ancient cultures and literatures. This attitude represents a variant comparable to 'old is good' (cf. also Schäublein, pp. 318-19). This attitude towards the Orient is found as early as Herodotus, but in Hellenistic times it became the fashion to admire the exotic oriental nations who by then had become better known. Therefore, in *Ap.* 1.28-29, Josephus makes a connection between the Jewish culture and that of other oriental nations in comparison with the Greeks. For this reason we can also assume that Josephus found it more expedient to refer solely to the ancient Jewish scriptures as authorities for his account in *The Jewish Antiquities*.

Finally, we may perhaps be able to receive some assistance from *Ap.* for understanding the significance of the actual use of such a great number of non-biblical references in *Ant.* For it is clear that also in *Ap.*, the Mosaic code and the Jewish Bible play the predominant role in support of the defence of Judaism. And all the other numerous sources which Josephus draws upon here serve to support and substantiate the Jewish cause which is basically unravelled by the biblical scriptures. Thus, there is reason to assume that the same applies to *Ant.* The biblical books are Josephus' basis, and compared with them, the non-biblical texts are not equally important sources, but merely supporting, secondary material, which is why they are not mentioned by Josephus in his principal statements regarding the basis of *Ant.*

Thus, it may be possible to understand that in *Ant.* as a whole, especially *Ant.* 12-20, Josephus draws on a number of non-biblical sources without directly stating this in the introduction and conclusion of the work. But what then about *Ant.* 1-11? Can these books justifiably be said to be a translation of the biblical books on which they are based? No, a translation in the modern sense of the word is out of the question. It is more likely that here we encounter a paraphrase or in many cases a downright rewriting of the biblical material. As mentioned above, Josephus systematized his biblical sources. He coordinates the books of Samuel and Kings with the books of Chronicles, and now and then he even incorporates material from the books of the Prophets in this synthesis. He links the Hebrew version of the Bible together with the often strongly divergent version in the Septuagint, or other Greek translations which remind one of the Septuagint. He places canonical and noncanonical material together. He systematizes the great amount of legal materal found in the second to fifth books of the Pentateuch. He shortens the bibli-

cal rendering; for example, he omits controversial material such as the story about the Golden Calf and the story about Moses when he destroyed the first set of the Law Tablets. He expands the account, as seen from the above, partly by introducing new material of a non-Jewish origin where it serves to support the narrative, and party with 'oral' Jewish material of haggadic as well as halakhic nature. One example of this kind of Jewish narrative subject matter (haggadah) is the story of Moses' campaign in Ethiopia. First and foremost, however, Josephus endows the Old Testament material with his own literary style and tone of language, which must be described as being typically Hellenistic, because he draws attention to important characters and presents them giving particular interest to the psychological, erotic, dramatic, tragic and pathetic features in the story. Abraham, Joseph, Moses, Saul, David, Solomon and other important Jewish persons are portrayed in a Hellenistic light as great Greco-Roman intellectuals, lawgivers, wise men and generals. Moreover, as mentioned above, many of the stories, in particular the stories of Joseph, Samson and Esther, are transformed into Hellenistic short stories or small novels. . . . In this way, Josephus radically transforms the biblical subject matter. In the light of this, one cannot speak of a translation in the modern sense of the word.

Nevertheless, this is precisely what Josephus does. And on top of this, he claims that in his 'translation', he has neither 'added to' nor 'omitted' anything. If we are to accept these statements of Josephus as sincere and honest, we are forced to undertake a closer deliberation concerning the conceptions applied here. One possibility we have already mentioned, namely that Josephus was not stating the truth or that he was simply thoughtless. This view dominates the classical conception of Josephus. . . . Another possibility is that we are dealing with rhetorical formulae, a kind of literary topos, insufficient with regard to contents, the purpose of which was to achieve a (albeit empty) publicity for Josephus' work. . . . A third possibility, which is related to the second, is as proposed by van Unnik (1978, pp. 26-40), viz. that one can assume that Josephus' use of these formulae is intended to emphasize his objectivity and impartiality. They are then interpreted as a parallel to Tacitus' expression, 'sine ira et studio' (without negative and positive preconceptions). A fourth possibility is that Josephus does not make a clear distinction between the written and the oral 'scripture', 'law' or Torah . . . , as a fifth possibility, assumes that by using these formulae Josephus particularly adopts an oriental historiographical tradition in which the emphasis is placed on the ancient sacral texts for the historical rendering.

As implied, these explanations do not all exclude each other, and in several of them we take hold of important and correct assumptions. Before we resort to this kind of explanation, however, we do owe it to Josephus and to ourselves to consider whether there are other possibilities for the understanding of these expressions. What could have Josephus meant by 'translating', 'adding' and 'omitting'?

If one maintains that Josephus was personally responsible for both the principal expressions and the manner in which they are realized in *Ant.*, it is obvious that he used the word 'translation' in a way which differs from how it is understood by readers today. However, in his preface to *Ant.*, Josephus gives us a hint as to how the term should be understood. In *Ant.* 1.10-13, he refers to the Septuagint as a predecessor and model for *Ant.* In modern interpretation, the Septuagint is seen just as much as an interpretative paraphrase (a type of exegesis or midrash), as a translation of the Old Testament. This also applies to the ancient translations of biblical texts from Hebrew to Aramaic, the so-called Targumim. Apparently, a translation as it is generally understood today, has a different connotation than it had in the Jewish communities in Palestine and the Diaspora in early Roman times, i. e. before the Bar Kokhba rebellion (132-135), before Mishnah (c. 200) and before Aquila made a literal translation of the Hebrew Bible into Greek (c. 120-140). It appears that at the time, a translation was more a question of rendering the essential contents of a text as it was understood by the translator rather than literally transposing it from one language to another. This conception was probably also an underlying factor in Philo's allegorical renderings of the biblical books which were published during the first half of the first century CE [Christian Era], approximately one generation before Josephus. The same idea can be traced in the contemporary eschatological interpretation of the biblical scriptures made by the community at Qumran. Finally, this tendency is found among the earliest Christian writers, who, simultaneously with Josephus, in the books of the New Testament, translated and expounded parts of the Old Testament in eschatological and typological fashion.

This is the light in which Josephus' 'exact translation' of the Bible can and should be seen. For Josephus, a 'translation' seems to have meant such an attempt to render the essential contents of the text. All of *Ant.* testifies to the fact that Josephus—if not in theory, at any rate in practice—distinguished between the contents of the texts and their external composition. Moreover, he seems to have believed that the contents of the texts were not touched by the external changes made in the formulation. The essence of this discussion—if we follow our reconstruction of Josephus' idea—is that in *Ant.*, Josephus intended to render the contents of the biblical books exactly and correctly. And he attempted to do this not merely in spite of but indeed by virtue of his Hellenistic transformation and modernization of their form, his interpretative systematizing of the texts, his omissions and additions. In reality, in *Ant.*, we encounter a preacher and a prophet, who presents the contents of the biblical books in a renewed, topical version of divine truth for his Hellenistic contemporaries to accept or reject.

In support of our understanding of Josephus' words, we have found agreement with the meaning of a 'translation' of the Bible in usage contemporary to Josephus. Secondly, there can hardly be any doubt that by this interpretation we have understood Josephus' own view on the matter. In *Ant.* 4.196-198, he comments on his rendering of the Mosaic code and asserts that precisely by his systematized change of the text, he has rendered everything exactly as Moses himself had given it. Finally, this understanding

readily falls into line with *Ant.*' s main purpose as an apologetic work. . . .

During the discussion concerning *Ant.*'s treatment of the biblical books, we have been continually referred to Josephus as an apologist and preacher. We have observed that he makes radical changes in editing his sources. However, the question arises whether this drastic editorial work results in a maltreatment of the sources. How does Josephus in fact treat his sources? This question is of decisive importance for how we may use *Ant.* as a historical source.

Fortunately, this question is more easily answered than the preceding ones. In the course of recent decades, numerous investigations of this matter have been undertaken, e. g. Josephus' treatment of Genesis, 1 and 2 Samuel, Esther, the Aristeas letter and 1 Maccabees. There is an astonishing degree of unanimity in these investigations which point to the following conclusions. Josephus treats his sources cautiously and carefully as far as the factual contents are concerned. But, with regard to the linguistic, stylistic form and concerning the composition he works freely. Here, he becomes the philologist, he cultivates style in each sentence, he polishes syntax and experiments with vocabulary. Here, he works with sketches of people, the composition and the narrative sequence whereby he introduces features from Hellenistic novel writing. Over and above this freedom with regard to language, style and composition, we have already been able to observe how Josephus readily supplements his main sources and elaborates on them by means of additional material from 'oral' Jewish tradition, quotations from Greco-Roman literature, official documents, geographical, topographical and archaeological information, legends, etc. Finally, in these investigations, time and again, we have been able to ascertain that Josephus' paraphrase and elaboration of the main sources coincide with his own apologetic interests and at the same time make his own interests topical. It is particularly surprising, however, that this radical process of editing rarely interferes with the substance of the main sources, or alters the facts. Once Josephus' literary leanings and professional tendencies have been defined, it is not difficult to separate his editing, and, so to speak, extricate the main source from these layers of 'wrapping'. Besides, investigations of the way in which Josephus uses *Bell.* in *Ant.* point in the same direction. So, we may state that today there is a high degree of clarity with regard to how Josephus treats his sources.

Ant., then, is a work which stands apart from others as an apologetic and missionary rendering of the holy scriptures of the Jewish people, at once presenting the Jewish religion and the history of the Jewish people. In saying this, something decisive has also been said with regard to the aim of *Ant.* In the foregoing paragraphs we have been compelled to touch upon this subject repeatedly, for the aim of the work appears clearly from the way in which Josephus treats his sources in *Ant.* Here, he adduces an impressive number of documents, quotations and references, all of which serve the purpose of supporting and strengthening the statements in the holy scriptures of the Jewish people. So, the idea is that the biblical scriptures must be trustworthy not only because they are ancient, but also because they are confirmed by a series of non-Jewish sources. In line with this, Josephus addresses himself to non-Jewish readers and in general, it is his purpose to convince them of the truth and value of the ancient Jewish scriptures, religion and history.

This overall aim which we can derive from *Ant.* as a whole is in agreement with Josephus' own words where he more specifically expresses his purpose. This applies, first, to the quite general expressions he uses in his introduction to *Ant.*, where (*Ant.* 1.5) he states:

> And now I have undertaken this present work in the belief that the whole Greek-speaking world will find it worthy of attention.

This also applies to *Ap.*, where the introduction makes references to *Ant.*:

> In the history of our *Antiquities*, most excellent Epaphroditus, I have, I think, made sufficiently clear to any who may peruse that work the extreme antiquity of our Jewish race, the purity of the original stock, and the manner in which it established itself in the country which we occupy to-day. That history embraces a period of five thousand years (*Ap.* 1.1).

Here, it is emphasized that *Ant.* is a documentation of the antiquity of the Jewish people, their special history and their right to the land of Palestine. The purpose of the work is even more clearly stated in *Ant.* 14.186, where Josephus explains why he cites a number of Roman documents which testify to the privileges granted to the Jewish people throughout the years:

> And here it seems to me necessary to make public all the honours given our nation and the alliances made with them by the Romans and their emperors, in order that the other nations may not fail to recognize that both the kings of Asia and of Europe have held us in esteem and have admired our bravery and loyalty.

The motive for Josephus' citing the pro-Jewish documents is thus the existing animosity against the Jewish people; cf. *Ant.* 14.187 where Josephus says that 'many persons, out of enmity to us' refuse to believe in the genuineness of these documents. Indeed, in *Bell.* 1.2, Josephus even speaks about many historians' 'hatred of the Jews'. This explanation of the purpose of citing the pro-Jewish documents is disclosed even more clearly in *Ant.* 16.174-178, which concludes a series of similar documents.

> Now it was necessary for me to cite these decrees since this account of our history is chiefly meant to reach the Greeks in order to show them that in former times we were treated with all respect and were not prevented by our rulers from practising any of our ancestral customs but, on the contrary, even had their co-operation in preserving our religion and our way of honouring God. And if I frequently mention these decrees, it is to reconcile the other nations to us and to remove the causes for hatred which have taken root in thoughtless persons among us as well as among them (Ant. 16.174-175).

In this passage, it is made crystal clear that Josephus' mo-

tive for citing these decrees is the mutual enmity between Jews and 'Greeks' (heathens or non-Jews) and the hatred of the latter towards the Jewish people. It is equally clear—first by citing the pro-Jewish decrees, but secondly also with *Ant.* in its entirety—that the purpose is to defend the Jewish people and their rights in the Roman Empire.

Thus, the aim of *Ant.* may in fact be said to be national apologetic and in that sense the aim is the same as that of *Bell.* To this may be added, as we have already seen in preceding paragraphs, a clearly defined interest in presenting Judaism as an honourable and attractive religion. When Josephus emphasizes the antiquity of Judaism, he points in this direction, likewise, when he underlines its religious content and the high level of it (cf. esp. *Ant.* 1.15, 18-26, which stress the dignity and purity of the Mosaic concept of God). Moreover, it should be mentioned that Josephus correspondingly accentuates the moral essence of Judaism and its teaching of God's justice. Thus, Josephus describes Judaism as an attractive religion centred around a sublime conception of God and around moral capability and virtue (aretē). By this, it was probably Josephus' intention to solicit sympathy and understanding, indeed perhaps even approval, for Judaism as a religion.

Likewise, the Hellenization of Judaism and of the history of the Jewish people indicates this missionary tendency. Josephus often 'translates' the biblical concept of God by well-known Hellenistic expressions, e. g. 'The divine' (to theion), 'the daemonic' (to daimon), 'necessity' (to chreon), 'destiny' (hē haimarmenē), 'providence' (hē pronoia), 'fate' (hē tychē), etc. The three classical Jewish schools—the Sadducees, the Pharisees and the Essenes— are depicted by Josephus as being philosophical tendencies similar to the Greek, e. g. the Stoics. Likewise, Josephus portrays the Jewish heroes in a Hellenistic light. Abraham is portrayed as a wise man and philosopher; Moses as the ideal lawgiver—creator of the ideal political-moral constitution; David as the great hero and king of warriors; Solomon, again, as a philosopher and the ideal prince of peace. The stories of Abraham, Joseph, Moses, Samson and Esther have all the features of Hellenistic short stories and novels. Presumably, the intention was to solicit the favour of the Greek readers of *Ant.* All of the Jewish religion and history is presented as an ancient and venerable heritage of wisdom (sophia) and virtue (aretē) which are ideals for all people. So, the intention of *Ant.* is to defend Judaism and the Jewish people and, at the same time, to argue for their cause. . . .

As we have noted, the work is addressed to 'the whole Greek-speaking world' or merely to the 'Greeks', i. e. to those in the Roman empire who have a knowledge of Greek, in other words, all of the educated persons in that part of the world. Thus, *Ant.*, unlike *Bell.*, is hardly primarily addressed to the government and the ruling class in Rome, although this audience also plays a role for Josephus in *Ant.* Therefore, we must reject the hypotheses advanced, especially by Laqueur, Case and S.J.D. Cohen, that *Ant.* presupposes a new dangerous situation for the Jewish people who are threatened by anti-Jewish measures on the part of Domitian, and therefore the work is primarily addressed to the Roman government in a political and apologetical style. A deterioration like this in the situation of the Jewish people in the early 90s cannot in fact be proved on the basis of existing sources, and by postulating that the aim of this work is primarily political-apologetical one violates *Ant.* Nor is *Ant.* first and foremost addressed to the Jewish people or its leaders as assumed, for example, by Migliario. The Jews cannot be excluded from the public for which *Ant.* is intended, but it is completely senseless to imagine that they were the primary target for the work. In the first place, *Ant.* is addressed to two wide circles of readers in the Greco-Roman world: on the one hand, the vast non-Jewish public which was neutral towards the Jews and Judaism, and on the other, the numerous and influential circles which were favourably disposed towards and interested in Judaism. The anti-Semites of the ancient world presumably constitute an important element in explaining why *Ant.* was committed to writing, but they should probably not be included among the circles whom Josephus expected to be readers of his work. Surely, he did not hope that he would be in a position to convince them. But that applied to the two other groups which were also exposed to agitation from the anti-Semites. We may assume, therefore, that in defence of Judaism and the Jewish people, *Ant.* is primarily addressed to the first named group of neutrals and, perhaps, also to the government in Rome, whereas *Ant.* as a work of agitation and as a missionary work in favour of Judaism is intended, particularly, for the second of the two groups mentioned. Towards the former, Josephus wished to counteract the activities of the anti-Semites, and towards the latter, he wished to consolidate and strengthen the sympathy which its members already nourished towards Judaism. . . .

Vita

In our discussion . . . of *Ant.*, it was mentioned that apparently *Vita* was written in continuation of this work and, at any rate, published together with it. In *Ant.* 20.259-261, Josephus gives a brief résumé of the contents of *Ant.*, and in *Ant.* 20.262-265, he credits himself with having done what no one else, neither Jew nor Gentile, could have done. Josephus writes that by his compatriots he is acknowledged as the greatest with regard to Jewish learning. As far as Greek language and literature are concerned he has strenuously acquired a fairly good knowledge, although he never found it within his power to attain a good pronunciation. Besides, the Jews do not attach any importance to the learning of foreign languages. Anyone, indeed even a slave, can learn them. No, the Jewish people have the greatest respect and admiration for one who has an exact knowledge of the law and is able to translate it correctly and interpret the holy scriptures. So, this is what matters and apart from Josephus, only a very few have been able to do it. Therefore, as he writes in *Ant.* 20.266, it would perhaps be of interest to his readers for him to recount briefly his lineage and life while there are still persons living who can disprove or prove his statements. Josephus starts the final paragraph of *Ant.* by saying 'with this', that is to say with *Vita*, he intends to conclude his *Antiquities*.

Therefore, *Ant.* 20.262-267 leaves very little doubt that

Vita was published as a part of *Ant.*, perhaps as an appendix. This assumption, is also confirmed by the concluding remarks in *Vita*:

> Such are the events of my whole life; from them let others judge as they will of my character. Having now, most excellent Epaphroditus, rendered you a complete account of our antiquities, I shall here for the present conclude my narrative (*Vita* 430).

Also in this passage—exactly as in *Ant.* 20.266-267—*Vita* manifests itself as a part of *Ant.* Thus, the literary origin and dating of *Vita* must be assumed to be the same as that of *Ant.*

This conclusion is valid regardless of how one dates the dual work *Ant.-Vita.* We have quite simply followed the information given us by Josephus at the end of *Ant.* 20, and on the basis of this information, we have dated both of these works to the year 93-94.

However, a brief comment made by the Byzantine author, Photius in the 10th century has given rise to extremely daring hypotheses. *Vita* 359-360 presupposes that King Agrippa II is no longer living, and the above mentioned Photius informs us that the king died in the third year of Emperor Trajan, i.e. in the year 100-101 (Bibliotheka, Codex 33). On the assumption that this is true, a number of authors, headed by Laqueur, have resorted to redating not only *Vita*, but *Ant.* as well, since both of these works, as we have asserted, are literarily connected. The consequence of this redating is that Josephus' own dating of *Vita* in *Ant.* 20.267 must be rejected. In order to explain all of these circumstances some have constructed a complicated hypothesis which is fundamentally based on the assumption that Josephus continually revised his works and altered their tendency to agree with the political situation which prevailed at any given time. . . . Then, *Ant.* 20.267 is presumed to have its origin in an earlier edition of *Ant.*, an edition which, it should be noted, was published without *Vita*. Moreover, this presupposes that Josephus was so indolent and thoughtless that in later editions of *Ant.*, he did not care, or was not able, to correct the dating in the first edition. Finally, it presupposes that *Vita* was not added to *Ant.* until an edition which appeared after 100-101, since it is also asserted that the main reason for the writing of *Vita* was the work of Justus of Tiberias which is purported to have contained a devastating criticism of Josephus' activities in Galilee and of his writings, and this work did not appear until after the death of Agrippa II. . . .

Vita is the shortest of Josephus' works and comprises only one book. It begins with an account of the author's ancestry and lineage (1-6). This is followed by a brief description of his childhood, youth and education (7-12), and a more lengthy narrative of his journey to Rome (13-16). The following passage (17-27) describes the situation in Jerusalem on Josephus' return from Rome. This account is even longer and one is aware of the fact that the author has arrived at events of importance and interest. The following brief passage (28-29) tells us about Josephus being appointed as leader in Galilee. *Vita* 30 describes Josephus' journey to Galilee, and the following lengthy section (31-

411) gives us an account in great detail about Josephus' activities in Galilee from the autumn of 66 to the spring of 67 when Vespasian arrived at Ptolemais. This section runs parallel with *Bell.* 2. (457)562-3.34, which is shortened especially at the beginning, and then considerably expanded, in particular, where the actual period in Galilee is concerned. This section also concludes with a reference to *Bell.* where the reader is told that he will be able to find a continuation of the story (*Vita* 412). *Vita* 413 is a transitional passage leading on to the brief account of Josephus' life after the year 67. This section is introduced by a narrative of events in Judaea from the years 67-71 (414-421) and continues with a brief mention of Josephus' life in Rome after the year 71 (422-429). Thereafter, *Vita* concludes with a short passage (430) which is quoted above in section 4 a. . . .

A study of the contents of *Vita* and its disposition necessarily leads on to the question of the theme of this curious little book. This question becomes even more urgent if we take another look at *Ant.* 20.266 which describes the contents of *Vita* as being 'to recount briefly my lineage and the events of my life'. In response to this, in *Vita* 430 we find: 'Such are the events of my whole life'. Thus, *Vita* itself claims to be a biography which covers all of Josephus' life. But the text of *Vita* does not readily fulfil this programme. . . . On the contrary, it manifests itself as a thorough account of Josephus' activities in Galilee, embellished with a number of brief autobiographical notes which are given by way of introduction and conclusion of this account. How can we explain this relationship?

Naturally, the matter is linked together with the question of the aim of *Vita* and it can hardly be solved completely without an answer to this question. But at this point some tentative comments can be made. In theory, there are two possibilities for the explanation. Either *Vita* is not a true autobiography, but rather something other than it pretends to be, or *Vita* should be understood to be an autobiography of a very special nature in which everything of importance is centred around a decisive climax in the life of the author. . . .

It has already become necessary for us to consider the question of the aim of *Vita*. It could scarcely have been the main purpose of *Vita* to defend Josephus against accusations of having been responsible for revolts against Rome made by Galilee, or parts of Galilee, and their defection from Agrippa II, since neither in *Bell.* nor in *Vita* does Josephus conceal his participation and leading role in the War. Nor can *Vita* as a whole be interpreted as a defence against accusations made by Justus of Tiberias or other persons, whether these are to be seen as accusations of having abused his position as general in Galilee to commit tyranny and to gain personal advantages, of having molested Justus and his family or accusations of having presented an untruthful account of the history of the war in *Bell.* None of these hypotheses is capable of presenting an exhaustive explanation of the entire contents of *Vita*, and therefore they must be abandoned.

Instead, I am convinced that the aim of *Vita* can be understood most clearly and defined by way of *Ant.* 20.265-267, and in the light of this, from the introductions to *Bell.* and

Ant., by Josephus' apologetic comments on his writings in *Ap.* 1.47-56, and by a few other references. In *Ant.* 20.262-265, Josephus stresses his unexcelled Jewish learning—his knowledge of the law and his ability to translate and interpret the holy scriptures—as the decisive prerequisite why he and he alone of his contemporaries was able to compose a work like *Ant.* But this prerequisite is precisely linked with his 'lineage' ('genos') which, as stated in *Ant.* 20.266, he will 'recount' in *Vita*. The connection between these two factors is stated explicitly in *Ap.*:

> Nevertheless, certain despicable persons have essayed to malign my history [*Bell.*], taking it for a prize composition such as is set to boys at school. What an extraordinary accusation and calumny! Surely they ought to recognize that it is the duty of one who promises to present his readers with actual facts first to obtain an exact knowledge of them himself, either through having been in close touch with the events, or by inquiry from those who knew them. That duty I consider myself to have amply fulfilled in both my works. In my *Antiquities*, as I said, I have given a translation of our sacred books; being a priest and of priestly ancestry (*genos*), I am well versed in the philosophy of these writings (*Ap.* 1.53-54).

Thus, Josephus' qualifications for being able to accomplish this 'translation' are to be found in his status as a priest and his priestly lineage. This connection is already implied in *Bell.* 1.3 where, by way of introducing himself, in addition to his identity and his participation in the War, Josephus emphasizes the fact that he is a priest. Finally, . . . Josephus also emphasized the connection between his priestly status and his knowledge of the scriptures:

> a priest himself and of priestly descent (*eggonos*),
> he was not ignorant of the prophecies in the sacred books (*Bell.* 3.352).

So, in his own eyes, Josephus' dignity as a priest was of vital importance to his capacity as a writer. But it is this very dignity which is explained in he introductory passages of *Vita*. Therefore, we can assume that part of the aim of *Vita* is to give a detailed account of Josephus' qualifications as an author.

In the light of this, it may be assumed that the remainder of *Vita* has a similar aim. We have previously observed how Josephus stresses the fact that it is important for a historian to have experienced in person the events about which he writes. Not only in *Bell.*, but also in the introduction to *Ant.* and first and foremost in *Ap.*, Josephus stresses that in adherence to the classical historiographical principles, the foremost duty of the historical writer is to narrate the important historical events in which he himself participated. Therefore, it should be considered whether Josephus in *Ant.* 20.266 and *Vita* 430 was not touching on the same theme, which means that the events in his life, which he here discusses, can be interpreted as the historically significant events he himself witnessed. Naturally, these events are in particular reference to the Jewish-Roman War, but here again primarily the War in Galilee in which Josephus actively participated. Therefore, the events of his life which Josephus speaks of in *Ant.* 20.266 and *Vita* 430 can be interpreted as referring primarily to the historical events in his life which he has already recounted in *Bell.*, and which he will elaborate on in *Vita.* This interpretation is supported by *Vita* 357-358, where Josephus actually reproaches Justus of Tiberias for not being present in person either in Galilee (Jotapata) or in Jerusalem.

On the basis of these deliberations, Josephus may be presumed to have had a dual purpose in writing *Vita.* One aim was to establish his priestly heritage which made it possible for him to compose *Ant.* (and his other works) on the basis of the holy scriptures. The other aim was to tell us about his own participation in the Jewish War, since this is his fundamental and decisive prerequisite for writing contemporary history, primarily *Bell.*

If we interpret *Vita* in this way, a connection is made between the contents of *Vita* on the one hand, and the placement of the book in the complete literary production of Josephus on the other; a connection which Josephus himself has taken great pains to emphasize by publishing *Vita* together with *Ant.* Thus *Vita* no longer stands as an obscure appendix to *Ant.*, an incomplete autobiography, let alone as an apologetic excursus which is difficult to understand. Then, *Vita* comes forth as a genuine autobiography, albeit an autobiography of a very special nature, since it is dependent upon the unusual history of the author's life and his writings which the biography will serve to elucidate and justify. . . .

Against Apion

Ap., which comprises two books, is the last of Josephus' works, at least the last known and handed down. While it is true that we do not know precisely when it was written, since there are several references in it to *Ant.*, it must have been composed later than *Ant.*, i.e. after 93-94.

The title, *Contra Apionem* (*Against Apion*), was not designated by Josephus. He makes no mention whatsoever of a name for this work. The title which is used today originates from tradition, since after the death of Josephus, when the work was being copied, at one point or another it was given this designation. Moreover, it is not a very well chosen title, since only in the second book are there any remarks about and against the person Apion, who was a Greek orator and author from Alexandria who lived at the same time as Philo in the first half of the first century. The first book of *Ap.* defends Judaism by other means. A title such as Against the Greeks or In Defence of Judaism would have corresponded better with the contents of *Ap.* and with Josephus' intentions. . . .

In the introduction, 1.1-5, Josephus outlines the reason for the work as being that 'a considerable number of persons' will not believe what he has stated in *Antiquities*, but instead are 'influenced by the malicious calumnies of certain individuals'. They claim that the Jewish people are not an ancient race because they are not mentioned in Greek literature. Josephus intends to refute this conception, partly by proving that the Jews actually are mentioned by Greek authors, and partly by explaining why, all the same, this is so seldom the case.

He begins with the latter and thereby he attempts to reverse the accusations against the Jewish people converting them into an attack on Greek historiography. In *Ap.* 1.6-27, Josephus attempts to prove that Greek culture, literature and historical writing are, in fact, of later date, and likewise dependent upon oriental culture. He also claims that the Greek historical writings are full of errors and contradictions; furthermore, that these are partly due to the fact that the Greeks did not keep public annals and records on which the historians could rely, and partly owing to the Greeks' preference for literary expression and rhetorical style.

In the following paragraphs, *Ap.* 1.28-46, it is asserted that on the contrary, the oriental peoples, among them the Jews, had long ago appointed experts to keep continuous records of historical events. Josephus cites the Jewish Canon as an example.

The next section, *Ap.* 1.47-56, is an excursus in which Josephus, in continuation of his remarks on the Jewish Canon, speaks about his own *Bell.* as an example of eyewitnessed, and therefore reliable historical writing. This section concludes in his formulating of his own two principles on translation, that is to say rendering of documents, and personal experience as being the basis of reliable writing of history.

In *Ap.* 1.57-72, Josephus explains that the reason why the Greeks do not mention the Jews is the fact that the Jewish people are an inland nation who cultivate their land, and it was not possible for the maritime Greeks to establish contact with them. Naturally, the absence of this contact does not go to prove that the Jews were a young nation. For there are many other peoples, especially the Egyptians and the Phoenicians, who mentioned the Jews at an early date.

Thereafter, Josephus cites a number of accounts and quotations from the Egyptian author Manetho, from Phoenician and other sources and from the Babylonian author Berosus. The purpose of all these citations is to testify to the agreement between the statements in these sources and the contents of the Jewish scriptures.

Having done this, Josephus can take hold of his next objective, which is to testify to the fact that the Jewish people actually are mentioned by several Greek authors. Among them, he counts Pythagoras, Herodotus, Aristotle and, especially, Hecataeus of Abdera who is purported to have written a whole book about the Jews (c. 330 BCE [Before the Christian Era]). All of these authors and many others are cited by Josephus in *Ap.* 1.161-218.

This concludes the first main section of *Ap.*, the testimony to the antiquity of the Jewish people, and now Josephus can commence on his next topic, which consists of repudiating a number of accusations made against Judaism and the Jewish people.

In the beginning, in *Ap.* 1.219-287, Josephus deals with Manetho, who had written that originally the Jews were a crowd of lepers and afflicted people who were driven out of Egypt. Josephus employs the method of first minutely paraphrasing and quoting this Manetho and then analyzing the text quoted, whereupon he tears it apart by pointing out its intrinsic contradictions and disagreement with other known facts.

Having finished with Manetho, Josephus subjects similar presentations made by the Greek authors Chaeremon and Lysimachus to the same treatment, as seen in *Ap.* 1.288-319. Hereafter, the first book of *Ap.* ends rather abruptly.

Ap. 2 is introduced by a résumé of the first book, and a programme for the second, 2.1-7, in which particular attention is given to a refutation of Apion's accusations against the Jews.

The first half of *Ap.* 2 deals with Apion. It starts with his account of Moses and the Jews in Egypt and from there goes on, especially to Apion's claim that the Jews in Alexandria did not have citizenship in that city. This is one of the most famous passages in *Ap.* It is followed by an indignant rejection of a whole series of anti-Semitic slander stories which Apion is said to have circulated. First, the story about the Jews having worshiped the head of an ass in the Temple in Jerusalem. Then, the story about the Jews having fattened, slain and devoured an innocent Greek, and followed by a few other stories of the same kind. Josephus sums up this series of stories by citing a number of assertions made on the part of Apion that Judaism must be false since the Jewish people have experienced so many misfortunes, and since they have not produced very many men of genius, etc. Fortunately, however, Josephus can conclude this violent dispute with Apion by relating that this dire enemy of the Jewish people suffered a well-deserved painful death. This is a widely used stereotype motive, a topos often encountered in Jewish (and later Christian) apologetic literature.

The second major section in *Ap.* 2 contains the famous account of the 'Jewish constitution', in which Josephus explains the main principles and fundamental ideas in the Mosaic code. This is the place where Josephus introduces the expression 'theocracy' (theokratia)—which does not occur in any other place in all of the Greek literature—to describe the special nature of the Jewish political system. He pronounces Moses to be the world's first lawgiver, and also emphasizes the conception of God as the seed of Judaism, while at the same time, he emphasizes the moral principles as fundamental in the Jewish religion.

In the final major section of *Ap.* 2, Josephus compares the Mosaic code with Greek lawgiving and religion. Already in the preceding paragraph, he asserted that at first the Greeks had learnt something from the Jewish conception of God, thus e. g. Pythagoras, Plato and the Stoics, and Josephus continues this line of thought here. He is able to point out some analogies between the Mosaic code and the laws of Plato, and he is also able to maintain that both the Greek philosophers and the masses in the Greco-Roman cities appear to have imitated the laws of Moses. At the same time, Josephus maintains that the Jewish laws are more demanding than the Greek, and that the Jews observe the law to a higher degree than do the Greeks. Although Josephus often states that it is not his intention to criticize the religion of others, here, he is not able to restrain a traditional Jewish accusation against the 'ridicu-

lous' Greek worship of gods, which is another set feature, a topos, in Jewish (and early Christian) apologetic literature.

Josephus sums up *Ap.* with yet another reference to *Ant.*, where the reader will be able to find a more comprehensive account of the Mosaic code and the Jewish 'constitution'. Once more he gives a résumé of the contents of and he points out that the goal of the Mosaic code is love, not hate. Thereafter, he concludes by proudly proclaiming that Judiaism has truly brought this and may other beautiful ideas into the world. A dedication to Epaphroditus brings the work to a close. . . .

The theme of *Ap.* is obviously the controversy between Judaism and Greek civilization. For Josephus personally, this controversy expressed itself in the Greek criticism and rejection of *Ant.* This obviously corresponds with a Greek criticism of *Bell.* which should be seen in its relationship with Josephus' own criticism of Greek historiography in *Ap.* 1.6-46. However, this controversy is not only apparent in *Ap.*, but also, as we have previously observed, it appears in the earlier works, *Bell.* and *Ant.* Josephus makes similar criticisms of the Greek writing of history both in *Bell.* (1.1-3, 6-8) and in *Ant.* (1.1-4). Thus, Josephus by his writings is situated in the firing line of a far greater conflict between the Jews and the non-Jewish world. *Bell.* 1.2 speaks openly about the 'hatred of the Jews' as a motive of some of the Greek historical writers—rivals of Josephus—who had written accounts of the Jewish Roman War. And as we have noted previously, *Ant.* 14.187 and 16.174-175 state that the enmity and hatred of the Jewish people was a decisive cause for Josephus to write *Ant.*

Thus, the controversy between Josephus and contemporary, rival Greek authors which we hear about in *Ap.* 1.1-2 belongs in the context of suspicion, polemics and hatred which so strongly influenced the relationship between Jews and non-Jews ('Greeks') during the centuries around the beginning of the common era. . . . Likewise, we have emphasized that one of the purposes of *Bell.* and *Ant.* was to contribute to the preservation of, or to re-establish the legal and political status of the Jews in these cities. With regard to this matter, in *Ap.*, we receive definite information concerning the conditions in Alexandria (*Ap.* 2.33-78; cf. *Bell.* 2.487-499; *Ant.* 18.257-261; and Philo's works, Flaccus and Legatio ad Gaium). Apion is said to contest the rights and privileges of the Jewish population in this city, whereas Josephus defends them.

During the period from Antiochus IV Epiphanes (175-164 BCE), but with particular reference to the establishment of the Hasmonaean supremacy at the end of the second century BCE and until the revolt of Bar Kokhba (132-135 CE), an unrelenting conflict raged between Jews and 'Greeks'. It was fought in all parts of the Greco-Roman world, in the motherland of Palestine and in the widespread Diaspora. Moreover, it was fought on several levels and by many means. It took place economically and politically as in Caesarea and Alexandria. It took place militarily as in the Hasmonaean period of expansion and in the year 66-67 CE, and it took place ideologically and literarily, as seen in the works of Josephus and Philo. This overall conflict is the theme of *Ap.*

This work provides us with an insight into the mutual contempt and degradation which dominated the relationship between 'Greeks' and Jews. We also observe that apparently this controversy was part of an even greater struggle between Hellenism and the Orient; cf. *Ap.* 1.28-46, where Josephus ranks Judaism on a par with the great oriental phalanx with which he confronts the Greek civilization.

This conflict between contemporary Jews and non-Jews is the motive and theme of *Apion* and, as we have pointed out in the previous sections, it also determines the earlier works, *Bellum* and *Antiquities* great extent. . . .

The aim and circle of readers of *Ap.* may be determined to be the same as those of *Ant.* Like that which applies to this work, the aim and readers of *Ap.* are also twofold. The work addresses itself partly to the far-reaching circles in the Greco-Roman world which remained neutral in the controversy between the Jews and the 'Greeks' in order to prevent and avert the effects which the anti-Semitic attacks on the Jews might cause. But, *Ap.* also addresses itself to the groups which were favourably inclined to Judaism with the intention of defending and interpreting the religion which they found attractive. Moreover, we can probably assume that here and there Josephus particularly aims at the government in Rome for the same reason as applies to the first group mentioned. On the other hand, there is nothing to indicate that he had a Jewish audience in mind, a theory advanced by Migliario. Nevertheless, the decisive group aimed at is definitely those who were interested in Judaism. They constitute partly an important group of allies of the Jewish people in the Greco-Roman world, and partly they are potential converts. It is obviously for their benefit that Josephus describes Judaism as the true philosophy which is testified and revered by the best Greek philosophers and historians. It is for them that he portrays Moses as the ideal and earliest lawgiver. It is probably also this group which gives Josephus occasion to embellish to such an extent the Jewish proselytism and mission. His criticism of the Greek worship of their gods also belongs in this context. All of these features indicate and testify to the fact that *Ap.* is primarily a work of missionary literature, a work of apologetic and propaganda of 'hortatory' nature, primarily addressed to the 'Gentiles', who were interested in the Jewish faith, in an effort to attract them even closer to Judaism as 'God-fearing' or as actual proselytes. . . .

Thus, *Ap.* can be regarded as the key to all of Josephus' writings. The primary factor in these is scarcely Josephus' role in the Jewish War, his surrender to the Romans, or his emperor prophecy with all that this seems to have secured for him in the way of privileges. Nor can it be his controversies with other Jews such as Justus of Tiberias or Jonathan the Weaver, of Cyrene, no matter how essential these may appear to be. Nor can it be the presumed instability of Josephus' career, status and income, as assumed by the Laqueur school. But it is the political and spiritual status of the Jewish people and of Judaism in the Greco-Roman world which constitutes the central theme in all of Josephus' works. Outwardly, his main political aim is to re-establish, maintain and secure the rights and position of the Jewish people within the Roman Empire

in the precarious situation following the War in 66-70 (74). Inwardly, among the Jewish people, he tries to promote a degree of openness towards and cooperation with Rome as well as the Greco-Roman, Hellenistic civilization. Furthermore, with regard to morals and religion, Josephus endeavoured to preserve and expand Judaism as a meaningful and influential 'philosophy' in the world at the time. All these features come to the fore in *Ap.*, and viewed in the light of *Ap.*, they also become apparent in *Bell.* and *Ant.* In all his works, it is essential for Josephus to counteract the 'hatred of the Jews', to secure the rights of the Jewish people and to present Judaism in such a way that its appeal to the non-Jews is clearly evident.

FURTHER READING

Farmer, William Reuben. "Josephus." In his *Maccabees, Zealots, and Josephus*, pp. 11-23. New York: Columbia University Press, 1956.

> Examines Josephus's *Jewish War* against first-century documents in order to arrive at a reliable picture of the events of the Jewish war.

Pines, Shlomo. *An Arabic Version of the Testamonium Flavium and Its Implications.* Jerusalem: Jerusalem Academy Press, 1971, 87 p.

> Etymological discussion that compares the Agapius Arabic version of the Testamonium, the extant Josephan Greek text, and Eusebius's rendering in his *Historia Ecclesiastica* and *Demonstratio*, contending that all three agree in their titling of Jesus as the "anointed," but leave the question of his messiahship open to interpretation.

Schwartz, Daniel R. "Studies in Josephus and Judean Chronology." In his *Studies in the Jewish Backround of Christianity*, pp. 155-282. Tübingen: J. C. B. Mohr (Paul Siebeck), 1992.

> Investigates Josephus's use of sources and their chronological problems, especially in relation to the Roman emperors, the Herods, and Pontius Pilate.

Schwartz, Seth. *Josephus and Judean Politics.* Leiden: E. J. Brill, 1990, 256 p.

> Examines Josephus's portrayal of the political factors influencing the Jewish priesthood, the Pharisees, Rabbinical Judaism, and the Herodians after the year 70.

Sterling, Gregory E. "The *Antiquitates Judaicae* of Josephos." In his *Historiography and Self-Definition*, pp. 226-310. Leiden: E. J. Brill, 1992.

> Explores the literary techniques, historiographical traditions, sources, and objectives of Josephus's *Jewish Antiquities*.

Villalba I Varneda, Pere. *The Historical Method of Flavius Josephus.* Leiden: E. J. Brill, 1986, 295 p.

> Studies the methodology and literary genre of *Jewish War* and *Jewish Antiquities*, with particular emphasis on the causes of various events and the speeches of several historical figures.

Williamson, G. A. *The World of Josephus.* London: Secker & Warburg, 1964, 318 p.

Detailed overview of "Josephus' world—the world that helped to make him what he was, the world of geography, of history, of religion, of thought, of circumstance."

Njáls saga

c. 1280

(Also known as *Brennu-Njáls Saga* and *Njála*.) Icelandic saga.

INTRODUCTION

Njáls saga is the longest and the most sophisticated of Iceland's family sagas. Like other sagas of this genre, *Njáls saga* recounts a series of dramatic events set in Iceland during the early Medieval period, centering on the travels and exploits of prominent families. Scholars maintain that, unlike other family sagas, which were composed and elaborated over generations, *Njáls saga* was created by an individual author of exceptional skill. Rather than focusing on historical fact, as did most other saga writers, the author of *Njáls saga* devised his plot from a number of oral and written sources, manipulating the material to suit his own style, ideology, and artistic vision. According to Gwyn Jones, *Njáls saga* "is . . . a work of realistic fiction which uses history with superb skill for its own creative purposes. Its ultimate concern is with something which transcends historical fact or tradition—and that is human destiny."

Plot and Major Characters

Although *Njáls saga* was written in the latter portion of the thirteenth century, it recalls events that occurred as early as the year 1000. Its plot is highly complex and involves six hundred characters, ranging from the sinister to the comic. The two heroes of the saga are Gunnar, a powerful warrior much like Sigfried of heroic legend, and Njáll, an acclaimed lawyer, chieftain, and advisor to Gunnar. Structurally, *Njáls saga* is divided into two major sections with the first centering on Gunnar's heroic life and death and the second telling of Njáll's life, his family, and their deaths. In the opening chapters of the saga Gunnar marries Hallgerður, who later provokes two great blood feuds, the first being with Berþóra, the wife of Njáll, and the second with Gunnar's enemies, Skammkell, Otkell, and Morður Valgarðsson, men who are jealous of Gunnar's accomplishments. Because of his wife's actions, Gunnar is provoked into murdering numerous prominent individuals and, as a result, is sentenced to three years of exile. Refusing to leave Iceland, Gunnar is murdered in his home at Hliðarendi. The second part of *Njáls saga* concerns an equally devastating feud between Njáll's sons and the family of Þráinn Sigfússon. The story climaxes with the burning of Njáll and his family in their home by Flosi, a reluctant enemy whose family had been dishonored by Njáll's sons. In what some critics regard as a continuation of the second part, and others consider a separate third section of the saga, Njáll's son-in-law Kári escapes and eventually follows Flosi to Rome, where both men are absolved of their sins, and the two become reconciled.

Major Themes

Njáls saga treats several themes typical of the heroic age, specifically, subjection to fate, fascination with and the glorification of the heroic individual, and the importance of defending one's honor through blood revenge. Critics of *Njáls saga* have praised its prevailing mood of fatalism, observing that not only does it significantly contribute to the vivid evocation of ancient Icelandic life but also functions as an important structural device; they have found that the author's repeated emphasis on fate, through dreams, omens, prophecies, and portents lends credibility and unity to the saga's complicated plot. For example, the prophesy that Hallgerður's beauty would cause great suffering later makes her violent acts of vengeance seem unavoidable. Midway through *Njáls saga*, however, with a detailed account of Iceland's conversion to Christianity, the saga's mood of pagan fatalism gives way to a Christian belief in providence. At the same time, the action shifts from the heroic Gunnar to the Christian Njáll and his family. Moreover, the theme of honor prevalent in the first half of the saga, while still generating violence in the second portion of the work, is gradually discredited and replaced by a sense of Christian forbearance, thus allowing for *Njáls saga*'s peaceful conclusion. Such modulations in theme have led many scholars to interpret *Njáls saga* as a homily in which the author glorifies the hero but condemns the violence and suffering generated by heroic conduct, preferring instead a Christian society governed by law, order, humility, and grace.

Critical Reception

Historians have discovered twenty-four *Njáls saga* manuscripts—a high number given the work's antiquity, and a testament to the saga's widespread popularity during the Middle Ages. Despite such early approval, *Njáls saga* was not printed until 1772, long after the printing of other family sagas, and was not translated into a modern language until 1841, when a Danish translation was made by N. M. Petersen. Critics of *Njáls saga*, citing its many historical inconsistencies, long failed to acknowledge it as a significant work of literature, asserting that it was simply pieced together from two lost sagas—the putative *Gunnar's saga* and a supposed earlier *Njáll's saga*. It was not until the early twentieth century that many notable Icelandic critics, led by Einar Ólafur Sveinsson, began to recognize *Njáls saga* as a valuable and original work of art skillfully written by an unknown author who consciously manipulated historical events. Since the 1955 English translation by Carl F. Bayerschmidt and Lee M. Hollander, English-language criticism of *Njáls saga* has flourished. Many scholars have drawn comparisons between it and other well-known ancient works, including the *Iliad*, *Beowulf*, and the *Song of Roland*, noting similarities in structure, theme, and overall content. Others, such as W. H. Auden, have lauded *Njáls saga* as a significant literary achievement, maintaining that it accomplished a realistic and dramatically convincing narrative structure centuries before the development of similar types of prose fiction in the West.

PRINCIPAL ENGLISH TRANSLATIONS

Njáls saga   (translated by Carl F. Bayerschmidt and Lee M. Hollander)   1955
Njáls saga   (translated by Magnus Magnusson and Hermann Pálsson)   1960

CRITICISM

Gwyn Jones   (essay date 1954)

SOURCE: "The Greatest of Sagas," *The Times Literary Supplement*, No. 2760, December 24, 1954, p. 836.

[*In the following essay, Jones lauds* Njáls saga *as "a work of realistic fiction which uses history with superb skill for its own creative purposes."*]

There has never been any doubt among Icelanders that the greatest of all sagas is that **Brennu-Njáls Saga** which for almost one hundred years has been known to the English reader in Dasent's pioneer rendering, **The Story of Burnt Njal**. It is permissible, even proper, to have a favourite elsewhere: the chivalric and sentimental reader may respond more warmly to the fine feeling and noble situations of *Laxdœla Saga;* those who love high poetry and fierce adventure will always find *Egils Saga* irresistible; while the passionate regard of many Icelanders for the saga of the crossed and outlawed Grettir is a moving revelation of how a people may find its soul mirrored and its fate expressed in the tale of one man. But if we are seeking one work to demonstrate the achievement of Saga, *Njála* (to give it its title of affection) will be that work. Far more than any of its rivals it has claims to be the national epic of Iceland.

First, *Njála* by its place in the chronological record as well as by its literary excellence marks the culmination of saga art. This had developed from the historical works of the twelfth century, sometimes annalistic, sometimes legendary and edifying, but at no time productive of a literary masterpiece. Throughout the thirteenth century we observe how the creative artist is gaining on the historian, and how with freedom comes an increasing mastery of style and matter. Snorri Sturluson's *Egils Saga* is one great landmark, *Njála* another. In the former the incomparable historian of the North showed what might be done with historical and traditional material pragmatically and artistically treated. The first part of his saga, telling of King Harald Fairhair and Thórólf Kveldúlfsson, of their friendship, estrangement and quarrel, and how the king slew his great retainer jealously (and yet with justification), was a model of narrative and character-drawing not to be surpassed by any later writer in the saga kind; but the life of the poet Egill, to which this is the prelude, is memorable rather for the brilliance of its episodes than for sustained power. Then, half a century later, about 1280, the south of Iceland produced the nameless master whose absolute control of his material, together with his perfected prose style, led to such a triumph of realistic narrative art as *Njála.*

It may well have appeared to the authors and schools of late thirteenth-century Iceland that the remote south or south-east had contributed less than its share to the corpus of saga. Compared with the firths of the west and northwest it had, indeed, produced virtually nothing. Or at least nothing that has been preserved. The Vatnajökull and Markarfljót, Fljótshlíth and Thórsmörk, were not on the saga map. To anyone who knows what the sagas mean to the Icelandic landscape, and what that landscape means to the sagas the thought is a startling one. It is hardly an exaggeration to say that *Njála* gave this part of Iceland a soul, so that for to-day's traveller each place-name there is hallowed by its past, while his every stride strikes a tragic or heroic echo from its stones. Consider the lovely hillslope of Hlítharendi, Gunnar's home, where the wandering channels of Markriver carve the black sands of the seaward plain and the horizon dies behind the purple tusks of the Westmann Islands and the cloud-hung glaciers of the Eyjafjall. It was here, as *Njála* tells us, that the outlawed Gunnar rode down to his exile, and was thrown from his horse so that his face was turned again towards home, and cried (though he knew that his life depended on his going away): "Lovely is the hillside, so that it has never looked so lovely to me, the cornfields white and the homefield mown—and I will ride back home and never leave it." And so he did, and so he died, and is part of the scene for ever. It would be easy to adduce a long list of places where the *landvœttir* or land-spirits had never found a dwelling but for *Njála.*

Then *Njála* is the picture of an age. Just as *War and Peace* includes within its world not only the Bezukhovs, the Rostovs, the Bolkonskis and the Kuragins, but peasant, soldier, clerk and seamstress, Berthier and Kutuzov, Tsar and Emperor, and even Platon Karataev's dog, so *Njála* has room not only for Njáll and his sons and for such southern families as are their enemies or friends, but for all the leading men of Iceland too, Snorri Godi, Gudmund the Mighty, Skapti Thoroddsson, and further afield for the kings and earls of Norway, Denmark, Orkney and Ireland; for hucksters, beggar-women, farmers and sailors, and even for the hound Sám whose dying howl announced Gunnar's approaching doom. There are some twenty-five fully drawn characters, and these are surrounded by scores of shrewdly delineated lesser persons who between them give us the very feel of the great days of the Republic. Nor is the picture one of a confined society. If the young Icelanders are farmers' sons, they are many of them peasant princes too, who have rubbed shoulders with kings and noblemen and louted to none of them. The heartland of the saga is Iceland, from the deep rifts of Thingvellir to the southern ice-sheet; but its events reach out over northern and western Europe. Paradoxically, it is the more Icelandic for its awareness of the world outside. The heartland shows truer against the wide horizons.

It follows that *Njála* is a full book. The main theme is never suspended: the burning of Njáll, all that preceded it and all that was fated to follow, these are before us from the first sentences to the last. But this sequence of cause and event is enriched by much else. *Njála* is the saga of law *par excellence;* it is rich in constitutional history; the story of the conversion to Christianity is amply presented. The law, the constitution, and the change of faith are essential to the private histories of the characters. *Njála* is not an historical thesis which needs human heroes; it is a work of realistic fiction which uses history with superb skill for its own creative purposes. Its ultimate concern is with something which transcends historical fact or tradition—and that is human destiny. So the old religion and the new are needed, and prophecy and the supernatural, together with ingredients noble and mean, wise and foolish, important and petty, and sometimes ambiguous. These are presented directly through human beings, their thoughts, motives, and actions. For the most part the saga is heroic or tragic, yet from time to time the note may be homely or comic, the pointing and counterpointing is most delicate. What men do, and why they do it, and what happens to them—these are the problems cogitated and the issues displayed. *Njála* proceeded not only from a skilled hand but from a richly stored mind. Its author was markedly influenced by *Laxdœla,* and was learned in earlier sagas generally; he was well versed in historical records, both genealogical and narrative, native and foreign; the lawbooks he had at his fingers' ends, and his knowledge of patristic and other religious literature was extensive. To this book-learning he could add a wealth of oral tradition whose volume and variety we are only now coming to appreciate.

His main concern, as has been said, was with human destiny. The hero of the first third of the saga is Gunnar, one of the noblest men that ever lived in Iceland. It was his fortune (and misfortune) to marry the beautiful, spoiled, and trouble-bent Hallgerd. "She was fair-haired, and so dowered with it that she might hide herself in it; but she was prodigal and fierce-hearted." Many men had died because of her, this perilous maiden who grew worse after marriage; and Gunnar was the dearest sacrifice to her imperious and enigmatic temper. She involved him against his will in so many feuds that eventually two-score of his enemies besieged him in his house. Only his wife and mother were with him, but he held them off till his bowstring was cut through. It was now that he asked for two locks of his wife's long hair, to twist into a new string; and it was now with her snake-tongue that she tauntingly denied him his request. Soon he was dead, after one of the unforgettable defences in heroic literature; but Hallgerd lived on to embroil the sons of Njáll more deeply in a new feud which would lead to an even more destructive climax.

Njáll was Gunnar's best friend, an older man with a houseful of turbulent sons, including the troll-ugly, homicidal Skarphedinn. Time and time again he was able to save Gunnar from the disasters in which Hallgerd's pride and greed engulfed him. He was a wise and peace-loving man, loyal and magnanimous, at once blest and racked by his ability to read the future. Not that he was a blind fatalist: men, he knew, had their choice of action, but that choice once made Njáll knew what must follow. Thus he foresaw Gunnar's death if he would not go abroad, and the moment came when he foresaw his own. The most unbearable of all the burdens laid on him by his wisdom and foresight was when his son Skarphedinn came home to tell him that he had killed his foster-brother Höskuld.

> "Bitter tidings these," says Njáll, "and bad to hear, for indeed this grief touches me so close that I think it would have been better to lose two of my sons and have Höskuld live."
>
> "It is some excuse for you," says Skarphedinn, "that you are an old man, and it is only to be expected that it would touch you close."
>
> "No less than my age," says Njáll, "is the fact that I know better than you what will follow."
>
> "What will follow?" asks Skarphedinn.
>
> "My death," says Njáll, "and my wife's death, and the death of all my sons."

The duty of vengeance for Höskuld fell upon Flosi from ice-girt Svínafell. He hoped to avoid bloodshed, but events and personalities proved too strong for this. It was Flosi's destiny that, hate the task as he would, he must burn Njáll and all his family indoors. It is because he accepted his destiny that he is *sögulegt,* worth telling about. Even at the burning he wishes to spare all save the slayers of Höskuld. He calls the women and children and all the servants out to safety, and they go. Then, as the hall blazes, he begs Njáll to come out too.

> "I have no wish to come out," answers Njáll, "for I am an old man and little fitted to avenge my sons, and I will not live my life in shame."
>
> The Flosi spoke to Bergthóra [Njáll's wife]: "Come out, lady, for I would not for anything burn you indoors."
>
> "I was given to Njáll young," said Bergthóra, "and it was my promise to him that we should share the same fate."

And so, their destiny accepted, as Gunnar and Flosi had accepted theirs, they perish by the fire, and all their sons, fierce and terrible men, perish too. Yet the burning of Bergthórshvoll, as Flosi only too well knew, was "a great and ill deed" which could solve nothing. The balances sway anew, and now it is Kári, Njáll's son-in-law, whose infant son had also died in the fire, who inherits the sacred and inalienable duty of a bloody revenge. For years Kári hunted down the burners, in Iceland and abroad. All other men took atonement in time, but he took none. Atonement came in the end when his ship was cast away on the coast near Svínafell. He reached Flosi's home in the storm, a helpless man, seeking safety, and as he came inside the house his foe knew him and sprang up to meet him, and kissed him, and set him down in the high seat by his side. And we know that all the vast orchestration of the saga has been leading to this last clear note of reconciliation. Suddenly there is no more to be said. "And there I end Burnt-Njáll's saga."

Njála is a book big and rich enough to be most things to most men. It exists magnificently at the level of an adventure story (which is where most of us first meet it); while for riper minds it provides a noble descant on the theme of our human mystery. It has always been held a document of high importance for students of the Saga Age in Iceland, of the Heroic Age of Germania, or of epical, heroic and tragic literature in general, but its final excellence is in itself and for itself, neither borrowed from comparisons nor based on scholastic utility. It is a book big enough to offer assurance and achieve inevitability. Gunnar will be killed, Njáll will be burned, Flosi and Kári will be reconciled. These events, we know, are not to be evaded; but they must not be hurried on, or anticipated either. For *Njála*'s massive certainty thrives on a shimmering interplay of yea and nay, of hopes raised and poised and raised again, then dashed. How easily the slaying of Höskuld could have been compounded. At how many points the tragic action seems to be arrested and might be diverted. "If only," we say, "if only—." For this is life itself moving before us, the moment hardly to be determined when the casual hardens into the inescapable. Yet for the author, his

plan is so sure that he need neither loiter nor hasten over its unfolding.

Events must be seen in true perspective, people in their right context. Before we meet Gunnar, for example, we must appreciate the deep fatality that lies in Hallgerd, his wife-to-be. Only then can we see his predicament as his friends and neighbours saw it. There is an elaborate pattern of action and thought which displays the wisdom and unselfishness of Njáll and the dignity of his wife Bergthóra, and this we must study in full before we feel the horror and pity of their destruction. And if Flosi is to command our respect and win our affection, we must understand how a good man may be left not with a choice between right and wrong, but with a sick decision as to what is bad and what still worse. And in the author's grand design all these things are related to the social, legal, political and religious issues of their day.

It was said earlier in this article that *Njála* was written about the year 1280, at a time when the saga-writers had evolved by long practice what has often been regarded as the perfect *oral* style of story-telling. It has been preserved in very early manuscripts indeed, so that we feel ourselves close to the missing archetype. It is now just twenty-one years ago since Professor Einar Ol. Sveinsson published

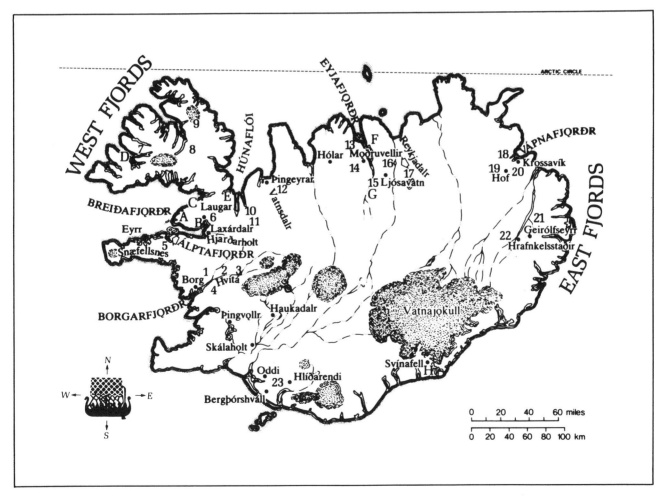

A map of Iceland showing the locations of various sagas. The site of Njáls saga *is indicated by the number twenty-three.*

325

his first study of the saga and argued against the theory then prevalent of a saga built by accretion on the foundations of two lost and independent sagas about Gunnar and Njáll, and with a long textual history behind it. Instead, he saw *Njála* as a saga written once and for all by a single author, and this view, with all that it implies for our notion of the origin and development of saga literature, has now gained almost universal credence. In 1943 appeared his *Á Njálsbúð* a substantial work of criticism of *Njála* as a work of art. In 1952 and 1953 respectively were published the Icelandic and English versions of his study of the *Njála* manuscripts. And now we have the edition itself, with a comprehensive apparatus, produced in the noble style of the Íslenzk Fornrit series from Reykjavík. If any saga from the classical period at once challenged and deserved the erudition, the taste, and the devotion which the Professor of Icelandic Literature in the University of Iceland has lavished upon his task, it was surely that which has now received them, *Brennu-Njáls Saga,* of all sagas greatest, of all sagas best.

Carl F. Bayerschmidt and Lee M. Hollander   (essay date 1955)

SOURCE: Introduction to *Njál's Saga*, translated by Carl F. Bayerschmidt and Lee M. Hollander, American-Scandinavian Foundation, 1955, pp. 1-15.

[*Bayerschmidt and Hollander are American scholars and translators of Norse literature. Below, the critics discuss Njáls saga's historical context and authorship, noting in particular the author's realistic characterizations. They assert that "nowhere else in medieval literature, with the possible exception of Chaucer, can be found a comparable wealth of real persons, not just types, such as we possess in this and similar sagas."*]

"Never, surely, has the art of story telling, in subsequent centuries, reached the perfection attained by the Icelanders before the invention of printing. Leaving aside the long genealogical lists, so important to the early Icelanders, but rather tedious to a modern reader, I have never found anything to compare with them. And what finer example of this art without art than the *Story of Burnt Njal*? I read it for the first time in the midst of the scenes where the events took place. All the Icelandic sagas, and this one in particular, spoil one for the reading of contemporary tales. The people 'come alive' of themselves by what they say and do; one is completely unconscious of any narrator. And in the *Njáls saga*, when the reader comes to Chapters 127 and 128, which tell of the burning of Njál, his wife, and his sons, at Bergthórsknoll, by Flosi and his band of one hundred and twenty men, he will recognize, I think, that perfection in the art of story telling was reached . . . centuries before there was any talk, in the western world, at least, of its being an art."

Thus writes James Norman Hall in his autobiography, *My Island Home*. Though connoisseurs may take exception to some of the distinguished novelist's statements and may insist that several other sagas excel the *Njáls saga* as works of art, it remains true that *Njála* (as the Icelanders fondly call it) has been by all odds the most famous Icelandic saga and the best loved in ancient as well as in modern times. No other saga offers so many stirring scenes, such a gallery of memorable personages subtly yet dramatically portrayed. And though there are dull pages there are many that no one can read unmoved.

Of the size of a modern novel, it is nevertheless far less perspicuous than a novel of similar length by reason of the great variety of its contents and—this must be admitted—the excessive number of characters. Also, the connection of events is not as plain as we are accustomed to have it made for us. . . .

It stands to reason that no summary can give a just idea of the merits of a literary monument. In the case of the medieval novels we call sagas, perhaps more than in any other branch of literature, a proper evaluation is possible only if the audience for which it was intended is kept in mind—and there is substantial agreement that literature, of whatever kind, presupposes a public. The sagas, then, written by cloister-taught men at the writing desk, certainly were intended for being read aloud to the assembled inmates of lonely farms during the long winter evenings, as is still the case in Iceland. There were no towns, villages, or hamlets with their diversions. This serves to explain the uniformly "unbookish," artless style, the general decency of tone, even the contents, of the typical "family saga." The common interests of such gatherings also account for the attention given in them to the affairs of the chieftains, their ancestry and feuds (we all like to hear of the doings of "our betters"), and also explain why we are told only incidentally of the occupations and hardships of everyday life familiar to all and so not worth telling. The wonder is that in a country so purely agrarian and so remote from the centers of civilization standards were so high. For there was no leisure class with aristocratic tastes and habits, as was the case in central and southern Europe, and to a lesser degree in Scandinavia, during the Middle Ages. Naturally, there were leaders, notably the *godis*, whose half-clerical, half-worldly authority generally was inherited. But nobody was above manual labor; for instance we read in our saga that the newly made *godi* Hoskuld Thráinsson had got up at daybreak of a fine morning before anyone in the household to sow the grain on his infield, when the sons of Njál came upon him.

Furthermore, though there were in those days not nearly as many lines of interest as in modern times, nevertheless there obtained a certain mobility and more of an intellectual life of sorts, even in the lower strata of society, than in the caste- and priest-ridden Europe of the early Middle Ages. We hear of excellent husbandmen successful in cattle and sheep raising which, in addition to fishing, at all times has been the mainstay of the economic life of the island. Some were skillful builders, carpenters, smiths. Others were bored by the settled life in the country and became seafaring merchants trading with all the shorelands of the western world. The "younger sons" of the landed proprietors normally went abroad, visiting relatives in Norway and the Western Isles from which their forbears had come, or else attached themselves to the courts of princes, serving them in peace and war as skalds, councilors, ambassadors. Then, granted a return to their native land, they contributed, by the recital at firesides and assemblies of their varied experiences, to the broadening of their less fortunate countrymen. Frequent gatherings at marriages and *arvels,* the local and quarterly assemblies, and the yearly Althing helped to break the monotony of hard lives. At these the sports of wrestling, horsefighting, and ball games were indulged in, and minds were exercised in the study and practice of the law, in all its fine points, and by the widespread cultivation of the arts of skaldic composition and narration. Thus, spared the senseless turmoil of constant feudal wars, notwithstanding its isolation the population of the island was kept free from stagnating intellectually, at least till the late Middle Ages.

Probably the most popular of all entertainments, whether in the Orient or the Occident, has been the art of storytelling. In the case of Scandinavia we know that the preservation and recital of local history was cultivated from the oldest times, particularly in western and southern Norway, from which the bulk of the population of Iceland is derived. With the introduction of Christianity there (*ca.* 1000 A.D.) more and more of this material found its way to parchment, once the clerics had set the example with their chronicles and works of edification. The earliest preserved Icelandic manuscript, scraps of sermons, dates from *ca.* 1150, but no doubt writing was practiced as soon as the Church was organized in the first century. But how did the saga literature as we know it come into being?

There has been scholarly controversy about the number of intermediate stages to be presupposed. The Free Prose theory posits that current oral tradition was transferred directly to parchment without significant modifications; the Book Prose theory, that men skillful in composition deliberately set themselves the task of shaping and welding together the material of tradition, amplifying or shortening to suit the needs of the case or their own taste. Against the latter view it has been urged that the undeniable sameness of style, of treatment, and even of subject matter, pervading all saga literature certainly bespeaks nearness to oral tradition. The upholders of the Book Prose theory reply that all these features, once the characteristics of saga narration had been evolved and fixed, no more belonged to the individual "authors" of the sagas than, say, did the typical turns of the ballad or the tags of the medieval folk epic; that authorship in our sense, with its conscious striving for self-expression and originality in theme and language, is not to be expected in saga literature.

However that may be, in the case of the *Njáls saga*, at least, there can be no doubt that its author had on his desk the manuscripts of a number of earlier sagas and helped himself liberally from them. This is shown by the presence of unmistakable verbal similarities and of whole passages demonstrably more organic in them. Thus the episode of Thangbrand's mission, much we are told about the Battle of Clontarf, and some passages dealing with juridical procedure are, as differences in style indicate, lifted bodily from written sources now lost. Indications also point to that being the case with much of the genealogical material. On the other hand, there is a notable absence of local tradition that might have been handed down orally, which

is surprising when we realize that some of these local events must have lived on in the memory of men: witness a number of skaldic verses composed in the middle of the thirteenth century which presuppose a knowledge of these happenings.

There has been controversy also on the unity of our saga in particular. From the olden times on down to the middle of the last century it was accepted in good faith as one of the "classical" sagas and enjoyed for what it was worth. Then, under the influence of the critical views concerning authorship and unity, notably of the Homeric poems and the *Nibelungenlied,* doubts began to be entertained. The great Icelandic scholar Gudbrandur Vígfússon proved conclusively that, far from being one of the old sagas, *Njála* on the contrary is the latest of the great family sagas and must have been written toward the end of the thirteenth century. He also propounded the theory that as we have it the saga is inferior and a composite, essentially, of two original, independent sagas, a *Gunnars saga* and a *Njáls saga,* pieced together in a perfunctory fashion by some compiler who also provided a few introductory chapters and a conclusion.

This view, notwithstanding isolated protests, prevailed with some modifications until the 1920's, when investigation demonstrated that after all the saga is the work of one author, both in conception and style; and that it actually does hang together very well, though the causal connection frequently is obscured by the inclusion of more or less irrelevant matter—matter which evidently interested the author or which he thought would interest his audience. The latter includes the rather adolescent accounts of the adventures of Hrút, Gunnar, and the sons of Njál in foreign parts, accounts clearly borrowed from the *Fornaldarsogur* type of stories then in vogue in which the supernatural and martial elements predominate; and the excessive space given to the law and to genealogy, much to the detriment of our enjoyment of the saga as a work of art. Still, one must bear in mind that our more stringent conception of the unity of action and of perspective was foreign to the Middle Ages.

Few will relish the details and long-winded recapitulations of the many lawsuits, caviar though they may be to the legally minded. Nevertheless, account must be taken of the fact that the details in the last action which fill the inordinately long Chapter 142 and following chapters, were of exceeding importance, involving practically all the leading families of the republic. One may also claim some artistic purpose served through the growing dramatic tension built up by the duel of wits and fine points of the law between Flosi's legal adviser Eyjólf on the one hand and Thórhall, the disciple of Njál, on the other. Being spared none of the legal details we feel as though we were bodily present at the trial as the prosecutor drones on with his legal formulas, as witnesses are summoned, and juries are challenged, until the legal bag is emptied of all its tricks and the ultima ratio of the sword is invoked.

Similarly the genealogies, excessive even for an Icelandic saga, with their pursuit of ancestry both on the sword and the spindle side into dim antiquity, are a bore just like those of the Bible. But for societies at a certain stage of development they are poetry, each name calling to mind the glorious deeds of a forbear and giving legitimacy and standing to the descendant. Thus our author is concerned to have us know that the personages in his story are people of note and not just anybody.

Scanning the saga for other clues to the author's personality we are struck by the unusually large role he assigns to the supernatural, from dreams and visions of the second-sighted to the Christian miracle in its crassest medieval form. He does not seem to boggle at any of it, whether clearly heathen or Christian; which, to be sure, parallels the attitude of the Icelandic Church which for a long time was remarkably tolerant of heathen practices and beliefs. The opinion may be hazarded that to our ethical sense some of the saga "miracles" are by far more offensive than heathen magic. Thus, to mention only two cases, we are shocked to hear Ámundi praise the Lord for restoring his eyesight in order to let him see to kill the man who refused to pay him wergild. Nor do we see why, of all persons, the sardonic and aggressive Skarphedin should have the sign of the cross burned on his shoulders and back. And the medieval Church might approve, but we do not, Flosi's and Kári's pilgrimage to Rome to obtain absolution for valorous deeds the author well knew were demanded of them by their pre-Christian code of morality.

There is one aspect of the supernatural, common to be sure to all saga literature, which calls for a remark. Nearly all important events are foreshadowed in some way by dreams, portents, even mere surmises of the foreknowing. Whereas the practice of modern story-telling (most overtly in the detective novel) calls for suspense and not disclosing the real connection till the final denouement, the saga "gives it all away" from the first; nor does this cause our interest to flag in the least. On the contrary, our curiosity is if anything whetted more keenly to see if what is foretold really will come to pass, and how. To give one example from our saga: In the very first chapter the wise Hrút, on being asked by his brother how he likes his niece Hallgerd, first hesitates, then answers, "Beautiful this maiden certainly is, and many are likely to suffer for it; but I don't know whence thief's eyes have come into our kin," thus prognosticating the violent deaths of her three husbands and the brazen large-scale theft coming many years—and many pages—later. That is, the epic device of prognosis, used similarly in scores of places, very effectively holds the story together.

In apparent contrast to this predilection for the supernatural, and side by side with it, is the cool realism of the saga and its restrained and impartial treatment of the characters. The narrator takes no sides, lets their deeds speak for themselves. Avarice, vengefulness, jealousy, deceitfulness, are found not only in the rogues, nor are their counterparts confined only to the just. The erotic element, where it does appear, is treated with the hard hands of the farmer. No sentimentality is wasted on it. Take what we moderns would call the case of love at first sight between Gunnar and Hallgerd. Twice a widow, the experienced Hallgerd boldly accosts Gunnar at the Althing. She is attracted by his stately appearance and the fame of his warlike exploits abroad (much, we would love to think, like

Desdemona by Othello's) and Gunnar is not unresponsive to her charms. "They talked together aloud," whereupon Gunnar abruptly proposes marriage. Without indicating her feelings she refers him to her relatives, and the match is made. There is not a hint of love-making, of the shy awakening of affection. We conclude that the author is uninfluenced, at least in this respect, by the rising tide of chivalric Romanticism from the south which soon was to spell the end of saga writing. But that does not mean he is obtuse to the tender bonds of feeling between husband and wife, as witness the simple touching words of Bergthóra declining to leave her husband in their burning home: "As a young woman I was married to Njál and vowed that one fate should befall us both."

Neither this evident lack of interest in the erotic, on the one hand, nor his love for a good fight on the other, allows us to infer that the author was, or was not, a cleric; though the thought lies near that he must have been connected with the former cloister of Thykkvibær at the mouth of the Skaptá River in southern Iceland. He certainly displays an intimate acquaintance with that region of formidable, glacier-fed rivers, their sandy and swampy flood plains, and the mountains, particularly of what is now called the West Skaptafells district, whereas his information about the western and eastern quarters of the island is more sketchy and often inaccurate. The vagueness of his references to the shorelands of Britain, central Europe, and especially those of Norway, render it unlikely that he ever was abroad.

In general he is an indifferent observer of things as compared with his intense preoccupation with human nature and its manifestations. In this field his skill in portraying living men and women has given us an unexampled wealth of striking characters and unforgettable, unhackneyed scenes. It is that, more than the recital of the bold deeds of heroes like Hrút, Gunnar, Skarphedin, and Kári, which accounts for the popularity of this saga with mature readers.

That Njál seemed to the author the central character is evident from the last words of the saga: "And here we conclude the saga of the Burning of Njál." Naturally, this outrage left a deep impression and no doubt, together with the great lawsuit arising out of it, formed the core of the otherwise rather scanty traditions of the Southern Quarter. Njál's character is not as easy to grasp as we would deem at first sight. Though he is fundamentally a man of peace, we discern in his counsels that after all he has first and foremost the welfare of his own kin at heart. And tragically it is this very concern that leads to their complete annihilation, for all he does to forestall it. The words of the Eddic *Hóvamól* come to mind:

> Middling wise   every man should be;
>   beware of being too wise!
> His fate let no one   beforehand know
>   who would keep his heart from care.

Inseparable from Njál, also, is his younger friend, Gunnar of Hlídarendi, the shining and ideal hero without a blemish—so much so, in fact, as to be somewhat colorless—a man who dislikes the shedding of blood but is a match for many when aroused. It is just such a nature as his, open-hearted and guileless, that needs the friendship and counsel of the prescient Njál.

If Gunnar is of a good-natured disposition, wishing to be a friend of all, Skarphedin cares not a whit how many enemies he makes by his taunts. His dark looks and grim aspect inspire fear in others. One is reminded of the demonic Hagen of the *Nibelungenlied* who forges on with his company to certain destruction in the land of the Huns even after, and just because of, the dire prophecy of the water sprites that not one of his host will escape the carnage there. Like him, Skarphedin, fatalistic and scornful of death, though convinced in his soul that destruction is inevitable, yields to the counsel of his aged father to await the enemy within doors rather than fight outside.

His antagonist Flosi is a born leader: moderate, circumspect, resourceful in planning, and resolute in carrying out what he resolves on though it may be repugnant to him. His inner struggle is revealed in his encounter with Hildigunn, and also when he fatally misinterprets Njál's gift of a silken gown as a spiteful hint of lack of manhood in being amenable to a compromise rather than fight it out.

Few distinct features except irreconcilableness are discernible in the character of the avenger, the heroic Kári. Even more than Gunnar he is idealized to the point of colorlessness. He comes alive as a person only where, in a deliberate attempt to relieve the absolutely single-minded pursuit of vengeance, the author associates him, in a Don Quijote-Sancho Panza-like alliance with the rabbit-hearted braggart Bjorn, him of the keen vision and the swift feet who in a fight shields himself behind Kári.

Of the less admirable characters, we cannot fail to remember the insanely jealous Thjóstólf, the cantankerous, bickering liar Skamkel, the contriving, smooth Mord who sows fatal discord between bosom friends out of sheer deviltry, or the insolent scoundrel Hrapp.

Women play a small but decisive role in the saga. There is the weak, shallow-minded Unn; the libidinous and masterful Queen Gunnhild; the matronly but vengeful and disdainful Bergthóra; the demanding Hildigunn, whose passionate grief over the loss of her husband unsettles a man like Flosi; and especially the enigmatic and highly complex Hallgerd, whose long golden hair is the first thing mentioned about her and whose refusal of it to Gunnar nearly the last, the woman who after having been the wife of heroes like Glúm and Gunnar lands in the arms of Hrapp. She is not so much evil as unstable or "mixed," as the saga has it. Pleasure-loving and selfish, she cannot stand any lack of provisions and sends her first husband to his death for them and in her third marriage has her slave steal them from a neighbor. It would be a complete misunderstanding, both of her character and the situation, to regard that act as one of revenge on Otkel and Skamkel who have turned down ignominiously Gunnar's request to buy provisions from them.

Undeniably, the scene is overcrowded with a multitude of characters. Many do not stay long enough on it for us to get acquainted with them. But there is rich, pulsing life in the altercations, the plottings, the parleyings, the Althing deliberations, for which these multitudes form the foil.

Nowhere else in medieval literature, with the possible exception of Chaucer, can be found a comparable wealth of real persons, not just types, such as we possess in this and similar sagas. Indeed, we would have to go back to Greek tragedy and forward to the drama of the sixteenth and seventeenth centuries to equal it in Europe.

But perhaps the crowning glory of *Njála* is its style. The style of the sagas, or rather their manner (but they are inseparable), has been likened to a snow-covered volcano in whose depths glow the fires of fierce passion but whose surface is cold and calm. A deceptive bland simplicity bridges over deep chasms of hidden hatreds, raging jealousy. Only by some chance remark, perhaps, do we glimpse what is beneath. Tight-lipped understatement, by all means, rather than overstatement, is the rule. Never a full-mouthed explosion of pent-up emotions familiar to us from the baroque drama.

Essentially, this manner is dramatic. Few chapters in our saga but are enlivened, or actually carried, by dialogue; hardly an episode but contains a climax or else the resolution of unbearable tension, all in that curiously nervous yet subdued fashion, spiced with apposite saws and proverbs, which is one of the secrets of saga style. Nor is this manner as "artless" as one approaching it for the first time might suppose. Rather, it is the culmination of a century, or centuries, of growth. In the older sagas (those from the beginning of the thirteenth century) there is utter simplicity verging on bareness. Increasing practice in the narrative art, together with the influence of southern chivalry and the Church, gradually soften this abruptness and laconicalness adding a measure of color and warmth. Yet the "classic" style of the best sagas never exhibits the verbosity and preciosity of the later clerico-romantic style. In many famous passages of *Njála* perhaps the optimum is reached. This style, universally admired, never successfully imitated, is the despair of translators, though it may flatter us to think that the more natural idiom of today may afford better possibilities of suggesting the original than did the artificial and ponderous vehicles of earlier periods, especially since we now know the distinction between the unlabored prose and the heavily archaic manner of the verse.

It remains to speak of the verse material. Let us admit that the greater number of the skaldic stanzas are not of a particularly high quality. Neither are they, barring the snatches attributed to Thórhild, Thráin, and Snorri, genuinely contemporary with the personages purported to have spoken them. More substantial and forceful by far are the unquestionably genuine verses found in the episode dealing with Thangbrand's mission. The "Song of the Valkyries" (probably from the beginning of the 11th century) belongs to an entirely different category and, indeed, is one of the most striking lays of Norse antiquity, one remembered in the Orkneys till within recent time. It is a gloomy prophecy of the outcome of the great Battle of Clontarf, fought between the forces of old King Brján of Munster and King Sigtrygg of Dublin and his viking allies: "Few lays in Old Norse literature compare with the 'Song of the Valkyries' in somber power and dark magnificence. Thoroughly in harmony with the great carnage presaged is the gruesome picture of the loom; and terribly splendid, the vision of the red dawn with its cloud rack, incarnadined by the blood of warriors, into which the battle maidens issue forth, riding on wild horses to join the fray" [L. M. Hollander, *Old Norse Poems,* 1936].

W. H. Auden (essay date 1956)

SOURCE: "Concrete and Fastidious," *The New Statesman & Nation*, Vol. LII, No. 1338, November 3, 1956, pp. 551-52.

[*Often considered the poetic successor of W. B. Yeats and T. S. Eliot, Auden is also highly regarded for his literary criticism. As a committed follower of Christianity, he considered it necessary to view art in the context of moral and theological absolutes. Thus, he regarded art as a "secondary world" which should serve a definite purpose within the "primary world" of human history. Here, Auden lauds Icelandic literature, particularly* Njáls saga, *for its prose form and realistic portrayal of early Icelandic society.*]

Disinfected of all polemical associations, "social realism" could be a useful descriptive term for a certain kind of literature. To call a writer a social realist would mean that, whether writing real or feigned history, he deliberately confined his portrayal of human nature to those aspects which individuals reveal to each other through their deeds, their words and their looks. There is, of course, a great deal more to human nature than this. There is much which a man is unwilling or unable to reveal about himself to others, though others, through their own subjective experiences, can imagine some of it, but all this the social realist deliberately excludes.

He also, so far as it is possible, deliberately excludes himself from his narrative. He may possess, or believe that he does, a truer grasp of the real significance of their actions than his characters themselves, he may see them, for instance, as the unwitting agents of Divine Providence or the forces of History but, if so, he keeps his opinions to himself. In his narrative, cause, motive, effect, are what his characters think they are. Similarly, his own moral values may be very different from those of the society he is describing, but the only overt moral judgments he will express are those which his characters pass on each other.

This combination of impersonal narration plus the exclusion of all subjective elements of dream and fancy gives all social realist works certain literary qualities in common. In all of them, the variation in character lies within the human range and is consistent with the society to which the character belongs: the best are not demi-gods, the worst are not devils. Secondly, individuals will be presented in their social context which influences their character but never wholly commands it: kings are always distinguishable from peasants, but all kings are not seriousminded, nor all peasants comic clowns. Lastly, their speech, from its most elevated to its lowest, lies within the range of credible conversation. It follows from this that, though it is possible to write social realist works in verse, provided that the poet uses a mixed or middle style, prose is the natural and proper medium, and a prose, moreover, which is as free as possible from all rhetorical schematisation and metaphorical elaboration. Social realism is not, of course, the only or necessarily the best kind of literature. It seems, however, to be the latest kind to evolve and in some ways, perhaps, it is the most grown-up.

The Icelandic Sagas are one of the most extraordinary phenomena in cultural history, not because they are so good but because of the kind of goodness which they exhibit. Had the Icelanders of the Middle Ages gone on writing verse epics like *The Battle of Maldon* or turned to ballads, we might admire them as much but we should not be so astonished. What they actually did, however, was to produce a socially realist literature centuries before any other part of Europe even attempted such a thing, and of a quality which, within its limited scale, has never been surpassed.

So long as one does not claim that, given their circumstances, the Icelanders were bound to write as they did, there is some point in considering the ways in which, compared with their contemporaries in the rest of Europe, their life was peculiar. The majority of the settlers were of aristocratic origin who had left Scandinavia because they wished neither to be ruled nor to rule but to be independent. They had inherited the warrior *ethos* of their class, but their profession was no longer fighting or conquering subject peoples. They might from time to time go on pirate raids but such expeditions were interludes in their daily life of farming and fishing. Some might own larger and better farms than others, but there were no great feudal landowners with their private armies. We hear of the existence of slaves but not of a leisure class which considers work beneath its dignity. Living on a small, not very fertile, island, far from the main centres of political, religious and intellectual activity, their interests were bound to be parochial. Everyone, to some degree, knew everyone else, and world events aroused less interest than the doings of the neighbours.

Granted the wish to write in a socially realistic way, it is clearly easier for a writer to succeed in such a society than in a larger and less homogeneous one, for the social realist is necessarily confined to a kind of life of which he has first-hand intimate knowledge. If he attempts to deal with people and societies which he does not really know, he will either conventionalise or produce a lifeless and ponderous documentation. Throughout the Sagas one is conscious of first-hand experience. In the literature of societies with a slave-servant class, members of the lower orders generally appear either as faithful retainers who only exist in and for their masters, or as comic rogues, or, as in the Courtly Romances, they are ignored. But the slave Melkof in *Njál's Saga* is as real an individual as his mistress Hallgerd.

> When Gunnar had gone Hallgerd came to speak with the slave Melkof. [We have previously been told that he was "Irish and a man very much disliked."]
>
> "I have thought of an errand for you," she said. "I want you to ride to Kirkby."
>
> "What am I to do there?" he asked.
>
> "You are to steal enough food to load two horses, and be sure to take butter and cheese and then set fire to the storehouse. They will all believe it happened through carelessness and no one will be thinking of a theft."
>
> The slave said: "I have done bad things, but never was I a thief."
>
> "You don't say!" answered Hallgerd. "You act as though you were an honourable man and yet you have been both a thief and a murderer. And don't you dare refuse or I shall have you killed."
>
> He believed he knew her well enough to know that she would do so: so he took two horses, placed packsaddles on them, and rode to Kirkby.

An even more remarkable example of emancipation from literary convention is the portrait of Bjorn the White. He is introduced as a henpecked husband and a braggart of the Parolles type and the reader naturally expects a comic dénouement in which his cowardice is exposed. But something quite different happens.

> Kári then went and took his stand under a projecting crag and Bjorn asked: "Where shall I stand now?"
>
> Kári answered: "You can choose one of two things: either stand behind me and use your shield to protect yourself, if necessary, or else mount your horse and ride away as fast as you can."
>
> "That I don't want to do," said Bjorn, "and for a number of reasons. In the first place, if I ride away, malicious tongues might say that I left you in the lurch out of cowardice, and, in the second place, I know what a catch they think they have in me, so two or three would pursue me. No! I prefer to stand by you and defend myself with you."

And he does. Nobody without first-hand experience would have dared, when describing events in a culture to which physical courage was the supreme virtue, to present a character who is neither absolutely brave nor absolutely a coward but brave—and cowardly—to a certain degree.

First-hand knowledge of a small homogeneous society is not enough by itself to produce social realism; if it were, it would be one of the most primitive *genres*. It also requires a humanist attitude of mind which has rid itself of superstition, that is to say, of the notion that God intervenes directly in events so that their only significance and importance lies in their providential meaning. It is the development of this mentality, centuries before the rest of Europe, that remains so inexplicable about the Icelanders. Thus, in *Njál's Saga*, which was almost certainly put into its present shape by a cleric, there is an account of the conversion of Iceland to Christianity. One would expect to find, and anywhere else in the same age one would find, an account in black and white. All the Christians would be heroes, all pagans villains. In the struggle between them all the miracles would be on the Christian side and victory for the Faith would be a foregone conclusion. But we are given nothing of this sort. Thangbrand, the missionary sent by King Olaf, may, it is true, carry a crucifix instead of a shield when he defeats his pagan challenger, but his victory does not seem particularly miraculous because we have already been shown that he is a great warrior. Nor does such magical assistance as he gets make him a superman: he is nearly destroyed by the counter-magic of a heathen sorcerer and withdraws before he has completed his job.

> Thangbrand discussed with Gest the advisability of travelling to the firths further west, but Gest advised against it, saying that there lived men who were very hard and difficult to deal with—"But if it is ordained that this faith is to gain strength, then it is likely to be accepted at the Althing. . . . You are the one who has done most to promote it, even though it may be granted to others to introduce it into the laws.

Not long after the Althing meets.

> Both sides went to the Law-Mount, and Christians as well as heathens named witnesses and declared their former community of laws dissolved. . . . The Christians chose as their lawspeaker Hall of Sida, but he went to Thorgeir, the *godi* of Ljosovatn, and gave him three marks of silver in order that he proclaim what the law should be. This, however, was a very risky step, because Thorgeir was still a heathen.
>
> That entire day Thorgier lay with a cloak spread over his head so that no one might speak to him. The following day all assembled before the Law-Mount.
>
> Then Thorgeir asked to be heard and spoke:"It seems to me that our affairs have come to a dangerous pass if we do not all have one and the same law. If the laws are torn asunder, then security can no longer prevail, and we cannot afford to incur that danger. Now, therefor, I shall ask both heathens and Christians whether they

will abide by the laws I shall proclaim." All agreed to that.

> "This is the foundation of our laws," he said, "that all men in this land are to be Christians and that they are no longer to worship idols, nor expose children, nor eat horse-meat. If any man is found guilty of these practices, he shall be condemned to outlawry, but if he carries them on in secret, there shall be no punishment involved."

Though the Christian party includes some bad-hats like Mord Valgardsson and killers like Skarphedin Njalsson, it is supported by most of the wisest and most level-headed members of the community like Njál himself, Hall of Sida and Flosi, and the unbiased reader can see good secular reasons why they should.

The pagan culture of Iceland had been a shame culture in which it was a matter of personal honour and duty to avenge injuries and insults to oneself or to one's kin. The attempt to replace the private blood-feud by public law and arbitration had been only partially successful because there was in Iceland no single authority powerful enough to enforce the acceptance of a legal decision by anyone who, out of pride or passion, chose to reject it.

I have met people who dislike the Sagas and, though I do not share their dislike, I can understand why. I know of no other literature in which the characters seem, by our standards, so sane and their actions so lunatic. The code by which they live puts the society at the mercy of its most violent members and the havoc wrought by the malicious and the hot-headed is out of all proportion to their numbers. One row between two housewives—one of the curious things about Icelandic society seems to have been the complete inability of the husbands to keep their wives in order—can result in a whole chain of murders. With what a surprise and relief one reads of someone, like Snorri, ignoring an insult.

Under the circumstances a religion like Christianity which replaced shame by guilt and valued love of one's neighbour above courage would, apart from any theological or spiritual considerations, make an appeal to common sense.

Any work of art is the joint product of a sensibility and a medium of expression, and one reason, at least, why social realism did not appear outside of Iceland until much later was the lack, elsewhere, of an adequate prose instrument. The Saga writers were fortunate in two respects. Poetry in Scandinavia had become a highly specialised esoteric art of immense technical virtuosity, highly allusive and rhetorical, and, consequently, very limited in its subject-matter. A northern writer who wished to tell an intelligible story was bound to tell it in prose because it would have been impossible to tell it in skaldic verse. Secondly, thanks to the geographical remoteness of Scandinavia, classical Latin and the whole rhetorical tradition that went with it had had little influence upon the northern languages. The speeches of the lawyers at the Althing would have seemed childishly naive to Cicero; on the other hand, a piece of concrete narrative like the story of Gunnar's death could not have been written in Ciceronian Latin.

In the rest of Europe verse had remained a much looser medium, the formal demands of which were not severe enough to prevent its narrative use, but sufficient to prevent a thorough-going realism. At the same time, particularly in those countries which had been part of the Roman Empire, the Roman notion of what prose should be like persisted despite the changes that had taken place in the Latin tongue. Gregory of Tours, for example, seems to have been after the same kind of historical story-telling as the Icelandic historians but the Latin at his disposal was always getting in his way.

The prose of the Sagas, especially the dialogue, is not easy to translate. It is not a high style like that of epic; on the other hand, it is not an unbuttoned go-as-you-please style but the language of an aristocratic society with a great respect for forms and its own dignity. In their new translation of *Njál's Saga*, Messrs. Bayerschmidt and Hollander have been able to profit from modern textual scholarship and a reading public which can tolerate an unbowdlerised version. I am inclined to feel, however, that Dasent's translation, despite some archaisms, may be closer in spirit to the original. In their laudable wish not to be quaint, the present translators sometimes fall into colloquialisms which are equally anachronistic because their associations are irrevocably modern and local, phrases, for example, like "You're a brick" or "That's mighty good of you." (Once, very oddly, they allow themselves the impossible archaism "caitiff wretch.") More seriously, they write what may be called standard American English. An American, when he is not being consciously hard-boiled and slangy, writes sentences which are slower in rhythm and more latinate in diction than an Englishman. Thus the translators write "Father has retired" where an Englishman would have written "Father has gone to bed"; where Dasent has "Such words of comfort had he for them all, and others still more strong," they have "With such exhortations and with other words even more indomitable he encouraged them."

Needless to say, I am not trying to suggest that American English is in any way inferior to British English as a language: I do believe, however, that in attempting to reproduce the terseness of Icelandic, a British translator has a certain innate advantage. But this may be prejudice and, in any case, it is as easy to criticise a translation, however good, as it is hard to make one, however bad.

I wish the translators had supplied genealogical maps and trees. I do not agree with their opinion, given in the introduction, that genealogies are boring, but for a modern reader they are easier to follow in a visual form, and, boring or not, it is impossible to follow a tale of blood-feuds without a clear knowledge of the kin relationships. The canvas in *Njál's Saga* is unusually large and I would advise anyone reading it for the first time to construct his own genealogical diagrams as he goes along.

Magnus Magnusson (essay date 1960)

SOURCE: Introduction to *Njal's Saga*, translated by Magnus Magnusson and Hermann Pálsson, Penguin Books, 1960, pp. 9-31.

[*An Icelandic historian and scholar, Magnusson has written several books about Norse literature, including* Iceland Saga *(1987). In the following excerpt, he views* Njáls saga *from historical, social, and political perspectives. Magnusson also addresses the saga's major sources, its treatment of paganism and Christianity, its characters, and its overall aesthetic value.*]

Njal's Saga is the mightiest of all the classical Icelandic sagas. It was written in Iceland by an unknown author in the last quarter of the thirteenth century—somewhere around the year 1280, as nearly as can be deduced; and, from the outset, it has always been regarded as the greatest of the vast, uneven, and (to the English-speaking world, alas) largely unfamiliar prose literature of Iceland in the Middle Ages. Its early popularity can be seen from the fact that more vellum manuscripts of *Njal's Saga* have survived than of any other saga (twenty-four, some of them very fragmentary). Succeeding generations of Icelanders have endorsed this immediate affection, and the reputation of the saga has emerged enhanced from 150 years of rigorous scholarly examination.

Njal's Saga is an epic prose narrative about people— people who lived in Iceland, intensely and often violently, some 300 years before this saga was written. It would be as misleading to call it a history as to call it an historical novel. The saga is broadly based on authenticated historical event, its material is drawn from oral traditions and occasional written records, but it is given life and force and significant artistic shape by the creative genius of its anonymous author. The original manuscript of the saga has not survived; the earliest extant MS. is from c. 1300, that is to say approximately twenty years later. . . .

Readers unfamiliar with Old Icelandic literature may find it helpful to be shown *Njal's Saga* in its historical perspective; for it was written at a crucial period of Iceland's early history, both literary and political, which had an important effect on its composition.

Iceland was discovered and settled by land-hungry Norsemen late in the ninth century A.D. —some 400 years before *Njal's Saga* was written. It was the last convulsive movement of peoples in the great Scandinavian migrations that had already sent Viking ships to Russia, to the British Isles, to France, even to North Africa. But Iceland, let it be said, was never a Viking nation, in the popular conception. This new nation, a composite of settlers from Scandinavia and the Norse colonies in Ireland and the Hebrides, numbering at most perhaps 60,000, quickly established a unique parliamentary commonwealth (in 930), which finally broke down only a few years before *Njal's Saga* was born. It is difficult to believe that the author was not affected by the events of his lifetime—the years of savage internal strife, murderous intrigues, and ruthless self-seeking power-politics that led, in 1262, to the loss of the independence that her pioneers had created. It had been an independence based on law and the rights of the individual—'With laws shall our land be built up but with lawlessness laid waste,' as Njal says in Chapter 70. In an age where his land had indeed been laid waste by lawlessness, the author could look back to an age which must have seemed truly heroic in comparison, when a man's

pride and honour were more dearly prized possessions than wealth or even life itself. There was strife enough between men, yes; but it was strife over human principles, not politics.

Alongside the progressive deterioration of civil order and integrity in Iceland there had been a compensatory development of literary awareness. Vernacular prose-writing in Iceland started in the early years of the twelfth century, functional and fragmentary at first, but growing steadily in output, in craftsmanship and stature and artistry. The written language was exercised strenuously and extensively on all the familiar subjects of medieval literature— saints' lives, historical chronicling, treatises, translations of foreign books on religion, philosophy, poetry, education, astronomy, travel. . . . But as well as this mass of 'applied' learned and literary activity, of what one might call 'official' literature, there was evolving a unique type of literary entertainment called saga. By the end of the twelfth century, sagas were being written about life in Iceland from the earliest stages of her history down to contemporary times, as well as biographies of the past and present kings of Norway. Saga-writing grew apace throughout the thirteenth century, with such great achievements as *Heimskringla, Egil's Saga, Laxdæla Saga,* and *Gisli's Saga* as well as a host of others; and at the apex (but not the end) of saga development came *Njal's Saga.* It was an age of writing with no disengagement between literature and life; Snorri Sturluson (1179-1241) was the leading political figure of his day as well as a great historian, poet, and saga-writer. The author of *Njal's Saga,* too, seems, on the internal evidence of the saga, to have been urgently aware of the larger events of his own day.

This awareness of his times is constantly reflected in the saga, superficially in the numerous echoes of contemporary persons and events, but more significantly in the capacity of his experience. And when he came to apply his own personal experience to the major tragic issues of the tenth century, the essential craftsman's tools were already to hand—a literary form sufficiently developed to contain this tragedy, and a literary language sufficiently sophisticated to express his own complexity, his irony, his vivid observation, his dark and brooding intelligence of fate. . . .

Modern readers may find the saga-technique, with its impersonal economy of style and consistent lack of explanation of motive, a little strange at first, before they are acclimatized to it. It certainly has difficulties for us that never existed for the contemporary audience, and a few comments about the more obvious saga characteristics may help the reader to overcome this initial awkwardness.

First of all, there are certain narrative conventions that the thirteenth-century audience was fully conditioned to expect and to appreciate. Newcomers to the saga are formally introduced ('There was a man called . . .') and given a brief character-sketch and genealogy. The character-sketch is both perfunctory and final; from then on, the reader is expected to draw his own conclusions about the personality as it becomes revealed in action, speech, or silence—never by interior analysis. The genealogies tend to be much longer. To us they may seem tedious and intrusive at times, but they were in fact much the more significant source of information, because the contemporary audience could not only recognize the family characteristics of a person and deduce character from the quality of pedigree, but could fit him or her into a known historical context, through familiarity with other sagas. . . . To take only one example: the drum-rolling genealogy of Mord Valgardsson (Chapter 25) is one of the best in the whole saga—the catalogue of picturesquely-named Viking heroes in his pedigree is impeccable; yet Mord is a rogue. The forceful family characteristics of heroic rivalry and tough self-reliance have degenerated into foxy cunning and plausibility; but at the same time Mord's ancestry helps to explain both his urge for revenge (to regain a dwindled authority) and his importance to the other characters in the saga.

From these genealogies, the reader is expected to untangle the intricate relationships by blood and marriage which dictated loyalties and actions. The author was able to take for granted a detailed knowledge of historical and social background, and did not require to stress the aspects which prove significant—such as, for instance, the crucial, prevading conceptions of honour, of luck, of fate, of nobility of character. Behaviour which may seem to us inexplicable, and which is given no explanation by the author, was often the peremptory response to these conventions.

'Honour' is a word that occurs with great frequency in the Icelandic sagas, but in none more so than in *Njal's Saga.* Any slight, real or imagined, to one's honour or to the honour of one's family had to be revenged, with either blood or money. It is a little pathetic, now, to read how vulnerable these men were to calls on their honour; it was fatally easy to goad them into action to avenge some suspicion of an insult. Without realizing this, it is impossible to feel the appalling pressure which Hildigunn put on her uncle Flosi with her elaborate, almost formal, taunts in Chapter 116; but it is essential to recognize it to be able to visualize Flosi's stiff-legged, suspicious, bristling approach to the abortive peace-meeting with Njal and his sons at the Althing (Chapter 123).

The legal system in Iceland was at best an uneasy substitute for revenge. Too often legal actions brought by a dead man's kinsmen against the killer were thwarted by the intricacy of court procedure, and then the only alternative to further violence was mutually-agreed arbitration. Even when a verdict of guilty was brought, it was still the duty of the plaintiff to execute the sentence; the state had no power to enforce outlawry.

'Luck' is another word which has wider connotations in *Njal's Saga* than is usual in our day. Good luck or ill luck was inherent in every individual, and ultra-sensitive men, like Njal or Hrut, could detect it in others, like an aura. Skarp-Hedin is 'ill-starred', but Kari is 'lucky'. Some men were doomed to bring ill luck to all they touched—Hrapp, for instance. One's luck was an inescapable part of the complex pattern of fate.

The concept of Fate plays an important part in *Njal's Saga.* The action is swept along by a powerful under-current of fate, and Njal's fierce struggle to alter its course heightens the conflict of personalities. Njal was prescient; he could see aspects of the future, blurred glimpses illuminated by sudden ambiguous shafts of knowledge. He was not a fatalist in the heathen sense—a man content to accept what fate had in store, but careful to meet it like a man. It is only when Christianity and its effects begin to filter into the saga that Njal achieves peace with his own fate.

In addition to fate, the saga has constant recourse to the supernatural. Some have complained that this in some way 'spoils' the bleak realism of the saga. But it is important to remember that in the thirteenth century and earlier, these manifestations of the supernatural were wholeheartedly believed in—ghosts, prophecies, dreams, hallucinations, fetches, portents. The audience believed in them, and the story-teller believed in them. In the second place, this supplied the author with an accepted and valuable literary device. By means of prophecy and visions, he could adumbrate future events without compromising his suspense effect or the conventional chronological presentation of the narrative. And later, by underlining the eventual truth of these prophecies, the author could tighten the strand of narrative.

In effect, the supernatural elements are used as the tissues that knit the sprawling material of the saga into firm structural units; they provide interior tension within the solid tripartite construction of the saga (Chapters 1-81; 82-132; 133-end).

The author could also use the known social fabric to create subtleties of behaviour which we might overlook. Formal hospitality was an integral part of this social structure, and the occasional breaches of the etiquette of giving and accepting hospitality had enormous significance. It is fitting that *Njal's Saga* should end with the formal test of Flosi's character through his capacity for hospitality, when his enemy, Kari, deliberately goes to his house for shelter. . . .

[*Njal's Saga*] paints a vivid and unforgettable picture of a living society—men and women at work and at leisure, a quiet self-reliant rural community through which occasional violence erupts brutally. Hoskuld Hvitaness-Priest is killed on a brilliant spring morning as he sows seed in his cornfield. No one, not even the least significant characters, exists without relation to this society; men die making charcoal, or trading, or carting dried fish, or herding livestock. The land itself, mountain, river, and pasture, is constantly before our eyes, the land that sustained and conditioned this people, the land that held Gunnar's heart in thrall. The land has not changed; today one can go by car from Reykjavik to the 'Njal country' and back in a single day, and recognize with a shock of pleasure the places described by the author.

Within this busy and active society, conceptions that are alien to us nowadays fit naturally and without strain. The formalities of betrothal and divorce, of lawsuits and challenges, of horse-fights and religious life, of manners and morals—all these emerge gently and clearly. The tenth-century farmhouse takes shape through the slow accumulation of incidental description, the pattern of clothing and weapons, wealth and poverty, power and subservience, unfolds before our eyes.

There is no need to say much about the system of laws. There are strong indications that the author of *Njal's Saga* used some written law code as his model for the extensive legal matter in the saga—and not always accurately, at that. This is a rather specialized subject, and it would be unnecessary to annotate the occasional discrepancies. The picture of the law system at work is in general a true one.

But perhaps a few words on the social and political context may be useful.

Some sixty years after the settlement of Iceland began, the Icelandic state was established with the institution of the 'Althing' (General Assembly). Previously there had only been local assemblies, as in other Scandinavian communities, under local chieftains; they were judicial rather than legislative. But in 930 the leading chieftains of Iceland founded the Althing, having commissioned a legal expert to prepare a special code of laws for the new state, based on Norwegian law.

The Althing was held annually in the open air for two weeks late in June at Thingvellir ('Assembly Plains'), and was the main judicial, legislative, and social event of the year. Those who attended it were accommodated in semi-permanent 'booths'—stone-and-turf enclosures which were temporarily furnished (often most lavishly) and roofed with cloth for occupation. Constitutional and judicial authority was in the hands of the chieftains, who combined religious and secular power and had the title of *goði*'—priest-chieftain. There were thirty-nine of them in Iceland at this time, and their status was largely hereditary, depending on the wealth and influence of their ancestors who had settled in Iceland; but the office could be bought, sold, divided, and even temporarily borrowed, as well as inherited (cf. Chapters 109 and 141).

Their function as heathen priests seems for the most part to have been rather perfunctory; their real power lay in wealth, in kinship, and in the personal allegiance of their followers. Paganism in Iceland seems to have been rather a diffuse religion. Belief in the existence of spirits was widespread, and the careful pagan took pains not to offend them; these spirits were thought to live in stones or groves or waterfalls and were sometimes propitiated by gifts of food—they were the 'natural geniuses' of the place. In addition to this, Icelanders believed in gods—a loose hierarchy of supra-mortals whom they liked to make friends with, rather than worship. In Iceland, Thor seems to have been the staple god. The gods were not all-powerful themselves; they were subject to impersonal, indifferent Fate, and to the same vices and virtues as mankind is.

The priest-chieftains were responsible for the upkeep of temples, which were used for sacrifices; but the degree of devotion shown varied very much according to the individual. It is clear that belief in the gods was weakening right from the earliest settlement of Iceland, although men continued to believe in the *idea* of a god. Many of the original settlers had come into contact with Christianity in Ireland; some of them were already baptized Christians,

others were to a greater or lesser degree familiar with it. One of the first settlers, Helgi the Lean, half Norse and half Irish, 'believed in Christ but invoked Thor for sea-journeys and times of crisis'; he named his farm Kristness. Throughout the tenth century formal paganism was on the decline, and contact with Christianity abroad increased; which partly, at least, explains how the conversion of Iceland to Christianity in the year 1000 was achieved without bloodshed (cf. Chapters 100-5). There was a Christian mission to Iceland early in the 980s which seems to have had considerable effect on men's minds, although it ended rather abruptly after blood had been spilt.

Christianity, once accepted by Althing decree, did not seem to make much immediate difference to Iceland. If anything, violence increased for a time. The pagan standards of conduct were based not so much on religion as on the old Germanic social code of self-reliance, personal loyalty to one's leader, and obligations to one's kin . . . a code of ethics best expounded in the tenth-century *Hávamál* poems ('The Words of the High One'). Immortality was conceived of in terms not of another life, but of fame; and the conception of Valhalla, where slain warriors feasted with Odin and prepared for the last great battle, was purely a literary one that never seems to have had any great effect on popular belief. Under Christianity, the moral code in Iceland did not change at once; but its tensions may well have been increased.

Nor did the social structure of Iceland change immediately. The priest-chieftains retained their titles and authority, which many of them reinforced by becoming leaders of the Church. But it did have one effect that seems to have been far-reaching: it hastened the decline of the individual free-holding farmer.

All the original settlers who came to Iceland during the period of the settlements became land-owning farmers. They brought with them some dependants and followers, but most of the farm-work was done for them by slaves, who were plentiful—mainly captives taken during Viking raids.

Slaves were owned body and soul by their masters; but in Iceland they had rather more sympathetic treatment—even certain legal privileges—than was common elsewhere. The sagas record many instances in the early days of slaves being given their freedom and even some land of their own as well. Slavery gradually decreased in Iceland during the tenth century, for whereas in the early days there had been land for all and no need to work, now free-men could no longer get themselves land cheaply or for nothing, and had to take jobs to keep themselves. Furthermore, the market in slaves diminished and it became as cheap to employ labour as to own it. Slaves could buy their freedom for half their market value, the rest to be paid later on the instalment system. Slavery continued in Iceland on a rapidly diminishing scale until early in the twelfth century, but continued elsewhere in Scandinavia for another two centuries. Probably the ultimately telling factor was the ban, under Christianity, on the practice of exposing children at birth (cf. Chapter 105); this robbed the slave-owner of his favourite means of controlling the slave birth-rate and thus easing his household costs (there is only one recorded instance of a slave being castrated).

Throughout the tenth century the free-holding farmer was the core of the community. Iceland was an aristocratic state, certainly, even though it was not considered an indignity to do farm-work (*Njal's Saga* is full of examples of this). The chieftains administered the country through the political authority and laws that they had themselves created and which they could easily frustrate when it served their purpose to do so.

But the power of the chieftains rested ultimately on the freeholding farmer. Each chieftain had a varying number of supporters; householders of a certain standard of wealth were bound by law to adhere to a chieftain, but they could freely choose to which chieftain in their Quarter they gave their allegiance. They paid him temple-dues and were committed to attend the Althing to support him or, in lieu of that, pay him a tax to defray the expenses of the Althing visit; in return, the chieftain was committed to give his followers protection and help. The chieftain was no less dependent on his followers than they on him (cf. Chapter 107, where Mord Valgardsson is seen to be losing authority and wealth because his followers are transferring their allegiance to Hoskuld Hvitaness-Priest).

With the advent of the Church in Iceland, the social structure changed to the extent that landlordism on a large scale came into being (there is no evidence of it in the tenth century, but that is not necessarily conclusive). The Church quickly began to amass ownership of land which was let to tenant farmers, and a new dimension was added to the conception of power. Previously, chieftains had derived power from a mutual relationship with their followers; now their power began to grow independent of goodwill. Furthermore, once the system of power through temple-allegiance broke down under Christianity, the potential bounds of power were extended; for previously a chieftain's followers were drawn from those who lived within a reasonable distance, at least, of the temple to which they subscribed.

The Church, thrustful and demanding, added a new factor to the ceaseless jockeying for power and influence that goes on in any community. In addition to arousing savage internal disputes in Iceland, it opened the way for external interference, for the Church connected Iceland with the outside world far more than it had been before. It brought Iceland within the power-range of Scandinavia; for instance, Bishop Gudmund, during his long struggles with chieftains at the beginning of the thirteenth century, invoked the assistance and authority of the archbishop of Norway.

Gradually the chieftains became more and more ambitious, more and more arrogant in their attitude to the law and their dealings with each other. By the beginning of the thirteenth century effective power throughout the land had been gathered into the grasp of some half dozen families. The violent disputes that arose in Iceland gave the rulers of Norway, who for centuries had wanted to get their hands on Iceland, the opportunity to intervene. Chieftains who tried to extend their power over the whole

of Iceland used the Norwegian throne as an ally—only to find themselves fatally mortgaged to it. Finally, in 1262, came the inevitable end of the republic; the Althing, under heavy pressure, agreed to pay tax and allegiance to the crown of Norway. It has taken Iceland nearly seven centuries to regain that independence.

These comments refer, of course, only to social and political changes caused by the Church. They ignore the many beneficial effects of the early Church in Iceland, particularly the part it played in developing Icelandic literature, not only through the introduction of writing but by the early exercise of literary ability.

One of the questions about *Njal's Saga* most frequently argued is—'How true is it?' Some have thought it practically pure fiction, others practically verbatim truth, even down to the dialogues.

The Burning of Bergthorsknoll is undoubtedly a historical fact, corroborated by earlier written sources—by, for instance, *Landnámabók* (Book of Settlements), the early-twelfth-century historical account of Iceland's first settlers and their descendants; and excavations close to the site of the present farm at Bergthorsknoll have proved that certain buildings—outhouses, probably—were burned down there hundreds of years ago, although exact dating has not been possible. Probably, Njal's home stood on exactly the same spot as the present farm, on top of a low swelling mound on the sea-level plain of the Land-Isles on the south coast.

The author of *Njal's Saga* clearly made use of a number of written sources (many of them traceable) for some of the saga material—the account of the conversion of Iceland to Christianity in the year 1000, for instance (which is so like a straight 'lift' from another document that scholars have occasionally thought the account to be a later interpolation in the saga); the account of the Battle of Clontarf outside Dublin in 1014; the elaborate, confusing, and sometimes incorrect legal formulae; the genealogies, and background material for many of the subsidiary characters. He can be proved to have known and often made use of material from other sagas written in the thirteenth century.

Some of his information also came to him embedded in the occasional verses in the saga. None of them has any great literary merit, and on linguistic and stylistic grounds few of them are thought by scholars to be as old as the events of the saga; but many of them were undoubtedly composed before the saga was written—thereby suggesting the existence of flourishing oral traditions that were being occasionally replenished from the imagination. It is, however, curious that some of the verses contain information that is contradictory to the narrative; for instance, the verse ascribed to Gunnar in his burial-mound (Chapter 78), which is thought to antedate the writing of the saga, says unequivocally that Gunnar refused to leave Iceland because he was reluctant to yield to his enemies. This gives a very different account from the aesthetic, almost lyrical, version in the saga itself.

Indeed, it can be shown that he used his sources with considerable freedom and occasional mistakes, which can be accounted for by both garbled oral traditions and the natural tendency of an author to manipulate material for aesthetic purposes. His version of the institution of the Fifth Court, for instance, is obviously distorted and misdated, an attempt to make this historic event an integral part of the saga—and perhaps to give Njal a larger role in Iceland's history than he actually played. The chronology of events in the saga is at times wildly inconsistent and cannot bear too close a scrutiny . . . ; the author has sacrificed the calendar to give his narrative greater impact and significance. There are also some striking similarities to certain events of the thirteenth century—burnings, battles, disputes, even individual wounds. Some scholars have claimed that the whole pattern of dispute is unmistakably thirteenth-century—the gathering of huge bands of men on great cross-country marches, the immense mobilizations of fighting men for the crises. Some of the very minor characters are perhaps entirely fictitious and their names are obviously spurious. The late Barði Guðmundsson wrote numerous articles (recently published posthumously under the title *Njal's Saga's Author*) brilliantly elaborating the thesis that most of the events described in the saga were inspired by thirteenth-century events in which the alleged author had played a conspicuous part. However, the really important thing is that, whether or not all these people lived and behaved in the way described by the author, in *Njal's Saga* they all have a vivid and unquestionable life of their own.

From thirteenth-century sources it is clear that sagas were regarded at the time as what one might call 'serious entertainment'. Contemporary writers were fully aware of the distortions that time can create in the memories of things past, and were not particularly concerned about it.

Where strict historical accuracy could be vouchsafed, by reference to contemporary witnesses, it was valued; but artistic values were no less warmly appreciated where historicity could not be claimed—and *Njal's Saga* unlike some others, makes no explicit claim to historical truth.

The distinction is obvious from a saga like *Sverrir's Saga,* for instance. This is a contemporary Icelandic account of the life of King Sverrir of Norway (1152-1202), compiled by a friend of the king's under the king's personal guidance; and in a later Introduction the point is specifically made that the historicity of the saga cannot be doubted, because of the reliability and immediacy of its sources—'it could not have become garbled by oral tradition'. But the Icelandic historian Styrmir the Learned (d. 1245), writing an Epilogue to *Saint Olaf's Saga,* said, 'You can accept from this composed saga whatever you think most likely, for in old sagas many things are confused. This is only to be expected where oral tradition alone supplies the material. . . . I expect that holy King Olaf would not be offended by any inaccuracies in the saga, for it has been written in order to entertain others rather than to criticize the king or out of any malice.'

An Icelandic scribe who wrote out a copy of *Thidrek's Saga* probably at the same time as *Njal's Saga* was being composed had much to say about sagas as serious entertainment in an Introduction. Their value, he thought, was both moral and practical.

'Sagas about worthy men', he wrote, 'are useful to know, because they show us noble deeds and brave feats, whereas ill-deeds are manifestations of indolence; thus, such sagas point the distinction between good and evil for those who wish to understand it.'

Further: 'With sagas one man can gladden many an hour, whereas most entertainments are difficult to arrange; some are very costly, some cannot be enjoyed without large numbers of people, some only entertain a very few people for a brief time, and some entail physical danger. But saga entertainment or poetry costs nothing and holds no dangers, and one man can entertain as many or as few as wish to listen; it is equally practicable night or day, by light or in darkness.'

Such were the literary ideas in circulation at the time that *Njal's Saga* was being composed.

They can be seen in actual practice in the following incident which occurred in the year 1258 in Iceland, and which was recorded in the contemporary *Sturlunga Saga:* it tells how a certain Thorgils Skardi came to the farmhouse at Hrafnagill one evening in that year. When he arrived, his host asked him what entertainment he would prefer—saga-reading or ballad-dancing. Thorgils asked what sagas were available, and was told that the saga of Archbishop Thomas á Beckett was at hand, amongst others. This is the one that Thorgils chose, 'for he loved him more than any other holy man'. (This saga, or versions of it at least, survives to this day in several manuscripts.)

The emphasis on *reading* aloud is interesting, for it suggests that the sagas were specifically designed for public, rather than private, reading. It also suggests an explanation of the characteristics of oral style which some scholars have found in the sagas; what appears to be a transcription of an existing oral tale is much more likely to have been a deliberate simulation of the earlier oral style. Formal story-telling had developed into formal saga-reading many years before *Njal's Saga* was written, and the saga bears constant marks of the concern the author showed for the listener as well as the reader.

As 'serious entertainment', *Njal's Saga* is pre-eminent. It is primarily the work of an author, not a historian. As Professor Turville-Petre of Oxford has put it, 'It was not the author's purpose to write a work of history, but rather to use an historical subject for an epic in prose.'

Perhaps, in the last resort of definition, we might call *Njal's Saga* a homily. Throughout the saga there is a bitter conflict between the forces of good and evil; physical violence is the symptom of this constant friction. In the saga, evil is consistently generated by self-aggrandisement, by the attempt to gain power or wealth. Mord Valgardsson is the most obvious example of this; it is Mord's envy of men who stand in his way, like Gunnar of Hlidarend with his fame and wealth, and Hoskuld Hvitaness-Priest with his growing authority, that motivates his destructive scheming. Hrut's journey to Norway to claim an inheritance, and his unscrupulous way of gaining his fortune (by consenting to be the elderly Queen Mother's lover) frustrate his promising marriage to Unn—who, in her second marriage, gives birth to Mord Valgardsson; and that ill-starred marriage is made possible by the money that Gunnar forcibly took from Hrut as a dowry back-claim. Hrapp's bribing of the weak-willed Thrain Sigfusson (Chapter 88) causes the clash with the Njalssons that leads to Thrain's death. Hildigunn's arrogant insistence that Hoskuld must get a chieftaincy before she will consent to marry him, and Njal's manipulation of the Constitution to achieve this, provoke Mord to malevolent enmity. Greed for money (the bait that proved fatal to Eyjolf Bolverksson) and for power invariably has disastrous consequences.

It is the unfailing source of evil in *Njal's Saga*; and it is significant that greed and power-lust were such potent causes of the civil disruption that racked Iceland in the thirteenth century and led to her loss of independence in 1262.

But money in itself could never assuage the misfortunes created by money; not even the unheard-of treble compensation awarded for the death of Hoskuld Hvitaness-Priest could placate the ugly hostilities that were aroused by the killing.

In this homily, the only answer to the violence aroused by evil is active will towards good. Christianity comes to Iceland half-way through the action; and it is the Christian virtues of self-sacrifice and humility that eventually stem the tide of evil, not the pagan virtues of heroism and pride. Njal, with his weird pagan prescience and his complex intelligence, is powerless against the doom he foresees for his friend Gunnar and himself, and only broadens the scope of catastrophe by his efforts to avert it; it is only when he resigns himself to the new God, when he abandons his devious scheming and sacrifices himself and his violent sons in the fire at Bergthorsknoll, that the possibility of resolution emerges. Flosi, goaded beyond endurance by taunts at his manhood, lets his smarting pride control his actions; it is only when he sees the incredible self-sacrifice of his father-in-law, Hall of Sida, who humbly confesses his 'lack of heroism' and is prepared to waive compensation for his son's death in order to end the violence—it is only then that Flosi's good qualities reassert themselves. From then on, he lets Kari butcher his followers without retaliation, until at last Kari is ready for a reconciliation (after a pilgrimage to Rome).

Ultimately, there is an indictment of violence, and of the way of life that fostered it. Behind the rather wistful vision of past heroism lies recognition of the endless strife it provoked. It was pride that helped to spread the poison of violence, the affronted pride even of good men like Gunnar; such fierce preoccupation with honour was bound to lead to bloodshed. Throughout the saga 'good' men and 'worthy' men try hard to settle disputes peacefully, to find solutions that satisfy the 'honour' of all concerned; but too often their efforts are frustrated by someone's pride. We can see this operating at its baldest in Chapter 91: Njal knows that his sons' quarrel with Thrain will have disastrous effects, but he realizes, too, that they have mortgaged their pride by making the quarrel public, and that therefore he must help them get public satisfaction. His contribution is merely to prearrange fresh provocation for

the inevitable killing. It is a pattern of behaviour all too familiar, even today.

It would, however, be quite wrong to offer the impression that this is what *Njal's Saga* is 'about'—a Christian morality. It is a facile and dangerous satisfaction to peddle some subjective interpretation of a great work. At best, one can only indicate what one believes were central attitudes. *Njal's Saga* has been vigorously quarried in the past for material to fit some theory or other, for there are any amount of 'telling' sentences with which to support a favourite cause. But it is the *completeness* of the saga that really matters; its artistry, not its argument.

Its prose has a taut epigrammatic terseness that has often proved hard to reproduce in English. It is cool, impersonal, objective, easy-paced; only in sudden explosions of harsh dialogue does the effortless lope of the narration change its unhurried stride.

And yet, under this studied urbanity, tensions gather like muscles rippling under skin; a shade of emphasis here—just a matter of word-order, so hard to transfer from an inflected language like Icelandic to an uninflected one—or a flash of irony there, breaking momentarily through the detachment. In the midst of such economy, one spendthrift sentence can speak volumes: 'two ravens flew with them all the way' (Chapter 79) as Skarp-Hedin and Hogni set out at night to avenge Gunnar; 'the fire still burned fitfully, flaring up and sinking again' (Chapter 130) as the superstitious Burners peered through the smoke and heard the voice of Skarp-Hedin chanting a verse amidst the dying flames.

One can be dramatic without exclamation marks. The author uses dialogue extensively throughout the narrative, and all the climaxes are compellingly visualized—Skarp-Hedin skimming over the ice to cut down Thrain (Chapter 92), the Njalssons marching grimly from booth to booth at the Althing seeking support (Chapter 119), Kari's eruption into the earl's hall in Orkney to kill Gunnar Lambason (Chapter 155), Bergthora storming at her sons at table to goad them into avenging an insult (Chapter 44). The scenes are innumerable; many of them could be transferred directly to the stage with scarcely an added word of dialogue—these whiplash retorts, these silences, these slow deliberate formalities that are a prelude to violence. And yet, nothing is given too much prominence; each event, each episode, each act (to use once again the theatre analogy that suggests itself so often) is subdued into its proper place in the Grand Design.

The author's constructional ability is remarkable. The saga has a deep, powerful, subtly varied rhythm that keeps the action moving with unhurried fluency. It could be likened to a storm; a series of ominous gusts of wind disturbing a calm day, an atmosphere growing more and more charged with a brooding promise of thunder. However often the saga relapses into calmness and peace—as for instance with the successive episodes of Gunnar's life, 'and now there was peace for a while'—the irresistible rhythm of approaching storm takes control again. Gradually the rhythm gathers speed, the intervals of calm become fewer and farther between. There is a superbly sustained climax of storm from Chapter 108 to Chapter 145; and then, at last, it begins to blow itself out.

All this is done with great sureness of touch. So, too, are the contrast between light and shade in the narrative, the variations of mood. From the death of Gunnar we plunge into the light-hearted adventures of the younger Njalssons abroad, a brief escape that gradually becomes shadowed with trouble. From the savage avenging fury of Kari with Thorgeir Skorar-Geir we turn to the ironic comedy of Bjorn of Mork, the cowardly braggart who does not quite suffer the humiliation we expect. There is a constant interplay of battle and debate, a long thrust-and-parry court drama (surely the first court-room drama in European literature?) followed hard by an uproar of battle.

But above all, the saga is rich beyond belief in its characters. They spring to life in a few vivid sentences; some, like the old woman Sæunn in Chapter 124, are only glimpsed in a paragraph—but with what telling effect. Others, like Njal and Skarp-Hedin, Gunnar and Flosi, Hallgerd and Bergthora, grow with the saga, deepening and broadening until we seem to know them like neighbours. Consider the subtle ageing of Njal over the last forty years of his life, how he seems physically to shrink, how his intellectual vigour quietly fades into the frail resignation of the octogenarian; and yet we are hard put to it to remember exactly *how* the effect is achieved. Watch how Skarp-Hedin becomes more and more committed to his restless, contemptuous role as the frustrated Viking, the elder son who never left his father's home; the ugly mouth, the constant scornful grin, the unnatural pallor relieved in anger by burning spots of red—all these are gradually heightened until at the end he is almost a nightmare figure as he stalks through the Althing, brutal, sardonic, terrible, and doomed. And yet, in death (what a delicate touch, this) the terror of his presence vanishes, we are told; it is as if death has released the appalling tensions that possessed his soul during the last years of his grim life, and we see again the person as we first met him in the saga—courageous, manly, quick-tongued, rather likeable.

Gunnar is on a different plane. He is never allowed to dominate in the way Njal does. His portrait, like that of Kari, has a blurred, romantic wash; he is the hero without peer, the knight on the tapestry. And like the true hero of old, he is never more alive than when meeting his death.

It is, of course, essential to the balance of the saga that Gunnar (and Kari) should engage our sympathies with less immediacy than do Njal (and Flosi); but within these necessary limits Gunnar is more complex than he appears at first glance. Behind his fantastic ability in battle and his courage is his concern at taking life (Chapter 54), behind his willingness to be guided by Njal is a deep, secret stubbornness. He is not, as one might think, a hero who happens to be a farmer; he is a farmer who happens to be a hero—and a reluctant one, at that.

The secondary characters—and what a host of them there is—are never perfunctory. How subtly individual they are: Hogni, Gunnar's son, slow and honest, who has to be carefully nursed by Skarp-Hedin into avenging his father, but who will then be diverted from vengeance only with the greatest reluctance; that most engaging villain Hrapp, irrepressibly insolent even at the moment of death; Thorhall Asgrimsson, so profoundly emotional that his whole body is affected by stress—violent swoons, a crippling boil whose brutal lancing releases his surging lust for revenge; Hrut, gracefully maturing into wisdom after his saddening youth; Bergthora, harsh but at the last gentle as she deliberately accompanies her husband to death.

The women of *Njal's Saga*, in fact, have no less significance than the men, although there are not many of them. No attempt is made to romanticize them; they are forceful, intensely individual, unforgettably real. Staid old scholars have argued with frenzied passion about Hallgerd, the enigmatic, dishonest, ravishing Hallgerd; some have rushed to her defence with such zeal that they have even accused the author of the saga of bias against her.

And then there is Njal himself, the benevolent farmer-sage with the Celtic name of Neil. His restless brooding brain behind his bland beardless face dominates the saga, even long after his death. This is Njal's saga, and he is worthy of it.

Hallberg notes the atmosphere in which *Njáls saga* was written:

Christianity had long since been introduced officially, but its spirit had not yet been able to permeate the Icelanders' view of life. Moral values wavered uncertainly in the gap between two systems of norms. The political situation acquired its impress from the ruthless feuds between powerful chieftains. No one could be sure of life and limb; peril lurked in all quarters, even from one's own kinsmen. In such an age it was dangerous to cling to illusions. Men's attitudes became sober and skeptical. It is this mode of thought and conduct to which saga style has given ultimate expression.

Peter Hallberg, in his The Icelandic Saga, *University of Nebraska Press, 1962.*

Denton Fox   (essay date 1963)

SOURCE: "*Njáls Saga* and the Western Literary Tradition," *Comparative Literature*, Vol. 15, No. 4, Fall, 1963, pp. 289-310.

[*In the following essay, Fox compares* Njáls saga *with other notable European epics, praising it for its historical accuracy and aesthetic merit, and noting in particular the saga's structural unity.*]

Most of the vast literature which has grown up around *Njáls saga*, the most important of the Icelandic family sagas, has been quite properly concerned with the problems of its origin, its historical accuracy, and its relation to the other sagas. My intention here, however, is to isolate the saga from its Icelandic literary background, and to consider it both *in vacuo* and as a work in the Western literary tradition. This approach plainly has great limitations and hazards, but it seems to me, for two reasons, to be legitimate. The first is simply the pragmatic reason that comparison of *Njáls saga* with other historically unrelated works throws a great deal of light on the saga. The other is that it seems to me unfortunate that *Njáls saga* in particular, and the Icelandic family sagas in general, are so commonly overlooked by non-specialists and play such a small role in what we loosely call our European literary tradition. I hope, by examining *Njáls saga* in the general context of European literature, to establish its claim to be, in W. P. Ker's words, "one of the great prose works of the world" [*Epic and Romance,* 1897].

The time-honored label applied to *Njáls saga* is "epic." If one takes this cliché seriously, and compares the saga with some of the great European epics—the *Iliad,* the *Odyssey, Beowulf,* the *Song of Roland*—remarkable similarities can be found, even though the five works are in many ways so disparate that it appears rash to group them together. On the most general level, they obviously present five different but by no means completely dissimilar versions of heroic conduct—the way in which a warrior should act. More tangible, however, is the question of the relationship between each of these works and its historical background. If we leave aside the saga, for a moment, it is clear that each of the other four works has a kernel of historical truth—the (or at least *a*) Trojan War, the raids and wars of the Danes, Geats, and Swedes, the fight at Roncesvalles—but that the poems themselves are fictions, not histories. All of the poems, however, take a very serious attitude toward historical truth, and are, in fact, pseudohistories of important earlier events in which the ancestors of the poet and his audience took part. The societies which produced the Homeric poems, *Beowulf,* and *Roland* were all societies moving away from what has been termed the "heroic age," and in each of these epics the poet is looking back towards a world which he feels to be both similar to and different from his own; the characters he creates are of his own race and their way of living is not altogether unlike that of his contemporaries, but the epic characters lived in an age when significant individual action was much more possible.

If we turn back to *Njáls saga,* we find a number of striking similarities. The saga obviously has a kernel of historical truth—some of the events in it are historical (for example, the introduction of Christianity into Iceland and the Battle of Clontarf), and many of its characters are historical figures—but it is equally obvious that the saga as a whole is not true. On the other hand, the saga, even more than the epic poems, is clearly designed so that it will appear to its audience to be history. There is also a chronological similarity with the epic poems; the historical events in *Njáls saga* took place between two hundred and fifty and three hundred years before the saga was written (the events are dated about the year 1000, and the saga is now supposed to have been composed about 1280). What is more significant is that, at the time the saga was composed Iceland, like the societies which produced the epic poems, was moving away from a heroic age. The thirteenth century in Iceland, the age of the Sturlungs, was bloody and violent enough for any taste, but it was a time of diminishing political liberty. Power was no longer distributed among

a great many independent farmers, as it had been before, but was concentrated in the hands of a few families, and later, after the loss of Icelandic independence in 1262-64, relinquished to Norway.

Njáls saga is, on the surface, most obviously unlike the epic poems in the formal aspects of its style and structure, but here, too, comparison is valuable. The fact that the saga is a prose work should not blind us to the strong resemblance between its style and the Homeric style. Auerbach's excellent remarks on Homer give an equally exact description of the saga:

> the Homeric style knows only a foreground, only a uniformly illuminated, uniformly objective present . . . the basic impulse of the Homeric style [is] to represent phenomena in a fully externalized form, visible and palpable in all their parts, and completely fixed in their spatial and temporal relations [Erich Auerbach, *Mimesis,* tr. W. R. Trask, 1953].

Related to this general resemblance are some more specific resemblances. One is the lack of suspense (the eventual fates of the chief characters are not concealed), common to both *Njáls saga* and Homer—and to *Beowulf* and *Roland*—which is derived from the impulse "to represent phenomena in a fully externalized form, visible and palpable in all their parts." Another is the complete self-effacement of the poet or narrator in all these works, and the exclusive concentration on objective phenomena. Syntactic parataxis, a dominant feature of *Beowulf* and *Roland* and occurring also very clearly in Homer and in the saga, is related to this self-effacement—reflecting the author's reluctance to insert his own explanatory or subordinating connectives. Still another related characteristic is the extremely traditional and unidiosyncratic style of all these works. Like epic poetry, though to a lesser degree, the sagas have their own formulae, set phrases which are repeated whenever the appropriate situation recurs.

The four epic poems present similar problems of structure and unity. The *Odyssey,* even if we overlook the so-called "Telemachia," seems superficially to have several subjects: the first half deals with a fabulous voyage, the second half describes the domestic and political difficulties faced by a returning king. *Beowulf* breaks into two parts: Beowulf 's fights with the Grendel ménage and with the dragon. The two parts not only have different antagonists, but also essentially different protagonists: the young Beowulf, a hero seeking glory in a foreign land; and the old Beowulf, a king defending his people. The *Song of Roland* has, quite literally, two protagonists and two antagonists, since Roland maims Marsilion and dies little more than halfway through the poem, leaving the stage free for the war between Charlemagne and Baligant. The *Iliad* is a slightly different case, since it does not break in the middle, but Wolf and his followers have shown us that the unity of the poem is at least disputable; Achilles, for instance, appears in less than half of the twenty-four books.

The degree to which a single author was responsible for each of these poems is still being disputed, and perhaps always will be. But it is coming to be more and more a matter of agreement that the poems as they stand, whatever their origins may be, are nonetheless works of remarkable unity, and that the apparent breaks in their structures are actually highly functional. Each of the poems is constructed differently; but, at the risk of oversimplification, one may observe that the apparently broken but actually unified structure corresponds to the apparently double but actually single subject: the hero as an individual (Roland, or the young Beowulf, for instance), and the hero as a member of society (Charlemagne, the old Beowulf).

Njáls saga, like the epic poems, seems to have some structural flaws. Not only is the saga sharply divided into two main parts—the first covering Gunnar's life and death, and the second dealing with Njal's family, their death, and the revenge taken for them—but even within these parts there are many apparent digressions. In the tradition of the Homeric analysts, it has often been held that the saga was unskillfully soldered together from two hypothetical earlier sagas, one of which had Gunnar for its hero and the other Njal. The comparison with the epic poems, however, suggests that it is possible that the saga has a genuine unity. Argument by analogy here is, of course, worthless; the demonstration of unity must rest solely on analysis of the saga. But the analogy is still useful, since it indicates that an apparently disjointed subject matter has repeatedly been an ingredient in works of epic scope and unity.

Although the saga breaks very obviously into two main parts, it can also be divided more precisely into five sections. Chapters 1-27, which form an introduction, deal principally with the assorted marital problems of Hrut and of his niece, Hallgerda, but also introduce the two main characters, Gunnar and Njal. Chapters 28-80 cover Gunnar's life: his growing prosperity, his marriage with Hallgerda, the quarrel between Hallgerda and Bergthora, Njal's wife, the manslaughter into which Gunnar is forced, the sentence of exile which is passed upon him, his refusal to go abroad, and his death, after he is trapped in his house by his enemies. In the third section, Chapters 81-106, many of the characters go abroad and there are various quarrels and killings, but there is finally a period of peace and quiet. It is in this section that the introduction of Christianity is described. Chapters 107-130, the fourth section, tell how Njal's sons are stirred up by Mord Valgardsson to kill Hauskuld, Njal's foster son, and how, as a consequence, Njal with his family is trapped in his house and burned alive, the sole survivor being Kari, Njal's son-in-law. The last section, Chapters 131-159, describes the revenge which Kari takes and his final reconciliation with Flosi, who had been the leader of Njal's enemies.

This short summary shows the large number of different actions included in the saga, but also suggests an at least rudimentary overall structure. The first two sections are clearly parallel to the third and fourth: the first and third sections are both introductory, giving a general picture of Iceland (and even of a larger area, since much of the action in these sections takes place abroad), while the second and the fourth sections describe how a man or family turns, not entirely by intention, to manslaughter, and as a result is trapped at home and killed. But we must look more closely at each of the five sections before we can determine the real structure of the saga.

The principal character of the first chapters is Hrut. The saga tells how he goes abroad to Norway, enters into an affair with Queen Gunnhilda, the king's mother, has a successful battle against vikings, is held in much honor by the king, and finally, having won wealth and glory, leaves Gunnhilda to return to Iceland. Upon his return he marries a woman named Unna, but the match turns out to be disastrous; Hrut, because of a curse laid on him by Gunnhilda, is unable to consummate the marriage, and Unna divorces him. He later incurs disgrace when Gunnar intimidates him into returning her dowry.

Hrut has very little connection with the main plot; like Unna, he drops completely out of the saga well before Gunnar's death. But it is clear that Hrut's career parallels and forecasts Gunnar's. Gunnar, at the beginning of the second section, goes to Norway and wins some battles against vikings. Like Hrut, Gunnar becomes a friend of kings and also enters into an amorous relationship (though a chaster one than Hrut's) with a kinswoman of the ruler of Norway. When he returns to Iceland, a wealthy and a famous man, his first action, again like Hrut, is to marry. His wife, Hallgerda, is the cause of many troubles and, ultimately, of his death. The parallel between Hrut and Gunnar is obvious enough, once it is pointed out, and the author of the saga has, very cleverly, done just that. After Unna's divorce, her father brings a suit against Hrut for the return of her dowry; Hrut counters this by challenging her father to a single combat. Unna's father saves his life but loses much honor by refusing the challenge and abandoning his claim to the dowry. Later in the saga Gunnar, on Unna's behalf, brings another suit against Hrut for the dowry, but, after making a mistake in legal procedure, uses against Hrut the same device that Hrut had used against Unna's father, a challenge to single combat. Hrut's reaction is the same—a sensible but shameful refusal, and a relinquishing of the dowry. It is neatly underlined that Gunnar is the parallel and successor of Hrut.

The other important character of the first section is Hallgerda; although she is of no importance to the plot until she marries Gunnar in the beginning of the second section, the saga devotes nine chapters to her early life. This is provided, not to establish her character, which is simple enough, being all superlatives—very beautiful, very proud, and very unscrupulous—but again to furnish parallels to the main action. Hallgerda has two husbands before Gunnar, and is responsible for the deaths of both of them. We are shown that her destiny is to be death to her husbands and are given the first two terms of an ascending three-term sequence. Her first husband is killed as she wishes, and there are no important repercussions; her second husband is killed against her consent, though she is still the ultimate cause of his death, and her own foster father loses his life in the affair. Hallgerda will be responsible in many ways for the killing of her third husband, Gunnar, and the troubles which she starts will grow far beyond her control and will have great repercussions.

These parallels make it abundantly clear that there is a close structural bond between the introductory section and the rest of the saga. But an equally important aspect of this opening section is the sort of world which it shows. In some respects this world is identical with the Iceland which we see in other sagas, a harsh and unfriendly country, yet one loved by its inhabitants; a land where the individual is all-important and where constant self-assertion is necessary for honorable survival. The main principle of order is the bond of kinship or of friendship between men, but even this bond, with the duty of revenge that it entails, leads often to violence. One aspect of this world which *Njáls saga* stresses is its paganism; it is no accident that Swan, the powerful and sinister magician who can conjure up mists and fogs at will, is described in the introductory section. Another aspect of this world, important throughout the saga, is the law—both the complicated legal code itself and the annual judicial assembly, the *Althing*. The saga opens with a description of Mord Fiddle, a great lawyer; and the legal theme continues to get so much attention that critics have complained of the "excessive space given to the law . . . the details and long-winded recapitulations of the many lawsuits" [Introduction to *Njál's saga,* tr. Bayerschmidt and Hollander, 1955]. As it appears in the beginning of the saga, the law is ambivalent: on the one hand, it is a useful and necessary principle of order; on the other, it is inadequate, since it can not only be perverted by a clever lawyer but also over-ridden by brute force, as in the cases of Hrut's and Gunnar's challenges to single combat.

This world has implicit in it a number of problems, and the rest of the saga is concerned with these problems. There is the problem of the law, its justness, its power, and the proper attitude of man towards it; there is also the problem, ultimately a related one, of the validity of paganism. But the most general and most important problem is how man should act in such a world—whether it is possible for him to maintain in every sense his honor and his individuality, and at the same time to live a peaceful and prosperous life. A crucial question, of course, is what "honor" means; and this question, which will reappear constantly in different forms throughout the saga, is already raised and provisionally answered in the introductory section. In an incident which seems a complete digression, Hrut stops at a friend's house just after he has been divorced. There are some children playing in the room who act out the divorce scene; one boy says repeatedly, "I will be Mord, and summon thee to lose thy wife because thou hast not slept with her." After this great insult violence is imminent. Hrut's brother indeed strikes the boy,

> but Hrut said, 'Come hither to me,' and the boy did so. Then Hrut drew a ring from his finger and gave it to him, and said, 'Go away, and try no man's temper henceforth.' Then the boy went away saying, 'Thy manliness I will bear in mind all my life.' From this matter Hrut got great praise . . .

We see here the ancient concept of honor, which demanded violent retribution for any insult, and especially for any insult which cast aspersions on one's manhood, could come into conflict with and be superseded by a higher honor. But the solution may not always be this easy.

The second section of the saga, in which Gunnar's life and death are related, deals at length with the question of the proper reaction to insult or injury. This section opens with the description of the vendetta between Hallgerda, Gunnar's wife, and Bergthora, Njal's wife, an extended and brilliant symbol for the great chain of revenge which at once held together and held down the early Germanic peoples. Hallgerda and Bergthora quarrel, and Hallgerda has one of her servants, Kol, kill one of Bergthora's servants. Bergthora arranges to have Kol killed, Hallgerda has Kol's slayer killed, and the chain stretches on. The victims are of progressively higher rank, until at last one of Gunnar's relatives is killed. At this point, it seems inevitable that Gunnar must join battle with Njal's family. But all through this long series of killings Gunnar and Njal have maintained their friendship, and have quietly paid wergilds to atone for the deaths their wives have caused. At the end, Gunnar does not even demand payment for his dead relative, but simply lets the matter ride until Njal finally presses a wergild upon him.

[*Njáls saga*] is neither true factual history nor historical allegory, but it is still hard to avoid the conclusion that its author was seriously concerned with history.

—*Denton Fox*

In this episode, Gunnar successfully passes through his trial. He manages to avoid violence and yet to keep his honor undiminished. But this is possible only because he has to do with Njal, who is another man of good will; later he will not be so fortunate. During the rest of this section of the saga, Gunnar gets more and more embroiled in quarrels which are not of his own making, but which he cannot avoid. From one standpoint, he seems to be an ideal hero; as the sister of one of his enemies remarks, "Gunnar is slow to be drawn into quarrels, but a hard hitter if he cannot avoid them" (Chapter 58). But, although he never gives offense and always attempts to settle disputes peacefully, his enemies continually put him in situations where he must fight or proclaim himself a coward. For all his reluctance and dislike of bloodshed, he is driven to kill more and more men, until he finally kills two men from the same family, even though Njal, who is gifted with the second sight, has warned him that this will lead to his death.

The final result of Gunnar's slayings is that he is sentenced at the Althing to go abroad for three years, under penalty of being declared an outlaw. Njal shows Gunnar what alternatives he has. If he goes abroad, "Thou wilt come back with great glory, and live to be an old man, and no man here will then tread on thy heel; but if thou dost not fare away . . . then thou wilt be slain here in the land" (Chapter 74). So Gunnar prepares to leave Iceland, saying that he will never return. But, as he is riding down to the ship, he looks back at his home and makes his famous speech: "Fair is the Lithe; so fair that it has never seemed to me so fair; the corn fields are white to harvest, and the home mead is mown; and now I will ride back home, and not fare abroad at all" (Chapter 75). And so he stays in Iceland, and is killed.

A weariness from perpetually extricating himself from trouble, a love of his home, perhaps even the human tendency towards self-destruction which the saga so constantly illustrates all enter into his decision to remain. But I think there is another and more important reason. He is Gunnar of Lithend; if he left Iceland he would lose part of his name and part of his identity, and become a homeless wanderer with no position or honor except what he could take by violent means from other men. He feels, perhaps, that if he accepts the sentence of exile, he will be admitting that it was just, and will also be seeking refuge in flight from his enemies. Essentially, Gunnar is faced with a sophisticated version of the classic Germanic choice—he must give up his honor or his life. It is no accident that at this point in the saga we are given two other examples of men who consciously accept death rather than incur dishonor. Just before a battle, Gunnar has a prophetic dream which shows beyond any doubt that his brother, Hjort, will be killed. Gunnar tells Hjort to ride away from the battle, but Hjort says, "I will not do that; though I know my death is sure, I will stand by thee still" (Chapter 62). Then there is a Norwegian, Thorir, the son-in-law of one of Gunnar's enemies, who at first declines to join in an attack on Gunnar. But his mother-in-law taunts him with being a coward, so he gives away his possessions and says to her, "I will go with thy husband, and neither of us two shall come back."

The theme of honor is brought to a climax at Gunnar's death scene, when Gunnar, alone except for his wife and mother, is trapped in his house, surrounded by enemies. There are three parts of this episode which are particularly noteworthy. Mord Valgardsson, the worst of Gunnar's enemies, suggests twice that they set fire to the house and burn Gunnar in it, but is twice rebuked for this evil idea by his comrades. This passage, which raises the question of whether or not any moral distinction is possible between different forms of slaying, is important mainly because it looks forward to the later episode in which Njal actually is burned alive. In another significant section, Gunnar reaches through the window to get one of the arrows which have been shot at him, saying, "it will be a shame to them if they get a hurt from their own weapons" (Chapter 77). His mother warns him against this, but he persists and wounds one of his enemies with the arrow. The result is that the besiegers believe Gunnar to have run out of arrows, and press the attack more fiercely. Gunnar here acts from wanton pride, which is very unusual for him, and this pride is clearly condemned, both by his mother's rebuke and by the course of events, since his action hastens his own death.

But the most important part of this episode is the famous section in which Gunnar breaks his bowstring and asks his wife to twist together two locks of her hair for a replacement " 'Does aught lie on it?' she says. 'My life lies on it,' he said; 'for they will never come to close quarters with me if I can keep them off with my bow.' " Then Hallgerda reminds Gunnar of a slap on the face which he had given

her long ago, for ample cause, and refuses his request. As a result, Gunnar's enemies are able to close with him and kill him. This is clearly the culmination of the whole first half of the saga, both emotionally and thematically, and it is appropriate that Hallgerda figures so prominently. Hallgerda, who is always shown as bloodily preoccupied with preserving her own extreme form of personal honor, is both a representative and caricature of the old heroic ethos. When she refuses to provide Gunnar with a bowstring, one feels that she may be modeling herself on Brunhild. But in the context of the saga, Hallgerda is merely contemptible, and, since she causes her husband's death and then runs away, her pride is revealed to be simple selfishness. When she reappears briefly later in the saga, again as a trouble-maker, we are inclined to agree with the character who calls her "either a hag . . . or a whore."

In the first half of the saga, then, the two central characters are Hallgerda and Gunnar. Hallgerda demonstrates the essential unattractiveness of a single-minded preoccupation with personal honor, and Gunnar shows how it is impossible for any man, no matter how well-intentioned and slow to anger, to live in a society whose only non-materialistic value is a narrow concept of honor (largely something as simple as the imperative: "A man must revenge injuries") without losing either his self-respect or his life. Gunnar's death is the indictment of the whole society.

After his death, the focus of the saga changes sharply. One of the most obvious changes, of course, is that there is a new protagonist; Gunnar is replaced by Njal. And yet this is not quite accurate, for the proper equivalent to Gunnar is not the single man, Njal, but Njal together with his family. Along with this, there is a corresponding shift in theme away from the heroic individual and towards men who are bound together by love and duty. As far as character goes, the equivalent to Gunnar would be Njal's son, Skarphedinn, who is equally valiant, if surlier. But Skarphedinn is distinctly subservient to Njal, and Njal is so little a great warrior that his enemies accuse him, because of his beardlessness, of being effeminate.

Njal's character is described accurately when he is first introduced into the saga:

> He was so great a lawyer, that his match was not to be found. Wise too he was, and foreknowing and foresighted. Of good counsel, and ready to give it, and all that he advised men was sure to be the best for them to do. Gentle and generous, he unravelled every man's knotty points who came to see him about them [Chapter 20].

Although any great sage in early Iceland would also be a great lawyer, it is still interesting that this aspect of Njal is stressed so heavily throughout the saga. As we have already seen, the law is ambivalent, being in theory a force for order but in practice often a force working towards disorder. Njal quibbles and takes refuge in technicalities as often as any man, but he makes his basic relationship to the law clear when he says, "it will never do to have no law in the land," and especially when he quotes the proverb, "with law shall our land be built up and settled, and with lawlessness wasted and spoiled." This is quite literally true; for the law, which could provide public and permanent settlements for feuds, was almost the only way to escape the endless revenge which devastated the country. Njal is clearly a proponent of the law as a principle of order which can, at least potentially, overrule the prevailing anarchy of lawless individuals.

In the third section of the saga, there appears another principle of order, Christianity, to buttress the law. Chapters 100-105 form an apparent digression in which the introduction of Christianity into Iceland is related. The climax of the episode is the description of the assembly where the Christian and heathen parties confront each other and dissolve their old community of law, amid great uproar and imminent violence. The Christian party then takes the bold step of asking a heathen, Thorgeir, to say what the law shall be. After deliberating for a day, Thorgeir speaks:

> It seems to me as though our matters were come to a dead lock, if we are not all to have one and the same law; for if there be a sundering of the laws, then there will be a sundering of the peace, and we shall never be able to live in the land . . . This is the beginning of our laws, that all men shall be Christian here in the land . . .

Far from being a digression, this section is actually one of the central points of the saga, for it is here that the two great suprapersonal forces for good are bound together. And the first Icelander mentioned as being in favor of Christianity is Njal, so that he becomes a representative of Christianity as well as of law.

The author of the saga scrupulously avoids any oversimplification; he shows, on the one hand, that the law does not lead regularly or even frequently to justice, and, on the other, that the Christianization of Iceland does not produce anything like a Christian community. The missionary who converts the Icelanders is simply a thug, and the Christianity which he brings supplants the system of blood revenge only very sporadically. In the chapter following the description of the acceptance of Christianity, we are told how a blind man is miraculously given back his sight so that he can kill his father's slayer. But it becomes clear that the account of the conversion of Iceland has some very genuine significance if we consider Hauskuld Thrainsson, whose story is related in the parts of the saga which immediately precede and follow the introduction of Christianity.

Hauskuld Thrainsson is the son of a man whom Skarphedinn, Njal's son, had killed. When Njal meets the boy, after the killing, he gives him a ring and asks, "Knowest thou what brought thy father to his death?" Hauskuld replies, "I know that Skarphedinn slew him; but we need not keep that in mind, when an atonement has been made for it, and a full price paid for him" (Chapter 94). This answer impresses Njal so much that he adopts Hauskuld as a foster son and takes him into his house; but it is of course the direct opposite of the proper attitude of a son towards his father's slayer, under the old code. (The conversation is reminiscent of Hrut's actions towards the boy who insults him; since both scenes involve a man talking to a boy and giving him a ring, we may assume an intentional parallel.) Njal's sons and Hauskuld become inseparable friends; but

eventually men, principally the evil Mord Valgardsson, attempt to break their friendship by spreading slander and lies. Njal's sons are finally seduced into killing Hauskuld, who makes no attempt to defend himself, but instead says to his assailants, "God help me, and forgive you!" (Chapter 111).

In the same section of the saga, then, we have both the account of the historical conversion of Iceland and the concrete example, the patently Christian life and death of Hauskuld. But Hauskuld is not merely an exemplary figure; he is also crucial to the plot. He is killed by Njal's sons without the knowledge of their father, which in itself is unusual and ominous; when Njal hears what has happened, he prophesies that this deed will cause the death of himself and his wife and all his sons. (The gift of prophecy often functions as a literary device to reveal the relationship between immediate cause and future effect.) As the saga continues, Njal and his family are, in fact, killed by Hauskuld's avengers. Njal underlines the magnitude of the sin that has been committed in killing such a man when he says, "I loved Hauskuld more than my own sons, and when I heard that he was slain, methought the sweetest light of my eyes was quenched, and I would rather have lost all my sons, and that he were alive" (Chapter 122).

The fourth section of the saga, in which the fall of Njal and his family is recorded, is in many ways an obvious parallel to the second section, the fall of Gunnar. In both cases the protagonists come into great hazard as a result of homicide; in both cases there is a settlement of the dispute at the annual legal assembly which provides a temporary reprieve but is later broken; and in both cases the protagonists are trapped in their houses by their assembled enemies and killed. But it is the contrasts between the two sections which are the most instructive. One major difference is that Njal's death seems so much more predestined than Gunnar's. Gunnar chooses his own death when he decides to break the legal settlement and remain in Iceland; after Hauskuld's death, Njal and his sons have really no chance to escape. The settlement that is made between them and Hauskuld's avengers is broken immediately, and through no fault of theirs. Then there is a long series of ominous supernatural portents (Chapters 124, 125, 127) which further increases the sense of inevitability. With Gunnar, the emphasis was on the heroic individual and his choice; with Njal, on the effects of sin and the relationship between man and fate. As a corollary, Njal's slayers are portrayed as not really villainous. Their leader, Flosi, is anything but vindictive; and, though he commits the terrible sin of burning Njal, he shows clearly that he does this only because he is compelled to, when he says:

> Now there are but two choices left, and neither of them good. One is to turn away, and that is our death; the other, to set fire to the house, and burn them inside it; and that is a deed which we shall have to answer for heavily before God, since we are Christian men ourselves; but still we must take to that counsel [Chapter 128].

But the main contrast between the two sections is in the death scenes themselves. Njal's death is explicitly Christian. He says, during the burning:

Keep up your hearts, nor utter shrieks, for this is but a passing storm, and it will be long before ye have another such; and put your faith in God, and believe that he is so merciful that he will not let us burn both in this world and the next [Chapter 129].

When Njal and his wife lie down to die, they cross themselves and commend their souls to God. The neighbors who search for the bodies after the burning find that Njal and his wife are completely unburnt, and that Njal's body shines with a surpassing radiance. These miracles have no special novelty, but their obvious literary function is further emphasized by the contrast with the pagan supernaturalism of the scene in which Gunnar, after his death, is seen sitting in his cairn reciting skaldic poetry.

Even more striking is the distinctive tone of Njal's death. Gunnar's wife wantonly caused the death of her husband; Njal's wife, when she is offered a chance to leave the burning house in safety, says, "I was given away to Njal young, and I have promised him this, that we would both share the same fate." A curious gentleness and love runs through the whole scene, massacre though it is. Even Skarphedinn, the greatest warrior of Njal's sons, and a figure who generally verges on the sinister, with his saturnine mockery and his desperate courage, appears in a new light at his death. The love which he shows for his friend, Kari, and his desire to save Kari's life at the cost of his own make psychologically plausible the later scene where his body is found branded with two crosses. "All men said that they thought that it was better to be near Skarphedinn dead than they weened, for no man was afraid of him" (Chapter 132).

Njal's death is the crest of the second and higher wave of the saga. But, if it is a graver and more resounding event than Gunnar's death, it is less tragic. Gunnar died in an atmosphere of betrayal, a single man fighting against a hostile world. Njal and his family, trapped inside their burning house, are surprisingly neither tragic nor pathetic; they are fated, but they have mastered their fate by being at peace with it. If their death is in part a defeat of law and wisdom (for Njal, at least, is entirely guiltless), it is still not an inevitable and universal defeat. One feels that the world has changed since Gunnar's death, so that it is now conceivable that a man could live a long and honorable life. The change is not a large one, for the duty of blood revenge is still paramount, the law is still ineffectual, and Christianity is intermittent and superficial; but there is nonetheless a distant glimpse of a rational and merciful order underlying the world.

After Njal's death the predictable cycle starts again. Njal's friends make an attempt to gain revenge through the law, this is frustrated, and there is the inevitable bloodshed. But, although the course of action seems on the surface to be conventional and stereotyped, the reality is very different. This is partly due to the characters of the two men chiefly involved, Kari and Flosi. Kari, who first entered the saga, appropriately, as the rescuer of Njal's sons when they were abroad, and who later married one of Njal's daughters, is the only man who escaped from the burning house. He is the third hero of the saga, and in some ways he combines in himself both Njal and Gunnar—Njal because of the family connection and because he carries on the fight against Njal's enemies, Gunnar because of a marked similarity of character. Like Gunnar, Kari is a man of even temper but also a uniquely skillful and valiant fighter. The writer of the saga underlines the resemblance by making a character remark that Kari is "that man . . . who most resembles Gunnar in all respects." Flosi, the leader of the house burners, is Kari's opponent and should be the villain of the piece, but is actually an entirely sympathetic character, being "the merriest of men, and the best of hosts, and it is so said that he had most of the chieftain in him of all the men of his time" (Chapter 146). He never boasts about the house burning, nor does he ever show fear of its consequences.

Circumstances have forced these two good men into violent conflict; through Flosi, Kari lost not only Njal, his father-in-law, and Njal's sons, his closest friends, but also his only son, a small boy who was killed in the fire. Both by temperament and by all the customs of the land, Kari is bound to seek revenge, and a tragic conclusion, in which one or both of the two men are killed, appears to be inevitable. But, by considerable art, and especially by making Kari act in an extremely interesting way, the writer of the saga works towards an entirely different solution. Kari is so grief-stricken that he cannot sleep and is intent on revenge. When a settlement is arranged between some of Njal's friends and the burners, Kari refuses to accept any financial compensation and exempts himself from the truce. But on the other hand, he is curiously restrained. He speaks constantly of Njal and Skarphedinn, but "he never abused his foes, and never threatened them." He does manage to kill a good number of his enemies, but all under special circumstances which put him in a very favorable light. On one occasion, he and a single companion come across fifteen of their enemies asleep in the open country. They wake them, wait for them to arm, and then attack, killing five and putting the other ten to flight. On another occasion, after both Kari and his enemies have left Iceland, he lands in Orkney and goes up to an earl's hall, where he hears one of his enemies boasting about the burning of Njal. Kari goes alone into the hall, kills the man in the midst of his friends, and comes out again. Sometimes he refrains from slaughter even when he has his enemies in his power.

Kari's restraint, or perhaps more precisely his nonchalance and complete lack of bloodthirstiness, is shown very clearly by his attitude towards his allies. When the settlement is made between Njal's friends and the burners, one man, Thorgeir, joins Kari in exempting himself from the truce. The two fight as allies for a while, and then an intermediary tries to persuade Thorgeir to come to terms with his enemies. Thorgeir is unwilling to accept a settlement, but Kari browbeats him into it, and deprives himself of any support. Kari now takes for his companion a man named Bjorn, a henpecked and cowardly boaster and an ingratiatingly ridiculous character. Kari, who apparently derives as much amusement from Bjorn as the reader does, has several fights while Bjorn stands behind him and alternatively congratulates himself on his bravery and wonders how he can safely run away. Bjorn creates a change of mood; after he appears, it becomes very difficult to take Kari's revenge seriously. This change towards a lighthearted tone is apparent even in the happy ending of Bjorn's story. Kari, before he leaves Iceland, praises him and finds him a protector. Afterwards, "Bjorn was thought to be much more of a man than he had been before" (Chapter 151).

Flosi, who has a rather passive role in this part of the saga, shows even more restraint than Kari, and is in many ways surprisingly similar to him. Like Kari, he refuses on one occasion to kill an enemy who attacks him and then falls into his power (Chapter 136). He has the same courage, the same equable disposition, and the same reluctance to threaten or abuse his enemies. Once when Kari kills one of Flosi's men, Flosi says only, "Kari hath not done this without a cause; he is in no atonement with us, and he only did what he had a right to do" (Chapter 155). Flosi underlines his kinship with Kari when he remarks, "There are few men like Kari, and I would that my mind were shapen altogether like his" (Chapter 147).

Before coming to the end of the saga, the climactic meeting between Kari and Flosi, we should consider two structurally significant matters.

One is the character, Hall of the Side (Hallr Þorsteinsson or Siðu-Hallr), Flosi's father-in-law. Hall, who never takes any major part in the action, appears first in the section which describes the introduction of Christianity; he is the man who welcomes the missionary to Iceland, and is generally the leader of the Christian party. We see him again briefly when Flosi is avenging Hauskuld; "a wise man and good-hearted" (Chapter 119), he begs Flosi to accept a peaceful settlement and succeeds in patching up a temporary truce. But his most significant appearance is during the great fight at the Althing between the party of his son-in-law, Flosi, and the party of Njal's avengers. After Hall and his sons are attacked by the avengers and retreat, Hall says, "This is a sad state of things when the whole host of men at the Thing fight, and I would . . . that we begged us help even though that be brought against us by some men, and that we part them" (Chapter 145). Hall tries to stop the fight, and persists even after his son is killed by one of the avengers, until, with assistance, he manages again to bring about a temporary truce. The next day, during the assembly, he stands up and, after saying, "I shall now show that I am a man of little courage," asks for a permanent settlement. Later, when the negotiations are going badly, Hall says:

> All men know what a grief I have suffered in the loss of my son Ljot; many will think that he would be valued dearest of all those men who have fallen here; but I will do this for the sake of an atonement—I will put no price on my son, and yet will come forward and grant both pledges and peace to those who are my adversaries [Chapter 145].

There is obviously a close parallel between Hall and Hauskuld Thrainsson. Both lead exemplary Christian lives and go dramatically against one of the most important obligations of the old morality, the duty to revenge the deaths of one's relatives. But the parallel does not hold completely. Hauskuld's actions lead him to his death, but Hall's actions prove to be very wise even from the most mundane viewpoint. The speech in which he offers to forego any reparations for his son is greeted with great applause; and later everyone at the assembly contributes towards a gift, so that he actually receives an immensely large wergild. Like the figure of Bjorn, Hall marks the change of mood which has come into the saga, the movement towards comedy and peace. Hall also forms a bridge between Hauskuld and Kari; if his character is parallel to Hauskuld's, his situation is parallel to Kari's, for both men have had their sons killed by their enemies. At this point in the saga Kari's policy of revenge seems to put him in direct opposition to Hall, but Hall's actions give us a strong hint of Kari's final decision.

The other structurally significant matter which needs to be considered is the description of the Battle of Clontarf, the famous battle that Brian Boru fought against Earl Sigurd of the Orkneys and King Sigtrygg of Dublin on Good Friday, 1014. This bit of history has only a tenuous connection with the plot of the saga—fifteen of the burners are killed fighting under Earl Sigurd—but is thematically very important. The historical significance of the battle need not concern us here; in the saga it is a conflict between the Irish, representatives of virtue, mercy, and Christianity, and the Scandinavians of Ireland and the islands, representatives of treachery, murder, and anti-Christianity. As one example out of a great many, we may consider the two joint leaders of a viking force, Brodir and Ospak. Brodir, a Christian apostate, a worshipper of devils (or of heathen gods) and a magician, tries to kill Ospak by a treacherous trap and then meets his death in the battle, fighting on the Scandinavian side. Ospak, a heathen, vows to accept Christianity if he escapes Brodir's trap, and after he does escape is baptized and fights in the battle on Brian's side. The issues of the battle are made very plain, and it is repeatedly emphasized that it is not just an ordinary human fight. In no other part of the saga is the supernatural so prominent; there are at least thirteen miracles and portents (such as showers of blood), and the author of the saga inserts at this point the famous "Darraðarljóð" (the original of Thomas Gray's "The Fatal Sisters"), describing the Valkyries weaving a web of battle. What we have in this historical interlude, then, is a full-scale, concrete representation of the fight between good and evil that rages throughout the saga, made explicitly cosmological by the supernatural references, and carried out in terms familiar in the rest of the saga: good is represented by Christianity, mercy (Brian is accustomed to pardon a man three times for the same offense), and loyalty; bad by bloodthirstiness, ravenous self-aggrandizement, and disloyalty. There is even an obvious parallel between the battle and the first part of the saga; Kormlada, the mother of King Sigtrygg and the instigator of the battle, closely resembles Hallgerda; she is very beautiful, often-married (and responsible for the death of at least one of her husbands), and extremely vindictive.

After the forces of good have won this crucial battle, the author needs only a few pages to show the triumph of good in the main plot, and to close the saga. Flosi makes a pilgrimage to Rome, is absolved, and returns to Iceland;

Kari, some time later, does the same. But on his return Kari is shipwrecked, and cast up on the coast of Iceland, in a snowstorm, at a place near Flosi's house. When Kari goes to Flosi and throws himself on his mercy, Flosi greets him warmly, they come to a complete reconciliation, and Kari spends the winter with him. The final, masterful, touch is that, since Kari's wife has died, Flosi gives to him in marriage his niece, Hildigunna, "whom Hauskuld . . . had had to wife" (Chapter 159). By this marriage Kari and Flosi are welded indissolubly into the same family, and Kari becomes the successor of the saintly Hauskuld.

These last pages complete the pattern of the saga. We see Kari as the final hero, uniting in himself the figures of the heroic individual, Gunnar, and the man of justice and Christianity, Njal, but finding for himself a new solution, and one which involves life, not death. There is very clearly a meaningful pattern here. But we must be cautious of easy oversimplifications; the most characteristic quality of the saga's author is his desire to do full justice to the complexity of life. Kari is not a simple exemplary figure; his decision to become reconciled with the leader of his son's killers comes only after he has revenged himself on a good many men. And, while there is little doubt that his reconciliation is the final answer to the problems of human life which are raised in the saga, this does not cancel out the earlier answers, Gunnar's heroic death and Njal's noble martyrdom. There is also another trap into which we may fall. It is dangerously easy to distort the saga by imposing on it anachronistically our own moral standards. We are apt to think that Christianity is good, blood revenge bad, and the two absolutely incompatible. But matters were not so simple for the author of the saga. As Dorothy Whitelock has said of Anglo-Saxon England, "the duty of protecting one's kindred, or one's lord, or one's man, and of exacting retribution from the slayer and his kindred if any of these were killed, was not superseded by Christianity" [*The Audience of Beowulf*, 1951]. If the author of the saga sees a clash between Christianity and revenge, and gives the final preference to Christianity, he also recognizes that revenge could be a very pressing duty and, in a land of uncertain legal sanctions, to some extent a commendable one.

We have seen how the saga is meticulously organized spatially, so to speak, with parallel but contrasting characters and scenes. But it may also be useful to look at its chronological and historical aspects. The saga, of course, is neither true factual history nor historical allegory, but it is still hard to avoid the conclusion that its author was seriously concerned with history. In the first part of the saga we see two sides of the old heroic age: Gunnar, an individual fighting valiantly against certain death, and Hallgerda, a figure of selfish and murderous pride. Then, in the middle of the saga, there is the long description of the introduction of Christianity into Iceland, followed by a declining emphasis on heroic individualism. From that point on, there is increasing attention to Christianity and Christian virtues, leading up to the great triumph of Christianity, the battle of Clontarf, and then the reconciliation between Kari and Flosi. The author of the saga seems to be putting into dramatic form the essence of early Icelandic history. Like the other major European epics, *Njáls saga* presents

a civilization, a true picture of man and society in their historical as well as their timeless aspects.

Einar Ólafur Sveinsson   (essay date 1966)

SOURCE: *Njál's Saga: A Literary Masterpiece*, edited and translated by Paul Schach, University of Nebraska Press, 1971, 210 p.

[*An Icelandic author and educator, Sveinsson is the foremost scholar of* Njáls saga *and the author of several books on the subject, including* Njáls Saga: A Literary Masterpiece *(1966). In the following excerpt from that work, Sveinsson examines* Njáls saga's *many characters, especially the women.*]

I

The Danish literary critic Paul V. Rubow has estimated that *Njáls saga* contains twenty-five carefully and skillfully executed character portraits [*Smaa Kritiske Breve*, 1936]. That is a considerable number, and yet it is somewhat too low rather than too high. In addition to these full-length portraits, there are sketches of at least a dozen men and women which are as distinctive as the main char-

A page from the Njáls saga *manuscript known as* Reykjabók, *dated around 1300.*

acters of many another saga that does not approach the richness of *Njála* in this respect. And finally we meet a host of individuals who appear briefly, some of them only once or twice, but who leave a distinct image on the mind of the reader. Even more impressive than the number of characters, however, is the consummate skill and profound understanding with which they are portrayed. In some cases the author shows us a picture of the external appearance of his characters; in all cases he affords us a description of their internal nature, of their mental disposition and temperament. To be sure, we may sometimes have questions regarding the true motives of the characters when under strong emotional stress. As examples we might mention Gunnar's fatal decision to defy the law and return home instead of going into exile (chapter 75), or Flosi's sudden change of heart following the slaying of Höskuldur Hvítanessgoði (chapter 123). It is also difficult to understand Skarphéðinn completely. But in all these cases we will arrive at a satisfactory understanding if we read the saga thoughtfully and with an open mind. In so doing we must be careful not to jump to conclusions regarding any of the characters on the basis of the first impression or of a single episode. It is necessary to keep in mind everything a character says and does, without subtracting anything from or adding anything to the author's account. And it goes without saying that we must not indulge in speculation regarding the historical reliability of this or that scene or character.

Not a few scholars have been so led astray by their search for historical truth in the saga that they quite failed to see the characters as the author depicted them. Some critics have been unable to resist the evidence and influence of other sources, which cast a false and confusing light on the characters of *Njáls saga*, with the result that the account in *Njála* was often not fully understood and appreciated. Others have tried to fill in what they felt to be missing features of some of the character portraits. Still others became so impressed with or engrossed in this or that incident that they arrived at distorted, fragmentary views of certain characters which are substantially different from the composite pictures that are revealed by a careful consideration of their total role in the saga. In *Njáls saga* especially it is essential to see the characters in their totality. All of the widely scattered and seemingly contradictory words and deeds of a given character must be brought together; each must be examined in the light of the others in order, if possible, to find the common denominator. Only when the critic has exhausted every effort in this direction is he justified in trying to assess the degree of success achieved by the author in his character portrayals. We must not forget that what sometimes seem to the casual reader to be artistic flaws and inconsistencies in the character portraits can well be the author's intentional revelation of disharmonies and incongruities in the complex natures of the characters themselves.

And finally, we must constantly remind ourselves that all attempts to "rehabilitate" or plead the cause of a particular character in the saga are futile. All we can (and must) do is to make an honest effort to see and understand the author's characters as he portrayed them. The only question we are permitted to ask is: Are the character portraits

artistically good or faulty? If the characters are well drawn, we must accept them as they are, whether or not we are pleased with these pictures of our saga heroes.

II

The first question which arises when we begin the review of the host of characters in *Njála* is this: Which characters emerge from this "shadow army" sufficiently to assume distinct individuality and the appearance of real living beings? To be sure, it is not difficult to find certain types among them or to divide them into groups on the basis of common characteristics; and yet, when compared with each other, each one is found to have his own individual stamp.

Although a spiritual affinity exists between an author and his characters, he has to maintain a certain degree of artistic objectivity and impartiality toward them. Thus in a sense he exists both inside and outside of his characters. This affinity tends to bring the character closer, and if it is very strong and personal, there is a danger that the characters may get out of focus and become blurred. On the other hand, if the author's objectivity and impartiality predominate, his characters recede into the distance and his sympathy may be transformed into cold, heartless comprehension or at best into uncertainty or ambivalence. In some authors, both sympathy and comprehension yield to feelings of aversion and animosity, and under the undue influence of such feelings they may create characters not unlike the stock villains in modern detective thrillers.

The author of *Njála* is not entirely free of such bias; his sympathies are rather unevenly distributed among his many children. But we must not blame him for this until we have considered the possible causes or reasons for his partiality. The division of characters in *King Lear* into "good guys" and "bad guys" is no less striking; there too we find men of the most noble qualities beside monsters in human form.

Actually, the author of *Njála* has been seriously criticized for his one-sided character depiction in connection with only four persons in the saga: on the one hand there is Hallgerður, who is treated rather harshly, and on the other hand, there are the three shining heroes, Gunnar of Hlíðarendi, Kári Sölmundarson, and Höskuldur Hvítanessgoði. . . .

As early as 1700, or perhaps even earlier, we find Icelandic poets expressing mixed feelings toward Hallgerður and Gunnar. Aside from this, the Norwegian novelist and critic Hans E. Kinck was probably the first to assail the portrait of Gunnar as we find it in *Njáls saga* ["Et par ting om ættesagaen," *Festskrift til Gerhard Gran*, 1916]. It seems clear that this picture of Gunnar got under his skin. And Sigurður Guðmundsson, who sought in his *Skírnir* to trace the history of this saga hero and the development of the Gunnar legend, goes so far as to say that the author's fondness for his warrior-hero vitiated the saga ["Gunnar á Hlíðarenda," *Skírnir*, 1918]. At the same time, Sigurður is able to appreciate the ethical refinement of the character portrait and the high esteem it has enjoyed for this reason. And I suspect that the view is quite generally held that the strong romantic radiance which has fallen on Gunnar has distorted the human dimensions of his image to a greater or lesser degree.

I am afraid that such views have been strengthened by the suspicion that not everything which is related about Gunnar is historically correct, and that his portrait and personality bear the stamp of a later age. But as we have already noted, historical inaccuracies are of importance only if they are detrimental to the verisimilitude of the literary work. And such suspicions regarding historical inaccuracies in the portrayal of a character have nothing to do with the aesthetic enjoyment of a work of literature. Even if the anachronisms or the transgressions against the spirit of the times are obvious, narrative and character depiction can be so excellent that the historical inaccuracies fade into the background. Who would dream of making a fuss about the fact that *Antony and Cleopatra* bears little resemblance to the Egypt of the Ptolemys? All that matters is the excellence of the character portraits themselves. Of course the portrait of Gunnar is not realistic, but realism is not the only form of art. It is also artistic to be able to expand the dimensions of a man in a poetic manner. This character portrait is enveloped by an idealistic, romantic radiance—but let us not forget that this contributes to the poetic beauty of the picture. Gunnar is endowed with those characteristics which, because of the nature of his role in the story, he must not lack; and what is even more important, his portrait still bears the stamp of a real human being, the appearance of a living man, despite the romantic radiance surrounding it. And above all, Gunnar's portrait possesses a unique and unmistakable individuality. The more I study this portrait, the more deeply impressed I become with its gentleness, as it emerges from the narrative, and with the author's interpretation of Gunnar's sensitivity and self-control, of his competitive spirit and conscientiousness, and of the fine nuances of these traits of character. Gunnar of Hlíðarendi is the most modern of all the characters of the saga. He is what we might call a man of the nineteenth century. Is it not strange that so many people today find it difficult to recognize and accept him for what he is?

The depiction of Kári, on the other hand, seems to me to have suffered much more from romantic influence. This character portrait lacks richness. And yet even here we are sometimes surprised to discover unsuspected traits, such as his ironic sense of humor. But if we read the story in its entirety, we can see that the author had good reasons for depicting Kári as he did. . . .

Höskuldur Hvítanessgoði is a character I should not like to have missing from the saga. Many persons object to this character portrayal because, they maintain, no one like that could have lived in Iceland during the eleventh century. In this they are probably correct, although it is difficult to measure the remarkably strong influence of new currents such as Christianity on certain individuals, especially when these spiritual currents are just beginning to become effective. But men like Höskuldur certainly did exist in Iceland during the thirteenth century—not many, to be sure, but some. From the point of view of our own day this character portrait seems unrealistic and unnatural; indeed, it seems almost incredible. But all of this tells us nothing about its authenticity. Truth is often stranger than fiction, and real events sometimes impress us as improbable when utilized in fiction. For the thread of the story the figure of Höskuldur is essential. Without it, the tragedy in the life of Njáll and Skarphéðinn would not be nearly so profound and dreadful as it is. And finally, there is great poetic beauty in this character portrait.

III

Because they contrast so markedly with the remaining twenty-two major characters, these three portraits add to the broad diversity of the saga. Character portrayals in which the colors are more blended, and in which the author's curiosity and his sympathy with his characters are in balance, are less strongly molded and colored by his idealism. "Paint me as I am," said Cromwell, "wart and all." These words must not, of course, be taken at face value, for the photograph is scarcely the highest form of art. But properly understood, they possess a certain validity: a picture should reveal and not conceal the characteristic features of the subject. Even the wart is worth including insofar as it can be given some artistic significance and if it does not conflict with the nature and purpose of the work. A good example of this is the beardlessness of Njáll—an apparently trifling detail, which nevertheless plays an important role in the story. Another example is the paleness of Skarphéðin's face. Similarly, small incidents can be filled with great meaning, as for instance the description of Þórhallur Ásgrímsson when he learned of the burning of Njáll: His body became swollen; a stream of blood gushed from both ears and could not be checked. He fell down unconscious, and then the bleeding stopped. His deep grief and desire for revenge are revealed (and find momentary release) in this manner, and these feelings also, it seems, later on cause his foot ailment, which cannot be cured until he is on the field of battle.

In *Njáls saga* Verðandi prevails. Events approach, pass by, and continue on their swift, unrelenting course. Willingly or unwillingly men become involved and are swept along. Sometimes the stream of events lifts them up toward the light and the sun, and sometimes it drags them down into the depths. It brings them happiness which is never completely exhausted, and inflicts wounds which never heal. Most of the people in the saga are consistent within themselves; their basic character does not change under the stress and strain of life, but merely responds to challenge. But sometimes the onslaughts of life have a permanent effect on the mental and emotional life of individuals; their basic character is not altered, but the course of their inner life is changed. The most remarkable examples of such character development are Hallgerður and Njáll.

This process of genesis and evolution is not simple; it is not merely a matter of stimulus and response. Events are brought about by many causes. The provocations and motives which impel a man to perform a single deed are usually many and varied. Events are brought forth through the combined force of a whole complex of external and internal causes. And it must not be forgotten that frequently these motives and stimuli occurred over a considerable span of time. Often new irritations aggravate old, encapsulated, half-forgotten wounds. And no form of hatred is more certain to erupt into violence than when old, repressed, smoldering resentments are inflamed by new provocations.

In the story of Gunnar we see a great warrior and hero who is more reluctant than others to kill, a man who is not easily provoked to fight, but who is most formidable when he cannot escape doing so. The heart of such a man is moved by many feelings and emotions which no one else is aware of. Finally all these precipitate the critical decision of his life: contrary to all expectations and driven by a powerful impulse, he defies the sentence of banishment imposed upon him by the General Assembly. He refuses to depart from his beautiful farm even though this should cost him his life. The reason may be that he has grown weary of living, but another passage in the story suggests that he is unwilling to capitulate to his enemies.

In the story of Flosi following the slaying of Höskuldur Hvítanessgoði we can discern a mind in conflict with itself. We can sense the storm which rages there as Flosi rides away from his farm, Vorsabær, to attend the Assembly; later all signs seem to point toward a peaceful reconciliation. But then mere trifles suffice to rekindle the smoldering anger so that it gains the upper hand. At still another place in the saga we see a Norwegian who knows that death awaits him if he settles in Iceland; yet he does so, even though he certainly does not want to die. We see Eyjólfur Bölverksson, who becomes Flosi's chief advocate at the trial following the burning of Njáll. He well knows that it will seal his own doom, and yet Flosi's golden arm ring and harsh demands are more persuasive than this certain knowledge. These men act as though under a spell which has deprived them of their normal manner of behavior. The author of *Njáls saga* doubtless knew stories of spells and enchantments which robbed men of their will power or drove them into actions which were contrary to their nature. But he no doubt had also seen and experienced such inconsistencies and incongruities in human thought and behavior. *Njáls saga* is very much concerned with the role of the will in human life.

As in *Njáls saga*, psychological struggle and emotional conflict are very much in evidence in the dramas of Racine and Corneille. But here everything is out in the open. The audience sees and hears everything on the stage; the characters do not hesitate to express themselves freely. In *Njála*, too, many individual incidents and utterances bear unmistakable and memorable witness to the inner struggle of the characters. But the reader is not given a constant insight into their minds and hearts; rather, he is given brief views or glimpses of what is going on there. And what he perceives is not a logical debate, but a blind storm of passion. It sometimes seems to the reader as if he were gazing into the twilight, where half or fully concealed forces and unknown motives are at work no less than those which are fully apparent. Sometimes he may doubt that this or that person really understands himself. Modern psychology has helped us to gain a deeper comprehension of such matters through a better understanding of the subconscious and of other related factors. And writers today have learned much from psychology. But the author of *Njála*

had to depend entirely on his own observations and insights and on his artistic instinct.

All of this tends to make it more difficult for the reader to understand many of the saga characters. To be sure, all of the characters are drawn with clear and distinct lines, and each portrait possesses an inner consistency. But a relatively large number of these men and women are of a complex and puzzling nature, and a great deal is said about them in the saga. It is quite obvious that the author was strongly attracted to them, and that he put forth every effort to portray them. His people are not like the characters of Sophocles or Menander, but Hallgerður and Lady Macbeth would have had a great deal to talk about, even though their fates and passions were not the same. But that is a long story, and I cannot attempt to tell it here.

IV

It may be that people who are used to the psychological analyses of modern literature will find some of the preceding statements strange or surprising. They may regard the comments in the saga about the motives, feelings, and thoughts of the characters somewhat meager. And at first they may think that what has already been said here about the character portraits in *Njála* is overstated or exaggerated.

It is true enough that the psychological analyses in *Njála* are few and modest in extent. The thoughts and feelings of the characters are not dissected before the reader. To be sure, the reader is now and then given a glimpse into the mind and heart of a character, but this is something quite different from the modern stream of consciousness technique. The statements about the characters of *Njáls saga* constitute portraits in the literal sense of the word. The author wishes to portray his people as they are, as living entities in all the struggles and vicissitudes of life. The inner character, the internal nature of the people, is the nucleus, of course, for it is from this internal nature of a man that the forces derive which exert an influence on the outer world, on other individuals and events.

As is customary in the Icelandic sagas of national heroes, the author gives us a preliminary description of his characters when he introduces them into his story. Farther along in the saga, at the most suitable places, he lets us know something about their thoughts and feelings. But these revelations never turn into psychological analyses. For the most part, the people are depicted from the outside. We know what they are from the way they appear, from what they do and say, and from what others say about them. Frequently the basic characteristics of an individual are revealed through his dealings with others. In this method of relative or indirect character delineation the author of *Njáls saga* has achieved a degree of skill that may be called consummate. One minor incident can suffice to characterize many persons. This is a narrative technique which the author of *Njála* learned from earlier masters of the art of saga writing. It is a technique which reminds us somewhat of modern stage plays, especially those in which the characters are not permitted to indulge in lyric effusion and introspective monologues. The techniques of the saga writer are narrowly circumscribed by convention. But once a writer has mastered these techniques, he can achieve considerable success in depicting the inner motives of even the most complex and puzzling characters. Psychological analysis tends to encroach upon artistic convention, and artistic convention threatens to dull analysis. When the artist succeeds in reconciling the demands of both, he may be destined to create a literary work of exceptional merit.

V

. . . [Let us look at] the wide range of people portrayed. We see here men and women from all walks of life and from all social classes. We find a host of aristocrats with the rank of *goði,* and yet each one is different from the rest: Höskuldur Dala-Kollson, Mörður gígja, Mörður Valgarðsson, Gizur hvíti, Hjalti Skeggjason, Skafti Þóroddsson, Snorri goði, Flosi, Hallur of Síða, Guðmundur ríki, and many more. There is no sharp line of demarcation drawn between these *goðar* on the one hand and chieftains without authority and farmers on the other hand, and this includes both prosperous landowners and farmers of more modest means. In addition there are household servants, sheepherders and farmhands, freedmen and thralls. With this last group, the character depictions tend to be somewhat sketchier, drawn with a few, but usually clear, strokes; and Þórður leysingjason (the agnomen means "son of a freed thrall") and the farmhand Atli stand out clearly as individuals. There are also a number of Norwegians, most of them rather indifferent. Of the landlopers, the most memorable is Kaupa-Héðinn, whose coarse picture the author drew with genuine relish. And finally, there are bands of vagrants and beggars, a nameless mass, from which no individuals emerge. But even so, these masses are teeming with life and activity. The spread in age among the characters is equally large. At Bergþórshvoll lives the ancient crone Sæunn, half senile and yet prescient; her intriguing portrait is drawn with sadness blended with humor. At the other extreme is the boy Þórður, the son of Kári, who refuses to leave his grandmother in the burning house. As in the Icelandic sagas generally, however, the majority of the characters are adults, neither very young nor very old.

I shall not attempt to give a survey here of the traits of character of all the distinctive persons in the saga, but I cannot refrain from pointing out that to a certain degree these persons can be divided into groups according to their attitudes toward life and other qualities without in any way detracting from their unique individuality. I have already alluded to the fact that artistically portrayed characters of earlier poetic works can become models for later writers, and that large numbers of individuals are thus created who bear a certain family resemblance to each other. Thus Njáll has certain features in common with Óðinn, while Skarphéðinn belongs to the group I called the dark-haired heroes, and Gunnar and Helgi and several others can be classified among the blond champions. Gunnar and Kári are colored by a certain romantic light, and thus they have much in common with some of the splendid warriors of *Laxdœla,* although the colors in *Njála* are more subdued. But there are other attributes too which differentiate the characters and character portraits in *Njála.* First of all there is a striking difference between the men of thought

and the men of action (and there is an exceptionally large number of sages and wise men: Hrútur, Mörður gígja, Skafti Þóroddsson, Mörður Valgarðsson, Snorri goði, Hallur of Síða, Þórhallur Ásgrímsson, Eyjólfur Bölverksson, and above all Njáll himself). Equally obvious is another division: that between men and women who possess will power and who discipline themselves in accordance with their ethical views, and those who lack moral scruples and restraints. All of the evil-doers belong to the latter group. It must be clear to all who have given the matter serious thought that to the author of *Njáls saga* this distinction is of the utmost importance in the life of man.

I shall mention two additional groups or types of characters, of lesser importance, and yet not unworthy of note. Several persons are endowed with the faculty of self-criticism and the ability to express this criticism in a mocking or ironic manner. Skarphéðinn possesses this ability, as do Atli and Hrappur also—both of whom quite candidly characterize themselves as rascals. Njáll too is able to scoff at himself: when he lies down to await death in his flaming house, it is with the comment that he has long had the reputation of being fond of ease.

And finally, at two points in the story the conflict between wishful thinking and reality is the focal point of character portrayal. In the case of Björn of Mörk this is quite obvious, but the conflict also provides the key for an understanding of Skammkell. Regarded from this point of view, his thoughts and desires are clearly revealed to us. It is interesting to note that men who are basically so unlike each other as Skammkell and Björn share the qualities of self-adulation and braggadocio. Their similarity in this respect is underscored by their use of similar words in similar situations. On one occasion Skammkell says to his friend Otkell (chapter 49): "I shall go out with you, for we have to be clever about this. I want to be nearest to you when your need is greatest." The conversation between Kári and Björn runs as follows (chapter 151): "What plan shall we adopt now? I want to see how clever you are," said Kári. Björn replied, "Do you think it important for us to be clever?" "Yes, indeed," said Kári. "Then you will discover," said Björn, "that I am not lacking in cleverness any more than in hardihood." These words of Björn shed light on the character of Skammkell.

VI

With such a large number of character portraits in a single work, an author runs the risk of having them turn into a sort of chaotic picture gallery. But the author of *Njáls saga* avoids this danger through his skill in arrangement and composition. A clear distinction is made between leading and secondary characters, and the saga naturally tells us more about the former than the latter. The figure of Njáll towers above all other people in the saga, but he shares the stage with Gunnar in the first part and with Skarphéðinn, Hallgerður, Bergþóra, and Mörður in the second part of the trilogy. In the final part of the story Kári and Flosi share the interest of the reader between them. The other characters come and go depending on the role they have to play in a given scene. We might say that the spotlight is constantly focused on the main characters, but only occasionally and momentarily on the minor ones.

Quite often two characters are seen side by side, such as Hrútur and Höskuldur, or Njáll and Gunnar, and then one of them is usually a man of wisdom while the other is a man of action. Or else we find two warriors together, such as Gunnar and Kolskeggur, or Skarphéðinn and his brothers (both of whom together have the role of one man, in accordance with Olrik's "law of twins"). In such cases one of the two warriors has the center of the stage while the other serves as a sort of foil by means of which the dominant member of the pair is more fully characterized. From time to time, however, the spotlight also falls on the lesser character, so that we likewise get a good idea of his character. An example of this is Helgi Njálsson, who stands in the shadow of his brother Skarphéðinn during the greater part of the story. But when Helgi makes his voyage abroad, he occupies the center of the stage, and the reader almost has the feeling that he sees in him a rejuvenated Njáll. The portrait of Helgi which we are shown in this episode is both pleasing and fascinating.

Often little is required to delineate the secondary characters. One person wakes the other by arousing his sympathy or antipathy, and from this interplay both come to life. Thus dead names momentarily assume the features of living beings, and in turn quicken others, until the entire shadow host of *Njáls saga* has come to life. Each time they return to the stage, the supporting characters are made to reveal more about themselves until their portraits are complete.

From what has been said, it might seem that these characters are like pampered children, who simply accept everything which is given to them, and that the author can do with them as he pleases. But this, strangely enough, is not the case. Every significant work of art maintains a mysterious independence in relationship to its creator. It develops from its nucleus in accordance with laws which are difficult for the artist to master or to change. And so it happens that the author of *Njáls saga* becomes entranced and enchanted by his children, and they run away with him. We see in *Njála* how some of the secondary characters acquire intriguing peculiarities or become involved in striking incidents which arouse our interest in them and increase their power of attraction over us. Svanur of Svanshóll is not merely wicked; he also possesses magic powers, which cast a strange supernatural aura over him. In the picture of Earl Hákon we find the gift of second sight added to the sympathy and antipathy of the kings' sagas, and this added feature renews and retouches the entire portrait. Almost everything that is said about Þórhallur Ásgrímsson is intended to make him memorable and unique; no one reacts so strangely to the death of Njáll as he does.

Some of the minor characters are even more demanding of the author and the reader than these. Hrappur was intended, of course, to become an outlaw in Norway, and the composition and economy of the story require that this incident be related rather briefly. But the author soon becomes so intrigued with this villainous creature of his that he devotes two precious chapters to him. Björn of Mörk was supposed to add a light touch to the saga, which needs comedy at that point. At first the author is a bit hard on

Björn, but he soon takes a fancy to him; by the time he finishes this episode, he has created a masterpiece of character portrayal. It is not at all unusual for great artists to lose control over their creations; a good example is Shylock the Jew, who strives with might and main and overwhelms the comedy about the merchant of Venice.

VII

The author of *Njála* is a great idealist. Like Boileau, he would call a cat a cat and Rollet a villain. But the phenomena of human life can have a strong attraction for him, the repulsive ones no less than the pleasing ones. Some of the most remarkable character portraits in the saga show this balance. If the author's sympathy for his characters is sometimes not very strong, his curiosity and desire to see and understand are so much the stronger.

Good examples of this are the four chief villains of the saga: Þjóstólfur, Hrappur, Skammkell, and Mörður. All are branded with the same mark: they lack moral checks and restraints, and live according to the view that they have a right to do as they please. Idealists around the turn of the century had a distrust of these character portraits, but nowadays at least we know that such people do exist. Except for this one common characteristic, however, these villains are quite unique.

Hrappur and Þjóstólfur are both homeless, unruly fellows who never hesitate to resort to violence if they feel that someone has stepped on their toes. Hrappur is an adventurous fellow, ingratiating or impudent as the situation demands, mealy-mouthed or loudmouthed, eager to seize every opportunity for pleasure—a ladies' man who thinks only of the passing moment. He does not hesitate to indulge every sensual desire, and for this reason he is constantly on the run, trying to escape the consequences. There is nothing to indicate that he is not content with this sort of life, and he is shrewd and slippery as an eel when it comes to wriggling out of just punishment. He is shameless, impious (he is the only atheist in the whole story), and malicious, and he dies with words of scorn about himself on his lips.

Whereas Hrappur can be smooth and polished, Þjóstólfur is always coarse and bristling. He is a turbulent fellow who can't avoid clashing with people wherever he happens to be. He is endowed with a certain primitive loyalty, and this loyalty together with a fear of several men are the only things which keep him somewhat in check. He does not hesitate to swing his huge, heavy-shafted ax, and he too is in the habit of indulging every impulse. But there is one desire that cannot be fulfilled. As the poet Grímur Thomsen expressed it:

> Hallgerðar hann engum unni,
> og eigi mátti hann sjálfur njóta;
> þeir, sem ástir hennar hljóta,
> hans fá koss af öxarmunni.

> ("Hallgerð's love he granted no one, and he himself could not win her favor; those who did gain her love received the kiss of his ax.")

This deed of jealousy, his killing of Glúmur, does not bring him the fulfillment of his wishes. His slaying of

Hallgerð's two husbands does not gain him her favor. The deeds of this man of action are the useless and worthless outlets for his desires, and their very senselessness destroys him inwardly. Hrút's sword stroke comes none too soon.

Skammkell is not the most imposing rascal in the story, but his description is certainly not the least remarkable. He is somewhat harder to understand than the first two. Skammkell is dishonest and malicious, and constantly tries to harm others even though he himself does not gain anything (or even hope to gain anything) by it. And yet he has little in common with the conventional villains of popular mystery novels or romantic tales who bear little resemblance to living human beings and who do evil for no apparent reason. Skammkel's evil deeds have valid motives. Let us take a look at the saga.

In chapter 49 Gunnar comes to the farm Kirkjubær to offer Otkell compensation for Hallgerð's theft. Skammkell is already there, and when Otkell and his men go out, Skammkell says the following words, which have already been quoted in part: "I shall go out with you, for we have to be clever about this. I want to be nearest to you when your need is greatest as it now is. I advise you to act important." First of all, we must consider the sliminess in these words of Skammkell about his trustworthiness and his desire to help. His words are those of a hypocrite, and here, as so often is the case with hypocrites, we find truth blended with falsehood. Skammkell wants Gunnar's visit to Kirkjubær to turn out badly; indeed, he wishes him every possible kind of disgrace—if for no other reason than that Gunnar enjoys great fame and popularity. At first blush this may seem to be a strange explanation, and yet envy is reason enough for ill will—at any rate in real life, if not in fiction. Skammkell pretends to be Otkel's friend, and in the end they are actually both killed together; yet he never is concerned about protecting Otkell from danger as a friend would do—at least once in a while. And this fact is significant, for it suggests that there are other concerns which are of greater importance to Skammkell than the good fortune and happiness of Otkell.

The similarity which we have already observed between the words of Skammkell and those of Björn of Mörk afford us a glimpse into the hidden recesses of Skammkel's mind. As strange as it may seem at first glance, his manner of thinking is not completely unrelated to that of Björn. He is a sullen daydreamer. He dresses up reality with lies and wishful thinking, but he lacks Björn's kindness and nobleness of heart and harmless boasting. He jumps at every opportunity to attempt to make his desires come true; in so doing he confuses reality with his own lies, and this makes him a most dangerous man.

Skammkell dreams of men who are independent and defiant, men from whom the most famous warriors seek help but receive nothing but haughty repudiation, men who make a litigant offer them every possible redress and then subject him to humiliation and send him away with nothing accomplished. The men Skammkell identifies himself with in his daydreams are hard-bitten and proud. They thunder out a scornful summons to their enemies to appear at the General Assembly for trial, ride them down and bloody them with their spurs, and laugh at them as they go racing off. These men are killers, proud, unrelenting, and cruel—chieftains with great authority who terrorize people through their overwhelming power.

Skammkell himself is only an average man, if that. He has no outstanding qualities of excellence. He is despised and disdained—and that is the source of his cruelty and vengefulness. Far from being a warrior, he is actually a coward, as one can see best from the fact that he takes to his bed ill at the General Assembly at the very time Otkel's suit for theft against Gunnar is on the agenda. By contrast, he is quite cocky during the journey to summon Gunnar, and when Otkell rides Gunnar down and wounds him with his spurs, he is transported with delight, for his daydreams are being fulfilled. He is so beside himself that the thought of danger does not cross his mind.

Skammkell himself is neither a champion nor a chieftain. But he has Otkell, and through his friendship for Otkell he can experience vicariously the pleasure of being a hero and a chieftain. To be sure, this has its drawbacks. It is possible for Otkell to flex his muscles because of his relationship to the people of Mosfell, but in reality he often has to be prodded into action. Otkell is not averse to peace and reconciliation, and at such times Skammkell has to intervene as best he can. He musters all of his shrewdness and shamelessness to convince Otkell of the defects of Gunnar's offers of redress, and in the end he succeeds in bringing Gunnar's attempted settlement to naught. Through his visit to Mosfell, Skammkell is able to compel matters to go as he wishes. Upon returning he lies unblushingly and with great enthusiasm: "There is no need to speak softly about this case. . . . They also thought it of the greatest importance that you behaved so boldly. . . ."

Skammkell is terribly eager for something big and exciting to happen—quarrels, summonses to appear in court, killings. He is quite enchanted by such matters. And when reality threatens to grow dull, Skammkell is prepared to brighten it up with his untruths. Mörður Valgardsson, the other liar in the story, can always distinguish between truth and fiction, but I am not sure that this is the case with Skammkell. Dishonesty has penetrated to the very heart of this perverse daydreamer.

Unlike Skammkell, Mörður generally does not meddle in other people's affairs, but he too sometimes has to be prodded into action. He is a clever man, skillful at maneuvering on the chessboard of life. For him the end justifies the means, and he has no compunctions about cold-bloodedly destroying his enemies, the innocent as well as the guilty. He can take swift action or bide his time as the occasion demands. He is endowed with a certain magnetic force; everyone is favorably impressed by what he says, and few can resist believing him. He is pleasant to get along with socially. He loves his wife as dearly as his own eyes, and shows concern for her kinsmen. This certainly does not make him a psychological puzzle. The only thing that is difficult to understand about him is the motives for some of his actions, especially for the evil he sows between the sons of Njáll and Höskuldur Hvítanessgoði.

Jóhann Sigurjónsson in his play *Løgneren* (*The Liar*) explained the slander which Mörður carries back and forth between Höskuldur and the Njálssons on the basis of two motives: the struggle for power and jealousy. But it is like carrying coals to Newcastle to employ two of the strongest passions of the human heart at one and the same time. A double motive tends to have a weakening effect when either one of the two would be quite sufficient. The author of *Njála* employs a different method: he has the past intensify the present. Mörður has harbored a grudge against Njáll ever since he unsuccessfully supported Gunnar's enemies, and he has harbored rancor toward Skarphéðinn ever since Skarphéðinn humiliated him by compelling him to grant self-judgment to Gunnar's son Högni (chapter 79). Additional hatred is engendered through the fact that Höskuldur has begun to draw some of his thing-men away from him to his newly-created *goðorð*.

When his father, Valgarður inn grái, incites Mörður to destroy Höskuldur and the sons of Njáll, he reminds him of the money Skarphéðinn forced him to pay after Gunnar's death (chapter 107). Mörður had twice accepted money in return for his support of Gunnar's enemies, and he freely admitted his avariciousness to Þorgeir Otkelsson (chapter 67: "It is well known that I never refuse money . . ."). And yet it would be absurd to regard his love of money as the basic cause of his enmity toward Gunnar or to assume that he joined Gunnar's enemies out of greed (and that his hatred for Gunnar was secondary to it). The opposite is the truth. Money helped to influence him to take part in these cases, but the underlying motive was his animosity toward Gunnar. This may seem strange at first, but it can easily be shown to be true.

Gunnar had done his kinswoman Unnur, the mother of Mörður, a great favor at the risk of his own life: he had reclaimed from her former husband, Hrútur, her share of their property—a large amount of money, which had made her a very desirable match (chapter 24). When Unnur offered Gunnar a share of the money in payment, he refused to accept it; "but he asserted that he felt he had a greater claim for future support on her and her kinsmen than on anyone else. And Unnur agreed with him." The cruel irony of this is soon revealed.

Now Valgarður grái (chapter 25) makes a proposal of marriage to Unnur, and she marries him "without consulting any of her kinsmen. But Gunnar and Njáll and many others disapproved of this, for he was a malicious and unpopular man." A coolness develops between Unnur and her kinsmen. A feeling of ingratitude turns this coolness into secret animosity. This is a strange and noteworthy situation. No one hates Skarphéðinn with more unrelenting fury than Grani Gunnarsson, the very person whose life he once spared and whose father's slaying he had avenged. Good deeds can lead to ingratitude as well as to gratitude, to hatred as well as to love. And it is not at all certain that the hatred of ingratitude is any quicker to die out than the love of gratitude.

From Valgarður nothing else was to be expected than animosity and resentment toward Gunnar. Gunnar had affronted him by disapproving of his marriage. And Mörður could hardly escape being poisoned by the venomous at-

mosphere which prevailed in his home as he was growing up. Thus it is scarcely a matter of chance that when he was fully grown, "he treated his kinsmen badly, but Gunnar worst of all." Later (chapter 46) we read that "he bitterly envied Gunnar of Hlíðarendi." Envy is a common emotion, which all human beings know and understand. Although some writers might hesitate to call it by its right name, that is not the case with the author of *Njála*.

VIII

Finnur Jónsson somewhere comments that in *Njáls saga* all human passions have a free rein except the love of man and woman. No one would ever suggest that *Njála* is a love story such as *Laxdœla* or *Gunnlaugs saga* or *Kormaks saga*. And yet it does have something to say about this human relationship.

In *Kormaks saga* the author depicts the development of the love of Kormakur and Steingerður—at first as delicate as the dust on the wings of a butterfly, not unmixed with playful teasing, and then, quite suddenly, powerful and ardent. At one place in *Njála* the author would have had an excellent opportunity to do something similar: during the courtship of Njál's foster son, Höskuldur Þráinsson, when Flosi asks his niece Hildigunnur whether she wishes to accept him as her husband.

> She said she was a proud woman—"and I am not certain that this proposal is advisable for me, since such men are involved—and that all the more so, since this man does not have a *goðorð*. You promised me that you would not marry me to anyone who was not a chieftain."
>
> "That is sufficient reason," said Flosi, "for me to reject the proposal, if you do not wish to marry Höskuldur."
>
> "I didn't say," she replied, "that I don't want to marry Höskuldur if they provide him with a *goðorð*. But otherwise I won't consider it."

Hildigunn's pride is described extremely well, but the affection which is obviously already beginning to awaken between her and Höskuldur does not cast its faint warming light over the scene, nor is there any hint of encouragement or good-natured teasing in her expression as she makes her stipulations. But what could this great narrative artist not have made of this scene if he had been in the mood to do so! I must confess that I do not know whether the resulting portrait of Hildigunnur would have been any better than the cold, aristocratic picture he has created, but it would have been more humanly appealing.

Nor does this saga show the glorious beauty of passion, as we find it revealed in some of the Eddic poems, in *Tristrams saga*, or in *Laxdœla*. The author of *Njála* had the story of Guðrún Ósvífursdóttir, the heroine of *Laxdœla saga*, in mind when he created the portrait of Hallgerður—but what a difference there is between them.

Passion can blaze with pure, clear flames. We see something of this in the grief of Hildigunnur over the death of Höskuldur. But usually it seems to smolder down deep and flash out through the dross and slag, a searing fire that consumes and destroys more than it warms and illuminates. One need only think of the affair between Hrútur and Queen Gunnhildur, of the hurtful relationship between Hrútur and Unnur, or of the misfortune which resulted from the three marriages of Hallgerður, to cite but a few examples. At first blush we might feel inclined to attribute this to the ascetic spirit of the Middle Ages, which had such a deep-rooted aversion to the "lusts of the flesh." A closer view of the matter, however, shows that this explanation is not satisfactory. Something quite different is involved here, something that goes back to the life experience of the author rather than to the spirit of an age. It is just as though everything were enveloped in the grayness of pessimism, so that this great passion is revealed in its vehemence but not in its colorful beauty and splendor. In this connection I cannot help thinking of another writer who during a certain period of his life seems to have been seized by a similar kind of pessimism. The author of *Hamlet* seems to have been strangely obsessed with the idea of the corruption of the flesh, of defilement and incest, when he wrote about problems of human existence in that work. And I doubt whether more is known about the reasons for his pessimism than for that of the author of *Njála.*

This grayness, which often darkens the colors in *Njáls saga*, is in no way prejudicial to the breadth and diversity of the subject matter. Indeed, matters are discussed here which occur seldom or never in other sagas. A story such as that of the married life of Hallgerður, for example, is not frequently encountered in saga literature. Most saga writers would have made a wide circle around such a problem, which is far more difficult to cope with successfully than, for instance, the story of Helga in fagra in *Gunnlaugs saga*. Episodes such as the affair between Hrútur and Queen Gunnhildur are very infrequent in the *Íslendingasögur* (even though they might not seem so strange to people today), and yet this episode is so essential to the story that the author endows it with sorcery. Scarcely any other saga author would have attempted a story such as that which Unnur tells her father about her experiences with Hrútur, and many a writer of later times would have hesitated to do so.

Njáls saga is a story for men. This is not to suggest that the author did not expect to have women among his audience, but he wrote from a man's point of view, with a man's understanding—and lack of understanding—of women. It is difficult to say what is gained and what is lost thereby without weighing off one against the other. *Njáls saga* lacks the leniency and sensitivity of *Laxdœla* in regard to women. Although the author of *Njála* was a peace-loving and conciliatory man, the saga mentions only one woman who tries to prevent hostility: that is Hróðný, who dissuades her brother Ingjaldur from joining the attack against Njáll (chapter 124). But there were special reasons for this, and Hróðný made no attempt to dissuade her brother from fighting against the enemies of Njáll. On the contrary, she was actually exposing him to danger by persuading him to withdraw from the plot against Njáll. One of the most effective scenes in the entire story is the one in which Hildigunnur incites her uncle Flosi to avenge the death of her husband. It must be borne in mind that the author himself embraces the concept of honor which gives rise to her taunting words, as do almost all the characters

in his story. Thus there is no cause for censuring Hildigunnur on this score.

Here, then, we have an example of how women incite men to vengeance and thus stir up active hostility. . . . Sometimes it seems as though an idea like that of Pandora crossed the author's mind when he wrote about women such as Gunnhildur, Hallgerður, Guðrún náttsól, and Kormlöð. It is strange, therefore, that, with the exception of the two killings by Hallgerð's foster father, Þjóstólfur (chapters 11 and 17), there is no violence in *Njála* caused by the jealousy of two men in love with the same woman.

During the lifetime of Hallgerður there is one period which contrasts markedly with the rest, and that is her marriage to Glúmur. This period is characterized by a warmth and a remarkable candor and a tender congeniality such as occurs only rarely in the story. Something of this feeling is found in the words spoken by Gizur hvíti about the love of Mörður Valgarðsson for his wife (chapter 135), and especially in the union between Njáll and Bergþóra. So powerful can this harmony between husband and wife become that Hallgerður, during her marriage with Glúmur, is able to keep herself under control, and Bergþóra never transgresses a certain limit in her behavior. The most magnificent scene in the saga which is inspired by the love of man and woman and which glorifies their unity of heart and mind is the one in which Bergþóra refuses to leave Njáll in their burning house (chapter 129).

IX

Although some women might feel that the author of *Njáls saga* has treated their sex unfairly, most would probably be pleased at the large number of magnificent and splendid and memorable female characters he has included among his store of character portraits.

Many women are mentioned in the saga, and some of them, of course, are little more than names. This is true of Njál's daughters Helga and Þorgerður, and of his daughters-in-law Þórhildur and Ástríður of Djúpárbakki, as well as of Bergljót, the kinswoman of Earl Hákon. Somewhat more distinct are the pictures which emerge of the chieftain's daughter, Þórhalla Ásgrímsdóttir; Hildigunnur læknir (the Healer); and Þórhildur skáldkona (the Poetess); and Þorgerður, the daughter of Glúmur and Hallgerður. There are several examples of kindhearted women who were easily beguiled by men, such as Ormhildur, the kinswoman of Gunnar (chapter 71); Guðrún, the daughter of Guðbrandur í Dölum in Norway (chapter 87); and Guðrún náttsól, who had a fondness for foreigners (chapters 61 and 64). Two excellent chapters are devoted to Hróðný, the friend of Njáll and mother of his son Höskuldur; and Valgerður, the mistress of the house at Mörk, is also described vividly and in considerable detail.

Then there are the full-length portraits of the main women characters: Unnur, the daughter of Mörður gígja; Queen Gunnhildur of Norway; Hallgerður; Bergþóra; Hildigunnur; and Kormlöð, the mother of King Sigtryggur of Ireland. All of them are proud and passionate except Unnur, who seems broken in spirit because of her ill-starred marriage to Hrútur. The two queens are mature women, eager to enjoy life and wield power; both of them could have belonged to the life of the Renaissance. There is a certain grandeur about Gunnhildur. In her character we find voluptuousness and love of comfort strangely blended with harshness and cruelty, but the dominant trait in her personality is her insatiable sensual desire. She keeps Hrútur in her castle much as Tannhäuser was kept in the Mountain of Venus. But in time he grows more and more quiet and takes to thinking about returning home, and she begins to suspect that there is another woman in the game. She accuses him of having a sweetheart in Iceland, but he denies it. The thought rankles in her mind, and when they take leave of each other, she puts her arms about his neck and kisses him. Then she puts a curse on Hrút's union with her unknown rival and concludes with these words: "Neither of us has conducted himself well. You did not trust me . . . and I have laid a spell on you." Hrútur laughs and goes away.

Kormlöð is in many ways the opposite of Gunnhildur. She permits her son Sigtryggur to use her as a decoy both for Sigurður, Earl of Orkney, and for the viking Bróðir. She seems to be quite unconcerned about the possible outcome of this crafty scheming, and would quite likely not have been displeased if the two had come to blows on her account. She herself seems to be motivated by no other desires except for power and above all for revenge against her divorced husband, King Brjánn. She was good, the saga says, in all those qualities which were not subject to her will, but utterly wicked in everything which was subject to it.

Let us turn from these two women to two others, who resemble them in certain respects, but who are much more appealing: Hildigunnur and Bergþóra. The initial descriptions of these women are similar. The author tells us that Bergþóra was "a spirited and high-minded woman, but somewhat harsh-natured," and he says that Hildigunnur was "a spirited and very beautiful woman. She was more skillful at needlework than most women. She was very cruel and harsh-natured, but noble when that was called for." The two women have the qualities of spirit, loyalty, and harshness of nature in common, although the harsh nature of Hildigunnur is somewhat more strongly emphasized, and in addition she is called cruel. There is no doubt what the author had in mind here: her desire for revenge for the slaying of Höskuldur, which is not satisfied with the most honorable settlement short of blood vengeance.

Because of her beauty and skill in handicraft, Hildigunnur is a desirable match, just as Unnur was because of her beauty and courteous behavior, and this is scarcely surprising. In the description of Bergþóra, however, there is no mention of beauty, and Hallgerður can tell her to her face without contradiction that she has turtle-back nails on every finger. But everything about Hildigunnur is lovely.

The word "harsh-natured" can have various meanings, but the events of the saga define Hildigunn's character more precisely. When Höskuldur with his companions comes to ask for her hand in marriage, we get to see the pride of a woman who was descended from one of the greatest aristocratic families of Iceland and who was

reared in one of the most majestic regions of that beautiful country, remote from the more densely settled areas. She hears a faint murmur from those far-distant places; but her spirit is molded by the magnitude and solitude of nature, and she demands of her suitor that distinction with which only a chieftaincy can endow him. A strange coolness lies over the beginning of their courtship; the loveliness of youth and the awakening fondness for each other are enveloped in a cold veil.

The saga does not deprive Hildigunnur of her loveliness, but reveals her finest qualities. She gets along splendidly with Bergþóra, despite the fact that both of them are strong personalities. The saga shows how her love for Höskuldur somewhat mellows her pride: she wants her husband to move to another district when an estrangement develops between him and the Njálssons in order to prevent more serious trouble, but Höskuldur refuses to do so despite his gentle nature. Later the saga shows her grief for her dead husband, and here her harshness comes to the fore, and her fierceness, which demands vengeance. The author judges this cruelty severely, as though it had gone somewhat too far, but the account of these events is remarkably good, and Hildigunn's emotions are revealed in all their beauty and glory. And even when her passions are most intense, as she taunts her uncle Flosi, she does not lose her aristocratic bearing.

Hildigunnur is mentioned only once more in the story: at the very end she is married to Kári Sölmundarson. Doubtless this was a historical fact, which the author felt he could not dispute or avoid mentioning. But this marriage is not so romantic as other things which the saga relates about her, and the author quite neglects to explain how this proud woman could bring herself to marry one of the slayers of her first husband. It is almost as though the hand that holds the pen has grown weary. And yet it should be pointed out that this event is in no way at variance with the main theme of this part of the story; on the contrary, it is the very focus of it. It was not possible to find more cogent proof of complete reconciliation than the fact that Kári was able to win the hand of Hildigunnur in marriage.

Actually the author undertook a larger and much more difficult task in his portrayal of Bergþóra. From the Christian point of view, to be sure, Hildigunn's desire for revenge is blameworthy; but it is fully in accord with the pagan concept of honor and thus a fitting theme for heroic poetry and prose of all times. Within this frame of reference it does not offend our aesthetic sensibilities. Quite the opposite, however, is the case with Bergþóra, whose portrait reveals blemishes from both the aesthetic and ethical points of view. And yet the author succeeds in convincing the reader that she is the greatest woman character in his story.

He does not endow her with physical beauty, nor with proud lineage or the manifestly noble bearing of Hildigunnur. Rather, she is described as impetuous and revengeful, and she even brings about the death of several persons without regard for possibly dangerous consequences. She can easily be irritated, and "rages," as the saga puts it, when she grows angry. These incidents are generally described with a touch of good-natured irony, and this contributes greatly to the clarity with which her portrait is developed.

There is nothing crafty or cunning about Bergþóra. She is simple and straightforward. Her revengefulness is completely natural and fully in harmony with the pagan mode of thought. She is sensitive to everything that concerns the honor of herself, her husband, her sons, and her household. She does not bear a grudge long, nor is she cruel, judged by the standards of her own day. She is the personification of fidelity, a good mistress of the house, and radiates a vital warmth, so that the servants declare that they would rather perish (if that should be necessary) in the home of Bergþóra and Njáll than anywhere else.

Bergþóra commits a potentially dangerous offense by being harshly discourteous to Hallgerður while the latter is a guest in her home. This does not arise from common surliness, but from a lack of self-control. (Bergþóra has borne a feeling of antipathy toward Hallgerður from the first moment she saw her, if not earlier, and now this feeling finds the opportunity to express itself.) And yet Bergþóra does have a certain self-control and a feeling of propriety. This is demonstrated by the fact that under sufficiently grave circumstances she refuses to permit herself to be provoked. When Hallgerður boasts of the slaying of Bergþóra's menservants, Bergþóra makes no attempt to conceal her anger; but when Hallgerður causes the death of Þórður leysingjason and sends a messenger to inform her of this, the saga states that "Bergþóra declared that she would not use abusive language against Hallgerður, since that would not be suitable vengeance for such a terrible act." Here we see the difference between the two women. In a similar situation Hallgerður would have "raged." Bergþóra can distinguish the significant from the insignificant; she seems to know instinctively when it is out of place to rant and rave. The response must be suitable to the provocation. Her loftiness of feeling helps her to achieve moderation.

Bergþóra's magnanimity is also demonstrated in other ways. When Njáll learns about Otkel's refusal to sell hay and food to Gunnar (chapter 47), he gives vent to his indignation and displeasure. But Bergþóra immediately says, "What's the use of talking so much about such things? It would be much more manly to give him both hay and food, since you are short of neither." To which Njáll replies, "You are quite right." And when her rival, Hróðný, brings the body of Höskuldur, her son and Njál's, to Bergþórshvoll and asks for help, it is far from Bergþóra's nature to treat her cruelly because of jealousy. The situation demands something quite different from resentment over the paternity of Höskuldur. Instead, she immediately goads her sons to avenge the slaying of their half brother: "You men amaze me. You kill people for little reason, but now you stew about it and chew it over until nothing will come of it."

A casual reading of the saga can well evoke the feeling that Bergþóra dominates her husband. Njáll sometimes "strives mightily at sitting still," while Bergþóra not infrequently "storms" or "rages," as the author puts it. But the more closely we study the saga, the more obvious it be-

comes that this is far from the truth. To be sure, Bergþóra is highly regarded by her family and her servants, and she enjoys considerable authority within the household. This can best be seen, perhaps, in her curt comment to Atli (chapter 36): "I am Njál's wife, and I have as much authority in hiring servants as he does." But when the stakes are high, she is always sensitive to the will of her husband and never goes further on her own volition than he would forgive her for doing.

In the final event of her life Bergþóra attains her moment of perfection. Whatever was offensive or detrimental disappears, and the noblest qualities in her character come forth. Now that so much is at stake, she can afford to put them to good account. She and her husband and their sons are inside the flaming house at Bergþórshvoll. The women and children and servants are permitted to go outside, and their daughters-in-law and their daughter Helga take leave of their husbands. Flosi has Njáll and Bergþóra called to the door.

> "I want to offer to permit you to come out," said Flosi, "for you do not deserve to burn."
>
> Njáll replied, "I have no wish to go outside, for I am an old man now, and poorly fitted to avenge the death of my sons, and I do not want to live in shame."
>
> Flosi then said to Bergþóra, "You come out, Bergþóra, for I do not want you to burn under any circumstances."
>
> Bergþóra replied, "I was given to Njáll in marriage when young, and I promised him then that we would share the same fate."
>
> Then they both went back in.
>
> Bergþóra said, "What shall we do now?"
>
> "Let us go to bed," replied Njáll, "and lie down. I have long been fond of my ease."
>
> Then they lay down in the bed and placed the little boy, Kári's son Þórður, who did not want to be parted from his grandmother, between them. Then they made the sign of the cross over themselves and the boy and commended their souls to God, and that was the last they were heard to speak.

Where are now the turtle-back fingernails, the silly anger at trifles, the vehemence and raging? There is no trace of them left. All that remains is dignity, greatness, and beauty.

Thus the author takes leave of Bergþóra. With the exception of Kormlöð—and she seems to have been taken over almost unchanged from another work (*Brjáns saga*)— Hildigunnur and Valgerður, the housemistress at Mörk, are the last women characters to be described in the saga. I have already pointed out with what understanding the author depicted Hildigunnur at the end of the story. Valgerður is certainly not lenient with her husband, Björn; and yet, when he returns home from his expedition with Kári after having dispatched three men and having been wounded himself, the stern features of her face soften into a smile. We are left with the impression that the author's attitude toward women mellows as time passes. His own spirit is purified through the writing of the saga.

Richard F. Allen   (essay date 1971)

SOURCE: *Fire and Iron: Critical Approaches to "Njáls Saga,"* University of Pittsburgh Press, 1971, 254 p.

[*In the following essay, Allen discusses such important themes as law, violence, paganism, Christianity, and the vengeful woman in* Njáls saga.]

It is possible to derive underlying themes of *Njáls saga* from the form of the saga itself as it appears in perspective, a perspective distant enough to comprehend certain other works. The main curve of the saga suggests comparisons with other works and suggests as well the patterns of the human spirit which inform these works. As the themes emerge they are seen to comprise a polarity of forces, at times hostile, at times complementary to one another. Clusters of symbols (events, figures, sayings) align themselves in the direction of one pole or another. Belonging to these clusters are the so-called inserts (the chapters about the conversion, the Battle of Clontarf) and a supposed fault (the excessively long passages of law). Without them the fundamental themes of the saga would fail to be delineated clearly.

At the farthest distance from *Njáls saga* the events that remain impressed upon the memory are Gunnarr's last stand and the Burning. Each presents the image of men defending what they have inherited, and made, and held together, their families and their farmsteads, against foes determined to bring them down. Standing a little closer, one can perceive the outlines of the two great law processes that flank the Burning, the one where Flosi spurns the settlement offered him, the other where the suits of the Burners and of Njáll's supporters break down into general conflict. Gunnarr's last stand is also preceded by law processes and followed by violence, but on a lesser scale. In terms of the excitement which the saga generates it is natural to speak of events leading up to Gunnarr's death and Njáll's Burning, but in terms of the whole structure of this saga it is useful to think of events as leading down through stages of violence and disorder and attempted settlements to the baleful vision of the flames and ashes at Bergþórshváll. The Burning must have been a truly spectacular event, visible for miles around the flat and sandy plain where Bergþórshváll stands. As a vision it was all too real, and it stamped itself on the minds of the Icelanders as a most memorable event in a stirring age. As the central vision of the saga it seems a symbol for the failure of law and for a destruction of order which men have not been able to prevent.

Such symbols are the center of other heroic works. The destruction of Troy by fire and plunder is apparently the nucleus of fact about which a whole epic cycle accrued. In a later heroic age the Germanic peoples had no cities of their own to burn, but their principal legends preserve memories of kingly halls destroyed by fire. The *Beowulf*-poet, even as he tells of the building of Heorot, broods over its coming destruction in flames. From his allusions it appears that Heorot burned because well-meaning plans, in-

tended as in *Njáls saga* to lay old feuds to rest, only worked to awaken them to greater fury. The old poem, the *Bjarkamál,* and the late *Hrólfs saga Kraka* call up the heroic defense of Hrólfr's warriors within his burning castle at Leire, where Heorot had stood. The various strands of the story of the Volsungs, as it was remembered to the north and south in Germanic lands, have as main events the overwhelming of men in their halls, often by fire: "Guðrún Gjúki's daughter avenged her brothers, as has been told. First she killed the sons of Atli and then she put Atli to death and burned the hall and all the retainers. About that is said this poem." These words introduce the *Atlakviða* and the sons whom Guðrún kills are of course her own sons too. The figure of the vengeful woman who will be satisfied by nothing less than complete and, indeed, insensate revenge appears in these tales. They find a final expression in the *Nibelungenlied.* There the drive towards the utter destruction of men cannot be controlled. It rages unchecked—mighty kings and heroes are helpless to prevent or stay it—until the "she-devil" (*vâlandinne*), Kriemhild (the counterpart of Guðrún above), sees her brothers and the Burgundians annihilated along with the best part of Etzel's and Dietrich's men as well. This version of the story above all others expresses the fear (but the dreadful longing too) that has fascinated the Germanic peoples—the fear and yet the desire to behold the catastrophic end of all things. The *Voluspá,* is the poem that gives mythic expression to this concern with the fate of the world which man inhabits. It tells and foretells the course of the world, of its creation from primeval chaos, of its dissolution into flames and darkness in the great battle between the gods and their foes from hell, of the mysterious rebirth of the world into a green land waiting to be peopled. The potency of these images has remained undiminished to the present day—their recent notorious association with the doom of the Third Reich was all too real.

It has been remarked that the heroic legends of the Germanic peoples celebrate defeats and never victories [Bertha S. Phillpotts, *Edda and Saga,* 1931]. Even in historical times the two most famous Norwegian kings, Óláfr Tryggvason and St. Óláfr Haraldsson, were appreciated as much for having met their ends in properly spectacular debacles as for any of their other achievements. But a defeat worthy of celebration also implies a resistance heroic and sustained enough to live on as an example to later men. If in *Njáls saga* Gunnarr's death and the Burning of Njáll represent notable victories for forces of disorder, as the slaughter of tens of thousands at the end of the *Nibelungenlied* certainly does, nevertheless the poem and the saga (and other poems and sagas remembering the defeats of men) are victories of another sort. Out of destruction they create; they begin to make the memories of disaster understandable and endurable even in the act of preserving them. Those wrought with the greatest art (and *Njáls saga* belongs in that company) are triumphs of narrative organization, enduring achievements of the human will.

Gunnarr's defeat in defense of his house—it is actually pulled apart about him—and the reduction of Bergþórshváll to ashes are the central images of that saga which, more than any other, deals with the efforts of men to rule themselves by law and their own good will. That these events did happen shows that the efforts failed. But in the structure of the saga as a whole they by no means stand for a complete failure—indeed, the recuperative powers of men are defined in this saga by their ability, finally, to cope with these events. The men of Iceland, as represented in *Njáls saga*, go a long way into the darkness. The Burning itself threatens to lead to outspreading and uncontainable conflicts. But these are purged in the great battle at the Althing and there is hope they will not accumulate and fester anew. The settlements that are finally reached remain unbroken because men, willing good in God's name, follow Hallr of Síða's example and intercede to temper the old code. From this point on the course of the saga emerges, gradually, from a world of strife to the final peace of Kári's reconciliation with Flosi, a peace made firm by his marriage to Hildigunnr, the very woman who incited Flosi to the Burning. At a very great distance, the curve of the saga resembles that of the mythic poem, *Voluspá,* where the world of gods and men falls apart into the blaze and extinction of *ragnarok* only to reemerge into a new light. The curve of *Njáls saga* is shallower. Neither Gunnarr's death nor the Burning destroys the society pictured in the saga, although both shake it. The order that appears at the end is not the emergence of a newly born society but a restoration of the old society, scarcely transformed by but at least now open to the new light and revelation of Christianity.

I have meant to suggest by my phrasing and examples that into *Njáls saga* are displaced the patterns associated with myths of creation and the night journey. It is true that many distinctive motifs of these patterns, even as they may occur in displaced form, do not appear. These patterns stand far back from the realistic and semihistorical genre of the saga and this original statement will be modified in the course of discussion. But it is here where such a discussion must begin. These patterns are associated with (and in myth they signify) the establishment, growth, and maturation of the human consciousness, with the concomitant development of individual will and capacity for creative ordering. In heroic myth where the emerging awareness and will senses itself threatened by a return to or upheaval of those regions whence it came, the interplay between forces is portrayed as a struggle. It is a struggle between dark, bloody, engulfing forces from a chaotic realm, forces represented as belonging to a female chthonic side of nature, against powers with a masculine signature, often incorporated into a single hero, a figure of light, with will and strength to dare overcome and rule his opponent. The presence of this struggle (the delineation and explication of which is important to the development of the human spirit), although it is displaced into a realistic narrative, is one reason for the power which a work like *Njáls saga* can exert even through translation. The pattern of such a fundamental narrative structure appeals to and awakens counterparts in the psyche (archetypes) that are themselves charged with feeling. Since a single event or symbol belonging to an archetype may awaken the entire pattern, or contain it, brief moments, even phrases, in narrative may become the focal points of all the intensity and significance of that narrative.

But the sagas are a long way from the myths briefly

touched upon above, a long way with respect both to their mode of presentation and to the state of man's consciousness that they reflect. Creation myths, with their theme of the dividing of heaven and earth from a primordial female chaos (or monster), and the night journey, with its descent into darkness of the hero who fights the dragon and emerges with greater wisdom, are myths that represent man and mankind at a youthful and adolescent stage of awareness and capacity for self-rule. In these stages men, and the heroes who represent them, are not only assaulted but are often overwhelmed and defeated by the forces that threaten what they have built up. Beowulf rids Heorot of the fear of Grendel; with God's light to show him the way he overcomes Grendel's dangerous mother, but he cannot avail against the dragon and the dragon's fire in his final fight. His death is the end of his people. *Voluspá,* the *Volsunga saga,* and the *Nibelungenlied,* which in spite of the late date of their final preservation and recomposition in widely separated lands may be considered to have evolved from matters and concerns shared by the Germanic peoples, demonstrate the appeal of narrative processes that drive on to complete and terrible destruction. In *Njáls saga,* the reminder that Hallgerðr is descended directly from Sigurðr the dragon-slayer calls up into the saga the complex of emotions associated with the old poetry and legends.

But the sagas show man with a firmer grip on himself than is reflected in the older tales. Things do get out of hand, of course, again and again, but the process is checked before an utter breakdown is reached. G. R. Levy has remarked that the sagas present a "mature vision of the human will resisting calamity" [*The Sword from the Rock,* 1953]. The pattern that informs *Njáls saga* is implicit in this remark. It is a sustained effort of men, mindful of their origins and history, to maintain their society against whatever threatens to disrupt it, an effort by men whose race had the courage, will, and confidence to explore, conquer, and settle the lands from the North Cape to Sicily, from the Volga basin to North America. The vision of the saga is twofold here, for it comments not only on the men of Iceland's saga age but on the Icelanders of the thirteenth century. In commemorating the men of the past it warms and sustains the men of the present. Much has been written to say that the sagas are a continuation and final expression of the Germanic heroic age. But the sagas do not represent a continuation only of the old heroic spirit, the willingness to choose between the evil choices, to embrace defeat for the sake of fame, to die well and by dying well to live in fame which never dies. Certainly, the sagas do glow with that light shifted from the legendary poems into the prose histories of Icelanders. The old heroic celebration of man's unyielding will was noble and remains noble in the sagas. But what is equally impressive, and new, is the increased capacity of men to absorb disaster, to continue the story after the hall has burned and the heroes have fallen. The sagas show that man's ability to cope has grown stronger and this strengthening is an altering of, a coming to terms with, the fears and powers that shaped the earlier myths and legends.

The old fears of failure remain. But disheartening as Gunnarr's death indeed is and disastrous as the Burning is, the society depicted in **Njáls saga** has the strength to respond and carry on. Njáll's cause is taken up by his kinsmen; the following suits involve and embroil most of the island's mighty men and their followers. But even then, Hallr of Siða, with his willingness to forego compensation for his son Ljótr, pulls men back from the brink.

That men realize, early in the saga, what may eventually be at stake is seen in Gunnarr's immediate response to Hallgerðr's mischief-making. Invited to Bergþórshváll she has been insulted over a question of seating arrangements which Njáll's wife, Bergþóra, has provocatively established. Hallgerðr taunts Bergþóra with Njáll's beardlessness; Bergþóra insultingly replies. Hallgerðr appeals to Gunnarr:

> "It will be little use to me," says Hallgerðr, "to have married the man who is the most valiant in Iceland, if you will not revenge this, Gunnarr." He sprang up and leaped across the table and said, "I will go home, and it is most suitable that you should bandy words with your servants, but not in another man's household. Besides I am deeply obliged to Njáll and I will not be made a fool by your incitements." (ch. 35)

The two women, however, egging on lesser men, do stir up major trouble, and it is perhaps difficult now to appreciate the extent to which Gunnarr and Njáll must labor to keep the peace and maintain self-control. The wise, older lawyer and the vigorous, attractive hero working together are barely able to ward off the first major threat to their peace, a threat insistently brought to bear by proud and intemperate women. This is an image which is presented in its purest form in these first series of "escalations" in which Gunnarr is involved, but it may be discerned throughout the saga [Theodore M. Andersson, *The Icelandic Family Saga: An Analytic Reading,* 1967].

In **Njáls saga** women align themselves with those forces which drag men to death, which disrupt their agreements and their daily lives, which press them on to the narrow path between shame on the one side and death on the other which so many saga heroes walk. And because the saga-man's vision, although centered in a realistic narrative, embraced a wider spectrum than has been open to recent realistic narrative, other powers of the forces of order and disorder come into view in the glimpses and more-than-glimpses **Njáls saga** gives of the apocalyptic and demonic realms. Discussion of the women and discussion of the wonders in **Njáls saga** belong together, but they must be put off until one more approach is made to the central experience which underlies this work.

The problems which the Icelanders had to cope with were both within and without them. Their primary experience and task was the settling of the land itself—of imposing on an unpopulated, remote, and volcanic island, rich enough but not overflowing with natural resources, the forms of human culture. But these forms could not be successfully established and maintained unless men imposed order upon themselves, unless they could find means to contain within certain limits the vigor, the rashness, the aggressiveness, and the malice which were within them (as they are within all men) and which were (malice excepted)

qualities expressive of the will and confidence of the Norsemen. The need to control these qualities is recognized in Njáll's famous remark, which repeats an ancient legal proverb. " 'With laws shall our land be built up, but with lawlessness destroyed.' " It is important to understand that Njáll is not as much invoking a concept of legal justice as a concept of the forms which are needed to guide the actions of men. It is the tragedy of Gunnarr, and of the lawyer, Njáll, that the law to which they try to submit their hopes and passions is inadequate to contain them. In fact the original law of **Njáls saga**, the secular law untempered by the ethical commands of Christianity, cannot possibly bring about the building up Njáll speaks of so long as it is principally an elaborate substitute for blood revenge and so long as it is buffeted and misused by little men who are motivated by envy and malice and who must be opposed on their own terms.

The weapons men have at their disposal to effect the settlement and building of the land—and these are self-control and the system of laws—are two-edged. Gunnarr and Njáll go to great lengths to hold themselves in check and for both men the extent of their efforts is tragically defined by the magnitude of the fate which overtakes them when these efforts fail. Gunnarr wonders if something is not the matter with him because he is more reluctant to kill than other men. The result of this admirable reluctance—the saga represents it as admirable in the saga's own terms as well as ours—is simply to goad Gunnarr's enemies to further attempts to provoke him. When these attempts ultimately succeed—for Gunnarr is bound by the code of honor of the times—better men of good will are dragged in against Gunnarr and the result is that the man who represents all that is best about the old heroic society is outlawed from it and put to death by men who acknowledge their admiration for him. *Gísla saga* and *Grettis saga* present a similar pattern.

Njáll's story may similarly be seen as a lifelong striving, courageous and doomed, to avert the fate he sees before him. But each step he takes, settling quarrels, concluding alliances, adopting potential enemies, contracting worthy marriages, only ensures that the eventual collapse of his efforts will be all the more thorough. As long as men have only two courses of action by which to follow up an insult or injury—monetary settlement (either through legal judgment or arbitration) and blood revenge—the building up of the land through law will always threaten to devolve into violence and disaster. What is needed is a sanction that will permit men honorably to cease to seek revenge.

As I have suggested, it is not entirely accurate to read **Njáls saga**, or to summarize its major themes, as one of law striving against lawlessness. The saga makes it all too clear that the law itself can be used and misused as an aggressive and personal weapon. Njáll himself is introduced as a man "of sound and benevolent counsel and all advice which he gave men turned out well" (ch. 20). But he is not above manipulating the law for his own family's benefit, although it may be argued that the nation also benefits from his maneuvering. Njáll has sought to marry his foster son, Hoskuldr, to Flosi's niece Hildigunnr. She is a proud woman who does not wish to marry any man who is not a chieftain, and Flosi respects this wish. Njáll tries to buy a chieftainship for Hoskuldr, but has no success. He then embarks on an intricate scheme to induce his countrymen to establish additional chieftainships:

> Summer now passes until the Althing. That summer there were great disputes at the Thing. Many men came to consult with Njáll as was their wont. But he gave counsel in men's suits in an unlikely manner so that the pleas of both defense and prosecution came to nought. From this arose a great strife, when suits could not be brought to a conclusion, and men rode home from the Althing unreconciled. (ch. 97)

At the next Althing the situation is the same and men say they prefer to settle their quarrels with weapons. Njáll expresses dismay at the thought and acknowledges the responsibility which the great chieftains and wise men like himself have when complaints must be satisfied. He proposes a Fifth Court to be established over the four existing Quarter Courts to function as a court of appeals. This plan is accepted; the court is established and with it additional chieftainships, one of which goes to Hoskuldr. Njáll stipulates that " 'in this court it shall so be, that if one side pleads correctly and the other incorrectly, the judgment shall go to that side which proceeds correctly in its plea' " (ch. 97). This is a point that is to be crucial to later events and which again reveals that the justice of the decision which may be reached through the forms is not the primary concern of the great lawyer. In the saga the establishment of the Fifth Court, a highly important development in Icelandic history, is represented as having come forth from Njáll's desire to get a good marriage for his foster son (see ch. 4). It is a large reshaping of the Icelandic constitution for the sake of a personal aim, although the reshaping is a useful one and the aim (to erase the enmity between Njáll's kin and Hoskuldr's) is by no means a selfish one.

But Njáll here does use his knowledge of the law as a personal weapon to manipulate the chiefs who are more powerful than he. In other contexts, it is possible to see that the law cannot only be used aggressively, but that it is indeed agression itself in a sublimated form. The last statement is virtually self-evident when one examines the wergild provisions of Icelandic law, which appear prominently in *Njáls saga* and which are similar to fines established for the slaying of men in Germanic law. Here a man's death is simply equated with so much money (or goods), depending on his rank. For a man of any standing the standard compensation in *Njáls saga* is two hundred ounces of silver, the equivalent of the value of sixty-four milk cows. The force of this equation is made clear in an example cited by Hakon Melberg of the father who refused compensation for his slain son, saying he did not wish to carry his son around in his purse. The executive authority had an obvious interest in the institution of wergild, not only because it helped dampen and control feuding between clans but because it provided money for the state as well—in Norwegian law the king partook of any fines levied at the assemblies and in Iceland the Law Speaker received a half-share of any fines levied at the Althing. Power can be seen as taking form around the institutions set up to deal with manslaughter cases and other

disputes, and James Bryce has noted the unique course this process took in Iceland: "Of Iceland, indeed, one may say that so far from the State creating the Law, the Law created the State—that is to say, such State organizations as existed came into being for the sake of deciding lawsuits" [James Bryce, "Primitive Iceland," *Studies in History and Jurisprudence,* 1901]. This statement too embodies some of the meaning of "With law shall our land be built." But it is important to remember that no central authority existed in Iceland for enforcing the decision of the law courts. That was left to the parties concerned.

Since a great deal of the law (and all of it that is represented in *Njáls saga* as being the law of the land) is concerned with defining the occasions when one may feel insulted or injured by another and with outlining the procedures to be followed in law suits, it is possible to say that the law is aggression projected outward and codified. The more complicated its structure, the more potential violence it contains; the more elaborate its provisions for appeals and the more extended its capacities for dealing with complicated quarrels, the more extensive the violence that will be released if these procedures break down, as they do break down in *Njáls saga.* This process and the one-to-one equivalence of law and money to aggression become plain in the vivid confrontation between Flosi and the Njálssons which takes place before the Burning.

This . . . is the scene where Flosi, who has brought suit against the Njálssons and Kári for the slaying of Hoskuldr, faces them over the great heap of silver which the arbitrators have pledged as an extra-ordinary compensation. Indeed Snorri the Priest, in announcing the decision, has asked the entire assembly, from the great chieftains to the farmers in their followings, to contribute, " 'for the sake of God' " (ch. 123), something to make up the six-hundred ounces of silver that has been set as the atonement for Hoskuldr. The pile of money thus symbolizes the stake and interest the whole national assembly has in bringing about a peaceful settlement through established legal means and it is associated with the might and interest of the Christian God.

After it is collected, Njáll takes a silk cloth and a pair of boots and places them on top of the pile. He then goes back to his booth, announces the satisfactory conclusion of the case, and pleads with his sons not to spoil it. Skarpheðinn grins. The critical scene then gets under way as both parties line up opposite one another in the Court of Legislature with the gifts and silver between them:

> Flosi entered the Court of Legislature to behold the money and said, "This sum is great and good and well paid out, as is to be expected." Then he took up the cloak and asked who might have given it, but no man answered him. Again he waved the cloak and asked who might have given it, and laughed, and no man answered. Flosi said, "Is it that none of you know who owned this garment, or do you not dare to tell me?" (ch. 123)

Flosi . . . is trapped. He desires to accept this settlement but he is bound to blood revenge by his niece's incitement. The cloak offers the opportunity. Not only might it remind him of the bloody cloak of Hoskuldr which Hildigunnr in her passion flung about him, it may also suggest a slight to Flosi's manliness because such valuable garments were worn for show by man and woman alike. There is perhaps a suggestion that he is being overpaid, almost bribed by the anxious men not to take up arms. His irritation may be further stirred by the thought that the Njálssons have gotten off relatively easily in the amount which they personally had to contribute. There is, moreover, an undercurrent of feeling here that somehow it is unmanly to agree to a peaceful settlement. It is one of the concerns of *Njáls saga* to show that manliness can be embodied in restraint as well as violence. But here restraint is no longer possible—it is obvious from what follows that if Flosi does not act to break the settlement, Skarpheðinn will. And, partly because of the unspoken anxiety that such peaceful proceedings are somehow less manly than open hostilities and partly because there was one sure way to provoke men beyond endurance, the agreement is shattered by an exchange of sexual insults:

> Skarpheðinn said, "Who do you think gave it?" Flosi said, "If you want to know that, then I will tell you what I think—this is my guess, that your father gave it, the beardless man—because many who see him do not know whether he is a man or a woman." Skarpheðinn said, "It is ill done to taunt him in his old age when no manly man has done that before. You can know this, that he is a man, because he has gotten sons with his wife. Few of our kinsmen have so lain unatoned for beside our house that we have not avenged them." Then Skarpheðinn took back the silk cloak and tossed a pair of blue breeches to Flosi and said that he'd have more need of them. Flosi said, "And why will I need them more?" Skarpheðinn said, "Because of this—if you're the bride of the Svínafell Troll, as they say, and every ninth night he uses you as a woman." Flosi then kicked the money and said he would not have a penny of it and said that now one thing or the other would be—that Hoskuldr should remain unatoned for, or else that for him they would take blood revenge. (ch. 123)

The pile of silver has represented, or rather, it *is* in palpable form the most complex agreement yet seen in *Njáls saga.* It is intended to contain and control the long chain of passion and violence that has slowly linked itself together and grown in strength ever since Njáll's wife, Bergþóra, insulted Gunnarr's wife, Hallgerðr: ever since Þráinn Sigfússon took part in the murder of Þórðr Freedmansson, the Njálssons' foster-father. Flosi's mocking words to Njáll, "the beardless man," rake up the old insult first composed by Hallgerðr and repeated by her in her last appearance in the saga (ch. 91). By using it Flosi associates himself with the pride and spitefulness of Hallgerðr. By using it, and thus by ensuring that Hildigunnr's desire for blood revenge will be fulfilled, he becomes an agent of these women and for the forces that these women harbor. When he kicks the pile of silver all the hopes and painfully constructed agreements of the men are broken down. One could not ask for a more concrete or vivid symbol for the relationship between money and aggression. The structure he spurns lapses back to its primal form which is violence.

Just as the pile of silver embodied the most far-reaching settlement attempted in the saga, so its kicking apart leads directly to the most terrible event of the saga, the Burning.

The men of good will in *Njáls saga* have struggled to keep a hold on the matters that so closely affect their lives. Underlying this effort to maintain order—and such is its force in the saga that through long episodes its time units may best be defined in terms of the yearly cycle of events that are brought to focus and judged upon at the Althing—underlying this effort is the Icelanders' own experience in settling and maintaining their land. This experience, this participation in bringing the world of man to a land where none before had dwelt, was preserved in the *Landnámabók,* celebrated in the sagas, and made visible each summer in the gathering together at Thingvellir, the impressive site of the Althing. Here suits were decided upon, laws made or altered, news exchanged and stories told. The assembly helped maintain a cultural and linguistic unity in an island whose geography and difficult communications might otherwise have led to a drifting apart of the settlers.

Perhaps the very view of things as they appear from Thingvellir may have imparted to the men gathered there a sense of the issues involved in the making of a nation. It is not possible to say what conscious effect this view worked upon the medieval Icelanders, although it is certain that the man who composed *Njáls saga* was thoroughly familiar with Thingvellir and could perhaps expect his audience to provide their own landscape from their own knowledge. But for men today the landscape at Thingvellir can awaken feelings that are not altogether dependent on the wealth of history and heroic saga that pass in review. It is a proper intuition and critical sense that leads Einar Ól. Sveinsson to begin his book, *Á Njálsbúð,* with an evocation of this landscape and with an appeal to the memories it calls up, for this is where a book about *Njáls saga* should begin. But even apart from the memories, the landscape itself is meaningful, as Ari Bouman has noted [in *Patterns in Old English and Old Icelandic Literature,* 1962], for by itself it is a vast image of the situation in which civilized and civilizing man has ever found himself. . . .

The land itself is no passive thing, but felt to be alive, inhabited by a variety of spirits, both friendly and unfriendly, trolls, giants, apparitions, and the animated dead that live on in their barrows and venture about the countryside. The land itself contains forces that can destroy all man has built up—devastating flash floods, the result of volcanic activity beneath glaciers, and volcanic outbursts, some of which are among the greatest ever recorded. It is a tribute to the steady nerves, even obliviousness, of the saga-men, that these phenomena are scarcely noted in the family sagas. Perhaps they had to be accepted as a portion of fate, for absolutely nothing can be done to avoid or resist them. Indeed a laconic reminder of the indifference shown towards men by the gods responsible for such activity is said to have helped persuade the Althing to forsake them for Christianity. As the assembly debated and was at the point of rupture over whether to maintain the old pagan ways or to adopt the new religion,

> a man came running and said that the earth-fire

had come up in Olfus and would overrun the farmstead of Þoroddr the Priest. Then the heathen men spoke up, saying, "It is no wonder that the gods become angry at such debates." Then Snorri the Priest said, "What were the gods angry at when the lava burned on which we are now standing?" After that men went from the Law Rock.

But dry and sensible as Snorri's remark is, it recognizes that the very ground on which the Althing met had originated in some form of preternatural convulsion. In *Njáls saga* an incident occurs that similarly links the vulcanism of the land to the resentful powers of the pagan gods. On his mission of conversion, Þangbrandr is stalked by one Galdra-Heðinn, a wizard of sorts:

> The heathen men struck a bargain with him that he should contrive the deaths of Þangbrandr and his company. Galdra-Heðinn went up onto Arnastakk Heath and there performed a great sacrifice. Then when Þangbrandr was riding westwards, the earth burst apart beneath his horse, but he leaped from the horse and came up safely on the edge of the brink, but the earth swallowed the horse with all its gear and they never saw him again. Then Þangbrandr praised God. (ch. 101)

If the saga-men kept a stiff upper lip about the natural perils of their land, other Icelanders must have been more talkative, for Saxo Grammaticus passes on reports of malignant springs, mountains that belch forth flames, tumbling glaciers, pestilent floods, and moaning spirits of the damned. The thirteenth-century Norwegian work, *The King's Mirror,* remarks in one passage that the fruitful earth must be called living but as for Iceland, the fires there which feed upon the stones must be the fires of hell itself and the ice and cold of the land the cold of hell itself, made visible to men as a divine warning: "But now no one can deny what he sees before his own eyes, since we hear exactly the same things about the tortures of hell as those which one can see on the island called Iceland: for there are vast and boundless fire, overpowering frost and glaciers, boiling springs, and violent ice-cold streams." But, since God rules over all, the "devil can, therefore, injure no one to such an extent that he is consumed either by the fires of death which he has kindled and continues to maintain by means of dreadful earthquakes, or by such other fiendish enmity or malignity as he delights in. For he is allowed to do nothing more than the task at hand." In such a context Morðr's wish to burn Gunnarr within, the fire Flosi sets to Bergþórshváll, and the words of Njáll, "and trust in this, that God is merciful and he will not let us burn both in this world and the next" (ch. 129), link themselves to the much greater drama contained in the Christian vision.

It is probably not necessary to pursue further the point that the land harbored powerful spirits and was itself alive, although Snorri's patriotic tale in *Heimskringla* should be mentioned where the mountain giants and animal spirits of Iceland frighten away the warlock emissary of King Óláfr (these guardians are incorporated into the present-day Icelandic national emblem). One might also recall the myth in Snorri's *Edda* in which the gods fashion the heavens and the earth from the body of the frost giant Ymir.

To sum up, *Njáls saga* embodies and is built about an experience fundamental to the life of the Icelanders, that of governing their behavior by formal (if not always rational) procedures, of imposing law upon their actions. This experience became visible for a representative body of the population at the district assemblies and especially at the yearly great assembly at the Althing. In its turn the experience recapitulates and is analogous to the building up of the Icelandic nation. It reenacts the moment in their history when this people undertook in separate groups and by separate decisions to settle on the empty land, to press upon it the pattern of their culture. And this process in turn is analogous to the fundamental human experience, which each culture and each individual undergoes, of a coming to self-awareness, of a building up and a maintaining of a conscious integrity against whatever works to tear apart and dissolve that structure.

The myths, symbols, and motifs associated with the complex of patterns shaping the polarity that develops between this integrity and its adversaries align themselves with powers represented as belonging to masculine or feminine realms. The land and sea with their capacity to absorb and give rebirth take on a feminine valence; so also do the threats that come from the land and the sea. That which tills the land and builds upon it and seeks to wrest the shape of the land to its will falls on the masculine side. In *Njáls saga*—a saga which as it goes along more and more clearly presents a dialectic between conserving and destroying forces—it is therefore at least appropriate that those forces which fall on the destroying side should, in general, line up with elements belonging to the female world and that those forces which fall on the masculine side are those which strive to maintain order. Njáll and Gunnarr, Kári at the story's end, and the great men of good will, chieftains like Snorri the Priest and Hallr of Síða, even the turbulent Þangbrandr who brings tidings of the might of God the Father, all act to strengthen the society in which they move and to ensure its continuance, either through actual legislation that affects the entire country or by endeavoring to settle the quarrels set in motion by women, or by both. In back of the smaller men who oppose them and in back of the events that overtake them may often be discerned the figures of vengeful women and other powers, supernatural, associated with the land itself. Even Skarpheðinn's love of battle and Flosi's vehemence, which are kinds of a male pride of force, join to satisfy Hildigunnr's wish for blood revenge. Gunnarr has few faults, but one of them is an occasional hastiness of decision, an impulsive rashness which offsets his usual self-control. This impulsiveness plays a large part in two of his fateful decisions where, in effect, he hands himself over into the power of present or future foes. In the one this impulsiveness is called forth by Hallgerðr; in the other by the beauty of the land itself.

Gunnarr's courtship of Hallgerðr is a hasty one indeed. It begins when Hallgerðr, in a reversal of the custom, makes the first move:

> One day as Gunnarr went from the Law Rock,

he passed below the Mosfell booth. Then he saw some women coming from the opposite direction and they were well dressed. She who was in the lead was the best arrayed. And when they met, she at once greeted Gunnarr. He took her greeting well and asked who she was. She said her name was Hallgerðr and that she was the daughter of Hoskuldr Dala-Kollsson. She spoke boldly to him and asked him to tell about his travels; he said he would not deny her that. They sat down and talked. She was dressed so that she wore a red tunic which was handsomely decorated; she had over this a scarlet cloak trimmed with lacework down to its hem. Her hair fell to her bosom and was both rich and fair. Gunnarr was in his princely clothes which King Haraldr Gormsson had given him. He had the ring on his arm which was the gift of Earl Hákon. They talked aloud and at length. It came about that he asked whether she was unmarried. She says that that was so—"and there are not many who'd risk it," says she. "Do you think there's no match good enough for you?" says Gunnarr. "It's not that," she says, "but I will be particular about my choice." "How would you answer if I ask for you?" says Gunnarr. "You won't have that in mind," she says. "But I do," Gunnarr says. "If such a notion has occurred to you," Hallgerðr says, "then go and talk with my father." Then they ended their talk. (ch. 33)

The scene is a fine one, with both figures dressed to play their roles. Gunnarr, home from his triumphant adventures, wearing his noble garments and the gold ring of the Norwegian ruler, is virtually a prince, or as near to it as an Icelander can become. Hallgerðr by now is a fully mature woman—the description again dwells on her remarkable hair and perhaps suggests the strong element of sexuality residing in her. Such vivid patches of color remain in one's memory precisely because they are infrequent. Gunnarr, even Gunnarr in his princely robes, will become a victim of this woman's pride and it is tempting to see in the color of her dress the red naturally associated with blood and, in some instances of Norse lore, with falsity.

Gunnarr goes "at once" (þegar) to ask his old foes, Hoskuldr and Hrútr, for Hallgerðr's hand. Hrútr tries to warn Gunnarr of Hallgerðr's mixed nature. When Gunnarr suspects that their former enmity is affecting his description, Hrútr replies, "It is not that; it is more that I see you cannot prevent yourself." And when Gunnarr says that Hallgerðr seems willing, Hrútr comments, "I see that this must be, because this is a marriage of desire for you both, and you two will risk the most, whatever happens" (ch. 33). Although Hrútr spells out to Gunnarr all her faults, they end by sending for Hallgerðr and letting her declare her own betrothal. Njáll, when he hears the news, is greatly displeased. "From her will come great trouble when she comes here to the east," he predicts. Hallgerðr has brought out in Gunnarr an unexpected hastiness—it belongs to the larger theme of excess that runs through the saga. Hrútr's remarks show that he regards Gunnarr as a man not in control of himself (Hrútr, thanks to his experience with Queen Gunnhildr, has some knowledge of such matters). Gunnarr has given way to impulse and desire and he will bring to his home at Hlíðarendi a woman who

in Njáll's words will be a continual source of trouble, of "all the trouble" (allt it illa) if Njáll's words are translated literally.

After this, it is not a complete surprise when Gunnarr, once more at a crucial moment in his life, suddenly yields to impulses that perhaps have been stirring ever since a sentence of exile has been passed upon him. Gunnarr bids farewell to his people and rides off from Hlíðarendi, bound away from Iceland. But his horse stumbles and Gunnarr has to jump from the saddle: "His gaze was turned towards the hillside and the farmstead at Hlíðarendi and he said, "Fair is the hillside, so that never has it seemed so fair to me, the bright fields and the mown meadows, and I will ride back home and never go away" (ch. 75). So at the last moment Gunnarr is led by fate (the omen of the horse's stumbling) and by his own inner desire to turn back to the land which in its way has created Gunnarr and defined him. To him the land seems infused with beauty, a beauty that must come from the projection upon it of his own desire to stay. Never has it seemed so fair to him; it is as if the land lures him back, and, indeed, that is all the explanation we get from him in life. The close bond between the heroes of the sagas and the very land itself appears at this moment and is given expression. It is a rare, almost isolated, revelation in the sagas that this attraction existed and was felt. The fascination and compelling force of the scene is acknowledged by its fame—it is probably the best known and most frequently cited incident in all of saga literature, and this fact partly obscures how unusual it is. It is not adequate to say that the saga-man is here simply adorning, disguising, and diverting attention away from the undeniable fact that Gunnarr is breaking his word and the law of the land. Nor is it simply a rationalization uttered by Gunnarr to excuse his suddenly formed but long brewing resolve to go back and face his enemies, although that is part of the explanation for his speech. Neither explanation accounts for the force of the scene, for the fascination it exerts, and for the arrest of attention it compels.

This force is one of archetypal potency in two senses, both because it awakens thoughts of other heroes in similar predicaments and because it presents a picture in itself highly significant. Gunnarr in turning back turns back to face his enemies as all heroes must—no hero can run away. Gunnarr himself says so, for after his death his son and Skarpheðinn see him awake in his burial mound, exultantly singing that "rather will he wish to die than yield, rather die than yield." One thinks of Roland turning back from the shelter of the pass at Roncesvalles to face the pagan host, proudly refusing to summon help and dying at last on the slopes overlooking the lands his king had conquered. (Gunnarr sends his men away to finish the harvest; it is possible to see reshaped in the pair of Gunnarr and Kolskeggr the lineaments of Roland and Oliver). In a later tradition, Melville's Ahab comes to mind as he brings the Pequod up into the wind blowing away from the White Whale and sails back to face that great foe. Gunnarr's action belongs to all heroic literature. The image the saga-man's point of view provides at this moment shows in a static picture the same pattern, the hero turned around to face the region where he knows he will have to fight, here the hillside and the house of Hlíðarendi. Gunnarr's return to the land raises, contains, and satisfies unspoken but profound feelings because it reunites polarities—the hero with his masculine will and strength turns back to the fair land, the alluring land, which attracts him as Hallgerðr did when he first saw her, the land from which he came and in which he will be buried. Ari Bouman even suggests that Gunnarr returns because he cannot give up Hallgerðr, and although on the surface this seems highly unlikely—there is little love lost between Gunnarr and Hallgerðr at the end of their marriage—in another way Bouman's observation is true, for Hallgerðr and the land belong to the same complex of forces and they exercise over Gunnarr an identical allurement. The hero fulfills himself by urging himself back to his home, his wife, his mother, and his land, all of which are by him in his last fight, one of which betrays him. Denton Fox sees that Gunnarr would not be himself if he went away. Although fame and fortune and a long life are prophesied for him should he abide by his sentence of exile, overseas he would be just another man. But in Iceland he is Gunnarr of Hlíðarendi, and his true fame and his real identity rest in that and in the defense he will make of his home, the last stand of the hero becoming a highly compact symbol of the defense of order and the settled land that is the major concern of *Njáls saga.*

Although Gunnarr is declared an outlaw at the end, he has stood for restraint and good will. When these become outraged beyond endurance, his defense becomes a retribution to those who worked to undo him and his best hopes. It is a famous defiance. It stands as a warning to future men and women who wish to raise strife against strong men and stir up trouble in the land. " 'His defense will endure in memory so long as the land is lived in' " (*byggt*) merges with and uses the same verb as " 'With laws shall our land be built up' " (*byggja*). At the same time Gunnarr fulfills the other half of the saying, " 'and by lawlessness destroyed,' " for he does break his word and in going back dooms himself. The situation thus attracts to itself values and themes of great complexity, but they complement, rather than contradict, one another.

In these two scenes, that of Gunnarr's meeting with Hallgerðr and that of his turning back to Hlíðarendi, there may be discerned the polarities of *Njáls saga* which at once attract, struggle with, and define each other. They emerge far more sharply, however, in the wonders and the furious women as the appearances of the former and the wishes of the latter come to be more and more bound together. Female trouble-making, turbulent men, pagan mischief, strange wonders, and hostile terrain first come together when Hallgerðr sends Þjóstólfr, her foster-father, to seek safety with her maternal uncle, Svanr. Þjóstólfr has just killed Hallgerðr's first husband. Svanr is the uncle who is "well skilled in wizardry . . . and an extremely difficult man to have dealings with" (ch. 10). When Svanr hears the news of the killings, he exclaims, "Such I call men, who do not shrink from anything . . ." (ch. 12). In Svanr's exclamation is that equation of vehemence with manliness which the saga endeavors to modify. The kinsmen of Hallgerðr's unfortunate husband send a raiding party after Þjóstólfr, but Svanr baffles the attackers by conjuring up a magic fog:

> Ósvífr said, "Svanr will have caused this, and it would be well if nothing worse follows." A little later a great darkness came before their eyes so that they saw not, and they fell off their horses and lost their horses and stumbled into swamps, and some into the woods so that they came near to suffering injury. They lost their weapons. (ch. 12)

This happens three times before the men give up and ride away to seek compensation from Hallgerðr's father. It is tempting to see in the men benighted by the wizard's fog and gone astray in the morasses and woods a symbol of the predicament of men in pagan Iceland unable to avail against this combination of vengefulness and magic, in a plight where the land itself seems against them.

Svanr's close connection with the land can be seen in the manner of his death, which the saga-man reports in his best neutral style:

> The news became known from north in Bjarnarfjord, that Svanr had rowed out in spring to go fishing, and a great east wind had come upon the crew and driven them up at Veiðilaus and there they perished. But those fishermen who were at Kaldbak thought they saw Svanr going into Kaldbakhorn Mountain and he was well received there. But others denied the story and said there was nothing to it. But all knew this, that he was never seen again dead or alive. (ch. 14)

The dark side of pagan Iceland stands behind Svanr. Þjóstólfr, whom he shelters, is the first of the malicious little men, hard to restrain and swift to carry out the urgings of proud women, and, in fact, there is something peculiarly close in his attachment to his foster daughter, Hallgerðr, and in his evident jealousy of her husbands.

[The saga genre] developed after the breakdown of the epic synthesis but . . . it still remains close enough to this synthesis that it can contain in organic fashion much of the epic vision. It is a genre that, professing to be history, contains the adventure of romance, the fated course of heroes, the humor and self-criticism of comedy, all in a linear and self-restoring form.

—*Richard F. Allen*

The side of lawful dealings and good will obtains powerful reinforcements when it is strengthened with the power of the Christian God whom Þangbrandr brings to Iceland. He tells Hallr of Síða of the angel Michael who in his mercy lets the good weigh more heavily than the bad. This is a crucial and new idea, one that can liberate the Icelanders from the bloody cycles of revenge to which their customs have committed them. Þangbrandr brings off a number of miracles to demonstrate the might of the new God. In them can be seen what Christianity is overcoming—shrieking heathen women casting spells, malicious ambushers, berserks unstoppable by fire or sword, wizards like Svanr, all that darkened the older days with sorcery, blood, and vengefulness. But once the force of Christianity is placed behind the men of good will and wisdom (Njáll is one of the first converts), the conflicts in the saga intensify. From here on the conflict is no longer one between desirable and undesirable tendencies in a society of men. It becomes a widening one in which events in Iceland and elsewhere become specifically linked with a conflict of good with evil. This conflict is made visible in the wonders. In the part of *Njáls saga* following the conversion they become spectacular unveilings of the apocalyptic and demonic realms. The use of them to underlie the conflict of men and to reveal a struggle of good against evil is unusual in the context of saga conventions. Although there are some parallels (such as the succession of good and bad dream women who appear to Gísli in his saga), marvelous happenings in saga literature often function to provide local color or appear as folklore elements routinely associated with given situations. They are part of the normal experience of the men and women who inhabit the sagas. But the happenings to be discussed here are no ordinary wonders; they are forcefully shaped and related; they endure in memory; and they gather up and symbolize major themes of the saga.

Unusual portents often accompany the climactic events of sagas. But the one that portends the Burning is extraordinary indeed and strikingly reveals what powers Flosi is committed to once he has resolved that "we shall ride to Bergþórshváll with our entire company to attack the Njálssons with fire and iron and not turn away before they all are dead" (ch. 124). Time then passes.

> At Reykir in Skeið lived Runólfr Þorsteinsson. His son was named Hildiglúmr. One Sunday night Hildiglúmr went outdoors; it was twelve weeks before winter began. He heard a tremendous crash and to him it seemed that both earth and heaven shook. He looked westward then; he thought he saw a ring and a fiery glare about it and in the ring a man on a grey horse. The man passed over swiftly and he was riding hard. In his grasp he had a burning brand; he rode so close to Hildiglúmr that he could plainly see him. The rider was black as pitch. Hildiglúmr heard him speak these words with a great voice:
>
> > I ride a horse,
> > with icy mane
> > and dripping forelock,
> > the evil-working mount.
> > Fire at the brand's tip
> > and poison in between;
> > so fares Flosi's plan
> > as this burning brand;
> > so fares Flosi's plan
> > as this burning brand.
>
> Then the rider hurled the brand eastward to-

wards the mountains and a great fire leapt up to meet it so that Hildiglúmr felt he could not see beyond to the mountains. He thought the rider held on eastwards beneath the fire and vanished out of sight. Then Hildiglúmr went in and to his room and there lost consciousness for a long time, but finally came out of his faint. He remembered all that had happened earlier. He told his father and his father told him to tell Hjalti Skeggjason. Hildiglúmr went and told him. "You have seen a witchride," says Hjalti, "and that ever comes before great events." (ch. 125)

The nightmarish apparition speaks for itself; the black rider with his horse at once icy and fiery is a rider from demonic realms. The ominous pronouncement and the vision of the land convulsed with fire and poison awaken thoughts of the *ragnarok,* the whelming of the created world by supernatural foes and monsters from hell as it is told in Snorri's *Edda* and the *Voluspá.* In Christian commentary the figure of the horse and rider gathered to itself similar associations; the rider was equated with the mind and soul of man, the horse with the body, with appetites and passions, with woman. The rider who lost control of his horse would be carried headlong to damnation. Such commentary would well fit Hildiglúmr's remarkable vision, which reveals that the headlong course of Flosi's plan, driven as it is by Hildigunnr's urgings, can no longer be headed off or stayed. Finally the vision recalls the earlier times in the saga when horses played their part in letting loose the passions of men. Gunnarr first resorts to killing after Otkell on a runaway horse has ridden him down (ch. 53); his next great feud begins when matters get out of hand at a horsefight (into which another Hildigunnr has incited the Kolsson brothers, ch. 58). The significance of the careering horse bearing its rider along has thus partly been established within the saga itself. All these things may be kept in mind as Flosi sets out to take fire and iron to the Njálssons at Bergþórshváll.

The bodies of Njáll and Bergþóra are unburned when they are recovered from the ashes, for which miracle (*jartegn*) all praise God. And Hjalti Skeggjason speaks for all when he says that "Njáll's countenance and body seem so bright to me that never have I seen a dead man's body so bright" (ch. 132). This phenomenon, of course, frequently surrounds and preserves the bodies of martyrs and holy men. Flosi and his band have burned to death a saintly man; nor is there any reason to suppose that this episode is an interpolation or is out of harmony with the rest of the saga. What is best and most memorable about Njáll—his good will, generosity, and lifelong effort to uphold the orderly conduct of life—is associated with the Christianity that has begun to play its part in the island's affairs.

It is not surprising then that the Burners are summoned to retribution by a more than human power. Flosi dreams at Svínafell one night that a man who calls himself Iron-Grim comes out of the cliffs of Lomágnúpr, calling out the names of men. In the list are many Burners and other men besides. When Flosi asks Iron-Grim where he is going, Iron-Grim replies that he is going to the Althing, where " 'First I shall clear [*ryðja*] the jury, and then the courts, and then the field for battle.' " Then, as Flosi tells it to Ketill of Mork, he " 'struck his staff downwards and there was a great crash; Iron-Grim then reentered the mountain but I was filled with dread.' " Ketill does not have to ponder long before he can tell Flosi, " 'It is my foreboding that they will be doomed men who were summoned' " (ch. 133). Flosi's dream has been adapted from the *Dialogues* of Gregory the Great, as Einar Ól. Sveinsson has shown, and adapted well. Iron-Grim is another figure from the demonic world, accompanied like the witch-rider with appropriate sound effects, swallowed up like Svanr by the mountain. He is a spirit of battle and strife and he is travelling to the Althing where his presence will soon be felt. In his words one hears the actual lapsing of the procedures of law back to the primitive strife from which they arose; the technical phrases *ryðja kvið, ryðja dóm*—"to challenge a jury or judge"—merge with the primal force of the verb, to clear, to strip away, even to conquer. Iron-Grim will strip the facade from the forms of law to lay bare the field for slaughter. Yet at the same time he is under some constraint, for in summoning the men who are doomed to die, Iron-Grim is announcing the judgment of God who now rules the fates. His summons looks forward beyond the battle at the Althing to the great event which dominates the close of *Njáls saga*, the Battle of Clontarf. And there the hand and might of God are made manifest.

The Battle of Clontarf was fought near Dublin on April 23, 1014, a Good Friday. The Irish were led by Brian Boruma, the Irish High-King, against forces commanded by King Mælmordha of the Leinstermen and by King Sigtryggr Silkbeard, ruler of the Norsemen who controlled Dublin. As *Njáls saga* represents it, Sigtryggr's ambitions are inflamed by his mother, Queen Kormloð. "She was a very beautiful woman and well endowed in all those natural gifts not hers to determine, but it was a saying of men that she was completely evil in all things which were within her power to determine" (ch. 154). Kormloð was married to King Brian, but divorced him, and now she is filled with hatred for him (ch. 154). The issue at stake in the Battle of Clontarf was really the Leinstermen's determination "to maintain their independence against the high king," but the victory of Brian, even though he was killed, also put an end to the ambitions of the Dublin Norse. But in memory and tradition the issues became much wider. The battle became a decisive clash of the free and Christian Irish against hosts of the enslaving Northmen, an outright victory of Christianity over the heathen foes who had so long tried to usurp the Irish lands. An epic tradition grew up about the event and it is evident that *Njáls saga* drew on a lost saga about Brian or Earl Sigurðr for much of its material in these chapters (ch. 154-57).

The presentation of this battle near the end of the saga gives rise to a curious effect. The saga is driving to its close—Kári has almost exhausted his missions of revenge, and both Kári and Flosi with his men are travelling by separate ways to Rome to be absolved there. But as the saga nears its close and as one senses that the various strands are being brought together, at the same time the scale of events widens immensely. There is a strong tension generated between the compressive, concluding drive of the narrative and the sudden expansion of the saga's vision which now embraces the clash of nations and supernatural powers. The reader's concern with the quarrels of

Icelanders is led on to an involvement with this great battle where the forces that have clashed behind and through the actors in the saga emerge and battle with one another on a much vaster scale.

Flosi has been taken into Earl Sigurðr of Orkney's retinue. When Sigurðr joins King Sigtryggr a number of the Burners follow him, but Sigurðr insists that Flosi make his pilgrimage to Rome (ch. 157). Sigurðr sails to Ireland and there "fifteen men from the Burners fell in Brian's Battle" (ch. 157). But as accompanying portents have shown, Brian's Battle was a triumph of Christianity over its foes. Its significance is announced in terms that suggest comparison with Judgment Day itself. When one viking, Bróðir, once a Christian but now a relapsed and most cunning sorcerer, asks his brother, Óspakr, the meaning of frightful omens that have bedeviled Bróðir and his men (ch. 156), Óspakr answers:

> "When the blood rained upon you, that means that you will shed the blood of many men, both of your own and others. And when you heard the great din, it means that the world's shattering will be revealed to you; you will all die suddenly. And when the weapons attacked you, that means battle will come. And when the ravens attacked you, they were those demons whom you once believed in and they will drag you to the torments of hell." (ch. 156)

Not one to ignore his own predictions, Óspakr embraces Christianity and goes off to join King Brian. Bróðir joins the Norsemen and it will be he who takes King Brian's life. The fall of the saintly king before such a foe shows what forces have met on this field. The saga-man feels no need to state the unspoken parallel between the King of the Irish and the much higher King who also died on Good Friday.

When the Burners fall, fighting on the wrong side, in such a battle as this, an absolute judgment is made of the Burning. In Icelandic terms to resort to burning was a shameful and desperate act, one of the acts to which the strong term, *niðings-verk,* was applied. The death of fifteen of the Burners in the Battle of Clontarf implies that it was an evil act as well, at least implies that they met their proper deserts in a battle where there is no doubt whose side the God of Battles favors.

The Clontarf episode, far from being a clumsy digression for the sake of its own interest, an interpolation that disrupts the end of the saga by its expansion of a tradition about the fate of the Burners there, is instead a clear discovery in more-than-human form of the powers that have used men as their agents. The final shaping of this strife into a powerful image is presented in the *Darraðarljóð,* the poem which is the great coda to the tale of the Battle of Clontarf. In this, the powers that have men in their grip appear as the Valkyries who weave a frightful web. The rule that gives shape and order to men's lives is seen in the metaphor of the war-weaving loom as an interplay of bloody and opposing pulls driven together by force. If God rules the final outcome, nevertheless these powers out of an older pagan world still preside over the fates of individual men. Christianity has provided men with a vision that at once encompasses and surpasses these powers but it has not destroyed them, and thus it is not inconsistent that they are allowed to have the final say.

> On Good Friday it so happened at Caithness that a man named Dorruðr went outside. He saw that twelve riders rode together up to a certain bower and there they all disappeared. He went up to the bower and looked in a window which was there and saw that there were women within and that they had set up a loom. Men's heads were used for weights, and men's guts for weft and warp, a sword for the beater, and an arrow for the shuttle. They were chanting verses. (ch. 157)

The poem they chant is in an old heroic meter although some of its phrasings resemble the glittering diction of the skalds. Two stanzas will suffice to give an idea of its substance:

> Hildr goes to weave the warweb,
> Hjorþrimul with her,
> Sanngríðr and Svipul,
> And with swords unsheathed.
> Spear shall clash,
> Shield shall break;
> The battle-axe shall bite the shield.
>
> And sorrow will await the Irish,
> Sorrow that will never
> In men's memories grow old.
> Now the web is woven
> And the field is reddened.
> Sorrowful tidings of the fall of men
> Will go about the land. (ch. 157, sts. 3, 9)

It is obvious that the Valkyries (for so they are revealed to be in their singing) are determining the outcome of the battle and of separate events within it by weaving their "web of war," for this phrase, if it is not the actual meaning conveyed by *vefr darraðar* (a kenning for the banner on a battle standard), is what is certainly implied by their activity. When they are finished the women tear the cloth from the loom and each keeps a piece of it. "They mounted their horses and rode, six to the south and six to the north" (ch. 157). The action suggests the polarity of contending forces that have been woven together to make the battle.

As aftershocks following an earthquake, the weaving of this web and the battle this weaving fashioned are accompanied by lesser marvels. In some of them the motif of the engulfing earth or sea appears:

> At Thvattriver the priest saw on Good Friday a deep sea gulf beside the altar and he saw therein many dreadful things and for a long time afterwards he was not able to sing the holy services.
>
> This occurrence happened in Orkney, that Hárekr thought he saw Earl Sigurðr and some men with him. Hárekr took his horse and rode to meet the Earl and men saw that they met and rode beneath a certain hill. They never appeared again and no trace was found of Hárekr. (ch. 157)

The deep anxieties of men rise to the surface here and take shape. The priest by the monstrous gulf opening before him, unable to sing the services whose words form appeals to the power and mercy of God, is a good symbol for the predicament of man awed and terrified by what he sees within himself. Man needs the forms and laws he himself creates; he needs the power of the heaven-dwelling God within him to hold back what threatens to sweep him away.

The *Darraðarljóð* completes and underscores the shift of modes that occurs in the Clontarf episode of the saga, the shift from a narrative centered upon the realistic actions of men to a narrative still so centered but whose boundaries have been flung wide open to admit the vision of the great powers that have informed the action of the saga. The poem is a confirmation of this shift. In form it contrasts with the stanzas of skaldic verse which have appeared elsewhere. In style its heavily stressed phrases and the characteristic alliterations intensify those same qualities that do indeed resound in the regular prose rhythms and word linkings of this saga. The *Darraðarljóð* is in auditory terms a climactic resolution of the heroic and preternatural themes that are suggested in the very sound itself of the prose instrument that is commanded by the composer of *Njáls saga.* And the inclusion of such a poem brings *Njáls saga* closer to the realm of the legendary sagas where other poems in Eddic meters are found along with abundant manifestations of the supernatural. This broadening of vision at the end of *Njáls saga* is not unlike the process in Aeschylus's *Agamemnon* to which Maud Bodkin refers:

> In the choral odes of the play, when the visible action and conflict of individual wills is suspended, we become aware of an action "lifted out of time and space on to the plane of the universal." On the invisible scene, "as though on a higher stage, uncurtained in the choral part," appear Hybris and Peitho, Nemesis and Ate, mythical shapes representing the forces concerned in the human drama.

In the *Darraðarljóð* the wondrous is brought together with the women weaving the web of strife. Sinister queens stand at both the beginning and the end of the saga. Women begin the trouble in *Njáls saga* and they continue to incite it. Into them are displaced vaster destructive forces that in an impersonal way are sensed by the myth-making mind as feminine. Having looked at some of the wonders of the saga, one must turn to the women, since they go together.

Images of women as troublemakers and as creatures keenly aware that insult and injury to their men and kindred must be paid for appear often, not only in *Njáls saga* but in other sagas and other records as well. There is undoubtedly an historical base to such images. Tacitus gives us a picture of the German women whose heroic pleadings rally their men from the edge of defeat. It is not too far a step from that to the image of a single woman furiously inciting men to avenge a fallen kinsman. Such is the image preserved in the Eddic poems where such vengeance was "felt as a vindication of the fame of the deceased. We can deduce this by noting that the emphasis is always laid on the slain, not on the slayer" [Bertha S. Phillpotts, *Edda*

A depiction of Njál battling evil, in an Icelandic manuscript of Njáls saga *dated around 1300.*

and Saga]. Women are more mindful, perhaps, of the fame and reputation of the family that has been born out of them, of the plight they are left in when the protectors of the family are slain. For fame they are willing to sacrifice individual members. There is a certain sacredness about the duty of revenge and the task of whetting, of inciting men to the attack, is carried out with ritualistic care. Terror, fear, and awe accompany such moments, especially when men become overwhelmed by the force speaking through such a woman. The *Nibelungenlied* does not surpass the portrait of a fury-possessed woman such as is beheld in Fredegund in the pages of Gregory's *History of the Franks.* The awe inspired by a woman dedicated to revenge is still detectable in the admiring remarks made at the end of *Harðar saga ok Hólmverja* where Horðr's fame is assured because

> Four and twenty men were killed in revenge for
> Horðr. For none of them was atonement offered.
> The sons of Horðr and his kinsmen and in-laws
> killed some, and Hróarr killed others. And most
> of them were killed through the counsel of
> Þorborg Grimkell's-daughter. . . . After no
> other single man in Iceland had so many men
> been killed in revenge and all unatoned for.

But there is a change from the situation found in the Eddic poetry to that in the sagas. The figure of the avenging female loses some of her numinous qualities. Along with and in place of a woman who fulfills a traditional role appear proud, touchy, and willful individuals, women who act out of a sense of personal pique and desire, not out of familial service to the "sacred duty of revenge." The contrast between the older and the newer types is seen in *Njáls saga* between Hallgerðr, who wishes to use Gunnarr to glorify herself, and Hildigunnr, who uses Flosi as an instrument to avenge her fallen husband. Her concern is not with her own reputation but with Hoskuldr's.

It is reasonable to believe that some of the examples of such women and some of the instances of whetting to revenge found in the sagas reflect historical truth. But with a motif as persistent as this one, central in the cycles of heroic poems, one which occurs frequently in the family sagas and which is a marked feature of the legendary sagas, it must be recognized that this motif has become a standard narrative component because it satisfied otherwise unexpressed concerns, that it may act as a screen which at once conceals and utters certain perceptions which cannot otherwise be articulated.

One explanation is that the figure of the vengeful woman is an outward projection of man's own uneasy awareness of the divided state within him, that it is a mechanism whereby the blame and guilt for his failures to control his passions (and for his desire for such failures) can be shifted to an outside cause. Maud Bodkin has referred to "a sense of man's terror of that weakness in himself which he projects upon the type figure of women" [*Archetypal Patterns in Poetry,* 1963]. E. R. Dodds has described the process in more general terms and has pointed out that in Homeric poetry motivation and explanations for man's impulsive acts are provided for by an elaborate system of terms for forces which are felt to possess man from the outside: "When a character acts in a manner contrary to the system of conscious dispositions which he is said to 'know,' his action is not properly his own, but has been dictated to him. In other words, unsystematised, nonrational impulses, and the acts resulting from them, tend to be excluded from the self and ascribed to alien origin" [*The Greeks and the Irrational,* 1951]. Men first perceive the structure of their own passions and desires thrown outward upon the world; they have to perceive them outwardly before they can again take them into themselves and thus become introspectively aware of what indeed resides in them.

Thus the women in the saga, who are portrayed as characters in their own right, also fulfill an impersonal role. They embody the conflicting passions and social dilemmas that exist within the culture, the culture of which the sagas are a partial expression. There is the conflict between the natural reluctance of men to risk their lives (for life is dear) and their duty to avenge their kindred. There is the conflict between shame that follows for not taking forthright vengeance and the disapproval that accrues about those who will break and not abide by the settlements of men. The actions of Gunnarr and Njáll and other men of good will are designed to strengthen the system of laws, to enhance the status of those who prefer to talk rather than to kill. But the law by which Njáll hopes to build up the land is not strong enough to resist the pressures that are brought to bear upon it from men and women whose pride, shortsightedness, rashness, and sheer malice conspire against it. Moreover, the old system of atonements and arbitration was in itself, as has been seen, based on a rationalization and sublimation of the original violence it sought to govern and hence was apt, in times of instability, to revert to its original state. Halfway through the saga, the desire of men to build up a land through an ordered pattern of life (a pattern in terms of which the old recourse to feud and fighting is seen as lawlessness) receives powerful reinforcement with the introduction of Christianity. Mercy, forgiveness, and the thought that reward and vengeance are the Lord's (" 'He will not let us burn both in this world and the next' ") have a power in them that strengthens the hand of men willing good. And as a consequence, the women who represent and speak for the older order are thrown over to and linked with the pagan world where powers of darkness and evil stir. It must be emphasized that this is an impersonal process of representing divisions and polarities within the human mind, divisions which are, of course, made objective and all too real in human deeds and the pattern of human culture. When I speak of men who wish to build up the land, I mean the men and women who together did in fact settle Iceland and wrought the culture that has, through great times and hard times and many changes, endured to the present day. This is the culture that produced the sagas and the sagas remember many deeds of ancestors, but they cast these deeds into forms not untouched by the force of myth. A distinction has to be made between these men as they appear as historical characters in *Njáls saga* and as their figures are used as representative types; between these women as the saga preserves their individual persons and as the saga manipulates them under cover of traditional motifs to embody forces. And it must be remembered that at times the myth and the reality did merge and could not be distinguished. Hildigunnr, the proud but cautious bride who wishes her husband to live with her in the land east away from his dangerous kinsmen (ch. 97) grows easily into the Hildigunnr who with priestlike deliberation and long-considered savage passion incites her uncle to blood revenge.

This great scene stands for all the other times women have stirred up trouble in *Njáls saga* and it is the culmination of the theme. This moment is reached when Flosi and his men ride to visit Hildigunnr, his niece, after the brutal slaying of her husband, Hoskuldr Hvitaness-Priest. Flosi has been talking with his kinsmen and allies who have urged him to accept the generous offers of settlement that Njáll and the others are sure to make. Flosi is ill at ease when he comes to make the visit to the widowed Hildigunnr—he knows what is going to happen, that she will egg him on to blood revenge in such terms that he cannot shirk from that course. But custom and courtesy oblige him to submit himself to her passion. There is an atmosphere of compulsion and ritual inevitability in what follows.

Hildigunnr has ordered the house swept, the tapestries hung up, and the high seat set at the table for Flosi. She goes to meet him:" 'Be welcome, kinsman; my heart is rejoiced at your arrival.' Flosi said, 'We'll eat the noon meal here and ride on' " (ch. 116). Flosi's curt and nervous reply to Hildigunnr's formal greeting reveals his uneasiness. He walks into the room where the meal is set and throws the high seat away from him, which Hildigunnr had set there to remind him that he is the head of her family. Flosi says,

> "I am neither a king nor an earl, and there is no need to furnish a high seat for me and no need to mock me." Hildigunnr stood close by and said, "That is too bad, if you are displeased because we did this with sincere intentions." Flosi said, "If you have sound intentions towards me, they will declare themselves if they are good and they will condemn themselves if they are evil." Hildigunnr laughed a cold laugh and said, "This is still off the mark; we will come closer before things are settled."

The towel Hildigunnr gives Flosi is full of holes and one end has been ripped away, a token, Sveinsson notes, of Hildigunnr's abandonment and loss [Einar Ól. Sveinsson, *Fornrit*, 1954]. Flosi uses the tablecloth instead. But the action so far, as Hildigunnr has hinted, has only been preliminary. The issues come out into the open as the men eat:

> Then Hildigunnr came into the room and stepped before Flosi, brushed her hair from her eyes and wept. Flosi said, "You are low in spirits now, niece, since you are weeping. Nevertheless it is proper that you should weep for a good man." "What action now or support shall I have from you?" she says. Flosi said, "I will prosecute your case as far as the law permits or strive for that settlement which good men will see is honorable to us in every respect." She said, "Hoskuldr would have taken blood revenge for you, if he had had this suit to take up on your behalf." Flosi answered, "You are not lacking in savageness, and it is clear what you want."

Hildigunnr reminds him that Flosi's brothers had taken blood revenge on Árnorr Ornólfsson for an injury to their father less grave than that Hoskuldr suffered:

> Hildigunnr then went from her room and opened up her clothes chest. She took out the cloak which Flosi had given to Hoskuldr and in that cloak Hoskuldr had been slain. She had preserved it with all its blood. Silently she went up to Flosi. Flosi was finished and the dishes had been cleared. Then Hildigunnr flung the cloak over Flosi; the blood poured down all about him. Then she spoke: "You gave this cloak to Hoskuldr, Flosi; now I give it back to you. In this cloak he was slain. I call God and good men to witness that I conjure you by all the might of thy Christ and by thy manliness and by thy valor to revenge all wounds which he had on his dead body, or else be called a contemptible wretch [*níðingr*] by every man." Flosi hurled the cloak back into her face and said, "Monster that you are, you wish that we should take up what will turn out the worst for all of us. 'Cold are the

counsels of women.' " Flosi was so shaken that
at times his face turned red as blood, then pale
as grass, then blue-black as death [*blár sem hel*].
(ch. 116)

These similes account for three out of the one hundred
forty-eight to be found in thirty-two family sagas and the
degree of Flosi's agitation may be judged from the fact
that this is the only such triple occurrence in these sagas.
In the last there is a buried mythological reference, for
Snorri tells us of the goddess Hel, the goddess of the dead,
that "she is half blue-black and half flesh-colored, whereby she is easily recognized, and rather lowering and
fierce." Flosi's face is stamped with the colors of fear and
death whose power he is now forced to serve. The epithet
Flosi flings at Hildigunnr in his dismay and anger—"you
are the greatest monster (*þú ert it mesta forað*)"
—curiously fits the assertion that women, pagan powers,
the land, and perilous places gather together in an archetypal cluster of symbols. For the primary meaning of *forað*
was a dangerous place, a precipice, abyss, or swamp,
meanings which it still retains in modern Icelandic. Perhaps the meanings, "monster," "ogre," developed because
unpleasant creatures often dwell in such places. So considered, the epithet here draws to it associations of the
swamps in which Svanr's blinded foes stumble, the cliff-
sides that open up to receive Svanr and Iron-Grim, perhaps the deep sea gulf (*sjávardjúp*) that appeared before
the altar at Thvattriver. Whether such associations were
intended by the saga-man or consciously made by his audience is another question; one doubts that they were, although the use of the word, with its double meaning, may
have released certain affects. But the possibility is latent
in the saga for such an association.

Hildigunnr's incitement has been a stirring up of the
strongest appeals to old custom and man's sense of shame
and it has been a summoning of more-than-human poten-
cies. Covered with his nephew's blood, called *níðingr* to
his face in the presence of his men, urged by the power of
the strongest god Hildigunnr can think of, the new Christ,
Flosi is committed to the course he knows is the worst for
all. Hildigunnr's reference to Christ certainly seems an
ironic touch. Flosi is urged on in Christ's name to avenge
the man who died with a prayer on his lips that God forgive his slayers. That Hildigunnr refers to "your Christ"
makes it reasonably certain that she still speaks and acts
in the name of the older gods. In fact, the blood-drenched
cloak she wrathfully flings about her uncle may even be
intended to evoke the scarlet or purple robe that the
Roman soldiers, who were also of the old order, fling
about Christ in mockery before his crucifixion. Flosi is no
Christ-figure, but he is struggling to understand the new
religion—his reluctance and words show that, for under
the old code his obligation to avenge Hoskuldr was clear
and certain. And Hildigunnr's passionate gesture is, like
the mocking investiture of Christ, a condemnatory one as
well; the course Hildigunnr dictates is a course that should
surely bring death upon Flosi's own head in turn. But except for Hildigunnr's curious reference to Christ, there is
no word or phrase to indicate whether or not the saga-man
intended his audience to draw such a parallel or whether
or not he expected that it could. That the parallel does sug-

gest itself, however, is an indication of how critical this
scene is.

" 'Cold are the counsels of women' "—that wisdom, uttered at one of the most dramatic moments of the saga,
awakens echoes of its own. Hildigunnr's whetting must
lead to the Burning and the consequences of that threaten
to break apart the system of law and ordered agreements
which give form, sense, and security to the national life.
In fact both sides recognize that whatever the decision is
at the Althing, it is one that cannot possibly be enforced
by legal means and the suit will break down into the violence it is attempting to contain. Snorri the Priest admits
this in a pretrial agreement he makes with Ásgrímr
Elliða-Grímsson whose men and whose son, the great lawyer Þórhallr, are supporting the suits of Njáll's kinsmen
and friends against the Burners. Snorri predicts:

"It is likely that you will be prosecuting the case
vigorously while they will defend themselves in
a like manner, and neither of you will concede
the other's right. Then you will not be able to
bear them and will attack them. And that will
be the only way left because they wish to repay
your loss of lives with further shame and the
death of your kinsmen with dishonor." It
seemed to them that Snorri was urging them on
somewhat. (ch. 139)

And he can think of no solution but to set dead against
dead. In the course of drawing up a battle plan he says,
" 'and when you have killed as many of them on the other
side as I think you can afford to pay atonement fees for
and still retain your chieftainships and rights to residence,
then I will jump in with all my men and part you.' "

In a sense then the great law processes that follow are but
an elaborate series of technical maneuverings over a foregone conclusion—that neither side will accept the decision. The law has become an inadequate instrument—the
law that was designed not so much to determine the rights
and wrongs of the issues it decided but designed rather to
impose a correct form on the way settlements were to be
reached. It is obvious in the suits that conviction depends
on the correctness of procedure in the charge and not on
whether the charge can be proven. There is no question
that Flosi has led a party to burn the Njálssons within
their house; the question is whether witnesses to the act
can be correctly summoned and the jury correctly
charged. Thus, when a verdict actually is given against
Flosi, after a long series of technical quibblings and reversals themselves reversed by brilliant lawyering behind the
scenes, the result is somehow irrelevant and hardly emphasized. Indeed the moment of victory for Njáll's party
is quickly overturned, when Flosi appeals the verdict to
the Fifth Court on the grounds of a procedural irregulari-
ty, a result of a carefully prepared scheme of Flosi's lawyer. The Burners in the climactic suit actually become the
prosecutors for a brief moment until Þórhallr quickly in-
stitutes a countersuit charging Flosi with bribing his lawyer to defend him. All this maneuvering is exciting and in
its own way it is the analogue of the bloody escalations
which have developed in earlier feuds, but it evades the
central issue. The court and the law have failed, had to fail
given the structure of the law, to make a satisfactory pro-

nouncement on the tragic and terrible events of the saga—that Njáll and his sons were burned to death within their house after the brutal slaying of Flosi's nephew. The Burning above all has been a desperate and heinous act and the pronouncements the law makes upon it must have some relevance to the right and wrong of the matter if the law to which men submit themselves is to make any sense at all. If the law cannot cope with this central event, it must either be strengthened by new means or altered; otherwise, the land-destroying lawlessness that Njáll had feared will have prevailed.

The lengthy repetitions of the legal formulas work to stave off the issue in another fashion. They come to have a solemn, almost incantory effect, as if by their impressive phrasing and very sound they may ward off the trouble that is brooding over the assembly, as if through the sheer virtuosity of words they could soothe the violence at the same time that they summon witnesses to it. The effect is not unlike that of some of the magical charms and alliterative vows used to make pacts binding and to call down curses on oath-breakers. At least, this is my conjecture why so much legal matter is present here and repeated verbatim at such length. For present readers many of these passages may become tedious and they are easily skipped over. It is obvious, nevertheless, that they are there by deliberation. Earlier trial scenes have prepared the audience for such procedures and made it familiar with the terminology. And when he wants to, the saga-man is perfectly capable of a summary:

> Ásgrímr and his men had the other suits for the Burning put in motion and they went forward. (ch. 143)

> Then Morðr named witnesses and stated those four charges which he had prepared against Flosi and Eyjólfr, and Morðr used all the same words in his statement of the charge as he had previously used in his citation. (ch. 144)

If extended passages of legal prose are present, the reason is that the saga-man wanted them to be. Perhaps his particular audience delighted in the full panoply of technicalities (no other saga so revels in such swathes of law)—and perhaps a truly skilled speaker could make all the matter of summoning and charging exciting and effective. There is, moreover, a certain satiric force and grim humor in the spectacle of all this frantic, windy, and death-laden lawyering. But I think the reason advanced above is also part of the explanation, that the law is used almost as magic in an attempt to ward off the inevitable conflict. In a saga so concerned with man's attempt to rule himself, it is appropriate that the law itself appears as a final barrier of words thrown up against the conflict that is rapidly approaching.

The conflict breaks into the open when Morðr, who with Þórhallr's backstage advice has skillfully conducted the case through all its stages, makes a final and fatal blunder, a blunder involving a technicality which Njáll himself had carefully stipulated at the time he established the rules governing the Fifth Court. The way is open for Flosi's party to bring up their countercharges and have a sentence of outlawry proclaimed against their foes. Possibly Morðr

has deliberately blundered—he has been an agent for disorder all along and he has little love for the men whose suit he has been obliged to conduct. He disappears into the tumult which he has served so well. There is a glimpse of him pressing Flosi's men and then without any comment he is out of the saga just as Hallgerðr was allowed to vanish without any formal notice. This outbreak of battle is a striking scene where the procedures in the land's highest court suddenly revert to passion and war. The high feelings and hatreds and irreconcilable festering grievances hitherto pent in are purged and cancelled in the violence that follows. Their nature and this process of purgation are symbolized in the remarkable moment after Þórhallr, laid up in bed with an infected leg, hears the news of Morðr's blunder:

> Now it should be told that the messenger comes to Þórhallr and tells him what had happened, that they would all be made outlaws and that the manslaughter suit was voided. And when Þórhallr heard that, he was so moved that he could not speak a word. He sprang up from his bed and seized with both hands the spear Skarpheðinn had given him and drove it into his leg. Flesh and the core of the boil were on the spear as he dug it out of his leg. Such a gush of blood and pus followed that it fell across the floor in a stream. Þórhallr went out of the booth without limping and strode so vigorously that the messenger could not follow him. He fared on until he came to the Fifth Court. Then he ran into Grímr the Red, a kinsman of Flosi. As soon as they met. Þórhallr laid out with his spear against Grímr's shield and cleft it apart. The spear went on through Grímr and came out between his shoulders. Þórhallr cast him off the spear, dead. (ch. 145)

The large clash of armed men which this act sets off is final evidence that the old code has been broken down. The spectacle of so many men warring with one another on the plains dedicated to the making and upholding of law shows what the long chain of grievances and quarrels, begun decades before, has led to. And although this battle may even accounts there is no hope that the process will not begin anew unless some shift of values is made. For the law, even when it worked by substituting itself for violence, never quite dispelled the shame and anger roused by insult and injury. And because the law is a substitute for violence, it is compromised, for violence is at its base. Perhaps this is what Snorri the Priest alludes to when he draws up his forces to halt Flosi's retreat. Flosi asks him why Snorri is barring their way to a safe retreat:" 'I am not causing your way to be barred,' says Snorri, 'but I know who is and will tell you without being asked, that Þorvaldr Crop-Beard and Kolr are bringing this about' " (ch. 145). The reference is a somewhat confused allusion to an incident recorded in the *Íslandingabók*. Þorvaldr had burned his brother Gunnarr alive in his house; Þorvaldr's grandfather had murdered a thrall named Kolr in the early days of the settlement. For this he had been outlawed and the money from the land where Kolr's corpse was found had been appropriated for the use of the Althing. Snorri's reference may be a reminder that to the Althing itself a trace still clings of these two base and contemptible crimes, that the Althing is partly sustained by an outlaw's forfeit property. At least it is an admission that the spirits of criminal and victim still haunt the Althing.

But the old ways are not wholly restored after the battle is ended. Hallr of Síða's generous offer to let his son lie unatoned is the act that shifts the mind of the assembly. It is an act of forgiveness, for Hallr a gesture of great sacrifice and for the nation a new wisdom. Although foreshadowed in the gestures of Hrútr and the good will Gunnarr and Njáll nurture between them, it is here given public and dramatic sanction. It is the act that shifts the saga itself onto an upward path that leads, eventually, to the reconciliation between Kári and Flosi and to Kári's marriage with Hildigunnr. For the structure of *Njáls saga* is a structure that leads beyond the tragic events which are its points of greatest intensity and deepest sorrow. The curtain does not fall upon the figures of men mournfully praising the fallen Gunnarr, or sorrowfully and wonderingly discovering the unharmed bodies amid the ashes at Bergþórshváll. Such scenes bring to mind the final scenes of dramatic tragedy.

But it is perhaps well to remember that tragedy was once part of a larger cycle that ended in comedy. Saga preserves this larger structure. It is capable of focusing to a tragic point, but it rarely ends there. Reports of vengeance and eventual settlement follow the death of major figures. These reports are nearly always present, although they can be shaped so as to give rise to markedly different effects. Some sagas, as W. P. Ker and Bertha Phillpotts have noted, avoid the fatal consequences towards which they seem to have been travelling, come to a reconciliatory end, or else die quietly away. A saga like *Laxdœla saga* ends with all passions exhausted and played out, on a note of tragic regret, in Guðrún's famous admission to her grandson, " 'I was the worst to him whom I loved most.' " In *Gísla saga* the sections of revenge and aftermath are very sharply curtailed and abortive. The saga's dramatic climax is the heroic last stand and death of Gísli which comes very shortly before the end. Grettir meets a fate very similar to that of Gísli, but his saga yields to the impulse to continue onwards to a lighter and more gentle ending. The adventure of Grettir's half-brother in Constantinople and his happy marriage to the Lady Spes comprise the story of a man of good luck. Here the saga form breaks into the realm of romance. The generic contrast between the sections is obvious, but was not, I think, felt as a lapse of taste or artistic control. This upward swing seen so clearly in *Grettis saga* is visible also in *Njáls saga* and confirms a tendency of the saga form. It is a tendency towards an expanding action at the end. The saga hero dies alone, but his figure is not an isolated one. About the bodies of the slain gather friends and kindred. A man's death involved all men in Iceland, or could nearly do so, as *Njáls saga* illustrates. And the men that gather about the slain have come not merely to pick up the pieces. Life goes on; there is a healing vigor in the society that emerges in the saga literature. It was a society that was able to sustain great losses, to appreciate what had been lost, and that could yet go on. It is only in *Njáls saga* that the mechanisms of atonement and settlement fail to check the cy-

cles of vengeance before they get so out of hand that a large disruption of much of the civil order is threatened, a disruption which the Battle at the Althing represents and portrays. But that threat too is finally contained. At the end Kári and Flosi are reconciled, and Hildigunnr married to Kári. The upswing concludes with a knitting together of the torn fabric of the island. It is a restoration of the old society, but in its restored form a society considerably changed and tempered, both by the experience it has endured and by the revelation of Christian mercy. There is an analogue here with the action of comedy which moves toward the birth of a new society and embraces old and new at the end in reconciliation and wedding. It is tempting to say that saga as a genre contains the stuff of tragedy in a comic form, and, indeed, W. P. Ker comes close to such an observation when, after reviewing the *Bandamanna saga,* he says that heroic narrative in Iceland was "a form which proves itself equally capable of Tragedy and Comedy" [*Epic and Romance,* 1896]. Perhaps one comes closer to an understanding of saga as genre if one considers that it developed after the breakdown of the epic synthesis but that it still remains close enough to this synthesis that it can contain in organic fashion much of the epic vision. It is a genre that, professing to be history, contains the adventure of romance, the fated course of heroes, the humor and self-criticism of comedy, all in a linear and self-restoring form. After fatal events, men could take measure of themselves and go on. The extent of the calamities they faced, the sternness with which they were expected to act, and the number of tales told about their heroic deeds were measures of the strength of their society.

At the end in *Njáls saga* the slowly rising curve along which Kári, Flosi, and Hildigunnr have made their way divides in two directions. The one direction goes with history and comes down to the listeners who are hearing the story. Curiously enough it is Kári, the striking heroic figure who first appeared upon the sea in his gleaming armor, whose line goes on into the world that the audience knows. By Hildigunnr Kári has children. A grandson, Kolbeinn, "was one of the most renowned men in that family" (ch. 159). The line goes on into the light of contemporary day. But for Flosi, whose strength served the destroying wrath of Hildigunnr, the line curves back into the realm of mystery and myth, back into that realm where all stories begin:

> Men say this, that such was the life's-ending of Flosi, that he fared abroad when he had become an old man to seek house timber. He was in Norway that winter. But in summer he was late in getting under way. Men told him that his ship was not seaworthy. Flosi said that it was good enough for an old and doomed man. He boarded that ship and put out to sea. Of that ship nothing was ever heard again. (ch. 159)

"Of that ship nothing was ever heard again." As so often in the sagas a few words awaken memories of far-off times and the old heroic days. Flosi's last seafaring is not unlike the last voyage of the legendary Danish king, Scyld Scefing, when, given to the ocean, he rides out in his funeral ship. And the Beowulf poet says:

*Men ne cunnon
secgan tō sōðe   selerǣdende
hǣleð under heofenum   hwā þǣm
hlǣste onfēng.*

[Men, the counsellors in the hall, the heroes beneath the heavens, could not truly say who received that ocean cargo.]

The treasure laden upon Scyld's ship is the tribute paid him by men who will maintain Scyld's strong-handed rule. Flosi, who in his way and time served the old order, vanishes, without praise, in a ship laden with timber for building anew. Flosi the old man disappears in the sea as all heroes must at sunset before they are reborn. His end is a token to men that what they have heard is not a history only. His end is a token that what they have heard they will hear again.

Paul Schach   (essay date 1984)

SOURCE: "Major Sagas about Icelanders," in *Icelandic Sagas*, Twayne Publishers, 1984, pp. 97-130.

[*In the excerpt below, Schach interprets* Njáls saga *as a homily in which its author stresses the virtues of Christianity and condemns the ineffective legal system of medieval Iceland.*]

Brennu-Njáls saga (The story of Njál of the burning) is the longest, the most profound, and the most powerful of the *Íslendinga sögur.* It is a trilogy with a preface of twenty chapters in which the author introduces several main characters and adumbrates one of the major conflicts of the saga. The first part is the story of a remarkable friendship between Njál, a wise and gentle, albeit devious, lawyer who has never wielded weapons, and Gunnar, a formidable warrior who is reluctant to kill. This story ends with the slaying of Gunnar in a heroic stand against an overwhelming number of assailants. The second part relates the conflict between Njál's sons and Thráin Sigfússon and Njál's constant but vain endeavor to make and preserve peace following Thráin's slaying. This story culminates in the death by burning of Njál and his family in their home. The final part of the saga relates the relentless quest of Njál's son-in-law Kári for vengeance against the burners and concludes with a reconciliation between Kári and Flosi, the leader of the burners.

A century ago A. U. Bååth declared that the author of *Njála* had the final words of his saga in mind before he set the first ones down on parchment [*Studier öfver Kompositionen i Några Isländska Ättsagor,* 1895]. This coherence and tightness of composition were achieved through the structural device of complex plot interlace and the rhetorical technique of foreshadowing, which is employed with greater skill, variety, and density in *Njála* than in any other saga. Dreams, visions, warnings, predictions, premonitions, omens, portents, taunts and introductory character sketches are artfully used to anticipate the future, heighten suspense, and connect widely separated events.

In the first chapter, for example, Hallgered is introduced as a tall, beautiful child with long, silken hair. When her father Höskuld asks his brother Hrút whether he does not think she is beautiful, he replies, "That girl is beautiful enough, and many will suffer because of it. But I cannot understand how thief's eyes have come into our family." In chapter 48, Hallgerd sends a slave to steal cheese from a neighbor, and the ensuing feud eventually leads to her husband Gunnar's destruction. Hallgerd's first two husbands were killed by her foster father for slapping her face. When Gunnar slaps her for instigating this theft, she says that she will remember the slap and repay it if possible. During Gunnar's last stand—he is in his home at Hlídarendi with Hallgerd and his mother Rannveig—his bowstring is cut asunder.

> He said to Hallgerd, "Let me have two strands of your hair, and you and mother twist them into a bowstring for me."
>
> "Does it mean something to you?" she asked.
>
> "It means my life," he said, "for they will never overcome me as long as I can use my bow."
>
> "In that case," she said, "I shall remind you of the slap on the cheek. I do not care at all how long you hold out."
>
> "Each earns fame in his own way," said Gunnar. "You will not be asked again."
>
> Rannveig said, "Your behavior is evil, and your shame will long endure." (chap. 77)

No less remarkable than the tight structure and complex texture of *Njála* are the memorable characters the author has created. Einar Ólafur Sveinsson devoted over two-thirds of his monograph on this saga to a discussion of these fascinating men and women and to an analysis of the author's techniques of character delineation and development [*Njáls Saga,* 1966]. A few of the characters are painted in black and white, but most of them are complex, being portrayed in various shades of gray.

More than most saga writers, the author of *Njála* expressed his own opinion of his characters through the technique of having one individual pass judgment on the behavior of another. After Gunnar has slain a man named Thorgeir Otkelsson, Njál succeeds in bringing about an arbitration, according to which Gunnar and his brother Kolskegg agree to go abroad for three years. When at the last minute Gunnar unexpectedly decides to remain in Iceland and urges Kolskegg to do likewise, his loyal brother declares, "I shall not act basely (*níðast*) in this or in any other matter in which people trust me" (chap. 75). Kolskegg goes abroad, never to return; Gunnar rides home to Hlídarendi, thus giving Hallgerd the opportunity of repaying him for the slap on her cheek.

It is not surprising that a work of such magnitude as *Njáls saga* should have been subjected to differing interpretations. An older generation of scholars believed firmly in its historical veracity, and some went so far as to declare Ari Thorgilsson in error when his sober recording of facts differed from the literary treatment of them in the saga [*The Book of the Icelanders,* 1930]. It is clear that the author made use of historical sources. In *Landnámabók* we read that a man named Njál was burned to death with seven other persons in his home at Bergthórshvol, and there is archaeological evidence to support this statement. *Landnámabók* also records Gunnar's death at Hlídarendi as well as a fight between Gunnar and some farmers at Knafahólar and Gunnar's killing of two enemies named Otkel and Skammkel [*Íslendinga sögur,* 1953]. A surprisingly large number of major characters, however, are not mentioned in historical sources, and some of them, at least, must be regarded as fictitious.

A comparison of the sparse historical records with the treatment of them in *Njála* is revealing. The historical Njál appears to have been an obscure farmer whose name was remembered only because of the horrible manner of his death. The author of *Njála* imaginatively embellished the meager historical account of this event with details borrowed from descriptions of burnings recorded in *Sturlunga saga.* In the skirmish at Knafahólar, Gunnar and his band (*lið*) killed an Icelander and two Norwegians, and Gunnar's brother Hjört and a manservant were slain. From this event, the author created three fights, in which Gunnar himself dispatched over twenty men. In his final battle, Gunnar was aided by another man; in the saga, he has to fight unaided, as is proper for saga heroes. It is obvious that the author dealt freely with his materials for the purpose of expanding the dimensions of his heroes, and some readers will doubtless feel that he went too far in this. Even greater distortion is found in his treatment of Skapti Thóroddsson. We recall that Skapti around 1005 improved the constitution by establishing the appellate court known as the *fimmtardómr* and making it difficult for chieftains to blame their crimes on henchmen. In the saga, credit for this is given to Njál, and Skapti is denigrated and degraded into a ridiculous figure who is taunted at the General Assembly. By contrast, Gudmund the Mighty, who appears in a dubious light in the earlier works, is portrayed very favorably in *Njála.*

More recently there has been a tendency to regard *Njáls saga* as a *roman á clef,* in which the author thinly disguised contemporary happenings and prominent persons, including himself. Certain events and individuals in *Njála,* it is true, have close correspondences in *Sturlunga saga,* and the author did derive inspiration and information from that history. Furthermore, the significance of the saga for contemporary times was so great that, according to Heusler, copies were made of it before the author had had time to eliminate minor errors in a final revision [*Die Geschichte vom weisen Njál,* 1914]. The careful development of two central themes in the work, however, indicates that *Njála* is much more than a mere literary reflection of the contemporary scene.

There is better reason to interpret *Njáls saga* as a homily as, among others, Magnus Magnusson and Hermann Pálsson have done [*Njáls Saga,* 1960]. In the first part of the saga (chaps. 21-81), which takes place during pagan times, there is much talk about fate and honor. Early in the second part (chaps. 82-132), the author inserted a digression in the form of a detailed description of the conversion (chaps. 100-105), after which the pagan concept of fate, at least in Njál's mind, is transformed into the Christian belief in providence. Three years after the conversion, Ámundi the Blind, illegitimate son of Höskuld Njálsson,

miraculously has his sight restored long enough to wreak vengeance on his father's slayer (chap. 106). We are reminded of the skaldic stanza by Earl Rögnvald about the slaughter of Saracens in *Orkneyinga saga* ("This was God's doing") and of the prophet Samuel's anointment of King Sverrir's hands for hatred against his enemies.

A deeper understanding of Christianity is demonstrated by Njál's foster son Höskuld. After the killing of Thráin by Njál's sons to avenge indignities suffered because of him in Norway, Njál fosters Thráin's son Höskuld in the hope of averting further killing. When Höskuld is fully grown, the villain Mörd, who plotted Gunnar's death, through insidious slander convinces Njál's sons and Kári that Höskuld intends to kill them all in vengeance for Thráin's death. As Höskuld goes out to sow grain on a spring morning, they attack him from ambush. Without attempting to strike back, Höskuld sinks to his knees with these words on his lips, "May God help me and forgive you." "This was the only thing," the author tells us, "that grieved Njál so deeply that he could never speak about it without being moved to tears" (chap. 111). These words are an echo of a passage in Snorri's *Prose Edda* describing the grief of the gods, and especially of Odin, at the slaying of the innocent god Baldur [Sveinsson, *Njáls Saga*].

Njál, who has long known the manner of his own death (chap. 55), now reveals that Höskuld's slaying will bring disaster to his wife and their sons as well, and Flosi ominously declares that "seeds of evil have been sown, and they will yield evil" (chap. 115). Höskuld's widow Hildigunn implores her uncle Flosi in the name of his Christ to exact blood vengeance for her husband or else be called a "vile wretch (*niðingr*)" by all men (chap. 117). From this point on, the author presents a crescendo of pagan portents interspersed with Christian sentiments until the tragedy reaches its climax. When all efforts at arbitration fail, Flosi rides to Bergthórshvol with 120 followers. Despite the fact that Njál's people can hold them off out of doors, Njál insists that they enter the house. Reluctantly, Flosi orders the building to be set on fire, "for this," he says, "is a great responsibility before God, since we are Christian men ourselves" (chap. 128).

Soon the roof is ablaze, and Njál consoles the frightened women: "Take heart and speak no words of despair, for this will be only a brief storm, and it will be long before another one like it comes. Have faith in God's mercy, for he will not let us burn in both this world and the next" (chap. 129). The reason for Njál's insistence that his people enter the house is now clear: inexorable pagan fate in his mind has been transformed into benign Christian providence, and he regards the destruction of himself and his family as an act of penance for the slaying of his spiritual son Höskuld (38).

The women, children, and servants are now permitted to leave the house. Flosi, who feels obligated to kill only Njál's sons and Kári, begs Njál and his wife Bergthóra to come out also. Njál refuses because, he says, he is too old to avenge his sons and unwilling to live in shame for not doing so. Bergthóra, who has often been strong-willed and abrasive, replies to Flosi with quiet dignity, "I was married to Njál when young. I promised him that we should endure the same fate." They lie down, cross themselves, commend their souls to God, and calmly await death. After the fires have died down, it is found that their son Skarphédin, the fiercest of warriors, has burned two marks of the cross on his body, and Hjalti Skeggjason declares that Njál's countenance and body "have a radiance such as I have never seen before on a dead man's body" (chap. 132). All present agree that that is so.

The prosecution of the burners ends in a mistrial, and a bloody battle breaks out at the General Assembly. With the help of several other chieftains, Snorri godi separates the two sides and later initiates arbitration. The turning point in the bitter wrangling comes when Hall of Sída, whose son Ljót was killed in the fighting, in a spirit of Christian humility and magnanimity foregoes compensation for his son and yet pledges peace to his adversaries. Heavy fines are imposed on Flosi and all the other burners, and they are ordered to leave the country, some for three years and some for life. Kári, who alone has escaped alive from the burning, excludes himself from the settlement and launches a fearful campaign of vengeance, during which he kills twenty of Flosi's men, the last one in Wales. Flosi makes no attempt to retaliate.

At this point the author inserted a second digression into his story. In the Battle of Clontarf, which is fought on Good Friday, fourteen of Flosi's remaining fifteen followers are killed while fighting against the Christian King Brján of Ireland. Although the king himself is slain, his army is victorious. This dramatic interlude, preceded by portents and attended by marvels, is one of the finest examples of the medieval digression *ad aliud extra materiam*, that is, to something outside the story proper. Just as the conversion episode marked the beginning of the conflict between paganism and Christianity, the Battle of Clontarf signifies its conclusion.

The second theme in *Njáls saga* is stated by Njál himself in the form of a well-known proverb: "With laws shall our land be built up, but with lawlessness laid waste" (chap. 70). The author, who probably completed his book about 1290, had lived to see Njál's prophecy fulfilled. The barbarous cruelty and the disregard for and subversion of the law during the Sturlung Age doubtless whetted his curiosity about legal problems and procedures. From a lawbook, he filled page after page with minute descriptions of intricate legal moves and countermoves. Occasionally he was so intent on copying legal formulae correctly that he failed to substitute the names of his characters for the name *Jón* (that is, *N.N.*) in the codex (see chap. 141). Despite all the legalistic rigamarole, however, not one lawsuit is carried to a successful conclusion in this saga. Settlement of quarrels is usually achieved by extralegal means through arbitration, but powerful individuals thwart such settlements by refusing to abide by the terms imposed (Gunnar) or by excluding themselves from the agreement (Kári). Ironically the prosecution of the burners fails in the appellate court established (according to the story) by Njál himself, the wisest lawyer of his day (for the purpose of securing a chieftaincy for his foster son Höskuld in order to facilitate Höskuld's marriage to Hildigunn). The second theme of *Njáls saga* can thus be defined as an indictment of the

legal system of medieval Iceland and a condemnation of the ruthless men who subverted it for selfish reasons.

Gunnar lived and died by the sword in accordance with the pagan heroic code of his day. Njál failed because he relied entirely on his own finite wisdom and on his cleverness in manipulating the law. As in *Heiðarvíga saga*, final reconciliation in *Njála* can be achieved only through the practical application of Christian ethics. Just as he skillfully brought together the many strands of his convoluted plot, the author of *Njála* thus neatly combined the two main themes of his story. After receiving absolution of their sins in Rome, Kári and Flosi too are reconciled. The reconciliation is sealed and symbolized by a marriage between Kári and Hildigunn.

From a cursory reading of *Njála,* we might gain the impression that the author was trying to imitate the simple language of oral tales. His style is more lucid and fluent than that of most sagas, but its cadences and nuances, as Einar Ólafur Sveinsson has emphasized, are not those of everyday speech [*Njáls Saga*]. Unfortunately, the simple but sophisticated language of *Njála* cannot be reproduced in English because of its inflexible word order. The style of *Njála* can be approximated in German, but some Icelanders feel that only Latin is adequate for the satisfactory translation of this and other sagas.

FURTHER READING

Allen, Richard F. *Fire and Iron: Critical Approaches to "Njáls saga."* Pittsburgh: University of Pittsburgh Press, 1971, 254 p.

> Discusses *Njáls saga*'s origins, style, content, language, and major themes while maintaining that *Njáls saga* is a coherent work written by a single author.

Byock, Jesse L. *Feud in the Icelandic Saga.* Berkeley: University of California Press, 1982, 293 p.

> Detailed discussion of feud in *Njáls saga* and other Icelandic works.

Clark, George. "*Beowulf* and *Njálssaga*." In *Proceedings of the First International Saga Conference, University of Edinburgh,* edited by Peter Foote, Hermann Pálsson, and Desmond Slay, pp. 66-87. London: The Viking Society for Northern Research, 1973.

> Examines "the aesthetic and . . . literary-historical implications of a *Beowulf* analogue imbedded in the text of *Njálssaga*."

Clover, Carol J. "Open Composition: The Atlantic Interlude in *Njáls saga*." In *Sagas of the Icelanders: A Book of Essays,* edited by John Tucker, pp. 280-91. New York: Garland Publishing, 1989.

> Affirms *Njáls saga*'s flexible narrative structure through an examination of the numerous foreign journeys contained within the text.

Foote, Peter G. and Wilson, David M. "The Free." In their *The Viking Achievement: A Survey of the Society and Culture of Early Medieval Scandinavia,* pp. 79-122. New York: Praeger Publishers, 1970.

Describes the social and political environment of medieval Iceland.

Hallberg, Peter. *The Icelandic Saga.* Translated by Paul Schach. Lincoln: University of Nebraska Press, 1962, 179 p.

Describes the social and political environment of medieval Iceland.

General overview of Icelandic saga literature focusing on the sagas' early development and common themes.

Hieatt, Constance B. "Hrútr's Voyage to Norway and the Structure of *Njála*." In *Sagas of the Icelanders: A Book of Essays,* edited by John Tucker, pp. 272-79. New York: Garland Publishing, 1989.

Asserts that Hrútr's voyage to Norway, presented in the introduction of *Njáls saga,* is significant to the work's overall structure.

Judd, William E. "Valgerðr's Smile." *Scandinavian Studies* 56, No. 3 (Summer 1984): 203-12.

Maintains that the Kári and Bjorn interlude in *Njáls saga* was intended as an argument against the heroic ideal.

Lönnroth, Lars. *"Njáls saga": A Critical Introduction.* Berkeley: University of California Press, 1976, 275 p.

Investigates the oral composition and social background of *Njáls saga.*

———. "Indoctrination in the Icelandic Saga." In *The Nor-dic Mind: Current Trends in Scandinavian Literary Criticism,* edited by Frank Egholm Andersen and John Weinstock, pp. 305-18. Lanham, Md.: University Press of America, 1986.

Contends that *Njáls saga*'s author took a nonobjective stance in his depiction of the Icelandic social structure.

Miller, William Ian. "The Central Feud in *Njáls saga.*" In *Sagas of the Icelanders: A Book of Essays,* edited by John Tucker, pp. 292-322. New York: Garland Publishing, 1989.

Recounts the blood feud between the Sígfussons and the Njálssons, maintaining that Skarpheðinn's motive for killing Höskuldr was political.

Sveinsson, Einar Ólafur. *"Njáls saga": A Literary Masterpiece.* Edited and translated by Paul Schach. Lincoln: University of Nebraska Press, 1971, 210 p.

Study of *Njáls saga*'s sources and aesthetic merits, specifically its principal characters and overall philosophy.

Thomas, R. George. "Some Exceptional Women in the Sagas." *Saga-Book* XIII, No. V (1952-53): 307-27.

Investigates the social role of women during the time in which the family sagas were written, focusing on some of the more unconventional female characters in the sagas.

CLASSICAL AND MEDIEVAL LITERATURE CRITICISM

INDEXES

Literary Criticism Series
Cumulative Author Index

Literary Criticism Series
Cumulative Topic Index

CMLC Cumulative Nationality Index

CMLC Cumulative Title Index

CMLC Cumulative Critic Index

How to Use This Index

The main references

```
Calvino, Italo
    1923-1985.....CLC 5, 8, 11, 22, 33, 39,
                               73; SSC 3
```

list all author entries in the following Gale Literary Criticism series:

BLC = *Black Literature Criticism*
CLC = *Contemporary Literary Criticism*
CLR = *Children's Literature Review*
CMLC = *Classical and Medieval Literature Criticism*
DA = *DISCovering Authors*
DC = *Drama Criticism*
HLC = *Hispanic Literature Criticism*
LC = *Literature Criticism from 1400 to 1800*
NCLC = *Nineteenth-Century Literature Criticism*
PC = *Poetry Criticism*
SSC = *Short Story Criticism*
TCLC = *Twentieth-Century Literary Criticism*
WLC = *World Literature Criticism, 1500 to the Present*

The cross-references

```
See also CANR 23; CA 85-88;
    obituary CA 116
```

list all author entries in the following Gale biographical and literary sources:

AAYA = *Authors & Artists for Young Adults*
AITN = *Authors in the News*
BEST = *Bestsellers*
BW = *Black Writers*
CA = *Contemporary Authors*
CAAS = *Contemporary Authors Autobiography Series*
CABS = *Contemporary Authors Bibliographical Series*
CANR = *Contemporary Authors New Revision Series*
CAP = *Contemporary Authors Permanent Series*
CDALB = *Concise Dictionary of American Literary Biography*
CDBLB = *Concise Dictionary of British Literary Biography*
DLB = *Dictionary of Literary Biography*
DLBD = *Dictionary of Literary Biography Documentary Series*
DLBY = *Dictionary of Literary Biography Yearbook*
HW = *Hispanic Writers*
JRDA = *Junior DISCovering Authors*
MAICYA = *Major Authors and Illustrators for Children and Young Adults*
MTCW = *Major 20th-Century Writers*
SAAS = *Something about the Author Autobiography Series*
SATA = *Something about the Author*
YABC = *Yesterday's Authors of Books for Children*

Literary Criticism Series
Cumulative Author Index

A.
See Arnold, Matthew

A. E. . . . . TCLC **3, 10**
See also Russell, George William
See also DLB 19

A. M.
See Megged, Aharon

A. R. P-C
See Galsworthy, John

Abasiyanik, Sait Faik   1906-1954
See Sait Faik
See also CA 123

Abbey, Edward   1927-1989 . . . . . . CLC **36, 59**
See also CA 45-48; 128; CANR 2, 41

Abbott, Lee K(ittredge)   1947- . . . . . . CLC **48**
See also CA 124; DLB 130

Abe, Kobo   1924-1993 . . . . . CLC **8, 22, 53, 81**
See also CA 65-68; 140; CANR 24; MTCW

Abelard, Peter   c. 1079-c. 1142 . . . CMLC **11**
See also DLB 115

Abell, Kjeld   1901-1961 . . . . CLC **15**
See also CA 111

Abish, Walter   1931- . . . . CLC **22**
See also CA 101; CANR 37; DLB 130

Abrahams, Peter (Henry)   1919- . . . . . CLC **4**
See also BW 1; CA 57-60; CANR 26;
DLB 117; MTCW

Abrams, M(eyer) H(oward)   1912-. . . CLC **24**
See also CA 57-60; CANR 13, 33; DLB 67

Abse, Dannie   1923-. . . . . CLC **7, 29**
See also CA 53-56; CAAS 1; CANR 4;
DLB 27

Achebe, (Albert) Chinua(lumogu)
1930- . . . . . CLC **1, 3, 5, 7, 11, 26, 51, 75;**
BLC; DA; WLC
See also BW 2; CA 1-4R; CANR 6, 26;
CLR 20; DLB 117; MAICYA; MTCW;
SATA 38, 40

Acker, Kathy   1948- . . . . CLC **45**
See also CA 117; 122

Ackroyd, Peter   1949-. . . . . CLC **34, 52**
See also CA 123; 127

Acorn, Milton   1923-. . . . . CLC **15**
See also CA 103; DLB 53

Adamov, Arthur   1908-1970 . . . . . . CLC **4, 25**
See also CA 17-18; 25-28R; CAP 2; MTCW

Adams, Alice (Boyd)   1926- . . . CLC **6, 13, 46**
See also CA 81-84; CANR 26; DLBY 86;
MTCW

Adams, Douglas (Noel)   1952- . . . CLC **27, 60**
See also AAYA 4; BEST 89:3; CA 106;
CANR 34; DLBY 83; JRDA

Adams, Francis   1862-1893 . . . . . . NCLC **33**

Adams, Henry (Brooks)
1838-1918 . . . . TCLC **4, 52; DA**
See also CA 104; 133; DLB 12, 47

Adams, Richard (George)
1920- . . . . CLC **4, 5, 18**
See also AITN 1, 2; CA 49-52; CANR 3,
35; CLR 20; JRDA; MAICYA; MTCW;
SATA 7, 69

Adamson, Joy(-Friederike Victoria)
1910-1980 . . . . CLC **17**
See also CA 69-72; 93-96; CANR 22;
MTCW; SATA 11, 22

Adcock, Fleur   1934-. . . . . CLC **41**
See also CA 25-28R; CANR 11, 34;
DLB 40

Addams, Charles (Samuel)
1912-1988 . . . . CLC **30**
See also CA 61-64; 126; CANR 12

Addison, Joseph   1672-1719 . . . . LC **18**
See also CDBLB 1660-1789; DLB 101

Adler, C(arole) S(chwerdtfeger)
1932- . . . . CLC **35**
See also AAYA 4; CA 89-92; CANR 19,
40; JRDA; MAICYA; SAAS 15;
SATA 26, 63

Adler, Renata   1938-. . . . . CLC **8, 31**
See also CA 49-52; CANR 5, 22; MTCW

Ady, Endre   1877-1919 . . . . TCLC **11**
See also CA 107

Aeschylus
525B.C.-456B.C. . . . . CMLC **11; DA**

Afton, Effie
See Harper, Frances Ellen Watkins

Agapida, Fray Antonio
See Irving, Washington

Agee, James (Rufus)
1909-1955 . . . . TCLC **1, 19**
See also AITN 1; CA 108;
CDALB 1941-1968; DLB 2, 26

Aghill, Gordon
See Silverberg, Robert

Agnon, S(hmuel) Y(osef Halevi)
1888-1970 . . . . CLC **4, 8, 14**
See also CA 17-18; 25-28R; CAP 2; MTCW

Aherne, Owen
See Cassill, R(onald) V(erlin)

Ai   1947-. . . . . CLC **4, 14, 69**
See also CA 85-88; CAAS 13; DLB 120

Aickman, Robert (Fordyce)
1914-1981 . . . . CLC **57**
See also CA 5-8R; CANR 3

Aiken, Conrad (Potter)
1889-1973 . . . CLC **1, 3, 5, 10, 52; SSC 9**
See also CA 5-8R; 45-48; CANR 4;
CDALB 1929-1941; DLB 9, 45, 102;
MTCW; SATA 3, 30

Aiken, Joan (Delano)   1924-. . . . . CLC **35**
See also AAYA 1; CA 9-12R; CANR 4, 23,
34; CLR 1, 19; JRDA; MAICYA;
MTCW; SAAS 1; SATA 2, 30, 73

Ainsworth, William Harrison
1805-1882 . . . . NCLC **13**
See also DLB 21; SATA 24

Aitmatov, Chingiz (Torekulovich)
1928-. . . . . CLC **71**
See also CA 103; CANR 38; MTCW;
SATA 56

Akers, Floyd
See Baum, L(yman) Frank

Akhmadulina, Bella Akhatovna
1937-. . . . . CLC **53**
See also CA 65-68

Akhmatova, Anna
1888-1966 . . . . CLC **11, 25, 64; PC 2**
See also CA 19-20; 25-28R; CANR 35;
CAP 1; MTCW

Aksakov, Sergei Timofeyvich
1791-1859 . . . . NCLC **2**

Aksenov, Vassily   . . . . CLC **22**
See also Aksyonov, Vassily (Pavlovich)

Aksyonov, Vassily (Pavlovich)
1932-. . . . . CLC **37**
See also Aksenov, Vassily
See also CA 53-56; CANR 12

Akutagawa Ryunosuke
1892-1927 . . . . TCLC **16**
See also CA 117

Alain   1868-1951 . . . . TCLC **41**

Alain-Fournier . . . . TCLC **6**
See also Fournier, Henri Alban
See also DLB 65

Alarcon, Pedro Antonio de
1833-1891 . . . . NCLC **1**

Alas (y Urena), Leopoldo (Enrique Garcia)
1852-1901 . . . . TCLC **29**
See also CA 113; 131; HW

Albee, Edward (Franklin III)
1928- . . . . . . CLC **1, 2, 3, 5, 9, 11, 13, 25,**
53; DA; WLC
See also AITN 1; CA 5-8R; CABS 3;
CANR 8; CDALB 1941-1968; DLB 7;
MTCW

Alberti, Rafael   1902- . . . . CLC **7**
See also CA 85-88; DLB 108

Alcala-Galiano, Juan Valera y
See Valera y Alcala-Galiano, Juan

Alcott, Amos Bronson   1799-1888 . . NCLC **1**
See also DLB 1

Alcott, Louisa May
1832-1888 . . . . NCLC **6; DA; WLC**
See also CDALB 1865-1917; CLR 1;
DLB 1, 42, 79; JRDA; MAICYA;
YABC 1

Aldanov, M. A.
See Aldanov, Mark (Alexandrovich)

Aldanov, Mark (Alexandrovich)
1886(?)-1957 . . . . TCLC **23**
See also CA 118

Aldington, Richard 1892-1962...... **CLC 49**
See also CA 85-88; DLB 20, 36, 100

Aldiss, Brian W(ilson)
1925- .... **CLC 5, 14, 40**
See also CA 5-8R; CAAS 2; CANR 5, 28;
DLB 14; MTCW; SATA 34

Alegria, Claribel 1924-........... **CLC 75**
See also CA 131; CAAS 15; HW

Alegria, Fernando 1918-.......... **CLC 57**
See also CA 9-12R; CANR 5, 32; HW

Aleichem, Sholom .... **TCLC 1, 35**
See also Rabinovitch, Sholem

Aleixandre, Vicente 1898-1984 ... **CLC 9, 36**
See also CA 85-88; 114; CANR 26;
DLB 108; HW; MTCW

Alepoudelis, Odysseus
See Elytis, Odysseus

Aleshkovsky, Joseph 1929-
See Aleshkovsky, Yuz
See also CA 121; 128

Aleshkovsky, Yuz .... **CLC 44**
See also Aleshkovsky, Joseph

Alexander, Lloyd (Chudley) 1924- .. **CLC 35**
See also AAYA 1; CA 1-4R; CANR 1, 24,
38; CLR 1, 5; DLB 52; JRDA; MAICYA;
MTCW; SATA 3, 49

Alfau, Felipe 1902-.............. **CLC 66**
See also CA 137

Alger, Horatio, Jr. 1832-1899..... **NCLC 8**
See also DLB 42; SATA 16

Algren, Nelson 1909-1981 .... **CLC 4, 10, 33**
See also CA 13-16R; 103; CANR 20;
CDALB 1941-1968; DLB 9; DLBY 81,
82; MTCW

Ali, Ahmed 1910-.............. **CLC 69**
See also CA 25-28R; CANR 15, 34

Alighieri, Dante 1265-1321 .... **CMLC 3**

Allan, John B.
See Westlake, Donald E(dwin)

Allen, Edward 1948-.............. **CLC 59**

Allen, Roland
See Ayckbourn, Alan

Allen, Sarah A.
See Hopkins, Pauline Elizabeth

Allen, Woody 1935-........... **CLC 16, 52**
See also AAYA 10; CA 33-36R; CANR 27,
38; DLB 44; MTCW

Allende, Isabel 1942-.... **CLC 39, 57; HLC**
See also CA 125; 130; HW; MTCW

Alleyn, Ellen
See Rossetti, Christina (Georgina)

Allingham, Margery (Louise)
1904-1966 .... **CLC 19**
See also CA 5-8R; 25-28R; CANR 4;
DLB 77; MTCW

Allingham, William 1824-1889 ... **NCLC 25**
See also DLB 35

Allison, Dorothy E. 1949-........ **CLC 78**
See also CA 140

Allston, Washington 1779-1843.... **NCLC 2**
See also DLB 1

Almedingen, E. M. .... **CLC 12**
See also Almedingen, Martha Edith von
See also SATA 3

Almedingen, Martha Edith von 1898-1971
See Almedingen, E. M.
See also CA 1-4R; CANR 1

Almqvist, Carl Jonas Love
1793-1866 .... **NCLC 42**

Alonso, Damaso 1898-1990 .... **CLC 14**
See also CA 110; 131; 130; DLB 108; HW

Alov
See Gogol, Nikolai (Vasilyevich)

Alta 1942-...................... **CLC 19**
See also CA 57-60

Alter, Robert B(ernard) 1935-...... **CLC 34**
See also CA 49-52; CANR 1

Alther, Lisa 1944-.............. **CLC 7, 41**
See also CA 65-68; CANR 12, 30; MTCW

Altman, Robert 1925-............ **CLC 16**
See also CA 73-76; CANR 43

Alvarez, A(lfred) 1929-......... **CLC 5, 13**
See also CA 1-4R; CANR 3, 33; DLB 14,
40

Alvarez, Alejandro Rodriguez 1903-1965
See Casona, Alejandro
See also CA 131; 93-96; HW

Amado, Jorge 1912-..... **CLC 13, 40; HLC**
See also CA 77-80; CANR 35; DLB 113;
MTCW

Ambler, Eric 1909-............ **CLC 4, 6, 9**
See also CA 9-12R; CANR 7, 38; DLB 77;
MTCW

Amichai, Yehuda 1924-...... **CLC 9, 22, 57**
See also CA 85-88; MTCW

Amiel, Henri Frederic 1821-1881 .. **NCLC 4**

Amis, Kingsley (William)
1922- .. **CLC 1, 2, 3, 5, 8, 13, 40, 44; DA**
See also AITN 2; CA 9-12R; CANR 8, 28;
CDBLB 1945-1960; DLB 15, 27, 100, 139;
MTCW

Amis, Martin (Louis)
1949- .... **CLC 4, 9, 38, 62**
See also BEST 90:3; CA 65-68; CANR 8,
27; DLB 14

Ammons, A(rchie) R(andolph)
1926- .... **CLC 2, 3, 5, 8, 9, 25, 57**
See also AITN 1; CA 9-12R; CANR 6, 36;
DLB 5; MTCW

Amo, Tauraatua i
See Adams, Henry (Brooks)

Anand, Mulk Raj 1905-........... **CLC 23**
See also CA 65-68; CANR 32; MTCW

Anatol
See Schnitzler, Arthur

Anaya, Rudolfo A(lfonso)
1937- .... **CLC 23; HLC**
See also CA 45-48; CAAS 4; CANR 1, 32;
DLB 82; HW 1; MTCW

Andersen, Hans Christian
1805-1875 .. **NCLC 7; DA; SSC 6; WLC**
See also CLR 6; MAICYA; YABC 1

Anderson, C. Farley
See Mencken, H(enry) L(ouis); Nathan,
George Jean

Anderson, Jessica (Margaret) Queale
.... **CLC 37**
See also CA 9-12R; CANR 4

Anderson, Jon (Victor) 1940- .... **CLC 9**
See also CA 25-28R; CANR 20

Anderson, Lindsay (Gordon)
1923-...................... **CLC 20**
See also CA 125; 128

Anderson, Maxwell 1888-1959 ..... **TCLC 2**
See also CA 105; DLB 7

Anderson, Poul (William) 1926- .... **CLC 15**
See also AAYA 5; CA 1-4R; CAAS 2;
CANR 2, 15, 34; DLB 8; MTCW;
SATA 39

Anderson, Robert (Woodruff)
1917-...................... **CLC 23**
See also AITN 1; CA 21-24R; CANR 32;
DLB 7

Anderson, Sherwood
1876-1941 .... **TCLC 1, 10, 24; DA;**
SSC 1; WLC
See also CA 104; 121; CDALB 1917-1929;
DLB 4, 9, 86; DLBD 1; MTCW

Andouard
See Giraudoux, (Hippolyte) Jean

Andrade, Carlos Drummond de ...... **CLC 18**
See also Drummond de Andrade, Carlos

Andrade, Mario de 1893-1945..... **TCLC 43**

Andrewes, Lancelot 1555-1626 .... **LC 5**

Andrews, Cicily Fairfield
See West, Rebecca

Andrews, Elton V.
See Pohl, Frederik

Andreyev, Leonid (Nikolaevich)
1871-1919 .... **TCLC 3**
See also CA 104

Andric, Ivo 1892-1975 .... **CLC 8**
See also CA 81-84; 57-60; CANR 43;
MTCW

Angelique, Pierre
See Bataille, Georges

Angell, Roger 1920-.............. **CLC 26**
See also CA 57-60; CANR 13, 44

Angelou, Maya
1928- .... **CLC 12, 35, 64, 77; BLC; DA**
See also AAYA 7; BW 2; CA 65-68;
CANR 19, 42; DLB 38; MTCW;
SATA 49

Annensky, Innokenty Fyodorovich
1856-1909 .... **TCLC 14**
See also CA 110

Anon, Charles Robert
See Pessoa, Fernando (Antonio Nogueira)

Anouilh, Jean (Marie Lucien Pierre)
1910-1987 ...... **CLC 1, 3, 8, 13, 40, 50**
See also CA 17-20R; 123; CANR 32;
MTCW

Anthony, Florence
See Ai

Anthony, John
See Ciardi, John (Anthony)

Anthony, Peter
See Shaffer, Anthony (Joshua); Shaffer,
Peter (Levin)

Anthony, Piers 1934-............. **CLC 35**
See also AAYA 11; CA 21-24R; CANR 28;
DLB 8; MTCW

Antoine, Marc
See Proust, (Valentin-Louis-George-Eugene-) Marcel

Antoninus, Brother
See Everson, William (Oliver)

Antonioni, Michelangelo 1912- ..... **CLC 20**
See also CA 73-76

Antschel, Paul 1920-1970...... **CLC 10, 19**
See also Celan, Paul
See also CA 85-88; CANR 33; MTCW

Anwar, Chairil 1922-1949 .... **TCLC 22**
See also CA 121

Apollinaire, Guillaume .. **TCLC 3, 8, 51; PC 7**
See also Kostrowitzki, Wilhelm Apollinaris de

Appelfeld, Aharon 1932- .... **CLC 23, 47**
See also CA 112; 133

Apple, Max (Isaac) 1941-....... **CLC 9, 33**
See also CA 81-84; CANR 19; DLB 130

Appleman, Philip (Dean) 1926-..... **CLC 51**
See also CA 13-16R; CAAS 18; CANR 6, 29

Appleton, Lawrence
See Lovecraft, H(oward) P(hillips)

Apteryx
See Eliot, T(homas) S(tearns)

Apuleius, (Lucius Madaurensis)
125(?)-175(?) .... **CMLC 1**

Aquin, Hubert 1929-1977......... **CLC 15**
See also CA 105; DLB 53

Aragon, Louis 1897-1982....... **CLC 3, 22**
See also CA 69-72; 108; CANR 28; DLB 72; MTCW

Arany, Janos 1817-1882........ **NCLC 34**

Arbuthnot, John 1667-1735.......... **LC 1**
See also DLB 101

Archer, Herbert Winslow
See Mencken, H(enry) L(ouis)

Archer, Jeffrey (Howard) 1940- .... **CLC 28**
See also BEST 89:3; CA 77-80; CANR 22

Archer, Jules 1915- .... **CLC 12**
See also CA 9-12R; CANR 6; SAAS 5; SATA 4

Archer, Lee
See Ellison, Harlan

Arden, John 1930- .... **CLC 6, 13, 15**
See also CA 13-16R; CAAS 4; CANR 31; DLB 13; MTCW

Arenas, Reinaldo
1943-1990 ...:.......... **CLC 41; HLC**
See also CA 124; 128; 133; HW

Arendt, Hannah 1906-1975 .... **CLC 66**
See also CA 17-20R; 61-64; CANR 26; MTCW

Aretino, Pietro 1492-1556 .... **LC 12**

Arghezi, Tudor.................... **CLC 80**
See also Theodorescu, Ion N.

Arguedas, Jose Maria
1911-1969 .... **CLC 10, 18**
See also CA 89-92; DLB 113; HW

Argueta, Manlio 1936-........... **CLC 31**
See also CA 131; HW

Ariosto, Ludovico 1474-1533........ **LC 6**

Aristides
See Epstein, Joseph

Aristophanes
450B.C.-385B.C.... **CMLC 4; DA; DC 2**

Arlt, Roberto (Godofredo Christophersen)
1900-1942 .... **TCLC 29; HLC**
See also CA 123; 131; HW

Armah, Ayi Kwei 1939-.... **CLC 5, 33; BLC**
See also BW 1; CA 61-64; CANR 21; DLB 117; MTCW

Armatrading, Joan 1950-.......... **CLC 17**
See also CA 114

Arnette, Robert
See Silverberg, Robert

Arnim, Achim von (Ludwig Joachim von Arnim) 1781-1831 .... **NCLC 5**
See also DLB 90

Arnim, Bettina von 1785-1859.... **NCLC 38**
See also DLB 90

Arnold, Matthew
1822-1888 ..... **NCLC 6, 29; DA; PC 5; WLC**
See also CDBLB 1832-1890; DLB 32, 57

Arnold, Thomas 1795-1842 ...... **NCLC 18**
See also DLB 55

Arnow, Harriette (Louisa) Simpson
1908-1986 .... **CLC 2, 7, 18**
See also CA 9-12R; 118; CANR 14; DLB 6; MTCW; SATA 42, 47

Arp, Hans
See Arp, Jean

Arp, Jean 1887-1966.............. **CLC 5**
See also CA 81-84; 25-28R; CANR 42

Arrabal
See Arrabal, Fernando

Arrabal, Fernando 1932- ... **CLC 2, 9, 18, 58**
See also CA 9-12R; CANR 15

Arrick, Fran.................... **CLC 30**

Artaud, Antonin 1896-1948 ..... **TCLC 3, 36**
See also CA 104

Arthur, Ruth M(abel) 1905-1979.... **CLC 12**
See also CA 9-12R; 85-88; CANR 4; SATA 7, 26

Artsybashev, Mikhail (Petrovich)
1878-1927 .... **TCLC 31**

Arundel, Honor (Morfydd)
1919-1973 .... **CLC 17**
See also CA 21-22; 41-44R; CAP 2; SATA 4, 24

Asch, Sholem 1880-1957 .... **TCLC 3**
See also CA 105

Ash, Shalom
See Asch, Sholem

Ashbery, John (Lawrence)
1927- ...... **CLC 2, 3, 4, 6, 9, 13, 15, 25, 41, 77**
See also CA 5-8R; CANR 9, 37; DLB 5; DLBY 81; MTCW

Ashdown, Clifford
See Freeman, R(ichard) Austin

Ashe, Gordon
See Creasey, John

Ashton-Warner, Sylvia (Constance)
1908-1984 .... **CLC 19**
See also CA 69-72; 112; CANR 29; MTCW

Asimov, Isaac
1920-1992 ...... **CLC 1, 3, 9, 19, 26, 76**
See also BEST 90:2; CA 1-4R; 137; CANR 2, 19, 36; CLR 12; DLB 8; DLBY 92; JRDA; MAICYA; MTCW; SATA 1, 26, 74

Astley, Thea (Beatrice May)
1925- .... **CLC 41**
See also CA 65-68; CANR 11, 43

Aston, James
See White, T(erence) H(anbury)

Asturias, Miguel Angel
1899-1974 .... **CLC 3, 8, 13; HLC**
See also CA 25-28; 49-52; CANR 32; CAP 2; DLB 113; HW; MTCW

Atares, Carlos Saura
See Saura (Atares), Carlos

Atheling, William
See Pound, Ezra (Weston Loomis)

Atheling, William, Jr.
See Blish, James (Benjamin)

Atherton, Gertrude (Franklin Horn)
1857-1948 .... **TCLC 2**
See also CA 104; DLB 9, 78

Atherton, Lucius
See Masters, Edgar Lee

Atkins, Jack
See Harris, Mark

Atticus
See Fleming, Ian (Lancaster)

Atwood, Margaret (Eleanor)
1939- ..... **CLC 2, 3, 4, 8, 13, 15, 25, 44; DA; PC 8; SSC 2; WLC**
See also AAYA 12; BEST 89:2; CA 49-52; CANR 3, 24, 33; DLB 53; MTCW; SATA 50

Aubigny, Pierre d'
See Mencken, H(enry) L(ouis)

Aubin, Penelope 1685-1731(?)........ **LC 9**
See also DLB 39

Auchincloss, Louis (Stanton)
1917- .... **CLC 4, 6, 9, 18, 45**
See also CA 1-4R; CANR 6, 29; DLB 2; DLBY 80; MTCW

Auden, W(ystan) H(ugh)
1907-1973 ...... **CLC 1, 2, 3, 4, 6, 9, 11, 14, 43; DA; PC 1; WLC**
See also CA 9-12R; 45-48; CANR 5; CDBLB 1914-1945; DLB 10, 20; MTCW

Audiberti, Jacques 1900-1965 ...... **CLC 38**
See also CA 25-28R

Auel, Jean M(arie) 1936-.......... **CLC 31**
See also AAYA 7; BEST 90:4; CA 103; CANR 21

Auerbach, Erich 1892-1957 .... **TCLC 43**
See also CA 118

Augier, Emile 1820-1889 .... **NCLC 31**

August, John
See De Voto, Bernard (Augustine)

Augustine, St. 354-430.......... **CMLC 6**

Aurelius
See Bourne, Randolph S(illiman)

Austen, Jane
1775-1817 .... **NCLC 1, 13, 19, 33; DA;
WLC**
See also CDBLB 1789-1832; DLB 116

Auster, Paul 1947- .... **CLC 47**
See also CA 69-72; CANR 23

Austin, Frank
See Faust, Frederick (Schiller)

Austin, Mary (Hunter)
1868-1934 .... **TCLC 25**
See also CA 109; DLB 9, 78

Autran Dourado, Waldomiro
See Dourado, (Waldomiro Freitas) Autran

Averroes 1126-1198 .... **CMLC 7**
See also DLB 115

Avison, Margaret 1918- .... **CLC 2, 4**
See also CA 17-20R; DLB 53; MTCW

Axton, David
See Koontz, Dean R(ay)

Ayckbourn, Alan
1939- .... **CLC 5, 8, 18, 33, 74**
See also CA 21-24R; CANR 31; DLB 13;
MTCW

Aydy, Catherine
See Tennant, Emma (Christina)

Ayme, Marcel (Andre) 1902-1967... **CLC 11**
See also CA 89-92; CLR 25; DLB 72

Ayrton, Michael 1921-1975 .... **CLC 7**
See also CA 5-8R; 61-64; CANR 9, 21

Azorin .... **CLC 11**
See also Martinez Ruiz, Jose

Azuela, Mariano
1873-1952 .... **TCLC 3; HLC**
See also CA 104; 131; HW; MTCW

Baastad, Babbis Friis
See Friis-Baastad, Babbis Ellinor

Bab
See Gilbert, W(illiam) S(chwenck)

Babbis, Eleanor
See Friis-Baastad, Babbis Ellinor

Babel, Isaak (Emmanuilovich)
1894-1941(?) .... **TCLC 2, 13**
See also CA 104

Babits, Mihaly 1883-1941 .... **TCLC 14**
See also CA 114

Babur 1483-1530 .... **LC 18**

Bacchelli, Riccardo 1891-1985 ..... **CLC 19**
See also CA 29-32R; 117

Bach, Richard (David) 1936- ...... **CLC 14**
See also AITN 1; BEST 89:2; CA 9-12R;
CANR 18; MTCW; SATA 13

Bachman, Richard
See King, Stephen (Edwin)

Bachmann, Ingeborg 1926-1973 ..... **CLC 69**
See also CA 93-96; 45-48; DLB 85

Bacon, Francis 1561-1626 .... **LC 18**
See also CDBLB Before 1660

Bacovia, George .... **TCLC 24**
See also Vasiliu, Gheorghe

Badanes, Jerome 1937- .... **CLC 59**

Bagehot, Walter 1826-1877 ...... **NCLC 10**
See also DLB 55

Bagnold, Enid 1889-1981 .... **CLC 25**
See also CA 5-8R; 103; CANR 5, 40;
DLB 13; MAICYA; SATA 1, 25

Bagrjana, Elisaveta
See Belcheva, Elisaveta

Bagryana, Elisaveta
See Belcheva, Elisaveta

Bailey, Paul 1937- .... **CLC 45**
See also CA 21-24R; CANR 16; DLB 14

Baillie, Joanna 1762-1851 .... **NCLC 2**
See also DLB 93

Bainbridge, Beryl (Margaret)
1933- .... **CLC 4, 5, 8, 10, 14, 18, 22, 62**
See also CA 21-24R; CANR 24; DLB 14;
MTCW

Baker, Elliott 1922- .... **CLC 8**
See also CA 45-48; CANR 2

Baker, Nicholson 1957- .... **CLC 61**
See also CA 135

Baker, Ray Stannard 1870-1946... **TCLC 47**
See also CA 118

Baker, Russell (Wayne) 1925- ...... **CLC 31**
See also BEST 89:4; CA 57-60; CANR 11,
41; MTCW

Bakhtin, M.
See Bakhtin, Mikhail Mikhailovich

Bakhtin, M. M.
See Bakhtin, Mikhail Mikhailovich

Bakhtin, Mikhail
See Bakhtin, Mikhail Mikhailovich

Bakhtin, Mikhail Mikhailovich
1895-1975 .... **CLC 83**
See also CA 128; 113

Bakshi, Ralph 1938(?)- .... **CLC 26**
See also CA 112; 138

Bakunin, Mikhail (Alexandrovich)
1814-1876 .... **NCLC 25**

Baldwin, James (Arthur)
1924-1987 ...... **CLC 1, 2, 3, 4, 5, 8, 13,
15, 17, 42, 50, 67; BLC; DA; DC 1;
SSC 10; WLC**
See also AAYA 4; BW 1; CA 1-4R; 124;
CABS 1; CANR 3, 24;
CDALB 1941-1968; DLB 2, 7, 33;
DLBY 87; MTCW; SATA 9, 54

Ballard, J(ames) G(raham)
1930- .... **CLC 3, 6, 14, 36; SSC 1**
See also AAYA 3; CA 5-8R; CANR 15, 39;
DLB 14; MTCW

Balmont, Konstantin (Dmitriyevich)
1867-1943 .... **TCLC 11**
See also CA 109

Balzac, Honore de
1799-1850 .... **NCLC 5, 35; DA; SSC 5;
WLC**
See also DLB 119

Bambara, Toni Cade
1939- .... **CLC 19; BLC; DA**
See also AAYA 5; BW 2; CA 29-32R;
CANR 24; DLB 38; MTCW

Bamdad, A.
See Shamlu, Ahmad

Banat, D. R.
See Bradbury, Ray (Douglas)

Bancroft, Laura
See Baum, L(yman) Frank

Banim, John 1798-1842 .... **NCLC 13**
See also DLB 116

Banim, Michael 1796-1874 ...... **NCLC 13**

Banks, Iain
See Banks, Iain M(enzies)

Banks, Iain M(enzies) 1954- .... **CLC 34**
See also CA 123; 128

Banks, Lynne Reid .... **CLC 23**
See also Reid Banks, Lynne
See also AAYA 6

Banks, Russell 1940- .... **CLC 37, 72**
See also CA 65-68; CAAS 15; CANR 19;
DLB 130

Banville, John 1945- .... **CLC 46**
See also CA 117; 128; DLB 14

Banville, Theodore (Faullain) de
1832-1891 .... **NCLC 9**

Baraka, Amiri
1934- .... **CLC 1, 2, 3, 5, 10, 14, 33;
BLC; DA; PC 4**
See also Jones, LeRoi
See also BW 2; CA 21-24R; CABS 3;
CANR 27, 38; CDALB 1941-1968;
DLB 5, 7, 16, 38; DLBD 8; MTCW

Barbellion, W. N. P. .... **TCLC 24**
See also Cummings, Bruce F(rederick)

Barbera, Jack 1945- .... **CLC 44**
See also CA 110

Barbey d'Aurevilly, Jules Amedee
1808-1889 .... **NCLC 1**
See also DLB 119

Barbusse, Henri 1873-1935 .... **TCLC 5**
See also CA 105; DLB 65

Barclay, Bill
See Moorcock, Michael (John)

Barclay, William Ewert
See Moorcock, Michael (John)

Barea, Arturo 1897-1957 .... **TCLC 14**
See also CA 111

Barfoot, Joan 1946- .... **CLC 18**
See also CA 105

Baring, Maurice 1874-1945 .... **TCLC 8**
See also CA 105; DLB 34

Barker, Clive 1952- .... **CLC 52**
See also AAYA 10; BEST 90:3; CA 121;
129; MTCW

Barker, George Granville
1913-1991 .... **CLC 8, 48**
See also CA 9-12R; 135; CANR 7, 38;
DLB 20; MTCW

Barker, Harley Granville
See Granville-Barker, Harley
See also DLB 10

Barker, Howard 1946- .... **CLC 37**
See also CA 102; DLB 13

Barker, Pat 1943- .... **CLC 32**
See also CA 117; 122

Barlow, Joel 1754-1812 .... **NCLC 23**
See also DLB 37

Barnard, Mary (Ethel) 1909- .... **CLC 48**
See also CA 21-22; CAP 2**

Barnes, Djuna
1892-1982 ... **CLC 3, 4, 8, 11, 29; SSC 3**
See also CA 9-12R; 107; CANR 16; DLB 4,
9, 45; MTCW

Barnes, Julian 1946-.............. **CLC 42**
See also CA 102; CANR 19; DLBY 93

Barnes, Peter 1931- .... **CLC 5, 56**
See also CA 65-68; CAAS 12; CANR 33,
34; DLB 13; MTCW

Baroja (y Nessi), Pio
1872-1956 .... **TCLC 8; HLC**
See also CA 104

Baron, David
See Pinter, Harold

Baron Corvo
See Rolfe, Frederick (William Serafino
Austin Lewis Mary)

Barondess, Sue K(aufman)
1926-1977 .... **CLC 8**
See also Kaufman, Sue
See also CA 1-4R; 69-72; CANR 1

Baron de Teive
See Pessoa, Fernando (Antonio Nogueira)

Barres, Maurice 1862-1923 .... **TCLC 47**
See also DLB 123

Barreto, Afonso Henrique de Lima
See Lima Barreto, Afonso Henrique de

Barrett, (Roger) Syd 1946- .... **CLC 35**
See also Pink Floyd

Barrett, William (Christopher)
1913-1992 .... **CLC 27**
See also CA 13-16R; 139; CANR 11

Barrie, J(ames) M(atthew)
1860-1937 .... **TCLC 2**
See also CA 104; 136; CDBLB 1890-1914;
CLR 16; DLB 10, 141; MAICYA;
YABC 1

Barrington, Michael
See Moorcock, Michael (John)

Barrol, Grady
See Bograd, Larry

Barry, Mike
See Malzberg, Barry N(athaniel)

Barry, Philip 1896-1949.......... **TCLC 11**
See also CA 109; DLB 7

Bart, Andre Schwarz
See Schwarz-Bart, Andre

Barth, John (Simmons)
1930- ...... **CLC 1, 2, 3, 5, 7, 9, 10, 14,
27, 51; SSC 10**
See also AITN 1, 2; CA 1-4R; CABS 1;
CANR 5, 23; DLB 2; MTCW

Barthelme, Donald
1931-1989 ..... **CLC 1, 2, 3, 5, 6, 8, 13,
23, 46, 59; SSC 2**
See also CA 21-24R; 129; CANR 20;
DLB 2; DLBY 80, 89; MTCW; SATA 7,
62

Barthelme, Frederick 1943-........ **CLC 36**
See also CA 114; 122; DLBY 85

Barthes, Roland (Gerard)
1915-1980 .... **CLC 24, 83**
See also CA 130; 97-100; MTCW

Barzun, Jacques (Martin) 1907- .... **CLC 51**
See also CA 61-64; CANR 22

Bashevis, Isaac
See Singer, Isaac Bashevis

Bashkirtseff, Marie 1859-1884 ... **NCLC 27**

Basho
See Matsuo Basho

Bass, Kingsley B., Jr.
See Bullins, Ed

Bass, Rick 1958-................ **CLC 79**
See also CA 126

Bassani, Giorgio 1916-............. **CLC 9**
See also CA 65-68; CANR 33; DLB 128;
MTCW

Bastos, Augusto (Antonio) Roa
See Roa Bastos, Augusto (Antonio)

Bataille, Georges 1897-1962 .... **CLC 29**
See also CA 101; 89-92

Bates, H(erbert) E(rnest)
1905-1974 .... **CLC 46; SSC 10**
See also CA 93-96; 45-48; CANR 34;
MTCW

Bauchart
See Camus, Albert

Baudelaire, Charles
1821-1867 ..... **NCLC 6, 29; DA; PC 1;
WLC**

Baudrillard, Jean 1929-........... **CLC 60**

Baum, L(yman) Frank 1856-1919 ... **TCLC 7**
See also CA 108; 133; CLR 15; DLB 22;
JRDA; MAICYA; MTCW; SATA 18

Baum, Louis F.
See Baum, L(yman) Frank

Baumbach, Jonathan 1933-...... **CLC 6, 23**
See also CA 13-16R; CAAS 5; CANR 12;
DLBY 80; MTCW

Bausch, Richard (Carl) 1945- ...... **CLC 51**
See also CA 101; CAAS 14; CANR 43;
DLB 130

Baxter, Charles 1947-......... **CLC 45, 78**
See also CA 57-60; CANR 40; DLB 130

Baxter, George Owen
See Faust, Frederick (Schiller)

Baxter, James K(eir) 1926-1972 .... **CLC 14**
See also CA 77-80

Baxter, John
See Hunt, E(verette) Howard, Jr.

Bayer, Sylvia
See Glassco, John

Beagle, Peter S(oyer) 1939-......... **CLC 7**
See also CA 9-12R; CANR 4; DLBY 80;
SATA 60

Bean, Normal
See Burroughs, Edgar Rice

Beard, Charles A(ustin)
1874-1948 .... **TCLC 15**
See also CA 115; DLB 17; SATA 18

Beardsley, Aubrey 1872-1898 ..... **NCLC 6**

Beattie, Ann
1947-.... **CLC 8, 13, 18, 40, 63; SSC 11**
See also BEST 90:2; CA 81-84; DLBY 82;
MTCW

Beattie, James 1735-1803 .... **NCLC 25**
See also DLB 109

Beauchamp, Kathleen Mansfield 1888-1923
See Mansfield, Katherine
See also CA 104; 134; DA

Beaumarchais, Pierre-Augustin Caron de
1732-1799 .... **DC 4**

**Beauvoir, Simone (Lucie Ernestine Marie
Bertrand) de**
1908-1986 .... **CLC 1, 2, 4, 8, 14, 31, 44,
50, 71; DA; WLC**
See also CA 9-12R; 118; CANR 28;
DLB 72; DLBY 86; MTCW

Becker, Jurek 1937-............ **CLC 7, 19**
See also CA 85-88; DLB 75

Becker, Walter 1950-............. **CLC 26**

Beckett, Samuel (Barclay)
1906-1989 ...... **CLC 1, 2, 3, 4, 6, 9, 10,
11, 14, 18, 29, 57, 59, 83; DA; WLC**
See also CA 5-8R; 130; CANR 33;
CDBLB 1945-1960; DLB 13, 15;
DLBY 90; MTCW

Beckford, William 1760-1844 .... **NCLC 16**
See also DLB 39

Beckman, Gunnel 1910-........... **CLC 26**
See also CA 33-36R; CANR 15; CLR 25;
MAICYA; SAAS 9; SATA 6

Becque, Henri 1837-1899........ **NCLC 3**

Beddoes, Thomas Lovell
1803-1849 .... **NCLC 3**
See also DLB 96

Bedford, Donald F.
See Fearing, Kenneth (Flexner)

Beecher, Catharine Esther
1800-1878 .... **NCLC 30**
See also DLB 1

Beecher, John 1904-1980.......... **CLC 6**
See also AITN 1; CA 5-8R; 105; CANR 8

Beer, Johann 1655-1700............. **LC 5**

Beer, Patricia 1924-.............. **CLC 58**
See also CA 61-64; CANR 13; DLB 40

Beerbohm, Henry Maximilian
1872-1956 .... **TCLC 1, 24**
See also CA 104; DLB 34, 100

Begiebing, Robert J(ohn) 1946-..... **CLC 70**
See also CA 122; CANR 40

Behan, Brendan
1923-1964 .... **CLC 1, 8, 11, 15, 79**
See also CA 73-76; CANR 33;
CDBLB 1945-1960; DLB 13; MTCW

Behn, Aphra
1640(?)-1689 .... **LC 1; DA; DC 4; WLC**
See also DLB 39, 80, 131

Behrman, S(amuel) N(athaniel)
1893-1973 .... **CLC 40**
See also CA 13-16; 45-48; CAP 1; DLB 7,
44

Belasco, David 1853-1931 .... **TCLC 3**
See also CA 104; DLB 7

Belcheva, Elisaveta 1893- .... **CLC 10**

Beldone, Phil "Cheech"
See Ellison, Harlan

Beleno
See Azuela, Mariano

Belinski, Vissarion Grigoryevich
1811-1848 .... **NCLC 5**

Belitt, Ben 1911-. . . . . **CLC 22**
See also CA 13-16R; CAAS 4; CANR 7;
DLB 5

Bell, James Madison
1826-1902 . . . . **TCLC 43; BLC**
See also BW 1; CA 122; 124; DLB 50

Bell, Madison (Smartt) 1957- . . . . . . **CLC 41**
See also CA 111; CANR 28

Bell, Marvin (Hartley) 1937-. . . . . **CLC 8, 31**
See also CA 21-24R; CAAS 14; DLB 5;
MTCW

Bell, W. L. D.
See Mencken, H(enry) L(ouis)

Bellamy, Atwood C.
See Mencken, H(enry) L(ouis)

Bellamy, Edward 1850-1898 . . . . . . **NCLC 4**
See also DLB 12

Bellin, Edward J.
See Kuttner, Henry

Belloc, (Joseph) Hilaire (Pierre)
1870-1953 . . . . **TCLC 7, 18**
See also CA 106; DLB 19, 100, 141;
YABC 1

Belloc, Joseph Peter Rene Hilaire
See Belloc, (Joseph) Hilaire (Pierre)

Belloc, Joseph Pierre Hilaire
See Belloc, (Joseph) Hilaire (Pierre)

Belloc, M. A.
See Lowndes, Marie Adelaide (Belloc)

Bellow, Saul
1915- . . . . . . **CLC 1, 2, 3, 6, 8, 10, 13, 15,
25, 33, 34, 63, 79; DA; SSC 14; WLC**
See also AITN 2; BEST 89:3; CA 5-8R;
CABS 1; CANR 29; CDALB 1941-1968;
DLB 2, 28; DLBD 3; DLBY 82; MTCW

Belser, Reimond Karel Maria de
1929- . . . . **CLC 14**

Bely, Andrey . . . . **TCLC 7**
See also Bugayev, Boris Nikolayevich

Benary, Margot
See Benary-Isbert, Margot

Benary-Isbert, Margot 1889-1979 . . . **CLC 12**
See also CA 5-8R; 89-92; CANR 4;
CLR 12; MAICYA; SATA 2, 21

Benavente (y Martinez), Jacinto
1866-1954 . . . . **TCLC 3**
See also CA 106; 131; HW; MTCW

Benchley, Peter (Bradford)
1940- . . . . **CLC 4, 8**
See also AITN 2; CA 17-20R; CANR 12,
35; MTCW; SATA 3

Benchley, Robert (Charles)
1889-1945 . . . . **TCLC 1**
See also CA 105; DLB 11

Benedikt, Michael 1935- . . . . **CLC 4, 14**
See also CA 13-16R; CANR 7; DLB 5

Benet, Juan 1927-. . . . . **CLC 28**
See also CA 143

Benet, Stephen Vincent
1898-1943 . . . . **TCLC 7; SSC 10**
See also CA 104; DLB 4, 48, 102; YABC 1

Benet, William Rose 1886-1950 . . . **TCLC 28**
See also CA 118; DLB 45

Benford, Gregory (Albert) 1941-. . . . **CLC 52**
See also CA 69-72; CANR 12, 24;
DLBY 82

Bengtsson, Frans (Gunnar)
1894-1954 . . . . **TCLC 48**

Benjamin, David
See Slavitt, David R(ytman)

Benjamin, Lois
See Gould, Lois

Benjamin, Walter 1892-1940 . . . . . **TCLC 39**

Benn, Gottfried 1886-1956. . . . . **TCLC 3**
See also CA 106; DLB 56

Bennett, Alan 1934- . . . . **CLC 45, 77**
See also CA 103; CANR 35; MTCW

Bennett, (Enoch) Arnold
1867-1931 . . . . **TCLC 5, 20**
See also CA 106; CDBLB 1890-1914;
DLB 10, 34, 98

Bennett, Elizabeth
See Mitchell, Margaret (Munnerlyn)

Bennett, George Harold 1930-
See Bennett, Hal
See also BW 1; CA 97-100

Bennett, Hal . . . . **CLC 5**
See also Bennett, George Harold
See also DLB 33

Bennett, Jay 1912-. . . . . **CLC 35**
See also AAYA 10; CA 69-72; CANR 11,
42; JRDA; SAAS 4; SATA 27, 41

Bennett, Louise (Simone)
1919- . . . . **CLC 28; BLC**
See also BW 2; DLB 117

Benson, E(dward) F(rederic)
1867-1940 . . . . **TCLC 27**
See also CA 114; DLB 135

Benson, Jackson J. 1930-. . . . . **CLC 34**
See also CA 25-28R; DLB 111

Benson, Sally 1900-1972 . . . . **CLC 17**
See also CA 19-20; 37-40R; CAP 1;
SATA 1, 27, 35

Benson, Stella 1892-1933. . . . . **TCLC 17**
See also CA 117; DLB 36

Bentham, Jeremy 1748-1832 . . . . . **NCLC 38**
See also DLB 107

Bentley, E(dmund) C(lerihew)
1875-1956 . . . . **TCLC 12**
See also CA 108; DLB 70

Bentley, Eric (Russell) 1916-. . . . . . . **CLC 24**
See also CA 5-8R; CANR 6

Beranger, Pierre Jean de
1780-1857 . . . . **NCLC 34**

Berger, Colonel
See Malraux, (Georges-)Andre

Berger, John (Peter) 1926- . . . . . . **CLC 2, 19**
See also CA 81-84; DLB 14

Berger, Melvin H. 1927- . . . . **CLC 12**
See also CA 5-8R; CANR 4; CLR 32;
SAAS 2; SATA 5

Berger, Thomas (Louis)
1924- . . . . **CLC 3, 5, 8, 11, 18, 38**
See also CA 1-4R; CANR 5, 28; DLB 2;
DLBY 80; MTCW

Bergman, (Ernst) Ingmar
1918- . . . . **CLC 16, 72**
See also CA 81-84; CANR 33

Bergson, Henri 1859-1941 . . . . **TCLC 32**

Bergstein, Eleanor 1938-. . . . . **CLC 4**
See also CA 53-56; CANR 5

Berkoff, Steven 1937-. . . . . **CLC 56**
See also CA 104

Bermant, Chaim (Icyk) 1929- . . . . . . **CLC 40**
See also CA 57-60; CANR 6, 31

Bern, Victoria
See Fisher, M(ary) F(rances) K(ennedy)

Bernanos, (Paul Louis) Georges
1888-1948 . . . . **TCLC 3**
See also CA 104; 130; DLB 72

Bernard, April 1956- . . . . **CLC 59**
See also CA 131

Berne, Victoria
See Fisher, M(ary) F(rances) K(ennedy)

Bernhard, Thomas
1931-1989 . . . . **CLC 3, 32, 61**
See also CA 85-88; 127; CANR 32;
DLB 85, 124; MTCW

Berrigan, Daniel 1921-. . . . . **CLC 4**
See also CA 33-36R; CAAS 1; CANR 11,
43; DLB 5

Berrigan, Edmund Joseph Michael, Jr.
1934-1983
See Berrigan, Ted
See also CA 61-64; 110; CANR 14

Berrigan, Ted. . . . . **CLC 37**
See also Berrigan, Edmund Joseph Michael,
Jr.
See also DLB 5

Berry, Charles Edward Anderson 1931-
See Berry, Chuck
See also CA 115

Berry, Chuck. . . . . **CLC 17**
See also Berry, Charles Edward Anderson

Berry, Jonas
See Ashbery, John (Lawrence)

Berry, Wendell (Erdman)
1934- . . . . **CLC 4, 6, 8, 27, 46**
See also AITN 1; CA 73-76; DLB 5, 6

Berryman, John
1914-1972 . . . . . . **CLC 1, 2, 3, 4, 6, 8, 10,
13, 25, 62**
See also CA 13-16; 33-36R; CABS 2;
CANR 35; CAP 1; CDALB 1941-1968;
DLB 48; MTCW

Bertolucci, Bernardo 1940- . . . . **CLC 16**
See also CA 106

Bertrand, Aloysius 1807-1841 . . . . **NCLC 31**

Bertran de Born c. 1140-1215. . . . . **CMLC 5**

Besant, Annie (Wood) 1847-1933 . . . **TCLC 9**
See also CA 105

Bessie, Alvah 1904-1985. . . . . **CLC 23**
See also CA 5-8R; 116; CANR 2; DLB 26

Bethlen, T. D.
See Silverberg, Robert

Beti, Mongo. . . . . **CLC 27; BLC**
See also Biyidi, Alexandre

Betjeman, John
1906-1984 .... CLC **2, 6, 10, 34, 43**
See also CA 9-12R; 112; CANR 33;
CDBLB 1945-1960; DLB 20; DLBY 84;
MTCW

Bettelheim, Bruno 1903-1990 ...... CLC **79**
See also CA 81-84; 131; CANR 23; MTCW

Betti, Ugo 1892-1953 .... TCLC **5**
See also CA 104

Betts, Doris (Waugh) 1932-.... CLC **3, 6, 28**
See also CA 13-16R; CANR 9; DLBY 82

Bevan, Alistair
See Roberts, Keith (John Kingston)

Beynon, John
See Harris, John (Wyndham Parkes Lucas)
Beynon

Bialik, Chaim Nachman
1873-1934 .... TCLC **25**

Bickerstaff, Isaac
See Swift, Jonathan

Bidart, Frank 1939- .... CLC **33**
See also CA 140

Bienek, Horst 1930-............ CLC **7, 11**
See also CA 73-76; DLB 75

Bierce, Ambrose (Gwinett)
1842-1914(?) ...... TCLC **1, 7, 44**; DA;
SSC **9**; WLC
See also CA 104; 139; CDALB 1865-1917;
DLB 11, 12, 23, 71, 74

Billings, Josh
See Shaw, Henry Wheeler

Billington, (Lady) Rachel (Mary)
1942- .... CLC **43**
See also AITN 2; CA 33-36R; CANR 44

Binyon, T(imothy) J(ohn) 1936- .... CLC **34**
See also CA 111; CANR 28

Bioy Casares, Adolfo
1914- .... CLC **4, 8, 13**; HLC
See also CA 29-32R; CANR 19, 43;
DLB 113; HW; MTCW

Bird, C.
See Ellison, Harlan

Bird, Cordwainer
See Ellison, Harlan

Bird, Robert Montgomery
1806-1854 .... NCLC **1**

Birney, (Alfred) Earle
1904- ....CLC **1, 4, 6, 11**
See also CA 1-4R; CANR 5, 20; DLB 88;
MTCW

Bishop, Elizabeth
1911-1979 ..... CLC **1, 4, 9, 13, 15, 32**;
DA; PC **3**
See also CA 5-8R; 89-92; CABS 2;
CANR 26; CDALB 1968-1988; DLB 5;
MTCW; SATA 24

Bishop, John 1935-............... CLC **10**
See also CA 105

Bissett, Bill 1939-............... CLC **18**
See also CA 69-72; CAAS 19; CANR 15;
DLB 53; MTCW

Bitov, Andrei (Georgievich) 1937-... CLC **57**
See also CA 142

Biyidi, Alexandre 1932-
See Beti, Mongo
See also BW 1; CA 114; 124; MTCW

Bjarme, Brynjolf
See Ibsen, Henrik (Johan)

Bjornson, Bjornstjerne (Martinius)
1832-1910 .... TCLC **7, 37**
See also CA 104

Black, Robert
See Holdstock, Robert P.

Blackburn, Paul 1926-1971 ...... CLC **9, 43**
See also CA 81-84; 33-36R; CANR 34;
DLB 16; DLBY 81

Black Elk 1863-1950 .... TCLC **33**
See also CA 144

Black Hobart
See Sanders, (James) Ed(ward)

Blacklin, Malcolm
See Chambers, Aidan

Blackmore, R(ichard) D(oddridge)
1825-1900 .... TCLC **27**
See also CA 120; DLB 18

Blackmur, R(ichard) P(almer)
1904-1965 .... CLC **2, 24**
See also CA 11-12; 25-28R; CAP 1; DLB 63

Black Tarantula, The
See Acker, Kathy

Blackwood, Algernon (Henry)
1869-1951 .... TCLC **5**
See also CA 105

Blackwood, Caroline 1931- .... CLC **6, 9**
See also CA 85-88; CANR 32; DLB 14;
MTCW

Blade, Alexander
See Hamilton, Edmond; Silverberg, Robert

Blaga, Lucian 1895-1961 .... CLC **75**

Blair, Eric (Arthur) 1903-1950
See Orwell, George
See also CA 104; 132; DA; MTCW;
SATA 29

Blais, Marie-Claire
1939- .... CLC **2, 4, 6, 13, 22**
See also CA 21-24R; CAAS 4; CANR 38;
DLB 53; MTCW

Blaise, Clark 1940-............... CLC **29**
See also AITN 2; CA 53-56; CAAS 3;
CANR 5; DLB 53

Blake, Nicholas
See Day Lewis, C(ecil)
See also DLB 77

Blake, William
1757-1827 ..... NCLC **13, 37**; DA; WLC
See also CDBLB 1789-1832; DLB 93;
MAICYA; SATA 30

Blasco Ibanez, Vicente
1867-1928 .... TCLC **12**
See also CA 110; 131; HW; MTCW

Blatty, William Peter 1928-........ CLC **2**
See also CA 5-8R; CANR 9

Bleeck, Oliver
See Thomas, Ross (Elmore)

Blessing, Lee 1949-............... CLC **54**

Blish, James (Benjamin)
1921-1975 .... CLC **14**
See also CA 1-4R; 57-60; CANR 3; DLB 8;
MTCW; SATA 66

Bliss, Reginald
See Wells, H(erbert) G(eorge)

Blixen, Karen (Christentze Dinesen)
1885-1962
See Dinesen, Isak
See also CA 25-28; CANR 22; CAP 2;
MTCW; SATA 44

Bloch, Robert (Albert) 1917-....... CLC **33**
See also CA 5-8R; CANR 5; DLB 44;
SATA 12

Blok, Alexander (Alexandrovich)
1880-1921 .... TCLC **5**
See also CA 104

Blom, Jan
See Breytenbach, Breyten

Bloom, Harold 1930- .... CLC **24**
See also CA 13-16R; CANR 39; DLB 67

Bloomfield, Aurelius
See Bourne, Randolph S(illiman)

Blount, Roy (Alton), Jr. 1941- ..... CLC **38**
See also CA 53-56; CANR 10, 28; MTCW

Bloy, Leon 1846-1917............. TCLC **22**
See also CA 121; DLB 123

Blume, Judy (Sussman) 1938-... CLC **12, 30**
See also AAYA 3; CA 29-32R; CANR 13,
37; CLR 2, 15; DLB 52; JRDA;
MAICYA; MTCW; SATA 2, 31

Blunden, Edmund (Charles)
1896-1974 .... CLC **2, 56**
See also CA 17-18; 45-48; CAP 2; DLB 20,
100; MTCW

Bly, Robert (Elwood)
1926- .... CLC **1, 2, 5, 10, 15, 38**
See also CA 5-8R; CANR 41; DLB 5;
MTCW

Bobette
See Simenon, Georges (Jacques Christian)

Boccaccio, Giovanni
1313-1375 .... CMLC **13**; SSC **10**

Bochco, Steven 1943-............. CLC **35**
See also AAYA 11; CA 124; 138

Bodenheim, Maxwell 1892-1954 ... TCLC **44**
See also CA 110; DLB 9, 45

Bodker, Cecil 1927- .... CLC **21**
See also CA 73-76; CANR 13, 44; CLR 23;
MAICYA; SATA 14

Boell, Heinrich (Theodor) 1917-1985
See Boll, Heinrich (Theodor)
See also CA 21-24R; 116; CANR 24; DA;
DLB 69; DLBY 85; MTCW

Boerne, Alfred
See Doeblin, Alfred

Bogan, Louise 1897-1970..... CLC **4, 39, 46**
See also CA 73-76; 25-28R; CANR 33;
DLB 45; MTCW

Bogarde, Dirk .... CLC **19**
See also Van Den Bogarde, Derek Jules
Gaspard Ulric Niven
See also DLB 14

Bogosian, Eric 1953- .... CLC **45**
See also CA 138

Bograd, Larry 1953-.............. **CLC 35**
See also CA 93-96; SATA 33

Boiardo, Matteo Maria 1441-1494 .... **LC 6**

Boileau-Despreaux, Nicolas
1636-1711 .... **LC 3**

Boland, Eavan (Aisling) 1944-... **CLC 40, 67**
See also CA 143; DLB 40

Boll, Heinrich (Theodor)
1917-1985 .... **CLC 2, 3, 6, 9, 11, 15, 27, 39, 72; WLC**
See also Boell, Heinrich (Theodor)
See also DLB 69; DLBY 85

Bolt, Lee
See Faust, Frederick (Schiller)

Bolt, Robert (Oxton) 1924-........ **CLC 14**
See also CA 17-20R; CANR 35; DLB 13;
MTCW

Bomkauf
See Kaufman, Bob (Garnell)

Bonaventura................... **NCLC 35**
See also DLB 90

Bond, Edward 1934-....... **CLC 4, 6, 13, 23**
See also CA 25-28R; CANR 38; DLB 13;
MTCW

Bonham, Frank 1914-1989........ **CLC 12**
See also AAYA 1; CA 9-12R; CANR 4, 36;
JRDA; MAICYA; SAAS 3; SATA 1, 49,
62

Bonnefoy, Yves 1923-....... **CLC 9, 15, 58**
See also CA 85-88; CANR 33; MTCW

Bontemps, Arna(ud Wendell)
1902-1973 .... **CLC 1, 18; BLC**
See also BW 1; CA 1-4R; 41-44R; CANR 4,
35; CLR 6; DLB 48, 51; JRDA;
MAICYA; MTCW; SATA 2, 24, 44

Booth, Martin 1944-............. **CLC 13**
See also CA 93-96; CAAS 2

Booth, Philip 1925-............... **CLC 23**
See also CA 5-8R; CANR 5; DLBY 82

Booth, Wayne C(layson) 1921- ..... **CLC 24**
See also CA 1-4R; CAAS 5; CANR 3, 43;
DLB 67

Borchert, Wolfgang 1921-1947 ..... **TCLC 5**
See also CA 104; DLB 69, 124

Borel, Petrus 1809-1859........ **NCLC 41**

Borges, Jorge Luis
1899-1986 ... **CLC 1, 2, 3, 4, 6, 8, 9, 10,
13, 19, 44, 48, 83; DA; HLC; SSC 4;
WLC**
See also CA 21-24R; CANR 19, 33;
DLB 113; DLBY 86; HW; MTCW

Borowski, Tadeusz 1922-1951...... **TCLC 9**
See also CA 106

Borrow, George (Henry)
1803-1881 .... **NCLC 9**
See also DLB 21, 55

Bosman, Herman Charles
1905-1951 .... **TCLC 49**

Bosschere, Jean de 1878(?)-1953... **TCLC 19**
See also CA 115

Boswell, James
1740-1795 .... **LC 4; DA; WLC**
See also CDBLB 1660-1789; DLB 104, 142

Bottoms, David 1949-............ **CLC 53**
See also CA 105; CANR 22; DLB 120;
DLBY 83

Boucicault, Dion 1820-1890...... **NCLC 41**

Boucolon, Maryse 1937-
See Conde, Maryse
See also CA 110; CANR 30

Bourget, Paul (Charles Joseph)
1852-1935 .... **TCLC 12**
See also CA 107; DLB 123

Bourjaily, Vance (Nye) 1922- .... **CLC 8, 62**
See also CA 1-4R; CAAS 1; CANR 2;
DLB 2

Bourne, Randolph S(illiman)
1886-1918 .... **TCLC 16**
See also CA 117; DLB 63

Bova, Ben(jamin William) 1932-.... **CLC 45**
See also CA 5-8R; CAAS 18; CANR 11;
CLR 3; DLBY 81; MAICYA; MTCW;
SATA 6, 68

Bowen, Elizabeth (Dorothea Cole)
1899-1973 ...... **CLC 1, 3, 6, 11, 15, 22;
SSC 3**
See also CA 17-18; 41-44R; CANR 35;
CAP 2; CDBLB 1945-1960; DLB 15;
MTCW

Bowering, George 1935-........ **CLC 15, 47**
See also CA 21-24R; CAAS 16; CANR 10;
DLB 53

Bowering, Marilyn R(uthe) 1949-... **CLC 32**
See also CA 101

Bowers, Edgar 1924- .... **CLC 9**
See also CA 5-8R; CANR 24; DLB 5

Bowie, David .... **CLC 17**
See also Jones, David Robert

Bowles, Jane (Sydney)
1917-1973 .... **CLC 3, 68**
See also CA 19-20; 41-44R; CAP 2

Bowles, Paul (Frederick)
1910- .... **CLC 1, 2, 19, 53; SSC 3**
See also CA 1-4R; CAAS 1; CANR 1, 19;
DLB 5, 6; MTCW

Box, Edgar
See Vidal, Gore

Boyd, Nancy
See Millay, Edna St. Vincent

Boyd, William 1952-........ **CLC 28, 53, 70**
See also CA 114; 120

Boyle, Kay
1902-1992 ..... **CLC 1, 5, 19, 58; SSC 5**
See also CA 13-16R; 140; CAAS 1;
CANR 29; DLB 4, 9, 48, 86; DLBY 93;
MTCW

Boyle, Mark
See Kienzle, William X(avier)

Boyle, Patrick 1905-1982......... **CLC 19**
See also CA 127

Boyle, T. C.
See Boyle, T(homas) Coraghessan

Boyle, T(homas) Coraghessan
1948- .... **CLC 36, 55**
See also BEST 90:4; CA 120; CANR 44;
DLBY 86

Boz
See Dickens, Charles (John Huffam)

Brackenridge, Hugh Henry
1748-1816 .... **NCLC 7**
See also DLB 11, 37

Bradbury, Edward P.
See Moorcock, Michael (John)

Bradbury, Malcolm (Stanley)
1932- .... **CLC 32, 61**
See also CA 1-4R; CANR 1, 33; DLB 14;
MTCW

Bradbury, Ray (Douglas)
1920- ... **CLC 1, 3, 10, 15, 42; DA; WLC**
See also AITN 1, 2; CA 1-4R; CANR 2, 30;
CDALB 1968-1988; DLB 2, 8; MTCW;
SATA 11, 64

Bradford, Gamaliel 1863-1932..... **TCLC 36**
See also DLB 17

Bradley, David (Henry, Jr.)
1950- .... **CLC 23; BLC**
See also BW 1; CA 104; CANR 26; DLB 33

Bradley, John Ed(mund, Jr.)
1958- .... **CLC 55**
See also CA 139

Bradley, Marion Zimmer 1930-..... **CLC 30**
See also AAYA 9; CA 57-60; CAAS 10;
CANR 7, 31; DLB 8; MTCW

Bradstreet, Anne 1612(?)-1672 ... **LC 4; DA**
See also CDALB 1640-1865; DLB 24

Bragg, Melvyn 1939-............. **CLC 10**
See also BEST 89:3; CA 57-60; CANR 10;
DLB 14

Braine, John (Gerard)
1922-1986 .... **CLC 1, 3, 41**
See also CA 1-4R; 120; CANR 1, 33;
CDBLB 1945-1960; DLB 15; DLBY 86;
MTCW

Brammer, William 1930(?)-1978 .... **CLC 31**
See also CA 77-80

Brancati, Vitaliano 1907-1954..... **TCLC 12**
See also CA 109

Brancato, Robin F(idler) 1936-..... **CLC 35**
See also AAYA 9; CA 69-72; CANR 11;
CLR 32; JRDA; SAAS 9; SATA 23

Brand, Max
See Faust, Frederick (Schiller)

Brand, Millen 1906-1980 .... **CLC 7**
See also CA 21-24R; 97-100

Branden, Barbara .... **CLC 44**

Brandes, Georg (Morris Cohen)
1842-1927 .... **TCLC 10**
See also CA 105

Brandys, Kazimierz 1916-......... **CLC 62**

Branley, Franklyn M(ansfield)
1915- .... **CLC 21**
See also CA 33-36R; CANR 14, 39;
CLR 13; MAICYA; SAAS 16; SATA 4,
68

Brathwaite, Edward (Kamau)
1930- .... **CLC 11**
See also BW 2; CA 25-28R; CANR 11, 26;
DLB 125

Brautigan, Richard (Gary)
1935-1984 .... **CLC 1, 3, 5, 9, 12, 34, 42**
See also CA 53-56; 113; CANR 34; DLB 2,
5; DLBY 80, 84; MTCW; SATA 56

Author Index

Braverman, Kate 1950- .... **CLC 67**
See also CA 89-92

Brecht, Bertolt
1898-1956 ...... **TCLC 1, 6, 13, 35; DA; DC 3; WLC**
See also CA 104; 133; DLB 56, 124; MTCW

Brecht, Eugen Berthold Friedrich
See Brecht, Bertolt

Bremer, Fredrika 1801-1865 ..... **NCLC 11**

Brennan, Christopher John
1870-1932 .... **TCLC 17**
See also CA 117

Brennan, Maeve 1917- .... **CLC 5**
See also CA 81-84

Brentano, Clemens (Maria)
1778-1842 .... **NCLC 1**

Brent of Bin Bin
See Franklin, (Stella Maraia Sarah) Miles

Brenton, Howard 1942- .... **CLC 31**
See also CA 69-72; CANR 33; DLB 13; MTCW

Breslin, James 1930-
See Breslin, Jimmy
See also CA 73-76; CANR 31; MTCW

Breslin, Jimmy .... **CLC 4, 43**
See also Breslin, James
See also AITN 1

Bresson, Robert 1907- .... **CLC 16**
See also CA 110

Breton, Andre 1896-1966... **CLC 2, 9, 15, 54**
See also CA 19-20; 25-28R; CANR 40; CAP 2; DLB 65; MTCW

Breytenbach, Breyten 1939(?)- .. **CLC 23, 37**
See also CA 113; 129

Bridgers, Sue Ellen 1942- .... **CLC 26**
See also AAYA 8; CA 65-68; CANR 11, 36; CLR 18; DLB 52; JRDA; MAICYA; SAAS 1; SATA 22

Bridges, Robert (Seymour)
1844-1930 .... **TCLC 1**
See also CA 104; CDBLB 1890-1914; DLB 19, 98

Bridie, James .... **TCLC 3**
See also Mavor, Osborne Henry
See also DLB 10

Brin, David 1950- .... **CLC 34**
See also CA 102; CANR 24; SATA 65

Brink, Andre (Philippus)
1935- .... **CLC 18, 36**
See also CA 104; CANR 39; MTCW

Brinsmead, H(esba) F(ay) 1922- .... **CLC 21**
See also CA 21-24R; CANR 10; MAICYA; SAAS 5; SATA 18

Brittain, Vera (Mary)
1893(?)-1970 .... **CLC 23**
See also CA 13-16; 25-28R; CAP 1; MTCW

Broch, Hermann 1886-1951....... **TCLC 20**
See also CA 117; DLB 85, 124

Brock, Rose
See Hansen, Joseph

Brodkey, Harold 1930-............ **CLC 56**
See also CA 111; DLB 130

Brodsky, Iosif Alexandrovich 1940-
See Brodsky, Joseph
See also AITN 1; CA 41-44R; CANR 37; MTCW

Brodsky, Joseph .. **CLC 4, 6, 13, 36, 50; PC 9**
See also Brodsky, Iosif Alexandrovich

Brodsky, Michael Mark 1948- ..... **CLC 19**
See also CA 102; CANR 18, 41

Bromell, Henry 1947-.............. **CLC 5**
See also CA 53-56; CANR 9

Bromfield, Louis (Brucker)
1896-1956 .... **TCLC 11**
See also CA 107; DLB 4, 9, 86

Broner, E(sther) M(asserman)
1930-...................... **CLC 19**
See also CA 17-20R; CANR 8, 25; DLB 28

Bronk, William 1918-............. **CLC 10**
See also CA 89-92; CANR 23

Bronstein, Lev Davidovich
See Trotsky, Leon

Bronte, Anne 1820-1849......... **NCLC 4**
See also DLB 21

Bronte, Charlotte
1816-1855 ... **NCLC 3, 8, 33; DA; WLC**
See also CDBLB 1832-1890; DLB 21

Bronte, (Jane) Emily
1818-1848 .... **NCLC 16, 35; DA; PC 8; WLC**
See also CDBLB 1832-1890; DLB 21, 32

Brooke, Frances 1724-1789 .... **LC 6**
See also DLB 39, 99

Brooke, Henry 1703(?)-1783 .... **LC 1**
See also DLB 39

Brooke, Rupert (Chawner)
1887-1915 .... **TCLC 2, 7; DA; WLC**
See also CA 104; 132; CDBLB 1914-1945; DLB 19; MTCW

Brooke-Haven, P.
See Wodehouse, P(elham) G(renville)

Brooke-Rose, Christine 1926- ...... **CLC 40**
See also CA 13-16R; DLB 14

Brookner, Anita 1928- ...... **CLC 32, 34, 51**
See also CA 114; 120; CANR 37; DLBY 87; MTCW

Brooks, Cleanth 1906- .... **CLC 24**
See also CA 17-20R; CANR 33, 35; DLB 63; MTCW

Brooks, George
See Baum, L(yman) Frank

Brooks, Gwendolyn
1917- ...... **CLC 1, 2, 4, 5, 15, 49; BLC; DA; PC 7; WLC**
See also AITN 1; BW 2; CA 1-4R; CANR 1, 27; CDALB 1941-1968; CLR 27; DLB 5, 76; MTCW; SATA 6

Brooks, Mel.................... **CLC 12**
See also Kaminsky, Melvin
See also DLB 26

Brooks, Peter 1938-.............. **CLC 34**
See also CA 45-48; CANR 1

Brooks, Van Wyck 1886-1963...... **CLC 29**
See also CA 1-4R; CANR 6; DLB 45, 63, 103

Brophy, Brigid (Antonia)
1929-.................. **CLC 6, 11, 29**
See also CA 5-8R; CAAS 4; CANR 25; DLB 14; MTCW

Brosman, Catharine Savage 1934-.... **CLC 9**
See also CA 61-64; CANR 21

Brother Antoninus
See Everson, William (Oliver)

Broughton, T(homas) Alan 1936- ... **CLC 19**
See also CA 45-48; CANR 2, 23

Broumas, Olga 1949-.......... **CLC 10, 73**
See also CA 85-88; CANR 20

Brown, Charles Brockden
1771-1810 .... **NCLC 22**
See also CDALB 1640-1865; DLB 37, 59, 73

Brown, Christy 1932-1981........ **CLC 63**
See also CA 105; 104; DLB 14

Brown, Claude 1937- .... **CLC 30; BLC**
See also AAYA 7; BW 1; CA 73-76

Brown, Dee (Alexander) 1908- .. **CLC 18, 47**
See also CA 13-16R; CAAS 6; CANR 11; DLBY 80; MTCW; SATA 5

Brown, George
See Wertmueller, Lina

Brown, George Douglas
1869-1902 .... **TCLC 28**

Brown, George Mackay 1921-.... **CLC 5, 48**
See also CA 21-24R; CAAS 6; CANR 12, 37; DLB 14, 27, 139; MTCW; SATA 35

Brown, (William) Larry 1951-...... **CLC 73**
See also CA 130; 134

Brown, Moses
See Barrett, William (Christopher)

Brown, Rita Mae 1944-..... **CLC 18, 43, 79**
See also CA 45-48; CANR 2, 11, 35; MTCW

Brown, Roderick (Langmere) Haig-
See Haig-Brown, Roderick (Langmere)

Brown, Rosellen 1939-............ **CLC 32**
See also CA 77-80; CAAS 10; CANR 14, 44

Brown, Sterling Allen
1901-1989 .... **CLC 1, 23, 59; BLC**
See also BW 1; CA 85-88; 127; CANR 26; DLB 48, 51, 63; MTCW

Brown, Will
See Ainsworth, William Harrison

Brown, William Wells
1813-1884 .... **NCLC 2; BLC; DC 1**
See also DLB 3, 50

Browne, (Clyde) Jackson 1948(?)-... **CLC 21**
See also CA 120

Browning, Elizabeth Barrett
1806-1861 ..... **NCLC 1, 16; DA; PC 6; WLC**
See also CDBLB 1832-1890; DLB 32

Browning, Robert
1812-1889 .... **NCLC 19; DA; PC 2**
See also CDBLB 1832-1890; DLB 32; YABC 1

Browning, Tod 1882-1962 .... **CLC 16**
See also CA 141; 117

Bruccoli, Matthew J(oseph) 1931- .. **CLC 34**
See also CA 9-12R; CANR 7; DLB 103

Cage, John (Milton, Jr.) 1912- ..... **CLC 41**
See also CA 13-16R; CANR 9

Cain, G.
See Cabrera Infante, G(uillermo)

Cain, Guillermo
See Cabrera Infante, G(uillermo)

Cain, James M(allahan)
1892-1977 .... **CLC 3, 11, 28**
See also AITN 1; CA 17-20R; 73-76;
CANR 8, 34; MTCW

Caine, Mark
See Raphael, Frederic (Michael)

Calasso, Roberto 1941- .... **CLC 81**
See also CA 143

Calderon de la Barca, Pedro
1600-1681 .... **LC 23; DC 3**

Caldwell, Erskine (Preston)
1903-1987 .... **CLC 1, 8, 14, 50, 60**
See also AITN 1; CA 1-4R; 121; CAAS 1;
CANR 2, 33; DLB 9, 86; MTCW

Caldwell, (Janet Miriam) Taylor (Holland)
1900-1985 .... **CLC 2, 28, 39**
See also CA 5-8R; 116; CANR 5

Calhoun, John Caldwell
1782-1850 .... **NCLC 15**
See also DLB 3

Calisher, Hortense
1911- .... **CLC 2, 4, 8, 38; SSC 15**
See also CA 1-4R; CANR 1, 22; DLB 2;
MTCW

Callaghan, Morley Edward
1903-1990 .... **CLC 3, 14, 41, 65**
See also CA 9-12R; 132; CANR 33;
DLB 68; MTCW

Calvino, Italo
1923-1985 ..... **CLC 5, 8, 11, 22, 33, 39,
73; SSC 3**
See also CA 85-88; 116; CANR 23; MTCW

Cameron, Carey 1952- .... **CLC 59**
See also CA 135

Cameron, Peter 1959-............. **CLC 44**
See also CA 125

Campana, Dino 1885-1932........ **TCLC 20**
See also CA 117; DLB 114

Campbell, John W(ood, Jr.)
1910-1971 .... **CLC 32**
See also CA 21-22; 29-32R; CANR 34;
CAP 2; DLB 8; MTCW

Campbell, Joseph 1904-1987 .... **CLC 69**
See also AAYA 3; BEST 89:2; CA 1-4R;
124; CANR 3, 28; MTCW

Campbell, (John) Ramsey 1946- .... **CLC 42**
See also CA 57-60; CANR 7

Campbell, (Ignatius) Roy (Dunnachie)
1901-1957 .... **TCLC 5**
See also CA 104; DLB 20

Campbell, Thomas 1777-1844 .... **NCLC 19**
See also DLB 93

Campbell, Wilfred................ **TCLC 9**
See also Campbell, William

Campbell, William 1858(?)-1918
See Campbell, Wilfred
See also CA 106; DLB 92

Campos, Alvaro de
See Pessoa, Fernando (Antonio Nogueira)

Camus, Albert
1913-1960 .... **CLC 1, 2, 4, 9, 11, 14, 32,
63, 69; DA; DC 2; SSC 9; WLC**
See also CA 89-92; DLB 72; MTCW

Canby, Vincent 1924-............. **CLC 13**
See also CA 81-84

Cancale
See Desnos, Robert

Canetti, Elias 1905- ...... **CLC 3, 14, 25, 75**
See also CA 21-24R; CANR 23; DLB 85,
124; MTCW

Canin, Ethan 1960-............... **CLC 55**
See also CA 131; 135

Cannon, Curt
See Hunter, Evan

Cape, Judith
See Page, P(atricia) K(athleen)

Capek, Karel
1890-1938 ..... **TCLC 6, 37; DA; DC 1;
WLC**
See also CA 104; 140

Capote, Truman
1924-1984 ...... **CLC 1, 3, 8, 13, 19, 34,
38, 58; DA; SSC 2; WLC**
See also CA 5-8R; 113; CANR 18;
CDALB 1941-1968; DLB 2; DLBY 80,
84; MTCW

Capra, Frank 1897-1991........... **CLC 16**
See also CA 61-64; 135

Caputo, Philip 1941-............. **CLC 32**
See also CA 73-76; CANR 40

Card, Orson Scott 1951- .... **CLC 44, 47, 50**
See also AAYA 11; CA 102; CANR 27;
MTCW

Cardenal (Martinez), Ernesto
1925- .... **CLC 31; HLC**
See also CA 49-52; CANR 2, 32; HW;
MTCW

Carducci, Giosue 1835-1907....... **TCLC 32**

Carew, Thomas 1595(?)-1640........ **LC 13**
See also DLB 126

Carey, Ernestine Gilbreth 1908-.... **CLC 17**
See also CA 5-8R; SATA 2

Carey, Peter 1943-............ **CLC 40, 55**
See also CA 123; 127; MTCW

Carleton, William 1794-1869...... **NCLC 3**

Carlisle, Henry (Coffin) 1926-...... **CLC 33**
See also CA 13-16R; CANR 15

Carlsen, Chris
See Holdstock, Robert P.

Carlson, Ron(ald F.) 1947-........ **CLC 54**
See also CA 105; CANR 27

Carlyle, Thomas 1795-1881 .. **NCLC 22; DA**
See also CDBLB 1789-1832; DLB 55

Carman, (William) Bliss
1861-1929 .... **TCLC 7**
See also CA 104; DLB 92

Carnegie, Dale 1888-1955 .... **TCLC 53**

Carossa, Hans 1878-1956........ **TCLC 48**
See also DLB 66

Carpenter, Don(ald Richard)
1931- .... **CLC 41**
See also CA 45-48; CANR 1

Carpentier (y Valmont), Alejo
1904-1980 .... **CLC 8, 11, 38; HLC**
See also CA 65-68; 97-100; CANR 11;
DLB 113; HW

Carr, Emily 1871-1945.......... **TCLC 32**
See also DLB 68

Carr, John Dickson 1906-1977 ...... **CLC 3**
See also CA 49-52; 69-72; CANR 3, 33;
MTCW

Carr, Philippa
See Hibbert, Eleanor Alice Burford

Carr, Virginia Spencer 1929-....... **CLC 34**
See also CA 61-64; DLB 111

Carrier, Roch 1937-........... **CLC 13, 78**
See also CA 130; DLB 53

Carroll, James P. 1943(?)-........ **CLC 38**
See also CA 81-84

Carroll, Jim 1951- .... **CLC 35**
See also CA 45-48; CANR 42

Carroll, Lewis .... **NCLC 2; WLC**
See also Dodgson, Charles Lutwidge
See also CDBLB 1832-1890; CLR 2, 18;
DLB 18; JRDA

Carroll, Paul Vincent 1900-1968.... **CLC 10**
See also CA 9-12R; 25-28R; DLB 10

Carruth, Hayden 1921- .... **CLC 4, 7, 10, 18**
See also CA 9-12R; CANR 4, 38; DLB 5;
MTCW; SATA 47

Carson, Rachel Louise 1907-1964... **CLC 71**
See also CA 77-80; CANR 35; MTCW;
SATA 23

Carter, Angela (Olive)
1940-1992 ...... **CLC 5, 41, 76; SSC 13**
See also CA 53-56; 136; CANR 12, 36;
DLB 14; MTCW; SATA 66;
SATA-Obit 70

Carter, Nick
See Smith, Martin Cruz

Carver, Raymond
1938-1988 ... **CLC 22, 36, 53, 55; SSC 8**
See also CA 33-36R; 126; CANR 17, 34;
DLB 130; DLBY 84, 88; MTCW

Cary, (Arthur) Joyce (Lunel)
1888-1957 .... **TCLC 1, 29**
See also CA 104; CDBLB 1914-1945;
DLB 15, 100

Casanova de Seingalt, Giovanni Jacopo
1725-1798 .... **LC 13**

Casares, Adolfo Bioy
See Bioy Casares, Adolfo

Casely-Hayford, J(oseph) E(phraim)
1866-1930 .... **TCLC 24; BLC**
See also BW 2; CA 123

Casey, John (Dudley) 1939-........ **CLC 59**
See also BEST 90:2; CA 69-72; CANR 23

Casey, Michael 1947-.............. **CLC 2**
See also CA 65-68; DLB 5

Casey, Patrick
See Thurman, Wallace (Henry)

Casey, Warren (Peter) 1935-1988 ... **CLC 12**
See also CA 101; 127

Casona, Alejandro................. **CLC 49**
See also Alvarez, Alejandro Rodriguez

Cornwell, David (John Moore)
    1931- . . . . CLC 9, 15
    See also le Carre, John
    See also CA 5-8R; CANR 13, 33; MTCW

Corrigan, Kevin . . . . CLC 55

Corso, (Nunzio) Gregory 1930-. . . CLC 1, 11
    See also CA 5-8R; CANR 41; DLB 5, 16;
    MTCW

Cortazar, Julio
    1914-1984 . . . . . . CLC 2, 3, 5, 10, 13, 15,
                              33, 34; HLC; SSC 7
    See also CA 21-24R; CANR 12, 32;
    DLB 113; HW; MTCW

Corwin, Cecil
    See Kornbluth, C(yril) M.

Cosic, Dobrica 1921- . . . . CLC 14
    See also CA 122; 138

Costain, Thomas B(ertram)
    1885-1965 . . . . CLC 30
    See also CA 5-8R; 25-28R; DLB 9

Costantini, Humberto
    1924(?)-1987 . . . . CLC 49
    See also CA 131; 122; HW

Costello, Elvis 1955- . . . . CLC 21

Cotter, Joseph Seamon Sr.
    1861-1949 . . . . TCLC 28; BLC
    See also BW 1; CA 124; DLB 50

Couch, Arthur Thomas Quiller
    See Quiller-Couch, Arthur Thomas

Coulton, James
    See Hansen, Joseph

Couperus, Louis (Marie Anne)
    1863-1923 . . . . TCLC 15
    See also CA 115

Court, Wesli
    See Turco, Lewis (Putnam)

Courtenay, Bryce 1933- . . . . CLC 59
    See also CA 138

Courtney, Robert
    See Ellison, Harlan

Cousteau, Jacques-Yves 1910- . . . . . . CLC 30
    See also CA 65-68; CANR 15; MTCW;
    SATA 38

Coward, Noel (Peirce)
    1899-1973 . . . . CLC 1, 9, 29, 51
    See also AITN 1; CA 17-18; 41-44R;
    CANR 35; CAP 2; CDBLB 1914-1945;
    DLB 10; MTCW

Cowley, Malcolm 1898-1989 . . . . CLC 39
    See also CA 5-8R; 128; CANR 3; DLB 4,
    48; DLBY 81, 89; MTCW

Cowper, William 1731-1800 . . . . . . NCLC 8
    See also DLB 104, 109

Cox, William Trevor 1928- . . . CLC 9, 14, 71
    See also Trevor, William
    See also CA 9-12R; CANR 4, 37; DLB 14;
    MTCW

Cozzens, James Gould
    1903-1978 . . . . CLC 1, 4, 11
    See also CA 9-12R; 81-84; CANR 19;
    CDALB 1941-1968; DLB 9; DLBD 2;
    DLBY 84; MTCW

Crabbe, George 1754-1832 . . . . NCLC 26
    See also DLB 93

Craig, A. A.
    See Anderson, Poul (William)

Craik, Dinah Maria (Mulock)
    1826-1887 . . . . NCLC 38
    See also DLB 35; MAICYA; SATA 34

Cram, Ralph Adams 1863-1942 . . . . TCLC 45

Crane, (Harold) Hart
    1899-1932 . . . . TCLC 2, 5; DA; PC 3;
                                               WLC
    See also CA 104; 127; CDALB 1917-1929;
    DLB 4, 48; MTCW

Crane, R(onald) S(almon)
    1886-1967 . . . . CLC 27
    See also CA 85-88; DLB 63

Crane, Stephen (Townley)
    1871-1900 . . . . . . TCLC 11, 17, 32; DA;
                                        SSC 7; WLC
    See also CA 109; 140; CDALB 1865-1917;
    DLB 12, 54, 78; YABC 2

Crase, Douglas 1944- . . . . CLC 58
    See also CA 106

Crashaw, Richard 1612(?)-1649 . . . . . . LC 24
    See also DLB 126

Craven, Margaret 1901-1980 . . . . . . CLC 17
    See also CA 103

Crawford, F(rancis) Marion
    1854-1909 . . . . TCLC 10
    See also CA 107; DLB 71

Crawford, Isabella Valancy
    1850-1887 . . . . NCLC 12
    See also DLB 92

Crayon, Geoffrey
    See Irving, Washington

Creasey, John 1908-1973 . . . . CLC 11
    See also CA 5-8R; 41-44R; CANR 8;
    DLB 77; MTCW

Crebillon, Claude Prosper Jolyot de (fils)
    1707-1777 . . . . LC 1

Credo
    See Creasey, John

Creeley, Robert (White)
    1926- . . . . . CLC 1, 2, 4, 8, 11, 15, 36, 78
    See also CA 1-4R; CAAS 10; CANR 23, 43;
    DLB 5, 16; MTCW

Crews, Harry (Eugene)
    1935- . . . . CLC 6, 23, 49
    See also AITN 1; CA 25-28R; CANR 20;
    DLB 6; MTCW

Crichton, (John) Michael
    1942- . . . . CLC 2, 6, 54
    See also AAYA 10; AITN 2; CA 25-28R;
    CANR 13, 40; DLBY 81; JRDA;
    MTCW; SATA 9

Crispin, Edmund . . . . CLC 22
    See also Montgomery, (Robert) Bruce
    See also DLB 87

Cristofer, Michael 1945(?)- . . . . CLC 28
    See also CA 110; DLB 7

Croce, Benedetto 1866-1952 . . . . . . TCLC 37
    See also CA 120

Crockett, David 1786-1836 . . . . NCLC 8
    See also DLB 3, 11

Crockett, Davy
    See Crockett, David

Croker, John Wilson 1780-1857 . . NCLC 10
    See also DLB 110

Crommelynck, Fernand 1885-1970 . . CLC 75
    See also CA 89-92

Cronin, A(rchibald) J(oseph)
    1896-1981 . . . . CLC 32
    See also CA 1-4R; 102; CANR 5; SATA 25,
    47

Cross, Amanda
    See Heilbrun, Carolyn G(old)

Crothers, Rachel 1878(?)-1958 . . . . . TCLC 19
    See also CA 113; DLB 7

Croves, Hal
    See Traven, B.

Crowfield, Christopher
    See Stowe, Harriet (Elizabeth) Beecher

Crowley, Aleister . . . . TCLC 7
    See also Crowley, Edward Alexander

Crowley, Edward Alexander 1875-1947
    See Crowley, Aleister
    See also CA 104

Crowley, John 1942- . . . . CLC 57
    See also CA 61-64; CANR 43; DLBY 82;
    SATA 65

Crud
    See Crumb, R(obert)

Crumarums
    See Crumb, R(obert)

Crumb, R(obert) 1943- . . . . CLC 17
    See also CA 106

Crumbum
    See Crumb, R(obert)

Crumski
    See Crumb, R(obert)

Crum the Bum
    See Crumb, R(obert)

Crunk
    See Crumb, R(obert)

Crustt
    See Crumb, R(obert)

Cryer, Gretchen (Kiger) 1935- . . . . . . CLC 21
    See also CA 114; 123

Csath, Geza 1887-1919 . . . . TCLC 13
    See also CA 111

Cudlip, David 1933- . . . . CLC 34

Cullen, Countee
    1903-1946 . . . . . . TCLC 4, 37; BLC; DA
    See also BW 1; CA 108; 124;
    CDALB 1917-1929; DLB 4, 48, 51;
    MTCW; SATA 18

Cum, R.
    See Crumb, R(obert)

Cummings, Bruce F(rederick) 1889-1919
    See Barbellion, W. N. P.
    See also CA 123

Cummings, E(dward) E(stlin)
    1894-1962 . . . . . . CLC 1, 3, 8, 12, 15, 68;
                                      DA; PC 5; WLC 2
    See also CA 73-76; CANR 31;
    CDALB 1929-1941; DLB 4, 48; MTCW

Cunha, Euclides (Rodrigues Pimenta) da
    1866-1909 . . . . TCLC 24
    See also CA 123

Cunningham, E. V.
See Fast, Howard (Melvin)

Cunningham, J(ames) V(incent)
1911-1985 .... **CLC 3, 31**
See also CA 1-4R; 115; CANR 1; DLB 5

Cunningham, Julia (Woolfolk)
1916- .... **CLC 12**
See also CA 9-12R; CANR 4, 19, 36;
JRDA; MAICYA; SAAS 2; SATA 1, 26

Cunningham, Michael 1952- .... **CLC 34**
See also CA 136

Cunninghame Graham, R(obert) B(ontine)
1852-1936 .... **TCLC 19**
See also Graham, R(obert) B(ontine)
Cunninghame
See also CA 119; DLB 98

Currie, Ellen 19(?)- .... **CLC 44**

Curtin, Philip
See Lowndes, Marie Adelaide (Belloc)

Curtis, Price
See Ellison, Harlan

Cutrate, Joe
See Spiegelman, Art

Czaczkes, Shmuel Yosef
See Agnon, S(hmuel) Y(osef Halevi)

D. P.
See Wells, H(erbert) G(eorge)

Dabrowska, Maria (Szumska)
1889-1965 .... **CLC 15**
See also CA 106

Dabydeen, David 1955- .... **CLC 34**
See also BW 1; CA 125

Dacey, Philip 1939- .... **CLC 51**
See also CA 37-40R; CAAS 17; CANR 14,
32; DLB 105

Dagerman, Stig (Halvard)
1923-1954 .... **TCLC 17**
See also CA 117

Dahl, Roald 1916-1990..... **CLC 1, 6, 18, 79**
See also CA 1-4R; 133; CANR 6, 32, 37;
CLR 1, 7; DLB 139; JRDA; MAICYA;
MTCW; SATA 1, 26, 73; SATA-Obit 65

Dahlberg, Edward 1900-1977... **CLC 1, 7, 14**
See also CA 9-12R; 69-72; CANR 31;
DLB 48; MTCW

Dale, Colin. .... **TCLC 18**
See also Lawrence, T(homas) E(dward)

Dale, George E.
See Asimov, Isaac

Daly, Elizabeth 1878-1967........ **CLC 52**
See also CA 23-24; 25-28R; CAP 2

Daly, Maureen 1921- .... **CLC 17**
See also AAYA 5; CANR 37; JRDA;
MAICYA; SAAS 1; SATA 2

Daniel, Samuel 1562(?)-1619....... **LC 24**
See also DLB 62

Daniels, Brett
See Adler, Renata

Dannay, Frederic 1905-1982 ...... **CLC 11**
See also Queen, Ellery
See also CA 1-4R; 107; CANR 1, 39;
DLB 137; MTCW

D'Annunzio, Gabriele
1863-1938 .... **TCLC 6, 40**
See also CA 104

d'Antibes, Germain
See Simenon, Georges (Jacques Christian)

Danvers, Dennis 1947- .... **CLC 70**

Danziger, Paula 1944- .... **CLC 21**
See also AAYA 4; CA 112; 115; CANR 37;
CLR 20; JRDA; MAICYA; SATA 30,
36, 63

Dario, Ruben 1867-1916 .... **TCLC 4; HLC**
See also CA 131; HW; MTCW

Darley, George 1795-1846 .... **NCLC 2**
See also DLB 96

Daryush, Elizabeth 1887-1977.... **CLC 6, 19**
See also CA 49-52; CANR 3; DLB 20

Daudet, (Louis Marie) Alphonse
1840-1897 .... **NCLC 1**
See also DLB 123

Daumal, Rene 1908-1944........ **TCLC 14**
See also CA 114

Davenport, Guy (Mattison, Jr.)
1927- .... **CLC 6, 14, 38**
See also CA 33-36R; CANR 23; DLB 130

Davidson, Avram 1923-
See Queen, Ellery
See also CA 101; CANR 26; DLB 8

Davidson, Donald (Grady)
1893-1968 .... **CLC 2, 13, 19**
See also CA 5-8R; 25-28R; CANR 4;
DLB 45

Davidson, Hugh
See Hamilton, Edmond

Davidson, John 1857-1909....... **TCLC 24**
See also CA 118; DLB 19

Davidson, Sara 1943- .... **CLC 9**
See also CA 81-84; CANR 44

Davie, Donald (Alfred)
1922- .... **CLC 5, 8, 10, 31**
See also CA 1-4R; CAAS 3; CANR 1, 44;
DLB 27; MTCW

Davies, Ray(mond Douglas) 1944- .. **CLC 21**
See also CA 116

Davies, Rhys 1903-1978........... **CLC 23**
See also CA 9-12R; 81-84; CANR 4;
DLB 139

Davies, (William) Robertson
1913- ..... **CLC 2, 7, 13, 25, 42, 75; DA;**
WLC
See also BEST 89:2; CA 33-36R; CANR 17,
42; DLB 68; MTCW

Davies, W(illiam) H(enry)
1871-1940 .... **TCLC 5**
See also CA 104; DLB 19

Davies, Walter C.
See Kornbluth, C(yril) M.

Davis, Angela (Yvonne) 1944- ...... **CLC 77**
See also BW 2; CA 57-60; CANR 10

Davis, B. Lynch
See Bioy Casares, Adolfo; Borges, Jorge
Luis

Davis, Gordon
See Hunt, E(verette) Howard, Jr.

Davis, Harold Lenoir 1896-1960.... **CLC 49**
See also CA 89-92; DLB 9

Davis, Rebecca (Blaine) Harding
1831-1910 .... **TCLC 6**
See also CA 104; DLB 74

Davis, Richard Harding
1864-1916 .... **TCLC 24**
See also CA 114; DLB 12, 23, 78, 79

Davison, Frank Dalby 1893-1970 ... **CLC 15**
See also CA 116

Davison, Lawrence H.
See Lawrence, D(avid) H(erbert Richards)

Davison, Peter (Hubert) 1928- ..... **CLC 28**
See also CA 9-12R; CAAS 4; CANR 3, 43;
DLB 5

Davys, Mary 1674-1732............. **LC 1**
See also DLB 39

Dawson, Fielding 1930- .... **CLC 6**
See also CA 85-88; DLB 130

Dawson, Peter
See Faust, Frederick (Schiller)

Day, Clarence (Shepard, Jr.)
1874-1935 .... **TCLC 25**
See also CA 108; DLB 11

Day, Thomas 1748-1789............. **LC 1**
See also DLB 39; YABC 1

Day Lewis, C(ecil)
1904-1972 .... **CLC 1, 6, 10**
See also Blake, Nicholas
See also CA 13-16; 33-36R; CANR 34;
CAP 1; DLB 15, 20; MTCW

Dazai, Osamu .... **TCLC 11**
See also Tsushima, Shuji

de Andrade, Carlos Drummond
See Drummond de Andrade, Carlos

Deane, Norman
See Creasey, John

de Beauvoir, Simone (Lucie Ernestine Marie
Bertrand)
See Beauvoir, Simone (Lucie Ernestine
Marie Bertrand) de

de Brissac, Malcolm
See Dickinson, Peter (Malcolm)

de Chardin, Pierre Teilhard
See Teilhard de Chardin, (Marie Joseph)
Pierre

Dee, John 1527-1608 .... **LC 20**

Deer, Sandra 1940-................ **CLC 45**

De Ferrari, Gabriella .... **CLC 65**

Defoe, Daniel
1660(?)-1731 .... **LC 1; DA; WLC**
See also CDBLB 1660-1789; DLB 39, 95,
101; JRDA; MAICYA; SATA 22

de Gourmont, Remy
See Gourmont, Remy de

de Hartog, Jan 1914- .... **CLC 19**
See also CA 1-4R; CANR 1

de Hostos, E. M.
See Hostos (y Bonilla), Eugenio Maria de

de Hostos, Eugenio M.
See Hostos (y Bonilla), Eugenio Maria de

Deighton, Len . . . . CLC 4, 7, 22, 46
See also Deighton, Leonard Cyril
See also AAYA 6; BEST 89:2;
CDBLB 1960 to Present; DLB 87

Deighton, Leonard Cyril 1929-
See Deighton, Len
See also CA 9-12R; CANR 19, 33; MTCW

Dekker, Thomas 1572(?)-1632 . . . . . . LC 22
See also CDBLB Before 1660; DLB 62

de la Mare, Walter (John)
1873-1956 . . TCLC 4, 53; SSC 14; WLC
See also CDBLB 1914-1945; CLR 23;
DLB 19; SATA 16

Delaney, Franey
See O'Hara, John (Henry)

Delaney, Shelagh 1939- . . . . CLC 29
See also CA 17-20R; CANR 30;
CDBLB 1960 to Present; DLB 13;
MTCW

Delany, Mary (Granville Pendarves)
1700-1788 . . . . LC 12

Delany, Samuel R(ay, Jr.)
1942- . . . . CLC 8, 14, 38; BLC
See also BW 2; CA 81-84; CANR 27, 43;
DLB 8, 33; MTCW

De La Ramee, (Marie) Louise 1839-1908
See Ouida
See also SATA 20

de la Roche, Mazo 1879-1961 . . . . . . CLC 14
See also CA 85-88; CANR 30; DLB 68;
SATA 64

Delbanco, Nicholas (Franklin)
1942- . . . . CLC 6, 13
See also CA 17-20R; CAAS 2; CANR 29;
DLB 6

del Castillo, Michel 1933- . . . . CLC 38
See also CA 109

Deledda, Grazia (Cosima)
1875(?)-1936 . . . . TCLC 23
See also CA 123

Delibes, Miguel . . . . CLC 8, 18
See also Delibes Setien, Miguel

Delibes Setien, Miguel 1920-
See Delibes, Miguel
See also CA 45-48; CANR 1, 32; HW;
MTCW

DeLillo, Don
1936- . . . . . CLC 8, 10, 13, 27, 39, 54, 76
See also BEST 89:1; CA 81-84; CANR 21;
DLB 6; MTCW

de Lisser, H. G.
See De Lisser, Herbert George
See also DLB 117

De Lisser, Herbert George
1878-1944 . . . . TCLC 12
See also de Lisser, H. G.
See also BW 2; CA 109

Deloria, Vine (Victor), Jr. 1933- . . . . CLC 21
See also CA 53-56; CANR 5, 20; MTCW;
SATA 21

Del Vecchio, John M(ichael)
1947- . . . . CLC 29
See also CA 110; DLBD 9

de Man, Paul (Adolph Michel)
1919-1983 . . . . CLC 55
See also CA 128; 111; DLB 67; MTCW

De Marinis, Rick 1934- . . . . CLC 54
See also CA 57-60; CANR 9, 25

Demby, William 1922- . . . . . . CLC 53; BLC
See also BW 1; CA 81-84; DLB 33

Demijohn, Thom
See Disch, Thomas M(ichael)

de Montherlant, Henry (Milon)
See Montherlant, Henry (Milon) de

Demosthenes 384B.C.-322B.C. . . . CMLC 13

de Natale, Francine
See Malzberg, Barry N(athaniel)

Denby, Edwin (Orr) 1903-1983 . . . . . CLC 48
See also CA 138; 110

Denis, Julio
See Cortazar, Julio

Denmark, Harrison
See Zelazny, Roger (Joseph)

Dennis, John 1658-1734 . . . . LC 11
See also DLB 101

Dennis, Nigel (Forbes) 1912-1989 . . . . CLC 8
See also CA 25-28R; 129; DLB 13, 15;
MTCW

De Palma, Brian (Russell) 1940- . . . . CLC 20
See also CA 109

De Quincey, Thomas 1785-1859 . . . NCLC 4
See also CDBLB 1789-1832; DLB 110

Deren, Eleanora 1908(?)-1961
See Deren, Maya
See also CA 111

Deren, Maya . . . . CLC 16
See also Deren, Eleanora

Derleth, August (William)
1909-1971 . . . . CLC 31
See also CA 1-4R; 29-32R; CANR 4;
DLB 9; SATA 5

de Routisie, Albert
See Aragon, Louis

Derrida, Jacques 1930- . . . . CLC 24
See also CA 124; 127

Derry Down Derry
See Lear, Edward

Dersonnes, Jacques
See Simenon, Georges (Jacques Christian)

Desai, Anita 1937- . . . . CLC 19, 37
See also CA 81-84; CANR 33; MTCW;
SATA 63

de Saint-Luc, Jean
See Glassco, John

de Saint Roman, Arnaud
See Aragon, Louis

Descartes, Rene 1596-1650 . . . . LC 20

De Sica, Vittorio 1901(?)-1974 . . . . . CLC 20
See also CA 117

Desnos, Robert 1900-1945 . . . . TCLC 22
See also CA 121

Destouches, Louis-Ferdinand
1894-1961 . . . . CLC 9, 15
See also Celine, Louis-Ferdinand
See also CA 85-88; CANR 28; MTCW

Deutsch, Babette 1895-1982 . . . . CLC 18
See also CA 1-4R; 108; CANR 4; DLB 45;
SATA 1, 33

Devenant, William 1606-1649 . . . . . . LC 13

Devkota, Laxmiprasad
1909-1959 . . . . TCLC 23
See also CA 123

De Voto, Bernard (Augustine)
1897-1955 . . . . TCLC 29
See also CA 113; DLB 9

De Vries, Peter
1910-1993 . . . . CLC 1, 2, 3, 7, 10, 28, 46
See also CA 17-20R; 142; CANR 41;
DLB 6; DLBY 82; MTCW

Dexter, Martin
See Faust, Frederick (Schiller)

Dexter, Pete 1943- . . . . CLC 34, 55
See also BEST 89:2; CA 127; 131; MTCW

Diamano, Silmang
See Senghor, Leopold Sedar

Diamond, Neil 1941- . . . . CLC 30
See also CA 108

di Bassetto, Corno
See Shaw, George Bernard

Dick, Philip K(indred)
1928-1982 . . . . CLC 10, 30, 72
See also CA 49-52; 106; CANR 2, 16;
DLB 8; MTCW

Dickens, Charles (John Huffam)
1812-1870 . . . . . NCLC 3, 8, 18, 26; DA;
WLC
See also CDBLB 1832-1890; DLB 21, 55,
70; JRDA; MAICYA; SATA 15

Dickey, James (Lafayette)
1923- . . . . CLC 1, 2, 4, 7, 10, 15, 47
See also AITN 1, 2; CA 9-12R; CABS 2;
CANR 10; CDALB 1968-1988; DLB 5;
DLBD 7; DLBY 82, 93; MTCW

Dickey, William 1928- . . . . CLC 3, 28
See also CA 9-12R; CANR 24; DLB 5

Dickinson, Charles 1951- . . . . CLC 49
See also CA 128

Dickinson, Emily (Elizabeth)
1830-1886 . . NCLC 21; DA; PC 1; WLC
See also CDALB 1865-1917; DLB 1;
SATA 29

Dickinson, Peter (Malcolm)
1927- . . . . CLC 12, 35
See also AAYA 9; CA 41-44R; CANR 31;
CLR 29; DLB 87; JRDA; MAICYA;
SATA 5, 62

Dickson, Carr
See Carr, John Dickson

Dickson, Carter
See Carr, John Dickson

Didion, Joan 1934- . . . . . CLC 1, 3, 8, 14, 32
See also AITN 1; CA 5-8R; CANR 14;
CDALB 1968-1988; DLB 2; DLBY 81,
86; MTCW

Dietrich, Robert
See Hunt, E(verette) Howard, Jr.

Dillard, Annie 1945- . . . . CLC 9, 60
See also AAYA 6; CA 49-52; CANR 3, 43;
DLBY 80; MTCW; SATA 10

Dillard, R(ichard) H(enry) W(ilde)
1937- . . . . CLC 5
See also CA 21-24R; CAAS 7; CANR 10;
DLB 5

Dillon, Eilis 1920-. . . . . CLC 17
See also CA 9-12R; CAAS 3; CANR 4, 38;
CLR 26; MAICYA; SATA 2, 74

Dimont, Penelope
See Mortimer, Penelope (Ruth)

Dinesen, Isak. . . . . CLC 10, 29; SSC 7
See also Blixen, Karen (Christentze
Dinesen)

Ding Ling. . . . . CLC 68
See also Chiang Pin-chin

Disch, Thomas M(ichael) 1940-. . . CLC 7, 36
See also CA 21-24R; CAAS 4; CANR 17,
36; CLR 18; DLB 8; MAICYA; MTCW;
SAAS 15; SATA 54

Disch, Tom
See Disch, Thomas M(ichael)

d'Isly, Georges
See Simenon, Georges (Jacques Christian)

Disraeli, Benjamin 1804-1881 . . NCLC 2, 39
See also DLB 21, 55

Ditcum, Steve
See Crumb, R(obert)

Dixon, Paige
See Corcoran, Barbara

Dixon, Stephen 1936-. . . . . CLC 52
See also CA 89-92; CANR 17, 40; DLB 130

Dobell, Sydney Thompson
1824-1874 . . . . NCLC 43
See also DLB 32

Doblin, Alfred . . . . TCLC 13
See also Doeblin, Alfred

Dobrolyubov, Nikolai Alexandrovich
1836-1861 . . . . NCLC 5

Dobyns, Stephen 1941-. . . . . CLC 37
See also CA 45-48; CANR 2, 18

Doctorow, E(dgar) L(aurence)
1931- . . . . . CLC 6, 11, 15, 18, 37, 44, 65
See also AITN 2; BEST 89:3; CA 45-48;
CANR 2, 33; CDALB 1968-1988; DLB 2,
28; DLBY 80; MTCW

Dodgson, Charles Lutwidge 1832-1898
See Carroll, Lewis
See also CLR 2; DA; MAICYA; YABC 2

Dodson, Owen (Vincent)
1914-1983 . . . . CLC 79; BLC
See also BW 1; CA 65-68; 110; CANR 24;
DLB 76

Doeblin, Alfred 1878-1957. . . . . . . TCLC 13
See also Doblin, Alfred
See also CA 110; 141; DLB 66

Doerr, Harriet 1910- . . . . CLC 34
See also CA 117; 122

Domecq, H(onorio) Bustos
See Bioy Casares, Adolfo; Borges, Jorge
Luis

Domini, Rey
See Lorde, Audre (Geraldine)

Dominique
See Proust, (Valentin-Louis-George-Eugene-)
Marcel

Don, A
See Stephen, Leslie

Donaldson, Stephen R. 1947-. . . . . . . CLC 46
See also CA 89-92; CANR 13

Donleavy, J(ames) P(atrick)
1926- . . . . CLC 1, 4, 6, 10, 45
See also AITN 2; CA 9-12R; CANR 24;
DLB 6; MTCW

Donne, John
1572-1631 . . . . LC 10, 24; DA; PC 1
See also CDBLB Before 1660; DLB 121

Donnell, David 1939(?)-. . . . . CLC 34

Donoso (Yanez), Jose
1924- . . . . CLC 4, 8, 11, 32; HLC
See also CA 81-84; CANR 32; DLB 113;
HW; MTCW

Donovan, John 1928-1992 . . . . CLC 35
See also CA 97-100; 137; CLR 3;
MAICYA; SATA 29

Don Roberto
See Cunninghame Graham, R(obert)
B(ontine)

Doolittle, Hilda
1886-1961 . . . . . CLC 3, 8, 14, 31, 34, 73;
DA; PC 5; WLC
See also H. D.
See also CA 97-100; CANR 35; DLB 4, 45;
MTCW

Dorfman, Ariel 1942-. . . . CLC 48, 77; HLC
See also CA 124; 130; HW

Dorn, Edward (Merton) 1929-. . . CLC 10, 18
See also CA 93-96; CANR 42; DLB 5

Dorsan, Luc
See Simenon, Georges (Jacques Christian)

Dorsange, Jean
See Simenon, Georges (Jacques Christian)

Dos Passos, John (Roderigo)
1896-1970 . . . . . . CLC 1, 4, 8, 11, 15, 25,
34, 82; DA; WLC
See also CA 1-4R; 29-32R; CANR 3;
CDALB 1929-1941; DLB 4, 9; DLBD 1;
MTCW

Dossage, Jean
See Simenon, Georges (Jacques Christian)

Dostoevsky, Fedor Mikhailovich
1821-1881 . . . . . . NCLC 2, 7, 21, 33, 43;
DA; SSC 2; WLC

Doughty, Charles M(ontagu)
1843-1926 . . . . TCLC 27
See also CA 115; DLB 19, 57

Douglas, Ellen
See Haxton, Josephine Ayres

Douglas, Gavin 1475(?)-1522. . . . . . . LC 20

Douglas, Keith 1920-1944 . . . . TCLC 40
See also DLB 27

Douglas, Leonard
See Bradbury, Ray (Douglas)

Douglas, Michael
See Crichton, (John) Michael

Douglass, Frederick
1817(?)-1895 . . . . NCLC 7; BLC; DA;
WLC
See also CDALB 1640-1865; DLB 1, 43, 50,
79; SATA 29

Dourado, (Waldomiro Freitas) Autran
1926- . . . . CLC 23, 60
See also CA 25-28R; CANR 34

Dourado, Waldomiro Autran
See Dourado, (Waldomiro Freitas) Autran

Dove, Rita (Frances)
1952- . . . . CLC 50, 81; PC 6
See also BW 2; CA 109; CAAS 19;
CANR 27, 42; DLB 120

Dowell, Coleman 1925-1985. . . . . . . CLC 60
See also CA 25-28R; 117; CANR 10;
DLB 130

Dowson, Ernest Christopher
1867-1900 . . . . TCLC 4
See also CA 105; DLB 19, 135

Doyle, A. Conan
See Doyle, Arthur Conan

Doyle, Arthur Conan
1859-1930 . . . . . . TCLC 7; DA; SSC 12;
WLC
See also CA 104; 122; CDBLB 1890-1914;
DLB 18, 70; MTCW; SATA 24

Doyle, Conan 1859-1930
See Doyle, Arthur Conan

Doyle, John
See Graves, Robert (von Ranke)

Doyle, Roddy 1958(?)-. . . . . CLC 81
See also CA 143

Doyle, Sir A. Conan
See Doyle, Arthur Conan

Doyle, Sir Arthur Conan
See Doyle, Arthur Conan

Dr. A
See Asimov, Isaac; Silverstein, Alvin

Drabble, Margaret
1939- . . . . CLC 2, 3, 5, 8, 10, 22, 53
See also CA 13-16R; CANR 18, 35;
CDBLB 1960 to Present; DLB 14;
MTCW; SATA 48

Drapier, M. B.
See Swift, Jonathan

Drayham, James
See Mencken, H(enry) L(ouis)

Drayton, Michael 1563-1631. . . . . LC 8

Dreadstone, Carl
See Campbell, (John) Ramsey

Dreiser, Theodore (Herman Albert)
1871-1945 . . . . TCLC 10, 18, 35; DA;
WLC
See also CA 106; 132; CDALB 1865-1917;
DLB 9, 12, 102, 137; DLBD 1; MTCW

Drexler, Rosalyn 1926- . . . . CLC 2, 6
See also CA 81-84

Dreyer, Carl Theodor 1889-1968. . . . CLC 16
See also CA 116

Drieu la Rochelle, Pierre(-Eugene)
1893-1945 . . . . TCLC 21
See also CA 117; DLB 72

Drop Shot
See Cable, George Washington

Droste-Hulshoff, Annette Freiin von
1797-1848 . . . . NCLC 3
See also DLB 133

Drummond, Walter
See Silverberg, Robert

Drummond, William Henry
1854-1907 . . . . TCLC 25
See also DLB 92

Drummond de Andrade, Carlos
  1902-1987 .... **CLC 18**
  See also Andrade, Carlos Drummond de
  See also CA 132; 123

Drury, Allen (Stuart) 1918-....... **CLC 37**
  See also CA 57-60; CANR 18

Dryden, John
  1631-1700 ... **LC 3, 21; DA; DC 3; WLC**
  See also CDBLB 1660-1789; DLB 80, 101,
  131

Duberman, Martin 1930-.......... **CLC 8**
  See also CA 1-4R; CANR 2

Dubie, Norman (Evans) 1945-...... **CLC 36**
  See also CA 69-72; CANR 12; DLB 120

Du Bois, W(illiam) E(dward) B(urghardt)
  1868-1963 ...... **CLC 1, 2, 13, 64; BLC;**
                                    DA; WLC
  See also BW 1; CA 85-88; CANR 34;
  CDALB 1865-1917; DLB 47, 50, 91;
  MTCW; SATA 42

Dubus, Andre 1936-... **CLC 13, 36; SSC 15**
  See also CA 21-24R; CANR 17; DLB 130

Duca Minimo
  See D'Annunzio, Gabriele

Ducharme, Rejean 1941-.......... **CLC 74**
  See also DLB 60

Duclos, Charles Pinot 1704-1772 ..... **LC 1**

Dudek, Louis 1918- .... **CLC 11, 19**
  See also CA 45-48; CAAS 14; CANR 1;
  DLB 88

Duerrenmatt, Friedrich
  .... **CLC 1, 4, 8, 11, 15, 43**
  See also Duerrenmatt, Friedrich
  See also DLB 69, 124

Duerrenmatt, Friedrich
  1921-1990 ...... **CLC 1, 4, 8, 11, 15, 43**
  See also Duerrenmatt, Friedrich
  See also CA 17-20R; CANR 33; DLB 69,
  124; MTCW

Duffy, Bruce (?)-................ **CLC 50**

Duffy, Maureen 1933- .... **CLC 37**
  See also CA 25-28R; CANR 33; DLB 14;
  MTCW

Dugan, Alan 1923- .... **CLC 2, 6**
  See also CA 81-84; DLB 5

du Gard, Roger Martin
  See Martin du Gard, Roger

Duhamel, Georges 1884-1966 .... **CLC 8**
  See also CA 81-84; 25-28R; CANR 35;
  DLB 65; MTCW

Dujardin, Edouard (Emile Louis)
  1861-1949 .... **TCLC 13**
  See also CA 109; DLB 123

Dumas, Alexandre (Davy de la Pailleterie)
  1802-1870 .... **NCLC 11; DA; WLC**
  See also DLB 119; SATA 18

Dumas, Alexandre
  1824-1895 .... **NCLC 9; DC 1**

Dumas, Claudine
  See Malzberg, Barry N(athaniel)

Dumas, Henry L. 1934-1968 ..... **CLC 6, 62**
  See also BW 1; CA 85-88; DLB 41

du Maurier, Daphne
  1907-1989 .... **CLC 6, 11, 59**
  See also CA 5-8R; 128; CANR 6; MTCW;
  SATA 27, 60

Dunbar, Paul Laurence
  1872-1906 ...... **TCLC 2, 12; BLC; DA;**
                            PC 5; SSC 8; WLC
  See also BW 1; CA 104; 124;
  CDALB 1865-1917; DLB 50, 54, 78;
  SATA 34

Dunbar, William 1460(?)-1530(?) .... **LC 20**

Duncan, Lois 1934-............... **CLC 26**
  See also AAYA 4; CA 1-4R; CANR 2, 23,
  36; CLR 29; JRDA; MAICYA; SAAS 2;
  SATA 1, 36, 75

Duncan, Robert (Edward)
  1919-1988 .... **CLC 1, 2, 4, 7, 15, 41, 55;**
                                        PC 2
  See also CA 9-12R; 124; CANR 28; DLB 5,
  16; MTCW

Dunlap, William 1766-1839 .... **NCLC 2**
  See also DLB 30, 37, 59

Dunn, Douglas (Eaglesham)
  1942-..................... **CLC 6, 40**
  See also CA 45-48; CANR 2, 33; DLB 40;
  MTCW

Dunn, Katherine (Karen) 1945-..... **CLC 71**
  See also CA 33-36R

Dunn, Stephen 1939- .... **CLC 36**
  See also CA 33-36R; CANR 12; DLB 105

Dunne, Finley Peter 1867-1936.... **TCLC 28**
  See also CA 108; DLB 11, 23

Dunne, John Gregory 1932-........ **CLC 28**
  See also CA 25-28R; CANR 14; DLBY 80

Dunsany, Edward John Moreton Drax
      Plunkett 1878-1957
  See Dunsany, Lord; Lord Dunsany
  See also CA 104; DLB 10

Dunsany, Lord................... **TCLC 2**
  See also Dunsany, Edward John Moreton
  Drax Plunkett
  See also DLB 77

du Perry, Jean
  See Simenon, Georges (Jacques Christian)

Durang, Christopher (Ferdinand)
  1949-..................... **CLC 27, 38**
  See also CA 105

Duras, Marguerite
  1914- ...... **CLC 3, 6, 11, 20, 34, 40, 68**
  See also CA 25-28R; DLB 83; MTCW

Durban, (Rosa) Pam 1947-........ **CLC 39**
  See also CA 123

Durcan, Paul 1944-............ **CLC 43, 70**
  See also CA 134

Durrell, Lawrence (George)
  1912-1990 .... **CLC 1, 4, 6, 8, 13, 27, 41**
  See also CA 9-12R; 132; CANR 40;
  CDBLB 1945-1960; DLB 15, 27;
  DLBY 90; MTCW

Dutt, Toru 1856-1877.......... **NCLC 29**

Dwight, Timothy 1752-1817...... **NCLC 13**
  See also DLB 37

Dworkin, Andrea 1946- .... **CLC 43**
  See also CA 77-80; CANR 16, 39; MTCW

Dwyer, Deanna
  See Koontz, Dean R(ay)

Dwyer, K. R.
  See Koontz, Dean R(ay)

Dylan, Bob 1941- ...... **CLC 3, 4, 6, 12, 77**
  See also CA 41-44R; DLB 16

Eagleton, Terence (Francis) 1943-
  See Eagleton, Terry
  See also CA 57-60; CANR 7, 23; MTCW

Eagleton, Terry .... **CLC 63**
  See also Eagleton, Terence (Francis)

Early, Jack
  See Scoppettone, Sandra

East, Michael
  See West, Morris L(anglo)

Eastaway, Edward
  See Thomas, (Philip) Edward

Eastlake, William (Derry) 1917-..... **CLC 8**
  See also CA 5-8R; CAAS 1; CANR 5;
  DLB 6

Eberhart, Richard (Ghormley)
  1904- .... **CLC 3, 11, 19, 56**
  See also CA 1-4R; CANR 2;
  CDALB 1941-1968; DLB 48; MTCW

Eberstadt, Fernanda 1960-........ **CLC 39**
  See also CA 136

Echegaray (y Eizaguirre), Jose (Maria Waldo)
  1832-1916 .... **TCLC 4**
  See also CA 104; CANR 32; HW; MTCW

Echeverria, (Jose) Esteban (Antonino)
  1805-1851 .... **NCLC 18**

Echo
  See Proust, (Valentin-Louis-George-Eugene-)
  Marcel

Eckert, Allan W. 1931- .... **CLC 17**
  See also CA 13-16R; CANR 14; SATA 27,
  29

Eckhart, Meister 1260(?)-1328(?) .. **CMLC 9**
  See also DLB 115

Eckmar, F. R.
  See de Hartog, Jan

Eco, Umberto 1932-........... **CLC 28, 60**
  See also BEST 90:1; CA 77-80; CANR 12,
  33; MTCW

Eddison, E(ric) R(ucker)
  1882-1945 .... **TCLC 15**
  See also CA 109

Edel, (Joseph) Leon 1907-...... **CLC 29, 34**
  See also CA 1-4R; CANR 1, 22; DLB 103

Eden, Emily 1797-1869 .... **NCLC 10**

Edgar, David 1948-.............. **CLC 42**
  See also CA 57-60; CANR 12; DLB 13;
  MTCW

Edgerton, Clyde (Carlyle) 1944- .... **CLC 39**
  See also CA 118; 134

Edgeworth, Maria 1767-1849...... **NCLC 1**
  See also DLB 116; SATA 21

Edmonds, Paul
  See Kuttner, Henry

Edmonds, Walter D(umaux) 1903- .. **CLC 35**
  See also CA 5-8R; CANR 2; DLB 9;
  MAICYA; SAAS 4; SATA 1, 27

Edmondson, Wallace
  See Ellison, Harlan

Eschenbach, Wolfram von
   See Wolfram von Eschenbach

Eseki, Bruno
   See Mphahlele, Ezekiel

Esenin, Sergei (Alexandrovich)
   1895-1925 .... **TCLC 4**
   See also CA 104

Eshleman, Clayton   1935- .... **CLC 7**
   See also CA 33-36R; CAAS 6; DLB 5

Espriella, Don Manuel Alvarez
   See Southey, Robert

Espriu, Salvador   1913-1985 .... **CLC 9**
   See also CA 115; DLB 134

Espronceda, Jose de   1808-1842 ... **NCLC 39**

Esse, James
   See Stephens, James

Esterbrook, Tom
   See Hubbard, L(afayette) Ron(ald)

Estleman, Loren D.   1952- .... **CLC 48**
   See also CA 85-88; CANR 27; MTCW

Eugenides, Jeffrey   1960(?)- .... **CLC 81**
   See also CA 144

Euripides   c. 485B.C.-406B.C. .... **DC 4**
   See also DA

Evan, Evin
   See Faust, Frederick (Schiller)

Evans, Evan
   See Faust, Frederick (Schiller)

Evans, Marian
   See Eliot, George

Evans, Mary Ann
   See Eliot, George

Evarts, Esther
   See Benson, Sally

Everett, Percival L.   1956- .... **CLC 57**
   See also BW 2; CA 129

Everson, R(onald) G(ilmour)
   1903- .... **CLC 27**
   See also CA 17-20R; DLB 88

Everson, William (Oliver)
   1912- .... **CLC 1, 5, 14**
   See also CA 9-12R; CANR 20; DLB 5, 16;
   MTCW

Evtushenko, Evgenii Aleksandrovich
   See Yevtushenko, Yevgeny (Alexandrovich)

Ewart, Gavin (Buchanan)
   1916- .... **CLC 13, 46**
   See also CA 89-92; CANR 17; DLB 40;
   MTCW

Ewers, Hanns Heinz   1871-1943 ... **TCLC 12**
   See also CA 109

Ewing, Frederick R.
   See Sturgeon, Theodore (Hamilton)

Exley, Frederick (Earl)
   1929-1992 .... **CLC 6, 11**
   See also AITN 2; CA 81-84; 138; DLBY 81

Eynhardt, Guillermo
   See Quiroga, Horacio (Sylvestre)

Ezekiel, Nissim   1924- .... **CLC 61**
   See also CA 61-64

Ezekiel, Tish O'Dowd   1943- .... **CLC 34**
   See also CA 129

Fadeyev, A.
   See Bulgya, Alexander Alexandrovich

Fadeyev, Alexander .... **TCLC 53**
   See also Bulgya, Alexander Alexandrovich

Fagen, Donald   1948- .... **CLC 26**

Fainzilberg, Ilya Arnoldovich   1897-1937
   See Ilf, Ilya
   See also CA 120

Fair, Ronald L.   1932- .... **CLC 18**
   See also BW 1; CA 69-72; CANR 25;
   DLB 33

Fairbairns, Zoe (Ann)   1948- .... **CLC 32**
   See also CA 103; CANR 21

Falco, Gian
   See Papini, Giovanni

Falconer, James
   See Kirkup, James

Falconer, Kenneth
   See Kornbluth, C(yril) M.

Falkland, Samuel
   See Heijermans, Herman

Fallaci, Oriana   1930- .... **CLC 11**
   See also CA 77-80; CANR 15; MTCW

Faludy, George   1913- .... **CLC 42**
   See also CA 21-24R

Faludy, Gyoergy
   See Faludy, George

Fanon, Frantz   1925-1961 ..... **CLC 74; BLC**
   See also BW 1; CA 116; 89-92

Fanshawe, Ann .... **LC 11**

Fante, John (Thomas)   1911-1983 ... **CLC 60**
   See also CA 69-72; 109; CANR 23;
   DLB 130; DLBY 83

Farah, Nuruddin   1945- .... **CLC 53; BLC**
   See also BW 2; CA 106; DLB 125

Fargue, Leon-Paul   1876(?)-1947 ... **TCLC 11**
   See also CA 109

Farigoule, Louis
   See Romains, Jules

Farina, Richard   1936(?)-1966 .... **CLC 9**
   See also CA 81-84; 25-28R

Farley, Walter (Lorimer)
   1915-1989 .... **CLC 17**
   See also CA 17-20R; CANR 8, 29; DLB 22;
   JRDA; MAICYA; SATA 2, 43

Farmer, Philip Jose   1918- .... **CLC 1, 19**
   See also CA 1-4R; CANR 4, 35; DLB 8;
   MTCW

Farquhar, George   1677-1707 .... **LC 21**
   See also DLB 84

Farrell, J(ames) G(ordon)
   1935-1979 .... **CLC 6**
   See also CA 73-76; 89-92; CANR 36;
   DLB 14; MTCW

Farrell, James T(homas)
   1904-1979 .... **CLC 1, 4, 8, 11, 66**
   See also CA 5-8R; 89-92; CANR 9; DLB 4,
   9, 86; DLBD 2; MTCW

Farren, Richard J.
   See Betjeman, John

Farren, Richard M.
   See Betjeman, John

Fassbinder, Rainer Werner
   1946-1982 .... **CLC 20**
   See also CA 93-96; 106; CANR 31

Fast, Howard (Melvin)   1914- ...... **CLC 23**
   See also CA 1-4R; CAAS 18; CANR 1, 33;
   DLB 9; SATA 7

Faulcon, Robert
   See Holdstock, Robert P.

Faulkner, William (Cuthbert)
   1897-1962 ..... **CLC 1, 3, 6, 8, 9, 11, 14,
   18, 28, 52, 68; DA; SSC 1; WLC**
   See also AAYA 7; CA 81-84; CANR 33;
   CDALB 1929-1941; DLB 9, 11, 44, 102;
   DLBD 2; DLBY 86; MTCW

Fauset, Jessie Redmon
   1884(?)-1961 .... **CLC 19, 54; BLC**
   See also BW 1; CA 109; DLB 51

Faust, Frederick (Schiller)
   1892-1944(?) .... **TCLC 49**
   See also CA 108

Faust, Irvin   1924- .... **CLC 8**
   See also CA 33-36R; CANR 28; DLB 2, 28;
   DLBY 80

Fawkes, Guy
   See Benchley, Robert (Charles)

Fearing, Kenneth (Flexner)
   1902-1961 .... **CLC 51**
   See also CA 93-96; DLB 9

Fecamps, Elise
   See Creasey, John

Federman, Raymond   1928- ...... **CLC 6, 47**
   See also CA 17-20R; CAAS 8; CANR 10,
   43; DLBY 80

Federspiel, J(uerg) F.   1931- .... **CLC 42**

Feiffer, Jules (Ralph)   1929- .... **CLC 2, 8, 64**
   See also AAYA 3; CA 17-20R; CANR 30;
   DLB 7, 44; MTCW; SATA 8, 61

Feige, Hermann Albert Otto Maximilian
   See Traven, B.

Fei-Kan, Li
   See Li Fei-kan

Feinberg, David B.   1956- .... **CLC 59**
   See also CA 135

Feinstein, Elaine   1930- .... **CLC 36**
   See also CA 69-72; CAAS 1; CANR 31;
   DLB 14, 40; MTCW

Feldman, Irving (Mordecai)   1928- .... **CLC 7**
   See also CA 1-4R; CANR 1

Fellini, Federico   1920-1993 .... **CLC 16**
   See also CA 65-68; 143; CANR 33

Felsen, Henry Gregor   1916- .... **CLC 17**
   See also CA 1-4R; CANR 1; SAAS 2;
   SATA 1

Fenton, James Martin   1949- .... **CLC 32**
   See also CA 102; DLB 40

Ferber, Edna   1887-1968 .... **CLC 18**
   See also AITN 1; CA 5-8R; 25-28R; DLB 9,
   28, 86; MTCW; SATA 7

Ferguson, Helen
   See Kavan, Anna

Ferguson, Samuel   1810-1886 ..... **NCLC 33**
   See also DLB 32

Ferling, Lawrence
   See Ferlinghetti, Lawrence (Monsanto)

Fosse, Robert Louis   1927-1987
See Fosse, Bob
See also CA 110; 123

Foster, Stephen Collins
1826-1864 . . . . NCLC 26

Foucault, Michel
1926-1984 . . . . CLC 31, 34, 69
See also CA 105; 113; CANR 34; MTCW

Fouque, Friedrich (Heinrich Karl) de la Motte
1777-1843 . . . . NCLC 2
See also DLB 90

Fournier, Henri Alban   1886-1914
See Alain-Fournier
See also CA 104

Fournier, Pierre   1916- . . . . CLC 11
See also Gascar, Pierre
See also CA 89-92; CANR 16, 40

Fowles, John
1926- . . . . CLC 1, 2, 3, 4, 6, 9, 10, 15, 33
See also CA 5-8R; CANR 25; CDBLB 1960
to Present; DLB 14, 139; MTCW;
SATA 22

Fox, Paula   1923- . . . . CLC 2, 8
See also AAYA 3; CA 73-76; CANR 20,
36; CLR 1; DLB 52; JRDA; MAICYA;
MTCW; SATA 17, 60

Fox, William Price (Jr.)   1926- . . . . . CLC 22
See also CA 17-20R; CAAS 19; CANR 11;
DLB 2; DLBY 81

Foxe, John   1516(?)-1587 . . . . LC 14

Frame, Janet . . . . CLC 2, 3, 6, 22, 66
See also Clutha, Janet Paterson Frame

France, Anatole . . . . TCLC 9
See also Thibault, Jacques Anatole Francois
See also DLB 123

Francis, Claude   19(?)- . . . . CLC 50

Francis, Dick   1920- . . . . CLC 2, 22, 42
See also AAYA 5; BEST 89:3; CA 5-8R;
CANR 9, 42; CDBLB 1960 to Present;
DLB 87; MTCW

Francis, Robert (Churchill)
1901-1987 . . . . CLC 15
See also CA 1-4R; 123; CANR 1

Frank, Anne(lies Marie)
1929-1945 . . . . TCLC 17; DA; WLC
See also AAYA 12; CA 113; 133; MTCW;
SATA 42

Frank, Elizabeth   1945- . . . . CLC 39
See also CA 121; 126

Franklin, Benjamin
See Hasek, Jaroslav (Matej Frantisek)

Franklin, Benjamin   1706-1790. . . LC 25; DA
See also CDALB 1640-1865; DLB 24, 43,
73

Franklin, (Stella Maraia Sarah) Miles
1879-1954 . . . . TCLC 7
See also CA 104

Fraser, (Lady) Antonia (Pakenham)
1932- . . . . CLC 32
See also CA 85-88; CANR 44; MTCW;
SATA 32

Fraser, George MacDonald   1925- . . . . CLC 7
See also CA 45-48; CANR 2

Fraser, Sylvia   1935- . . . . CLC 64
See also CA 45-48; CANR 1, 16

Frayn, Michael   1933- . . . . . . CLC 3, 7, 31, 47
See also CA 5-8R; CANR 30; DLB 13, 14;
MTCW

Fraze, Candida (Merrill)   1945- . . . . . CLC 50
See also CA 126

Frazer, J(ames) G(eorge)
1854-1941 . . . . TCLC 32
See also CA 118

Frazer, Robert Caine
See Creasey, John

Frazer, Sir James George
See Frazer, J(ames) G(eorge)

Frazier, Ian   1951- . . . . CLC 46
See also CA 130

Frederic, Harold   1856-1898 . . . . . . NCLC 10
See also DLB 12, 23

Frederick, John
See Faust, Frederick (Schiller)

Frederick the Great   1712-1786 . . . . . . LC 14

Fredro, Aleksander   1793-1876 . . . . . NCLC 8

Freeling, Nicolas   1927- . . . . CLC 38
See also CA 49-52; CAAS 12; CANR 1, 17;
DLB 87

Freeman, Douglas Southall
1886-1953 . . . . TCLC 11
See also CA 109; DLB 17

Freeman, Judith   1946- . . . . CLC 55

Freeman, Mary Eleanor Wilkins
1852-1930 . . . . TCLC 9; SSC 1
See also CA 106; DLB 12, 78

Freeman, R(ichard) Austin
1862-1943 . . . . TCLC 21
See also CA 113; DLB 70

French, Marilyn   1929- . . . . . . CLC 10, 18, 60
See also CA 69-72; CANR 3, 31; MTCW

French, Paul
See Asimov, Isaac

Freneau, Philip Morin   1752-1832 . . NCLC 1
See also DLB 37, 43

Freud, Sigmund   1856-1939 . . . . TCLC 52
See also CA 115; 133; MTCW

Friedan, Betty (Naomi)   1921- . . . . . . CLC 74
See also CA 65-68; CANR 18; MTCW

Friedman, B(ernard) H(arper)
1926- . . . . CLC 7
See also CA 1-4R; CANR 3

Friedman, Bruce Jay   1930- . . . . CLC 3, 5, 56
See also CA 9-12R; CANR 25; DLB 2, 28

Friel, Brian   1929- . . . . CLC 5, 42, 59
See also CA 21-24R; CANR 33; DLB 13;
MTCW

Friis-Baastad, Babbis Ellinor
1921-1970 . . . . CLC 12
See also CA 17-20R; 134; SATA 7

Frisch, Max (Rudolf)
1911-1991 . . . . . CLC 3, 9, 14, 18, 32, 44
See also CA 85-88; 134; CANR 32;
DLB 69, 124; MTCW

Fromentin, Eugene (Samuel Auguste)
1820-1876 . . . . NCLC 10
See also DLB 123

Frost, Frederick
See Faust, Frederick (Schiller)

Frost, Robert (Lee)
1874-1963 . . . . CLC 1, 3, 4, 9, 10, 13, 15,
26, 34, 44; DA; PC 1; WLC
See also CA 89-92; CANR 33;
CDALB 1917-1929; DLB 54; DLBD 7;
MTCW; SATA 14

Froude, James Anthony
1818-1894 . . . . NCLC 43
See also DLB 18, 57

Froy, Herald
See Waterhouse, Keith (Spencer)

Fry, Christopher   1907- . . . . CLC 2, 10, 14
See also CA 17-20R; CANR 9, 30; DLB 13;
MTCW; SATA 66

Frye, (Herman) Northrop
1912-1991 . . . . CLC 24, 70
See also CA 5-8R; 133; CANR 8, 37;
DLB 67, 68; MTCW

Fuchs, Daniel   1909-1993 . . . . CLC 8, 22
See also CA 81-84; 142; CAAS 5;
CANR 40; DLB 9, 26, 28; DLBY 93

Fuchs, Daniel   1934- . . . . CLC 34
See also CA 37-40R; CANR 14

Fuentes, Carlos
1928- . . . . . . CLC 3, 8, 10, 13, 22, 41, 60;
DA; HLC; WLC
See also AAYA 4; AITN 2; CA 69-72;
CANR 10, 32; DLB 113; HW; MTCW

Fuentes, Gregorio Lopez y
See Lopez y Fuentes, Gregorio

Fugard, (Harold) Athol
1932- . . . . CLC 5, 9, 14, 25, 40, 80; DC 3
See also CA 85-88; CANR 32; MTCW

Fugard, Sheila   1932- . . . . CLC 48
See also CA 125

Fuller, Charles (H., Jr.)
1939- . . . . CLC 25; BLC; DC 1
See also BW 2; CA 108; 112; DLB 38;
MTCW

Fuller, John (Leopold)   1937- . . . . CLC 62
See also CA 21-24R; CANR 9, 44; DLB 40

Fuller, Margaret . . . . NCLC 5
See also Ossoli, Sarah Margaret (Fuller
marchesa d')

Fuller, Roy (Broadbent)
1912-1991 . . . . CLC 4, 28
See also CA 5-8R; 135; CAAS 10; DLB 15,
20

Fulton, Alice   1952- . . . . CLC 52
See also CA 116

Furphy, Joseph   1843-1912 . . . . TCLC 25

Fussell, Paul   1924- . . . . CLC 74
See also BEST 90:1; CA 17-20R; CANR 8,
21, 35; MTCW

Futabatei, Shimei   1864-1909 . . . . . . TCLC 44

Futrelle, Jacques   1875-1912 . . . . . . TCLC 19
See also CA 113

G. B. S.
See Shaw, George Bernard

Gaboriau, Emile   1835-1873 . . . . . . NCLC 14

Gadda, Carlo Emilio   1893-1973 . . . . CLC 11
See also CA 89-92

Gaddis, William
   1922-....... **CLC 1, 3, 6, 8, 10, 19, 43**
   See also CA 17-20R; CANR 21; DLB 2;
   MTCW

Gaines, Ernest J(ames)
   1933-..........**CLC 3, 11, 18; BLC**
   See also AITN 1; BW 2; CA 9-12R;
   CANR 6, 24, 42; CDALB 1968-1988;
   DLB 2, 33; DLBY 80; MTCW

Gaitskill, Mary 1954-............ **CLC 69**
   See also CA 128

Galdos, Benito Perez
   See Perez Galdos, Benito

Gale, Zona 1874-1938 .... **TCLC 7**
   See also CA 105; DLB 9, 78

Galeano, Eduardo (Hughes) 1940-... **CLC 72**
   See also CA 29-32R; CANR 13, 32; HW

Galiano, Juan Valera y Alcala
   See Valera y Alcala-Galiano, Juan

Gallagher, Tess 1943-.... **CLC 18, 63; PC 9**
   See also CA 106; DLB 120

Gallant, Mavis
   1922-.......... **CLC 7, 18, 38; SSC 5**
   See also CA 69-72; CANR 29; DLB 53;
   MTCW

Gallant, Roy A(rthur) 1924- .... **CLC 17**
   See also CA 5-8R; CANR 4, 29; CLR 30;
   MAICYA; SATA 4, 68

Gallico, Paul (William) 1897-1976 ... **CLC 2**
   See also AITN 1; CA 5-8R; 69-72;
   CANR 23; DLB 9; MAICYA; SATA 13

Gallup, Ralph
   See Whitemore, Hugh (John)

Galsworthy, John
   1867-1933 .... **TCLC 1, 45; DA; WLC 2**
   See also CA 104; 141; CDBLB 1890-1914;
   DLB 10, 34, 98

Galt, John 1779-1839........... **NCLC 1**
   See also DLB 99, 116

Galvin, James 1951-............. **CLC 38**
   See also CA 108; CANR 26

Gamboa, Federico 1864-1939...... **TCLC 36**

Gann, Ernest Kellogg 1910-1991.... **CLC 23**
   See also AITN 1; CA 1-4R; 136; CANR 1

Garcia, Cristina 1958- .... **CLC 76**
   See also CA 141

Garcia Lorca, Federico
   1898-1936 .... **TCLC 1, 7, 49; DA;
               DC 2; HLC; PC 3; WLC**
   See also CA 104; 131; DLB 108; HW;
   MTCW

Garcia Marquez, Gabriel (Jose)
   1928-.... **CLC 2, 3, 8, 10, 15, 27, 47, 55;
            DA; HLC; SSC 8; WLC**
   See also Marquez, Gabriel (Jose) Garcia
   See also AAYA 3; BEST 89:1, 90:4;
   CA 33-36R; CANR 10, 28; DLB 113;
   HW; MTCW

Gard, Janice
   See Latham, Jean Lee

Gard, Roger Martin du
   See Martin du Gard, Roger

Gardam, Jane 1928-............. **CLC 43**
   See also CA 49-52; CANR 2, 18, 33;
   CLR 12; DLB 14; MAICYA; MTCW;
   SAAS 9; SATA 28, 39, 76

Gardner, Herb................... **CLC 44**

Gardner, John (Champlin), Jr.
   1933-1982 ..... **CLC 2, 3, 5, 7, 8, 10, 18,
                 28, 34; SSC 7**
   See also AITN 1; CA 65-68; 107;
   CANR 33; DLB 2; DLBY 82; MTCW;
   SATA 31, 40

Gardner, John (Edmund) 1926-..... **CLC 30**
   See also CA 103; CANR 15; MTCW

Gardner, Noel
   See Kuttner, Henry

Gardons, S. S.
   See Snodgrass, W(illiam) D(e Witt)

Garfield, Leon 1921-............. **CLC 12**
   See also AAYA 8; CA 17-20R; CANR 38,
   41; CLR 21; JRDA; MAICYA; SATA 1,
   32, 76

Garland, (Hannibal) Hamlin
   1860-1940 .... **TCLC 3**
   See also CA 104; DLB 12, 71, 78

Garneau, (Hector de) Saint-Denys
   1912-1943 .... **TCLC 13**
   See also CA 111; DLB 88

Garner, Alan 1934-.............. **CLC 17**
   See also CA 73-76; CANR 15; CLR 20;
   MAICYA; MTCW; SATA 18, 69

Garner, Hugh 1913-1979.......... **CLC 13**
   See also CA 69-72; CANR 31; DLB 68

Garnett, David 1892-1981.......... **CLC 3**
   See also CA 5-8R; 103; CANR 17; DLB 34

Garos, Stephanie
   See Katz, Steve

Garrett, George (Palmer)
   1929-.................**CLC 3, 11, 51**
   See also CA 1-4R; CAAS 5; CANR 1, 42;
   DLB 2, 5, 130; DLBY 83

Garrick, David 1717-1779 .... **LC 15**
   See also DLB 84

Garrigue, Jean 1914-1972 .... **CLC 2, 8**
   See also CA 5-8R; 37-40R; CANR 20

Garrison, Frederick
   See Sinclair, Upton (Beall)

Garth, Will
   See Hamilton, Edmond; Kuttner, Henry

Garvey, Marcus (Moziah, Jr.)
   1887-1940 .... **TCLC 41; BLC**
   See also BW 1; CA 120; 124

Gary, Romain .... **CLC 25**
   See also Kacew, Romain
   See also DLB 83

Gascar, Pierre .... **CLC 11**
   See also Fournier, Pierre

Gascoyne, David (Emery) 1916- .... **CLC 45**
   See also CA 65-68; CANR 10, 28; DLB 20;
   MTCW

Gaskell, Elizabeth Cleghorn
   1810-1865 .... **NCLC 5**
   See also CDBLB 1832-1890; DLB 21

Gass, William H(oward)
   1924- ... **CLC 1, 2, 8, 11, 15, 39; SSC 12**
   See also CA 17-20R; CANR 30; DLB 2;
   MTCW

Gasset, Jose Ortega y
   See Ortega y Gasset, Jose

Gautier, Theophile 1811-1872 ..... **NCLC 1**
   See also DLB 119

Gawsworth, John
   See Bates, H(erbert) E(rnest)

Gaye, Marvin (Penze) 1939-1984 ... **CLC 26**
   See also CA 112

Gebler, Carlo (Ernest) 1954-....... **CLC 39**
   See also CA 119; 133

Gee, Maggie (Mary) 1948-........ **CLC 57**
   See also CA 130

Gee, Maurice (Gough) 1931-....... **CLC 29**
   See also CA 97-100; SATA 46

Gelbart, Larry (Simon) 1923- ... **CLC 21, 61**
   See also CA 73-76

Gelber, Jack 1932-........**CLC 1, 6, 14, 79**
   See also CA 1-4R; CANR 2; DLB 7

Gellhorn, Martha (Ellis) 1908-.. **CLC 14, 60**
   See also CA 77-80; CANR 44; DLBY 82

Genet, Jean
   1910-1986 ... **CLC 1, 2, 5, 10, 14, 44, 46**
   See also CA 13-16R; CANR 18; DLB 72;
   DLBY 86; MTCW

Gent, Peter 1942-................ **CLC 29**
   See also AITN 1; CA 89-92; DLBY 82

Gentlewoman in New England, A
   See Bradstreet, Anne

Gentlewoman in Those Parts, A
   See Bradstreet, Anne

George, Jean Craighead 1919-...... **CLC 35**
   See also AAYA 8; CA 5-8R; CANR 25;
   CLR 1; DLB 52; JRDA; MAICYA;
   SATA 2, 68

George, Stefan (Anton)
   1868-1933 .... **TCLC 2, 14**
   See also CA 104

Georges, Georges Martin
   See Simenon, Georges (Jacques Christian)

Gerhardi, William Alexander
   See Gerhardie, William Alexander

Gerhardie, William Alexander
   1895-1977 .... **CLC 5**
   See also CA 25-28R; 73-76; CANR 18;
   DLB 36

Gerstler, Amy 1956-............. **CLC 70**

Gertler, T. .... **CLC 34**
   See also CA 116; 121

Ghalib 1797-1869 .... **NCLC 39**

Ghelderode, Michel de
   1898-1962 .... **CLC 6, 11**
   See also CA 85-88; CANR 40

Ghiselin, Brewster 1903- .... **CLC 23**
   See also CA 13-16R; CAAS 10; CANR 13

Ghose, Zulfikar 1935-............. **CLC 42**
   See also CA 65-68

Ghosh, Amitav 1956- .... **CLC 44**

Giacosa, Giuseppe 1847-1906 ...... **TCLC 7**
   See also CA 104

Gibb, Lee
See Waterhouse, Keith (Spencer)

Gibbon, Lewis Grassic .... TCLC 4
See also Mitchell, James Leslie

Gibbons, Kaye 1960- .... CLC 50

Gibran, Kahlil
1883-1931 .... TCLC 1, 9; PC 9
See also CA 104

Gibson, William 1914- .... CLC 23; DA
See also CA 9-12R; CANR 9, 42; DLB 7;
SATA 66

Gibson, William (Ford) 1948- ... CLC 39, 63
See also AAYA 12; CA 126; 133

Gide, Andre (Paul Guillaume)
1869-1951 .... TCLC 5, 12, 36; DA;
SSC 13; WLC
See also CA 104; 124; DLB 65; MTCW

Gifford, Barry (Colby) 1946- .... CLC 34
See also CA 65-68; CANR 9, 30, 40

Gilbert, W(illiam) S(chwenck)
1836-1911 .... TCLC 3
See also CA 104; SATA 36

Gilbreth, Frank B., Jr. 1911- .... CLC 17
See also CA 9-12R; SATA 2

Gilchrist, Ellen 1935- .. CLC 34, 48; SSC 14
See also CA 113; 116; CANR 41; DLB 130;
MTCW

Giles, Molly 1942- .... CLC 39
See also CA 126

Gill, Patrick
See Creasey, John

Gilliam, Terry (Vance) 1940- .... CLC 21
See also Monty Python
See also CA 108; 113; CANR 35

Gillian, Jerry
See Gilliam, Terry (Vance)

Gilliatt, Penelope (Ann Douglass)
1932-1993 .... CLC 2, 10, 13, 53
See also AITN 2; CA 13-16R; 141; DLB 14

Gilman, Charlotte (Anna) Perkins (Stetson)
1860-1935 .... TCLC 9, 37; SSC 13
See also CA 106

Gilmour, David 1949- .... CLC 35
See also Pink Floyd
See also CA 138

Gilpin, William 1724-1804 .... NCLC 30

Gilray, J. D.
See Mencken, H(enry) L(ouis)

Gilroy, Frank D(aniel) 1925- .... CLC 2
See also CA 81-84; CANR 32; DLB 7

Ginsberg, Allen
1926- ...... CLC 1, 2, 3, 4, 6, 13, 36, 69;
DA; PC 4; WLC 3
See also AITN 1; CA 1-4R; CANR 2, 41;
CDALB 1941-1968; DLB 5, 16; MTCW

Ginzburg, Natalia
1916-1991 .... CLC 5, 11, 54, 70
See also CA 85-88; 135; CANR 33; MTCW

Giono, Jean 1895-1970 .... CLC 4, 11
See also CA 45-48; 29-32R; CANR 2, 35;
DLB 72; MTCW

Giovanni, Nikki
1943- ...... CLC 2, 4, 19, 64; BLC; DA
See also AITN 1; BW 2; CA 29-32R;
CAAS 6; CANR 18, 41; CLR 6; DLB 5,
41; MAICYA; MTCW; SATA 24

Giovene, Andrea 1904- .... CLC 7
See also CA 85-88

Gippius, Zinaida (Nikolayevna) 1869-1945
See Hippius, Zinaida
See also CA 106

Giraudoux, (Hippolyte) Jean
1882-1944 .... TCLC 2, 7
See also CA 104; DLB 65

Gironella, Jose Maria 1917- .... CLC 11
See also CA 101

Gissing, George (Robert)
1857-1903 .... TCLC 3, 24, 47
See also CA 105; DLB 18, 135

Giurlani, Aldo
See Palazzeschi, Aldo

Gladkov, Fyodor (Vasilyevich)
1883-1958 .... TCLC 27

Glanville, Brian (Lester) 1931- ...... CLC 6
See also CA 5-8R; CAAS 9; CANR 3;
DLB 15, 139; SATA 42

Glasgow, Ellen (Anderson Gholson)
1873(?)-1945 .... TCLC 2, 7
See also CA 104; DLB 9, 12

Glassco, John 1909-1981 .... CLC 9
See also CA 13-16R; 102; CANR 15;
DLB 68

Glasscock, Amnesia
See Steinbeck, John (Ernst)

Glasser, Ronald J. 1940(?)- .... CLC 37

Glassman, Joyce
See Johnson, Joyce

Glendinning, Victoria 1937- .... CLC 50
See also CA 120; 127

Glissant, Edouard 1928- .... CLC 10, 68

Gloag, Julian 1930- .... CLC 40
See also AITN 1; CA 65-68; CANR 10

Glowacki, Aleksander 1845-1912
See Prus, Boleslaw

Gluck, Louise (Elisabeth)
1943- .... CLC 7, 22, 44, 81
See also Glueck, Louise
See also CA 33-36R; CANR 40; DLB 5

Glueck, Louise .... CLC 7, 22
See also Gluck, Louise (Elisabeth)
See also DLB 5

Gobineau, Joseph Arthur (Comte) de
1816-1882 .... NCLC 17
See also DLB 123

Godard, Jean-Luc 1930- .... CLC 20
See also CA 93-96

Godden, (Margaret) Rumer 1907- ... CLC 53
See also AAYA 6; CA 5-8R; CANR 4, 27,
36; CLR 20; MAICYA; SAAS 12;
SATA 3, 36

Godoy Alcayaga, Lucila 1889-1957
See Mistral, Gabriela
See also BW 2; CA 104; 131; HW; MTCW

Godwin, Gail (Kathleen)
1937- .... CLC 5, 8, 22, 31, 69
See also CA 29-32R; CANR 15, 43; DLB 6;
MTCW

Godwin, William 1756-1836 ...... NCLC 14
See also CDBLB 1789-1832; DLB 39, 104,
142

Goethe, Johann Wolfgang von
1749-1832 .... NCLC 4, 22, 34; DA;
PC 5; WLC 3
See also DLB 94

Gogarty, Oliver St. John
1878-1957 .... TCLC 15
See also CA 109; DLB 15, 19

Gogol, Nikolai (Vasilyevich)
1809-1852 .... NCLC 5, 15, 31; DA;
DC 1; SSC 4; WLC

Goines, Donald
1937(?)-1974 .... CLC 80; BLC
See also AITN 1; BW 1; CA 124; 114;
DLB 33

Gold, Herbert 1924- .... CLC 4, 7, 14, 42
See also CA 9-12R; CANR 17; DLB 2;
DLBY 81

Goldbarth, Albert 1948- .... CLC 5, 38
See also CA 53-56; CANR 6, 40; DLB 120

Goldberg, Anatol 1910-1982 .... CLC 34
See also CA 131; 117

Goldemberg, Isaac 1945- .... CLC 52
See also CA 69-72; CAAS 12; CANR 11,
32; HW

Golden Silver
See Storm, Hyemeyohsts

Golding, William (Gerald)
1911-1993 .... CLC 1, 2, 3, 8, 10, 17, 27,
58, 81; DA; WLC
See also AAYA 5; CA 5-8R; 141;
CANR 13, 33; CDBLB 1945-1960;
DLB 15, 100; MTCW

Goldman, Emma 1869-1940 ...... TCLC 13
See also CA 110

Goldman, Francisco 1955- .... CLC 76

Goldman, William (W.) 1931- .... CLC 1, 48
See also CA 9-12R; CANR 29; DLB 44

Goldmann, Lucien 1913-1970 ...... CLC 24
See also CA 25-28; CAP 2

Goldoni, Carlo 1707-1793 .... LC 4

Goldsberry, Steven 1949- .... CLC 34
See also CA 131

Goldsmith, Oliver
1728-1774 .... LC 2; DA; WLC
See also CDBLB 1660-1789; DLB 39, 89,
104, 109, 142; SATA 26

Goldsmith, Peter
See Priestley, J(ohn) B(oynton)

Gombrowicz, Witold
1904-1969 .... CLC 4, 7, 11, 49
See also CA 19-20; 25-28R; CAP 2

Gomez de la Serna, Ramon
1888-1963 .... CLC 9
See also CA 116; HW

Goncharov, Ivan Alexandrovich
1812-1891 .... NCLC 1

Gregor, Arthur 1923- .... CLC 9
See also CA 25-28R; CAAS 10; CANR 11;
SATA 36

Gregor, Lee
See Pohl, Frederik

Gregory, Isabella Augusta (Persse)
1852-1932 .... TCLC 1
See also CA 104; DLB 10

Gregory, J. Dennis
See Williams, John A(lfred)

Grendon, Stephen
See Derleth, August (William)

Grenville, Kate 1950- .... CLC 61
See also CA 118

Grenville, Pelham
See Wodehouse, P(elham) G(renville)

Greve, Felix Paul (Berthold Friedrich)
1879-1948
See Grove, Frederick Philip
See also CA 104; 141

Grey, Zane 1872-1939 .... TCLC 6
See also CA 104; 132; DLB 9; MTCW

Grieg, (Johan) Nordahl (Brun)
1902-1943 .... TCLC 10
See also CA 107

Grieve, C(hristopher) M(urray)
1892-1978 .... CLC 11, 19
See also MacDiarmid, Hugh
See also CA 5-8R; 85-88; CANR 33;
MTCW

Griffin, Gerald 1803-1840 .... NCLC 7

Griffin, John Howard 1920-1980.... CLC 68
See also AITN 1; CA 1-4R; 101; CANR 2

Griffin, Peter .... CLC 39

Griffiths, Trevor 1935- .... CLC 13, 52
See also CA 97-100; DLB 13

Grigson, Geoffrey (Edward Harvey)
1905-1985 .... CLC 7, 39
See also CA 25-28R; 118; CANR 20, 33;
DLB 27; MTCW

Grillparzer, Franz 1791-1872...... NCLC 1
See also DLB 133

Grimble, Reverend Charles James
See Eliot, T(homas) S(tearns)

Grimke, Charlotte L(ottie) Forten
1837(?)-1914
See Forten, Charlotte L.
See also BW 1; CA 117; 124

Grimm, Jacob Ludwig Karl
1785-1863 .... NCLC 3
See also DLB 90; MAICYA; SATA 22

Grimm, Wilhelm Karl 1786-1859 .. NCLC 3
See also DLB 90; MAICYA; SATA 22

Grimmelshausen, Johann Jakob Christoffel
von 1621-1676 .... LC 6

Grindel, Eugene 1895-1952
See Eluard, Paul
See also CA 104

Grossman, David 1954- .... CLC 67
See also CA 138

Grossman, Vasily (Semenovich)
1905-1964 .... CLC 41
See also CA 124; 130; MTCW

Grove, Frederick Philip .... TCLC 4
See also Greve, Felix Paul (Berthold
Friedrich)
See also DLB 92

Grubb
See Crumb, R(obert)

Grumbach, Doris (Isaac)
1918- .... CLC 13, 22, 64
See also CA 5-8R; CAAS 2; CANR 9, 42

Grundtvig, Nicolai Frederik Severin
1783-1872 .... NCLC 1

Grunge
See Crumb, R(obert)

Grunwald, Lisa 1959- .... CLC 44
See also CA 120

Guare, John 1938- .... CLC 8, 14, 29, 67
See also CA 73-76; CANR 21; DLB 7;
MTCW

Gudjonsson, Halldor Kiljan 1902-
See Laxness, Halldor
See also CA 103

Guenter, Erich
See Eich, Guenter

Guest, Barbara 1920- .... CLC 34
See also CA 25-28R; CANR 11, 44; DLB 5

Guest, Judith (Ann) 1936- .... CLC 8, 30
See also AAYA 7; CA 77-80; CANR 15;
MTCW

Guild, Nicholas M. 1944-......... CLC 33
See also CA 93-96

Guillemin, Jacques
See Sartre, Jean-Paul

Guillen, Jorge 1893-1984......... CLC 11
See also CA 89-92; 112; DLB 108; HW

Guillen (y Batista), Nicolas (Cristobal)
1902-1989 ..... CLC 48, 79; BLC; HLC
See also BW 2; CA 116; 125; 129; HW

Guillevic, (Eugene) 1907-......... CLC 33
See also CA 93-96

Guillois
See Desnos, Robert

Guiney, Louise Imogen
1861-1920 .... TCLC 41
See also DLB 54

Guiraldes, Ricardo (Guillermo)
1886-1927 .... TCLC 39
See also CA 131; HW; MTCW

Gunn, Bill .... CLC 5
See also Gunn, William Harrison
See also DLB 38

Gunn, Thom(son William)
1929- .... CLC 3, 6, 18, 32, 81
See also CA 17-20R; CANR 9, 33;
CDBLB 1960 to Present; DLB 27;
MTCW

Gunn, William Harrison 1934(?)-1989
See Gunn, Bill
See also AITN 1; BW 1; CA 13-16R; 128;
CANR 12, 25

Gunnars, Kristjana 1948-......... CLC 69
See also CA 113; DLB 60

Gurganus, Allan 1947- .... CLC 70
See also BEST 90:1; CA 135

Gurney, A(lbert) R(amsdell), Jr.
1930- .... CLC 32, 50, 54
See also CA 77-80; CANR 32

Gurney, Ivor (Bertie) 1890-1937... TCLC 33

Gurney, Peter
See Gurney, A(lbert) R(amsdell), Jr.

Gustafson, Ralph (Barker) 1909-.... CLC 36
See also CA 21-24R; CANR 8; DLB 88

Gut, Gom
See Simenon, Georges (Jacques Christian)

Guthrie, A(lfred) B(ertram), Jr.
1901-1991 .... CLC 23
See also CA 57-60; 134; CANR 24; DLB 6;
SATA 62; SATA-Obit 67

Guthrie, Isobel
See Grieve, C(hristopher) M(urray)

Guthrie, Woodrow Wilson 1912-1967
See Guthrie, Woody
See also CA 113; 93-96

Guthrie, Woody................. CLC 35
See also Guthrie, Woodrow Wilson

Guy, Rosa (Cuthbert) 1928-........ CLC 26
See also AAYA 4; BW 2; CA 17-20R;
CANR 14, 34; CLR 13; DLB 33; JRDA;
MAICYA; SATA 14, 62

Gwendolyn
See Bennett, (Enoch) Arnold

H. D. .... CLC 3, 8, 14, 31, 34, 73; PC 5
See also Doolittle, Hilda

Haavikko, Paavo Juhani
1931- .... CLC 18, 34
See also CA 106

Habbema, Koos
See Heijermans, Herman

Hacker, Marilyn 1942- .... CLC 5, 9, 23, 72
See also CA 77-80; DLB 120

Haggard, H(enry) Rider
1856-1925 .... TCLC 11
See also CA 108; DLB 70; SATA 16

Haig, Fenil
See Ford, Ford Madox

Haig-Brown, Roderick (Langmere)
1908-1976 .... CLC 21
See also CA 5-8R; 69-72; CANR 4, 38;
CLR 31; DLB 88; MAICYA; SATA 12

Hailey, Arthur 1920- .... CLC 5
See also AITN 2; BEST 90:3; CA 1-4R;
CANR 2, 36; DLB 88; DLBY 82; MTCW

Hailey, Elizabeth Forsythe 1938-... CLC 40
See also CA 93-96; CAAS 1; CANR 15

Haines, John (Meade) 1924-....... CLC 58
See also CA 17-20R; CANR 13, 34; DLB 5

Haldeman, Joe (William) 1943-..... CLC 61
See also CA 53-56; CANR 6; DLB 8

Haley, Alex(ander Murray Palmer)
1921-1992 .... CLC 8, 12, 76; BLC; DA
See also BW 2; CA 77-80; 136; DLB 38;
MTCW

Haliburton, Thomas Chandler
1796-1865 .... NCLC 15
See also DLB 11, 99

Herriot, James 1916- .... CLC 12
See also Wight, James Alfred
See also AAYA 1; CANR 40

Herrmann, Dorothy 1941- .... CLC 44
See also CA 107

Herrmann, Taffy
See Herrmann, Dorothy

Hersey, John (Richard)
1914-1993 .... CLC 1, 2, 7, 9, 40, 81
See also CA 17-20R; 140; CANR 33;
DLB 6; MTCW; SATA 25;
SATA-Obit 76

Herzen, Aleksandr Ivanovich
1812-1870 .... NCLC 10

Herzl, Theodor 1860-1904 .... TCLC 36

Herzog, Werner 1942- .... CLC 16
See also CA 89-92

Hesiod c. 8th cent. B.C.- .... CMLC 5

Hesse, Hermann
1877-1962 .... CLC 1, 2, 3, 6, 11, 17, 25,
69; DA; SSC 9; WLC
See also CA 17-18; CAP 2; DLB 66;
MTCW; SATA 50

Hewes, Cady
See De Voto, Bernard (Augustine)

Heyen, William 1940- .... CLC 13, 18
See also CA 33-36R; CAAS 9; DLB 5

Heyerdahl, Thor 1914- .... CLC 26
See also CA 5-8R; CANR 5, 22; MTCW;
SATA 2, 52

Heym, Georg (Theodor Franz Arthur)
1887-1912 .... TCLC 9
See also CA 106

Heym, Stefan 1913- .... CLC 41
See also CA 9-12R; CANR 4; DLB 69

Heyse, Paul (Johann Ludwig von)
1830-1914 .... TCLC 8
See also CA 104; DLB 129

Hibbert, Eleanor Alice Burford
1906-1993 .... CLC 7
See also BEST 90:4; CA 17-20R; 140;
CANR 9, 28; SATA 2; SATA-Obit 74

Higgins, George V(incent)
1939- .... CLC 4, 7, 10, 18
See also CA 77-80; CAAS 5; CANR 17;
DLB 2; DLBY 81; MTCW

Higginson, Thomas Wentworth
1823-1911 .... TCLC 36
See also DLB 1, 64

Highet, Helen
See MacInnes, Helen (Clark)

Highsmith, (Mary) Patricia
1921- .... CLC 2, 4, 14, 42
See also CA 1-4R; CANR 1, 20; MTCW

Highwater, Jamake (Mamake)
1942(?)- .... CLC 12
See also AAYA 7; CA 65-68; CAAS 7;
CANR 10, 34; CLR 17; DLB 52;
DLBY 85; JRDA; MAICYA; SATA 30,
32, 69

Hijuelos, Oscar 1951- ...... CLC 65; HLC
See also BEST 90:1; CA 123; HW

Hikmet, Nazim 1902(?)-1963 .... CLC 40
See also CA 141; 93-96

Hildesheimer, Wolfgang
1916-1991 .... CLC 49
See also CA 101; 135; DLB 69, 124

Hill, Geoffrey (William)
1932- .... CLC 5, 8, 18, 45
See also CA 81-84; CANR 21;
CDBLB 1960 to Present; DLB 40;
MTCW

Hill, George Roy 1921- .... CLC 26
See also CA 110; 122

Hill, John
See Koontz, Dean R(ay)

Hill, Susan (Elizabeth) 1942- .... CLC 4
See also CA 33-36R; CANR 29; DLB 14,
139; MTCW

Hillerman, Tony 1925- .... CLC 62
See also AAYA 6; BEST 89:1; CA 29-32R;
CANR 21, 42; SATA 6

Hillesum, Etty 1914-1943 .... TCLC 49
See also CA 137

Hilliard, Noel (Harvey) 1929- ...... CLC 15
See also CA 9-12R; CANR 7

Hillis, Rick 1956- .... CLC 66
See also CA 134

Hilton, James 1900-1954 .... TCLC 21
See also CA 108; DLB 34, 77; SATA 34

Himes, Chester (Bomar)
1909-1984 .... CLC 2, 4, 7, 18, 58; BLC
See also BW 2; CA 25-28R; 114; CANR 22;
DLB 2, 76; MTCW

Hinde, Thomas .... CLC 6, 11
See also Chitty, Thomas Willes

Hindin, Nathan
See Bloch, Robert (Albert)

Hine, (William) Daryl 1936- .... CLC 15
See also CA 1-4R; CAAS 15; CANR 1, 20;
DLB 60

Hinkson, Katharine Tynan
See Tynan, Katharine

Hinton, S(usan) E(loise)
1950- .... CLC 30; DA
See also AAYA 2; CA 81-84; CANR 32;
CLR 3, 23; JRDA; MAICYA; MTCW;
SATA 19, 58

Hippius, Zinaida .... TCLC 9
See also Gippius, Zinaida (Nikolayevna)

Hiraoka, Kimitake 1925-1970
See Mishima, Yukio
See also CA 97-100; 29-32R; MTCW

Hirsch, E(ric) D(onald), Jr. 1928- ... CLC 79
See also CA 25-28R; CANR 27; DLB 67;
MTCW

Hirsch, Edward 1950- .... CLC 31, 50
See also CA 104; CANR 20, 42; DLB 120

Hitchcock, Alfred (Joseph)
1899-1980 .... CLC 16
See also CA 97-100; SATA 24, 27

Hitler, Adolf 1889-1945 .... TCLC 53
See also CA 117

Hoagland, Edward 1932- .... CLC 28
See also CA 1-4R; CANR 2, 31; DLB 6;
SATA 51

Hoban, Russell (Conwell) 1925- .. CLC 7, 25
See also CA 5-8R; CANR 23, 37; CLR 3;
DLB 52; MAICYA; MTCW; SATA 1, 40

Hobbs, Perry
See Blackmur, R(ichard) P(almer)

Hobson, Laura Z(ametkin)
1900-1986 .... CLC 7, 25
See also CA 17-20R; 118; DLB 28;
SATA 52

Hochhuth, Rolf 1931- .... CLC 4, 11, 18
See also CA 5-8R; CANR 33; DLB 124;
MTCW

Hochman, Sandra 1936- .... CLC 3, 8
See also CA 5-8R; DLB 5

Hochwaelder, Fritz 1911-1986 ..... CLC 36
See also CA 29-32R; 120; CANR 42;
MTCW

Hochwalder, Fritz
See Hochwaelder, Fritz

Hocking, Mary (Eunice) 1921- ..... CLC 13
See also CA 101; CANR 18, 40

Hodgins, Jack 1938- .... CLC 23
See also CA 93-96; DLB 60

Hodgson, William Hope
1877(?)-1918 .... TCLC 13
See also CA 111; DLB 70

Hoffman, Alice 1952- .... CLC 51
See also CA 77-80; CANR 34; MTCW

Hoffman, Daniel (Gerard)
1923- .... CLC 6, 13, 23
See also CA 1-4R; CANR 4; DLB 5

Hoffman, Stanley 1944- .... CLC 5
See also CA 77-80

Hoffman, William M(oses) 1939- ... CLC 40
See also CA 57-60; CANR 11

Hoffmann, E(rnst) T(heodor) A(madeus)
1776-1822 .... NCLC 2; SSC 13
See also DLB 90; SATA 27

Hofmann, Gert 1931- .... CLC 54
See also CA 128

Hofmannsthal, Hugo von
1874-1929 .... TCLC 11; DC 4
See also CA 106; DLB 81, 118

Hogan, Linda 1947- .... CLC 73
See also CA 120

Hogarth, Charles
See Creasey, John

Hogg, James 1770-1835 .... NCLC 4
See also DLB 93, 116

Holbach, Paul Henri Thiry Baron
1723-1789 .... LC 14

Holberg, Ludvig 1684-1754 .... LC 6

Holden, Ursula 1921- .... CLC 18
See also CA 101; CAAS 8; CANR 22

Holderlin, (Johann Christian) Friedrich
1770-1843 .... NCLC 16; PC 4

Holdstock, Robert
See Holdstock, Robert P.

Holdstock, Robert P. 1948- .... CLC 39
See also CA 131

Holland, Isabelle 1920- .... CLC 21
See also AAYA 11; CA 21-24R; CANR 10,
25; JRDA; MAICYA; SATA 8, 70

Holland, Marcus
See Caldwell, (Janet Miriam) Taylor
(Holland)

Hollander, John 1929- . . . . . . **CLC 2, 5, 8, 14**
See also CA 1-4R; CANR 1; DLB 5;
SATA 13

Hollander, Paul
See Silverberg, Robert

Holleran, Andrew 1943(?)- . . . . **CLC 38**
See also CA 144

Hollinghurst, Alan 1954- . . . . **CLC 55**
See also CA 114

Hollis, Jim
See Summers, Hollis (Spurgeon, Jr.)

Holmes, John
See Souster, (Holmes) Raymond

Holmes, John Clellon 1926-1988. . . . **CLC 56**
See also CA 9-12R; 125; CANR 4; DLB 16

Holmes, Oliver Wendell
1809-1894 . . . . **NCLC 14**
See also CDALB 1640-1865; DLB 1;
SATA 34

Holmes, Raymond
See Souster, (Holmes) Raymond

Holt, Victoria
See Hibbert, Eleanor Alice Burford

Holub, Miroslav 1923- . . . . **CLC 4**
See also CA 21-24R; CANR 10

Homer c. 8th cent. B.C.- . . . . . **CMLC 1; DA**

Honig, Edwin 1919- . . . . **CLC 33**
See also CA 5-8R; CAAS 8; CANR 4;
DLB 5

Hood, Hugh (John Blagdon)
1928- . . . . **CLC 15, 28**
See also CA 49-52; CAAS 17; CANR 1, 33;
DLB 53

Hood, Thomas 1799-1845. . . . . . . **NCLC 16**
See also DLB 96

Hooker, (Peter) Jeremy 1941- . . . . . **CLC 43**
See also CA 77-80; CANR 22; DLB 40

Hope, A(lec) D(erwent) 1907- . . . . **CLC 3, 51**
See also CA 21-24R; CANR 33; MTCW

Hope, Brian
See Creasey, John

Hope, Christopher (David Tully)
1944- . . . . **CLC 52**
See also CA 106; SATA 62

Hopkins, Gerard Manley
1844-1889 . . . . **NCLC 17; DA; WLC**
See also CDBLB 1890-1914; DLB 35, 57

Hopkins, John (Richard) 1931- . . . . . **CLC 4**
See also CA 85-88

Hopkins, Pauline Elizabeth
1859-1930 . . . . **TCLC 28; BLC**
See also BW 2; CA 141; DLB 50

Hopkinson, Francis 1737-1791 . . . . . . **LC 25**
See also DLB 31

Hopley-Woolrich, Cornell George 1903-1968
See Woolrich, Cornell
See also CA 13-14; CAP 1

Horatio
See Proust, (Valentin-Louis-George-Eugene-)
Marcel

Horgan, Paul 1903- . . . . **CLC 9, 53**
See also CA 13-16R; CANR 9, 35;
DLB 102; DLBY 85; MTCW; SATA 13

Horn, Peter
See Kuttner, Henry

Hornem, Horace Esq.
See Byron, George Gordon (Noel)

Horovitz, Israel 1939- . . . . **CLC 56**
See also CA 33-36R; DLB 7

Horvath, Odon von
See Horvath, Oedoen von
See also DLB 85, 124

Horvath, Oedoen von 1901-1938. . . **TCLC 45**
See also Horvath, Odon von
See also CA 118

Horwitz, Julius 1920-1986. . . . . **CLC 14**
See also CA 9-12R; 119; CANR 12

Hospital, Janette Turner 1942- . . . . . **CLC 42**
See also CA 108

Hostos, E. M. de
See Hostos (y Bonilla), Eugenio Maria de

Hostos, Eugenio M. de
See Hostos (y Bonilla), Eugenio Maria de

Hostos, Eugenio Maria
See Hostos (y Bonilla), Eugenio Maria de

Hostos (y Bonilla), Eugenio Maria de
1839-1903 . . . . **TCLC 24**
See also CA 123; 131; HW

Houdini
See Lovecraft, H(oward) P(hillips)

Hougan, Carolyn 1943- . . . . **CLC 34**
See also CA 139

Household, Geoffrey (Edward West)
1900-1988 . . . . **CLC 11**
See also CA 77-80; 126; DLB 87; SATA 14,
59

Housman, A(lfred) E(dward)
1859-1936 . . . . . . **TCLC 1, 10; DA; PC 2**
See also CA 104; 125; DLB 19; MTCW

Housman, Laurence 1865-1959 . . . . . **TCLC 7**
See also CA 106; DLB 10; SATA 25

Howard, Elizabeth Jane 1923- . . . **CLC 7, 29**
See also CA 5-8R; CANR 8

Howard, Maureen 1930- . . . . . **CLC 5, 14, 46**
See also CA 53-56; CANR 31; DLBY 83;
MTCW

Howard, Richard 1929- . . . . . . **CLC 7, 10, 47**
See also AITN 1; CA 85-88; CANR 25;
DLB 5

Howard, Robert Ervin 1906-1936. . . **TCLC 8**
See also CA 105

Howard, Warren F.
See Pohl, Frederik

Howe, Fanny 1940- . . . . **CLC 47**
See also CA 117; SATA 52

Howe, Julia Ward 1819-1910 . . . . . **TCLC 21**
See also CA 117; DLB 1

Howe, Susan 1937- . . . . **CLC 72**
See also DLB 120

Howe, Tina 1937- . . . . **CLC 48**
See also CA 109

Howell, James 1594(?)-1666 . . . . **LC 13**

Howells, W. D.
See Howells, William Dean

Howells, William D.
See Howells, William Dean

Howells, William Dean
1837-1920 . . . . **TCLC 7, 17, 41**
See also CA 104; 134; CDALB 1865-1917;
DLB 12, 64, 74, 79

Howes, Barbara 1914- . . . . **CLC 15**
See also CA 9-12R; CAAS 3; SATA 5

Hrabal, Bohumil 1914- . . . . **CLC 13, 67**
See also CA 106; CAAS 12

Hsun, Lu . . . . **TCLC 3**
See also Shu-Jen, Chou

Hubbard, L(afayette) Ron(ald)
1911-1986 . . . . **CLC 43**
See also CA 77-80; 118; CANR 22

Huch, Ricarda (Octavia)
1864-1947 . . . . **TCLC 13**
See also CA 111; DLB 66

Huddle, David 1942- . . . . **CLC 49**
See also CA 57-60; DLB 130

Hudson, Jeffrey
See Crichton, (John) Michael

Hudson, W(illiam) H(enry)
1841-1922 . . . . **TCLC 29**
See also CA 115; DLB 98; SATA 35

Hueffer, Ford Madox
See Ford, Ford Madox

Hughart, Barry 1934- . . . . **CLC 39**
See also CA 137

Hughes, Colin
See Creasey, John

Hughes, David (John) 1930- . . . . **CLC 48**
See also CA 116; 129; DLB 14

Hughes, (James) Langston
1902-1967 . . . **CLC 1, 5, 10, 15, 35, 44;**
BLC; DA; DC 3; PC 1; SSC 6; WLC
See also AAYA 12; BW 1; CA 1-4R;
25-28R; CANR 1, 34; CDALB 1929-1941;
CLR 17; DLB 4, 7, 48, 51, 86; JRDA;
MAICYA; MTCW; SATA 4, 33

Hughes, Richard (Arthur Warren)
1900-1976 . . . . **CLC 1, 11**
See also CA 5-8R; 65-68; CANR 4;
DLB 15; MTCW; SATA 8, 25

Hughes, Ted
1930- . . . . **CLC 2, 4, 9, 14, 37; PC 7**
See also CA 1-4R; CANR 1, 33; CLR 3;
DLB 40; MAICYA; MTCW; SATA 27,
49

Hugo, Richard F(ranklin)
1923-1982 . . . . **CLC 6, 18, 32**
See also CA 49-52; 108; CANR 3; DLB 5

Hugo, Victor (Marie)
1802-1885 . . **NCLC 3, 10, 21; DA; WLC**
See also DLB 119; SATA 47

Huidobro, Vicente
See Huidobro Fernandez, Vicente Garcia

Huidobro Fernandez, Vicente Garcia
1893-1948 . . . . **TCLC 31**
See also CA 131; HW

Hulme, Keri 1947- . . . . **CLC 39**
See also CA 125

Hulme, T(homas) E(rnest)
1883-1917 . . . . **TCLC 21**
See also CA 117; DLB 19

Hume, David 1711-1776. . . . . **LC 7**
See also DLB 104

James, Andrew
See Kirkup, James

James, C(yril) L(ionel) R(obert)
1901-1989 . . . . CLC 33
See also BW 2; CA 117; 125; 128; DLB 125;
MTCW

James, Daniel (Lewis) 1911-1988
See Santiago, Danny
See also CA 125

James, Dynely
See Mayne, William (James Carter)

James, Henry
1843-1916 . . . . . . TCLC 2, 11, 24, 40, 47;
DA; SSC 8; WLC
See also CA 104; 132; CDALB 1865-1917;
DLB 12, 71, 74; MTCW

James, Montague (Rhodes)
1862-1936 . . . . TCLC 6
See also CA 104

James, P. D. . . . . CLC 18, 46
See also White, Phyllis Dorothy James
See also BEST 90:2; CDBLB 1960 to
Present; DLB 87

James, Philip
See Moorcock, Michael (John)

James, William 1842-1910 . . . . . TCLC 15, 32
See also CA 109

James I 1394-1437 . . . . LC 20

Jameson, Anna 1794-1860 . . . . NCLC 43
See also DLB 99

Jami, Nur al-Din 'Abd al-Rahman
1414-1492 . . . . LC 9

Jandl, Ernst 1925- . . . . CLC 34

Janowitz, Tama 1957- . . . . CLC 43
See also CA 106

Jarrell, Randall
1914-1965 . . . . CLC 1, 2, 6, 9, 13, 49
See also CA 5-8R; 25-28R; CABS 2;
CANR 6, 34; CDALB 1941-1968; CLR 6;
DLB 48, 52; MAICYA; MTCW; SATA 7

Jarry, Alfred 1873-1907 . . . . TCLC 2, 14
See also CA 104

Jarvis, E. K.
See Bloch, Robert (Albert); Ellison, Harlan;
Silverberg, Robert

Jeake, Samuel, Jr.
See Aiken, Conrad (Potter)

Jean Paul 1763-1825 . . . . NCLC 7

Jeffers, (John) Robinson
1887-1962 . . . . CLC 2, 3, 11, 15, 54; DA;
WLC
See also CA 85-88; CANR 35;
CDALB 1917-1929; DLB 45; MTCW

Jefferson, Janet
See Mencken, H(enry) L(ouis)

Jefferson, Thomas 1743-1826 . . . . NCLC 11
See also CDALB 1640-1865; DLB 31

Jeffrey, Francis 1773-1850 . . . . . . NCLC 33
See also DLB 107

Jelakowitch, Ivan
See Heijermans, Herman

Jellicoe, (Patricia) Ann 1927- . . . . . . CLC 27
See also CA 85-88; DLB 13

Jen, Gish . . . . CLC 70
See also Jen, Lillian

Jen, Lillian 1956(?)-
See Jen, Gish
See also CA 135

Jenkins, (John) Robin 1912- . . . . . . CLC 52
See also CA 1-4R; CANR 1; DLB 14

Jennings, Elizabeth (Joan)
1926- . . . . CLC 5, 14
See also CA 61-64; CAAS 5; CANR 8, 39;
DLB 27; MTCW; SATA 66

Jennings, Waylon 1937- . . . . CLC 21

Jensen, Johannes V. 1873-1950 . . . . TCLC 41

Jensen, Laura (Linnea) 1948- . . . . . . CLC 37
See also CA 103

Jerome, Jerome K(lapka)
1859-1927 . . . . TCLC 23
See also CA 119; DLB 10, 34, 135

Jerrold, Douglas William
1803-1857 . . . . NCLC 2

Jewett, (Theodora) Sarah Orne
1849-1909 . . . . TCLC 1, 22; SSC 6
See also CA 108; 127; DLB 12, 74;
SATA 15

Jewsbury, Geraldine (Endsor)
1812-1880 . . . . NCLC 22
See also DLB 21

Jhabvala, Ruth Prawer
1927- . . . . CLC 4, 8, 29
See also CA 1-4R; CANR 2, 29; DLB 139;
MTCW

Jiles, Paulette 1943- . . . . CLC 13, 58
See also CA 101

Jimenez (Mantecon), Juan Ramon
1881-1958 . . . . TCLC 4; HLC; PC 7
See also CA 104; 131; DLB 134; HW;
MTCW

Jimenez, Ramon
See Jimenez (Mantecon), Juan Ramon

Jimenez Mantecon, Juan
See Jimenez (Mantecon), Juan Ramon

Joel, Billy . . . . CLC 26
See also Joel, William Martin

Joel, William Martin 1949-
See Joel, Billy
See also CA 108

John of the Cross, St. 1542-1591 . . . . LC 18

Johnson, B(ryan) S(tanley William)
1933-1973 . . . . CLC 6, 9
See also CA 9-12R; 53-56; CANR 9;
DLB 14, 40

Johnson, Benj. F. of Boo
See Riley, James Whitcomb

Johnson, Benjamin F. of Boo
See Riley, James Whitcomb

Johnson, Charles (Richard)
1948- . . . . CLC 7, 51, 65; BLC
See also BW 2; CA 116; CAAS 18;
CANR 42; DLB 33

Johnson, Denis 1949- . . . . CLC 52
See also CA 117; 121; DLB 120

Johnson, Diane 1934- . . . . CLC 5, 13, 48
See also CA 41-44R; CANR 17, 40;
DLBY 80; MTCW

Johnson, Eyvind (Olof Verner)
1900-1976 . . . . CLC 14
See also CA 73-76; 69-72; CANR 34

Johnson, J. R.
See James, C(yril) L(ionel) R(obert)

Johnson, James Weldon
1871-1938 . . . . TCLC 3, 19; BLC
See also BW 1; CA 104; 125;
CDALB 1917-1929; CLR 32; DLB 51;
MTCW; SATA 31

Johnson, Joyce 1935- . . . . CLC 58
See also CA 125; 129

Johnson, Lionel (Pigot)
1867-1902 . . . . TCLC 19
See also CA 117; DLB 19

Johnson, Mel
See Malzberg, Barry N(athaniel)

Johnson, Pamela Hansford
1912-1981 . . . . CLC 1, 7, 27
See also CA 1-4R; 104; CANR 2, 28;
DLB 15; MTCW

Johnson, Samuel
1709-1784 . . . . LC 15; DA; WLC
See also CDBLB 1660-1789; DLB 39, 95,
104, 142

Johnson, Uwe
1934-1984 . . . . CLC 5, 10, 15, 40
See also CA 1-4R; 112; CANR 1, 39;
DLB 75; MTCW

Johnston, George (Benson) 1913- . . . CLC 51
See also CA 1-4R; CANR 5, 20; DLB 88

Johnston, Jennifer 1930- . . . . CLC 7
See also CA 85-88; DLB 14

Jolley, (Monica) Elizabeth 1923- . . . CLC 46
See also CA 127; CAAS 13

Jones, Arthur Llewellyn 1863-1947
See Machen, Arthur
See also CA 104

Jones, D(ouglas) G(ordon) 1929- . . . . CLC 10
See also CA 29-32R; CANR 13; DLB 53

Jones, David (Michael)
1895-1974 . . . . CLC 2, 4, 7, 13, 42
See also CA 9-12R; 53-56; CANR 28;
CDBLB 1945-1960; DLB 20, 100; MTCW

Jones, David Robert 1947-
See Bowie, David
See also CA 103

Jones, Diana Wynne 1934- . . . . CLC 26
See also AAYA 12; CA 49-52; CANR 4,
26; CLR 23; JRDA; MAICYA; SAAS 7;
SATA 9, 70

Jones, Edward P. 1950- . . . . CLC 76
See also BW 2; CA 142

Jones, Gayl 1949- . . . . CLC 6, 9; BLC
See also BW 2; CA 77-80; CANR 27;
DLB 33; MTCW

Jones, James 1921-1977 . . . . CLC 1, 3, 10, 39
See also AITN 1, 2; CA 1-4R; 69-72;
CANR 6; DLB 2; MTCW

Jones, John J.
See Lovecraft, H(oward) P(hillips)

Jones, LeRoi . . . . CLC 1, 2, 3, 5, 10, 14
See also Baraka, Amiri

Jones, Louis B. . . . . CLC 65
See also CA 141

Jones, Madison (Percy, Jr.) 1925- ... **CLC 4**
See also CA 13-16R; CAAS 11; CANR 7

Jones, Mervyn 1922- .... **CLC 10, 52**
See also CA 45-48; CAAS 5; CANR 1;
MTCW

Jones, Mick 1956(?)- .... **CLC 30**
See also Clash, The

Jones, Nettie (Pearl) 1941- .... **CLC 34**
See also BW 2; CA 137

Jones, Preston 1936-1979 .... **CLC 10**
See also CA 73-76; 89-92; DLB 7

Jones, Robert F(rancis) 1934-....... **CLC 7**
See also CA 49-52; CANR 2

Jones, Rod 1953- .... **CLC 50**
See also CA 128

Jones, Terence Graham Parry
1942- .... **CLC 21**
See also Jones, Terry; Monty Python
See also CA 112; 116; CANR 35; SATA 51

Jones, Terry
See Jones, Terence Graham Parry
See also SATA 67

Jones, Thom 1945(?)- .... **CLC 81**

Jong, Erica 1942-...... **CLC 4, 6, 8, 18, 83**
See also AITN 1; BEST 90:2; CA 73-76;
CANR 26; DLB 2, 5, 28; MTCW

Jonson, Ben(jamin)
1572(?)-1637 .... **LC 6; DA; DC 4; WLC**
See also CDBLB Before 1660; DLB 62, 121

Jordan, June 1936-......... **CLC 5, 11, 23**
See also AAYA 2; BW 2; CA 33-36R;
CANR 25; CLR 10; DLB 38; MAICYA;
MTCW; SATA 4

Jordan, Pat(rick M.) 1941- .... **CLC 37**
See also CA 33-36R

Jorgensen, Ivar
See Ellison, Harlan

Jorgenson, Ivar
See Silverberg, Robert

Josephus, Flavius c. 37-100 ...... **CMLC 13**

Josipovici, Gabriel 1940-........ **CLC 6, 43**
See also CA 37-40R; CAAS 8; DLB 14

Joubert, Joseph 1754-1824 .... **NCLC 9**

Jouve, Pierre Jean 1887-1976...... **CLC 47**
See also CA 65-68

Joyce, James (Augustine Aloysius)
1882-1941 ...... **TCLC 3, 8, 16, 35; DA;
SSC 3; WLC**
See also CA 104; 126; CDBLB 1914-1945;
DLB 10, 19, 36; MTCW

Jozsef, Attila 1905-1937.......... **TCLC 22**
See also CA 116

Juana Ines de la Cruz 1651(?)-1695 ... **LC 5**

Judd, Cyril
See Kornbluth, C(yril) M.; Pohl, Frederik

Julian of Norwich 1342(?)-1416(?) .... **LC 6**

Just, Ward (Swift) 1935- .... **CLC 4, 27**
See also CA 25-28R; CANR 32

Justice, Donald (Rodney) 1925- .. **CLC 6, 19**
See also CA 5-8R; CANR 26; DLBY 83

Juvenal c. 55-c. 127 .... **CMLC 8**

Juvenis
See Bourne, Randolph S(illiman)

Kacew, Romain 1914-1980
See Gary, Romain
See also CA 108; 102

Kadare, Ismail 1936- .... **CLC 52**

Kadohata, Cynthia................. **CLC 59**
See also CA 140

Kafka, Franz
1883-1924 .... **TCLC 2, 6, 13, 29, 47, 53;
DA; SSC 5; WLC**
See also CA 105; 126; DLB 81; MTCW

Kahn, Roger 1927-............... **CLC 30**
See also CA 25-28R; CANR 44; SATA 37

Kain, Saul
See Sassoon, Siegfried (Lorraine)

Kaiser, Georg 1878-1945 .... **TCLC 9**
See also CA 106; DLB 124

Kaletski, Alexander 1946- .... **CLC 39**
See also CA 118; 143

Kalidasa fl. c. 400- .... **CMLC 9**

Kallman, Chester (Simon)
1921-1975 .... **CLC 2**
See also CA 45-48; 53-56; CANR 3

Kaminsky, Melvin 1926-
See Brooks, Mel
See also CA 65-68; CANR 16

Kaminsky, Stuart M(elvin) 1934- ... **CLC 59**
See also CA 73-76; CANR 29

Kane, Paul
See Simon, Paul

Kane, Wilson
See Bloch, Robert (Albert)

Kanin, Garson 1912-............. **CLC 22**
See also AITN 1; CA 5-8R; CANR 7;
DLB 7

Kaniuk, Yoram 1930-............ **CLC 19**
See also CA 134

Kant, Immanuel 1724-1804 ...... **NCLC 27**
See also DLB 94

Kantor, MacKinlay 1904-1977 ...... **CLC 7**
See also CA 61-64; 73-76; DLB 9, 102

Kaplan, David Michael 1946- ...... **CLC 50**

Kaplan, James 1951- .... **CLC 59**
See also CA 135

Karageorge, Michael
See Anderson, Poul (William)

Karamzin, Nikolai Mikhailovich
1766-1826 .... **NCLC 3**

Karapanou, Margarita 1946-....... **CLC 13**
See also CA 101

Karinthy, Frigyes 1887-1938 ...... **TCLC 47**

Karl, Frederick R(obert) 1927-..... **CLC 34**
See also CA 5-8R; CANR 3, 44

Kastel, Warren
See Silverberg, Robert

Kataev, Evgeny Petrovich 1903-1942
See Petrov, Evgeny
See also CA 120

Kataphusin
See Ruskin, John

Katz, Steve 1935-............... **CLC 47**
See also CA 25-28R; CAAS 14; CANR 12;
DLBY 83

Kauffman, Janet 1945-........... **CLC 42**
See also CA 117; CANR 43; DLBY 86

Kaufman, Bob (Garnell)
1925-1986 .... **CLC 49**
See also BW 1; CA 41-44R; 118; CANR 22;
DLB 16, 41

Kaufman, George S. 1889-1961..... **CLC 38**
See also CA 108; 93-96; DLB 7

Kaufman, Sue .... **CLC 3, 8**
See also Barondess, Sue K(aufman)

Kavafis, Konstantinos Petrou 1863-1933
See Cavafy, C(onstantine) P(eter)
See also CA 104

Kavan, Anna 1901-1968...... **CLC 5, 13, 82**
See also CA 5-8R; CANR 6; MTCW

Kavanagh, Dan
See Barnes, Julian

Kavanagh, Patrick (Joseph)
1904-1967 .... **CLC 22**
See also CA 123; 25-28R; DLB 15, 20;
MTCW

Kawabata, Yasunari
1899-1972 .... **CLC 2, 5, 9, 18**
See also CA 93-96; 33-36R

Kaye, M(ary) M(argaret) 1909-..... **CLC 28**
See also CA 89-92; CANR 24; MTCW;
SATA 62

Kaye, Mollie
See Kaye, M(ary) M(argaret)

Kaye-Smith, Sheila 1887-1956..... **TCLC 20**
See also CA 118; DLB 36

Kaymor, Patrice Maguilene
See Senghor, Leopold Sedar

Kazan, Elia 1909-........... **CLC 6, 16, 63**
See also CA 21-24R; CANR 32

Kazantzakis, Nikos
1883(?)-1957 .... **TCLC 2, 5, 33**
See also CA 105; 132; MTCW

Kazin, Alfred 1915- .... **CLC 34, 38**
See also CA 1-4R; CAAS 7; CANR 1;
DLB 67

Keane, Mary Nesta (Skrine) 1904-
See Keane, Molly
See also CA 108; 114

Keane, Molly.................... **CLC 31**
See also Keane, Mary Nesta (Skrine)

Keates, Jonathan 19(?)-........... **CLC 34**

Keaton, Buster 1895-1966 .... **CLC 20**

Keats, John
1795-1821 ... **NCLC 8; DA; PC 1; WLC**
See also CDBLB 1789-1832; DLB 96, 110

Keene, Donald 1922- .... **CLC 34**
See also CA 1-4R; CANR 5

Keillor, Garrison .... **CLC 40**
See also Keillor, Gary (Edward)
See also AAYA 2; BEST 89:3; DLBY 87;
SATA 58

Keillor, Gary (Edward) 1942-
See Keillor, Garrison
See also CA 111; 117; CANR 36; MTCW

Keith, Michael
See Hubbard, L(afayette) Ron(ald)

Keller, Gottfried 1819-1890....... **NCLC 2**
See also DLB 129

Kellerman, Jonathan 1949- .... **CLC 44**
See also BEST 90:1; CA 106; CANR 29

Kelley, William Melvin 1937-...... **CLC 22**
See also BW 1; CA 77-80; CANR 27;
DLB 33

Kellogg, Marjorie 1922-.......... **CLC 2**
See also CA 81-84

Kellow, Kathleen
See Hibbert, Eleanor Alice Burford

Kelly, M(ilton) T(erry) 1947-....... **CLC 55**
See also CA 97-100; CANR 19, 43

Kelman, James 1946-............ **CLC 58**

Kemal, Yashar 1923- .... **CLC 14, 29**
See also CA 89-92; CANR 44

Kemble, Fanny 1809-1893 .... **NCLC 18**
See also DLB 32

Kemelman, Harry 1908-........... **CLC 2**
See also AITN 1; CA 9-12R; CANR 6;
DLB 28

Kempe, Margery 1373(?)-1440(?) ..... **LC 6**

Kempis, Thomas a 1380-1471 .... **LC 11**

Kendall, Henry 1839-1882....... **NCLC 12**

Keneally, Thomas (Michael)
1935- ...... **CLC 5, 8, 10, 14, 19, 27, 43**
See also CA 85-88; CANR 10; MTCW

Kennedy, Adrienne (Lita)
1931- .... **CLC 66; BLC**
See also BW 2; CA 103; CABS 3;
CANR 26; DLB 38

Kennedy, John Pendleton
1795-1870 .... **NCLC 2**
See also DLB 3

Kennedy, Joseph Charles 1929-...... **CLC 8**
See also Kennedy, X. J.
See also CA 1-4R; CANR 4, 30, 40;
SATA 14

Kennedy, William 1928-... **CLC 6, 28, 34, 53**
See also AAYA 1; CA 85-88; CANR 14,
31; DLBY 85; MTCW; SATA 57

Kennedy, X. J................... **CLC 42**
See also Kennedy, Joseph Charles
See also CAAS 9; CLR 27; DLB 5

Kent, Kelvin
See Kuttner, Henry

Kenton, Maxwell
See Southern, Terry

Kenyon, Robert O.
See Kuttner, Henry

Kerouac, Jack ..... **CLC 1, 2, 3, 5, 14, 29, 61**
See also Kerouac, Jean-Louis Lebris de
See also CDALB 1941-1968; DLB 2, 16;
DLBD 3

Kerouac, Jean-Louis Lebris de 1922-1969
See Kerouac, Jack
See also AITN 1; CA 5-8R; 25-28R;
CANR 26; DA; MTCW; WLC

Kerr, Jean 1923-................ **CLC 22**
See also CA 5-8R; CANR 7

Kerr, M. E. .... **CLC 12, 35**
See also Meaker, Marijane (Agnes)
See also AAYA 2; CLR 29; SAAS 1

Kerr, Robert .... **CLC 55**

Kerrigan, (Thomas) Anthony
1918- .... **CLC 4, 6**
See also CA 49-52; CAAS 11; CANR 4

Kerry, Lois
See Duncan, Lois

Kesey, Ken (Elton)
1935- ...... **CLC 1, 3, 6, 11, 46, 64; DA;
WLC**
See also CA 1-4R; CANR 22, 38;
CDALB 1968-1988; DLB 2, 16; MTCW;
SATA 66

Kesselring, Joseph (Otto)
1902-1967 .... **CLC 45**

Kessler, Jascha (Frederick) 1929-.... **CLC 4**
See also CA 17-20R; CANR 8

Kettelkamp, Larry (Dale) 1933- .... **CLC 12**
See also CA 29-32R; CANR 16; SAAS 3;
SATA 2

Keyber, Conny
See Fielding, Henry

Keyes, Daniel 1927-.......... **CLC 80; DA**
See also CA 17-20R; CANR 10, 26;
SATA 37

Khayyam, Omar
1048-1131 .... **CMLC 11; PC 8**

Kherdian, David 1931-........... **CLC 6, 9**
See also CA 21-24R; CAAS 2; CANR 39;
CLR 24; JRDA; MAICYA; SATA 16, 74

Khlebnikov, Velimir .... **TCLC 20**
See also Khlebnikov, Viktor Vladimirovich

Khlebnikov, Viktor Vladimirovich 1885-1922
See Khlebnikov, Velimir
See also CA 117

Khodasevich, Vladislav (Felitsianovich)
1886-1939 .... **TCLC 15**
See also CA 115

Kielland, Alexander Lange
1849-1906 .... **TCLC 5**
See also CA 104

Kiely, Benedict 1919-.......... **CLC 23, 43**
See also CA 1-4R; CANR 2; DLB 15

Kienzle, William X(avier) 1928- .... **CLC 25**
See also CA 93-96; CAAS 1; CANR 9, 31;
MTCW

Kierkegaard, Soren 1813-1855.... **NCLC 34**

Killens, John Oliver 1916-1987..... **CLC 10**
See also BW 2; CA 77-80; 123; CAAS 2;
CANR 26; DLB 33

Killigrew, Anne 1660-1685.......... **LC 4**
See also DLB 131

Kim
See Simenon, Georges (Jacques Christian)

Kincaid, Jamaica 1949- ... **CLC 43, 68; BLC**
See also BW 2; CA 125

King, Francis (Henry) 1923-..... **CLC 8, 53**
See also CA 1-4R; CANR 1, 33; DLB 15,
139; MTCW

King, Martin Luther, Jr.
1929-1968 .... **CLC 83; BLC; DA**
See also BW 2; CA 25-28; CANR 27, 44;
CAP 2; MTCW; SATA 14

King, Stephen (Edwin)
1947- .... **CLC 12, 26, 37, 61**
See also AAYA 1; BEST 90:1; CA 61-64;
CANR 1, 30; DLBY 80; JRDA; MTCW;
SATA 9, 55

King, Steve
See King, Stephen (Edwin)

Kingman, Lee.................... **CLC 17**
See also Natti, (Mary) Lee
See also SAAS 3; SATA 1, 67

Kingsley, Charles 1819-1875 ..... **NCLC 35**
See also DLB 21, 32; YABC 2

Kingsley, Sidney 1906-........... **CLC 44**
See also CA 85-88; DLB 7

Kingsolver, Barbara 1955-...... **CLC 55, 81**
See also CA 129; 134

Kingston, Maxine (Ting Ting) Hong
1940- .... **CLC 12, 19, 58**
See also AAYA 8; CA 69-72; CANR 13,
38; DLBY 80; MTCW; SATA 53

Kinnell, Galway
1927- .... **CLC 1, 2, 3, 5, 13, 29**
See also CA 9-12R; CANR 10, 34; DLB 5;
DLBY 87; MTCW

Kinsella, Thomas 1928- .... **CLC 4, 19**
See also CA 17-20R; CANR 15; DLB 27;
MTCW

Kinsella, W(illiam) P(atrick)
1935- .... **CLC 27, 43**
See also AAYA 7; CA 97-100; CAAS 7;
CANR 21, 35; MTCW

Kipling, (Joseph) Rudyard
1865-1936 ...... **TCLC 8, 17; DA; PC 3;
SSC 5; WLC**
See also CA 105; 120; CANR 33;
CDBLB 1890-1914; DLB 19, 34, 141;
MAICYA; MTCW; YABC 2

Kirkup, James 1918- .... **CLC 1**
See also CA 1-4R; CAAS 4; CANR 2;
DLB 27; SATA 12

Kirkwood, James 1930(?)-1989 ...... **CLC 9**
See also AITN 2; CA 1-4R; 128; CANR 6,
40

Kis, Danilo 1935-1989 .... **CLC 57**
See also CA 109; 118; 129; MTCW

Kivi, Aleksis 1834-1872 .... **NCLC 30**

Kizer, Carolyn (Ashley)
1925- .... **CLC 15, 39, 80**
See also CA 65-68; CAAS 5; CANR 24;
DLB 5

Klabund 1890-1928............. **TCLC 44**
See also DLB 66

Klappert, Peter 1942-............. **CLC 57**
See also CA 33-36R; DLB 5

Klein, A(braham) M(oses)
1909-1972 .... **CLC 19**
See also CA 101; 37-40R; DLB 68

Klein, Norma 1938-1989 .... **CLC 30**
See also AAYA 2; CA 41-44R; 128;
CANR 15, 37; CLR 2, 19; JRDA;
MAICYA; SAAS 1; SATA 7, 57

Klein, T(heodore) E(ibon) D(onald)
1947- .... **CLC 34**
See also CA 119; CANR 44

Kleist, Heinrich von
    1777-1811 .... **NCLC 2, 37**
    See also DLB 90

Klima, Ivan 1931-................ **CLC 56**
    See also CA 25-28R; CANR 17

Klimentov, Andrei Platonovich 1899-1951
    See Platonov, Andrei
    See also CA 108

Klinger, Friedrich Maximilian von
    1752-1831 .... **NCLC 1**
    See also DLB 94

Klopstock, Friedrich Gottlieb
    1724-1803 .... **NCLC 11**
    See also DLB 97

Knebel, Fletcher 1911-1993....... **CLC 14**
    See also AITN 1; CA 1-4R; 140; CAAS 3;
    CANR 1, 36; SATA 36; SATA-Obit 75

Knickerbocker, Diedrich
    See Irving, Washington

Knight, Etheridge
    1931-1991 .... **CLC 40; BLC**
    See also BW 1; CA 21-24R; 133; CANR 23;
    DLB 41

Knight, Sarah Kemble 1666-1727 ..... **LC 7**
    See also DLB 24

Knowles, John
    1926- .... **CLC 1, 4, 10, 26; DA**
    See also AAYA 10; CA 17-20R; CANR 40;
    CDALB 1968-1988; DLB 6; MTCW;
    SATA 8

Knox, Calvin M.
    See Silverberg, Robert

Knye, Cassandra
    See Disch, Thomas M(ichael)

Koch, C(hristopher) J(ohn) 1932- ... **CLC 42**
    See also CA 127

Koch, Christopher
    See Koch, C(hristopher) J(ohn)

Koch, Kenneth 1925- .... **CLC 5, 8, 44**
    See also CA 1-4R; CANR 6, 36; DLB 5;
    SATA 65

Kochanowski, Jan 1530-1584........ **LC 10**

Kock, Charles Paul de
    1794-1871 .... **NCLC 16**

Koda Shigeyuki 1867-1947
    See Rohan, Koda
    See also CA 121

Koestler, Arthur
    1905-1983 .... **CLC 1, 3, 6, 8, 15, 33**
    See also CA 1-4R; 109; CANR 1, 33;
    CDBLB 1945-1960; DLBY 83; MTCW

Kogawa, Joy Nozomi 1935-....... **CLC 78**
    See also CA 101; CANR 19

Kohout, Pavel 1928-.............. **CLC 13**
    See also CA 45-48; CANR 3

Koizumi, Yakumo
    See Hearn, (Patricio) Lafcadio (Tessima
    Carlos)

Kolmar, Gertrud 1894-1943...... **TCLC 40**

Konrad, George
    See Konrad, Gyoergy

Konrad, Gyoergy 1933- ...... **CLC 4, 10, 73**
    See also CA 85-88

Konwicki, Tadeusz 1926-..... **CLC 8, 28, 54**
    See also CA 101; CAAS 9; CANR 39;
    MTCW

Koontz, Dean R(ay) 1945-......... **CLC 78**
    See also AAYA 9; BEST 89:3, 90:2;
    CA 108; CANR 19, 36; MTCW

Kopit, Arthur (Lee) 1937- .... **CLC 1, 18, 33**
    See also AITN 1; CA 81-84; CABS 3;
    DLB 7; MTCW

Kops, Bernard 1926-.............. **CLC 4**
    See also CA 5-8R; DLB 13

Kornbluth, C(yril) M. 1923-1958.... **TCLC 8**
    See also CA 105; DLB 8

Korolenko, V. G.
    See Korolenko, Vladimir Galaktionovich

Korolenko, Vladimir
    See Korolenko, Vladimir Galaktionovich

Korolenko, Vladimir G.
    See Korolenko, Vladimir Galaktionovich

Korolenko, Vladimir Galaktionovich
    1853-1921 .... **TCLC 22**
    See also CA 121

Kosinski, Jerzy (Nikodem)
    1933-1991 .... **CLC 1, 2, 3, 6, 10, 15, 53,
                                                    70**
    See also CA 17-20R; 134; CANR 9; DLB 2;
    DLBY 82; MTCW

Kostelanetz, Richard (Cory) 1940- .. **CLC 28**
    See also CA 13-16R; CAAS 8; CANR 38

Kostrowitzki, Wilhelm Apollinaris de
    1880-1918
    See Apollinaire, Guillaume
    See also CA 104

Kotlowitz, Robert 1924-........... **CLC 4**
    See also CA 33-36R; CANR 36

Kotzebue, August (Friedrich Ferdinand) von
    1761-1819 .... **NCLC 25**
    See also DLB 94

Kotzwinkle, William 1938- ... **CLC 5, 14, 35**
    See also CA 45-48; CANR 3, 44; CLR 6;
    MAICYA; SATA 24, 70

Kozol, Jonathan 1936-............ **CLC 17**
    See also CA 61-64; CANR 16

Kozoll, Michael 1940(?)- .... **CLC 35**

Kramer, Kathryn 19(?)- .... **CLC 34**

Kramer, Larry 1935- .... **CLC 42**
    See also CA 124; 126

Krasicki, Ignacy 1735-1801 ...... **NCLC 8**

Krasinski, Zygmunt 1812-1859 .... **NCLC 4**

Kraus, Karl 1874-1936........... **TCLC 5**
    See also CA 104; DLB 118

Kreve (Mickevicius), Vincas
    1882-1954 .... **TCLC 27**

Kristeva, Julia 1941- .... **CLC 77**

Kristofferson, Kris 1936-.......... **CLC 26**
    See also CA 104

Krizanc, John 1956-.............. **CLC 57**

Krleza, Miroslav 1893-1981........ **CLC 8**
    See also CA 97-100; 105

Kroetsch, Robert 1927- ...... **CLC 5, 23, 57**
    See also CA 17-20R; CANR 8, 38; DLB 53;
    MTCW

Kroetz, Franz
    See Kroetz, Franz Xaver

Kroetz, Franz Xaver 1946- .... **CLC 41**
    See also CA 130

Kroker, Arthur 1945-............ **CLC 77**

Kropotkin, Peter (Aleksieevich)
    1842-1921 .... **TCLC 36**
    See also CA 119

Krotkov, Yuri 1917-.............. **CLC 19**
    See also CA 102

Krumb
    See Crumb, R(obert)

Krumgold, Joseph (Quincy)
    1908-1980 .... **CLC 12**
    See also CA 9-12R; 101; CANR 7;
    MAICYA; SATA 1, 23, 48

Krumwitz
    See Crumb, R(obert)

Krutch, Joseph Wood 1893-1970.... **CLC 24**
    See also CA 1-4R; 25-28R; CANR 4;
    DLB 63

Krutzch, Gus
    See Eliot, T(homas) S(tearns)

Krylov, Ivan Andreevich
    1768(?)-1844 .... **NCLC 1**

Kubin, Alfred 1877-1959 .... **TCLC 23**
    See also CA 112; DLB 81

Kubrick, Stanley 1928-............ **CLC 16**
    See also CA 81-84; CANR 33; DLB 26

Kumin, Maxine (Winokur)
    1925- .... **CLC 5, 13, 28**
    See also AITN 2; CA 1-4R; CAAS 8;
    CANR 1, 21; DLB 5; MTCW; SATA 12

Kundera, Milan
    1929- .... **CLC 4, 9, 19, 32, 68**
    See also AAYA 2; CA 85-88; CANR 19;
    MTCW

Kunitz, Stanley (Jasspon)
    1905- .... **CLC 6, 11, 14**
    See also CA 41-44R; CANR 26; DLB 48;
    MTCW

Kunze, Reiner 1933-............. **CLC 10**
    See also CA 93-96; DLB 75

Kuprin, Aleksandr Ivanovich
    1870-1938 .... **TCLC 5**
    See also CA 104

Kureishi, Hanif 1954(?)-.......... **CLC 64**
    See also CA 139

Kurosawa, Akira 1910-............ **CLC 16**
    See also AAYA 11; CA 101

Kushner, Tony 1957(?)- .... **CLC 81**
    See also CA 144

Kuttner, Henry 1915-1958........ **TCLC 10**
    See also CA 107; DLB 8

Kuzma, Greg 1944-................ **CLC 7**
    See also CA 33-36R

Kuzmin, Mikhail 1872(?)-1936 .... **TCLC 40**

Kyd, Thomas 1558-1594....... **LC 22; DC 3**
    See also DLB 62

Kyprianos, Iossif
    See Samarakis, Antonis

La Bruyere, Jean de 1645-1696...... **LC 17**

Lacan, Jacques (Marie Emile)
    1901-1981 .... CLC **75**
    See also CA 121; 104

Laclos, Pierre Ambroise Francois Choderlos
    de 1741-1803 .... NCLC **4**

Lacolere, Francois
    See Aragon, Louis

La Colere, Francois
    See Aragon, Louis

La Deshabilleuse
    See Simenon, Georges (Jacques Christian)

Lady Gregory
    See Gregory, Isabella Augusta (Persse)

Lady of Quality, A
    See Bagnold, Enid

La Fayette, Marie (Madelaine Pioche de la
    Vergne Comtes 1634-1693...... LC **2**

Lafayette, Rene
    See Hubbard, L(afayette) Ron(ald)

Laforgue, Jules 1860-1887....... NCLC **5**

Lagerkvist, Paer (Fabian)
    1891-1974 .... CLC **7, 10, 13, 54**
    See also Lagerkvist, Par
    See also CA 85-88; 49-52; MTCW

Lagerkvist, Par
    See Lagerkvist, Paer (Fabian)
    See also SSC 12

Lagerloef, Selma (Ottiliana Lovisa)
    1858-1940 .... TCLC **4, 36**
    See also Lagerlof, Selma (Ottiliana Lovisa)
    See also CA 108; CLR 7; SATA 15

Lagerlof, Selma (Ottiliana Lovisa)
    See Lagerloef, Selma (Ottiliana Lovisa)
    See also CLR 7; SATA 15

La Guma, (Justin) Alex(ander)
    1925-1985 .... CLC **19**
    See also BW 1; CA 49-52; 118; CANR 25;
    DLB 117; MTCW

Laidlaw, A. K.
    See Grieve, C(hristopher) M(urray)

Lainez, Manuel Mujica
    See Mujica Lainez, Manuel
    See also HW

Lamartine, Alphonse (Marie Louis Prat) de
    1790-1869 .... NCLC **11**

Lamb, Charles
    1775-1834 .... NCLC **10**; DA; WLC
    See also CDBLB 1789-1832; DLB 93, 107;
    SATA 17

Lamb, Lady Caroline 1785-1828.. NCLC **38**
    See also DLB 116

Lamming, George (William)
    1927- .... CLC **2, 4, 66**; BLC
    See also BW 2; CA 85-88; CANR 26;
    DLB 125; MTCW

L'Amour, Louis (Dearborn)
    1908-1988 .... CLC **25, 55**
    See also AITN 2; BEST 89:2; CA 1-4R;
    125; CANR 3, 25, 40; DLBY 80; MTCW

Lampedusa, Giuseppe (Tomasi) di ... TCLC **13**
    See also Tomasi di Lampedusa, Giuseppe

Lampman, Archibald 1861-1899 .. NCLC **25**
    See also DLB 92

Lancaster, Bruce 1896-1963....... CLC **36**
    See also CA 9-10; CAP 1; SATA 9

Landau, Mark Alexandrovich
    See Aldanov, Mark (Alexandrovich)

Landau-Aldanov, Mark Alexandrovich
    See Aldanov, Mark (Alexandrovich)

Landis, John 1950- .... CLC **26**
    See also CA 112; 122

Landolfi, Tommaso 1908-1979... CLC **11, 49**
    See also CA 127; 117

Landon, Letitia Elizabeth
    1802-1838 .... NCLC **15**
    See also DLB 96

Landor, Walter Savage
    1775-1864 .... NCLC **14**
    See also DLB 93, 107

Landwirth, Heinz 1927-
    See Lind, Jakov
    See also CA 9-12R; CANR 7

Lane, Patrick 1939- .... CLC **25**
    See also CA 97-100; DLB 53

Lang, Andrew 1844-1912 .... TCLC **16**
    See also CA 114; 137; DLB 98, 141;
    MAICYA; SATA 16

Lang, Fritz 1890-1976 .... CLC **20**
    See also CA 77-80; 69-72; CANR 30

Lange, John
    See Crichton, (John) Michael

Langer, Elinor 1939- .... CLC **34**
    See also CA 121

Langland, William
    1330(?)-1400(?) .... LC **19**; DA

Langstaff, Launcelot
    See Irving, Washington

Lanier, Sidney 1842-1881 .... NCLC **6**
    See also DLB 64; MAICYA; SATA 18

Lanyer, Aemilia 1569-1645 .... LC **10**

Lao Tzu .... CMLC **7**

Lapine, James (Elliot) 1949- .... CLC **39**
    See also CA 123; 130

Larbaud, Valery (Nicolas)
    1881-1957 .... TCLC **9**
    See also CA 106

Lardner, Ring
    See Lardner, Ring(gold) W(ilmer)

Lardner, Ring W., Jr.
    See Lardner, Ring(gold) W(ilmer)

Lardner, Ring(gold) W(ilmer)
    1885-1933 .... TCLC **2, 14**
    See also CA 104; 131; CDALB 1917-1929;
    DLB 11, 25, 86; MTCW

Laredo, Betty
    See Codrescu, Andrei

Larkin, Maia
    See Wojciechowska, Maia (Teresa)

Larkin, Philip (Arthur)
    1922-1985 .... CLC **3, 5, 8, 9, 13, 18, 33,**
                                        39, 64
    See also CA 5-8R; 117; CANR 24;
    CDBLB 1960 to Present; DLB 27;
    MTCW

Larra (y Sanchez de Castro), Mariano Jose de
    1809-1837 .... NCLC **17**

Larsen, Eric 1941- .... CLC **55**
    See also CA 132

Larsen, Nella 1891-1964 ..... CLC **37**; BLC
    See also BW 1; CA 125; DLB 51

Larson, Charles R(aymond) 1938-... CLC **31**
    See also CA 53-56; CANR 4

Latham, Jean Lee 1902-......... CLC **12**
    See also AITN 1; CA 5-8R; CANR 7;
    MAICYA; SATA 2, 68

Latham, Mavis
    See Clark, Mavis Thorpe

Lathen, Emma................... CLC **2**
    See also Hennissart, Martha; Latsis, Mary
    J(ane)

Lathrop, Francis
    See Leiber, Fritz (Reuter, Jr.)

Latsis, Mary J(ane)
    See Lathen, Emma
    See also CA 85-88

Lattimore, Richmond (Alexander)
    1906-1984 .... CLC **3**
    See also CA 1-4R; 112; CANR 1

Laughlin, James 1914-........... CLC **49**
    See also CA 21-24R; CANR 9; DLB 48

Laurence, (Jean) Margaret (Wemyss)
    1926-1987 .. CLC **3, 6, 13, 50, 62**; SSC **7**
    See also CA 5-8R; 121; CANR 33; DLB 53;
    MTCW; SATA 50

Laurent, Antoine 1952- .... CLC **50**

Lauscher, Hermann
    See Hesse, Hermann

Lautreamont, Comte de
    1846-1870 .... NCLC **12**; SSC **14**

Laverty, Donald
    See Blish, James (Benjamin)

Lavin, Mary 1912-...... CLC **4, 18**; SSC **4**
    See also CA 9-12R; CANR 33; DLB 15;
    MTCW

Lavond, Paul Dennis
    See Kornbluth, C(yril) M.; Pohl, Frederik

Lawler, Raymond Evenor 1922- .... CLC **58**
    See also CA 103

Lawrence, D(avid) H(erbert Richards)
    1885-1930 .... TCLC **2, 9, 16, 33, 48**;
                                DA; SSC **4**; WLC
    See also CA 104; 121; CDBLB 1914-1945;
    DLB 10, 19, 36, 98; MTCW

Lawrence, T(homas) E(dward)
    1888-1935 .... TCLC **18**
    See also Dale, Colin
    See also CA 115

Lawrence of Arabia
    See Lawrence, T(homas) E(dward)

Lawson, Henry (Archibald Hertzberg)
    1867-1922 .... TCLC **27**
    See also CA 120

Lawton, Dennis
    See Faust, Frederick (Schiller)

Laxness, Halldor.................. CLC **25**
    See also Gudjonsson, Halldor Kiljan

Layamon fl. c. 1200-............ CMLC **10**

Laye, Camara 1928-1980 ... CLC **4, 38**; BLC
    See also BW 1; CA 85-88; 97-100;
    CANR 25; MTCW

Layton, Irving (Peter) 1912- . . . . . **CLC 2, 15**
See also CA 1-4R; CANR 2, 33, 43;
DLB 88; MTCW

Lazarus, Emma 1849-1887. . . . . . . **NCLC 8**

Lazarus, Felix
See Cable, George Washington

Lazarus, Henry
See Slavitt, David R(ytman)

Lea, Joan
See Neufeld, John (Arthur)

Leacock, Stephen (Butler)
1869-1944 . . . . **TCLC 2**
See also CA 104; 141; DLB 92

Lear, Edward 1812-1888 . . . . **NCLC 3**
See also CLR 1; DLB 32; MAICYA;
SATA 18

Lear, Norman (Milton) 1922- . . . . . **CLC 12**
See also CA 73-76

Leavis, F(rank) R(aymond)
1895-1978 . . . . **CLC 24**
See also CA 21-24R; 77-80; CANR 44;
MTCW

Leavitt, David 1961- . . . . **CLC 34**
See also CA 116; 122; DLB 130

Leblanc, Maurice (Marie Emile)
1864-1941 . . . . **TCLC 49**
See also CA 110

Lebowitz, Fran(ces Ann)
1951(?)- . . . . **CLC 11, 36**
See also CA 81-84; CANR 14; MTCW

le Carre, John . . . . **CLC 3, 5, 9, 15, 28**
See also Cornwell, David (John Moore)
See also BEST 89:4; CDBLB 1960 to
Present; DLB 87

Le Clezio, J(ean) M(arie) G(ustave)
1940- . . . . **CLC 31**
See also CA 116; 128; DLB 83

Leconte de Lisle, Charles-Marie-Rene
1818-1894 . . . . **NCLC 29**

Le Coq, Monsieur
See Simenon, Georges (Jacques Christian)

Leduc, Violette 1907-1972 . . . . **CLC 22**
See also CA 13-14; 33-36R; CAP 1

Ledwidge, Francis 1887(?)-1917 . . . **TCLC 23**
See also CA 123; DLB 20

Lee, Andrea 1953- . . . . **CLC 36; BLC**
See also BW 1; CA 125

Lee, Andrew
See Auchincloss, Louis (Stanton)

Lee, Don L. . . . . **CLC 2**
See also Madhubuti, Haki R.

Lee, George W(ashington)
1894-1976 . . . . **CLC 52; BLC**
See also BW 1; CA 125; DLB 51

Lee, (Nelle) Harper
1926- . . . . **CLC 12, 60; DA; WLC**
See also CA 13-16R; CDALB 1941-1968;
DLB 6; MTCW; SATA 11

Lee, Julian
See Latham, Jean Lee

Lee, Larry
See Lee, Lawrence

Lee, Lawrence 1941-1990. . . . . **CLC 34**
See also CA 131; CANR 43

Lee, Manfred B(ennington)
1905-1971 . . . . **CLC 11**
See also Queen, Ellery
See also CA 1-4R; 29-32R; CANR 2;
DLB 137

Lee, Stan 1922- . . . . **CLC 17**
See also AAYA 5; CA 108; 111

Lee, Tanith 1947- . . . . **CLC 46**
See also CA 37-40R; SATA 8

Lee, Vernon . . . . **TCLC 5**
See also Paget, Violet
See also DLB 57

Lee, William
See Burroughs, William S(eward)

Lee, Willy
See Burroughs, William S(eward)

Lee-Hamilton, Eugene (Jacob)
1845-1907 . . . . **TCLC 22**
See also CA 117

Leet, Judith 1935- . . . . **CLC 11**

Le Fanu, Joseph Sheridan
1814-1873 . . . . **NCLC 9; SSC 14**
See also DLB 21, 70

Leffland, Ella 1931- . . . . **CLC 19**
See also CA 29-32R; CANR 35; DLBY 84;
SATA 65

Leger, Alexis
See Leger, (Marie-Rene Auguste) Alexis
Saint-Leger

Leger, (Marie-Rene Auguste) Alexis
Saint-Leger 1887-1975. . . . . . . **CLC 11**
See also Perse, St.-John
See also CA 13-16R; 61-64; CANR 43;
MTCW

Leger, Saintleger
See Leger, (Marie-Rene Auguste) Alexis
Saint-Leger

Le Guin, Ursula K(roeber)
1929- . . . . **CLC 8, 13, 22, 45, 71; SSC 12**
See also AAYA 9; AITN 1; CA 21-24R;
CANR 9, 32; CDALB 1968-1988; CLR 3,
28; DLB 8, 52; JRDA; MAICYA;
MTCW; SATA 4, 52

Lehmann, Rosamond (Nina)
1901-1990 . . . . **CLC 5**
See also CA 77-80; 131; CANR 8; DLB 15

Leiber, Fritz (Reuter, Jr.)
1910-1992 . . . . **CLC 25**
See also CA 45-48; 139; CANR 2, 40;
DLB 8; MTCW; SATA 45;
SATA-Obit 73

Leimbach, Martha 1963-
See Leimbach, Marti
See also CA 130

Leimbach, Marti . . . . **CLC 65**
See also Leimbach, Martha

Leino, Eino . . . . **TCLC 24**
See also Loennbohm, Armas Eino Leopold

Leiris, Michel (Julien) 1901-1990 . . . **CLC 61**
See also CA 119; 128; 132

Leithauser, Brad 1953- . . . . **CLC 27**
See also CA 107; CANR 27; DLB 120

Lelchuk, Alan 1938- . . . . **CLC 5**
See also CA 45-48; CANR 1

Lem, Stanislaw 1921- . . . . **CLC 8, 15, 40**
See also CA 105; CAAS 1; CANR 32;
MTCW

Lemann, Nancy 1956-. . . . . **CLC 39**
See also CA 118; 136

Lemonnier, (Antoine Louis) Camille
1844-1913 . . . . **TCLC 22**
See also CA 121

Lenau, Nikolaus 1802-1850 . . . . . . **NCLC 16**

L'Engle, Madeleine (Camp Franklin)
1918- . . . . **CLC 12**
See also AAYA 1; AITN 2; CA 1-4R;
CANR 3, 21, 39; CLR 1, 14; DLB 52;
JRDA; MAICYA; MTCW; SAAS 15;
SATA 1, 27, 75

Lengyel, Jozsef 1896-1975. . . . . **CLC 7**
See also CA 85-88; 57-60

Lennon, John (Ono)
1940-1980 . . . . **CLC 12, 35**
See also CA 102

Lennox, Charlotte Ramsay
1729(?)-1804 . . . . **NCLC 23**
See also DLB 39

Lentricchia, Frank (Jr.) 1940-. . . . . . **CLC 34**
See also CA 25-28R; CANR 19

Lenz, Siegfried 1926- . . . . **CLC 27**
See also CA 89-92; DLB 75

Leonard, Elmore (John, Jr.)
1925- . . . . **CLC 28, 34, 71**
See also AITN 1; BEST 89:1, 90:4;
CA 81-84; CANR 12, 28; MTCW

Leonard, Hugh
See Byrne, John Keyes
See also DLB 13

Leopardi, (Conte) Giacomo (Talegardo
Francesco di Sales Save
1798-1837 . . . . **NCLC 22**

Le Reveler
See Artaud, Antonin

Lerman, Eleanor 1952-. . . . . **CLC 9**
See also CA 85-88

Lerman, Rhoda 1936-. . . . . **CLC 56**
See also CA 49-52

Lermontov, Mikhail Yuryevich
1814-1841 . . . . **NCLC 5**

Leroux, Gaston 1868-1927. . . . . **TCLC 25**
See also CA 108; 136; SATA 65

Lesage, Alain-Rene 1668-1747. . . . . . . **LC 2**

Leskov, Nikolai (Semyonovich)
1831-1895 . . . . **NCLC 25**

Lessing, Doris (May)
1919- . . . . . **CLC 1, 2, 3, 6, 10, 15, 22, 40;
DA; SSC 6**
See also CA 9-12R; CAAS 14; CANR 33;
CDBLB 1960 to Present; DLB 15, 139;
DLBY 85; MTCW

Lessing, Gotthold Ephraim
1729-1781 . . . . **LC 8**
See also DLB 97

Lester, Richard 1932-. . . . . **CLC 20**

Lever, Charles (James)
1806-1872 . . . . **NCLC 23**
See also DLB 21

Leverson, Ada 1865(?)-1936(?) .... **TCLC 18**
See also Elaine
See also CA 117

Levertov, Denise
1923- ...... **CLC 1, 2, 3, 5, 8, 15, 28, 66**
See also CA 1-4R; CAAS 19; CANR 3, 29;
DLB 5; MTCW

Levi, Jonathan .... **CLC 76**

Levi, Peter (Chad Tigar) 1931- ..... **CLC 41**
See also CA 5-8R; CANR 34; DLB 40

Levi, Primo
1919-1987 .... **CLC 37, 50; SSC 12**
See also CA 13-16R; 122; CANR 12, 33;
MTCW

Levin, Ira 1929- .... **CLC 3, 6**
See also CA 21-24R; CANR 17, 44;
MTCW; SATA 66

Levin, Meyer 1905-1981 .... **CLC 7**
See also AITN 1; CA 9-12R; 104;
CANR 15; DLB 9, 28; DLBY 81;
SATA 21, 27

Levine, Norman 1924- .... **CLC 54**
See also CA 73-76; CANR 14; DLB 88

Levine, Philip 1928-.. **CLC 2, 4, 5, 9, 14, 33**
See also CA 9-12R; CANR 9, 37; DLB 5

Levinson, Deirdre 1931- .... **CLC 49**
See also CA 73-76

Levi-Strauss, Claude 1908- .... **CLC 38**
See also CA 1-4R; CANR 6, 32; MTCW

Levitin, Sonia (Wolff) 1934- .... **CLC 17**
See also CA 29-32R; CANR 14, 32; JRDA;
MAICYA; SAAS 2; SATA 4, 68

Levon, O. U.
See Kesey, Ken (Elton)

Lewes, George Henry
1817-1878 .... **NCLC 25**
See also DLB 55

Lewis, Alun 1915-1944........... **TCLC 3**
See also CA 104; DLB 20

Lewis, C. Day
See Day Lewis, C(ecil)

Lewis, C(live) S(taples)
1898-1963 ..... **CLC 1, 3, 6, 14, 27; DA;
WLC**
See also AAYA 3; CA 81-84; CANR 33;
CDBLB 1945-1960; CLR 3, 27; DLB 15,
100; JRDA; MAICYA; MTCW;
SATA 13

Lewis, Janet 1899- .... **CLC 41**
See also Winters, Janet Lewis
See also CA 9-12R; CANR 29; CAP 1;
DLBY 87

Lewis, Matthew Gregory
1775-1818 .... **NCLC 11**
See also DLB 39

Lewis, (Harry) Sinclair
1885-1951 ..... **TCLC 4, 13, 23, 39; DA;
WLC**
See also CA 104; 133; CDALB 1917-1929;
DLB 9, 102; DLBD 1; MTCW

Lewis, (Percy) Wyndham
1884(?)-1957 .... **TCLC 2, 9**
See also CA 104; DLB 15

Lewisohn, Ludwig 1883-1955...... **TCLC 19**
See also CA 107; DLB 4, 9, 28, 102

Lezama Lima, Jose 1910-1976 ... **CLC 4, 10**
See also CA 77-80; DLB 113; HW

L'Heureux, John (Clarke) 1934-.... **CLC 52**
See also CA 13-16R; CANR 23

Liddell, C. H.
See Kuttner, Henry

Lie, Jonas (Lauritz Idemil)
1833-1908(?) .... **TCLC 5**
See also CA 115

Lieber, Joel 1937-1971............. **CLC 6**
See also CA 73-76; 29-32R

Lieber, Stanley Martin
See Lee, Stan

Lieberman, Laurence (James)
1935- .... **CLC 4, 36**
See also CA 17-20R; CANR 8, 36

Lieksman, Anders
See Haavikko, Paavo Juhani

Li Fei-kan 1904-................. **CLC 18**
See also CA 105

Lifton, Robert Jay 1926-.......... **CLC 67**
See also CA 17-20R; CANR 27; SATA 66

Lightfoot, Gordon 1938-.......... **CLC 26**
See also CA 109

Lightman, Alan P. 1948- .... **CLC 81**
See also CA 141

Ligotti, Thomas 1953- .... **CLC 44**
See also CA 123

Liliencron, (Friedrich Adolf Axel) Detlev von
1844-1909 .... **TCLC 18**
See also CA 117

Lima, Jose Lezama
See Lezama Lima, Jose

Lima Barreto, Afonso Henrique de
1881-1922 .... **TCLC 23**
See also CA 117

Limonov, Eduard................. **CLC 67**

Lin, Frank
See Atherton, Gertrude (Franklin Horn)

Lincoln, Abraham 1809-1865..... **NCLC 18**

Lind, Jakov .... **CLC 1, 2, 4, 27, 82**
See also Landwirth, Heinz
See also CAAS 4

Lindbergh, Anne (Spencer) Morrow
1906- .... **CLC 82**
See also CA 17-20R; CANR 16; MTCW;
SATA 33

Lindsay, David 1878-1945 .... **TCLC 15**
See also CA 113

Lindsay, (Nicholas) Vachel
1879-1931 .... **TCLC 17; DA; WLC**
See also CA 114; 135; CDALB 1865-1917;
DLB 54; SATA 40

Linke-Poot
See Doeblin, Alfred

Linney, Romulus 1930- .... **CLC 51**
See also CA 1-4R; CANR 40, 44

Linton, Eliza Lynn 1822-1898.... **NCLC 41**
See also DLB 18

Li Po 701-763 .... **CMLC 2**

Lipsius, Justus 1547-1606 .... **LC 16**

Lipsyte, Robert (Michael)
1938- .... **CLC 21; DA**
See also AAYA 7; CA 17-20R; CANR 8;
CLR 23; JRDA; MAICYA; SATA 5, 68

Lish, Gordon (Jay) 1934-......... **CLC 45**
See also CA 113; 117; DLB 130

Lispector, Clarice 1925-1977...... **CLC 43**
See also CA 139; 116; DLB 113

Littell, Robert 1935(?)- .... **CLC 42**
See also CA 109; 112

Little, Malcolm 1925-1965
See Malcolm X
See also BW 1; CA 125; 111; DA; MTCW

Littlewit, Humphrey Gent.
See Lovecraft, H(oward) P(hillips)

Litwos
See Sienkiewicz, Henryk (Adam Alexander
Pius)

Liu E 1857-1909 .... **TCLC 15**
See also CA 115

Lively, Penelope (Margaret)
1933- .... **CLC 32, 50**
See also CA 41-44R; CANR 29; CLR 7;
DLB 14; JRDA; MAICYA; MTCW;
SATA 7, 60

Livesay, Dorothy (Kathleen)
1909- .... **CLC 4, 15, 79**
See also AITN 2; CA 25-28R; CAAS 8;
CANR 36; DLB 68; MTCW

Livy c. 59B.C.-c. 17 .... **CMLC 11**

Lizardi, Jose Joaquin Fernandez de
1776-1827 .... **NCLC 30**

Llewellyn, Richard .... **CLC 7**
See also Llewellyn Lloyd, Richard Dafydd
Vivian
See also DLB 15

Llewellyn Lloyd, Richard Dafydd Vivian
1906-1983 .... **CLC 80**
See also Llewellyn, Richard
See also CA 53-56; 111; CANR 7;
SATA 11, 37

Llosa, (Jorge) Mario (Pedro) Vargas
See Vargas Llosa, (Jorge) Mario (Pedro)

Lloyd Webber, Andrew 1948-
See Webber, Andrew Lloyd
See also AAYA 1; CA 116; SATA 56

Llull, Ramon c. 1235-c. 1316..... **CMLC 12**

Locke, Alain (Le Roy)
1886-1954 .... **TCLC 43**
See also BW 1; CA 106; 124; DLB 51

Locke, John 1632-1704 .... **LC 7**
See also DLB 101

Locke-Elliott, Sumner
See Elliott, Sumner Locke

Lockhart, John Gibson
1794-1854 .... **NCLC 6**
See also DLB 110, 116

Lodge, David (John) 1935-........ **CLC 36**
See also BEST 90:1; CA 17-20R; CANR 19;
DLB 14; MTCW

Loennbohm, Armas Eino Leopold 1878-1926
See Leino, Eino
See also CA 123

MacDonald, George 1824-1905 . . . . . TCLC 9
See also CA 106; 137; DLB 18; MAICYA;
SATA 33

Macdonald, John
See Millar, Kenneth

MacDonald, John D(ann)
1916-1986 . . . . **CLC 3, 27, 44**
See also CA 1-4R; 121; CANR 1, 19;
DLB 8; DLBY 86; MTCW

Macdonald, John Ross
See Millar, Kenneth

Macdonald, Ross . . . . . CLC 1, 2, 3, 14, 34, 41
See also Millar, Kenneth
See also DLBD 6

MacDougal, John
See Blish, James (Benjamin)

MacEwen, Gwendolyn (Margaret)
1941-1987 . . . . CLC 13, 55
See also CA 9-12R; 124; CANR 7, 22;
DLB 53; SATA 50, 55

Machado (y Ruiz), Antonio
1875-1939 . . . . TCLC 3
See also CA 104; DLB 108

Machado de Assis, Joaquim Maria
1839-1908 . . . . TCLC 10; BLC
See also CA 107

Machen, Arthur . . . . TCLC 4
See also Jones, Arthur Llewellyn
See also DLB 36

Machiavelli, Niccolo 1469-1527 . . LC 8; DA

MacInnes, Colin 1914-1976 . . . . . CLC 4, 23
See also CA 69-72; 65-68; CANR 21;
DLB 14; MTCW

MacInnes, Helen (Clark)
1907-1985 . . . . CLC 27, 39
See also CA 1-4R; 117; CANR 1, 28;
DLB 87; MTCW; SATA 22, 44

Mackay, Mary 1855-1924
See Corelli, Marie
See also CA 118

Mackenzie, Compton (Edward Montague)
1883-1972 . . . . CLC 18
See also CA 21-22; 37-40R; CAP 2;
DLB 34, 100

Mackenzie, Henry 1745-1831 . . . . NCLC 41
See also DLB 39

Mackintosh, Elizabeth 1896(?)-1952
See Tey, Josephine
See also CA 110

MacLaren, James
See Grieve, C(hristopher) M(urray)

Mac Laverty, Bernard 1942- . . . . CLC 31
See also CA 116; 118; CANR 43

MacLean, Alistair (Stuart)
1922-1987 . . . . CLC 3, 13, 50, 63
See also CA 57-60; 121; CANR 28; MTCW;
SATA 23, 50

Maclean, Norman (Fitzroy)
1902-1990 . . . . CLC 78; SSC 13
See also CA 102; 132

MacLeish, Archibald
1892-1982 . . . . CLC 3, 8, 14, 68
See also CA 9-12R; 106; CANR 33; DLB 4,
7, 45; DLBY 82; MTCW

MacLennan, (John) Hugh
1907-1990 . . . . CLC 2, 14
See also CA 5-8R; 142; CANR 33; DLB 68;
MTCW

MacLeod, Alistair 1936- . . . . CLC 56
See also CA 123; DLB 60

MacNeice, (Frederick) Louis
1907-1963 . . . . CLC 1, 4, 10, 53
See also CA 85-88; DLB 10, 20; MTCW

MacNeill, Dand
See Fraser, George MacDonald

Macpherson, (Jean) Jay 1931- . . . . . . CLC 14
See also CA 5-8R; DLB 53

MacShane, Frank 1927- . . . . CLC 39
See also CA 9-12R; CANR 3, 33; DLB 111

Macumber, Mari
See Sandoz, Mari(e Susette)

Madach, Imre 1823-1864 . . . . NCLC 19

Madden, (Jerry) David 1933- . . . . CLC 5, 15
See also CA 1-4R; CAAS 3; CANR 4;
DLB 6; MTCW

Maddern, Al(an)
See Ellison, Harlan

Madhubuti, Haki R.
1942- . . . . CLC 6, 73; BLC; PC 5
See also Lee, Don L.
See also BW 2; CA 73-76; CANR 24;
DLB 5, 41; DLBD 8

Madow, Pauline (Reichberg) . . . . CLC 1
See also CA 9-12R

Maepenn, Hugh
See Kuttner, Henry

Maepenn, K. H.
See Kuttner, Henry

Maeterlinck, Maurice 1862-1949 . . . TCLC 3
See also CA 104; 136; SATA 66

Maginn, William 1794-1842 . . . . . . NCLC 8
See also DLB 110

Mahapatra, Jayanta 1928- . . . . CLC 33
See also CA 73-76; CAAS 9; CANR 15, 33

Mahfouz, Naguib (Abdel Aziz Al-Sabilgi)
1911(?)-
See Mahfuz, Najib
See also BEST 89:2; CA 128; MTCW

Mahfuz, Najib . . . . CLC 52, 55
See also Mahfouz, Naguib (Abdel Aziz
Al-Sabilgi)
See also DLBY 88

Mahon, Derek 1941- . . . . CLC 27
See also CA 113; 128; DLB 40

Mailer, Norman
1923- . . . . . . CLC 1, 2, 3, 4, 5, 8, 11, 14,
28, 39, 74; DA
See also AITN 2; CA 9-12R; CABS 1;
CANR 28; CDALB 1968-1988; DLB 2,
16, 28; DLBD 3; DLBY 80, 83; MTCW

Maillet, Antonine 1929- . . . . CLC 54
See also CA 115; 120; DLB 60

Mais, Roger 1905-1955 . . . . TCLC 8
See also BW 1; CA 105; 124; DLB 125;
MTCW

Maistre, Joseph de 1753-1821 . . . . NCLC 37

Maitland, Sara (Louise) 1950- . . . . . . CLC 49
See also CA 69-72; CANR 13

Major, Clarence
1936- . . . . CLC 3, 19, 48; BLC
See also BW 2; CA 21-24R; CAAS 6;
CANR 13, 25; DLB 33

Major, Kevin (Gerald) 1949- . . . . CLC 26
See also CA 97-100; CANR 21, 38;
CLR 11; DLB 60; JRDA; MAICYA;
SATA 32

Maki, James
See Ozu, Yasujiro

Malabaila, Damiano
See Levi, Primo

Malamud, Bernard
1914-1986 . . . . . . CLC 1, 2, 3, 5, 8, 9, 11,
18, 27, 44, 78; DA; SSC 15; WLC
See also CA 5-8R; 118; CABS 1; CANR 28;
CDALB 1941-1968; DLB 2, 28;
DLBY 80, 86; MTCW

Malaparte, Curzio 1898-1957 . . . . . TCLC 52

Malcolm, Dan
See Silverberg, Robert

Malcolm X . . . . CLC 82; BLC
See also Little, Malcolm

Malherbe, Francois de 1555-1628 . . . . . LC 5

Mallarme, Stephane
1842-1898 . . . . NCLC 4, 41; PC 4

Mallet-Joris, Francoise 1930- . . . . . . CLC 11
See also CA 65-68; CANR 17; DLB 83

Malley, Ern
See McAuley, James Phillip

Mallowan, Agatha Christie
See Christie, Agatha (Mary Clarissa)

Maloff, Saul 1922- . . . . CLC 5
See also CA 33-36R

Malone, Louis
See MacNeice, (Frederick) Louis

Malone, Michael (Christopher)
1942- . . . . CLC 43
See also CA 77-80; CANR 14, 32

Malory, (Sir) Thomas
1410(?)-1471(?) . . . . LC 11; DA
See also CDBLB Before 1660; SATA 33, 59

Malouf, (George Joseph) David
1934- . . . . CLC 28
See also CA 124

Malraux, (Georges-)Andre
1901-1976 . . . . . . CLC 1, 4, 9, 13, 15, 57
See also CA 21-22; 69-72; CANR 34;
CAP 2; DLB 72; MTCW

Malzberg, Barry N(athaniel) 1939- . . . CLC 7
See also CA 61-64; CAAS 4; CANR 16;
DLB 8

Mamet, David (Alan)
1947- . . . . CLC 9, 15, 34, 46; DC 4
See also AAYA 3; CA 81-84; CABS 3;
CANR 15, 41; DLB 7; MTCW

Mamoulian, Rouben (Zachary)
1897-1987 . . . . CLC 16
See also CA 25-28R; 124

Mandelstam, Osip (Emilievich)
1891(?)-1938(?) . . . . TCLC 2, 6
See also CA 104

Mander, (Mary) Jane 1877-1949 . . . TCLC 31

Mandiargues, Andre Pieyre de. . . . . . CLC 41
See also Pieyre de Mandiargues, Andre
See also DLB 83

Mandrake, Ethel Belle
See Thurman, Wallace (Henry)

Mangan, James Clarence
1803-1849 . . . . NCLC 27

Maniere, J.-E.
See Giraudoux, (Hippolyte) Jean

Manley, (Mary) Delariviere
1672(?)-1724 . . . . LC 1
See also DLB 39, 80

Mann, Abel
See Creasey, John

Mann, (Luiz) Heinrich   1871-1950. . . TCLC 9
See also CA 106; DLB 66

Mann, (Paul) Thomas
1875-1955 . . . . TCLC 2, 8, 14, 21, 35, 44;
DA; SSC 5; WLC
See also CA 104; 128; DLB 66; MTCW

Manning, David
See Faust, Frederick (Schiller)

Manning, Frederic   1887(?)-1935 . . . TCLC 25
See also CA 124

Manning, Olivia   1915-1980 . . . . . . CLC 5, 19
See also CA 5-8R; 101; CANR 29; MTCW

Mano, D. Keith   1942- . . . . CLC 2, 10
See also CA 25-28R; CAAS 6; CANR 26;
DLB 6

Mansfield, Katherine
. . . . TCLC 2, 8, 39; SSC 9; WLC
See also Beauchamp, Kathleen Mansfield

Manso, Peter   1940- . . . . CLC 39
See also CA 29-32R; CANR 44

Mantecon, Juan Jimenez
See Jimenez (Mantecon), Juan Ramon

Manton, Peter
See Creasey, John

Man Without a Spleen, A
See Chekhov, Anton (Pavlovich)

Manzoni, Alessandro   1785-1873 . . NCLC 29

Mapu, Abraham (ben Jekutiel)
1808-1867 . . . . NCLC 18

Mara, Sally
See Queneau, Raymond

Marat, Jean Paul   1743-1793 . . . . LC 10

Marcel, Gabriel Honore
1889-1973 . . . . CLC 15
See also CA 102; 45-48; MTCW

Marchbanks, Samuel
See Davies, (William) Robertson

Marchi, Giacomo
See Bassani, Giorgio

Margulies, Donald. . . . . CLC 76

Marie de France   c. 12th cent. -. . . . CMLC 8

Marie de l'Incarnation   1599-1672. . . . LC 10

Mariner, Scott
See Pohl, Frederik

Marinetti, Filippo Tommaso
1876-1944 . . . . TCLC 10
See also CA 107; DLB 114

Marivaux, Pierre Carlet de Chamblain de
1688-1763 . . . . LC 4

Markandaya, Kamala . . . . CLC 8, 38
See also Taylor, Kamala (Purnaiya)

Markfield, Wallace   1926-. . . . . CLC 8
See also CA 69-72; CAAS 3; DLB 2, 28

Markham, Edwin   1852-1940 . . . . . TCLC 47
See also DLB 54

Markham, Robert
See Amis, Kingsley (William)

Marks, J
See Highwater, Jamake (Mamake)

Marks-Highwater, J
See Highwater, Jamake (Mamake)

Markson, David M(errill)   1927- . . . . CLC 67
See also CA 49-52; CANR 1

Marley, Bob. . . . . CLC 17
See also Marley, Robert Nesta

Marley, Robert Nesta   1945-1981
See Marley, Bob
See also CA 107; 103

Marlowe, Christopher
1564-1593 . . . . . LC 22; DA; DC 1; WLC
See also CDBLB Before 1660; DLB 62

Marmontel, Jean-Francois
1723-1799 . . . . LC 2

Marquand, John P(hillips)
1893-1960 . . . . CLC 2, 10
See also CA 85-88; DLB 9, 102

Marquez, Gabriel (Jose) Garcia. . . . . CLC 68
See also Garcia Marquez, Gabriel (Jose)

Marquis, Don(ald Robert Perry)
1878-1937 . . . . TCLC 7
See also CA 104; DLB 11, 25

Marric, J. J.
See Creasey, John

Marrow, Bernard
See Moore, Brian

Marryat, Frederick   1792-1848 . . . . NCLC 3
See also DLB 21

Marsden, James
See Creasey, John

Marsh, (Edith) Ngaio
1899-1982 . . . . CLC 7, 53
See also CA 9-12R; CANR 6; DLB 77;
MTCW

Marshall, Garry   1934- . . . . CLC 17
See also AAYA 3; CA 111; SATA 60

Marshall, Paule
1929- . . . . CLC 27, 72; BLC; SSC 3
See also BW 2; CA 77-80; CANR 25;
DLB 33; MTCW

Marsten, Richard
See Hunter, Evan

Martha, Henry
See Harris, Mark

Martin, Ken
See Hubbard, L(afayette) Ron(ald)

Martin, Richard
See Creasey, John

Martin, Steve   1945- . . . . CLC 30
See also CA 97-100; CANR 30; MTCW

Martin, Violet Florence
1862-1915 . . . . TCLC 51

Martin, Webber
See Silverberg, Robert

Martindale, Patrick Victor
See White, Patrick (Victor Martindale)

Martin du Gard, Roger
1881-1958 . . . . TCLC 24
See also CA 118; DLB 65

Martineau, Harriet   1802-1876. . . . NCLC 26
See also DLB 21, 55; YABC 2

Martines, Julia
See O'Faolain, Julia

Martinez, Jacinto Benavente y
See Benavente (y Martinez), Jacinto

Martinez Ruiz, Jose   1873-1967
See Azorin; Ruiz, Jose Martinez
See also CA 93-96; HW

Martinez Sierra, Gregorio
1881-1947 . . . . TCLC 6
See also CA 115

Martinez Sierra, Maria (de la O'LeJarraga)
1874-1974 . . . . TCLC 6
See also CA 115

Martinsen, Martin
See Follett, Ken(neth Martin)

Martinson, Harry (Edmund)
1904-1978 . . . . CLC 14
See also CA 77-80; CANR 34

Marut, Ret
See Traven, B.

Marut, Robert
See Traven, B.

Marvell, Andrew
1621-1678 . . . . LC 4; DA; WLC
See also CDBLB 1660-1789; DLB 131

Marx, Karl (Heinrich)
1818-1883 . . . . NCLC 17
See also DLB 129

Masaoka Shiki. . . . . TCLC 18
See also Masaoka Tsunenori

Masaoka Tsunenori   1867-1902
See Masaoka Shiki
See also CA 117

Masefield, John (Edward)
1878-1967 . . . . CLC 11, 47
See also CA 19-20; 25-28R; CANR 33;
CAP 2; CDBLB 1890-1914; DLB 10;
MTCW; SATA 19

Maso, Carole   19(?)- . . . . CLC 44

Mason, Bobbie Ann
1940- . . . . CLC 28, 43, 82; SSC 4
See also AAYA 5; CA 53-56; CANR 11,
31; DLBY 87; MTCW

Mason, Ernst
See Pohl, Frederik

Mason, Lee W.
See Malzberg, Barry N(athaniel)

Mason, Nick   1945-. . . . . CLC 35
See also Pink Floyd

Mason, Tally
See Derleth, August (William)

Mass, William
See Gibson, William

Masters, Edgar Lee
    1868-1950 . . . . . . **TCLC 2, 25; DA; PC 1**
See also CA 104; 133; CDALB 1865-1917;
    DLB 54; MTCW

Masters, Hilary 1928- . . . . **CLC 48**
See also CA 25-28R; CANR 13

Mastrosimone, William 19(?)- . . . . . . **CLC 36**

Mathe, Albert
See Camus, Albert

Matheson, Richard Burton 1926- . . . **CLC 37**
See also CA 97-100; DLB 8, 44

Mathews, Harry 1930- . . . . **CLC 6, 52**
See also CA 21-24R; CAAS 6; CANR 18,
    40

Mathias, Roland (Glyn) 1915- . . . . . . **CLC 45**
See also CA 97-100; CANR 19, 41; DLB 27

Matsuo Basho 1644-1694 . . . . **PC 3**

Mattheson, Rodney
See Creasey, John

Matthews, Greg 1949- . . . . **CLC 45**
See also CA 135

Matthews, William 1942- . . . . **CLC 40**
See also CA 29-32R; CAAS 18; CANR 12;
    DLB 5

Matthias, John (Edward) 1941- . . . . . . **CLC 9**
See also CA 33-36R

Matthiessen, Peter
    1927- . . . . **CLC 5, 7, 11, 32, 64**
See also AAYA 6; BEST 90:4; CA 9-12R;
    CANR 21; DLB 6; MTCW; SATA 27

Maturin, Charles Robert
    1780(?)-1824 . . . . **NCLC 6**

Matute (Ausejo), Ana Maria
    1925- . . . . **CLC 11**
See also CA 89-92; MTCW

Maugham, W. S.
See Maugham, W(illiam) Somerset

Maugham, W(illiam) Somerset
    1874-1965 . . . . . . **CLC 1, 11, 15, 67; DA;**
                       SSC 8; WLC
See also CA 5-8R; 25-28R; CANR 40;
    CDBLB 1914-1945; DLB 10, 36, 77, 100;
    MTCW; SATA 54

Maugham, William Somerset
See Maugham, W(illiam) Somerset

Maupassant, (Henri Rene Albert) Guy de
    1850-1893 . . . . **NCLC 1, 42; DA; SSC 1;**
                                 WLC
See also DLB 123

Maurhut, Richard
See Traven, B.

Mauriac, Claude 1914- . . . . **CLC 9**
See also CA 89-92; DLB 83

Mauriac, Francois (Charles)
    1885-1970 . . . . **CLC 4, 9, 56**
See also CA 25-28; CAP 2; DLB 65;
    MTCW

Mavor, Osborne Henry 1888-1951
See Bridie, James
See also CA 104

Maxwell, William (Keepers, Jr.)
    1908- . . . . **CLC 19**
See also CA 93-96; DLBY 80

May, Elaine 1932- . . . . **CLC 16**
See also CA 124; 142; DLB 44

Mayakovski, Vladimir (Vladimirovich)
    1893-1930 . . . . **TCLC 4, 18**
See also CA 104

Mayhew, Henry 1812-1887 . . . . . . **NCLC 31**
See also DLB 18, 55

Maynard, Joyce 1953- . . . . **CLC 23**
See also CA 111; 129

Mayne, William (James Carter)
    1928- . . . . **CLC 12**
See also CA 9-12R; CANR 37; CLR 25;
    JRDA; MAICYA; SAAS 11; SATA 6, 68

Mayo, Jim
See L'Amour, Louis (Dearborn)

Maysles, Albert 1926- . . . . **CLC 16**
See also CA 29-32R

Maysles, David 1932- . . . . **CLC 16**

Mazer, Norma Fox 1931- . . . . **CLC 26**
See also AAYA 5; CA 69-72; CANR 12,
    32; CLR 23; JRDA; MAICYA; SAAS 1;
    SATA 24, 67

Mazzini, Guiseppe 1805-1872 . . . . **NCLC 34**

McAuley, James Phillip
    1917-1976 . . . . **CLC 45**
See also CA 97-100

McBain, Ed
See Hunter, Evan

McBrien, William Augustine
    1930- . . . . **CLC 44**
See also CA 107

McCaffrey, Anne (Inez) 1926- . . . . . . **CLC 17**
See also AAYA 6; AITN 2; BEST 89:2;
    CA 25-28R; CANR 15, 35; DLB 8;
    JRDA; MAICYA; MTCW; SAAS 11;
    SATA 8, 70

McCann, Arthur
See Campbell, John W(ood, Jr.)

McCann, Edson
See Pohl, Frederik

McCarthy, Charles, Jr. 1933-
See McCarthy, Cormac
See also CANR 42

McCarthy, Cormac . . . . **CLC 4, 57**
See also McCarthy, Charles, Jr.
See also DLB 6

McCarthy, Mary (Therese)
    1912-1989 . . . **CLC 1, 3, 5, 14, 24, 39, 59**
See also CA 5-8R; 129; CANR 16; DLB 2;
    DLBY 81; MTCW

McCartney, (James) Paul
    1942- . . . . **CLC 12, 35**

McCauley, Stephen (D.) 1955- . . . . . **CLC 50**
See also CA 141

McClure, Michael (Thomas)
    1932- . . . . **CLC 6, 10**
See also CA 21-24R; CANR 17; DLB 16

McCorkle, Jill (Collins) 1958- . . . . . . **CLC 51**
See also CA 121; DLBY 87

McCourt, James 1941- . . . . **CLC 5**
See also CA 57-60

McCoy, Horace (Stanley)
    1897-1955 . . . . **TCLC 28**
See also CA 108; DLB 9

McCrae, John 1872-1918 . . . . **TCLC 12**
See also CA 109; DLB 92

McCreigh, James
See Pohl, Frederik

McCullers, (Lula) Carson (Smith)
    1917-1967 . . . . **CLC 1, 4, 10, 12, 48; DA;**
                         SSC 9; WLC
See also CA 5-8R; 25-28R; CABS 1, 3;
    CANR 18; CDALB 1941-1968; DLB 2, 7;
    MTCW; SATA 27

McCulloch, John Tyler
See Burroughs, Edgar Rice

McCullough, Colleen 1938(?)- . . . . . . **CLC 27**
See also CA 81-84; CANR 17; MTCW

McElroy, Joseph 1930- . . . . **CLC 5, 47**
See also CA 17-20R

McEwan, Ian (Russell) 1948- . . . **CLC 13, 66**
See also BEST 90:4; CA 61-64; CANR 14,
    41; DLB 14; MTCW

McFadden, David 1940- . . . . **CLC 48**
See also CA 104; DLB 60

McFarland, Dennis 1950- . . . . **CLC 65**

McGahern, John 1934- . . . . **CLC 5, 9, 48**
See also CA 17-20R; CANR 29; DLB 14;
    MTCW

McGinley, Patrick (Anthony)
    1937- . . . . **CLC 41**
See also CA 120; 127

McGinley, Phyllis 1905-1978 . . . . . . **CLC 14**
See also CA 9-12R; 77-80; CANR 19;
    DLB 11, 48; SATA 2, 24, 44

McGinniss, Joe 1942- . . . . **CLC 32**
See also AITN 2; BEST 89:2; CA 25-28R;
    CANR 26

McGivern, Maureen Daly
See Daly, Maureen

McGrath, Patrick 1950- . . . . **CLC 55**
See also CA 136

McGrath, Thomas (Matthew)
    1916-1990 . . . . **CLC 28, 59**
See also CA 9-12R; 132; CANR 6, 33;
    MTCW; SATA 41; SATA-Obit 66

McGuane, Thomas (Francis III)
    1939- . . . . **CLC 3, 7, 18, 45**
See also AITN 2; CA 49-52; CANR 5, 24;
    DLB 2; DLBY 80; MTCW

McGuckian, Medbh 1950- . . . . **CLC 48**
See also CA 143; DLB 40

McHale, Tom 1942(?)-1982 . . . . **CLC 3, 5**
See also AITN 1; CA 77-80; 106

McIlvanney, William 1936- . . . . **CLC 42**
See also CA 25-28R; DLB 14

McIlwraith, Maureen Mollie Hunter
See Hunter, Mollie
See also SATA 2

McInerney, Jay 1955- . . . . **CLC 34**
See also CA 116; 123

McIntyre, Vonda N(eel) 1948- . . . . . **CLC 18**
See also CA 81-84; CANR 17, 34; MTCW

McKay, Claude . . . . . **TCLC 7, 41; BLC; PC 2**
See also McKay, Festus Claudius
See also DLB 4, 45, 51, 117

McKay, Festus Claudius 1889-1948
See McKay, Claude
See also BW 1; CA 104; 124; DA; MTCW;
WLC

McKuen, Rod 1933- . . . . CLC 1, 3
See also AITN 1; CA 41-44R; CANR 40

McLoughlin, R. B.
See Mencken, H(enry) L(ouis)

McLuhan, (Herbert) Marshall
1911-1980 . . . . CLC 37, 83
See also CA 9-12R; 102; CANR 12, 34;
DLB 88; MTCW

McMillan, Terry (L.) 1951- . . . . . CLC 50, 61
See also CA 140

McMurtry, Larry (Jeff)
1936- . . . . CLC 2, 3, 7, 11, 27, 44
See also AITN 2; BEST 89:2; CA 5-8R;
CANR 19, 43; CDALB 1968-1988;
DLB 2; DLBY 80, 87; MTCW

McNally, T. M. 1961- . . . . CLC 82

McNally, Terrence 1939- . . . . . CLC 4, 7, 41
See also CA 45-48; CANR 2; DLB 7

McNamer, Deirdre 1950- . . . . CLC 70

McNeile, Herman Cyril 1888-1937
See Sapper
See also DLB 77

McPhee, John (Angus) 1931- . . . . . . CLC 36
See also BEST 90:1; CA 65-68; CANR 20;
MTCW

McPherson, James Alan
1943- . . . . CLC 19, 77
See also BW; CA 25-28R; CAAS 17;
CANR 24; DLB 38; MTCW

McPherson, William (Alexander)
1933- . . . . CLC 34
See also CA 69-72; CANR 28

McSweeney, Kerry . . . . CLC 34

Mead, Margaret 1901-1978 . . . . CLC 37
See also AITN 1; CA 1-4R; 81-84;
CANR 4; MTCW; SATA 20

Meaker, Marijane (Agnes) 1927-
See Kerr, M. E.
See also CA 107; CANR 37; JRDA;
MAICYA; MTCW; SATA 20, 61

Medoff, Mark (Howard) 1940- . . . CLC 6, 23
See also AITN 1; CA 53-56; CANR 5;
DLB 7

Medvedev, P. N.
See Bakhtin, Mikhail Mikhailovich

Meged, Aharon
See Megged, Aharon

Meged, Aron
See Megged, Aharon

Megged, Aharon 1920- . . . . CLC 9
See also CA 49-52; CAAS 13; CANR 1

Mehta, Ved (Parkash) 1934- . . . . CLC 37
See also CA 1-4R; CANR 2, 23; MTCW

Melanter
See Blackmore, R(ichard) D(oddridge)

Melikow, Loris
See Hofmannsthal, Hugo von

Melmoth, Sebastian
See Wilde, Oscar (Fingal O'Flahertie Wills)

Meltzer, Milton 1915- . . . . CLC 26
See also AAYA 8; CA 13-16R; CANR 38;
CLR 13; DLB 61; JRDA; MAICYA;
SAAS 1; SATA 1, 50

Melville, Herman
1819-1891 . . . . NCLC 3, 12, 29, 45; DA;
SSC 1; WLC
See also CDALB 1640-1865; DLB 3, 74;
SATA 59

Menander
c. 342B.C.-c. 292B.C. . . . . CMLC 9; DC 3

Mencken, H(enry) L(ouis)
1880-1956 . . . . TCLC 13
See also Hatteras, Owen
See also CA 105; 125; CDALB 1917-1929;
DLB 11, 29, 63, 137; MTCW

Mercer, David 1928-1980 . . . . CLC 5
See also CA 9-12R; 102; CANR 23;
DLB 13; MTCW

Merchant, Paul
See Ellison, Harlan

Meredith, George 1828-1909 . . . TCLC 17, 43
See also CA 117; CDBLB 1832-1890;
DLB 18, 35, 57

Meredith, William (Morris)
1919- . . . . CLC 4, 13, 22, 55
See also CA 9-12R; CAAS 14; CANR 6, 40;
DLB 5

Merezhkovsky, Dmitry Sergeyevich
1865-1941 . . . . TCLC 29

Merimee, Prosper
1803-1870 . . . . NCLC 6; SSC 7
See also DLB 119

Merkin, Daphne 1954- . . . . CLC 44
See also CA 123

Merlin, Arthur
See Blish, James (Benjamin)

Merrill, James (Ingram)
1926- . . . . CLC 2, 3, 6, 8, 13, 18, 34
See also CA 13-16R; CANR 10; DLB 5;
DLBY 85; MTCW

Merriman, Alex
See Silverberg, Robert

Merritt, E. B.
See Waddington, Miriam

Merton, Thomas
1915-1968 . . . . CLC 1, 3, 11, 34, 83
See also CA 5-8R; 25-28R; CANR 22;
DLB 48; DLBY 81; MTCW

Merwin, W(illiam) S(tanley)
1927- . . . . . . CLC 1, 2, 3, 5, 8, 13, 18, 45
See also CA 13-16R; CANR 15; DLB 5;
MTCW

Metcalf, John 1938- . . . . CLC 37
See also CA 113; DLB 60

Metcalf, Suzanne
See Baum, L(yman) Frank

Mew, Charlotte (Mary)
1870-1928 . . . . TCLC 8
See also CA 105; DLB 19, 135

Mewshaw, Michael 1943- . . . . CLC 9
See also CA 53-56; CANR 7; DLBY 80

Meyer, June
See Jordan, June

Meyer, Lynn
See Slavitt, David R(ytman)

Meyer-Meyrink, Gustav 1868-1932
See Meyrink, Gustav
See also CA 117

Meyers, Jeffrey 1939- . . . . CLC 39
See also CA 73-76; DLB 111

Meynell, Alice (Christina Gertrude Thompson)
1847-1922 . . . . TCLC 6
See also CA 104; DLB 19, 98

Meyrink, Gustav . . . . TCLC 21
See also Meyer-Meyrink, Gustav
See also DLB 81

Michaels, Leonard 1933- . . . . CLC 6, 25
See also CA 61-64; CANR 21; DLB 130;
MTCW

Michaux, Henri 1899-1984 . . . . . . CLC 8, 19
See also CA 85-88; 114

Michelangelo 1475-1564 . . . . LC 12

Michelet, Jules 1798-1874 . . . . NCLC 31

Michener, James A(lbert)
1907(?)- . . . . CLC 1, 5, 11, 29, 60
See also AITN 1; BEST 90:1; CA 5-8R;
CANR 21; DLB 6; MTCW

Mickiewicz, Adam 1798-1855 . . . . . NCLC 3

Middleton, Christopher 1926- . . . . . . CLC 13
See also CA 13-16R; CANR 29; DLB 40

Middleton, Stanley 1919- . . . . CLC 7, 38
See also CA 25-28R; CANR 21; DLB 14

Migueis, Jose Rodrigues 1901- . . . . . CLC 10

Mikszath, Kalman 1847-1910 . . . . . TCLC 31

Miles, Josephine
1911-1985 . . . . CLC 1, 2, 14, 34, 39
See also CA 1-4R; 116; CANR 2; DLB 48

Militant
See Sandburg, Carl (August)

Mill, John Stuart 1806-1873 . . . . . NCLC 11
See also CDBLB 1832-1890; DLB 55

Millar, Kenneth 1915-1983 . . . . CLC 14
See also Macdonald, Ross
See also CA 9-12R; 110; CANR 16; DLB 2;
DLBD 6; DLBY 83; MTCW

Millay, E. Vincent
See Millay, Edna St. Vincent

Millay, Edna St. Vincent
1892-1950 . . . . . . TCLC 4, 49; DA; PC 6
See also CA 104; 130; CDALB 1917-1929;
DLB 45; MTCW

Miller, Arthur
1915- . . . . CLC 1, 2, 6, 10, 15, 26, 47, 78;
DA; DC 1; WLC
See also AITN 1; CA 1-4R; CABS 3;
CANR 2, 30; CDALB 1941-1968; DLB 7;
MTCW

Miller, Henry (Valentine)
1891-1980 . . . . CLC 1, 2, 4, 9, 14, 43;
DA; WLC
See also CA 9-12R; 97-100; CANR 33;
CDALB 1929-1941; DLB 4, 9; DLBY 80;
MTCW

Miller, Jason 1939(?)- . . . . CLC 2
See also AITN 1; CA 73-76; DLB 7

Miller, Sue 1943- . . . . CLC 44
See also BEST 90:3; CA 139

Miller, Walter M(ichael, Jr.)
1923- . . . . **CLC 4, 30**
See also CA 85-88; DLB 8

Millett, Kate 1934- . . . . **CLC 67**
See also AITN 1; CA 73-76; CANR 32;
MTCW

Millhauser, Steven 1943- . . . . **CLC 21, 54**
See also CA 110; 111; DLB 2

Millin, Sarah Gertrude 1889-1968 . . **CLC 49**
See also CA 102; 93-96

Milne, A(lan) A(lexander)
1882-1956 . . . . **TCLC 6**
See also CA 104; 133; CLR 1, 26; DLB 10,
77, 100; MAICYA; MTCW; YABC 1

Milner, Ron(ald) 1938- . . . . **CLC 56; BLC**
See also AITN 1; BW; CA 73-76;
CANR 24; DLB 38; MTCW

Milosz, Czeslaw
1911- . . . **CLC 5, 11, 22, 31, 56, 82; PC 8**
See also CA 81-84; CANR 23; MTCW

Milton, John 1608-1674 . . . **LC 9; DA; WLC**
See also CDBLB 1660-1789; DLB 131

Minehaha, Cornelius
See Wedekind, (Benjamin) Frank(lin)

Miner, Valerie 1947- . . . . **CLC 40**
See also CA 97-100

Minimo, Duca
See D'Annunzio, Gabriele

Minot, Susan 1956- . . . . **CLC 44**
See also CA 134

Minus, Ed 1938- . . . . **CLC 39**

Miranda, Javier
See Bioy Casares, Adolfo

Miro (Ferrer), Gabriel (Francisco Victor)
1879-1930 . . . . **TCLC 5**
See also CA 104

Mishima, Yukio
. . . . **CLC 2, 4, 6, 9, 27; DC 1; SSC 4**
See also Hiraoka, Kimitake

Mistral, Frederic 1830-1914 . . . . . . **TCLC 51**
See also CA 122

Mistral, Gabriela . . . . **TCLC 2; HLC**
See also Godoy Alcayaga, Lucila

Mistry, Rohinton 1952- . . . . **CLC 71**
See also CA 141

Mitchell, Clyde
See Ellison, Harlan; Silverberg, Robert

Mitchell, James Leslie 1901-1935
See Gibbon, Lewis Grassic
See also CA 104; DLB 15

Mitchell, Joni 1943- . . . . **CLC 12**
See also CA 112

Mitchell, Margaret (Munnerlyn)
1900-1949 . . . . **TCLC 11**
See also CA 109; 125; DLB 9; MTCW

Mitchell, Peggy
See Mitchell, Margaret (Munnerlyn)

Mitchell, S(ilas) Weir 1829-1914 . . **TCLC 36**

Mitchell, W(illiam) O(rmond)
1914- . . . . **CLC 25**
See also CA 77-80; CANR 15, 43; DLB 88

Mitford, Mary Russell 1787-1855 . . **NCLC 4**
See also DLB 110, 116

Mitford, Nancy 1904-1973 . . . . **CLC 44**
See also CA 9-12R

Miyamoto, Yuriko 1899-1951 . . . . . **TCLC 37**

Mo, Timothy (Peter) 1950(?)- . . . . . . **CLC 46**
See also CA 117; MTCW

Modarressi, Taghi (M.) 1931- . . . . . . **CLC 44**
See also CA 121; 134

Modiano, Patrick (Jean) 1945- . . . . . **CLC 18**
See also CA 85-88; CANR 17, 40; DLB 83

Moerck, Paal
See Roelvaag, O(le) E(dvart)

Mofolo, Thomas (Mokopu)
1875(?)-1948 . . . . **TCLC 22; BLC**
See also CA 121

Mohr, Nicholasa 1935- . . . . . . **CLC 12; HLC**
See also AAYA 8; CA 49-52; CANR 1, 32;
CLR 22; HW; JRDA; SAAS 8; SATA 8

Mojtabai, A(nn) G(race)
1938- . . . . **CLC 5, 9, 15, 29**
See also CA 85-88

Moliere 1622-1673 . . . . **LC 10; DA; WLC**

Molin, Charles
See Mayne, William (James Carter)

Molnar, Ferenc 1878-1952 . . . . **TCLC 20**
See also CA 109

Momaday, N(avarre) Scott
1934- . . . . **CLC 2, 19; DA**
See also AAYA 11; CA 25-28R; CANR 14,
34; MTCW; SATA 30, 48

Monette, Paul 1945- . . . . **CLC 82**
See also CA 139

Monroe, Harriet 1860-1936 . . . . . . **TCLC 12**
See also CA 109; DLB 54, 91

Monroe, Lyle
See Heinlein, Robert A(nson)

Montagu, Elizabeth 1917- . . . . **NCLC 7**
See also CA 9-12R

Montagu, Mary (Pierrepont) Wortley
1689-1762 . . . . **LC 9**
See also DLB 95, 101

Montagu, W. H.
See Coleridge, Samuel Taylor

Montague, John (Patrick)
1929- . . . . **CLC 13, 46**
See also CA 9-12R; CANR 9; DLB 40;
MTCW

Montaigne, Michel (Eyquem) de
1533-1592 . . . . **LC 8; DA; WLC**

Montale, Eugenio 1896-1981 . . . **CLC 7, 9, 18**
See also CA 17-20R; 104; CANR 30;
DLB 114; MTCW

Montesquieu, Charles-Louis de Secondat
1689-1755 . . . . **LC 7**

Montgomery, (Robert) Bruce 1921-1978
See Crispin, Edmund
See also CA 104

Montgomery, L(ucy) M(aud)
1874-1942 . . . . **TCLC 51**
See also AAYA 12; CA 108; 137; CLR 8;
DLB 92; JRDA; MAICYA; YABC 1

Montgomery, Marion H., Jr. 1925- . . **CLC 7**
See also AITN 1; CA 1-4R; CANR 3;
DLB 6

Montgomery, Max
See Davenport, Guy (Mattison, Jr.)

Montherlant, Henry (Milon) de
1896-1972 . . . . **CLC 8, 19**
See also CA 85-88; 37-40R; DLB 72;
MTCW

Monty Python . . . . **CLC 21**
See also Chapman, Graham; Cleese, John
(Marwood); Gilliam, Terry (Vance); Idle,
Eric; Jones, Terence Graham Parry; Palin,
Michael (Edward)
See also AAYA 7

Moodie, Susanna (Strickland)
1803-1885 . . . . **NCLC 14**
See also DLB 99

Mooney, Edward 1951- . . . . **CLC 25**
See also CA 130

Mooney, Ted
See Mooney, Edward

Moorcock, Michael (John)
1939- . . . . **CLC 5, 27, 58**
See also CA 45-48; CAAS 5; CANR 2, 17,
38; DLB 14; MTCW

Moore, Brian
1921- . . . . **CLC 1, 3, 5, 7, 8, 19, 32**
See also CA 1-4R; CANR 1, 25, 42; MTCW

Moore, Edward
See Muir, Edwin

Moore, George Augustus
1852-1933 . . . . **TCLC 7**
See also CA 104; DLB 10, 18, 57, 135

Moore, Lorrie . . . . **CLC 39, 45, 68**
See also Moore, Marie Lorena

Moore, Marianne (Craig)
1887-1972 . . . . **CLC 1, 2, 4, 8, 10, 13, 19,
47; DA; PC 4**
See also CA 1-4R; 33-36R; CANR 3;
CDALB 1929-1941; DLB 45; DLBD 7;
MTCW; SATA 20

Moore, Marie Lorena 1957-
See Moore, Lorrie
See also CA 116; CANR 39

Moore, Thomas 1779-1852 . . . . **NCLC 6**
See also DLB 96

Morand, Paul 1888-1976 . . . . **CLC 41**
See also CA 69-72; DLB 65

Morante, Elsa 1918-1985 . . . . **CLC 8, 47**
See also CA 85-88; 117; CANR 35; MTCW

Moravia, Alberto . . . . . . **CLC 2, 7, 11, 27, 46**
See also Pincherle, Alberto

More, Hannah 1745-1833 . . . . **NCLC 27**
See also DLB 107, 109, 116

More, Henry 1614-1687 . . . . **LC 9**
See also DLB 126

More, Sir Thomas 1478-1535 . . . . . . **LC 10**

Moreas, Jean . . . . **TCLC 18**
See also Papadiamantopoulos, Johannes

Morgan, Berry 1919- . . . . **CLC 6**
See also CA 49-52; DLB 6

Morgan, Claire
See Highsmith, (Mary) Patricia

Morgan, Edwin (George) 1920- . . . . . **CLC 31**
See also CA 5-8R; CANR 3, 43; DLB 27

Nabokov, Vladimir (Vladimirovich)
1899-1977 ..... CLC 1, 2, 3, 6, 8, 11, 15,
23, 44, 46, 64; DA; SSC 11; WLC
See also CA 5-8R; 69-72; CANR 20;
CDALB 1941-1968; DLB 2; DLBD 3;
DLBY 80, 91; MTCW

Nagai Kafu .... TCLC 51
See also Nagai Sokichi

Nagai Sokichi 1879-1959
See Nagai Kafu
See also CA 117

Nagy, Laszlo 1925-1978 .... CLC 7
See also CA 129; 112

Naipaul, Shiva(dhar Srinivasa)
1945-1985 .... CLC 32, 39
See also CA 110; 112; 116; CANR 33;
DLBY 85; MTCW

Naipaul, V(idiadhar) S(urajprasad)
1932- .... CLC 4, 7, 9, 13, 18, 37
See also CA 1-4R; CANR 1, 33;
CDBLB 1960 to Present; DLB 125;
DLBY 85; MTCW

Nakos, Lilika 1899(?)- .... CLC 29

Narayan, R(asipuram) K(rishnaswami)
1906- .... CLC 7, 28, 47
See also CA 81-84; CANR 33; MTCW;
SATA 62

Nash, (Frediric) Ogden 1902-1971 .. CLC 23
See also CA 13-14; 29-32R; CANR 34;
CAP 1; DLB 11; MAICYA; MTCW;
SATA 2, 46

Nathan, Daniel
See Dannay, Frederic

Nathan, George Jean 1882-1958 ... TCLC 18
See also Hatteras, Owen
See also CA 114; DLB 137

Natsume, Kinnosuke 1867-1916
See Natsume, Soseki
See also CA 104

Natsume, Soseki .... TCLC 2, 10
See also Natsume, Kinnosuke

Natti, (Mary) Lee 1919-
See Kingman, Lee
See also CA 5-8R; CANR 2

Naylor, Gloria
1950- .... CLC 28, 52; BLC; DA
See also AAYA 6; BW; CA 107; CANR 27;
MTCW

Neihardt, John Gneisenau
1881-1973 .... CLC 32
See also CA 13-14; CAP 1; DLB 9, 54

Nekrasov, Nikolai Alekseevich
1821-1878 .... NCLC 11

Nelligan, Emile 1879-1941 .... TCLC 14
See also CA 114; DLB 92

Nelson, Willie 1933- .... CLC 17
See also CA 107

Nemerov, Howard (Stanley)
1920-1991 .... CLC 2, 6, 9, 36
See also CA 1-4R; 134; CABS 2; CANR 1,
27; DLB 6; DLBY 83; MTCW

Neruda, Pablo
1904-1973 ..... CLC 1, 2, 5, 7, 9, 28, 62;
DA; HLC; PC 4; WLC
See also CA 19-20; 45-48; CAP 2; HW;
MTCW

Nerval, Gerard de 1808-1855 ...... NCLC 1

Nervo, (Jose) Amado (Ruiz de)
1870-1919 .... TCLC 11
See also CA 109; 131; HW

Nessi, Pio Baroja y
See Baroja (y Nessi), Pio

Nestroy, Johann 1801-1862 ...... NCLC 42
See also DLB 133

Neufeld, John (Arthur) 1938- ...... CLC 17
See also AAYA 11; CA 25-28R; CANR 11,
37; MAICYA; SAAS 3; SATA 6

Neville, Emily Cheney 1919- .... CLC 12
See also CA 5-8R; CANR 3, 37; JRDA;
MAICYA; SAAS 2; SATA 1

Newbound, Bernard Slade 1930-
See Slade, Bernard
See also CA 81-84

Newby, P(ercy) H(oward)
1918- .... CLC 2, 13
See also CA 5-8R; CANR 32; DLB 15;
MTCW

Newlove, Donald 1928- .... CLC 6
See also CA 29-32R; CANR 25

Newlove, John (Herbert) 1938- ..... CLC 14
See also CA 21-24R; CANR 9, 25

Newman, Charles 1938- .... CLC 2, 8
See also CA 21-24R

Newman, Edwin (Harold) 1919- .... CLC 14
See also AITN 1; CA 69-72; CANR 5

Newman, John Henry
1801-1890 .... NCLC 38
See also DLB 18, 32, 55

Newton, Suzanne 1936- .... CLC 35
See also CA 41-44R; CANR 14; JRDA;
SATA 5, 77

Nexo, Martin Andersen
1869-1954 .... TCLC 43

Nezval, Vitezslav 1900-1958 ...... TCLC 44
See also CA 123

Ng, Fae Myenne 1957(?)- .... CLC 81

Ngema, Mbongeni 1955- .... CLC 57
See also CA 143

Ngugi, James T(hiong'o) .... CLC 3, 7, 13
See also Ngugi wa Thiong'o

Ngugi wa Thiong'o 1938- ..... CLC 36; BLC
See also Ngugi, James T(hiong'o)
See also BW; CA 81-84; CANR 27;
DLB 125; MTCW

Nichol, B(arrie) P(hillip)
1944-1988 .... CLC 18
See also CA 53-56; DLB 53; SATA 66

Nichols, John (Treadwell) 1940- .... CLC 38
See also CA 9-12R; CAAS 2; CANR 6;
DLBY 82

Nichols, Leigh
See Koontz, Dean R(ay)

Nichols, Peter (Richard)
1927- .... CLC 5, 36, 65
See also CA 104; CANR 33; DLB 13;
MTCW

Nicolas, F. R. E.
See Freeling, Nicolas

Niedecker, Lorine 1903-1970 .... CLC 10, 42
See also CA 25-28; CAP 2; DLB 48

Nietzsche, Friedrich (Wilhelm)
1844-1900 .... TCLC 10, 18
See also CA 107; 121; DLB 129

Nievo, Ippolito 1831-1861 .... NCLC 22

Nightingale, Anne Redmon 1943-
See Redmon, Anne
See also CA 103

Nik.T.O.
See Annensky, Innokenty Fyodorovich

Nin, Anais
1903-1977 ...... CLC 1, 4, 8, 11, 14, 60;
SSC 10
See also AITN 2; CA 13-16R; 69-72;
CANR 22; DLB 2, 4; MTCW

Nissenson, Hugh 1933- .... CLC 4, 9
See also CA 17-20R; CANR 27; DLB 28

Niven, Larry .... CLC 8
See also Niven, Laurence Van Cott
See also DLB 8

Niven, Laurence Van Cott 1938-
See Niven, Larry
See also CA 21-24R; CAAS 12; CANR 14,
44; MTCW

Nixon, Agnes Eckhardt 1927- ...... CLC 21
See also CA 110

Nizan, Paul 1905-1940 .... TCLC 40
See also DLB 72

Nkosi, Lewis 1936- .... CLC 45; BLC
See also BW; CA 65-68; CANR 27

Nodier, (Jean) Charles (Emmanuel)
1780-1844 .... NCLC 19
See also DLB 119

Nolan, Christopher 1965- .... CLC 58
See also CA 111

Norden, Charles
See Durrell, Lawrence (George)

Nordhoff, Charles (Bernard)
1887-1947 .... TCLC 23
See also CA 108; DLB 9; SATA 23

Norfolk, Lawrence 1963- .... CLC 76
See also CA 144

Norman, Marsha 1947- .... CLC 28
See also CA 105; CABS 3; CANR 41;
DLBY 84

Norris, Benjamin Franklin, Jr.
1870-1902 .... TCLC 24
See also Norris, Frank
See also CA 110

Norris, Frank
See Norris, Benjamin Franklin, Jr.
See also CDALB 1865-1917; DLB 12, 71

Norris, Leslie 1921- .... CLC 14
See also CA 11-12; CANR 14; CAP 1;
DLB 27

North, Andrew
See Norton, Andre

North, Anthony
See Koontz, Dean R(ay)

North, Captain George
See Stevenson, Robert Louis (Balfour)

North, Milou
See Erdrich, Louise

Northrup, B. A.
See Hubbard, L(afayette) Ron(ald)

Orton, Joe .... CLC 4, 13, 43; DC 3
See also Orton, John Kingsley
See also CDBLB 1960 to Present; DLB 13

Orton, John Kingsley 1933-1967
See Orton, Joe
See also CA 85-88; CANR 35; MTCW

Orwell, George
.... TCLC 2, 6, 15, 31, 51; WLC
See also Blair, Eric (Arthur)
See also CDBLB 1945-1960; DLB 15, 98

Osborne, David
See Silverberg, Robert

Osborne, George
See Silverberg, Robert

Osborne, John (James)
1929- .... CLC 1, 2, 5, 11, 45; DA; WLC
See also CA 13-16R; CANR 21;
CDBLB 1945-1960; DLB 13; MTCW

Osborne, Lawrence 1958- .... CLC 50

Oshima, Nagisa 1932- .... CLC 20
See also CA 116; 121

Oskison, John Milton
1874-1947 .... TCLC 35
See also CA 144

Ossoli, Sarah Margaret (Fuller marchesa d')
1810-1850
See Fuller, Margaret
See also SATA 25

Ostrovsky, Alexander
1823-1886 .... NCLC 30

Otero, Blas de 1916-1979......... CLC 11
See also CA 89-92; DLB 134

Otto, Whitney 1955-.............. CLC 70
See also CA 140

Ouida .... TCLC 43
See also De La Ramee, (Marie) Louise
See also DLB 18

Ousmane, Sembene 1923- .... CLC 66; BLC
See also BW; CA 117; 125; MTCW

Ovid 43B.C.-18th cent. (?)... CMLC 7; PC 2

Owen, Hugh
See Faust, Frederick (Schiller)

Owen, Wilfred (Edward Salter)
1893-1918 ...... TCLC 5, 27; DA; WLC
See also CA 104; 141; CDBLB 1914-1945;
DLB 20

Owens, Rochelle 1936-............ CLC 8
See also CA 17-20R; CAAS 2; CANR 39

Oz, Amos 1939- ... CLC 5, 8, 11, 27, 33, 54
See also CA 53-56; CANR 27; MTCW

Ozick, Cynthia
1928- .... CLC 3, 7, 28, 62; SSC 15
See also BEST 90:1; CA 17-20R; CANR 23;
DLB 28; DLBY 82; MTCW

Ozu, Yasujiro 1903-1963.......... CLC 16
See also CA 112

Pacheco, C.
See Pessoa, Fernando (Antonio Nogueira)

Pa Chin
See Li Fei-kan

Pack, Robert 1929-............... CLC 13
See also CA 1-4R; CANR 3, 44; DLB 5

Padgett, Lewis
See Kuttner, Henry

Padilla (Lorenzo), Heberto 1932-... CLC 38
See also AITN 1; CA 123; 131; HW

Page, Jimmy 1944-................ CLC 12

Page, Louise 1955-............... CLC 40
See also CA 140

Page, P(atricia) K(athleen)
1916- .... CLC 7, 18
See also CA 53-56; CANR 4, 22; DLB 68;
MTCW

Paget, Violet 1856-1935
See Lee, Vernon
See also CA 104

Paget-Lowe, Henry
See Lovecraft, H(oward) P(hillips)

Paglia, Camille (Anna) 1947-...... CLC 68
See also CA 140

Paige, Richard
See Koontz, Dean R(ay)

Pakenham, Antonia
See Fraser, (Lady) Antonia (Pakenham)

Palamas, Kostes 1859-1943 .... TCLC 5
See also CA 105

Palazzeschi, Aldo 1885-1974...... CLC 11
See also CA 89-92; 53-56; DLB 114

Paley, Grace 1922-.... CLC 4, 6, 37; SSC 8
See also CA 25-28R; CANR 13; DLB 28;
MTCW

Palin, Michael (Edward) 1943-..... CLC 21
See also Monty Python
See also CA 107; CANR 35; SATA 67

Palliser, Charles 1947-............ CLC 65
See also CA 136

Palma, Ricardo 1833-1919....... TCLC 29

Pancake, Breece Dexter 1952-1979
See Pancake, Breece D'J
See also CA 123; 109

Pancake, Breece D'J............... CLC 29
See also Pancake, Breece Dexter
See also DLB 130

Panko, Rudy
See Gogol, Nikolai (Vasilyevich)

Papadiamantis, Alexandros
1851-1911 .... TCLC 29

Papadiamantopoulos, Johannes 1856-1910
See Moreas, Jean
See also CA 117

Papini, Giovanni 1881-1956....... TCLC 22
See also CA 121

Paracelsus 1493-1541.............. LC 14

Parasol, Peter
See Stevens, Wallace

Parfenie, Maria
See Codrescu, Andrei

Parini, Jay (Lee) 1948- .... CLC 54
See also CA 97-100; CAAS 16; CANR 32

Park, Jordan
See Kornbluth, C(yril) M.; Pohl, Frederik

Parker, Bert
See Ellison, Harlan

Parker, Dorothy (Rothschild)
1893-1967 .... CLC 15, 68; SSC 2
See also CA 19-20; 25-28R; CAP 2;
DLB 11, 45, 86; MTCW

Parker, Robert B(rown) 1932-...... CLC 27
See also BEST 89:4; CA 49-52; CANR 1,
26; MTCW

Parkes, Lucas
See Harris, John (Wyndham Parkes Lucas)
Beynon

Parkin, Frank 1940-.............. CLC 43

Parkman, Francis, Jr.
1823-1893 .... NCLC 12
See also DLB 1, 30

Parks, Gordon (Alexander Buchanan)
1912- .... CLC 1, 16; BLC
See also AITN 2; BW; CA 41-44R;
CANR 26; DLB 33; SATA 8

Parnell, Thomas 1679-1718 .... LC 3
See also DLB 94

Parra, Nicanor 1914-........ CLC 2; HLC
See also CA 85-88; CANR 32; HW; MTCW

Parrish, Mary Frances
See Fisher, M(ary) F(rances) K(ennedy)

Parson
See Coleridge, Samuel Taylor

Parson Lot
See Kingsley, Charles

Partridge, Anthony
See Oppenheim, E(dward) Phillips

Pascoli, Giovanni 1855-1912 ..... TCLC 45

Pasolini, Pier Paolo
1922-1975 .... CLC 20, 37
See also CA 93-96; 61-64; DLB 128;
MTCW

Pasquini
See Silone, Ignazio

Pastan, Linda (Olenik) 1932- ...... CLC 27
See also CA 61-64; CANR 18, 40; DLB 5

Pasternak, Boris (Leonidovich)
1890-1960 ...... CLC 7, 10, 18, 63; DA;
PC 6; WLC
See also CA 127; 116; MTCW

Patchen, Kenneth 1911-1972... CLC 1, 2, 18
See also CA 1-4R; 33-36R; CANR 3, 35;
DLB 16, 48; MTCW

Pater, Walter (Horatio)
1839-1894 .... NCLC 7
See also CDBLB 1832-1890; DLB 57

Paterson, A(ndrew) B(arton)
1864-1941 .... TCLC 32

Paterson, Katherine (Womeldorf)
1932- .... CLC 12, 30
See also AAYA 1; CA 21-24R; CANR 28;
CLR 7; DLB 52; JRDA; MAICYA;
MTCW; SATA 13, 53

Patmore, Coventry Kersey Dighton
1823-1896 .... NCLC 9
See also DLB 35, 98

Paton, Alan (Stewart)
1903-1988 ...... CLC 4, 10, 25, 55; DA;
WLC
See also CA 13-16; 125; CANR 22; CAP 1;
MTCW; SATA 11, 56

Paton Walsh, Gillian 1937-
See Walsh, Jill Paton
See also CANR 38; JRDA; MAICYA;
SAAS 3; SATA 4, 72

Paulding, James Kirke   1778-1860. . NCLC 2
See also DLB 3, 59, 74

Paulin, Thomas Neilson   1949-
See Paulin, Tom
See also CA 123; 128

Paulin, Tom . . . . CLC 37
See also Paulin, Thomas Neilson
See also DLB 40

Paustovsky, Konstantin (Georgievich)
1892-1968 . . . . CLC 40
See also CA 93-96; 25-28R

Pavese, Cesare   1908-1950 . . . . TCLC 3
See also CA 104; DLB 128

Pavic, Milorad   1929- . . . . CLC 60
See also CA 136

Payne, Alan
See Jakes, John (William)

Paz, Gil
See Lugones, Leopoldo

Paz, Octavio
1914- . . . . CLC 3, 4, 6, 10, 19, 51, 65;
DA; HLC; PC 1; WLC
See also CA 73-76; CANR 32; DLBY 90;
HW; MTCW

Peacock, Molly   1947-. . . . . CLC 60
See also CA 103; DLB 120

Peacock, Thomas Love
1785-1866 . . . . NCLC 22
See also DLB 96, 116

Peake, Mervyn   1911-1968 . . . . CLC 7, 54
See also CA 5-8R; 25-28R; CANR 3;
DLB 15; MTCW; SATA 23

Pearce, Philippa . . . . CLC 21
See also Christie, (Ann) Philippa
See also CLR 9; MAICYA; SATA 1, 67

Pearl, Eric
See Elman, Richard

Pearson, T(homas) R(eid)   1956- . . . . CLC 39
See also CA 120; 130

Peck, Dale   1968(?)- . . . . CLC 81

Peck, John   1941- . . . . CLC 3
See also CA 49-52; CANR 3

Peck, Richard (Wayne)   1934- . . . . . . CLC 21
See also AAYA 1; CA 85-88; CANR 19,
38; JRDA; MAICYA; SAAS 2; SATA 18,
55

Peck, Robert Newton   1928-. . . . CLC 17; DA
See also AAYA 3; CA 81-84; CANR 31;
JRDA; MAICYA; SAAS 1; SATA 21, 62

Peckinpah, (David) Sam(uel)
1925-1984 . . . . CLC 20
See also CA 109; 114

Pedersen, Knut   1859-1952
See Hamsun, Knut
See also CA 104; 119; MTCW

Peeslake, Gaffer
See Durrell, Lawrence (George)

Peguy, Charles Pierre
1873-1914 . . . . TCLC 10
See also CA 107

Pena, Ramon del Valle y
See Valle-Inclan, Ramon (Maria) del

Pendennis, Arthur Esquir
See Thackeray, William Makepeace

Penn, William   1644-1718 . . . . LC 25
See also DLB 24

Pepys, Samuel
1633-1703 . . . . LC 11; DA; WLC
See also CDBLB 1660-1789; DLB 101

Percy, Walker
1916-1990 . . . . CLC 2, 3, 6, 8, 14, 18, 47,
65
See also CA 1-4R; 131; CANR 1, 23;
DLB 2; DLBY 80, 90; MTCW

Perec, Georges   1936-1982 . . . . CLC 56
See also CA 141; DLB 83

Pereda (y Sanchez de Porrua), Jose Maria de
1833-1906 . . . . TCLC 16
See also CA 117

Pereda y Porrua, Jose Maria de
See Pereda (y Sanchez de Porrua), Jose
Maria de

Peregoy, George Weems
See Mencken, H(enry) L(ouis)

Perelman, S(idney) J(oseph)
1904-1979 . . . CLC 3, 5, 9, 15, 23, 44, 49
See also AITN 1, 2; CA 73-76; 89-92;
CANR 18; DLB 11, 44; MTCW

Peret, Benjamin   1899-1959 . . . . TCLC 20
See also CA 117

Peretz, Isaac Loeb   1851(?)-1915 . . . TCLC 16
See also CA 109

Peretz, Yitzhok Leibush
See Peretz, Isaac Loeb

Perez Galdos, Benito   1843-1920 . . . TCLC 27
See also CA 125; HW

Perrault, Charles   1628-1703 . . . . LC 2
See also MAICYA; SATA 25

Perry, Brighton
See Sherwood, Robert E(mmet)

Perse, St.-John . . . . CLC 4, 11, 46
See also Leger, (Marie-Rene Auguste) Alexis
Saint-Leger

Peseenz, Tulio F.
See Lopez y Fuentes, Gregorio

Pesetsky, Bette   1932-. . . . . CLC 28
See also CA 133; DLB 130

Peshkov, Alexei Maximovich   1868-1936
See Gorky, Maxim
See also CA 105; 141; DA

Pessoa, Fernando (Antonio Nogueira)
1888-1935 . . . . TCLC 27; HLC
See also CA 125

Peterkin, Julia Mood   1880-1961. . . . CLC 31
See also CA 102; DLB 9

Peters, Joan K.   1945-. . . . . CLC 39

Peters, Robert L(ouis)   1924-. . . . . CLC 7
See also CA 13-16R; CAAS 8; DLB 105

Petofi, Sandor   1823-1849. . . . . NCLC 21

Petrakis, Harry Mark   1923-. . . . . CLC 3
See also CA 9-12R; CANR 4, 30

Petrarch   1304-1374. . . . . PC 8

Petrov, Evgeny . . . . TCLC 21
See also Kataev, Evgeny Petrovich

Petry, Ann (Lane)   1908- . . . . . . CLC 1, 7, 18
See also BW; CA 5-8R; CAAS 6; CANR 4;
CLR 12; DLB 76; JRDA; MAICYA;
MTCW; SATA 5

Petursson, Halligrimur   1614-1674 . . . . LC 8

Philipson, Morris H.   1926-. . . . . CLC 53
See also CA 1-4R; CANR 4

Phillips, David Graham
1867-1911 . . . . TCLC 44
See also CA 108; DLB 9, 12

Phillips, Jack
See Sandburg, Carl (August)

Phillips, Jayne Anne   1952- . . . . . CLC 15, 33
See also CA 101; CANR 24; DLBY 80;
MTCW

Phillips, Richard
See Dick, Philip K(indred)

Phillips, Robert (Schaeffer)   1938-. . . CLC 28
See also CA 17-20R; CAAS 13; CANR 8;
DLB 105

Phillips, Ward
See Lovecraft, H(oward) P(hillips)

Piccolo, Lucio   1901-1969. . . . . CLC 13
See also CA 97-100; DLB 114

Pickthall, Marjorie L(owry) C(hristie)
1883-1922 . . . . TCLC 21
See also CA 107; DLB 92

Pico della Mirandola, Giovanni
1463-1494 . . . . LC 15

Piercy, Marge
1936- . . . . CLC 3, 6, 14, 18, 27, 62
See also CA 21-24R; CAAS 1; CANR 13,
43; DLB 120; MTCW

Piers, Robert
See Anthony, Piers

Pieyre de Mandiargues, Andre   1909-1991
See Mandiargues, Andre Pieyre de
See also CA 103; 136; CANR 22

Pilnyak, Boris . . . . TCLC 23
See also Vogau, Boris Andreyevich

Pincherle, Alberto   1907-1990 . . . CLC 11, 18
See also Moravia, Alberto
See also CA 25-28R; 132; CANR 33;
MTCW

Pinckney, Darryl   1953- . . . . CLC 76
See also CA 143

Pindar   518B.C.-446B.C. . . . . CMLC 12

Pineda, Cecile   1942-. . . . . CLC 39
See also CA 118

Pinero, Arthur Wing   1855-1934 . . . TCLC 32
See also CA 110; DLB 10

Pinero, Miguel (Antonio Gomez)
1946-1988 . . . . CLC 4, 55
See also CA 61-64; 125; CANR 29; HW

Pinget, Robert   1919- . . . . CLC 7, 13, 37
See also CA 85-88; DLB 83

Pink Floyd . . . . CLC 35
See also Barrett, (Roger) Syd; Gilmour,
David; Mason, Nick; Waters, Roger;
Wright, Rick

Pinkney, Edward   1802-1828 . . . . . NCLC 31

Pinkwater, Daniel Manus   1941-. . . . CLC 35
See also Pinkwater, Manus
See also AAYA 1; CA 29-32R; CANR 12,
38; CLR 4; JRDA; MAICYA; SAAS 3;
SATA 46, 76

Pinkwater, Manus
See Pinkwater, Daniel Manus
See also SATA 8

Pinsky, Robert 1940- .... **CLC 9, 19, 38**
See also CA 29-32R; CAAS 4; DLBY 82

Pinta, Harold
See Pinter, Harold

Pinter, Harold
1930- ..... **CLC 1, 3, 6, 9, 11, 15, 27, 58,**
73; DA; WLC
See also CA 5-8R; CANR 33; CDBLB 1960
to Present; DLB 13; MTCW

Pirandello, Luigi
1867-1936 ...... **TCLC 4, 29; DA; WLC**
See also CA 104

Pirsig, Robert M(aynard)
1928- .... **CLC 4, 6, 73**
See also CA 53-56; CANR 42; MTCW;
SATA 39

Pisarev, Dmitry Ivanovich
1840-1868 .... **NCLC 25**

Pix, Mary (Griffith) 1666-1709 .... **LC 8**
See also DLB 80

Pixerecourt, Guilbert de
1773-1844 .... **NCLC 39**

Plaidy, Jean
See Hibbert, Eleanor Alice Burford

Planche, James Robinson
1796-1880 .... **NCLC 42**

Plant, Robert 1948- .... **CLC 12**

Plante, David (Robert)
1940- .... **CLC 7, 23, 38**
See also CA 37-40R; CANR 12, 36;
DLBY 83; MTCW

Plath, Sylvia
1932-1963 ..... **CLC 1, 2, 3, 5, 9, 11, 14,**
17, 50, 51, 62; DA; PC 1; WLC
See also CA 19-20; CANR 34; CAP 2;
CDALB 1941-1968; DLB 5, 6; MTCW

Plato 428(?)B.C.-348(?)B.C.... **CMLC 8; DA**

Platonov, Andrei .... **TCLC 14**
See also Klimentov, Andrei Platonovich

Platt, Kin 1911- .... **CLC 26**
See also AAYA 11; CA 17-20R; CANR 11;
JRDA; SAAS 17; SATA 21

Plick et Plock
See Simenon, Georges (Jacques Christian)

Plimpton, George (Ames) 1927-..... **CLC 36**
See also AITN 1; CA 21-24R; CANR 32;
MTCW; SATA 10

Plomer, William Charles Franklin
1903-1973 .... **CLC 4, 8**
See also CA 21-22; CANR 34; CAP 2;
DLB 20; MTCW; SATA 24

Plowman, Piers
See Kavanagh, Patrick (Joseph)

Plum, J.
See Wodehouse, P(elham) G(renville)

Plumly, Stanley (Ross) 1939- ...... **CLC 33**
See also CA 108; 110; DLB 5

Plumpe, Friedrich Wilhelm
1888-1931 .... **TCLC 53**
See also CA 112

Poe, Edgar Allan
1809-1849 ..... **NCLC 1, 16; DA; PC 1;**
SSC 1; WLC
See also CDALB 1640-1865; DLB 3, 59, 73,
74; SATA 23

Poet of Titchfield Street, The
See Pound, Ezra (Weston Loomis)

Pohl, Frederik 1919- .... **CLC 18**
See also CA 61-64; CAAS 1; CANR 11, 37;
DLB 8; MTCW; SATA 24

Poirier, Louis 1910-
See Gracq, Julien
See also CA 122; 126

Poitier, Sidney 1927- .... **CLC 26**
See also BW; CA 117

Polanski, Roman 1933- .... **CLC 16**
See also CA 77-80

Poliakoff, Stephen 1952- .... **CLC 38**
See also CA 106; DLB 13

Police, The .... **CLC 26**
See also Copeland, Stewart (Armstrong);
Summers, Andrew James; Sumner,
Gordon Matthew

Pollitt, Katha 1949- .... **CLC 28**
See also CA 120; 122; MTCW

Pollock, (Mary) Sharon 1936-...... **CLC 50**
See also CA 141; DLB 60

Pomerance, Bernard 1940-........ **CLC 13**
See also CA 101

Ponge, Francis (Jean Gaston Alfred)
1899-1988 .... **CLC 6, 18**
See also CA 85-88; 126; CANR 40

Pontoppidan, Henrik 1857-1943 ... **TCLC 29**

Poole, Josephine .... **CLC 17**
See also Helyar, Jane Penelope Josephine
See also SAAS 2; SATA 5

Popa, Vasko 1922- .... **CLC 19**
See also CA 112

Pope, Alexander
1688-1744 .... **LC 3; DA; WLC**
See also CDBLB 1660-1789; DLB 95, 101

Porter, Connie (Rose) 1959(?)- ..... **CLC 70**
See also CA 142

Porter, Gene(va Grace) Stratton
1863(?)-1924 .... **TCLC 21**
See also CA 112

Porter, Katherine Anne
1890-1980 ...... **CLC 1, 3, 7, 10, 13, 15,**
27; DA; SSC 4
See also AITN 2; CA 1-4R; 101; CANR 1;
DLB 4, 9, 102; DLBY 80; MTCW;
SATA 23, 39

Porter, Peter (Neville Frederick)
1929- .... **CLC 5, 13, 33**
See also CA 85-88; DLB 40

Porter, William Sydney 1862-1910
See Henry, O.
See also CA 104; 131; CDALB 1865-1917;
DA; DLB 12, 78, 79; MTCW; YABC 2

Portillo (y Pacheco), Jose Lopez
See Lopez Portillo (y Pacheco), Jose

Post, Melville Davisson
1869-1930 .... **TCLC 39**
See also CA 110

Potok, Chaim 1929- ...... **CLC 2, 7, 14, 26**
See also AITN 1, 2; CA 17-20R; CANR 19,
35; DLB 28; MTCW; SATA 33

Potter, Beatrice
See Webb, (Martha) Beatrice (Potter)
See also MAICYA

Potter, Dennis (Christopher George)
1935- .... **CLC 58**
See also CA 107; CANR 33; MTCW

Pound, Ezra (Weston Loomis)
1885-1972 ...... **CLC 1, 2, 3, 4, 5, 7, 10,**
13, 18, 34, 48, 50; DA; PC 4; WLC
See also CA 5-8R; 37-40R; CANR 40;
CDALB 1917-1929; DLB 4, 45, 63;
MTCW

Povod, Reinaldo 1959-........... **CLC 44**
See also CA 136

Powell, Anthony (Dymoke)
1905- .... **CLC 1, 3, 7, 9, 10, 31**
See also CA 1-4R; CANR 1, 32;
CDBLB 1945-1960; DLB 15; MTCW

Powell, Dawn 1897-1965 .... **CLC 66**
See also CA 5-8R

Powell, Padgett 1952-............ **CLC 34**
See also CA 126

Powers, J(ames) F(arl)
1917- .... **CLC 1, 4, 8, 57; SSC 4**
See also CA 1-4R; CANR 2; DLB 130;
MTCW

Powers, John J(ames) 1945-
See Powers, John R.
See also CA 69-72

Powers, John R. .... **CLC 66**
See also Powers, John J(ames)

Pownall, David 1938-............ **CLC 10**
See also CA 89-92; CAAS 18; DLB 14

Powys, John Cowper
1872-1963 .... **CLC 7, 9, 15, 46**
See also CA 85-88; DLB 15; MTCW

Powys, T(heodore) F(rancis)
1875-1953 .... **TCLC 9**
See also CA 106; DLB 36

Prager, Emily 1952-............. **CLC 56**

Pratt, E(dwin) J(ohn)
1883(?)-1964 .... **CLC 19**
See also CA 141; 93-96; DLB 92

Premchand .... **TCLC 21**
See also Srivastava, Dhanpat Rai

Preussler, Otfried 1923-.......... **CLC 17**
See also CA 77-80; SATA 24

Prevert, Jacques (Henri Marie)
1900-1977 .... **CLC 15**
See also CA 77-80; 69-72; CANR 29;
MTCW; SATA 30

Prevost, Abbe (Antoine Francois)
1697-1763 .... **LC 1**

Price, (Edward) Reynolds
1933- .... **CLC 3, 6, 13, 43, 50, 63**
See also CA 1-4R; CANR 1, 37; DLB 2

Price, Richard 1949- .... **CLC 6, 12**
See also CA 49-52; CANR 3; DLBY 81

Prichard, Katharine Susannah
1883-1969 .... **CLC 46**
See also CA 11-12; CANR 33; CAP 1;
MTCW; SATA 66

Priestley, J(ohn) B(oynton)
1894-1984 .... **CLC 2, 5, 9, 34**
See also CA 9-12R; 113; CANR 33;
CDBLB 1914-1945; DLB 10, 34, 77, 100,
139; DLBY 84; MTCW

Prince 1958(?)- .... **CLC 35**

Prince, F(rank) T(empleton) 1912- .. **CLC 22**
See also CA 101; CANR 43; DLB 20

Prince Kropotkin
See Kropotkin, Peter (Aleksieevich)

Prior, Matthew 1664-1721 .... **LC 4**
See also DLB 95

Pritchard, William H(arrison)
1932- .... **CLC 34**
See also CA 65-68; CANR 23; DLB 111

Pritchett, V(ictor) S(awdon)
1900- .... **CLC 5, 13, 15, 41; SSC 14**
See also CA 61-64; CANR 31; DLB 15,
139; MTCW

Private 19022
See Manning, Frederic

Probst, Mark 1925- .... **CLC 59**
See also CA 130

Prokosch, Frederic 1908-1989.... **CLC 4, 48**
See also CA 73-76; 128; DLB 48

Prophet, The
See Dreiser, Theodore (Herman Albert)

Prose, Francine 1947-............. **CLC 45**
See also CA 109; 112

Proudhon
See Cunha, Euclides (Rodrigues Pimenta) da

Proulx, E. Annie 1935- .... **CLC 81**

Proust, (Valentin-Louis-George-Eugene-)
Marcel
1871-1922 ... **TCLC 7, 13, 33; DA; WLC**
See also CA 104; 120; DLB 65; MTCW

Prowler, Harley
See Masters, Edgar Lee

Prus, Boleslaw................. **TCLC 48**
See also Glowacki, Aleksander

Pryor, Richard (Franklin Lenox Thomas)
1940- .... **CLC 26**
See also CA 122

Przybyszewski, Stanislaw
1868-1927 .... **TCLC 36**
See also DLB 66

Pteleon
See Grieve, C(hristopher) M(urray)

Puckett, Lute
See Masters, Edgar Lee

Puig, Manuel
1932-1990 ... **CLC 3, 5, 10, 28, 65; HLC**
See also CA 45-48; CANR 2, 32; DLB 113;
HW; MTCW

Purdy, Al(fred Wellington)
1918- .... **CLC 3, 6, 14, 50**
See also CA 81-84; CAAS 17; CANR 42;
DLB 88

Purdy, James (Amos)
1923- .... **CLC 2, 4, 10, 28, 52**
See also CA 33-36R; CAAS 1; CANR 19;
DLB 2; MTCW

Pure, Simon
See Swinnerton, Frank Arthur

Pushkin, Alexander (Sergeyevich)
1799-1837 ...... **NCLC 3, 27; DA; WLC**
See also SATA 61

P'u Sung-ling 1640-1715 .... **LC 3**

Putnam, Arthur Lee
See Alger, Horatio, Jr.

Puzo, Mario 1920- .... **CLC 1, 2, 6, 36**
See also CA 65-68; CANR 4, 42; DLB 6;
MTCW

Pym, Barbara (Mary Crampton)
1913-1980 .... **CLC 13, 19, 37**
See also CA 13-14; 97-100; CANR 13, 34;
CAP 1; DLB 14; DLBY 87; MTCW

Pynchon, Thomas (Ruggles, Jr.)
1937- ..... **CLC 2, 3, 6, 9, 11, 18, 33, 62,**
72; DA; SSC 14; WLC
See also BEST 90:2; CA 17-20R; CANR 22;
DLB 2; MTCW

Q
See Quiller-Couch, Arthur Thomas

Qian Zhongshu
See Ch'ien Chung-shu

Qroll
See Dagerman, Stig (Halvard)

Quarrington, Paul (Lewis) 1953-.... **CLC 65**
See also CA 129

Quasimodo, Salvatore 1901-1968 ... **CLC 10**
See also CA 13-16; 25-28R; CAP 1;
DLB 114; MTCW

Queen, Ellery.................. **CLC 3, 11**
See also Dannay, Frederic; Davidson,
Avram; Lee, Manfred B(ennington);
Sturgeon, Theodore (Hamilton); Vance,
John Holbrook

Queen, Ellery, Jr.
See Dannay, Frederic; Lee, Manfred
B(ennington)

Queneau, Raymond
1903-1976 .... **CLC 2, 5, 10, 42**
See also CA 77-80; 69-72; CANR 32;
DLB 72; MTCW

Quevedo, Francisco de 1580-1645.... **LC 23**

Quiller-Couch, Arthur Thomas
1863-1944 .... **TCLC 53**
See also CA 118; DLB 135

Quin, Ann (Marie) 1936-1973....... **CLC 6**
See also CA 9-12R; 45-48; DLB 14

Quinn, Martin
See Smith, Martin Cruz

Quinn, Simon
See Smith, Martin Cruz

Quiroga, Horacio (Sylvestre)
1878-1937 .... **TCLC 20; HLC**
See also CA 117; 131; HW; MTCW

Quoirez, Francoise 1935-........... **CLC 9**
See also Sagan, Francoise
See also CA 49-52; CANR 6, 39; MTCW

Raabe, Wilhelm 1831-1910 .... **TCLC 45**
See also DLB 129

Rabe, David (William) 1940-... **CLC 4, 8, 33**
See also CA 85-88; CABS 3; DLB 7

Rabelais, Francois
1483-1553 .... **LC 5; DA; WLC**

Rabinovitch, Sholem 1859-1916
See Aleichem, Sholom
See also CA 104

Radcliffe, Ann (Ward) 1764-1823 .. **NCLC 6**
See also DLB 39

Radiguet, Raymond 1903-1923 .... **TCLC 29**
See also DLB 65

Radnoti, Miklos 1909-1944 .... **TCLC 16**
See also CA 118

Rado, James 1939-............... **CLC 17**
See also CA 105

Radvanyi, Netty 1900-1983
See Seghers, Anna
See also CA 85-88; 110

Raeburn, John (Hay) 1941-........ **CLC 34**
See also CA 57-60

Ragni, Gerome 1942-1991 .... **CLC 17**
See also CA 105; 134

Rahv, Philip 1908-1973 .... **CLC 24**
See also Greenberg, Ivan
See also DLB 137

Raine, Craig 1944-............... **CLC 32**
See also CA 108; CANR 29; DLB 40

Raine, Kathleen (Jessie) 1908- ... **CLC 7, 45**
See also CA 85-88; DLB 20; MTCW

Rainis, Janis 1865-1929 .... **TCLC 29**

Rakosi, Carl..................... **CLC 47**
See also Rawley, Callman
See also CAAS 5

Raleigh, Richard
See Lovecraft, H(oward) P(hillips)

Rallentando, H. P.
See Sayers, Dorothy L(eigh)

Ramal, Walter
See de la Mare, Walter (John)

Ramon, Juan
See Jimenez (Mantecon), Juan Ramon

Ramos, Graciliano 1892-1953 ..... **TCLC 32**

Rampersad, Arnold 1941-......... **CLC 44**
See also CA 127; 133; DLB 111

Rampling, Anne
See Rice, Anne

Ramuz, Charles-Ferdinand
1878-1947 .... **TCLC 33**

Rand, Ayn
1905-1982 ...... **CLC 3, 30, 44, 79; DA;**
WLC
See also AAYA 10; CA 13-16R; 105;
CANR 27; MTCW

Randall, Dudley (Felker)
1914- .... **CLC 1; BLC**
See also BW; CA 25-28R; CANR 23;
DLB 41

Randall, Robert
See Silverberg, Robert

Ranger, Ken
See Creasey, John

Ransom, John Crowe
1888-1974 .... **CLC 2, 4, 5, 11, 24**
See also CA 5-8R; 49-52; CANR 6, 34;
DLB 45, 63; MTCW

Rao, Raja 1909- .... **CLC 25, 56**
See also CA 73-76; MTCW

Raphael, Frederic (Michael)
1931- .... CLC **2, 14**
See also CA 1-4R; CANR 1; DLB 14

Ratcliffe, James P.
See Mencken, H(enry) L(ouis)

Rathbone, Julian 1935- .... CLC **41**
See also CA 101; CANR 34

Rattigan, Terence (Mervyn)
1911-1977 .... CLC **7**
See also CA 85-88; 73-76;
CDBLB 1945-1960; DLB 13; MTCW

Ratushinskaya, Irina 1954- .... CLC **54**
See also CA 129

Raven, Simon (Arthur Noel)
1927- .... CLC **14**
See also CA 81-84

Rawley, Callman 1903-
See Rakosi, Carl
See also CA 21-24R; CANR 12, 32

Rawlings, Marjorie Kinnan
1896-1953 .... TCLC **4**
See also CA 104; 137; DLB 9, 22, 102;
JRDA; MAICYA; YABC 1

Ray, Satyajit 1921-1992....... CLC **16, 76**
See also CA 114; 137

Read, Herbert Edward 1893-1968.... CLC **4**
See also CA 85-88; 25-28R; DLB 20

Read, Piers Paul 1941- ...... CLC **4, 10, 25**
See also CA 21-24R; CANR 38; DLB 14;
SATA 21

Reade, Charles 1814-1884 .... NCLC **2**
See also DLB 21

Reade, Hamish
See Gray, Simon (James Holliday)

Reading, Peter 1946- .... CLC **47**
See also CA 103; DLB 40

Reaney, James 1926- .... CLC **13**
See also CA 41-44R; CAAS 15; CANR 42;
DLB 68; SATA 43

Rebreanu, Liviu 1885-1944 .... TCLC **28**

Rechy, John (Francisco)
1934- .... CLC **1, 7, 14, 18; HLC**
See also CA 5-8R; CAAS 4; CANR 6, 32;
DLB 122; DLBY 82; HW

Redcam, Tom 1870-1933 .... TCLC **25**

Reddin, Keith.................... CLC **67**

Redgrove, Peter (William)
1932- .... CLC **6, 41**
See also CA 1-4R; CANR 3, 39; DLB 40

Redmon, Anne................... CLC **22**
See also Nightingale, Anne Redmon
See also DLBY 86

Reed, Eliot
See Ambler, Eric

Reed, Ishmael
1938- ... CLC **2, 3, 5, 6, 13, 32, 60; BLC**
See also BW; CA 21-24R; CANR 25;
DLB 2, 5, 33; DLBD 8; MTCW

Reed, John (Silas) 1887-1920 ..... TCLC **9**
See also CA 106

Reed, Lou.................... CLC **21**
See also Firbank, Louis

Reeve, Clara 1729-1807 .... NCLC **19**
See also DLB 39

Reid, Christopher (John) 1949-..... CLC **33**
See also CA 140; DLB 40

Reid, Desmond
See Moorcock, Michael (John)

Reid Banks, Lynne 1929-
See Banks, Lynne Reid
See also CA 1-4R; CANR 6, 22, 38;
CLR 24; JRDA; MAICYA; SATA 22, 75

Reilly, William K.
See Creasey, John

Reiner, Max
See Caldwell, (Janet Miriam) Taylor
(Holland)

Reis, Ricardo
See Pessoa, Fernando (Antonio Nogueira)

Remarque, Erich Maria
1898-1970 .... CLC **21; DA**
See also CA 77-80; 29-32R; DLB 56;
MTCW

Remizov, A.
See Remizov, Aleksei (Mikhailovich)

Remizov, A. M.
See Remizov, Aleksei (Mikhailovich)

Remizov, Aleksei (Mikhailovich)
1877-1957 .... TCLC **27**
See also CA 125; 133

Renan, Joseph Ernest
1823-1892 .... NCLC **26**

Renard, Jules 1864-1910 .... TCLC **17**
See also CA 117

Renault, Mary.............. CLC **3, 11, 17**
See also Challans, Mary
See also DLBY 83

Rendell, Ruth (Barbara) 1930- .. CLC **28, 48**
See also Vine, Barbara
See also CA 109; CANR 32; DLB 87;
MTCW

Renoir, Jean 1894-1979 .... CLC **20**
See also CA 129; 85-88

Resnais, Alain 1922-.............. CLC **16**

Reverdy, Pierre 1889-1960 .... CLC **53**
See also CA 97-100; 89-92

Rexroth, Kenneth
1905-1982 ...... CLC **1, 2, 6, 11, 22, 49**
See also CA 5-8R; 107; CANR 14, 34;
CDALB 1941-1968; DLB 16, 48;
DLBY 82; MTCW

Reyes, Alfonso 1889-1959 .... TCLC **33**
See also CA 131; HW

Reyes y Basoalto, Ricardo Eliecer Neftali
See Neruda, Pablo

Reymont, Wladyslaw (Stanislaw)
1868(?)-1925 .... TCLC **5**
See also CA 104

Reynolds, Jonathan 1942- .... CLC **6, 38**
See also CA 65-68; CANR 28

Reynolds, Joshua 1723-1792 .... LC **15**
See also DLB 104

Reynolds, Michael Shane 1937- .... CLC **44**
See also CA 65-68; CANR 9

Reznikoff, Charles 1894-1976 .... CLC **9**
See also CA 33-36; 61-64; CAP 2; DLB 28,
45

Rezzori (d'Arezzo), Gregor von
1914- .... CLC **25**
See also CA 122; 136

Rhine, Richard
See Silverstein, Alvin

Rhodes, Eugene Manlove
1869-1934 .... TCLC **53**

R'hoone
See Balzac, Honore de

Rhys, Jean
1890(?)-1979 .... CLC **2, 4, 6, 14, 19, 51**
See also CA 25-28R; 85-88; CANR 35;
CDBLB 1945-1960; DLB 36, 117; MTCW

Ribeiro, Darcy 1922- .... CLC **34**
See also CA 33-36R

Ribeiro, Joao Ubaldo (Osorio Pimentel)
1941- .... CLC **10, 67**
See also CA 81-84

Ribman, Ronald (Burt) 1932- .... CLC **7**
See also CA 21-24R

Ricci, Nino 1959-................. CLC **70**
See also CA 137

Rice, Anne 1941- .... CLC **41**
See also AAYA 9; BEST 89:2; CA 65-68;
CANR 12, 36

Rice, Elmer (Leopold)
1892-1967 .... CLC **7, 49**
See also CA 21-22; 25-28R; CAP 2; DLB 4,
7; MTCW

Rice, Tim 1944- .... CLC **21**
See also CA 103

Rich, Adrienne (Cecile)
1929- .... CLC **3, 6, 7, 11, 18, 36, 73, 76;
PC 5**
See also CA 9-12R; CANR 20; DLB 5, 67;
MTCW

Rich, Barbara
See Graves, Robert (von Ranke)

Rich, Robert
See Trumbo, Dalton

Richards, David Adams 1950-...... CLC **59**
See also CA 93-96; DLB 53

Richards, I(vor) A(rmstrong)
1893-1979 .... CLC **14, 24**
See also CA 41-44R; 89-92; CANR 34;
DLB 27

Richardson, Anne
See Roiphe, Anne Richardson

Richardson, Dorothy Miller
1873-1957 .... TCLC **3**
See also CA 104; DLB 36

Richardson, Ethel Florence (Lindesay)
1870-1946
See Richardson, Henry Handel
See also CA 105

Richardson, Henry Handel......... TCLC **4**
See also Richardson, Ethel Florence
(Lindesay)

Richardson, Samuel
1689-1761 .... LC **1; DA; WLC**
See also CDBLB 1660-1789; DLB 39

Schneider, Leonard Alfred 1925-1966
See Bruce, Lenny
See also CA 89-92

Schnitzler, Arthur
1862-1931 . . . . **TCLC 4; SSC 15**
See also CA 104; DLB 81, 118

Schor, Sandra (M.) 1932(?)-1990 . . . **CLC 65**
See also CA 132

Schorer, Mark 1908-1977 . . . . **CLC 9**
See also CA 5-8R; 73-76; CANR 7;
DLB 103

Schrader, Paul (Joseph) 1946- . . . . . **CLC 26**
See also CA 37-40R; CANR 41; DLB 44

Schreiner, Olive (Emilie Albertina)
1855-1920 . . . . **TCLC 9**
See also CA 105; DLB 18

Schulberg, Budd (Wilson)
1914- . . . . **CLC 7, 48**
See also CA 25-28R; CANR 19; DLB 6, 26,
28; DLBY 81

Schulz, Bruno
1892-1942 . . . . **TCLC 5, 51; SSC 13**
See also CA 115; 123

Schulz, Charles M(onroe) 1922- . . . . **CLC 12**
See also CA 9-12R; CANR 6; SATA 10

Schumacher, E(rnst) F(riedrich)
1911-1977 . . . . **CLC 80**
See also CA 81-84; 73-76; CANR 34

Schuyler, James Marcus
1923-1991 . . . . **CLC 5, 23**
See also CA 101; 134; DLB 5

Schwartz, Delmore (David)
1913-1966 . . . . . . **CLC 2, 4, 10, 45; PC 8**
See also CA 17-18; 25-28R; CANR 35;
CAP 2; DLB 28, 48; MTCW

Schwartz, Ernst
See Ozu, Yasujiro

Schwartz, John Burnham 1965- . . . . **CLC 59**
See also CA 132

Schwartz, Lynne Sharon 1939- . . . . . **CLC 31**
See also CA 103; CANR 44

Schwartz, Muriel A.
See Eliot, T(homas) S(tearns)

Schwarz-Bart, Andre 1928- . . . . **CLC 2, 4**
See also CA 89-92

Schwarz-Bart, Simone 1938- . . . . **CLC 7**
See also CA 97-100

Schwob, (Mayer Andre) Marcel
1867-1905 . . . . **TCLC 20**
See also CA 117; DLB 123

Sciascia, Leonardo
1921-1989 . . . . **CLC 8, 9, 41**
See also CA 85-88; 130; CANR 35; MTCW

Scoppettone, Sandra 1936- . . . . **CLC 26**
See also AAYA 11; CA 5-8R; CANR 41;
SATA 9

Scorsese, Martin 1942- . . . . **CLC 20**
See also CA 110; 114

Scotland, Jay
See Jakes, John (William)

Scott, Duncan Campbell
1862-1947 . . . . **TCLC 6**
See also CA 104; DLB 92

Scott, Evelyn 1893-1963 . . . . **CLC 43**
See also CA 104; 112; DLB 9, 48

Scott, F(rancis) R(eginald)
1899-1985 . . . . **CLC 22**
See also CA 101; 114; DLB 88

Scott, Frank
See Scott, F(rancis) R(eginald)

Scott, Joanna 1960- . . . . **CLC 50**
See also CA 126

Scott, Paul (Mark) 1920-1978 . . . . **CLC 9, 60**
See also CA 81-84; 77-80; CANR 33;
DLB 14; MTCW

Scott, Walter
1771-1832 . . . . **NCLC 15; DA; WLC**
See also CDBLB 1789-1832; DLB 93, 107,
116; YABC 2

Scribe, (Augustin) Eugene
1791-1861 . . . . **NCLC 16**

Scrum, R.
See Crumb, R(obert)

Scudery, Madeleine de 1607-1701 . . . . . **LC 2**

Scum
See Crumb, R(obert)

Scumbag, Little Bobby
See Crumb, R(obert)

Seabrook, John
See Hubbard, L(afayette) Ron(ald)

Sealy, I. Allan 1951- . . . . **CLC 55**

Search, Alexander
See Pessoa, Fernando (Antonio Nogueira)

Sebastian, Lee
See Silverberg, Robert

Sebastian Owl
See Thompson, Hunter S(tockton)

Sebestyen, Ouida 1924- . . . . **CLC 30**
See also AAYA 8; CA 107; CANR 40;
CLR 17; JRDA; MAICYA; SAAS 10;
SATA 39

Secundus, H. Scriblerus
See Fielding, Henry

Sedges, John
See Buck, Pearl S(ydenstricker)

Sedgwick, Catharine Maria
1789-1867 . . . . **NCLC 19**
See also DLB 1, 74

Seelye, John 1931- . . . . **CLC 7**

Seferiades, Giorgos Stylianou 1900-1971
See Seferis, George
See also CA 5-8R; 33-36R; CANR 5, 36;
MTCW

Seferis, George . . . . **CLC 5, 11**
See also Seferiades, Giorgos Stylianou

Segal, Erich (Wolf) 1937- . . . . **CLC 3, 10**
See also BEST 89:1; CA 25-28R; CANR 20,
36; DLBY 86; MTCW

Seger, Bob 1945- . . . . **CLC 35**

Seghers, Anna . . . . **CLC 7**
See also Radvanyi, Netty
See also DLB 69

Seidel, Frederick (Lewis) 1936- . . . . . **CLC 18**
See also CA 13-16R; CANR 8; DLBY 84

Seifert, Jaroslav 1901-1986 . . . . . **CLC 34, 44**
See also CA 127; MTCW

Sei Shonagon c. 966-1017(?) . . . . . . **CMLC 6**

Selby, Hubert, Jr. 1928- . . . . . **CLC 1, 2, 4, 8**
See also CA 13-16R; CANR 33; DLB 2

Selzer, Richard 1928- . . . . **CLC 74**
See also CA 65-68; CANR 14

Sembene, Ousmane
See Ousmane, Sembene

Senancour, Etienne Pivert de
1770-1846 . . . . **NCLC 16**
See also DLB 119

Sender, Ramon (Jose)
1902-1982 . . . . **CLC 8; HLC**
See also CA 5-8R; 105; CANR 8; HW;
MTCW

Seneca, Lucius Annaeus
4B.C.-65 . . . . **CMLC 6**

Senghor, Leopold Sedar
1906- . . . . **CLC 54; BLC**
See also BW; CA 116; 125; MTCW

Serling, (Edward) Rod(man)
1924-1975 . . . . **CLC 30**
See also AITN 1; CA 65-68; 57-60; DLB 26

Serna, Ramon Gomez de la
See Gomez de la Serna, Ramon

Serpieres
See Guillevic, (Eugene)

Service, Robert
See Service, Robert W(illiam)
See also DLB 92

Service, Robert W(illiam)
1874(?)-1958 . . . . . . **TCLC 15; DA; WLC**
See also Service, Robert
See also CA 115; 140; SATA 20

Seth, Vikram 1952- . . . . **CLC 43**
See also CA 121; 127; DLB 120

Seton, Cynthia Propper
1926-1982 . . . . **CLC 27**
See also CA 5-8R; 108; CANR 7

Seton, Ernest (Evan) Thompson
1860-1946 . . . . **TCLC 31**
See also CA 109; DLB 92; JRDA; SATA 18

Seton-Thompson, Ernest
See Seton, Ernest (Evan) Thompson

Settle, Mary Lee 1918- . . . . **CLC 19, 61**
See also CA 89-92; CAAS 1; CANR 44;
DLB 6

Seuphor, Michel
See Arp, Jean

Sevigne, Marie (de Rabutin-Chantal) Marquise
de 1626-1696 . . . . **LC 11**

Sexton, Anne (Harvey)
1928-1974 . . . . **CLC 2, 4, 6, 8, 10, 15, 53;**
DA; PC 2; WLC
See also CA 1-4R; 53-56; CABS 2;
CANR 3, 36; CDALB 1941-1968; DLB 5;
MTCW; SATA 10

Shaara, Michael (Joseph Jr.)
1929-1988 . . . . **CLC 15**
See also AITN 1; CA 102; DLBY 83

Shackleton, C. C.
See Aldiss, Brian W(ilson)

Shacochis, Bob . . . . **CLC 39**
See also Shacochis, Robert G.

Shacochis, Robert G. 1951-
See Shacochis, Bob
See also CA 119; 124

Shaffer, Anthony (Joshua) 1926-.... **CLC 19**
See also CA 110; 116; DLB 13

Shaffer, Peter (Levin)
1926- .... **CLC 5, 14, 18, 37, 60**
See also CA 25-28R; CANR 25;
CDBLB 1960 to Present; DLB 13;
MTCW

Shakey, Bernard
See Young, Neil

Shalamov, Varlam (Tikhonovich)
1907(?)-1982 .... **CLC 18**
See also CA 129; 105

Shamlu, Ahmad 1925- .... **CLC 10**

Shammas, Anton 1951-............ **CLC 55**

Shange, Ntozake
1948- .... **CLC 8, 25, 38, 74; BLC; DC 3**
See also AAYA 9; BW; CA 85-88; CABS 3;
CANR 27; DLB 38; MTCW

Shanley, John Patrick 1950-....... **CLC 75**
See also CA 128; 133

Shapcott, Thomas William 1935- ... **CLC 38**
See also CA 69-72

Shapiro, Jane.................... **CLC 76**

Shapiro, Karl (Jay) 1913- .. **CLC 4, 8, 15, 53**
See also CA 1-4R; CAAS 6; CANR 1, 36;
DLB 48; MTCW

Sharp, William 1855-1905 .... **TCLC 39**

Sharpe, Thomas Ridley 1928-
See Sharpe, Tom
See also CA 114; 122

Sharpe, Tom.................... **CLC 36**
See also Sharpe, Thomas Ridley
See also DLB 14

Shaw, Bernard.................... **TCLC 45**
See also Shaw, George Bernard

Shaw, G. Bernard
See Shaw, George Bernard

Shaw, George Bernard
1856-1950 .... **TCLC 3, 9, 21; DA; WLC**
See also Shaw, Bernard
See also CA 104; 128; CDBLB 1914-1945;
DLB 10, 57; MTCW

Shaw, Henry Wheeler
1818-1885 .... **NCLC 15**
See also DLB 11

Shaw, Irwin 1913-1984...... **CLC 7, 23, 34**
See also AITN 1; CA 13-16R; 112;
CANR 21; CDALB 1941-1968; DLB 6,
102; DLBY 84; MTCW

Shaw, Robert 1927-1978 .... **CLC 5**
See also AITN 1; CA 1-4R; 81-84;
CANR 4; DLB 13, 14

Shaw, T. E.
See Lawrence, T(homas) E(dward)

Shawn, Wallace 1943- .... **CLC 41**
See also CA 112

Sheed, Wilfrid (John Joseph)
1930- .... **CLC 2, 4, 10, 53**
See also CA 65-68; CANR 30; DLB 6;
MTCW

Sheldon, Alice Hastings Bradley
1915(?)-1987
See Tiptree, James, Jr.
See also CA 108; 122; CANR 34; MTCW

Sheldon, John
See Bloch, Robert (Albert)

Shelley, Mary Wollstonecraft (Godwin)
1797-1851 .... **NCLC 14; DA; WLC**
See also CDBLB 1789-1832; DLB 110, 116;
SATA 29

Shelley, Percy Bysshe
1792-1822 .... **NCLC 18; DA; WLC**
See also CDBLB 1789-1832; DLB 96, 110

Shepard, Jim 1956-.............. **CLC 36**
See also CA 137

Shepard, Lucius 1947- .... **CLC 34**
See also CA 128; 141

Shepard, Sam
1943- .... **CLC 4, 6, 17, 34, 41, 44**
See also AAYA 1; CA 69-72; CABS 3;
CANR 22; DLB 7; MTCW

Shepherd, Michael
See Ludlum, Robert

Sherburne, Zoa (Morin) 1912-...... **CLC 30**
See also CA 1-4R; CANR 3, 37; MAICYA;
SAAS 18; SATA 3

Sheridan, Frances 1724-1766........ **LC 7**
See also DLB 39, 84

Sheridan, Richard Brinsley
1751-1816 ... **NCLC 5; DA; DC 1; WLC**
See also CDBLB 1660-1789; DLB 89

Sherman, Jonathan Marc.......... **CLC 55**

Sherman, Martin 1941(?)- .... **CLC 19**
See also CA 116; 123

Sherwin, Judith Johnson 1936-... **CLC 7, 15**
See also CA 25-28R; CANR 34

Sherwood, Frances 1940-.......... **CLC 81**

Sherwood, Robert E(mmet)
1896-1955 .... **TCLC 3**
See also CA 104; DLB 7, 26

Shiel, M(atthew) P(hipps)
1865-1947 .... **TCLC 8**
See also CA 106

Shiga, Naoya 1883-1971.......... **CLC 33**
See also CA 101; 33-36R

Shimazaki Haruki 1872-1943
See Shimazaki Toson
See also CA 105; 134

Shimazaki Toson................ **TCLC 5**
See also Shimazaki Haruki

Sholokhov, Mikhail (Aleksandrovich)
1905-1984 .... **CLC 7, 15**
See also CA 101; 112; MTCW; SATA 36

Shone, Patric
See Hanley, James

Shreve, Susan Richards 1939-...... **CLC 23**
See also CA 49-52; CAAS 5; CANR 5, 38;
MAICYA; SATA 41, 46

Shue, Larry 1946-1985............ **CLC 52**
See also CA 117

Shu-Jen, Chou 1881-1936
See Hsun, Lu
See also CA 104

Shulman, Alix Kates 1932- ...... **CLC 2, 10**
See also CA 29-32R; CANR 43; SATA 7

Shuster, Joe 1914- .... **CLC 21**

Shute, Nevil.................... **CLC 30**
See also Norway, Nevil Shute

Shuttle, Penelope (Diane) 1947- ..... **CLC 7**
See also CA 93-96; CANR 39; DLB 14, 40

Sidney, Mary 1561-1621 .... **LC 19**

Sidney, Sir Philip 1554-1586.... **LC 19; DA**
See also CDBLB Before 1660

Siegel, Jerome 1914- .... **CLC 21**
See also CA 116

Siegel, Jerry
See Siegel, Jerome

Sienkiewicz, Henryk (Adam Alexander Pius)
1846-1916 .... **TCLC 3**
See also CA 104; 134

Sierra, Gregorio Martinez
See Martinez Sierra, Gregorio

Sierra, Maria (de la O'LeJarraga) Martinez
See Martinez Sierra, Maria (de la
O'LeJarraga)

Sigal, Clancy 1926-................ **CLC 7**
See also CA 1-4R

Sigourney, Lydia Howard (Huntley)
1791-1865 .... **NCLC 21**
See also DLB 1, 42, 73

Siguenza y Gongora, Carlos de
1645-1700 .... **LC 8**

Sigurjonsson, Johann 1880-1919... **TCLC 27**

Sikelianos, Angelos 1884-1951 .... **TCLC 39**

Silkin, Jon 1930- .... **CLC 2, 6, 43**
See also CA 5-8R; CAAS 5; DLB 27

Silko, Leslie Marmon
1948- .... **CLC 23, 74; DA**
See also CA 115; 122

Sillanpaa, Frans Eemil 1888-1964... **CLC 19**
See also CA 129; 93-96; MTCW

Sillitoe, Alan
1928- .... **CLC 1, 3, 6, 10, 19, 57**
See also AITN 1; CA 9-12R; CAAS 2;
CANR 8, 26; CDBLB 1960 to Present;
DLB 14, 139; MTCW; SATA 61

Silone, Ignazio 1900-1978 .... **CLC 4**
See also CA 25-28; 81-84; CANR 34;
CAP 2; MTCW

Silver, Joan Micklin 1935- .... **CLC 20**
See also CA 114; 121

Silver, Nicholas
See Faust, Frederick (Schiller)

Silverberg, Robert 1935- .... **CLC 7**
See also CA 1-4R; CAAS 3; CANR 1, 20,
36; DLB 8; MAICYA; MTCW; SATA 13

Silverstein, Alvin 1933- .... **CLC 17**
See also CA 49-52; CANR 2; CLR 25;
JRDA; MAICYA; SATA 8, 69

Silverstein, Virginia B(arbara Opshelor)
1937- .... **CLC 17**
See also CA 49-52; CANR 2; CLR 25;
JRDA; MAICYA; SATA 8, 69

Sim, Georges
See Simenon, Georges (Jacques Christian)

Simak, Clifford D(onald)
1904-1988 . . . . **CLC 1, 55**
See also CA 1-4R; 125; CANR 1, 35;
DLB 8; MTCW; SATA 56

Simenon, Georges (Jacques Christian)
1903-1989 . . . . . . **CLC 1, 2, 3, 8, 18, 47**
See also CA 85-88; 129; CANR 35;
DLB 72; DLBY 89; MTCW

Simic, Charles 1938-. . . **CLC 6, 9, 22, 49, 68**
See also CA 29-32R; CAAS 4; CANR 12,
33; DLB 105

Simmons, Charles (Paul) 1924-. . . . . **CLC 57**
See also CA 89-92

Simmons, Dan 1948-. . . . . **CLC 44**
See also CA 138

Simmons, James (Stewart Alexander)
1933- . . . . **CLC 43**
See also CA 105; DLB 40

Simms, William Gilmore
1806-1870 . . . . **NCLC 3**
See also DLB 3, 30, 59, 73

Simon, Carly 1945-. . . . . **CLC 26**
See also CA 105

Simon, Claude 1913-. . . . . . . **CLC 4, 9, 15, 39**
See also CA 89-92; CANR 33; DLB 83;
MTCW

Simon, (Marvin) Neil
1927- . . . . **CLC 6, 11, 31, 39, 70**
See also AITN 1; CA 21-24R; CANR 26;
DLB 7; MTCW

Simon, Paul 1942(?)- . . . . **CLC 17**
See also CA 116

Simonon, Paul 1956(?)- . . . . **CLC 30**
See also Clash, The

Simpson, Harriette
See Arnow, Harriette (Louisa) Simpson

Simpson, Louis (Aston Marantz)
1923- . . . . **CLC 4, 7, 9, 32**
See also CA 1-4R; CAAS 4; CANR 1;
DLB 5; MTCW

Simpson, Mona (Elizabeth) 1957-. . . **CLC 44**
See also CA 122; 135

Simpson, N(orman) F(rederick)
1919- . . . . **CLC 29**
See also CA 13-16R; DLB 13

Sinclair, Andrew (Annandale)
1935- . . . . **CLC 2, 14**
See also CA 9-12R; CAAS 5; CANR 14, 38;
DLB 14; MTCW

Sinclair, Emil
See Hesse, Hermann

Sinclair, Iain 1943-. . . . . **CLC 76**
See also CA 132

Sinclair, Iain MacGregor
See Sinclair, Iain

Sinclair, Mary Amelia St. Clair 1865(?)-1946
See Sinclair, May
See also CA 104

Sinclair, May. . . . . **TCLC 3, 11**
See also Sinclair, Mary Amelia St. Clair
See also DLB 36, 135

Sinclair, Upton (Beall)
1878-1968 . . . . . . **CLC 1, 11, 15, 63; DA;
WLC**
See also CA 5-8R; 25-28R; CANR 7;
CDALB 1929-1941; DLB 9; MTCW;
SATA 9

Singer, Isaac
See Singer, Isaac Bashevis

Singer, Isaac Bashevis
1904-1991 . . . . **CLC 1, 3, 6, 9, 11, 15, 23,
38, 69; DA; SSC 3; WLC**
See also AITN 1, 2; CA 1-4R; 134;
CANR 1, 39; CDALB 1941-1968; CLR 1;
DLB 6, 28, 52; DLBY 91; JRDA;
MAICYA; MTCW; SATA 3, 27;
SATA-Obit 68

Singer, Israel Joshua 1893-1944 . . . **TCLC 33**

Singh, Khushwant 1915-. . . . . **CLC 11**
See also CA 9-12R; CAAS 9; CANR 6

Sinjohn, John
See Galsworthy, John

Sinyavsky, Andrei (Donatevich)
1925- . . . . **CLC 8**
See also CA 85-88

Sirin, V.
See Nabokov, Vladimir (Vladimirovich)

Sissman, L(ouis) E(dward)
1928-1976 . . . . **CLC 9, 18**
See also CA 21-24R; 65-68; CANR 13;
DLB 5

Sisson, C(harles) H(ubert) 1914-. . . . . **CLC 8**
See also CA 1-4R; CAAS 3; CANR 3;
DLB 27

Sitwell, Dame Edith
1887-1964 . . . . **CLC 2, 9, 67; PC 3**
See also CA 9-12R; CANR 35;
CDBLB 1945-1960; DLB 20; MTCW

Sjoewall, Maj 1935-. . . . . **CLC 7**
See also CA 65-68

Sjowall, Maj
See Sjoewall, Maj

Skelton, Robin 1925-. . . . . **CLC 13**
See also AITN 2; CA 5-8R; CAAS 5;
CANR 28; DLB 27, 53

Skolimowski, Jerzy 1938- . . . . **CLC 20**
See also CA 128

Skram, Amalie (Bertha)
1847-1905 . . . . **TCLC 25**

Skvorecky, Josef (Vaclav)
1924- . . . . **CLC 15, 39, 69**
See also CA 61-64; CAAS 1; CANR 10, 34;
MTCW

Slade, Bernard. . . . . **CLC 11, 46**
See also Newbound, Bernard Slade
See also CAAS 9; DLB 53

Slaughter, Carolyn 1946-. . . . . **CLC 56**
See also CA 85-88

Slaughter, Frank G(ill) 1908- . . . . . . **CLC 29**
See also AITN 2; CA 5-8R; CANR 5

Slavitt, David R(ytman) 1935-. . . . **CLC 5, 14**
See also CA 21-24R; CAAS 3; CANR 41;
DLB 5, 6

Slesinger, Tess 1905-1945 . . . . **TCLC 10**
See also CA 107; DLB 102

Slessor, Kenneth 1901-1971. . . . . **CLC 14**
See also CA 102; 89-92

Slowacki, Juliusz 1809-1849 . . . . . **NCLC 15**

Smart, Christopher 1722-1771. . . . . . . **LC 3**
See also DLB 109

Smart, Elizabeth 1913-1986. . . . . **CLC 54**
See also CA 81-84; 118; DLB 88

Smiley, Jane (Graves) 1949- . . . . **CLC 53, 76**
See also CA 104; CANR 30

Smith, A(rthur) J(ames) M(arshall)
1902-1980 . . . . **CLC 15**
See also CA 1-4R; 102; CANR 4; DLB 88

Smith, Betty (Wehner) 1896-1972. . . **CLC 19**
See also CA 5-8R; 33-36R; DLBY 82;
SATA 6

Smith, Charlotte (Turner)
1749-1806 . . . . **NCLC 23**
See also DLB 39, 109

Smith, Clark Ashton 1893-1961 . . . . **CLC 43**
See also CA 143

Smith, Dave. . . . . **CLC 22, 42**
See also Smith, David (Jeddie)
See also CAAS 7; DLB 5

Smith, David (Jeddie) 1942-
See Smith, Dave
See also CA 49-52; CANR 1

Smith, Florence Margaret
1902-1971 . . . . **CLC 8**
See also Smith, Stevie
See also CA 17-18; 29-32R; CANR 35;
CAP 2; MTCW

Smith, Iain Crichton 1928- . . . . **CLC 64**
See also CA 21-24R; DLB 40, 139

Smith, John 1580(?)-1631 . . . . **LC 9**

Smith, Johnston
See Crane, Stephen (Townley)

Smith, Lee 1944-. . . . . **CLC 25, 73**
See also CA 114; 119; DLBY 83

Smith, Martin
See Smith, Martin Cruz

Smith, Martin Cruz 1942-. . . . . **CLC 25**
See also BEST 89:4; CA 85-88; CANR 6,
23, 43

Smith, Mary-Ann Tirone 1944-. . . . . **CLC 39**
See also CA 118; 136

Smith, Patti 1946- . . . . **CLC 12**
See also CA 93-96

Smith, Pauline (Urmson)
1882-1959 . . . . **TCLC 25**

Smith, Rosamond
See Oates, Joyce Carol

Smith, Sheila Kaye
See Kaye-Smith, Sheila

Smith, Stevie. . . . . **CLC 3, 8, 25, 44**
See also Smith, Florence Margaret
See also DLB 20

Smith, Wilbur A(ddison) 1933-. . . . . . **CLC 33**
See also CA 13-16R; CANR 7; MTCW

Smith, William Jay 1918- . . . . **CLC 6**
See also CA 5-8R; CANR 44; DLB 5;
MAICYA; SATA 2, 68

Smith, Woodrow Wilson
See Kuttner, Henry

Smolenskin, Peretz 1842-1885.... **NCLC 30**

Smollett, Tobias (George) 1721-1771 .. **LC 2**
  See also CDBLB 1660-1789; DLB 39, 104

Snodgrass, W(illiam) D(e Witt)
  1926- .... **CLC 2, 6, 10, 18, 68**
  See also CA 1-4R; CANR 6, 36; DLB 5;
  MTCW

Snow, C(harles) P(ercy)
  1905-1980 ...... **CLC 1, 4, 6, 9, 13, 19**
  See also CA 5-8R; 101; CANR 28;
  CDBLB 1945-1960; DLB 15, 77; MTCW

Snow, Frances Compton
  See Adams, Henry (Brooks)

Snyder, Gary (Sherman)
  1930- .... **CLC 1, 2, 5, 9, 32**
  See also CA 17-20R; CANR 30; DLB 5, 16

Snyder, Zilpha Keatley 1927- ...... **CLC 17**
  See also CA 9-12R; CANR 38; CLR 31;
  JRDA; MAICYA; SAAS 2; SATA 1, 28,
  75

Soares, Bernardo
  See Pessoa, Fernando (Antonio Nogueira)

Sobh, A.
  See Shamlu, Ahmad

Sobol, Joshua.................. **CLC 60**

Soderberg, Hjalmar 1869-1941 .... **TCLC 39**

Sodergran, Edith (Irene)
  See Soedergran, Edith (Irene)

Soedergran, Edith (Irene)
  1892-1923 .... **TCLC 31**

Softly, Edgar
  See Lovecraft, H(oward) P(hillips)

Softly, Edward
  See Lovecraft, H(oward) P(hillips)

Sokolov, Raymond 1941-.......... **CLC 7**
  See also CA 85-88

Solo, Jay
  See Ellison, Harlan

Sologub, Fyodor .... **TCLC 9**
  See also Teternikov, Fyodor Kuzmich

Solomons, Ikey Esquir
  See Thackeray, William Makepeace

Solomos, Dionysios 1798-1857 ... **NCLC 15**

Solwoska, Mara
  See French, Marilyn

Solzhenitsyn, Aleksandr I(sayevich)
  1918- ...... **CLC 1, 2, 4, 7, 9, 10, 18, 26,
                              34, 78; DA; WLC**
  See also AITN 1; CA 69-72; CANR 40;
  MTCW

Somers, Jane
  See Lessing, Doris (May)

Somerville, Edith 1858-1949 ...... **TCLC 51**
  See also DLB 135

Somerville & Ross
  See Martin, Violet Florence; Somerville,
  Edith

Sommer, Scott 1951- .... **CLC 25**
  See also CA 106

Sondheim, Stephen (Joshua)
  1930- .... **CLC 30, 39**
  See also AAYA 11; CA 103

Sontag, Susan 1933-... **CLC 1, 2, 10, 13, 31**
  See also CA 17-20R; CANR 25; DLB 2, 67;
  MTCW

Sophocles
  496(?)B.C.-406(?)B.C..... **CMLC 2; DA;
                                            DC 1**

Sorel, Julia
  See Drexler, Rosalyn

Sorrentino, Gilbert
  1929- .... **CLC 3, 7, 14, 22, 40**
  See also CA 77-80; CANR 14, 33; DLB 5;
  DLBY 80

Soto, Gary 1952-........ **CLC 32, 80; HLC**
  See also AAYA 10; CA 119; 125; DLB 82;
  HW; JRDA

Soupault, Philippe 1897-1990 ...... **CLC 68**
  See also CA 116; 131

Souster, (Holmes) Raymond
  1921- .... **CLC 5, 14**
  See also CA 13-16R; CAAS 14; CANR 13,
  29; DLB 88; SATA 63

Southern, Terry 1926- .... **CLC 7**
  See also CA 1-4R; CANR 1; DLB 2

Southey, Robert 1774-1843 ...... **NCLC 8**
  See also DLB 93, 107, 142; SATA 54

Southworth, Emma Dorothy Eliza Nevitte
  1819-1899 .... **NCLC 26**

Souza, Ernest
  See Scott, Evelyn

Soyinka, Wole
  1934- .... **CLC 3, 5, 14, 36, 44; BLC;
                              DA; DC 2; WLC**
  See also BW; CA 13-16R; CANR 27, 39;
  DLB 125; MTCW

Spackman, W(illiam) M(ode)
  1905-1990 .... **CLC 46**
  See also CA 81-84; 132

Spacks, Barry 1931-............. **CLC 14**
  See also CA 29-32R; CANR 33; DLB 105

Spanidou, Irini 1946-............. **CLC 44**

Spark, Muriel (Sarah)
  1918- .... **CLC 2, 3, 5, 8, 13, 18, 40;
                              SSC 10**
  See also CA 5-8R; CANR 12, 36;
  CDBLB 1945-1960; DLB 15, 139; MTCW

Spaulding, Douglas
  See Bradbury, Ray (Douglas)

Spaulding, Leonard
  See Bradbury, Ray (Douglas)

Spence, J. A. D.
  See Eliot, T(homas) S(tearns)

Spencer, Elizabeth 1921-......... **CLC 22**
  See also CA 13-16R; CANR 32; DLB 6;
  MTCW; SATA 14

Spencer, Leonard G.
  See Silverberg, Robert

Spencer, Scott 1945-............. **CLC 30**
  See also CA 113; DLBY 86

Spender, Stephen (Harold)
  1909- .... **CLC 1, 2, 5, 10, 41**
  See also CA 9-12R; CANR 31;
  CDBLB 1945-1960; DLB 20; MTCW

Spengler, Oswald (Arnold Gottfried)
  1880-1936 .... **TCLC 25**
  See also CA 118

Spenser, Edmund
  1552(?)-1599 .... **LC 5; DA; PC 8; WLC**
  See also CDBLB Before 1660

Spicer, Jack 1925-1965 ...... **CLC 8, 18, 72**
  See also CA 85-88; DLB 5, 16

Spiegelman, Art 1948-............ **CLC 76**
  See also AAYA 10; CA 125; CANR 41

Spielberg, Peter 1929-............. **CLC 6**
  See also CA 5-8R; CANR 4; DLBY 81

Spielberg, Steven 1947-.......... **CLC 20**
  See also AAYA 8; CA 77-80; CANR 32;
  SATA 32

Spillane, Frank Morrison 1918-
  See Spillane, Mickey
  See also CA 25-28R; CANR 28; MTCW;
  SATA 66

Spillane, Mickey .... **CLC 3, 13**
  See also Spillane, Frank Morrison

Spinoza, Benedictus de 1632-1677 .... **LC 9**

Spinrad, Norman (Richard) 1940-... **CLC 46**
  See also CA 37-40R; CAAS 19; CANR 20;
  DLB 8

Spitteler, Carl (Friedrich Georg)
  1845-1924 .... **TCLC 12**
  See also CA 109; DLB 129

Spivack, Kathleen (Romola Drucker)
  1938- .... **CLC 6**
  See also CA 49-52

Spoto, Donald 1941-............. **CLC 39**
  See also CA 65-68; CANR 11

Springsteen, Bruce (F.) 1949- ...... **CLC 17**
  See also CA 111

Spurling, Hilary 1940-............ **CLC 34**
  See also CA 104; CANR 25

Squires, (James) Radcliffe
  1917-1993 .... **CLC 51**
  See also CA 1-4R; 140; CANR 6, 21

Srivastava, Dhanpat Rai 1880(?)-1936
  See Premchand
  See also CA 118

Stacy, Donald
  See Pohl, Frederik

Stael, Germaine de
  See Stael-Holstein, Anne Louise Germaine
  Necker Baronn
  See also DLB 119

Stael-Holstein, Anne Louise Germaine Necker
  Baronn 1766-1817 .... **NCLC 3**
  See also Stael, Germaine de

Stafford, Jean 1915-1979 ... **CLC 4, 7, 19, 68**
  See also CA 1-4R; 85-88; CANR 3; DLB 2;
  MTCW; SATA 22

Stafford, William (Edgar)
  1914-1993 .... **CLC 4, 7, 29**
  See also CA 5-8R; 142; CAAS 3; CANR 5,
  22; DLB 5

Staines, Trevor
  See Brunner, John (Kilian Houston)

Stairs, Gordon
  See Austin, Mary (Hunter)

Stannard, Martin 1947-.......... **CLC 44**
  See also CA 142

Stanton, Maura 1946- .... **CLC 9**
  See also CA 89-92; CANR 15; DLB 120

Stanton, Schuyler
   See Baum, L(yman) Frank

Stapledon, (William) Olaf
   1886-1950 .... TCLC 22
   See also CA 111; DLB 15

Starbuck, George (Edwin) 1931-.... CLC 53
   See also CA 21-24R; CANR 23

Stark, Richard
   See Westlake, Donald E(dwin)

Staunton, Schuyler
   See Baum, L(yman) Frank

Stead, Christina (Ellen)
   1902-1983 .... CLC 2, 5, 8, 32, 80
   See also CA 13-16R; 109; CANR 33, 40;
   MTCW

Stead, William Thomas
   1849-1912 .... TCLC 48

Steele, Richard 1672-1729 .... LC 18
   See also CDBLB 1660-1789; DLB 84, 101

Steele, Timothy (Reid) 1948-...... CLC 45
   See also CA 93-96; CANR 16; DLB 120

Steffens, (Joseph) Lincoln
   1866-1936 .... TCLC 20
   See also CA 117

Stegner, Wallace (Earle)
   1909-1993 .... CLC 9, 49, 81
   See also AITN 1; BEST 90:3; CA 1-4R;
   141; CAAS 9; CANR 1, 21; DLB 9;
   DLBY 93; MTCW

Stein, Gertrude
   1874-1946 ...... TCLC 1, 6, 28, 48; DA;
   WLC
   See also CA 104; 132; CDALB 1917-1929;
   ' DLB 4, 54, 86; MTCW

Steinbeck, John (Ernst)
   1902-1968 ...... CLC 1, 5, 9, 13, 21, 34,
   45, 75; DA; SSC 11; WLC
   See also AAYA 12; CA 1-4R; 25-28R;
   CANR 1, 35; CDALB 1929-1941; DLB 7,
   9; DLBD 2; MTCW; SATA 9

Steinem, Gloria 1934-............. CLC 63
   See also CA 53-56; CANR 28; MTCW

Steiner, George 1929-............. CLC 24
   See also CA 73-76; CANR 31; DLB 67;
   MTCW; SATA 62

Steiner, K. Leslie
   See Delany, Samuel R(ay, Jr.)

Steiner, Rudolf 1861-1925 .... TCLC 13
   See also CA 107

Stendhal 1783-1842.... NCLC 23; DA; WLC
   See also DLB 119

Stephen, Leslie 1832-1904 .... TCLC 23
   See also CA 123; DLB 57

Stephen, Sir Leslie
   See Stephen, Leslie

Stephen, Virginia
   See Woolf, (Adeline) Virginia

Stephens, James 1882(?)-1950...... TCLC 4
   See also CA 104; DLB 19

Stephens, Reed
   See Donaldson, Stephen R.

Steptoe, Lydia
   See Barnes, Djuna

Sterchi, Beat 1949-............... CLC 65

Sterling, Brett
   See Bradbury, Ray (Douglas); Hamilton,
   Edmond

Sterling, Bruce 1954-............. CLC 72
   See also CA 119; CANR 44

Sterling, George 1869-1926 ...... TCLC 20
   See also CA 117; DLB 54

Stern, Gerald 1925- .... CLC 40
   See also CA 81-84; CANR 28; DLB 105

Stern, Richard (Gustave) 1928-... CLC 4, 39
   See also CA 1-4R; CANR 1, 25; DLBY 87

Sternberg, Josef von 1894-1969..... CLC 20
   See also CA 81-84

Sterne, Laurence
   1713-1768 .... LC 2; DA; WLC
   See also CDBLB 1660-1789; DLB 39

Sternheim, (William Adolf) Carl
   1878-1942 .... TCLC 8
   See also CA 105; DLB 56, 118

Stevens, Mark 1951- .... CLC 34
   See also CA 122

Stevens, Wallace
   1879-1955 .... TCLC 3, 12, 45; DA;
   PC 6; WLC
   See also CA 104; 124; CDALB 1929-1941;
   DLB 54; MTCW

Stevenson, Anne (Katharine)
   1933- .... CLC 7, 33
   See also CA 17-20R; CAAS 9; CANR 9, 33;
   DLB 40; MTCW

Stevenson, Robert Louis (Balfour)
   1850-1894 .... NCLC 5, 14; DA;
   SSC 11; WLC
   See also CDBLB 1890-1914; CLR 10, 11;
   DLB 18, 57, 141; JRDA; MAICYA;
   YABC 2

Stewart, J(ohn) I(nnes) M(ackintosh)
   1906- .... CLC 7, 14, 32
   See also CA 85-88; CAAS 3; MTCW

Stewart, Mary (Florence Elinor)
   1916- .... CLC 7, 35
   See also CA 1-4R; CANR 1; SATA 12

Stewart, Mary Rainbow
   See Stewart, Mary (Florence Elinor)

Stifter, Adalbert 1805-1868 ...... NCLC 41
   See also DLB 133

Still, James 1906-................ CLC 49
   See also CA 65-68; CAAS 17; CANR 10,
   26; DLB 9; SATA 29

Sting
   See Sumner, Gordon Matthew

Stirling, Arthur
   See Sinclair, Upton (Beall)

Stitt, Milan 1941-................ CLC 29
   See also CA 69-72

Stockton, Francis Richard 1834-1902
   See Stockton, Frank R.
   See also CA 108; 137; MAICYA; SATA 44

Stockton, Frank R. .... TCLC 47
   See also Stockton, Francis Richard
   See also DLB 42, 74; SATA 32

Stoddard, Charles
   See Kuttner, Henry

Stoker, Abraham 1847-1912
   See Stoker, Bram
   See also CA 105; DA; SATA 29

Stoker, Bram .... TCLC 8; WLC
   See also Stoker, Abraham
   See also CDBLB 1890-1914; DLB 36, 70

Stolz, Mary (Slattery) 1920-....... CLC 12
   See also AAYA 8; AITN 1; CA 5-8R;
   CANR 13, 41; JRDA; MAICYA;
   SAAS 3; SATA 10, 71

Stone, Irving 1903-1989............ CLC 7
   See also AITN 1; CA 1-4R; 129; CAAS 3;
   CANR 1, 23; MTCW; SATA 3;
   SATA-Obit 64

Stone, Oliver 1946-............... CLC 73
   See also CA 110

Stone, Robert (Anthony)
   1937- .... CLC 5, 23, 42
   See also CA 85-88; CANR 23; MTCW

Stone, Zachary
   See Follett, Ken(neth Martin)

Stoppard, Tom
   1937- ...... CLC 1, 3, 4, 5, 8, 15, 29, 34,
   63; DA; WLC
   See also CA 81-84; CANR 39;
   CDBLB 1960 to Present; DLB 13;
   DLBY 85; MTCW

Storey, David (Malcolm)
   1933- ....CLC 2, 4, 5, 8
   See also CA 81-84; CANR 36; DLB 13, 14;
   MTCW

Storm, Hyemeyohsts 1935-......... CLC 3
   See also CA 81-84

Storm, (Hans) Theodor (Woldsen)
   1817-1888 .... NCLC 1

Storni, Alfonsina
   1892-1938 .... TCLC 5; HLC
   See also CA 104; 131; HW

Stout, Rex (Todhunter) 1886-1975 ... CLC 3
   See also AITN 2; CA 61-64

Stow, (Julian) Randolph 1935- .. CLC 23, 48
   See also CA 13-16R; CANR 33; MTCW

Stowe, Harriet (Elizabeth) Beecher
   1811-1896 .... NCLC 3; DA; WLC
   See also CDALB 1865-1917; DLB 1, 12, 42,
   74; JRDA; MAICYA; YABC 1

Strachey, (Giles) Lytton
   1880-1932 .... TCLC 12
   See also CA 110; DLBD 10

Strand, Mark 1934- ......CLC 6, 18, 41, 71
   See also CA 21-24R; CANR 40; DLB 5;
   SATA 41

Straub, Peter (Francis) 1943- ...... CLC 28
   See also BEST 89:1; CA 85-88; CANR 28;
   DLBY 84; MTCW

Strauss, Botho 1944- .... CLC 22
   See also DLB 124

Streatfeild, (Mary) Noel
   1895(?)-1986 .... CLC 21
   See also CA 81-84; 120; CANR 31;
   CLR 17; MAICYA; SATA 20, 48

Stribling, T(homas) S(igismund)
   1881-1965 .... CLC 23
   See also CA 107; DLB 9

Tate, (John Orley) Allen
1899-1979 . . . . **CLC 2, 4, 6, 9, 11, 14, 24**
See also CA 5-8R; 85-88; CANR 32;
DLB 4, 45, 63; MTCW

Tate, Ellalice
See Hibbert, Eleanor Alice Burford

Tate, James (Vincent) 1943- . . . **CLC 2, 6, 25**
See also CA 21-24R; CANR 29; DLB 5

Tavel, Ronald 1940- . . . . **CLC 6**
See also CA 21-24R; CANR 33

Taylor, Cecil Philip 1929-1981 . . . . . **CLC 27**
See also CA 25-28R; 105

Taylor, Edward 1642(?)-1729. . . . **LC 11; DA**
See also DLB 24

Taylor, Eleanor Ross 1920- . . . . **CLC 5**
See also CA 81-84

Taylor, Elizabeth 1912-1975 . . . **CLC 2, 4, 29**
See also CA 13-16R; CANR 9; DLB 139;
MTCW; SATA 13

Taylor, Henry (Splawn) 1942- . . . . . . **CLC 44**
See also CA 33-36R; CAAS 7; CANR 31;
DLB 5

Taylor, Kamala (Purnaiya) 1924-
See Markandaya, Kamala
See also CA 77-80

Taylor, Mildred D. . . . . **CLC 21**
See also AAYA 10; BW; CA 85-88;
CANR 25; CLR 9; DLB 52; JRDA;
MAICYA; SAAS 5; SATA 15, 70

Taylor, Peter (Hillsman)
1917- . . . . . . **CLC 1, 4, 18, 37, 44, 50, 71;
SSC 10**
See also CA 13-16R; CANR 9; DLBY 81;
MTCW

Taylor, Robert Lewis 1912- . . . . **CLC 14**
See also CA 1-4R; CANR 3; SATA 10

Tchekhov, Anton
See Chekhov, Anton (Pavlovich)

Teasdale, Sara 1884-1933 . . . . **TCLC 4**
See also CA 104; DLB 45; SATA 32

Tegner, Esaias 1782-1846 . . . . **NCLC 2**

Teilhard de Chardin, (Marie Joseph) Pierre
1881-1955 . . . . **TCLC 9**
See also CA 105

Temple, Ann
See Mortimer, Penelope (Ruth)

Tennant, Emma (Christina)
1937- . . . . **CLC 13, 52**
See also CA 65-68; CAAS 9; CANR 10, 38;
DLB 14

Tenneshaw, S. M.
See Silverberg, Robert

Tennyson, Alfred
1809-1892 . . **NCLC 30; DA; PC 6; WLC**
See also CDBLB 1832-1890; DLB 32

Teran, Lisa St. Aubin de . . . . **CLC 36**
See also St. Aubin de Teran, Lisa

Teresa de Jesus, St. 1515-1582 . . . . . . **LC 18**

Terkel, Louis 1912-
See Terkel, Studs
See also CA 57-60; CANR 18; MTCW

Terkel, Studs . . . . **CLC 38**
See also Terkel, Louis
See also AITN 1

Terry, C. V.
See Slaughter, Frank G(ill)

Terry, Megan 1932- . . . . **CLC 19**
See also CA 77-80; CABS 3; CANR 43;
DLB 7

Tertz, Abram
See Sinyavsky, Andrei (Donatevich)

Tesich, Steve 1943(?)- . . . . **CLC 40, 69**
See also CA 105; DLBY 83

Teternikov, Fyodor Kuzmich 1863-1927
See Sologub, Fyodor
See also CA 104

Tevis, Walter 1928-1984 . . . . **CLC 42**
See also CA 113

Tey, Josephine . . . . **TCLC 14**
See also Mackintosh, Elizabeth
See also DLB 77

Thackeray, William Makepeace
1811-1863 . . . . **NCLC 5, 14, 22, 43; DA;
WLC**
See also CDBLB 1832-1890; DLB 21, 55;
SATA 23

Thakura, Ravindranatha
See Tagore, Rabindranath

Tharoor, Shashi 1956- . . . . **CLC 70**
See also CA 141

Thelwell, Michael Miles 1939- . . . . . **CLC 22**
See also CA 101

Theobald, Lewis, Jr.
See Lovecraft, H(oward) P(hillips)

Theodorescu, Ion N. 1880-1967
See Arghezi, Tudor
See also CA 116

Theriault, Yves 1915-1983 . . . . **CLC 79**
See also CA 102; DLB 88

Theroux, Alexander (Louis)
1939- . . . . **CLC 2, 25**
See also CA 85-88; CANR 20

Theroux, Paul (Edward)
1941- . . . . **CLC 5, 8, 11, 15, 28, 46**
See also BEST 89:4; CA 33-36R; CANR 20;
DLB 2; MTCW; SATA 44

Thesen, Sharon 1946- . . . . **CLC 56**

Thevenin, Denis
See Duhamel, Georges

Thibault, Jacques Anatole Francois
1844-1924
See France, Anatole
See also CA 106; 127; MTCW

Thiele, Colin (Milton) 1920- . . . . **CLC 17**
See also CA 29-32R; CANR 12, 28;
CLR 27; MAICYA; SAAS 2; SATA 14,
72

Thomas, Audrey (Callahan)
1935- . . . . **CLC 7, 13, 37**
See also AITN 2; CA 21-24R; CAAS 19;
CANR 36; DLB 60; MTCW

Thomas, D(onald) M(ichael)
1935- . . . . **CLC 13, 22, 31**
See also CA 61-64; CAAS 11; CANR 17;
CDBLB 1960 to Present; DLB 40;
MTCW

Thomas, Dylan (Marlais)
1914-1953 . . . **TCLC 1, 8, 45; DA; PC 2;
SSC 3; WLC**
See also CA 104; 120; CDBLB 1945-1960;
DLB 13, 20, 139; MTCW; SATA 60

Thomas, (Philip) Edward
1878-1917 . . . . **TCLC 10**
See also CA 106; DLB 19

Thomas, Joyce Carol 1938- . . . .**CLC 35**
See also AAYA 12; BW; CA 113; 116;
CLR 19; DLB 33; JRDA; MAICYA;
MTCW; SAAS 7; SATA 40

Thomas, Lewis 1913-1993 . . . . **CLC 35**
See also CA 85-88; 143; CANR 38; MTCW

Thomas, Paul
See Mann, (Paul) Thomas

Thomas, Piri 1928- . . . . **CLC 17**
See also CA 73-76; HW

Thomas, R(onald) S(tuart)
1913- . . . . **CLC 6, 13, 48**
See also CA 89-92; CAAS 4; CANR 30;
CDBLB 1960 to Present; DLB 27;
MTCW

Thomas, Ross (Elmore) 1926- . . . . . . **CLC 39**
See also CA 33-36R; CANR 22

Thompson, Francis Clegg
See Mencken, H(enry) L(ouis)

Thompson, Francis Joseph
1859-1907 . . . . **TCLC 4**
See also CA 104; CDBLB 1890-1914;
DLB 19

Thompson, Hunter S(tockton)
1939- . . . . **CLC 9, 17, 40**
See also BEST 89:1; CA 17-20R; CANR 23;
MTCW

Thompson, James Myers
See Thompson, Jim (Myers)

Thompson, Jim (Myers)
1906-1977(?) . . . . **CLC 69**
See also CA 140

Thompson, Judith . . . . **CLC 39**

Thomson, James 1700-1748 . . . . **LC 16**

Thomson, James 1834-1882 . . . . . . **NCLC 18**

Thoreau, Henry David
1817-1862 . . . . . . **NCLC 7, 21; DA; WLC**
See also CDALB 1640-1865; DLB 1

Thornton, Hall
See Silverberg, Robert

Thurber, James (Grover)
1894-1961 . . . **CLC 5, 11, 25; DA; SSC 1**
See also CA 73-76; CANR 17, 39;
CDALB 1929-1941; DLB 4, 11, 22, 102;
MAICYA; MTCW; SATA 13

Thurman, Wallace (Henry)
1902-1934 . . . . **TCLC 6; BLC**
See also BW; CA 104; 124; DLB 51

Ticheburn, Cheviot
See Ainsworth, William Harrison

Tieck, (Johann) Ludwig
1773-1853 . . . . **NCLC 5**
See also DLB 90

Tiger, Derry
See Ellison, Harlan

Tilghman, Christopher 1948(?)- . . . . . **CLC 65**

Tillinghast, Richard (Williford)
1940- .... **CLC 29**
See also CA 29-32R; CANR 26

Timrod, Henry 1828-1867 .... **NCLC 25**
See also DLB 3

Tindall, Gillian 1938- .... **CLC 7**
See also CA 21-24R; CANR 11

Tiptree, James, Jr. .... **CLC 48, 50**
See also Sheldon, Alice Hastings Bradley
See also DLB 8

Titmarsh, Michael Angelo
See Thackeray, William Makepeace

Tocqueville, Alexis (Charles Henri Maurice
Clerel Comte) 1805-1859..... **NCLC 7**

Tolkien, J(ohn) R(onald) R(euel)
1892-1973 .... **CLC 1, 2, 3, 8, 12, 38;**
DA; WLC
See also AAYA 10; AITN 1; CA 17-18;
45-48; CANR 36; CAP 2;
CDBLB 1914-1945; DLB 15; JRDA;
MAICYA; MTCW; SATA 2, 24, 32

Toller, Ernst 1893-1939 .... **TCLC 10**
See also CA 107; DLB 124

Tolson, M. B.
See Tolson, Melvin B(eaunorus)

Tolson, Melvin B(eaunorus)
1898(?)-1966 .... **CLC 36; BLC**
See also BW; CA 124; 89-92; DLB 48, 76

Tolstoi, Aleksei Nikolaevich
See Tolstoy, Alexey Nikolaevich

Tolstoy, Alexey Nikolaevich
1882-1945 .... **TCLC 18**
See also CA 107

Tolstoy, Count Leo
See Tolstoy, Leo (Nikolaevich)

Tolstoy, Leo (Nikolaevich)
1828-1910 ...... **TCLC 4, 11, 17, 28, 44;**
DA; SSC 9; WLC
See also CA 104; 123; SATA 26

Tomasi di Lampedusa, Giuseppe 1896-1957
See Lampedusa, Giuseppe (Tomasi) di
See also CA 111

Tomlin, Lily...................... **CLC 17**
See also Tomlin, Mary Jean

Tomlin, Mary Jean 1939(?)-
See Tomlin, Lily
See also CA 117

Tomlinson, (Alfred) Charles
1927- .... **CLC 2, 4, 6, 13, 45**
See also CA 5-8R; CANR 33; DLB 40

Tonson, Jacob
See Bennett, (Enoch) Arnold

Toole, John Kennedy
1937-1969 .... **CLC 19, 64**
See also CA 104; DLBY 81

Toomer, Jean
1894-1967 ...... **CLC 1, 4, 13, 22; BLC;**
PC 7; SSC 1
See also BW; CA 85-88;
CDALB 1917-1929; DLB 45, 51; MTCW

Torley, Luke
See Blish, James (Benjamin)

Tornimparte, Alessandra
See Ginzburg, Natalia

Torre, Raoul della
See Mencken, H(enry) L(ouis)

Torrey, E(dwin) Fuller 1937- .... **CLC 34**
See also CA 119

Torsvan, Ben Traven
See Traven, B.

Torsvan, Benno Traven
See Traven, B.

Torsvan, Berick Traven
See Traven, B.

Torsvan, Berwick Traven
See Traven, B.

Torsvan, Bruno Traven
See Traven, B.

Torsvan, Traven
See Traven, B.

Tournier, Michel (Edouard)
1924- .... **CLC 6, 23, 36**
See also CA 49-52; CANR 3, 36; DLB 83;
MTCW; SATA 23

Tournimparte, Alessandra
See Ginzburg, Natalia

Towers, Ivar
See Kornbluth, C(yril) M.

Townsend, Sue 1946- .... **CLC 61**
See also CA 119; 127; MTCW; SATA 48,
55

Townshend, Peter (Dennis Blandford)
1945- .... **CLC 17, 42**
See also CA 107

Tozzi, Federigo 1883-1920....... **TCLC 31**

Traill, Catharine Parr
1802-1899 .... **NCLC 31**
See also DLB 99

Trakl, Georg 1887-1914........... **TCLC 5**
See also CA 104

Transtroemer, Tomas (Goesta)
1931- .... **CLC 52, 65**
See also CA 117; 129; CAAS 17

Transtromer, Tomas Gosta
See Transtroemer, Tomas (Goesta)

Traven, B. (?)-1969............. **CLC 8, 11**
See also CA 19-20; 25-28R; CAP 2; DLB 9,
56; MTCW

Treitel, Jonathan 1959- .... **CLC 70**

Tremain, Rose 1943-.............. **CLC 42**
See also CA 97-100; CANR 44; DLB 14

Tremblay, Michel 1942-........... **CLC 29**
See also CA 116; 128; DLB 60; MTCW

Trevanian (a pseudonym) 1930(?)-... **CLC 29**
See also CA 108

Trevor, Glen
See Hilton, James

Trevor, William
1928- .... **CLC 7, 9, 14, 25, 71**
See also Cox, William Trevor
See also DLB 14, 139

Trifonov, Yuri (Valentinovich)
1925-1981 .... **CLC 45**
See also CA 126; 103; MTCW

Trilling, Lionel 1905-1975 .... **CLC 9, 11, 24**
See also CA 9-12R; 61-64; CANR 10;
DLB 28, 63; MTCW

Trimball, W. H.
See Mencken, H(enry) L(ouis)

Tristan
See Gomez de la Serna, Ramon

Tristram
See Housman, A(lfred) E(dward)

Trogdon, William (Lewis) 1939-
See Heat-Moon, William Least
See also CA 115; 119

Trollope, Anthony
1815-1882 ...... **NCLC 6, 33; DA; WLC**
See also CDBLB 1832-1890; DLB 21, 57;
SATA 22

Trollope, Frances 1779-1863 ..... **NCLC 30**
See also DLB 21

Trotsky, Leon 1879-1940......... **TCLC 22**
See also CA 118

Trotter (Cockburn), Catharine
1679-1749 .... **LC 8**
See also DLB 84

Trout, Kilgore
See Farmer, Philip Jose

Trow, George W. S. 1943-......... **CLC 52**
See also CA 126

Troyat, Henri 1911-.............. **CLC 23**
See also CA 45-48; CANR 2, 33; MTCW

Trudeau, G(arretson) B(eekman) 1948-
See Trudeau, Garry B.
See also CA 81-84; CANR 31; SATA 35

Trudeau, Garry B................. **CLC 12**
See also Trudeau, G(arretson) B(eekman)
See also AAYA 10; AITN 2

Truffaut, Francois 1932-1984....... **CLC 20**
See also CA 81-84; 113; CANR 34

Trumbo, Dalton 1905-1976 .... **CLC 19**
See also CA 21-24R; 69-72; CANR 10;
DLB 26

Trumbull, John 1750-1831....... **NCLC 30**
See also DLB 31

Trundlett, Helen B.
See Eliot, T(homas) S(tearns)

Tryon, Thomas 1926-1991 .... **CLC 3, 11**
See also AITN 1; CA 29-32R; 135;
CANR 32; MTCW

Tryon, Tom
See Tryon, Thomas

Ts'ao Hsueh-ch'in 1715(?)-1763....... **LC 1**

Tsushima, Shuji 1909-1948
See Dazai, Osamu
See also CA 107

Tsvetaeva (Efron), Marina (Ivanovna)
1892-1941 .... **TCLC 7, 35**
See also CA 104; 128; MTCW

Tuck, Lily 1938-................. **CLC 70**
See also CA 139

Tu Fu 712-770.................... **PC 9**

Tunis, John R(oberts) 1889-1975 ... **CLC 12**
See also CA 61-64; DLB 22; JRDA;
MAICYA; SATA 30, 37

Tuohy, Frank..................... **CLC 37**
See also Tuohy, John Francis
See also DLB 14, 139

Tuohy, John Francis 1925-
See Tuohy, Frank
See also CA 5-8R; CANR 3

Turco, Lewis (Putnam) 1934- ... **CLC 11, 63**
See also CA 13-16R; CANR 24; DLBY 84

Turgenev, Ivan
1818-1883 ...... **NCLC 21; DA; SSC 7;**
WLC

Turner, Frederick 1943-.......... **CLC 48**
See also CA 73-76; CAAS 10; CANR 12,
30; DLB 40

Tusan, Stan 1936-................ **CLC 22**
See also CA 105

Tutu, Desmond M(pilo)
1931- .... **CLC 80; BLC**
See also BW; CA 125

Tutuola, Amos 1920- ... **CLC 5, 14, 29; BLC**
See also BW; CA 9-12R; CANR 27;
DLB 125; MTCW

Twain, Mark
... **TCLC 6, 12, 19, 36, 48; SSC 6; WLC**
See also Clemens, Samuel Langhorne
See also DLB 11, 12, 23, 64, 74

Tyler, Anne
1941- .... **CLC 7, 11, 18, 28, 44, 59**
See also BEST 89:1; CA 9-12R; CANR 11,
33; DLB 6; DLBY 82; MTCW; SATA 7

Tyler, Royall 1757-1826.......... **NCLC 3**
See also DLB 37

Tynan, Katharine 1861-1931 .... **TCLC 3**
See also CA 104

Tytell, John 1939- .... **CLC 50**
See also CA 29-32R

Tyutchev, Fyodor 1803-1873 ..... **NCLC 34**

Tzara, Tristan .... **CLC 47**
See also Rosenfeld, Samuel

Uhry, Alfred 1936-................ **CLC 55**
See also CA 127; 133

Ulf, Haerved
See Strindberg, (Johan) August

Ulf, Harved
See Strindberg, (Johan) August

Ulibarri, Sabine R(eyes) 1919- ..... **CLC 83**
See also CA 131; DLB 82; HW

Unamuno (y Jugo), Miguel de
1864-1936 .... **TCLC 2, 9; HLC; SSC 11**
See also CA 104; 131; DLB 108; HW;
MTCW

Undercliffe, Errol
See Campbell, (John) Ramsey

Underwood, Miles
See Glassco, John

Undset, Sigrid
1882-1949 .... **TCLC 3; DA; WLC**
See also CA 104; 129; MTCW

Ungaretti, Giuseppe
1888-1970 .... **CLC 7, 11, 15**
See also CA 19-20; 25-28R; CAP 2;
DLB 114

Unger, Douglas 1952-............ **CLC 34**
See also CA 130

Unsworth, Barry (Forster) 1930-.... **CLC 76**
See also CA 25-28R; CANR 30

Updike, John (Hoyer)
1932- ...... **CLC 1, 2, 3, 5, 7, 9, 13, 15,**
23, 34, 43, 70; DA; SSC 13; WLC
See also CA 1-4R; CABS 1; CANR 4, 33;
CDALB 1968-1988; DLB 2, 5; DLBD 3;
DLBY 80, 82; MTCW

Upshaw, Margaret Mitchell
See Mitchell, Margaret (Munnerlyn)

Upton, Mark
See Sanders, Lawrence

Urdang, Constance (Henriette)
1922- .... **CLC 47**
See also CA 21-24R; CANR 9, 24

Uriel, Henry
See Faust, Frederick (Schiller)

Uris, Leon (Marcus) 1924-....... **CLC 7, 32**
See also AITN 1, 2; BEST 89:2; CA 1-4R;
CANR 1, 40; MTCW; SATA 49

Urmuz
See Codrescu, Andrei

Ustinov, Peter (Alexander) 1921-.... **CLC 1**
See also AITN 1; CA 13-16R; CANR 25;
DLB 13

V
See Chekhov, Anton (Pavlovich)

Vaculik, Ludvik 1926- .... **CLC 7**
See also CA 53-56

Valenzuela, Luisa 1938-... **CLC 31; SSC 14**
See also CA 101; CANR 32; DLB 113; HW

Valera y Alcala-Galiano, Juan
1824-1905 .... **TCLC 10**
See also CA 106

Valery, (Ambroise) Paul (Toussaint Jules)
1871-1945 .... **TCLC 4, 15; PC 9**
See also CA 104; 122; MTCW

Valle-Inclan, Ramon (Maria) del
1866-1936 .... **TCLC 5; HLC**
See also CA 106; DLB 134

Vallejo, Antonio Buero
See Buero Vallejo, Antonio

Vallejo, Cesar (Abraham)
1892-1938 .... **TCLC 3; HLC**
See also CA 105; HW

Valle Y Pena, Ramon del
See Valle-Inclan, Ramon (Maria) del

Van Ash, Cay 1918-.............. **CLC 34**

Vanbrugh, Sir John 1664-1726 ...... **LC 21**
See also DLB 80

Van Campen, Karl
See Campbell, John W(ood, Jr.)

Vance, Gerald
See Silverberg, Robert

Vance, Jack .... **CLC 35**
See also Vance, John Holbrook
See also DLB 8

Vance, John Holbrook 1916-
See Queen, Ellery; Vance, Jack
See also CA 29-32R; CANR 17; MTCW

Van Den Bogarde, Derek Jules Gaspard Ulric
Niven 1921-
See Bogarde, Dirk
See also CA 77-80

Vandenburgh, Jane .... **CLC 59**

Vanderhaeghe, Guy 1951- .... **CLC 41**
See also CA 113

van der Post, Laurens (Jan) 1906- ... **CLC 5**
See also CA 5-8R; CANR 35

van de Wetering, Janwillem 1931- .. **CLC 47**
See also CA 49-52; CANR 4

Van Dine, S. S. .... **TCLC 23**
See also Wright, Willard Huntington

Van Doren, Carl (Clinton)
1885-1950 .... **TCLC 18**
See also CA 111

Van Doren, Mark 1894-1972..... **CLC 6, 10**
See also CA 1-4R; 37-40R; CANR 3;
DLB 45; MTCW

Van Druten, John (William)
1901-1957 .... **TCLC 2**
See also CA 104; DLB 10

Van Duyn, Mona (Jane)
1921- .... **CLC 3, 7, 63**
See also CA 9-12R; CANR 7, 38; DLB 5

Van Dyne, Edith
See Baum, L(yman) Frank

van Itallie, Jean-Claude 1936-....... **CLC 3**
See also CA 45-48; CAAS 2; CANR 1;
DLB 7

van Ostaijen, Paul 1896-1928 ..... **TCLC 33**

Van Peebles, Melvin 1932- ...... **CLC 2, 20**
See also BW; CA 85-88; CANR 27

Vansittart, Peter 1920-............ **CLC 42**
See also CA 1-4R; CANR 3

Van Vechten, Carl 1880-1964 ...... **CLC 33**
See also CA 89-92; DLB 4, 9, 51

Van Vogt, A(lfred) E(lton) 1912-..... **CLC 1**
See also CA 21-24R; CANR 28; DLB 8;
SATA 14

Varda, Agnes 1928- .... **CLC 16**
See also CA 116; 122

Vargas Llosa, (Jorge) Mario (Pedro)
1936- .... **CLC 3, 6, 9, 10, 15, 31, 42;**
DA; HLC
See also CA 73-76; CANR 18, 32, 42; HW;
MTCW

Vasiliu, Gheorghe 1881-1957
See Bacovia, George
See also CA 123

Vassa, Gustavus
See Equiano, Olaudah

Vassilikos, Vassilis 1933-......... **CLC 4, 8**
See also CA 81-84

Vaughn, Stephanie................. **CLC 62**

Vazov, Ivan (Minchov)
1850-1921 .... **TCLC 25**
See also CA 121

Veblen, Thorstein (Bunde)
1857-1929 .... **TCLC 31**
See also CA 115

Vega, Lope de 1562-1635........... **LC 23**

Venison, Alfred
See Pound, Ezra (Weston Loomis)

Verdi, Marie de
See Mencken, H(enry) L(ouis)

Verdu, Matilde
See Cela, Camilo Jose

Wallace, David Foster 1962- .... **CLC 50**
See also CA 132

Wallace, Dexter
See Masters, Edgar Lee

Wallace, Irving 1916-1990 ...... **CLC 7, 13**
See also AITN 1; CA 1-4R; 132; CAAS 1;
CANR 1, 27; MTCW

Wallant, Edward Lewis
1926-1962 .... **CLC 5, 10**
See also CA 1-4R; CANR 22; DLB 2, 28;
MTCW

Walpole, Horace 1717-1797 .... **LC 2**
See also DLB 39, 104

Walpole, Hugh (Seymour)
1884-1941 .... **TCLC 5**
See also CA 104; DLB 34

Walser, Martin 1927- .... **CLC 27**
See also CA 57-60; CANR 8; DLB 75, 124

Walser, Robert 1878-1956 .... **TCLC 18**
See also CA 118; DLB 66

Walsh, Jill Paton .... **CLC 35**
See also Paton Walsh, Gillian
See also AAYA 11; CLR 2; SAAS 3

Walter, William Christian
See Andersen, Hans Christian

Wambaugh, Joseph (Aloysius, Jr.)
1937- .... **CLC 3, 18**
See also AITN 1; BEST 89:3; CA 33-36R;
CANR 42; DLB 6; DLBY 83; MTCW

Ward, Arthur Henry Sarsfield 1883-1959
See Rohmer, Sax
See also CA 108

Ward, Douglas Turner 1930- .... **CLC 19**
See also BW; CA 81-84; CANR 27; DLB 7,
38

Ward, Peter
See Faust, Frederick (Schiller)

Warhol, Andy 1928(?)-1987 .... **CLC 20**
See also AAYA 12; BEST 89:4; CA 89-92;
121; CANR 34

Warner, Francis (Robert le Plastrier)
1937- .... **CLC 14**
See also CA 53-56; CANR 11

Warner, Marina 1946- .... **CLC 59**
See also CA 65-68; CANR 21

Warner, Rex (Ernest) 1905-1986.... **CLC 45**
See also CA 89-92; 119; DLB 15

Warner, Susan (Bogert)
1819-1885 .... **NCLC 31**
See also DLB 3, 42

Warner, Sylvia (Constance) Ashton
See Ashton-Warner, Sylvia (Constance)

Warner, Sylvia Townsend
1893-1978 .... **CLC 7, 19**
See also CA 61-64; 77-80; CANR 16;
DLB 34, 139; MTCW

Warren, Mercy Otis 1728-1814... **NCLC 13**
See also DLB 31

Warren, Robert Penn
1905-1989 .... **CLC 1, 4, 6, 8, 10, 13, 18,
39, 53, 59; DA; SSC 4; WLC**
See also AITN 1; CA 13-16R; 129;
CANR 10; CDALB 1968-1988; DLB 2,
48; DLBY 80, 89; MTCW; SATA 46, 63

Warshofsky, Isaac
See Singer, Isaac Bashevis

Warton, Thomas 1728-1790........ **LC 15**
See also DLB 104, 109

Waruk, Kona
See Harris, (Theodore) Wilson

Warung, Price 1855-1911........ **TCLC 45**

Warwick, Jarvis
See Garner, Hugh

Washington, Alex
See Harris, Mark

Washington, Booker T(aliaferro)
1856-1915 .... **TCLC 10; BLC**
See also BW; CA 114; 125; SATA 28

Washington, George 1732-1799...... **LC 25**
See also DLB 31

Wassermann, (Karl) Jakob
1873-1934 .... **TCLC 6**
See also CA 104; DLB 66

Wasserstein, Wendy
1950- .... **CLC 32, 59; DC 4**
See also CA 121; 129; CABS 3

Waterhouse, Keith (Spencer)
1929- .... **CLC 47**
See also CA 5-8R; CANR 38; DLB 13, 15;
MTCW

Waters, Roger 1944- .... **CLC 35**
See also Pink Floyd

Watkins, Frances Ellen
See Harper, Frances Ellen Watkins

Watkins, Gerrold
See Malzberg, Barry N(athaniel)

Watkins, Paul 1964- .... **CLC 55**
See also CA 132

Watkins, Vernon Phillips
1906-1967 .... **CLC 43**
See also CA 9-10; 25-28R; CAP 1; DLB 20

Watson, Irving S.
See Mencken, H(enry) L(ouis)

Watson, John H.
See Farmer, Philip Jose

Watson, Richard F.
See Silverberg, Robert

Waugh, Auberon (Alexander) 1939-.. **CLC 7**
See also CA 45-48; CANR 6, 22; DLB 14

Waugh, Evelyn (Arthur St. John)
1903-1966 ...... **CLC 1, 3, 8, 13, 19, 27,
44; DA; WLC**
See also CA 85-88; 25-28R; CANR 22;
CDBLB 1914-1945; DLB 15; MTCW

Waugh, Harriet 1944- .... **CLC 6**
See also CA 85-88; CANR 22

Ways, C. R.
See Blount, Roy (Alton), Jr.

Waystaff, Simon
See Swift, Jonathan

Webb, (Martha) Beatrice (Potter)
1858-1943 .... **TCLC 22**
See also Potter, Beatrice
See also CA 117

Webb, Charles (Richard) 1939- ...... **CLC 7**
See also CA 25-28R

Webb, James H(enry), Jr. 1946-.... **CLC 22**
See also CA 81-84

Webb, Mary (Gladys Meredith)
1881-1927 .... **TCLC 24**
See also CA 123; DLB 34

Webb, Mrs. Sidney
See Webb, (Martha) Beatrice (Potter)

Webb, Phyllis 1927- .... **CLC 18**
See also CA 104; CANR 23; DLB 53

Webb, Sidney (James)
1859-1947 .... **TCLC 22**
See also CA 117

Webber, Andrew Lloyd .... **CLC 21**
See also Lloyd Webber, Andrew

Weber, Lenora Mattingly
1895-1971 .... **CLC 12**
See also CA 19-20; 29-32R; CAP 1;
SATA 2, 26

Webster, John 1579(?)-1634(?) .... **DC 2**
See also CDBLB Before 1660; DA; DLB 58;
WLC

Webster, Noah 1758-1843 .... **NCLC 30**

Wedekind, (Benjamin) Frank(lin)
1864-1918 .... **TCLC 7**
See also CA 104; DLB 118

Weidman, Jerome 1913- .... **CLC 7**
See also AITN 2; CA 1-4R; CANR 1;
DLB 28

Weil, Simone (Adolphine)
1909-1943 .... **TCLC 23**
See also CA 117

Weinstein, Nathan
See West, Nathanael

Weinstein, Nathan von Wallenstein
See West, Nathanael

Weir, Peter (Lindsay) 1944- .... **CLC 20**
See also CA 113; 123

Weiss, Peter (Ulrich)
1916-1982 .... **CLC 3, 15, 51**
See also CA 45-48; 106; CANR 3; DLB 69,
124

Weiss, Theodore (Russell)
1916- .... **CLC 3, 8, 14**
See also CA 9-12R; CAAS 2; DLB 5

Welch, (Maurice) Denton
1915-1948 .... **TCLC 22**
See also CA 121

Welch, James 1940- .... **CLC 6, 14, 52**
See also CA 85-88; CANR 42

Weldon, Fay
1933(?)- .... **CLC 6, 9, 11, 19, 36, 59**
See also CA 21-24R; CANR 16;
CDBLB 1960 to Present; DLB 14;
MTCW

Wellek, Rene 1903- .... **CLC 28**
See also CA 5-8R; CAAS 7; CANR 8;
DLB 63

Weller, Michael 1942- .... **CLC 10, 53**
See also CA 85-88

Weller, Paul 1958- .... **CLC 26**

Wellershoff, Dieter 1925- .... **CLC 46**
See also CA 89-92; CANR 16, 37

Welles, (George) Orson
1915-1985 .... **CLC 20, 80**
See also CA 93-96; 117

Wellman, Mac 1945- .... **CLC 65**

Wellman, Manly Wade 1903-1986 . . **CLC 49**
See also CA 1-4R; 118; CANR 6, 16, 44;
SATA 6, 47

Wells, Carolyn 1869(?)-1942 . . . . . . **TCLC 35**
See also CA 113; DLB 11

Wells, H(erbert) G(eorge)
1866-1946 . . . . **TCLC 6, 12, 19; DA;
SSC 6; WLC**
See also CA 110; 121; CDBLB 1914-1945;
DLB 34, 70; MTCW; SATA 20

Wells, Rosemary 1943-. . . . . **CLC 12**
See also CA 85-88; CLR 16; MAICYA;
SAAS 1; SATA 18, 69

Welty, Eudora
1909- . . . . . . **CLC 1, 2, 5, 14, 22, 33; DA;
SSC 1; WLC**
See also CA 9-12R; CABS 1; CANR 32;
CDALB 1941-1968; DLB 2, 102;
DLBY 87; MTCW

Wen I-to 1899-1946 . . . . **TCLC 28**

Wentworth, Robert
See Hamilton, Edmond

Werfel, Franz (V.) 1890-1945 . . . . . . **TCLC 8**
See also CA 104; DLB 81, 124

Wergeland, Henrik Arnold
1808-1845 . . . . **NCLC 5**

Wersba, Barbara 1932-. . . . . **CLC 30**
See also AAYA 2; CA 29-32R; CANR 16,
38; CLR 3; DLB 52; JRDA; MAICYA;
SAAS 2; SATA 1, 58

Wertmueller, Lina 1928- . . . . **CLC 16**
See also CA 97-100; CANR 39

Wescott, Glenway 1901-1987. . . . . . . **CLC 13**
See also CA 13-16R; 121; CANR 23;
DLB 4, 9, 102

Wesker, Arnold 1932- . . . . **CLC 3, 5, 42**
See also CA 1-4R; CAAS 7; CANR 1, 33;
CDBLB 1960 to Present; DLB 13;
MTCW

Wesley, Richard (Errol) 1945-. . . . . . . **CLC 7**
See also BW; CA 57-60; CANR 27; DLB 38

Wessel, Johan Herman 1742-1785 . . . . **LC 7**

West, Anthony (Panther)
1914-1987 . . . . **CLC 50**
See also CA 45-48; 124; CANR 3, 19;
DLB 15

West, C. P.
See Wodehouse, P(elham) G(renville)

West, (Mary) Jessamyn
1902-1984 . . . . **CLC 7, 17**
See also CA 9-12R; 112; CANR 27; DLB 6;
DLBY 84; MTCW; SATA 37

West, Morris L(anglo) 1916-. . . . . **CLC 6, 33**
See also CA 5-8R; CANR 24; MTCW

West, Nathanael
1903-1940 . . . . **TCLC 1, 14, 44**
See also CA 104; 125; CDALB 1929-1941;
DLB 4, 9, 28; MTCW

West, Owen
See Koontz, Dean R(ay)

West, Paul 1930- . . . . **CLC 7, 14**
See also CA 13-16R; CAAS 7; CANR 22;
DLB 14

West, Rebecca 1892-1983 . . **CLC 7, 9, 31, 50**
See also CA 5-8R; 109; CANR 19; DLB 36;
DLBY 83; MTCW

Westall, Robert (Atkinson)
1929-1993 . . . . **CLC 17**
See also AAYA 12; CA 69-72; 141;
CANR 18; CLR 13; JRDA; MAICYA;
SAAS 2; SATA 23, 69; SATA-Obit 75

Westlake, Donald E(dwin)
1933- . . . . **CLC 7, 33**
See also CA 17-20R; CAAS 13; CANR 16,
44

Westmacott, Mary
See Christie, Agatha (Mary Clarissa)

Weston, Allen
See Norton, Andre

Wetcheek, J. L.
See Feuchtwanger, Lion

Wetering, Janwillem van de
See van de Wetering, Janwillem

Wetherell, Elizabeth
See Warner, Susan (Bogert)

Whalen, Philip 1923- . . . . **CLC 6, 29**
See also CA 9-12R; CANR 5, 39; DLB 16

Wharton, Edith (Newbold Jones)
1862-1937 . . . . . . **TCLC 3, 9, 27, 53; DA;
SSC 6; WLC**
See also CA 104; 132; CDALB 1865-1917;
DLB 4, 9, 12, 78; MTCW

Wharton, James
See Mencken, H(enry) L(ouis)

Wharton, William (a pseudonym)
. . . . **CLC 18, 37**
See also CA 93-96; DLBY 80

Wheatley (Peters), Phillis
1754(?)-1784 . . . . **LC 3; BLC; DA; PC 3;
WLC**
See also CDALB 1640-1865; DLB 31, 50

Wheelock, John Hall 1886-1978 . . . . **CLC 14**
See also CA 13-16R; 77-80; CANR 14;
DLB 45

White, E(lwyn) B(rooks)
1899-1985 . . . . **CLC 10, 34, 39**
See also AITN 2; CA 13-16R; 116;
CANR 16, 37; CLR 1, 21; DLB 11, 22;
MAICYA; MTCW; SATA 2, 29, 44

White, Edmund (Valentine III)
1940- . . . . **CLC 27**
See also AAYA 7; CA 45-48; CANR 3, 19,
36; MTCW

White, Patrick (Victor Martindale)
1912-1990 . . **CLC 3, 4, 5, 7, 9, 18, 65, 69**
See also CA 81-84; 132; CANR 43; MTCW

White, Phyllis Dorothy James 1920-
See James, P. D.
See also CA 21-24R; CANR 17, 43; MTCW

White, T(erence) H(anbury)
1906-1964 . . . . **CLC 30**
See also CA 73-76; CANR 37; JRDA;
MAICYA; SATA 12

White, Terence de Vere 1912-. . . . . . . **CLC 49**
See also CA 49-52; CANR 3

White, Walter F(rancis)
1893-1955 . . . . **TCLC 15**
See also White, Walter
See also CA 115; 124; DLB 51

White, William Hale 1831-1913
See Rutherford, Mark
See also CA 121

Whitehead, E(dward) A(nthony)
1933- . . . . **CLC 5**
See also CA 65-68

Whitemore, Hugh (John) 1936-. . . . . **CLC 37**
See also CA 132

Whitman, Sarah Helen (Power)
1803-1878 . . . . **NCLC 19**
See also DLB 1

Whitman, Walt(er)
1819-1892 . . . . . **NCLC 4, 31; DA; PC 3;
WLC**
See also CDALB 1640-1865; DLB 3, 64;
SATA 20

Whitney, Phyllis A(yame) 1903-. . . . **CLC 42**
See also AITN 2; BEST 90:3; CA 1-4R;
CANR 3, 25, 38; JRDA; MAICYA;
SATA 1, 30

Whittemore, (Edward) Reed (Jr.)
1919- . . . . **CLC 4**
See also CA 9-12R; CAAS 8; CANR 4;
DLB 5

Whittier, John Greenleaf
1807-1892 . . . . **NCLC 8**
See also CDALB 1640-1865; DLB 1

Whittlebot, Hernia
See Coward, Noel (Peirce)

Wicker, Thomas Grey 1926-
See Wicker, Tom
See also CA 65-68; CANR 21

Wicker, Tom . . . . **CLC 7**
See also Wicker, Thomas Grey

Wideman, John Edgar
1941- . . . . **CLC 5, 34, 36, 67; BLC**
See also BW; CA 85-88; CANR 14, 42;
DLB 33

Wiebe, Rudy (Henry) 1934-. . . **CLC 6, 11, 14**
See also CA 37-40R; CANR 42; DLB 60

Wieland, Christoph Martin
1733-1813 . . . . **NCLC 17**
See also DLB 97

Wieners, John 1934-. . . . . **CLC 7**
See also CA 13-16R; DLB 16

Wiesel, Elie(zer)
1928- . . . . **CLC 3, 5, 11, 37; DA**
See also AAYA 7; AITN 1; CA 5-8R;
CAAS 4; CANR 8, 40; DLB 83;
DLBY 87; MTCW; SATA 56

Wiggins, Marianne 1947-. . . . . **CLC 57**
See also BEST 89:3; CA 130

Wight, James Alfred 1916-
See Herriot, James
See also CA 77-80; SATA 44, 55

Wilbur, Richard (Purdy)
1921- . . . . **CLC 3, 6, 9, 14, 53; DA**
See also CA 1-4R; CABS 2; CANR 2, 29;
DLB 5; MTCW; SATA 9

Wild, Peter 1940-. . . . . **CLC 14**
See also CA 37-40R; DLB 5

Wilde, Oscar (Fingal O'Flahertie Wills)
1854(?)-1900 . . . . **TCLC 1, 8, 23, 41; DA;
SSC 11; WLC**
See also CA 104; 119; CDBLB 1890-1914;
DLB 10, 19, 34, 57, 141; SATA 24

Wolff, Sonia
See Levitin, Sonia (Wolff)

Wolff, Tobias (Jonathan Ansell)
1945- . . . . **CLC 39, 64**
See also BEST 90:2; CA 114; 117; DLB 130

Wolfram von Eschenbach
c. 1170-c. 1220 . . . . **CMLC 5**
See also DLB 138

Wolitzer, Hilma 1930- . . . . **CLC 17**
See also CA 65-68; CANR 18, 40; SATA 31

Wollstonecraft, Mary 1759-1797 . . . . . **LC 5**
See also CDBLB 1789-1832; DLB 39, 104

Wonder, Stevie . . . . **CLC 12**
See also Morris, Steveland Judkins

Wong, Jade Snow 1922- . . . . **CLC 17**
See also CA 109

Woodcott, Keith
See Brunner, John (Kilian Houston)

Woodruff, Robert W.
See Mencken, H(enry) L(ouis)

Woolf, (Adeline) Virginia
1882-1941 . . . . . . **TCLC 1, 5, 20, 43; DA;**
SSC 7; WLC
See also CA 104; 130; CDBLB 1914-1945;
DLB 36, 100; DLBD 10; MTCW

Woollcott, Alexander (Humphreys)
1887-1943 . . . . **TCLC 5**
See also CA 105; DLB 29

Woolrich, Cornell 1903-1968 . . . . **CLC 77**
See also Hopley-Woolrich, Cornell George

Wordsworth, Dorothy
1771-1855 . . . . **NCLC 25**
See also DLB 107

Wordsworth, William
1770-1850 . . . . **NCLC 12, 38; DA; PC 4;**
WLC
See also CDBLB 1789-1832; DLB 93, 107

Wouk, Herman 1915- . . . . **CLC 1, 9, 38**
See also CA 5-8R; CANR 6, 33; DLBY 82;
MTCW

Wright, Charles (Penzel, Jr.)
1935- . . . . **CLC 6, 13, 28**
See also CA 29-32R; CAAS 7; CANR 23,
36; DLBY 82; MTCW

Wright, Charles Stevenson
1932- . . . . **CLC 49; BLC 3**
See also BW; CA 9-12R; CANR 26;
DLB 33

Wright, Jack R.
See Harris, Mark

Wright, James (Arlington)
1927-1980 . . . . **CLC 3, 5, 10, 28**
See also AITN 2; CA 49-52; 97-100;
CANR 4, 34; DLB 5; MTCW

Wright, Judith (Arundell)
1915- . . . . **CLC 11, 53**
See also CA 13-16R; CANR 31; MTCW;
SATA 14

Wright, L(aurali) R. 1939- . . . . **CLC 44**
See also CA 138

Wright, Richard (Nathaniel)
1908-1960 . . . . **CLC 1, 3, 4, 9, 14, 21, 48,**
74; BLC; DA; SSC 2; WLC
See also AAYA 5; BW; CA 108;
CDALB 1929-1941; DLB 76, 102;
DLBD 2; MTCW

Wright, Richard B(ruce) 1937- . . . . . . **CLC 6**
See also CA 85-88; DLB 53

Wright, Rick 1945- . . . . **CLC 35**
See also Pink Floyd

Wright, Rowland
See Wells, Carolyn

Wright, Stephen 1946- . . . . **CLC 33**

Wright, Willard Huntington 1888-1939
See Van Dine, S. S.
See also CA 115

Wright, William 1930- . . . . **CLC 44**
See also CA 53-56; CANR 7, 23

Wu Ch'eng-en 1500(?)-1582(?) . . . . **LC 7**

Wu Ching-tzu 1701-1754 . . . . **LC 2**

Wurlitzer, Rudolph 1938(?)- . . . **CLC 2, 4, 15**
See also CA 85-88

Wycherley, William 1641-1715 . . . . **LC 8, 21**
See also CDBLB 1660-1789; DLB 80

Wylie, Elinor (Morton Hoyt)
1885-1928 . . . . **TCLC 8**
See also CA 105; DLB 9, 45

Wylie, Philip (Gordon) 1902-1971 . . . **CLC 43**
See also CA 21-22; 33-36R; CAP 2; DLB 9

Wyndham, John
See Harris, John (Wyndham Parkes Lucas)
Beynon

Wyss, Johann David Von
1743-1818 . . . . **NCLC 10**
See also JRDA; MAICYA; SATA 27, 29

Yakumo Koizumi
See Hearn, (Patricio) Lafcadio (Tessima
Carlos)

Yanez, Jose Donoso
See Donoso (Yanez), Jose

Yanovsky, Basile S.
See Yanovsky, V(assily) S(emenovich)

Yanovsky, V(assily) S(emenovich)
1906-1989 . . . . **CLC 2, 18**
See also CA 97-100; 129

Yates, Richard 1926-1992 . . . . . **CLC 7, 8, 23**
See also CA 5-8R; 139; CANR 10, 43;
DLB 2; DLBY 81, 92

Yeats, W. B.
See Yeats, William Butler

Yeats, William Butler
1865-1939 . . . . . **TCLC 1, 11, 18, 31; DA;**
WLC
See also CA 104; 127; CDBLB 1890-1914;
DLB 10, 19, 98; MTCW

Yehoshua, A(braham) B.
1936- . . . . **CLC 13, 31**
See also CA 33-36R; CANR 43

Yep, Laurence Michael 1948- . . . . . . **CLC 35**
See also AAYA 5; CA 49-52; CANR 1;
CLR 3, 17; DLB 52; JRDA; MAICYA;
SATA 7, 69

Yerby, Frank G(arvin)
1916-1991 . . . . **CLC 1, 7, 22; BLC**
See also BW; CA 9-12R; 136; CANR 16;
DLB 76; MTCW

Yesenin, Sergei Alexandrovich
See Esenin, Sergei (Alexandrovich)

Yevtushenko, Yevgeny (Alexandrovich)
1933- . . . . **CLC 1, 3, 13, 26, 51**
See also CA 81-84; CANR 33; MTCW

Yezierska, Anzia 1885(?)-1970 . . . . . **CLC 46**
See also CA 126; 89-92; DLB 28; MTCW

Yglesias, Helen 1915- . . . . **CLC 7, 22**
See also CA 37-40R; CANR 15; MTCW

Yokomitsu Riichi 1898-1947 . . . . . . **TCLC 47**

Yonge, Charlotte (Mary)
1823-1901 . . . . **TCLC 48**
See also CA 109; DLB 18; SATA 17

York, Jeremy
See Creasey, John

York, Simon
See Heinlein, Robert A(nson)

Yorke, Henry Vincent 1905-1974 . . . **CLC 13**
See also Green, Henry
See also CA 85-88; 49-52

Young, Al(bert James)
1939- . . . . **CLC 19; BLC**
See also BW; CA 29-32R; CANR 26;
DLB 33

Young, Andrew (John) 1885-1971 . . . . **CLC 5**
See also CA 5-8R; CANR 7, 29

Young, Collier
See Bloch, Robert (Albert)

Young, Edward 1683-1765 . . . . **LC 3**
See also DLB 95

Young, Marguerite 1909- . . . . **CLC 82**
See also CA 13-16; CAP 1

Young, Neil 1945- . . . . **CLC 17**
See also CA 110

Yourcenar, Marguerite
1903-1987 . . . . **CLC 19, 38, 50**
See also CA 69-72; CANR 23; DLB 72;
DLBY 88; MTCW

Yurick, Sol 1925- . . . . **CLC 6**
See also CA 13-16R; CANR 25

Zabolotskii, Nikolai Alekseevich
1903-1958 . . . . **TCLC 52**
See also CA 116

Zamiatin, Yevgenii
See Zamyatin, Evgeny Ivanovich

Zamyatin, Evgeny Ivanovich
1884-1937 . . . . **TCLC 8, 37**
See also CA 105

Zangwill, Israel 1864-1926 . . . . **TCLC 16**
See also CA 109; DLB 10, 135

Zappa, Francis Vincent, Jr. 1940-1993
See Zappa, Frank
See also CA 108; 143

Zappa, Frank . . . . **CLC 17**
See also Zappa, Francis Vincent, Jr.

Zaturenska, Marya 1902-1982 . . . . **CLC 6, 11**
See also CA 13-16R; 105; CANR 22

Zelazny, Roger (Joseph) 1937- . . . . . **CLC 21**
See also AAYA 7; CA 21-24R; CANR 26;
DLB 8; MTCW; SATA 39, 57

Zhdanov, Andrei A(lexandrovich)
1896-1948 . . . . **TCLC 18**
See also CA 117

Zhukovsky, Vasily 1783-1852 . . . . **NCLC 35**

Ziegenhagen, Eric . . . . **CLC 55**

Zimmer, Jill Schary
See Robinson, Jill

Zimmerman, Robert
See Dylan, Bob

Zindel, Paul 1936- . . . . **CLC 6, 26; DA**
See also AAYA 2; CA 73-76; CANR 31;
CLR 3; DLB 7, 52; JRDA; MAICYA;
MTCW; SATA 16, 58

Zinov'Ev, A. A.
See Zinoviev, Alexander (Aleksandrovich)

Zinoviev, Alexander (Aleksandrovich)
1922- . . . . **CLC 19**
See also CA 116; 133; CAAS 10

Zoilus
See Lovecraft, H(oward) P(hillips)

Zola, Emile (Edouard Charles Antoine)
1840-1902 . . . . . . **TCLC 1, 6, 21, 41; DA;**
WLC
See also CA 104; 138; DLB 123

Zoline, Pamela 1941- . . . . **CLC 62**

Zorrilla y Moral, Jose 1817-1893 . . **NCLC 6**

Zoshchenko, Mikhail (Mikhailovich)
1895-1958 . . . . **TCLC 15; SSC 15**
See also CA 115

Zuckmayer, Carl 1896-1977. . . . . . . **CLC 18**
See also CA 69-72; DLB 56, 124

Zuk, Georges
See Skelton, Robin

Zukofsky, Louis
1904-1978 . . . . **CLC 1, 2, 4, 7, 11, 18**
See also CA 9-12R; 77-80; CANR 39;
DLB 5; MTCW

Zweig, Paul 1935-1984. . . . . **CLC 34, 42**
See also CA 85-88; 113

Zweig, Stefan 1881-1942 . . . . **TCLC 17**
See also CA 112; DLB 81, 118

Literary Criticism Series
Cumulative Topic Index

This index lists all topic entries in the Gale Literary Criticism Series *Classical and Medieval Literature Criticism, Contemporary Literary Criticism, Literature Criticism from 1400 to 1800, Nineteenth-Century Literature Criticism,* and *Twentieth-Century Literary Criticism.*

Topic Index

CMLC Cumulative Nationality Index

CMLC Cumulative Title Index

Title Index

Title Index

Title Index

CMLC Cumulative Critic Index

Critic Index

Critic Index

Critic Index

Critic Index

Critic Index

ISBN 0-8103-2434-2